A Window on Their World

A Window on Their World

The Court Diary of Rabbi Ḥayyim Gundersheim
Frankfurt am Main, 1773–1794

Edward Fram

Hebrew Union College Press
Cincinnati, Ohio

The publication of this book was made possible through a grant from the George und Franziska Speyer'sche Hochschulstiftung, Frankfurt am Main.

Layout: Marzel A.S — Jerusalem
Cover design: Kelby Bowers

Library of Congress Cataloging-in-Publication Data
Gundersheim, Hayyim, d. 1795.
A window on their world : the court diary of Rabbi Ḥayyim Gundersheim,
Frankfurt am Main 1773-1794 / [edited and commented by] Edward Fram.
p. cm.
Includes bibliographical references and index.
ISBN 978-0-87820-253-9
1. Gundersheim, Ḥayyim, d. 1795—Diaries. 2. Rabbis—Germany—Frankfurt am Main—Diaries. 3. Jewish judges—Germany—Frankfurt am Main—Diaries. 4. Rabbinical courts—Germany—History—18th century. 5. Germany—Biography. I. Fram, Edward. II. Title.
BM755.G865A3 2012
296.092--dc23 2011030597

For my son,

David,

who brings his family great joy in the present
and gives us great hope for the future.

Contents

Preface

Georg Heuberger, my predecessor, who sadly passed away on 7 November 2010, initiated the editing and publication of a Hebrew manuscript from the collection of the Jewish Museum of Frankfurt when he was Managing Director of the Commission for the Research of the History of Frankfurt Jewry. By way of various contacts, this complex project was begun under the patronage of the Commission's supporting body, the City of Frankfurt. We sincerely thank the City of Frankfurt am Main for its contribution.

The successful completion of the edition is now at hand. It contains a collection of decisions of a unique historical source, the Frankfurt rabbinical court, the *beyt din*, from the second half of the eighteenth century. This collection offers insights into Jewish life during that time which we cannot obtain from any other source. Therefore, I am very glad that such significant source material regarding the history of Frankfurt Jewry is being published at the end of my sixth year on the Commission.

I would like to thank Professor Edward Fram of Ben-Gurion University of the Negev, Beer Sheva, Israel, who pursued this project with stamina and commitment. I would also like to thank the numerous colleagues and friends listed in his acknowledgments who supported him in this undertaking. Special thanks are due to Ben-Gurion University of the Negev for financial support of the publication, as well as to Professor Michael A. Meyer, chair of the Publications Committee at Hebrew Union College Press and International President of the Leo Baeck Institute, for agreeing to publish the volume.

I would also like to thank our Chief Curator and Deputy Director at the Jewish Museum Frankfurt, Dr. Johannes Wachten, who, with his immense knowledge, took care of this important research project at the museum.

The multilingual nature of this work has made publication difficult and complex. A substantial subvention towards the printing costs came from the Georg und Franziska Speyer'sche Hochschulstiftung. Through this support the Foundation has yet again demonstrated its deep appreciation for the mission of the Commission for the Research of the History of Frankfurt Jewry. For this I would like to thank the Foundation and its directors, in particular Professor Dr. Salomon Korn.

Professor Dr. Raphael Gross
Director Jewish Museum
Frankfurt am Main

Acknowledgments

The preparation of this work was only possible because of the efforts and good will of a number of people. The idea of transcribing this manuscript began with the Jüdisches Museum in Frankfurt and its founding director, the late Georg Heuberger. The Kommission zur Erforschung der Geschichte der Frankfurter Juden approved the plan and it and the Museum helped see to it that it came about. Johannes Wachten, deputy director of the Museum, together with my friend and colleague, the late Robert Liberles, approached me about preparing the transcription. I agreed to do so without really realizing how much was involved or appreciating the richness of what was before me. Johannes and Bob took a deep and ongoing interest in this project for which I am profoundly grateful.

My student Rivka Sendik prepared a preliminary electronic transcription of the manuscript. Her efforts made it far easier for me to continue the work and her own fine Masters' thesis that was based on this material alerted me to some of the historical questions that could emerge from further research.

Eventually it was necessary for me to move beyond photocopies and examine the manuscript itself. Again, the Jüdisches Museum was fully supportive of my efforts. It was at this point that I came to appreciate and rely on the sage advice of Johannes Wachten and his colleague at the Museum, Michael Lenarz. Time and time again they helped me decipher words that I could not read or begin to understand, aided my appreciation of the historical context of these documents, and told me of sources that I did not even know existed. I returned to Frankfurt a number of times during the course of this project and each time, even late into night when everyone else had gone home, they were there to help. Their assistance was not limited to my visits to the Museum. Their immediate responses to my e-mails and extra efforts to check material and consult with experts beyond the confines of the Museum added immeasurably to the value of this work. Their skill, patience, and friendship made it possible to continue to move on. The index of German words that appears at the end of the transcription was only possible with their help.

At the Central Archives for the History of the Jewish People in Jerusalem, Hadassah Assouline introduced me to Shlomo Ettlinger's genealogical study of Frankfurt Jewry and Aryeh Segall's transcription of the Frankfurt *pinqas* or communal record book. Segall's meticulous, but unfortunately as yet unpublished transcription, translation, and notation of the *pinqas* allowed me to include corollary material that I would probably never have had the skill to deal with. All transcriptions of material from the Frankfurt *pinqas* that appear here in the appendices are taken directly from Segall's work that was transferred into electronic form by the Germania Judaica project under the directorship of Yisrael Yuval. My thanks to Yaakov Guggenheim for providing me with an electronic copy of the material. Segall's work is published here with the expressed, written consent of the Central Archives for the History of the Jewish People. I thank the director of the archives, Ms. Assouline, for this and her ongoing suggestions of where to look for what.

The Library of The Jewish Theological Seminary has allowed me access to manuscripts and some — but not all — of its archival material connected with this topic and I thank the institution and its staff, particularly Rabbi Jerry Schwarzbard, for their assistance. As the reader will soon see, the manuscript that is the focus of this study is very much connected to The Seminary and it is published here courtesy of The Library of the Jewish Theological Seminary.

I have also used manuscript material from the YIVO archival collection in New York. Manuscript material from the collection is published here with the expressed consent of the YIVO Institute for Jewish Research, New York.

Colleagues and friends who have sat in the same libraries and archives and/or worked on similar types of material have offered me their time and expertise. Jay Berkovitz is working on his own transcription of material from the rabbinic court of Metz from approximately the same time period and we have been able to compare notes along the way. Noa Shashar has provided me with more than a few tips and manuscript materials to examine. Verena Kasper-Marienberg has been most generous in sharing her own research and made it clear to me how crucial archival material in Vienna is to understanding the history of Frankfurt Jewry. Debra Kaplan made numerous suggestions for improvements in my summaries of cases and the introduction. Yehoshafat Popp helped with the identification of German terms that so often appear in this manuscript in Hebrew characters. Morris Faierstein and Chava Turniansky helped resolve a number of problems in Yiddish terms. Sharon Liberman Mintz was kind enough to suggest material for the dust jacket of this volume. My thanks to each and every one of them.

Sonja Rethy, managing editor of the Hebrew Union College Press, has been ever so patient with online editing and has helped improve the final product. I am most appreciative of her efforts, patience, and wisdom. Arieh Marzel's expertise in typesetting has made the final product a reality.

Publication of the work was made possible through a generous grant from the Georg und Franziska Speyer'sche Hochschulstiftung. Again, Johannes Wachten's efforts in this regard as in so many others were crucial and they are just another example of how this project could never have been completed without his help.

Thanks too to the Jüdisches Museum's current director, Raphael Gross, for his support of our request for funding. Supplementary publication funds were provided by the Faculty of Humanities and Social Sciences and the Office of the Rector at my home institution, Ben-Gurion University of the Negev.

I have done my best to make sure that all references are as accurate as possible. Neither the Hebrew Union College Press nor I can bear responsibility for the persistence or accuracy of URLs for third-party internet websites that I have referred to and we do not guarantee that the contents of such websites are or will remain accurate or appropriate. As for what appears between the covers of this book, any work of this length that has been prepared by one person is bound to have its errors. I have done my best to limit them and I am responsible for those that remain.

Rules of Style

Names of persons who lived in late eighteenth-century Frankfurt have generally been written as they appear in the index to M. Horovitz's *Die Inschriften des alten Friedhofs der israelitischen Gemeinde zu Frankfurt a.M.* (Frankfurt: J. Kauffmann, 1901; referred to here by its Hebrew title, *Abney zikkaron*). The goal of the transliteration of personal and family names has been to make it as easy as possible for those interested in locating further information about these individuals in the existing literature to do so. Shlomo Ettlinger's *Ēlē tōldōt* used a rather idiosyncratic transliteration system of personal names that has not been taken into account here. Some adjustments have been made that reflect modern English usage. Since English does not generally employ an umlaut, Bär has become Ber and Löb has become Leb. Biblical names with accepted English forms have been given in English rather than German style (i.e., Isaac not Isak; Solomon rather than Salomon). The *J* that often represents the Hebrew letter *yod* in German usage has been replaced with a *Y* (e.g., Juzpa has become Yuzpa) although biblical names beginning with the letter *yod* that have accepted forms in English have generally been retained (Joel and not Yoel). The *Ch* that was used by Horovitz to represent the Hebrew letter *ḥet* has been rendered here as *ḥ* (Ḥayyim rather than Chajim and Pinḥas not Pinchas). Transliteration of Hebrew names from other historical periods and Hebrew words have followed the rules for transliteration in *The Jewish Encyclopedia* (New York: Funk and Wagnalls, 1907) with two adjustments: the *vav* is shown as a *v* rather than a *w* and the *quf* is represented by a *q*. To ease in recognition, place names have not always been transliterated exactly. Thus, for example, Frankfurt appears here in its Hebrew transliteration as *Franqfurṭ* rather than *Ferʾanqefurṭ*.

Introduction

Among the holdings of the Jüdisches Museum in Frankfurt am Main is a collection of 210 loose paper folios hand-written in Hebrew characters and catalogued as manuscript B1986/288.[1] Most of its leaves are 19.8 x 16 cm in size with writing on both sides of the paper, but there are some smaller sheets. Twelve pages are blank on one side, and two are blank on both sides. According to the numbering in the upper corners of the pages, the manuscript once consisted of at least 247 folios. The first 39 leaves, however, have been missing from the collection from at least the early 1920s.[2]

The manuscript was written by multiple hands, all Ashkenazic semi-cursives typical of the late early modern period.[3] It was composed in rabbinic Hebrew, and peppered with Yiddish as well as German words transliterated into Hebrew characters. A number of pages were written entirely in Yiddish and/or transliterated German.

An index at the end of the manuscript makes it clear that the complete collection contained at least 254 documents, but the extant material offers only 220, almost all dated in Frankfurt between 1773 and 1794. The files are generally arranged in chronological order. Two pagination systems in parts of the manuscript and a seemingly mistaken internal cross-reference suggest that the collection was once "closed" and later "reopened" when new material was added.[4]

---

1. A description of the manuscript was prepared by Dr. Johannes Wachten, Chief Curator and Deputy Director of the Jüdisches Museum in Frankfurt, on 19 November 1990.
2. Two pages are numbered as folio 60 and there are two pages without pagination, one between folios 143 and 144 and a second between folios 232 and 233. Folio 117 is missing and folios 236 and 237 are blank on both sides. Regarding the manuscript in the 1920s, see Yaᶜaqov Koppel Duschinsky, "Sefer maᶜaseh beyt din de-q[ehillat] q[odesh] Franqfurṭ y[agen] ᶜ[aleyha] e[lohim] mi-shannat [5]429 ᶜad [5]499," *Ha-ẓofeh le-ḥokmat Yisraʾel* 10 (1926): 106–15.
3. In at least one case, two scribes contributed to the writing of the same document (see Ḥayyim Gundersheim, Jewish Theological Seminary, Adler MS. 935 [New York], no. 99; all numbered references refer to this edition — the diary itself is not numbered). My observation on the period of the handwriting is based on a comparison with the Frankfurt *Memorbuch*, MS. Heb. 1092, The National Library of Israel (Jerusalem), and Pinqas Franqfurṭ, MS. 4°662, The National Library of Israel (Jerusalem). The *Memorbuch* is available online at http://jnul.huji.ac.il/dl/mss/heb1092/index_eng.html, accessed 26 April 2009.
4. On fol. 48b there is a cross-reference to fol. 128b. The relevant material does not appear there, but rather on fol. 240b. Fol. 241 sports a second pagination (129) and this double pagination continues in the index to the collection on fols. 242–44 (earlier labeled as fols. 130–32). This

Although the manuscript emanated from Frankfurt and is now in Frankfurt, it has not always been in Frankfurt. According to Charles Duschinsky, who used the document and described it in an article published in 1926, the material was purchased by the British bibliophile and collector Elkan Nathan Adler "a few years earlier" in Jerusalem and was brought to London.[5] It was assigned shelf-number 935 in the Adler manuscript collection, and when Adler sold much of his library to The Jewish Theological Seminary in 1923 MS. 935 was to be transferred to New York City with the rest of the material.[6] However, Duschinsky had borrowed manuscripts from Adler before the sale and they remained with Duschinsky in London when Adler's collection was shipped to New York. On 14 June 1923 Duschinsky wrote to Professor Alexander Marx, librarian of The Jewish Theological Seminary, and informed him that he held two manuscripts that had belonged to Adler. Duschinsky asked that he be allowed to retain the manuscripts "for a little while" so he could continue to work on them. Marx replied to Duschinsky on 27 June 1923, "I have no objection to your retaining the manuscripts you are using a little longer, but I would be obliged, if you would give me the number of the second one."[7] Less than three weeks later Duschinsky informed Marx that the second manuscript was Adler MS. 935.[8]

Time passed and on 30 March 1925 Marx wrote to Duschinsky asking him

---

suggests that at one time the manuscript had only 132 folios. Folios 1–127 were the body of the text, fols. 128–29 were an appendix of sorts, and there was an index to the collection on folios 130–32. When new material was added to the collection, it was placed after fol. 127, continuing the body of the text. These new folios were numbered consecutively from 128 through 239. When the text was complete, the appendix was again placed at the end (now fols. 240b–241a), and the index followed, renumbered as fols. 241b–247a.

5. Duschinsky, "Sefer maʿaseh beyt din," 110. Duschinsky used the manuscript and transcribed a section of it in his earlier article, "The Rabbinate of the Great Synagogue, London, from 1756–1842," *Jewish Quarterly Review* 11, no. 3 (1921): 345–50 (reprinted as *The Rabbinate of the Great Synagogue, London, from 1756–1842*, with a new bibliographical note by Ruth Lehmann [Farnborough: Gregg, 1971], 254–59).

6. According to Cecil Roth, *Encyclopaedia Judaica*, 2d ed. (Detroit: Macmillan, 2007), s.v. "Adler, Elkan Nathan," Adler was forced to sell his collection "in order to make good the embezzlements of a business associate." Regarding the manuscript, see Elkan Nathan Adler, *Catalogue of Hebrew Manuscripts in the Collection of Elkan Nathan Adler* (Cambridge: Cambridge University Press, 1921), 23. Also see illustration no. 56 in the catalogue showing fol. 187a of the manuscript with the shelf-number in the Adler collection in the top left corner of the page.

7. Letter from Marx to Duschinsky, 27 June 1923 (Duschinsky File [in process], Alexander Marx Collection, ARC 80 [New York: Jewish Theological Seminary]). All subsequent references to correspondence between Duschinsky, his family, and Marx, are found in this file. According to the archivist of The Jewish Theological Seminary, Ms. Ellen Kastel, as of August 2009 the Alexander Marx file was still incomplete.

8. Letter from Duschinsky to Marx, 12 July 1923. In his 1926 article Duschinsky wrote that the

when he would return the manuscripts. In June of that year Duschinsky returned one of the manuscripts via the mail — insuring it for £25! — but on 16 June 1925 he wrote to Marx asking to extend the loan of MS. Adler 935 "for a few more months." Duschinsky explained, "I have made extensive notes from it and also copied part and should like to work it out as soon as I can."[9] Marx responded on 6 July 1925, "As to MS. 935, I shall be glad to extend the time for another three months, but then I would like to get it."

By 1927 someone in the library of The Jewish Theological Seminary noted that Adler MS. 935 was not in the collection, and the manuscript was listed as "missing."[10] Duschinsky and Marx continued to correspond through the 1920s and 1930s about books and other topics, yet the extant correspondence between them in the Alexander Marx Files in The Library of The Jewish Theological Seminary of America in New York makes no further reference to Adler MS. 935.[11]

The fate of Adler MS. 935 in the ensuing years remains unclear, but in the 1970s the manuscript resurfaced and was purchased in London by a Frankfurt art dealer who sold it to the Frankfurt municipal archives in 1981.[12] In 1986 the manuscript was transferred from the archives to the Jüdisches Museum, another municipal facility in Frankfurt, where it became MS. B1986/288.[13] As of this writing (July

---

Adler collection had been transferred to The Jewish Theological Seminary and specifically thanked Marx for lending Adler MS. 935 to him ("Sefer maʿaseh beyt din," 110 n. 2).

9. The information about the insurance appears in a letter from Duschinsky to Marx, 6 June 1925.

10. Rabbi Jerry Schwarzbard, Special Collections Librarian of The Jewish Theological Seminary, informed me of the listing of the manuscript as missing in an electronic letter, 27 November 2007.

11. Charles Duschinsky died in London in July 1944. On 14 June 1946 Professor Marx wrote to Mr. (Albi?) Rosenthal of Oxford and requested that he ask the Duschinsky family about three manuscripts that had belonged to Elkan Adler that Marx believed were in the Duschinsky estate. Elkan Adler died only on 15 September 1946, and thus Marx's inquiry of Duschinky's heirs about Adler material was presumably about items that Marx thought The Seminary had acquired in 1923. The manuscripts Marx was referring to were not itemized in the extant correspondence, and without further information it is impossible to say with certainty that Adler MS. 935 was among them. Rosenthal showed the letter to the Duschinsky family, and on 30 June 1946 Duschinsky's widow signed a letter to Marx in the name of the family denying The Seminary's claim. Marx maintained The Seminary's rights to the material in a letter to Mrs. Duschinsky dated 16 October 1946, but there is no evidence that he took the matter any further.

12. Johannes Wachten, electronic letters to the author, 27 November 2007, 13 June 2008, and 29 July 2009. In his letter of 29 July 2009 Dr. Wachten informed me that the dealer, with whom he had spoken in the previous few days, declined to reveal the name of the person from whom he had purchased the manuscript.

13. Johannes Wachten, electronic letter to the author, 13 June 2008.

2009), The Jewish Theological Seminary has requested the return of the manuscript but this has yet to take place.[14]

The manuscript represents a type of source material that has not been integrated into the study of early modern European Jewry: the decisions and rulings of rabbinic courts (Heb., sg. *beyt din*; pl., *battey din*).[15] Rabbinic courts were an integral part of Jewish life during this and earlier periods, and there are a number of extant records of *battey din* from early modern Europe, mainly but not exclusively from the second half of the eighteenth century.[16] These include various types of proceedings from relatively large Jewish communities, such as this manuscript from Frankfurt, and others from Altona, Amsterdam, Metz, and Prague, as well as records from smaller centers such as Niedernai, Romanswiller, and Kępno.[17]

---

14. Since I assume that the manuscript will eventually be returned to The Jewish Theological Seminary, I have referred to it throughout as Adler MS. 935. A microfilm copy of the manuscript is in the Central Archive for the History of the Jewish People (Jerusalem), film HM2/5872.
15. For now, see Jay Berkovitz, "Civil Law and Justice in the Rabbinic Tribunals of 18th Century Metz," in *Iggud: Selected Essays in Jewish Studies* (Jerusalem: Magnes, 2008), 87–99, as well as his "Acculturation and Integration in Eighteenth-Century Metz: The Circuitous Path to Modernity," *Jewish History* (2010), http://www.springerlink.com/content/rn54u021283115j1/fulltext.pdf; Andreas Gotzmann, *Jüdische Autonomie in der Frühen Neuzeit: Recht und Gemeinschaft im deutschen Judentum*, Hamburger Beiträge zur Geschichte der deutschen Juden 32 (Göttingen: Wallstein, 2008), particularly 255, 269–72, and 473; David H. Horowitz, "Fractures and Fissures in Jewish Communal Autonomy in Hamburg, 1710–1782," Ph.D. diss. (Columbia University, 2010); and to a very limited extent, Maoz Kahana, "Me-Pra'g le-Presburg: ketibah hilkatit be-ʿolam mishtaneh me-ha-'Nodaʿ be- Yehudah' el ha-'Ḥata"m sofer' 1720–1839," Ph.D. diss. (Hebrew University, 2010), p. 131.
16. There seems to have been a plethora of rabbinic courts in the sixteenth and seventeenth-century Ottoman Empire, but, according to Yosef Hacker, "Gebulteyha shel ha-ʾoṭonomyah ha-yehudit: ha-shippuṭ ha-ʿaẓmi ha-yehudi be-ʾimperyah ha-ʿotmaʾnit be-meʾot ha-16 — ha-18," in *Transition and Change in Modern Jewish History, Essays Presented in Honor of Shmuel Ettinger*, ed. S. Almog et al. (Jerusalem: Shazar, 1987), 381, no records from these courts are known to have survived.
17. A subject search of the electronic catalogue of The Institute for Microfilmed Hebrew Manuscripts (Jerusalem) for the Hebrew term "beyt din" and a visit to the Central Archives for the History of the Jewish People in Jerusalem easily reveals more. Almost all such records remain in manuscript, although some have been published. Among them are eight rulings of the rabbinic court of Tiktin from the seventeenth century, published by Mordechai Nadav, *Pinqas qahal Ṭiqṭin 381–566*, vol. 2 (Jerusalem: Israel Academy of Sciences and Humanities, 1999), 7–12; material from the Cracow rabbinic court from the seventeenth century published by P.H. Wettstein, *Mi-pinqasey ha-qahal be-Qeraʾqaʾ* (Breslau: S. Schottländer, 1900), and from the late seventeenth century and first half of the eighteenth century in P.H. Wettstein, "Dibrey ḥefeẓ mi-pinqasey ha-qahal be-Qeraʾqaʾ," *Meʾasef* (St. Petersburg) 1 (1902): 36–37, 51–52. Eighteen decisions of the Amsterdam rabbinic court were published by Yosef Kaplan, "Pesaqim mi-beyt ha-din shel ha-qehillah ha-sefardit — ha-porṭugaʾlit be-ʾAmsṭerdam be-meʾah ha-shemonah

The Frankfurt *beyt din* kept records by order of the Jewish community. A communal ordinance of 1754 demanded that judges of the rabbinic court maintain a "protocol" of the claims and counterclaims of litigants who came before them.[18] The court was to prepare a written summary of the main arguments of both sides before issuing its verdict, which was to be signed by each member of the court. These protocols were to be held in a special room maintained for the *beyt din* by the community, the key to which was held by the head of the court.[19]

This manuscript is not such a protocol. It often notes that a full record of the case at hand can be found "in the book of claims" (*qunṭres ha-ṭaᶜanot*) that is "before us," presumably in the court's room.[20] The decisions are not signed by each of the judges, but in almost every entry there is a list of the judges who decided the case with an ever so modest "and me" (*ve-ʾani*) at the end.[21] Finally, the manuscript

---

ᶜesreh u-mashmaᶜutam ha-hisṭorit — ḥebratit," *Studies on the History of Dutch Jewry* 5 (1988): 41–54 (kindly referred to me by Dr. Evelyne Oliel-Grausz). Material from the Prague rabbinic court from the years 1682 and 1683 was published by Simon Adler, "Das älteste Judicial-Protokoll des jüdischen Gemeinde-Archives in Prag (1682)," *Jahrbuch der Gesellschaft für Geschichte der Juden in der Čechoslovakischen Republik* 3 (1931): 220–52 (my thanks to Dr. Michael Silber for pointing out this reference to me). Adler lists thousands of pages of unpublished material from Prague from the years between 1682 and 1779 (p. 253 n. 1). Also see Adler's "Aus den Judizialakten des XVIII. Jahrhunderts. Bilder aus dem täglichen Leben der Juden in Prag," *Jahrbuch der Gesellschaft für Geschichte der Juden in der Čechoslovakischen Republik* 8 (1936), 411–20. Professor Jay Berkovitz is currently preparing an edition of the Metz records tentatively titled *Protocols of Justice*. Markus Horovitz in his *Frankfurter Rabbinen: ein Beitrag zur Geschichte der israelitischen Gemeide*, 2d ed., with a supplement by Josef Unna (Hildesheim: Georg Olms, 1972), 194 (in Hebrew, *Rabbaney Franqfurṭ*, with a supplement by Joseph Unna, translated by Joshua Amir [Jerusalem: Mossad Harav Kook, 1972], 137–38 with n. 6), noted that he had what he termed a protocol of the Frankfurt rabbinic court ("Protokollbuch") from the second half of the eighteenth century. This appears to be folder 77–78, Collection of Rabbinical and Historical Manuscripts (RG 128), YIVO Archives, New York (henceforth YIVO MS. RG 128 [folder 77–78]). From time to time portions of court records appear in rabbinic responsa. See, for example, Solomon Luria, *Sheʾelot u-teshubot ha-Maharsha"l* (Jerusalem: Oẓar ha-sefarim, 1969), no. 21.

18. Records were maintained earlier as well, and the author seems to have had access to them (see Gundersheim, Adler MS. 935, nos. 253, 254). Responses and counterclaims were part of the judicial process in Frankfurt. See, for example, nos. 40, 41.
19. See Żydowski Instytut Historyczny (ŻIH), MS. 517 (Warsaw), fols. 13b-14a (no. 67), ordinances of the Frankfurt Jewish community from 1754. The manuscript, described in the typescript catalogue of Franciszka (Ephraim) Kupfer and Stefan Strelcyn, *Katalog rękopisow orientalnych ze zbiorów polskich*, vol. 4, Rękopisy hebrajskie i aramejskie, Zakład Orientalistaki PAN (Warsaw), is available on film as HM2/5912 at the Central Archives for the History of the Jewish People.
20. See, for example, Gundersheim, Adler MS. 935, no. 120.
21. Exceptions can be found in nos. 43, 44, 53, 77, 79, 89, and 90, where Gundersheim's name is

appears to have been held in the author's possession, for he recorded the dates of his children's births on one of the last pages of the collection, presumably not something that one would do in a public record book.[22] This is a personal record of the court's rulings and decisions prepared by a longtime member of the Frankfurt judiciary, Rabbi Ḥayyim Gundersheim (d. 1795).[23]

Gundersheim was first appointed as a rabbinic judge (Heb. sg., *dayyan*; pl., *dayyanim*) in Frankfurt about 1767, when he was probably in his late twenties, and remained on the court until his death in 1795.[24] Given that the manuscript was written by multiple hands, it would seem that Gundersheim did not prepare the entire copy. Nonetheless, the constant use of the word "me" to refer to himself suggests that the material was prepared specifically for him or copied from his own papers.

In creating his diary Gundersheim routinely listed the names of the litigants and their legal representatives (if any), as well as what he believed to be their principle claims and the court's verdict. He noted the names of people who came to testify on behalf of litigants (or at least those whose testimony he deemed worthy of including), as well as the other judges who heard the case with him, the names of relevant court officials present at the proceedings, and the date of the court's ruling. Unless copying a precedent useful in a case before him, Gundersheim only

---

spelled out. Such use of "me" in the signature was not unique. Rabbi Nathan Maas also referred to himself as "me" in his personal papers (see below p.94 and YIVO MS. RG128 [folder 77–78], fol. 67a).

22. Gundersheim, Adler MS. 935, fol. 247b. It was a common custom among both Jews and Christians to record significant family dates (e.g., births, deaths) in an important personal volume such as a bible or prayer book. Another example of this from the Jewish community of the early eighteenth century can be found in The Jewish Theological Seminary's copy of *Shulḥan ʿaruk*, Yoreh deʿah (Cracow, 1594) on the verso side of the title page, the first page of the introduction, and the last page of the volume.

23. See Gundersheim, Adler MS. 935, no. 194, in which the author of the manuscript signed his name as "ve-ʾani" ("and me"). The same document can be found in the Frankfurt archives in German (here Appendix 6). In the German version all the signatories are the same as in no. 194 except for one: the "ve-ʾani" has been replaced by Hayum Gondersheim, or Rabbi Ḥayyim Gundersheim.

24. Gundersheim's entry in the Frankfurt *Memorbuch* noted that he was a judge for 28 years (Frankfurt *Memorbuch*, fol. 350a). This would place his first appointment to the court in about 1767. The earliest record listed in the index to the diary is from 1769. Given that his parents married on 2 July 1738 (see Shlomo Ettlinger, *Ēlē tōldōt*, P/237, Central Archives for the Jewish People (Jerusalem), 17.5.1804; cf., 4.5.1769, where he listed the date of their marriage as "um 1742" [about 1742]), he could not have been more than in his late twenties when he was first appointed to the court.

recorded cases that he himself heard or had a role in.[25] Gundersheim was not alone in keeping a personal court diary. His colleague on the court and head of the yeshiva in Frankfurt, Rabbi Nathan Maas (d. 1796), also maintained such a record, and it appears that they had access to each other's files.[26] Gundersheim's record does not contain every case that he heard during his tenure on the court.[27]

Ḥayyim Gundersheim was very much a member of the elite of Frankfurt Jewry, and not just by dint of his rabbinic scholarship.[28] Rabbi Ḥayyim's great-grandfather was Ḥayyim Gundersheim of Mainz, a military supplier who entered into a partnership with the court Jew Leffman Behrens in 1697. The elder Ḥayyim Gundersheim later worked with Behrens's grandson, Gumpert Behrens, supplying food and goods to the troops of the Elector of Hannover.[29] Ḥayyim Gundersheim of Mainz's son and Rabbi Ḥayyim's grandfather, Hirsch Gundersheim (d. 1771), was a preceptor (*gabbaʾy*) of charitable funds in the Frankfurt Jewish community and was involved in the search for the chief rabbi of Frankfurt in 1759.[30] A supplier

---

25. See Gundersheim, Adler MS. 935, no. 254. No. 37 appears to be an exception to this, but the circumstances of its copying (see the following note) suggest that this text may have found its way into the collection at least in part due to chance.
26. Gundersheim (or the scribe) noted that no. 37 was copied from the notebook of the head of the rabbinic court, Rabbi Nathan Maas. This corresponds to YIVO MS. RG 128 (folder 77–78), fol. 114a. Gundersheim appears as "me" in another document on this very page of the YIVO manuscript, and that case is the same as no. 227 in Gundersheim's collection. It may well be that Maas copied the latter case, or had it copied, from Gundersheim's files. Also see Horovitz, *Rabbaney Franqfurṭ*, 137.
27. See YIVO MS. RG 128 (folder 77–78), fols. 64a–66a, 66b–67a, for material that does not appear in Gundersheim's diary even though Gundersheim was listed as a member of the judicial panel.
28. There were two other Ḥayyim Gundersheims in Frankfurt whose lives overlapped with the *dayyan* Ḥayyim Gundersheim, both of whom were the sons of Hirsch Gundersheims. One died in the summer of 1756 or 1757, apparently as a very young man (Markus Horovitz, *Abney zikkaron: ha-ketab ve-ha-miktab* [Frankfurt: J. Kauffmann, 1901], no. 2917; Horovitz recorded the year as 1757, but 22 Tammuz [20 July], the date of death recorded by Horovitz from the gravestone, did not fall on a Tuesday in 1757 — although it in did in 1756). The other Ḥayyim Gundersheim was the *dayyan*'s paternal uncle, who died in the autumn of 1791 after having been sick "for much of his life" (*rob yamav*; Frankfurt *Memorbuch*, fol. 327b; Horovitz, no. 3078, with the correction of Ettlinger, *Ēlē tōldōt*, 13.10.1791).
29. Rabbi Ḥayyim Gundersheim's great-grandfather was in Frankfurt between 1705 and 1710. On his activities, see Bernd Schedlitz, *Leffmann Behrens: Untersuchungen zum Hofjudentum in Zeitalter des Absolutismus* (Hildesheim: August Lax, 1984), 89–90, with n. 7, as well as Adolf Kober, "Die Reichsstadt Köln und die Juden in den Jahren 1685–1715: Ein Beitrag zur Geschichte der jüdischen Hoffaktoren," *Monatsschrift für Geschichte und Wissenschaft des Judentums* 75 (1931): 419–20, and Lionel Kochan, *The Making of Western Jewry, 1600–1819* (London: Palgrave, 2004), 102.
30. See Aryeh Segall, ed. and comp., Ḥomer le-pinqas ha-qahal (Franqfurṭ), Personal Papers of Aryeh Segall (Central Archives for the History of the Jewish People, Jerusalem), no. 463 (1759).

of war materials, in 1764 he had the savvy and financial wherewithal to turn to the Imperial Aulic Court (*Reichshofrat*) in Vienna, the highest court of the Holy Roman Empire, to obtain rights for his son Shene'ur Ziskind Gundersheim (d. 1802), who was then the chief rabbi in the Trier region ("Oberrabbiner im Erzstift Trier").[31] Upon his death in April 1771, Hirsch Gundersheim was posthumously granted the title of *ḥaber* (lit., "friend;" here signifying a layman who had knowledge of rabbinic law and practice) by his son and Rabbi Ḥayyim's paternal uncle, Rabbi Shene'ur Ziskind.[32]

Rabbi Shene'ur Ziskind served as rabbi in the Trier region for over 35 years and became head of its rabbinic court. In 1794 the French invaded Koblenz, where Rabbi Shene'ur Ziskind lived. The French occupation of much of the Rhineland was characterized by plundering, violence, and exploitation of the local population. Presumably because of this Rabbi Shene'ur Ziskind fled the region and returned to his native Frankfurt.[33] Soon after his return, he served as a member of the

31. Michael Brocke and Julius Carlebach, eds., *Biographisches Handbuch der Rabbiner: Die Rabbiner der Emanzipationszeit in den deutschen, böhmischen und grosspolnischen Ländern 1781–1871,* arranged by Carsten Wilke (Munich: K.G. Saur, 2004), no. 0630 (p. 396), noted that Hirsch's efforts in this matter began in Frankfurt already in 1763. I have also relied on the research of Dr. Verena Kasper-Marienberg of Karl-Franzens-Universität (Graz) who has generously shared her findings with me.

32. See Horovitz, *Abney zikkaron*, no. 3410. Also see Frankfurt *Memorbuch*, fol. 232b. On the title "*ḥaber*," see Israel Jacob Yuval, *Ḥakamim be-doram* (Jerusalem: Magnes, 1988), 280–81, 341. The posthumous conferring of titles in Jewish communities in the German lands goes back at least to the Middle Ages (see Avraham [Rami] Reiner, "Eben she-katub ʿaleha: to'arey ha-nifṭarim be-maẓebot beyt ha-ʿalmin be-Wirẓburg 1147–1346," *Tarbiz* 78, no. 1 [December 2008]: 126–32, and on a later period, Israel Jacob Yuval, "Taqqanot neged ribbuy gerushin be-Germanyah be-me'ah ha-15," *Zion* 48 [1983]: 182 n. 16). While not an everyday occurrence in late eighteenth-century Frankfurt, it was not an uncommon way of bestowing honor on the deceased and granting some solace (and/or honor) to the survivors (see, for example, Horovitz, *Abney zikkaron*, nos. 3410 [1771], 3417 [1771], and 4447 [1804], and Mordechai Breuer, *Ohaley Torah: ha-yeshibah, tabnitah ve-toledoteyha* [Jerusalem: Shazar, 2003], 392–93 n. 48, regarding the significance of the practice). The custom was not unique to Frankfurt (see M. Weinberg, *Die Memorbücher der jüdischen Gemeinden in Bayern*, 2 vols. [Frankfurt: S. Neumann, 1937], 218 no. 3). However, not everyone wanted such titles. Rabbi Nathan Maas specifically asked that no title be posthumously conferred on him (see Horovitz, *Abney zikkaron*, no. 4228 [1796], as well as Frankfurt *Memorbuch*, fol. 345a), as did Leb Schwarzschild (Frankfurt *Memorbuch*, fol. 457a).

33. On the French Revolutionary Wars in this region, see Jacques Godechot, *La grande nation: l'expansion révolutionnaire de la France dans le monde de 1789 à 1799*, 2d ed. (Paris: Aubier, 1983), 183–85, and on the treatment of the local population, T.C.W. Blanning, *The French Revolution in Germany* (Oxford: Clarendon, 1983), 83–127. According to the *Memorbuch* (fol. 392b), the ongoing war was the reason Shene'ur Ziskind left Koblenz. On Shene'ur Ziskind Gundersheim, see the material cited in Brocke and Carlebach, *Biographisches Handbuch*,

rabbinic court and published a lengthy commentary on a portion of Rabbi Joseph Caro's *Shulḥan ʿaruk.*[34] Another of Rabbi Ḥayyim's paternal uncles, Zeligman Gundersheim (d. 1819), was a butcher by trade and a member of the Jewish communal leadership in Frankfurt in the mid-1790s. He married the daughter of the head of the rabbinic court of Hannover.[35]

Rabbi Ḥayyim's father, Yuzpa, or Jozef, Gundersheim (d. 1804) held various leadership roles in the Frankfurt Jewish community for over thirty years.[36] Already in the late 1760s he was a *gabbaʾy,* and by 1774 his son was signing his own name as "Ḥayyim son of the 'administrator and leader' [*parnas ve-manhig*], the honorable Yuzpa."[37] Yuzpa continued to serve the community, and in 1790 he addressed the crown prince on behalf of the Jewish community during the festivities surrounding the coronation of Leopold II in Frankfurt.[38] He and two others presented Emperors Leopold II (1790) and Franz II (1792) with gifts from the Jewish community during their coronation ceremonies. He also had an audience with Franz II and his advisers that was said to have lasted "a few hours."[39] Rabbi Ḥayyim's mother, Zippora (d. 1769), was the daughter of a communal lay leader in Düsseldorf, and Relcha, Ḥayyim's first wife, was the daughter of Aaron Lehren, another member of the Jewish communal leadership in Frankfurt.[40]

---

no. 0630. Brocke and Carlebach dated his return to Frankfurt to 1796. On his tenure on the Frankfurt court, which began after his nephew Rabbi Ḥayyim's death, see Horovitz, *Rabbaney Franqfurṭ*, 170, as well as Segall, Pinqas Frankfurṭ, no. 532 (1799).

34. Sheneʾur Ziskind Gundersheim, *Sefer meqor ḥayyim ve-sefer tifʾeret Ẓebi* (Offenbach: Ẓebi Hirsch Segal and Son, 1798). Sheneʾur Gundersheim mentioned his service on the Frankfurt rabbinic court in the unpaginated introduction. He was appointed to his position on the court on 21 February 1796 (JTS MS. 3672 [New York], fol. 24a).

35. See Segall, Pinqas Frankfurṭ, no. 452 (1794). Regarding his profession and marriage, see Ettlinger, *Ēlē tōldōt*, 11.6.1819; and death, Horovitz, *Abney zikkaron*, no. 4970. Another uncle, Moses Gundersheim, a merchant, was born in 1753, married in 1790, and later divorced. He died in 1826 (*Ēlē tōldōt*, 15.7.1826).

36. See Segall, Pinqas Frankfurṭ, nos. 412, 413 (1766), 418, 469 (1767), 421 (1768), 429, 431 (1769 [by which time he was appointed *gabbaʾy*]), 435 (1772), 436 (1787), 446 (1793), 452 (1794), 479, 483 (1779), 486, 487 (1782), 490b (1787), and 499 (1788).

37. Gundersheim, Adler MS. 935, no. 44 (1774).

38. Horovitz, *Rabbaney Franqfurṭ*, 166–67. The Golden Bull of Charles IV (1356; http://www.fordham.edu/halsall/source/goldenbull.html, accessed 6 March 2011) established that the Emperor be elected in Frankfurt. From 1562 until 1792 the Emperor was also crowned in Frankfurt.

39. See Frankfurt *Memorbuch*, fol. 401a. Also see I. Kracauer, *Geschichte der Juden in Frankfurt a.M. (1150–1824)*, vol. 2 (Frankfurt: Kauffmann, 1927), 312–14. On the Jews of Frankfurt paying homage to the Emperor, see Stephan Wendehorst, "Imperial Spaces as Jewish Spaces — The Holy Roman Empire, the Emperor and the Jews in the Early Modern Period. Some Preliminary Observations," *Jahrbuch des Simon-Dubnow-Instituts* 2 (2003): 452–53.

40. See Frankfurt *Memorbuch*, fol. 224a, regarding his mother, and fol. 301a, with respect to his

Rabbi Ḥayyim Gundersheim himself had a small family. He married his first wife, Relcha, on 30 December 1764 and she died in May 1786.[41] There appear to have been no (surviving?) children from the marriage. On 28 February 1787 Rabbi Ḥayyim married the daughter of the late Samuel Flörsheim, Brendela (d. 1819) — who had not previously been married — in nearby Bockenheim (about 4 kilometers northwest of the Jewish area of Frankfurt, and from 1895 a part of Frankfurt).[42] Together they had two children.[43] Gundersheim suffered from chronic leg problems, but, according to the Frankfurt *Memorbuch* (a communal memorial book listing and telling of the deceased; entries were generally paid for by surviving relatives who probably provided content for the entry as well) he still managed to be among the first to the synagogue morning and night, a sign that he remained mobile.[44] Rabbi Ḥayyim died on 28 May 1795, soon after having been appointed to a new term on the court.[45]

Rabbi Ḥayyim Gundersheim did not spend his entire day on the court, for being a judge was not a full-time position. Indeed, most of the court decisions in Gundersheim's diary were written in the evening, which suggests that the court convened late in the day or at night, leaving judges time for other pursuits.[46]

first wife.

41. On the date of the marriage, see JTS MS. 3672, fol. 31b. On her date of death, see Frankfurt *Memorbuch*, fol. 301a.
42. With respect to the date of Brendela's death, see Horovitz, *Abney zikkaron*, no. 4945, and Frankfurt *Memorbuch*, fol. 453a.
43. See JTS MS. 3672, fol. 125a. At the end of this manuscript Gundersheim recorded that his daughter Hannah was born on 19 Tevet 5550 (5 January 1790), and his son Moses on 27 Tammuz 5552 (17 July 1792; Gundersheim, Adler MS. 935, fol. 247b). Moses died in 1799 (see Ettlinger, *Ēlē tōldōt*, 28.5.1795).
44. See Frankfurt *Memorbuch*, fol. 350a. For a brief but very helpful introduction to *Memorbücher* as a genre, see Siegmund Salfeld, *Das Martyrologium des Nürnberger Memorbuches* (Berlin: Leonhard Simion, 1898), ix-xiv. On the Frankfurt *Memorbuch*, see Cecil Roth, *The Frankfurt Memorbuch* (Jerusalem: Jewish National and University Library, 1965). A useful tool for finding information about some of the individuals mentioned in the Frankfurt *Memorbuch* is Tzvia Koren-Loeb, "Das Memorbuch zu Frankfurt am Main: Erschließung und Kommentierung ausgewählter Themenkreise," Ph.D. diss. (Universität Duisburg-Essen, 2008). It is available online at http://duepublico.uni-duisburg-essen.de/servlets/DocumentServet?id=18193&lang=en, accessed 20 January 2010. Payment by family members is mentioned in almost every entry in the Frankfurt *Memorbuch*. See too, case no. 150 in Gundersheim's diary.
45. Regarding his reappointment, see Segall, Pinqas Franqfurṭ, no. 494 (4 March 1795).
46. Although rabbinic courts are supposed to convene only during the day (*Shulḥan ʿaruk*, Ḥoshen mishpaṭ 5.2), the number of records written at night suggests that the Frankfurt court either met at night or wrote its decisions in the evening. Convening in the evening was not unique, for in Poznań the rabbinic court met after the evening prayers (see Anna Michałowska-Mycielska, *The Jewish Community: Authority and Social Control in Poznań and*

Although an ordinance from the mid-seventeenth century decreed that judges receive an annual salary for "lost time" (*sekar baṭṭalah*), that is, time that they could have spent doing other things, this arrangement appears not to have been in force in the second half of the eighteenth century.[47] Community records from 1754 stipulated that judges receive *sekar baṭṭalah* for each case that they heard rather than a guaranteed salary.[48] Payment was made by the litigants and was generally prorated based upon the value of the case. Except for property purchases, both sides paid equal amounts to the court.[49]

With the judiciary more of a sideline than a primary source of income, *dayyanim* had to find a means of earning a living, and many did so in the field of education. Gundersheim was the "second" or vice-chair of a study hall (*kloysz*) that had been established in Frankfurt through an endowment by Leb Reiss (d. 1778).[50]

Swarzędz, 1650–1793, trans. Alicja Adamowicz, Bibliotheca Judaica 3 [Wrocław: Wydawnictwo Uniwersytetu Wrocławskiego, 2008], 127). In Prague, the court met between the afternoon and the evening prayers (Gutmann Klemperer, "The Rabbis of Prague: A History of the Rabbinate of Prague from the Death of Rabbi Loewe b. Bezalel ['The High Rabbi Loew'] to the Present [1609–1879]," *Historia Judaica* 12–13 [1950–51]: 76).

47. See Segall, Pinqas Frankfurṭ, no. 273 (1658). Also see Rivka Sendik, "Beyn din le-pesher: peᶜiluto shel beyt ha-din be-qehillat Franqfurṭ ᶜa[l] n[ahar] Mayn be-maḥaẓit ha-sheniyyah shel ha-meʾah ha-shemonah ᶜesreh," M.A. thesis (Ben-Gurion University of the Negev, 2000), 66. On the payment of judges in general, see Jacob Katz, *Masoret u-mashber: ha-ḥebrah ha-yehudit be-moẓaʾey yemey ha-beynayyim* (Jerusalem: Bialik Institute, 1958), 120.

48. In Brody (Galicia) in approximately the 1730s, rabbinic judges appear not to have received any form of payment for their judicial services, not even for "lost time" (introduction of Jacob Landau to the responsa of his father, Ezekiel Landau, *Sheʾelot u-teshubot nodaᶜ be-Yehudah ha-shalem*, Oraḥ ḥayyim, ed. Jacob Ehrnfeld et al. [Ashkelon: Machon Yerushalayim, 1994], 32). Whether the rabbinic judges in Brody were all part of the local *kloysz* and payment from the *kloysz* was viewed as including remuneration for their judicial services requires further investigation.

49. ŻIH MS. 517, fol. 20b, no. 95. Also see Gundersheim, Adler MS. 935, no. 36, where the payment was specifically termed "*sekar baṭṭalah*" (the *shammash* or court beadle also received payment in this case). Examples of payment receipts from this period can be found in YIVO MS. RG 128 (folder 77–78) attached to fol. 170b, and on an unpaginated slip that was placed in this YIVO manuscript but belongs to case no. 248 in the Gundersheim diary.

50. On the establishment of this *kloysz*, see Frankfurt *Memorbuch*, fol. 259b, as well as Horovitz, *Abney zikkaron*, no. 3603. On the history of the institution of the *kloysz* and possible parallels in the Christian community, see Elchanan Reiner, "Hon, maᶜamad ḥebrati ve-talmud Torah: ha-qeloyz be-ḥebrah ha-yehudit be-mizraḥ eyropah," *Zion* 58, no. 3 (1993): 290–99. Regarding the *kloysz* in early modern Germany, see Herman Pollack, *Jewish Folkways in Germanic Lands (1648–1806)* (Cambridge, Mass.: M.I.T. Press, 1971), 72–73; Breuer, *Ohaley Torah*, 25–26, 301–3, 306–8; and Monika Preuss, *Gelehrte Juden: Lernen als Frömmigkeitsideal in der frühen Neuzeit*, Hamburger Beiträge zur Geschichte der Deutschen Juden 31 (Göttingen: Wallstein, 2007), 43–127. Reiss's *kloysz* was not the first *kloysz* in Frankfurt, for Glikl bat Leb of Hamlen's son

Gundersheim's efforts as a teacher and mentor were the first accomplishments listed in his entry in the *Memorbuch.* He was said to have spent each day until noon (presumably not on the Sabbath and Festivals) in the study hall teaching Talmud and commentaries to the children of the poor.[51] He was also said to have given of his own time and money to assist these children. In this, Gundersheim seems to have been helped by his first wife, Relcha, who was also said to have helped poor yeshiva students.[52]

Gundersheim's extra-judicial activities were not unique among his judicial colleagues in Frankfurt. Rabbi Jacob Schames (d. 1785) spent his days teaching, and died while living in the Samson Wertheim *kloysz* where presumably he was head of the study hall.[53] Rabbi Abraham Trier (d. 1794) served as head of the Scheyer *kloysz* and later the Wertheim *kloysz.*[54] Another member of the court, Rabbi Mendele Lilg (d. 1790), spent "about thirty years" in the study hall teaching youngsters, including Rabbi Moses Sofer (1762–1839; later known as "Ḥata″m Sofer," an acronym for one of his works) who would gain great fame as the rabbi of Bratislava (Pressburg) and as a leading advocate of traditional Jewish life in the face of the advent of Reform Judaism.[55] Rabbi Mendel Samst (d. 1815), who also served on the Frankfurt judiciary, eventually became the leader of the Reiss

studied in a Frankfurt *kloysz* (see Glikl bat Leb of Hamlen, *Glikl zikronot 1691–1719*, edited and translated by Chava Turniansky [Jerusalem: Shazar, 2006], 451; also see Reiner, 298–99). For a student's point of view on life in the Frankfurt *kloysz*, see the material cited and translated in Simḥah Assaf, *Meqorot le-toledot ha-ḥinuk be-Yisraʾel*, vol. 1, ed. Shmuel Glick (Jerusalem: Jewish Theological Seminary, 2002), 383–90. Regarding the position of "second" in the *kloysz*, see document no. 226 in this collection.

51. See Frankfurt *Memorbuch*, fol. 350a. Poor students were an integral part of the *kloysz* in early eighteenth-century Mannheim (see Assaf, *Meqorot le-toledot ha-ḥinuk*, vol. 1, 257, no. 17). Whether this was true in the Reiss *kloysz* as well, I do not know.

52. See her entry in the Frankfurt *Memorbuch*, fol. 301a. The wives of other leaders of yeshivas also seem to have helped their husbands. For example, see Horovitz, *Abney zikkaron*, no. 3894, the gravestone of Yentela, wife of Rabbi Nathan Maas, as well as Frankfurt *Memorbuch*, fol. 299b.

53. See Frankfurt *Memorbuch*, fol. 295a. In the Wertheim *kloysz*, the rabbi who headed the institution was given the right to live in the *kloysz* (see Gundersheim, Adler MS. 935, no. 226). Also see Koren-Loeb, "Das Memorbuch zu Frankfurt," 605–6.

54. See Gundersheim, Adler MS. 935, no. 226. Both Trier and Schames were termed *"ab beyt din be-qeloyz"* (head of the rabbinic court of the *kloysz*; see Horovitz, *Abney zikkaron*, nos. 3964, 4130, as well as in the Frankfurt *Memorbuch*). There is no evidence that there was a rabbinic court in the *kloysz* and, in this context, the term "ab beyt din" may have meant "head" or "president" of the *kloysz* (see Elchanan Reiner, "Hon, maʿamad ḥebrati ve-talmud Torah," 310–12 with notes 52, 57; cf., Preuss, *Gelehrte Juden*, 130–31).

55. See Frankfurt *Memorbuch*, fol. 317a. A native of Frankfurt, Sofer explicitly counted Lilg among his teachers (see Moses Sofer, *Sefer ḥata″m sofer* [Oraḥ ḥayyim], reprint, 1895 [Jerusalem: Meqor, 1970], no. 156).

study hall after having been in the Kann *kloysz*.[56] Although members of the *battey din* were typically involved in educational endeavors, this did not prevent them from taking other jobs to supplement their incomes. For example, Rabbi Lezer Wallau (d. 1821) was an agent in the transaction of the sale of a house, for which he received compensation.[57] Rabbis Meʾir Schiff (d. 1807), Trier, and Zanvil Trach (d. 1796) argued a case before the court on behalf of charitable causes (although it is not clear that they received remuneration for this), while Trier received payment in exchange for performing certain unspecified rites in a benefactor's memory.[58]

In addition to teaching young people, Gundersheim led a study group in Talmud presumably made up of adult men. The group strove to complete the entire corpus of the Babylonian Talmud and, according to the *Memorbuch*, they succeeded in finishing "a number" of the Six Talmudic Orders.[59] Gundersheim also gave public sermons and had interests beyond Talmud and Jewish law that are said to have included Hebrew grammar.[60] His entry in the *Memorbuch* conveys an image of a man who, while not the leading talmudic scholar of his age, was accomplished in rabbinic literature and well-liked by his community.[61] This image is reinforced

---

56. See Frankfurt *Memorbuch*, fol. 445a, as well as Horovitz, *Abney zikkaron*, no. 4810 (1815), and Koren-Loeb, "Das Memorbuch zu Frankfurt," 595.
57. See Gundersheim, Adler MS. 935, nos. 195 and 59. On Wallau, see Brocke and Carlebach, *Biographisches Handbuch*, no. 1823, as well as Horovitz, *Rabbaney Franqfurṭ*, 236.
58. Gundersheim, Adler MS. 935, no. 59. Also see no. 52, where Schiff argued a case for his sister. Again, it is not clear that he was paid for this. Schiff, who was the head of the Reiss *kloysz* at the time of his death, served on the court for almost 40 years (see Frankfurt *Memorbuch*, fol. 416b, as well as the material in Brocke and Carlebach, *Biographisches Handbuch*, no. 1582, and his gravestone in Michael Brocke, *Der alte jüdische Friedhof zu Frankfurt am Main: unbekannte Denkmäler und Inschriften* [Sigmaringen: J. Thorbecke, 1996], 390–93). On Trach, see Frankfurt *Memorbuch*, fol. 354a, as well as Brocke and Carlebach, no. 0323. Regarding Trier and his benefactor, see Gundersheim, Adler MS. 935, no. 140.
59. It is not clear whether this was part of Gundersheim's responsibilities in the *kloysz*. If this was an "extra activity," it is not known whether he received payment for it. Teaching classes for free was a notable activity in contemporary Frankfurt and no mention was made of Gundersheim having done this gratis (cf., the entry for Ziskind Stern [d. 1802] in Frankfurt *Memorbuch*, fol. 390a). This study group was not connected to the now popular *daf yomi* (lit., "daily folio") form of Talmud study that only began in the 1920s.
60. In the Lemle Reinganum *kloysz* established in early eighteenth-century Mannheim, Hebrew grammar was an accepted part of the curriculum (see Assaf, *Meqorot le-toledot ha-ḥinuk*, vol. 1, 256, no. 12).
61. Even well-liked people could be the object of malicious comments made in the course of a dispute. Jacob Schwab, a yeshiva student from outside of Frankfurt, came to study for the rabbinate in a Frankfurt yeshiva or *kloysz* ("jüdische Universität"). At some point he was accused of inappropriate behavior, including profaning the Sabbath. In response, he lashed out against Rabbis Meʾir Schiff and Ḥayyim Gundersheim, presumably in their capacities as leaders of the

by a postscript in one of the cases in Gundersheim's diary. In April 1780, two days after the court had given its decision in a liability case, Gundersheim accompanied Feitel of Kassel to the synagogue where he was to take an oath regarding money he denied owing a local Frankfurt resident. That Gundersheim, rather than one of the other two judges who heard the case, accompanied the deponent to the synagogue — as happened in other instances — suggests that Gundersheim was seen as the junior member of the court entrusted with doing some of the court's more mundane tasks.[62] That being said, Gundersheim had sufficient personal skills to convince Feitel to relent on his claims and meet with the head of the court, Rabbi Nathan Maas, to work out a compromise between him and his legal adversary.

The Judiciary

Ḥayyim Gundersheim served on the rabbinic court during a rather unusual, if not anomalous, period in the legal history of the Jewish community in early modern Frankfurt. From at least the 1620s the community had used an electoral college of lay leaders to appoint judicial panels. Each year the court was dissolved and a new court was selected, often composed of the same members.[63] This arrangement continued through the seventeenth century, albeit with intermittent delays in making appointments.[64] In 1697 the community expanded the court system by establishing a second tribunal, as was done in other relatively large Jewish communities such as Prague and Cracow.[65] The two Frankfurt courts did not sit simultaneously but consecutively, each for about half a year.[66] Each court had a president or head

Reiss *kloysz*. See Verena Kasper, "Die Frankfurter Judengemeinde und der Reichshofrat unter Joseph II. (1765–1790)," Ph.D. diss. (Graz: Karl-Franzens-Universität, 2009), 665–66.

62. Gundersheim, Adler MS. 935, no. 122. Also see nos. 65, 107, and 213. In the latter case it was also Gundersheim who was asked by the other members of the court to leave the proceedings to ask a legal question of Rabbi Pinḥas Horowitz.

63. Segall, Pinqas Frankfurṭ, no. 111 (May 1621). Segall noted that this was the earliest extant ordinance from Frankfurt calling for the annual dissolution of the court (n. 9). It gives no reason as to why the court was to be disbanded annually.

64. See Segall, Pinqas Frankfurṭ, nos. 177–79 (1635–1638), 181–82 (1639–1640), 186–92 (1641–47), 194 (1654), 195, (1657), 196–99 (1659–62), 301 (1670), 303–4 (1671, 1673), 306–9 (1674–78), 309a–b (1681–82), 312–14 (1683–85), 316–19 (1686–89), and 349–56 (1691–98).

65. See Simḥah Assaf, *Battey ha-din ve-sidreyhem aḥarey ḥatimat ha-talmud* (Jerusalem: n.p., 1924), 49–50. Cracow had three courts that dealt with different issues based on the value/nature of the case. In addition, in the summer of 1683 the Cracow community renewed a privilege to a local guild that empowered it to establish courts to judge its own members (see Wettstein, "Dibrey ḥefeẓ," 31–32).

66. Segall, Pinqas Frankfurṭ, no. 355 (1697). Previously, an extra court had been added for the period of the Frankfurt commercial fair (see no. 110 [1621]).

of the court (*ab beyt din*), although the chief rabbi of Frankfurt was the head of the rabbinic judicial system by dint of his position.[67] At the end of a full year, the community made new appointments to both courts. The rotation of courts was not unknown in contemporary Jewish communities. In the 1730s, and perhaps for some time before and thereafter, there were four rotating rabbinic tribunals in the Galician town of Brody (presently in Ukraine). Each tribunal had an *ab beyt din* and sat for a week. After four weeks the rotation began anew.[68]

In 1754 the community reissued its ordinances regarding the appointment of judges. The use of an electoral college continued with four *parnasim*, three preceptors of communal funds (*heqesh gabbaʾim*), and twelve members of the community at large chosen by sortition.[69] Community members (*baʿaley batim*) had to have a net worth of over 3,000 guldens, be over the age of thirty, have been married for at least three years, and could not be closely related to one of the other electors in order to be eligible to be selected.[70] The electoral college was to meet each Hebrew month of Adar (late February, early March) to appoint twelve *dayyanim*, six regular judges and six alternates.[71] The appointment of alternates was important because litigants could be related to members of the court, forcing certain judges to recuse themselves.[72] Moreover, the community recognized that, in the course of life, dis-

67. This was not unique to Frankfurt. See Assaf, *Battey ha-din ve-sidreyhem*, 49.

68. See the introduction of Jacob Landau to his father's responsa (Landau, *Responsa*, 32; the material was cited by N.M. Gelber, *Toledot yehudey Brody*, vol. 6 of *ʿArim ve-imahot be-Yisraʾel*, ed. Y.L. Maimon [Jerusalem: Mossad Harav Kook, 1955], 55 with n. 30). Jacob noted that his father was in his early twenties when first appointed to the court. Since Ezekiel Landau was born in 1713 this would make the observation valid for at least about the mid-1730s.

69. The use of lots to choose an electoral college that would then make further choices had parallels in both Jewish and non-Jewish systems of government in earlier periods. See my *Ideals Face Reality: Jewish Law and Life in Poland, 1550–1655*, Monographs of the Hebrew Union College 21 (Cincinnati: Hebrew Union College Press, 1997), 39; Nicolai Rubinstein, *The Government of Florence Under the Medici (1434 to 1494)*, 2d ed. (Oxford: Clarendon, 1997), 4–5 with n. 4; and Robert Finaly, *Politics in Renaissance Venice* (New Brunswick, N.J.: Rutgers University Press, 1980), 141–43. According to a view in the Talmud, the seventy elders chosen by Moses were also picked by lot (see B.T., *Sanhedrin* 17a) but they were not chosen to be an electoral college. On the Church's opposition to the use of lots in ecclesiastical elections, see Thomas Aquinas, *Summa Theologiae*, vol. 40, ed. and trans. T. F. O'Aleara and M. J. Duffy (London: Blackfriars, 1964), 67–69.

70. In the mid-1780s, the scribe Isaac Schiff was paid 200 guldens per annum and provided with food. When Schiff declared that he did not want to eat with his employer, he was given an extra 2 guldens per week for food (see Gundersheim, Adler MS. 935, no. 217). Although Schiff said that the food allowance was inadequate, this anecdote gives some sense of what income and expenses were and makes it clear that 3,000 guldens was a large sum.

71. ŻIH MS. 517, fol. 13b, no. 66.

72. See, for example Gundersheim, Adler MS. 935, no. 117, in which Gundersheim recused himself.

putes and hard feelings could arise between families and individuals, and litigants might feel that a particular judge was less than impartial towards them. Thus each of the parties had the right to disqualify one — but not more than one — of the judges on a tribunal if a litigant felt that the judge "hated him."[73]

This arrangement for the selection of judges soon broke down. In December 1768 the leadership declared that on 22 January 1769 the nineteen lay leaders would gather to elect only nine judges, six regular members of the two rabbinic courts and three alternates.[74] These would be the last elections for more than a quarter of a century.[75]

The failure of the community to appoint *dayyanim* for over twenty-five years does not mean that there were no active rabbinic tribunals staffed by knowledgeable jurists in Frankfurt during this time — Rabbi Ḥayyim Gundersheim's diary and other sources show that there most definitely were.[76] In the fall of 1779, in 1781, in the spring of 1785, and in 1793 there was a full complement of six judges plus the chief rabbi of Frankfurt, Pinḥas (Phinehas) Horowitz (d. 1805), functioning in the community.[77] At least four *dayyanim* appointed in 1769 died before elections were held again in March 1795: Rabbis Anshel Zunz (d. 1775), Isaac Meʾir Schwarzschild (d. 1777), Jacob Schames (d. 1785), and Mendele Lilg (d. 1789).[78] For a while the community may have relied on alternates; later they may have made ad hoc appointments to meet ongoing needs.[79] One way or another, the Frankfurt

Also see nos. 49, 50, 110, and 118.

73. ŻIH MS. 517, fol. 25b, no. 115.

74. Again, four of the electors were to be *parnasim*, three to be preceptors, and twelve, householders, according to the same conditions laid out in 1754 (Segall, Pinqas Frankfurṭ, no. 425 [1768]). This was not the only arrangement for choosing judges that the Frankfurt Jewish community had known. In 1633 the community had a somewhat different procedure but this too relied on an electoral college for choosing the most worthy candidates (see Segall, Pinqas Frankfurṭ, no. 176 [1633]).

75. In March 1795, the communal leadership noted that there had not been a formal selection of *dayyanim* for over twenty-five years (see Segall, Pinqas Frankfurṭ, no. 494 [4 March 1795]; also see Horovitz, *Rabbaney Franqfurṭ*, 169, as well as Gotzmann, *Jüdische Autonomie*, 242). Why elections did not take place remains a matter of speculation (see Horovitz, *Rabbaney Franqfurṭ*, 169).

76. I have used the term "jurist" here and throughout to refer to judges or decisors and *not* to all those who might have received advanced legal training.

77. Regarding members of the court during 1779, 1781, 1785, and 1793, see Segall, Pinqas Frankfurṭ, no. 483 (1779); Horovitz, *Rabbaney Franqfurṭ*, 155 with no. 19; Gundersheim, Adler MS. 935, no. 139; YIVO MS. RG 128 (folder 77–78), fol. 56b; and Appendix 3.

78. On Schames and Lilg, see Brocke and Carlebach, *Biographisches Handbuch*, nos. 1571 and 1115.

79. Rabbis Lezer Wallau and Mendele Samst (d. 1815, see Brocke and Carlebach, *Biographisches Handbuch*, no. 1551) first appeared in Gundersheim's diary in 1778. Samst's entry in the

Jewish community maintained a pool of judges — all of whom were male as Jewish law does not allow females to be members of the judiciary — who serviced the community.[80]

During the early period of Gundersheim's tenure on the court there seems to have been a constant shuffling of tribunals. In the summer of 1774 Gundersheim sat on the court with Rabbis Abraham Trier and Meʾir Schiff. Earlier in the year he had been with Rabbis Meʾir Schwarzschild and Abraham Trier. Later in the year he would serve with Rabbis Anshel Zunz and Jacob Schames.[81] Perhaps Gundersheim was still just an alternate. With time this juggling of judicial panels abated, and by the mid-1780s Gundersheim was fairly consistently sitting with Rabbis Meʾir Schiff and Nathan Maas.[82] From the community's perspective this arrangement may not have been ideal, and may well explain a clause in the 1795 appointment of judges that demanded a return to rotating the composition of rabbinic courts every six months based on a lottery.[83]

With the exception of the head of the rabbinic court, Rabbi Pinḥas Horowitz, who was a native of Czortków (today in Ukraine) and had served in a number of eastern European communities before coming to Frankfurt in 1772, all the *dayyanim* on the Frankfurt rabbinic court with whom Gundersheim served were members of well-established Frankfurt families. The Trach family arrived in Frankfurt in the mid-seventeenth century, as did the Samst, Trier, Maas, Schames, and Schwarzschild clans.[84] The Schiff family may have arrived in the late sixteenth

---

Memorbuch (fol. 445a) noted that he was a member of the rabbinic court for almost 40 years. This would put his first appointment in the 1770s. Both Wallau and Samst received full appointments in 1795 (see Segall, Pinqas Frankfurṭ, no. 494).

80. The requirement that judges be male can be found in *Shulḥan ʿaruk*, Ḥoshen mishpaṭ 7.4 with the sources cited by Rabbi Elijah ben Solomon Zalman of Vilnius, *Biʾur ha-Gera"ʾ* (Jerusalem: Machon Shulhan Melakim, 2004), n. 14.
81. See Gundersheim, Adler MS. 935, nos. 38–48.
82. Gundersheim, Adler MS. 935, nos. 186–200. According to a communal decision taken in the fall of 1770, when Maas was appointed acting rabbi of Frankfurt, he was specifically exempted from sitting on the court in cases worth less than 50 reichstalers (cited in Horovitz, *Rabbaney Franqfurṭ*, 140 n. 11).
83. There were years in which Gundersheim heard cases for more than six months of the year (see, for example, 1776 or 1781). He could have been an alternate during these periods, or perhaps the six month rule was not always followed. Nevertheless, Gundersheim's presence on judicial panels often occurred in "bunches" (e.g., January, February, March or October, November, December, January).
84. See Alexander Dietz, *Stammbuch der Frankfurter Juden. Geschichtliche Mitteilungen über die Frankfurter jüdischen Familien von 1349–1849, nebst einem Plane der Judengasse* (Frankfurt: J. St. Goar, 1907), 308, regarding the Trach family; 23 (Samst); 308 (Trier); 189–90 (Maas); 253 (Schames) and 279 (Schwarzschild). An English translation of this work was published as

century, and Rabbi Mendele Lilg's ancestors had resided in Frankfurt from at least the late sixteenth century.[85] In fact, Gundersheim's family was perhaps the most recent of the arrivals. Moreover, all of the judges appear to have been appointed from the ranks of the talmudic academy rather than from among those who had gained practical experience working in the courts as representatives of litigants.[86] This suggests that the contemporary community continued to place a premium on talmudic scholarship rather than on the bureaucratic skills that well-experienced advocates who appeared before the court may have acquired.

Litigants, Their Representatives, and Their Cases

The Frankfurt rabbinic court was used by individuals from diverse socio-economic rungs of society — from maidservants without resident rights to the wealthiest members of the *Judengasse* (lit., "the Jewish lane") such as the Mai (May) and Rothschild families.[87] This does not mean that both individual Jews and the Jewish community itself did not turn to non-Jewish courts, for they certainly did, as will be discussed; but the broad-based use of the court in Frankfurt was in marked contrast to the character of the rabbinic court in contemporary Metz. There, as Jay Berkovitz has shown, those who came before the *beyt din* were disproportionately from the communal and rabbinic elites and their families.[88]

Women, married and single, were major litigants before the Frankfurt court, both as plaintiffs and defendants. They were involved in estate claims, commercial and real estate transactions, contract disputes and requests for payment of their

---

The Jewish Community of Frankfurt: A Genealogical Study 1349–1849, trans. Frances Martin (Camelford: Vanderher, 1988).

85. On the Schiffs, see Dietz, *Stammbuch der Frankfurter Juden*, 257–58; on the Lilg family, see Ettlinger, *Ēlē tōldōt*, 18.7.1789, 3.3.1744, 27.10.1726, 15.6.1677, 28.1.1654, um 1623 (Isaac Bachrach-Mendele), 23.8.1599.

86. In some early modern non-Jewish societies (e.g., Castile, Portugal, imperial magistrates in eighteenth-century Prussia) judges were also generally appointed from the academy (i.e., universities) rather than from among advocates (see Richard L. Kagan, *Lawsuits and Litigants in Castile, 1500–1700* [Chapel Hill: University of North Carolina Press, 1981], 76, 177 with n. 41). A much different model existed in early modern Venice, where aristocratic status rather than legal training or experience was a requirement for judicial appointment. On the system in Venice and its rationales, see James E. Shaw, *The Justice of Venice: Authorities and Liberties in the Urban Economy 1550–1700* (Oxford: Oxford University Press, 2006), 11–18.

87. On the wealth of the Mai and Rothschild families in the year 1800, see Dietz, *Stammbuch der Frankfurter Juden*, 197.

88. See Jay Berkovitz, *Protocols of Justice: The Pinkas of the Metz Rabbinic Court 1771–1789* (Leiden: Brill, forthcoming).

marriage contracts.[89] At least one woman, Glikhe, widow of Meʾir Flörsheim, acted as the administrator of her late husband's estate, a position that may have brought her before the court more than the one time mentioned in Gundersheim's diary.[90] However, perhaps with the exception of one case involving a dispute over fees between various matchmakers, in all instances in which married women litigated before the courts they did so either with their husbands or with the expressed written consent of their husbands.[91] Married women were legally subservient to their husbands, and they appear not to have been permitted to undertake legal action independently except in the case of divorce proceedings. It was only single women, whether spinsters or widows, who approached the court independently. Single women whose fathers had died or who had attained a level of independence had no one to control them; widows were freed from their husbands' control through death.[92]

The *beyt din* may not have been anxious to address this legal handicap of married women even in cases when a husband was disabled and unable to grant his wife expressed consent to conduct a transaction or manage familial assets. Neta Wezlar appears to have been unable to speak or give legally acceptable instructions during much of a lengthy illness that afflicted him the last 13 years of his life until his death in August 1784.[93] His wife, Rechle Wezlar, wanted to sell some of her husband's properties during the period of his incapacitation, and to do so she approached the non-Jewish authorities in Wetzlar for help.[94] The royal commis-

89. For example, Gundersheim, Adler MS. 935, nos. 121, 164, 242 (estates); 74 (commercial); 66, 155, 186 (real estate); 150, 151 (contracts); 138, 143 (marriage contracts).
90. Gundersheim, Adler MS. 935, no. 176.
91. Gundersheim, Adler MS. 935, nos. 164 and 211; cf., no. 39.
92. Life-long single women lived in the Frankfurt Jewish community, but determining their numbers requires further research. In contemporary non-Jewish society their numbers reached about 10–20% of all women and these numbers tended to be greater in towns than in villages (see Maryanne Kowaleski, "Singlewomen in Medieval and Early Modern Europe: The Demographic Perspective," in *Singlewomen in the European Past, 1250–1800*, ed. Judith Bennett, Amy Froide [Philadelphia: University of Pennsylvania Press, 1999], 53–54; also see Sheilagh Ogilvie, *A Bitter Living: Women, Markets, and Social Capital in Early Modern Germany* [Oxford: Oxford University Press, 2003], 40–54). Regarding unmarried women in Württemberg (near Stuttgart), Ogilvie noted that only half of the unmarried women in their late twenties lived with their parents, and that as these women grew older they were less likely to live with their parents or be servants in the homes of others (270–72).
93. Frankfurt *Memorbuch*, fol. 292b.
94. It is unknown whether Rechle petitioned the rabbinic court or the Jewish community before turning to the authorities in Wetzlar. According to Neta's entry in the Frankfurt *Memorbuch*, while he was well he had had dealings with the non-Jewish authorities regarding Jewish prisoners (fol. 292b) and perhaps Rechle was able to build on these connections.

sion in Wetzlar assigned her rights over the properties, which she sold in 1779, leaving the rabbinic court to recognize formally her circumvention of communal authority.[95] The rabbinic court seems to have learned a lesson. A few years later, in August 1782, Rechle's son successfully approached the court on her behalf, winning an assurance that her upcoming sale of property would be recognized.[96]

Although some litigants in Frankfurt approached the court directly, most realized that they did not have the necessary skills and experience to advance their cases or to respond effectively to the various charges against them. To meet the needs of litigants, a cadre of more than a dozen legal representatives served the Frankfurt Jewish community during the period covered by Gundersheim's diary. Though there was some talmudic opposition to the use of representation, by the late Middle Ages it had become commonplace, and at least one listing in the Frankfurt *Memorbuch* praised someone for performing this function during his lifetime.[97]

There is no information regarding the formal training of such legal representatives (all of whom were male), yet it would seem that all who served in this capacity had extensive training in rabbinic texts.[98] Moses Auch was said to have studied with "great rabbis" when he was young and Herz Ulf was described as having gone from yeshiva to yeshiva to learn from different teachers.[99] Meʾir Maas studied

---

95. Gundersheim, Adler MS. 935, nos. 111, 112, and 124.
96. Gundersheim, Adler MS. 935, no. 155.
97. On talmudic opposition to the use of representation see B.T., *Shabuʿot* 31a. For a general overview of the use of representation in Jewish law, see Assaf, *Battey ha-din ve-sidreyhem*, 95–99; Nahum Rakover, *Ha-sheliḥut ve-ha-harshaʾah be-mishpaṭ ha-ʿibri* (Jerusalem: Mossad Harav Kook, 1972), 308–36; Aaron Kirschenbaum, "Representation in Litigation in Jewish Law," *Diné Israel* 6 (1975): xxv–xli, particularly n. 71; Yedidya Dinari, *Ḥakmey Ashkenaz be-shalhey yemey ha-beynayyim: darkeyhem ve-kitbeyhem be-halakah* (Jerusalem: Bialik Institute, 1984), 128–32; and Eric Zimmer, *Harmony and Discord: An Analysis of the Decline of Jewish Self-Government in 15th Century Central Europe* (New York: Yeshiva University Press, 1970), 84. On opposition to legal representation in late sixteenth and early seventeenth-century Frankfurt, see Sendik, "Beyn din le-pesher," 44. Praise is found in the *Memorbuch* entry for Zalman Geiger (fol. 251b), who acted as a representative. Even if this praise was scripted and paid for by family members, they nonetheless appear to have taken pride in his work.
98. I have not included in this list of representatives learned sons who represented their fathers and mothers. Sometimes such sons were indeed well-experienced advocates (e.g., Gundersheim, Adler MS. 935, no. 84), but in other instances there is nothing to suggest that they performed this function for anyone but their family (for example, no. 57 with Frankfurt *Memorbuch*, fol. 257b, and no. 129 with Frankfurt *Memorbuch*, fol. 437b, both cases of sons who represented their widowed mothers, and no. 70 with Frankfurt *Memorbuch*, fol. 451b, a case of a son who represented his father).
99. Frankfurt *Memorbuch*, fols. 384b and 292b.

with scholars and the leading rabbis of the generation were said to have sung his praises.[100] Beyond their early training, these men all continued to study as adults and some even taught Talmud in the community. Leb Schwarzschild was among the first to study in the Reiss *kloysz* and later continued his studies in the Kann study hall. He also taught a Talmud class for youth.[101] Benedit Hanau also studied in the Reiss study hall.[102] Meʾir Maas was said not only to have studied but to have taught Talmud and to have had many students, while Aaron Scheyer participated in the group that studied the Talmud daily with the goal of eventually completing it from beginning to end — the very same group that Gundersheim once led.[103]

What differentiated these individuals from members of the court often may have been a matter of chance. Leb Schwarzshild was described as having studied day and night, but immediately after his marriage his house burned down and he lost his wealth. This severe setback must have affected his studies. Eventually Schwarzshild followed his father as the community's scribe, but he never became a judge.[104] Zalman Geiger was an ascetic who not only fasted but was said to have afflicted his body with various forms of self-mortification from his youth to his old age.[105] A man who acted in such a fashion may not have been considered an acceptable candidate for the bench. Meʾir Maas's brother Rabbi Nathan Maas sat on the court, and his appointment precluded Meʾir's.[106] Each of these individuals was learned enough to prepare cases for others and present them to the court, but they never became judges themselves. Beyond personal circumstances, local politics may also have prevented otherwise qualified candidates from being appointed to the court. One can also not rule out the possibility that local politics could serve in an individual's favor; Gundersheim's own appointment to the court may have been influenced by his father's position in the community.[107]

Given that Moses Auch appeared in more than fifty cases recorded by Gundersheim, one would assume that he and other representatives received remuneration for their services. Gundersheim's diary provides no information

100. Frankfurt *Memorbuch*, fol. 317b.
101. Frankfurt *Memorbuch*, fol. 457a.
102. Frankfurt *Memorbuch*, fol. 413a.
103. Frankfurt *Memorbuch*, fol. 317b, regarding Maas, and fol. 264a with respect to Scheyer.
104. Frankfurt *Memorbuch*, fol. 457a as well as fol. 340b regarding his taking his father's place in 1794 after the period of mourning. His father had been the scribe since 1741.
105. Frankfurt *Memorbuch*, fol. 251b.
106. On the prohibition of two brothers sitting together on the same court, see *Shulḥan ʿaruk*, Ḥoshen mishaṭ 7.9.
107. Given that the Gundersheims were not an old Frankfurt family, Rabbi Ḥayyim's father may have had a particular interest in seeing his son on the rabbinic court and enjoying the prestige and legitimization that came with it.

about this. If representatives were paid, there was either too much competition, not enough litigation, and/or the remuneration for such services was not enough to support full-time work. Auch, who presumably also appeared in cases not mentioned by Gundersheim, was said to have been very busy trying to support his family in a number of ways and was described in his entry in the *Memorbuch* as "a poor man."[108] Perhaps Auch's financial situation was due to mismanagement of funds or an unexpected business loss, but his experience suggests that one of the busiest legal representatives of his time may not have been paid enough to maintain a comfortable way of life for himself and his family.

Not every learned person in the community became a legal representative. Abraham Flesch was described in his entry in the *Memorbuch* as an expert in some sections of the Talmud as well as in rabbinic authorities. Towards the end of his life he stopped working and dedicated himself to study and prayer, but there is no evidence that he represented others before the court.[109] Moses Fulda was also said to have been a scholar of Jewish law who had great familiarity with the Talmud and rabbinic authorities. However, he had to make a living, and being a legal representative was not one of the ways that he chose to do so.[110] Mordecai Adler, son of Rabbi Nathan Adler, was said to have both studied and taught Talmud, rabbinic literature, and rabbinic legal authorities, yet he too had to work to support his family.[111] These men were fine scholars and, like Gundersheim and some of those who served as legal representatives, were often given the honorific title *moreynu* ("our teacher") after their deaths; yet they made their livings outside of the courtroom.[112] Perhaps their counsel was never sought out. As yet, there is insufficient information on how representatives were chosen to be sure.

The men and women who appeared before Gundersheim and his colleagues generally had representation. In some instances the record reflects that the litigant was present before the court together with his or her representative; in other instances, the representative was formally empowered by the litigant and appeared before the court alone, even though the litigant was a Frankfurt resident.[113] Yet, representation was not seen as a necessity by Jewish law, the community, or individuals. The community did not provide representation for those who could

108. Frankfurt *Memorbuch*, fol. 384b.
109. Frankfurt *Memorbuch*, fol. 289a.
110. Frankfurt *Memorbuch*, fol. 369b.
111. Frankfurt *Memorbuch*, fol. 436b.
112. Zalman Geiger (Frankfurt *Memorbuch*, fol. 251b) and Herz Ulf (fol. 292b) were both posthumously honored with the title *moreynu*.
113. In Gundersheim, Adler MS. 935, no. 51, fol. 54b, the litigant appeared before the court with his representative. In no. 40, he did not.

not afford it, and in some cases litigants with representation disputed their cases against those without. The court did not see this as an advantage that disqualified the proceedings. Thus, Gumpel Mai was represented by Moses Auch in his dispute with Sorle, widow of Me᾿ir Schuster, over repairs to be made to a house, while she represented herself and her children.[114] Ẓipper Levy, a maidservant in Frankfurt who apparently came from Eibingen (about 65 kilometers west of Frankfurt), represented herself in her dispute, but her protagonist, from Eibingen, did not. Perhaps in these cases the individuals without representation could not afford it.[115] Courts were not the exclusive domains of professionals.

A number of areas of Jewish law occupied the Frankfurt rabbinic court.[116] Approximately five per cent of the cases described by Gundersheim dealt with rituals that required a rabbinic court, such as *ḥaliẓah*, a quasi-divorce between a childless widow and her late husband's brother (see Deut. 25.5–10).[117] In another matter Jacob Reiss passed away leaving his widow pregnant with their first child. It so happened that a boy was born, and it was the court's responsibility to decide what should be done. According to the Torah, if the first-born child of a woman was a vaginally delivered male, he had to be redeemed by the father from a *kohen* (priest) for five silver coins (see Ex. 13.13, Num. 18.15–16). In this case, the obligation to redeem the boy remained even though the father had died. The question was who would redeem him? The matter was brought before the court, which not only decided what would be done but saw to it that its decision was carried out.[118]

Similarly, when the community wished to reconstruct the local hospice, communal leaders consulted the rabbinic courts for advice on how to build the structure. Rabbis were not architects or engineers, but they were experts in Jewish ritual law. Even in contemporary times, male members of the priestly caste (*kohanim*) were prohibited from becoming ritually impure through contact with the dead,

---

114. Gundersheim, Adler MS. 935, no. 79. Also see nos. 186, 171, and 207.

115. Gundersheim, Adler MS. 935, no. 81. Also see no. 240; cf., however, nos. 63 and 121. In case no. 63 all four of the maidservants had representation, but this was a dispute over lottery winnings and, believing that they were assured of some income, they may have felt confident that they could pay any legal fees. In case no. 121, the maidservant had representation in her claims for back wages, expenses, et al., against the estate of her former employer. Here there may have been too much at stake not to hire a representative.

116. Private ritual queries related to the laws of menstruation or questions of kashrut were brought to individual rabbis rather than rabbinic courts. The court did deal with a matter of communal concern connected to the laws of ritual purity (*niddah*; see Gundersheim, Adler MS. 935, no. 191; YIVO MS. RG 128 [folder 77–78], fols. 113a–b).

117. In general on the scope of the court's activity, see Sendik, "Beyn din le-pesher," 22–33.

118. Gundersheim, Adler MS. 935, no. 37.

except for their own next of kin (i.e., parents, wife, children, brother, and sister).[119] This included not only direct contact with a corpse, but also being under the same roof as the dead. Since it was assumed that there would often be bodies in a hospice, and also because the building bordered the cemetery, rabbis were consulted about how to build the structure in a way that limited the spread of ritual impurity.[120] The rabbis provided detailed instructions on how to do so, and the lay leadership saw to it that these guidelines were carried out in ongoing consultation with the rabbinic court.

The court also heard various types of disputes between Jews who adhered to the demands of Jewish law and brought their litigation in labor disputes (e.g., conditions of employment and demands for payment), commercial transactions, and contracts before the *beyt din*. These types of cases represent about 20% of the files in Gundersheim's diary. The expertise of the Frankfurt court was also recognized beyond the borders of the town. When a dispute over a dowry arose between Mendel Wertheim of Worms and his prospective son-in-law, Ḥayyim Leb of Fürth, the case was brought to the Frankfurt court even though the original marriage agreement had been signed in Worms (about 70 km. southwest of Frankfurt) before local leaders. Apparently the Frankfurt *beyt din* was viewed by Jews in nearby communities as an authoritative and neutral venue to attain justice.[121]

The non-Jewish political leadership too, including the Imperial government in Vienna, turned to the Frankfurt rabbinic court.[122] In about 1781 there were approximately 50 Jewish families in Illereichen-Altenstadt (near Ausburg).[123] The community had a cantor who seems to have fulfilled some rabbinic tasks (he is

---

119. See Lev. 21.1–4, *Shulḥan ʿaruk*, Yoreh deʿah 374.4.

120. Gundersheim, Adler MS. 935, no. 252. The problem of ritual impurity in public areas had been raised earlier in the century in the Frankfurt Jewish community as well as in other Jewish communities of the early modern period. See David Malkiel, "Law and Architecture: The Pollution Crisis in the Italian Ghetto," *European Journal of Jewish Studies* 4, no. 2 (2010): 255–76, with specific reference to Frankfurt on 268–69.

121. See Gundersheim, Adler MS. 935, no. 38.

122. See Gundersheim, Adler MS. 935, nos. 188 and 194 (with appendix 6). Note too that the Vice Chancellor of the Palatinate of Mannheim turned to the chief rabbi of Frankfurt for a clarification of the parameters of Jewish law (see below 59). Non-Jewish authorities consulting with rabbinic leaders also took place in contemporary Prague. On this see Sharon Flatto, *The Kabbalistic Culture of Eighteenth-Century Prague: Ezekiel Landau and His Contemporaries* (Oxford: Littman Library of Jewish Civilization, 2010), 51.

123. There were 51 Jewish families in Illereichen-Altenstadt in 1789 (see *Pinqas ha-qehillot: enẓiqlopediyah shel ha-yishubim ha-Yehudiyyim le-min hivvasdam ve-ʿad le-ʾaḥar shoʾat milḥemet ha-ʿolam ha-sheniyyah*, vol. 1 *Germanyah — Baʾvʾaryah*, ed. Baruch Ophir in collaboration with Chasia Turtel-Aberzhanska and Shlomo Schmiedt [Jerusalem: Yad Vashem, 1972], 605–6). I have assumed that there were about 50 families 9 years earlier.

termed a *moreh ẓedeq*, lit. "an instructor of the right way," as well as a *sheliaḥ ẓibbur*, a "cantor"). When the community decided to terminate his employment, a dispute broke out between the two sides.[124] With no rabbi in town, the case was brought before the regional rabbi (*rab ha-medinah*) about 100 kilometers away in Wallerstein, Rabbi Simḥah Bunim Rappaport.[125] However, the Jews of Illereichen-Altenstadt were displeased with Rappaport's decision and appealed to the local non-Jewish authorities. Appeals to the non-Jewish authorities suggest that the frequency with which the decisions of Jewish courts were overturned was high enough to convince individuals that it was worth the time, effort, and money necessary to launch such legal actions. Instead of dealing with this case themselves, the authorities in Schwaben asked the *beyt din* in Frankfurt (over 300 kilometers from Illereichen-Altenstadt) to review Rappaport's ruling. The Frankfurt *dayyanim* sat in a full court of seven with Rabbi Pinḥas Horowitz at their head to consider their response.[126]

Beyond such cases, trusts and estates were a central component of Gundersheim's experience on the court. The court dealt with disputes between heirs, appointed and discharged guardians, and, if necessary, could itself act as a guardian.[127] The *beyt din* also oversaw the liquidation of estates and the distribution of funds to beneficiaries.[128] The sale of the assets of minors or the young by guardians required court permission, and in some instances the court did not give its assent until it had obtained consent from the wards.[129] The court also ruled with respect to custody and child support.[130] Questions regarding distribution from charitable trusts were also brought before the court.[131] Guardianship, trusts, and estates represent about one-fifth of the cases described by Gundersheim.

In addition to deciding legal questions, the court had a number of administrative

---

124. The appellant was an eastern European Jew who may have had different perceptions about appealing to the non-Jewish authorities than the local Jews.
125. On Rappaport, see the approbations to his *Sefer ḥiddushey halakot Rashba"z ʿal masseket Giṭṭin* (Fürth: Isaac ben Leb Buchbinder, 1779), as well as Daniel J. Cohen, "Irgguney 'beney ha-medinah' be-Ashkenaz be-meʾot ha-17 ve-ha-18," Ph.D. diss. (Jerusalem: Hebrew University, 1967), table 6, p. 407. Also see Sendik, "Beyn din le-pesher," 21. With regard to the office of regional rabbi, see Cohen, 157–164, 175–81.
126. Gundersheim, Adler MS. 935, no. 139.
127. See, for example, Gundersheim, Adler MS. 935, nos. 61 and 138. No. 128 is an example of guardians being discharged after the ward had come of age. Cf., however, nos. 164 and 168.
128. Gundersheim, Adler MS. 935, no. 149.
129. Gundersheim, Adler MS. 935, nos. 113 and 214.
130. Gundersheim, Adler MS. 935, no. 138.
131. For example, Gundersheim, Adler MS. 935, nos. 225, 234, and 235.

functions. In one instance the *beyt din* clarified one of its earlier rulings.[132] In another, when someone lost a debt note, the court had to approve its reissue.[133] At one point the court was asked to quell unspecified rumors about a Jewish servant's son that had arisen in the wake of testimony.[134] The court also acted as a trustee holding obligatory notes until a particular action was carried out, and then transferred them to the payee.[135]

Beyond such administrative roles, the court had a "constitutional" function in the community. When the community had questions related to Jewish law or the meaning of communal ordinances, it turned to the court for clarifications.[136] For example, in late November 1766 the community enacted an ordinance forbidding the playing of cards (with some exceptions), late night drinking of wine, beer, and coffee in groups in private homes, and attendance at concerts and comedies. Those who violated the ordinance were to seek a penance from the head of the rabbinic court and were threatened with a fine, half of which would go to the community and half to the authorities.[137] The community warned that those who violated the ordinance would be turned over to the non-Jewish authorities, in the hope that this would ensure the collection of the fine. Making good on threats was more difficult than making them, but by giving the non-Jewish authorities an interest in the matter the Jewish community created a more credible threat and thus enhanced its own authority. But turning a Jew over to the non-Jewish authorities was not a simple matter in Jewish law. To quell any doubts about the legitimacy of the ordinance it was specifically noted that the two rabbinic courts and the president of the court were present when the ordinance was enacted. Not only did the court acknowledge that *halakah* permitted this, but asserted it was a mitzvah to turn such a person over to the authorities for collection of the fine and due punishment.[138] While the Frankfurt rabbinate did not enact the ordinance, their interpretation of it gave it legitimacy.

---

132. Gundersheim, Adler MS. 935, nos. 43 and 44.
133. Gundersheim, Adler MS. 935, no. 43.
134. Gundersheim, Adler MS. 935, no. 240.
135. Gundersheim, Adler MS. 935, no. 60.
136. See, for example, Gundersheim, Adler MS. 935, nos. 100 and 170. This was a known function of rabbinic courts in the Ashkenazic world. See Katz, *Masoret u-mashber*, 99 with n. 9.
137. See Segall, Pinqas Frankfurṭ, no. 412, as well as Mordecai Nadav, "Pinqas qahal Franqfurṭ de-Mayn," *Kiryat Sefer* 31 (1955–56): 513, and Gotzmann, *Jüdische Autonomie*, 254. There is no evidence in Gundersheim's diary of Jews actually being forced to pay such fines to the authorities, yet material from the first half of the seventeenth century shows that this rule had been enforced (see I. Kracauer, "Beiträge zur Geschichte der Frankfurter Juden im dreisßigjährigen Kriege," *Zeitschrift für die Geschichte der Juden in Deutschland* 3 [1889]: 341–42).
138. Cf. *Shulḥan ʿaruk*, Ḥoshen mishpaṭ 388.

One particular case is helpful in delineating the scope of the Frankfurt rabbinic court's powers in this field.[139] Sometime before 1782, the Frankfurt Jewish community appointed Shoʾel (Saul?) ben Shalom Katz of Poland as cantor (*ḥazzan*). The terms of his appointment are not completely known, but he appears to have been given a residence and his wife enjoyed the use of a place in the women's section of the synagogue.[140] From the perspective of the Jewish communal leadership of Frankfurt, the cantor was an employee who was "indentured to the community."[141]

By the summer of 1782 there were rumors that Shoʾel was behaving inappropriately, and the communal leadership turned to the rabbinic court for instruction on what practical steps should be taken to prevent Shoʾel from continuing in his ways. The record does not itemize what exactly it was that Shoʾel was doing, but, given that the court ordered him to stay away from women, presumably womanizing was part of the problem.[142]

However, over the long term, the court's attempts at effecting behavior modification through its order were not successful, for in September 1789 the communal leadership was again consulting with the rabbinic court concerning Shoʾel. The *beyt din* had little new to suggest to improve Shoʾel's behavior, and ordered him to fulfill the guidelines it had set out for him in 1782. However, given Shoʾel's continued lapses, the court prohibited him from leading prayers during the period of the High Holy Days for the next four years.[143] Only after four years would it consider reinstating him.[144] Suitability to serve as a representative of the Jewish community on the High Holy Days was a matter of Jewish law and, at least in the realm of rituals that affected the community, the court had the right to give a practical ruling and impose it on Jewish society.[145]

Unfortunately for all concerned, Shoʾel was not able to follow the directives that he had been given by the court, and in early 1793 he was accused of impregnating his female servant, a charge that he and his supporters denied. The court was again asked by the community to deal with Shoʾel's case. The court, with its full complement of six judges plus Rabbi Pinḥas Horowitz, noted that from a purely halakic perspective it did not have the right to disqualify Shoʾel from being the

139. On this case, also see Sendik, "Beyn din le-pesher," 75–78.

140. Segall, Pinqas Frankfurṭ, no. 446 (1793).

141. The phrase "*meshuʿabadey qahal*" occurs in ŻIH MS. 517, fol. 13b (no. 65). The rabbinic court specifically stated that the rules outlined in these ordinances applied to Shoʾel (see Appendix 3, no. 445).

142. Gundersheim, Adler MS. 935, no. 153.

143. Gundersheim, Adler MS. 935, no. 224, and Segall, Pinqas Frankfurṭ, no. 439 (1789).

144. See YIVO MS. RG 128 (folder 77–78), fol. 70b, cited here at the end of Appendix 3.

145. See *Shulḥan ʿaruk*, Oraḥ ḥayyim 581.1 with Isserles's comments.

communal cantor because there were no witnesses to substantiate the accusations against him. Technically speaking the charges were hearsay, and, therefore, Jewish law could not provide a basis for firing him. The only source that the court could muster for removing Shoʾel from his position was a communal ordinance from 1754 regarding inappropriate behaviors or traits attributed to communal functionaries.[146] The court was the interpreter of the community's regulations, and it ruled that the community had the right to dismiss Shoʾel on the basis of its by-laws; but the court was not responsible for the implementation of communal ordinances and it did not have the authority to fire Shoʾel.[147] Rabbis did not rule the Jewish community in Frankfurt; laymen did. This was neither unique nor new and rabbis accepted it.[148] It was up to the community to terminate Shoʾel, and, with the *beyt din*'s opinion in hand, they did.[149]

The rabbinic court placed checks on the abuse of communal authority while at the same time strengthening legitimate communal control. This does not mean that the court could never take the initiative in certain issues, particularly those related to ritual. There had been a tradition that post-partum women not ritually immerse until at least the forty-first day after the birth of a boy and the eighty-first day after the birth of a girl.[150] This was an old custom in some German communities, including Frankfurt, where already Rabbi Alexander Suslin ha-Kohen (d. 1349) had noted it as the practice.[151] However, this was not the only custom with respect to post-partum ritual purification.[152] Rabbis Joseph Caro (Safed, d. 1575)

---

146. ŻIH MS. 517, fol. 13b (no. 65), cited in Appendix 3.

147. The court interpreted other documents as well, such as wills (see Gundersheim, Adler MS. 935, no. 225). There were other models for the interpretation of communal ordinances in Jewish communities. In this regard, see Aviad Hacohen, "Parshanut taqqanot ha-qahal be-mishpaṭ ha-ʿibri," Ph.D. diss. (Jerusalem: Hebrew University, 2003), 40–59.

148. In early modern Poland too, it was laymen who ruled communities, not rabbis (see my, *Ideals Face Reality*, 38–47). In Spanish-Portuguese Jewish communities in western Europe, lay leaders usurped the rabbis' role in the judicial field (see Menachem Elon, *Ha-mishpaṭ ha-ʿibri toledotav, meqorotav, ʿeqronotav*, 3d ed., vol. 1 [Jerusalem: Magnes, 1992], 32 n. 104; Hacker, "Gebulteyha shel ha-ʾoṭonomyah ha-yehudit," 352–54). In Amsterdam rabbis would recover this right later in the century (see Yosef Kaplan, "Pesaqim mi-beyt ha-din," 2–9).

149. Segall, Pinqas Frankfurṭ, nos. 445 and 446 (both from 1793).

150. Cf., Lev. 12.1–8.

151. The title page of the 1571 (Cracow) edition of the *Sefer ha-aggudah* labels the author as "Rabbi Aleksander ha-Kohen ... from Frankfurt." Also see Horovitz, *Rabbaney Franqfurṭ*, 5. As for the reference to these customs, see Aleksander Suslin Ha-kohen, *Sefer ha-aggudah*, vol. 2, ed. Eleazar Brizel (Jerusalem: n.p., 1966), 190, with reference to Aleksander Suslin Ha-Kohen, *Sefer ha-aggudah* (1571; reprint, New York: Abraham Cik, 1959), Niddah, no. 18. Also see Joseph Juspa Nördlingen Hahn, *Yosef omeẓ*, reprint, 1928 (Jerusalem: n.p., 1965), 343.

152. On the history of the custom see Yitzhak (Eric) Zimmer, "Yemey ha-ṭohar shel ha-yoledet," in

and Moses Isserles (Cracow, d. 1572) had both endorsed an alternative view in their *Shulḥan ʿaruk*, the very work that the Frankfurt *beyt din* had told the Prince of Corvey in 1769 was the standard Jewish legal code worldwide.[153] Caro and Isserles allowed a woman to immerse anytime seven days after the birth of a boy or fourteen days after the birth of a girl if the woman had gone seven consecutive days without seeing vaginal blood or staining. Isserles, whose comments generally reflected Polish — if not German — Jewish customs, acknowledged that his view was not the only legal view and specifically noted that in communities where the custom was to wait until after the fortieth or eightieth day before immersing women should maintain the local custom.[154] However, observance of the old, stringent practice seems to have been eroding; indeed in mid-eighteenth-century Metz Rabbi Jonathan Eybeschütz (rabbi of Metz 1741–50, d. 1764) had tried to abolish it.[155] The rabbinic court of Frankfurt tried to maintain the local custom and responded with a Yiddish language edict that threatened those who did not observe it, whether in Frankfurt or its environs, with a public denunciation as violators of local custom.[156]

Another aspect of law that the court dealt with was taxation. In addition to

---

ʿOlam ke-minhago noheg (Jerusalem: Shazar, 1996), 220–39, especially 236–37. In the fifteenth century, Rabbi Joseph Colon was asked about this practice of German Jews (see his *Sefer sheʾelot u-teshubot Mahari"q ha-yeshanot* [Jerusalem: Oraysoh, 1988], no. 144). Colon noted that the custom could be found in the early fourteenth-century work of Yeḥiel ben Yequtiʾel ha-Rofeʾ, yet the nineteenth-century editor of this book noted in a letter to his publisher that there was no reference to this custom in the text (Yeḥiʾel ben Yequtiʾel Anau, *Sefer tanyaʾ rabbati*, ed. Shimʿon Horowitz [Warsaw: I. Goldman, 1879], fol. 3b). Jacob Molin, *Sefer Mahari"l: Minhagim*, ed. Shelomoh Spitzer (Jerusalem: Machon Yerushalayim, 1989), 595 no. 5, who was active in nearby Mainz in the first half of the fifteenth-century, maintained that a woman should not immerse until the forty-second or eighty-second day respectively. His position does not necessarily mean that this was the accepted custom in his time and place. In the second half of the sixteenth century, Rabbi Moses Isserles was aware of communities that followed the 40/80 rule. See his *Sheʾelot u-teshubot ha-Rema"ʾ*, ed. Asher Siev (Jerusalem: Feldheim, 1970), no. 94, as well as his comment in *Shulḥan ʿaruk* , Yoreh deʿah 194.1.

153. Caro and Isserles were certainly not the first to support a shorter waiting period. See the material cited by Caro in his *Beyt Yosef*, Yoreh deʿah 194.1. On the Frankfurt *beyt din*'s statement to the Prince of Corvey, see YIVO MS. RG 128 (folder 77–78), fol. 90a (translated here on pp. 65–66).

154. *Shulḥan ʿaruk*, Yoreh deʿah 194.1. As to when people could be informed that they did not have to observe the custom, see Isserles, *Responsa*, no. 94. The rabbis of Frankfurt cited Isserles's view that local custom must be maintained as a proof for their claims (Gundersheim, Adler MS. 935, no. 191).

155. See Zimmer, "Yemey ha-ṭohar," 239.

156. Gundersheim, Adler MS. 935, no. 191. Violators were also warned of further, and presumably harsher, yet unspecified, punishments.

questions of who was responsible for paying what on jointly owned properties, the financial self-assessment of members that the community used as the basis for determining an individual's tax liability was easily given to abuse.[157] To stem such abuses, the community enacted ordinances to try to strengthen tax assessors and encourage people to declare their net worth accurately. In the course of their work, the communal leadership turned to the court to see if their enactment was, in essence, "constitutional."[158]

The court was well-aware of the importance of tax collection to communal survival in Frankfurt, but it also knew that there were mutterings in the community about uneven assessments some years earlier. Literally using the fear of God to impose order on the system, in 1789 the court took action to try to protect all sides. It made tax assessors take a solemn oath to be impartial in performing their duties and composed a warning to be read in all synagogues advising householders of the importance of proper self-assessment. The court also equipped tax assessors with a letter to be read to individuals before they declared their net worth. Any party failing to act honestly was threatened with dire punishment, while those who acted in good faith were promised they would merit seeing the redemption of Israel and enjoy a life of peace.[159] Gundersheim left only a handful of taxation cases, but they reflect the court's important role within the community. Administrative and interpretive matters represent about 15% of the records that Gundersheim maintained.

The largest category of cases recorded in Gundersheim's diary — about 40% of all actions — dealt with real estate. The court not only finalized the sale of houses and issued a record of the sale to the buyer, but it received bids from individuals who wished to purchase property that was for sale.[160] When the community wanted to sell real property, it, too, through its representatives, had to appear before the court to complete the transaction.[161] There were also numerous sales

---

157. The problem was also addressed by the Frankfurt rabbinic synod of 1603 (see Markus Horovitz, *Die Frankfurter Rabbinerversamlung vom Jahre 1603* [Frankfurt: M. Slobotzky, 1897], 21–22).

158. See Gundersheim, Adler MS. 935, no. 227. Also see the discussion in Sendik, "Beyn din lepesher," 69–75.

159. Gundersheim, Adler MS. 935, nos. 228 and 229.

160. See Gundersheim, Adler MS. 935, no. 53. Technically speaking, sales of homes were sales of the right to live in the house and the obligations that came with it (e.g., payment of taxes), rather than a transfer of real property, since Jews did not own the land on the *Judengasse* (see Gerald Soliday, *A Community in Conflict: Frankfurt Society in the Seventeenth and Early Eighteenth Centuries* [Hanover, N.H.: University Press of New England, 1974], 196). The court did not issue proof of sale notes when individuals bought property from the community (see, for example, no. 92), for the court record itself was deemed to be sufficient. Regarding bids, see, for example, nos. 53, 58, and 73.

161. See, for example, Gundersheim, Adler MS. 935, nos. 101, 120, and 144.

of seats in the men's and women's sections of the synagogues that were concluded before the court. Houses, and seats in the synagogue, were often owned by multiple parties each of whom might have had a half or a quarter share.[162] Although use of the property had to be shared, houses were not fully divided or equipped for separate living and only one person could sit on a seat in the synagogue at any given time. Moreover, living on the ground floor was perceived as preferable to living on the upper floors, probably due to the convenience of easy access to the street, kitchen, and storage cellar in an age in which there were no elevators. Besides, the outhouse was also on the ground floor or in the cellar.[163] Since partial ownership of real property represented partial ownership of the entire holding rather than a specific section of the building or seat, equity demanded that space be shared evenly and that each party enjoy the opportunity to live in the "good" parts of the house or sit in a synagogue seat according to his or her share.

Although modern arbitrators might take practical considerations into account when resolving legal conundrums, personal needs such as one party requiring the lower floor due to infirmity or young children — concerns that might have been used to resolve to whom to give priority — had no independent standing in the Ashkenazic tradition with respect to questions of ownership.[164] To resolve the problem of use of the property in an impartial fashion, it was the accepted practice to rotate living spaces in the house — or use of the seat in the synagogue — at set intervals.[165] To determine who would live where when, the court administered a lottery.[166]

The use of sortilege to divide property seemed to have had biblical antecedents,

162. See, for example, Gundersheim, Adler MS. 935, no. 82.

163. See Gundersheim, Adler MS. 935, no. 70. The question of access to the toilet was an issue the court had to deal with a number of times. See nos. 70, 105, and 174.

164. The biblical verse "and you shall do what is just and good in the eyes of God" (Deut. 6.18) was invoked by Rabbi Moses ben Naḥman (known as Naḥmanides, 1191–ca. 1270; Gerona, Land of Israel), in his biblical commentary, to incorporate a broad range of social concerns into the legal process, but he did not include these sorts of practical concerns in the division of property (Moses ben Naḥman, *Perush ha-Torah*, ed. Ḥayyim Dov Chavel [Jerusalem: Mossad Harav Kook, 1962], Deut. 6.18). See too, B.T., *Baba᾽ meẓiᶜa᾽* 108a, regarding this verse in a very specific aspect of property law. In Gundersheim's diary, Deut. 6.18 was invoked in praise of compromise (see no. 176). Someone might have suggested interpreting the verse "you will get up before the elderly" (Lev. 19.32) as a justification for moving upstairs when the elderly needed to live on the ground floor, but I have not found such a reading.

165. Barbara Goodwin, *Justice by Lottery*, 2d ed. (Exeter: Imprint Academic, 2005), 69, has argued that given joint ownership, "rotation is the just method of distribution for 'exclusive-use' durables."

166. The court was not the only institution in the community to use a lottery to determine matters. The community used a lottery to select officials, as mentioned earlier, and charitable trusts

for according to the scriptural account the Land of Israel was divided among the tribes by lot (see Num. 26.52–56, Josh. 18.6). However, the biblical lottery allocated as yet unclaimed land, granting full ownership to people over land that had no owner.[167] The Frankfurt lottery divided the use of real property between undisputed proprietors, each of whose stake in the possession was not altered by sortition.

It is possible that Frankfurt Jewry clung to the very simplest reading of Proverbs, "The lot will end litigation and separate between the mighty" (18.18). It was a fair system for allocating the use of shared real property, and if the Jews of Frankfurt saw an aspect of the Divine in such lotteries as is implied in the lottery involving Jonah (1.7), then it was hardly arbitrary.[168] Such a view had further biblical antecedents in another verse in Proverbs, "The lots may be cast into the lap, but the issue depends wholly on the Lord" (16.33), a view shared by many in the non-Jewish community.[169] But neither these nor any other verses were ever

---

also used lotteries to decide who would receive funds (see Gundersheim, Adler MS. 935, no. 225).

167. In B.T., *Baba᾽ batra᾽* 106b, sortition was used for a division of outright ownership, not a sharing of real property.

168. The thrust of biblical stories was that there was an aspect of the Divine, when sortilege was used, which both brought things that were hidden to light (e.g., 1 Sam. 14.41–45 with Rashi's comments) and determined what course of action should be taken (e.g., Num. 33.54; 34.13). A talmudic rabbi stated that "one does not cut his finger below [i.e., in this world] unless it was declared above, as it is said, 'The steps of man are ordered' [Ps. 37.23] 'and how can man understand his way'" (Prv. 20.24; B.T., *Ḥullin* 7b).

169. Although Thomas Aquinas specifically saw the *sors divisoria* ("sortilege of allotment") that was used to divide property as based on chance and without supernatural significance, medieval Christian societies generally believed that lotteries were a means of invoking the divine, a perception that continued into the sixteenth century among both Catholics and Protestants (see Aquinas, *Summa Theologiae*, 95.8, pp. 65–69, and on general perceptions, Neil Duxbury, *Random Justice: On Lotteries and Legal Decision-Making* [Oxford: Clarendon, 1999], 17–20). Indeed, John Calvin (d. 1564) understood the verse from Proverbs as a message to man "that it is not by their own power that pebbles are cast into the lap and drawn out, but the one thing that could have been attributed to chance He testifies to come from Himself" (Jean Calvin, *Institutes of the Christian Religion*, ed. John T. McNeill, trans. Ford Lewis Battles, in collaboration with the editor, and a committee of advisers, The Library of Christian Classics 20 [Philadelphia: Westminster Press, 1960], 205). Keith Thomas pointed out that a major shift took place in the early seventeenth century among Puritans, who denied that sortilege was an act of divine providence, or at least not more than any other act. Thomas noted that it took some time for this view to become widely accepted, but it represented a major break with the past and was a step toward a new age (see Keith Thomas, *Religion and the Decline of Magic: Studies in Popular Beliefs in Sixteenth and Seventeenth Century England* [London: Weidenfeld and Nicholson, 1971], 119–24). It is not clear whether the litigants who came before the rabbinic

invoked in Gundersheim's diary to support the practice. For the jurist's diary, the use of lotteries was simply a fact of daily life.[170]

The lottery completed, the court specified the exact areas of the house each party had a right to and stated the exact dates on which the rotation would take place. Usually after three years each side would move into the other (or another) section of the house, thus assuring an equitable sharing of space.[171] Even when no lottery was required, the court was a place to turn when disputes arose between tenants in common with regard to renovations or the right of passage within the house.[172]

Although by ordinance of the Jewish community the Frankfurt rabbinic court was required to render its decision within three days of having heard a claim, how long the entire legal process generally took remains unclear.[173] Gundersheim only recorded the date decisions were given, not the date on which a case was first brought before the court. In one case it appears that it took the court at least two weeks from the beginning of the proceedings until it gave its decision.[174] It is hard to say whether this was typical, for court proceedings could involve a number of steps. For example, Meʾir Segal lent money to an individual in 1766 and received a contract itemizing the agreement. Some years later a fire wiped out Segal's possessions, including the contract. To protect himself, Segal approached the court and asked that it instruct the Jewish community to reissue his contract. Because the borrower openly admitted her debt and the community had a record of the original transaction this would seem to have been a simple matter. Still, the court questioned Segal, summoned the borrower and questioned her, called for repre-

---

court and the *dayyanim* who administered the lottery in Frankfurt in the last half of the eighteenth century had yet taken this step (see the following note).

170. Rabbi Yaʾir Bachrach (d. 1702; Worms, Metz) perceived honest lotteries as subject to Divine will (Yaʾir Bachrach, *Ḥavat Yaʾir* [Frankfurt: Johannes Faust, 1699], no. 61). The responsum makes mention of prayer before a lottery and even noted that one might pray to win the lottery and that such prayer might be efficacious. This suggests that Bachrach did not view this as simply an aleatory act (see Thomas, *Religion and the Decline of Magic*, 120). There were other views among early modern rabbis regarding contemporary lotteries, see, for example, Benjamin Slonik, *Sheʾelot u-teshubot masaʾat Binyamin* (Vilnius: Abraham Ẓebi Katzenellenbogen, 1894), no. 7, who lived in late sixteenth, early seventeenth-century Poland.

171. An example of this is found in Gundersheim, Adler MS. 935, no. 47. A lottery with regard to seats in the synagogue is found in no. 85.

172. See Gundersheim, Adler MS. 935, no. 70.

173. ŻIH MS. 517, no. 67.

174. Gundersheim, Adler MS. 935, no. 108. One of the litigants died on 23 March 1778, and the ruling was given two weeks later on 7 April. There were multiple claimants in the case and perhaps the case continued to be argued after this individual's death. It is also possible that the court took more than two weeks to decide this matter.

sentatives of the community to come before it, and questioned someone who had lent the borrower money after Segal had. There were also negotiations between Segal and the second lender. Gundersheim did not record the date on which the proceedings began, so there is no way of telling how long the entire process took. But, because the summoning of one individual was dependent on the answers of the previous individual it may have taken some time.[175] In another instance a party was asked to bring proofs for its claims, and it took about two weeks for them to produce the names of two witnesses who would testify on their behalf. Before the court summoned the two individuals, it called the other litigant before it so that he could hear the testimony.[176] All this took time.

Despite this wealth of information, any attempt to extrapolate from Gundersheim's diary to the overall activities of the Frankfurt rabbinic court should be made with great caution. Gundersheim's diary reflects that he was present at only one divorce case.[177] A second divorce is discussed in case no. 179 and a third in case no. 221. Three divorces over a 20 year span would suggest that divorce was a rarity in Frankfurt, yet other material from the period contains a (partial?) list of 30 female residents of Frankfurt who were divorced from 1772–1805, including five divorces that took place in 1787 when Gundersheim was active on the court.[178] Divorce was clearly hardly a rarity.[179] Perhaps Gundersheim was not present at the divorces that took place during his years on the court, or perhaps he chose not to record them. One way or another, Gundersheim's records do not reflect the full scope of the court's activity.

Jews in the Courts of Non-Jews

"And these are the laws that you will put before them." (Ex. 21.1)

The rabbinic understanding of this verse was summed up by the great medieval exegete Rabbi Solomon ben Isaac (known by the acronym Rashi, d. 1105; Northern France) who relied on earlier sources when he made his comments on the last words of the verse:

175. See Gundersheim, Adler MS. 935, no. 43.
176. Gundersheim, Adler MS. 935, no. 67.
177. The case appears in the index to all cases in the diary (fol. 241b, from 1769) but the full record has not survived.
178. JTS MS. 3672, fols. 118b–123a.
179. Bodleian Library, MS. Opp. 730 (Oxford University). A scribe's record book from between 1672 and 1706 lists 76 divorces he participated in, almost all of which took place in Frankfurt.

> "Before them" and not before non-Jews.[180] And even if you knew that in a specific legal matter they [i.e., non-Jews] judge just as Jewish law does, do not bring it to their courts for one who brings cases between Jews before non-Jews profanes the name of God and gives added cause to praise the name of idolatry [in the name of which the non-Jewish courts administer justice],[181] as it is said, "Because their rock is not like our Rock that our enemies should judge us" (Deut. 32.31),[182] that is, it is a testimony to the superiority of their creed when our enemies are judges [over us].

The normative legal ramifications of this view were ensconced in Jewish law in Rabbi Joseph Caro's sixteenth-century authoritative legal code, *Shulḥan ʿaruk*, where he wrote,

> It is prohibited to be judged before judges who are idolaters or in their courts, even in a matter that they judge in consonance with Jewish law ... and anyone who brings their case before them is wicked and it is as if he cursed and insulted and raised a hand against the Torah of Moses, peace be upon him.[183]

With the loss of Jewish autonomy in the post-Temple period, the jurisdiction of non-Jewish authorities in both civil and criminal matters generally trumped that of Jewish courts. Nevertheless, the custom of respecting the corporate autonomy of the Jews, particularly in civil suits, had a long history in the European lands.[184] Roman Imperial legislation had recognized the rights of Jews to judge themselves in matters of civil law, and in the High Middle Ages this was codified in

180. See B.T., *Giṭṭin* 88b.

181. See *Pentateuch with Targum Onkelos, Haphtaroth and Prayers for Sabbath and Rashi's Commentary (Exodus)*, translated and annotated by M. Rosenbaum et al. (London: Shapiro, Vallentine and Co., 1930), 108.

182. I have translated this verse as it has been understood in Jewish tradition (see Targum Onkelos Deut. 32.31 as well as Ex. 21.22). For a possible better reading, see E. A. Speiser, "The Stem *PLL* in Hebrew," *Journal of Biblical Literature* 82, no. 3 (September 1963): 303–4. Cf., however, *Deuteronomy (Debarim): The Traditional Hebrew Text with the New JPS Translation*, with commentary by Jeffrey Tigay (Philadelphia: Jewish Publication Society, 1996), 310, where this interpretation was rejected and a different reading was offered (see n. 132).

183. *Shulḥan ʿaruk*, Ḥoshen mishpaṭ 26.1. Also see Elon, *Ha-mishpaṭ ha-ʿibri*, 13–18.

184. See the material cited by David Shohet, *The Jewish Court in the Middle Ages*, reprint, 1931, Studies in Jewish Jurisprudence (New York: Hermon, 1974), 110; Katz, *Masoret u-mashber*, 121–22; and Elon, *Ha-mishpaṭ ha-ʿibri*, 16 with n. 49. The situation in the Ottoman Empire was much different (see Hacker, "Gebulteyha shel ha-ʾoṭonomyah ha-yehudit," 359–65, 381–88). By and large Jewish courts lost their right to deal with criminal matters during the Middle Ages.

the German lands through charters issued to Jewish communities.[185] This held firm in the Holy Roman Empire during most of the early modern period, for the Empire — which continued to exist until 1806 — had an interest in maintaining a strong Jewish community.[186] Non-Jewish authorities ostensibly had no say over Jewish rituals such as Sabbath observance or kosher food, and although in some times and places questions of personal status (e.g., marriage, divorce) were within the jurisdiction of the non-Jewish authorities, it appears that Jews rarely turned to them for rulings in these matters.[187]

The Jewish community of Frankfurt received the right to judge its own members according to Jewish law in 1366. However, in his directive to the mayor (*Schultheiß*) of Frankfurt, Charles IV (d. 1378) stipulated that such cases must be worth the Emperor's while from a monetary point of view, suggesting that the royal court had a financial interest in the workings of the Jewish court.[188] Already during

185. See Guido Kisch, "Relations Between Jewish and Christian Courts in the Middle Ages," in *Louis Ginzberg Jubilee Volume on the Occasion of His Seventieth Birthday*, ed. Alexander Marx et al. (New York: Jewish Publication Society, 1945), 201–17 (English section), as well as his *The Jews in Medieval Germany: A Study of Their Legal and Social Status*, 2d ed. (New York: Ktav, 1970), 100–3.

186. On the Imperial Court's interest in the Jewish community, particularly in Frankfurt, see Soliday, *A Community in Conflict*, 190. For a thought-provoking view regarding the interests of absolute rulers in maintaining Jewish courts, see Andreas Gotzmann, "At Home in Many Worlds? Thoughts About New Concepts in Jewish Legal History," *Jahrbuch des Simon-Dubnow-Instituts* 2 (2003): 413–36.

187. Gotzmann, *Jüdische Autonomie*, 258–59, argued that the non-Jewish authorities could exert influence even in religious questions through their interpretation of statutes, privileges, etc. Although the Hapsburg state began to consider marriage to be a civil matter in 1783, in the Holy Roman Empire it remained an ecclesiastical matter (see Judith von Schmädel, "The History of Marriage Law in Austria and Germany: From Sacrament to Civil Contract," *Hitotsubashi Journal of Law and Politics* 37 [2009]: 43; on the Hapsburg state, see Lois Dubin, "Jewish Women, Marriage Law, and Emancipation: The Civil Divorce of Rachele Morschene in Late Eighteenth-Century Trieste," in *Acculturation and Its Discontents: The Italian Jewish Experience Between Exclusion and Inclusion*, ed. David Myers et al. [Toronto: University of Toronto Press, 2008], 119–20). Nevertheless, the Hamburg government maintained that it had the final say in marriage and divorce (see David H. Horowitz, "Fractures and Fissures," 74–75). Alexandr Putík, "The Prague Jewish Community in the Late 17th and Early 18th Centuries," *Judaica Bohemiae* 35 (1999), 27, noted that Jewish marriage and divorce were within the jurisdiction of the Archbishop of Prague, however, in practice, Jews did not make appeals to him. Nevertheless, such appeals were not unheard of in medieval Aragon where the non-Jewish authorities maintained this right (see Elka Klein, *Jews, Christian Society, and Royal Power in Medieval Barcelona* [Ann Arbor: University of Michigan Press, 2006], 158).

188. See Georg Ludwig Kriegk, *Frankfurter Bürgerzwiste und Zustände im Mittelalter: Ein auf urkundlichen Forschungen beruhender Beitrag zur Geschichte des deutschen Bürgerthums* (Frankfurt: J. D. Sauerländer, 1862), 426.

the medieval period in various European settings, tax collecting or other economic benefits were an important reason for supporting some form of Jewish autonomy.[189] In 1614 during the Fettmilch uprising the Jews were expelled from Frankfurt, but they soon returned after Imperial commissioners executed the leaders of the revolt in 1616.[190] The rights, obligations, and restrictions on the Jews of Frankfurt were itemized in 1617 and included permission for Jews to regulate their own judicial affairs in civil suits through the Jewish communal leadership and their rabbis. Ostensibly this was granted to relieve the leadership of Frankfurt from having to deal with the "unruly Jews" who were said to have brought their petty concerns to the mayor and magistrates every day (*tägliches*). Nevertheless, the magistrates demanded that crimes and "other important matters" (*Frevel und andere wichtige Sachen*) involving Jews be brought before them.[191] The magistrates also remained a court of appeal for internal Jewish disputes.[192]

---

189. On medieval France and England, see Salo Baron, *The Jewish Community*, vol. 1 (Philadelphia: Jewish Publication Society, 1942), 244–45; on medieval Aragon, see Yom Tov Assis, *The Golden Age of Aragonese Jewry: Community and Society in the Crown of Aragon, 1213–1327* (London: Littman, 1997), 17, 32, 48. On France from the sixteenth to eighteenth centuries, see Jay Berkovitz, *Rites and Passages: The Beginnings of Modern Jewish Culture in France, 1650–1860* (Philadelphia: University of Pennsylvania Press, 2004), 21, and on Poland, Israel Halperin, *Pinqas vaᶜad arbᶜa arazot*, revised and edited by Israel Bartal, with an introduction by Shmuel Ettinger (Jerusalem: Bialik Institute, 1990), xvi–xviii. On the interests of the Empire, see R. Po-chia Hsia, "The Jews and the Emperor," in *State and Society in Early Modern Austria*, ed. Charles Ingrao (West Lafayette: Purdue University Press, 1994), 74, and Christopher Friedrichs, *The Early Modern City, 1450–1750* (London: Longman, 1995), 311.

190. Regarding the expulsion and the readmission of the Jews, see the material cited by Gotzmann, *Jüdische Autonomie*, 304 n. 19. The Fettmilch revolt should not be seen solely as an anti-Jewish attack. On misunderstandings about the nature of the uprising in both German and Jewish historiography, see Christopher Friedrichs, "Politics or Pogrom? The Fettmilch Uprising in German and Jewish History," *Central European History* 19, no. 2 (June 1986): 186–228.

191. See Johann Jacob Schudt, *Jüdische merckwürdigkeiten: Vorstellende was sich curieuses und denckwurdiges in den neuern Zeiten bei einigen Jahr-hunderten mit denen in alle IV. Theile der Welt sonderlich durch Teutschland zerstreuten Juden zugetragen*, vol. 3, reprint, 1714 (Berlin: Louis Lamm, 1922), 1601–2, section 98. Section 100 (1602–3) notes that cases of murder, manslaughter, and "other important matters" (*und andere wichtige Sachen*) were to be brought before the magistrates. There is a brief legal and demographic history of the *Judengasse* until 1709 in Cilli Kasper-Holtkotte, *Die jüdische Gemeinde von Frankfurt/Main in der Frühen Neuzeit: Familien, Netzwerke und Konflikte eines jüdischen Zentrums* (Göttingen: De Gruyter, 2010), 17–21.

192. On Jews before the Frankfurt magistrates in the mid-eighteenth century, see Gabriela Schlick, "Zur Rolle der reichsstädtischen Gerichtsbarkeiten in den Alltagsbeziehungen der Frankfurter Juden im 18. Jahrhundert," in *Die Frankfurter Judengasse: Jüdisches Leben in der frühen Neuzeit*, ed. Fritz Backhaus et al. (Frankfurt: Societät, 2006), 171–85, particularly 180–81, regarding procedure and a case between Jews.

Frankfurt was an Imperial city and as such it enjoyed special status in the Empire as a separate legislative, administrative, and judicial unit.[193] The Emperor guaranteed this special status and it gave him the right to intervene in the affairs of these cities, including in disputes between individuals.[194] This also afforded residents of Imperial cities, Jews among them, the opportunity to turn directly to the *Reichshofrat* in Vienna — well beyond the reach of the *beyt din* and the Jewish community. There was little the Jewish communal leadership could do about this, even regarding disputes that were ostensibly internal Jewish matters.

The prohibition and rabbinic invective against turning to the courts of non-Jews, and the Frankfurt Jewish community's rights of self-adjudication not withstanding, many Jews did whatever they could to get what they believed was or could be theirs. Jews in Frankfurt as well as in Strasbourg and other areas in the German lands, having lived under multiple jurisdictions for centuries, were practiced in manipulating this situation to their advantage.[195] Sometimes Jews took their concerns directly to the non-Jewish courts; in other cases they appealed the

193. Peter Johanek, "Imperial and Free Towns of the Holy Roman Empire City-States in Pre-Modern Germany," in *A Comparative Study of Thirty City-State Cultures: An Investigation Conducted by the Copenhagen Polis Centre*, ed. Mogens Herman Hansen, Historik-Filosofiske Skrifter 21 (Copenhagen: Kongelige Danske Videns Kabernes Selskab, 2000), 306.

194. Imperial Cities were among the most loyal supporters of the Emperor, yet this did not prevent them from challenging his authority and trying to expand their own (see John Gagliardo, *Reich and Nation: The Holy Roman Empire as Idea and Reality, 1763–1806* [Bloomington: Indiana University Press, 1980], 11–12). On the other hand, the Emperor's role as protector of Jewish rights gave him additional grounds for intervening in the affairs of these cities (see Hsia, "The Jews and the Emperor," 79).

195. On multiple jurisdictions in the German lands and their Jewish residents, see Friedrich Battenberg, "Zur Rechtsstellung der Juden am Mittelrhein in Spätmittelalter und früher Neuzeit," *Zeitschrift für Historische Forschung* 6 (1979): 130–31, 138–43, 153–63. On Strasbourg, see Debra Kaplan, "Kooperation und Konflikt. Elässische Juden, Herrschaft und Recht im Spiegel der Reichskammergerichtsprozesse des 16. Jahrhunderts," in *Juden im Recht: Neue Zugänge zur Rechtsgeschichte der Juden im alten Reich*, ed. Andreas Gotzmann and Stephan Wendehorst, Zeitschrift für Historische Forschung Supplement 39 (Berlin: Dunckert & Humblot, 2007), 339–40, 346. On other areas of the German speaking lands, see Azriel Shohet, *ʿIm ḥilufey tequfot: reʾshit ha-haskalah be-yahadut Germanyah* (Jerusalem: Mosad Bialik, 1960), 72–73. There may have been other addresses to appeal cases as well, such as the Faculty of Law at the University of Vienna. On law faculties as appellate courts in the eighteenth century, see John P. Dawson, *A History of Lay Judges* (Cambridge, Mass.: Harvard University Press, 1960), 109. Law faculties were especially used when the case was not appropriate for the Imperial court. With respect the extent of the use of this method of appeal (not specifically by Jews), see Ulrich Falk, *Consilia. Studien zur Praxis der Rechtsgutachten in der Frühen Neuzeit* (Frankfurt: Vittorio Klostermann, 2006), 21–24. My thanks to Dr. Monika Preuss for this reference and to Prof. Dr. Falk for providing me with a copy of his work.

decisions of the *beyt din* to the non-Jewish authorities, and in other cases individuals brought non-Jewish officials into Jewish courts, something that *halakah* also prohibited.[196]

The problem of Jews going to non-Jewish courts was not new or unique to Frankfurt. Although in twelfth-century France there seems to have been some accommodation for a Jew taking a co-religionist to the courts of non-Jews if both parties agreed to do so of their own accord, Guido Kisch wrote regarding medieval Germany that, "There is, in fact, not a single instance of a Jew's bringing suit against a fellow-Jew in a non-Jewish court, not even as the result of mutual agreement or of a Jewish defendant's refusing to appear before a Jewish court."[197] Even if Kisch was correct, this situation did not continue. Already in the fourteenth century there were Jews in the German lands who brought their disputes to non-Jewish courts, and during the fifteenth century there were both rabbinic scholars and lay people who did so.[198] As Roman Law advanced in late fifteenth and sixteenth-century Germany and displaced canon law, Jews probably found it less and less objectionable to enter non-Jewish courts and the practice continued.[199] Cases between Jews

---

196. For examples of outside intervention, see Gundersheim, Adler MS. 935, nos. 111, 112, 124, and 155. The non-Jewish authorities also became involved in cases in eighteenth-century Hamburg (see David H. Horowitz, "Fractures and Fissures," 118–27). The right to appeal the decisions of rabbinic courts to the non-Jewish authorities was also found in smaller communities such as Münster (Westphalia), where jurisdiction was in the hands of a bishop (Carl Rixen, *Geschichte und Organisation der Juden im ehemaligen Stifte Münster* [Münster: Westfälischen Vereinsdruckerei, 1906], 50; my thanks to Dr. Monika Preuss for bringing this source to my attention). On the prohibition in Jewish law, see Isserles's comments on *Shulḥan ʿaruk*, Ḥoshen mishpaṭ 26.1.

197. Kisch, *The Jews in Medieval Germany*, 173. There were cases of Jews who were unhappy with the decisions of Jewish courts and appealed to the non-Jewish authorities (see, for example, Simha Goldin, *Ha-yiḥud ve-ha-yaḥad: ḥidat hisardutan shel ha-qebuẓot ha-yehudiyyot be-yemey ha-beynayyim* [Tel Aviv: Hakibbutz Hameuchad, 1997], 134). Regarding Rabbi Jacob ben Meʾir (Rabbeynu Tam) and the twelfth-century ordinance attributed to him allowing litigation before a non-Jewish court if both parties agreed to it, see Louis Finkelstein, *Jewish Self-Government in the Middle Ages*, 2d ed. (New York: Feldheim, 1964), 155–56 with n. 1 on p. 156. By the mid-sixteenth century, the *halakah* specifically rejected this position (*Shulḥan ʿaruk*, Ḥoshen mishpaṭ 26.1). Jewish law made provisions for litigation in non-Jewish courts if a defendant refused to obey Jewish courts (26.2).

198. On the fourteenth century, see Zvi Avneri, "Peniyyah le-ʿerkkaʾot," *Zion* 25 (1960): 57–61. Regarding the fifteenth century, see Zimmer, *Harmony and Discord*, 85–89, who also noted that rabbis allowed Jewish litigants to approach non-Jewish courts if there was no local rabbinic court.

199. During the Middle Ages, canon law had served as the principle source for judicial rulings and clerics were often involved in arbitration (see James Q. Whitman, *The Legacy of Roman Law*

were brought before the *Reichshofrat* in the second half of the sixteenth century, into the seventeenth century, and beyond.[200]

Jews taking their cases to non-Jewish courts became so widespread that it prompted a response from the rabbinic leadership of the German lands.[201] In August 1603 a regional synod held in Frankfurt noted that "it is [a] common offense among the people of our generation to refuse to obey Jewish law and even to compel opposing litigants to present themselves before secular courts." The synod not only instituted a prayer to be said publicly on each Sabbath regarding the matter, but threatened to ostracize those who took their disputes to non-Jewish courts. More practically, the synod set up five regional courts, including one in Frankfurt, to try and deal with intractable individuals who could not be disciplined by their own communities due to their wealth and influence.[202] In 1675 the Jewish community in Frankfurt took further measures to address the problem, and while they may have had some short term success, in the long run they seem to have solved little.[203]

---

in the German Romantic Era: Historical Vision and Legal Change [Princeton, N.J.: Princeton University Press, 1990], 10).

200. Hsia, "The Jews and the Emperor," 72. See Barbara Staudinger, "'Gelangt an eur kayserliche Majestät mein allerunderthenigistes Bitten' Handlungsstrategien der jüdischen Elite am Reichshofrat im 16. und 17. Jahrhundert," in *Hofjuden und Landjuden: Jüdisches Leben in der Frühen Neuzeit*, ed. Sabine Hödl et al. (Berlin: Philo, 2004), 153–56, regarding the number of cases brought by Jews in the Holy Roman Empire to the *Reichshofrat* between 1559 and 1670 (not all these cases were intra-Jewish disputes). Also see Anette Baumann, "Jüdische Reichskammergerichtsprozesse aus den Reichsstädten Frankfurt und Hamburg. Eine quantitative Annäherung," in *Juden im Recht: Neue Zugänge zur Rechtsgeschichte der Juden im Alten Reich*, ed. Andreas Gotzmann et al., Zeitschrift für Historische Forschung Supplement 39 (Berlin: Duncker & Humblot, 2007), 296–316, as well as Kasper, "Die Frankfurter Judengemeinde," 399–418, 597–620, for examples from approximately the last third of the eighteenth century.

201. See Kasper-Holtkotte, *Die jüdische Gemeinde von Frankfurt*, 95–106.

202. Horovitz, *Die Frankfurter Rabbinerversamlung*, 20–21. See Finkelstein, *Jewish Self-Government*, 257–58, for a somewhat abbreviated "free translation." Also see Eric Zimmer, *Jewish Synods in Germany During the Late Middle Ages* (New York: Yeshiva University Press, 1978), 79–80, 147–54; Volker Press, "Kaiser Rudolf II. und der Zusammenschluß der deutschen Judenheit: Die sogenannte Frankfurter Rabbinerverschwörung von 1603 und ihre Folgen," in *Zur Geschichte der Juden im Deutschland des späten Mittelalters und der frühen Neuzeit*, ed. Alfred Haverkamp (Stuttgart: Anton Hiersemann, 1981), 248–52; and Birgit Klein, "Die 'Frankfurter Rabbinerversammlung' von 1603: Vorgeschichte, Verordnungen, Folgen," in *Die Frankfurter Judengasse: Jüdisches Leben in der frühen Neuzeit*, ed. Fritz Backhaus et al. (Frankfurt: Societät, 2006), 167–68. I have been unable to locate a copy of the prayer.

203. Azriel Shohet, *ʿIm ḥilufey tequfot*, 72, with appendix on pp. 261–63. Also see Kasper-Holtkotte, *Die jüdische Gemeinde von Frankfurt*, 106, n. 61.

Jews going to non-Jewish courts was a problem that caught the attention of Jewish leaders beyond the Empire as well.[204] In 1653 the Jewish leadership in Poznań threatened to punish Jews who appealed the judgments of Jewish courts in non-Jewish courts.[205] Similarly, in Lithuania in the summer of 1673 the Jewish national council ordered the excommunication of anyone who appealed the decision of Jewish courts to the non-Jewish authorities or brought their cases to non-Jewish courts rather than Jewish courts.[206] In 1692 a local act in the L'viv region noted that cases between Jews were to be tried in Jewish courts. However, by 1740, if not earlier, Jews could be found going to non-Jewish courts for justice.[207]

Jews from Frankfurt appeared before the *Reichshofrat* in numbers that were well-beyond their proportion of the general population.[208] So many Jews in late eighteenth-century Frankfurt took their litigation against each other to non-Jewish courts that it prompted Rabbi Nathan Maas to complain about the damage this did to the status of the Jewish community and the image of the Jew in the eyes of non-Jews.[209] And it was not only laypeople who took their cases to the non-Jewish

204. See Katz, *Masoret u-mashber*, 122–23 with n. 36.

205. Michałowska-Mycielska, *The Jewish Community*, 134, 243.

206. Simon Dubnow, ed., *Pinqas ha-medinah o pinqas vaʿad ha-qehillot ha-raʾshiyyot bi-medinat Liṭaʾ: qobeẓ taqqanot u-pesaqim mi-shenat [5]383 ʿad shenat [5]521* (Berlin: Ayanot, 1925), no. 690, also cited by Michałowska-Mycielska, 243.

207. See Zbigniew Pazdro, *Organizacya i praktyka żydowskich sądów podwojewodzinskich w okresie 1740–1772 r.* (L'viv: Nakładem Funduszu Konkursowego, 1903), 8–9; also see there no. 35 (pp. 208–11) where in December 1754 Rabbi Chaim Szymchowicz sued the Jewish community of L'viv in a non-Jewish court for payment of his salary. Also see Moshe Rosman, "The Role of Non-Jewish Authorities in Resolving Conflicts within Jewish Communities in the Early Modern Period," *Political Studies Review* 12, no. 3–4 (Fall 2000): 59–62.

208. According to Eva Ortlieb,"Frankfurt vor dem Reichshofrat," in *Die Reichsstadt Frankfurt als Rechts- und Gerichtslandschaft im Römisch-Deutschen Reich*, ed. Anja Amend et al. (Munich: Oldenbourg, 2008), 65, in appeals to the *Reichshofrat* involving Frankfurt residents, approximately 35% of the plaintiffs and 20% of the defendants were Jews. Frankfurt had about 32,000 residents in 1700, and, in the early part of the eighteenth century, approximately 3,000 Jews (see Soliday, *A Community in Conflict*, 53–60). The total population of Frankfurt declined in the middle of the second half of the eighteenth century before rising again in the 1790s. See Hans Mauersberg, *Wirtschafts- und Sozialgeschichte zentraleuropäischer Städte in neuerer Zeit* (Göttingen: Vandenhoeck & Ruprecht, 1960), 54, who estimated the total population of Frankfurt as 32,318 (1751–55), 30,027 (1771–75), and 35,322 (1796–1800). The methodological difficulties of these calculations are discussed by Mauersberg (48–55) and neatly summarized in English by Soliday (33–40, esp. 35). On the Jewish population in Frankfurt in the early modern period, also see Josef Unna, *Statistik der Frankfurter Juden bis zum Jahre 1866* (Frankfurt: Israelitischen Gemeide Frankfurt, 1931), 11. I have not found an estimate of the number of Jews in Frankfurt in the late eighteenth century.

209. Nathan Maas, *Sefer binyan Shelomoh (Sanhedrin)* (Offenbach: Abraham Poppers, 1784), fol. 112a, cited by Sendik, "Beyn din le-pesher," 90.

authorities. In some instances the Jewish community itself turned to the Frankfurt magistrates to try to enforce its rulings.[210] Members of the Jewish communal leadership and the rabbinic elite as well brought their disputes before the courts of non-Jews. Perhaps the most extreme example of this involved Rabbi Nathan Adler in 1779. Adler, the scion of an old Frankfurt family and teacher of Rabbi Moses Sofer, refused to heed warnings from both the community and its rabbinic courts not to hold private prayer services for his circle of followers, but to attend the established synagogues. Adler's obstinacy resulted in his being excommunicated.[211] The confrontation escalated and the matter was brought before the non-Jewish authorities in Frankfurt and, ultimately, to the *Reichshofrat,* which ruled in favor of the Jewish community.[212] Similarly, a disagreement between two of the most established families in the *Judengasse*, the Kulp and Kann families, began within the Jewish community in 1749 and was in the Frankfurt courts by 1750.[213] And the matter did not stop there. In the same year it came before the Emperor, and then continued to weave its way through municipal and Imperial courts into the late 1760s.[214]

Again, such behavior was not unique to Frankfurt. In contemporary Altona, Rabbi Zalman Emden, son of one of the foremost rabbis of the eighteenth century, Rabbi Jacob Emden (d. 1776), filed a *supplik* ("petition") with the king asking that his dispute with the executors of his father's estate be heard before the royal courts.

---

210. The community turned to the Frankfurt authorities for support in their ruling against the Wertheimer family regarding an appointment in the family *kloysz*. While the Frankfurt authorities supported the community in this instance, once the case moved beyond the *Judengasse*, Zachariah Wertheimer was able to appeal to the Emperor. See Kasper, "Die Frankfurter Judengemeinde," 150–51.

211. On Adler, see the biographical material cited by Rachel Elior, "Natan Adler ve-ha-ʿedah ha-ḥasidit be-Franqforṭ: ha-ziqah beyn ḥaburot ḥasidiyyot be-mizraḥ eyropah u-be-merkazah be-meʾah ha-18," *Zion* 59, no. 1 (1994): 31 n. 1, as well as 32–33 and the references in the notes there. A somewhat abbreviated version of the article appeared in English as "Rabbi Nathan Adler of Frankfurt and the Controversy Surrounding Him," in *Mysticism, Magic, and Kabbalah in Ashkenazi Judaism: International Symposium Held in Frankfurt a.M.*, ed. Karl Erich Grözinger, Joseph Dan (Berlin: W. de Gruyter, 1995), 223–42.

212. See Horovitz, *Rabbaney Franqfurṭ*, 155. While Horovitz noted that it is not clear which of the sides first took the case beyond the Jewish community, once it was out of the community both parties became involved.

213. On the two families, see Dietz, *Stammbuch der Frankfurter Juden*, 174–77, and 159–66. On the case, see I. Kracauer, "Die Kulp-Kannschen Wirren. Ein Beitrag zur Geschichte der jüdischen Gemeinde in Frankfurt a.M. im XVIII. Jahrhundert," *Archiv für Frankfurts Geschichte und Kunst* Series 3, no. 10 (1910): 135–212, and more specifically regarding the case coming before the Frankfurt magistrates, 152–54.

214. Kracauer, "Die Kulp-Kannschen Wirren," 161–63, 195–205.

Although the authorities rejected the request and ordered the case back to the Jewish community, the plea reinforces the fact that even members of the rabbinic elite could turn to non-Jewish courts if they believed it to be in their best interest.[215]

Given the number and nature of the Jews who brought their cases to non-Jewish courts, it is not surprising that there was some confusion among the non-Jewish authorities regarding the demands of Jewish law with respect to Jews bringing intra-Jewish litigation before the courts of non-Jews. In 1781 the authorities in Frankfurt, acting on behalf of the Vice Chancellor of the Palatinate of Mannheim, asked the chief rabbi of Frankfurt what issues, according to Jewish law, Jews *had* to bring before Jewish courts and what litigation could be brought before non-Jewish courts.[216]

Responding in late December 1781, Rabbi Pinḥas Horowitz was careful to recognize explicitly the legitimacy of the non-Jewish courts and the fairness of their decisions. Jewish tradition maintained that non-Jews were commanded to establish a system of courts as part of the Noachide laws, and Horowitz admitted that the local authorities maintained just and fair courts.[217] Be that as it may, Horowitz noted that the Torah specifically commanded Jews to bring their cases before their own courts, not the courts of non-Jews.

The Torah's commandment notwithstanding, Horowitz acknowledged that there were "many people in our generation" who brought their monetary cases before non-Jewish courts. Horowitz believed that such people turned to non-Jewish courts for practical reasons, because they "wanted to attain money that the Torah had not granted them," that is to say, they thought that it would be to their advantage to try their cases in non-Jewish courts. Horowitz declared that such

215. See Staatsarchive, MS. AHW/121/3 (Hamburg), fol. 42b. Emden's actions forced the community to respond a number of times to the king's courts. The community used a professional to do so and incurred expenses (see fol. 43a). I thank Ms. Noa Shashar for sharing her transcription of the material with me.

216. Institut für Stadtgeschichte Frankfurt am Main, Ugb D33 (Frankfurt), fol. 30b. My thanks to Professor Andreas Gotzmann for pointing out this source to me. The record contains both the Hebrew original and the German translation. A portion of the German translation of Horowitz's letter that appears in the manuscript was published by Professor Gotzmann in his *Jüdische Autonomie*, 472–73. Gotzmann also discussed the background to the letter (465–73).

217. On the establishment of courts as one of the Noachide laws, see B.T., *Sanhedrin* 56a–b, one of the sources cited by Horowitz. Cf., Yom Tov Assis, "Yehudey Sefarad be-ʿerkkaʾot ha-goyyim (ha-meʾot ha-13 ve-ha-14)," in *Tarbut ve-ḥebrah be-toledot Yisraʾel be-yemey ha-benayyim: qobeẓ maʾamarim le-zikro shel Ḥayyim Hillel Ben-Sasson*, ed. Reuben Bonfil et al. (Jerusalem: Shazar, 1989), 404, who noted that Jews in medieval Christian Spain believed the courts of non-Jews to be corrupt and susceptible to bribery.

people were violating Jewish law just "like anyone who eats food that is prohibited to us or marries a woman who is prohibited to us based on the Torah."[218]

Horowitz stressed that there were specific areas of the law concerning which all Jews turned to Jewish courts. Prohibited relationships, marriage and divorce, ritual matters such as permitted and prohibited foods, laws of the synagogue and its use, as well as wills and estates, were matters that Horowitz declared were always brought before Jewish courts, although there is little question that his claim that *all* Jews *always* brought these matters to Jewish courts was exaggerated. In contemporary Frankfurt, the Sichel brothers acknowledged that they had taken their dispute over their father's estate to the non-Jewish courts before they brought it to the *beyt din*.[219] A few years earlier, an extended period of rancor between a husband and wife brought the couple before the non-Jewish authorities before they ultimately came to a financial settlement in June 1760.[220] In another instance in the mid-1770s, Yuzpa Trier had to pay his three unmarried sisters-in-law to entice them to appear in the Frankfurt rabbinic court in a dispute over a number of issues, including their father's estate.[221]

Horowitz's statement was hyperbole, perhaps strategically aimed at strengthening, or at least not weakening, the community's right to continue to judge its own members — but hyperbole none the less.

Jews appearing in non-Jewish courts has often been thought to be a harbinger of change, pending modernization, and the collapse of Jewish communal authority. Yet Jews in the medieval Muslim world took matters to Muslim courts as a

218. A Jewish preacher in fourteenth-century Saragossa greatly expanded on the grievous nature of the sin (see Baḥye ben Asher, *Rabbeynu Baḥye bi'ur ʿal ha-Torah*, vol. 2, ed. Ḥayyim Dov Chavel [Jerusalem: Mossad Harav Kook, 1967], Ex. 21.1). The work appears in English translation as Baḥye ben Asher, *Midrash Rabbeinu Bachya, Torah Commentary*, vol. 4, trans. and annotated by Eliyahu Munk (Jerusalem: n.p., 1998), 1123–5.

219. The *beyt din* would not take the matter up until the Sichels produced a release from the non-Jewish court (see Gundersheim, Adler MS. 935, no. 236). One of Horowitz's own undated responsa dealt with the case of a Jewish family that took a dispute over an inheritance to the non-Jewish authorities, although the case may not have been from Frankfurt (see Pinḥas Horowitz, *Sefer she'elot u-teshubot gibʿat Pinḥas* [Józefów: B. Zetzer, 1875], no. 71). For an example of an important Jewish family from Berlin bringing an inheritance dispute before the non-Jewish authorities in the first half of the seventeenth century, see Birgit Klein, "Erbinnen in Norm und Praxis: Fiktion und Realität im Erbstreit der Familien Liebmann-von Geldern," in *Juden im Recht: Neue Zugänge zur Rechtsgeschichte der Juden im Alten Reich*, ed. Andreas Gotzmann, Stephan Wendehorst, Zeitschrift für Historische Forschung Supplement 39 (Berlin: Duncker & Humblot, 2007), 163–205.

220. On this dispute between Kalman Sichel and his "dear wife" Breinlen, see JTS, MS. 3967 (New York), fol. 10a–b. The couple seems to have separated but not divorced.

221. See Gundersheim, Adler MS. 935, no. 41 (fol. 46a).

matter of course, and there, rabbis made accommodations for this practice.[222] In the sixteenth and seventeenth centuries too, Jews routinely found their way to Ottoman courts.[223] Jews in Christian Spain also brought internal matters such as monetary disputes before royal courts.[224] No less an authority than Rabbi Solomon ibn Adret (d. 1310, Barcelona), one of the leading halakists of Christian Spain, appeared before the royal court in an internal Jewish matter.[225] In these contexts, Jews going to non-Jewish courts was not a sign of the collapse of the traditional community. German Jews bringing their intra-Jewish cases to non-Jewish courts was significant because they had generally not done so during the medieval period. Nonetheless, the process which led to this change was a long one and not a sudden development.

Still, the problem of Jews taking their disputes to non-Jewish courts should not be overstated. Gundersheim's diary shows that hundreds of Jews who lived in the Frankfurt *Judengasse* continued to bring their cases to Jewish courts. Litigants who brought their suits before the *beyt din* appear to have had confidence in the court, and in some instances they seem to have almost run to it. When Benedict Mai sold an unspecified amount of wine to Leb Oppenheim, Mai's father-in-law, Yudaʾ Kulp, objected and would not give Oppenheim access to the goods that were held in his possession. The case, which involved leading families in the *Judengasse*, was heard by the court so quickly that events were referred to as having taken place "last Monday."[226] Some litigants may have been committed to rule of law in

222. See S. D. Goitein, *A Mediterranean Society: The Jewish Communities of the Arab World as Portrayed in the Documents of the Cairo Geniza*, vol. 2 (Berkeley: University of California Press, 1967), 398–402; Marina Rustow, *Heresy and the Politics of Community: The Jews of the Fatimid Caliphate* (Ithaca: Cornell University Press, 2008), 72 with n. 12; Gideon Libson, *Jewish and Islamic Law: A Comparative Study of Custom During the Geonic Period*, Harvard Series in Islamic Law (Cambridge, Mass.: Islamic Legal Studies Program, Harvard Law School, 2003), 80–91; Uriel I. Simonsohn, "Overlapping Jurisdictions: Confessional Boundaries and Judicial Choice Among Christians and Jews Under Early Muslim Rule," Ph.D. diss. (Princeton University, 2008), 253–301.

223. See Hacker, "Gebulteyha shel ha-ʾoṭonomyah ha-yehudit," 381–82, and most recently, Yaron Ben-Naeh, *Jews in the Realms of the Sultans: Ottoman Jewish Society in the Seventeenth Century* (Tübingen: Morh Siebeck, 2008), 237–43.

224. Assis, "Yehudey Sefarad be-ʿerkkaʾot ha-goyyim," 408–23; Elka Klein, *Jews, Christian Society, and Royal Power*, 158.

225. Elka Klein, *Jews, Christian Society, and Royal Power*, 155–58.

226. Gundersheim, Adler MS. 935, no. 40, fol. 44a. According to Dietz, *Stammbuch der Frankfurter Juden*, 197, Benedict Mai would become the third richest man in the *Judengasse* by 1800 and his assets would be more than twice that of Mayer Amschel Rothschild. While he may not have enjoyed wealth in the 1770s when this case took place, both Oppenheim and Kulp were men of considerable wealth (see both their gravestones as recorded in Horovitz, *Abney zikkaron*,

the traditional Jewish context; others may have had faith in the ability of the *beyt din* and the Jewish community to administer and enforce justice. Still others may not have had the means to take their cases out of the community. The role of legal representatives in inducing litigants to take their claims to one court or another is also not known.[227] Lacking the full records of the rabbinic courts in Frankfurt as well as a good understanding of the role of representation, and without a study of the Frankfurt municipal records, the complete story of Jewish litigation in the second half of the eighteenth century cannot yet be told.[228]

Practical Authority of the Frankfurt Rabbinic Court

In an environment in which members of the community turned to non-Jewish courts, the rabbinic court itself could not assume that its rulings would be carried out and took steps to insure that its verdicts would be followed.[229] In almost all the litigation that was heard by the tribunals Rabbi Ḥayyim Gundersheim sat on, litigants were obligated to sign an agreement that they would "affirm and abide by" (*le-asher u-le-qayyem*) the court's decision before the court would consider the case.[230] Non-compliance with the terms of the agreement could bring about excommunication and fines. Such conditions had been imposed on litigants in the fifteenth century in matters of arbitration, but in the late eighteenth century the rabbinic court in Frankfurt imposed this condition both on court-brokered compromises and on legal decisions.[231]

In some cases Gundersheim noted that the litigants had executed the rulings

---

nos. 3806 and 3887, respectively). Oppenheim had also served in the communal leadership (see Segall, Pinqas Frankfurṭ, no. 421 [1768]).

227. In general the role of representation in the creation of litigation in the Jewish community requires investigation. C.W. Brooks, *Pettyfoggers and Vipers of the Commonwealth: The "Lower Branch" of the Legal Profession in Early Modern England*, Cambridge Studies in English Legal History (Cambridge: Cambridge University Press, 1986), 115, noted that "the question of whether lawyers create lawsuits or lawsuits lawyers is a classic chicken-or-egg dilemma," although in sixteenth-century England it was "clear that the lawsuits came first."

228. Verena Kasper, *Die Frankfurter jüdische Gemeinde am Reichshofrat in josephinischer Zeit (1765–90)*, Schriftenreihe des Centrums für Jüdische Studien 19 (Vienna: Studienverlag, forthcoming), will be a significant step in this direction with respect to Frankfurt Jews in the *Reichshofrat*.

229. See the comments of Zimmer, *Harmony and Discord*, 102–3.

230. See, for example, Gundersheim, Adler MS. 935, nos. 41, 42, 45, among many others. Mosheh Frank, *Qehillot Ashkenaz u-battey dineyhen* (Tel Aviv: Dvir, 1937), 30–31, noted that in the fifteenth century *battey din* also demanded that litigants formally obligate themselves to accept the court's verdict before they would judge the case.

231. On the fifteenth century, see Zimmer, *Harmony and Discord*, 71. Court-ordered compromises

of the court and even noted the date on which this occurred. In a dispute that ended with a relatively modest settlement (5 guldens) it would seem that payment was made on the spot, but this was not always the case, even when the amounts disputed were small.[232] Threats notwithstanding, in some instances both individuals and the community failed to fulfill what the court had obligated them to do.[233] One individual who did not comply with the court's ruling later needed to return to the court to transact a sale of property. He found that the *beyt din* would not process his transaction until he did what the court had asked of him some years earlier.[234] Here the court self-policed its ruling. Elsewhere Gundersheim noted that a ruling of the court was followed, but execution was not particularly swift. In a familial dispute the court heard in 1774 its ruling was issued on 1 April of that year, yet the parties did not comply with the ruling until some four months later. Only on 27 July did the two sides come before Gundersheim to make the necessary transfer of payment and undertake the obligations the court had imposed on them.[235] Perhaps there were some mitigating circumstances in this particular case which had to do with one of the parties being engaged to be married. In another case, a complicated estate dispute that had already been taken to the non-Jewish courts, and then, apparently at the behest of the parties, withdrawn and taken to the Jewish courts, a decision was given by the court in March 1791.[236] Four days later, the parties were back in court involved in negotiations that lasted for two days. After a further two days the court gave its second decision on the matter. Execution of the court's orders by the parties took place within eleven days of the final decision.[237]

In a number of cases the court required that one of the litigants take an oath as a way of insuring that their claims were indeed true. To swear falsely was not just a crime against society, but made God, whose Name was invoked in the act of taking the oath, an accomplice in the crime.[238] Rabbis took the matter extremely seriously, and before someone deponed an oath they were told of the immediate and terrible

---

were not simply an equal division of what was being disputed. See, for example, Gundersheim, Adler MS. 935, no. 121.

232. Gundersheim, Adler MS. 935, no. 71.

233. Gundersheim, Adler MS. 935, nos. 41 and 71. Also see no. 62 where the parties came to a compromise after the court had made its decision. These sources were cited by Sendik, "Beyn din le-pesher," 64.

234. Gundersheim, Adler MS. 935, no. 199 with no. 171. Also see Sendik, "Beyn din le-pesher," 64.

235. Gundersheim, Adler MS. 935, no. 41 (postscript on fol. 47a).

236. Gundersheim, Adler MS. 935, no. 236.

237. See Gundersheim, Adler MS. 935, no. 237, with postscript.

238. See Jacob Milgrom, *Leviticus 1–16: A New Translation with Introduction and Commentary*, The Anchor Bible, vol. 3 (New York: Doubleday, 1991), 336, 337, 367–68.

consequences that a false oath would have for the individual, his family, and the People of Israel.[239] Taking an oath required a ceremony separate from the court proceedings, and in one case it took about a month after the court imposed an oath on a litigant for it to be administered.[240] In another instance, in which one of the parties was from Worms, the deponent preferred to come to a compromise with the claimant — which in this case took approximately five months — rather than take an oath.[241]

In at least one instance the court was unable to impose its ruling on individuals who were hardly on the fringes of rabbinic culture. In the course of a financial dispute in early 1778, the court ordered the children of Rabbi Meʾir Schwarzschild (who had been a *dayyan* on the Frankfurt *beyt din*) to take an oath regarding their father's debts. To this end, "soon after the court ruling," Gundersheim accompanied them to the synagogue where he was to administer the oath. According to the court's ruling, the plaintiff, Joel Bing, had the right to decide which of Schwarzschild's children should take the oath, and asked that one of the daughters do so. She refused. There in the synagogue Gundersheim reminded her that the court had given Bing the right to choose who would take the oath, but still she refused. Unable to overcome the impasse, the parties left the synagogue. At some point, the community became involved and ordered that Schwarzschild's son take the oath, which he did about six months after the original court order. Thus the court's order was only partially fulfilled, for Bing had lost one of the privileges the court had granted him.[242]

Echoes of the at times tenuous authority of the rabbinic court can be heard in the response of the *beyt din* of Frankfurt to a question asked of it by the non-Jewish authorities in Corvey regarding two Jews from the town of Höxter, over 200 kilometers north of Frankfurt (today in North-Rhine Westphalia).[243] At stake was

239. See B.T., *Shabuʿot* 38b–39a; Maimonides, *Code of Law*, Laws of Oaths 11.15; *Shulḥan ʿaruk*, Ḥoshen mishpaṭ 87.20, 21. See the postscript in Gundersheim, Adler MS. 935, no. 65, from which it appears that a different form of threat may have been used in contemporary Frankfurt.

240. Gundersheim, Adler MS. 935, no. 65.

241. Gundersheim, Adler MS. 935, no. 62 with postscript. The delay could have been due to the physical distance between the litigants. The defendant was a merchant who had been in Frankfurt during one of the commercial fairs and may have returned home or traveled elsewhere (he had representation and was not personally present in court) either before or after the court's decision.

242. Gundersheim, Adler MS. 935, nos. 105 and 107.

243. For a survey of the history of the Jews in the Corvey region during the early modern period, see Jörg Deventer, *Das Abseits als sicherer Ort? Jüdische Minderheit und christliche Gesellschaft im Alten Reich am Beispiel der Fürstabtei Corvey (1550–1807)*, Forschungen zur Regionalgeschichte 21 (Paderborn: Ferdinand Schöningh, 1996). While this work focuses on the seventeenth

whether a Jew in whose house public prayers took place could prevent someone who did not want to share in the public expenses of prayer — such as renting space and the hiring of a cantor — from entering his house to pray, and also whether this person could use communal utensils for making matzos.[244] Presumably lacking any form of local rabbinic leadership, the Jews took their disagreement to the local non-Jewish authorities.

That Jews in this small town turned to the non-Jewish authorities may not be noteworthy, for already in the fifteenth century, in some small communities in the German lands that had no rabbinic court, rabbis accepted the fact that litigants took their cases to the non-Jewish authorities.[245] The community in Höxter may have fit this model and, indeed, in the second half of the seventeenth century, disputes between Jews seem to have been submitted to the non-Jewish legal authorities in Corvey. In a number of instances in the seventeenth century the authorities referred such questions to the rabbinic court in Hildesheim, with which the Jewish community in Corvey maintained a connection.[246] However, for as yet unknown reasons, in the second half of the eighteenth century a number of cases between Jews in Corvey were sent by the non-Jewish authorities to the Frankfurt rabbinic court.[247]

In early April 1769, soon after Rabbi Gundersheim had joined the rabbinic court of Frankfurt, the *beyt din* composed a very detailed Hebrew language response to the ruler of Höxter, the Prince of Corvey.

> We have agreed to answer in the matter of the claims and disputes between Me'ir Levi and Yuqab Herz and his wife of Höxter that was sent to us by our lord, the pious Prince of Corvey, may the Lord increase his splendor, that we, the rabbinic court, should deal with the matter and rule on the law according to the religion of our Holy Torah.[248] First, we would like

century, there is a discussion of the status of the Jews in the eighteenth century as well. Regarding Jews in Höxter in earlier periods, see Diethard Aschoff, "Höxter," in *Germania Judaica*, ed. Arye Maimon, vol. 3.1 (Tübingen: Mohr, 1987), 567.

244. My thanks to Mr. Michael Lenarz and Dr. Johannes Wachten for identifying this town called "He'qsher" in Hebrew. According to the document, the local authorities would not allow the Jews to build a synagogue in Höxter but they were allowed "to pray in a room" in a private house (YIVO MS. RG 128 [folder 77–78], fol. 87a). Also see Deventer, *Das Abseits als sicherer Ort?*, 108 with n. 123, and page 109 dealing with a somewhat earlier period.

245. See Zimmer, *Harmony and Discord*, 88.

246. See Deventer, *Das Abseits als sicherer Ort?*, 116–19.

247. Also see Gundersheim, Adler MS. 935, no. 161.

248. On the possible identity of Me'ir Levi and the person who may have been the leader of the Jewish community (*Obervorsteher*), see Deventer, *Das Abseits als sicherer Ort?*, 113. Also see

> to thank God, who in our servitude has not abandoned us and who has given us favor in the eyes of kings and rulers who protect us under their wings to strengthen our religion and customs according to our holy Torah, including what we have received in the Oral Torah as everything has been explained to us in the Talmud. And it [i.e., the Oral Torah] is what one person received from another back to our teacher Moses, may his memory be a blessing. Also the decrees and ordinances made by our Sages, may their memories be a blessing, who came after the Talmud, whose ordinances and decrees spread and were accepted in all Jewish communities. And our laws are outlined for us briefly in all the matters listed above by the volumes of *Shulḥan ʿaruk* which the entire House of Israel relies on, as our eyes see. For our lord, the pious Prince of Corvey, may his splendor be increased, requested that we rule in the matter of the above mentioned claims and disputes and [he will] support our ruling in this. And for this we give praise to God, be He blessed, for the past and pray for the future that we should find favor and mercy in the eyes of our lord the prince, that he remain diligent in guarding our welfare. And on account of this may our lord, the pious prince, may his splendor be increased, as well as his ministers and advisers live long and may their days and years be spent in peace, tranquility, and rest and may there be peace and tranquility in their courts and castles and in their days may Israel and Judah be in the territory of Benjamin at Zelzah (1 Sam. 10.2) forever ... and certainly since we have seen that with the greatest kindness our lord, the pious prince, may his splendor be increased, will spread his mercy on them and he wishes to protect their well being and our religion, the Jewish religion, and therefore, it is clear that they [the Jews of Höxter] are obliged to protect their well being together and to pray to God, may He be blessed. And just as we pray for the peace of the great man, our lord, the pious prince, may his splendor be raised, with all his ministers and advisers that their days and years in power may be lengthened and may they always succeed in their ways and treat all those under their rule with mercy and pity and in their days may we merit that a redeemer may come to Zion in joy. Amen.[249]

Given the explanation of basic Jewish concepts such as the Oral Torah, the relatively simple argumentation that characterizes the legal discussion in the response,

---

the material cited in Wolfgang Leesch, *Inventar des Archivs der Stadt Höxter*, Inventare der nichtstaatlichen Archive Westfalens. Neue Folge 1 (Münster: Aschendorff, 1961), 63, no. 4.

249. YIVO MS. RG 128 (folder 77–78), fols. 90a-b, 92b. The material is cited by permission of the YIVO Institute for Jewish Research, New York.

and the almost obeisant praise of the local prince, this letter appears have been written in Hebrew and translated into German for the prince or his deputies. However, a legal brief written but one day earlier by the very same Frankfurt rabbinic court for translation into German and transmission to the *Reichshofrat* in Vienna contains none of this sort of praise for the ruler.[250] Moreover, the Prince of Corvey, for whom the rabbis of Frankfurt prayed so fervently in this letter, was none other than a Benedictine monk, Philipp von Spiegel zu Desenberg, Abbot of the Imperial Abbey of Corvey from 1758–76.[251]

The seventeenth and eighteenth centuries were periods of significant change in the German lands and their environs.[252] Already in late seventeenth-century Berlin, the Prussian state began to consolidate its power by interfering in the internal workings of Jewish communities.[253] This continued in the early eighteenth century when the authority of rabbinic courts was restricted to cases less than 100 reichstalers in value, while disputes involving greater sums were to be referred to the *Kammergericht*, the Prussian supreme court.[254] In 1730 Frederick Wilhelm (d. 1740) abolished Jewish judicial autonomy, further concentrating power in state hands.[255] In the age of absolutism, because the state sought to remove all competition, Frederick Wilhelm's actions were not confined to the Jews; he also canceled the right of nobles to judge their serfs and disbanded the courts of guilds.[256] The trend extended beyond the German lands, for in 1734 the Metz Parliament limited the jurisdiction of the rabbinic courts over Jews, leaving Jewish courts as places of

250. YIVO MS. RG 128 (folder 77–78), fol. 85a–b. Verena Kasper has kindly confirmed for me that a German translation of the text is extant in the records of the *Reichshofrat* in Vienna.

251. A portrait of Philipp from the abbot gallery of the castle in Corvey is reproduced in Peter Ilisch and Arnold Schwede, *Das Münzwesen im Stift Corvey 1541–1794*, Studien und Quellen zur Westfälischen Geschichte 58, Veröffentlichungen der Historischen Kommission für Westfalen 11 (Paderborn: Bonifatius, 2007), 523. A coin minted by the Abbey in 1759 described Philipp as "prince and abbot of Corvey" (see http://www.muenzauktion.com/hoelscher/pic/081025006bz.jpg, accessed 19 March 2009 or in Ilisch and Schwede, 537).

252. On the impending change, see Selma Stern, *The Court Jew*, trans. Ralph Weiman (Philadelphia: Jewish Publication Society, 1950), 178–79.

253. David Sorkin, *The Transformation of German Jewry, 1780–1840* (New York: Oxford University Press, 1987), 44.

254. Azriel Shohet, *ʿIm ḥilufey tequfot*, 83.

255. Azriel Shohet, *ʿIm ḥilufey tequfot*, 86, as well as Mordechai Breuer, "The Early Modern Period," in *German-Jewish History in Modern Times*, ed. Michael Meyer and Michael Brenner, trans. William Templer (New York: Columbia University Press, 1996), 254. On legal reform in Prussia, see Selma Stern, *Der Preussische Staat und die Juden*, vol. 3.1 (Tübingen: Mohr Siebeck, 1971), 111–33, especially, 117–20.

256. Azriel Shohet, *ʿIm ḥilufey tequfot*, 86.

voluntary arbitration of disputes.[257] Change came more slowly to the Holy Roman Empire and to Frankfurt, but the rabbinic leadership was most likely well-aware of what was happening around it.

While the differences between the two letters addressed to Vienna and Höxter within a day of each other may have been a matter of convention, the Frankfurt rabbinic court's exuberance in praising the Prince of Corvey may reflect their joy not only in receiving a case between Jews from the non-Jewish legal system, but in the secular authority's promise to enforce the rabbinic court's decision ("the pious Prince of Corvey ... who requested that we rule in the matter ... and [he will] support our ruling in this. And for this we give praise to God, be He blessed"). Presumably the Abbot of Corvey and/or his deputies did not want to deal with a case involving Jewish religious life. Yet, in returning the case to the Jewish community and promising to enforce the *beyt din*'s decision, they bolstered the prestige of the rabbinic court in a period when the authority of such courts was being questioned.[258]

Court Records as Historical Sources

Court records are quite different than rabbinic responsa, a literature that has proven itself to be a rich cache of information for the history of Jewish law as well as for reconstructing daily life.[259] Responsa (pl.; sing., responsum) are ostensibly the written answers, generally of individual scholars of rabbinic law, to questions addressed to them by those facing legal conundrums and/or situations that were

257. See Berkovitz, *Rites and Passages*, 20.

258. When Rabbi Pinḥas Horowitz was asked a question by the magistrates of Frankfurt in 1781, he opened with praise for the non-Jewish officials "... who honored me through our lords, the great local rulers, to ask my opinion in matters of our religion ... and I freed up time to answer because of this honor ..." (Frankfurt Ugb D33, fol. 30b). Horowitz was not profuse in his praise of the officials, but then he was not asked to decide a case but rather to clarify the law. Case no. 161 from November 1782 in Gundersheim's diary was also sent to the Frankfurt rabbinic court by the non-Jewish authorities (*hoch löbliche Juden Kommission*) in Corvey, and Gundersheim's record of the court's decision is without any praise for the prince. However, this text was Gundersheim's personal record of the case and not the court's official response to the authorities.

259. The relevant literature in the fields of Jewish law and history extends beyond the scope of a footnote. An attempt to begin to summarize the material was made by Peter Haas, *Responsa: Literary History of a Rabbinic Genre* (Atlanta: Scholars Press, 1996), 14–19. Some of the shortcomings of his efforts are pointed out by Haym Soloveitchik, "Responsa: Literary History and Basic Literacy," review of *Responsa: The Literary History of a Rabbinic Genre* by Peter Haas, *AJS Review* 24, no. 2 (1999): 343–57.

perceived to be without clear precedents or directives in legal codes.[260] Queries could deal with almost any matter of Jewish law (*halakah*) applicable in the post-Temple age, from matters of ritual observance to legal procedure. In general, the greater the reputation of the jurist and the greater the perceived dilemma the more likely he was to receive queries from beyond his community.

Asking legal questions of individuals who were recognized as legal authorities was in no way unique to Jewish society. In Roman times, the Emperor and magistrates were asked specific questions on technical points of law and responded with rescripts.[261] This practice continued in the medieval church with decretals, and has its parallel in the Muslim world in *fatāwā*.[262]

The jurisdiction of rabbinic courts was far more circumscribed than that of individual decisors. Even with its great reputation — few courts in any historical period could boast the likes of Rabbis Pinḥas Horowitz, Nathan Maas, and Meʾir Schiff — the *beyt din* in Frankfurt did not receive cases from those who lived outside of the town unless the cases were somehow tied to Frankfurt (e.g., real property), there was difficulty reaching a decision elsewhere, or the court received a request to deal with a matter from the non-Jewish authorities.[263] This was in keeping with a long-standing tradition in Jewish communities in the German lands which prohibited rabbis or heads of courts from extending their jurisdiction over those who were normally subject to different authorities.[264]

In theory, anyone could address a question to a rabbi, but, more often than not, an individual would have formal inquiries written up by other rabbis who would take the facts of the case and rework them into the language of rabbinic discourse before presenting them to a rabbinic decisor for his decision.[265] Thus, responsa

260. Responsa could be written by courts as well, although this was far less common. See for example, Bodleian Library, MS. Mich. 465 (Oxford University), fol. 54a, for a procedural question addressed to a court and responded to in 1687. No location was specified.

261. See Peter Heather, *The Fall of the Roman Empire: A New History of Rome and the Barbarians* (New York: Oxford University Press, 2006), 108–9.

262. On decretals, James Brundage, *Medieval Canon Law* (London: Longman, 1995), 53, and, on *fatāwā*, Joseph Schacht, *An Introduction to Islamic Law* (Oxford: Clarendon, 1964), 73–75.

263. See Gundersheim, Adler MS. 935, nos. 139, 161, and 188 with introduction, for examples of non-Jewish authorities turning to the Frankfurt rabbinic court. No. 38 deals with a matter from Worms that local authorities appear to have been unable to settle.

264. See Finkelstein, *Jewish Self-Government*, 263 no. 13.

265. On the reworking of material, also see Frank, *Qehillot Ashkenaz*, 90–91. Ashkenazic rabbis in earlier generations generally accepted queries from judges and not litigants. In this regard, see Dinari, *Ḥakmey Ashkenaz be-shalhey yemey ha-beynayyim*, 233–34, with n. 18, as well as Moses Mintz, *Sheʾelot u-teshubot Rabbeynu Mosheh Minẓ*, ed. Yonatan Shraga Domb (Jerusalem: Machon Yerushalayim, 1991), end of no. 28, and Yaʿaqov Koppel Duschinsky, "Toledot R' David Oppenheymer," *Ha-ẓofeh le-ḥakmat Yisraʾel* 5 and 6 (1921–22): 208–23. The phrase "*shalom*

were almost always written by the elite for the elite. As noted, court cases could be initiated by anyone, and Gundersheim's diary contains cases brought by people from various strata of life, including the impoverished.[266] In such cases the elite of the court were were often addressed directly by individuals who probably lacked any sort of formal education, and the members of the court likely responded to these individuals directly as well.

Like jurists in other cultures who received questions on specific points of law or legal procedure, rabbinic decisors (Heb., *poseq*; pl., *poseqim*) generally accepted information as received and responded accordingly. Rabbis were not invested with investigative powers, and the distances involved often made any protracted questioning impractical. Nevertheless, *poseqim*, particularly when dealing with commercial matters, often quizzed local business people in order to learn about common practices in the marketplace.[267] By contrast, the rabbinic court in Frankfurt did have the authority to investigate matters, and litigants took this as a given. In a case involving commissions on the sale of lottery tickets, one of the litigants informed the court through his advocate that he had not paid his agent the normal fees, but rather, higher ones. The legal representative did not prove this point by bringing witnesses or documents, but told the court they could find this out for themselves if they inquired with other lottery agents.[268] In other instances the court held multiple on-site inspections, and in one case members of the court determined which of certain house repairs were urgent and which were not.[269] In yet another case the court consulted with specialists from beyond the Jewish community to ascertain the facts of a case.[270] It also summoned individuals to answer questions if it saw fit to do so.[271]

ʿal dayyaney Yisraʾel" ("peace on the judges of Israel" [B.T., *Ketubbot* 50a]) was a common salutation in responsa of rabbis in early modern Europe, as a search in the Bar-Ilan Global Jewish Database (Responsa Project), ver. 16, shows. The reworking of the facts of the case by professionals for professionals was to be found in the Muslim world as well (see Muhammed Khalid Masud, Brinkely Messick, and David S. Powers, "Muftis, Fatwas, and Islamic Legal Interpretation," in *Islamic Legal Interpretation: Muftis and their Fatwas,* ed. Muhammed Khalid Masud, Brinkely Messick, and David S. Powers, Harvard Studies in Islamic Law [Cambridge, Mass.: Harvard University Press, 1996], 20).

266. See, for example, Gundersheim, Adler MS. 935, nos. 185 and 214.
267. Also see Pinḥas Horowitz, *Responsa*, no. 19, where the questioner collected information before sending his query.
268. See Gundersheim, Adler MS. 935, no. 68.
269. Gundersheim, Adler MS. 935, nos. 100, 101, 115. Regarding the home improvements, see no. 79. It is unclear who paid for these consultations.
270. This was true of the rabbinic court in Metz as well. See Berkovitz, *Protocols of Justice*.
271. See, for example, Gundersheim, Adler MS. 935, nos. 40, 67, 100, 114, and 135. On calling witnesses, see *Shulḥan ʿaruk*, Ḥoshen mishpaṭ 11.1. Also see Berkovitz, *Protocols of Justice*.

With the information in hand, the *poseq* would often craft a response in which he typically attempted to rely on a talmudic text he perceived to be applicable to the particular case, as well as on precedents in rabbinic interpretation, law, and, possibly, local custom. In the course of his discussion an astute respondent would not only advance his own thesis, but raise possible criticisms of his opinion before showing that such objections were either not pertinent to the situation or could not be sustained logically. This was an important part of the legal argument since the authority of a rabbi's ruling rested not only on his personal standing, but on how successfully he convinced the recipient(s) of his legal reasoning. Although rabbis may have discussed their decisions with students and colleagues before issuing them, responsa represent the opinions of the individuals who authored them.[272]

Court decisions were significantly different than responsa in that they represented the unified voice of a panel of rabbis. While there could be discussion and dissent behind closed doors, to the world outside the court presented a unified front. In keeping with the rules of *halakah*, an edict of the Jewish community in Frankfurt from 1754 explicitly stated that decisions had to be signed by all members of the court, even those who were in dissent.[273] Moreover, unlike responsa, court decisions did not have to be justified; the court simply had to inform litigants of its rulings.[274]

---

272. In the fifteenth century, even leading German rabbis consulted with colleagues from time to time before giving rulings (see Dinari, *Ḥakmey Ashkenaz be-shalhey yemey ha-beynayyim*, 40–47). Consultations were also common elsewhere in matters of personal status, particularly with respect to an *ʿagunah*, that is, a woman whose husband had disappeared and was presumed but not confirmed to be dead, or a woman who was given a questionable bill of divorce (*geṭ*). In such cases, often one rabbi authored a responsum and then sent it to at least two colleagues for their written agreement. The co-signers might add a minor addendum. See, for example, Joshua Höschel ben Joseph, *Sefer peney Yehoshuʿa ḥeleq sheni mi-sheʾelot u-teshubot* (L'viv: Zalman Leb Flekir, 1860), no. 53.

273. See *Shulḥan ʿaruk*, Ḥoshen misphaṭ 19.1–2. A rationale is suggested in Joshua Falk, *Sefer meʾirat ʿenayim* 19 n. 1. The Frankfurt communal ordinance threatened a *dayyan* who failed to sign the decision with a three year suspension (ŻIH MS. 517, fols. 25b–26a, no. 116). This was a long-standing rule in the community (see Segall, Pinqas Frankfurṭ, no. 320, section 30, from December 1674). In the seventeenth century, *dayyanim* were obligated to take an oath that they would follow the community's ordinances before they began their term on the bench (see no. 309b from 1682).

274. ŻIH MS. 517, no. 67. On the question of whether a rabbinic court must provide justification for its rulings, see Eliav Schochetman, "Ḥobat ha-hanmaqah be-mishpaṭ ha-ʿibri," *Shenaton ha-mishpaṭ ha-ʿibri* 6–7 (1979–80): 321–52 (with respect to this period, particularly 321–38), as well as *Shulḥan ʿaruk*, Ḥoshen mishpaṭ 14.4, 19.1–2. Failure to offer rationales in civil cases in early modern Castile led to an accusation that the court made its decisions arbitrarily (see Kagan, *Lawsuits and Litigants*, 27). I do not know whether there was such a feeling among the Jews of late eighteenth-century Frankfurt, but there could hardly have been much pressure for

This later point may have carried over from litigation between individuals to administrative matters as well. For example, the non-Jewish authorities in Vienna requested that the local Jewish community forward a question to Frankfurt, and in February 1785 the leaders of the Frankfurt community presented the question to the *beyt din*.[275] The court was asked whether a child born in the first year of a couple's marriage had the right to inherit from its mother. In the twelfth century, Rabbi Jacob ben Meʾir (Northern France, d. 1171; known as Rabbeynu Tam) enacted an ordinance that if a woman died during the first year (or second according to some versions) of marriage, her dowry had to be returned to her father unless there were children from the union. The authorities in Vienna appear to have been asking for clarifications regarding the ordinance, particularly regarding the rights of the child.[276]

This was the sort of question to be found in the responsa literature. When rabbis were asked about the practical ramifications of the medieval ordinance connected to this issue, they offered detailed discussions of possible interpretations and dealt with the scope and applicability of the ordinance.[277] The rabbinic court of Frankfurt did not do this. It gave a terse ruling and no more. Perhaps this was all that was needed when responding to the non-Jewish authorities, but it offered the Jewish community of Vienna no way of explaining the rules of Jewish life to outsiders. Not surprisingly, less than six months later further questions related

rabbinic courts to provide such rationales. In contemporary local non-Jewish society courts did not divulge the reasons for their decisions to the parties involved, although a debate on the matter was taking place in legal circles and there was full disclosure in some cases in Hesse in the 1750s and 1760s. Still, courts in the German lands generally did not publish their judgments with rationales until the nineteenth century (John P. Dawson, *Judges: Oracles of the Law*, Thomas M. Cooley Lectures [Ann Arbor: University of Michigan Law School, 1968], 432–38, and 437–38 n. 21, specifically regarding Hesse; Hans-Peter Haferkamp, "The Science of Private Law and the State in Nineteenth Century Germany," *American Journal of Comparative Law* 56, no. 3 [Summer 2008]: 257–58).

275. Gundersheim, Adler MS. 935, no. 188.

276. On the ordinance, see *tosafot*, B.T., *Ketubbot* 47a–b, and the material cited by Ephraim Kupfer, ed., *Teshubot u-pesaqim meʾet ḥakhmey Ashkenaz ve-Ẓarefat* (Jerusalem: Mekize Nirdamim, 1973), no. 103 (pp. 162–63), and his discussion of the sources and the acceptance of the ordinance in appendix 3, pts. 1, 2 (pp. 316–19). Also see Israel Yuval, "Ha-hesdarim ha-kaspiyyim shel ha-nesuʾin be-Ashkenaz be-yemey ha-beynayyim," in *Dat ve-kalkalah*, ed. Menahem Ben-Sasson (Jerusalem: Shazar, 1995), 199–201, and Aharon Shweka, "Ha-pulmus ʿal taqqanot Ṭoliṭulah be-yerushat ha-baʿal et ishto," *Tarbiz* 68, no. 1 (December 1998): 87–127, regarding a similar ordinance in medieval Toledo (see *Shulḥan ʿaruk*, Eben ha-ʿezer 118.8).

277. See, for example, Slonik, *Responsa*, nos. 11, 12, albeit material from late sixteenth-century Lithuania.

to medieval ordinances and the rules of inheritance came from the non-Jewish authorities in Vienna.[278]

The Frankfurt court also functioned differently than did individual rabbis in that, as mentioned, the court had to work within a defined schedule. This is not to suggest, though, that rabbinic decisors could ignore time restrictions, for many questions demanded immediate responses to prevent human suffering or economic loss.[279] In other instances circumstances forced the decisor to rush the writing of a decision, perhaps before he had time to finish or express all of his thoughts. Rabbis were often dependent on a messenger who was waiting at the door pressuring them to hand over the letter so that he could go on his way.[280] Although in the seventeenth and eighteenth centuries there was a regular postal service in the western portions of the Empire that could be used to send material between many centers, universal postal service had yet to be instituted.[281] Sometimes, too, questions were asked while a *poseq* was traveling, leaving him to answer without an opportunity

---

278. See Gundersheim, Adler MS. 935, no. 194.

279. Joel Sirkes, *She'elot u-teshubot ha-bayit ḥadash* (Frankfurt: Johan Vost, 1697), no. 90, related that his colleagues attending the fair late in the winter of 1632 asked him to return home and give his legal opinion on a certain matter. This gave him an opportunity to compose a well-considered responsum. Nothing suggests that members of the Frankfurt court had similar chances for reflection and research. In outlying communities the situation may have been different. Lay courts that offered arbitration were another matter (see Katz, *Masoret u-mashber*, 121, on these two latter issues).

280. This problem hampered rabbis in the German lands prior to the very late sixteenth century, and in eastern Europe for some time thereafter (see Dinari, *Ḥakmey Ashkenaz be-shalhey yemey ha-beynayyim*, 231, regarding the German lands in the fifteenth century). Although there was some form of orderly mail or courier service between sixteenth-century Cracow and an unspecified town (see Isserles, *Responsa*, no. 128 [p. 498]), rabbis were generally dependent on travelers who might take letters to their destinations for them (see, for example, Isserles, nos. 67 [p. 394; a case in which the letter arrived opened and damaged], 105 [p. 443], 106 [p. 446]; Me'ir ben Gedaliah, *She'elot ut-teshubot* [Venice: Bragadin, 1618], no. 49, who had no one to send the letter with). Obviously, wars could disrupt communications as is clear from Joshua Höschel ben Joseph, *Responsa* (pt. 2), no. 63. When rabbis began to avail themselves of the postal service of non-Jews requires further investigation. Some Jews appear to have been well-aware of the local postal schedule. A calendar of the Jewish year published in Fürth in 1757 noted the dates of departure of the mail, yet, according to Mosche Rosenfeld, ("Fürther jüdische Kalender," *Israelitische Kultusgemeinde Fürth*, September 1989, 32), of the 68 extant Hebrew calendars published for Fürth Jewry between 1737 and 1790, this was the only one to record this information. Also see Carlebach, *Palaces of Time*, 139.

281. On mail service in the Empire, see Klaus Beyrer, "The Mail-Coach Revolution: Landmarks in Travel in Germany between the Seventeenth and Nineteenth Centuries," *German History* 24, no. 3 [2006]: 375–83, and, far more extensively, Wolfgang Behringer, *Thurn und Taxis: Die Geschichte ihrer Post und ihrer Unternehmen* [Munich: Piper, 1990], 79–148).

to consult his books.[282] In an extreme case in the fifteenth century, a responsum was written as the decisor and his community faced imminent expulsion.[283]

The sending of a responsum did not mean that the *poseq* stopped work on his opinion.[284] Even if a responsum was sent, rabbis could rework their views in preparation for eventual copying by others or, in the era of print, for publication.[285] There could also be a give and take between the *poseq* and his colleagues, including the questioner.[286] Sometimes a rabbi reversed his

---

282. In the first half of the seventeenth century, Sirkes, *Responsa* (old), no. 100, noted that he wrote a responsum while at the fair in Lublin, where the only text he had access to was *Shulḥan ʿaruk*. He later rewrote his opinion (also see Joel Sirkes, *Sheʾelot u-teshubot ha-ba"ḥ ha-ḥadashot* [Koretz: Johan Anton Kreiger, 1785], nos. 56, 57). Just after the turn of the eighteenth century, Rabbi David Oppenheim twice noted that he was writing while away from his library (see Duschinsky, "Toledot R' David Oppenheymer," 247 n. 194, summarized in English in his "Rabbi David Oppenheimer: Glimpses of His Life and Activity, Derived from His Manuscripts in the Bodleian Library," *Jewish Quarterly Review* 20, no. 3 [1930]: 241).

283. See Dinari, *Ḥakmey Ashkenaz be-shalhey yemey ha-beynayyim*, 230 (Dinari's source should be corrected to Mintz, *Responsa*, no. 49a, p. 217). For many rabbis, making a copy of the responsum was part of the process. If time did not permit it, a copy of the responsum would have to be returned to the sender, copied for him by the recipient, or ultimately returned to the decisor's descendents for it to be included in his collected writings.

284. Rabbi Abraham Slonik noted that he had authored an opinion permitting a certain *ʿagunah* to remarry and showed it to colleagues at the fair in Lublin in 1639. Rabbis Yom Tov Lipman Heller, Meʾir ben Abraham Sack of L'viv, and Moses Mendels of Poznań agreed to the allowance, but Slonik continued to work on the responsum as new information became available. He returned to the matter to stave off the criticisms of a colleague and again, in 1646, when he learned that the deceased had had a second wife (and a child) in Frankfurt, and that the rabbinate there was uncertain as to whether the second wife could remarry (see Joshua Höschel ben Joseph, *Responsa* [pt. 2], no. 63).

285. See, for example, Mintz, *Responsa*, no. 34a, who seems to have made some editorial comments after having sent out his responsum. Rabbis not only reviewed but sometimes rewrote material that they had already sent out. In this regard, see Gershon Ashkenazi, *Sheʾelot u-teshubot ʿabodat ha-gershuni* (Frankfurt: n.p., 1699), introduction, with my, "Taqdim hilkati she-ʾeyno raʾuyi le-shemo," in *ʿAl pi ha-beʾer: meḥqarim be-hagut yehudit u-be-maḥshebet ha-halakah muggashim le-Yaʿaqob Blidstein*, ed. Uri Erlich et al. (Beer Sheva: Ben-Gurion University Press, 2008), 401–12.

286. Regarding the fifteenth century, see Dinari, *Ḥakmey Ashkenaz be-shalhey yemey ha-beynayyim*, 237; in the sixteenth century, see Jacob Weil, *Sheḥiṭot u-bediqot*, with notes by Ẓebi ben Isaac Jacob (Cracow: Isaac Prostitz, 1577), 38a–b, for a matter that was discussed orally and in which Isserles ultimately changed his mind; with respect to the seventeenth century, see Debra Kaplan, http://www.earlymodern.org/workshops/2006/kaplan/index.php?pid=34, accessed 5 February 2009. Sometimes authors/editors/publishers of responsa excluded such correspondance and only included the view of the rabbi whose responsa were being published (see Shmuel Glick, "ʿAl shinuyyim hashmaṭot ve-ẓenzurah penimit be-sifrey sheʾelot u-teshubot," *Quntres* 1, no. 1 [2009]: 69–70).

decision.[287] This was a luxury that courts generally did not enjoy, for unless new evidence came to light or the court made a blatant mistake, once a court made its decision, it was final.[288]

Issues discussed in responsa could easily parallel cases considered by rabbinic courts because judges on rabbinic panels often turned to *poseqim* for directions and clarifications. However, court records differ from responsa as a source of law and history in that they generally represent legal practice as opposed to authoritative opinions on points of law.[289] That is to say, while the authors of responsa intended their answers to be practical legal rulings that could and should be relied upon in practice, there is rarely any way of knowing whether their rulings were actually followed.[290] Perhaps in their own communities their rulings were enforced due to their authority as communal rabbis, but elsewhere *poseqim* had no means of

---

287. See Meʾir Katzenellenbogen's responsum in Judah ben Eliezer ha-Levi and Meʾir ben Isaac Katzenellenbogen Mintz, *Sefer sheʾelot u-teshubot Mahar"i Minẓ ve-Mahara"m Padovah*, reprint, 1882 (Jerusalem: n.p., 1980), no. 4. Katzenellenbogen's original response to Rabbi Benedit Ashkenazi of Bologna was given orally. Later, after consulting his books and the rabbinic court records on the case, Katzenellenbogen reversed his opinion.

288. Regarding new evidence, see B.T., *Sanhedrin* 31a; *Shulḥan ʿaruk*, Ḥoshen mishpaṭ 20; on a judge reversing his opinion if mistaken, see B.T., *Shabuʿot* 30b with Rashi's comments, and *Shulḥan ʿaruk*, Ḥoshen mishpaṭ 17.8. Also see *Shulḥan ʿaruk*, Ḥoshen mishpaṭ 25, with the very helpful summaries of Rabbi Shabbetai ben Meʾir ha-Kohen. In twelfth-century northern France, there seems to have been a possibility of appealing decisions to the outstanding rabbi of the age, Rabbeynu Tam (see Avraham [Rami] Reiner, "Battey ha-din be-Ẓarefat be-meʾah ha-shetaym ʿesreh: beyn rikkuz le-bizzur," in *ʿAl pi ha-beʾer: meḥqarim be-hagut yehudit u-be-maḥshebet ha-halakah muggashim le-Yaʿaqob Blidstein*, ed. Uri Erlich et al. [Beer Sheva: Ben-Gurion University Press, 2008], 568–74, 579–80, 585).

289. See Schochetman, "Ḥobat ha-hanmaqah," 338–45.

290. In this, responsa literature was significantly different than talmudic exegesis. Pinḥas Horowitz, *Responsa*, no. 6, in considering a practical matter, made specific reference to his theoretical writings, where he offered proofs for both sides of an issue. When asked to make a decision, on the other hand, he had different considerations and took a clear stand on the matter. Horowitz noted that a specific argument was good for theoretical discussions but not for practical rulings (*ṭob huʾ le-pilpulaʾ ve-loʾ le-maʿaseh*). Sometimes a decisor raised legal possibilities in the course of his responsum but stepped back from actually relying on them (*halakah ve-loʾ le-maʿaseh*; see, for example, Slonik, *Responsa*, no. 40). Such reticence could reflect a lack of independence on the part of the decisor (see Samuel Morell, *Precedent and Judicial Discretion: The Case of Joseph ibn Lev*, South Florida Studies in the History of Judaism 26 [Atlanta: Scholars Press, 1991], 9–14), but Slonik did not lack in self-confidence or independence of thought (see my, *My Dear Daughter: Rabbi Benjamin Slonik and the Education of Jewish Women in Sixteenth-Century Poland*, Monographs of the Hebrew Union College 33 [Cincinnati: Hebrew Union College Press, 2007], 116–28). In this case, hesitation to use such possibilities may well reflect his concerns about whether his legal hypotheses were fully worked out.

ensuring that their decisions were obeyed.[291] Barring information to the contrary, the historian must view responsa as the expressions of legal possibilities by highly qualified individuals rather than as an indication of what happened in practice. They were authoritative — at least in their author's view — but not practically binding. Courts were somewhat different.

Rabbinic courts were communal institutions, and Jewish communities such as that in late eighteenth-century Frankfurt were eager to maintain their authority.[292] As shown earlier, the rulings of the Frankfurt rabbinic court were not always promptly or exactly fulfilled, but there was an infrastructure designed to enforce these decisions.[293] The Frankfurt rabbinic court routinely threatened those who did not perform their obligations with fines, only half of which went to communal institutions; the other half was to go to the non-Jewish authorities.[294] From the perspective of the early modern state in which there was no effective tax collection system, a potential source of extra-ordinary income could not be ignored.[295] This gave the non-Jewish authorities a financial interest in seeing to it that the

291. The problem of enforcement was not unique to rabbis. Given the vast distances and relatively poor means of communication in the Holy Roman Empire, there were no guarantees that decisions of the Supreme Court of the Empire (*Reichskammergericht*) could be enforced in all of the Empire's territories (see Ralf-Peter Fuchs, "The Supreme Court of the Holy Roman Empire: The State of Research and the Outlook," *The Sixteenth Century Journal* 34, no. 1 [Spring 2003]: 10).

292. Maintaining separate courts was a way of maintaining Jewish identity. In general, on Jewish courts in the Middle Ages, see David Shohet, *The Jewish Court in the Middle Ages*, as well as some of the criticism leveled against Shohet's view on Jews in non-Jewish courts in Kisch, *The Jews in Medieval Germany*, 442 n. 4.

293. Regarding Frankfurt, see, for example, Segall, Pinqas Frankfurṭ, no. 320, section 30, where it was assumed that the preceptor (*gabbaʾy*) of the community would enforce court rulings.

294. See, for example, Gundersheim, Adler MS. 935, nos. 47, 51, 79, 82, and 212, among others. Also see Zimmer, *Harmony and Discord*, 101, and Kracauer, "Beiträge zur Geschichte der Frankfurter Juden," 350–51. From at least the fourteenth century the non-Jewish authorities in some German communities extracted a portion of the fines imposed by Jewish courts for themselves. Although Jewish communities were not always forthcoming in transferring such fines to the non-Jewish authorities, the authorities were not shy about seeking out what they believed to be theirs (see Frank, *Qehillot Ashkenaz*, 37–42; also see Katz, *Masoret u-mashber*, 113 with n. 3). This custom of dividing fines continued in other locales in Germany such as seventeenth-century Mannheim (see Leopold Löwenstein, *Geschichte der Juden in der Kurpfalz*, Beiträge zur Geschichte der Juden in Deutschland 1 [Frankfurt: J. Kauffmann, 1895], 77–78, no. 8, also cited in Azriel Shohet, *ʿIm ḥilufey tequfot*, 77). In eighteenth-century Poznań, fines for the breach of communal regulations also went in whole or in part to non-Jewish authorities (see Michałowska-Mycielska, *The Jewish Community*, 241–42).

295. See Soliday, *A Community in Conflict*, 189, regarding the magistrates of Frankfurt and their financial interest in the Jews during a somewhat earlier period. With regard to the difficulty of collecting taxes from territories beyond the emperor's own imperial towns, see Johanek,

verdicts of the Jewish courts were carried out, and added an additional threat of enforcement.

Given the jurisdictional jockeying that took place among Jews, litigants sometimes went beyond the community to advance their interests and circumvented the rulings of both individual rabbis and the court. Because of this, court records, responsa, and certainly a personal diary, may represent only a part of the history of a case; other sources both from beyond and within the Jewish community must be used to fill in.

For example, in 1789 there was a dispute regarding the appointment of the new head of the Scheyer study house in Frankfurt. The previous head of the *kloysz*, Rabbi Abraham Trier, had accepted an appointment to the Wertheim family *kloysz* and expected that his son, Rabbi Zalman Katz, would succeed him as head of the Scheyer study house. Trier was not simply being hopeful, for he had made his son's succession to the position of head of the Scheyer *kloysz* part of his agreement with the Wertheim study house. But the agreement did not go unchallenged. Rabbi Herz Zunz, who had served as the deputy head of the Scheyer *kloysz* for fourteen years, believed that he was next in line to lead the study house, and contested Katz's appointment before the Frankfurt rabbinic court.[296] The court record only deals with the dispute in the Scheyer study house, which is all that can be expected for that was all the court was asked to consider. Yet the previous head of the *kloysz*, Rabbi Jacob Schames, had died in 1785 and the administrator of the Wertheim *kloysz*, Zechariah Wertheim, had been petitioning the *Reichshofrat* from 1787 regarding appointments to his family's *kloysz*.[297] Had the position gone unfilled as a dispute worked its way through the non-Jewish courts? Did Imperial involvement in the workings of the Jewish community play a role in this case? A full examination of the matter requires looking beyond the records of the Frankfurt *beyt din*.[298]

Despite their shortcomings, court records have a number of advantages over responsa as historical records of events. *Poseqim* generally received their information from only one source, leaving them vulnerable to manipulation by questioners who may have had their own reasons for wording a question one way or another.[299]

"Imperial and Free Towns," 295. Also see Rudolf Vierhaus, *Germany in the Age of Absolutism*, trans. Jonathan Knudsen (Cambridge: Cambridge University Press, 1988), 108.

296. Gundersheim, Adler MS. 935, no. 226.

297. Kasper, "Die Frankfurter Judengemeinde," 107–11, 150–51, 212–24.

298. Preuss, *Gelehrte Juden*, shows how records from the non-Jewish authorities can inform the history of the *kloysz*, an institution that at first glance would appear to be very insular.

299. See Masud, Messick, and Powers, "Muftis, Fatwas and Islamic Legal Interpretation," 22, who point out that in the Islamic world questioners may have transmitted a selective rendering

Conversely, it was the responsibility of courts to hear all sides of a case in the presence of the other litigant(s), either directly from the parties involved or from their legal representatives.[300] Judgment could not be rendered without it. The author of a responsum had no such obligation, for his task was to answer the question as posed.[301]

This being said, the claims of litigants as reported by Gundersheim must also be considered carefully. The testimony, the discussion, and all the oral communication in the rabbinic court took place in Yiddish. Yet, in his personal records, Gundersheim almost always summarized arguments and testimony that he heard in Yiddish in Hebrew, a language in which he was proficient but almost certainly never had to speak.[302] Hebrew was the mother tongue of no one in Frankfurt, yet

---

of the facts. There is no reason to assume that such things did not occur in the Jewish world as well. On hearing only one side of the argument in Jewish law, see Schochetman, "Ḥobat ha-hanmaqah," 341. In the mid-sixteenth century, Rabbi Manoach ben Asher (northern Italian lands) cited an enactment made by Rabbi Ḥayyim ben Isaac of Vienna (fl. second half thirteenth century), and other leading rabbis, that a rabbi should never give a ruling without hearing both sides of the story. Rabbi Manoach appears to have believed that this extended beyond simple monetary disputes. See Rabbi Manoach's letter in Isserles, *Responsa*, no. 57, p. 273.

300. See B.T., *Sanhedrin* 7b; *Shabuᶜot* 31a; *Shulḥan ᶜaruk*, Ḥoshen mishpaṭ 13.6, 17.5. Despite this rule, there were attempts to justify hearing one side at a time in the late Middle Ages (see Dinari, *Ḥakmey Ashkenaz be-shalhey yemey ha-beynayyim*, 126–27; Zimmer, *Harmony and Discord*, 80). The use of written claims from both sides was possible (see *Shulḥan ᶜaruk*, Ḥoshen mishpaṭ 13.3) and in monetary matters it seems to have become an accepted practice in the medieval period in the German lands and northern France. The custom seems to have continued in some areas of sixteenth-century Poland but was later rejected. On the use of written testimony in monetary cases, see Abraham Fuss, "ᶜEdut be-ketab be-diney mamonot," *Shenaton ha-mishpaṭ ha-ᶜibri* 3–4 (1976–77): 327–39.

301. There were rabbinic authorities who refrained from giving an opinion in monetary disputes unless they personally heard the claims of each side, or a question came directly from the panel of judges who had heard the litigants (see Meʾir ben Gedaliah, *Responsa*, no. 22). This was in keeping with the ruling of Isserles in *Shulḥan ᶜaruk*, Ḥoshen mishpaṭ 17.5 (see too the sources and exceptions gathered by Abraham Eisenstadt in his *Pitḥey teshubah* [n. 11]).

302. Although Gundersheim cited some Yiddish testimony, he generally paraphrased such statements in Hebrew or referred to them without citing them. Gundersheim, Adler MS. 935, no. 65, includes testimony that was given in Yiddish but summarized in Hebrew. No. 121 makes references to testimony but does not quote it. No. 65 includes testimony given in Yiddish. It would appear that depositions were taken in Yiddish (see YIVO MS. RG 128 [folder 77–78]; there is no clear pagination in this section of the microfilm in the Central Archives for the History of the Jewish People [HM2/4447]; the Yiddish material appears after fol. 171a in the film). Examples of Yiddish testimony that appear in responsa literature from the fifteenth to seventeenth centuries were brought together in Shneur Zalman Shazar, "Gebiyyot ᶜedut be-lashon yidish be-sheʾelot u-teshubot," in *Orey dorot: meḥqarim ve-heʾarot le-toledot Yisraʾel*

it was the official language of rabbinic literature. Rabbis traditionally used it in correspondence with each other and in writing their legal views, but there is no evidence that they spoke it. Its use facilitated the expression of halakic concepts in familiar terms, but a purely literary language could not keep up with the vocabulary of daily life and thus impeded the recording of events in both court records and responsa.[303] Linguistic problems aside, ultimately it was impossible to use any language to capture in writing the expressions and gestures used by speakers before the court, signals that conveyed specific meanings in the context of the time and place in which they were made. As James Boyd White has asked,

> ... how little of what happens in any real utterance is reducible to the words uttered, let alone to the 'propositions' they are supposed to express, and how much lies in the gesture, in the relations between speaker and auditor, in their material context, in the understandings they share — understandings about the natural world, about human motives and capacities and dangers, about what needs to be said and what does not. The meaning of a sentence lies not only in what we tend to think of as the sentence itself, in the words, but in the context, verbal and nonverbal, out of which it is constructed.[304]

It was not only Gundersheim who reconstructed the events of the past. As noted, many of the litigants mentioned in Rabbi Gundersheim's diary — although usually not the poor — had legal representation. Then, as today, good counsel not only addressed the court in a highly stylized fashion, but shaped the arguments, claims, and counterclaims of their clients in order to promote and justify their interests.[305]

---

be-dorot ha-ʾaḥaronim, reprint, 1929 (Jerusalem: Mossad Bialik, 1971), 239–319. Such testimony was sometimes omitted in subsequent editions of a collection, presumably to save space (see Glick, "ʿAl shinuyyim hashmaṭot ve-ẓenzurah," 63). What appears to be a responsum written in Yiddish appears in the YIVO film of the abovementioned manuscript (MK 482.2) between folios 113 and 114. The Yiddish pages are not numbered and are of a different hand than the surrounding pages (the YIVO film of the manuscript is different than the Jerusalem film). The pages were once folded, suggesting that it was sent in the mail or by messenger. Unfortunately, I was not permitted to examine the original manuscript.

303. Gundersheim's use of German rather than Hebrew terms for many household items or parts of houses in nos. 79 and 243 is one example of the inability of eighteenth-century Hebrew to keep up with developments.

304. James Boyd White, *Justice as Translation: An Essay in Cultural and Legal Criticism* (Chicago: University of Chicago Press, 1990), xi–xii.

305. For a related perspective on how narrative was created to advance a client's interests in a specific type of legal document in sixteenth-century France, see Natalie Davis, *Fiction in the Archives: Pardon Tales and Their Tellers in Sixteenth-Century France* (Stanford: Stanford University Press, 1987).

Representatives chose which facts to include and which to ignore. They translated what their clients told them into the legal language used by the rabbinic court but, by its very nature, such "translation" was often imperfect.[306]

One must assume that *dayyanim* were not naive and that they were well-aware of the strategies used by counsel.[307] Nevertheless, the Frankfurt *Judengasse* was crowded, and local judges likely often knew litigants and the events at hand quite well. In some instances they could easily have been so close to the case and the values and pressures of their community that they may have missed such legal strategies or simply accepted them as self-evident.[308]

Responsa remain an indispensable source for Jewish legal history. It was here that decisors offered new interpretations of the law and defended their positions. This was the crucible in which legal innovations were not only suggested but substantiated. In responsa, rabbis had to explain their thinking and justify their insights to colleagues, and, if their work was published, to posterity. Here the development of Jewish law is most tangible. Such creativity may well have taken place in courts as well, but courts — at least the Frankfurt court — left almost no record of the legal reasoning that led to individual decisions. Although presumably Gundersheim and his colleagues deliberated on points of law and procedure before giving their decisions, legal justifications — not to mention legal reasoning — are almost totally absent from Gundersheim's diary. In the few instances where Gundersheim does discuss the legal process he is brief and makes almost no attempt to anchor decisions in legal sources, let alone to develop ideas.[309] As noted earlier, rabbinic courts did not have to state why they came to their conclusions. The legal argument so central to responsa literature has no parallel in Gundersheim's diary.[310]

---

306. The idea of "translation" and the recognition of the concomitant problems of presenting the story at hand in legal language belongs to James Boyd White, "An Old-Fashioned View of the Nature of Law," *Theoretical Inquiries in Law* 12, no. 1 (January 2011): 388.

307. The question of the trustworthiness of testimony, assuming that a witness did not perjure himself, is an entire sub-field in philosophy that has ramifications for historical inquiry as well. For a brief survey of some of the issues, see Jennifer Lackey, "Introduction," in *The Epistemology of Testimony*, ed. Jennifer Lackey and Ernest Sosa (Oxford: Clarendon, 2006), 1–7.

308. On such possibilities, see Harold Berman, *Law and Revolution: The Formation of the Western Legal Tradition* (Cambridge, Mass.: Harvard University Press, 1983), 157.

309. Gundersheim, Adler MS. 935, no. 180, is a rare example of the citation of legal sources in the manuscript. Cf., nos. 41 and 43 where rationales are given but no textual sources are offered.

310. Markus Horovitz noted that the rulings in the *Protokollbuche* (see above, n. 17) "were always clear [and] extensively and masterfully grounded" ("sind immer klar, erschöpfend und mit einer Meisterschaft begründet"), suggesting that these court records contained legal

With legal argumentation such a central component of responsa literature, authors as well as medieval copyists and early modern editors routinely edited out details that were extraneous to the legal discussion at hand.[311] The personal names of the litigants and other "players" in cases were often replaced with Reuben and Sarah, the Hebrew equivalents of John and Jane Doe. Sometimes actual place names were represented by Tiberias and Sephorris, towns in the Land of Israel during the talmudic period. Other sundry details that did not contribute to the argument, such as dates, were routinely omitted. Anonymity may have evolved to protect the identity of those involved in the case, which contributed to the transformation of responsa into a literature of timeless legal principles rather than a host of answers to specific questions, but this often left responsa a poor source for historical details.[312] Court documents were public records and they had to include specific details. Not surprisingly, Gundersheim's diary, a private record of public events, is full of place names, personal names, and dates. He did not record every personal name, particularly those of women, who were often referred to as "the wife of" so and so or "the daughter of" so and so, yet details were an integral part of the record.[313] This does not mean that court records or a personal diary are infallible historical sources. Gundersheim had the right to write what he pleased in his diary, and often noted that he was omitting some of the litigants' claims, presum-

discussions. While there are justifications given for a few court decisions in YIVO MS. RG 128 (folder 77–78), fols. 29a–b, 42a–b, they are relatively brief postscripts and are not integral parts of the decision.

311. The laconic nature of many responsa from medieval France and Germany was often the result of such editing; responsa were simply paraphrased. Once the tosafists (twelfth-thirteenth centuries) introduced dialectics into the halakic world, such discussions had to remain in the text, and the character of copying changed (see Haym Soloveitchik, *Shu"t ke-meqor hisṭori* [Jerusalem: Shazar, 1990], 11–12; Avraham Grossman, *Ḥakmey Ashkenaz ha-riʾshonim*, 2d ed. [Jerusalem: Magnes, 1989], 68, 154–57, as well as his *Ḥakmey Ẓarefat ha-riʾshonim: qoroteyhem, darkam be-hanagat ha-ẓibbur, yiẓiratam ha-ruḥanit* [Jerusalem: Magnes, 1995], 67, 243–44). On early modern editions, see Glick, "ʿAl shinuyyim hashmaṭot ve-ẓenzurah," 63. Many early modern collections were published posthumously, offering the opportunity for significant editing. When such a work was published there was little reason to keep the original manuscript, leaving precious few opportunities to discover what was altered.

312. Questions that appear in the responsa literature were routinely edited and shortened, making it difficult to know what was included in the original letter to the legal authority. If questioners erased the names of the litigants it may well have been to avoid the possibility of favoritism, or perhaps they had already been acculturated into the literary world of responsa.

313. One notable exception is the case of a woman who was required to undergo *ḥaliẓah* but married another man and had a child with him before she did (Gundersheim, Adler MS. 935, no. 221). The omission may have been to protect the identity of the sinner, but was more likely a function of the fact that she and her husband were both transients rather than local residents.

ably for reasons of space or personal preference, although he sometimes pointed out that such material could be found in official court records.[314] Nevertheless, specific details were part and parcel of his diary.

The use of responsa as historical sources is also hampered by a change in the genre during the late medieval and early modern period. From at least the fifteenth century on, responsa writing in the Ashkenazic world was not only a way of answering practical questions, but a form of rabbinic essay writing. From time to time rabbis used the question and answer format to raise a problem and answer it. Lacking an accepted genre for legal expositions, responsa filled the void.[315] After all, a question and answer is still a responsum, even if the questioner was none other than the writer who posed the question to himself. Not every author used responsa in this way, but a number of outstanding rabbis did, such as Rabbis Israel Isserlein (d. 1460, Marburg, Neustadt [near Vienna]), who used this method often, as well as Moses Isserles, Benjamin Slonik (d. after 1620, Lithuania), Yaʾir Bachrach (d. 1702, Worms), and, to a lesser exent, Pinḥas Horowitz.[316] Questioners also asked rabbis hypothetical questions in an attempt to expand the parameters of knowledge.[317] In some instances there are hints in the text that the question was indeed

314. As mentioned above, the court maintained what Gundersheim termed a record of claims (*qunṭres ha-ṭaᶜanot*) to which he often referred (see, for example, Gundersheim, Adler MS. 935, no. 79). This appears to have contained a complete record of the claims of each of the litigants, but the term may well refer to written claims submitted by the sides to the court (see no. 190, fol. 182b, line 15).

315. By the modern period, this had become such a normal feature of rabbinic responsa that Glick, "ᶜAl shinuyyim hashmaṭot ve-ẓenzurah," 45, described it as a characteristic of the literary genre. I have not investigated whether this phenomenon took place in the writings of rabbis in the early modern Sephardic world, but Professor Samuel Morell believes that it was not unknown there (electronic letter to the author, 12 September 2010). More than a century ago, scholars of Islam noticed that the question posed in a *fatwā* could well have been invented by the author (see Jakob Skovgaard-Petersen, *Defining Islam for the Egyptian State: Muftis and Fatwas of the Dār al-Iftā*, Social, Economic, and Political Studies of the Middle East and Asia 59 [Leiden: Brill, 1997], 11, 20–21). Skovgaard-Petersen suggested that the "risk of fictitious fatwas" may have caused scholars to prefer court records over fatwas as historical sources.

316. On Isserlein, see Shabbetay ben Meʾir ha-Kohen, *Siftey kohen* (Yoreh deᶜah) (Cracow: Meisels, 1646), 196 n. 20, and Dinari, *Ḥakmey Ashkenaz be-shalhey yemey ha-beynayyim*, 302–3. Isserles's famed responsum regarding a Sabbath wedding was written after the fact to justify his actions to his critics (Isserles, *Responsa*, no. 125, especially p. 488). With respect to Slonik, see my, *My Dear Daughter*, 123 n. 169, 132 n. 204. See Elchanan Reiner, "Maᶜaseh she-ʾirᶜa be-q[ehillat] q[odesh] Virmaysaʾ be-raᶜash ha-gadol shenat [5]396," *Haaretz* 6 October 2006: 4 (Culture and Literature Section), with respect to Bachrach. Also see Pinḥas Horowitz, *Responsa*, no. 59.

317. Talya Fishman, "Forging Jewish Memory: *Besamim Rosh* and the Invention of Pre-Emancipation Jewish Culture," in *Jewish History and Jewish Memory: Essays in Honor of Yosef*

theoretical, but one must assume that there were other instances when a questioner did not want to be turned away by a busy rabbi and therefore concealed that the question had been concocted.[318] As such, responsa of the period must be used as historical sources with extra caution.[319] By contrast, court cases, with their wealth of specific details, may be more valuable for reconstructing historical events.

A comparison of two entries in Rabbi Gundersheim's diary with the responsa of one of his colleagues is illustrative of some of the respective advantages and disadvantages of court records and responsa as sources of historical data.[320]

Rabbi Pinḥas Horowitz was an outstanding legal authority in his own right. Horowitz and Gundersheim knew each other well and from time to time they served on the court together. When Gundersheim died, it was Horowitz who eulogized him that very morning and posthumously bestowed on him the title of "*moreynu*."[321]

In an undated responsum, Horowitz considered the matter of someone who left 4,000 guldens to the community to be invested in a perpetual trust. In making the bequest, the donor had assumed a certain annual return on the principle and accordingly bequeathed specific amounts to various charitable causes. Unfortunately, the actual return on the investment was less than had been anticipated. There had also been a delay in investing the money and both factors led to a financial short-fall already in the first year.[322]

The question was which of the charitable causes should suffer the loss. In keeping with the nature of responsa writing, Horowitz dealt with the narrow legal

---

Hayim Yerushalmi, ed. Elisheva Carlebach, John Efron, and David Myers (Hanover, New Hampshire: Brandeis University Press, 1998), 75–76, very nicely placed this phenomenon into one of its historical contexts.

318. See Pinḥas Horowitz, *Responsa*, no. 5, in which the questioner specifically noted that his question was a practical matter (*halakah le-maʿaseh*) to which he needed a prompt answer. The need to alert Horowitz to this fact implies that the questioner believed that some people sent questions that were not.

319. The distinction between practical decisions and legal essays had ramifications in the legal world. This was expressed by Rabbi Shabbetay ben Meʾir ha-Kohen in the mid-seventeenth century (see above, n. 316). It has a parallel of sorts in English law in the difference between *ratio decidendi* and *obiter dictum*. The privileging of the former over the latter is an old one in English law and remains firm, although it has recently been suggested that *obiter dictum* should not be dismissed so easily (see Rupert Cross and J.W. Harris, *Precedent in English Law*, 4th ed., Clarendon Law Series [Oxford: Clarendon Press, 1991], 41, as well as the material cited by Neil Duxbury, *The Nature and Authority of Precedent* [Cambridge: Cambridge University Press, 2008], 70 n. 47, with his own comments on p. 3).

320. To the best of my knowledge, Gundersheim did not author any responsa.

321. See Gundersheim's entry in the Frankfurt *Memorbuch*, fol. 350a.

322. Pinḥas Horowitz, *Responsa*, no. 72.

issue at hand without mentioning who the benefactor was, when or where this took place, or what the exact nature of the bequest was. Nevertheless, the responsum offers some historical information, such as the amount of money involved, the expected and the actual return on the investment, and one of the classes of beneficiaries. Because this was a case that came before the court, this relatively meager yield of details can be significantly supplemented through an examination of Gundersheim's court diary.

In November 1781 the executors of this estate brought their questions to the rabbinic court on which both Gundersheim and Horowitz sat.[323] The opinion found in Horowitz's responsum was the very position taken by the court, yet the court record provides many more details than the rabbinic responsum.[324] Gundersheim's diary includes the names of the benefactor, the executors, the date, the various charitable causes involved, and the context of the case. The court record also provides an important corrective to Horowitz's responsum. While Horowitz referred to the benefactor as a male, the court record makes it clear that this was not so, for it was the late Brynla, widow of Neta Orschel, who bequeathed the funds. Gundersheim's version is supported both by the Frankfurt *Memorbuch* and Brynla's gravestone, both of which mention that she had bequeathed funds for charitable purposes.[325]

That the court record provides more information regarding the case is simply in keeping with the nature of the genre. It is to be expected that Rabbi Pinḥas Horowitz, or those who edited his responsa (for they were published posthumously), removed the name of the benefactor since it had no bearing on the legal matter at hand. Given that Hebrew has no neuter form, the masculine was the default and anonymous gender and it was used. In so doing Horowitz or his editor did no harm to the legal positions being discussed, but inadvertently highlighted one of the perils of using responsa as a source for historical data.[326]

A more troubling case from a methodological standpoint dealt with a deathbed

323. Gundersheim, Adler MS. 935, no. 140.

324. This responsum was written after the court gave its ruling. In discussing the delay in depositing the funds with the community, Horowitz noted, "I ruled that this should not be considered a loss ..." The use of the perfect tense suggests that a decision had already been given and Horowitz was using his responsum to explicate a point of law.

325. See Frankfurt *Memorbuch*, fol. 272a; for the gravestone, see Horovitz, *Abney zikkaron*, no. 3683. Both texts specifically noted that Brynla (in the later text referred to as Bryndela) left money for charitable purposes.

326. See Debra Kaplan, "Women and Worth: Female Access to Property in Early Modern Urban Jewish Communities," *Leo Baeck Institute Yearbook* 55 (2010): 98, who was able to make a proper assessment based on Gundersheim's diary.

will. In an undated responsum, Horowitz addressed the question of an unnamed individual who on his deathbed itemized how his assets should be divided, and appointed executors to carry out his will. Some of the funds were to be set aside as dowries for his children, while a significant sum was to be invested with the community in a perpetual fund that would provide proceeds to be distributed annually to charitable causes. The executors did not invest the funds but distributed money to the charities each year from the principal, allowing one of the executors to borrow what is termed "a huge sum" from the principal for his own needs. As time passed, two of the executors died and the extent of the misappropriation of funds became clear. Unfortunately for the estate, it could not make a full recovery from the estate of the executor who had expropriated the funds. There were not only insufficient funds to give to charity, but there was not enough money on hand to give the one remaining child of the benefactor a dowry. The question was, how should the losses be divided between the child and the charities?[327]

Horowitz was not the only one to deal with this question.[328] In the summer of 1775 this very case was brought to the rabbinic court in Frankfurt, and Horowitz and Gundersheim sat together on the judicial panel that considered it. Again, the court records are full of historical information that is missing from the responsum, including the name of the deceased (Leb Kann who died in 1766) and the executor who absconded with the money (none other than Leb's own brother, Jacob).[329] In the responsum, Horowitz ruled that there should be a 2:1 division of assets in favor of the orphan child. However, according to Gundersheim's record, the court ruled that there should be a 3:1 division of assets in favor of the orphan — and Horowitz was a party to the court's decision! The contradiction is startling, but revealing of the nature of early modern responsa literature.

Gundersheim listed the members of the panel that considered the matter of the Kann estate. In addition to himself and Horowitz, Rabbis Nathan Maas and Jacob Schames were also on the court.[330] Presumably each member of the court had a

327. Pinḥas Horowitz, *Responsa*, no. 69.
328. See Sendik, "Beyn din le-pesher," 83–85, who already noticed this parallel.
329. Gundersheim, Adler MS. 935, no. 59.
330. Given the talmudic rule that one may not have an even number of judges (*eyn beyt din shaqul*, see *Sanhedrin* 1.6; regarding B.T., *Sanhedrin* 7b, where an even number of judges seems to have been used, see the comments of Rabbi Joshua Falk, *Perishah*, Ḥoshen mishpaṭ 3 n. 10, who took it as axiomatic that there should not be an even number of judges), it is unclear why there were four judges on this panel. A number of other cases in Gundersheim's diary were also heard by four judges (e.g., nos. 59, 61, 108, 140, 143, 223, 242). This was not unknown in Frankfurt. In 1469 four scholars sat on a court of arbitration (see Zimmer, *Harmony and Discord*, 67–68). Regarding nearby Mainz in the medieval period, see the possibility raised in Ephraim Kanarfogel, "Religious Leadership During the Tosafist Period: Between the Academy

say in constructing the court's decision, and the majority of members believed that there should be a 3:1 division of assets. Apparently Horowitz disagreed, but, as noted earlier, Jewish law and a communal ordinance prohibited recording dissenting views in decisions.[331] Silenced by the *halakah* and the community, Horowitz used a responsum as a vehicle to express his own opinion. He made no mention of conflicting views about this matter on the court and was able to do so in good conscience, for the anonymity of the genre of responsa obfuscated any connection between his response and the actual case. The irony of it is that with the loss of court records, Horowitz's view as expressed in his responsum appeared to be the *only* opinion rather than the minority opinion. If Horowitz's literary maneuvering was in any way typical of responsa, court records provide an important corrective to the writings of individual rabbis.

In addition to the particular details of the cases recorded by Rabbi Gundersheim, information about daily life, living conditions, architecture, religious observance, communal self-government, and more are waiting to be gleaned from the folios of the diary. The goal of this project has been to make a historical source that has been long-neglected available to a wider audience. Also, in outlining biographical information about the author of the diary and the institution wherein he worked, I have tried to give the reader some background to the material and at the same time expand on a number of methodological issues involved in the use of court records as historical and legal sources.

The diary itself offers few, if any, hints of the massive political, social, and religious upheavals that were, at that time, looming on the horizon. On the eve of the nineteenth century, the Frankfurt *Judengasse* was still a very traditional place, and Rabbi Ḥayyim Gundersheim's diary provides a relatively clear window through which we can see into this lost world.

---

and the Rabbinic Court," in *Jewish Religious Leadership: Image and Reality*, vol. 1, ed. Jack Wertheimer (New York: Jewish Theological Seminary, 2004), 268 with n. 8, 276 n. 45. Some interesting possibilities are also raised from a reading of G.W. Paton and G. Sawer, "Ratio Decidendi and Obiter Dictum in Appellate Courts," *The Law Quarterly Review* 68 (October 1947): 462–65.

331. Cf., Gundersheim, Adler MS. 935, no. 37, where there was a clear disagreement among the *dayyanim*. However, this was a ritual matter rather than a decision in a dispute between two litigants.

The Court Diary of Rabbi Ḥayyim Gundersheim

Abbreviations and Non-Hebrew Terms

This manuscript uses numerous abbreviations and non-Hebrew terms. There is a glossary of Hebrew abbreviations on pages 573-81.In many instances abbreviations are specific to the case, such as an abbreviation of the name of one of the parties mentioned. In these instances the abbreviation is explained on first mention in each document in a footnote.

Although abbreviations are generally indicated in Hebrew through the use of an apostrophe or a quotation mark, there are numerous instances in the manuscript where this was not done. In these instances too, the abbreviation is explained on first mention in each document. A few unmarked abbreviations frequently recur in the manuscript. They are listed below but not glossed on each occurrence in the text. There are numerous mistakes in the spelling of Hebrew words throughout the manuscript. So long as the meaning of the word is clear in the original, there has been no attempt to annotate such errors.

Terms are explained in footnotes when it was felt that there was some room for misunderstanding. Non-Hebrew terms appear in a glossary on pages 585–603.

Individuals have generally been referred to in the introductions by their personal names. This reflects the style of the texts themselves which usually refer to people on a first name rather than last name basis after first mention. However, when two parties in the case have the same personal name, I used surnames for ease of identification.

...	חומר חסר (דף קטוע וכדומה)
[...]	אותיות לא ברורות
[אבג]	אפשרות להסביר אותיות לא ברורות או חסרות
{אבג}	אותיות מחוקות
(אבג)	אותיות המופיעות מחוץ לשורה (למעלה, למטה ובשוליים)
<אבג>	פתיחת ראשי תבות
הק	הקטן
יצו	ישמרהו צורו וגואלו, ישמרם צורם וגואלם
כ	כבוד
כה	כבוד הרב
לפק	לפרט קטן
נפ.	נפטר
צל	צלם (Kreuzer)
ר	רב, רבי
רט	רייכשטאלר

קצורים להפניות:

דייץ	Alexander Dietz. *Stammbuch der Frankfurter Juden*. Frankfurt: J. St. Goar, 1907.
מזכיר נשמות	י׳ ק׳ דושינסקי. ספר מזכיר נשמות דק״ק אָפָּפֶנבאך ע״נ מיין ועוד קהלות אחרות במדינת אשכנז. פרנקפורט תרפ״ד.
דושינסקי	Charles Duschinsky. *The Rabbinate of the Great Synagogue, London, from 1756-1842*. 1921. Reprinted with a bibliographic note by Ruth P. Lehmann. Farnborough: Gregg, 1971.
אלה תולדות	Shlomo Ettlinger. *Ēlē tōldōt*. CAHJP. P/237.
אבני זכרון	M. Horovitz. *Die Inschriften des alten Friedhofs der israelitischen Gemeinde zu Frankfurt a.M.* Frankfurt: J. Kauffmann, 1901.
לוינשטיין	Leopold Löwenstein. *Zur Geschichte der Juden in Fürth*. 1909-13, Hildesheim: Olms, 1974.
ספר הזכרונות	׳ספר הזכרונות׳ של קהילת פרנקפורט ע״נ מיין. הספריה הלאומית. ירושלים. כתב יד Heb. 1092
וכשטיין	Bernhard Wachstein. *Die Inschriften des alten Judenfriedhofes in Wien*. Vol. 2. Vienna: Braumüller, 1917.

❖ ❖ ❖

Fols. 1–39 are missing from the manuscript.

The Diary

Fol. 40a is blank.

No. 35[1]

Fol. 40b; Late 1773

Half a seat in the upper section of the synagogue that belonged to Solomon Spiegel was sold to Herz Zunz for 101 guldens (the other half of the seat belonged to Leb Spiegel) before a lower court (*beyt din qaṭan*). The sale was made with the express written consent of Solomon Spiegel's creditors. Herz was obligated to pay one-third of the amount due immediately and two-thirds in six equal payments, one every six months. The record is damaged and incomplete. See no. 36.

מ ע"ב

1. מעשה ב"ד קטן ב"ה
2. חצי מקום שלם ב[בה]"[כ] העליונה שהי' שייך לה"ה כ שלמה
3. ש[פיגל][2] כץ [א. ו]חצי השניי' מן מקום הנ"ל שייך לה"ה כ"ה
4. [ליב שפי]גיל כץ נמכר [ב]פנינו ע"פ כ' שלמה שפיגיל הנ"ל
5. [העומד ב]שליחות של כל הבע"ח שלו באשר שניתן לו כבר
6. [רשות מבע]"[ח] שלו כמבואר בק"ס שהוציע[.] לפנינו הנאמן כ"ה
7. [אנשיל פפאן] כץ שנעשה י"ט סיון תקלג לפק ונזכר עכשיו
8. ... שלמה הנ"ל בשליחות הבע"ח הנ"ל לה"ה התורנ[י]
9. [הירץ בן כ]"ה הדיין כ"ה אנשיל צונץ בעד סך אחד ומאה
10. [זהו' אין קונפונטצי]אהן מינץ אום דך זהו' פוס לשלם השליש[.]
11. [מדמי מכירה הנ"ל] תיכף בשעת מסירת החליטה ושני ש...
12. [הנותרים] מסך מאה {זהו'} ואחד זהו' דמי שכירות
13. [הנ"ל על ששה חצאי'] שנים זא"ז ומחויב ליתן ששה {..".}[ח"כ][3]
14. ...[ם] ח"כ הראשון יתחיל מיד אחר מ[סירת]

---

1. The cases are not numbered in the manuscript and numbering has been entered here for ease of reference. The first 34 cases mentioned in the index to Gundersheim's files (here pp. 523–35) are missing.
2. ההשלמות הן על פי תעודה מס' 36.
3. תוספת מעל השורה

15. ... שאר להאפותיקו מפורש שלא יצא
16. ... נתפרע אפי' אחד מן הזמני'
17. ... תקלד ל[פ]ק הק' נתן בלא"א כ"ה שלמה[1]
18. ... {. . ...}

No. 36

Fols. 41a–b; Sunday evening, 28 November 1773

The sale of half a seat in the upper men's section of the old synagogue (Altschule) mentioned in no. 35 was brought before a high court (*beyt din gadol*), apparently for its approval. There are some points of information here that are not found in the extant portion of no. 35. The seat was currently being used by David Gamburg. The availability of the seat was announced three times in the synagogue, presumably to attract the highest bid. Herz Zunz made the highest offer and was awarded the seat. The owner of the seat, Solomon Spiegel, appears not to have been present at the sale and was represented by Anshel Pfann. The terms of sale are itemized and the court declared the sale to be final. There is a postscript that the seller was obligated to pay court costs. The document is damaged and incomplete.

מא ע"א

1. מעשה ב"ד גדול[2] ב"ה
2. חצי מקום שלם בבה"כ ישן[3] העליונה {שהי} אשר כעת עומד עליו כ"ה דוד גמבורג
3. שהי' שייך לה"ה כ' שלמה שפיגיל כץ ו([א]שר)[4] חצי השניי' מן המקום הנ"ל ש[י]יך לה"ה [כ']...
4. ליב שפיגיל כץ הוכרז ע"פ כ' שלמה הנ"ל העומד בשליחות של [כ] הבע"ח
5. באשר שניתן לו כבר רשות מבע"ח שלו כמבואר בק"ס שהציע לפנינו ה[נאמן]
6. כ"ה אנשיל פפאן כץ שנעשה יט סיון תקלג לפק {ונמכר עכ} בבה"כ ישן
7. שלש פעמי' שכל מי שרוצה לקנותו יבוא לפנינו ב"ד גם הוכרז לפנינו ב"ד
8. שיפסקו המוסיפי' ולא הי' אחד שהי' פוסק כפי מה שפסק ה"ה התורני כ"ה [הירץ]
9. בן ה"ה הדיין כ"ה אנשיל צונץ נר"ו בכן מכרנו החצי מקום הנ"ל במעמד הנאמן כ"ה
10. אנשיל פפאן (הנ"ל)[5] בהרשאת כ' שלמה הנ"ל לה"ה התורני כ"ה הירץ הנ"ל בעד סך א[חד]
11. ומאה זהו' אין קונפונטציאהן מינץ אַ ך"ד זהו' פוס לשלם השליש מדמי מכרה הנ"ל

---

1. הרב נתן מז
2. ר' שו"ע חו"מ יד (א).
3. על בתי הכנסת הישן והחדש, ר' דייץ, עמ' 438.
4. תוספת מעל השורה
5. תוספת מעל השורה

12. תיכף בשעת מסירת החלוטה ושני שלישי' הנו[תרים מסך מ]אה ואחד זהו' דמ[י]..
13. מכירה הנ"ל על ששה חצאי שני' זא"ז ומחויב ליתן ש[שה] זמני' [..]' ו[.]מן יום ח'...
14. הראשון יתחיל {מיד} אחר מסירת החלטה וה...ישאר...
15. שלא יצא מחזקת מרא קמא כל זמן שלא נתפרע אפי...
16. במקום הנ"ל אשר הי' שייך מקדמת דנא לה"ה כ' שלמה ש[פיגל]...
17. לה"ה התורני כ"ה הירץ בן הדיין כ"ה אנשיל צונץ נ[ר"ו]...
18. ולצמיתת עלמין עם כל זכות וחזקה וכמו שהי'...
19. כץ בלי שום שיור כלל וכלל ורשא[י]...
20. להוריש ולהנחיל לה[ח]ליף להשכ[ין]...
21. איניש דר[ש]אי לעשות בשל[ו]...
22. חצי מקום הנ"ל לה"ה כ"ה הירץ...
23. מי שיהי' הן רבי' או יחיד...
24. לדבר והלב לחשוב ול[הרהר]...
25. אופן שיהי' דברי' ב[טלין]...
26. קיימין ולא יהי' חלין כל[ל]...

מא ע"ב

1. או ב"ד יצו או שום משפט שבעולם הן בדא"ה והן בד"י כ[י] דברי המערער הם בטלין ומבו[טלין]
2. {כחרס הנשבר בא} באשר שנעשה הכל ע"פ כ' שלמה שפיגל כץ הנ"ל וכתבנו וחתמנו זא[ת]
3. בתוקף מעשה [ב]"ד ובכח ב"ד יפה להיות ביד הלוקח ה"ה התורני כ"ה הירץ הנ"ל וי"א וב"כ
4. ...[לע]דות ולזכות ולראי' שיעמוד חצי מקו' הנ"ל ביד לוקח הנ"ל וי"א וב"כ בלי שום מוח[ה]
5. ...ל נעשה (פה פפ"ד)[1] אור ליו' ב' י"ד כסליו תקלד לפק
6. ...אותו על ששה חצאי שני' רצופי' זא"ז וזמן הראשון הוא חצי שנה אחר מסירת החלטה ואח"כ כל א
7. ...חצי שנה זא"ז עד כלות זמן ששה חצאי שני' הנ"ל ועל זמני' הנ"ל מחויב הלוקח כ' ליתן ששה ח"כ
8. ...ידו לאורדר
9. הלוקח ... הלווה בשביל המוכר
10. שמחויב המוכר [לי]תן שכר בטלה להאלופי' דייני' ולשמש סך והרשות ביד
11. ...לוקח הנ"ל ל[ח]כות כ...לשליש דמי מכירה שצריך לשלם בשעת מסירת החלטה וכ...
12. ...[נ]אמנות ע"י ההד... הלוקח הנ"ל ולראי' מהימנא באנו על החתום
13. ...
14. ... שטר אפותיקו ע"פ נאמני הקהלה כנהוג ואין צריך לכתוב מצרי'
15. ...דש שליט מבית
16. ... עם כל חזקותיו וזכיותיו ומצאיו ומבואיו
17. ...רעא עד רום רקיע כמו שבי' שייך

---

1. תוספת מעל השורה

No. 37

Fols. 42a–b; undated but dealing with an event that took place in 1763 or early 1764[1]

Jacob Reiss passed away while his wife was pregnant. His here unnamed wife subsequently gave vaginal birth to a son, her first child. According to Jewish law, such a son must be redeemed from a *kohen* (a member of a priestly family) after 30 days (see Exodus 13.13, Numbers 18.15–16). This was an obligation for the father to fulfill but, due to Jacob's death, this was impossible. Members of the court were asked what should be done now that the child was 30 days old. All three were of different minds on the matter and each opinion was duly recorded. The section concludes with a description of the ceremony that eventually took place. This particular record was copied from the notebook of the head of the rabbinic court, Rabbi Nathan Maas, whose view that the child should be redeemed immediately was followed. The text is damaged and incomplete and has been supplemented by the original found in the notebook of Rabbi Maas (YIVO MS. RG 128 [folder 77–78], fol. 114a; noted here in square brackets).

מב ע"א

1. העתק מפנקס הראש ב"ד ור"י כמהורר[2] נתן מז נר"ו
2. [מעש]ה שאירעו כאן ב"א ש{מ.} שמת בשמו ר' יעקב בן הירץ[3] רייס והניח אשתו מעוברת
3. ואח"כ המליטה בן זכר בכור פטר רחם לאמו ושאלה נשאל מאת ב"ד ה"ה הגאון
4. אב"ד מהורר אברהם נר"ו[4] והדיין התורני {כ} המופלא כ"ה יעקב שמש [ו]א[ני][5] ולאח[ר]
5. העי[ו]ן בדברי פוסקים הי' דעת אב"ד נר"ו לפדות[ו] התינק[6] עתה בלא ברכה [דהיינו]
6. שאם של התינק תתן חמש סלעים דמי {פידיונו} פדיונו במתנה כדי לפדותו א[ך מפני]
7. ספק יפדה התינק את עצמו עוד פעם לכשיגדיל ג"כ בלא ברכה ויתלה
8. התינק טס של כסף ויכתב עליו ספק פדוי ודעת התורני ר"י[7] הנ"ל [הי'] {שימ..}
9. שימתן עד שיגדל ויתלה התינק טס של כסף ויכתוב עליו שהוא בכור שאינו פד[וי]
10. ודעתי הי' שיפדה עתה התינק כדת {וכהילכתא}(וכהילכתו)[8] אף ב[ברכ]ה והיינו גם כן באופן
11. הנ"ל שתתן האם של התינק דמי {הפידיון} הפדיון [לתינוק] במתנה גמור[ה] ע"מ

---

1. Jacob Reiss died in April 1763 (see Ettlinger, 25.4.1763). His son must have reached 30 days of age in 1763 or early 1764.
2. כבוד מורנו הרב והגאון רב רבי
3. בנו של יעקב בן הירץ רייס נקרא על שמו, יעקב רייס, ונפטר כילד בשנת תקכ"ט (ר' אבני זכרון, מס' 3335).
4. הרב אברהם טריר שהיה אב"ד בקלויז (ר' הקדמה עמ' 77).
5. כאן רב נתן מז
6. צ"ל 'התינוק'
7. רב יעקב
8. תיקון מעל השורה

12. לפדותו דוקא ולא באופן אחר ולא תהי׳ דמי [הפדיון משל תינוק]
13. גם לא תתן האם במתנה סתמא [ב]לא ע״מ לפדות[ו / והמעיין בכתבי] הפוסקים
14. יבין הטעם ונחתנו אח״כ למינינא {ונמצא} ונמצא שר[בו דעת האו]מר[ים שי]עשו
15. הפדיון מיד ולענין ברכה לפי דעתינו הנ״ל [נ]מצ[א עכ״פ ע״פ רוב הדעו]ת [שאי]ן [לעשות]
16. ברכה עכשיו ונמצא עכשיו {כשיפצר כשתצטרך} כ[שתצטרף רוב הדיעות שצריך] לעש[ות]
17. כדעת הגא[ו]ן אב״ד נר״ו [אכן אח״כ הוקשה בעני הדיין ר״י]
18. הנ״ל דבר זה לומר שיע[ש]ה [שני פעמים הפדיון בלא ברכה / ולבטל תקנת חכמים / דעכ״פ]
19. פעם אחת מ[חויב בברכה / ומנ״ל למימר שלא יברך כלל / ובשביל זה הי׳ חוזר מדעתו]
20. ו[ט]פי ניחא ל[ו] להס[כ]י׳ לדעת[י הנ״ל / אכן הגאון אב״ד נר״ו בעבור שהי׳ אצלו עכ״פ]
21. [ה]ספק אמר [ל]ן ש[ק]בלה בידו מפ[י אביו ז״ל[1] / בכ״מ שיש ספק ברכה יאמר תחילה הפסוק]
22. ויברך דוד עד מעולם ועד [עולם[2] אשר קדשנו וכו׳ / דפסוק זה הוי כאלו אמר שם ומלכות[3] /]
23. ובשביל שאמר שקבלה ה[יא בידו / הנחנהו בדעתו ולא מחינון בידו / והסכמנו לעשות כן – –

מב ע״ב

1. ב״ה
2. אח״כ הלכנו אצל התינוק וזה ה[סד]ר אשר סדרנו האם של התינוק הי׳ נ[ו]תן
3. לה״ג אב״ד נר״ו החמשת סלעי׳ לזכות בהם לתינוק / וה״ג אב״ד נר״ו הי׳ זוכה
4. בהמעות והחזיק בהגבהה ע״מ לפדותו בהם אח״כ נוטל התינוק ואמר
5. זה הבן הוא בן בכור פטר רחם לאמו והקב״ה צוה לפדותו ואנחנו ב״ד
6. רוצי׳ לזכות את ה[ב]ן ולפדותו ואח״כ הי׳ נו[ת]ן התינוק לכהן ואח״כ נוטל
7. בידו דמי פדיונו והי׳ מושיט לכהן והי׳ אומר לו הילך חמשה סלעי׳ דמי
8. פדיונו ובשעת נתינת הדמי׳ עובר לעשייתן / הי׳ מברך ויברך דוד
9. עד מעולם ו[עד] עולם אשר קדשנו במצוותיו וציוונו על פדיון הבכור
10. וקודם לכן העמ[דנו על] השלחן פרי חדשי׳ כדי לברך ג״כ שהחיינו ונותן הדמי׳
11. לכהן בידו ונוטל [התינ]וק ממנו ואח״כ הי׳ כהן אומר ג״פ[4] בן זה הבכור פדוי
12. הוא [ואח״כ ה׳ מברך כל] אחד מאתנו ברכת בור[א] פרי הגפן כנהוג

No. 38

Wertheim v. Trach

Fols. 43a–b; Tuesday evening, 25 January 1774

A dispute over a dowry between Mendel Wertheim of Worms, the father of a bride,

---

1. שמעון בן יוסף טריר (אלה תולדות 4.12.1759).
2. דברי הימים א כ״ט, י
3. ר׳ שו״ת חתם סופר, או״ח ס׳ קנו.
4. גימל פעמים

and his prospective son-in-law, Ḥayyim Leb, son of the late Zalman Trach from Fürth, brought representatives of the parties to the Frankfurt court in the hope of reaching a settlement. The marriage had been delayed for some time (a preliminary marriage agreement had been signed in Worms before community leaders in the spring of 1772). The sides agreed to be bound by the decision of the Frankfurt court. The court arranged a compromise and the wedding was scheduled to take place about two months later. The text is damaged and incomplete.

מג ע"א

1. ב"ה
2. ע"ד טענות והפרשות שיש בין ה"ה התורני כ"ה מענדלי ווירטהיים
3. מן ק"ק ווירמש ובין חתנו המקושר הב"ח כ' חיים ליב בהמנוח[1] כ"ה זלמן
4. טראך מפירדא שה"ה כ' אהרן בן המנוח כ' מרדכי ז"ל מווירמש
5. הבא בכח והרשאה מספקת מחמיו כ"ה מענדלה הנ"ל וה"ה התורני
6. כ"ה משה אויך בהרשאת הב"ח כ' חיים ליב הנ"ל נתעצמו בטענו[']
7. לפנינו זה מול זה כמבואר בק"ה באריכות המונח לפנינו בענין הת
8. התקשרות של הבח[2] כ' ח"ל[3] הנ"ל עם בת {כ}של כ"ה מע[נ]דלי הנ"ל כמו ש...
9. לפנינו כ' אהרן הנ"ל תנאים ראשונים ההוקם בק"ק ווירמש ביו' ה' לגל[4]...
10. לספירה תקלב לפ"ק ע"י נאמני הקהלה שמה והנה אחרי שהצדדים
11. הנ"ל חתמו עצמם בתוקף קומפרמיס בח"ח ובקנס סך מסוים ל[אשר]
12. ולקיים כל אשר יצא מאתנו נזדקקנו להם ודברנו על לב הצדדים
13. הנ"ל לפשר בניהם ולקרב הזוג והר[כ]ינו א[ת] ראשם לדברינו ה"ה
14. הב"ח כ' חיים ליב הנ"ל בעצמו שבא לפנינו... אהרן הנ"ל
15. בכו"ה הנ"ל {שנ}שנתנו לפנינו בת"כ ובפ"...ם כפי שהתרצו ה...
16. בפנינו וכמבואר דהיינו הב"ח כ' חיים ליב [הנ"]ל יכניס לנדן כה"ר ...
17. כל מה שיש לו הן רב או מעט וה"ה התורני כ"ה מענדלי ווירטהיים יצו
18. יכנס לנדן בתו הבתולה מ' רעכלא קה"ח ס[ך ש]ני מאות זהו' במזומנים
19. בלי ניכוי פרוטה אחת מלבד הח"כ ש... מחל מב"ח ...
20. [זהו'] שמחויב להחזיר לו ג"כ...חנם ...
21. כח"ל[5] הנ"ל מחמיו כה"מ[6] הנ"ל ...
22. אותו כ"י [....] כ...
23. נר"ו יקבל הב"ח הנ"ל לאח[ר] ...
24. שנזכר[ת] בתוך התנאים ...

---

1. בן המנוח
2. הבחור חמד
3. חיים ליב
4. כנראה ל"ג בעומר שבאותה השנה נפל ביום ה' י"ח אייר.
5. כבוד חיים ליב
6. כבוד הרב מענדלי

25. קרקעות שהתחייב א"ע ...
26. רביעית בית שלו וחצי ...
27. מחויב ה"... הנ"ל לכנוס ...

מג ע"ב

1. ב"ה
2. בתנ"ר הנ"ל ושארי דברים התחייבו' משני צדדים הנזכרים
3. שמה יהי' הכל בתקפו והחתנה תהי' למז"ט בחדש אדר הסמוך
4. בלי {עיכוב} שום עיכוב וטענה ואמתלא שבעולם כל הנ"ל התרצו
5. הצדדים הנ"ל לפנינו ותקעו כפם בידינו על כל הנ"ל כנ"ל וכדי
6. שיהי' מאושר ויקוים כל הנ"ל בכל תוקף באנו אנחנו על החותם
7. בתוקף מעשה ב"ד ובכח ב"ד יפה יצא מאתנו אור ליו' ד' די
8. שבט תקלד לפק הק' נתן מז ר"י פה פפ"ד הק אנשיל צונץ ואני

No. 39

Fol. 43b; Sunday 6 February 1774(?)

The court arranged a compromise in a dispute between three matchmakers, each of whom claimed that they were owed fees for brokering the marriage of the son of Herz Gans and the daughter of the late Aaron Fulda. The text is damaged and incomplete but it is clear that both the Gans and Fulda families were obligated to make payment to at least two of the matchmakers.

9. ביו' א' דדי[1] שבט עשינו פשרה בין השדכנים ה"ה התורני כ"ה נתן אופנה וכ' אלי'
10. פולדא והאשה מ' יענטלה וואהל שכל א' תבע שדכנות מן השידוך שנעשה בין
11. בן של הירץ גנץ[2] ובין בת של המנוח כ"ה אהרן פולדא ז"ל ופסקנו ד"פ שכ' אלי' יקח
12. משני צדדי' ארבע זהו' ו[ה]אשה מ' יענטלה תקח משני צדדי' שלשה זהו' והמותרות
13. ... כאשר יא... בפנינו אין הוא בעצמו הי' לבד רק הוא מצוה לר'
14. ... {וגם הוא} לכן עשה כ' שמואל סופר הנ"ל אבל כ'
15. ... שאין לו ...ה עכשיו כלל מש"ה לא פסק לו מידי

1. בשנת תקל"ד כ"ד שבט נפל ביום שבת.
2. פייס, בנו של הירץ גנץ, נשא לאשה את גוטלה בת אהרן פולדא בסביבות שנת 1775 (ר' אלה תולדות 22.4.1816).

No. 40

Oppenheim v. Mai

Fols. 44a–b; undated, incomplete

Michael, Gumpel, and Benedict Mai (May), three brothers, jointly owned an unspecified quantity of wine that was held under lock and key by Yudaʾ Kulp, Gumpel Mai's father-in-law. With the express consent of his brothers, Benedict Mai negotiated the sale of the wine to Leb Oppenheim, but Kulp contested the sale. When Oppenheim's representatives arrived to collect the wine, Kulp refused to give it to them. Kulp maintained that he had initially made it clear that he wanted to purchase the wine at a specific price but had feigned disinterest when asked about the sale in order not to become involved in a bidding war. Both Oppenheim and Kulp had representation before the court and the respective advocates each made a number of specific arguments to support their clients' positions. The parties were asked to agree to be bound by the court's decision before the court would proceed.

In the course of its deliberations, the court summoned Benedict Mai and asked him a number of questions about the transaction. The court ruled in Oppenheim's favor but since Gumpel Mai was a partner in the holdings, the court gave Gumpel the right to keep his third of the wine (with an appropriate reduction in the amount paid by Oppenheim to the brothers), presumably so Gumpel could sell it to his father-in-law. If Gumpel decided not to keep his portion of the wine, then Oppenheim had rights to all the wine as originally contracted in the sale. The document is damaged and some information is missing.

מד ע"א

1. בה
2. ע"ד הפרשות וסכסוכים שיש בין הצדדים הנ"ל בין ה"ה הו"ה
3. פו"מ כ"ה ליב אופנהיים ובין ה"ה הוה[1] הנעלה כ' יודא קולפא
4. יצו ובין ה"ה הו"ה כ"ה גומפל מאיי סגל מחמת היין שהי' שייך
5. להני תלתא אחי ה"ה הוה כ' מיכאל והו"ה כ' גומפל הנ"ל וה"ה הו"ה
6. כ' בענדיט מאיי סג"ל והיין מונח תחת רשות כ' יודא קולפא ונמכר
7. לכ"ה ליב הנ"ל ע"י כ' בענדיט הנ"ל שאמר שהי' רשות לזה מן הנהו
8. תרי אחי מיכאל וכ' {בענדיט} (גומפל)[2] הנ"ל בעד מאה ושני רט והנה כל
9. אחד מהצדדים הנ"ל רוצה לזכות במקח היין ונתעצמו בטענותיהם
10. לפנינו והיינו שה"ה התורני כ"ה זלמן גייגר בהרשאת כ"ה ליב הנ"ל תבע

---

1. המפואר והחשוב
2. תיקון מעל השורה

11. לפנינו ואמר ש"כ בענדיט הביא לכ' ליב הנ"ל שני פעמים איין פרוב מהיין הנ"ל
12. וזה הי' אי אפשר בלי ידיעת כ"י[1] הנ"ל באשר שמונח בתוך רשות מסוגר וצריך
13. ליתן המפתח למקום שמונח היין וגם שאל לכ' בענדיט אם כ"י הנ"ל לא רצה ליקח
14. היין והשיב כ"ב[2] הנ"ל שלא רצה כי[3] הנ"ל ליקח היין והנה ביו' ב' העבר בא כ' בענד[יט]
15. הנ"ל לכה[4] ליב הנ"ל ופ[ס]ק עמו מחמת היין עד שנתרצו שניהם ומכר כ"ב הנ"ל
16. לכ"ה ליב הנ"ל היין בעד מאה ושני ר"ט ואמר כ"ב הנ"ל ל{כ"ה ליב} לאחר גמר
17. המקח באשר שכ"י הנ"ל לא רצה להניח עוד היין בתוך רשותו בכן יקח כה"ל[5] הנ"ל
18. היין היום עוד מתוך {מ}רשות כ"י הנ"ל וכן עשה כה"ל הנ"ל והוציא [ה]וצאת
19. ושלח בעל עגלה וב"מ ליקח היין ועכב כ"י הנ"ל ליתן לו בכן {ב}תובע
20. כ"ה זלמן הנ"ל באשר שהיין שלו {שלקח} שלקח מהאחי' המשותפי' ביין אל
21. יעכב כ"י הנ"ל מליתן לו {הרין} היין הנ"ל והתורני כ"ה משה אויך בהרשאת
22. כ"י הנ"ל בא לפנינו ואמר שכ' יודא הי' [פו]סק על היין כבר מאה {רט}רט קודם
23. המכירה לכה"ל הנ"ל רק כ' ב[ענ]דיט הנ"ל לא רצה להניח לו תיכף באותו
24. פעם משום שסבר שימכר ביוקר מזה הסכום ואם לאו לא ימכר ביותר
25. רצה להניח לו ולאח"כ עשה כ"י[6] את עצמו כאי[לו לא] יד[ע] רצה ליקח ה...
26. שלא יבוא להעלות דמי המקח אבל כוונתו הי['] ... שנעשה ...
27. יחזיק הוא היין באותו מקח וטוען כ"ה...
28. בדרכי הקני' רק בדברים בעלמא ...
29. סכום המקח שנעשה באשר שהיין מונח...

מד ע"ב

1. בה
2. וכדי לחקור הדבר שלחנו אחר המוכר כ' בענדיט ובא לפנינו ואמר שהי' לו
3. רשות מן אחיו כ' מיכאל וכ' גומפל הנ"ל ל{כ}מכור היין וגם אמר כ' בענדיט
4. הנ"ל ששאל קודם המכירה לאחיו כ' גומפל הנ"ל אם רוצה חמיו ליקח אותו
5. והשיב כ' גומפל הנ"ל שחמיו אינו רוצה ליקח {היין} אותו אפילו בשמונים
6. רט {וכ"מ} וכה"מ[7] הנ"ל עומד בטענותיו שאמר לו כ"ה {כ'} גומפל שמה שאמר
7. בשם חמיו (ולאח"כ גמר המקח לא בשום דרכי' הקנייי' רק [...] הי' דבר' בעלמא)[8] שלא רצה הוא מטעם אמתלא וכוונתו שנעשה סכום מקח ע"י אחר
8. ועל אותו מקח רצה חמיו ליקח [היין] עוד טען כה"מ הנ"ל בהרשאת כה[9]
9. גומפל הנ"ל באשר שכ' גומפל הנ"ל הוא {משותף} משותף ביין בכן רוצה

---

1. כבוד יודא
2. כבוד בענדיט
3. כבוד יודא
4. לכבוד הרב
5. כבוד הרב ליב
6. כבוד יודא
7. כבוד הרב משה
8. תוספת מעל השורה
9. כבוד הרב

10. הוא {חמיו ליקח ליתן על דמי השני שלישי יין לאחיו כ׳ מיכאל וכ׳ גומפל}
11. בעצמו ליקח היין בדמי מקח שנתן כה״ל הנ״ל ורוצה לשלם דמי שני שלישי׳ האחרי׳
12. לאחיו כ׳ מכאל וכ׳ בענדיט הנ״ל והאריכו הצדדים הנ״ל בטענותיהם וב[ת]שובתיה׳
13. זה מול זה וזה מול זה כמבואר באריכות מתוך ק״ה המונוח אצלינו
14. הנה אחרי שהצדדים הנ״ל חתמו עצמם בתוקף קומפרמיס {בטעות}
15. בח״ח ובקנס סך מסוים לאשר ולקיים את כל אשר יצא מאתנו נזדקקנו
16. להם ו{מצאנו} ודרשנו וחקרנו הדק היטיב בטענותיהם ובדברי ה[מ]ו[כ]ר
17. ומצאנו שהדין עם כ״ה ליב הנ״ל נגד טענות כ׳ יודא הנ״ל אכן מחמת זה
18. שטוען כ׳ גומפל הנ״ל שהוא רצה לזכות ביין מצאנו שאינו יוכל לזכות
19. רק בחלק שליש מהיין הנ״ל אבל בשני שלישים הנותרים שהי׳ שייכי׳
20. לאחיו כ׳ {גומפל} מיכאל וכ׳ בענדיט הנ״ל אין לו שום זכות כלל
21. וכלל {יצ}בכן אם כ׳ גומפל הנ״ל רצה לזכות {...} ב[ח]לק שליש מהיין
22. הנ״ל אזי הברירה על שני שלישי׳ נותרי׳ ביד כה״ל[1] אם רצה
23. להחזיק המקח לפי ערך סכום המקח שקנה מתחילה כל היין
24. ... ובאם כ׳ [גו]מפל הנ״ל לא רצה לזכות בחלק שליש מהיין
25. ...יזכה כה[״ל...] בכל המקח כמו שקנה מתחילה יצא מאתנו
26. ...לדל... שש[2] הק׳ אברהם טריר ואני

Fol. 45a is blank.

No. 41

Trier v. Schwarzschild

Fols. 45b–47a; Thursday 1 April 1774

Yuzpa Trier was married to (Leah) Hindele (née Schwarzschild) who had three unmarried sisters. The sisters' father, Leser, died and the unmarried sisters rented space (and presumably lived), according to court decisions issued in April 1766 and October/November 1767, in the Trier family house on Roter Hut (see Dietz, p. 455, no. 79). One of the sisters, Hindche, was now about to marry and this prompted the Triers to come to the court to settle outstanding issues (disputes with

1. כבוד הרב ליב
2. כנראה הרב מאיר שווארץ שילד

the remaining sisters would presumably be settled when they married).[1] Yuzpa, in large part based on the aforementioned court decisions, claimed that he was owed rent, taxes that he had paid for Hindche, a sum that Yuzpa had paid for his late father-in-law, court costs, and gravestone costs. In addition, Hindele was to have received a portion of her father's estate, and Yuzpa claimed that she had not yet received it. Yuzpa admitted to having received a total of 100 guldens for all his claims but was now seeking approximately 20 guldens more. Through her representative, Hindche countered that she should only be responsible for 25% of what was claimed against her. Moreover, Hindche noted that earlier court decisions had left Yuzpa responsible for a share of taxes and repairs that the sisters had paid. She added that there were additional costs related to the commemoration of her father's death that Yuzpa had not contributed to and that, in fact, Yuzpa owed her money. Yuzpa, who represented himself, offered various counterclaims and the court ultimately decided that Hindche must pay him 3 guldens. The court specifically noted that its decision had no bearing on Yuzpa's potential claims against the other sisters or theirs against him.

Yuzpa made an additional claim against Hindche and her prospective husband. Leser Schwarzschild's estate had an outstanding debt of 200 guldens. Following a court order, Yuzpa paid the current interest on the debt (5% per annum), but, upon marriage each daughter was to assume her share of the annual payment. Yuzpa requested that Hindche and her husband do so and to this end asked that they be ordered to set aside a portion of their house as collateral. Hindche argued that since she did not have residence rights in Frankfurt she should be considered as if she were still single and exempt from payment. Even if the court did not accept this argument, Hindche maintained that she should only have to pay 2.5 guldens a year and not 5 guldens. In this the court sided with Yuzpa.

A postscript from 27 July 1774 explains why the court sided with Yuzpa in this latter matter. It also notes that on that day Hindche made payment to Yuzpa and, through her representative, undertook her obligation to pay her share of the debt of her father's estate.

מה ע"ב

ב"ה
ע"ד הסכסוכי' והפרשות שבין ה"ה כ' יוזפא טריר הבא בכח
עצמו ובהרשאת אשתו מ' הינדלה בת המנוח כ' ליזר ש"ש ז"ל בין
אחות אשתו הבתולה הכלה מ' הינדכה בת המנוח כ' ליזר ז"ל
הנ"ל שהציעו טענותיו לפנינו ה"ה כ' יוזפא הנ"ל וה"ה כ"ה אנשיל

1. The two other sisters, Frummet and Merle, never married (see Horovitz, no. 4416, and Ettlinger, 27.12.1762).

6. פפאן בהרשאתה הכלה מ' הינדכה הנ"ל ו{ה"ה התורני} כמבואר
7. בק"ה באריכות המונח לפנינו והנה אחרי שהצדדי' הנ"ל
8. חתמו עצמם בתוקף קומפרמיס בח"ח ובקנס סך מסויים לאשר
9. ולקיים בכל אשר יצא מאתנו וגם קבלו עליהם לעשות פשר
10. דבר ביניהם ולאשר ולקיים כנ"ל בכן נזדקקנו להם ומצאנו על
11. כל פרט ופרט כמבואר להבא והיינו שכ' יוזפא הנ"ל הציע
12. לפנינו פסק ב"ד שיצא ביו' א' ל"ב למב"י תקד"ו לפ"ק[1] וגם מן ב'
13. מרחשון תקד"ח ושם נאמר שמחויבי' השלוש[.] אחיות
14. הבתולה מ' הינדכה הנ"ל ומ' מערלה ומ' פרומט בנות המונח
15. כ' ליזר הנ"ל לשלם לכ' יוזפא הנ"ל מחמת שכירות חלקי שנים
16. עשר בית צום רויט"ה הו"ט משך ד"ב חדושי' לפ"ע עשרה זהו'
17. לשנה העולה חי' זהו' א' ק"ש עוד מחויבי' לשלם שכר דירה
18. מבית הנ"ל מן שלשה שנים קודם הגורל שהאחיות הנ"ל [ב]חי'
19. בחלקו הנ"ל והיינו ... תק{נ}(ד)[2]"ה עד שנת תקד"ח כל שנה סך
20. ... ה"ה [כ"ה] אנשיל

מו ע"א

1. ב"ה
2. פפאן הנ"ל בשביל חלק שנים עשר בית הנ"ל ששכר מן כ' גרשון
3. ש"ס[3] העולה לשלשה שנים שלשי' ושבעה זהו' וחצי לפי פסק דין הנ"ל
4. עוד מחויבת לשלם לפי פסק דין הנ"ל מחמת תשלומן לגובי' כ"ב
5. זהו' עוד מחובי' לשלם לפי פ"ד הנ"ל מחמת תשלומן לג"ע שכ'
6. יוזפא שילם עבר[4] חמיו ז"ל אחד ועשרי' זהו' כ"ה צ"ל[5] שלשה רביע'
7. העולה ששה עשר זהו' ג' צ"ל עוד תובע כ' יוזפא הנ"ל
8. [ב]אשר שנזכר בפ"ד הנ"ל {מ} שכל מה שנמצא בעזבון חמיו ז"ל
9. הנ"ל שלא חלקו עדיין שמחויבת האחיות הנ"ל ליתן לאשת כ' יוזפא הנ"ל חלק שמינית ולא
10. קיבלה כלום בכן תובע כ' יוזפא הנ"ל חמשה זהו' ב[ע]ד חלקה ואמר שהי' שווה לכל הפחות כ"כ
11. עוד נזכר בפ"ד הנ"ל שמחויבת לשלם עשרה זהו' וחצי עבור הוצאות שהוציא כ' יוזפא הנ"ל עד
12. שכיפה האחיות הנ"ל לדון בד"י עוד מחויבת לשלם שלשה רביעית הוצאות עמידת מצבה לחמ[יו]
13. ז"ל העולה על חלקם שלשה זהו' ג' צל עוד מחויבת לישלם ההלוה ששלים כ' יוזפא הנ"ל שכר

---

1. בשנה זו ל"ב בעומר נפל ביום שבת.
2. תוספת מעל השורה
3. אולי צ"ל 'ש"ש' (שווארץ שילד); עיין אבני זכרון, מס' 4429. אביו, שמואל, היה גר ברויטה הוט (ר' אלה תולדות 2.10.1751).
4. צ"ל 'עבור'
5. על השימוש ב-'צ"ל' במקום 'Kreuzer' ר' לוח המטבעות ומידות.

14. בטילה לב"ד ולשמש עבור האחיות חמשה זהו' כל התביעות הנ"ל עולה מאה ועשרי' זהו' שלשי' צל
15. ועל זה קבל מאה זהו' בכן תובע כ' יוזפא הנ"ל המו(ת)[1]רות דהיינו עשרי' זהו' שלשי' צל וה"ה התורני
16. כ"ה אנשיל פפאן בהרשאת הכלה מ' היניכה[2] הנ"ל השיב באשר שלא תבע עכשיו רק ממנה לבדו שהול[ך]
17. עמו לדין בכן אין עלי' לשלם רק רביעית מתביעות מותרות הנ"ל וגם תבעה מן כ' יוזפא הנ"ל
18. באשר שנאמר בפ"ד הנ"ל שכל מה שתוציאו האחיות עבור בנין קלקול הבית ותוכל לברר ע"י
19. בעל מלאכות וכן מה שהוצרך לשלם עבור גרונד ציץ שנתרצה כ' יוזפא הנ"ל שיתן חלקו בכן
20. רוצה כה"א[3] הנ"ל בהרשאת הנ"ל לחשוב עם כ"י[4] הנ"ל והציע חשבן לפנינו מה ששילמו האחיות
21. לו עבור בדק הבית וגם גרונד ציץ העולה על חלק כ' יוזפא הנ"ל שמונה זהו' לח צל עוד
22. שילמו האחיות הנ"ל רוק שטאנד שאצינג מן חיי' אבי' ז"ל הנ"ל מן שנת תקך"ג ושנת תקך"ד (לפק) על חלקו
23. ד' זהו' יוד צל גם הוציאו הוצאות מחמת נר תמיד העולה על חלקו שלשה זהו' מ"ה צל עולה יחד
24. מחמת תביעות הנ"ל ששה עשר זהו' ל"ג צל שהוציאו האחיות ביחדיו בעבורו בכן תובעו
25. הכלה מ' היניכה הנ"ל חלק שליש מזה מן כ' יוזפא הנ"ל חמשה זהו' לא צל וכ' יוזפא הנ"ל השׁ[יב]
26. מה שתבע כה"א הנ"ל וחשב מחמת גרונד ציץ ובדק הבית רוצה לשל[ם]...מה שתב[עה]
27. מחמת שאצינג תעון[5] כי[6] הנ"ל באשר שהאחיות הנ"ל לא ...

מו ע"ב

1. שעמדו לפני ב"ד בשנת תקכ"ו מסתמא לא שילמו משלהם רק מעזבון חמיו ז"ל ומחמת הוצאות נר תמיד
2. השיב כ' יוזפא הנ"ל שאשתו ידע בוודא[7] שחצה[8] שנה ראשונה דהיינו קודם חלוקה היה [מדליק]ן נר
3. תמיד הנ"ל מעזבון חמיו ולאחר חלוקה הניחה אשתו מחלקה כל כך בעזבון אבי' כמו שמגיע על חלקה
4. לסייעת הדלקת נר תמיד הנ"ל ולאחר שחשבנו ודקדקנו היטיב בטענות הנ"ל מצנו[9] שמחויבת הכלה

1. תוספת מעל השורה
2. צ"ל 'הינכה' וכן בהמשך
3. כבוד הרב אנשיל
4. כבוד יוזפא
5. אולי צ"ל 'טוען'
6. כבוד יוזפא
7. צ"ל 'בוודאי'
8. צ"ל 'חצי'
9. צ"ל 'מצאנו'

5. מרת היניכה הנ״ל לשלם לכ׳ יוזפא הנ״ל שלשה זהו׳ ובזה המה פטורי׳ זה מזו וזו מזה מכל תבעות
6. הנ״ל דהיינו הכלה הבתולה מ׳ היניכה הנ״ל לבד אבל בין כ׳ יוזפא הנ״ל ושאר אחיות הפנויית הנ״ל
7. יקוב הדין ההר ביניהם עוד תובע כ׳ יוזפא הנ״ל באשר שנזכר בפ״ד הנ״ל וז״ל ומחמת קנין על רווחי׳
8. עשרה זהו׳ לשנה מן שני מאות זהו׳ שנשאר {שנשאר} עזבון חמיו עדיין חייב לגובי׳ פטורי׳
9. הפנויית אך כשירצה להנשא לאיש אחר אז מחויבת כל אחת ואחת מהפנויית כשיגיע
10. כשיגיע לנשואין לכנוס ג״כ באותו חוב של רווחים שוה בשוה עם כ׳ יוזפא מאותו יום [ו]הלאה
11. או שישלמו שני מאות זהו׳ הנ״ל עכ״ל וטעון׳ כ׳ יוזפא הנ״ל באשר שהבתולה מ היניכה הנ״ל באה
12. לכלל נישואין ומיועדת עתה לישא עם חתנה המקושר עמה בכן תקיים פס״ד הנ״ל לכנוס ג״כ
13. בחוב רווחי׳ הנ״ל לשלם מידי שנה בשנה חמשה זהו׳ ותובע כ׳ יוזפא הנ״ל שכמו שהי׳ מוכרח
14. הוא ואשתו לעשות ק״ס קודם חתנותו ולהשתעבד חלק שנים עשר מבית הנ״ל לגובי׳ לשלם
15. כל שנה סך עשרה זהו׳ רווחי׳ וכנ״ל כן תעשה הכלה מ היניכה הנ״ל ג״כ ק״ס על חלקה שנים
16. עשר מבית הנ״ל ולהשתעבד נכסים על חוב הנ״ל והיינו שווה בשווה עם כ״י[2] לשלם מידי
17. שנה בשנה סך חמשה זהו׳ מן רווחי׳ הנ״ל וכמ״ש בפ״[ד ה]נ״ל וה״ה התורני כה אנשיל פפאן
18. השיב באשר ... מ׳ היניכה הנ״ל אינה מחזיק עירונית כאן יש לה דין פנויי׳ ואף אם היא צריכה
19. ... מגיע עלי׳ רק חלק רביעית מן החוב רווחי׳ הנ״ל והאריכו בטענותיהם

מז ע״א

1. ובתשובתיהם ומצאנו שכדברי כ׳ יוזפא הנ״ל כן הוא שהכלה מ׳ היניכה הנ״ל מחויבת לכנוס ג״כ באותו
2. של רווחי׳ הנ״ל שוה בשוה עם כ׳ יוזפא הנ״ל והיינו שמחויבת לעשות ק״ס קודם חתנת ולהשתעבד חלקה
3. שנים עשר מבית הנ״ל לכ׳ יוזפא ואשתו הנ״ל לשלם חמשה זהו׳ כל שנה מיום נשואין שלה והלאה עד שתגיע
4. כל אחת ואחת משתי אחיות הפנויית מ׳ פרומט ומ׳ מערלה הנ״ל לכלל נשואין ג״כ ואז יקוב הדין ההר
5. ביניהם ובין הצדדים הנ״ל עוד תובע כ׳ יוזפא הנ״ל באשר ששתי אחיות הפנויית מ׳ פרומט ומ׳
6. מערלה הנ״ל עכב[ו] מהכלה מ׳ היניכה הנ״ל איהר קשט ובתוכה בגדים וחפצי׳ שלה מתו[3] חשד שחשדו את
7. הכלה הנ״ל שנטלה משלהם גם לקחו מתוך קישט הנ״ל משכן והחזירו ללוה ולקחו הפרעון סך
8. חמשי׳ ר״ט לעצמן והכלה מ׳ היניכה מרוצה להניח להם סך הנ״ל אם תחזירו לה שאר חפצי׳

1. צ״ל 'וטוען'
2. כבוד יוזפא
3. צ״ל 'מתוך'

9. שלה בכן תובע כ' יוזפא הנ"ל רביעית מן חמשי' ר"ט הנ"ל באשר שמגיע לו חלק רביעית מכל
10. עזבון חמיו ז"ל ואפשר שהעלימו ג"כ מעזבון חמיו וכה"א הנ"ל השיב מה שהישב[1] ומצאונו שאין
11. ממש בתביעה זו מן כ' יוזפא הנ"ל יצא מאתנו יו' ה' י"ב למב"י[2] תקל"ד הק מאיר שש
12. הק אברהם טריר כהן ואני
13. מה שפסקנו ד"פ מחמת רווחי' שכ"י[3] הנ"ל זוכה בטענותיו הוא שמצד השכל הי' יכול לתבוע
14. שהכלה הנ"ל תשלם לגובי' בראש חלק שליש מהקרן שני מאות זהו' שהי' חייב אבי' לגוב'
15. כמו שהי' כ' יוזפא הנ"ל מוכרח לשלם קודם חתנותו חלק המגיע לו בקרן וכמו שנזכר
16. בפס"ד מן תקדו או שתשלם היא לבד רווחי' מחלק קרן המגיע לה לשלם והמותרות
17. מחויבי' כ' יוזפא והכלה הנ"ל ליקח עליהם החוב והתשלומין רווחי' אך באשר שכ"י
18. הנ"ל לא תבע רק שהיא תכנוס עמו שוה בשוה בחוב הרווחי' הנ"ל לכך פסקנו שכדבר
19. כן הוא
20. כהיו' דלמטה קיימו הצדדי' הנ"ל את פס"ד הנ"ל ובאו לפני ה"ה התורני כ"ה אנשיל פפאן הנ"ל
21. בהרשאת הנ"ל וה"ה כ' יוזפא הנ"ל ובפני קיבל כ' יוזפא הנ"ל שלשה זהו' מכה"א[4] הנ"ל בהרשאת הנ"ל
22. וגם נעשה ק"ס עי'[5] נאמני הקהלה כנהוג כמבואר בפסק דין הנ"ל ולראיי' (ע"פ דרכן [.]' לפני)[6] חתמת[י] לשני צדדי'
23. נעשה פה פ"פ יו' ד' יט מנחם תקלד לפק

No. 42

Fol. 47b; Sunday evening, 24 April 1774

Four matchmakers — one married man, two bachelors, and one married woman — claimed fees for arranging the marriage of the son of Elchanan Katz of Frankfurt and the daughter of Berman Kohen of Friedberg. The Frankfurt court was asked to arrange a compromise among the matchmakers, which it did. The court investigated each of the claims and heard from Elchanan Katz before giving its decision. The names of the members of the court are not given.

---

1. צ"ל 'שהשיב'
2. בשנה זו י"ב לעומר חל ביום שישי ולא ביום חמישי. יתכן שפסק הדין הוצא בערב.
3. כבוד יוזפא
4. כבוד הרב אנשיל
5. על ידי
6. תוספת מעל השורה

מז ע״ב

1. בה
2. ע״ד הפרשות שיש בין הני צדדי דהיינו ה״ה האלוף וה״ק היקר כ׳ יוזפא ו[ו]עטרהַאן וה״ה הבחור כ׳
3. וואלף בהמנוח[1] מה״ר דוד טרויב ז״ל וה״ה הבחור כ׳ יעקב בכ״ה יהודא זעלקי זצ״ל מפייארשטארף
4. והאשה מ׳ קילכה אשת גבריאל מק״ק פ״ב שכל א׳ וא׳ רוצה לזכות בשכר שדכנות מהשידוך
5. שנעשה ונגמר שנתקשר בן של הו״ה היקר כ׳ אלחנן קאץ מפה עם בת הו״ה כ״ה בערמן כהן מק״ק
6. פרידבורג ולאחר שחתמו הצדדי׳ הנ״ל א״ע בתוקף קומפרמיס בח״ח ובקנס סך מסויים לחזק ולקיים
7. את הפשר אשר יצא מאתנו נזדקקנו להם וחקרנו בטענותיהם שהאריכו לפנינו גם שמענו את
8. פי הבעל דבר הו״ה היקר כ׳ אלחנן קאץ הנ״ל ומצאנו ע״ד פשר דבר שמשכר שדכנות
9. הנ״ל העולה משני הצדדים שלשי׳ וששה זהו׳ יקבל הו״ה כ׳ יוזפא הנ״ל ששה זהו׳ והבחור
10. כ׳ וואלף טרויב הנ״ל יקבל מהשדכנות הנ״ל שנים עשר זהו׳ והבחור כ׳ יעקב הנ״ל יקבל חמשה
11. עשר זהו׳ והאשה מ׳ קילכה הנ״ל תקבל שלשה זהו׳ יצא מאתנו אור ליו׳ ב ד״ט למב״י שנת
12. תקלד לפ״ק פה פ״פ דמיין

No. 43

Fols. 48a–b; Sunday evening, 24 July 1774

In 1776, Meʾir Segal loaned Hendele, widow of David Traub (d. 1763), 100 reichstalers at 6% per annum. The transaction was duly recorded by the community and Meʾir received a contract itemizing the agreement. According to Meʾir, the contract was subsequently destroyed in a fire; therefore he now came to the court asking that it order the community to reissue the loan document, backdated to 1766. Meʾir was able to substantiate his claim that he had made a loan to Hendele through the copy recorded in the communal record book. According to the record, the debt was to have been repaid in 1768, but Meʾir maintained that Hendele had never made payment on the loan or the interest. Hendele confirmed that this was true. The court inquired whether anyone had lent money to Hendele subsequent to Meʾir's loan. This was an important step because the reissue of the note would impinge on the rights of subsequent creditors. There was one such creditor, and while Joel Bing accepted that the original note had been destroyed, he questioned

1. בן המנוח

the assertion that no payment had ever been made. Joel initially objected to the reissue of the note but the court urged the parties to compromise and they did. Me'ir's claim on the accrued interest was reduced by 20 reichstalers (see, however, no. 44). The court ordered the community to reissue the note with reduced accrued interest and an addendum that this note replaced the earlier one lost in the fire.

There is a postscript that gives a rationale for the court's ruling. It notes that since the custom in Frankfurt was only to recognize contracts drawn up by the community, no note against Hendele other than Joel Bing's would have legal standing, for it was the only other note recorded by the community. As for oral transactions, they were always superseded by written transactions no matter which came first. The court relied on document no. 254 as a precedent in this matter. Also see no. 44.

מח ע"א

1. ב"ה
2. ה"ה התורני כ"ה מאיר בן המנוח כ"ה יעקב ישראל סגל ז"ל הציע לפנינו העתק ק"ס מפנקס הנאמני'
3. פה מן האשה מרת הענדלה אל' המנוח כמ"ה דוד טרויב שעשתה ק"ס בכא"ה ביו' ד' ז'
4. אייר תקד"ו והודית שחייב' לכ"ה מאיר הנ"ל סך מאה ר"ט בת"ע עם רווחי' עצ"ה ששה
5. למאה לשנה לשלם ולפרוע הקרן הנ"ל בכלות שתי שנים מהיום והרווחי' הנ"ל בכלות
6. כל שנה ושנה ועל הק"ס הנ"ל כתוב שנכתב ונמסר השטר ליד ר"מי[1] הנ"ל ואמר ר"מ הנ"ל
7. שאמת הוא שהי' השטר הנ"ל תחת [י]דו ו{וב}רשותו אבל אחר שנגע בו יד ה'
8. ונשרף בעו"ה ביתו שהי' דר בו נשרף בתוכה גם זה השטר עם שאר מטלטלי'
9. וחפצם וספרי' וכתבי' בכן ביקש מאתנו כ"ה מאיר הנ"ל לצוות לנאמני' הקהילה
10. עידי השטר הנ"ל לתקן ולחדש לו שטר מחדש מזמן ראשון מאחר שלא קיבל שום
11. פרוטה אחת דמי פירעון על השטר הנ"ל הן מקרן מאה רט הנ"ל הן מרווחים
12. שעולים מסך קרן הנ"ל מזמן השטר עד עתה ושגם האשה מ' הענדלה הנ"ל
13. [ה]ודה לדבריו שמעולם לא שילמה לו ע"ז השטר {ע"ע סך} שום פרוטה אחת
14. הן מקרן הנ"ל או מרווחי' העולים מזמן השטר ע"ע סך ארבעי' ושמונה ר"ט
15. ויותר ושאלנו את פי כה"מ הנ"ל אם לא ידע אם יש עוד ק"ס ושטר על
16. לוה שלו מזמן מא(ו)[2]חר מזמן [ה]שטר שלו הנ"ל והשיב שידע [ש]יש עוד שטר על
17. לוה שלו אחד מא(ו)[3]ח{ו}ר {ברשות}(לה"ה)[4] כ"ה יואל בינגא סג"ל אבל זולת זה אין על
18. הלוה שלו שטר מא(ו)[5]ח{ו}ר לשטר שלו כפי שנשמע מנאמני הקהלה פה ושלחנו
19. אחרי האשה מ' הענדלה הנ"ל והודית בפנינו שכל דברי כה"מ הנ"ל

---

1. רב מאיר
2. תוספת מעל השורה
3. תוספת מעל השורה
4. תוספת מעל השורה
5. תוספת מעל השורה

20. כני׳ היו ושלא שילמה פרוטה אחת על חובה שטר הנ״ל לא מקרן ולא מרווחי׳
21. ואמרה שיכתבו לכה״מ הנ״ל שטר חדש בכא״ה ואפי׳ מזמן ראשון שהיא
22. מאמין לו שנשרף השטר שהי׳ בידו ובאשר שנהוג פה שכל ק״ס ושטר שלא
23. נעשה ע״י נאמני הקהלה פה אין לו זכות וכח השטר בכן שלחנו אחרי
24. נאמני הקהלה ובא לפנינו ושאלנו אותם אם יש עוד שטר אם מאוחר מזמן
25. שטר הנ״ל על הק״ס שעשתה האשה הנ״ל (והשבו)[1] שלא נעשה שום שטר וק״ס
26. מהאשה הנ״ל מאוחר מזמן השטר הנ״ל זולת זה אותו שטר מאוחר שיש
27. ברשות כ״ה יואל בינגא הנ״ל ו[של]חנו אחר כ״ה יואל בינגא הנ״ל ובא
28. לפנינו ואמר שידע שהי׳ תחת כה״מ הנ״ל שטר אחד מן האשה מ׳
29. הענדלה הנ״ל ממאה רט קרן וגם מאמין לכה״מ [ה]נ״ל שנשרף הש[טר]
30. הנ״ל רק שהוא אינו מרוצה שיכתוב לו שטר ... מזמן ראש[ון]...
31. קרן

מח ע״ב

1. ב״ה
2. קרן ורווחי׳ כנ״ל באשר שלא ידע אם לא נפרע כלום מרווחי׳ ושאינו מאמין למלוה ולווה
3. שלא שילמה כלל וכלל מרוחי׳ פרוטה אחת ודברנו על לבם והתפשרו א״ע ה״ה כה״מ[2]
4. הנ״ל וה״ה כה״י[3] הנ״ל בפנינו שיוכתב לכה״מ הנ״ל שטר חדש מזמן ראשון בכא״ה
5. רק שיוכתב על שטר חדש א״ע שינוכה מרווחי׳ העולים מזמן השטר עד עתה
6. סך עשרי׳ רט גם התנה בפי׳ כה״י הנ״ל שלא יזיק לו פשר זה כלום אם יהי׳ לו
7. דו״ד על רווחים העולי׳ מזמן שטר הנ״ל ואחר שנעשה כל הנ״ל מצאנו ע״פ הדת
8. והדין לתקן ולהקים לכה״מ הנ״ל על הק״ס הנ״ל שטר מחודש מזמן הנ״ל בכן צווינו
9. בכח ב״ד יפה להנאמיני׳ עידי השטר לתקן ולחתו[4] השטר מחדש כפי משמעות הק״ס
10. הנ״ל מזמן הק״ס וקודם שימסרו לכה״מ הנ״ל יכתבו על השטר מע״ל שינוכה מדמי
11. רווחים העולים מסך קרן דמי השטר הנ״ל מזמן ק״ס הנ״ל ע״ע סך עשרים רט
12. זולת זה יהי׳ להשטר הלז כל תוקף ועוז בכא״ה כמו השטר הראשון בלי שום
13. פקפוק כלל והנאמני׳ יכתבו בתוך השטר קוד׳ שיכתבו הכל שריר וקים (בזה הלשון)[5] [נכ]תב
14. [ו]נמסר שטר זה פעם שנית ע״פ (ב״ד)[6] {בזה הלשון} תחת השטר שנשרף וכפי המבואר
15. בפסק ב״ד הנמסר לידינו יצא מאתננו אור ליו׳ ב׳ טוב מנחם תקל״ד לפק
16. ה״ק אברהם טריר כהן
17. ה״ק מאיר בלל״א כ״ה זלמן שיף כץ
18. ה״ק חיים בלל״א פ״ו כ״ה יוזפא גונדרשהיים

---

1. תוספת מעל השורה
2. כבוד הרב מאיר
3. כבוד הרב יואל
4. צ״ל ׳ולחתום׳
5. תוספת מעל השורה
6. תוספת מעל השורה

19. טעם מפסק דין הנ"ל באשר ש[ה"ה][1] מודה וגם מאוחר צוה לכתוב אין אנו חוששין בשביל
20. אחרי' אפשר שיש עוד [מלווים] אחרים על הלוה שאנו מחויבי' להם בכתב שטר זה ד"א
21. באשר שנהוג כאן שכל השטרות צריך להיות ע"י נאמני הקהלה דאל"כ לא מועיל כ[לו]ם
22. והם אומרי' שלא נעשה כלום ולמלוה ע"פ מאוחרן לא חיישינן דלא יגרע להן כלום דאפי' (מלוה ע"פ)[2] מוקדמין
23. אפ"ה אינו גובי' קודם מלוה בשטר מאוחר גם באינו פסק ב"ד כדומה לזה והעתקתי בדף קדח
24. ע"ב

No. 44

Fol. 49a; Monday 25 July 1774

Following the court's decision given the previous evening in the matter of Meʾir Segal's lost loan document (see no. 43), this record summarizes the decision and adds that Meʾir did not renounce his claim to the 20 reichstalers of interest that had accrued on Hendele's loan, but only gave precedence to Joel Bing's claims on this amount.

מט ע"א

1. ב"ה
2. ע"ד שיצא מאתנו ח"מ פסק ב"ד ביו' ב' טוב מנחם תקלד לפק ומבואר בתוכה שבאה לפנינו
3. האשה מ' הענדלה אשת ה"מ כמ"ה דוד טרויב ז"ל והודת בפנינו על העתק ק"ס שהציע
4. לפנינו ה"ה התורני נ"ה כ"ה מאיר ב"המנוח[3] כ"ה יעקב ישראל סגל ז"ל שעשתה האשה מ'
5. הענדלה הנ"ל ק"ס ביו' ד' זיין אייר תקד"ו בכא"ה והודית שחייבה לכה"מ[4] הנ"ל סך מאה
6. רט בת"ע עם רווחים עצ"ה ששה ממאה לשנה לשלם ולפרוע הקרן הנ"ל בכלות שתי
7. שנים מהיו' ולשלם הרווחים הנ"ל כל שנה ושנה וביקש מאתנו כה"מ הנ"ל לצוות לנאמני' עידי
8. עידי השטר לחתום ולתקן לו שטר חדש על ק"ס הנ"ל מזמן הנ"ל תחת שטר ראשון שנשרף
9. לו עם ביתו שהיה דר בו ר"נ והאשה מ' הענדלה הודית בפנינו שדברי כה"מ הנ"ל
10. הם נכונים וכני' ושהיא לא שילמה פרוטה אחת לכה"מ הנ"ל מדמי ק"ס הנ"ל לא מהקרן
11. ולא מהרווחים שעולים מזמן ק"ס הנ"ל ע"ע אמנם ע"פ (פשר)[5] שנעשה בין ה"ה כה"מ הנ"ל ובין
12. ה"ה ה"ק כ"ה יואל בינגא סגל שיש לו שטר מאוחר לזמן שטר כה"מ הנ"ל יצא מאתנו

1. האשה הענדלה
2. תוספת מעל השורה
3. בן המנוח
4. כבוד הרב מאיר
5. תוספת מעל השורה

13. שנכתוב ע״פ הנא = מני[1] שטר חדש על ק״ס הנ״ל מזמן ק״ס הנ״ל ושיוכתב על שטר
14. מע״ל שינוכה מדמי רווחים הנ״ל סך עשרים רט והותנה בפירוש שסך עשרי׳ רט
15. הנ״ל שינוכה מדמי רווחים הנ״ל הוא דוקא נגד ב״ח מאוחר כה״י בינגא הנ״ל
16. באם יבוא השטר הנ״ל ידי גביי׳ אמנם האשה מ׳ הענדלה הנ״ל מחויבת להשלים
17. ולפרוע אותו עשרי׳ רט לכ״ה מאיר הנ״ל אחרי שהודית בפנינו שלא שילמה
18. פרוטה אחת מהקרן ורווחים שעולים עד הנה ולראי׳ באנו ע״ה היו׳ יו׳ ב׳ טוב
19. מנחם תקלד לפק
20. ה״ק אברהם טריר כהן
21. ה״ק מאיר בן לאא כהרר[2] זלמן שיף כץ
22. ה״ק חיים בן פו״מ כ׳ יוזפא גונדרשהיים שליטא

No. 45

Buch v. Schuster

Fol. 49b; (based on its position between nos. 44 and 46, presumably 25 July) 1774

Moses Buch and Lemele Schuster dealt together in lottery tickets. Moses held a prize-winning ticket from a lottery in The Hague as well as one from the Hanau lottery. Lemele, apparently concerned that Moses held too many of the assets, asked Moses to give him the Hague ticket. Moses did so, but before they settled accounts, Moses died. About six weeks after Moses' death, his three brothers (Moses had not married) deposited the Hanau ticket with the court, claiming that Lemele still held the Hague ticket and owed the estate over 20 guldens. Lemele countered that he had returned the Hague ticket to Moses before his death and owed the estate only about 2 guldens. Both sides agreed to be bound by the court's decision, whether it be based on a compromise or the letter of the law. The end of the document is damaged and incomplete.[3]

מט ע״ב

1. ב״ה
2. ע״ד שבא לפנינו ה״ה התורני כ״ה אנשיל פפאן בהרשאת האחי׳ כ״ה אפרי׳ וכ׳
3. ליזר וכ׳ גדלי׳ בני המנוח כ׳ יעקב בוך ז״ל ותובע מן ה״ה הו״ה כ׳ לעמלי שוסטר כץ דמי טרע
4. טרעפיר מן תביעת האג״ישע לאט״ריע צעטיל העולה י״ד זהו׳ מ״ט צל והיינו מכח אחיהם

---

1. הסימן = מיועד לקרב בין האותיות שקצת רחוקות זו מזו כאן בכתב היד.
2. לאבי אדוני כבוד הרב רבי
3. This case is discussed in Schlick, "Zur Rolle der reichs städtischen Gerichtsbarkeiten," 182–85.

5. הב"ח היקר כ' משה ז"ל שהי' נושא ונותן במו"מ {לאטחיע} לאטריע צעטיל עם כ' לעמלי הנ"ל
6. והיו לכ"מ[1] ז"ל הנ"ל בידו אותו טרעפיר רביעת צעטיל האג הנ"ל מן סך הנ"ל וביקש כ' לעמלי
7. הנ"ל מן כ' משה ז"ל הנ"ל באותו פעם שיתן לו אותו טרעפר הנ"ל על חשבון באשר {שיש} שהי'
8. בידו באותו פעם זולת טרעפיר הנ"ל עוד אחד ושני רביעית טרעפיר מן הענוישא
9. לאטריע בכן יתן לו עד שיחשבו בהדדי ובאם מחויב כ' לעמלי הנ"ל לשלם לכ"מ הנ"ל מותרות
10. אז ישלם לו וכן יעשה (ונתן)[2] כ' משה ז"ל הנ"ל לכ"ל[3] הנ"ל אותו רביעית צעטיל בין כך נפטר הבחור
11. כ' משה ז"ל הנ"ל ו"חלי[ש][4] בכן רוצים להחזירם לו אותן הענוישא טרעפיר הנ"ל נגד זה
12. מחויב כ' לעמלי הנ"ל ליתן להם לאחר ניכוי כפי חשבונו מה שנשאר אחיהם כ"מ ז"ל הנ"ל
13. חייב לו מחויב כל הנ"ל ליתן להם סך כ' זהו' כ"ו צל והניחו האחי' הנ"ל אותו טרעפיר
14. מן הענוישא לאטריע הנ"ל לפנינו והו"ה כ' לעמלי הנ"ל השיב ששילם כבר דמי טרעפר
15. מן רביעית האג {הנ"ל} הנ"ל לאחיהם כ' משה ז"ל הנ"ל בחייו והא ראיי' שנטל אותו רביעית
16. צעטיל ממנו בכן אין עליו שום תביעה מחמת טרעפר מן האג הנ"ל אכן מחמת טרעפר
17. הענויש[ו]א אם ינוכה מסך העולה טרעפיר הנ"ל {מ.ן} מחמת חשבון שהציע לפנינו כ"י[5]
18. הנ"ל מגיע להם עוד א' זהו' נ"[ז] צל אחר שיחזירו לו אותו טרעפיר הנ"ל רוצה ליתן להם אותן
19. א' זהו' נ"[ז] צל הנ"ל והאריכו בטענותיהם זה מול זה וזה מול זה ובאשר שהצדדים הנ"ל
20. קיבלו ע"ע וחתמו את עצמם בתוקף קומפרמיס בח"ח ובקנס סך מסויים לאשר ולקיים
21. [א]ת כל אשר יצא מאתנו הן לדין הן לפשר בכן נזדקקנו להם ומצאנו עד"פ שכ' לעמלי הנ"ל
22. ...ת...האחי' הנ"ל סך ע... [נא] צל נגד זה יוחזר לו אותן טרעפר מן חד ושני
23. תביעות ה[ענוישא] ... המה פטורי' זה מזו וזו מזה מחמת תביעות הנ"ל
24. יצא [מאתנו] ... תקלד לפ"ק

No. 46

Kassel v. Halberstadt et al.

Fols. 50a–b; Monday 25 July 1774

In 1713 Anshel and Meʾir Kassel agreed to set aside 1000 reichstalers that they had received as part of an inheritance from their father. The money was to be invested,

1. כבוד משה
2. תוספת מעל השורה
3. כבוד לעמלי
4. האות האחרונה לא ברורה; אולי ר"ל 'ושבק חיים לכל ישראל'
5. כנראה שצ"ל 'כ"ל', דהיינו כבוד לעמלי

and each year sixty reichstalers were to be used to support poor brides and clothe needy children. In 1751 the brothers appeared before the court to modify their agreement, stipulating that each brother would from now on hold 500 reichstalers and guarantee a 6% annual return. This was reaffirmed in 1764, although, at that time, Me'ir's descendents claimed that Anshel's children were not fulfilling their obligation and had not set aside 500 reichstalers as Me'ir had done. Anshel's children — a married daughter and her husband and a widowed daughter — admitted that they had not done what was required of them and were willing to return to the earlier arrangement (the document is damaged in this section and one cannot say how much they were in arrears). The family asked the court to confirm the agreement between the parties. It also asked what should be done with the revenues that had accrued on the money that Me'ir had set aside, and what Anshel's children should do regarding payments that were in arrears and future obligations. The court was also asked to impose an arrangement for holding the funds, which it did, beginning with the coming year. The court noted that no funds could be disbursed without the knowledge of all parties and it created a mechanism for insuring that all sides of the family shared control of the funds.

נון ע"א

ע"ד שבא לפנינו ה"ה האלוף והתורני כ"ה אנשיל פפאן כץ בהרשאת יורשי' המנוח כ' יוקל קאסיל סגל ז"ל ה"ה הו"ה כ' מאיר וה"ה כ' גומפל סגל ובהרשאות יורשי' המנוח כ"ה בענדיט ב[ה]"מ כ"ה מאיר קאסיל ז"ל ה"ה הו"ה כ' שלמה וכ' זיסקינד ותובע את יורשי' המנוח כ"ה אנשיל קאסיל סגל ז"ל ה"ה האשה מרת גוטלה בת כ"ה אנשיל קאסיל ז"ל ומבעלה ה"ה הו"ה כ"ה איצק הלברשטאט יצו חתן ר"א[1] הנ"ל ומהאשה מרת {מעל} מערלה בת ר"א הנ"ל אל' המנוח כ"ה גדלי' רופא ז"ל והציע לפנינו העתק מהפנקס נאמנים הקהלה מק"ס שעשאו האחים הנ"ל כ"ה מאיר וכ"ה אנשיל ז"ל הנ"ל ביו' ה' יא מנחם תע"ג שחייבי' בע"ק[2] אלף רייכשטאהלר הבאים לידם מעזבון אביהם ז"ל[3] והמה בידם בת"ע עצ"ה על רווחים ממאה רט ששה רט לשנה והרווחים יפרעו בכל שנה לצורך עניית כלות וגם ללבוש בהם קופה ייגנן וגם הציע לפנינו העתק העתק[4] ממעשה ב"ד מן ח"י אדר תקי"א ששם נאמר בז"ה והיינו שמעתה התחייבי' האחים הנ"ל מחמת ק"ס ושטר הנזכר כל חד חמשה מאות רט בלי שום תורת ערבות קב[ל][5]נות כלל וכלל ורק כל חד חייב חייב[6] בפני עצמו חמשה מאות רט ודמי חוב

1. רבי אנשיל
2. בערבות קבלנות (ר' בהמשך שורות 12-13)
3. יוזבל קאסיל נפטר בשנת תע"ה (ר' אבני זכרון, מס' 1657).
4. כפילות במקור
5. כנראה שהיה 'ר' ו-'ל' נכתב מעליו.
6. כפילות במקור

14. הנ״ל הם על האחים ועל י״א תורת חוב גמור לשלם כפי המבואר בקס[1] ובהעתק
15. שטר הנ״ל וכו׳ ואמר כה״א[2] הנ״ל באשר שהחמשה מאות רט הנ״ל מן כ״ה מאיר הנ״ל המה
16. כעת תחת יד האשה מ׳ חייכה אל׳ ר׳ העניך האלי בת כ״ה מאיר ז״ל הנ״ל על
17. רווחים ששה ממאה לשנה ורווחי׳ מחולקי׳ כל שנה לדבר טוב בידיעת שאר קרובי׳
18. כמבאור בפסק ב״ד ההוקם אור ליו׳ ב׳ טוב אדר ראשון תקכ״ד כיצד ינהגו
19. בגביית ובחלוקת הרווחים הנ״ל אמנם החמשה מאות רט שחייבי׳ יורשי׳ המנוח כ״ה
20. אנשיל ז״ל הנ״ל וי״א הנ״ל כפי ק״ס ופס״ד הנ״ל [אחר]י כן ג״כ לשלמו הרווחים מידי שנה
21. בשנה שלשים רט לצורך [ד]בר טוב הנ״ל וכנ״ל תבע כה״א[3] הנ״ל בהרשאות הנ״ל
22. את היורשי׳ כ״ה אנשיל ז״ל הנ״ל שתשלמו ג״כ מידי שנה בשנה הרווחים כדי לקיים
23. דבר טוב הנ״ל ולהתנהג באותן הרווחי׳ על אופן המבאור במעשה ב״ד הנ״ל
24. מחמת הרווחים מחמש[ה] מאות רט אשר תחת יד יורשי׳ כה״א הנ״ל וכנ״ל וה״ה
25. התורני כ״ה מאיר לוי בהרשאת האשה מ׳ גוטלה ובעלה הו״ה כ״ה איצק הלברשטא[ט]
26. הנ״ל ובהרשאות האשה מרת מערלה א׳ ר׳ גדלי׳ רופא יורשים המנוח כ״ה אנשיל קאסיל
27. סגל ז״ל הנ״ל הודה בפנינו שהמה חייבי׳ עדיין הקרן מ[ת״]ק רט ולא נתפרע ע...
28. כלום מהקרן רק הרווחים עד עתה המה היה מחלקי׳ בעצ...מע[שיו] המה מ...לשלם...

נון ע״ב

1. ב״ה
2. מידי שנה בשנה מעתה ועד עולם לצורך דבר טוב הנ״ל ועל אופן המבואר בפס״ד הנ״ל וגם אופן
3. חלוקת הרווחי׳ הנ״ל לד״ט הנ״ל המה מרוצים ג״כ להתנהג בהם על אופן המבואר בפסד[4] הנ״ל כיצד
4. יתנהגו עם רווחים מחמשה מאות רט שהמה ביד יורשי׳ המנוח כ״ה מאיר ז״ל הנ״ל / והנה אחרי
5. שהצדדים הנ״ל נתנו עיניהם עלינו ב״ד וביקשו מאתנו לפרוש להם כיצד ינהגו בחלוקת
6. רווחי׳ הנ״ל וליתן להם תוקף מעשה ב״ד על כל הנ״ל בכן נזדקקנו להם ומצאנו שמעשה ב״ד ההוקם
7. חי׳ אדר תקי״א הוא בתקפו בכל תוקף ועוז הנאמר שם על הקרן מחמשה מאות שחייב
8. כ״ה אנשיל ז״ל הנ״ל וי״א וב״כ הקרן מת״ק רט להיורשי׳ לשלם ולפרוע רווחים מידי שנה
9. בשנה שלשים רט לצורך ד״ט וכל זמן שלא נכתב תברא על הקרן ת״ק רט הנ״ל החוב
10. קרן מת״ק רט הנ״ל הוא בתקפו ועל הרווחים שעברו עד ר״ה הב״ע שנת תקל״ה
11. פטורים היורשי׳ כה״א הנ״ל מליתן שום פרוטה מהרווחים הנ״ל וגם אינם
12. צריכן ליתן חשבון על הרווחי׳ שעברו עד ר״ה הב״ע שנת תקל״ה הנ״ל אכן מר״ה
13. תקל״ה הב״ע ולהבא צריכן ליתן היורשי׳ מכה״א[5] ז״ל הנ״ל דהיינו ה״ה הו״ה כ״ה איצק

---

1. בקומפרמיס
2. כבוד הרב אנשיל
3. כבוד הרב אנשיל (פפאן)
4. בפסק דין
5. כבוד הרב אנשיל

14. הלברשטאט וזוגותו מ' גוטלה והאשה מ' מערלה הנ"ל כל אחד סך חמשה עשר רט
15. שהם יחד שלשים רט כל שנה ושנה וגם קוויטונג מהיורשי' כ' יוקל ז"ל הנ"ל ומיורשי'
16. כ"ה בענדיט קאסיל ז"ל הנ"ל ויונח בתוך קלפי מסוגרת בשני שלעסיר מחולפי'
17. ולכל שלאס מפתח אחד והקלפי תהיה בשנה ראשונה משנת תקל"ה הסומך
18. ביד הו"ה כ"ה משה[1] בכ"י[2] קאסיל הנ"ל ומפתח ומפתח[3] אחד ביד יורשי' כה"ב[4]
19. קאסיל הנ"ל ומפתח אחד ביד יורשי כה"א ובשנה שנייה תהיי' הקלפי ביד יורשי המנוח
20. כ"ה בענדיט קאסיל ז"ל הנ"ל ומפתח אחד ביד יורשי' כ' יוקל קאסיל ז"ל הנ"ל ומפתח
21. אחד ביד יורשי' המנוח כה אנשיל קאסיל הנ"ל ובשנה השלישית תהי' הקלפי ביד
22. יורשי' כה"א הנ"ל ושני המפתחות יהי' ביד יורשי' כה"ב הנ"ל וביד יורשי' כה"א
23. הנ"ל קאסיל הנ"ל וכן חוזר חלילה לעולם והרווחים הנ"ל יחולק בכל שנה לצורך
24. ד"ט הנ"ל ולא יוציאו שום אחד משלשה כתות הנ"ל שום הוצאות לד"ט הנ"ל אם לאו
25. בדעת כולם כה יקום וכה יהי' לדור דורים ו[גוף] מעשה ב"ד הלז יונח ביד יורשי'
26. כ' יוקל הנ"ל דהיינו ביד הו"ה כ' משה הנ"ל ומחויב כ' משה הנ"ל ליתן העתק מקויים
27. ליורשי כה"א הנ"ל והעתק מקוים ליורשי כ"ה בענדיט הנ"ל כל הנ"ל ניתן לכתוב בתוקף
28. מעשה ב"ד ובכח [ב"ד] יפה בכל תוקף ועוז שבעולם כאילו נעשה בבי דינא
29. ... ולראי' בא[נו על] החותם היו' יו' ב' טוב מנחם תקל"ד לפ"ק ה"ק מאיר ש"ש[5]

No. 47

Landau v. Wetterhahn

Fols. 51a–52a; Sunday 7 August 1774

A dispute broke out between the descendents of two widows who had once lived in the Wetterhahn house over who had the right to live in or rent out the lower floor of the building. Houses often had multiple owners, yet the areas of ownership were not clearly divided. Thus, the question was, "who had the right to live where?" Given the convenience of access, people generally appear to have preferred living on the ground floor. Tevele Landau, who inherited half of the house from his late sister, Rösle, widow of Lipman Schwarzschild, produced a document from 1751 according to which the two widows agreed to use a lottery to determine who would live where for a certain period of time.[6] After six years, they were to exchange

1. היה ליוקל קאסיל בן בשם משה (ר' אבני זכרון, מס' 4117). לא ברור למה הוא לא מוזכר לעיל.
2. בן כבוד יוקל
3. כפילות במקור
4. כבוד הרב בענדיט
5. חסרה שורה במקור
6. Rösle Schwarzschild survived her husband (see Ettlinger, 28.9.1771) and was predeceased by her son, Ber,

living quarters. Following the 1751 lottery the lower floor was to revert to Tevele in the summer of 1774, and he came to the court to force Yuzpa Wetterhahn, whose mother had also lived in the house, to vacate the area. Tevele was aware that he might not win his point in court and, through his representative, argued that even if the 1751 lottery was not accepted, Yuzpa had lived in the lower half of the house for three years since the death of his mother and Tevele's turn had come. Yuzpa's representative responded that the lottery of 1751 was no longer binding because Yuzpa's mother had had no ownership in the house and therefore her actions could not obligate those who did. Yuzpa rejected Tevele's claims for equitable treatment since Tevele had never shown any desire to move onto the lower level. Yuzpa asked the court to hold a new lottery. The court agreed with Yuzpa, but first had to obtain the consent of Yuzpa's brother who also owned a share of the house. That done, the court held a new lottery and determined that Tevele Landau would have use of the lower level for three years beginning from the date of the decision. The parties were to rotate their living quarters every three years. The court also specified what areas of the house were to be shared by the parties.[1]

נא ע״א

1. ב״ה
2. ע״ד שבא לפנינו ה״ה התורני כ״ה משה אויק בהרשאות ה״ה הו״ה כ׳ טעבלי לנדויא
3. ששייך לו החצי בית צום וועטרהאַן והציע לפנינו כתב גורל מחילוקי דירות הנעשה בין
4. האשה המנוח מ׳ בילה אל׳ כ״ה לימא וועטרהאַן ז״ל ובין האשה המונוח מ׳ רייזלה {אל׳} אל׳ המנוח כ׳
5. ליפמן ש״ש[2] ז״ל אחותו כ״ט[3] הנ״ל ביו׳ ויו תמוז תק[י״א] ואח״כ אחר העדרת אל׳ ריזלה הנ״ל נתחזק הגורל
6. בין האשה מ׳ בילא ובין הו״ה כ״ט הנ״ל ולפי הגורל וחילוקי דירות הנ״ל מגיע דירה התחתונה
7. מר״ח אלול הבע״ל על ששה שנים רצופים לכ׳ טעבלי לנדויא ולכ׳ יוזפא ווע[ט]רהאַן בן
8. המנוח כ״ה לימא ז״ל הנ״ל הדירה העליונה בכן תבע כה״מ[4] הנ״ל מן כ׳ יוזפא הנ״ל
9. שיפנה שטח התחתונה לשוכר של כ״ט הנ״ל והוא ידור בשטח העליונה באשר שנזכר
10. בגורל הנ״ל שנעשה הגורל הנ״ל שיהי׳ חוזר חלילה ע״ע ואף לי״א וב״כ ואף אם לא יזכה
11. בזה מ״מ באשר שכ׳ יוזפא הנ״ל הי׳ דר בשטח התחתונה לאחר מיתת אמה מ׳ בילה הנ״ל
12. ע״ע שלשה שני׳ דהיינו משנת תקלא עד שנת תקלד בכן מגיע עכ״פ לכ׳ טעבלי הנ״ל

---

who died in 1764 without having married and without progeny (see Ettlinger, 28.12.1764). This allowed Tevele to inherit from his sister.

1. A discussion of the case appears at http://www.earlymodern.org/citation.php?citKey=15&docKey=e, accessed 27 May 2007.
2. שווארצשילד
3. כבוד טעבלי
4. כבוד הרב משה

13. ג״כ דירה התחתונה כמו שהי׳ דר בו כ״י[1] הנ״ל וה״ה כ״ה זלמן גייגר בהרשאות
14. הו״ה כ״י וועטרהאַן השיב שאותו כתב גורל וחילוקי דירות הנעשה מן אל׳ בילה הנ״ל
15. בטלה עכשיו שמתה האשה מ׳ בילה הנ״ל באשר שלא הי׳ בידה לעשות על י״א וב״כ
16. הואיל שלא הי׳ לה חלק בחצי בית הנ״ל לא מכח יד העליונה ולא במיגר אל׳ רק שהית׳ דר
17. בו בשכירות כמו שהציע לפנינו כה״ז[2] הנ״ל כתב וסילוק השבעות כתובת׳ וגם ת״ר
18. מן כ׳ יוזפא הנ״ל ומבואר מתוכם שהי׳ דר האל׳ מ׳ בילה הנ״ל בחצי בית הנ״ל בשכירות
19. שהי׳ צריכה ליתן לבניה בכן נתבטל הגורל עכשיו ומה שהי׳ דר בשטח התחתונה
20. כ׳ יוזפא הנ״ל לאחר מיתת אמו שלשה שני׳ לא גרע זכות בזה עבור שלא מיחה לו כ״ט הנ״ל
21. {בוואד} בוודאי מחל לו ב[ו]כן[3] תבע כה״ז הנ״ל שיעשו ב״ד גורל מחדש ביניהם והאריכו
22. הצדדים הנ״ל {בפני.נו..} בפנינו כמבואר הכל בק״ה המונח לפנינו ובעבור
23. שהצדד׳ הנ״ל

נא ע״ב

1. ב״ה
2. שהצדדים הנ״ל חתמו עצמם בתוקף קומפרמיס בח״ח ובקנס סך מסויים להקדש
3. ולשררה יר״ה לאשר ולקיים את כל אשר יצא מאתנו נזדקקנו להם ומצאנו שאין לכ״ט הנ״ל
4. שום זכות יותר מכ׳ יוזפא הנ״ל בשטח התחתונה מחמת הגורל הנ״ל וגם לא מחמת ה״ג
5. ה״ג[4] שישנו שהי׳ דר בו כ״י הנ״ל בלי גורל חדש בכן צריכי׳ שני הצדדים הנ״ל לעשות
6. מעתה גורל חדש על חלוקת דירות בית הנ״ל ביניהם והתרצו הצדדים הנ״ל שאנחנו
7. ב״ד ח״מ נעשה גורל מחדש (על חלוקות בית הנ״ל)[5] ביניהם ושלחנו אחר כ׳ ישי בה״מ כ״ה
8. לימא וועטרהאן ז״ל הנ״ל שיש לו ג״כ חלק רביעית בבית הנ״ל ובא לפנינו ואמר שהוא
9. מרוצה ג״כ בחלוקות דירות וגורל שנעשה אנחנו ח״מ על אופן שהתרצו הצדדים הנ״ל
10. בכן נזדקקנו להם והפלנו גורל ביניהם בפני כ״ה זלמן הנ״ל בהרשאות כ׳ יוזפא הנ״ל
11. וכ׳ ישי הנ״ל ובפני כה״מ הנ״ל בהרשאת כ׳ טעבלי הנ״ל ועלה ע״פ הגורל שטח מטה
12. על שלשה שני׳ רצופי׳ מיו׳ דלמטה לכ׳ טעבלי לנדויא הנ״ל ושטח מעלה להאחים כ׳ יוזפא
13. וכ׳ ישי הנ״ל והיינו מן ר״ח אלול תקלד עד ר״ח אלול תקלז הבע״ל יהי׳ לה״ה הו״ה כ׳ טעבלי
14. לנדויא ששייך לו החצי מבית הנ״ל ולי״א וב״כ בית החורף למטה על הארץ עם הסוכה
15. שני שטאָק הויך שני חדרים זה מול זה עם הויז עהרן עוד שלשה שטאק הויך חדר׳
16. לצד הרחוב עוד חדר אחד ארבע שטאק הויך לצד הרחוב ואותו חצי עליי׳
17. שאינינו בתוכה הקעמרכה האָלץ האף תחת הסוכה ומרתף הפנימי ולהאחים כ׳
18. יוזפא וכ׳ ישי הנ״ל שיש להם חצי שניי׳ מבית הנ״ל יהי׳ להם ולי״א וב״כ על משך
19. שלשה שנים הנ״ל חד{.} שטאק הויך שני חדרי׳ זה מול זה עם הויז עהרן אונד גענגלכה
20. שלושה שטאק הויך חדר אחד לצד החומה עוד חדר אחד ארבע שטאק לצד
21. החומה ואותו חצי עליי׳ עם הקעמרכה שבתוכה האלץ הויף תחת בית החורף דלמט[ה]

---

1. כבוד יוזפא
2. כבוד הרב זלמן
3. אולי צ״ל ׳ובכן׳
4. הסגת גבול; כפילות במקור
5. סוגריים במקור

22. ומרתף החיצון שתחת הרחוב ומשך חג הסוכות ישתמשו שני הדייר' הנ"ל בסוכה שוה
23. בשוה גם בהויז עהרן התחתון ישתמשו תמיד שוה בשוה ובכלות זמן שלשה שנים הנ"ל
24. ... אחרים רצופים בלי שום שהיי' ודחיי' שבעול'

נב ע"א

1. ב"ה
2. והיינו מן ר"ח אלול תקל"ז עד ר"ח אלול תק"מ הבע"ל יהי' להאחי' הנ"ל וליא[1] וב"כ שטח מטה וכנ"ל
3. לכ"ט[2] הנ"ל וליא[3] וב"כ שטח מעלה וכנ"ל וחוזר חלילה עד עולם משלשה לשלשה שני' כה יהי' וכה
4. יקום ע"ע ובאנו אנחנו ב"ד ח"מ ליתן לחולקת הדירות וגורל הנ"ל כל תוקף ועוז כתוקף מעשה
5. ב"ד ובכ"ח ב"ד יפה ולראי חתמנו היו' יו' א' א' דר"ח אלול שנת תקלד לפק
6. הק אברהם טריר כהן הק מאיר שיף ואני

No. 48

Rindskopf v. Pflegerin

Fols. 52b–53a; Wednesday 26 October 1774

Solomon Kronberg wished to purchase goods on credit from Ber Rindskopf. However, Ber claimed that he did not know Solomon and demanded a guarantor. Solomon offered his mother-in-law, Beyla Pflegerin, as guarantor and Ber sent a messenger to Beyla to confirm this, which she did. When Solomon failed to pay his debt, Ber turned to Beyla for payment. Beyla, a widow who represented herself in this matter, admitted to agreeing to guarantee the loan but made a number of claims with respect to the circumstances of her consent. She also admitted that neither she nor her son-in-law could currently pay the loan. The court spoke to both parties in search of a compromise. Ultimately Beyla was ordered to pay one-third of the debt in two installments. The text includes an addendum that the writer forgot to include when first summarizing the court's decision. According to the addendum, if Solomon's fortunes improved, he would have to pay the full amount that Ber claimed.

---

1. וליורשיהם אחריהם
2. לכבוד טעבלי
3. וליורשיו אחריו

נב ע״ב

1. ב״ה
2. ע״ד שבא לפנינו ה״ה התורני כ״ה משה אויך בהרשאות כ׳ פער ר״ק ותבע את
3. האשה מרת בילה פלעגרן אל׳ כ׳ קוסיל מן אופיבאך[1] סך שלשים וששה זהו׳ ארבעי׳
4. צל באשר שחתנה כ׳ שלמה קראני בורג לקח בהקפה מן כ׳ פער הנ״ל כפי סך
5. הנ״ל וכ׳ פער הנ״ל לא היה רוצה ליתן לכ׳ שלמה הנ״ל באשר שלא היה
6. מכירו ואמר כ׳ שלמה הנ״ל שחמותו מ׳ בילה תהי׳ ערב בעדו וע״ז שלח
7. כ׳ פער הנ״ל שליח אחד להאשה מ׳ בילה ושאלה אם תרצה להיות
8. ערב והשיבה שכ׳ פער הנ״ל יתן לו איך בין אייער צילר וע״ז נתן
9. כ׳ פער הנ״ל לחתנה כ׳ שלמה הנ״ל כפי סך ל״ו זהו׳ מם צל וכ׳ שלמה
10. הנ״ל לא שילם כלום לכ׳ פער בכן תבע מן האשה מרת בילה סך דמי הנ״ל
11. והאשה מ׳ בילה הנ״ל {הנ״ל} השיבה שאמת הדבר שכ׳ פער הנ״ל שלח אצלה
12. בחור {אצלה} אחד בבית כ׳ משה דייץ ושואלת אותה אם רוצה להיות
13. ערב והשיבה במהירות הן אבל לא ידעה על כמה וכמה שלקח חתנה
14. ממנו וגם לפני זה כבר היה חתנה נושא ונותן עם כ׳ פער הנ״ל
15. בלי ערבות ובפעם הזאת שלח כ׳ פער הנ״ל ושאל לה בלי ידיעת
16. חתנה הנ״ל ועוד טוענת האשה מ׳ בילה הנ״ל מה שיכירו הב״ד שמחויבת
17. לשלם יתן לה זמן כי אין לה עכשיו מעות לישלם מיד ועוד טוענת האשה
18. מ׳ בילה הנ״ל שאותו סחורה שלקח חתנה מן כ׳ פער הנ״ל נלקח ממנו
19. על השוק והיה לו סכנה בדבר ועל אופן הזה וודאי לא הית׳ ערב עוד
20. טענה שחתנה הנ״ל אין לו לשלם כעת הזאת וכאשר יצא במדינת
21. מגענצא נגד ב״ח שלו שלא לעשות בו נגישה לשלם עד כלות ששה שנים
22. והאריכו הצדדים הנ״ל בטענותיהם כמבאור מתוך ק״ה המונח לפנינו
23. ובאשר שהצדדים חתמו עצמם בתוקף קומפרמיס בח״ח ובקנס לאשר
24. ולקיים אשר יצא מאתונו[2] נזדקקנו להם ודברנו על לב הצדדים הנ״ל
25. לעשות פשר דבר ביניהם והרכינו את ראשם לדברינו וחתמו עצמם
26. הצדדים הנ״ל דהיינו כ״ה משה יאך[3] בהרשאות הנ״ל והאשה מרת בילה הנ״ל
27. ליקים בכל תוקף [ועו]ז כפי הפשר שיצא מאתנו גם על גוף החוב

נג ע״א

1. נגד גוף הלוה הנ״ל בכן נזדקקנו לפשרה ומצאנו שהאשה הנ״ל תשלם
2. בשביל כל החוב הנ״ל סך שנים עשר זהו׳ י״ג צל שתשלם החצי מן י״ב זהו׳ י״ג צל הנ״ל
3. עכשיו וחצי שניי׳ של דמי פשר הנ״ל על יריד פסח הסומך הבע״ל ואז
4. אין שום תביעה לכ׳ פער הנ״ל מחמת חוב לא על כ׳ שלמה הנ״ל
5. ולא על חמותו האשה מ׳ בילה הנ״ל יצא מאתנו יו׳ ד׳ כ״א מרחשון תקל״ה
6. ———

1. על קוסיל מן אופיבאך (אופנבאך), ר׳ דושינסקי, ספר מזכיר נשמות, עמ׳ 49, מס׳ 340.
2. ר״ל ׳מאתנו׳
3. צ״ל ׳אויך׳

7. נשכח מלכתוב אכן אם ירחיב ה׳ את גבולו של כ׳ שלמה הנ״ל לפי ראות עיני הב״ד
8. אזי מחויב להשלים לה״ה כ׳ פער הנ״ל כל מה שחייב לו מתביעתו הנ״ל
9. הק׳ יעקב שמש : הק׳ אנשיל צונץ : הק׳ חיים בפו״מ כ׳ יוזפא גונדרשהיי׳
10. שליטא

No. 49

Fol. 53b; Sunday evening, 30 October 1774

The court confirmed the sale of two half-seats in the old portion of the men's section of the synagogue by the estate of Aaron Orschel to Simeon Rindskopf. Both half-seats were sold after the customary public announcement that the seats were for sale. One-third of the price was paid immediately, one-third was due in six months, and the final third was due six months later, as was the common practice. Rabbi Isaac Meʾir Schwarzschild was related to Simeon and recused himself from signing the agreement. He was replaced by Rabbi Zanvil Trach whose absence from the court at the time of the transaction resulted in a minor change in the language of the document signed by members of the court.

נג ע״ב

1. ב״ה
2. אור ליו׳ ב׳ ד״ו מרחשון קהלת לפק מכרנו חצי מקו׳ בעז״א ישן בהויף שולי[1]
3. אשר עמד עליו כעת כ׳ לאזי אורשל שהי׳ שייך לה״ה המנוח כ׳ אהרן אורשל
4. מכרנו אחר הכרזה כנהוג לה״ה הו״ה כ׳ שמעון ר״ק בעד סך מאה וחמשי׳ זהו׳ כ
5. כנהוג לשלם שליש מיד נגד מסירת חלטה ושני שלישי׳ הנותרי׳ על ששה
6. חצאי שנה רצופי׳ זא״ז אין קונפונטציאהנש מינץ אויף דעם 24 *f* פוס
7. עוד מכרנו באותו מעמד חצי מקו׳ בעז״א ישן אשר עומד עליו כעת הב״ח
8. כ׳ הירש בהמנוח כ״א[2] אורשל שהי׳ שייך להמנוח כ׳ אהרן אורשל הנ״ל {לכ״ה}
9. לכ׳ שמעון ר״ק הנ״ל בעד תשעי׳ זהו׳ על אופן הנ״ל כמבואר הכל מתוך
10. מעשה ב״ד שהקמת[י] עליהם נעשה בפני כמ״ה מאיר שש[3] וכ״א[4] טריר ואני
11. ובאשר שכמ״ה מאיר הנ״ל הוא פסול עדות קורבה עם כ״ש[5] הנ״ל לא חתם ה

---

1. ר׳ דייץ, עמ׳ 439.
2. בן המנוח כבוד אייזק
3. שווארצשילד
4. כבוד אברהם
5. כבוד שמעון; שרלה בת פער רינדסקופף היתה אלמנותו של מענדלי שווארצשילד (אבני זכרון, מס׳ 3114); מענדלי היה אחיו של הרב מאיר (ר׳ אבני זכרון, מס׳ 3211).

12. הוא את מעשה ב"ד ר"ק[1] הדיין כ"ה זנוויל טראך חתם עצמו {במקו}
13. תחתיו {ולכך} ולפי שר"ז[2] הנ"ל לא הי' במעמד בשעת מכירה לכך {לא} כתוב[3] במב"ד
14. בפני ב"ד ולא בפנינו ב"ד

No. 50

Fol. 53b; Thursday evening, 24 November 1774

Rabbi Ḥayyim Gundersheim recorded that he signed a court document confirming the sale of half of the Schwarze Tür house by the heirs of Anshel Strauss to Anshel Flörsheim for 2750 guldens. The sale was transacted in the "small court." Gundersheim was not a member of this court, but since Rabbi Nathan Maas recused himself due to a familial connection with Flörsheim, Gundersheim took Maas's place in signing the document.

15. ———
16. אור ליו' ויו' ך"ב כסליו קהלת לפק חתמת[י] מעשה ב"ד קטן על חצי בית פנימי צור ש
17. שווארציטיר שהי' שייך ליתמי ה"ה המנוח כ' אנשיל שטרויס ונמכר לפני ב"ד לכ' אנשיל
18. בהמנוח[4] כ הירץ פלערשהיים ז"ל בעד עשרי' ושבעה מאות {זהו'} וחמשי' זהו' לשלם כנהוג
19. ובאשר שהדיין ר"י כמ"ה נתן מז הי' פסול קורבה עם לוקח הנ"ל[5] חתמת[י] במקומו את
מעשה ב"ד

Fol. 54a is blank.

1. לא ברור למה יש גרשיים.
2. רבי זנוויל
3. האות כף מהמילה 'כתוב' נכתב מעל המילה 'לא'.
4. בן המנוח
5. יענדלה, אשת הרב מז, היתה בתו של מיכאל פלערשהיים (ר' אבני זכרון, מס' 3894), אחיו של אנשיל (ר' אבני זכרון, מס' 3004).

No. 51

Sichel v. Oppenheimer

Fols. 54b–56a; Monday 20 March 1775

Anshel Sichel sued the estate of Yosle Oppenheimer for over 1300 guldens, claiming that Yosle had owed Anshel's grandfather, the late Herz Sichel, funds for both goods and rent. To substantiate his claim, Anshel produced a number of notes payable from Yosle as well as copies of account books. The guardians of Yosle's estate countered that Anshel owed the estate almost 600 guldens for various notes and goods that he had taken on credit. Through their representative, the guardians of Yosle's estate rejected all claims for payment for back rent, arguing that the account book of Herz's estate could not be relied upon and that the notes payable were out of date. The record notes a claim that Herz's estate had made a deal with Yosle during his lifetime that it would reduce the rent due if he made efforts to collect debts that were owed to Herz's estate. Yosle did so but bad specie in the payment to the estate led to a further dispute. The sides sought a compromise and agreed to be bound by the court's decision. As in many of the of court records, the court stipulated that if the parties failed to abide by the court's ruling they would have to pay a fine both to the community and to the non-Jewish authorities. Ultimately Yosle's estate was ordered to pay 18 guldens to Anshel and to return a pledge that Anshel had once left with Yosle.

This decision, like a number of other rulings in the collection, was signed by four judges.[1]

נד ע"ב

ב"ה

ע"ד שבא לפנינו ה"ה התורני כ"ה אנשיל פפאן כץ בהרשאות ובמעמד ה"ה הו"ה כ' אנשיל זיכל יצו ותבע מן העזבון המנוח כ"ה יוזלי אופנהיים סך שלשה עשר מאות וארבעים ותשעה זהו' כ"ח צל והציע לפנינו חשבן קונטא קוראנט שהעתק מתוך פנקס אפטרופסי' מעזבון אביו זקנו כ' הירץ זיכל ז"ל מה שנזכר שם שכה"י[2] ז"ל לקח מעזבון א"[ז][3] ז"ל הנ"ל סחורת העולה סך י"א מאות ס"א זהו' מ"ז צל גם העלה בחשבון כ' אנשיל הנ"ל מחמת שכירות הבית שהיה חייב כה"י ז"ל לעזבון הנ"ל מן שמונה שני' וחצי שדר כה"י ז"ל הנ"ל בחצי בית מן א"ז ז"ל הכל העולה י"א מאות זהו' והיינו מן שלשה שנים ראשוני' מן כסליו תקך"ב עד

---

1. See Introduction, p. 85 n. 330.
2. שכבוד הרב יוזלי
3. אנשיל זיכל

10. כסליו תקדה כל שנה ושנה שמונים וחמשה זהו׳ וכמו שהציע לפנינו שני ח״כ
11. משכירות הבית מח״י כה״י[1] ז״ל על אורדר כ׳ הירץ זיכל ההוקמו מן ה׳ כסליו
12. תקכ״ב על שני שנים ועל שלשה שנים כל אחד מסך פ״ה זהו׳ וח״כ השלישי
13. אמר כ״א הנ״ל שנאבד אבל עדיין חייב כה״י ז״ל לשלם על חמשה שנים
14. [ו]חצי שאחריהם והיינו מן כסליו תקדה עד סיון תקלמד לפק תובע
15. שכירות כל שנה שני מאות זהו׳ נמצא עולה יחד מחמת שכירות הבית
16. וכנ״ל ומחמת סחורות וכנ״ל עשרים וחמשה מאות וששה עשר זהו׳ מ״ז צל
17. ולאחר שינכה מזה בחשבונו מה שהעתק מפנקס הנ״ל ששילם כה״י ז״ל
18. להאפט = רופסי׳[2] הנ״ל במזומנים ט׳ מאות ול״ד זהו׳ ך״ב צל וגם העלה
19. שלקח {כל אחד} (כ״א)[3] הנ״ל בעצמו מן כה״י ז״ל יוד ראָלין יוכטן בעד שני מאות
20. ושנים עשר זהו׳ נ״ד צל בהקפה וגם מחשיב לפדות המשכן שהשכין כ״א אצל
21. כה״י ז״ל הנ״ל ל״ב אבנים טובות עם א׳ גדול על עשרים זהו׳ עולה יחד
22. י״א מאות וס״ז זהו׳ ט״ז צל ולאחר שנכה בחשבונו י״א מאות וס״ז זהו׳
23. ט״ז צל מסך ך״ה מאות וט״ז זהו׳ מ״ז צל עולה הנשאר י״ג מאות מ״ט זהו׳
24. ך״ח צל שתובע כ׳ אנשיל הנ״ל מעזבון הנ״ל וגם המשכון [מ]ן אבנים טובת
25. הנ״ל יוחזר לכ״א אנשיל[4] הנ״ל בחנם ודמי פדיי׳ שהם עשרים זהו׳ ינכה
26. מתביעה שלו הנ״ל [מ]ה״ה האלופים אפטר[ו]פסים מעזבון המנוח

נה ע״א

1. כה״י ז״ל הנ״ל ה״ה הו״ה כ׳ אברלי ווימפע בהרשאות אפטרופס כמ״ה מאיר ש״ש[5]
2. נרו[6] והאפטרופס האחר כ׳ ליב אופנהיים בעצמו השיבו על מה שתבע כ׳
3. אנשיל הנ״ל והעלה בחשבונו מחמת שכירות הבית שלאו כלום הואל[7] שלא
4. נזכר בפנקס אפטרופסי׳ וגם אינו בידו ח״כ ושטר שכירות הבית
5. ע״ז ושני ח״כ ישנים שהוציא הם כבר עבר זמנם ומסתמא כבר פרע
6. הכל בין שטרת הבית בין שאר דבר ואם כדברי כ״א הנ״ל מפני
7. מה לא תבע אותם בחייו באשר שכה״י ז״ל היה גברא דאית [ה]וצא[ו]ת
8. דינא ואדרבה האפטרופסי׳ הציעו חשבן לפנינו מכתב יד המנוח
9. כ״ה יוזל ז״ל הנ״ל שכ״א הנ״ל נשאר חייב לכה״י ז״ל הנ״ל סך חמשה מאות
10. ותשעי׳ וששה זהו׳ וב[תו]כה נזכר מה שכ׳ אנשיל הנ״ל חייב לכה״י ז״ל
11. פ״ב זהו׳ על שלשה ח״[מ][8] מן כ״א וכמו שהציעו האפטרופסי׳ השלשה ח״מ
12. לפנינו ובתוכן נכלל ג״כ השני מאות ושני׳ עשר זהו׳ בעד י[ו]כטן הנ״ל
13. וה״ה כ׳ אנשיל הנ״ל השיב מחמת שכירות הבית משלשה שנים ראשוני׳

---

1. כבוד הרב יוזלי
2. הסימן = מיועד לקרב בין האותיות שקצת רחוקות זו מזו כאן.
3. תוספת מעל השורה; כבוד אנשיל
4. כפילות במקור
5. שווארצשילד
6. נטריה רחמנא ופרקיה
7. יש כמה אפשרויות כאן: או שצ״ל ׳הואיל׳ או שהלמד מיותר וצ״ל ׳הוא׳ או שהוא רצה לכתוב ׳הוא הואיל׳.
8. חילופי מכתבים

14. הי״הי[1] שלשה ח״כ האחד אבד ושני ח״כ הציע לפנינו בכן אין מן הצוי[2]
15. לזכות בפנקס אפטרופסי׳ ועל חמשה שנים וחצי אינם יכולים לעשות
16. ח״כ באשר שלא יכולים לפרוט הסך דמי שכירות כי נתרצו האפטרופס[י׳]
17. עם כה״י ז״ל על אופן מה אם יתאמץ כה״י ז״ל בגביית חובות מן העזבון
18. כ׳ הירץ הנ״ל יהי׳ שכירות הבית לשנה מאה רט ובאם לא יתן שני
19. מאות לשנה ומש״כ לא היה יכולם להקים ח״כ על שכירות הבית ואמר
20. כ׳ אנשיל הנ״ל שכה״י ז״ל לא פעל כלום בגביית חובת ומ״ה חשב בחשבונ[ו]
21. שני מאות זהו׳ לשנה ומה שטענו האפטרופסי׳ שמא פרע כה״י ז״ל
22. השיב כ״א שהוא ביקש ממנו כמה וכמה פעמים לחשוב עמו אצל הא
23. האפטרופסי׳ ולא היה יוכל להיבא לכך ומכ״ש שלא פרע כלום ולפי
24. חשבן של כה״י ז״ל שהציע האפטרופסי׳ אדרבה הי׳ כ״א נשאר חייב
25. לכה״י ז״ל סך כמה וכמה מאות וכנ״ל ומה״ת יהי׳ נתן לכ״א מעות אבל
26. באמת הוא שכל החשבן שעשה כה״י ז״ל הוא פרוע וגם השלשה ח״מ מן
27. פ״ב זהו׳ פרוע הם והאריך בתשובותיו ע״[ד] תבעו האפט[רו]פס[י׳]

נה ע״ב

1. באשר שכה״י ז״ל גבה חוב השייך לעזבון (הנ״ל)[3] מן קארטי מנו״ו סך קל״ג זהו׳ ומאותו
2. מעות יחסרו מחמת מטבעות רעי׳ שהוצריך לגבות הי׳ הפסד במעות הנ״ל
3. יוד רט[4] וכה״י ז״ל היה חושב בחשבונו במילוי בכן מגיע לעזבון כה״י ז״ל יוד רט
4. וכ׳ אנשיל הנ״ל השיב שאותו מטבעות היה בתוך מעות אחרת שגבה
5. כה״י ז״ל חוב אחר שלא הזכיר בחשבונו וטוען כ׳ אנשיל הנ״ל שכה״י ז״ל
6. אמר[5] = לו שיש תחת ידו עוד שמונים רט שגבה ולא נזכר בפנקס אפטרופסי׳
7. ולאחר שיחשוב עם כ״א הנ״ל רוצה ליתן לו המעות ולא חישב ולא נתן
8. לו כלום בכן תובע כ״א הנ״ל הנ״ל[6] אותן מעות מעזבון כה״י ז״ל וה(א)[7]ריכו
9. הצדדים הנ״ל בטענותיהם ובתשובותיהם על כל פרט ופרט כמבואר
10. באריכות מתוך ק״ה המונח לפנינו והנה אחרי שהצדדים הנ״ל חתמו
11. עצמם בתוקף קומפרמיס בח״ח ובקנס מסויים לשררה ירה[8] ולהקדש
12. לאשר ולקיים את אשר יצא מאתנו גם קבלו עליהם בכל חומר ובקנס
13. כנ״ל ונתנו עיניהם עלינו ב״ד ח״מ לעשות פשר דבר ביניהם בכן נזדקקנו
14. להם ועיינו ודקדקנו בחשבונים הדק היטיב ומצאנו דרך פשר דבר
15. לטובת היתומם ולזכות המנוח כה״י ז״ל ולטובת כ״א הנ״ל להשוותם על
16. צד הממוצע אשר מצאנו אחר החקירה והעיון בטענותיהם שמחמת

---

1. הגרשיים במקור; כנראה שצ״ל ׳היו׳
2. לא ברור מה כוונת הדברים.
3. תוספת מעל השורה
4. 10 רייכשטאלר
5. המילה ׳אמר׳ היא מחוץ לשורה.
6. כפילות במקור
7. תוספת מעל השורה
8. ירום הודו

17. כל טענת ותביעות שיש להצדדים הנ״ל זה על זה וזה על זה וכנ[״ל]
18. מחויבים האפטרופסי׳ מעזבון כה״[י] אופנהיים ז״ל הנ״ל להחזיר
19. המשכון אבנים טובת שהוא תחת ידם מחותם ונכתב עליו משכון
20. בעד עשרים זהו׳ יחזירו האפטרופסי׳ לכ׳ אנשיל זיכל הנ״ל בחנם
21. ונוסף על זה מחויבים האפטרופסי׳ הנ״ל ליתן לכ׳ אנשיל הנ״ל מעזבון
22. כה״י ז״ל הנ״ל שמונה עשר זהו׳ זהו׳[1] במזומונים ובזה פטורים ומסולקים
23. הצדדים הנ״ל זה מזה וזה מזה מכל טענות ותביעות הנ״ל וגם הח״כ
24. והח״מ[2] הנ״ל מזה ומזה בטילם ומבוטלים וחלילה לשום אדם עוד לערער
25. ולטעונן מכל הענין [הנ״ל] עד יום דלמטה כי הכל חשבנו ושקלנו כל הטענות
26. פרוטי...פשר גם הנ״ל הכל מסולק ומבוטל כ״ז יצא מאתנו

נו ע״א

1. יו׳ ב חי א״ש קהלת לפק הג׳ אב״ד נר״ו והדיין כ״ה אברהם טריר
2. והדיין כ״ה זנוויל טראך ואני

No. 52

Fols. 56b–57a; Sunday 26 March 1775

Herz Adler (d. November 1774) predeceased his wife, Esther, who now came to the court to arrange the payment of her marriage contract. In 1743 Esther had agreed to forgo a portion of her marriage contract of 1705 guldens in favor of any surviving children of the union. At that time she also received a written promise that she would have the right to continue to live in a portion of Herz's house (if he would have one) for the duration of her widowhood. Now that Herz had died, Esther's brother, Rabbi Meʾir Schiff, who was often a member of the court, asked the court to search out any descendents of the deceased and receive their consent to pay Esther her marriage contract. Meʾir also asked that the court inquire of Herz's children and obtain their consent to excuse their mother/mother-in-law from taking the oath generally required of women collecting their marriage contracts (see *Ketubbot* 9.8). The court did so and the heirs waived any objections.

---

1. כפילות במקור
2. והחילופי מכתבים

נו ע"ב

1. ב"ה
2. ע"ד שבא לפנינו ה"ה התורני הדיין כ"ה מאיר שיף כץ בהרשאת אחותו האשה מ' אסתר אל' המנוח
3. כ' הירץ אדליר ז"ל והציע לפנינו שטר ת"א ההוקמו בין האשה מ' אסתר הנ"ל ובין בעלה המנוח
4. כ' הירץ ז"ל הנ"ל ביו' ד' ר"ח אלול תק"ג ושם נאמר וז"ל ובשנה שלישית ומשם ואיליך הדין ח
5. חוזר ל[ע]ינו אם תעדר היא ח"ו הבעל יורש את אשתו ואם יעדר הוא ח"ו תקחי כתובת' ותוספ'
6. משלם ובין הכל יחד סך שבעה עשרה מאות וחמשה זהו' רק שתניחי ותוותרי לז"ק שיהי' להם יחד חלק
7. רביעית מתוספ' וכו' גם אם יקנה כ"ה הירץ לעצמו בית שלם או חצי בית או רביעית בית
8. אזי יהי' לה מיגר אל' ברביעית בית עכ"ל וטעון כהר"מ[1] הנ"ל מאחר שבעלה הנ"ל נעדר ושחל"[ב]י[2] בכן
9. מגיע לה מחמת כתובת' ותוספ' לאחר ניכוי חלק רביעית מתוס' לז"ק סך חמשה עשרה מאות שמוני' וא'
10. ואחד זהו' טו צל ובעלה כ' הירץ ז"ל הנ"ל הניח אחריו מטלטלין דהיינו כלי תשמיש מעבל וכלי בית
11. כסף וזהוב וקרקעות הניח אחריו שלשה שמינית שהי' שייך לכ' הירץ הנ"ל ורביעית בית
12. נתן לחותנו כ' אלחנן פוקס בשיור יד העליונה לו ולאשתו על כל ימי חיי' בכן ביקש כהר"מ הנ"ל
13. שיחליטו הב"ד לאל' הנ"ל כל מה שהניח אחריו בעלה ז"ל הנ"ל הן בקרקעות והן במטלטלין וכנ"ל לפרעון ש
14. שטר כתובת' ותוספ' הנ"ל לחלוטין גמורין ולצמיתת עלמין ורוצה כהר"מ הנ"ל שנשלחו אנחנו ב"ד
15. ח"מ אחרי כל י"ח וחתנה כ' אלחנן פוקס הנ"ל באשר שהם גדולי' ובני דעת ואמרו שמרוצי' בכך במה
16. שיחליטו הב"ד את כל מה שהניח אחריו אביהם וחמיו כ"ה ז"ל הנ"ל בעזבונו לאמם מ' אסתר הנ"ל
17. לחלוטין גמורין ולצמיתת עלמין וגם שנשאלו להם אם רוצי' למחלה ולפ[ט]רה מהשבעת כתובה
18. ותוספ' וכן עשינו ושלחנו אחרי כל היורשי' כנ"ל ובא לפנינו ה"ה החתן כ' ליזר בן המנוח כ"ה
19. אדליר כ"ץ ז"ל הנ"ל וה"ה האשה מ' ריזכה ובעלה כ' אלחנן פוקס יצ"ו הנ"ל בת וחתן כ' הירץ ז"ל הנ"ל
20. והבתולה מ' צערלה בת כ' הירץ ז"ל הנ"ל וענו ואמרו כולם בהודאה גמורה ובנפש חפצה ובדעת ש

1. כבוד הרב מאיר
2. שבק חיים לכל בית ישראל

21. שלימה ומיוש[בת] ופטרו ומחלו במחילה גמורה ומיושבת מלהשביע את אמם וחמותו הנ"ל השבעת
22. כתובת' ותוספ' הנהוג פה וביקשו מאתנו ב"ד ח"מ להחליט את כל מה שהניח אחריו אביהם
23. וחמיו ז"ל הן בקרקעות והן במטלטלין וכנ"ל לאמם ולחמותו מ' אסתר הנ"ל לפירעון שטר כתובת'
24. ותוספ' לחלוטין גמורין ולצמיתת עלמין וליתר תוקף ועוז עשו כל היורשי' הנ"ל וכנ"ל ק"ג ע"[ס][1] בכא"ה לפנינו
25. ב"ד על כל הנ"ל בכן פטרנו אותה מהשבעת כתובת' ותוס' הנהוג פה בתוקף מעשה ב"ד ובכח ב"ד
26. יפה נגד יוצאי חלצי' וחתנה הנ"ל וי"א וב"כ גם חלטנו לחלוטין גמורין ולצמיתת עלמין את כל
27. מה שהניח אחריו כ' הירץ אדליר ז"ל הנ"ל הן קרקעות מטלטלין מעבל כלי בית כסף לאל' מ' אסתר
28. הנ"ל לפירעון כתובת' ותוספ' נגד י"ח וחתנה הנ"ל ומעתה אין יכולין כל י"ח וחתן הנ"ל הם
29. וי"א [ו]ב"כ (לערער)[2] ולטעון שום טענה ועירער יהי' מה שיהי' או מכל מה ש[יכל] נגד האל' הנ"ל וב"כ

נז ע"א

1. ב"ה
2. ואל יזדקק להם שום ב"ד לא בדא"ה ולא בד"י כי הכל נעשה ברצון נפשם ובדעתם
3. חפצה ומיושבת ובכח ב"ד יפה וכנ"ל וכאילו נעשה בפני ב"ד חשוב וראוי
4. והנעשה נעשה היו' יו' א' דד א"ש קהלת לפק

No. 53

Fols. 57b–58b; Sunday evening, 21 May 1775

Pescha, the widow of Aaron Orschel (d. April 1774), and her stepdaughter, Brendele, sold half a house on the Trommel lot after a period of open bidding. The house was offered for sale a number of times in both the old and new synagogues as well as before the court. Bids were to be submitted to the court. This document is a record of the sale to the highest bidder, Avrele Wimpfen, and it itemizes the conditions of sale. One condition was that the sellers had the right to continue to live in the house or rent it out until the beginning of the Hebrew month of Nissan 1778 (29 March). A copy of the record of sale was to be given to the new owner. Also see no. 54.

---

1. על סודר
2. תוספת מעל השורה

נז ע״ב

1. ב״ה
2. החצי בית צור טרום[1] שהי׳ שייך להמנוח כ׳ אהרן אורשל ז״ל
3. הוכרז ע״פ האשה מ׳ פעסכה אל׳ המנוח כ׳ אהרן ז״ל[2] הנ״ל
4. ובתה חו[ר]גתה מ׳ ברענדלה בבהכ״י וחדש זמן זמנא טובא
5. שכל מי שרוצה לקנות יבוא לפני ב״ד ויכרז לפני ב״ד עד
6. שיפסקו המוסיפן גם הוכרז לפנינו ב״ד ע״פ צוואת
7. הקהל [יצו] וע״פ האשה מ׳ פעסכה ובתה הנ״ל ולא הי׳ שום
8. אחד שהי׳ פוסק בעד חצי בית הנ״ל כפי מה שפוסק
9. ה״ה הו״ה כ׳ אברלי ווימפא סגל בכן מכרנו החצי בית
10. הנ״ל במעמד כ׳ יוסף בכ״ח[3] שטי[ב]ל בהרשאת האשה
11. אל׳ הנ״ל וב״ח מ׳ ברענדל הנ״ל לה״ה[4] כ׳ אברלי ווימפא
12. סגל הנ״ל בעד סך ארבעה אלופי׳ זהובי׳ לשלם אותם
13. אין קונפונטציאהנש מינץ אויף דען כד זהו׳ פוס והיינו
14. שעל כל סך דמי מקח הנ״ל יתן הלוקח כ׳ אברלי הנ״ל
15. בשעת מסירת החלוטה שבעה ח״כ על אורדר האשה מ׳
16. פעסכה ובתה מ׳ ברענדלה הנ״ל והיינו ח״כ אחד
17. מסך אלף זהו׳ לשלם אותו בחדש חשון תקלו לפק
18. הסמוך הבע״ל ועוד ששה ח״כ {לא} על אורדר הנ״ל כל
19. אחד {עם} מסך חמשה מאות זהו׳ לשלם אותם כל אחד
20. ואחד שמונה ימי׳ אחר יריד פה והיינו בששה ירידי׳
21. רצופי׳ וסמוכי׳ זא״ז ויריד ר[אשון] יהי׳ ביריד פסח
22. תקלו הבעל[5] גם נשאר החצי בי[ת] ה[...ל]אפותקו מפורש
23. שלא יצא מחזקת מרא קמא כל זמן שלא נתפרע אפי׳ אחד
24. מן הח״כ הנ״ל ויתן[ו]קן ע״ז שטר אפותקו ע״פ נאמני הקהלה
25. כנהוג גם הותנו בתנאי גמור {בתנאי} כתנאי בנגוב״ר
26. בכא״ה שאף שהקנין החצי בית הנ״ל צור טרום נקנה
27. מעכשיו לחלוטין גמורין להלוקח הנ״ל מ״מ שיירו המוכרי׳ הנ״ל
28. הנ״ל לעצמן

נח ע״א

1. ב״ה
2. הנ״ל לעצמן הפירות מחצי בית הנ״ל עד ניסן תקלח הבע״ל
3. ולא שעד בכלל ואין להלוקח הנ״ל הפירות מחצי בית הנ״ל

---

1. Trommel = (ע׳ דייץ, עמ׳ 478)
2. ר׳ דייץ, עמ׳ 312.
3. כנראה בן כבוד חיים (ר׳ אבני זכרון, מס׳ 3810).
4. להרב החכם
5. הבא עלינו לטובה

4. עד כלות זמן הנ"ל ורשאי המוכרי' הנ"ל לדור ולהשתמש
5. בעצמם באותו חצי בית גם להשכיר החצי בית הנ"ל לכל מי
6. שירצה על זמן הנ"ל ודמי שכירות יהי' להמוכרי' הנ"ל
7. ואין הלוקח יכול למחות בם ומעתה החצי בית הנ"ל אשר
8. הי' שייך מקדמת דנא להמנוח כ' אהרן אורשל ז"ל מעכשיו
9. לה"ה הו"ה כ' אברלי ווימפא סגל הנ"ל וי"א וב"כ לחלוטין
10. גמורין ולצמיתת עלמין כל ארכו ורחבו עם כל חזקותיו
11. וזכיותיו ומצאיו ומבואי' ומצריו וחצריו ומרתפות ועליות
12. עומקו ורומא מתהום {רקיע} ארעא עד תהום רקיע וכמו
13. שהי' שייך מקדמת לה"ה המנוח כ' אהרן אורשל ז"ל הנ"ל
14. בלי שום שיור כלל זולת שיור פירות על זמן הנ"ל וכנ"ל
15. ורשאי כה[1] אברלי הנ"ל וי"א וב"כ לעשות עם חצי בית
16. להוריש ולהנחיל להחליף להשכין למכור {ולהשכין} ולהשכיר
17. וליתן במתנה כאות נפשו ורצונו ככל אינש דרשאי לעשות
18. בשלו בלי מוחה כלל ואחר {שני} שנתפרע כל הח"כ הזמני'
19. הנ"ל שייך מעכשיו החצי בית הנ"ל לה"ה כ' אברלי הנ"ל וי"א
20. וב"כ בשופי גמור בלי שום עורר וטוען יהי' המערער
21. מי שיהי' הן רבי' או יחיד יהי' טענה מה שיהי' או בכל
22. אופן שיהי' מכל מה שהפה יוכל לדבר והלב לחשוב
23. ולהרהר וכל מי שיערער אחר מכירה הנ"ל יהי' מי שיהי'
24. או באיזה אופן שיהי' דברי' בטלים ומבוטלי' כחרס
25. הנשבר כאפס וכאין יחשב לא שרירין ולא קיימין ולא יהי'
26. חלין כלל וכלל וכטוען אחר מעשה ב"ד הגודל[2] ולא יזדקק
27. שום קהל או ב"ד יצו או שום משפט שבעולם לדבריו
28. המערער הן בדא"ה

נח ע"ב

1. ב"ה
2. המערער הן דבא"ה והן בד"י כי דברי המערער הם בטלי'
3. ומבוטלי' באשר שנעשה הכל ע"פ הקהל יצו וע"פ האשה
4. מ' פעסכה ובתה חורגתה מ' ברענדלה אל' ובת כ'
5. {אהרן} אהרן אורשל הנ"ל וכתבנו וחתמנו זאת בתוקף
6. מעשה ב"ד {וכ}ובכח {מעשה} ב"ד יפה להיות ביד לוקח
7. ה"ה הו"ה כ' אברלי ווימפא סגל הנ"ל וי"א וב"כ לעדות
8. ולזכות ולראי' שיעמוד חצי בית הנ"ל עם כל חזקותיו
9. וזכיותיו ביד הלוקח הנ"ל וי"א וב"כ בלי שום מוחה כלל

---

1. כבוד הרב
2. צ"ל 'הגדול'

10. נעשה פפי[1] דמיין אור ליו' ב לז למב"י קהלת לפק
11. הק' מאיר בן כ"ה זלמן [ש]יף
12. הק' אברהם טריר כהן
13. הק' חיים בפו"מ כ"ה יוזפא גונדרשהיים

No. 54

Fols. 59a–60a; Sunday evening, 28 May 1775

Pescha, the widow of Aaron Orschel, and her stepdaughter, Brendele, inherited from their late husband/stepfather land on the Trommel lot on which "half a house" stood. They were to receive income on the house itself when Pescha's sister-in-law, Breinle, died. Pescha and her stepdaughter decided to sell the current and future assets, and the sale was announced in both the old and new synagogues as well as before the court. The court recorded the sale of the assets to the highest bidder, noted the terms of sale, and itemized the rights of the purchaser, Leb Oppenheim. Also see no. 53.

נט ע"א

1. ב"ה
2. החצי בית צור טרופל[2] שהי' שייך גוף הקרקע לה"ה המנוח
3. כ' אהרן אורשל ז"ל והפירות מחצי בית שייכי' להאשה מ'
4. בריינלה אל' המנוח כ' נטע אורשל ז"ל כל זמן שהי' בחיי' ולאח"כ
5. הי' שייך הפירות ג"כ להמנוח כ אהרן אורשל ז"ל הנ"ל
6. הוכרז ע"פ האשה מ' פעסכה אל' המנוח כ' אהרן אורשל ז"ל
7. הנ"ל ובתה חורגתה מ' ברענדלה בת המנוח כ' אהרן ז"ל
8. הנ"ל בבהכ"י וחדש זמן זמני' טובא שכל מי שרוצה לקנות
9. {הגוף} חצי בית הנ"ל והיינו גוף הקרקע מהיו' והפירות
10. בכלות חיי' האשה מ' בריינלה הנ"ל וכנ"ל יבוא לפני ב"ד
11. גם הוכרז לפנינו ב"ד ח"מ ע"פ צוואת קהל יצו וע"פ האשה
12. מ' פעסכה ובתה הנ"ל עד שיפסקו המוסיפי' ולא הי'
13. שום אחד שהי' פוסק {כפי} בעד חצי בית הנ"ל כפי
14. מה שפסק ה"ה הו"ה פו"מ כ"ה ליב אופנהיי' בכן מכרנו
15. החצי בית הנ"ל דהיינו גוף הקרקע מעכשיו ולאחר העדרת
16. האשה מ' בריינלה הנ"ל ח"ו אף הפירות מחצי בית הנ"ל

1. פרנקפורט
2. לא מוכר בית בשם הזה; כנראה שצ"ל 'טרומל'.

17. במעמד כ' יוסף בכ"חי[1] שטיבל בהרשאת האשה ובתה הנ"ל
18. להה[2] {פ} הו"ה פו"[מ] כ"ה ליב אופנהיי' הנ"ל בעד סך שני אלופי'
19. ושבעה מאות זהו' לשלם אותם אין קונפונטציאהנש מינץ
20. אויף דען כ"ד זהו' פוס והיינו לשלם השליש מסך דמי
21. מכירה הנ"ל תיכף בשעת מסירת החלוטה ושני שלישי'
22. הנותרי' מדמי מכירה הנ"ל ישלם על ששה חצאי שני' רצופי'
23. וסמוכי' זא"ז מיו' מסירת החלוטה ומחויב הלוקח כ"ה ליב הנ"ל
24. ליתן ששה ח"כ על זמני' הנ"ל לאורדר האשה מ' פעסכה וב"ח
25. מ' ברענדלה הנ"ל גם נשא[ר] החצי בית הנ"ל לאפותיקו
26. מפורש שלא יצא מחזקת מרא קמא כל זמן שלא נתפר[ע]
27. אפי' אחד מן

נט ע"ב

1. ב"ה
2. אפי' אחד מן הח"כ הנ"ל ויתוקן ע"ז שטר אפותיקו ע"י
3. נאמני הקהלה כנהוג ומעתה החצי בית הנ"ל אשר הי'
4. שייך מקדמת דנא להמנוח כ' אהרן אורשל שייך הגוף
5. מעכשיו {והפ} ובכלות חיי' האשה מ' בריינלה הנ"ל אף
6. לה"ה הו"ה פו"מ כ"ה ליב אופנהיי' הנ"ל וי"א וב"כ לחלוטין
7. גמורין ולצמיתת עלמן כל ארכו ורחבו עם כל חזקותיו
8. וזכיותיו ומוצאיו ומובאיו ומצריו וחצריו ומרתפות ועליות
9. עמקא {ורחבו} ורומא מתהום ארעא עד {תה}ום (רום)[3] רקיע וכמו
10. שהי' שייך מקדמת להמנוח כ' אהרן אורשל ז"ל הנ"ל
11. בלי שום שיור כלל ורשאי כ"ה ליב הנ"ל וי"א וב"כ לעשות
12. עם חצי בית הנ"ל להוריש ולהנחיל להחליף להשכין למכור
13. ולהשכיר וליתן {במתה} במתנה כאות נפשו ורצונו ככל
14. אינש דרשאי לעשות בשלו בלי מוחה כלל ואחר שנתפרע
15. כל הח"כ הנ"ל שייך {מ}הגוף מעכשיו ומזמן הנ"ל אף הפיר'
16. מחצי בית הנ"ל לה"ה הו"ה פו"מ כ"ה ליב אופנהיי' וי"א וב"כ
17. בשופי גמור בלא שום עורר וטוען כלל יהי' המערער מי
18. שיהי' הן רבים או יחיד יהי' טענה מה שיהי' או
19. בכל אופן שיהי' {או בכל אופן} מכל מה שהפה יוכל
20. לדבר והלב לחשוב ולהרהר וכל מי שיערער אחר
21. מכירה הנ"ל יהי' מי שיהי' או באיזה אופן שיהי'
22. דברי' בטלי' ומבוטלי' כחרס הנשבר כאפס וכאין יחשב
23. לא שרירן ולא קיימן ולא יהי' חלין כלל וכלל וכטוען אחר

---

1. כנראה בן כבוד חיים
2. להרב החכם
3. תוספת מעל השורה

24. מעשה ב"ד הגודל[1] ולא יזדקק שום קהל או ב"ד יצו
25. או שום משפט שבעולם לדברי המערער הן בדא"ה
26. והן בד"י כי דברי המערער הם בטלי' ומבוטלי'
27. באשר שנעשה

סמך ע"א

1. ב"ה
2. שנעשה הכל ע"פ הקהל יצו וע"פ האשה מ' פעסכה ובתה
3. חורגתה מ' ברענדלה אל' ובת כ אהרן אורשל ז"ל הנ"ל
4. וכתבנו וחתמנו זאת בתוקף מעשה ב"ד ובכח ב"ד
5. יפה להיות ביד לוקח ה"ה הו"ה פו"מ כ"ה ליב אופנהיי'
6. הנ"ל וי"א וב"כ לעדות ולזכות לראי' {מהימנא} שיעמוד
7. גוף חצי בית הנ"ל והפירות כנ"ל עם כל חזקותיו וזכיותיו
8. ביד לוקח הנ"ל וי"א וב"כ בלי שום מוחה כלל נעשה פ"פ דמיין
9. או[2] ליו' ב מ"ד למב"י קהלת לפק הק' יצחק מאיר שווארץ שיל[ד]
10. הק' אברהם טריר כהן
11. {הק מאיר בלאא[3] בן כה זלמן שיף}
12. הק' חיים בפומ[4] כ יוזפא גונדרשהיי' יצו

No. 55

Fols. 60b–60c; Monday evening, 29 May 1775

One-third of an open plot of land on the Hinter Kranaich lot on which a house had once stood was put up for sale by the community. The sale was announced in the old and new synagogues. The sale was also announced before the court and bids were to be submitted to the court. Unlike in documents nos. 53 and 54, this document notes that the non-Jewish authorities ordered the Jewish community to take bids on the property. It also notes that the original owner, David Heichelom (Heichelsheim[?]), agreed to the sale. The space was sold to a widow, Merle Braunschweig, who was the highest bidder (also see no. 58). The document notes the exact location of the land, records the terms of sale, and the rights and obligations of the owner.

1. צ"ל 'הגדול'
2. צ"ל 'אור'
3. בן לאדוני אבי
4. בן פרנס ומנהיג

סמך ע"ב

1. ב"ה
2. שליש מן פלאטץ שהי' עומד עליו בית פנימי צור הינדר קראניך
3. דהיינו אותו בית שהי' עומד על צד ימין בכניסה מהרחוב לבתי'
4. פנימי' אותו שליש פלאטץ הנ"ל שהי' שייך לה"ה כ' דוד הייכלום
5. הוכרז {לפנינו ב"ד ח"מ} בבהכ"י וחדש זמן זמני' טובא ע"פ צוואת
6. הקהל יצו בפקודת הש[ר]רה יר"ה שכל מי שרוצה לקנות יבוא
7. לפנינו ב"ד גם הוכרז לפנינו ב"ד ח"מ ע"פ צוואת הקהל יצו
8. וברצון כ דוד הייכלום עד שיפסקו המוסיפי' ולא הי' שום
9. אחד שהי' פוסק כפי מה שפסקה האשה הקצינה מ' מערלה
10. בר{ונשוויג} אל' המנוח מ[ה'] משה ברונשוויג ז"ל בכן מכרנו שליש פלאטץ
11. הנ"ל להקצינה מ' מערלה הנ"ל בעד סך שבעה מאות ושמוני' ואחד
12. זהו' לשלם אותם אין קונפונטציאהנש מינץ אויף דען כ"ד זהו'
13. פוס והיינו לשלם שליש מסך דמי מכירה הנ"ל תכף בשעת
14. מסירת החלוטה ושני שלי' הנותרי' מסך דמי מכירה הנ"ל תשלם
15. על ששה חצאי שני' רצופי' וסמוכי' זא"ז מיו' מסירת החלוטה
16. ומחויבת האשה מ' מערלה הנ"ל ליתן ששה ח"כ על זמני' הנ"ל גם נשאר
17. אותו פלאטץ הנ"ל לאפותיקו מפורש שלא יצא מחזקת מרא קמא כל זמן
18. שלא נתפרע אפי' אחד מן הח"כ ויתוקן ע"ז שטר אפותיקו
19. ע"י נאמני הקהלה כנהוג ומעתה אותו שליש פלאטץ הנ"ל שהי' שייך מקדמת
20. לכ' דוד הייכלום יצו שייך מעכשיו להאשה הקצינה מ' מערלה הנ"ל וי"א
21. וב"כ לחלוטין גמורין ולצמיתת עלמן כל ארכו ורחבו עם כל חזקותיו
22. וזכיותיו ומוצאיו ומובאיו ומצריו ומרתפות וחצריו עומקא ורומא
23. מתהום ארעא עד רום רקיע וכמו שהי' שייך מקדמת לה"ה כ' דוד
24. הייכלום בלי שום שיור כלל ורשאי האשה מ' מערלה הנ"ל וי"א וב"כ
25. לעשות עם שליש פלאטץ הנ"ל לקנות ולהרוס להוריש ולהנחיל להחליף להשכין
26. למכור ולהשכיר וליתן במתנה כאות נפשה וכרצונה ככל אינש דרשאי
27. לעשות בשלו בלי מוחה כלל ולאחר שנתפרע כל הח"כ הנ"ל שייך
28. מעכשיו שליש פלאטץ [הנ"ל] להאשה היקרה מ' מערלה הנ"ל וי"א וב"כ
29. בשופי גמור

סמך ע"ג[1]

1. ב"ה
2. בשופי גמור בלי שום עורר וטוען כלל יהי' המערער מי שיהי' הן רבי'
3. או יחיד יהי' טענה מה שיהי' או בכל אופן שיהי' מכל מה שהפה
4. יוכל לדבר והלב לחשוב ולהרהר וכל מי שיערער אחר מכירה הנ"ל
5. יהי' מי שיהי' או באיזה אופן שיהי' דברי' בטלי' ומבוטלי' כחרס

---

1. על עמוד זה מופיעה שוב המילה 'סמך' ולכן קראנו לעמ' זה ע"ג.

הנשבר כאפס וכאין יחשב לא שרירן ולא קיימין ולא יהי׳ חלין כלל וכלל וכטוען אחר מעשה ב״ד הגודלי[1] ולא יזדקק שום קהל או ב״ד יצו או שום משפט שבעולם לדברי המערער הן בדא״ה והן {בד״י} בד״י כי דברי המערער הם בטלי׳ ומבוטלי׳ באשר שנעשה הכל ע״פ הקהל יצו וברצון כ׳ דוד הייכלום הנ״ל וכתבנו וחתמנו זאת בתוקף מעשה ב״ד ובכח ב״ד יפה להיות ביד לוקח ה״ה האשה מ׳ מערלה אל׳ כמהורר[2] משה ברונשוויג ז״ל וי״א וב״כ לעדות ולזכות ולראי׳ שיעמוד אותו שליש פלאטץ הנ״ל עם כל חזקותיו וזכיותיו ביד לוקח הנ״ל וי״א וב״כ בלי שום מוחה כלל נעשה פ״פ דמיין אור ליו׳ ג׳ מ״ה למב״י קהלת לפק הק׳ מאיר שווארץ שילד הק׳ אברהם טריר כהן הק׳ חיים בפו״מ כ׳ יוזפא גונדרשהיי׳ שליטא

No. 56

Fols. 60d–61a; Monday evening, 29 May 1775

The sale of a quarter of a house on the Goldener Apfel lot by the heirs of Rechle, widow of Moses Fulda, was recorded by the court. By order of the community, the sale was announced in the synagogues a number of times so that all those interested in bidding on the property could do so. The quarter of the house was ultimately sold to Isaac Sinzheim, who was about to marry (see Dietz, p. 287), for 560 guldens. Isaac was ordered to pay one-third of the purchase price immediately and the remaining two-thirds in six equal post-dated installments, each payment due in six month intervals. A copy of the document was to be given to Isaac Sinzheim as proof of his purchase.

סמך ע״ד[3]

ב״ה רביעת בית פנימי צור גולדני אפפל שהי׳ שייך להאשה מ׳ רעכלה אל׳ המנוח כ״ה משה ב״כ פער פולדא ז״ל הוכרז (בבהכ״י וחדש)[4] ע״פ צוות הקהל יצו וברצון יורשי העזבון של האשה הנ״ל בבהכ״י וחדש זמן זמני׳ טובא שכל מי שרוצה לקנות יבוא לפנינו ב״ד גם הוכרז לפנינו ב״ד ח״מ עד שיפסקו ה

1. צ״ל ׳הגדול׳
2. כבוד מורנו הרב והגאון רב רבי
3. ר׳ הערה בעמוד הקודם.
4. תוספת מחוץ לשורה

7. המוסיפין ולא הי' שום אחד שהי' פוסק כפי מה
8. שפסק הבחור החתן כ אייזק בכ"ה שמעון זינצהיים
9. בכן מכרנו רביעת בית פנימי הנ"ל להבחור כ' אייזק
10. הנ"ל בעד סך חמשה מאות וששי' זהו' לשלם אותם אין
11. קונפונטציאהנש מינץ אויף דען ד"ד (זהו')[1] פוס והיינו לשלם השליש
12. מסך דמי מכירה הנ"ל תיכף בשעת מסירת החלוטה ושני
13. שלישי' הנותרי' מסך דמי מכירה הנ"ל ישלם על ששה {שני'}
14. חצאי שני' רצופי' וסמוכי' זא"ז מיו' מסירת החלוטה ומחויב
15. הלוקח כ' אייזק הנ"ל ליתן ששה ח"כ על זמני' הנ"ל גם נשאר
16. הרביעת בית הנ"ל לאפותיקו מפורש שלא יצא מחזקת מרא
17. קמא כל זמן שלא נתפרע אפילו אחד מן הח"כ הנ"ל ויתוקן
18. ע"ז שטר אפותיקו ע"י נאמני הקהלה כנהוג ומעתה הרביעת
19. בית פנימי הנ"ל שהי' שייך מקדמת להאשה מ' רעכלה ז"ל
20. הנ"ל שייך מעכשיו להבחור החתן כ' אייזק הנ"ל וי"א וב"כ
21. לחלוטין גמורין ולצמיתת עלמן כל ארכו ורחבו עם כל חזקותיו
22. וזכיותיו ומוצאיו ומובאיו ומצריו וחצריו ומרתפות ועליות
23. עומקא ורומא מתהום ארעא עד רום רקיע וכמו שהי' שייך
24. מקדמת להאשה מ' רעכלה ז"ל הנ"ל בלי שום שיור כלל {וש} ורשאי כ'
25. אייזק הנ"ל וי"א וב"כ לעשות עם רביעת בית הנ"ל להוריש
26. ולהנחיל להחליף ולהשכין למכור ולהשכיר וליתן במתנה כאות
27. נפשו ככל איניש

סא ע"א

1. ב"ה
2. נפשו ככל איניש דרשאי לעשות בשלו בלי שום מוחה כלל
3. ולאחר שנתפרע כל הח"כ הנ"ל שייך מעכשיו הרביעת בית
4. הנ"ל להבחור החתן כ' אייזק הנ"ל בכ"ה שמעון זינצהיי'
5. הנ"ל וי"א וב"כ בשופי גמור בלי שום עורר וטוען כלל
6. יהי' המערער מי שיהי' הן יחיד או רבי' יהי' טענה מה
7. שיהי' או בכל אופן שיהי' מכל מה שהפה יוכל לדבר
8. והלב לחשוב {ולהרהי} ולהרהר וכל מי שיערער אחר מכירה
9. הנ"ל יהי' מי שיהי' או באיזה אופן שיהי' דברי' בטלי'
10. ומבוטלי' כחרס הנשבר כאפס וכאין יחשב לא שרירן ולא
11. קיימין ולא יהי' חלין כלל וכלל וכטוען אחר מעשה ב"ד הגדול
12. ואל יזדקק שום קהל או ב"ד יצו או שום משפט שבעולם
13. לדברי המערער הן בדא"ה והן בד"י כי דברי המערער
14. הם בטלי' ומבוטלי' באשר שנעשה הכל ע"פ צוות הקהל

---

1. תוספת מעל השורה

15. יצו וברצון יורשי האשה מ׳ רעכלה ז״ל הנ״ל וכתבנו וחתמ[נו]
16. זאת בתוקף מעשה ב״ד ובכח ב״ד יפה להיות ביד
17. לוקח הבחור החתן כ׳ אייזק הנ״ל וי״א וב״כ לעדות
18. ולזכות {לראי׳} לראי׳ שיעמוד הרביעת בית פנימי הנ״ל עם
19. כל חזקותיו וזכיותיו ביד לוקח הנ״ל וי״א וב״כ בלי שום
20. מוחה כלל נעשה פ״פ דמיין אור ליו׳ ג׳ מ״ה למב״י קהלת לפק
21. הק׳ יצחק מאיר שווארץ שילד הק׳ אברהם טריר כהן
22. הק׳ חיים בפו״מ כ׳ יוזפא גונדרשהיי׳ שליטא

No. 57

Maas v. Maas

Fols. 61b–63b; Tuesday 13 June 1775

Leser Maas challenged the right of his sister-in-law, Esther, widow of Leser's late brother, Zanvil, to give half of a house on the Drei Römer lot in which she currently lived to her son, Yuzpa, who was about to marry. Leser maintained that he and Zanvil had inherited the property from their mother, Hindele, and that therefore, because he owned half of it, Esther no right to give any more than a quarter of the house to her son. Moreover, Leser claimed that Esther had been living in the entire half of the house since Zanvil's death 12 years earlier and had never paid him rent for use of his share of the house. Through his representative, Leser asked the court to determine the amount of back rent that Esther should now pay.

Yuzpa, who represented his mother in her presence, questioned his uncle Leser's right to one quarter of the house and produced a contract to prove that his father, Zanvil, had purchased one quarter of the house from his and Leser's mother and her husband, Zalman Landau (Hindele had remarried after her husband, Solomon Maas's death) in 1725. As such, Leser only had rights to one eighth of the house. Yuzpa further claimed that Leser owed Esther money because he never contributed to the cost of repairs to the house or to taxes. Yuzpa also claimed that Leser had not shared in paying the debts of Hindele's estate and that he had not participated in the repayment of debts owed by a second deceased brother, Seligmann, who had died childless and whose outstanding debt of 35 guldens had been paid by Esther. Yuzpa argued that if Leser wanted to inherit from the estate he would have to share in the obligations of both Hindele and Seligmann's estates. Regarding the back rent, Yuzpa noted that his grandmother and her husband had lived in the half house with Zanvil's family for about 25 years, beginning in 1725, without ever having made a payment to Zanvil for use of the quarter of the house that belonged to him. Yuzpa now asked the court to place a value on this and obligate Hindele's estate to pay back rent to Zanvil's heirs.

Leser disputed the validity of the contract of sale for a number of reasons, including that there was no mention of the amount that the house was to be sold for. Through his representative he raised a number of counterclaims disputing his obligation to pay Esther for the various debts, although he admitted to owing her for back taxes and was willing to pay his share of the repair costs if she would swear that they were the correct sums.

Ultimately the two sides asked the court to suggest a compromise that all parties agreed to be bound by.

סא ע"ב

1. ב"ה
2. ע"[ד] שבא לפנינו ה"ה התורני כ"ה משה אויך בהרשאת הב"ח מ"ז[1] כ' ליזר בהמנוח[2]
3. כ' שלמה מז ז"ל ותבע מן האשה מ' אסתר אל' המנוח כ"ה זנוויל מז מאחר
4. שפסקה ליתן לנדן בנה החתן כ' יוזפא יצו החצי בית צור דרייא רעמר
5. שדרה בה עתה האשה מ' אסתר הנ"ל וטעון כהר"מ[3] הנ"ל באשר שחצי בית הנ"ל
6. נפל להני תרי אחיי לכ"ה זנוויל מז ז"ל הנ"ל וי"א ולאחיו כ' ליזר הנ"ל מכח ירושת
7. אמם מ' הינדלה אל' המנוח כ' זלמן לנדויא ז"ל בכן שייך החצי מחצי בית
8. הנ"ל דהיינו רביעית מבית שלם הנ"ל {שנפל לבעלה} וכל הנ"ל ואין כח ב
9. ביד האשה מ' אסתר הנ"ל לתת לבנה החתן הנ"ל רק רביעית מבית שלם
10. הנ"ל שנפל לבעלה וי"א וב"כ ולא החצי בית הנ"ל גם תבע כהר"מ הנ"ל
11. בהרשאות הנ"ל מאחר שלפי הנ"ל אין מגיע לה בבית הנ"ל מכח בעלה ז"ל
12. הנ"ל רק רביעית והיא דרה בכל חצי בית הנ"ל זה שנים עשר שנים ולא
13. נתנה פרוטה אחת שכירות לכ"ל[4] הנ"ל בעד רביעית בית שלם המגיע
14. לו על חלק ירושתו בכן תבע כהר"מ שישלם האשה הנ"ל שכירות מי"ב שנים
15. מרביעי' בית שלם המגיע לכ"ל לחלק ירושתו ויכירו וישומו הב"ד לפי ראות –
16. עניהם כמה שכירות שתתן האשה מ' אסתר הנ"ל ועל משך זמן הנ"ל לכ"ל הנ"ל
17. וה"ה החתן כ' יוזפא בן המנוח כ"ה זנוויל הנ"ל בהרשאת אמו מ' אסתר
18. הנ"ל ובמעמדה השיב על טענות כהר"מ הנ"ל והציע לפנינו גומ[ף][5] שטר
19. מכירה שמכרו אם זקנתו מ' הינדלה והדר בעלה כ' זלמן לנדויא
20. ז"ל הנ"ל רביעי' מבית שלם הנ"ל לאביו כה"ז[6] ז"ל הנ"ל ההוקם ר"ח אלול

---

1. אולי 'מלמד זקן' (ר' אבני זכרון, מס' 3755). יש כאן משחק על שם המשפחה, מז.
2. בן המנוח
3. כבוד הרב משה
4. לכבוד ליזר
5. כנראה שצ"ל 'גוף'
6. כבוד הרב זנוויל

21. תפ״ה לפק ולא הניחה אחריהם בעזבונו רק רביעי׳ מבית שלם הנ״ל ואין
22. לכ׳ ליזר הנ״ל תביעה מחמת חלקו מכח ירושת אמו רק חלקו ברביעי׳ בית הנ״ל ולא
23. מגיע ע״ח ר{״}ק חלק שמינית מבית שלם הנ״ל עוד טוען כ׳ יוזפא הנ״ל בהרשאות אמו
24. הנ״ל מאחר שכ׳ ליזר הנ״ל רוצה לזכות מה שמגיע לו ע״[ח] מירושת אמו ז״ל הנ״ל בכן מחויב
25. כ״ל הנ״ל לשלם ג״כ כפי חלקו החצי מהחובות שהניח אחריהם אמו ובעלה ז״ל הנ״ל והציע
26. לפנינו כי׳[1] הנ״ל שט״ח שחייבת אם זקנתו מ׳ הינדלה הנ״ל אם האחי׳ הנ״ל לנכדה
27. יתמי

סב ע״א

1. ב״ה
2. יתמי המנוח כ״ה זנוויל ז״ל הנ״ל סך שני מאות זהו׳ לשלם ולפרוע שעה א׳ קודם מותה
3. ההקום[2] ד״י מרחשון תקי״ב בכן תובע מן כ״ל[3] הנ״ל באם רוצה לזכות חצי מעזבון שהניח
4. אמו אחריו שישלם ג״כ החצי משט״ח הנ״ל דהיינו מאה זהו׳ קרן וגם רווחי׳ מכ״ג שני׳
5. עוד טוען כ״י[4] הנ״ל מאחר ששילמה אמו מ׳ אסתר הנ״ל על שט״ח מסך מאה רט שהי׳ חייב
6. כ׳ זלמן לנדויא באוה״ב[5] לשלם לכ״ה משה שיף ההוקם יו׳ ויו יוד אלול תע״ו לפק לערך מאה
7. זהו׳ במזומני׳ ועל המותרות נתנה ח״כ מידה שהיא תשלם ג״כ לזמ[ני׳] והאשה מ׳ אסתר
8. הנ״ל הוכרחה לעשות כן לפי שכ׳ איצק שיף יורשו של כ״ה משה שיף הנ״ל שהי׳ בידו
9. שט״ח הנ״ל הי׳ מוחה בהאשה מ׳ אסתר הנ״ל זה לפני י״ב שני׳ שרצה לכנוס בחצי
10. בית הנ״ל לדור בה עד שהתרצה א״ע לשלם שט״ח הנ״ל וכנ״ל ושט״ח הושליש
11. ביד כ״ה כ״ה[6] אנשיל פפאן כץ עד שתשלם כל דמי שט״ח הנ״ל בכן תובע כי׳ הנ״ל
12. שכ[״ל] הנ״ל ישלם לא״מו[7] מ׳ אסתר החצי מסך מאה רט דהיינו חמשי׳ רט ושט״ח הנ״ל הציע לפנינו
13. התורני כ״ה אנשיל פפאן הנ״ל עוד הציע לפנינו כי׳ הנ״ל כתב ראי׳ מן כ׳ זלמן פולדא משותף
14. בבית הנ״ל ההוקם ר״ח כסליו תקכ״ג ששילמה אמו מ׳ אסתר הנ״ל לכ׳ זלמן הנ״ל סך נ״ח זהו׳ זץ[8] מחמת
15. קרונדצינץ מהעבר מה שהגיע על חצי בית הנ״ל וגם הביא לפנינו כ״ז[9] הנ״ל שאמר ואמר שדבריו
16. כני׳ הם {בכן תובע} ובאמת הוא ח״י בכן תובע כ״י הנ״ל שישלם כ״ל הנ״ל לאמו הנ״ל מה שמגיע
17. ע״ח דהיינו ארבעה עשר זהו׳ ל״א צל והוא חלק רביעי׳ מהסך חמשי׳ ושמונה זהו׳ זץ הנ״ל עוד תבע

---

1. כבוד יוזפא
2. צ״ל ׳ההוקם׳
3. כבוד ליזר
4. כבוד יוזפא
5. ר׳ י׳ בכרך, חות יאיר, ח״א, ס׳ עח וגם י׳ ריישר, ספר שאלות ותשובות שבות יעקב, חלק א, העלי תע״ט, ס׳ קנה.
6. כפילות במקור
7. גרשיים במקור, כנראה בטעות (ר׳ לעיל סא ע״ב, שורה 17).
8. ז צ״ל
9. כבוד זלמן

18. כ״י הנ״ל באשר שאמו מ׳ אסתר הנ״ל שילמה קרונדצנץ כל שנה ושנה מן חצי בית הנ״ל משנת
19. תקך״ג וע״ע שהוא י״ג שנים והיינו כל שנה צריך ליתן מן בית שלם קרונדצנץ סך שנים עשר
20. זהו׳ ורביעי׳ או[י]ף דעם ך״[ד] זהו׳ פוס ולאחר שירדנו החשבן מגיע ע״ח שמינית מן כ״ל הנ״ל
21. במשך י״ג שנים הנ״ל אויף דעם כ״ד זהו׳ פוס עשרים ואחד זהו׳ מ״א צל גם תובע כ״י
22. הנ״ל והציע לפנינו חשבן ממה שהוציאו אמו הנ״ל ומשותפה בבית הנ״ל ה״ה כ׳ זלמן פולדא הנ״ל מזמן
23. שבאת אמו בחצי בית הנ״ל ע״ע בבדק הבית ולפי חשבון זה מגיע על חלק אמו שהוציאה סך ששים ואחד
24. זהו׳ ז׳ צל בכן תובע מן כ״ל שישלם לאמו חלק רביעי׳ מסך דמי בדק הבית הנ״ל והביא לפנינו ה״ה
25. כ׳ זלמן פולדא הנ״ל ואמר שאמת הוא שהוציאו ביחד ב״כ כפי הנזכר בחשבן עוד טען כ״י
26. הנ״ל ואמר מאחר שאמו זקנה מ׳ הינדלה הניח׳ אחרי׳ בשעת פטירתו שני בני׳ בשמם דודו כ׳ ליזר
27. הנ״ל וכ׳ זעליגמן מלבד אביו {מ}כ״ה זנוויל ז״ל הנ״ל שמת כבר בחיי׳ והוא שאותו נמצא ברביעית
28. בית הנ״ל שהניח׳ אם זקנתו מ׳ הינדלה בעזבונו וכנ״ל הי׳ שלשה יורשי׳ כל אחד יורש שלישת
29. מרביעית

סב ע״ב

1. ב״ה
2. מרביעית בית הנ״ל רק לאח״כ שנעדר גם כ׳ זעליגמן בלי ז״ק חזר ונפל חלקו שליש מרביעי׳
3. בית הנ״ל לירושה לפני דודו כ׳ ליזר ולכי״י הנ״ל מכח אביו כ״ה זנוו[י]ל הנ״ל וכי׳ הציע לפנינו
4. שני ח״כ מדודו כ׳ זעליגמן ז״ל הנ״ל שהי׳ חייב לאמו מ׳ אסתר הנ״ל אחד מסך עשרי׳ זהו׳ ההוקם –
5. ג׳ מנחם תקי״ג פראלא[עג]יהר׳ טוב תשרי תקי״ד על יריד פסח הסמוך תקי״ד ואחד מסך חמשה
6. עשר זהו׳ ההוקם יו׳ ג׳ ויו מרחשון תקט״ו העולה יחד שלושים וחמשה זהו׳ בכן אם דודו
7. כ[ל]׳ הנ״ל רוצה לזכות בחצי ורביעי׳ בית הנ״ל והוא מכח ירושת דודו כ׳ זעליגמן ז״ל הנ״ל
8. ג״כ מחיוב כ״ל הנ״ל ג״כ לשלם החצי מסך דמי ח״כ הנ״ל שהוא שבעה עשר זהו׳ וחצי גם תבע כ״י
9. הנ״ל בהרשאת הנ״ל שכ׳ ליזר הנ״ל ישלם החצי מהחוב מה שהי׳ חייבי׳ אמו זקנתו מ׳ הינדלה –
10. ובעלה כ״ז[2] לנדויא לגובי׳ יצו כיון שבא לירש החצי מה שהניח׳ אחריהם ועל מה שתבע כה״מ[3]

---

1. ולכבוד יוזפא
2. כבוד זלמן
3. כבוד הרב משה

11. או[י]ך הנ"ל מחמת שכירות הבית מרביעי' בית שדרה בה אמו מ' אסתר הנ"ל משך שני' עשר שני' בחצי
12. בית הנ"ל שתשלם אמו שכירות הבית {מחוב מרביעי'}לפי שומא שישומא הב"ד השיב כ"י הנ"ל
13. באשר שהאריך כבר בטענותיו שרביעי' מבית הנ"ל הי' שייך כבר לאביו ז"ל הנ"ל לחלוטין מחודש
14. אלול שנת תפ"ה לפק וכנ"ל ואביו חורגו כ"ז ואשתו אמו ז"ל הי' דרי בכל חצי בית גם משנת
15. תפ"ה ועד עת פטירתם שהוא לערך כ"ה שני' ולא נתנו שום פרוטה אחת לאביו כ"ה זנוויל
16. ז"ל הנ"ל בכן תובע כ"י הנ"ל בהרשאת אמו הנ["ל] מרביעית בית הנ"ל ממשך זמן הנ"ל ויכירו
17. וישומו הב"ד כמה שכירות מגיע לה לישלם כל הנ"ל החצי מדמי שכירות זה המוטל על עזבונם
18. הנ"ל מאחר שרוצה דודו כ"ל הנ"ל לירש החצי מכח ירושת אמו ז"ל הנ"ל וה"ה כ"ה משה אויך
19. בהרשאת הנ"ל השיב וטוען [על] שטר מכירה על רביע' בית הנ"ל שהציע לפנינו כי'
20. הנ"ל שלאו שטר שכה"זי הנ"ל לא הי' לו חזקה אצל הגובין יצו ו[מעש]ה הי' [נו]תנם לו שטר
21. מכירה כדי שיהי' לו לחזקה אצל הגובין יצו אבל לא מכרו לו רביעית בית הנ"ל
22. והא ראי' שלא נזכר בתוך שטר מכירה הסך דמי מכירה וגם יש ראי' ממה שהונח
23. שטר ביד גובי' ואין ביד כה"ז וי"א ועוד ראי' שמשנת תקי"ב עד שנת תקך"ג לקחו
24. הגובי' שכירות מחצי בית וגם יש תיקון הקלה[2] שעל כל מכירה צריך להיו' חלטה[3] ביד
25. לוקח בכן יציע כי' הנ"ל להחלוטה לפני ב"ד ואם לא יציע שטר בטל הוא כנ"ל ועל
26. מה שתובע כי' הנ"ל דמי שכירות הבית מן כ"ה שני' מחמת שדרין בחצי בית הנ"ל כ' זלמן
27. לנדויא וא[ש]תו ז"ל הנ"ל וכנ"ל השיב כה"[מ] כיון שכבר טוען שאינו ממש בשטר
28. מכירה הנ"ל וכנ"ל בכן אינו יוכל לתבוע שכירות ממה שאינו שלו ואף אם השטר
29. מכירה יה[י]' בתקפו טעון כהר"[מ][4] שמא נפרע כבר דמי שכירות הנ"ל ועל מה
30. שתבע כ"י הנ"ל מחמת שט"ח מן שני מאות זהו' מן אמו זקנתה הנ"ל מ' הינדלה
31. הנ"ל

סג ע"א

1. ב"ה
2. הנ"ל ונכדה יתמי כ"ה זנוויל הנ"ל וכנ"ל השיב כהר"מ הנ"ל שאפשר שיוכל להיות שהאשה
3. מ' הינדלה הנ"ל עדיין לא נשבעת שבוע' כתובת' ותוס' המוטל עלי' בכן לא חל שבועדה[5] על רביעית
4. בית הנ"ל וכ"י הנ"ל השיב ע"ז שוודאי נשבעת אמו זקנה ז"ל הנ"ל על כתובת' כנהוג פה והביא

---

1. כבוד הרב זנוויל
2. צ"ל 'הקהלה'
3. כנראה שצ"ל 'החלטה'
4. כבוד הרב משה
5. כנראה שצ"ל 'שעבודה'

5. לפנינו התורני כ"ה ישראל פלומבורג[1] מק"ק אויביבאך ואמר כה"י[2] הנ"ל שיש תחת ידו כתב ראי' מהשבעת
6. כתובה שעשת' האשה מ' הינדלה ז"ל הנ"ל ועל מה שתבע כ"י הנ"ל מחמת שט"ח מסך מאה רט וכנ"ל השיב
7. כהר"מ מאחר שכ' ליזר הנ"ל לא הי' ידע מזה השטר בכן לא הי' לה להאשה מ' אסתר הנ"ל לפרוע שט"ח הנ"ל שלא
8. מדעתא ומה ששילמה עשת' מעצמה ואין עליו לשלם לה אפי' פרוטה אחת לפירעון שט"ח הנ"ל / ועל מה שתבע
9. כ"י הנ"ל מחמת קרונדצינץ השיב כהר"מ שאמת הוא שכ"ל[3] הנ"ל מחויב לשלם ג"כ חלקו קרונדצינץ רק שתנכה
10. האשה מ' אסתר הנ"ל סך דמי קרונדצינץ הנ"ל ממה שמחויבת היא לשלם מ' שכירות הבית לכ"ל הנ"ל ממשך
11. י"ב שנים וכנ"ל ומה שתבע כ"י הנ"ל מחמת ח"כ מדודו כ' זעליגמן ז"ל הנ"ל השיב כהר"מ מאן ייא[מ]ר
12. שחתמת ידו ממש הוא וגם שמא פרע ומה שתבע כ"י הנ"ל שישלם כ' ליזר הנ"ל החצי מה שהוא חייב'
13. הזוג כ' זלמן לנדויא ואמו מ' הינדלה ז"ל הנ"ל גובי' השיב כהר"מ ששיעבוד הגובי' הוא על קרקאות[4]
14. של כ"ל הנ"ל והפירות שייכי' לכ' ליזר על כל ימי חיי' ומחמת דמי בדק הבית שהוציאה האשה מ' אסתר
15. הנ"ל ש[ת]בע כ"י הנ"ל מן כ"ל הנ"ל השיב כהר"מ שתשבע כמה הוציא' ויתן כ"ל הנ"ל חלקו המגיע עליו
16. והאריכו הצדדי' הנ"ל בטענותיהם ובתשובתיהם זה מול זה וזה מול זה בכל פרט ופרט כמבואר בק"ה
17. המונח לפנינו ובאשר שהצדדי' הנ"ל חתמו עצמם בתוקף קומפריס בח"ח ובקנס סך מסוים לאשר
18. ולקיי' הפס"ד מה שיצא מאתנו וגם נתנו הצדדי' הנ"ל עיניהם עלינו ב"ד ח"מ בענין תביע' דמי שכירות
19. הבית שיש ביניהם והיינו מה שתבע כ"י הנ"ל בהרשאת הנ"ל מן כ"ל הנ"ל דמי שכירות ממשך כ"ה שנים
20. שדרו הזוג כז"ל[5] ואשתו ז"ל הנ"ל וכנ"ל וכן מה שתבע כ"ל הנ"ל מהאשה מ' אסתר הנ"ל דמי שכירות ממשך

---

1. כנראה הרב ישראל בלומבורג (ר' מזכיר נשמות, מס' 404, 406).
2. כבוד הרב ישראל
3. שכבוד ליזר
4. צ"ל 'קרקעות'
5. כבוד זלמן לנדויא

21. י״ב שנים וכנ״ל לעשות פשר דבר ביניהם ומה שיצא מאתנו דך פ״ד[1] על שני תביעות קבלו עליהם הצדדי׳
22. הנ״ל בכל חומר ובקנס סך מסויים כנזכר בקומפרמיס המונח אצלינו בכן נזדקקנו להם ועיינו
23. ודקדקנו הדק היטיב בטענותיהם ובתשובתיהם ובשטרות שהציע לפנינו ומצאנו ששטר
24. מכירה שהציע לפנינו כ״י הנ״ל {של..ך} שמכרו האשה מ׳ הינדלה והדר בעלה כז״ל הנ״ל רביעית
25. מבית שלם הנ״ל לבנם כה״ז הנ״ל הוא בכחו ובגבורתם וכתוקף כל שטרי מכירת –
26. העשוי׳ בישראל ואין ממש במה שבאן[2] שההר״מ הנ״ל לבטל השטר מכירה [הנ]״ל ומעתה
27. אינו מגיע לכ׳ ליזר הנ״ל מכח ירושת אמו ז״ל הנ״ל בבית הנ״ל רק חלק שמינית מבית שלם
28. הנ״ל ועל מה שתבע כהר״מ הנ״ל ברשאת[3] הנ״ל דמי שכירות מהאשה מ״א[4] הנ״ל בשביל שררה
29. בחצי בית הנ״ל משך י״ב שנים מצאנו דרך פשר דבר לאחר ש[ינ]וכה האשה מ״א ...
30. סך דמי

סג ע״ב

1. ב״ה
2. סך דמי קרונדצינץ ששילמה כדת לכ״ז[5] פולדא הנ״ל ר״ח כסליו תקך״ג גם על חלק שמינית
3. לשלם על כ״ל הנ״ל וכנ״ל וגם מה שהוציאה לאח״כ כל שנה ושנה משנת תקך״ג ע״ע
4. שהוא לערך י״ג שנים וכנ״ל על כל חצי בית ה[נ]״ל ונכלל בתוכה חלק שמינית מן כ״ל הנ״ל
5. וגם אחר שינוכה האשה מרת אסתר מה שהוציאו דמי בדק הבית ג״כ על חלק שמינית
6. של כל הנ״ל וכמו שהציע לפנינו חשבן וכנ״ל וגם לאחר [ש]ינוכה מחמת מה –
7. שמצאנו דרך פשר דבר על מה שחייב׳ עזבון כ׳ זלמן ואשתו ז״ל הנ״ל לשלם לה
8. להאשה מ׳ אסתר הנ״ל מחמת תב[י]עת שכירות הבית מרביע בית ממשך כ״ה שנים שדרו
9. בו כז״ל הנ״ל ואשתו וגם מ[׳] תביעת החצי מחמת שני ח״כ מ״כ[6] זעליגמן מַז הנ״ל וכנ״ל
10. מצאנו שנשארה עדיין התחייבות על האשה מ״א[7] הנ״ל לשלם ולפרוע מחמת שכירות הבית
11. בשביל חלק שמינית סך ששי׳ זהו׳ ומעתה אם כ׳ ליזר הנ״ל חצי לזכות ולהחזיק עצמו במה
12. שמגיע לו בבית א׳ בתורת ירושתה מאמו מ׳ הינדלה יכול לירש חלק שמינית
13. מבית שלם הנ״ל נגד זה מחויב כ״ל הנ״ל לשלם ליתמי כה״ז[8] הנ״ל מחמת
14. דמי שט״ח מ[ס]ך שני מאות זהו׳ סך מאה זהובי׳ ע״ח וגם מחויב לשלם כ״ל הנ״ל להאשה
15. מ׳ אסתר הנ״ל מחמת מה ששילמה שט״ח מן משה שיף מסך מאה רט ומגיע ע״ח כ״ל הנ״ל

---

1. כנראה שצ״ל ׳דרך פ<שר> ד<בר>׳
2. אולי צ״ל ׳שטען׳
3. צ״ל ׳בהרשאת׳
4. מרת אסתר
5. כבוד זלמן
6. מן כבוד
7. מרת אסתר
8. כבוד הרב זנוויל

16. לשלם חמשי׳ רט וינוכה מזה ששי׳ זהו׳ שחייבת האשה מ׳ אסתר הנ״ל מחמת שכירות
17. הבית וכנ״ל וגם מוטי׳ על כ״ל הנ״ל לשלם החצי מהחוב שחייבי׳ כ׳ זלמן לנדויא
18. ואשתו אמו ז״ל להאלופי׳ הקציני׳ גובין יצו יצא מאתנו יו׳ ג׳ ט״ו סיון קהל״ת לפק
19. הק׳ אברהם טריר כהן
20. הק׳ זנוויל טראך
21. הק׳ חיי׳ בפו״מ כ״ה יוזפא גונדרשהיי׳

No. 58

Fols. 64a–64b; Wednesday evening, 21 June 1775

One-sixth of a plot where a house had once stood on the Kranich Hinterhaus lot was sold by Model Hass for 152 guldens to his daughter Merle, widow of Moses Braunschweig.[1] Merle had purchased a third of the land on the Kranich Hinterhaus lot just a few weeks earlier (see no. 55). As in other sales, there was a public announcement of the sale in the synagogues. The rights and obligations of the buyer are itemized.

סד ע״א

1. ב״ה
2. חלק שישית מן פלאטץ שהי׳ עומד עליו בית פנימי צור הינדר קראניך
3. דהיינו אותו בית שהי׳ עומד על צד ימין בכניסה מהרחוב מבתי׳
4. הפנימי׳ אותו חלק שישית פלאטץ הנ״ל שהי׳ שייך לה״ה כ׳ מאדל הז
5. יצו הוכרז בבהכ״י {..} וחדש זמן זמני׳ טובא ע״פ כ׳ מאדל הז
6. הנ״ל שכל מי שרוצה לקנותו יבא לפנינו ב״ד גם הוכרז לפנינו
7. ב״ד ח״מ עד שיפסקו המוסיפי׳ ולא הי׳ שום אחד שהי׳ פוסק
8. כפי מה שפסקה האשה הקצינה מ׳ מערלה אל׳ המנוח מה״[ר] משה [.]
9. ברונשוויג ז״ל[2] בכן מכרנו שישית פלאטץ הנ״ל להקצינה מ׳ מערלה
10. הנ״ל בעד סך מאה {ש}חמשי׳ ושני׳ זהו׳ לשלם אותם אין קונפונט[/]
11. ציאהנש מינץ אויף דען כ״ד זהו׳ פוס והיינו לשלם שליש מסך דמי
12. מכירה הנ״ל תיכף בשעת מסירת החלוטה ושני שלישי׳ הנותרי׳
13. מסך דמי {ר} מכירה הנ״ל תשלם על ששה חצאי שני׳ רצופי׳ וסמוכי׳ זא״ז
14. מיו׳ מסירת החלוטה ומחויבת האשה מ׳ מערלה הנ״ל ליתן ששה ח״כ
15. על זמני׳ הנ״ל גם נשאר אותו חלק שישית פלאטץ הנ״ל לאפותיקו
16. מפורש שלא יצא מחזקת מרא קמא כל זמן שלא נתפרע אפילו אחד

---

1. See Horovitz, *Abney zikkaron*, no. 3547.
2. במצבת מערלה כתוב לגבי בעלה, ׳ג״ע מהור״ר משה ברוינשוויג סג״ל׳ וכן בספר הזכרונות, רנב ע״ב.

17. מן הח״כ הנ״ל ויתוקן ע״ז שטר אפותיקו ע״י נ״ה כנהוג ומעתה
18. אותו שישית פלאטץ הנ״ל שהי׳ שייך מקדמת לה״ה כ׳ מאדל הַז [יצו]
19. שייך מעכשיו להאשה הקצינה מ׳ מערלה הנ״ל וי״א וב״כ לחלוטין
20. גמורין ולצמיתת עלמן כל ארכו ורחבו עם כל חזקותיו וזכיותיו
21. ומוצאיו ומובאיו ומצריו ומרתפות וחצריו עומקא ורומא מ
22. מתהום ארעא עד רום רקיע וכמו שהי׳ שייך מקדמת לה״ה
23. כ׳ מאדל הז יצו בלי שום שיור כלל ורשאי האשה מ מערלה
24. הנ״ל וי״א וב״כ לעשות עם שישית פלאטץ הנ״ל לקנות ולהרוס להוריש
25. ולהנחיל להחליף להשכין למכור ולהשכר וליתן במתנה כאות
26. נפשה וכרצונה ככל אינש דרשאי לעשות בשלו בלי מוחה כלל
27. ול[א]חר שנתפרע כל הח״כ שייך מעכשיו חלק שישית פלאטץ הנ״ל
28. להאשה

סד ע״ב

1. ב״ה
2. להאשה היקרה מ׳ מערלה הנ״ל וי״א וב״כ בשופי גמור בלי שום
3. עורר וטוען כלל יהי׳ המערער מי שיהי׳ הן רבי׳ או יחיד
4. יהי׳ טענה שיהי׳ או בכל אופן שיהי׳ מכל מה שהפה יוכל
5. לדבר והלב לחשב ולהרהר וכל מי שיערער אחר מכירה הנ״ל
6. יהי׳ מי שיהי׳ או באיזה אופן שיהי׳ דבריו בטלי׳ ומבוטלי׳
7. כחרס הנשבר כאפס וכאין יחשב לא שרירן ולא קיימין ולא
8. יהי׳ חלין כלל וכלל וכטוען אחר מעשה ב״ד הגדול ולא
9. יזדקק שום קהל או ב״ד יצו או שום משפט שבעולם לדברי
10. המערער הן בדאה[2] והן בדי[3] כי דברי המערער הן בטלי׳
11. ומבוטלי׳ באשר שנעשה הכל ע״פ וברצון כ׳ מאדל הז הנ״ל
12. וכתבנו וחתמנו זאת בתוקף מעשה ב״ד ובכח ב״ד יפה
13. להיות ביד הלוקח לה״ה האשה מ׳ מערלה אל׳ המנוח מה״[ר]
14. משה ברונשוויג ז״ל הנ״ל וי״א וב״כ לעדות ולזכות ולראי׳
15. שיעמוד אותו חלק שישית פלאטץ הנ״ל עם כל חזקותיו
16. וזכיותיו ביד לוקח הנ״ל וי״א וב״כ בלי שום מוחה כלל נעשה
17. פה פפדמיין[4] אור ליו׳ ה׳ כ״ד סיון קהלת לפק
18. ה״ק אברהם טריר כהן | הק׳ מאיר {שי} בלא״א כ׳ זלמן שיף |
19. ה״ק חיים בפו״מ כ יוזפא גונדרשהיי׳ שליטא

---

1. מרת
2. בדיני אומות העולם
3. בדיני ישראל
4. פרנקפורט דמיין

Fol. 65a is blank.

No. 59

Fols. 65b–66b; Tuesday 1 August 1775

On Monday 2 Tammuz (5)666 (9 June 1766), Leb Kann made a deathbed will wherein he ordered that funds from his estate be given to his heirs and that 13,000 guldens be used to create a perpetual fund the income from which was to be used for charitable purposes.[1] Three guardians were appointed to oversee the funds, one of whom, Leb's brother Jacob, managed the assets. In November 1774 Jacob Kann died. An examination of his accounts revealed that Leb's funds had never been invested and that Jacob, who had been a communal leader and was honored at the time of his death, had misappropriated assets. Jacob himself died deep in debt and Leb's estate had no possibility of full recovery.[2] When a second guardian also died, the lone surviving guardian approached the court asking that it decide who should suffer the losses: the charitable causes or Leb's son, Ber, who had yet to receive his portion of the estate. The position of the charities was argued by three individuals who were often members of the court: Rabbis Meʾir Schiff, Abraham Trier, and Zanvil Trach.

The court calculated that 39,000 guldens were owed to Ber. The court ruled that 75% of all assets of Leb Kann's estate, whether held by the guardian or whether in Jacob Kann's estate, should be given to Ber Kann, and 25% to the charitable causes (except for rent income due on the family home that was exclusively Ber's because he owned the house). Leb had stipulated that the charitable funds were to be used for (1) distribution to the needy before Passover, (2) support of those studying Torah and needy brides, and (3) distribution to needy family members and those studying Torah on the anniversary of Leb's death. The court instructed the guardian how to divide the funds between each of these charitable causes. The court also ordered that two more guardians immediately be appointed to oversee Leb's estate. Also see nos. 61, 88, Appendix 1, the *Responsa* of Rabbi Pinḥas Horowitz, no. 69, YIVO MS. RG 128 (folder 77–78), fols. 46b–47a, and the introduction, pages 84–86.

1. According to his gravestone (Horovitz, *Abney zikkaron*, no. 3240), Leb Kann died that very day. Information on the epitaph partially corroborates what is written here. Regarding the perpetual fund, see Dietz, p. 423.
2. See the entry in the Frankfurt *Memorbuch*, fol. 247b.

סה ע״ב

1. בס״ד
2. הן הקריב לפנינו ה״ה ג״ע האלוף והקצין כ״ה פער קליף יצו אפטרופוס של היותם[1] ה״ה הב״ח כ׳ פער[2]
3. בן גיסו פו״מ המנוח כ״ה ליב במוהר׳ איצק קן ז״ל במעמד גיסו של הב״ח כ׳ פער הנ״ל ה״ה האלוף
4. הקצין התורני כ״ה מאדל ברונשוויג סג״ל והציע לפנינו {העתק מקודם מ}גוף צוואת שכ״מ של
5. כ״ה ליב ז״ל הנ״ל הנעשה יו׳ ב׳ ב׳ תמוז תקכ״ו לפ״ק והנה באשר שעכשיו אחר פטירת
6. חבירא האפטרופסי׳ ה״ה ג״ה המנוח כ״ה אייזיק רייז ז״ל וה״ה פו״מ ה״ר יעקב במוהר׳ איצק קן
7. ז״ל לא נשאר בעזבון כ״ה ליב הנ״ל רק חלק חלק היותם[3] הנ״ל מה שמגיע לו ע״פ צוואה הנ״ל מחמת
8. נדוניתו עם חלק ירושתו כי שארי יורשי׳ המנוח כ״ה ליב הנ״ל כולם קיבלו כבר חלקם המגיע
9. להם ע״פ צוואה הנ״ל עם חלק ירושתו גם נשאר עדיין בעזבון הנ״ל סך מעות שצווה המנוח
10. כ״ה ליב הנ״ל בהצוואה הנ״ל ליתן אותו ביד בטוח לקיים לדורי דורת ולעשות מהרווחים
11. דבר טוב המבואר שם העולה יחד לסך שלשה עשר אלפי׳ זהו׳ ואף שנאמר שם שקודם
12. כל יותן ביד בטוח סך חמשת אלפי׳ זהו׳ וכו׳ גם אחר שיקויים מה שפסק לבניו ולבנותיו
13. קודם שירדו לנחלה יותן עוד סך שמונת אלפי׳ זהובי׳ ביד בטוח מ״מ אמר כהרר[4] פער
14. הנ״ל בשם ר״י[5] הנ״ל שלא הי׳ עוברי׳ על בל תאחר לפי דעתו במה שלא קיימו דברי המת
15. כהווייתן הואיל ולפי דבריהם נתנו כל שנה לדבר טוב כפי הצוואה הנ״ל והנה אחר ש
16. שנפטר ר׳ יעקב הנ״ל נמצא בחשבונות של העזבו[נו]ת כ״ה ליב הנ״ל שנשאר ביד ר״י הנ״ל
17. סך עצום קרוב לעשרי׳ ושלשת אלפי׳ זהו׳ קצת על ח״כ מה שנתחייב כבר לאחיו הנ״ל על
18. רווחי׳ מימי חיים חיותו וקצת ממה שהחזיק בידו אחת אל אחת אחר פטירת כ״ה ליב הנ״ל
19. מעזבונו וידוע ומפורס׳ עכשיו שר״י הנ״ל נשאר אחריו בעל חוב עצום ואין עזבון מגיע ל
20. לפרוע כל חובותיו ואפשר אפילו עד החצי לא יגיעו בכן ביקשו מאתנו להזדקק להם (ולדון)[6] על
21. מי יוחל ההפסד מה שיופסד מהחוב {של} שחייב ר״י הנ״ל בעזבון הנ״ל ולא יגיע לפרעון
22. אם על הדבר טוב הנ״ל או על היותם[7] הנ״ל גם שאלו כ״ה פער הנ״ל באשר שנמצא בעזבון
23. הנ״ל עוד חובות שהמה בחזקת אבודים לדון על מי יגיע ההפסד והנה ה״ה התורני כה׳

1. צ״ל ׳היתום׳ וכן כתוב בכ״י יווא.
2. ר׳ דושינסקי, מזכיר נשמות, עמ׳ 60-61, המזכיר שבמותו בער גם השאיר כספים לצדקה.
3. צ״ל ׳היתום׳ וכן כתוב בכ״י יווא.
4. כבוד הרב רבי
5. רבי יעקב
6. תוספת מעל השורה
7. צ״ל ׳היתום׳

24. מאיר מז בהרשאת האפטרופוס כ"ה פער הנ"ל טען לפנינו (לזכות היותם[1] כ' פער הנ"ל)[2] באשר שר"י הנ"ל הי' נותן
25. הדבר טוב כל שנה ושנה בכן אותו מעות שחייב ר"י הכל יחשב לגוף דבר טוב ויהי' כל
26. ההפסד על הד"ט ולפחות יפסיד לפי החשבון באשר שעדיין לא נפרש חלק היותם[3] מן חלק
27. דב"ט גם טעון באשר שמבואר בהצוואה הנ"ל שפסק שפסק[4] נדוניא לבנו הנ"ל ואחר שיותן
28. כנ"ל אח"כ יותן סך שמונות אלפי' זהו' צורך דבר ט דבר טוב[5] המבואר שם בכן עכ"פ
29. יש להיתום בנדוניא שלו דין קדימה על הד"ט של שמונת אלפי' הנ"ל וה"ה האלופי' הדייני'
30. ה"ה כ"ה אברהם טריר כ"ץ וכ"ה זנוויל טרך וכ"ה מאיר שיף הם הגובי' בשמותם בהצוואה
31. להיות תוך לומדי תורה שיש לו חלקם מן רווחי' של ד"ט ההוא הם (עמדו)[6] להפך בזכות דבר טוב
32. ולטעון בעדו והשיבו על דברי הרר[7] מאיר באשר שבצוואה{ומה}מבואר שם שקודם

סו ע"א

1. בס"ד
2. שקודם ירדו לנחלה יותן הד"ט של שמונת אלפי' זהו' הנ"ל וכבר הי' יורדים לנחלה בכן נשאר חוב
3. וד"ט על עזבון הנ"ל בחוב גמור על מה שנטלן בתורת ירושה העולה לסך עצום יותר מגוף דב"ט
4. ואחר שהאריכו בטענותיהם נזדקקנו להם ודקדקנו בלשון הצוואה והנה אחרי שהאפטרופוס
5. כ"ה פער הנ"ל הציעו לפנינו חשבונות ופנקסאות ואינ[פ]וטאריוס[8] מעזבון גיסו המנוח כ"ה ליב הנ"ל
6. וממה שנשאר עכשיו בעזבון הנ"ל ח"כ גלאנטרי יובעלין וספרי' מטלטלין אובליגאצ[י]אהן מחצר ד"ש[9] יר"ה
7. והנה אינפוטאריום ומה שהניח לפנינו האפטרופוס הו"ה ג"ץ כ"ה פער קליף מכל מה שיש כעת
8. בעזבון המנוח כ"ה ליב קן ז"ל מה ששייך להיותם[10] פער ולד"ט ונמצא חלק מן אובליגאצאהן מחצר

1. צ"ל 'היתום'
2. תוספת מעל השורה
3. צ"ל 'היתום'
4. כפילות במקור
5. כפילות במקור
6. תוספת מעל השורה
7. הרב רבי
8. צ"ל 'אינפנטאריום'
9. דער שררה(?)
10. צ"ל 'להיתום'

9. ד"ש יר"ה עולה לסך אחד עשר אלפי' ושלוש מאות זהו' מזומני' וח"כ שיש תחת יד האפטרופס כ
10. כה"פי הנ"ל עולה לסך ששת אלפי' מאה וחמשי' וששה זהו' גלאנטריע ויובעלין שיש תחת יד ה
11. האפטרופס הנ"ל השוה לפי דבריו סך שני אלפי' ושמוני' וארבע זהו' מה שמונח בעין בעזבון
12. ר"י מעזבון ר"ל[2] הנ"ל מן סחורות ברוך זהוב[3] שטרות ח"כ מלבד ח"כ משכירות הבית על ר' מאיר
13. ר"ש[4] עולה לפי דבריו סך ד' אלפי' ושולוש מאות וחמישים זהו' מה שנשאר ר"י הנ"ל חייב בעזבון
14. כה"ל[5] הנ"ל עולה לסך עשרי' ושלשת אלפי' שני מאות ושלושים זהו' עוד יש חובות אחרי' שהם
15. בתורת אבודים עולה לסך שני אלפי' מאה וששה עשר זהו' קופת כסף עומד בעין בעזבון
16. ר"י הנ"ל ספרי' ומטלטלים מלבד קרקעות וכוס של זהוב ושארי זהוב הנפרטים בצוואה ועיינו
17. ודקדקנו הדק היטיב בחשבון מה שמגיע להיתום כ' פער הנ"ל ע"פ הצוואה הנ"ל הן מחמת
18. נדוני' הן מחמת חלק ירושתו עם רווחי' שהי' עולה עד עכשיו ובאשר שאי אפשר לדקדק
19. בחשבונו עד תומין ועוכלא העלינו לפי דעתינו מתוך החשבונות שמגיע להיות[6] פער הנ"ל
20. מעזבון אביו כ"ה ליב ז"ל סך שלשים ותשעה אלפי' זהובי' מלבד ממה שמבואר בהצוואה ש
21. שהקרקעות והזהוב המבואר שם שיהי' להיתום הנ"ל ובאשר שלדברי' טובי' המבוארי'
22. בצוואה שייך שלושה עשר אלפי זהובי' בכן מצאנו שכל מה שנמצא בעזבון כ"ה ליב ז"ל הן
23. מזומני' ח"כ אובליגאצ[י]אהן הנ"ל שטרות כסף יובעלין גלאנדריע ספרי' ושאר מטלטלי' וחובות
24. חוץ קרקעות והזהוב הנ"ל ששייך להיותם[7] לבד כולם יחולקו לארבעה חלקי' דהיינו להיותם[8] שלשה
25. חלקים ולהד"ט חלק אחד בכן הן מן אובליגאציאהן ושטרות וח"כ הן מה שעדיין ביד האפטרו=
26. =פס כ"ה פער הנ"ל והן מה שמונח ונמצא בעזבון ר"י הנ"ל יחולק כל פרט ופרט לארבע ח
27. חלקי' ושייך שלשה חלקי' מכל אחד להיותם[9] פער וחלק אחד לדברי' טובי' וככה יהי'
28. החלוקה של כסף ויובעלין וספרי' ושארי מטלטלין יהי' מה שיהי' הכל יחולק לארבע חלקים

---

1. כבוד הרב פער
2. רבי ליב
3. אולי 'Bruchgold'
4. רויטשילד
5. כבוד הרב ליב
6. צ"ל 'להיתום'
7. צ"ל 'להיתום'
8. צ"ל 'להיתום'
9. צ"ל 'להיתום'

29. ולהיותם[1] פער שייך שלשה חלקי' ולדבר טוב חלק אחד וכה"ג מה שיבא לגוביי[נן] הן מהחוב
30. של ר"י והן משארי חובות הכל יחולק כנ"ל לפער שלשה חלקי' ולדברי' טובי' חלק אחד חוץ מ
31. מח"כ

סו ע"ב

1. בע"ה
2. מח"כ של שכירות הבית מסך מאה ושישי' וחמישה זהו' על ר' מאיר ר"ש המונח בעזבון ר"י[2] זה שייך
3. להיותם[3] פער לבד מאחר שהבית שייך ג"כ לו לבד כנ"ל ובאשר שהשלשה עשר אלפי' זהו'
4. של דברי' טובי' הנ"ל הם נחלקים בצוואה על שלשה עניני' והיינו הראשון מן סך ה' אלפי' זהו' יותן
5. הרווחי' לחלק לעניי' כל שנה ושנה עבור אפיית מצות ולשלוח להם בשר ויין על י"ט של פסח והשני
6. סך חמשת אלפי' יותנו הרווחי' כל שנה לסיועת לומדי תורה ולסיועת ה"כ וע"פ סידור שיצא מן
7. ה"[ג] אב"ד נרו[4] בצרוף הב"ד יצו כמבואר שם וכאשר כבר עשינו סידור חלוקה לזה אשתקד
8. וכמבואר בפס"ד שיצא מאתנו ט"ו טבת תקל"ד לפ"ק והשלישית סך שלשת אלפי זהו' יחולק מידי
9. שנה בשנה ביו' יארצייט של המנוח כ"ה ליב הנ"ל ללומדי תורה ולעזר' קרובי' אליו ממשפחתו ובאשר
10. שאין יד כולם שווים בכן יחולק כל פרט ופרט לפי {עין} (ערך דהיינו)[5] שיחולק לשלשה עשר חלקים ושייך ל
11. לדבר טוב הראשון חמשה חלקי' שלשה עשר מכל פרט ופרט וכהנ"ל לדב"ט השני ולהשלישית
12. שלשה חלקי' שלשה עשר ובאשר שכבר נחלק בשנה זו קודם פסח העבר דב"ט הראשון וכן
13. ביו' היארצייט העבר של שנה זו נחלק דב"ט השלישי לפ"ע בין קודם החלוקת של כ"ל[6] הנ"ל יותן
14. ג"כ לדבר טוב השני לפ"ע דהיינו מאה ושלשה זהו' (מן ר"ח תמוז דאשתקד עד ר"ח תמוז העבר)[7] ויחולק בין לומדי תורה ולה"כ לכל אחד

1. צ"ל 'להיתום'
2. ר' יעקב
3. צ"ל 'להיתום'
4. נטריה רחמנא ופרקיה
5. תוספת מעל השורה
6. כבוד ליב
7. תוספת מעל השורה

15. לפ״ע המבואר בפס״ד הנ״ל דהיינו לד״ט (מלומדי׳)[1] המחצה לפ״ע כל (...)[2] הרווחי׳ אשר עלה מן כל העזבון מיו׳ פ׳

16. פטירת ר״י עד ר״ח תמוז הסומך העבר בין שכבר באו לידי גובינא ובין מה שעדיין יבוא

17. להבא לידי גוביינא שייך הכל להיותם[3] הנ״ל לבד והרווחי׳ שנעלה מן ר״ח תמוז הסמוך הנ״ל

18. ואילך יחולק ביניהם ככל העזבון הנ״ל דהיינו להיותם[4] ג׳ חלקי׳ ולד״ט חלק אחד כנ״ל וכאשר

19. שהמנוח כ״ה ליב הנ״ל מינה בצוואתו הנ״ל מתחילה שלשה אפטרופסי׳ ועכשיו לא נשאר רק

20. אחד מהן בחיים חיותו בכן מצאנו שיתמנו מאתנו עוד שני אפטרופסי׳ אצל כ״ה פער

21. קליף הנ״ל לפקח על דברי׳ טובי׳ הנ״ל ולמהר להביאו לידי גוביינא ולעשותם למעות מזומני׳ ואז

22. יונח ביד בטוח כפי המבואר בהצוואה והיינו הנראה בטוח לפ[י ר]אות עינינו ב״ד

23. {יצא מאתנו} ומה {שיש עוד}(שיהי׳)[5] לדב״ט הנ״ל (איזה)[6] עירעור וטענה {על}(... אותם)[7] יורשי המנוח כה״ל ז״ל

24. הנ״ל שכבר נטלו חלקם בשלימות יקוב הדין את ההר ביניהם יצא מאתנו[8]

25. יו׳ ג׳ ה׳ אב קהלת לפק הג׳ אב״ד נרו׳

26. ור״י מהורר[9] נתן מז נרו׳

27. והדיין מהו׳ יעקב שמש נרו׳

28. ואני

Fol. 67a is blank.

---

1. תוספת מעל השורה
2. תוספת מעל השורה
3. צ״ל ׳להיתום׳
4. צ״ל ׳להיתום׳
5. תוספת מעל השורה
6. תוספת מעל השורה
7. תוספת מעל השורה
8. בכ״י יוו״א כתוב כאן, ׳יצא מאתנו ב״ד ח״מ בתורת פסק דין גמור ולראי׳ באנו על החתום׳. אמנם, שמות הדיינים חסרים מכ״י יוו״א.
9. מורנו הגדול ורבנו רבי

No. 60

Schwarzschild v. Fuchs

Fols. 67b–68a; Monday evening, 7 August 1775

Avrele Schwarzschild rented half of the Luchs house from Jonah Gamburg. The lease was due to expire in October 1775. In the summer of 1775, Jonah contracted to rent the space to Meʾir Fuchs and his son, Elchanan, for a three year period beginning when Avrele's lease expired. Avrele contested the right of the Fuchses to rent out the house that he was living in. Although the claim was not made against Jonah Gamburg, he did appear before the court with the rental agreement in hand and maintained that Avrele's continued residence in the space would cause him great damage.

Through his representative, Avrele contested the Fuchses' claims but ultimately both parties asked the court to impose a compromise. According to the court's instructions Avrele would relinquish his claims and leave the house when his lease expired in exchange for payment from the Fuchses.

סז ע"ב

1. ב"ה
2. הן היו' הקריב לפנינו ה"ה התורני כ"ה אברלי בן הדיין כמהו' מאיר
3. ש"ש[1] נרו' שדר כעת בחצי בית הנקרא צום לוקס בשכירות מן ה"ה התורני
4. כ"ה יונה גמבורג יצו וטען מצרנות באשר שהוא מצרן בחצי בית הנ"ל ורוצה
5. לסלק השוכרי' החצי בית הנ"ל ה"ה התורני כ"ה מאיר ובנו כ' אלחנן פוקס ששכרו
6. חצי בית הנ"ל מן כ"ה יונה הנ"ל על משך שלשה שני' מן ר"ח חשון שנת תקל"ו הבע"ל
7. עד ר"ח חשון תקלט לפק הבע"ל והשוכרי' הנ"ל השיבו שכ"ה אברלי הנ"ל
8. אבד זכותו מצרנות שלו במה שהמתין כל כך ולא בא בזמנו לאחר שהודיעו
9. לו המשכיר והאריכו בטענותיהם ובתשובתיהם זה מול זה וזה מול זה
10. כאשר מבואר הכל באריכות בק"ה אשר הי' מונח לפנינו וה"ה התורני כ"ה
11. יונה גמבורג ששייך לו החצי בית הנ"ל והשכיר אותו להשוכרי' הנ"ל על משך
12. זמן הנ"ל הציע לפנינו שטר שכירות ההוקם בינו ובין השוכרי' הנ"ל ביו'
13. ב' ה' תמוז קהלת לפק ונוסף על שטר שכירות הנ"ל אמר כ"ה יונה הנ"ל
14. שהוא והשוכרי' הנ"ל תקעו כפם זה לזה לחזק ולקיי' שכירות הנ"ל על אופני'
15. המבוארי' בשטר שכירות שהציע לפנינו וטען בקבלנא רבא נגד המצרן
16. כ"ה אברלי הנ"ל ואמר שגרם לו היזיק גדול אם נשאר עוד בחצי הנ"ל
17. לדור בו והאריך בטענותיהם כמבואר בק"ה וה"ה המצרן כ"ה אברלי הנ"ל
18. ומורשא שלו ה"ה התו' כ"ה משה אויך השיבו נגד טענות כ' אלחנן

---

1. שווארצשילד

19. ומורשא שלו ה"ה התו' כ"ה אהרן שייאר יצו ונגד כ"ה יונה גמבורג הנ"ל על
20. כל פרט ופרט באריכות ובאשר שהשוכרי' הנ"ל והמצרן הנ"ל נתנו עניהם
21. עלינו ב"ד ח"מ ותוקעו כפם בידינו לעשות פשר דבר ביניהם דהיינו
22. באופן שהמצרן כ"ה אברלי הנ"ל ימחול על זכות מצרנות שלו נגד
23. זה יתנו לו להשוכרי' הנ"ל סך כפי ראות ענינו ב"ד גם חתמו
24. א"ע המצרן והשוכרי' הנ"ל ע"ז בקומפרמיס המונח אצלינו לחזק ולקיים
25. בכל חומר ובקנס סך מסוים את אשר יצא מאתנו דרך פשר דבר בכן
26. נזדקקנו להם ויצא מאתנו דרך פ"ד שהשטר שכירות מחצי בית הנ"ל [צו]ם
27. לוקס ההוקם בין ה"ה המשכיר כ"ה יונה הנ"ל ובין ה"ה השוכרי' כ"ה מאיר ובנו
28. כ' אלחנן פוקס הנ"ל על משך זמן הנ"ל הוא בתוקפו ובגבורת[י]' ואין לה"ה
29. כ"ה אברלי {כ}הנ"ל שום טענה ועירעור נגד שטר שכירות הנ"ל יהי'
30. מה שיהי' הן בדא"ה והן בד"י בכן מחויב כ"ה אברלי הנ"ל לפנות הבית
31. הנ"ל בלי

סח ע"א

1. ב"ה
2. הנ"ל בלי עיכוב בכלות זמן שכירתו דהיינו ר"ח מרחשון תקלו הבע"ל
3. כדי שיכלו השוכרי' הנ"ל לכנוס ולדור בו נגד זה מחויבי' השוכרי' כ"ה
4. מאיר ובנו כ"ה אלחנן הנ"ל ליתן יחדיו לכ"ה אברלי הנ"ל תיכף ומיד סך
5. חמשה זהו' וגם יתנו השוכרי' כה מאיר ובנו כ' אלחנן הנ"ל שלשה ח"כ
6. מ"חי על אורדר כ"ה אברלי הנ"ל כ"א מסך חמשה זהו' שעול' יחד חמשה
7. עשר זהו' לשלם אותם על שלשה שני' רצופי' וסמוכי' זא"ז וזמן תשלומין
8. ח"כ הראשון יהי' ר"ח מרחשון שנת תקלזין הבע"ל ואותן ח"כ הנ"ל יהא
9. מונחי' ביד ב"ד עד שיפנה כ"ה אברלי הנ"ל החצי בית להשוכרי' הנ"ל
10. ואח"כ יומסר השלשה ח"כ הנ"ל לכ"ה אברלי הנ"ל יצא מאתנו אור ליו'
11. ג י"ב מנחם קהלת לפק הדיין כ"ה אברהם טריר כץ
12. והדיין כ"ה זנוויל טראך
13. ואני

Fols. 68b–69a are blank.

1. מחתימת ידם; אולי כתוב 'מ"חי'

No. 61

Fol. 69b; Sunday 27 August 1775

After dealing with the misappropriation of funds from the estate of Leb Kann (see no. 59), the court appointed two new guardians to join the one surviving guardian in the task of investing funds from Leb's estate for charitable purposes. The court noted that these two individuals were well-established financially and had always followed the court's rulings. The court empowered the guardians to do as they deemed necessary to further the interest of the charities. The guardians and their own estates were given legal immunity from any charges that might be brought against them with respect to their administration of the charitable funds. Also see no. 119.

סט ע"ב

1. ב"ה
2. באשר שכבר יצא מאתנו ב"ד ח"מ ביו' ג ה' אב העבר אודות הדבר
3. טוב של המנוח פו"מ כ"ה ליב ב"מ איצק קן שהי' מצווה בצוואת שכ"מ להניח
4. סך מסוים לקרן קיימת ביד בטוח לדורי דורת לעלות רווחים ושם
5. נאמר כדת מה לעשות ברווחי' העולי' {ח"כ} גם העמיד שלשה אפטרופסי'
6. בצוואה שם וכעת שנעדרו שני אפטרופסי' ושחל"י לזאת יצא מאתנו ב"ד
7. שיתמנו עוד שני אפטרופסי' אצל האפטרופס שלישי ה"ה הו"ה גע[1] כ"ה
8. בער קליף ושיפקחו שלשתן יחד בעיני פקיחא על הדב"ט לקיים הצוואת
9. שכ"מ בכל תוקף וכמבואר בפס"ד הנ"ל וכד חזינא דלית טבא דליהווי
10. אפטרופס על דב"ט הנ"ל עם כ"ה פער הנ"ל רק הני תרי גברי יקירא ה"ה הו"ה
11. כ"ה יוזל באמבורג וה"ה הו"ה כ"ה מאדל ברונשוויג סג["]ל חתן המנוח המנדב
12. כ"ה ליב הנ"ל[2] וחקרנו ושאלנו עליהם דגברי מעלי' הם {וש}ועשירי' ומשופעי'
13. בנכסיהן ומהינ' וחכימא ושמעו דינא ולא קבלו עליהם שמתא דרבנן בכן
14. אנחנו ב"ד ח"מ [.רשינו] והשלטון ויהיבנא רשותא לה"ה הו"ה כ"ה יוזל באמבורג
15. ולה"ה הו"ה לכ"ה מאדל הנ"ל לאסכויי' על הד"[ב]טובי' הנ"ל עם [ה"ה] האפטרופס
16. כ"ה פער קליף הנ"ל ויזכו בשביל הדב"ט הנ"ל ויהפכו בזכותו ויכניסו
17. נכסיו ופירותיו ב...מוחזק מה שמגיע לחלק דב"ט מעזבון כ"ה ליב ז"ל
18. הנ"ל הן מזומני' הן ח"כ אובליגאציאהן שטרות כסף יובעלן גלאנדריע ספרי'
19. ושאר מטלטלין וחובות ויקיימו כפי המבואר בפס"ד הנ"ל {וש}ורשות בידם
20. לישא {ויל}וליתן להכניס ולהוציא לצורך דב"ט הנ"ל כפי רצונם וכמבואר
21. בצוואה הנ"ל שהעתקנו ונתנו בידם ושום איניש לא ימחה בידם לע[שות]
22. דבר קטן או גדול או לגרוע כחם בין לזכות בין לחובה רק עשיית[ם]

---

1. גבאי צדקה
2. ר' אבני זכרון, מס' 5124.

23. י[ה]י׳ בכל תוקף ועוז ככל שאר אפטרופסי׳ הנעשין בישראל
24. בכא״ה ופטרנו הני תלתא אפטרופסי׳ הנ״ל וי״א וב״כ מכל אלה ושבועה
25. ושמתא ומן כל טענות ועירעור שבעולם {בעסק} (בשביל)[1] דב״ט הנ״ל יהי׳ מה שיהי׳
26. נגד מי שיהי׳ הן רבי׳ או יחיד או באיזה אופן שיהי׳ הן {בדא״ה והן} בדאה[2]
27. והן בד״י רק כל הנאמנת יהי׳ להאפטרופסי׳ הנ״ל וי״א וב״כ וכתבנו וחתמנו
28. זאת בתוקף מעשה ב״ד ובכח ב״ד יפה להיות ביד האלופי׳ אפטרופסי׳
29. הנ״ל וי״א וב״כ לעדות ולראי׳ נעשה פה פ״פורט דמיין היו׳ יו׳ א ב׳
30. דר״ח אלול קהלת לפק הג׳ אב״ד נרו׳ והדיין מהו׳ נתן מז נרו׳ {הדיין מהו׳}
31. והדיין מהו׳ יעקב שמש נרו׳ ואני

Page 70a is blank.

No. 62

Weiselveiler v. Adler

Fols. 70b–71a; Thursday 17 August 1775

A merchant from Holland who had silk clothes for sale visited Frankfurt during the 1774 fall fair and invited Kalman Weiselveiler to come to see him about purchasing his goods. According to Kalman, when he arrived, Feis Adler of Worms was already with the merchant in his room and Kalman waited for him to leave. As Adler left the room, Feis told Kalman that he could not meet the trader's asking price for the clothes and suggested that they enter into a partnership to acquire the goods. Kalman agreed, but stipulated that he would control two-thirds of the partnership and Feis one-third. According to Kalman, Feis agreed to these conditions with a handshake and then concluded the negotiations with the Dutch trader. Kalman claimed that Feis purchased the goods for 1800 guldens but failed to share the profits with him. Through his representative he now sued Feis for what he claimed was two-thirds of the profits, 600 guldens.

Feis, who was acting on behalf of orphans, counterclaimed that the agreement with Kalman was only talk and was never formally concluded. He maintained that

1. תוספת מעל השורה
2. בדיני אומות העולם

his discussion with Kalman was predicated on Kalman purchasing the goods, and that there was no talk of what would follow if Feis purchased them. Feis also noted that he himself did not purchase the goods. Rather, Moses Rüsselsheim did, and only later did they enter into an agreement. Since Feis was unable to prove his claims, the court ordered him to take an oath that he was telling the truth. If he did so, he would be free from Kalman's claims against him.

There is a postscript from early 1776 noting that Feis informed Rabbi Gundersheim that he had come to a compromise with Kalman, the specifics of which are not recorded here. Gundersheim sent a messenger of the court to Kalman to ascertain that this was so. Once confirmed, Feis was absolved of all claims against him and presumably also of the need to take the oath.

ע ע״ב

1. ב״ה
2. ע״ד שבא לפנינו ה״ה התורני כ״ה וואלף בוריך סגל בהרשאת ה״ה
3. הו״ה כ׳ קלמן ווייסלויילר ותובע מן הב״ח כ׳ פייס אדליר מק״ק ווירמש ה
4. הנושא ונותן עבור יתומי המנוח כמ״ה פער אדליר כץ ז״ל סך ששה
5. מאות זהו׳ והיינו שבאשר ביריד ר״ה העבר נזדמן כאן סוחר אחד
6. מן האלאנד בבית אושפיז שיש בתוכו חנות של כ׳ פייס הנ״ל והי׳ לו
7. מיני מלבושי׳ ובגדים של משי למכור ויקרא אליו כ׳ קלמן הנ״ל לקנותו וכשבא
8. אצלו כ׳ קלמן הנ״ל ראה שכ׳ פייס הנ״ל הי׳ בתוך החדר והמתן עד
9. צאתו ובצאתו אמר כ׳ פייס לכ׳ קלמן שפסק על מלבושי׳ לסוחר
10. סך חמשה (עשר)[1] מאות זהו׳ ולא רצה הסוחר אכן שסבר בדעתו שיכולין
11. ליתן עוד מאה זהו׳ ורוצה להשתתף עם כ׳ קלמן הנ״ל וכ׳ קלמן הנ״ל
12. השיב שאי אפשר לו להשתתף שוה בשוה רק באופן שיהי׳ לו
13. ב׳ שלישי׳ בריווח ולכ׳ פייס לא יהי׳ רק שליש אחד וע״ז נתרצו יחד
14. בת״כ וכשראה אותם ג״כ כ׳ קלמן הנ״ל נושא ונותן עם כ׳ פייס הנ״ל
15. עבור הבגדים הנ״ל והנה אח״כ נתוודע לכ׳ קלמן שכ׳ פייס הנ״ל
16. קנה אותם בעד סך ח״י מאות זהו׳ בכן תובע ב׳ שלישי׳ ריווח שעולה
17. לששה מאות זהו׳ {וה...} וה״ה התו[רני] כ״ה משה אויך השיב בהרשאת
18. הב״ח כ׳ פייס ובהרשאת אפטרופסי׳ דיתמי הנ״ל שכ׳ קלמן
19. הנ״ל הי׳ מתרצה להשתתף עם כ׳ פייס הנ״ל שבאם יקנה (הוא)[2] אותם
20. אזי יתן לכ׳ פייס הנ״ל חלקו בריווח והיינו החצי {בית}אמנם ההי[פך]
21. דהיינו באם שיקנה כ׳ פייס אותם שיותן לכ׳ {פייס} קלמן חלק
22. ריווח {..} (זה)[3] לא נזכר בדבריהם גם [ל]א הי׳ רק {חלק} דברי׳ בעלמא
23. בלי ח״כ {ג״כ} גם טען כ׳ פייס הנ״ל שלא קנה אותם המלבושי׳ הנ״ל

1. תוספת מעל השורה
2. תוספת מעל השורה
3. תוספת מעל השורה

24. רק אח"כ בא כ"ה {פייס} משה ריסל(ס)[1]היים וקנה אותם ובשעת קניי' לא הי'
25. דעתו לא על כ' פייס {ולא על} הנ"ל ופשיטא על כ' קלמן הנ"ל רק אחר המו"מ
26. השתתף כ"ה משה הנ"ל עם כ' פייס הנ"ל בכן אין לכ' {קלמן הנ"ל} קלמן
27. הנ"ל שום תביעה

עא ע"א

1. ב"ה
2. שום תביעה והאריכו בטענותיהם {ובתשוב} כמבואר הכל בק"ה
3. המונח לפנינו ובאשר שהצדדי' הנ"ל חתמו עצמם בתוקף קומפרמיס
4. בכא"ה בח"ח ובקנס סך מסוים לאשר ולקיים כפי הפס"ד שיצא מ
5. מאתנו בכן נזדקקנו להם ומצאנו שישבע כ' פייס הנ"ל ע"ד המקו'
6. ב"ה וע"ד ב"ד בלי ערמה ומרמה והוראת היתר שבעולם שכדבריו
7. כן הוא דהיינו הברירה[2] בידו לישבע שלא השתתף בת"כ עם
8. כ' קלמן הנ"ל על אופן שטען כ' קלמן הנ"ל באם שיקנה כ' פייס
9. הנ"ל שצריך ליתן חלק ריווח לכ' קלמן הנ"ל או שישבע {כ"ה פייס}
10. {הנ"ל}שכ"ה משה ריסלסהיים קנה לעצמו הבגדי' בלי שותפת
11. עם כ' פייס הנ"ל יצא מאתנו יו' ה' כ"א מנחם קהלת לפק
12. הדיין מהו' נתן מז נרו' והדיין מהו' יעקב שמש נרו'
13. ואני
14. באשר שבא אלי[3] (הב"ח)[4] כ' פייס אדליר מק"ק ווירמש הנמע"ל ואמר לי שהתפשר א"ע עם כ'
15. קלמן ווייסווילר מחמת תביעות הנ"ל על סך ידוע ביניהם שיתן {כ' פייס הנ} לכ'
16. קלמן הנ"ל ושלחתי אל כ' קלמן הנ"ל שלוחי בידינא לשאול אם כני' דבריו והשיב לי השליח
17. ב"ד שאמת כדבריו בכל פטור ומסולק (כ' פייס)[5] הית[..] של יתמי המנוח כ' פער אדליר כץ ז"ל
18. וי"א וב"כ מן כ' קלמן ווייסווילר הנ"ל וי"א וב"כ מחמת תביעות הנ"ל ולראי' באתי על
19. החתום יו' ג' טז שבט תקלמד ויו לפק[6]

No. 63

Fol. 71b; Thursday evening, 7 December 1775

Three female servants, none of whom are named in the document, had a

1. תוספת מעל האות הא
2. צ"ל 'הברירה'
3. כנראה הרב חיים גונדרשהיים
4. תוספת מעל השורה
5. תוספת מעל השורה
6. בשנה זו ט"ז שבט היה ביום ב'

disagreement with a fourth regarding the division of 120 guldens in a winning lottery ticket. The three women argued that since the fourth woman only purchased her share in the ticket a day before the draw, she should not share in the winnings, a claim disputed by the fourth woman. All the women had representation before the court which arranged a compromise in the matter.

עא ע״ב

1. ב״ה
2. שנת תקל״ויו
3. אור ליו׳ ויו עשק׳[1] טו כסליו באו לפנינו ה״ה התו׳ כ״ה משה אויך סגל וכ׳ שמואל סופר
4. ונתעצמו בטענותיהם בהרשאת ארבעה משרתת שהי׳ להם טרעפר בתוך
5. מ[י]נצר[2] לאטרע מסך קך זהו׳ ואחת {ממנה} ממשרתת לא הי׳ עושה שותפו׳
6. רק יום אחד לפני הצוג והאחרות הי׳ רוצה לדחות אותה מליתן לה חלקה
7. רביעית מסך שלשי׳ זהו׳ המגיע ע״ח {ונעשו}(עשינו)[3] פשרה ביניהם שאותה משרתת
8. יהי׳ לה כ״ב זהו׳ וחצי ע״ח והמותרות יהי׳ לשלשה אחרות ביחדיו

No. 64

Hammel v. Oppenheim

Fol. 71b; Sunday evening, 10 December 1775

Feis Hammel claimed that Elijah (Elkan?) Oppenheim owed him 15½ guldens for a lottery ticket that he had taken from him. Elijah did not dispute having taken the ticket, but wanted Feis to take an oath that he had not sold him the ticket after he already knew the winning numbers in the draw (apparently Elijah did not have a winning ticket). Elijah also wanted Feis to swear that the amount he was claiming was indeed correct. The court arranged a compromise: Elijah paid Feis 11¼ guldens and Feis did not have to take an oath.

9. אור ליו׳ ב חי כסליו שנת תקלמ״ויו לפק {נעשו}(עשינו)[4] פשרה בין ה״ה כ׳ פייס האמיל
10. ובין הב״ח כ׳ אלי׳ אופנהיי׳ [.] בעניין שכ׳ פייס תבע ממנו טו זהו׳ וחצי בעד צעטל
11. אין דער פרידבורגר אונד וירצבורגר אמפא לאטרע שלקח כ״א[5] הנ״ל ממנו

---

1. ערב שבת קודש
2. כנראה על שם העיר שבה התנהלה ההגרלה.
3. תוספת מעל השורה
4. תוספת מעל השורה
5. כבוד אלי׳

12. וכ' אלי' הנ"ל השיב שישבע כ' פייס הנ"ל שלא הטעה אותו במכירת צעטל (והיינו)[1] שלאחר
13. שנודע לו (כבר)[2] הנומר' מן הצוג {עדיין} (לאח"כ)[3] מכר לו צעטל וגם ישבע אם מגיע לו כל כך (כמו שתבע)[4] ולאחר
14. שאנח[נו] (רוצי')[5] להטל {יו} על כ' פייס הנ"ל קבלת חרם התפש[רו] א"[ע] שיתן כ' אלי' הנ"ל י"א זהו' ורביעי'
15. ...[מ]סולקי' זה מזה וזה מזה מהו' יעקב שמש וכ"ה מאיר שיף ואני

No. 65

Kassel v. Bing

Fols. 72a–b; Sunday 10 December 1775

Leb Kassel approached the court without representation and claimed that Anshel Bing and his son, Seligmann, owed him funds they had promised him as part of a compromise reached in settling the estate of Jacob Wett. While Leb brought a witness to support his claim, Seligmann, who represented himself and his father, denied the claim and the context of the witness's testimony. After the parties agreed to be bound by the court's decision, the court ordered that one of the Bings must swear that their version of the events was correct and the other must affirm it. If they would do so, they would be absolved from paying Leb. The court gave Leb the right to decide which of the Bings would take the oath. An addendum records that Seligmann took an oath about a month (7 January 1776) after the court's ruling and Anshel affirmed it.

עב ע"א

1. ב"ה
2. ע"ד שבא לפנינו ה"ה הו"ה כ"ה ליב קאסיל סג"ל ותבע מן ה"ה הו"ה כ' אנשיל ובנו כ'
3. זעליגמן בינגא יצו סך ששה עשר קרלינר באשר שבשעת פשר שנעשה בין כ"ה
4. ליב הנ"ל ובין כ אנשיל ובנו הנ"ל בירושת המנוח כ' יעקב קעט ז"ל התרצו אב
5. ובנו הנ"ל ליתן לכ"ה ליב שמונה זקוקי' כסף ולא קיבלו מהם בכן חשב כ"ה ליב הנ"ל
6. ותבע בעד כל זקוק שני קרלינר העולה לשמונה זקוקי' סך טז קרלינר

---

1. תוספת מעל השורה
2. תוספת מעל השורה
3. תוספת מעל השורה
4. תוספת מעל השורה
5. תוספת מעל השורה

7. גם הביא כ"ה ליב הנ"ל עד אחד שהי' בשעת פשר והגיד לפנינו בתע'[1]
8. אם לא יו"ע וז"ל בשעת גמר הפשר אמר כ' זעליגמן הנ"ל וואן איך גוט פערטיג
9. וואהר עם השררה יר"ה זוא האט ער ווידר צוגניסן עכ"ל וה"ה כ' זעליגמן הנ"ל
10. השיב בשבילו ובהרשאת אביו כ' אנשיל הנ"ל שבשעת גמר פשר לא דיברו
11. כלל מכסף רק ביו' שלאחריו תבע כ"ה ליב הנ"ל ממנו שיתן לו ג"כ כסף וע"ז
12. השיב כ"ז[2] הנ"ל באם שיגמר בטוב עם השררה ירה[3] יתן לו ג"כ איזה דבר
13. מכסף לפי רצונו ולא הי' רק דרך השטאה בעלמא והאריכו הצדדי' הנ"ל
14. בטענותיהם ובתשובתיהם כמבואר מתוך ק"ה המונח לפיננו[4] ובאשר
15. שהצדדי' הנ"ל חתמו עצמם בתוקף קומפרמיס בח"ח ובקנס סך מ[סוים]
16. לאשר ולקיים הפס"ד שיצא מאתנו נזדקקנו להם ומצאנו [ש]כ' א[נשיל]
17. ובנו כ"ז הנ"ל ישבעו ע"ד המקו' ב"ה וע"ד ב"ד בלי עו"מ ובלי שום הוראת
18. היתר שבעולם שכדבריהם כן הוא שבשעת גמר [פ]שר לא דברו [...] ש
19. שיתנו לכ"ה ליב הנ"ל כסף והיינו שאחד מהם מאב ובנו הנ"ל ישבע
20. והשני יענה אמן והברירה מי שישבע יהי' ביד המשביע כ"ה ליב הנ"ל
21. יצא מאתנו יו' א' טוב כסליו תקלמד ויו לפק
22. מהו' מאיר ש"ש[5] נרו' וכ"ה אברהם טריר ואני
23. כהיו' דלמטה קימו ה"ה כ' אנשיל ובנו כ' זעליגמן בינגא את הפס"ד הנ"ל
24. ונשבע כ' זעליגמן ואביו ענה אמן על שבועתו במעמדי ובמעמד
25. השמש

עב ע"ב

1. ב"ה
2. השמש כ"ה הירץ וואָהל יצו לאחר שהטלתי חרם על כ"ה ליב קאסיל שהי' ג"כ
3. בשעת השבועה בכן פטורי' ומסולקי' כ' אנשיל ובנו כ' זעליגמן בינגא הנ"ל מן
4. כ"ה ליב הנ"ל {מן} מחמת תביעות הנ"ל והנעשה נעשה יו' ג' טוב טבת קלמד"ויו[6]

---

1. בתורת עדות
2. כבוד זעליגמן
3. ירום הודו
4. צ"ל 'לפנינו'
5. שווארצשילד
6. ר"ל 'תקלמד"ויו'

No. 66

Rindskopf v. Mai

Fols. 73a–74a; Wednesday evening, 27 December 1775

Rechle, the widow of Jacob Mai, rented living space from Ber Rindskopf. In 1764, Rechle agreed in writing to pay for certain types of repairs during the years of her rental. Now, some eleven years later, Ber brought suit against Rechle to collect 92 guldens, 39 kreuzers that he had spent making such repairs. Ber produced an itemized list of the charges and invoices from those who performed the repairs to support his claim.

Rechle had given power of attorney to Me'ir Oppenheim, who had also acted as her guarantor for any obligation to Ber that the court might impose. Me'ir in turn appointed Aaron Scheyer to represent Rechle. She did not deny owing Ber money, however, she produced a receipt from 1770 signed by Ber certifying that she had paid over 58 guldens to him for many of these repair costs. She disputed her responsibility for other charges and noted that Ber had erred in his calculations. She asked that Ber take an oath with respect to the charges he had submitted and the funds he had received from her. In addition, Rechle claimed to have a note from Ber regarding certain household items she had left in the house (the house was now being sold and apparently she had vacated it). She asked that these items be returned to her.

Ber explicitly stated he would return the household goods to Rechle. He also acknowledged he had issued receipts to Rechle but explained that, trusting her, he had given her the receipts before receiving payment but that payment was never made. Ber noted that one of the charges was not included in the 1764 agreement, which Rechle had agreed orally to pay when her lease was renewed in about 1770.

The court accepted the authenticity of the receipts, instated a compromise on one claim, and instructed Rechle to confirm,within 30 days, that she had not paid all of the claims that Ber made against her. Ber was ordered to take an oath that the charges he had listed were accurate. When these orders were fulfilled by both sides, Rechle was to pay Ber 29 guldens, 24 kruezers.

עג ע"א

1. ב"ה
2. ע"ד שבא לפנינו ה"ה הו"ה כ' פער ר"ק ותבע מן האשה מ' רייכלה אל' המנוח כ' יעקב מאיי ז"ל
3. והציע לפנינו חשבן מה שהוציא בבדק הבית בבית שהי' דר בתוכה בשכירות
4. העולה לסך תשעי' ושני' זהו' לט צל גם הראה לפנינו קונטא מן בעלי מלאכות ע[ל]

5. כל פרט ופרט שנזכר בחשבן [ע]וד הציע כ"פ[1] הנ"ל כ"י התחייבות מן האשה מ' רייכלה
6. הנ"ל ההוקם יד טבת תקך"[ז][2] שבתוכה התחייבה א"ע האשה הנ"ל לשלם לכ"פ
7. תיקוני בדק הבית שנזכרי' בתוך כ"י כנ"ל ובאשר שבחשבונו נזכרי' אותם ת
8. תיקוני' הנפרטי' בהתחייבות בכן מחויבת היא לשלם לו סך מן החשבן
9. הנ"ל וה"ה התורני כ"ה אהרן שייאר יצו בהרשאת הו"ה גע[3] כ"ה מאיר אופנהייי'
10. שיש לו כו"ה מן האשה מרת רייכלה הנ"ל וגם כהר"מ[4] הנ"ל נעשה ערב בשבילה
11. לשלם לכ' פער מה ש[ז]וכה בדין הציע לפנינו כ"י קוויטונג ההוקם כ"א
12. מרחשון תקלא לפק שקיבל כ"פ הנ"ל מן האשה הנ"ל דמי חשבן מן נ"ח זהו' ט"ו [צל]
13. עוד טען שנמצא טעות בחשבן שהציע עתה כ' פער לפני ב"ד באשר שבחשב[ן]
14. קוויטונג הנ"ל העלה כ"פ הנ"ל בעד טעפעטן יא זהו' ך צל ובתוך החשבן שהעלה
15. עתה לא חשב רק חמשה זהו' בכן אותו ששה זהו' {...} ך צל קיבל יותר מן
16. הראוי לו עוד טען כהרא[5] הנ"ל שהעלה כ"פ בחשבונו בעד מעס געלט אן טאַך
17. טעקר אונד שלויט פיגר עשרה זהו' וטוען כה"א הנ"ל שלא נזכר בהתחייבו'
18. שלה שיתן כ"פ בעבורה מעס געלט גם בכמה בתי' אין נותנין מעס געלט
19. והיא לא נתנה לו רשות לזה ואין עלי' לשלם עוד טען שהעלה כ"פ בחשבן
20. קוויטונג הנ"ל שלשה זהו' וחצי דש{.}צ{.} בית צו ווייסן לפי התחייבות
21. הנ"ל מחויב כ"פ הנ"ל להעמיד את הבית לזמנו ב{.}נותן {..} תיקונו ובאשר
22. שעתה נמכר הבית ואין מן הצורך לכ"פ ווישן צו לאזין בכן תובעת ה
23. הדמי' מחמת וויישן לחזרה ועל הנשאר עדיין מחשבן של כ' פער טען כהר"א[6]
24. הנ"ל בהרשאת הנ"ל שישבע כ"פ הנ"ל על חשבן צדק על כל פרט ופרט שה[עלה]
25. בחשבונו

עג ע"ב

1. ב"ה
2. על כל מה שהוציא הן על מה שנתפרע לו והן על מה שלא נתפרע לו עדיין ואז {תש...} תשלם
3. הנשאר עוד הציע לפנינו כה"א הנ"ל כ"י הודאה מן כ"פ הנ"ל שיש תחת ידו כמה כלי בית
4. השייכי' להאשה הנ"ל שנשארו עומד בבית הנ"ל וכמו שנפרט שם בכן תבע מן כ"פ הנ"ל
5. שיחזיר לה עכשיו בפנות הבית וכו' פער ר"ק השיב שחתימת יד מן קוויטונג הנ"ל
6. מן סך נח זהו' ורביעית הוא באמת חתימת ידו ממש אבל לא קיבל תשלומין ממנה
7. רק הוא נתן לה אותו קוויטונג והאמין לה שתפרע לו אבל לא קיבל כלום ממנה ועל
8. עשרה זהו' מעס געלט שהעלה בחשבונו השיב באמת בהתחייבות שלה לא נזכר
9. כלום שבאותו פעם עדיין לא נעשה מעס געלט רק לפני חמשה שני' בהתחדשו'
10. שכירות הבית ביניהם אמרה האשה מ' רייכלה הנ"ל לכ"פ הנ"ל שיעשה מעס

---

1. כבוד פער
2. יעקב מאיי נפטר י"ד בתשרי תקכ"ט (אלה תולדות 25.9.1768) ואם כן מדובר בהתחייבות שנעשתה בחיי בעלה.
3. גבאי צדקה
4. כבוד הרב מאיר
5. כבוד הרב אהרן
6. כבוד הרב אהרן

11. געלט ויפרע בשבילה ועל תביעת כלי בית שנזכר בהתחייבות כ״י שלו השיב
12. כ״פ הנ״ל שאמת הוא שעדיין הם בידם ומרוצה לחזירם לה והאריכו בטענותי
13. = הם ובתשובתיהם על כל פרט ופרט כמבואר מתוך ק״ה המונח לפנינו ובאשר
14. שחתמו הצדדי׳ הנ״ל א״ע בתוקף קומפרמיס בח״ח ובקנס סך מסויים לאשר ולקיי׳
15. כל אשר יצא מאתנו נזדקקנו להם ומצאנו שחתימת יד קוויטונג שהציע לפנינו
16. כה״א הנ״ל הוא בתקפו ואין ממש בטענות כ״פ נגד קוויטונג הנ״ל רק ש
17. שאנחנו ב״ד ח״מ נותנ[י׳] חרם על האשה מ׳ רייכלה הנ״ל שתודה מיו׳ דלמטה תוך שלשי׳
18. יום האמת הוא שלא שילמה הן כולו או מקצתה מה שנזכר בתוך קוויטונג הנ״ל
19. ובכן ינוכה סך נח זהו׳ טו צל מן סך חשבן תביעת כ״פ הנ״ל ובזה נכ[לל] מה שרוצה
20. לנכות {סך שלשה זהו׳ וחצי מחמת דמי הויז צו} כה״א הנ״ל סך ששה זהו׳ וחצי בשביל
21. דמי טעפעטן שהעלה יותר מן הראוי וכנ״ל ומה שרוצה לנכות סך שלשה זהו׳
22. וחצי מחמת דמי הויז צו וייסן וכנ״ל מצאנו שאין בו ממש ומה שטען כה״א הנ״ל ורוצה
23. לנכות סך עשרה זהו׳ דמי מע[ס] געלט נתנו עיניהם עלינו ב״ד לפשר אותם
24. ומצאנו דרך פשר שמחויבת האשה מ׳ רייכלה לשלם לכ׳ פער בעד דמי {..}
25. מעס געלט שהעלה סך חמשה זהו׳ בכן לאחר ניכוי דמי קוויטונג כנ״ל וגם
26. דמי

עד ע״א

1. ב״ה
2. דמי מעס געלט נשאר עוד עשרי׳ וארבע זהו׳ כ״ד צל ישבע כ׳ פער הנ״ל ע״ד
3. המקו׳ ב״ה וע״ד ב״ד בלי ערמה ומרמה ושום הוראות היתר שבעולם על חשבן צדק
4. על כל מה שהעלה בחשבונו שהוציא כל כך כמו שהעלה הן על מה שנתפרע לו
5. והן על מה שלא נתפרע עדיין ואז מחויבת האשה מ׳ רייכלה הנ״ל לשלם
6. לכ׳ פער הנ״ל סך עשרי׳ וארבע זהו׳ כ״ד צל הנ״ל נוסף על חמשה זהו׳ דמי
7. מעס געלט כפי פשר שמצאנו וכנ״ל שהם יחד עשרי׳ ותשעה זהו׳ כד צל
8. הנ״ל ומחויב כ׳ פער הנ״ל להחזיר להאשה מ׳ רייכלה הנ״ל אותן כלי בית
9. שנזכר בתוך כ״י הודאה שיש עדיין תחת יד כ׳ פער הנ״ל וכ[מו] ש
10. [ש]הודה בפנינו יצא מאתנו אור ליו׳ ה׳ ה׳ טבת שנת תיו קוף למד
11. ויו לפק ר״י ורב״ד מהו׳ נתן מז והדיין מהו׳ יעקב שמש ואני

Fol. 74b is blank.

No. 67

Sichel v. Bonn

Fols. 75a–77a; Wednesday evening, 3 January 1776

Yosle Sichel and Herz Bonn and sons owned adjacent houses: Yosle, the Schlüssel house, and the Bonns, the Weisse Gans house. The Bonns' construction of two drainage ditches, or gutters, for their toilet, and a wall between the properties, brought Yosle to the court. He claimed that because of the placement of the ditches part of the wall was solely on his property. Yosle wanted the Bonns to move the two ditches back further onto their property so that the entire wall could be placed half on Yosle's property and half on the Bonns' property.

Through their representative, the Bonns raised a number of arguments to support the status quo, including a statement that this was where the drainage pipes had always been. Based on remains of walls on the site dating from "the fire" (the *Judengasse* suffered a disasterous conflagration in 1711 and the Weisse Gans house was burned [see Dietz, p. 450, no. 48]), they also suggested that the current wall may be entirely on their property. Yosle's representative dismissed these and other claims, asserting that the remnants may have been parts of other structures. Yosle made an additional claim regarding the installation of a post on his side of the wall that the Bonns also disputed.

After hearing from each side, the court called a building expert who was recognized as such by the non-Jewish authorities (apparently a non-Jew) and sent him to examine the site. The court then asked the expert extensive questions and his answers appear to have been the basis for the court's decision in favor of the Bonns. The court made aspects of the settlement contingent on the Bonns bringing proof for their claim that the drainage ditches had always been in this spot. To this end, about three weeks later, the Bonns brought two witnesses to support their claim as noted in an addendum on fol. 77a. Sichel rejected the witnesses, stating that one of them was his enemy and should not to be accepted as a witness against him. Nevertheless, after warning the witnesses, presumably about the seriousness of giving false testimony, the court heard their testimony and gave Yosle the opportunity to respond to their statements. Since he did not, their testimony and the court's decision stood.

עה ע"א

1. ב"ה
2. ע"ד הפרשות בין ה"ה הו"ה ג"ה כ' הירץ בון ובנ[י]ו הו"ה כ' פתחי' וכ'
3. איצק מחזיקי בית צור ווייסה גנץ ובין הו"ה כ' {איצק} יוזלי זיכל מחזיק חצי בית

4. צור שליסל והיינו שה״ה כ׳ יוזלי הנ״ל תבע לפנינו באשר שבסוכה[1] של כ׳
5. הירץ בון הנ״ל העמידו שני קנאהלין לצורך בית המוצנע גם העמידו אחורי אותן
6. קנאהלין מחיצה שקורין שאטוואנד להפסיק בין הסוכה השייך לכ׳ הירץ
7. הנ״ל ובין פלאטץ של[ו] וארכה של המחיצה נמשך ומגיע עד סוף רוחב הכותל
8. הבנין העומד מפסקת בין {ה״ה} בית של כ׳ הירץ בון ובין פלאטץ {בין פ} שלו
9. ובאשר שאותו כותל המפסקת עומד על מקו׳ המשותף לשניהם והיינו החצי
10. רחבה עומד על גבול של כ״ה[2] הנ״ל והחצי אחרת על גבול של כ׳ יוזלי בכן ראוי
11. להעמיד מחיצה שאטוואנד הנ״ל באופן שמגיע סוף ארכה עד אמצע כותל
12. המפסקת כדי שיהא ג״כ עומד על גבול שניהם אבל עכשיו שהיא מגיע עד
13. סוף כותל המפסקת נמצא מחיצת שאטוואנד עומד על גבול של כ׳ יוזל לבד
14. בכן רוצה למחות בידם שיסלקו השני קנאהלין הנ״ל ממקו׳ שהם עומדי׳ עכשיו
15. ויכניסם יותר לתוך גבולם כדי ש[יוכל] להעמיד המחיצה שאטוואנד
16. אחריהם בענין שנמשך סוף ארכה עד אמצע כותל בנ[י]ן המפסקת הנ״ל וכ״ה
17. בענדיט הענא במעמד כ׳ פתחי׳ השיב בהרשאת כ׳ הירץ הנ״ל שכאן נמצא
18. כאן הי׳ שש[ני] קנאהלין הי׳ עומדי׳ במרתף משך כל רוחבם ע[3] עד סמוך
19. לחומה כמו שהם עכשיו ואכ[4] אי אפשר להעמיד מחיצה אחורי קנאהלין אם לא
20. באופן שמגיע ארכה עד סוף רוחב המפסקת כותל המפסקת בכן
21. מוכרח להיות אחת משתים אלה או שכ׳ הירץ הנ״ל הי׳ לו חזקה שמחצת
22. שאטוואנד צריך להיות בתוך גבול של כ׳ יוזלה או שבעלי מלאכה שהי׳ בונין
23. כותל המפסקת הי׳ מכניס והעמידו כ״כ הכותל המפסקת {הי׳ מכ}נסי׳ סמוך
24. לסוכה יותר מחצי רחבה לתוך גבול של כ״ה הנ״ל עד שמחיצת שאטוואנד עומדת
25. ג״כ על גבול שלו אף שמגיע סוף ארכה לסוף רוחב של הכותל המפסקת עוד
26. טען מאן יימר אפשר {ש}שכל אורך כותל המפסקת מתחילת׳ מהרח[ו]ב עד
27. {סוף} סופה לצד סוכה כולה נבנית על גבול שלו הביא ראי׳ לזה מן איזה
28. קורת חרבות שעדיין עומדי׳ בתוך פלאטץ אחור כותל המפסקת
29. שבאותו מקו׳

עה ע״ב

1. ב״ה
2. שבאותו מקו׳ הי׳ עומד הכותל מפסקת קודם שריפה וא״כ עומד עכשיו
3. כותל הבנין המפסקת על גבול שלו לבד עוד טען כ״ה בענדיט בהרשאת
4. הנ״ל והביא ראי׳ שיוכל {להיות} לראות מתו[ך] הקענטל שעדיין הוא בתוך הפלאטץ
5. מבתי׳ פנימי׳ שהי׳ עומדי׳ אחורי הבית של כ׳ הירץ ואותו קענטל נמשך בשוה
6. עם הקענטל בתוך הסוכה של הירץ בון ומסתמא המחיצה שאטוואנד הי׳ עומדי׳
7. אחורי קענטל ומזה נראה שהמחיצה שאטוואנד מגיע עד סוף רוחב כותל ה

---

1. כנראה שמדובר באיזור מאחרי הבית ששם היו מעמידים את הסוכה.
2. כבוד הירץ
3. כנראה שהסופר הפסיק ואז חזר בלי למחוק את האות.
4. ואם כן

8. המפסקת בינו ובין פלאטץ של כ׳ יוזלי וה״ה התורני כה אנשיל פפאן בהרשאת
9. כ׳ יוזלי ובמעמדו השיב שהכותל בנין המפסקת וודאי עומד על גב[ו]ל שניהם
10. בשוה ומה שהביא ראי׳ מן הקורת חרבות הנ״ל אין ראי׳ שהי׳ שם כותל ישנה
11. אפשר שבנין אחר הי׳ שם ובשביל כן הי׳ קורת הללו ומה שטען כ״ה בענדיט
12. הנ״ל שקנאהלין במרתף הי׳ כמו שהי׳ עכשיו השיב כהר״א[1] הנ״ל מאן יימר
13. אפשר שהי׳ מקודם דחוקי׳ ונכנסי׳ יותר לתוך גבול של כ״ה הנ״ל כדי {שיהא}
14. שאם ימשך הקנאהלין למעלה בתוך הסוכה ומעמידין מחיצת שאטוואנד
15. אחורי הקנאהלין מגיע המחיצה עד {סוף} אמצע רוחב הכותל בנ[י]ן המפסקת
16. הנ״ל עוד טען כ׳ יוזלי שאף אם הי׳ הקנאהלין למטה בתוך המרתף סמוך
17. לחומה כמו שהם עומדי׳ מ״מ אפשר למעלה בסוכה לא הי׳ כן מקודם רק הי׳
18. נמשך יותר ונכנס לתוך גבול של כ״ה הנ״ל מקו׳ מושב כ״ה[2] ר[3] והוקבעם ה
19. הקנאהלין למעלה ונעשה בשיפוע טרענטר כדי שיכולין השופכין למשוך
20. למט[ה] קנאהלין במרתף על ראי׳ שהביא כ״ה בענדיט מן קענטל הנ״ל השי[ב]
21. כהר״א מאן יימר שהקענטל בתוך הסוכה של כ״ה הנ״ל הי׳ נמשך בשוה עם
22. הקענטל של הפלאטץ אפשר שהקענטל שבתוך הסוכה הי׳ נמשך באלכסון
23. בתוך סוכה של כ״ה הנ״ל וכשנ[ב]נה הבית של כ״ה הנ״ל {עשר} עכשיו הי׳ מכסה
24. הסוכה ברצפת אבני׳ והי׳ משנה ג״כ הקענטל והעמיד אותו בשוה עם הקענ[טל]
25. שהיא בתוך הפלאטץ גם אפשר שהמחיצה שאטוואנד הי׳ עומד על הקענטל
26. עצמו והשופכין נמשכין באלכסון {לנק} לנקבי הקנאהלין וגם א״ת שמתחילה
27. הי׳ בשוה וגם המחיצה שאטוואנד הי׳ אחורי קענטל עדיין יוכל להיות
28. שהמחיצת

עו ע״א

1. ב״ה
2. שהמחיצת שאטוואנד הי׳ נבנת ומתחיל מאמצע כותל המפסקת עד
3. מקו׳ ב״ה[4] ומשם ואילך נעשה המחיצה אחורי קענטל והאריכו בטענותיהם
4. ובתשובתיהם כמו שמובאת מתוך ק״ה המונח לפנינו ואחר גמר טענותי׳
5. שלחנו אחר אומן המושבע מפי השררה ירה[5] לראות י׳[6] איכות הבנין הכותל
6. {הק} המפסקת וגם איכות הבנין הקנאהלי למטה במרתף ולמעלה בסוכה
7. וגם איכות העמדת קענטל הנ״ל וחקרנו אותו היטיב בדרישה וחק(י)[7]רה כפי
8. הנצרך לענינים ובאשר שהצדדי׳ הנ״ל חתמו עצמם בתוקף קומפרמיס
9. בח״ח ובקנס סך מסוים לאשר ולקיים כפי הפס״ד אשר יצא מאתנו

---

1. כבוד הרב אנשיל
2. כותל המפסקת (המפסיק); אולי צ״ל ׳ב״ה׳ (בית המוצנע)
3. לא ברור מה כוונת האות כאן. אולי טעות סופר שלא נמחקה.
4. בית המוצנע(?)
5. ירום הודו
6. לא ברור מה כוונת האות כאן. אולי טעות סופר שלא נמחקה.
7. תוספת מעל השורה

בכן נזדקקנו להם ומצאנו שהכותל בנין המפסקת בין {ה"ה} בית של כ"הירץ ובין פלאטץ של כ' יוזלה הנ"ל עומד על גבול שני' בשוה ומחמת הקנאהלין הנ"ל כמו שהי' עכשיו כה יהי' הבא ואין צריך כ"ה הירץ הנ"ל לסלק אותם והמחיצה שאטוואנד שאחורי קנאהלין יהי' על אופן המבואר להבא דהיינו עכ"פ כנגד כל משיכת הקענטל עד הקנאהלין רשאי כ' הירץ להעמיד המחיצה שאטוואנד אחורי הקענטל ומחמת אחורי קנאהל ממש באשר שאפשר שמקודם לא הי' אחורי הקנאהלין שו[ם] מחיצה בפני עצמו רק מחיצה של הקנאהל עצמו הי' למחיצת שאטוואנד בכן צריך כ' הירץ להביא ראי' שהי' שם מחיצה בפני עצמו ובאם לא הביא ראי' אינו רשאי להעמיד מחיצה שאטוואנד אחורי קנאהלין אך יעמיד המחיצה שאטוואנד על השפה של הקנאהלין ויעלה באופן שיהי' המחיצה העומד על השפה כנגד אמצע הכותל המפסקת אכן אינו מחויב כ' הירץ למעט בשביל כך חלל הנקב שבקנאהלין ואינו צריך להעמיד המחיצה על חלל הנקב {שבקנאהלין} אפי' כל שהוא אבל אם הביא ראי' שגם כנגד הקנאהלין הי' עומד המחיצה בפני עצמו אחורי הקנאהלין גם עתה רשאי לעשות כן ומן הקנאהלין ואילך עד בנין כותל המפסקת צריך ג"כ כ' הירץ להביא ראי' שהמחיצה שאטוואנד הי' נמשך בשוה מהמחיצה שאחורי קענטל עד כותל בנין המפסקת ואז יבנה גם עתה כמו כן אף שמגיע עד סוף רוחב הכותל המפסקת ובאם לא הביא ראי'

עו ע"ב

ב"ה

לא הביא ראי' אזי אינו רשאי לבנות המחיצות שאטוואנד מן הקנאהלין ואילך לצד הסוכה אלא באופן שיהי' נמשך ומגיע עד אמצע רוחב כותל המפסקת {ובאם לא הביא ראי'} עוד התעצמו לדין הצדדים הנ"ל והיינו שהתורני כ"ה אנשיל פפאן תבע {בהרש} בהרשאת הנ"ל באשר שהבנין כותל המפסקת הוא משותף לשניהם ועל אותו רוחב אותו כותל עומד לצד הרחוב עמוד של אבן לצד של פלאטץ של כ' יוזלה האבן הוא שווה עם הכותל ועל צד של כ' הירץ בון נכנס מאותו אבן איין פפאלץ בכן טען כה"א[1] בקבלנא רבה על שלא עשה כ' הירץ הנ"ל אותו אבן רחב יותר כדי שיכנס ג"כ איין פ פפאלץ[2] בתוך גבולו לצורך בית שלו בכן תובע או שיקלף חצי רוחב האבן שעומד על גבול כ' יוזלה כדי שגם כ' יוזלה יוכל לעמוד ג"כ איין רחב שיכניס ממנו איין פפאלץ לתוך גבול שלו או שישלם דמי' בעבורו וכ"ה בענדיט בהרשאת הנ"ל השיב שלא הי' ביכולתו לעשות איין פפאלץ שיכנוס בגבול של כ' יוזלה בלי ידיעת כ' יוזלה ובאם הוא יבנה ביתו יוכל לעשות איין פפאלץ מאבן סמוך לאבן העומד על

1. כבוד הרב אנשיל
2. Phalze=Pfahl

16. הכותל וכהר״א[1] השיב שהוא {בענין} (בנין)[2] ח[ל]קאה אם לא נעשה מאבן רחב
17. והאריכו בטענותיהם כנראה מתוך ק״ה המונח אצלינו ואחר חקירת
18. האומן הנ״ל גם בזה מצאנו שהדין עם כ׳ הירץ הנ״ל וכ׳ יוזלה הנ״ל יעשה
19. גם הוא אבן שקורין פפאלץ בפני עצמו סמוך לכותל המפסקת בת[וך]
20. גבול שלו כדי לכנוס פתח שלו בתוך אותו אבן ובאשר שהתרצה לפנינו
21. כ׳ פתחי׳ בטענותיו שאינו מבקש מן כ׳ יוזלה הנ״ל לשלם מה שמגיע
22. על חלקו מדמי אותן אבן שעמד על כותל המפסקת על גבול שניהם בכן
23. כפי מה שהתרצה כה יהי יצא מאתנו אור ליו׳ ה׳ י״ב טבת תקלו לפק
24. הדין ר״י ורב״ד מהו׳ נתן מז והדיין כ״ה מאיר שיף ואני

עז ע״א

1. ב״ה
2. באשר שיצא בפס״ד הלז מאתנו ח״מ יב טבת העבר שכ׳ הירץ בון
3. צריך להביא ראי׳ שהי׳ שם {אק}מקדם אחורי קנאהל מחיצה בפני
4. עצמו ושלא הי׳ המחיצה של קנאהל עצמו למחיצת שאטוואנד
5. עוד נאמר בפס״ד הלז שכ׳ הירץ הנ״ל צריך להביא ראי׳ שהמחיצה
6. שאטוואנד הי׳ נמשך בשוה ממחיצה שאחורי קענטל עד כותל
7. בנין המפסקת ואז יבנה גם עתה כמו כן גוף שמגיע עד
8. סוף רוחב כותל המפסקת ע״כ מה שיצא בפס״ד הלז ביו׳ הנ״ל
9. וכהיו׳ דלמטה הביא הו״ה ג״ה כ׳ הירץ בון הנ״ל שני עדי׳ שהי׳
10. לאחורי הקנאהל מחיצה בפני עצמו וגם המחיצה שאט
11. = וואנד הי׳ שוה במשכו עד כותל בנין המפסקת בכן רשות
12. גם עתה לכ׳ הירץ בון ובניו הנ״ל לבנות המחיצה שאטוואנד
13. מאחורי קענטל ואילך עד הכותל המפסקת בשוה אף שמגיע
14. המחיצה עד סוף רוחב כותל בנין המפסקת יצא מאתנו
15. אור יו׳ ב ר״ח שבט תקלמד ויו לפק ר׳ נתן מז ר׳ מאיר שיף ואנ[י]
16. קודם ששלחנו אחרי עדי׳ שהי׳ כ׳ ליב אוקס וכ״ה איצק [בינגא]
17. שלחנו אחר כ׳ יוזלה זיכל ובא לפנינו ואמרנו לו שנשאר
18. במעמד {שמיעת} (הגדת)[3] עדי׳ והשיב שאינו מרוצה בעדי׳ הנ״ל שכ״ה
19. איצק הנ״ל הוא שונא ממנו וכ׳ ליב אוקס לא ידע כלום ונס מאת[נו]
20. שלחנו אח״כ אחרי עדי׳ ובאו לפנינו ואיימנו עליהם והגיד[ו]
21. עדותם ולאח״כ חוזרנו ושלחנו אחר כ׳ יוזלה הנ״ל אם רצה
22. להשיב על דברי עדי׳ ולא רצה לבוא גמרנו פסק דין ע״פ עדי׳
23. הנ״ל כנ״ל

---

1. כבוד הרב אנשיל
2. תוספת מעל לשורה
3. תוספת מעל השורה

No. 68

Oppenheim v. Kassel

Fols. 77b–78a; Monday 8 January 1776

Simeon Oppenheim, in his mid-twenties and unmarried, entered into an agreement to sell lottery tickets supplied by Moses Kassel.[1] According to Simeon, Moses offered to pay him a set commission for each ticket that he sold, and Simeon had the right to return any unsold tickets. Simeon returned eighty-nine unsold tickets together with the proceeds from the eleven tickets that he did sell, less his commissions. The tickets involved were "last class" tickets and there was a winning one among those that he sold.[2] For this ticket Simeon demanded a higher commission. Moses countered that he had offered Simeon such generous terms because he expected him to sell significantly more tickets than he did.[3] Moses noted that it was not customary to give such a high commission to those who sold so few tickets. In addition, he noted that in returning the tickets just two days before the draw, Simeon had caused Moses financial harm because this series of lottery tickets could not be returned to the lottery management. The court ruled that Moses had to fulfill the conditions that were originally agreed upon and pay Simeon what he was owed in full.

עז ע"ב

ב"ה
ע"ד שבא לפנינו ה"ה התורני כ"ה אנשיל פפאן כץ בהרשאת
הבחור כ' שמעון בן הו"ה יוז[ב]ל אופנהיים ותבע מן הוה[4] כ' משה
בהמנוח[5] כ' בענדיט קאסיל ז"ל סך כ"ד זהו' ט"ז צל והציע לפנינו חשבן
ובתוכה מן תשעה ועשרי' מעצר לאטירע לעצטה קלאס קורש מן טרעפר
מן שלשת אלפי' א צל מן כל זהו' העולה לג אלפי' סך חמיש[י'] זהו'
כאשר קצץ עמו המקח בשעת שלקח ממנו סך מאה שלישי צעטל ואף שהחזיר
לו סך פ"ט שלישי' ולא מכר מהם רק י"א שלישי' אשר בתוכם הי' טרעפר

---

1. According to Dietz, p. 220, Oppenheim was born in 1751.
2. See Helma Houtman-De Smedt, "North-West Europe under the Spell of Lotteries and Lotto in the Eighteenth and Nineteenth Centuries," in *Lotteries in Europe: Five Centuries of History*, ed. Bernard Bruno (Brussels: Belgian National Lottery, [1994]), 137–85, particularly 142–45, as well as Roberto Garvía, "Syndication, Institutionalization, and Lottery Play," *American Journal of Sociology* 113.3 (November 2007), 617–22, esp. 621–22.
3. Tickets were not just offered within the Jewish community. A Jew (Reinganum) took out an ad in the Friday 24 August 1781 (Nr. 135) edition of the *Journal in Frankfurt am Main* newspaper advertising lottery tickets from various places that were for sale "in der Judengaβe No. 185."
4. המפואר והחשוב
5. בן המנוח

9. הנ"ל מ"מ מגיע לו מה שקצץ עמו כי כך {ע} התנה עמו בשבועה שלקח שכל מה
10. שלא {מכר} יוכל למכור שרשאי להחזיר לו ומחויב כ' משה לקבל אותם
11. לחזרה ואפי לא מכר רק א' או ב' הי' צריך ג"כ לשלם לו מה שקצץ
12. ולאחר שניכה מה שמחויב לשלם לכ' משה נשאר עוד כד זהו' [ט]ז[1]
13. כנ"ל וה"ה התורני כ"ה משה אויך בהרשאת כ' משה קאסיל הנ"ל השיב
14. שכ' שמעון התחיל לעסוק במו"מ מן לאטררע צעטל {בש}בתשעה ועשרי'
15. לאטירע העבר ולקח מן כ' משה הנ"ל מאה שלישי' צעטל מן מאה נומרת
16. וטוען אף שאין דרך למכור מאה נומרת מ"מ נתן לו מפני שסבר שכ'
17. שמעון ימכרו אותן ומש"ה פסק עמו ג"כ ליתן לו א צל קורש מן כ' זהו'
18. רק לאח"כ שני ימי' פר דען צוג החזיר כ' שמעון הנ"ל ש[2] שמוני' ותשעה
19. שלישי' מן הנ"ל והשאיר בידו רק י'א {טריל} טריטל בכן לא זו בלבד שאינו
20. מגיע לכ' שמעון הקורש שפסק עמו באשר שלא עסק כמנהוג[3] שארי קולעקטע[הרין]
21. שלא לקח רק י"א שלישי' כחד איניש דעלמא שאין לו קורש בשביל זה וכמו
22. שנוכל לחקור אצל שארי קולעקטעהרין נהוג במ"מ[4] זה ואדרבה תבע
23. מן כ' שמעון שהחזיר לו פ"ט דריטל הנ"ל שלא מכרו כ"מ[5] הנ"ל רק י"א מהם
24. ו"משכ הוכרח כ"מ הנ"ל להחזיק לעצמו השני קלאסה ראשוני' ובפרט באשר
25. שהי' המאה שלישי' מן מאה נומרת מתחלפי' אינם יוכל להחזירם לדערעקצאין
26. כמו שיכול אלו לקח השלישי' מן נומרת שאינם מתחלפי' וטוען שהב"ד יחק[רו] כן
27. אצל הקולעקטער

עח ע"א

1. ב"ה
2. אצל הקולעקטר הנושאי' ונותני' בזה בכן הי' לו הפסד באלו
3. שבעי' ושמונה {רט} (טריטל)[6] שתבע מן כ' שמעון כל אחד א רט העולה
4. שבעי' ושמונה רט שתבע מן כ' שמעון שישלם לו {ג"כ בפיר}
5. ואף שאמת הוא שהתנה כ' משה עם כ' שמעון הנ"ל שרשאי להחזיר היינו
6. כדרך שנוהגי' להחזיר וכדרך {הת[...]} התגרי' במו"מ אבל להחזיר
7. לו סכום הרבה כמו שהחזיר כ"ש[7] הנ"ל לא הי' דעתו בהכי שיתן
8. לו הקורש והאריכו הצדדים הנ"ל בטענותיהם ובתשובתיהם כ[מ]בואר
9. מתוך ק"ה המונח לפנינו ובאשר שהצדדים הנ"ל חתמו עצמם ב
10. בתוקף קומפרמיס בח"ח ובקנס סך מסוים לאשר ולקיים כפי
11. אשר יצא מאתנו נזדקקנו להם {ומצאנו} ולאחר שדרשנו וחקרנו

---

1. כנראה 'ט"ז צל' (ר' לעיל, שורה 4)
2. כנראה שהסופר התחיל את המילה, הפסיק ואז התחיל שוב בלי למחוק את האות.
3. צ"ל 'כמנהג' או 'כנהוג'
4. אולי צ"ל 'במו"מ' (ר' לקמן דף עח ע"א שורה 6)
5. כבוד משה
6. תוספת מעל השורה
7. כבוד שמעון

12. משארי תגרי' במו"מ מצאנו שמא[חר] שהתנה כ' שמעון הנ"ל עם
13. כ' משה הנ"ל שמה שנשאר בידו ולא ימכרנו שרשאי להחזיר ליד
14. כ משה הנ"ל בכן אין כל ממש מה שתבע כ' משה הנ"ל מן כ' שמעון הנ"ל
15. ואדברה[1] שכ' משה מחויב לשלם הקורש כפי מה שהתנה עמו
16. ומחויב לשלם לכ' שמעון כפי חשבנו שהציע כ' שמעון לפנינו
17. יצא מאתנו יו' ב' טז טבת תקלו לפק
18. הדיין מהו' יעקב שמש נרו' הדיין כ"ה מאיר שיף ואני

No. 69

Fol. 78b; Wednesday evening, 31 January 1776

The court offered a financial compromise between four matchmakers, three of whom were males and all of whom claimed to have had a hand in arranging the marriage of the son of the late Aaron Fulda and the daughter of the late Moses Fahrgass. There appears to have been a certain sum to be paid to the matchmakers, and the court was appointed to decide how it should be divided. An addition above the final line of the text suggests that the court may have made the payments to the individuals immediately.

עח ע"ב

1. ב"ה
2. אור ליו' ה' יא שבט (תקלו לפק)[2] עשינו פשר בין כ"ה נתן אופנה וכ' שמואל סופר
3. והאשה מ' קלערכה אשת כ"ה משה אויך והב"ח כ' ליב בן כ"ה גומפל
4. עמריך יצו שהתעצמו בטענותיהם על דבר שדכנות מהשידוך
5. שנעשה בן[3] (כ')[4] המנוח כ"ה פולדא[5] עם היתומה של המנוח כ' משה
6. פאהר גאס שכל אחד מהם רוצה לזכות בשדכנות העולה לב' זהו' וחצ[6]
7. ופסקנו עפ[7] פשר שיהי' לכ"ה נתן אופנה שמונה זהו' ולכ' שמואל
8. סופר שמונה זהו' ולכ' ליב עמריך יא ז[הו'] וחצי ולהאשה מ קלערכה
9. ה' זהו' וכה חלקנו ביניהם (תיכף)[8] ר יעקב שמש ר' מאיר שיף ואני

---

1. אולי צ"ל 'ואדרבה'
2. תוספת מתחת השורה
3. אולי צ"ל 'בין בן'
4. תוספת מעל השורה
5. אולי צ"ל 'אהרן פולדא' (ע' לעיל, מס' 39); אשתו של נתן אופנה היתה בתו של אהרן פולדא (ר' אבני זכרון, מס' 4897).
6. צ"ל 'וחצי'
7. על פי
8. תוספת מעל השורה

No. 70

Schotten v. Falk

Fols. 79a–b; Sunday evening, 11 February 1776

Leb Schotten owned half of a house on the Falke lot that was recently renovated. A quarter of the house was owned by Abram Hain and the remaining quarter was owned by Mordecai Falk, who was about to move into the upper floor. Mordecai wanted to install more storage space on the ground floor of the house but Leb and Abram objected, claiming that it would increase the chance of theft and block light into the kitchen. They also contended that there was sufficient storage space on the upper floor and there was no need to build more. Mordecai, who was represented by his son, countered that he needed the space and that it could be built in such a way that it would not block the light or compromise security. Mordecai also had concerns about people other than the husbands and wives from the upper level passing through the area on the lower floor to get to the toilets. Leb and Abram objected to such a restriction on any family member but agreed that servants and others would have to use the toilets in the cellar. The court allowed the building of the storage space for personal use on condition that it was built in such a way that it did not block the light. With respect to access to the toilets, the court sided with Mordecai noting that the view expressed by him was the accepted custom.

עט ע"א

1. ב"ה
2. ע"ד שבא לפנינו ה"ה התורני כ"ה משה אויך בהרשאת ובמעמד הו"ה
3. כ"ה ליב שאטין כץ מחזיק חצי בית {שלם} מבית שלם שנבנה מחדש
4. צום פאלקין והו"ה כ' אברם האין שיש לו רביעית מבית שלם הנ"ל
5. ורוצי' למחות באותו שיבוא לדור בשטח מעלה בבית הנ"ל שלא יעמד
6. שאנק אין הוט עהרנד למטה באשר שעל אותו צד שהוא פתח המרתף
7. וגם מדרגה שקורין שטעג אי אפשר להעמיד שם שא[נק] ובצד
8. השניי' לצד הקוך אם שם עומד השאנק שאפשר שעל ידי שיכול
9. לעמוד על השאנק ויכולי' לגנוב מן השאנק שהוא על הקוך למעלה וגם
10. אין יכולי' לעשותו באשר שמחשיך אור {אור} של הקוך וזולת אותו
11. שאנק יש לאותו שדר בשטח מעלה שענק הרבה כדי סיפוקו והב"ח
12. כ' זעלקלי בן כ' מרדכי פאלק כץ השיב בהרשאת אביו כ'
13. מרדכי הנ"ל ששייך לו רביעית מבית שלם הנ"ל שאותו שיבא
14. בשטח מעלה לדור בו יש לו רשות להעמיד שאנק בשטח {מעלה} מטה
15. {ל}אין הויז עהרנד שעכשיו אין לאותו שדר בשטח מעלה כדי סיפוקי
16. שענק למעלה באשר שמשך הקוך למעלה הוא על צד אחד כולו ואף

17. שיש על צד שנית איין שאנק מ״מ אינו כדי סיפוקו ומה שטען כ״ה
18. ליב שמתירא מפני גניב[ה] לאו כלום הוא שכל שאנק הוא סגור
19. ומסוגר ומה שהוא טוען שיחשך האור של הקוך השיב שיכולי׳ לעשות
20. שיהי׳ מגיע הגוב׳ עד הגאגאטר של הקוך שאינו מחשיך האור ב[צד]
21. עוד טען כ׳ זעלקלי׳ בהרשאת הנ״ל ורוצה למחות {ש}ביד אותו
22. שידור בשטח העליונה שאינו רשאי לילך דרך בית החורף למטה לבית
23. המוצנע העומד בסוכה רק הבעל בית עצמו ואשתו אבל לא בנו ובנ[י]
24. ביתו רק שילכו לב״ה העומד במרתף באשר שיש קפידא גדולה לאו[תו]
25. לאותו שידור

עט ע״ב

1. ב״ה
2. לאותו שידור בשטח מטה בבית החורף עם כל בני בית מן אותו שידור
3. בשטח העליונה הולכין דרך בית החורף מכמה טעמי׳ שהאריך וה״ה
4. כ״ה ליב וכ׳ אברם הנ״ל השיבו שאותו שידור בשטח העליונה רשאי׳
5. להל(ו)[1]ך דרך בית החורף לבית המוצנע שבסוכה הוא ואשתו ובניו
6. וב״ב י״ח {אבל לא משרתיו ואנשי׳ אחרי׳ שהם בביתו} באשר שבקושי
7. הוא לילך דרך המרתף אבל לא משרתיו ואנשי׳ אחרי׳ שהם בביתו
8. הם לבד צריכי׳ לילך לב״ה שבמרתף והאריכו הצדדי׳ הנ״ל בטענות׳
9. כמבואר בק״ה המונח אצלינו ולאחר שחתמו הצדדי׳ את עצמו
10. בתוקף קומפרמיס בח״ח ובקנס סך מסוים לאשר ולקיי׳ הפס״ד
11. אשר יצא מאתנו נזדקקנו להם ומצאנו שאותו שידור בשטח עליונה
12. רשאי׳ להעמיד אין הויז עהרנד למטה על צד של הקוך איין
13. שפייס שאנק להניח בתוכו מה שהוא לצורך עצמו ובני ביתו בלבד
14. שיגיע משך הגוב׳ {על} עד הגאגאטר של הקוך ולא יותר כדי שלא
15. יאפל האור של הקוך ומחמת הליכות הבית המוצנע שבסוכה
16. לאותו שידור בשט[ח] העליונה דרך בית החורף למטה מצאנו שאין
17. רשות לילך בית החורף לב״ה ר״ק[2] הבעל בית ואשתו כנהוג אבל
18. לא בניו ושאר בני ביתו יצא מאתנו אור ליו׳ ב׳ כ״ב שבט תקלו
19. הדיין ר״י מהו׳ נתן מז נרו׳ והדיין מהו׳ יעקב שמש נרו׳ ואני

---

1. תוספת מעל השורה
2. לא ברור למה יש גרשיים כאן.

No. 71

New Synagogue Fraternity v. Kassel

Fol. 80a; Thursday 15 February [1776]

The fraternity of the new synagogue sued Moses Kassel for 8 guldens, 3 kreuzers for dues in arrears for the years 1767–70. Through his representative, Moses responded that in 1767 he had informed the fraternity that he wished to leave the group since Jacob Emden, a personal enemy, had assumed a position of leadership. The fraternity agreed to the request but demanded dues. Moses noted that since the time he had informed them of his decision to leave he had not been invited to the fraternity's monthly class, was not allowed to say Kaddish on the anniversary of the death of his father, and was embarrassed by members of the fraternity. Given such treatment, Moses maintained that he owed the fraternity nothing. Through its representative, the fraternity denied all these charges. The court arranged a compromise according to which Moses was to pay the fraternity 5 guldens. The record notes that Moses paid the amount before the court, apparently on the day that the decision was given.

פ ע"א

1. ב"ה
2. יו' ה' ך"ה שבט עשינו פשר בין ה"ה החברא של בהכ"ח עליונה שהעמידו
3. ה"ה כ"ה אנשיל פפאן לפנינו שבהרשאתם ותבע מן כ' משה ב' המנוח
4. כ' בענדיט קאסיל ז"ל סך שמונה זהו' ג' צל שהי' בתוך החברא גם חת
5. חתם השטר שלהם שהציע לפנינו ולא שילם בשלשה שני' מחדש שבט
6. תקך"ז עד כסליו תק"ל לפק העולה שבועה מעות עם פפ"מ[1] סך הנ"ל וכמו
7. שהציע חשבן לפנינו וה"ה כ"ה משה אויך בהרשאת כ' משה השיב
8. שבשנת תקך"ז העבר הי' כ' יעקב עמדין גבאי בהחברא ומש"כ הי' כ' משה
9. רוצה לצאת מתוך החברא עבור שהוא שונאו ובני החברא הי' מרוצה
10. שיצא אבל כ' משה לא רצה לשלם ואח"כ לא הי' קוראו אותו בערב ר"ח
11. שנאסף החברא תמיד ללמוד השיעור גם ביו' יארצייט לא הניחו מלומר
12. קדיש וביזו אותו בכן אין עליו לשלם כלום והם הכחישו אותו שלהד"ם
13. בכל טענותיו ולאחר שחתמו הצדדי' הנ"ל לקיים הפשר שיצא מאתנו נ
14. נזדקקנו להם ומצאנו שישלם כ' משה הנ"ל חמשה זהו' להחברא וכן שילם
15. בפנינו נעשה ביו' הנ"ל מהו' יעקב שמש וכ"ה זנוויל טר[אך ואני]

---

1. לכאורה 'פרנקפורט דמיין' אבל לא ברור מה כוונת הדברים כאן. אולי קשור לשיעור דמי החבר.

No. 72

Schuster v. Reizcha, widow of Feis Deuz

Fol. 80b; Sunday 18 February 1776

A seat in the lower women's section of the synagogue that belonged jointly to the widow of Moses Schuster and the wife of Samuel Schuster (neither woman is mentioned by name in the record) was rented out for a year, beginning Passover 1776, to Reizcha, widow of Feis Deuz. Samuel challenged the renter's right to lease the space, claiming that he had abutter's rights based on his wife's use of an adjoining seat and his ownership of a second seat that was nearby. Reizcha, who like Samuel had no representation, responded that Samuel was late in claiming abutter's rights and only intended to rent the space out to someone else.[1] Moreover, Reizcha said that she had previously raised the issue of her renting the space with Samuel's wife, who had not objected. After Samuel affirmed that he would not lease the space out to anyone else during the coming year the court granted him the right to the space.

פ ע"ב

1. ב"ה
2. המקו' בע"נ התחתונה ששייכות לאל'[2] המנוח כ' משה בן המנוח כ' איצק שוסטר כץ
3. ז"ל ואשת[3] ה"ה כ' שמואל בן ה"ה המנוח כ"ה הענלה שוסטר כץ ז"ל עומדות כעת
4. בשכירות על הינטר שטאנד של מקו' הנ"ל ונשכרת עכשיו המקו' הנ"ל משך שנה
5. אחת מן פסח הבע"ל להאשה מ' רייצכה אל' המנוח כמ"ה פייס דייץ ז"ל וה"ה כ'
6. שמואל הנ"ל רוצה לזכות במקו' הנ"ל מדין מצרנות באשר שאשתו ששכרה כעת
7. ההינדר שטאנד יש לה זכות בגוף המקו' כשהמשכר לא בא לבה"כ כנהוג
8. גם המקו' הנ"ל היא בצד מקו' ששייך ממנו לכ' שמואל הנ"ל והאשה מ' רייצכה
9. הנ"ל טענה נגדו שדעת כ' שמואל לחזור ולהשכיר גוף המקו' הנ"ל לאחר' עוד ט
10. טענה שהיא שכרה המקו' הנ"ל ביו' ג' וכ' שמואל לא תבע אותה בשביל מצ
11. =רנות הנ"ל עד יו' ה' שלאחריו עוד טענה שכבר קודם ששכרה המקו' הנ"ל הודיע
12. אותה לאשת כ' שמואל הנ"ל שדעתה לשכור אותה אם רוצה {להעמיד}[להי']
13. עומדות בהינדרשטאנד ולא רצתה בכן אין לה דין מצרנות והאריכו ב
14. בטענותיהם ובאשר שהצדדי' הנ"ל חתמו עצמם בתוקף קומפרמיס ב
15. בכא"ה ל[א]שר ולקיים כפי הפס"ד שיצא מאתנו בכן נזדקקנו להם והנה אחר
16. שכ' שמואל הנ"ל קיבל בחרם בפנינו ב"ד שאשתו היא בעצמה תעמוד

---

1. Reizcha's gravestone (Horovitz, no. 3829) notes that she came to the synagogue early and left late, suggesting that she attended synagogue regularly.
2. בריינלה (ר' אלה תולדות 8.1.1773).
3. כנראה שארלה בת אנשיל מז (אבני זכרון, מס' 3905, נפטר תקמ"ו).

17. על גוף המקו׳ הנ״ל משך שנה הנ״ל [ול]׳א תעמיד אחרת במקומה בכן מצאנו
18. שכ׳ שמואל הנ״ל זכה בהמקו׳ הנ״ל מדין מצרנות יצא מאתנו יו׳
19. א ך״ח שבט תקלמד ויו לפק מהו׳ יעקב שמש ור זנוויל טראך ואני

Fol. 81a is blank.

No. 73

Fols. 81b–82a; Sunday evening, 25 February 1776

A seat in the upper men's section of the old synagogue that belonged to the children of the late Moses Schwab was sold to Tevele Stiefel after a period of public bidding. The seat sold for 412 guldens. The record specifies the exact location of the seat in the synagogue and the terms of sale.

פא ע״ב

1. ב״ה
2. מקו׳ שלם בבה״כ ישן עליונה אשר כעת עומד עליו כ׳ אנשיל בינגא שהי׳
3. שייך להמנוח כ׳ משה שוואב ז״ל הפונה לצד {מזתח} מזרח ומצד ימין
4. הוא כותל דרומי ומצד שמאל על מקו׳ סמוך לו עומד עליו כעת כ׳ געטשליך
5. שטרויז כץ אותו מקו׳ שלם הנ״ל הוכרז ע״פ צוות הקהל יצו בבה״כ ישן ו
6. וחדש זמן זמני׳ טובא שכל מי שרוצה לקנותו יבוא לפנינו ב״ד גם הוכרז
7. לפנינו ב״ד במעמד האפטרופסים דיתמי המנוח כ׳ משה שוואב ז״ל הנ״ל
8. ה״ה הו״ה כ׳ אברהם שוואב וה״ה כ׳ זלמן רויטשילד יצו ולא הי׳ אחד
9. שהי׳ פוסק כפי מה שפסק ה״ה הו״ה כ׳ טעבלי בהמנוח[2] כ׳ חיים שטיפל ז״ל
10. בכן מכרנו המקו׳ שלם הנ״ל במעמד האפוטרופסים הנ״ל לה״ה כ׳ טעבלי
11. שטיפל הנ״ל בעד סך ארבע מאות ושנים עשר זהובים אין קונפונטציאהנש
12. מינץ אויף דעם כד זהו׳ פוס לשלם (השליש)[3] מסך דמי מכירה הנ״ל תיכף בשעת
13. מסירת החלטה ושני {ה}שלישי׳ הנותרים מסך דמי מכירה הנ״ל על ששה
14. חצאי שנים רצופי׳ זא״ז מיו׳ מסירת חלטה הנ״ל ומחויב הלוקח כ׳ טעבלי
15. הנ״ל ליתן ששה ח״כ על זמנים הנ״ל גם נשאר מקו׳ שלם הנ״ל לאפותיקו מפורש
16. שלא יצא מחזקת מרא קמא כל זמן שלא נתפרע אפי׳ אחד מן הזמני׳ הנ״ל

---

1. תוספת מעל השורה
2. בן המנוח
3. תוספת מעל השורה

17. ומעתה המקו׳ שלם הנ״ל שהי׳ שייך מק[ד]מת דנא להמנוח לה[מ]נוחי כ׳ משה
18. שוואב ז״ל שייך מעכשיו להה״ה הו״ה כ׳ טעבלי שטיפל הנ״ל וי״א וב״כ
19. לחלוטין גמורין ולצמיתת עלמן עם כל זכות וחזקה וכמו שהי׳ שייך
20. מקדמא דנא להמנוח כ׳ משה שוואב ז״ל הנ״ל שייך בלי שום שיור כלל
21. וכלל ורשאי ה״ה כ׳ טעבלי הנ״ל וי״א וב״כ לעשות עם מקו׳ שלם הנ״ל
22. להוריש ולהנחיל להחליף להשכין למכור ולהשכיר וליתן במתנה כאות נפשו

פב ע״א

1. ב״ה
2. ורצונו בכל איניש דרשאי לעשות בשלו בלי מוחה כלל ואחר שנתפר[ע] כל
3. ח״כ מהזמני׳ הנ״ל שייך מעכשיו המקו׳ שלם הנ״ל להה״ה הו״ה כ׳ טעבלי׳ הנ״ל
4. וי״א וב״כ בשופי גמור בלי שום עורר וטוען יהי׳ המערער {מה} מי שיהי׳
5. הן רבי׳ או יחיד יהי׳ טענה מה שיהי׳ או בכל אופן שיהי׳ מכל מה שהפה
6. יוכל לדבר והלב לחשוב ולהרהר וכל מי שיערער אחר מכירה הנ״ל יהי׳ מי
7. שיהי׳ או באיזה אופן שיהי׳ דברי׳ בטלי׳ ומבוטלים כחרס הנשבר כאפס
8. וכאין יחשב לא שרירן ולא קיימין ולא יהי׳ חלין כלל וכלל וכטוען אחר מעשה
9. ב״ד הגדול ולא יזדקק שום קהל או ב״ד יצו או שום משפט שבעולם הן בדא״ה
10. והן בד״י כי דברי המערער הם בטלים ומבוטלים באשר שנעשה הכל ע״פ {צואת} צוות
11. הקהל יצו ובמעמד האפוטרופסי׳ הנ״ל וכתבנו וחתמנו זאת בתוקף מעשה
12. ב״ד ובכח ב״ד יפה להיות ביד הלוקח כ׳ טעבלי הנ״ל וי״א וב״כ לעשות ול[ז]כות
13. ולראיי׳ שיעמוד המקו׳ שלם הנ״ל ביד לוקח הנ״ל וי״א וב״כ בלי שום מוחה כלל
14. נעשה פה פ״פ דמיין אור ליו׳ ב׳ ויו אדר[2] תקלמד ויו לפק ר׳ נתן מז ר׳ יעקב שמש
15. ואני

No. 74

Schiff v. Shinka, widow of Koppel Cohen

Fols. 82b–83a; Monday 29 April 1776

Herz Schiff and his son, Zalman, claimed that Shinka, the widow of Koppel Cohen, owed them funds for two loans they had given her in the fall of 1775.[3] Their claim was based on notes they had recorded in their personal business diary (*pinqas*). Shinka was present in the court and, like the Schiffs, had representation. She dis-

1. כפילות במקור
2. ו׳ אדר חל ביום ג׳ בשנה זו
3. The name appears on her gravestone as "Shinla" rather than "Shinka" as the name appears here (Horovitz, no. 4513). Her husband, Koppel, died in late 1763 (Horovitz, no. 3154).

puted the conditions of the first loan and the amount of her liability, producing her own business diary to support her contentions. She denied ever having transacted the second loan and offered a possible explanation for how the Schiffs came to record it in their account book, an explanation rejected as implausible by the Schiffs. The court ordered Shinka to swear that her claims were correct. If she did, she would be free of the claims the Schiffs had made against her.

פב ע"ב

1. ב"ה
2. ע"ד שבא לפנינו ה"ה התורני כ"ה אנשיל פפאן כץ בהרשאת ובמעמד ה"ה הו"ה פו"מ כ"ה הירץ
3. ובנו הו"ה כ"ה זלמן שיף כץ ותבע מן האשה מ' שינכה אל' המנוח כ' קאפל כהן ז"ל סך מאה ו
4. ותשעי' ותשעה רט כ"ה צל אין טוב מעות והציע לפנינו חשבן צדק שהעתיקו מפנקסם ובחוב'
5. העלו ההפרש מסך שלשה מאות זהו' מינץ שקיבלה האשה הנ"ל דען{אי לפי} צוועלפט
6. זעפט[ע]מברי[1] העבר אין ט"מ והיא לא שילמה רק אין ש"[מ] בכן נשארה האשה הנ"ל עדיין
7. חייב ההפרש מסך הנ"ל שעולה שלשי' ושלשה רט למד צל אין ט"מ גם הניח לפנינו
8. פנקס של כ"ה הירץ ובנו הנ"ל שכתוב בתוכה שחייבת לשלם סך הנ"ל אין ט"מ עוד
9. העלה כ"ה הירץ הנ"ל בחשבונו סך שלשה מאות זהו' מינץ אין שפל מעות שקיבלה האשה
10. מ' שינכה הנ"ל ממנו דען איילפטן אוקטובר[2] העבר שלא שילמה כלום ע"ז וגם הראה ל
11. לפנינו פנקס שלו שנזכר בתוכה סך הנ"ל ביו' הנ"ל וטוען באשר שבנו כ"ה זלמן הנ"ל
12. שכח מלהעתק סך זה בפנקסו מתוך כך שכח ג"כ מלהעלות לחשבן כשחשב עם האשה
13. הנ"ל עד שבועה העבר שמצאו כ"ה הירץ הנ"ל בפנקס שלו בכן תבע עכשיו מן האשה
14. הנ"ל נמצא עולה יחד עם ההפרש הנ"ל סך מאה ותשעי' ותשעה רט כ"[א] צל אין ק"[ד] א' טית
15. זהו' י'[.] צל וה"ה התורני כ"ה משה אויך בהרשאת האשה הקצינה (מ' שינכה הנ"ל)[3] ובמעמדה השיב
16. בברי ובודאי שאינה חייבות כלום שהסך שלשה מאות זהו' מינץ שקיבלה האשה דען
17. צוועלפטה זעפט[עמ]בר העבר לא הי' אין ט"מ רק אין ש"מ רק כ[מ]ו שחישבה עמו אין
18. שפל מעות והרא[ת] לפנינו ג"כ פנקס שלה שלא נזכר בתוכה ט"מ ואותו סך
19. שלשה מאות זהו' מינץ שתבע כ"ה הירץ הנ"ל מן איילפטן אוקטובר השיבה שלא קיבלה כ
20. כלום {ממ[...]} ממנו וגם לא נזכר כלום לגמרי בפנקס שלה וטוענת שאפשר שבטעות
21. הכפיל כ"ה הירץ הנ"ל אותן שלשה מאות זהו' מן צוועלפט[ה] זעפטעמבר שני פעמי' ב

---

1. 12 בספטמבר
2. 11 באוקטובר
3. תוספת מעל השורה

22. בפנקס שלו וכה״א[1] הנ״ל השיב מכ[ח] הה[פר]ש שיש בין שני הסכומי׳ ניכר שאינו טעות שחד
23. מהם הוא אין ט״מ וחד אין ש״מ ועוד יש הפ[ר]ש בזמן והאריכו הצדדי׳ הנ״ל בטענותיהם
24. ובתשובתיהם כמבואר בק״ה המונח לפנינו והנה אחרי שהצדדי׳ הנ״ל חתמו
25. עצמם

פג ע״א

1. ב״ה
2. א״ע בתוקף קומפרמיס בח״ח ובקנס סך מסויים לאשר ולקיים הפס״ד שיצא מאתנו
3. נזדקקנו להם ומצאנו שתשבע האשה מ׳ שינכה הנ״ל ע״ד המקו׳ ב״ה וע״ד ב״ד בלי ע
4. ערמה ומרמה ושום הוראות היתר שבעולם שכדברי׳ כן הוא שיודעת בברי שאותו
5. סך שלשה מאות זהו׳ שקיבלה דען צוועלפטה זעפטעמבר הי׳ אין שפל מעות וגם
6. שלא קיבלה לגמרי אותו סך שלשה מאות זהו׳ מינץ שהעלה כ״ה הירץ הנ״ל בחשבונו
7. מן איילפטן אוקטובר ואז לאחר שתשבע כנ״ל פטורה ומסולקת האשה מ׳
8. שינכה הנ״ל מן כ״ה הירץ ובנו כ״ה זלמן הנ״ל מחמת תביעות הנ״ל
9. יצא מאתנו היו׳ יו׳ ב׳ ד״ה למב״י שנת תקלמד ויו לפק

No. 75

Fol. 83b; Undated

The court recorded the sale of a portion of the back section of the (Hinter) Kranich lot where a house had once stood. The plot was two-thirds owned by the "collectors of the community" (those who collected debts) and one-third by two brothers, Yishai and Joseph Wetterhahn. The availability of the land was announced in the old and new synagogues, and before the court, by order of the collectors of the community and was put up for bids. It was sold to the highest bidder, the aforementioned Yishai Wetterhahn, for 820 guldens. Since Yishai already owned one-sixth of the property he was only required to pay out about 683 guldens: approximately 546 guldens to the community and 136 to his brother. The terms of sale are itemized.

פג ע״ב

1. ב״ה
2. פלאטץ שלם שהי׳ עומד עליו בית שלם פנימי צום הינטר קראנך דהיינו אותו בית שהי׳ עומד על צד

1. וכבוד הרב אנשיל

3. שמאל בכניסה מבית החיצון לבתי׳ פנימי׳ אותו בית שלם הנ״ל הי׳ שייך שני שלישי׳ ליורשי האחי׳
4. המונחי׳ כ׳ ליזר וכ׳ איצק בני המונחי׳ כ׳ שמע׳ מז ז״ל ושליש מבית הנ״ל הי׳ שייך להאחי׳ כ׳ ישי וכ׳
5. יוזפא בני המנוח כ׳ לימא ווערטרהאַן ז״ל ועתה שייך שני שלישי׳ מן פלאטץ הנ״ל להאלופי׳
6. קציני׳ גובי׳ יצו ושליש האחד להני תרי אחי׳ כ׳ ישי וכ׳ יוזפא הנ״ל אותו פלאטץ הנ״ל הוכרז
7. בבה״כ ישן וחדש זמן זמני׳ טובא {שכל מי ש} ע״פ צוות הגובי׳ והני תרי אחי׳ הנ״ל שכל מי שרוצה לקנותו
8. יבוא לפנינו ב״ד גם הוכרז לפנינו ב״ד ח״מ עד שיפסקו המוסיפי׳ ולא הי׳ שום אחד שהי׳ פוסק
9. כפי מה שפסק ה״ה כ׳ ישי בהמנוחי[1] כ׳ לימא ווערטרהאַן הנ״ל בכן מכרנו פלאטץ שלם הנ״ל לה״ה
10. כ׳ ישי ווערטרהאן הנ״ל בעד סך שמונה מאות ועשרי׳ זהו׳ אין קונפונטציאהנש מינץ אויף
11. דעם ך״ד זהו׳ פוס והיינו שמחויב כ׳ ישי הנ״ל לשלם להאלופי׳ גובי׳ יצו תיכף נגד מסירת מעשה
12. ב״ד הל[ז] סך מאה ושמוני׳ ושתי׳ זהו׳ י״[ד] צל והסך שלשה מאות וששי׳ וארבעה זהו׳ ד״ו צל
13. הנותרי׳ ממה שמגיע עוד להאלופי׳ גובי׳ יצו ע״ח מסך דמי מכירה הנ״ל מחויב כ׳ ישי הנ״ל
14. לשלם להאלופי׳ גובי׳ יצו על ששה חצאי שני׳ רצופי׳ זא״ז מיו׳ מסירת מעשה ב״ד {...}
15. ועד[2] מני׳ הנ״ל מחויב ליתן ח״כ על אורדר האלופי׳ גובי׳ יצו ולאחיו כ׳ יוזפא הנ״ל מחויב כ״י[3] הנ״ל
16. לשלם תיכף נגד קבלת החלטה ממנו סך ארבעי׳ וחמשה זהו׳ לד צל ועל סך תשעי׳ ואחד
17. זהו׳ ששה צל הנותרי׳ שמגיע עוד לאחיו כ׳ יוזפא הנ״ל ע״ח מחויב כ׳ ישי הנ״ל לשלם לאחיו
18. הנ״ל על ששה חצאי שני׳ רצופי׳ זא״ז מיו׳ מסירת החלטה מאחיו הנ״ל וע״ז מחויב ליתן ששה ח״כ על
19. אורדר אחיו הנ״ל גם נשאר אותו פלאטץ שלם הנ״ל לאפותיקו מפורש שלא יצא מחזקת מרא קמא כל
20. זמן שלא נתפרע אפי׳ אחד מן הח״כ הנ״ל ויתוקן ע״ז שטר אפותיקו ע״י נאמני הקהלה כנהוג

---

1. בן המנוח
2. כנראה שאות זו משמשת כאן גם כ-׳ד׳ וגם כ-׳ז׳ והמילים הן ׳ועד זמנים׳.
3. כבוד ישי

No. 76

Fol. 84a contains only a few words, which are repeated at the beginning of fol. 84b.

פד ע"א

1. ב"ה
2. חצי פלאטץ מן פי[1]

No. 77

Fol. 84b; Sunday evening, 2 June 1776

A record of the sale of half a plot of land on the back section of the (Hinter) Pflug lot. The land was sold to the Jewish community by Seligmann Ulf and Rehal, widow of Moses Wohl, for 475 guldens. Seligmann and Rehal each held equal shares in the land and agreed to the sale. As in other instances there was a public bidding for the land, and it was sold to the highest bidder. The record details the site and the terms of payment.[2]

פד ע"ב

1. ב"ה
2. חצי פלאטץ מן פלאטץ שלם שהיה עומד עליו אחד מן הבתים פנימי' צום הינטר פלוג דהיינו אותו בית
3. שהיה עומד על צד ימין בכניסה מהרחוב לבתים פנימי' שהיה רביעית מן פלאטץ שלם הנ"ל לה"ה
4. כה[3] זעליגמן אולף יצו ורביעית השני מן פלאטץ הנ"ל היה שייך להאשה מ' רעהל אל' המנוח כ' משה
5. וואהל ז"ל אותו חצי פלאטץ הנ"ל הוכרז בבה"כ ישן וחדש זמן זמנים טובא ברצון כ"ה זעליגמן והאשה
6. מ' רעהל הנ"ל שכל מי שרוצה לקנותו יובא לפנינו ב"ד גם הוכרז לפנינו ב"ד ח"מ עד שיפסקו המוסיפי'
7. ולא היה שום אחד שהיה פוסק כפי מה שפסקו ה"ה האלופי' קציני' גובים יצו בכן מכרנו חצי

---

1. שאר הדף הוא ריק.
2. A copy with original signatures appears in YIVO MS. RG 128 (folder 77–78), fols. 170a–b, where there is also an itemization of the fees paid to the court.
3. כבוד הרב

8. פלאטץ הנ"ל לה"ה האלופים קצינים גובי' יצו בעד סך ארבע מאות ושבעים וחמשה זהו' אין קונפינציאהנש
9. מינץ אויף דען כ"ד זהו' פוס והיינו לשלם שליש מדמי מכירה הנ"ל בשעת קבלת מעשה ב"ד הלז ושני שלישי'
10. הנותרים מסך דמי המכירה הנ"ל לשלם על ששה חצאי שנים רצופי' זא"ז מיום שניתן להם מעשה ב"ד הלז
11. וכנהוג הקהלה פה ומעתה אותו חצי פלאטץ הנ"ל שהיה שייך מקדמת לה"ה כ"ה זעליגמן אולף הנ"ל ולהאשה
12. מ' רעהל הנ"ל שייך מעכשיו להאלופי' קצינם גובי' יצו לחלוטין גמורין ולצמיתות עלמון[1] כל ארכו ורחבו
13. עם כל חזקותיו וזכיותיו ומוצאויו[2] ומובאי' ומצרים ומרתפות וחצריו עומקא ורומא מתהום ארעא ועד
14. רום רקיע וכמו שהוא שייך מקדמת לה"ה כה זעליגמן אולף ולהאשה מרת רעהל הנ"ל בלי שום
15. שיור כלל ורשאי האלופי' קצינים גובי' יצו לעשות עם חצי פלאטץ הנ"ל לבנו[ת] ולהרוס להוריש להנחיל
16. להחליף להשכין למכור ולהשכיר כאות נפשם וכרצונם ככל אינש שרשאי לעשות בשלו בלי מוחה
17. כלל ולאחר שנתפרע כל סך דמי מכירה הנ"ל שייך מעכשיו חלק חצי פלאטץ הנ"ל האלופי'
18. קצינם ג[ו]בי' יצו בשופי' גמור בלי שום עורר וטוען כלל יהי' המערער מי שיהי' {מכל מה} הן רבים הן
19. או יחיד יהי' טענה מה שיהי' או בכל אופן שיהי' מכל מה שהפה יוכל לדבר והלב לחשוב ולהרהר
20. וכל מי שיערער אחר מכירה הנ"ל יהי' מי שיהיה או באיזה אופן שיהי' דבריו בטלים ומבוטלי'
21. כחרס הנשבר כאפס וכאין יחשוב לא שרירן ולא קיימין ולא יהי' חלין כלל וכלל וכטוען אחר
22. מעשה ב"ד הגדול ולא יזדקק שום קהל או ב"ד יצו או שום משפט שבעולם לדברי המערע[ר ה]ן
23. בדא"ה הן בד"י כי דברי המערער הן בטלין ומבוטלים באשר שנעשה הכל ברצון כ"ה
24. זעליגמן אולף והאשה מרת רעהל הנ"ל וכתבנו וחתמנו זאת בתוקף מעשה ב"ד ובכח ב"ד
25. יפה להיות ביד הלוקחי' האלופי' קצינים יצו לעדות ולזכות ולראי' שיעמוד אותו חלק
26. חצי פלאטץ הנ"ל עם כל חזקותיו וזכיותיו ביד לוקחים הנ"ל בלי שום מוחה כלל נעשה פה
27. פ"פ דמיין אור ליו' ב' טז סיון תקלמד ויו לפק
28. ה"ק יצחק מאיר ש"ש[3]

---

1. צ"ל 'עלמין' (בכ"י ייוו"א כתוב 'עלמן')
2. צ"ל 'מוצאיו' וכן בכ"י ייוו"א
3. שווארצשילד

29. ה"ק אברהם טריר כהן
30. ואני ה"ק חיים גונדרשהיים

No. 78

Sichel v. Flörsheim

Fols. 85a–b; Tuesday 3 September 1776

Yosle Sichel claimed that Moses Flörsheim had not paid him and/or his late brother, Lema, 69 guldens, 56 kreuzers for four different transactions, including a loan and the acquisition of goods, made over approximately the last 18 months. Yosle based one of his claims on entries in business diaries and another on a note that he had from Moses. Moses countered that he had had no dealings with the Sichel store since mid-December 1774, and that there were duplications as a result of a mistake in entering information. Thus, he maintained, he could not be charged twice for the same transaction. Moses also claimed that Yosle had used the clothing he had left with him as collateral without permission. According to Moses, Yosle had made such extensive use of it that he wore it out. Moses, therefore, no longer wanted it back but wanted to be paid for it. Both parties asked the court to offer a compromise, which it did. Yosle kept the clothing as partial payment against Moses' outstanding debt, and Moses was ordered to pay an additional 21 guldens, 24 kreuzers to Yosle.

פה ע"א

1. ב"ה
2. ע"ד שבא לפנינו ה"ה התורני כ"ה משה אויך בהרשאת הבחור כ' יוזלה בן
3. כ' איצק זיכל יצו ותבע מן הבחור החתן כ' משה בהמנוח[1] כ' לעמלי פלערש[היים]
4. ז"ל והציע לפנינו חשבן העולה לסך ששי' ותשעה זהו' חמשים וששה צל והיינו
5. כפי מה שהעתק מפנקסם שהציע לפנינו הי' כמר משה חייב בעד מה ש
6. שלקח בהקפה אחת {מ}לאחת מהחנות שהי' לכ"ה יוזלי ולאחיו כ' לימא
7. בשותפות עד עשרה בטבת שנת קהל"ת לפק עולה לסך ד"ג זהו' ד"ב צל א
8. {א.כ} אח"כ כשהי' כ' לימא ז"ל הנ"ל מוטל על ערש דוי ר"נ והי' החנות {ו..לה}
9. {החנות} לכ' יוזלי הנ"ל לבד לקח בהקפה כ' משה הנ"ל אחת לאחת עד י"ט אחרון
10. דפסח שנת הנ"ל בעד ד' זהו' ל"ב צל גם פודה כ' יוזלי הנ"ל משכונו
11. הלומ[..]' והיינו מלבוש שהשכין כ' משה הנ"ל בעד ט"ז זהו' ל"ד צל בכן

1. בן המנוח

12. תבע המעות דמי פדיי׳ ורוצה לחזור לו מלבוש שלו גם העלה בחשבון
13. הנ״ל והיצעי[1] כ״י מן כ׳ משה הנ״ל שחייב לכ׳ לימא ז״ל הנ״ל סך כ״ה זהו׳ כ״ח צל
14. ולא נזכר בכ״י שהוא עשה שנזכר בפנקס בכן תבע שניהם העומד יחד סך
15. ס״ט זהו׳ נ״ו צל והב״ח כ׳ משה הנ״ל הישב שהכל הוא סך ממה שנשאר בפנקס
16. חייב לכ׳ לימא הנ״ל בפנקס לערך ובמשמעות זמן של הכ״י שהוא עשרה בטבת
17. קהלת לפק בכל מה שהעלה ב{פנקס} בחשבונו עוד סך כ״ג זהו׳ ד״ב צל
18. שלקח בהקפה עד עשרה בטבת (קהלת לפק)[2] אינו כלום ועל מה שהעלה בחשבונו מן
19. עשרה בטבת ואילך מה שלקח כ׳ משה הנ״ל הישב כ״מ[3] הנ״ל שלא הי׳ בא
20. בבית מעשרה בטבת ואילך ולא לקח כלום ממנו ומחמת דמי פדיי׳ המלבוש
21. מן הלומ[..]׳ הישב כ׳ משה הנ״ל ותבע ממנו באשר שכ׳ יוזלה הנ״ל הי׳ משתמש
22. במלבוש ל{..} שלו שלא ברשות והלבישו עד שה׳ מכלה את המלבוש הנ״ל
23. בכן רוצה כ״מ הנ״ל להניחו ביד כ׳ יוזלה הנ״ל ושישלם לו מה שהוציא דהיינו
24. לערך ד״ח זהו׳ וחצי והאריכו הצדדי׳ הנ״ל בטענותיה׳ כמבואר מתוך
25. ק״ה המונח לפנינו ואחר שחתמנו הצדידים הנ״ל בתוקף קומפרמיס בח״ח ובקנס
26. סך מסוים לאשר לקיים כל אשר יצא מאיתנו ב״ד ח״מ גם נתנו עיניהם עלינו
27. ב״ד לפשר [ב]יניהם בכן נזדקקנו להם והנה מאחר שכ׳ יוזלי הנ״ל

פה ע״ב

1. ב״ה
2. התרצו עצמו לפנינו להחזיק המלבוש בעד עשרים זה׳ בכן מצאנו ע״פ פשר
3. שהב״ח כמר משה הנ״ל ישלם עוד לכ[4] יוזלי הנ״ל מכל תביעות הנ״ל ו[נג]ד חזרת כ[״י]
4. שלו סך עשרים ואחת זהו׳ כ״ד צל ובזה המה פטורים זה {...} מזה מן תביעות
5. הנ״ל והמלבוש שייך [ג״כ] לכ׳ יוזלי הנ״ל יצא מאתנו יו׳ ג׳ י״ט אלול שנת קולת לפק
6. הק׳ יעקב שמש
7. הק׳ מאיר שיף ואני

No. 79

Mai v. Sorle, widow of Me'ir Schuster

Fols. 86a–89a; Thursday 12 September 1776

A house on the Vorder Pfanne lot was owned jointly by Gumpel Mai and Sorle, widow of Me'ir Schuster, and her children. The house was in need of repairs and

1. צ״ל ׳והציע׳
2. תוספת מעל השורה
3. כבוד משה
4. לכבוד

the owners came before the court arguing over who should pay for what. The record does not itemize their opposing claims, but notes that their arguments were recorded in the court's record book. After each side obligated itself to abide by the court's ruling, the court prevailed upon them to accept a compromise according to which both owners had to bear equally the cost of items that were in "great need" of repair. The determination of what was pressing and what was not was made by the court after it inspected the entire house. Less urgent repairs would generally be two-thirds paid for by Gumpel and one third by Sorle and her children. The lengthy record itemizes the various repairs and payments that each side was obliged to make according to the court's decisions. The owners of the house were also involved in litigation with Moses Rothschild, and Gumpel agreed to bear this cost. Finally, Gumpel asked the court to order Sorle to stop keeping a store in her portion of the house. The court ruled that Sorle could continue to operate her store, but noted that she could not prevent Gumpel from opening a store in the house, even if he were to sell the same products that she did, unless she had privileges from the community protecting her from such incursions, or if Gumpel's undertakings infringed on communal ordinances. Also see no. 80.

פו ע"א

1. ב"ה
2. ע"ד {שבאו} ה[פ]רשות וסיכסוכי' שבין מחזיקי בית צום פאדר פפאן
3. והי[נו][1] [בין] ה"ה הו"ה כ' גומפיל מאיי סג"ל שיש לו החצי מבית שלם הנ"ל ובין ה
4. האשה הקצינה מ' סערלה אל' המנוח כ' מאיר בכ"א[2] שוסטר כץ ז"ל ובני
5. יתמי המנוח כ"מ[3] ז"ל הנ"ל שיש להם החצי שניי' מבית הנ"ל שנת[ע]צמו בטענותיהם
6. לפנינו מחמת הוצאת מבדק ותיקוני הבית הנ"ל שה"ה התרוני[4] כ"ה משה
7. אויך בהרשאת ובמעמד כ' גומפיל הנ"ל והאשה מ' סערלה הנ"ל בהרשאת
8. בני יתמי המנוח כ"מ ז"ל הנ"ל כמבואר בקונטרס הטענות המונח לפנינו
9. באריכות והנה אחרי שהצדדי' הנ"ל חתמו עצמם בתוקף קומפערמיס בח"ח
10. ובקנס סך מסוים חצי לשררה יר"ה וחצי להקדש לאשר ולקיי' כפי שיצא
11. מאתנו נזדקקנו להם ודברנו על לבם לעשות פשר דבר ביניהם על אופן
12. המבואר למטה והיינו מה שהוא תקון וצורך גדול לבית הנ"ל מחויבת ה
13. האשה מ' סערלה הנ"ל ובני' הנ"ל לשלם החצי מהוצאת ומה שהוא לצורך
14. קצת אינ' מחויבי' לשלם רק השליש מהוצאת (וש[ני] השלישי')[5] הנותרי' על כ' גומפיל הנ"ל

1. צ"ל 'והיינו'
2. בן כבוד אהרן (ר' דייץ, עמ' 272)
3. כבוד מאיר
4. צ"ל 'התורני'
5. תוספת מעל השורה

15. לבד וזה תלוי בדעת ובהכרת ב״ד ח״מ מה שהוא לפי דעתם והכרתם צו
16. צורך גדול והלכנו בבית הנ״ל וראינו הבית הנ״ל מדיוטא התחתונה לדיוטא
17. העליונה ודקדקנו הדק ה[י]טיב בטענותיהם ובתשובתיהם דרך פ״ד על
18. כל פרט ופרט כמבואר להבא והיינו מחמת החדר בית החורף חד שטאק
19. הויך לצד הרחוב שרצה כ׳ גומפיל הנ״ל לעשות בחדר הלז פענשטר
20. ראמין [חד]ושי׳ וגם שפיגל שייפין[1](#[2]מצאנו בהוצאת {...}) אזי מחויבת לשלם כל אוא[3] מהם החצי
21. (כל או״א החצי)[4] מהוצאת ובאם היא אינה מרוצה בהם וכ׳ גומפיל רוצה לעשות אותם
22. איז היא [אי]נה מחויבת לשלם רק מהוצאת[5] ועל כ״ג[6] הנ״ל שני שלישי׳
23. ומחמת דמי תיקון פענשטר פאסטן אונד ריגל בחדר הנ״ל מחויבת

פו ע״ב

1. ב״ה
2. האשה לשלם רק השליש מהוצאת ועל כל[7] (למותר)[8] החצי ומחמת דמי קורות חדשי׳
3. ועי״כ צריכין להרוס ולחזור ולבנות התנור מחדש מחויבת האשה לשלם החצי
4. בהוצאת אבל בעשיית אויף זאטץ על התנור אינה צריכה לשלם רק ה
5. השליש ולפתוח חלון בקוך סמוך לתנור מחויבי׳ לשלם כל או״א החצי מחמת ע
6. מה שרצה כ׳ גומפיל הנ״ל לעשות בתוך חדר הנ״ל נייאה שאנק התרצו א״ע
7. שני צדדי׳ הנ״ל לעשות שני אייכנה שאנק חדשי׳ וליתן אחד בחדר הלז
8. ואחד שני שטוק הויך בחדר שהוא לצד הרחוב והאשה הנ״ל תשלם בחד
9. שאנק החצי מהוצאת ובחד שאנק אינה צריכה לשלם רק השליש ומחמת
10. מה שרצה כ׳ גומפיל הנ״ל לפתוח ולעשות חלון איבר ליכט למעלה מן השאנק
11. בחדר הלז [כד][9] שנפל האור על המדרגה שקורין {שאנק} שטעק מצאנו
12. ע״פ ריצוי הצדידי׳ הנ״ל שנעשה חלון הנ״ל באופן כמבואר למטה והיינו
13. דוקא מן רונטה שייפין ובעשית אייזן גרי[מד][10] נגד החלון לצד המדרגה ואותו
14. שידור בחדר הלז רשאי לתלות [ל]פני[׳] נגד חלון הלז ווילון לבן והאשה
15. מ׳ סערלה תשלם להוצאת חלון ואייזן גרימד הנ״ל השליש ומשם סך אם
16. כ״ג הנ״ל רוצה לעשת עוד חל[ון] אחד בתוך הדלת אין על האשה הנ״ל

---

1. תוספת מעל השורה
2. תוספת המסומנת בסימון # מופיעה בדף הקודם פה ע״ב: # בהוצאות דמי ראמין חדשי׳ צריך לשלם כל או״א (תוספת מעל השורה: מה[...] הנ״ל) החצי אבל בהוצאות דמי שפיגל שייפן אם האשה הנ״ל מרוצה ג״כ לעשות שפיגל ש[ייפ]ן אזי מחויבת
3. אחד ואחד
4. תוספת מעל השורה
5. כנראה שצ״ל ׳רק כשליש מההוצאות׳
6. כבוד גומפיל
7. מהמילה ׳רק׳ ועד המילה ׳כל׳ המילים מצויות בתוך מסגרת אחת.
8. תוספת מעל המילים במסגרת
9. אולי צ״ל ׳כדי׳
10. אפשרות נוספת ׳גרימז׳

17. לשלם כלום בהוצאת אותו חלון בתוך הדלת הנ"ל ומחמת הוצאת בקלאדונג
18. האסקופה שתחת הדלת בחדר הלז גם {אין} אם[1] צריכין לתיקון הקורה ש
19. שתחת האסקופה הנ"ל מחויבת האשה הנ"ל לשלם החצי ומחמת
20. הוצאות בחדר שהוא לצד בתי' פנימי' בשטח הלז חד שטאק הויך
21. והיינו החדר הלז מחדש צו פרידרין אונד דיא פענשטר ראהמין
22. צו רעפרירין מחויבת האשה הנ"ל לשלם החצי מחמת הוצאות מן

פז ע"א

1. ב"ה
2. אקארד עם מויארער סך עשרי' וחמשה זהו' והיינו בשביל דש קאמין אב צו
3. ברעכין אונד דש פַיֵער ריכט על צד השני אין דיא קוך צו מאכין אונד
4. דען גוסשטיין אן פאדר אויפן צו זעצין דש אונטרשטה געין ג' שטאק הויך
5. אויף צו מאכין וגם איין קליינה וואשר שטיין אונד דען פאדער קעלר
6. [ל]פעמי' צו איבר ווארפן מצאנו שתשלם האשה בדמי אקארד הנ"ל עשרה
7. זהו' והמותרות ישלם כ' גומפיל הנ"ל גם התרצו עצמם הצדדים הנ"ל לעשות
8. בחדר הלז נגד החלון שהוא למעלה מן הפתח אייזה שטאנגי מבחוץ לחדר
9. על הוצאת שניהם בשוה גם התרצו עצמם לפנינו שני הצדדים הנ"ל
10. לעשות שני קוכין חדשי' חד שטאק הויך ושני שטאק הויך גם בשטח
11. מטה (מטה)[2] דיא קוך גם דש שענקעלכה בבית החורף למטה על הוצאת ש
12. שניהם בשוה ונכלל בזה לעשות טיפן שענק [ש]סגרי' למעלה על שני קוכין
13. הנ"ל על הוצאת שני ה'<צדדים> בשוה בשטח שני שטעג הויך לפתוח חלון
14. איבר ליכט מחדר בית החורף שהוא לצד הרחוב כדי שנפל האור
15. על המדרגה מצאנו שיתקון חלון הלז כנ"ל בשטח חד שטאק הויך בכל
16. אופין כנ"ל והאשה מ' סערלה תשלם השליש מהוצאת ומחמת דמי והעלאויפן
17. וואסר שטיין בשטח הלז מחויבת האשה לשלם החצי ומחמת גטיפלש
18. בחדרי' בשטח [.] המבואר למטה ומחמת החדר שהוא לצד בתים פנימי'
19. בשטח שני שטאק הויך הנ"ל התרצו שני ה'<צדדים> לעשות (דלת חדש על הוצאות =)[3]
(שניהם בשוה גם התרצו שניהם לעשות)[4] בחדר הלז
20. פענשטר ראהמין חדשי' עם בשליגש חדש גם שפיגל שייפן חדשי'
21. בקלאדנוג אייכנה די[.]סה בריטר וגם לעשות גטיפלש חדשי'
22. בשני חדרי' זה מול זה בשטח הלז גם לעשות בשטח מטה אין הויז
23. עהרנד [אר]בעה שענק חדשי' עם בשליגש חדש כדי שישתמש

---

1. תוספת מעל השורה
2. תוספת מעל השורה
3. תוספת מעל השורה
4. תוספת מתחת השורה

פז ע״ב

1. ב״ה
2. כדי שישתמש כ״א בשני שענק והותנה בינ[י]ה' שתשלם האשה (הנ״ל)[1] בהוצאת
3. כל הנ״ל שלשי' זהו' וה[מ]ותרות הוא על הוצאת כ״ג הנ״ל לבד ובזה פטורה
4. האשה הנ״ל מלשלם בתיקון החדרי' הללו שיתקן עוד כ״ג הנ״ל בתוך ה
5. חדרי' הללו רק תיקון הקורה שנמשך מחדש בתוך החדר לצד בתים פנימי'
6. בשטח שני שטאק הויך שמחויבת האשה לשלם החצי ומחמת מה שרצה
7. כ״ג הנ״ל לעשות בשטח שני שטאק הויך כירה חדשה ולשנות פייער ריכט
8. ולהעמיד עוד תנור אחד ולעשות שני בתי חורף זה מול זה מצאנו שהאשה
9. הנ״ל אינה מחויבת לשלם בכל זה רק חלק שליש מהוצאת ובשטח שלשה
10. שטאק הויך הדלת צו רעפירן גם דיא רעהררן מן גוס שטיין עד חד
11. שטאק הויך צו ציהן מחויבת האשה לשלם החצי מחמת הוצאת
12. התנור משלשה שטאק הויך אינה מחויבת האשה הנ״ל לשל[ם]
13. רק השליש ד' שטאק הויך המסגרת בדלת אם צריך תיקון מ
14. מחויבת האשה לשלם החצי מהוצאת גם לעשות דלת מסוגרת ב
15. {בעשיי'} בעליי' תשלם האשה החצי בשטח הת[ח]תון דיא הויז עהרנד
16. גם הויז טיהרן צו רעפירירן פלאטץ אן דער וואנד אחורי הצינור
17. אין הויז עהרנד צו מאכין דיא קוך למטה אוז(צו)[2]בעשרן בחדר בית ה
18. החורף למטה צו פרידרן בסוכה שאחורי בית החורף דיא פ
19. פלאטץ גם שטיינה קענטל צו רעפירירן [מ]חויבת האשה לשלם
20. החצי ומחמת תיקון גם לעשות פענשטר ראהמין וד[.ס]ה בריטר וגם
21. וגם לעשות חלון בדלת בבית החורף למטה מחויבת האשה

פח ע״א

1. ב״ה
2. לשלם החצי ומחמת מה שרצה כ״ה גומפיל הנ״ל לעשות בסוכה שאחורי בית
3. החורף איין זענק לאך עם זענק חביות במרתף תחת הסוכה כדי להסיר ה
4. הסלון הנמשך דרך בית החורף למטה אין הויז עהרנד מצאנו באשר לפי
5. דברי הצדדים הנ״ל הי' מקדם איין זענק לאך ולאח״כ חזרו מחזיקי בית
6. שהי' באותו פעם להמשיך צנור תוך בית החורף בכן יוכל להיות שעל
7. אופן זה יהי' יותר לטובת הבית בכן אם רצה כ״ג הנ״ל לשנות ולעשות
8. זענק פאס אינה מחויבת האשה הנ״ל לשלם בהוצאת רק השליש
9. ומחמת דמי אקארד מן הצימר מאן העולה ך״ד זהו' לעשות נייאה שטעג
10. פענשטר פאסטין זאמבט ריגל חד שטאק מחו[י]בת האשה הנ״ל לשלם
11. החצי ולעשות קולענדר במדרגה חד ושני שטאק הויך [מ]חויבת
12. האשה הנ״ל לשלם החצי ו[מ]ה שתבע כ' גומפיל הנ״ל מאחר שלאחר

1. תוספת מעל השורה
2. תוספת מעל השורה

13. ששה שנים בעת שיחליפו את דירתם וכמו שמבואר בכתב גורל
14. שהוקמו ביניהם מאתנו ב"ד ח"מ שיבוא כ' גומפיל הנ"ל בשטח
15. מעלה חד שטאק הויך וטען שיתוקון (אז)[1] התנור חדש בחדר חד שטאק
16. הויך שהוא לצד בתים פנימי' על הוצאת שניהם באשר שאין
17. תנור באותו חדר כל זמן שהחדר הלז ביד האשה הנ"ל מצאנו שבכלות
18. ששה שני' אם ירצה כ"ג הנ"ל להעמיד תנור חדש מחויבת האשה הנ"ל
19. לשלם השליש מהוצאת גם הותנו ביניהם בפני ב"ד שכל אחד ואחד
20. מהם אין רשאי לשנות בדירתו {שוב} שום דבר חדש [מ]שך זמן שדר בו
21. ובאם [י]שנו שום דבר שלא ברשות חבירו אשר מחויב בעת
22. הדירה

פח ע"ב

1. ב"ה
2. שיחליפו את דירתם לחז[ו]ר ולעמוד אותו על [מ]כונו הראשון כמו שהי' מקודם
3. גם מצאנו אם נתקלקל שוב דבר בגבול של כל או"א שלא יתקן אותו בלי
4. ידיעת חבירו ומכ"ש שלא לבנות דבר חדש זולת ידיעת חבירו וגם
5. הותנה בינהם שהבריח מדלת הבית יהי' פתוח בלילה ע"ז י"א שעות
6. ולאח"כ יהי' סגור חוץ לעת הצורך (גם התרצה)[2] א"ע כ' גומפיל לפנינו מחמת הוצאת
7. המשפט עם ר' משה רויטשילד [מ]ח[מ]ת עשיית בית ה[מ]וצנע בסוכה
8. שאחורי בית החורף למטה שהאשה הנ"ל תהי' פטורה מלשלם
9. כלום בהוצאת משפט הנ"ל ומחמת מה שתבע כ"ג הנ"ל ורוצה למחות
10. ביד האשה מ' סערלה הנ"ל להחזיק חנות של סחורת שלה שנשאה
11. ונתנה בהן עתה בבית הנ"ל מכמה טעמי' וכמו ש[מ]בואר בק"ה המונח
12. אצלינו ובאם לא יזכה בזה טען שגם הוא רוצה לעסוק ולעשות
13. חנות בגבולו [מ]אותן סחורות שהאשה הנ"ל ג"כ נושאה ונותנה בו
14. ותבע שהב"ד יפילו גורל ביניה' [מ]ששה לששה שני' מי מהם יחז
15. יחזיק החנות הנ"ל בבית הנ"ל מצאנו שכ"ג אינה יכולה למחות ביד
16. האשה להחזיק חנות [מ]סחורת שנשאה ונת[נה] בהן עתה בגבולה בבית
17. גם אינה יכולה האשה הנ"ל למחות ביד כ' גומפיל הנ"ל {לעש}ות להיות
18. נושא ונותן בסחורת שהיא אינה נושאת ונותנות בהן עתה בחנות
19. בבית הנ"ל בגבולו אכן מה שרוצה כ"ג לעסוק בחנות בבית הנ"ל בגבולו
20. [מ]אותן [מ]יני סחורת שנושאת ונותנות בהן כבר מצאנו אם לא יהי'
21. דבר זה נגד נהוג ותיקון הקהילה יע"א שב[מ]ק[ומו] עומד באשר שהיא כבר
22. מוחזקת לעסוק באותן סחורת בביתה וגם אם לא יהי' ל[ה]אשה הנ"ל
23. ובני' הנ"ל שט[ר]ו' וזכיות ע"ז שיכולה למחות בשותפה בבית הנ"ל

---

1. תוספת מעל השורה
2. תוספת מעל השורה

פט ע"א

1. ב"ה
2. אזי גם בזה אינה יכולה למחות האשה מ' סערלה הנ"ל ביד כ"ג הנ"ל
3. {ביד כ"ג} לעשות גם הוא חנות [מ]אותן סחורת בגבולו בבית הנ"ל
4. יצא מאתנו יו' דח אלול שנת קולת לפק הדיין ורב"ד הק' מאיר ש"ש[1]
5. הק' אברהם טריר כץ
6. ואני הק' חיים בפו"מ כ' יוזפא גונדרשהיים שליטא

No. 80

Fols. 89b–90a; Sunday evening, 25 August 1776

The owners of the outer Vorder Pfanne house dealt with in case no. 79 asked the court to determine who had the right to live in which half of the house when. To do so, the court cast a lot in the presence of both parties and determined that Gumpel Mai would have the lower section of the house for a six year period and Sorle, widow of Me'ir Schuster, and her children would have the upper section. At the end of six years, the owners were obliged to switch their living quarters for the following six year period. The court detailed the exact areas that would be controlled by each owner during each period, as well as their rights to pass here and there within the house. Although this case appears in the manuscript after no. 79, chronologically it preceded it.

פט ע"ב

1. ב"ה
2. ע"ד שבא לפנינו מחזיקי בית חיצון צור פאדרפפאַן ה"ה הו"ה כ' גומפל בהמנוח[2] כ"ה אהרן מאיי
3. ז"ל סג"ל וה"ה האשה מ' סערלה אל' המנוח כ' מאיר בכ"א[3] שוסטר (כץ)[4] ז"ל ובהרשאת בני' יתמי ה
4. המנוח של כ' מאיר ז"ל הנ"ל וביקשו מאתנו ב"ד ח"מ שנעשו חלוקה וגורל בבית הנ"ל על א
5. אופן שהתרצו הצדדי' הנ"ל והנה אחרי שהצדדי' חתמו עצמם בתוקף קומפרמיס
6. בח"ח ובקנס מסויים לאשר ולקיים כפי שיצא מאתנו נזדקקנו להם ועשינו גורל
7. ביניהם במעמד כ' גומפל והאשה מ' סערלה הנ"ל ועלה ע"פ הגורל ש[טח] מ

---

1. שווארצשילד
2. בן המנוח
3. בן כבוד אהרן (ר' דייץ, עמ' 272)
4. תוספת מעל השורה

8. מטה על ששה שני' רצופי' מיו' דלמטה לכ' גומפל הנ"ל[1] שיש לו החצי מבית של[ם] ה
9. הנ"ל ושטח מעלה להאשה מ' סערלה ובני' הנ"ל על משך זמן ששה שני' הנ"ל שיש להם
10. החצי שניי' מבית שלם הנ"ל והיינו מן י"א אלול תקלמד ויו לפק עד יא אלול תקמ"ב
11. יהי' לה"ה הו"ה כ"[ג][2] הנ"ל ולי"א ולב"כ {ב"כ} בית החורף למטה בשטח התחתון עם הסוכה
12. שאחורי בית החורף דיא קוך אין הויז עהרנד עם הויז עהרנד עם שאנק שבתוכה
13. גם שני שטעג הויך שני חדרי' זה מול זה עם הויז עהרנד ורשאי להעמיד שם
14. אין הויז עהרנד שני שטעג הויך ב{...} בשטח הנ"ל אצל האשה מ' סערלה ויא[3] וב"כ
15. אינה רשאי להעמיד שום דבר אין הויז עהרנד שני שטאק הויך משך זמן הנ"ל
16. רק יהי' להם המהלך לבד גם שלשה שטאק יהי' לכ' גומפל וי"א וב"כ על זמן הנ"ל חדר א'
17. לצד בתי' פנימי' עם הויז עהרנד מה שהוא בין הקלענדר מן השטעג והחדר הנ"ל ובתוך
18. החדר הלז יש חלון אחד שפונה לקעמרכה שאין (שהוא בין שני חדרי' בשטח הלז)[4] רשאי כ' גומפל הנ"ל להעמיד [שום]
19. דב[ר] נגד החלון או לתלות ווילון לפני חלון הלז גם [ו]רשאי כ' גומפל להשתמש אויף
20. דעם גוסשטיין שהוא בתוך הקאמין באותו שטח גם ארבע שטאק הויך יהי' לכ' גומפל
21. וי"א וב"כ על משך זמן הנ"ל החדר שהוא לצד הרחוב ובהויז עהרנד (בשטח הלז)[5] בשטח הלז ישתמשו
22. שניהם והעליי' יהי' לכ' גומפל לבד והמרתפות יהי' לכ' גומפל הנ"ל משך זמן הנ"ל אותו
23. מרתף שהוא תחת פרהויז געגין דיא שטעג אריבר והמרתף החיצון תחת ה
24. השטוב ולהאשה מ' סערלה ובני' שיש להם חצי' שניי' מבית שלם הנ"ל יה[יה לה]ם ולי"א וב"כ
25. על משך

צדיק ע"א

1. על משך זמן ששה שני' הנ"ל חד שטאק הויך שני חדרי' זה מול זה עם הויז עהרנד והקוך
2. וכל מה שבתוכה גם רשאה להעמיד שאנק אין הויז עהרנד סמוך לשטעג במקו' שהי' הקאמין
3. אבל כ' גומפל הנ"ל אין רשאה להעמיד שום דבר בשטח הלז רק יהי' לו המהלך לבד
4. משך זמן הנ"ל גם שלשה שטאק הויך יהי' להאשה ובני' הנ"ל חדר בית החורף שהוא
5. לצד הרחוב וגם דש קעמרכה שהוא בין החדרי' ואותו גוסשטיין שהוא בשטח הלז
6. ישתמשו שניהם ג' ד' שטעג הויך חדר א' לצד בתי' פנימי' ובהויז עהרנד בשטח
7. הלז ישתמשו (שניהם)[6] בשוה ומרתף אחד מן החיצוני' והיינו אותו מרתף שהוא לצד ימין מן

1. ר' לקמן, מס' 148, דף קלז ע"ב.
2. כבוד גומפל
3. ויורשיה אחריה
4. תוספת מעל השורה
5. תוספת מעל השורה
6. תוספת מעל השורה

8. השטעג ומן המרתפות הפנימי׳ המרתף פנימי ובימי חג הסוכות ישתמו[1] שניהם
9. בסוכה שאחורי בית החורף בשוה אבל חוץ ימי החג סוכות אין רשאי למי שידור
10. בשטח מעלה להשתמש כלל בסוכה אפי׳ להעמיד תרנגולי׳ בסוכה גם בבית
11. המוצנע ישתמשו שניהם בשוה ובאם שיותן להם רשות לבנות ב״ה[2] בהסוכה התרצו
12. שני הצדדי׳ שאותו שידור בשטח מטה אין רשאי למחות ביד אותו שידור בשטח מ
13. מעלה להלוך דרך בית החורף למטה לבית המוצנע העומד בסוכה והיינו דוקא
14. להב״ב עם אשתו ובניו ש[י׳ א]ת׳[3] אבל לא משרת ואנשי׳ אחרי׳ שהם בביתו ובכלות זמן
15. ששה שני׳ הנ״ל יתחלפו הדירות הנ״ל על אופן הנ״ל על משך ששה שני׳ אחרי׳ רצופי׳
16. והיינו מן יא תקמ״ב עד יא אלול תקמ״ח הבע״ל יהי׳ להאשה מ׳ סערלה (הנ״ל)[4] {וב}
וי״א וב״כ
17. שטח מטה וכנ״ל ולכ׳ גומפיל הנ״ל וי״א וב״כ שטח מעלה וכנ״ל וחוזר חלילה מששה
18. לששה שני׳ כה יהי׳ וכה יקוי׳ להם וליא׳[5] ולב״כ מעתה ועד עולם כל הנ״ל נעשה לפנינו
19. ב״ד ח״מ בתוקף מעשה ב״ד ובכח ב״ד יפה אור ליו׳ ב יא אלול תקלמד ויו לפק
20. הק׳ מאיר ש״ש[6] הק׳ אברהם טריר ואני

No. 81

Jacob ben Moses of Eibingen v. Ẓipper, daughter of Moses Levy

Fol. 90b; Thursday 19 September 1776

Jacob ben Moses of Eibingen claimed a 50 gulden penalty payment plus unspecified expenses from Ẓipper, daughter of Moses Levy, an unmarried maidservant in Frankfurt. Jacob claimed that in the summer of 1775 Ẓipper had agreed to marry him, and produced a contract to this effect that was signed by her brother-in-law, who was said to have acted as her representative in Eibingen, about 65 km. west of Frankfurt. The contract specifically stated that she had accepted the arrangement, and contained a penalty clause for failure to fulfill the agreement. Ẓipper denied that she had ever consented to the contract and claimed that her brother-in-law had never asked her about it. Neither side had representation. Although the contract was signed by witnesses, they were related to each other in the first degree (brothers) and were disqualified from acting together. One of the witnesses

1. צ״ל ׳ישתמשו׳
2. בית המוצנע
3. שיהיו אתם(?)
4. תוספת מעל השורה
5. וליורשיהם אחריהם
6. שווארצשילד

appeared before the Frankfurt court and confirmed that Ẓipper had agreed to the arrangement. The court appears to have tried to convince Ẓipper to marry Jacob, but she refused. Both sides agreed to be bound by the court's compromise and it fined Ẓipper 20 guldens and released her and her brother-in-law from any further obligation in the matter.

צ ע"ב

1. ב"ה
2. ע"ד שבא לפנינו ה"ה הב"ח כ' יעקב בר משה מאייבינגין ותבע מן הבתולה מ' צפ
3. בת משה לוי משרתת פה ותבע קנס חמשי' זהו' שנזכר בתנאי' שהציע לפנינו
4. ההוקם באייבינגין יו' א' ד' תמוז שנת קהלת לפק שגיסה כ' יוסף בר יהודא ח
5. חתום עצמו בכחה ושם נאמר ששאל אותה ואמרה הן וטען שבאמת הית' מרוצה ב
6. באותו פעם בכן תבע קנס הנ"ל גם הוצאות והבתולה מ' ציפר השיבה שהיא לא
7. הי' מרוצה בשידוך וגיסה כ' יוסף הנ"ל לא הי' שואלת אותה וגם היא לא חתמה
8. א"ע תחת התנאי' והאריכו בטענותיהם והנה התנאי' שהציע חתמו תחתיו
9. שני עדי' והם אחי' זה לזה ה"ה יצחק בר אורי שרגא ואחיו (יודא)[1] בר אורי שרגא וכ' יצחק
10. הי' לפנינו ואמר שהיא הית' מרוצה ושקיבלו עליהם ג"כ הב"ח והבתולה הנ"ל בק"ס
11. על השידוך כנהוג שם באייבינגין ובאשר שהצדדי' הנ"ל חתמו עצמם בתוקף קומפרמי'
12. ב[כ]א"ה לאשר ולקיים כפי אשר יצא מאתנו והנה אחר שדברנו על לבה לקרב
13. ולא לרחק אך בכל זה לא היה אפשר לנו להביאה לידי קירוב אמנם לרחק עליהם
14. בתוקף הנ"ל ובק"ס בפ"מ לאשר ולקיים כפי הפשר שיצא מאתנו בכן נזדקקנו ורחק
15. ולפשרה ומצאנו שהשידוך הוא בטל ומבוטל רק שהיא תתן להב"ח כ' יעקב הנ"ל סך
16. עשרי' זהו' ובזה היא וגם גיסה יוסף בר [י]ודא ז"ל המה פטורים ממנו הן מתביעית
17. ממון הן מחרם ונגד נתינות סך עשרי' זהו' הנ"ל מחויב הב"ח הנ"ל ליתן פטורי'
18. להבתולה ולגיסה הנ"ל בכא"ה יצא מאתנו יו' ה' [ו'] תשרי תקל"ז לפק
19. ר' יעקב שמש
20. ר' מאיר שיף
21. ואני

No. 82

Fols. 91a–92b; Wednesday evening, 5 December 1776

Zalman Haas, Samuel Landau, Abraham Emmerich, and Sender Rindskopf each owned various portions of two houses on the Silberne Kanne lot. Zalman and Samuel each owned half of a house, Abraham and Sender each owned one-quarter

---

1. תוספת מעל השורה

of each home. The owners asked the court to determine who should live where in the houses, when, and for how long. The court noted that one-quarter of a house was insufficient living space, and decided to consolidate Abraham and Sender's holdings in each house for the purposes of living space without compromising their ownership rights. Each would now have one-half of a house. A lottery determined that Abraham would have space in the outer house and Sender in the inner. They were to switch every six years. The court held a second lottery for the division of each house. Here the rotation would take place after every three years. The court also specified which areas of the houses each family could use.

צא ע"א

1. ב"ה
2. ע"ד שבאו לפנינו מחזיקי שני בתי' צור זילברנה קן חיצון ופנימי ה"ה התורני כ"ה
3. בענדיט הענא סג"ל בהרשאת הו"ה כ' זלמן הז ששייך לו החצי בית חיצון הנ"ל
4. והו"ה כ"ה שמואל לנדויא ששייך לו החצי בית פנימי הנ"ל וה"ה הבחי[1] כ' וואלף
5. בהרשאת הו"ה גץ[2] כ' אברהם עמריך ששייך לו רביעית מבית חיצון ופנימי
6. הנ"ל והב"ח{ור} כ' מרדכי בהרשאת הו"ה כ"ה סענדר ר"ק ששייך לו ג"כ רביעית
7. מבית חיצון ופנימי הנ"ל וביקשו מאתנו ב"ד ח"מ לעשות חלוקה וגורל ב
8. ביניהם בבתי' הנ"ל ועל אופן חלקי הדירות כפי שהתרצו הנ"ל בפנינו
9. וכה יהי' וכה יקו' ביניהם ועל י"א וב"כ מעתה ועד עולם והנה אחרי שהצדדי'
10. הנ"ל חתמו עצמם בתוקף קומפרמיס בח"ח ובקנס סך מסוים חצי לשררה
11. ירה[3] וחצי להקדש לאשר ולקיים כפי שיצא מאתנו נזדקקנו להם ומצאנו
12. שראוי להטיל בתחילה בין ה"ה גץ כ' אברהם עמריך הנ"ל ובין הו"ה כ"ה ס[4] הנ"ל
13. באשר ששייך לכ"א רק רביעית בית מפנימי וחיצון ורביעית בית כל אחד
14. בפני עצמו אינו ראוי לדירה בכן צריכן ליתן לכל אחד ואחד חצי בית או
15. מפנימי או מחיצון והיינו זמן מה {ל} יהי' לא' מהם דירת חצי בית חיצון
16. ולחבירו חצי בית פנימי ובכלות הזמן יחלפו דירתם על זמן כזה וכן ע
17. עשינו והפלנו גורל בין כ' אברהם עמריך הנ"ל ובין כ"ה סענדר ר"ק הנ"ל על
18. חילוף דירתם מבית חיצון ופנימי הנ"ל (על)[5] ששה שני' לששה שני' ועלה הגורל
19. דירת חצי בית חיצון הנ"ל לכ' אברהם עמריך הנ"ל על משך ששה שני' רצופי'
20. והיינו מר"ח טבת תקלמד זיין הבע"ל עד ר"ח טבת תקמ"ג ומשך אותן ששה
21. שני'

---

1. הבחור חמד
2. גבאי צדקה
3. ירום הודו
4. סענדר (המוזכר לעיל)
5. תוספת מעל השורה

צא ע"ב

1. ב"ה
2. שייך לה"ה כ"ה סענדר דירת חצי בית הפנימי ובכלות וי"ו שני' הנ"ל יתחלפו
3. דירת חצי בית הנ"ל ביניהם על משך ששה שני' אחרי' רצופי' והיינו מר"ח טבת
4. תקמ"ג עד ר"ח טבת תקמט יהי' לכ' אברהם עמריך הנ"ל דירת חצי בית פנימי ולכ"ה
5. סענדר ר"ק יהי' דירת חצי בית חיצון וחוזר חלילה משׁשה לששה שני' וכה
6. יהי' וכה יקום להם וי"א מעתה וע"ע ואח"כ הפלנו גורל בין מחזיקי בית פנימי
7. שלשה שני' על שלשה שני' למי שיהי' שטח מעלה ולמי שיהי' שטח מטה מבית פנימי
8. הנ"ל ועלה ע"פ הגורל שטח עליון לה"ה הו"ה כ' שמואל לנדויא הנ"ל על משך שלשה
9. שני' רצופי' מר"ח טבת תקלזין הבעל[1] עד ר"ח טבת תק"מ הב"ע ושטח התחתון
10. לכ"[ה] סענדר ר"ק הנ"ל על משך שלשה שני' הנ"ל ובכלת שלשה שני' הנ"ל יתחלפו
11. דירתם ושייך לכהר"ס[2] הנ"ל שטח עליון על שלשה שני' והיינו מן ר"ח טבת תק"מ עד
12. ר"ח טבת תקמג ושטח התחתון לכה"ש[3] לנדויא הנ"ל {ויא} וי"א הנ"ל על אותן ג' שני' הנ"ל
13. ואופן דירתם ושטח מעלה מעלה[4] ושטח מטה התרצו הצדדי' הנ"ל שיש לה' שייכות
14. בבית הפנימי שיהי' באופן זה והיינו מי שיהי' לו שטח התחתון שייך לו בית ה
15. החורף למטה עם הסוכה שאחורי בית החורף דיא קוך דש הויז עהרנד עם
16. השענק שבתוכה שני שטעג הויך שני חדרי' זה מול זה עם הויז עהרנד קוך
17. והשענק שבתוכה שלשה שטאק הויך חדר בית החורף עם קעמרכה לצד
18. בית החיצון ארבע שטעג הויך שני חדרי' לצד החומה ושני מרתפי' הפנימי ו
19. ולמי ששייך לו שטח שלמעלה יהי' דירתו חד שטעג הויך שני חדרי' זה מול זה
20. עם הויז עהרנד קוך שענק שלשה שטעג הויך חדר בית החורף עם ק
21. קמערכה לצד החומה ארבע שטעג הויך שני חדרי' לצד בית החיצון
22. שני מרתפו' החיצוני' והעליי' ישתמשו בשותפת ובימי חג הסוכות ישתמשו
23. שניהם בסוכה שאחורי בית החורף כה יקום ביניהם ולי"א וב"כ ובכלות
24. הששה שני' הנ"ל והיינו מן ר"ח טבת תקמ"ג לפק יתחלפו {א.בתים}
25. כה"ר

צב ע"א

1. ב"ה
2. כה"ס וכ"א[5] הנ"ל דירתם מחצי בית פנימי לחצי בית חיצון ובא יבוא כ"א עמריך
3. הנ"ל וי"א וב"כ בחצי בית פנימי וכנ["ל] על משך ששה שני' אחרי' רצופי'
4. וכנ"ל והיינו עד ר"ח טבת תקמ"ט וכנ"ל על אופן הנ"ל והיינו שלשה שני' ראשוני'
5. יהי' לכ"א שטח מטה וכנ"ל וכה"ש הנ"ל שטח מעלה וכנ"ל ושלשה שני' אחרוני' כ"א

---

1. הבא עלינו לטובה
2. לכבוד הרב סענדר
3. לכבוד הרב שמואל
4. כפילות במקור
5. וכבוד אברהם

6. הנ״ל שטח מעלה וכנ״ל וכה״ש שטח מטה וכנ״ל וחוזר חלילה ביניה׳ ולי״א וב״כ
7. וכן עשינו גורל בין מחזיקי בית החיצון הנ״ל (משלשה שני׳ על שלשה שני׳)[1] למי שיהי׳ שטח עליון ולמי
8. שטח התחתון ועלה ע״פ הגורל שטח התחתן על משך שלשה שני׳ רצופי׳ מר״ח
9. טבת הבעל[2] להו״ה כ״ה זלמן הז הנ״ל וי״א וב״כ ושטח עליון לכ׳ אברהם עמריך
10. הנ״ל וי״א וב״כ והיינו עד ר״ח טבת תק״מ לפק ומכאן ואילך עד ר״ח טבת תקמ״ג
11. יתחלפו {ויהי׳} דירתם ויהי׳ לכ׳ זלמן הז שטח עליון ולכ׳ אברהם עמריך שטח התחתן
12. ואופן חלקי הדירות משטח עליון והתחתון התרצו הצדדי׳ {ש} השייכים לבית חיצון
13. כמבואר והיינו מי ששייך לו דירה התחתונה יהי׳ לו בית החורף למטה בשטח
14. התחתון עם קוך הויז עהרנד עם השענק שבתוכם שני שטאק הויך שני
15. חדרי׳ זה מול זה עם הויז עהרנד קויך שלשה שטאק הוך חדר בית החורף
16. עם קעמרכה לצד בתי׳ פנימי׳ ד׳ שטאק הויך חדר לצד בתי׳ פנימי׳ שני
17. מרתפות הפנימי׳ ולמי [ש]ידור בשטח עליונה יהי׳ לו חד שטאק הוך שני חדרי׳
18. זה מול זה הויז עהרנד קוך והשע[נ]ק שבתוכה שלשה שטאק הויך חדר
19. {ביפ} בית החורף עם קעמרכה לצד הרחוב ארבע שטאק הויך חדר לצד
20. הרחוב ושני מרתפו׳ החיצוני׳ והעליי׳ ישתמשו בשותפו׳ גם בסוכת
21. החג בחג ישתמשו בשותפת בסוכה שבין בתים פנימי׳ לחיצוני׳ ובכלות
22. ששה שני׳ הנ״ל והיינו מן ר״ח טבת תקמ״ג לפק יתחלפו כ״א הנ״ל עם כה״ס הנ״ל
23. דירתם [מ]בית חיצן לפנימי וכנ״ל ובא יבוא כה״ס הנ״ל לחצי בית חיצון על משך
24. ששה שני׳ אחרי׳ וכנ״ל והיינו שלשה שני׳ ראשוני׳ מששה שני׳ יהי׳ הוא בשטח
25. עליון

צב ע״ב

1. ב״ה
2. עליון וכ׳ זלמן הז בשטח התחתן שלשה שני׳ אחרוני׳ יהי׳ כ״ה סענדר הנ״ל ב
3. בשטח התחתן וכ׳ זלמן הז בשטח עליון (וחוזר חלילה ביניהם וי״א וב״כ)[3] וכן יהא חוזר חלילה ביניהם על כל
4. הצדדים וי״א וב״כ ע״ע אשר יש להם שייכות בבית חיצון ופ[נימי] הנ״ל כמבואר במב״ד הלז
5. נעשה לפנינו ב״ד ח״מ בתקף מעשה ב״ד ובכח ב״ד יפה אור ליו׳ ה׳ ך״ד כסליו תקלזין
6. הדיין ור״י מה׳ נתן מז וכ״ה מאיר שיף ואני
7. ש ש[4]

---

1. תוספת מעל השורה
2. הבא עלינו לטובה
3. תוספת מעל השורה
4. לא ברור למה שתי האותיות נמצאות כאן ומה משמעותן במידה שיש.

No. 83

Gitle, widow of Anshel Bonn v. Zipche, widow of Lipman Deuz

Fol. 93a; Tuesday 17 December 1776

In 1773 the court gave a ruling to Anshel Bonn and Zipche, widow of Lipman Deuz, with respect to the sharing of space in the Rindsfuss house. Anshel died in 1774 and his widow, Gitle, continued to live in the house. Despite the previous ruling, the two widows became involved in a dispute over who had rights to sections of the cellar. The parties turned to the court and asked it to determine each side's rights in the matter. Although both sides obligated themselves to accept the court's ruling, the court urged them to accept a compromise, which they did.

צג ע״א

1. ב״ה
2. מאחר שכבר יצא פס״ד ד׳ אלול תקל״ג בין מחזיקי בית צום רינדשפוס דהיינו בין
3. כ׳ אנשיל בון מחזיק שני׳ שליש בית הנ״ל ובין האשה מ׳ ציפכה אל׳ המנוח כ׳ ליפמן דייץ
4. ז״ל מחזקת שלשי[1] בית הנ״ל (ושם)[2] נאמר אופן חלוקת דירתם ואופין חלוקת מרתפות ש
5. שבבית הנ״ל וכעת נתהוו עוד הפרשות וטענות אודות חלוקות המרתפות בין
6. האשה מ׳ גיטלה אלמנות[3] המנוח כ׳ אנשיל הנ״ל ובין האשה מ׳ ציפכה הנ״ל ובתחילה
7. חתמו עצמם בקומפרמיס לקיים כפי הדין אשר יצא מאיתנו ואח״כ פשרנו ב
8. ביניהם בריצו הצדדים הנ״ל ותקעו{.} כפם לפנינו לקיים בכל תוקף על א
9. אופן המבואר והיינו שהאשה מ׳ ציפכה הנ״ל תהי׳ לה עד כלות ששה שני׳
10. מחצי אלול העבר המרתף {העמ} אמצעי המתחיל מפתח אותו מרתף אמצעי עד מחיצה
11. המפסקת בינו ובין המרתף הפנימי שהוא אורך ארבעשר[4] מנעלי׳ ורוחב
12. תשעה מנעלי׳ והאשה מ׳ גיטלה הנ״ל תהי׳ לה משך זמן (הנ״ל)[5] המרתף הפנימי עד
13. מחיצה המפסקת בינו ובין מרתף האמצעי וגם יהי׳ לה מרתף החיצונה שהוא
14. תחת השטעג (אפתח הבית)[6] עד מחיצת מרתף האמצעי אורך אחד עשר מנעלי׳ ורוחב שלשה
15. מנעלי׳ והמהלך דהיינו המדרגה שיורדן עלי׳ למרתף החיצון ששייך להאשה
16. גיטלה הנ״ל ולמרתף אמצעי ששייך להאשה מ׳ ציפכה הנ״ל עם המקום פנוי
17. שלפני {המרתף} המרתפות ה[נ״ל] שנכלל ג״כ בתוך המהלך שייך לשניהם
18. להילוכן ואין שום אחד מדיורי בית הנ״ל רשאי להעמיד שום דבר הן על

---

1. צ״ל ׳שליש׳
2. תוספת מעל השורה
3. צ״ל ׳אלמנת׳
4. ארבע עשר
5. תוספת מעל השורה
6. תוספת מעל השורה

19. השטעג שעלי' הולכין לתוך שני מרתפות החיצונים הנ"ל והן באותו מקום פנוי
20. הנ"ל רק להילוך בלבד כל הנ"ל התרצו הצדדים הנ"ל לפנינו בת"כ ואנחנו
21. ב"ד ח"מ בתוקף מעשה ב"ד ובכח ב"ד יפה נתננו תוקף לזה שכה יהי'
22. וכה יקום משך ששה שני' הנ"ל ואין שום א' מהצדדי' הנ"ל יכול לערער ולבטל
23. כל הנ"ל יצא מאיתנו יו' ג' זין טבת תקלזין לפק הדיין מה' יעקב שמש
24. הדיין ור"י מה' נתן מז ומה' יעקב שמשי ואני

No. 84

Yentela, widow of Solomon Maas v. Estate of Jacob Buch

Fol. 93b; Tuesday 24 December 1776

Me'ir Maas approached the court representing his mother, Yentela, widow of Solomon Maas, and claimed that the estate of the late Jacob Buch owed the Maas estate 13.5 reichstalers. The basis for the claim was an entry in Solomon Maas's business diary from 1732 stating that Jacob had borrowed 35 reichstalers from him. Although Jacob paid off some of the debt, the claim was that 13.5 reichstalers had never been repaid. The Buch family said that they knew nothing of the debt and had no business diary of Jacob's to refer to. Their representative noted that even if there had been a debt, it was very possible that Jacob had repaid the loan in full and that Solomon Maas had forgotten to record it in his diary. Both sides agreed to a compromise solution according to which Jacob's widow paid Yentela 6 guldens, 45 kruezers.

צג ע"ב

1. ב"ה
2. ע"ד שבא לפנינו ה"ה הב"ח כ' מאיר בהמנוח[2] כ"ה שלמה מז ז"ל בהרשאת
3. אמו מ' יענטלה אל' המנוח כ"ה שלמה מז ז"ל ותבעה מן האל' ויורשי המנוח כ'
4. יעקב בוך ז"ל סך שלשה עשר רט וחצי והציע לפנינו הויבט פנקס מאביו כ"ה
5. שלמה הנ"ל וכתוב בתוכה שכ' יעקב ז"ל נשאר חייב עדיין משנת תצב סך
6. ל"ה רט ונתפרע {אלא} א"ל"א[3] עד שנשאר שנת תצה סך הנ"ל וה"ה התורני נ"ה כ"ה
7. אנשיל פפאן בהרשאת האל' ויורשי כ' יעקב ז"ל השיב שמעולם לא הי' שומעי'
8. מהחוב הלז ואף אם יהי' חוב הלז אמת שמא פרע כ' יעקב ז"ל הנ"ל ונשכח מלכתוב

---

1. שמו של הדיין יעקב שמש מופיע כאן פעמיים.
2. בן המנוח
3. אחד לאחד?

9. בפנקס של כ״ש[1] ז״ל הנ״ל הפירעון ומאביהם כ׳ יעקב ז״ל אין להם שום פנקס ש
10. שיוכלו לבדק אבל הם אינם יודעי׳ כלום מהחוב הלז והנה באשר שהצדדי׳ הנ״ל
11. חתמו עצמם בתוקף קומפרמיס והיינו האל׳ כ״ה שלמה מז ז״ל ושני בני׳ הב״ח כ׳
12. יחזקאל והבחור כ׳ מאיר הנ״ל והאל׳ כ׳ יעקב בוך ז״ל לאשר ולקיים הפשר שיצא
13. מאתנו בכן נזדקקנו להם ומצאנו ע״פ פשר שאל׳ כ׳ יעקב ז״ל הנ״ל תתן להאל׳ כ״ה
14. שלמה מז ז״ל הנ״ל סך ששה זהו׳ מ״ה צל ובזה פטורי׳ כל יורשי ואל׳ כ׳ יעקב הנ״ל
15. מן אל׳ ויורשי כ״ה שלמה ז״ל הנ״ל מחמת תביעת הנ״ל יצא מאתנו יו׳ ג יד
16. טבת תקלמד זיין לפק הק׳ יעקב שמש הק׳ ענוויל[2] טראך ואני

No. 85

Fol. 94a; Sunday evening, 29 December 1776

Hirsch Landau and Moses Flörsheim each owned half of a seat in the lower men's section of the here unspecified synagogue. They approached the court and asked that it draw a lot to determine who would have the right to use the entire seat during the coming year and who would have the right to use the seat the year thereafter. The alternating arrangement was to continue in the years to come.

צד ע״א

1. ב״ה
2. מחזיקי מקו׳ בע״א התחתון אשר עמד עלי[3] כעת ה״ה כ״ה הירש לאנדויא סג״ל דהיינו כ״ה
3. הירש הנ״ל מחזיק חצי מקו׳ הנ״ל וה״ה התורני כ״ה משה בן הו״ה ג״צ כ״ה מאיר
4. פלערשהיים יצו מחזיק חצי מקו׳ השני התרצו עצמם להפיל גורל ביניהם
5. מי שיהי׳ לו מקו׳ {השני} השלם הנ״ל שנה הסמוכה דהיינו מן פסח הסומך שנת
6. תקלמד זיין הבע״ל עד פסח שנת תקל״ח הבע״ל מי שיהי׳ לו מקו׳ שלם הנ״[ל]
7. מן פסח תקלח שנה אחת וכן יחזור חלילה ביניהם שנה בשנה עד עולם
8. וכה יהי׳ וכה יקו׳ בין י״א וב״כ מעתה ועד עולם וכהיו׳ הפלנו גורל
9. ביניהם ועלה הגורל מן פסח הסמוך שנת תקלזיין עד פסח שנת תקלח
10. לה״ה כ״ה משה הנ״ל ומן פסח תקלח עד פסח תקלט לה״ה כ״ה הירש הנ״ל
11. וככה יהי׳ חוזר חלילה שנה בשנה עד עולם להם ולי״א וב״כ וכתבנו
12. זאת בתוקף מעשה ב״ד ובכח ב״ד יפה נעשה אור ליו׳ ב׳ כף טבת
13. תקלמד זיין לפק
14. הדיין ור״י מ״ה נתן מז וכ״ה מאיר שיף ואני ר׳ חיים גונדרשהיים

---

1. כבוד שלמה
2. צ״ל ׳זענוויל׳
3. צ״ל ׳עליו׳

No. 86

Fols. 94b–96a; Thusday evening, 2 January 1777

The outer house on the Schwert lot was two-thirds owned by Me᾿ir Kassel and one-third owned by Moses Schloss. The owners agreed to renovate the house and divide it into three living areas. Me᾿ir had the right to rent out one-third of the renovated house. Construction costs would be divided according to percentage of ownership. The owners agreed that no repairs could be made to the house without the knowledge of both owners. They itemized the division of space and also made conditions as to the rights of those who would live in each area. The owners now approached the court and asked that it cast lots to determine who would get which section of the house for a three-year period. Every three years thereafter, the families were to rotate their living quarters as specified in the document.

צד ע״ב

ב״ה

כהי׳ דלמטה אנחנו ח״מ מחזיק בית חיצון צום שווע[פ]רט דהיינו לכ׳ משה בן המנוח כ׳ ליב שלאס שייך אחד מבית הנ״ל ולכ׳ מאירי[1] המנוח כ׳ יוקל קאסיל ז״ל שייך שני שליש מבית הנ״ל התרצו יחד מחמת חלוקת ביתנו הנ״ל לחלוק על שלשה חלקי דיורי׳ חלק הראשון חדר בית החורף גלייכן ערד עם הקוך והשענק שבתוכה חדר א׳ בית החורף שני שטעג הויך לצד הסוכה עם הקמין אך אין לו רשות למי שמגיע לו חלק זה להעמיד שום דבר שני שטעג הויך בתוך הויז עהרנד וחדר אחד לצד הסוכה שלשה שטעג הויך וחמשה שטעג הויך מחויבי׳ אנחנו לבנות עוד חדר קטן לפנות בתוכה [כ]ל כלי בית על חג הפסח לצד הרחוב בשותפות דהיינו כפי מה שמגיע לכל א׳ על חלקו בבית הנ״ל לכ׳ מאיר הנ״ל שני שלישים ולכ׳[2] שליש אחד ואותו חדר חדש יהי׳ שייך למי שמגיע לו חלק שליש הלז גם יהי׳ לו המרתף {שנפסין} שנכנסין בו מתוך הקוך ושטח המרתף היא תחת הסוכה ותחת בית החורף למטה עד מחיצה עם הפתח העומד בשטעג פון הינדר קעלר כל הנ״ל הוא חלק שליש אחד וחלק השני א׳ שטעג הויך שני בית החורף זה מול זה והשאנק שנכנס בתוך השטעג וחדר אחד ד׳ שטעג הויך לצד הסוכה וחמשה שטעג הויך דען פר שלאסנה באזין לצד הסוכה והמרתף האמצעי שמתחיל ממחיצה שבינו להחיצונה עד מחיצה שבינו לפנימי דרך השטעג של מרתף החיצון יהי׳ [..ל.] למרתף אמצעי הנ״ל אבל אין לו רשות להלך דרך {מסתף} מרתף הפנימי הנכנסין לו דרך קוך ומחויבי׳ אנחנו

---

1. חסרה המילה ׳בן׳
2. כנראה שיש להוסיף כאן ׳משה׳

צה ע"א

1. ב"ה
2. ומחויבי' אנחנו לבנות מחיצה בצד השטעג מן השטעג עד כותל הבית המפסקת ב
3. בינו לבין בית שבצידו ולעשות פתח באותו מחיצה כדי שמי שמגיע לו החיצון
4. יכנס בו דרך השטעג והמקו' הפנוי ההוא דהיינו עד אותו מחיצה הנ"ל
5. יהי' שייך למרתף אמצעי ואין לחיצון רק המהלך והוצאות בנין המחיצה יהי'
6. בשותפות כפי מה שמגיע לכל אחד על חלקו בבית כנ"ל ושאנק עם אייזנה
7. טיהר ויש לו רשות להשליך עץ שלו אויף דיא שטעג למרתף כל הנ"ל הוא חלק
8. שליש שני וחלק השלישי שני שטעג הויך חדר בית החורף לצד הרחוב עם
9. הקוך גם השענק העומדי' בהויז עהרנד וגוסשטרין[1] העומד שני שטעג הויך
10. יהי' בשותפת לשלשה ב"ב הדרי' בו ושלשה שטעג הויך חדר אחד לצד
11. הרחוב וד' שטעג הויך גם נעבין חדר ואותו מרתף שיש {בתנה} בתוכה קעלר
12. לאָך לצד הרחוב המגיע עד המחיצה החדשה הנ"ל ועץ שלו ישליך דרך אותו
13. קעלר לאָך אבל דרך השטעג כל הנ"ל הוא חלק השלישי ובירושה יתנו בינינו שרשות
14. ביד כ' מאיר קאסיל המחזיק שני שלישי בית הנ"ל וי"א וב"כ לעשות שני שלישי הנ"ל
15. לשני דיורי' או לדור עצמו בשלש[2] אחד ולהשכיר שליש אחד לכל מי שירצה ובימי
16. חג הסוכת ישתמש שלשה דיורי' בשווה בהסוכה ואינו יכול למחות אותו
17. שדר למטה דש עסין דורך דיא שטופף צו טראגין ובית הכסא יהי' ג"כ ב
18. בשותפת לשלשה דיורי' הנ"ל וגם הותנה דש שני שטעג הויך החדר בית
19. החורף לצד הסוכה וועלכה נאך ניט גטעבלט אונד טאפי ציהרט איזט
20. מחויבי' אנחנו טעבלין וטאפי צירן צו לאזין בשותפות לשום כל אחד
21. כפי מה שיגיע על חלקו כנ"ל גם שלשה שטעג הויך החדר לצד הרחוב
22. מחויבי' אנחנו אונטר שיידין צו לאזין בשותפת כפי מה שיגיע כ"א ע"ח כדי
23. דער דש חלק בקומט שני חדרי' הוט מזה החדר דיא טאפיטין וועלכה
24. בתוך חדרי' זיינין אין להם רשות אב צו רייסין [מ]וז הכל אין אורדינונג

צה ע"ב

1. ב"ה
2. בלייבין וגם הותנו שלתקן בדק הבית אין לא' מהם רשות לעשות שום דבר
3. בלי ידיעות {חביח} חבירו והוצאות התיקון יהי' לעולם עכ"א כפי חלקו בבית
4. כנ"ל והתרצו יחיד[3] להטיל גורל על שלשה דיורי' הנ"ל משלשה שני' על שלשה שני' למי
5. שיגיע לכל אחד משלשה חלקי דיורי' הנ"ל וככה יהי' חוזר חלילה עד עולם גם לי"א וב"כ
6. אך בפירוש הותנו בינינו בגוב"ר בכא"ה {לפתח"ל} לפתחזל[4] שאם יהי' כ' כ'[5] דוד

1. כנראה שצ"ל 'וגוסשטיין'
2. צ"ל 'שליש'
3. צ"ל 'יחד'
4. לפי תקנת חז"ל
5. כפילות במקור

7. בהמנוחי[1] כ׳ משה הירש הארן המחזיק עכשיו בשכירות חדר בית למטה רוצה
8. לפנות אותו חדר בית החורף שדר בו אזי יתחילה הגורל פסח שנת תקלזין
9. הסמוך הבעל[2] ובאם לא ירצה לפנות ולצאת מאותו חדר אזי לא יתחיל הגורל
10. רק מפסח תקלח הבעל ואז מחיב כ׳ משה הנ״ל לשלם לכ׳ מאיר הנ״ל משלישית
11. בית עד פסח תקלח הבעל דהיינו ח״ך[3] מסך ארבעי׳ וארבע זהו׳ וידור משנה ב׳
12. בדירתם כפי שהם דרי׳ עכשיו ועד פסח תקלח הבעל ואופן הגורל יהי׳ באופן זה
13. למי שמגיע לו הגורל בשלשה שני׳ ראשוני מעת התחלת הגורל הנ״ל כנ״ל השליש הראשון דהיינו
14. בית החורף התחתון הנ״ל עם שייך לו כנ״ל יהי׳ לו שלשה שני׳ שניי׳ שלייש
15. האמצעי דהיינו א׳ שטעג הויך ב׳ בית החורף עם השייך לו כנ״ל ושלשה שני׳
16. השלישים יהי׳ לו שליש השלישי דהיינו בית החורף ב׳ שטעג הויך לצד הרחוב
17. בעם השייך לו כנ״ל ומי שמגיע לו בשלשה שני׳ ראשוני׳ שליש האמצעי כנ״ל יהי׳ לו בשלשה
18. שני׳ שניי׳ שליש השלישי כנ״ל ובשלשה שני׳ שלישיים שליש הראשון כנ״ל ומי שמגיע לו
19. שלשה שני׳ ראשונים שליש השלישי כנ״ל יהי׳ בשלשה שנה שניי׳ שליש הראשון כנ״ל
20. ובשלשה שני׳ שלישיים שליש האמצעי כנ״ל וכן יחזור חלילה עד עולם כל הנ״ל קבלנו
21. לאשר ולקיי׳ בח״ח ובשדא[4] בת״כ בפ״מ ושלחא למהדר ביה מיומא דנן ולעלם ועל ב״כ
22. וי״א עד עולם כל הנ״ל קבלו עליהם הצדדי׳ הנ״ל ולראי באו ע״ה

צו ע״א

1. ב״ה
2. כהי׳ דלמטה הפלנו גורל כנזכר במעשה ב״ד במעמד ובריצוי הצדדי׳
3. כ׳ מאיר סג״ל וכ׳ משה הנמע״ל ועלה הגורל על שלשה שני׳ ראשוני׳ מעת {לעת}
4. התחלת גורל הנ״ל על אופן המבואר בגוף מעשה ב״ד הנ״ל שיהי׳ לכ׳
5. מאיר שליש הראשון הנ״ל ושליש השלישי הנ״ל לכ׳ משה שליש אמצעי הנ״ל
6. ושלשה שני׳ השניי׳ יהי׳ לכ׳ מאיר הנ״ל שליש הראשון ושליש האמצעי
7. ולכ׳ משה הנ״ל שליש השלישי כנ״ל ושלשה שני׳ השלישי׳ יהי׳ לכ׳ מאיר
8. הנ״ל שליש האמצעי כנ״ל ושליש השלישי כנ״ל ולכ׳ משה הנ״ל שליש (הראשון)[5] כנ״ל
9. וכן יחזור חלילה שלשה שני׳ לשלשה שני׳ כנזכר למעלה בגוף מעשה ב״ד
10. וכה יהי׳ וכה יקו׳ מעתה וע״ע הכל כנזכר בגוף מב״ד וכתבנו
11. וחתמנו זאת להיות ביד כל אחד {כל הנ״ל קבלו[.] הצדדי׳ הנ״ל בפנינו}
12. נעשה אור ליו׳ ויו ך״ו טבת תקלמדזיין לפק
13. ר נתן מז ר יעקב שמש ואני

---

1. בן המנוח
2. הבא עלינו לטובה
3. אולי ׳חלק עשרים׳ (20%)
4. ובשבועה דאורייתא
5. תוספת מעל השורה

No. 87

Fol. 96b; Wednesday evening, 1 January 1777

A record of the sale of three-quarters of a plot on the Vorder Schule lot on which a house once stood (see Dietz, p. 472, no. 167). The lot had been owned by Herz Schloss and was being sold to Joel Halle for 1501 guldens. As in other such records, the terms of sale are itemized with one-third of the sale price payable immediately and two-thirds payable in three semi-annual installments over the next 18 months. This was somewhat unusual since in most agreements the payments were spread out over 36 months. This was the first of three sales of real propery by Herz Schloss (also see nos. 89, 90), who died on 8 February 1777.[6]

צו ע"ב

1. ב"ה
2. שלשה רביעית מפלאטץ שהי' עומד עליו הבית חיצון צור פאדר
3. שוהל שהי' שייך לכ"ה הירץ במ"ה אהרן שלאס נרו[7] נמכר בפנינו
4. ב"ד ח"מ להו"ה כ' יואל האלי בעד סך חמשה {מאות} (עשר)[8] {ע.ה}מאות (ואחת)[9] זהו'
5. לשלם אין קונפיטנטציאהן מינץ אויף דעם ך"ד זהו' פוס והיינו
6. לשלם שליש מדמי מכירה הנ"ל תיכף נגד מסירת החלטה ושני שלישי'
7. הנותרי' על שלשה חצאי שני' זא"ז מיו' מסירת החלטה נגד ח"כ
8. ושטר אפותיקו לאורדרי נעשה אור ליו' ך"ג טבת תקלזין לפק
9. הק נתן בלא"א כ"ה שלמה מז"ל[10] ראש הישיבה פה פפ"ד
10. הק יעקב שמש
11. הק חיים בפו"מ כ' יוזפא גונדרשהיי' שליטא
12. בעד סך חמשה עשרי[11] ואחת זהו'[12]

6. Regarding the date of his death, see Ettlinger, 8.2.1777.
7. נטריה רחמנא ופרקיה
8. תוספת מעל השורה
9. תוספת מעל השורה
10. מז ז"ל
11. כנראה שצריך להוסיף כאן 'מאות'
12. לאור אי בהירות בשורה 4, יתכן שהסופר חזר על הסכום כאן.

No. 88

Samuel Fulda on Behalf of all Creditors of the Estate of Jacob Kann *v.* *Jacob ben Leb of Mannheim*

Fols. 97a–b; Thursday evening, 23 January 1777

Jacob ben Leb of Mannheim married a widow, Ẓipper, who had lived in Frankfurt. Before leaving Frankfurt, Ẓipper left a deposit with the Jewish community to guarantee her right of residency in the community. Sometime after the marriage, Jacob purchased merchandise from a Frankfurt resident, Jacob Kann, at least partially on credit. Kann passed away before the note was paid.

Samuel Fulda represented a group of local creditors who were owed funds by the estate of the late Jacob Kann (see no. 59 and Appendix 1). The creditors had the unpaid note for 70 reichstalers that Jacob ben Leb had given Kann. The impetus for this case was Ẓipper's request that the Frankfurt Jewish community return her deposit to her as she seems to have been prepared to relinquish her right to live in Frankfurt. The group of creditors argued that it should assume the rights that belonged to Jacob ben Leb of Mannheim with respect to these funds, including the right to inherit them should Ẓipper predecease him. Ẓipper, through local representation, contested the creditors' rights to the assets. The court ruled in favor of Ẓipper. The text also appears in YIVO MS. RG 128 (folder 77–78), fol. 42a–b, with minor variations but with an important addition: the legal rationale for the court's decision. This has been added here as a footnote at the end of the record.

צז ע"א

1. ב"ה
2. ע"ד שבאו לפנינו ה"ה התורני כ"ה משה אויך בהרשאות הו"ה התורני
3. כ"ה שמואל פולדא יצו בשביל כל הבעלי חובות מן המנוח כ"ה יעקב קן
4. ז"ל וטוען שנמצא בעזבון כ"ה יעקב קן ז"ל חוב אחד מן סך שבעי' רט
5. על כ"ה יוקב בן כ"ה ליב מקקי[1] מנהיים יע"א בעד סחורת שלקח כ"ה יוקב
6. הנ"ל מן ר' יעקב הנ"ל בעודו בחיים בהקיפו[2] לאחר שנשא אשתו [מ'] ציפר
7. אל' כ' מאיר שוואב ז"ל ונשאר עדיין חייב בעזבון הנ"ל ותבע כ"ה משה
8. אויך באשר שהאשה מ' ציפר הניחה ביד האלופי' גובי' יצו סך ידוע
9. על חזקת עירונית קודם נסיעתה מפה ועתה שתבעה האשה הנ"ל סך

1. מקהילת קודש
2. בכתב יד יוו"א כתוב 'בהקפה' וכן נראה.

10. המעות המעות[1] שהניחה ורצה לסלק עירונית בכן רוצה להחזיק בבעלי[2]
11. חובות הנ״ל על סך שבעי׳ ר״ט שנשאר עדיין חייב כ״ה יוקב הנ״ל בעזבון
12. הנ״ל ומחמת שהמעות שתג[בה][3] האשה הנ״ל זכה בה[4] בעלה כ״ה יוקב[5]
13. כדין נכסי מלוג הפירות בחיי׳ והקרן לאחר מותה ואותו זכות
14. רוצים להחזיק עצמם הבעלי חובות הנ״ל על גביית חוב הנ״ל
15. וה״ה התורני כ׳ מאיר מז בהרשאת ה״ה פו״מ כ״ה ליב אופנהיים
16. שיש לו כו״ה מן האשה מציפר ובעל[6] כ״ה יוקב הנ״ל מקק מנהיים יעא[7]
17. השיב שהאשה אינה מחויבת לשלם חובות בעלה גם בשעת שהניחה
18. המעות הנ״ל ביד גובי׳ לא הי׳ עו[מד] לגבית פירות אדרבה שצריכה
19. להוסיף על הפירות ולשלם עוד עבור עלים[8] שלה וגם עדיין הברירה
20. בידה להניח עדיין ביד הגובי׳ והאריכו בטענותיהם כמבואר
21. בק״ה המונח לפנינו ולאחר שחתמו עצמם בתוקף קומפרמיס בח״ח
22. ובקנס לאשר ולקיי׳ כל אשר יצא מאתנו והיינו ה״ה פו״מ כ״ה ליב אופנהיי׳
23. בכו״ה מן

צז ע״ב

1. ב״ה
2. בכו״ה מן האשה מ׳ ציפר ובעלה כ״ה יוקב הנ״ל והתורני כ״ה שמואל
3. פולדא הנ״ל בהרשאות הבעלי חובות מן העזבון הנ״ל בכן נזדקקנו להם
4. ומצאנו שהדין עם האשה מ׳ ציפר הנ״ל ואין לבעלי חובות שום זכות על מעות שהניח האשה הנ״ל בי״ד[9] הגובי׳ הנ״ל יצא מאתנו אור ליו׳ ויו טז
5. שבט תקלזין לפק[10]

---

1. כפילות במקור אבל לא בכ״י יוו״א.
2. בכתב יד יוו״א כתוב ׳רוצים להחזיקו הבעלי׳ וכן נראה.
3. וכן כתוב בכ״י יוו״א
4. בכתב יד יוו״א כתוב ׳בהם׳
5. בכתב יד יוו״א כתוב ׳יוקב הנ״ל׳
6. בכתב יד יוו״א כתוב ׳ובעלה׳
7. יגן עליה אלהים
8. בכתב יד יוו״א כתוב ׳עולים שלה׳. על פי אלה תולדות (23.11.1767) היו לציפר ומאיר שוואב ארבעה ילדים. אחד, יצחק, מת כילד בשנת 1761 וילד אחר, ליב, עבר לגור בדרמשטאדט (לא ברור באיזה שנה). חיים שוואב נולד בפרנקפורט בשנת 1755 והתחתן לראשונה רק בשנת 1795 (ר׳ אלה תולדות 10.11.1832 וגם 12.1.1805 וגם דייץ, עמ׳ 277) והמשיך לגור בפרנקפורט עד מותו בשנת 1832. בת בשם פראדכה נולדה בשנת 1765 ולא התחתנה עד שנת 1785. פראדכה ובעלה גרו בפרנקפורט (ר׳ אלה תולדות 1.10.1809).
9. לא ברור למה יש גרשיים כאן. בכתב יד יוו״א אין.
10. גם בכתכ יד יוו״א (מח ע״ב) שמות הדיינים לא מוזכרים אמנם הוסיף המחבר (כנראה הרב נתן מז): ׳טעם דין זה כי מה שפסקנו שאין הבע״ח יכולין לזכות {מחמת} ברחווי׳ מ׳‹חמת› שנכסי מלוג הם והפירות לבעל הלא הוא מבואר בח״מ ס׳ צ״ז סע׳ כ״ו שאין בע״ח גובה מנכסי מלוג {...} ופשיט׳ דאיירי {...} אפילו מפירות דאי מ[גוף פשי]ט׳ הלא שלה הוא וכן כתב בעה״ת הביאו ב״י ס׳ קי״א והסמ״ע והש״ך שם בריש הסימן וכ״כ ב״ש באה״ע ס׳ פ״ה סעי׳ יז ס״ק לט / ומחמת טענות הבע״ח {...} שמגיע להם אותו זכות שירשה הבעל ולכן אינו מניחם ליתנו לה לית׳ כיון שהוא לוה ביד הגובי׳ קודם [נשו]אין א״כ אין הבעל יורשה קודם שגבת׳ דה״ל ראוי

No. 89

Fol. 98a; Wednesday evening, 1 January 1777

A second sale of property by Herz Schloss on 1 January 1777 (see too no. 87). Herz sold his quarter share of a house on the Wetterhahn lot to Aaron Flesch for 800 (gulden? — the currency is not specified). The record itemizes the terms of payment. Also see no. 90.

צח ע״א

1. ב״ה
2. רביעית בית צום וועטרהאן שהי׳ שייך לה״ה כה הירץ במ״ה
3. אהרן שלאס נרו[1] נמכר בפנינו ב״ד ח״מ להו״ה כה אהרן פלעש בעד
4. סך שמונה מאות לשלם אין קונפינטציאהן מינץ אויף דעם כ״ד זהו׳
5. פוס והיינו לשלם שליש מדמי מכירה הנ״ל תיכף נגד מסירת חלטה ושני שלישי׳
6. הנותרי׳ על ששה חצאי שני׳ {זאת} זא״ז מיו׳ מסירת החלטה נגד ח״כ ושטר
7. אפותיקו (לאורדר)[2] נעשה אור ליו׳ ה׳ דג טבת תקלזין לפק הק׳ נתן מז
8. הקטן יעקב שמש הק׳ חיים גונדרשהיים שליטא

No. 90

Fol. 98a; Sunday evening, 5 January 1777

A further sale of property by Herz Schloss (see nos. 87 and 89), this time a seat in the lower women's section of the synagogue. The seat was currently occupied by the wife of Ḥayyim Schuster. The seat was sold to Herz Flesch for 475 guldens. The record outlines the terms of payment.

9. מקו׳ שלם בע״נ התחתונה אשר עומדות עלי׳ כעת אשת כ״ה חיים {שוסט}
10. שוסטר כך הפונה לצד מערב סמוך לכותל המפסקת בין אנשי׳ ובין ע״נ
11. ומצד ימין אותו מקום הנ״ל עומדת כעת אשת כ״ה נטע שוסטר אותו מק׳ שלם
12. הנ״ל שהי׳ שייך לכ״ה הירץ בהר״ב מ״ה אהרן שלאס נרו[3] נמכר בפנינו לה״ה
13. כ״ה הירץ פלעש יצו בעד סך ארבע מאות שבעי׳ וחמשה זהו׳ לשלם

ואין הבעל יורש בראוי כמבואר באה״ע סי׳ צדיק סוף סעי׳ א׳.

1. נטריה רחמנא ופרקיה
2. תוספת מעל השורה
3. נטריה רחמנא ופרקיה

14. אין קונפינטעץ יאהנש מינץ אויף ד״ד זהו׳ פוס והיינו ששלם השליש מסך דמי מכירה
15. הנ״ל תיכף נגד מסירת החלטה ושני השלישים הנותרי׳ ישלם על ששה חצאי
16. שני׳ רצופים זא״ז מיו׳ מסירת החלטה ומחיב[1] כ״ה הירץ ליתן ח״כ על זמני׳ הנ״ל
17. גם נשאר מקו׳ שלם לאפותיקו מפורש שלא יצא מחזקת מרא קמא כל זמן שלא
18. נתפרע אפי׳ אחד מן הזמני׳ הנ״ל נעשה אור ליו׳ ב ד׳ז טבת תקלזין לפק
19. הקטן נתן מז הק מאיר שיף הק חיים גונדרשהיים שליטא

No. 91

Fol. 98b; Sunday 18 May 1777

The record of the sale of one-eighth of a house on the Drei Römer lot on the Neugasse for 228 guldens. The portion of the house was sold by the Jewish community to Joseph Hammel, who was engaged to be married. The terms of payment are itemized.

צח ע״ב

1. ב״ה
2. חלק שמינית מבית שלם צור דרויא רעהמר אין דער נייאגאס שהי׳ שייך להאלופי׳
3. גובי׳ יצו נמכר בפנינו ב״ד ח״מ לה״ה הב״ח החתן כ׳ יוסף בהמנוח[2] כ״ה מרדכי האמיל סג״ל ז״ל
4. בעד שני מאות ועשרי׳ ושמונה זהו׳ אין קונפונטציאהנש מעות אויף דעם כ״ד זהו׳ פוס
5. והיינו לשלם שליש מדמי מכירה הנ״ל תיכף נגד מסירת מעשה ב״ד{הלז} ושני שלישי׳ ה
6. הנותרי׳ מדמי מכירה הנ״ל לשלם על ששה חצאי שני׳ רצופי׳ זא״ז מיו׳ מסירת מעשה
7. ב״ד ומחויב הלוקח הנ״ל ליתן ששה ח״כ לאורדר האלופי׳ גובי׳ יצו על משך זמני׳ הנ״ל
8. נעשה יו׳ א׳ י״א אייר תקלמדזיין לפק ר נתן מז ר׳ מאיר שיף ואני
9. ———

No. 92

Fol. 98b; Sunday evening, 18 May 1777

A quarter of the Hindin house plus a quarter of a structure that stood behind the

---

1. צ״ל ׳ומחויב׳
2. בן המנוח

house were sold by the Jewish community to Moses Oppenheim for 1500 guldens. A note at the bottom of the page states that it was the policy of the court not to give those who bought property from the community a copy of the court record as was normally done in real estate transactions between private individuals. When the community sold property the court record itself was deemed sufficient as proof of purchase.

10. רביעית בית חיצון (עם (רביעי')[1] בנין ב[קי]כה שעומד אחורי הבית בסוכה)[2] דיא הינדן שהי' שייך להאלופי' גובי' יצו נמכר בפנינו ב"ד ח"מ
11. לה"ה כ' משה בהמנוח[3] כ' שלמה אופנהיים ז"ל בעד סך חמשה עשר מאות זהו' אין
12. קונפונטציאהנש מינץ אויף דעם כ"ד זהו' פוס והיינו לשלם שליש מדמי מכירה
13. הנ"ל תיכף נגד מסירת מעשה ב"ד ושני שלישי' הנותרי' מדמי מכירה הנ"ל לשלם על ששה
14. חצאי שני' רצופי' זא"ז מיו' מסירת מעשה ב"ד ומחויב הלוקח כ' משה הנ"ל ליתן ששה ח"כ
15. על זמני' הנ"ל נעשה אור ליו' ב' יב אייר תקלמד זיין לפק ר"נ[4] ורמ"ש ואני
16. ———
17. במעשה ב"ד גדול כתבנו קודם וכתבנו וחתמנו זאת ובאשר שכפי הנהוג
18. פה קהלתנו יע"א שהמכירה הנעשה מן האלופי' גובי' יצו אין יותן להלוקח שטר
19. החלטה בפני עצמו כמו שארי מכירות הנעשה מאנשי' אחרי' בכן יהא תוקף
20. מעשה ב"ד הלז כאילו יש להלוקח גם שטר החלטה בפני עצמו

No. 93

Fol. 99a; Tuesday evening, 22 May 1777

A record of the sale of one-third of an inner house on the Weiße Leiter lot by the community to Me'ir Sichel who had recently married. The property was sold for 2660 guldens. The terms of the agreement include a clause protecting Ber Reiss, who was renting the space at the time of sale. Reiss was allowed to continue living in the house, but all rent from the time of sale forward accrued to Sichel. The court prohibited Sichel from raising Reiss's rent for the duration of his lease (until Passover 1779).

1. תוספת מעל שורת התוספת
2. תוספת מעל השורה
3. בן המנוח
4. כנראה רב נתן מז

צט ע"א

1. ב"ה
2. שליש בית פנימי צור ווייסה לאטר שהי' שייך להאלופי' קציני' גובי' יצו נמכר
3. בפנינו ב"ד דלמטה להחתן כ' מאיר בהמנוח[1] כ' זלמן זיכל ז"ל בעד סך
4. עשרי' וששה מאות וששי' זהו' לשלם אין קונפונטציאהנש מינץ אויף
5. דעם כ"ד זהו' פוס והיינו לשלם שליש מדמי מכירה תיכף נגד מסירת
6. מעשה ב"ד ושני שלישי' הנותרי' מדמי מכירה הנ"ל לשלם לששה חצאי שני'
7. רצופי' זא"ז מיו' מסירת מעשה ב"ד מחויב הלוקח הנ"ל ליתן ח"כ לאורדר
8. הגובי' יצו על זמני' הנ"ל גם נשאר שליש הבית הנ"ל לאפותיקו מפורש
9. כנהוג גם הותנה בפירוש בשעת מכירה כתנאי בגוב"ר בכא"ה לפתחז"ל
10. שכל מי שיקנה השליש בית הנ"ל אין רשאי להוציא השוכר כ' פער רייס יצו
11. משליש בית הנ"ל שדר בתוכה כעת משך זמן שכירתו והיינו עד פסח
12. תקלט הבע"ל רק שישאר בו כ"ה פער הנ"ל על דמי השכירות הקצוב ממנו אכן
13. דמי השכירות שייך להלוקח מהיו' דלמטה נעשה פה פפדמיין[2] אור ליו'
14. ויו טז אייר שנת תקלמד זיין לפק ר נתן מז ור' מאיר שיף ואני

No. 94

Fol. 99b; Sunday evening, 22 June 1777

Two quarters of two seats (i.e., one quarter of each seat) that were next to each other in the men's section of the old synagogue were sold to Gumpel Kann for 400 guldens. The record notes that the quarter-seats previously belonged to Jacob Kann, and presumably the proceeds of the sale were used to help satisfy his creditors (see no. 88). A condition of the sale was that the purchaser was not entitled to benefit from the seats until Passover 1778. This arrangement left one of the seats half-owned by Gumpel and half-owned by the heirs of Hirsch Gundersheim. The other seat was one-quarter owned by Gumpel, one-quarter owned by his brother, Ber, and one-half owned by the heirs of Hirsch Gundersheim (see no. 96). Since the seats were owned by more than one owner, the right to sit on a seat rotated annually as a means of attaining equitable access to the assets.

---

1. בן המנוח
2. פפרנקפורט דמיין

צט ע"ב

1. ב"ה
2. רביעית (מן כל אחד ואחד)[1] משני מקומות הסמוכי' בע"א שעומדי' עלי' כעת הו"ה כ"ה גומפל קן וכ' זעליג הז
3. שהי' שייכי' להמנוח ר יעקב קן ז"ל אשר רביעית האחרי' מכ"א מהמקומות הנ"ל שייכי' לכ"ה
4. גומפל הנ"ל ואחיו כ' פער בני המנוח כ"ה ליב קן ז"ל וחצי' הנותרי' מכ"א משני מקומות
5. הנ"ל שייכי' לבני המנוח כ' הירש גונדרשהיים ז"ל אותן שני רביעית הנ"ל שהי'
6. שייך לכ"ה יעקב קן ז"ל נמכר בפנינו להוה[2] גומפל קן הנ"ל בעד ארבע מאות
7. זהו' לשלם אין קונפונטצאהנש מינץ אויף דעם כ"ד זהו' פוס והיינו לשלם שליש
8. מסך דמי מכירה הנ"ל תיכף נגד מסירת החלטה ושני שלישי' מדמי מכירה הנ"ל לשלם
9. על ששה חצאי שני' זא"ז מיו' מסירת החלטה גם נשאר שני רביעית מקומות הנ"ל
10. לאפותיקו מפורש שלא יצא מחזקת מרא קמא כל זמן שלא נתפרע אפי' אחד מן הזמני'
11. הנ"ל ובפ[י]רוש הותנה בשעת מכירה שלא יהא להלוקח הפירות משני רביעית
12. מקומות הנ"ל עד פסח הבע"ל גם מחויב להחליף מחזיקי' שני מקומות כל שנה
13. נעשה אור ליו' ב' חי סיון תקלזיין לפק ר' נתן מז ר אברהם טריר ואני

No. 95

Fol. 99b; Sunday evening, 22 June 1777

A full seat in the middle women's section that had previously belonged to Jacob Kann was sold to Leb Menz for 503 guldens. As in the previous case (no. 94), the conditions of sale stipulated that the purchaser could not enjoy benefits from the seat until Passover 1778.

14. ————
15. מקו' שלם בע"נ התיכונה שהי' עומדות עלי' כעת אשת כ' ליב בהמנוח[3] כ' זעליגמן
16. מענץ ז"ל שהי' שייך להמנוח כ"ה יעקב קן ז"ל נמכר ב[פנינו] לה"ה כ' ליב
17. בהמנוח כ' זעליגמן מענץ הנ"ל בעד סך חמשה מאות ושלשה זהו' לשלם
18. כפי תיקון הקהלה גם הותנה בפירוש שלא יהא להלוקח הנ"ל הפירות
19. עד פסח הבע"ל נעשה אור ליו' ב' חי סיון תקלמדזין לפק
20. רנ"מ ר אברהם טריר וא[ני]

---

1. תוספת מעל השורה
2. להמפואר והחשוב
3. בן המנוח

No. 96

Fol. 100a; Wednesday 25 June 1777

A few days after Gumpel Kann purchased two quarter-seats in the men's section of the synagogue (no. 94), he came to the court and declared that he had purchased the two quarter-seats in partnership with his brother, Ber Kann, who was engaged to be married. Gumpel asked the court to issue a document to his brother affirming his declaration, which it did. The document was considered proof of ownership and gave Gumpel and Ber equal rights in the seats.

קוף ע"א

1. ב"ה
2. במותב בי תלתא כחדא הוינא ואתא לקדמנא ה"ה הו"ה כ"ה גומפל בהמנוח[1] פו"מ כ"ה ליב קן שהיה
3. לוקח אור ליו' ב' חי סיון שנת תקלזיין לפנינו בד[2] ח"מ (ע"י)[3] אכ[רזתא][4] כנהוג הרביעות מן כל אחד משני
4. מקומת הסמוכי' בבה"כ ישן העומדי' עליהם כעת כה גומפל הנ"ל והו"ה כ' זעליג הז שהי' שייכי'
5. לדודו המנוח ר' יעקב קן בהמנוח מ"ה איצק קן ז"ל בעד ארבא[5] מאות זהו' הנמכרי'
6. לפנינו ב"ד ח"מ מן בעלי חובת של ר' יעקב ז"ל הנ"ל על אופן וזמני' המבוארי' במעשה ב"ד
7. שנעשה ביו' הנ"ל {הנ"ל} והודה בפנינו ה"ה הו"ה כ"ה גומפל הנ"ל ביו' דלמטה שלקח משני רביעי'
8. מקומת הנ"ל בשותפות עם אחיו הב"ח החתן כ' פ[ע]ר בהמנוח כ"ה ליב קן ז"ל ושייך לאחיו ר'
9. פער הנ"ל מחצי משני רביעי' מקומות הנ"ל ולעצמו החצי משני רביעי' מקומת הנ"ל ואין לאחד
10. מהאחים הנ"ל שום זכות ברביעית שני מקומות הנ"ל יותר מחבירו ובקש מאתנו ב"ד ח"מ
11. ליתן לאחיו כ' פער הנ"ל מעשה ב"ד מהודאה הנ"ל ואחר ששמענו הודאה מפי כ"ה גומפל
12. הנ"ל נזדקקנו אנחנו ב"ד ח"מ לדבריו לזאת באנו אנחנו ליתן להב"ח החתן כ' פער הנ"ל
13. כתב ראי' על הודאה הנ"ל בתוקף מעשה ב"ד ובכח ב"ד יפה להיות ביד החתן כ' פער
14. הנ"ל לעדות ולזכות ולראיי' ששני רביעי' מקומות הנ"ל הם בהשותפות להאחים כה
15. {גומפל וכ' פער הנ"ל אותו זכות ויפוי כח הוא ג"כ לכ' פער הנ"ל על חלקו הנזכר

---

1. בן המנוח
2. בית דין
3. תוספת מעל השורה
4. אולי צ"ל 'הכרזתא'
5. צ"ל 'ארבע'

16. במעשה ב"ד הנ"ל שיש ביד כ"ה גומפל הנ"ל אותו זכות} גומפל וכ' פער הנ"ל ואין
17. לא' מהם שום זכות יותר מחבירו וכל תוקף מעשה ב"ד ושופר' דשטרי ויפוי כח הוא ג"כ
18. הנזכר במעשה ב"ד הנ"ל [ש]יי[...] כ"ה גומפל הנ"ל אותו זכות ויפוי הוא ג"כ לכ' פער הנ"ל
19. על חלקו משני רביעי' מקומות הנ"ל וכאילו (נכתב)[1] המעשה ב"ד הנ"ל ג"כ על שמו ולראי' באנו על
20. החותם היום יו' ד' ך סיון תקלמד זיין לפק ר נתן מז רא"ט ואני

No. 97

Fol. 100b; Sunday evening, 20 July 1777

A record of the sale of two half lots, one on the Kranich lot and the other on the Vorder Enge Tür tract. Houses had once stood on both parcels of land. The Enge Tür section plus half of the area being sold on the Kranich lot belonged to the community; the remaining quarter of the Kranich section belonged to the heirs of Ber Deuz. The entire package was purchased by Moses Sichel for 2250 guldens. The sale was ordered by the community with the agreement of the guardian of Ber Deuz's children. The conditions of sale are outlined with specific reference to a previous court decision and to an agreement made earlier in the year that had to be respected. These latter documents are not in this collection.

ק ע"ב

1. ב"ה
2. שני חצאי פלאטץ שהי' עומדי' עליהם שני בתי' החיצוני' הסמוכי' צור קראניך אונד צור
3. פאדר ענגה טיהר דהיינו רביעית פלאטץ מן פלאטץ שהי' עומד עליו הבית צום קר
4. קראניך (הנ"ל)[2] גם החצי פלאטץ שהי' עומד עליו הבית צור (פאדר)[3] ענגה טיהר הי' שייכי' להאלופי' גובי'
5. יצו והרביעית מן פלאטץ שהי' עומד עלי' הבית צום קראנך הנ"ל הי' שייך ליתמי המנוח
6. כ' פער דייץ ז"ל[4] נמכרו בפנינו ב"ד ח"מ ע"פ צוות הגובי' וברצון הו"ה פו"מ כ"ה
7. אברהם וויניג יצו אפטרפס דיתמי הנ"ל לה"ה החתן כ' משה בהמנוח[5] כ' זלמן זיכל
8. בעד סך עשרי' ושני' מאות וחמשי' זהו' לשלם אותם כפי תיקון הקהלה יע"א
9. והותנה בפי' בשעת מכירה כתנאי בגוב"ר בכא"ה לפתחז"ל שכל מי שלוקח שני
10. חצאי פלאטץ הנ"ל שמחויב לקיים הפס"ד שיצא ביו' ה' ך"ד ניסן תקלמד זיין לפק בין

---

1. תוספת מעל השורה
2. תוספת מעל השורה
3. תוספת מעל השורה
4. אולי פער בן דוד דייץ. אם כן, מדובר בשני יתומים, דוד ופרעדכה (ר' אלה תולדות 22.2.1760).
5. בן המנוח

11. מחזיקי פלאטץ צום קראניך הנ״ל ובין מחזיקי בית צום פאדר פאלקין גם מחויב
12. הלוקח לקיים הדברי׳ המבוארי׳ בק״ס הנעשה יו׳ ב׳ ד״ה סיון תקלמד זיין לפ״ק מן
13. כ׳ משה זנקווערט ומה שהתחייב שם פו״מ כ׳ אברלי ווימפא בענין הבנין צור
14. ענגי טיהר נעשה אור ליו׳ ב׳ טז תמוז תקל״ז רנ״מ ורמ״ש ואני

No. 98

Fol. 100b; Sunday evening, 27 July 1777

The record of the sale of a lot on the Vorder Schule tract on which a house once stood. The land was sold by the children of Lippman Schuster to Schönle, widow of their first cousin Moses Schuster, for 1601 guldens. The failure to note the terms of payment or the names of the judges who sat on the court is unusual in this diary.

15. ———
16. חצי פלאטץ מן פלאטץ שלם שהי׳ עומד עליו בית החיצון צור פאדר שוהל שהי׳ שייך
17. ליתמי המנוח כ׳ ליפמן ב״מ[1] שוסטר נמכר {בפנינו} (בפני)[2] ב״ד להאשה מ׳ שינלה אל׳ המנוח כ׳ משה
18. בן מרדכי שוסטר ז״ל בעד ששה עשר מאות ואחד זהו׳ לשלם אין קונפונטציאהנש מינץ
19. אויף דעם ד״ד זהו׳ כפי תיקון הקהלה נעשה אור ליו׳ ב׳ דג תמוז תקלמד זיין לפק

No. 99

Stern v. Hammel

Fol. 101a–103b; late Monday 28 July 1777 with an addendum from Wednesday 6 August 1777

Late in 1766, Mendel Hammel, a wine merchant, gave his daughter, Reichle, and her husband, Süsskind Stern, a "half a male's portion" contract, an agreement intended to insure daughters a share in familial wealth. Although the Torah excluded daughters from inheriting from their fathers when there were surviving sons (see Numbers 27.1–11), Ashkenazic Jews often wanted to include them and their husbands in the division of familial assets. To do so, fathers routinely gave

1. בן משה (ע״פ אלה תולדות 18.7.1761)
2. תוספת מעל השורה

their daughters or sons-in-laws a contract in which they obligated their estates either to give the bearer of the contract a very large lump sum or half of a male's portion in the estate. It was usually in the best interests of the surviving sons to pay the latter.

Almost five years after Mendel's death, Süsskind and his wife came to the court and claimed that they had not received their share of the estate. Süsskind represented himself and his wife, and demanded an accounting of the value of the estate including all profits that his brothers-in-law, David and Feivish, had made using the estate's assets, as well as profits made in the course of business when assets of the estate were used as capital. Through their representative, the brothers countered that the size of the estate was less than Süsskind believed because the brothers had become partners in the business during Mendel's lifetime and 50% of the business had already belonged to them before their father's demise. Mendel, who lived the last years of his life blind and housebound, had obligated himself, a moment before his death, to pay each of his sons 5000 guldens, effectively exhausting his estate and leaving nothing for Süsskind and his wife. Süsskind countered that this and other measures taken by Mendel were nothing more than improper transfer of assets and he protested their validity. While the court recognized the partnership, it limited its scope to assets held by Mendel on the very day that the partnership was created. Assets acquired by Mendel thereafter accrued to the estate. As for the two 5000 gulden gifts, the court maintained their legitimacy.

A further point of dispute was a letter of obligation written by Mendel in 1772 in which he promised to pay each of the three Stern children 50 reichstalers upon their marriage. One of the children died before having married and Süsskind claimed that he should inherit the child's rights and be paid the 50 reichstalers. Süsskind also asked that the funds for the other two children be deposited in a guaranteed fund and that profits accrue to the children. This was outright rejected by the brothers and the court, although David and Feivish offered of their own accord to set aside a surety to guarantee the payment of the obligation.

There are numerous other claims and counterclaims in the record, many of which stemmed from the failure to settle the estate. With many of the facts in the case in dispute, the court imposed oaths on each party regarding their respective claims. This done, the court was able to settle the matter of the estate, and most of the other matters were easily dealt with. The main reason for the addendum was Süsskind's discovery that Mendel had sold his house to his sons. Süsskind feared that the sons had never paid their father for the house, and thus Mendel had improperly transferred assets of the estate (i.e., the value of the house had been transferred to the sons without them having transferred anything back to the father/estate). The court ordered the brothers to swear that they had paid for the house and that its value was included in the valuation of the estate. The addendum also deals with the surety for David and Feivish's obligation to Süsskind's children, as well as the various oaths that were to be taken.

קא ע"א

1. ב"ה
2. ע"ד ריבת והפרשות שיש בין הצדדים ה"ה הו"ה כה זיסקינד בן ה"ה המנוח מה' אברם שטערן ז"ל ואשתו
3. מרת רייכלה בת המנוח כ' מענדלי האמיל ז"ל ובין הני תרי אחים הו"ה כ' דוד וב"ח כ' פייפש בני
4. המנוח כ' מענדלי האמיל סג"ל הנ"ל שה"ה כה זיסקינד הנ"ל בעצמו וה"ה התורני כה משה אויך
5. בהרשאת האחים הנ"ל נתן עצמו בטענותיהם לפנינו זה מול זה וזה מול זה כמבואר באר[י]כ[ות]
6. בקונטרוס הטענות המונח לפינינו ואחרי שהצדדים הנ"ל חתמו עצמם בתוקף קומפערמיס בח"ח ובקנס
7. סך מסוים חצי לשררה יר"ה וחצי להקדש {.}לאשר ולקיים ככל אשר יצא מאתנו בכן נזדקקנו להם
8. ומצאנו על כל פרט ופרט כמבואר להבא והיינו ה"ה כה זיסקינד הנ"ל הציע לפנינו שטר חצי
9. חלק זכר ההוקם ג' כסליו שנת תקך"ז ותובע מן האחים באשר שלא קיבל כלום אחר מיתת
10. חמיו לתשלומין שטר חח"ז הנ"ל בכן מה שיש כעת ביד האחים הנ"ל וגם מה שהציאו
11. האחים הנ"ל עבור צרכי בית לאחר מיתת חימוי[1] ז"ל (וגם מה)[2] שהרוויחו מיום מיתת חמיו הנ"ל עד עכשיו
12. שייך הכל בעזבון חמיו כי כל זמן שלא נתפרע ש[ח]"ח הנ"ל שייך בעזבון חמיו ולא להם
13. רק המה אפטרופסים על העזבון בכן תבע מן האחים הנ"ל שיעשו חשבון צדק לפני הב"ד
14. מעזבון אביהם חמיו ז"ל מה שהניח אחריו בעזבונו לאחר מותו וגם מה שהוציאו מהעזבון
15. הנ"ל ומה שהרוויחו עד עכשיו וישלמו לו שחח"ז שלו וה"ה התורני כה משה אויך הנ"ל
16. בהרשאת האחים הנ"ל השיב והציע לפנינו שטר שותפות ההוקם [ד'][3] תמוז תקל"ב ושם
17. נאמר איך שהודה כ' מענדלי האמיל ז"ל הנ"ל שכל היינות שהי' לו תחת ידו וירושתו
18. שייך לא[4] ולשני בניו כ' דוד וכ' פייפש הנ"ל יחד בשותפת דהיינו לכ[5] מענדלי ז"ל החצי
19. ולשני בניו החצי וגם בכל עסק משא ומתן שהי' לו עם יין שייך הכל בשותפת ועוד נאמר שם

---

1. צ"ל 'חמיו'
2. תוספת מעל השורה
3. ר' לקמן דף קא ע"ב ששם רשום שהשטר הוקם ב־ב' תמוז תקל"ב.
4. צ"ל 'לו'
5. לכבוד

20. שנתן כ׳ מענדלי ז״ל הנ״ל לשני בניו כל [די]ן תורת נאמנת מפורש נגד בנותיו ולוקחי בנותיו
21. בלי נתינת שום חשבון על כל מה שהיה תחת ידו ורשותן בחייו ובמותו עוד הציע לפנינו
22. שני שטרי חובת מן אביהם כ׳ מענדלי ז״ל הנ״ל שחייב את עצמו לשלם ולפרוע שעה
23. אחת קודם מותו לכל אחד מבניו סך חמשת אלפי׳ זהו׳ וטוען כה משה הנ״ל באשר שאביהם כ׳
24. מענדלי ז״ל הנ״ל סגין נהור וכלה בבית שמונה שנה קודם מותו ולא היה יוכל להרויח כלום
25. ובניו האחים הנ״ל [..]ה [...]׳ את אביהם והיה נושאין ונותנין וגם לעצמין היה להם סך
26. ידוע שהרוויחו והי׳ [י]רא בדבר כך על אחר מיתתו שבנותיו ולוקחי בנותיו באים לירש ממון
27. שלהם בכן היה נותן להם אביהם שטר שותפות קודם מותו עם נאמנות בכן
28. מה שהניח אחריו אביהם ז״ל על חלקו אין בו כדי לפרוע שטר חובת הנ״ל סך עשרת
29. אלפים זהו׳ שהוא מקודם לשט׳ החח״ז שתבע כהר״ר זיסקינד הנ״ל שהוא רק ירושה בעלמא
30. ומה שהרוויחו אח״כ הם לעצמם וכ׳ פייפש הנ״ל בעצמו בא לפנינו ואמר ג״כ כנ״ל
31. ואין שום זכות לכהר״ר זיסקינד מחמת שטר חצי חלק זכר הנ״ל

קא ע״ב

1. ב״ה
2. וכהר״ר זיסקינד הנ״ל חזר והושב שכל השטרות מחמיו על גיסו האחים הנ״ל הם שטרות ה{פ}(ב)[1]רחות
3. בעלמא מאחר מאחר[2] שהוא יודע {שלא} שלא היה לאחים הנ״ל מעות לעצמם בכן השטר
4. שותפות הוא הפרחה[3] וכן השטרי חובת הם ג״כ הפ(ב)[4]רחות כדי לה{פ}(ב)[5]ריח מבתו גם
5. אין הנאמנות הנזכר בשטר שותפות מועיל על אחר מיתתו בכן ישבעו האחים הנ״ל
6. כמה הניחו בשותפות ועוד בטענותיו שכל מה שהניח הוא אחר מיתתו יש לו תביעה
7. מכח שטחח״ז והאריכו בטענותיהם ובתשובתיהם ולאחר שדקדקנו אנחנו ב״ד ח״מ בשט[ר]
8. שותפות הנ״ל מצאנו שאין להאחים הנ״ל חלק ביין מכח שטר {שופ} שותפות שלהם
9. כי אם ביין שהיי׳ לאביהם באותו פעם בשעת שותפות וגם אם נמכר אותו [יין]
10. שהיה לאביהם באותו פעם ומדמי מכירה נלקח יינות אחירות היינות שייך
11. ג״כ בשותפות או אותו דמי היין הנ״ל בעצמו אכן אם לקח אביהם אחר שותפות
12. עוד יין ממעות ששייך לעצמו אין להאחים הנ״ל שותפות {באחתו} (באותו)[6] יין ובהיות כן מצאנו שמחויבי׳
13. האחים כ׳ דוד וכ׳ פייס הנ״ל לישבע ע״ד המקו׳ ב״ה וע״ד ב״ד בלי עו״מ ובלי שום הוראות
14. היתר שבעולם שמה שהניח אחריו אביהם ז״ל הן חלקו מה שמגיע לו ביין שהיה בעזבון

---

1. תוספת מעל השורה
2. כפילות במקור
3. צ״ל ׳הברחה׳
4. תוספת מעל השורה
5. תוספת מעל השורה
6. תוספת מעל השורה

15. כנ"ל הן שאר כל עזבונו שהניח אביהם ז"ל הן כסף ושוה כסף מטלטלין מכל מה שהפה
16. יוכל לדבר והלב לחשוב ולהרהר חוץ מקרקעות באשר שבלא"ה אין לכהר"ז[1] הנ"ל [שום] תביעה
17. מכח שטר חח"ז שלו שלא יגיע כל עזבונו הנ"ל לאחר ניכוי התשלומין מעזבונו לאחותם
18. מרת רעכלה סך שני מאות קרלינר כפי שטר ההוקם [ב'] תמוז תקל"ב וגם ל[א]חר ניכוי
19. מאה רט דמי השטר לשני ילדי' מן כהר"ז הנ"ל ההוקם ב[ב'] תמוז תקל"ב כמבואר למטה {...}
20. שעכ"פ לא יגיע עזבונו הנ"ל לאחר ניכוי כל הנ"ל יותר לסך עשרת אלפי' זהו' דמי שט"ח שלו
21. מאביהם ז"ל ולאחר שישבעו האחים הנ"ל כנ"ל פטורים ומסולקים האחים הנ"ל מן כהר"ז הנ"ל
22. מחמת תביעות שטח"ז הנ"ל עוד תבע כהר"ז הנ"ל והציע לפנינו שט"ח מן חמיו לשלשה ילדיו ה[הוקם]
23. ב' תמוז תקל"ב לשלם ולפרוע לזמן הנישאון של כאו"א סך חמשים ר"ט ובאשר שאחר[2] מן הי[לדים]
24. מת בכן הוא יורש אותן חמשים רט וסך מאה רט מהשני אחיו שהם בחיי' חיותם יותן ביד [ב]
25. בטוח ורווחים יהי' להילדים וכ"ה משה בהרשאות הנ"ל הישב באשר שנזכר בשמו
26. לשלם לזמן נישאון בכן אין חל זמן פירעון קודם שעת נישאון ואותו שמת קודם נישא[ון]
27. אין מגיע לו כלום ולא יוכל אביו כהר"ז הנ"ל לירש אותו גם אין מחויבם (האחים)[3] הנ"ל לשלם
28. לשני ילדים שהם בעודם בחיים חיותם סך מאה רט קודם שהגיע לזמן נישאון רק רוצי'
29. לעמוד בטחון על מאה רט הנ"ל לגבות להם לזמן נישאון של כל אחד ואחד סך חמשי'
30. רט אבל האחים אין מגיע להם כלום עוד הישיב כה"מ[4] הנ"ל מאחר כשהיו האחים
31. הנ"ל רוצים לעשות שידוך עם אחותים מרת רעכלה לא היה רוצים לפסוק לנדון שלה
32. יותר משני מאות ק"ט כפי שט"ח מאביהם ז"ל וכנ"ל ואמר כה"ז שיתנו יותר נגד זה
33. רוצה

קב ע"א

1. ב"[ה]
2. רוצה למחול על שטר חוב מבניו שיש לו מאביהם ז"ל ועל זה התרצו האחים ונתנו לאחותים יותר
3. לנדן בכן תבע כהר"מ הנ"ל מכהר"ז הנ"ל שישלם מאה ר"ט שהיה רוצה למחול וכהר"ז הנ"ל
4. הישיב באשר שנזכר שט"ח לילדים הנ"ל שעה אחת קודם מותו בכן חל הפירעון מיד
5. ומה שהיה רוצה למחול על השט"ח בשביל שהיה פירקם לנדן אחותם יותר המגיע לה השיב

1. כבוד הרב זיסקינד
2. צ"ל 'אחד'
3. תוספת מעל השורה
4. כבוד הרב משה

6. שאינו יוכל למחול חובת בנים והאריכו הצדדים בטענותיהם ומצאנו שהדין עם האחים
7. הנ"ל ואין כהר"ז הנ"ל יורש את הילד המת וכן לשני הילדים שהם בעודם בחיים אין
8. מגיע להם רווחים מסך מאה ר"ט של שט"ח הנ"ל רק לזמן הנישאון[1] של כל אחד ואחד
9. מהילדים מחויבם האחים הנ"ל לפרוע לכל אחד ואחד חמשים רט ובאשר שהאחים
10. התרצו עצמם לעמוד בטחון מסך מאה רט כדי שיכולים לגבות הילדים בזמן הנשואין
11. שלהם כה יהי' וכה יקום שיעמדו האחים הנ"ל בטחון הנראה לעיני ב"ד על סך מאה ר"ט
12. הנ"ל מה שתבעו האחים מן כהר"ז הנ"ל סך מאה ר"ט הנ"ל אין בו ממש עוד תבע
13. כהר"ז הנ"ל {סך מאה ר"ט הנ"ל} מהאחים תרי גיסיו הנ"ל עשרה חגרים שהלוה להם ואמר
14. בשעת הלואה ששייכים לבנו אברם שהניחה לו אמו ז"ל וכהר"מ הנ"ל השיב אמת הוא
15. שהלוה להם כהר"ז הנ"ל אכן הם רוצים להחזיק בהם על תביעות חשבון שהציע לפנינו
16. שחייב להם כהר"ז הנ"ל וכמבואר למטה וכהר"ז הנ"ל הישיב אחר שהי' מודיע להם
17. בשעת הלואה שהי' לאברם בנו אינם יכולים להחזיק עצמם בהם {ומצאנו מאחר שכבר
18. פסקנו [של]אחר קבלת חרם מן האחים הנ"ל וכנ"ל אין ל[כה"ז] הנ"ל שום תביעה על האחים
19. הנ"ל מכח שחח"ז וכאשר שהודה עכ"פ כהר"ז הנ"ל שחייב להאחים הנ"ל כפי סך עשרה
20. חגרים הנ"ל} עוד תבע כהר"ז הנ"ל שכר שדכנות מאחותים סך חי זהו' וחצי וכהר"מ הנ"ל
21. השיב שקודם שנעשה השידוך מאחותים אמר כהר"ז הנ"ל שרוצה למחול שדכנות רק שית[נו]
22. לו חצי ק"ט לאיש עני {...} וטעון עוד שאם יגיע השבוע לכ' פייס שיהפך השבעה על
23. כהר"ז הנ"ל עוד תבע כהר"ז הנ"ל והציע לפנינו חשבון מפנקס שלו שמכר סחורת בהקפה
24. לחמיו ז"ל וגם להאחים אחת אל אחת העולה סך י"ז זהו' ל"ג צל וכהר"מ הנ"ל הודה לו
25. [ו]טעון שינכה סך חשבון ממה שחייב להם על חשבון שהציע לפנינו האחים וכמבאור למטה
26. עוד (טען)[2] כהר"ז הנ"ל שיש ביד האחים הנ"ל ח"כ מסך מאה רט שהיה חייב לאביהם חמיו
27. ז"ל וזמן פריעון היה קודם [מותו] ופרע כ"ה[3] הנ"ל לחמיו בעודו בחיי' שבעי' רט ועל
28. השלושים רט שנשאר עוד חייב מחזיק עצמו בשביל שטר חח"ז שלו וכנ"ל בכן תבע
29. הח"כ הלז לחזרה וכהר"מ הנ"ל וגם האחים הנ"ל בעצמם השיב [וה]ציע לפנינו [ח]"כ הנ"ל עד
30. פראטעשט שנעשה לאחר מיתת אביהם ז"ל וסמך עצמם על דינא דמלכות שאינן
31. יכולין לטעון שום פריעון עוד השיבו עוד שאינן יודעים שפ[ר]ע כלום על ח"כ הנ"ל

קב ע"ב

1. ב"ה
2. רק שזה יודעים שקיבל אביהם ממנו שלשים רט אבל אינו ידוע להם אם היה על ח"כ הנ"ל
3. או על חוב אחר ו{כהר"ז הנ"ל השיב שישבעו שניהם ש"ד אם לא ידעו שנתפרע על ח"כ
4. שבעים רט וגם אומרי' נעשה הפראטעשט} עוד טען שאם יפסוק הב"ד דלא שייך בזה

1. צ"ל 'הנישואין'
2. תוספת מעל השורה
3. הפניה לזיסקינד

5. דינא דמלכות' אזי ישבע כהר"ז שאינו חייב יותר מסך שלשים רט על ח"כ הנ"ל
6. ויכלול בשבוע שלא נשאר עדיין חייב לאביהם ז"ל וכהר"ז הנ"ל השיב שישבעו שניהם
7. ש"ד אם לא ידעו שנתפרע על ח"כ הנ"ל שבעי' רט וגם א[ו]מ[רי'] נעשה הפראטעשט
8. [כהר"]ז טען באשר שח"כ הנ"ל הוא מאביהם ז"ל והם בעצמם יודעים שאביהם קיבל
9. ממנו סך שלשי' רט רק אינם יודעים אם על חוב זה או על חוב אחר א"כ לא היה להם
10. לעשות הפראטעשט מבלי הגיד לו מקודם בכן ישבעו על אופן המעשה של
11. הפראטעשט גם אם יהי' בתוקפו הוא מחזיק עצמו בשביל שטחח"ז שלו עוד תבע
12. כהר"מ הנ"ל והציע לפנינו ח"כ מן כהר"ז הנ"ל לשלם לתרי גיסו האחים הנ"ל מאה
13. זהו' וכהר"ז הנ"ל הישב אמת שחייב להאחים הנ"ל מאה זהו' מסך ח"כ הנ"ל רק
14. שרוצה להחזיק עצמו בשביל שטחח"ז שלו עוד תבע בהר"מ והציע לפנינו חשבן מה
15. שחייב כהר"ז הנ"ל לשלם עבור [יין] שלקח מחמיו ז"ל ומהאחים הנ"ל אחת לאחת העולה סך חמשה
16. חמשה[1] וחמשי' זהו' עוד תבע ארבעה מידות יין שלקח לשבעות העבר לחברו שלו עולה ד' ק"[ש] שהם
17. ביחד נ"ו זהו' א' קש[2] וכהר"ז השיב החוב שבא מחמת חמיו ז"ל רוצה להחזיק בשביל שטר
18. חח"ז שלו וגם על חוב שבא מחמת שלקח מהם ועוד באשר שיש לו חלק בעזבון חמיו ז"ל
19. מכח שטחח"ז שלו בכן גם הוא רוצה לשתות יין בחנם מחלק שיש לו ואם יזכה בזה
20. בטענותיו עכ"פ ישבעו האחים הנ"ל על חשבון צדק וכהר"מ הנ"ל השיב אם יפסוק
21. הב"ד שום שבוע עליהם שיהפכו השבועה על כהר"ז ואף מחמת שבעות החשבון
22. ישבע עכ"פ מה שיודע שחייב להם והאריכו הצדדים הנ"ל בטענותיהם [ובת]
23. ובתשובתיהם על כל פרט ופרט כמבואר בק"ה ומצאנו מאחר שכבר פסקנו שלאחר
24. שישבעו האחים אודת תביעות של כהר"ז מחמת {שטח"ת שלו} שטחח"ז שלו כנ"ל שוב
25. אין לכהר"ז הנ"ל שום תביעה עליהם מכח שטר חח"ז שלו ופשיטא שאין יוכל להחזיק
26. בשביל כך על שום תביעה מהם בכך הסך מאה זהו' דמי ח"כ שחייב כהר"ז הנ"ל
27. להאחים הנ"ל כנ"ל מחויב לשלם גם מחמת ח"כ מסך מאה רט שהי' חייב לאביהם
28. ז"ל מחויב כה זיסקינד הנ"ל עכ"פ לשלם להאחים הנ"ל סך שלשים רט ש{הו. .ה
29. שנשאר עדיין חייב על אח"כ ה} רק שינכה סך ארבע עשר זהו' ל"ג צל שהו. .ה
30. האחים שחייב לו מחמת סחורת וכפי חשבונו כנ"ל שהודה {מחוייב בחי"ב
31. הנ"ל} שנשאר עדיין חייב על ח"כ הלז ועל שבעים רט הנותרים מסך דמי ח"כ הלז
32. ישבע

קג ע"א

1. ב"ה
2. ישבע כהר"ז הנ"ל על דעת המקו' ב"ה ועל דעת ב"ד בלי ערמה ומרמה ובלי שום הוראות
3. היתר שבעולם על ארבעי' רט שהאחים טוענים בברי שנשאר עוד חייב על ח"כ
4. הנ"ל ויכלול בשבועתו גם על שלשים רט שאינם יודעים האחים הנ"ל אם לא פרע

---

1. כפילות במקור
2. קופשטוק

5. על ח"כ הלז שא"כ נפרע על ח"כ הנ"ל ומחמת עשרה חגרים שתבע כהר"ז שהלווה
6. והאחים הנ"ל וכנ"ל מצאנו שאין כח לכהר"ז להוציא מיד האחים הנ"ל עשרה חגרי' הנ"ל
7. כל זמן שלא נתפרע מה שמחויב לשלם כהר"ז להאחים הנ"ל וכנ"ל ומחמת מה שתבע
8. כהר"ז הנ"ל שכר שדכנות סך חי זהו' וחצי וכנ"ל מצאנו שישבע כהר"ז הנ"ל ע"י
9. היפוך שכדבריו כן הוא ואז יוכל לנכות סך חי זהו' וחצי הנ"ל ממה שמחויב לשלם
10. להם ומה שרוצים האחים הנ"ל להטיל עוד על כהר"ז הנ"ל שיכלול בשבועתו שלא
11. נשאר עדיין חייב לאביהם ז"ל מלבד סך דמי ח"כ הנ"ל וסך מאה רט מצאנו שאין
12. בו ממש ומחמת תביעות החשבון של סך נו זהו' ך צל שתבעו האחים וכהר"ז
13. הנ"ל היה מטיל עליהם שבועה שהחשבונם הוא צדק והם חזרו והפכה השבועה
14. עליו מצאנו שאין כח ביד האחים הנ"ל להפ[ו]ך השבוע עליו אך אם האחים
15. אינם רוצים לישבע על חשבון צדק אזי מחויב כהר"ז הנ"ל לשלם מה שברי
16. לו שחייב להם גם מחויב לשלם הארבע מידות יין הנ"ל ועל השאר מחויב
17. לקבל בחרם בפנינו ב"ד שאינו נודע שחייב להם יותר יצא מאתנו {אור
18. ליו'} יום ג' ד'ג תמוז תקלזיין לפק ר"ני ור"מ שיף ואני
19. אחרי שיצא מאתנו פס"ד הנ"ל חזרו ונתעצמו הצדדים הנ"ל בטענותיהם
20. לפנינו ותבע לפנינו כה"ר זיסקינד הנ"ל באשר שבפס"ד הלז הוטל שבועה על
21. האחים הנ"ל שלא הניח אביהם יותר מעשרת אלפים זהו' לאחר ניכוי ה
22. הנאמרים שם ונאמר שם ג"כ חוץ מקרקעות שע"ז אינם צריכי' לישבע[.] ו
23. וטוען כהר"ז באשר שנודע לו שחמיו ז"ל מכר החצי בית שלו [צו]ם קאמעה ל
24. לבניו האחים הנ"ל בכל צריכי' לישבע גם על דמי מכירה הנ"ל וכ"ה משה
25. אויך בהרשאת האחים הנ"ל הציע לפנינו שטר מכירה ההו[א] בחדש
26. תמוז תקל"ב שנזכר שם שאביהם ז"ל מכר להם החצי בית הנ"ל והודה
27. שכבר נפרע

קג ע"ב

1. ב[ע]"ה
2. שכבר נתפרע לו דמי מכירה מהם ועם כל זה לא הניח אחריו בעזבונו יותר
3. מסך עשרת אלפים זהו' דמי שט"ח שלהם וכנ"ל והאריכו בטענותיהם ומצאנו
4. שמחויבי' האחים הנ"ל לפרוש בשבועתם הנ"ל דבר זה בפירוש והיינו
5. שכל מה שהניח אביהם בעזבון הן מהיין שהי' שייך לאביהם על חלקו
6. וכנ"ל הן כסף ושוה כסף מטלטלין חובת מנימולי' וא"נ מכל מה שהפה
7. יוכל לדבר והלב לחשוב ולהרהר בצירֻוף דמי מכירה חצי בית הנ"ל
8. שהודה אביהם ז"ל שקיבל מהם לא יגיע יותר מסך עשרת אלפים זהו'
9. לאחר ניכוי וכנ"ל עוד טען כהר"מ הנ"ל בהרשאות הנ"ל על דבר הבטחון הנאמר
10. בפס"ד הנ"ל שמחויבם האחים להעמיד על סך מאה (רט)[2] לישלם לשני ילדי' מן כהר"ז הנ"ל
11. לזמן הנישאון שלהם לכ"א סך חמשים רט שהתחייבו את עצמם האחים הנ"ל לעשות

1. כנראה רב נתן מז
2. תוספת מעל השורה

12. ק"ס על סך מאה רט לשלם להילדי' כפי המוזכר בשט"ח שלהם והיינו כ' דוד הנ"ל
13. שהוא נשוי רוצה לעשות ק"ס {באשה} והדר בעלה וכ' פייס הנ"ל [ש]עדיין פנוי
14. רוצה לעשות ק"ס הנ"ל עכשיו וכשיבוא לכלל נישואון גם אשתו תעשה קנין קודם
15. שתכנס לחופה וכהר"ז אינה מרוצה בבטחון הלז רק שיניחו ביד שליש
16. כנ"ל ומצאנו שכמו שהתחייבו האחים בהעמדת בטחון וכנ"ל כה יהי' וכה
17. יקום עוד טעון כהר"ז הנ"ל מחמת השבועה המוטל עליו בפס"ד הנ"ל
18. מחמת ח"כ מסך מאה רט מחמיו שרוצה להפך השבועה על האחים הנ"ל
19. וכהר"מ הנ"ל השיב שמאחר שמחויב כהר"ז הנ"ל לו שבוע ע"י גילגול שלשים
20. רט וכנ"ל בפ"ז שוב אינו יכול להפוך השבוע ומצאנו שהדין עם כהר"ז
21. הנ"ל שישבעו האחים הנ"ל ע"י ההיפוך ע"ד המקו' ב"ה וע"ד ב"ד בלי ער"מ
22. ובלי שום הוראות היתר שבעולם שכדברהם כן הוא שאינם יודעים
23. שנתפרע כלום לאביהם ז"ל על ח"כ מסך מאה רט הנ"ל ושלישי[1] רט שקיבל
24. אביהם מן כהר"ז שאינם יודעים אם על חוב זה או על חוב אחר ולאחר
25. שישבעו האחים הנ"ל מחויב כהר"ז הנ"ל לשלם להם סך שבעים רט
26. נגד חזרת ח"כ הנ"ל עם פראטעשט מלבד הלשלים[2] רט שהודה כהר"ז
27. הנ"ל שחייב לאביהם עוד ומה שרוצה כהר"ז הנ"ל להפוך עוד השבועה
28. המוטל עליו ע"י היפוך בפס"ד הנ"ל עבור שדכנות וכנ"ל מצאנו ששוב
29. אינו יוכל להפוך יצא מאתנו יו' ד' ג' אב תקלמד זיין לפק מדיינם הנ"ל

No. 100

Fol. 104a; Sunday 26 October 1777

Among the lots in the Jewish section was one that had been the site of a hospital (or, perhaps more correctly, a hospice) until 1711 but had been abandoned for a number of years. The non-Jewish authorities ordered that the community sell the land, but there had once been a synagogue on the plot and the community did not know if the plot could be sold in its entirety since it had been the site of a holy place. The community also did not know exactly where on the lot the synagogue had stood, and turned to the court for a ruling in the matter. To locate where the synagogue had been, the court, with all seven members, including Rabbi Pinḥas Horowitz, instead of the usual three, sought out elder members of the community who might have remembered the old synagogue. Together, they visited the place to mark out the boundaries. The court allowed the sale of the entire site, but

1. צ"ל 'ושלשים'
2. צ"ל 'השלשים'

stipulated that the place where the synagogue had stood could not be used for any inappropriate purpose, such as a garbage dump, tannery, etc. As a condition of sale, it ordered that the purchaser place a marker indicating that a synagogue had once been there and that the site could not be used for any inappropriate purposes in the future. Also see nos. 101, 120, 133, 151, as well as Appendix 2.

קד ע"א

1. ב"[ה]
2. ע"ד ששאלנו מאת האלופי' הקציני' פו"מ יצו בצירוף האלופי' קציני' גובי' יצו להורות להם
3. אודות פלאטץ שהונוח חורבה ושממה זה כמה שני' ונקרא בפי כל הקדש פלאטץ שה
4. שהי' בנוי עליו ההקדש לחולאי' [כ]נ"ל ועתה מחמת פקודת השררה יר"ה רוצי' האלופי'
5. גובי' יצו למכור הפלאטץ הנ"ל ובאשר שבהיותו בנוי הי' בהקדש הנ"ל בית הכנסת
6. והם אין יודעי' מקומו בכן נפשם בשאלתם אם רשאי' למכור הפלאטץ שלם
7. הנ"ל ולאחר שחקרנו ודרשנו מזקני' שבדור על דברי זה בא לפנינו הזקן כ' ליזר
8. שנאפיר מק"ק העדרנום[1] ו{ש}הלכנו עמו על פלאטץ הנ"ל והראה אותנו המקום שהי'
9. בה"כ לפי זכרונו ולאחר כל הנ"ל נזדקקנו לדין ומצאנו שמותרי' למכור פלאטץ שלם
10. הנ"ל אפי' מקום בה"כ רק שמחוייבי' להתנות עם הלוקח פלאטץ הנ"ל שאין רשאי
11. להשתמש במקום בה"כ הנ"ל המבואר למטה בתשמיש מגונה וגנאי גם מחויב
12. הלוקח לעשות בתוך המקו' שהי' [בה"]כ {חקיק} חקיקה על אבן או על גבי כותל
13. לזיכרון שהי' עליו מקדמת דנא בה"כ ושלא ישתמשו בו תשמיש של גנאי ומקו'
14. בה"כ הי' לפי דברי זקן כ' ליזה הנ"ל למטה על הארץ מ[סו]ף בנין הבית
15. צו עלי פאנד הי' מתחיל בה"כ והי' מושך ברוחב וכלה עד מק' שנמשך דיא
16. אן טאכ[ס] וכפי מדה זו הי' מרובע בכל צדיו יצא מאתנו {אור ליו'} יו' א כה (תשרי תקל"ח)[2]
17. {שני ו...} והגאון אב"ד נרו[3] יאיר ור"י מה' נתן מז נ"[4] ומה' יעקב שמש נר'
18. וכ"ה אברהם טריר וכ"ה זנוויל טראך וכ"ה מאיר שיף ואני

---

1. היה איש בפרנקפורט בשם ליזר שנאפיר שנפטר בשנת תקל"ט והיה נקרא 'דער אלטה ליזר' (ר' אלה תולדות 4.10.1778). הוריו התחתנו בשנת תע"ח (ר' אלה תולדות 7.3.1738). על פי אטלינגר ליזר היה בערך בן 58 שנפטר. לא ידוע לי על קשר בין הליזר הזה והעיר העדרנום וספק אם בן אדם בגילו היה יכול לעזור לגבי מיקום בית הכנסת לפני השריפה.
2. תוספת מתחת השורה
3. נטריה רחמנא ופרקיה
4. כנראה קיצור ל'נטריה רחמנא ופרקיה'

No. 101

Residents of Hirschorn and Elefant lots v. Community

Fols. 104b–106a; Thursday evening, 30 October 1777

In the wake of the court's decision just a few days earlier to allow the community to sell an abandoned plot (see no. 100), some of those whose homes bordered the lot came to the court to protect their rights. They argued that any new building that might be built on the site would block their windows, windows that had been in place for some time and had not been blocked when a building had stood on the plot prior to 1711. There was also a claim that if any new building were placed too close to the existing houses it would interfere with drainage, as well as an issue concerning a cellar under one of the homes whose ventilation hole was in the open lot. Through its representative, the community countered that some of the buildings on the adjacent lots were illegal and that neighbors had encroached onto the vacant lot. The court went to the site a number of times, consulted with professionals, and examined old contracts and rulings as part of its information gathering. The house owners originally signed an agreement that they would accept the court's ruling, but later agreed, together with the community, to accept a compromise offered by the court. The court's compromise, including an order for the various sides to pay each other for certain rights/damages, reflects an attempt to balance the rights and interests of all parties involved. Also see nos. 100, 120, 133, and 151.

קד ע"ב

1. ב"ה
2. ע"ד הפרשות וסכסוכים שבין האלופים קצנים גובים יצו בעסק בנין הקדש פלאטץ ובין
3. מחזיקי בית צום הירש הארין ומחזיקי בית צום עלי פאנט שרבו טענות הצדדים הנ"ל בפנינו
4. והיינו ה"ה התורני כה וואלף בוריך סג"ל הוא המורשה שטען לזכות האלופים גובים
5. יצו וה"ה התורני כ"ה שמואל סופר בא בהרשאת מחזיקי עלי=פאנט וה"ה התורני
6. כ"ה משה אויך בהרשאת מחזיקי בית צום הירש=הארין והכל מבואר לפנינו
7. באריכות בק"ה המונח לפנינו והיינו שה"ה האלופים גובים יצו רוצים לפנות
8. הקדש פלאטץ הנ"ל מרחוב עד החומה המפסקת בין א"נ לנימולים הכל סמוך ממש
9. לכותלי בתים צום הירש הארין ועלי פאנד ו[מחזק]י בית צום הירש הארין רוצים למחות
10. בידם באשר שהחדרים הפנימים שלהם העומדים סמוך ודבוקים בבית של עלי
11. =פאנד מן א' שטעג הויך עד למעלה כל רום ביתם יש לה' חלונות הפתוחים [ע]ל
12. הקדש פלאטץ והמה מוחזקים באלו החלונות מכמה וכמה שנים בכן אין להם [רשו]ת
13. לבנות נגד החלונות הללו באמרם שגם בהיותו הקדש על עמדו לא הי' נגד החלונות

14. רק חצר ולא בנין עוד הביאו ראי' וטענו מחזיקי ה"ה[1] מן הצנור שיש על גג בין בית
15. צום ה"ה לבית צום עלי פאנד שמשום יורדין השופכין להקדש פלאטץ משם
16. ראי' שהי' אותו מקום פנוי בכן אין להם רשות לבנות הכותל בסמוך ולסלק הצנור
17. שלהם גם המחזיקי בית צום עלי פאנד רצים ל[מחות] ביד האלופים גובים יצו מלבנות
18. סמוך ממנו לכותל הירש הארין באשר שיש להם מרתף תחת בית צום ה"ה אשר
19. יצא חור מן הקדש פלאטץ לתוך המרתף הנ"ל להכניס הרוח במרתף בכן אין להם
20. רשות לסתום החור שלהם גם רוצים מחזיקי בית צום עלי פאנד למחות בהאלופי'
21. גובים יצו מלבנות סמוך לכותל דרום שלהם באשר שיש להם חלונות מלמטה
22. עד למעלה כל רום ביתם באותו כותל הפתוחים להקדש פלאטץ והם מוחזקים
23. ג"כ באלו החלונות מכמה וכמה שנים ומטעם זה גם מחזיקי בית צום ה"ה רוצים
24. למחות ביד{.}ם מלבנות סמוך לכותל דרומי של עלי פאנד הנ"ל באשר שבית החורף
25. התחתונה של ה"ה שהוא בתוך הבית צום עלי פאנד יש לו ג"כ חלונות להקדש
26. פלאטץ מכותל דרומי של בית עלי [פאנד] ומוחזקים כמו כן באלו החלונות מכמה וכמה
27. שנים עוד התעמצו לפנינו וטענו האלופים גובים יצו שהסוכה שעומד אחורי בית
28. צום עלי פאנד לצד מזרח עם הפלאטץ דאחורי הסוכה עד החומה המפסקת
29. בין הנימולים

קה ע"א

1. ב"ה
2. בין א"נ לנימולי' ולצד צפון ברוחב עד הבית צום קרעפס ובאורך עד החומה
3. המפסקת בין נימולי' לא"נ הנ"ל הכל שייך להקדש פלאטץ ושלא כדין החזיקו מחזיקי
4. בית (צום)[2] עלי פאנד בהסוכה הנ"ל כאשר טענו לפנינו באריכות ומחזיקי בית צום עלי פאנד
5. השיבו לא לבד שהסוכה הנ"ל שייך להם אלא אף הפלאטץ שאחורי הסוכה באורך
6. וברוחב הנ"ל עד ששה בויא שוך מהחומה המפסקת הנ"ל הכל שייך להם כאשר ה
7. האריכו בטענותיהם וכמבואר בק"ה המונח לפנינו ובאשר שמחזיקי בית צום ה"ה
8. ומחזיקי בית צום עליפאנד הנ"ל חתמו עצמם בתוקף קומפרמיס בח"ח ובקנס
9. סך מסוים חצי לשררה ירה[3] וחצי להקדש בתחילה לקיים כפ' הדין שיצא מאתנו
10. ואח"כ {[חזרו]} התרצו וחזרו וחתמו עצמם מחזיקי בתי' הנ"ל בחומר קומפרמיס וכנ"ל לקיי'
11. כפי הפשר שיצא מאתנו גם האלופי' גובי' יצו בהסכמת אלופי' קציני' פו"מ יצו התרצו
12. ג"כ ונתנו עיניהם על הב"ד לפשר ולבצוע ביניהם בכן נזדקקנו להם ואחר שהלכנו על
13. הקדש פלאטץ איזה פעמי' למראה עינינו בנין בתי' הנ"ל עם הקדש פלאטץ עם אומני'
14. לדרוש מהם על מהות ואיכות הבנין בתי' הנ"ל וגם ע"י כמה חקירות ודרישות שהי'
15. לנו הן ע"י גביות עדות מכמה אנשי' שבאו לפנינו והן ע"י שטרות ופסקי' ישני'
16. אשר הי' מונחי' לפנינו מצאנו שהבנין של הקדש פלאטץ יהי' על אופן המבואר והיינו ש
17. שרשאי' האלופי' גובי' יצו וב"כ לבנותו מרחוב ואילך סמוך ממש לכותל של בית צום
18. הירשהארן עד המקו' שנכנסו החלונות מצד הכותל בית צום הירש הארן לתוך ה

---

1. הירש הארין
2. תוספת מעל השורה
3. ירום הודו

19. הקדש פלאטץ ומאותו מק׳<ום> ואילך כל משך מק׳ נגד החלונות של בית ה״ה הנ״ל מחויבי׳
20. להרחיק בנין הכותל של הקדש פלאטץ לערך שני בויא שוך ורביעית כדי שיהא ריווח
21. עכ״פ בין הכותל של הקדש פלאטץ ובין כל החלונות של בית ה״ה מן חד שעטג
22. עד למעלה {על הגג} כל רום ביתם משך שמונה בויא שוך ובזה יהי׳ ג״כ החור ה
23. המרתף של עלי פאנד פתוח ובאו[תו] ריווח מן לערך שני שוך ורביעית הנ״ל
24. רשאי׳

קה ע״ב

1. ב״ה
2. רשאי׳ המחזיקי בתי׳ הנ״ל להמשיך הצנור שהוא למעלה על הגג בין שני בתי׳ הנ״ל
3. לירד השופכין לתוך ריווח הנ״ל אכן באופן ובתנאי שלא [י]זיקו השופכין לבנין ה
4. החדש של הקדש פלאטץ וגם שלא יזיקו להמרתף של עלי פאנד הנ״ל אבל אם יזיקו השופכין
5. ע״י כך בבנין חדש הנ״ל או במרתף הנ״ל מחויבי׳ האלופי׳ גובי׳ יצו וב״כ ומחזיקי בתי׳
6. צום ה״ה ועלי פאנד וי״א וב״כ בין שלשתם יחד לתקן באופן שלא יוזק שום אחד מהם
7. או להמשיך הצנור במק׳ אחר שלא יהא שום אחד משלשתן נזוק והוצאות מוטל
8. על שלשתן יחד שוה בשוה ובעבור שמחויבי׳ האלופי׳ גובי׳ יצו להניח פנוי שלא לבנות
9. בכן מחויבי׳ המחזיקי ה״ה לשלם וליתן להאלופי׳ גובי׳ יצו מדי שנה בשנה שני זה[ו]׳
10. והחיוב הלז מוטל עליהם ועל י״א וב״כ עד עולם ובכל זה גוף המקו׳ ריווח של ע
11. של ערך שני שוך ורביעית הנ״ל שייך להקדש פלאטץ רק שאינם רשאי׳ לבנותו ב
12. בשביל הרחקת מן החלונות הבית של ה״ה והחור של מרתף הנ״ל ומהמקו׳ ש
13. שכלי׳ החלונות של בית ה״ה הנ״ל בחדרי׳ הדבוקי׳ לבית עלי פאנד הנ״ל
14. רשאי׳ האלופי׳ גובי׳ יצו לבנות סמוך ממש לכותל דרומי של בית עלי פאנד
15. ולבנות נגד החלונות שיש למחזיקי בית עלי פאנד מתהום ארעא עד ר
16. {רום רקיע} למעלה ואף נגד בית החורף שיש למחזיקי הירש הארן בבית
17. צום עלי פאנד רשאי׳ ג״כ לבנות החלונות שישנו לצד דרומת ועוד יותר
18. נתנו רשות מחזיקי בית צום עלי פאנד מאחר שלמעלה שלשה שטאק הויך
19. בעלי פאנד נכנס בשטח ביתם לפני׳ לערך שני אמות בכן ניתן רשות
20. להאלופי׳ גובי׳ הנ״ל יצו וב״כ להרחיב בנינם מן הקדש פלאטץ על אותו ב
21. בליטה הנכנס הנ״ל עד למעלה כפי שירצו ומחמת הסוכה והפלאטץ שאחורי
22. בית עלי פאנד הן לצד צפון עד הבית צום קרעפס וכן לצד דרום כל משך
23. ארכו לרוח מזרחית עד החומה המפסקת בין א״נ לנימולי׳ ואף המקו׳ ש
24. שעומדות

קו ע״א

1. ב״ה
2. שעומדות עכשיו מוקף במחיצות נסרי׳ שייך הכל להאלופי׳ גובי׳ יצו ומחויבי׳
3. המחזיקי בית צום עליפאנד לסלק מחיצת נסרי׳ של הסוכה הנ״ל אכן כשרוצי׳ הא

4. ⸗לופי'[1] גובי' יצו וב"כ לבנות פלאטץ הנ"ל מחויבי' להרחיק שיעור הרחקה א
5. ארבע אמות מן כל החלונות של בית עליפאנד שהמה לצד מזרח מתהום ארעא
6. עד למעלה כל רום בית של עליפאנד לצד מזרח אך רשות נתונה למחזיקי
7. עליפאנד שבחג הסוכות רשאי' לעשות סוכה אחורי ביתם בתוך שיעור
8. הרחקה הנ"ל אף במחיצות נסרי' ולהשתמש בו כל ימי החג אבל מיד אחר סוכות
9. מחויבי' לסלקם והשני בתי כסאות שעומדי' כעת אצל ואחורי הסוכה הנ"ל ו
10. ומחזיק בהם מחזיקי הירש הארן ועליפאנד יחזיקו בהם גם להבא הם וי"א
11. וב"כ כמו שהי' עד עכשיו ויכולי' להלוך עליהם כמו עד עתה ומחמת מי ג
12. גשמי' של המגדול סביב השטעג של עליפאנד כמו שהי' נמשך עד עתה כן יהי'
13. להבא נגד כל הנ"ל מחויבי' האלופי' גובי' יצו ליתן למחזיקי בית צום עליפאנד
14. סך מאה רט ולמחזיקי בית צום הירש הארן סך עשרי' רט יצא מאתנו
15. אור ליו' ויו עשק[2] א' דר"ח מרחשון שנת תקלמד חית לפק
16. הדיין ור"י מה' נתן מז הדיין ר' מאיר שיף ואני

No. 102

Fol. 106b; undated[3]

The sale of one-sixth of an inner house on the Hinter Sonne lot by the community to Yeḥiʾel Scheyer, a cantor, for 800 guldens was confirmed by the court. Yeḥiʾel was given particularly good terms in that he was allowed to pay in eight semi-annual installments rather than the more common six.

קו ע"ב
1. ב"ה
2. חלק שישית מבית פנימי צור הינטר זוהן שהי' שייך להאלופי' קציני' גובי'
3. יצו נמכר מן האלופי' גובי' הנ"ל בהסכמת האלופי' קציני' פו"מ יצו לה"ה
4. התורני (ש"ץ)[4] כ"ה יחיאל שייאר[5] סגל בעד סך שמונה מאות זהו' לשלם
5. אין קונפונטציאהנש מינץ אויף דעם כ"ד זהו' פוס והיינו לשלם
6. שליש מסך דמי מכירה הנ"ל תיכף נגד מסירת מעשה ב"ד הלז ושני

---

1. כנראה שה-⸗ אמור לקשר בין סוף השורה הקודמת והשורה הזאת.
2. ערב שבת קדש
3. YIVO MS. RG 128 (folder 77–78), fol. 162a–b, labeled a "copy of the rabbinic court's original ruling" (*heʿateq mi-guf maʿaseh b[yet] d[in]*), is an act of the court transferring full ownership of a portion of this house to Yeḥiʾel Scheyer. It is dated 23 October 1777 but is not identical with the proceedings described here since the members of the court were not the same in both cases.
4. תוספת מעל השורה
5. בכתב יד נראה שכתוב 'שיישאר' אבל לא ברור עם הסופר ניסה לכתוב את האלף על השין השני.

שלישי' הנותרי' מסך דמי מכירה הנ"ל לשלם על שמונה חצאי שני' רצופי' וסמוכי' זא"ז מיו' מסירת מעשה ב"ד הלז ומחויב הלוקח כ"ה יחיאל הנ"ל ליתן שמונה[1] ח"כ לאורדר האלופי' גובי' הנ"ל על זמני' הנ"ל גם נשאר שישית בית הנ"ל לאפותיקו מפורש שלא יצא מחזקת מרא קמא כל זמן שלא נתפרע אפי' אחד מן הח"כ הנ"ל[2] ובאשר ששלחו האלופי' גובי' אלינו ב"ד לעשות מעשה ב"ד וליתן תוקף על מכירה הנ"ל נזדקקנו להם ועשינו מעשה ב"ד וחתמו עצמם הדייני' הדיין ור"י מה' נתן מז הדיין כ"ה מאיר שיף ואני

No. 103

Fol. 107a; Monday 15 December 1777

The record of sale of half a seat in the lower women's section that had belonged to Zalman Schiff[3] and was being sold by his heirs (also see no. 106). The seat was presently being used, but was not owned, by the daughter-in-law of a member of

1. המילה לא נמצאת בכ"י יו"א.
2. בכ"י ייו"א, קסב ע"א-ע"ב, מוסיפים, 'ויתוקן ע"ז שטר אפותיקו ע"י נאמני הקהלה כנהוג ומעתה השישית בית פנימי הנ"ל שהי' שייך מקדמת להאלופי' גובי' יצו שייך מעכשיו לה"ה כ"ה יחיאל שייאר הנ"ל וי"א וב"כ לחלוטין גמורין ולצמיתות עלמין כל ארכו ורחבו עם כל חזקותיו וזכיותיו ומוצאיו ומובאיו ומצריו וחצריו ומרתפות ועליות עומקא ורומא מתהום ארעא עד רום רקיעי וכמו שהיה שייך מקדמת להאלופי' גובי' יצו בלי שום שיור כלל ורשאי ה"ה כ"ה יחיאל הנ"ל וי"א וב"כ לעשות עם שישית בית הנ"ל להוריש ולהנחיל ולהשכין למכור ולהשכיר וליתן במתנה כאות נפשו ורצונו ככל איניש דרשאי לעשות בשלו בלי שום מוחה כלל ולאחר שנתפרע כל הח"כ הנ"ל שייך מעכשיו השישית בית הנ"ל לכ"ה יחיאל הנ"ל וי"א וב"כ בשופי גמור בלי שום עורר וטוען כלל יהי' המערער מי שיהי' הן יחיד או רבים יהי' טענה מה שיהי' או בכל אופן שיהי' מכל מה שהפה יוכל לדבר והלב לחשוב ולהרהר וכל מי שיערער אחר מכירה הנ"ל יהי' מי שיהי' או באיזה אופן שיהי' דבריו בטלי' ומבוטלי' כחרס הנשבר כאפס וכאין יחשב לא שרירין ולא קיימין ולא יהי' חלין כלל וכלל וכטוען אחר מעשה ב"ד הגדול ואל יזדקק שום קהל או ב"ד יצו או שום משפט שבעולם לדברי המערער הן בדא"ה הן בד"י כי דברי המערער הם בטלי' ומבוטלי' ובאשר שכפי הנהוג פה קהלתינו יע"א שהמכירה הנעשה מן האלופי' גובי' יצו אין בכי יותן להלוקח שטר חלטה בפני עצמו כמו שארי מכירות הנעשה מאנשי' אחרי' בכן יהא תוקף מעשה ב"ד הלז כאילו יש להלוקח הנ"ל גם שטר חלטה בפני עצמו וכבתנו וחתמנו כל הנ"ל בתוקף מעשה ב"ד ובכח ב"ד יפה להיות ביד הלוקח כ"ה יחיאל שייאר סגל הנ"ל לעדות [ע"ב] ולזכות ולראי' שיעמוד השישית בית פנימי הנ"ל עם כל חזקותיו וזכיותיו ביד לוקח הנ"ל וי"א בלי שום מוחה כלל פ"פ דמיין יו' ג' יא מרחשון תקלמד חית לפ"ק
   הדיין ור"י מ"ה נתן מאז נר"ו
   הדיין כ"ה חיים גונדרשהיים נר"ו
   הדיין כ"ה מענדלי זאמשט נר"ו'
   (ברשות YIVO Institute for Jewish Research, New York)
3. Zalman Schiff died on 31 March 1777 (see Horovitz, no. 4305).

the court, Rabbi Maas, who did not recuse himself from this case. Moses Rindskopf purchased the seat for 301 guldens for his son, Yosle, who was recently married.

קז ע"א

1. ב"ה
2. חצי מקו' בע"נ התחתונה שהי' עומדות עלי' כעת אשת התורני כ"ה מאיר
3. בן הדיין ור"י מה' נתן מז נרו' שהי' שייך להמנוח כ"ה זלמן במה' טעבלי שיף ז"ל
4. נמכר בפני ב"ד ע"פ יורשי המנוח כה"ז[1] ז"ל הנ"ל להו"ה כ"ה משה ב"י[2] רינדשקאפף
5. שלקח בעד בנו החתן כ' יוזלי בעד סך שלשה מאות ואחד זהו' לשלם
6. כתקון הקהלה יו' ב' טו כסליו שנתקל"ח לפק רנ"מ ואני ורמענדלה[3] ליל[ג]

No. 104

Hirschorn v. Benevolent Society for Visiting the Sick

Fol. 107a; Sunday evening, 30 November 1777

David Hirschorn had been an upstanding member of a society for visiting the sick for a number of years. When the society decided to expel him he went to court. The society responded through its representative that it had recently noticed that David had been ineligible for admission to the group for reasons not specified in the record. According to society members, the preceptors had hidden the matter of David's ineligibility and admitted him anyway. When members of the society found this out, they brought the issue before the group's leadership and it was decided to terminate Hirschorn's affiliation. The society was willing to refund the membership dues that Hirschorn had paid over the years. The court spoke to members of the society (perhaps to David as well) and ultimately the society paid David a settlement.

7. ע"ד שבא לפנינו ה"ה כ' דוד בהמנוח[4] כ' משה הירשהארין ותבע מן הגבאי'
8. דחברא ישן דביקור חולי' וטוען באשר שלפני איזה שני' הי' בא לתוך
9. החברא הנ"ל בהסכמת כמה אנשי' מהחברא כנהוג אצלם ומאותו
10. זמן עד עתה גם הי' לוקחי' ממנו שבוע מעות[5] וגם הלך למנין להתפלל

---

1. כבוד הרב זלמן
2. בן יוקב (ר' אבני זכרון, מס' 4305).
3. והרב מענדלה
4. בן המנוח
5. ר' לקמן, דף קנא ע"ב, שורה 7.

כשארי א{...} אנשי' דחברא הנ"ל ועתה שרוצי' להוציא אותו מן החברא שלא כדין וה"ה התורני כ"ה משה אויך בהרשאת אנשי החברא הנ"ל השיב באריכות שמתחילה הכניסו אותו נגד תיקון {הקהלה} החברא אותן הגבאי' שהי' באותו הפעם והעלימו הדב[ר] עד עכשיו שנודע ה הדבר ע"י גבאי' אחרי' שנתהוו עכשיו והביא הדבר לפני וועד אסיפה מן אנשי החברא ונגמר וגמרו ביניהם להוציא אותו מן ה החברא ושבוע מעות שקיבלו ממנו רוצה להחזירם לו ובאשר שע"י שדברנו על לבם לפשר קרניהם [ה]ר[כי]נו את ראשם לדברינו ונזדקקנו לפשר ומצאנו שאנשי החברא יתנו לכ' דוד הנ"ל סך ארבעי' וארבעה זהו' ואז אין לכ' דוד הנ"ל שום תביעה וזכיות בהחברא הנ"ל ובפנינו קיבל כ' דוד הנ"ל סך דמי פשר הנ"ל בכן פטור ומסולק החברא הנ"ל מן כ' דוד הנ"ל מכל תביעות הנ"ל יצא מאתנו אור ליו' ב ב דרחי[1] כסליו תקל"ח

No. 105

Bing v. Schwarzschild

Fol. 107b–108b; Monday evening, 5 January 1778

Joel Bing came to the court claiming that the estate of the late rabbinic judge Rabbi Meʾir Schwarzschild owed him approximately 11 guldens for various goods that Rabbi Meʾir had purchased during his lifetime, and which were recorded in Joel's business diary. Joel also sought rent going back to 1765 for space that Rabbi Meʾir had leased in a house that Joel had partial ownership in. Rabbi Meʾir's heirs denied any knowledge of the debts and argued that any obligations may well have been paid during Rabbi Meʾir's lifetime and, if they had not, Joel should certainly have collected some of the funds while Rabbi Meʾir was alive. They also noted that Rabbi Meʾir made no reference to any such debts in his will. Rabbi Meʾir's heirs took the opportunity of appearing before the court to request that Joel be prevented from entering their section of the house in the future. Joel lived in an adjacent house and regularly entered the heirs' house to use the privy. The heirs argued that since Joel rented the space to them, he did not have the right to enter as he pleased, especially since he had his own privy in the basement. The matter seems to have been important to Joel because he raised a number of legal possibilities to insure that he and his wife would have continued access to these facilities, however, the court accepted none of them. Regarding the debts, the court ordered the beneficiaries

1. דראש חודש

to swear that they knew nothing of them (see no. 107). If they would do so, they would be absolved of all claims against them.

קז ע"ב

1. ב"ה
2. ע"ד שתבע לפנינו ה"ה התורני כ"ה בענדיט הענא סג"ל בהרשאת הו"ה כ"ה יואל בינגא
3. ותבע מן יורשי המנוח כמ"ה מאיר שש[1] ז"ל לערך אחד עשר זהו' שנשאר חייב כמהר"מ[2]
4. הנ"ל לכ"ה יואל הנ"ל בעד סחורת שמכר לו אחת אל אחת וכמבואר ג"כ בפנקס
5. שלו עוד תבע כה"ב[3] הנ"ל בהרשאת הנ"ל שכירות הבית באשר שמאותו בית שלם
6. שהי' דר בו כמהר"מ הנ"ל ירשה בת של כ"ה יואל הנ"ל חלק שמונה עשר אחר פטירת
7. הב"ח כ"ה פער בהמנוח[4] כ' ליפמן שש[5] בשנת תקך"ה והיא הקנה לאבי' כ"ה יואל הנ"ל
8. אותו חלק הנ"ל וגם בשנת תקלמד לפק לקח כ"ה יואל הנ"ל עוד חלק שמונה עשר מבית
9. הנ"ל מן האשה מ' הינדלה אל' המנוח מה' דוד טרויפף ז"ל[6] ובכן שייך לכ"ה יואל
10. הנ"ל חלק תשיעית מן בית שלם הנ"ל וכמהר"מ הנ"ל הי' דר בבית שלם הנ"ל וגם השכיר
11. חדר אחד ולא שילם כלום לכ' יואל הנ"ל בחייו בכן תבע שכירות הבית כפי חלקו
12. בבית הנ"ל מן יורשי' הנ"ל כפי ערך מאה רט לשנה והיינו מן שנת תקכה עד שנת תק"ל
13. חלק שמונה עשר מן שכירות הנ"ל לשנה ומן שנת תק"ל עד פטירת כמהר"מ הנ"ל חלק
14. תשיעית מן שכירות הנ"ל כל שנה וה"ה התורני כ"ה אנשיל פפאן בהרשאת יורשי המנוח
15. כמהר"מ הנ"ל השיב שמא פרע מורישם לכ"ה יואל הנ"ל וכה"י[7] הנ"ל הי' לו לתבוע מן מורישם
16. כשהוא בחייו וגם בתוך הצוואה שעשה כמהר"מ הנ"ל לא הזכיר כלום מחוב זה מסתמא פרע
17. הכל עוד טען כה"א[8] הנ"ל בהרשאת הנ"ל ורוצה למחות ביד כ"ה יואל הנ"ל מלילך על
18. בית המוצנע העומד בבית פנימי הנ"ל למטה אין הויז עהרנד סמוך לבית החורף
19. באשר שהוא דר בבית החיצון ושיש לו בית המוצנע בבית במרתף שלו ואין לו ר
20. רשות להשתמש בבית המוצנע שהוא בבית פנימי מאחר שחלק שלו בבית פנימי
21. יושכר והוא יקבל דמי שכירות המגיע על חלקו וכ"ה בענדיט הנ"ל בהרשאת הנ"ל
22. השיב שבית פנימי וחיצון הי' שייך לאיש אחד כ' פער שש[9] ז"ל ומסתמא הוא הי'
23. משתמש ג"כ בבית המוצנע הפנימי וממנו הי' יורשי' וחולקי' שני בתי' בכן גם הם
24. רשאי' להלוך בבית המוצנע וגם חמיו המנוח כמ"ה משה שש ז"ל ואנשי' אחרי' הדרי'
25. בבית

1. שווארצשילד
2. כבוד מורנו הרב מאיר
3. כבוד הרב בענדיט
4. בן המנוח
5. שווארצשילד
6. = הענדלה אלמנת דוד בן סענדר טרויב, בתו של הרב מאיר שווארץ שילד
7. כבוד הרב יואל
8. כבוד הרב אנשיל
9. שווארצשילד

קח ע"א

1. ב"ה
2. בבית החיצון הולכי' ג"כ על בית המוצנע הנ"ל בכן הוא טוען טענת חזקה ואינם יכולי' למחות
3. בידו ואף אם לא יזכה בזה רוצה להשכ[י]ר חלק תשיעית שלו מן הבית הנ"ל באופן זה שכ"ה
4. יואל עם אשתו רשאי' לילך על בית המוצנע הנ"ל ובאם לא יזכה גם בזה הוא רוצה להיות
5. מצרן בשכירות (חצי)[1] הבית פנימי הנ"ל וה"ה כ"ה אנשיל הנ"ל השיב שמעולם לא הי' הולכי' מבית
6. חיצון לפנימי על בית המוצ[נ]ע הנ"ל ובאם חמיו כמ"ה משה ז"ל הנ"ל הי' הולך עליו לפעמי'
7. אפשר שחס עליו מפני כבודו ש[רו]{.} אחיו הגדול אדרבה שהמנוח כ"ה מאיר ז"ל בחייו
8. הי' מוחה ביד כ"ה יואל הנ"ל מלילך בו גם הניח מסגרת לפני ב"ה ומה שהלך בו כה"י
9. הנ"ל הי' באלמות ופשיטא שלאו חזקה היא והוסיף לטעון אף באם ישכיר כ"ה יואל הנ"ל
10. חלק תשיעית שלו מבית פנימי הנ"ל אין לו רשות לילך עליו ולהשתמש גם הוא בבית
11. המוצנע הנ"ל שהוא מרבה הנכנסין בו ובאם הוא רוצה להיות מצרן בשכירות חצי
12. בית צריך לדור הוא בעצמו בתוכה ולא להשכיר לאחרי' וגם מפני ששייך בבית
13. הנ"ל ליתמי של המנוח כ"ה חיים בכמהר"מ[2] הנ"ל לא שייך דינא דבר מצרן[3] והאריכו ה
14. הצדדי' הנ"ל בטענותיהם כמבואר הכל בק"ה המונח לפנינו ובאשר שהצדדי' הנ"ל
15. חתמו עצמם בתוקף קומפרמיס בח"ח ובקנס סך מסויים לאשר ולקיי' הפס"ד שיצא
16. מאתנו בכן נזדקקנו להם ומצאנו שאין לכ"ה יואל סג"ל הנ"ל טענות חזקה על הליכות
17. בית המוצנע הנ"ל ואינו רשאי להלוך בה ולהשתמש בבית המוצנע הנ"ל גם אם
18. ישכיר לאחרי' חלק [ת]שיעת שלו בבית הנ"ל הפנימי אין לו רשות להלוך ג"כ על בית
19. המוצנע הנ"ל ומחמת מה שטען כ"ה בענדיט הנ"ל בהרשאת הנ"ל ורוצה לזכות בחצי
20. בית הנ"ל לדור בעצמו מכח דינא דבר מצרן מצאנו שאין לנו עכשיו עסק בדין מצרנות
21. ואם ישכיר כ"ה אברלי הנ"ל את חצי' השניי' מן הבית הפנימי אזי יקוב הדין (את)[4] ההר
22. ההר ביניהם ומחמת תביעת ממון שתבע כ"ה יואל מיורשי המנוח כמהר"מ
23. הנ"ל הן מחמת דמי שכירות הבית וכנ"ל והן מחמת סחורת וכנ"ל מצאנו
24. שאחד

קח ע"ב

1. ב"ה
2. שאחד מן שלשה יורשי' הנ"ל והם כ"ה אברלי שש הנ"ל ואחיותיו מחויב לישבע ע"ד
3. המקו' ב"ה וע"ד ב"ד בלי עו"מ ובלי שום הוראות היתר שבעולם במעמד שני יורשי'
4. אחרי' הנ"ל והם מחויבי' לענות אחר השבועה כל אחד אף אני כמוה' שאין יודעי'
5. שחייב מורישם כמ"ה מאיר ז"ל הנ"ל לכ"ה יואל סג"ל הנ"ל הן מחמת דמי שכירות ה
6. הבית וכנ"ל והן מחמת סחורת כנ"ל ולאחר שישבעו כנ"ל אזי פטורי' ומסולקי'

---

1. תוספת מעל השורה
2. בן כבוד מורנו הרב מאיר
3. ע' באנציקלופדיה תלמודית, כרך ד, טורים קע"ה-קע"ו.
4. תוספת מעל השורה

7. היורשי׳ המנוח כמהר״מ הנ״ל מן כל תבי[ע]ות כ״ה יואל סגל הנ״ל יצא מאתנו
8. אור ליו׳ ג זיין טבת תקל[ח] לפק ר׳ נתן מז ורמ״ש ואני

No. 106

Fol. 108b; Sunday evening, 11 January 1778

Seven-sixteenths of a seat in the old synagogue that was currently being used by Abraham Braunschweig was sold by auction to the judge, Meʾir Schiff, by the beneficiaries of the estate of Zalman Schiff for 261 guldens. Presumably, Meʾir Schiff was himself a beneficiary of his father's estate, but he was forced to purchase the seat as a means of returning its full value to the estate. Also see no. 103.

9. שבעה חלקי ששה עשר מן המקו׳ שלם בבה״כ ישן שעומד עליו כעת הו״ה כ״ה אברהם
10. ברונשוויג שהי׳ שייך להמנוח כ״ה זלמן במ״ה טע[בל]י שיף כץ ז״ל נמכר בהכרזתא
11. ע״פ יורשי׳ כה״ז[1] שיף ז״ל הנ״ל בפנינו ב״ד להאלוף הדיין כ״ה מאיר בכה״ז[2]
12. שיף ז״ל בעד שני מאות וששי׳ ואחד זהו׳ לשלם כפי תיקון הקהלה נעשה
13. אור ליו׳ ב׳ יג טבת תקלחית לפק ר נתן מז ורמענדלה[3] זאמשט ואני

No. 107

Fol. 108b; Monday 15 or Wednesday 17 June 1778

Soon after the court's decision in the matter of *Bing* v. *Schwarzschild* (no. 105), Rabbi Gundersheim accompanied the son and two daughters of the late Rabbi Meʾir Schwarzschild to the synagogue where they were to swear that they had no knowledge of any debts their father owed to Joel Bing. Following the court's decision, the judge informed them that one of them could swear and the others could answer "amen" to the statement. The plaintiff was present and had the right to decide who should swear. Joel Bing asked that one of the daughters do so, but she refused and wanted her brother to swear instead. Rabbi Gundersheim reminded them that the plaintiff had the right to decide who would swear, but they did not budge and the parties left the synagogue that day without swearing to anything. The

---

1. כבוד הרב זלמן
2. בן כבוד הרב זלמן
3. ורב מענדלה

matter remained unresolved for almost half a year until the community ordered Avreli Schwarzschild to swear that he had no knowledge of the debts.

מחמת פס"ד הנ"ל הי' הולכי' ר' אברלי ותרי אחיותיו לבה"כ לישבע סמוך לאחי[1] יציאת הפס"ד והלכתי אף אני עמהם וכשבא אל השבועה אמרתי למשבע שהי' במעמד שם שהברירה בידו להשביע איזו שירצה מהיורשי' ויענה אחרי' אמן [אח]"כ ובחר המשביע אשת כ' אברלי ווימפא ולא הי' רצת' אלא אחי' ר אברלי ישבע והיא יענה על שבועתו ואמרתי שהדין עם המשביע שהברירה בידו ואם לא נשבעה הרני רוצה ליצא מבה"כ בלי שבועה והי' הדבר הזה תלוי' עד עכשיו שצווה הקהל שר[2] אברלי ישבע וכן הוו יו' ד' לעת ערב ך סיון תקל"[ז][3] נשבע ר אברלי ואחיותיו ענו אף אני כמו' במעמדי ובמעמד השמש ר דוד שש[4] לאחר שאיימנו עליהם ולאחר שקיבל מהמשביע ב[ח]רם {לקיים הפשר} בכן פטורי' היורשי' הנ"ל מכל טענות ותביעות הי[ורש'] [ל]שב[ע]

No. 108

Perlcha, widow of David Gamburg v. Oppenheim

Fols. 109a–110b; Tuesday 7 April 1778

Perlcha, widow of David Gamburg, approached the court asking that it discharge her from the estate of her husband and that she be paid the 3000 guldens she was due as part of her marriage contract (*ketubbah*). The situation was complicated by the fact that David left not only a widow but also three children, and remained in debt to at least nine creditors, including a child for whom he acted as guardian.[5] The assets of the estate could not meet the financial claims against it.

Perlcha's representative argued that perhaps David had paid his creditors during his lifetime. Even if he had not, his obligation to Perlcha predated obligations to other creditors, and therefore her claims against the estate had precedence.[6] The court ordered the community to deal with the assets of the estate, collect any

1. צ"ל 'לאחר'
2. שר'
3. כ' סיון נפל ביום ד' בשנת תקל"ז. לאור זה שהפסק שעליו מבוסס השבועה היה בטבת תקל"ח (ר' מס' 105) וגם הפסק דין הבא ביומן (מס' 106) הוא משנת תקל"ח ובאותו הדף, כנראה שנפלה כאן טעות ומדובר בכ' סיון תקל"ח (שנפל ביום ב' בשבוע) או יום ד' כ"ב סיון תקל"ח.
4. שווארצשילד
5. See Kaplan, "Women and Worth," 111.
6. See Pinqas Franqfurṭ, fol. 266a (no. 499), from late 1788.

outstanding debts owed to David, and to sell notes that could be sold. Still unable to satisfy all of the claims, the court offered a compromise in which most creditors received from a fifth to a quarter of the value of their claims and the widow was given rights to the half of the house that her husband had owned. She was also ordered to support her children for three years from the date of the decision. With the execution of the agreement, Perlcha was relieved of all responsibilities for her husband's estate.

The case was argued before the court, at least in part, no later than 23 March 1778, the date of death of one of the litigants. The court gave its decision on 7 April.

קט ע"א

1. ב"ה
2. ע"ד טענות והפרשות שהי' לפנינו בין האשה מ' פערלכה אל' המנוח כ"ה דוד
3. גמבורג ז"ל ובין שארי בעלי חובות מבעלה ז"ל הנזכרי' למטה שתבעו חובתם
4. לפנינו מן עזבון ר דוד ז"ל הנ"ל והיינו שה"ה התורני כ"ה אהרן שייער בהרשאת
5. האשה מ' פערלכה הנ"ל אל' המנוח הנ"ל ביקש מאתנו לסלק אותה מן עזבון ב
6. בעלה ולפרוע לה דמי כתובת' ותוספ"[ת הע]ולה לסך שלשת אלפי' זהו' ובעלי ח
7. חובות מן ר דוד הנ"ל ז"ל אף הם תבעו חובתם לפנינו והיינו המנוח ג"ה
8. כ"ה אלחנן אופנהיים ז"ל הי' תובע לפנינו בעודו בחיי' חיותו סך מאה רט
9. מינץ שנתן בהקפה לר דוד ז"ל קודם מותו וכפי שנכתב בפנקס שלו וכ"ה
10. אהרן שייאר הנ"ל השיב באשר שתביעות ע"פ הוא ושמא פרע וגם כתובת אשה
11. הוא קוד[ם] קודמת בגובינא גם ה"ה התורני כ"ה מאיר מז בהרשאת
12. הו"ה התורני כ"ה זכרי' ווירטהיים תבע והציע לפנינו ח"כ עם פראטוישט
13. מן ר דוד גמבורג ז"ל הנ"ל מסך שמוני' וארבע {זהו'} קרלינר לשלם לכ"ה זכרי'
14. הנ"ל לזמן [ד]י ימי' מן יב סיון תקלוי"ו ותוך רעשפעקט טעג מן זמן פירעון
15. ח"כ הנ"ל מת ר דוד ז"ל הנ"ל בכן תבע דמי ח"כ הנ"ל מן עזבונו ואף שקיבל ר זכרי'
16. הנ"ל לאחר מיתת ר' דוד ז"ל הנ"ל מן הו"ה ג"ץ ר משה המבורג סג"ל סך שני
17. מאות וחמשה זהו' שהי' שייכי' לעזבון ר' דוד ז"ל הנ"ל טוען ואומר שתפס זה
18. בשביל קאוויטציאהל בהענא ואין לנכות זה מדמי ח"כ הנ"ל וה"ה כ"ה אהרן הנ"ל מל[ב][1]
19. תשובתיו הנ"ל על תביעות ר' אלחנן ז"ל הוסיף להשיב שר[2] זכריה שלא כדין ת
20. תפס סך שני מאות וחמשה זהו' הנ"ל שלאחר מיתת ר דוד שייכי' לכל ב"ח
21. ובראש לכתובת אשה וגם הו"ה התורני כ"ה זיסקינד שטערן במ"ה אברה[ם]
22. שטערן ז"ל תבע מעזבון ר דוד ז"ל הנ"ל בשביל עצמו לערך מאה רט עב
23. עבור קינדר חמושי'[3] שהי' לו שותפות עם ר דוד ז"ל הנ"ל ועוד תבע כ"ה זיסקינד
24. הנ"ל אפטרופוס על יתום פער בהמנוח[4] כ' ליב גנץ ז"ל סך שני מאות ושבעי'

---

1. אולי חסרה אות 'ד' וצ"ל 'מלבד'
2. שרבי
3. כנראה שהכוונה לחומשים להוראה
4. בן המנוח

25. זהו' שהי' ביד כה"ד[1] הנ"ל שהי' ג"כ אפטרופוס על יתום הנ"ל וטוען כהר"ז[2] הנ"ל שנתן
26. לכ"ה דוד הנ"ל ז"ל חשבן על סך הנ"ל וגם ר' דוד עצמו הי' כותב בפנקס שלו
27. ובאשר

קט ע"ב

1. ב"ה
2. ובאשר שנאבד הפנקס של כ"ד[3] הנ"ל עם קונטא אינו יכול לברר / עוד באה לפנינו
3. האשה מ' סערלה אל' המנוח כ' מאיר שוסטר והציע לפנינו ח"כ שיש לה על ר דוד
4. הנ"ל מסך שני מאות זהו' עם פראטעשט הזמן פירעון הוא מגיע עד לאחר
5. מותו / עוד בא לפנינו הו"ה כ' נטע שוסטר ותבע לערך שבעי' זהו' שנשאר לו
6. חייב כה"ד ז"ל הנ"ל לפי פ[נקסו ע]וד תבע לפנינו כ"ה ברוך יפה בהרשאת ר'
7. ברוך עלזנס מן ק"ק[4] אופיבאך [ש]יש לו כו"ה מן הו"ה ג"ע כ"ה אלי' האלי מקק[5] המבורג
8. חוב בפנקסו על ר דוד ז"ל הנ"ל מסך שני' עשר מאות וחמשי' ואחד מארק בא[נן] ה
9. העולה למטבעות שלנו לערך סך עשרה מאות וששי' ושלשה זהו' דא צל גם ב
10. בא לפנינו התורני כ"ה משה אויך בהרשאת הו"ה כ"ה פייבלמן פלערשהיים שיש
11. לו כו"ה מוספקת מן כ' איצק בוכבינדר מן ק"ק פירדא יע"א {...} ותבע מעזבון הנ"ל סך שני מאות
12. ושבעי' ושמונה זהו' מחמת ספרי' שמסר לו ע"י בנו כ בונפט על מו"מ מחליפין ספרי' ש
13. שנגמר ביניהם ולא קיבל כלום מן ר' דוד רק ששילם ר דוד סך ארבע עשר זהו' דמי פראכט וטוען
14. שהם עדיין בעין בעזבון הנ"ל וכ"ה אהרן הנ"ל כנ"ל על כל אחד ואחד על תביעות פנקס שמא פרע
15. וגם גביית (דמי)[6] כתובת' ותוספ' הם קודמין לכל החובות הנ"ל והאריכו הצדדי' הנ"ל בטענותיהם
16. ולאחר שחתמו האל' הנ"ל ובעלי חובות הנ"ל בתוקף קומפרמיס בח"ח ובקנס סך מסויים חצי
17. לשררה יר"ה וחצי להקדש לאשר ולקיים הפשר שיצא מאתנו ב"ד ח"מ נזדקקנו להם וטרם כל הוכרחנו
18. למנות אפטרופסי' להתעסק בעזבון הנ"ל ונתנו עינינו על הנאמני' דקהלותינו יע"א להיו'
19. עינם פקיחא על העזבון ולמכור מה שעשוי למכור ולגבות החובות מכל מי שנשאר חייב לעזבון
20. הנ"ל ולהניח אח"כ אינפוטאריום לפנינו על כל מה שנמצא בעזבון וכן עשו והנה לפי א
21. אינפוטאריום שמונח לפנינו כבר נחסר והוציא מעזבון הנ"ל מעת פטירת כ"ה דוד

1. כבוד הרב דוד
2. כבוד הרב זיסקינד
3. כבוד דוד
4. קהילת קודש
5. מקהילת קודש
6. תוספת מעל השורה

22. ז"ל הנ"ל עד הנה שכבר חלפו ועברו איזה שני' הן למזונות האל' ובני' והן לשכירות הבית
23. וחנות ו[ש]ארי הוצאות עולה מה שהוציא לערך סך שלשה עשר מאות זהו' לד"ע[1] ומה שנשאר
24. עוד בעין עם חובות וחצי בית צום לוקס בשיור יד העליונה לר' יונה גמבורג יצו שיש עדיין
25. בתוך העזבון אינו מגיע לפירעון כתובת' ותוספ' ולזאת נזדקקנו לפשר ומצאנו
26. דרך פשר דבר

קי ע"א

1. ב"ה
2. שישלם לכל אחד מבעלי חובות הנ"ל מעזבון ר דוד הנ"ל כפי הנראה לעינינו ב"ד לפי ה
3. החוב שיש לו על העזבון הנ"ל וכמבואר והיינו ליורשי המנוח ג"ה כ"ה אלחנן אופנהי'
4. ז"ל הנ"ל יותן מעזבון ר דוד ז"ל הנ"ל סך שלשי' זהו' להו"ה התורני כ"ה זכר' וורטהי'
5. הנ"ל יותן סך מאה ושתיים זהו' וחמ[ישים ושת]ים צל מלבד מה שתפס כבר שני מאות
6. וחמשה זהו' שגם המה יחזיק לעצמו ... כ"ה זיסקינד שטערן בשביל מה שתבע
7. לעצמו סך מאה רט יותן לו מעזבון הנ"ל סך עשרי' ושתי' זהו' וחצי נגד זה יקבל ב
8. בחרם שכדבריו כן הוא ובשביל מה שתבע עבור יתום פער בן המנוח כ' ליב גנץ
9. ז"ל יותן מעזבון הנ"ל סך חמשי' וארבעה זהו' להאשה מ' סערלה אל' המנוח כ' מאיר
10. שוסטר ז"ל הנ"ל יו[..][2] יותן סך חמשי' זהו' להו"ה כ' נטע שוסטר סך עשרה {רט} זהו' וחצי
11. להו"ה ג"ע ר אלי' האלי מהמבורג סך מאה וששה זהו' חי צל[3] לכ"ה איצק בוק בינדר
12. מפירדא מצאנו ע"פ פשר שיותן לו סך תשעי' ושתים זהו' והיינו {.} הספרי' דפוס
13. פירדא שישנו עדיין בעזבון הנ"ל יותן לו כלכך[4] ספרי' העולה לסך תשעי' ושתי' זהו'
14. לפי מקח הקצוב ביניהם ברשימה המונח לפנינו ובבירה ביד האל' ליתן לו מ
15. מאיזה מין ספרי' שתרצה על מקח הקצוב ביניהם ולאחר תשלומין כל הנ"ל לבעלי
16. חובות הנ"ל וגם לאחר שישולם להו"ה ג"ע כ' יעקב עמדין סך דמי פשר שעשו
17. הבוררי' ה"ג אב"ד נרו' והדיין ור"י מה' נתן מז נרו' בריצוי הצדדי' כל הנשאר אח"כ
18. בעזבון כ"ה דוד גמבורג ז"ל הנ"ל יהי' להאל' מ פערלכי הנ"ל הן מזומני' כסף ושוה
19. כסף מטלטלין חובות נימולי' וא"נ כלי בית וגם חצי בית צום לוקס וכפי שהי' ש
20. שייך להמנוח כה[5] דוד ז"ל בשיור יד העליונה לאביו כ"ה יונה גמבורג יצו וכל מה
21. שנמצא בעזבון הנ"ל החלטנו לחלוטין גמורין להאל' הנ"ל לפרעון כתובת' ותוספ' ורשו[ת]
22. בידה לעשות בהעזבון הנ"ל כל מה שתרצה ככל איניש דרשאי לעשות בשלו בלי שום מ
23. מוחה כלל ופטורה ומסולקת מן בעלי חובות הנ"ל מכל תביעות הנ"ל גם פטרנו בפטור

1. 34 צ"ל
2. יתכן שהסופר רצה למחוק את האותיות האחרונות כאן.
3. 18 צ"ל
4. כל כך
5. כבוד הרב

24. גמור את האל׳ הנ״ל שלא תשבע על כתובת׳ ואין ליורשי בעלה וב״כ על האל׳ הנ״ל וי״א
25. וב״כ שום נדר או שבועה או ק״ח נגד זה מחויבת האשה להחזיק את שלשה
26. ילדי׳ שיש לה

קי ע״ב

1. ב״ה
2. ילדי׳ שיש לה מבעלה כ״ה דוד ז״ל הנ״ל ולהחיות אותם וליתן להם כל צ
3. צרכיהם משך שלשה שני׳ מיו׳ דלמטה יצא מאתנו דרך פשר דבר יו׳ גימל יוד
4. ניסן תקלמד חית לפק ה״ג אבדי[1] נרו׳ הדיין ור״י מה׳ נתן מז נרו׳ ו
5. והדיין מה׳ יעקב שמש נרו׳ ואני

No. 109

Fol. 110b; Monday 15 June 1778

Half of the outer house on the Fröhlicher Mann lot that was owned by the community was sold to Yeḥiʾel Cohen for 3800 guldens. The record notes that two leaders of the community, Susel Kulp and Avreli Wimpe, were aware of the sale.

קי ע״ב

6. חצי בית חיצון צום פריהליכה מונן שהי׳ שייך להאלופי׳ גובי׳ יצו
7. מכרו האלופי׳ גובי׳ יצו בידיעות גבאי הקהל יצו ה״ה פו״מ כ״ה זוסיל קולפא
8. ופו״מ כ׳ אברלי ווימפא סג״ל להו״ה ג״ע כ׳ יחיאל כהן בעד סך שלשי׳ ושמנה
9. מאות זהו׳ לשלם כפי תיקון הקהלה ואנחנו ב״ד דלמטה עשינו מעשה
10. ב״ד ביו׳ ב כ סיון תקלמד חית לפק ר נתן מז וריעקב[2] שמש ואני

No. 110

Fol. 110b; Sunday evening, 1 November 1778

The community sold half a house on the Vogelgesang lot to Meʾir Flörsheim for 3885 guldens. The record notes that Rabbi Eleazar Wallau signed the decision in place of Rabbi Nathan Maas, who was related to Meʾir Flörsheim.

---

1. אב בית דין
2. ורב יעקב

ק״י ע״ב

11. חצי בית פנימי צום פאגלש גזאנג {נמכר בפנינו ב״ד} שהי[1] שייך להאלופי׳
12. קציני׳ גובי׳ יצו נמכר בפנינו ב״ד לה״ה הו״ה פו״מ כ״ה מאיר ב״מ[2] פלערשהיים
13. בעד סך שלשת אלפי׳ ושמנה מאות ושמוני׳ וחמשה זהו׳ לשלם כפי תיקון
14. הקהלה נעשה אור ליו׳ ב יב מרחשון תק[ו]ף למד טית לפק ר מאיר שיף ואני
15. ובאשר ש[ר]ב״ד מה[3] נתן מז הוא קרוב פסול עדות עם הלוקח חת[ם] במקומו ר ליזר
16. וואלה

No. 111

Fol. 111a; Tuesday evening, 12 January 1779

A record of the sale of one-quarter of a house on the Roter Turm lot that, after it was announced in both synagogues that it was available for sale, was sold by Rechla, wife of Neta Wezlar, to Zechariah Wertheim for 900 reichstalers. The record notes that Rechla's husband had owned the house, but had passed it on to his wife through a here unspecified ruling by a royal commission in Wetzlar. According to his record in the Frankfurt *Memorbuch* (fol. 292b), Neta was very sick for 13 years before his death on 31 August 1784, and during most of these years he did not speak regarding mundane matters. Also see nos. 112, 124, and, particularly, no. 155.

קיא ע״א

1. ב״ה
2. רביעית בית פנימי צום רויטה טאהרן שהי׳ שייך לכ״ה נטע וועצלר כץ ולאח״כ
3. ע״י משפט פיסוטאציאהנש = קומ[ס]יאהן[4] מהקיסר יר״ה בוועצלר נחלט כל הקרקעות
4. שהי׳ שייך לכ״ה נטע הנ״ל לאשתו מ׳ רעכלה כפי המבואר בארהי טיב[5] מכתב שהיא
5. לפנינו ב״ד אותו רביעית בית הנ״ל לאחר שהוכרז בבהכיו״ח מכרה האשה
6. הנ״ל רביעית בית הנ״ל לפנינו ב״ד לכ״ה זכרי׳ ווירטהיים בעד סך
7. תשעה מאות רט לשלם לפי תיקון הקהלה נעשה אור ליו׳ ד׳ ך״ה טבתקלט[6] לפק
8. רנ״מ רמ״ש ואני

---

1. שהיה
2. בן משה
3. מורנו הרב
4. הועדה הזאת היתה אחראית על בדיקת האכלוסיה היהודית ברחוב היהודים (האכלוסיה לא היתה אמורה לעבור חמש מאות משפחות).
5. כנראה שצ״ל 'באר היטיב'
6. טבת תקל״ט

No. 112

Fol. 111a; Thursday evening, 28 January 1779

The sale of half a house on the Roter Turm lot to Gumprecht Freidberg was recorded by the court. As in record no. 111, the house was sold by Rechle, wife of Neta Wezlar, who received ownership of it through a government order. There was a period of open bidding for the house and ultimately it was sold to Gumprecht for 2475 guldens. The record specifically notes that full payment would be made before the first day of the Hebrew month of Iyyar that year (16 May 1779). Also see no. 124.

9. חצי בית החיצון צום רויטה טארן שהי׳ שייך לכ״ה נטע וועצלר כץ
10. ולאח״כ נחלט (החצי)[1] הבית הנ״ל ע״י משפט פיסיטאציאהנש קומיסיאהן מהקיסר
11. יר״ה לאשתו מ׳ רעכלה אותו חצי בית הנ״ל לאחר הכרזה מכרנו הב״ד {ח״מ}
12. הרשומי׳ למטה לכ״ה גומפריכט פ״ב[2] בן המנוח כ״ה משה פרידבורג ז״ל
13. בעד סך שני אלפי׳ וארבע מאות ושבעי׳ וחמשה זהו׳ לשלם כפי תיקון
14. הקהלה והותנו בפירוש {ש.ד} שעד ר״ח אייר הסמוך הבע״ל (ולא עד בכלל)[3] יהי׳ הפי[רעון]
15. מחצי בית הנ״ל להמוכרות[4] האשה מ׳ רעכלה הנ״ל נעשה אור ליו׳ ויו יב שבט
16. תקלטית לפק ר״י ורב״ד מה׳ נ״מ נר׳ והדיין רמ״ש ואני

No. 113

Fols. 111b–112a; Sunday evening, 10 October 1779

Abraham Schwab-Öttingen and Zalman Rothschild, guardians of the children of the late Moses Schwab-Öttingen, requested permission from the court to sell one-quarter of a house on the Scheuer lot that was owned by one of the children, Isaac Schwab-Öttingen. The guardians had used the house as collateral to obtain funds at interest to provide a dowry for Isaac's sister, Reizche. If this loan was not satisfied soon there would be additional charges against the estate. Local taxes and maintaince on the house were also reducing the value of the estate. The estate had

---

1. תוספת מעל השורה
2. פרידבורג
3. תוספת מעל השורה
4. צ״ל ׳להמוכרת׳

a portion in another house that had ongoing charges (i.e., repairs, taxes). Fearing that the holdings of the child would continue to erode, the guardians petitioned the court to sell the one-quarter of a house on the Scheuer lot and use the proceeds of the sale to pay off debts. They would then invest the remaining funds. Isaac himself appeared before the court and agreed to the proposed sale, and the court gave its approval. Isaac's older brother, Seligmann, had renounced any claims against his father's estate in 1773, but he held a loan for 500 guldens plus interest that was secured by the house. It is not clear from this record how this lien was dealt with. Also see no. 128.

קיא ע״ב

1. ב״ה
2. הן הקריבו לפנינו ב״ד ח״מ ה״ה הו״ה כ׳ אברהם בהמנוח[1] כ׳ זעליגמן
3. איטינגין וה״ה הו״ה כ׳ זלמן בהמנוח כ׳ קלמן רויטשילד יצו אפטרופס דיתמי
4. המנוח כ׳ משה בזעליגמן[2] איטינגן ז״ל וביקשו מאתנו ב״ד ח״מ ליתן להם
5. רשות למכור רביעית בית החיצון צום שייער שהוא בעזבון כ׳ משה ז״ל
6. הנ״ל והציעו דבריהם לפנינו באשר שאותו רביעית בית שייך להיתו׳
7. כ׳ איצק בהמנוח כ׳ משה ז״ל הנ״ל לבד שאחיו הגדול כ׳ זעליגמן סילק עצמו
8. מן עזבון אביו ז״ל הנ״ל ע״פ הפשר שנעשה (בינו)[3] ובין האפטרופסי׳ הנ״ל וכפי ה
9. הפטורי׳ שהציעו האפטרופסי׳ הנ״ל לפנינו ההוקם יו׳ א יג תמוז שנת
10. תקלג לפק בח״י של כ׳ זעליגמן הנ״ל וגם כ׳ זעליגמן (בא)[4] {הודה} לפנינו והודה על
11. הח״י של הפטורי׳ הנ״ל בכן אין לכ׳ זעליגמן הנ״ל ברביעית בית הנ״ל רק
12. אחר שיש עדיין לכ״ז[5] הנ״ל שט״ח בידו מסך חמשה מאות זהו׳ על רווחי׳
13. ו[מ]שועבד רביעית בית הנ״ל על סך חמשה מאות זהו׳ הנ״ל עם רווחי׳ ה
14. העולים ע״ז {ואם לא יפרעו עכשיו מחויבי׳ ליתן ג״כ רווחי׳ מחוב זה}
15. וזולת אותן חמשה מאות זהו׳ הנ״ל יש עוד שיעבוד על רביעית בית
16. הנ״ל על מה שלווי׳ האפטרופסי׳ לצורך הנדן היתומה רייצכה הנשואה
17. לכ״ה יוזפא הירש ואם לא יפרעו עכשיו מחויבי׳ ליתן ג״כ רווחי׳ מחוב הזה
18. מלבד מה שיש להם הוצאות מידי שנה בשנה על רביעית בית קרונד צונץ
19. וגם הוצאות לחזק בדק הבית והני גברא הפטרופסי׳[6] הנ״ל בפחד׳ יתבי ש
20. שבלי ספק עי״כ מכלה קרנא של גוף רביעית בית הנ״ל לזאת דעתם שרוצי׳
21. לימכר רביעית בית הנ״ל ולשלם כל החובות הנ״ל והנשאר במזומני׳
22. הוא שייך לכ׳ איצק הנ״ל לבד ויכולי׳ להתעסק להלוות בת״ע על רווחי׳

---

1. בן המנוח
2. כנראה שצ״ל: בן זעליגמן; ע׳ אבני זכרון, מס׳ 3463. שם מצוין שהיה גר בבית צום שייער.
3. תוספת מעל השורה
4. תוספת מעל השורה
5. כבוד זעליגמן
6. צ״ל ׳האפטרופסי׳׳

23. ושההוא בוודאי יותר טוב להיתום הנ"ל ואחר הצעות דבריהם הנ"ל ש
24. שלחנו אחר היתום כ' איצק הנ"ל ובא לפנינו ואמר שמרוצה בכל מה
25. שרוצי'

קיב ע"א
1. ב"ה
2. שרוצי' אפטרופסי' לעשות / ולאחר שמצאנו (ג"כ)[1] שדברי האפטרופסי' הנ"ל הם כני'
3. ולטובת היתום כ' איצק הנ"ל כדי שלא לכלה קרנא בכן ניתן {להם} רשות ל
4. להאפטרופסי' הנ"ל מאתנו ב"ד ח"מ למכור את רביעית בית הנ"ל ב
5. בתוקף מעשה ב"ד ובכח ב"ד יפה ואין שום אדם רשאי למחות בידיהם
6. או לערער על מכירתם וכל דברי המערער יהי' בטלין ומבוטלין ואל יזדקק להם
7. שום דינא הן בדא"ה והן בד"י כי הכל נעשה בריצוי היתום הנ"ל ובכח ב"ד יפה
8. נעשה פה פפ"ד אור ליו' ב ב דר"ח מרחשון תק"מ פק[2] רנ"מ ורמ"ש ואני

No. 114

Fol. 112a; Monday evening, 18 October 1779

The engagement of Ber Kann (son of the late Jacob Kann) to the daughter of Sussmann Rüsselsheim gave rise to a dispute between no less than eight matchmakers regarding who was entitled to collect how much for arranging the match. The disputants signed an agreement that bound them to accept the court's decision and the court investigated the matter with Ber, who was an orphan, and his bride's family before giving its ruling. The marriage never took place as Ber died in January 1780.[3]

9. קיב ע"א
10. בדבר השידוך הנעשה שנתקשר עצמו היתום הב"ח כ' פער בהמנוח[4] כ"ה יעקב
11. קן[5] עם בת הו"ה כ' זוסמן ריסלסהיים התעצמו ורבו השדכני' המבוארי לפנינו
12. ב"ד ח"מ מחמת דמי שדכנות ולאחר שחתמו עצמם השדכני' המבוארי' למטה
13. בתוקף קומפרמיס בח"ח ובקנס סך מסויים לאשר ולקיים כפי הפשר שיצא מאתנו
14. נזדקקנו להם ולאחר ששמענו פי המחותני' הנ"ל עשינו החלוקה ע"פ פשר ביניהם

---

1. תוספת מעל השורה
2. פרט קטן (ר"ל לפרט קטן)
3. See Horovitz, no. 4330, with Ettlinger's corrections (13.1.1780).
4. בן המנוח
5. מעל הקטע יש את המילים, 'ב"ח של הו"ה כ"ה מאדל [ד]לפ[ו]קה'. יש סימן להכניס את המילים כאן אחרי השם 'קן' אבל לא ברור איך הדברים משתלבים בתוך הדיון.

כמבואר והיינו להשמש התורני כ"ה דוד ששי[1] סך עשרי' ושבעה זהו' לה"ה כ' אייזק אוקס עם חמותו האשה אל' מ' בילה אופנהיים סך עשרי' ואחד זהו' ארבעי' צל לה"ה כ"ה ראובן הירצפעלד מן ק"ק אופיבאך סך שלשי' וששה זהו' לה"ה כ' דוד העכט א זהוב לכ' ברוך פויעלה מן ק"ק אופיבאך שלשה זהו' יוד צל להאל' גאלדכה שפיגל א זהוב להאל' עדיל האמיל א זהוב אשת ר שמואל טריר א זה' ובזה פטורי' ומסולקי' השדכני' זה מזה וזו מזו {ואל} ואין להשדכני' הנ"ל שום תביעה על בעלי דברי' המחותני' הנ"ל מחמת תביעות השדכנות הנ"ל יצא מאתנו אור ליו' ג' טית מרחשון תק"מ ר"נ מז ור"מ[2] שיף ואני

No. 115

Fols. 112b–114a; possibly Wednesday evening, 5 January 1780

Owners of the Papagei and Frosch houses, which were adjacent to each other, came to the court with a request that it divide the open space behind the houses so the owners could build a fence that would stretch from the sheds behind the houses back to the wall that separated the Jewish quarter from the rest of the town. The owners did not need to turn to the court, for they could have located the boundary marker between the houses themselves; however, this would have required removing all the garbage that had accumulated there and the owners did not want to do so. The record also notes that they could have brought documentation regarding their plots, such as earlier court documents, but they did not do this either. The record gives no reason as to why they chose not to do so, but it appears to be connected to a lack of desire on the part of all parties to clean up the garbage in the lots. Instead, they asked the court to consult with an expert and divide the land, although they agreed among themselves that this division would not preempt their rights based upon the boundary marking on the ground or what was recorded in their contracts. The court acceded to the request and hired a professional who was licensed by the non-Jewish authorities. The members of the court were present when he measured the space. The sides formally agreed to a number of rules with respect to the fence that would be built between the two properties, payment for it, and any future building on the open spaces.

1. שווארצשילד
2. רב מאיר

קיב ע"ב

1. ב"ה
2. ע"ד שבאו לפנינו מחזיקי שני בתי' הסמוכים צום פאפיגייא אונד צום פראש
3. ה"ה הו"ה כ"ה זלמן בהמנוח[1] כ' וואלף בינגא ז"ל ששייך לו הבית שלם צום פאפיגייא
4. הנ"ל וה"ה התורני כ"ה הירץ ואחיו כ"{ה} אהרן בני המנוח הדיין מה' אנשיל צונץ
5. זצ"ל ששייך לכ"א מאחי' הנ"ל רביעית בית צום פראש הנ"ל וה"ה הו"ה כ"ה משה שפניער
6. כץ ששייך לו ג"כ רביעית בית צום פראש הנ"ל וה"ה הוה[2] כ"ה חיים בהמנוח[3] כ"ה
7. משה שוסטר כץ ז"ל ששייך לו ג"כ רביעית צום פראש וביקשו מאתונו[4] ב"ד ח"מ ליתן להם
8. תוקף ועוד על חלוקת פלאטץ שהוא אחורי שני בתי' הנ"ל שיש לכ' זלמן מחזיק הבית
9. צום פאפיגייא הנ"ל חלקו כ[ולל] מחזיקו בית צום פראש הנ"ל ג"כ חלקם בו ועכשיו
10. התרצו השני מחזיקי' הנ"ל לחלוק הפלאטץ הנ"ל ולהעמיד מחיצת נסרים באמצע רוחב
11. הפלאטץ מן הסוכות שהם אחורי השני בתי' הנ"ל עד החומה המפסקת בין נימלי' לא"נ
12. ובפירוש הותנו ביניהם שאינם רוצים לפנות האשפה המונח על הפלאטץ כדי
13. לבדוק ע"י חפירת קויפף מויער הגבול של כל או"א מהבתי' בתוך הפלאטץ הנ"ל
14. הנ"ל וגם אינם רוצים להציע לפנינו הזכיות ומעשה ב"ד שיש ביד כל או"א על ה
15. על הפלאטץ הנ"ל רק המה רוצים מאתנו ב"ד ח"מ {ל.דוד} (למדוד)[5] הפלאטץ ע"י אומן
16. רוחב

קיג ע"א

1. רוחב של הפלאטץ ולחלק הפלאטץ על האשפה לפי שעה {בעמצ} באמצע שוה בשוה כדי
2. שכל או"א ממחזיקי הבתים הנ"ל יכול להשתמש ולבנות על חצי פלאטץ הנ"ל על אופן המבואר (המבואר)[6]
3. והותנו ביניהם בפירוש בכא"ה שבחלוקה זו לא יפסיד ולא יגרע לגמרי הזכיות שיש
4. לכאו"א ממחזיקי בתי' הנ"ל בפלאטץ הנ"ל הן ע"י מעשה ב"ד והן ע"י חפירות קויפף [מו]יער
5. בפנות האשפה שיברר עי"כ הגבול של כאו"א מבתים בתוך הפלאטץ והנה אחרי שמ(ח)[7]זיקי
6. בתים הנ"ל וחתמו עצמם בתוקף קומפרמיס בח"ח ובקנס סך מסויים חצי לשררה יר"ה ו
7. וחצי להקדש לאשר ולקיים כפי מה שיצא מאתנו נזדקקנו להם ולאחר שהלכנו על
8. הפלאטץ וראינו מדידת הפלאטץ הנ"ל שנעשה ע"י אומן המושבע מהשררה יר"ה נמצא

---

1. בן המנוח
2. המפואר והחשוב
3. בן המנוח
4. ר"ל 'מאתנו'
5. תוספת מעל השורה
6. תוספת מעל השורה. המילה 'המבואר' הראשונה אינה ברורה ויתכן שזו הסיבה שהסופר חזר עליה.
7. תוספת מעל השורה

9. שרוחב מן כל הפלאטץ של שני בתים הנ"ל בתחילתו והיינו מיד אחורי הסוכות שאחורי
10. שני בתים הנ"ל הוא אחד עשר מנעלי' ושבעה ומחצה צאהל ובסופו סמוך לחומה המפסקת
11. בין נימולי' לא"נ רוחב של כל הפלאטץ הוא עשרה מנעלי' וחצי (ומעתה)[1] ורשאי כל או"א ממחזיקי שני
12. בתי' הנ"ל לחלוק הפלאטץ הנ"ל באמצע רוחבו ולהעמיד מחיצת נסרי' מן אחורי הסוכות
13. עד החומה המפסקת בין נימולי' לא"נ על הוצאות ש[לו] בלי שום מוחה כלל על אופן שיגיע
14. לכל צד וצד ממחזיק בתי' הנ"ל שוה בשוה בפלאטץ הנ"ל והמחיצות נסרי' הנ"ל יהי' עומדות
15. על גבול שניהם בשוה ומאחר שא"א לבנות מחיצת נסרי' אם לא שיהי' נסמכי' על קורות
16. לזאת הישוו גם עצמם המחזיקי' הנ"ל שמי שרוצה לעשות מחיצות נסרי' יכול לבנות
17. על קורות {שיניח...}(שיניח)[2] למטה בקרקע הפלאטץ מתחילת הפלאטץ שהוא אחורי הסוכו'
18. עד החומה המפסקת הנ"ל וגם למעלה על מחיצת נסרי' הנ"ל יכול להניח קורות כדי

קיג ע"ב

1. {לסמוך עלי' בנין מחיצות החומה המפסקת הנ"ל וגם למעלה על מחיצות נסרי' הנ"ל}
2. יוכול {לבנות להניח קורות כדי} לסמוך עלי' בנין מחיצות נסרי' הנ"ל גם יכול להעמיד {ק...ת} (קורות)[3]
3. באמצע מלמעלה למטה כפי הצורך למחיצות נסרי' הנ"ל וכל הקורות הנ"ל יהי' ג"כ על
4. גבול שניהם שוה בשוה ורשאי ג"כ מי שיעמד מחיצת נסרי' לעשות למטה על הקרקע
5. כמין חומה קטנה להניח עליה' הקורות שיעשה למטה על הקרקע פלאטץ הנ"ל וכפי
6. הצורך להגבי' שלא ירקיבו הקורות וגם החומה קטנה הנ"ל יהי' על גבול שניהם שוה בשוה
7. ולאחר שהועמד מחיצת נסרי' הנ"ל רשאי לכל צד וצד להשתמש ולבנות בחלקו והיינו אותו
8. צד שהעמיד מחיצה הנ"ל על הוצאות שלו רשאי {...אחד למטה על } ({לסמוך בנין של...})[4] לסמוך
9. בנין שלו ע"ג מחיצה אכן בפי' (בפי')[5] הותנו בכא"ה שאינו רשאי לבנות כאו"א רק שטח אחד למטה על{.} הקרקע
10. וגג למעלה על גבה אבל לא שני חדרי' זה למעלה מזה אבל למטה על הקרקע רשאי לבנות כמה חדרי'

---

1. תוספת מעל השורה
2. תוספת מעל השורה
3. תוספת מעל השורה
4. תוספת מחוקה מעל השורה
5. תוספת מעל השורה; כנראה שהפעם הראשונה שכתב את המילה, המילה לא היתה ברורה ולכן חזר והוסיף אותה.

11. זה לפני' מזה וגג עליהם ומי שבונה כבינין הנ"ל צריך לתקן באופן שמי גשמי' והשופכי' מבנין הנ"ל יורדי'
12. לתוך גבולו גם אינו רשאי לכל או"א ממחזיקי' הנ"ל לעשות חפירה בתוך קרקע פלאטץ הנ"ל ובאם אח"כ
13. הצד השני רוצה ג"כ לבנות בחלקו ולסמוך על גבי מחיצה הנ"ל אזי מחויב לשלם לחבירו הבונה
14. מחיצה הנ"ל על הוצאותיו דמי חצי מחיצה כ"כ הצריך לבנין שלו שרוצה לבנות ולא יותר
15. ובאם אחד ממחזיקי בתי' הנ"ל רוצה לבנות על חלקי בנין קבע בנין בית ממש כשארי בתי'
16. בקהלתינו יע"א אזי {מחויב} (מחויב)[1] צד השני לסלק את הבנין העומד בחלקו מה שמעכב את חברו מלבנות
17. כראוי בנין קבע שלו וגם אם אותו שרצה להעמיד בנין קבע כנ"ל ואז צריך לפנות את
18. האשפה אשר מונח על הפלאטץ וביקש [מ]צד השני שגם הוא יפנה את חלקו המונח בגבולו כדי
19. שע"י כך יבורר יפה ע"י חפירת קויפף מויער הגבול {ש.גיע} (שיגיע)[2] לכאו"א ממחזיקי

קיד ע"א

1. בתי' הנ"ל בתוך הפלאטץ הנ"ל אזי מחויב חבירו ג"כ לסייע לפנות את האשפה מן כל הפלאטץ
2. הנ"ל על הוצאות שניהם שוה בשוה אבל הוצאות לסתור הבנין שהי' על האשפה בתוך גבול של
3. כאו"א הוא עליו לבד ואין על חבירו לשלם עמו כל הנ"ל התרצ[ו] עצמם המחזיקי שני בתי' הנ"ל
4. לפי שעה אכן בפירוש הותנו בכא"ה שלא יפסיד ולא יגרע כלל וכלל לכל צד וצד ממחזיקי
5. בתי' הנ"ל בחלוקת הנ"ל שום זכות שימצא לאחר כך לכאו"א הן ע"י חפירת קויפמויער או שארי
6. זכיות ויפוי כח שיש לכל אחד ממחזיקי בתי' הנ"ל וי"א וב"כ ע"י ראיות ומעשה ב"ד שיברר לזמנו
7. ואין כח לצד שכנגדו לבטל אותן מכח חזקה או שום טענה שבעולם מכח חלוקה ובנין הנ"ל כי
8. כל זכיות שיהי' לכל או"א נשאר בתקפו ובגבורתי' בלי שום טענה ואמתלא שבעולם יהי' מה
9. שיהי' או באיזה אופן שיהי' הן בדא"ה והן בד"י כל הנ"ל נעשו בפנינו ב"ד בריצוי כל הצדדי'
10. והיינו כ' זלמן וכ"ה הירץ הנ"ל בשביל עצמו ובהרשאת אחיו כ"{ה} אהרן הנ"ל וכ"ה משה הנ"ל וכ"ה חיים
11. הנ"ל וכתבנו וחתמנו זאת בתוקף מעשה ב"ד ובכח ב"ד יפה להיות ביד כל צד וצד לראי' נעשה

---

1. תוספת מעל השורה
2. תוספת מעל השורה

12. אור ליו' ה {.י} [וו] שבט תקמם לפק {מה שנכתב ב"[.] גם יוכל להעמיד קורות באמצע מלמעלה למטה
13. כפי הצורך מחיצת נסרי' שייך הנ"ל} רנמ[1] רמש[2] ואני

No. 116

Fol. 114b; Tuesday evening, 11 January 1780

A seat in the middle women's section of the synagogue was sold to Kalman Reiss. The seat had belonged to the late Leb Schloss, and the guardians of Leb's estate agreed to have the court sell the seat after an announcement of its availability. The seat was purchased by Kalman Reiss, whose wife had been using the seat, for 800 guldens. Kalman was one of the two guardians of the estate appointed by the community.

קיד ע"ב

1. ב"ה
2. מקו' שלם בע"נ התיכונה שעומדות עלי' כעת אשת הו"ה כ' קלמן רייס שהי' שייך להמנוח
3. כ' ליב ב"כ מרדכי שלאס ז"ל כמבואר בקנין חליפין הנעשה ביו' [ד]' א דר"ח כסליו תקמם[3] לפק
4. מכרנו בהכרזה ברשיון האפטרופסי' המנויי' ע"פ הקהל יצו על עזבון המנוח כ' ליב ז"ל
5. הנ"ל הו"ה כ' וואלף ב"ז[4] היידלבורג והו"ה (כ')[5] קלמן רייס להה"ה כ' קלמן רייס הנ"ל בעד סך שמונה
6. מאות זהו' לשלם כפי תיקון הקהלה אור ליו' ד' ה שבט תקמ"ם לפק רנ"מ ורמ"ש ואני

No. 117

Fol. 114b; Tuesday evening, 11 January 1780

The further sale of assets of the late Leb Schloss (see no. 116) included the sale of half a seat in the upper women's section of the syngagogue to Isaiah Lehren for

1. רב נתן מז
2. רב מאיר שיף
3. א' דר"ח כסליו (= ל' חשון) נפל ביום ג' בשנת תק"ם.
4. בן זעלקלי
5. תוספת מעל השורה

348 guldens. The purchaser was Rabbi Gundersheim's brother-in-law, forcing the judge to recuse himself. He was replaced by Rabbi Mendele Samst.

7. ———
8. חצי מקו' שלם בע"נ העליונה אשר עומדות עלי' כעת אשת אנשיל כל[1] זיכל אשר הי'
9. שייך להמנוח כ' ליב שלאס ז"ל הנ"ל מכרנו לגיסי כ"ה ישעי' לעהרן יצו בעד סך שלשה
10. מאות וארבעי' ושמונה זהו' לשלם כפי תיקון הקהלה ביו' הנ"ל רנ"מ ורמ"ש
11. ובמקומי חתם עצמו הוספה דיין ר מענדלי זאמשט יצו

No. 118

Fol. 114b; Sunday evening, 6 February 1780

Two seats in the synagogue, one in the men's section and one in the lower women's section, that belonged to Simeon Sinzheim of Vienna were sold by his wife, Bela, whom Sinzheim had empowered.[2] The seat in the women's section was sold to Abraham Emmerich for 1080 guldens, while the seat in the men's section of the old synagogue was sold to Anshel Hahn for 251 guldens. Rabbi Me'ir Schiff had married a member of the Sinzheim family and, as a relative of one of the parties, recused himself from the case.[3] Rabbi Mendele Lilg was added to the court to form the necessary quorum.

12. ———
13. מקו' שלם בע"נ התחתונה אשר עומדות עלי' כעת אשת כ' אברם האן ומצד ימין לאותו
14. מקו' עומדות כעת אשת כ' אלי' רייס ומצד שמאל עומדות אשת כ' וואלף בכ"ה זעלקלי היידל
15. = בורג מקו' שלם הנ"ל שהי' שייך לכ"ה שמעון זינצהיים מווינא נמכר בפני ב"ד דלמטה ע"פ ה
16. האשה מ' בילה אשת כ"ה שמעון הנ"ל שיש לה כו"ה (מספקת)[4] מבעלה למכרו לה"ה ג"ע כ' אברהם עמריך
17. בעד סך עשרה מאות ושמוני' זהו' לשלם כפי תיקון הקהלה יע"א
18. ועוד מקו' שלם בבה"כ ישן העליונה אשר עומד עלי' כעת כ' אנשיל ב"כ אברם האן
19. שהי' שייך לכ"ה שמעון זינצהיים הנ"ל נמכר בפני ב"ד דלמטה ע"פ אשתו וכנ"ל לכ' אנשיל

———

1. כנראה שהסופר כתב 'כל' במקום 'זיכל' והמילה היתה צריכה להימחק.
2. On this couple, see Bernhard Wachstein, *Die Inschriften des alten Judenfriedhofes in Wien*, Quellen und Forschungen zur Geschichte der Juden in Deutsch-Österreich 4.2 (Vienna: Braumüller, 1917), 400.
3. See Horovitz, no. 4899.
4. תוספת מעל השורה

ב"כ אברם האן הנ"ל בעד סך שני מאות וחמשי' ואחד זהו' לשלם כפי תיקון הקהלה יע"א שני מכירות אלו נעשה אור ליו' ב ב דר"ח אדר ראשון תקמם לפק רנ"מ ובמקו' רמ"ש שהי' קרוב חתום עצמו ר' (הוספה דיין)[1] מענדלי לילג {...} אחרי

No. 119

Fols. 115a–b; Thursday 2 March 1780

The late Leb Kann made provisions in his will to establish a charitable trust after his death. In 1775 the court appointed administrators over the fund, one of whom was Leb's son-in-law (see no. 61). The others were not related to the Kann family. Two of Leb's sons now approached the court asking that it appoint them as administrators of the trust and allow them to invest the funds differently than had been done in the past. The sons admitted that when the original appointments were made in 1775 they were not eligible to become guardians, for one son, Gumpel Kann, was not in Frankfurt and the other, Ber Kann, was not yet married. However, now that they were both eligible, they claimed that it was inappropriate to have administrators who were not blood relatives of the deceased. While two of the current guardians were willing to resign their positions, they specifically objected to the brothers' plans to invest the money in a different fashion and argued that there could be no safer investment than investing funds with the community as they had done. One of the administrators also objected to the appointment of the brothers as the sole guardians of the trust, and requested that he be informed of the distributions of funds. The court rejected the brothers' request and noted that the current administrators could not simply resign. The court, which included four judges instead of the usual three, agreed to appoint the older brother, Gumpel, to serve as an administrator of the fund, but noted that the investments of the trust were not to be changed.

קטו ע"א

ב"ה

ע"ד שבא לפנינו ה"ה התורני כה' אנשיל פפאן בהרשאת ובמעמד הני תרי אחי' הו"ה כה' גומפיל והו"ה כ"ה פער בני המנוח פו"מ כ"ה ליב במ"א[2] קן ז"ל וטענו לפנינו מחמת אפטרופסית על הדבר טוב שהניח אביהם כ"ה ליב ז"ל

---

1. תוספת מעל השורה
2. בן מורנו איצק

6. הנ"ל שמ[נ]ו אנחנו ב"ד ח"מ תרי אפטרופסי' ה"ה הו"ה כ"ה יוזל
7. באמבורג יצו וה"ה הו"ה כה' מאדל ברונשוויג סג"ל חתן
8. המנוח המנדב כה' ליב ז"ל הנ"ל עם האפטרופס שהי'
9. כבר הו"ה ג"ע כה' פער קליף יצו כמבואר בשטר
10. אפטרופסי' שיצאו מאתנו ב' דר"ח אלול {קהלת} קהלת לפק
11. וטענו הני תרי אחי' הנ"ל שבאותו פעם לא {היה} הי' אחד
12. מהם ראוי' לאפטרופס שכה' גומפיל הנ"ל לא הי' כאן אלא בקק[1]
13. קאסיל אצל חמיו וכ"ה פער הנ"ל עדיין לא היה נשוי אבל מעתה
14. שהם בעצמם ראוי' להיות אפטרופסי' והם יורשי' דאורייתא בכן לא מיבעי'
15. שאינו מן הראוי להיות אפטרופס' לאיש אחר אשר לא ממשפחתם והו{"}א כה' יוזל באמבורג
16. אלא אף גיסם ה"ה כ' מאדל ברונשוויג הנ"ל אין לו שום זכות לדבר בעסק דב"ט כ"ש
17. לפקח בו רק המה הני תרי אחי' לבד זוכי' להיות אפטרופסי' ועוד תבעו האחי'
18. הנ"ל באשר שכבר יצאו מאתנו ב"ד ביו' ג' ב' אב' קהלת לפק לאחר שיבאו מה ששייך
19. לדב"ט לידי גוביינא ולמעות מזומנים שיונח ביד בטוח כפי המבואר בצוואה
20. מכה' ליב ז"ל הנ"ל והיינו הנראה בטוח לפי ראות עינ[י]נו ב"ד והנה הני תרי
21. אפטרופסי' הנ"ל כה' יוזל וכה' מאדל דעתם ליתן עכשיו אחרי שהביאו לידו מעות
22. מז(ו)[2]מנים הקרן ביד האלופי' קציני' גובי' יצו להיות בידם לדורי דורת על [רווחי']
23. עצ"ה כנהוג והני תרי אחי' הנ"ל טענו ומיחו שלא להניח ביד הגובי' יצו וטענו
24. {שבצוואות} שבצוואת אביהם לא צוה שינח ביד הגובי' רק ביד בטוח והם רוצים
25. שינחו במקו' אחר שהוא בטוח יותר מכמה חששי' לפי דעתם שהאריכו בזה
26. בטענותם וה"ה {ה"ה} פ' הו"ה כ' מאדל ברונשוויג סג"ל בעצמו השיב
27. בשבילו ובהרשאת אפטרופס האחר ה"ה ו[.][3] הו"ה כ' יוזל באמבורג
28. יצו שבאמת המה {מ[ח]וצים} מרוצים לסלק את עצמם מן האפטרופסות

קטו ע"ב

1. ב"ה
2. {אבל מ}אבל מחמת (דמי)[4] דב"ט הנ"ל טענו שאין לך ביד בטוח יותר שיונח ביד הגובי'
3. ולא על שום אופן אחר יהי' באיזו אופן שיהי' כמו שהאריך בזה בטענות
4. עוד טען כה' מאדל לטובת ד"ט הנ"ל ומוחה טענות הני תרי אחי' הנ"ל לבד
5. לאפטרופסי' מכמה {ט.מי'} טעמי' שהאריך כה' מאדל לפנינו בק"ה עוד טען
6. שאף אם ב"ד ממנה אפטרופסי' לתרי אחי' הנ"ל מ"מ רוצה הוא להוי' לו {י'...}ידיעה
7. בעסק התחלקות הצדקה והאריכו בזה בטענותיהם ובאשר שהני תרי אפטרופסי'

---

1. בקהילת קודש
2. תוספת מעל השורה
3. לא ברור אם יש כאן עוד שתי אותיות או אם הסופר התחיל לכתוב משהו ואז מחק או עזב אותו.
4. תוספת מעל השורה

8. הנ"ל והני תרי אחי' הנ"ל חתמו עצמם בתוקף קומפרמיס בח"ח ובקנס סך {מסויים} (מסויים)[1]
9. לאשר ולקיים את אשר יצא מאתנו נזדקקנו להם ומצאנו שאינם רשאי' ואין יכולת ביד האפטרופס'
10. הו"ה כ' מאדל סג"ל וה"ה הו"ה כ' יוזל באמבורג כלל וכלל לסלק עצמם מהאפטרופסי' הנ"ל
11. ומחויבי' להתעסק באפטרופסית שלהם על הדבר טוב כמקדם ומחמת מה שתובעי'
12. הני תרי אחי' הנ"ל כה' גומפייל וכה' פער הנ"ל שהם רוצים להיות אפטרופסי'
13. מצאנו שאחד מהם לבד יהי' ג"כ אפטרופס עם האפטרופסים אחרי' הנ"ל
14. ונמנה מאתנו הגדול שבהם ה"ה הו"ה כ"ה גומפיל הנ"ל וכל תוקף שטר אפטרופס
15. שופרי דשטרי ייפוי כח הנזכר בשטר אפטרופסות ההוקם מאתנו ב"ד ח"מ ב'
16. דר"ח אלול קהלת לפק[2] שיש ביד הני אפטרופסי' הנ"ל ואותו זכות ויפוי כח
17. הוא ג"כ לכ"ה גומפיל הנ"ל וכאילו נכתב השטר אפטרופסות הנ"ל ג"כ על
18. שמו וסידור חלוקת הצדקה יתהנגו[3] כפי פסקי דינם שכבר יצא מאתנו
19. שהם עומדים בתקפם ובגבורתם (גם)[4] אחר {ה(גם גם)} העיון והדקדוק
20. היטב לטובת הדבר טוב מצאנו שהקרן של דבר טוב
21. מחויבי' להניח אצל האלופי' קצינים גובי' יצו על רווחי' (על צד)[5] היתר
22. כנהוג ולא על שום אופן אחר יהי' באיזו אופן שיהי' יצא מאתנו יו'
23. ה' כ"ה א"ר תקמם לפק הגאב"ד נר' ור"י מהנ"מ ורי"ש ואני

No. 120

Community v. Emden et al.

Fols. 116a–119a (there is no fol. 117); Monday 28 February 1780

The sale of the abandoned lot in the Jewish quarter (see no. 100) did not go smoothly. Approximately one year after the sale, the purchasers of the lot, Jacob Emden and Isaac Sinzheim, failed to make an installment on their payments. The community came to the court — on which six judges sat instead of the regular three — to force the purchasers to make payment. In response, Jacob and Isaac argued that the sale should be canceled because the community misled them with respect to the size of the lot. Through their representatives, Jacob and Isaac noted

1. תוספת מעל השורה
2. לפרט קטן
3. צ"ל 'יתנהגו'
4. תוספת מעל השורה
5. תוספת מעל השורה

that even if the court upheld the sale, given that the sale was being contested, the date of purchase should be adjusted from the original date of sale to the date of the present court's decision. This would affect the date of subsequent installments and give Jacob and Isaac more time to make their payments. The community rejected these claims and argued that the dimensions of the lot it had provided were simply estimates and not exact computations. They also noted that Jacob had visited the site before the sale, precisely when it was being measured, and that he must have been aware of this. Moreover, when bids were taken for the lot, the community's representative specifically said that the property was being sold without specific measurements being offered. Jacob and Isaac's agent was said to have acknowledged as much when he responded to another potential purchaser that he was purchasing the lot "as is." To buttress their point, the community revealed that the second highest bidder for the lot, who had offered just one gulden less than what Jacob and Isaac offered, specifically stated that he too was willing to buy the lot "as is." Finally, the community's representative noted that this sale did not benefit the communal leaders personally because the proceeds of the sale went directly to the community chest. He reminded the court that it was its responsibility to protect the interests of the community, particularly because it had ramifications for "orphans and widows."[6] The court upheld the original sale and ordered Jacob Emden and Isaac Sinzheim to make their payment on time.

קטז ע"א

1. ע"ד שבא לפנינו ה"ה התורני כ"ה אנשיל פפאן כ"ץ בהרשאת האלופי' קציני' גובי' יצו ותובע מן
2. הלקוחות שלקחו ההקדש פלאטץ בפני ב"ד אור ליו' ב' טז סיון תקלטית העבר ה"ה הו"ה ג"ץ וג"ה כ"ה
3. יעקב עמדן יצו וה"ה הו"ה ג"ץ כ"ה איצק זינצהיים סג"ל כמו שמבואר במעשה ב"ד ההוקם ע"ז בעצם
4. היום הנ"ל בכן תבע דמי מכירה הנ"ל דהיינו סך שליש מדמי מכירה הנ"ל גם על סך שני שלישי'
5. הנותרי' מדמי מכירה הנ"ל יתנו ח"כ על זמני' מיו' מכירה הנ"ל וכמו שנזכר במעשה ב"ד לה"ה ה
6. התורני כ"ה מאיר מז בהרשאת ה"ה כ"ה יעקב וכ"ה איצק הנ"ל השיב שאמת הוא שקנו בפני ב"ד
7. רק הם רוצים לבטל המקח לפי שלערך חצי שנה קודם מכירה הלך ר' {..} מאיר מז הנ"ל לגובי'

6. Arye Edrei, "Beyt din ke-avihem shel yetomim," *Diné Israel* 19 (1997–98), 5–40, deals with whether the talmudic rule that the court may help orphans in their litigations is an obligation on the court or whether it is a directive for the court to use its judgment and invoke the rule as it sees fit.

8. יצו בשליחות מן ה"ק ג"ע וג"ה כ"ה יעקב עמדין וג"ע כ"ה זעליג הז יצו לקנות הפלאטץ הנ"ל מן הגובי'
9. יצו ולשאול מדת רחבו ועמקו וגם מהותו {ו..} ונתנו לו הגובי' יצו באותו פעם בכתב בהתאספם
10. יחדיו מדת ארכו ורחבו של הפלאטץ וכמו שהציע כהר"מ הנ"ל אותו כתב לפנינו ב"ד ובאשר ש
11. שלא נמצא מדתו כן הן במידת ארכו והן במידת רחבו והיינו בכ"י הנ"ל נכתב שלשי' ושניים שוך
12. איזט פארני דיא ברייט וטענו הלוקחי' שאינו כי אם שלשי' וחצי גם נכתב בכ"י הנ"ל בזה"ל
13. היר נאך גיהטש ווידר גראד עכ"ל ומשמע אחורי העיקום נמצא הרוחב כמו פאר[ני]ן לצד {...}
14. הרחוב שני' ושלשים שוך ובאמת אחורי העיקום{.} אינו רוחב יותר מעשרי' ושמונה שוך ה
15. הראוי לבנין בתי' {ועוד נמצ.} ועוד נמצא כתוב בכ"י הנ"ל בזה"ל דער הינטר פלאטץ איזט
16. ברייט פיהר אונד פונפציג שוך עכ"ל ולשון בני אדם כוונת הינדר פלאטץ הוא לבנות עלי'
17. בית פנימי ובאמת המק' הראוי לבנין בית פנימי אין רחבו מצפון לדרום יותר מן עשרי'
18. ושמונה שוך וכמו שהאריך בזה בטענותיו המבואר בפראטיקאהל המונח אצלינו ובאשר שהקוני'
19. הנ"ל סמכו דעתם {ד} דוקא על כתוב הנ"ל וע"ז דוקא הם הי' קוני' ועכשיו שלא נמצא כן בטל

קטז ע"ב

1. המקח ורוצי' לחזור מהמקח הקדש פלאטץ הנ"ל לגמרי עוד טען הנ"ל (כהר"מ הנ"ל)[1] בהרשאת הנ"ל אף אם לא יזכה בטענותיו
2. והמקח יהי' קיים מ"מ אינו מחויבי' הלוקחי' הנ"ל ליתן הח"כ הנ"ל מיו' מכירה רק מיו' שיצא פסק ב"ד בין
3. הצדדים הנ"ל מאחר שהם (הי')[2] רוצי' לערער על המקח בכן אינו נגמר המקח רק מיו' שיצא פסק ב"ד
4. ביניהם וה"ה כ"ה אנשיל הנ"ל השיב בהרשאת הגובי' הנ"ל אפשר שאם י[מ]ד[ד]נו המצא תמצא פארני
5. רחבו שלשי' ושתיים שוך אך אפי' אם יהי' כדברי הלקוחות כ' יעקב וכ"ה איצק הנ"ל מ"מ הכתב
6. שנכתב בחדר הגובי' נכתב שלא בדיקדוק רק הקירוב גם על מה שנכתב בכתב יד מהגובי'
7. דער הינדר פלאטץ איזט ברייט חמשי' וארבע שוך כוונתם הי' עם הפלאטץ מה שהוא א
8. אחורי בית צום עלי פאנד ועם כל משך הרצועה הנמשכת מצד דרום ברוחב כל הפלאטץ {...}

1. תוספת מעל השורה
2. תוספת מעל השורה

9. {...עם...} עם אחורי עליפאנדין מצד צפון ואותו משך הוא באמת רחב חמשי'{.}
10. וארבע שוך בקירוב כי הפלאטץ אחורי בית עליפאנדין שייך ג"כ להקדש פלאטץ וכמבואר ב
11. בפס"ד שיצא בין המצרנים ובין ה"ה האלופי' גובי' יצו ר"ח מרשון[1] תקלח לפק[2] ויש ראי' לזה שכ' יעקב
12. הי' יודע שכוונתם כן מאחר שהוא הי' ג"כ קודם המכירה הנ"ל על ההקדש פלאטץ וזה הוא דבר
13. הנראה לעינים שאם לא הי' יחשב משך הרצועה הנ"ל עם אחורי עליפאנדין נחסר כמעט ה
14. החצר מחמשי' וארבע שוך הנ"ל והוא דבר הנראה כרגע בחוש הראי' וא"כ למה הי' לוקח אתו אלא
15. וודאי שגם כ' יעקב ידע {...} שכוונתו בכתב יד מהגובי' יצו הי' באותן חמשי'
16. וארבע שוך בצירוף אחורי עלעפאנט וסבר וקיבל הכל גם כ' יעקב הנ"ל הי' פעם אחת
17. קודם המכירה על הקדש פלאטץ באסיפת שארי גובי' יצו כשמדדו אותו ומסתמא ג"כ הי' ידע
18. איכות ואופן המידה ואפ"ה הי' לוקח אותו אח"כ אכן כל הנ"ל יגענו רק לרווחא במילתא
19. אבל בלא"ה עיקר טענותם שאינם משגיחם כלל על כתב יד שנכתב בחדר הגובי'
20. [ומ]ה שנעשה יותר מחצי שנה קודם {שטענו} שנעשה מכירה בב"ד באשר שכשנמכר ע"י ב"ד
21. שולחי' להב"ד יצו מסתמא שימכרו הפלאטץ הנ"ל ולא הי' מזכירים שם המדה כלל {וגם כמה לוקחים}
22. {שהי' שם בשעת מכירה לקנותו} וכן הי' באמת נמכר בב"ד סתם הקדש פלאטץ בלי {שום}
23. הזכרת שום מידה וגם כמה לוקחי' שהי' שם בשעת מכירה לקנותו ופסקו דמים הי' שואלי'
24. להב"ד המדה והב"ד הי' {א..ר} אומר בפירוש זיא פר קויפן אויף קיין מדה וגם ה"ה כ' דוד הע[כט]

אין דף קיז

קיח ע"א

1. שמש של האלופי' גובי' יצו שהי' שליח מן כ' יעקב וכה"א[3] הנ"ל ליקח הפלטץ
2. הנ"ל אצל הב"ד היה נשאל מן אחד שהיה ג"כ רוצה לקנות הפלאטץ
3. הנ"ל כמה וכמה מידות ארכו ורחבו והשיב כ' דוד הנ"ל ער
4. ווירט פר קויפט כמות שהוא וכיון שהוא היה שליח של הקוני' כ'
5. יעקב וכה"א ווינר הנ"ל בוודאי הם קוני' ג"כ הפלאטץ כמות שהוא
6. ולא היה סומכי' על כתב יד שנכתב בחדר הגובי' גם במעשה

---

1. צ"ל 'מרחשון'
2. ר' לעיל, מס' 101.
3. וכבוד הרב איצק

7. ב״ד לא נזכר כלל שום מדה הן מדת ארכו ורחבו של הפלאטץ הנ״ל
8. מכל הנ״ל מבואר שגם הקוני׳ כ׳ יעקב וכה״א הנ״ל לא סמכו על
9. כתב של חדר הגובי׳ רק ליקח הפלאטץ כמות שהוא ועכ״פ כיון
10. שהמכירה שנעשה בב״ד לא היה מזכירן שם המדה אדרבה
11. הב״ד אומר בפי׳ דיא פר קויפין אויף קיין מדה וע״ז כל הלוקחי׳
12. שהיה שם באותו פעם הי׳ פוסקי׳ דמי המקח בכן מחויבים כ׳
13. יעקב וכה׳ איצק הנ״ל שהי׳ לוקחי׳ באותו פעם בב״ד ע״י
14. שלוחי׳ כ׳ דוד הנ״ל ג״כ לקיים המקח ההקדש פלאטץ
15. כמות שהוא ובפרט שהיה שם לוקח אחד שהיה פסק רק
16. זהוב אחד פחות ממה שפסק כה׳ יעקב {כ} וכה׳ איצק הנ״ל
17. בלי שום ידיעה מכתב הנ״ל ורצה לקנותו בסתם כמות שהוא א״כ
18. גם קנין של הלוקחי׳ כ׳ יעקב וכה׳ איצק הנ״ל הוא ג״כ בזה האופן
19. וממילא כיון שהמקח קיים מחויבים ג״כ הלוקחי׳ להעמיד זמן ששה
20. ח״כ של טערמינין מיו׳ שרצה הגובי׳ למסור להם מעשה ב״ד
21. וכפי מאמרם הי׳ ביו׳ יט׳ סיון תקלט[ל] העבר עוד הוסיף כ׳
22. אנשיל הנ״ל וטען מאחר שהמשפט הנ״ל אינו מגיע להאלופי׳
23. גובי׳ יצו בעצמם רק הוא מגיע לכלל קהלתינו יע״א בכן מוטל

קיח ע״ב

1. ב״ה
2. על הב״ד יצו לחפש כל זכיות ולטעון לטובת קהלתינו יע״א שהוא נוגע
3. ליתומי׳ ואלמונות וה״ה ג״ה כ׳ יעקב הנ״ל וג״ע כ׳ איצק זינצהיים בעצמם
4. השיבו על טענות הראשונות של כ׳ אנשיל הנ״ל שמה {שנזק} שנזכר
5. בתוך כתב יד של הגובי׳ הינדר פלאטץ נקרא כל מה שראוי׳
6. לבנות עליו בתים וכמו שהאריכו בהוכחות {לפנ.נו} לפנינו בקונטרס
7. הטענות ומה שטען כ״ה אנשיל הנ״ל שכ׳ יעקב הנ״ל הי׳ ג״כ
8. על הפלאטץ בהתאספי׳ שארי אלופי׳ גובי׳ יצו בשעה שהי׳
9. עוסקי׳ במדידה השיב כ׳ יעקב הנ״ל שלא היה משגיח כלל על מה
10. שהיה עוסקי׳ גם לא היה כותבי׳ שם מזה באותו פעם ועל מה
11. שטען שהב״ד לא היה מזכירן בשעת מכירה שום מדה אדרבה
12. הם הי׳ אומרי׳ להלוקחי׳ שהיה {שואילן} שואלין להם המדה והשיבו דיא
13. פר קויפין אויף קיין מדה ע״ז השיבו כ״ה יעקב וכ׳ איצק הנ״ל
14. בעצמם בוודאי אם שאר אנשי׳ הי׳ לוקחי׳ לא היה יכולי׳ לערער
15. אבל הם הי׳ יודעים מהכתב של הגובי׳ ועלי׳ הי׳ סומכין ובשבלי[1]
16. זה לא היה שואלים על המדה אצל הב״ד ובאשר שלא מצאו המדה
17. שנזכר בכתב של הגובי׳ בכן המקח שלהם הוא בטל ואולי אם יופסק
18. מב״ד שהמקח קיים כבר טענו למעלה כיון שלא הי׳ {מקובלי׳} מקבלי׳

1. צ״ל ׳ובשביל׳

19. המעשה ב"ד מפני {שתעדם} (שדעדם)[1] היה שאין מחויבים לקיים המקח
20. בכן אין החיוב שלהם מן פרעון המקח חל כלל עד לאחר שיצא
21. מפי ב"ד לקיים המקח ואינו מחויבים להעמיד זמן ח"כ של טערמינין
22. רק מיו' שיצא פסק דין והאריכו עוד הצדדי' הנ"ל בטענותיהם
23. ובתשובתיהם כמבואר הכל בקונטרס הטענות המונח {לפני-נו} (לפנינו)[2]
24. ובאשר שהצדדי' הנ"ל חתמו עצמם בתוקף קומפרמיס בח"ח
25. ובקנס סך מסויים דחצי לשררה ירה[3] וחצי להקדש לאשר ולקיים

קיט ע"א

1. כל מה שיצאו {מאותונו} מאתונו[4] בכן נזדקקנו להם ומצאנו שהקנין של המעשה
2. ב"ד מההקדש פלאטץ הנ"ל הנעשה אור ליו' ב' טז' סיון תקלט נשאר
3. בתוקפו בכל האופני' ותנאי' המבוארי' שם ומחויבי' הלקוחות ג"ה [כ']
4. יעקב הנ"ל וגם כ"ה איצק הנ"ל לקיים הקנין ההוא וגם התשלומין
5. יהי' בכל האופנים המבוארי' שם גם מצאנו שהתחייבות שליש פרעון
6. של דמי מכירה היא מיו' יט' סיון העבר שבאותו יום הי' הגובים
7. רוצים ליתן להם המעשה ב"ד וגם מחויבים הלקוחות הנ"ל
8. להעמיד זמן של ששה ח"כ משני שלישי' {הנותר} הנותרי' מדמי מכירה
9. מזמן הנ"ל לשלם לזמני' המבוארי' שם יצא {מאותונו} (מאתנו)[5] יו' ב' ד"ב א"ר
10. תקמם לפק רנמ[6] וריש[7] וראט[8] ורזט[9] ורמש[10] ואני

No. 121

Bunla, a maidservant v. Estate of Schönle, widow of Jacob Menz

Fols. 119b–121a; Tuesday evening, 7 March 1780

Two individuals, named here only as Bunla and Nathan, approached the court through their representative and claimed that they were owed funds and goods by the late Schönle, widow of Jacob Menz. Bunla, who served as Schönle's maidservant,

---

1. תוספת מעל השורה; צ"ל 'שדעתם'.
2. תוספת מעל השורה
3. ירום הודו
4. ר"ל 'מאתנו'
5. תוספת מעל השורה
6. רב נתן מז
7. ורב יעקב שמש
8. ורב אברהם טריר
9. ורב זלמן טראך
10. ורב מאיר שיף

claimed back wages, expenses, and a number of items of clothing that she said Schönle had promised her in a deathbed will. Nathan claimed a monetary payment of 50 guldens. His relationship to the deceased is not made clear.

The heirs of the estate disputed the validity of the will and suggested that it was written when Schönle was not mentally competent. They admitted that Schönle always noted her payments to her maidservant in her business diary and that no payments had been registered since the previous summer. However, they disputed the amount of wages owed as well as Bunla's claims for reimbursement of living expenses.

During her lifetime, Schönle did needlework for others. Her heirs claimed that certain items she had been working on were missing and implied that Bunla had taken them. Bunla denied knowing anything about what had happened to these items, although she did admit to holding some items of Bunla's own clothing. For his part, Nathan admitted to holding a mirror that belonged to Schönle as collateral against what he believed he was owed. The two sides agreed to accept a court-imposed compromise. After examining the will and questioning the witnesses who had signed it, the court determined it to be valid. It awarded the plaintiffs most of the funds that they claimed as well as items of clothing for Bunla as mentioned in the will. The validation of the will resulted in Schönle's niece's husband approaching the court with a claim for his wife.

קיט ע"ב

1. ב"ה
2. ע"ד שבא לפנינו התורני כה' משה אויך בהרשאת משרתת מ' בונלה
3. שהית' משרתת אצל האשה המונחת מ' שינלה אל' כה' יעקל
4. מענץ ובהרשאת הבחור כה' נתן ותבע את כל היורשים
5. של בעלהי[1] והציע לפנינו צוואת שכ"מ מן האשה ז"ל הנ"ל ושם
6. נאמר בזה"ל משרתת בינלה זול (מן)[2] מיין שבת מלבוש נעבשט
7. וואוכין מלבושי' געבין אונד נון זהו' ש"ב[3] נתן זול מן
8. נ' זהו' געבין בכן תבע כהר"מ[4] הנ"ל בהרשא הנ"ל מן
9. היורשי' של האלמנה ז"ל הנ"ל לקיים הצוואה וה"ה התורני
10. כה' אנשיל פפאן בהרשאת ובמעמד היורשי' מן האשה ז"ל
11. הנ"ל השיב שבצוואה הנ"ל אינה מבואר שנעשה בדעת
12. צלולה ומיושבת בכן אינו כלום ואף א"ת שאינה צריכה
13. להיות כתוב בתוך הצוואה כך מ"מ צריכה להיות בשעת

1. השווה שורות 9 ו-10
2. תוספת מעל השורה
3. אולי 'שאר בשרה'
4. כבוד הרב משה

14. ציווה בדעת צלולה ומי יימר {שהי'ת'} שהית' בדעת בעת
15. הצוואה גם מי יימר שהיא עשת' מאחר שהיא לא כתבה רק
16. יטכה טאקטר הי' כתבה ואפשר החתימה כה"ג אינה ממנה
17. רק יטכה הנ"ל הי' חותמה והיא הית' גוסס והאריך בטענותי'
18. עוד שבמתנת שכמ'[1] במקצת בעי קנין ובלא קנין אינה מועיל {כלום}
19. כלום עוד תבע כהר"מ הנ"ל בהרשאת משרתת הנ"ל שכירת {...}
20. שלה מן זמן קיץ העבר שלא שילמה {ל.} לה האשה ז"ל הנ"ל שהוא שלשה רט
21. שכירת קונפונטציאהנש רט נאכט געלט וגם ש[ו]א אונד העמד וה"ה
22. כה' יעסל כהן בהרשאת ובמעמד שאר היורשי' השיב (שהאמת)[2] שנמצא כתוב
23. בפנקס של האשה ז"ל הנ"ל הפרעון מדמי שכירת {המשרש}
24. המשרתת הנ"ל על כל ז[מ]ני' שהי' אצלה רק מזמן קיץ העבר עדיין
25. לא נזכר פירען כלום בפנקס שלה אבל מ"מ אינו נזכר בתוכה כמה

קך ע"א

1. ב"ה
2. הי' שכירת ומן נאכט געלט לא מוזכר כלום בכן אין מחויבי' כלל לשלם נאכט
3. געלט ודמי שכירת יכירו הב"ד כמה מגיע לה הואיל שבני הבית שלה
4. הי' מועטי' עוד תבע כהר"מ הנ"ל שכירת וגם מזונות על זמן החורף
5. הלז באשר שמשרתת הנ"ל נשאר בבית של האשה ז"ל הנ"ל אחר
6. מיתת' חמשה שבועות והוצאה משלה לצרך מזונות עד לאח"כ
7. ששלחו היורשי' שמש קהל אצלה אונד איהר דיא {קא.ט} קאשט אויף
8. זאגין גלאזט באופן שיכרו הב"ד כמה יגיע לה רק המה מניחי'
9. אותה בבית החורף שתשמר העזבון שהוא בתוך הבית שני שטעג הויך
10. בכן תובע דמי שכירות הנ"ל מן הזמן חורף הלז ועוד יכירו הב"ד כמה מגיע לה
11. מחמת דמי מזונות של הזמן חורף הלז וכ"ה יעסל (הנ"ל)[3] בהרשאת הנ"ל השיב שאחר כלות
12. השלשי' לאחר מיתת האשה הנ"ל אמרו היורשי' והזהירו אותה לצאת
13. מן הבית הנ"ל ומה שיופסק לה ע"פ ב"ד רוצה לשלם והיא לא יצאה
14. מן הבית עד שיגיד לה ע"פ שמש הקהל שתצא מן הבית ואעפ"כ
15. עדיין היא בתוכה עוד תבע כה' אנשיל הנ"ל והציע רשימה
16. מן מטלטלין ומלבושי' ותבע לפי דברי כ' יוקב בינגא שדר באותה
17. בית שהי' דר בה האשה ז"ל שמטלטלין צריכה להיות תחת {יד.} ידה
18. ואיזה מלבושי' מה שנזכר בתוכה הלביש המשרתת הנ"ל וכ' משה הנ"ל
19. השיב בהרשאת על איזה מהם שהיא לא ידעה כלום ובאם מחפש אחריהם
20. ימצא עדיין ושהיא אינו שומר עלי' ועל קצתם הודה שעדיין בעין בידה
21. ועל גדול שפיגל שנרשם ברשימה הנ"ל השיב כהר"מ הנ"ל בהרשאת כ' נתן
22. הנ"ל ששייך לו שפיגל הנ"ל ש[ע]קל להאשה מ' {שינל.} שינלה ז"ל הנ"ל {.וד}

---

1. שכיב מרע
2. תוספת מעל השורה
3. תוספת מעל השורה

23. עוד תבע כה″א הנ″ל שנשאר עדיין לאחר מיתת האשה ז″ל הנ″ל
24. {מלא.ת} מלאכת נשי' משל אחרי' שהית' (עשה)[1] כשהיא בחיי' חיותה ואותן דברים
25. הית' מונחת אין שענקלכה {און} (זה)[2] מפתח הית' ביד המשרתת הנ″ל
26. ולאחר שבעה ימים ממיתתה {נתנ.} נתנה המשרתת הנ″ל כל מה
27. שהית' בו [מ]ש[ל] אחרת לאשת כ' יוסף שלאס בת אחי של האשה
28. ז″ל הנ″ל {לח.ו.} לחזור לכל אחד מה ששייך לו

קך ע″ב

1. ב″ה
2. ועכשיו אומרות אשת כ' יוסף הנ″ל שחסר מן המלאכת נשי' והיינו לפי
3. דבריו [ל]אשה אחת מן פרידבורג נאבד {להּ} לה מיטשכה מוזהב
4. מיט שפיצץ ואשת כ' ליב ש″ש[3] ג″כ איין מיטשכה פון אנדרי צייג
5. ועוד איין גאלדנר לא פפון וועלכר פיהלט וכה' משה הנ″ל השיב
6. שמעולם לא הניחה האשה ז″ל מלאכת נשי' בתוך השענקלכה
7. הנ″ל רק היא הית' מניחה אותם כל לילה בתוך חדר שלה
8. שהית' ישינה ולאחר מיתתה הוסגר החדר הלז ולאח″כ כשהאחרי'
9. הי' תובעי' את שלהם הולכת אשת כ' יוסף הנ″ל עם שאר
10. היורשי' ור' אנשיל הנ″ל ליטול אותה ורוצם למסור ולשלוח למשרתת
11. הנ″ל לחזור וליתן כל אחד מה שמגיע לה והשיבו המשרתת שאינו
12. רוצה בכן לא ידעה מכלום והאריכו הצדדי' הנ″ל בטענותי'
13. על כל פרט ופרט כמבואר באריכות בק″ה המונח לפנינו ואחרי
14. שהצדדי' הנ″ל חתמו עצמם בתחילה בתוקף קומפרמיס בח″ח
15. ובקנס סך מסויים לאשר ולקיים את אשר יצא {מאתנו} מאתנו
16. ואח″כ נתנו עינהם עלינו ב″ד לפשר ולבצע בינהם וקיבלו
17. עליהם לאשר ולקיים ג″כ בתוקף קומפרמיס כנ″ל נזדקקנו
18. להם ומצאנו על דרך פשר דבר שמחמת שכירות נאכט געלט שוא העמד מזמן
19. קיץ העבר ומזמן חורף הלז שכירות ודמי מזונות יותן מעזבון האשה מ' שינלה ז″ל
20. הנ″ל למשרתת שלה מ' בונלה הנ″ל סך שנים עשר זהו' ובזה פטורים היורשי'
21. מחמת תביעות שכירות (ודמי מזונות)[4] הנ″ל ומחמת המתנות שנזכר בצוואה (הנ″ל) {...למשרתת...מלבוש וגם}[5]
22. {מלבושי' של .. חול} הנ″ל אחר שדקדקנו בצוואה ולשון כתיבת וחתימת העדים ואחר שחקרנו
23. ודרשנו את פי העדים החתומים בצוואה הנ″ל מצאנו דרך פשר שיקוים {...לה
24. מעזבון הנ″ל סך שלשים וחמשה} ויותן למשרתת הנ″ל המלבושי' שנזכר בצוואה

---

1. תוספת מעל השורה
2. תוספת מעל השורה
3. שווארצשילד
4. תוספת מעל השורה
5. תוספת מעל השורה

25. שבת מלבוש וגם מלבושי' של חול אך מדמי [חמש]י' זהו' הנזכר ינוכה סך חמשה

קכא ע"א

1. ב"ה
2. עשר זהו' ויותן לה מעזבן הנ"ל סך שלשי' וחמשה זהו' נגד זה
3. פטורה ומסולקת המשרתת הנ"ל מכל תביעות היורשי' הנ"ל
4. ואין עלי' מן היורשי' שום {תביע.}תביעה רק אותן מטלטלין
5. שנזכר ברשימה שהודית שיש עדיין בעין תחת ידה תחזיר
6. ליורשי' הנ"ל מחמת {ו}סך חמשי' זהו' מתנה שצוה ליתן לכה' נתן
7. הנ"ל ינוכה שבעה זהו' ויותן לו מעזבון הנ"ל רק ארבעי' ושלשה זהו'
8. ובזה יחזור כ' נתן הנ"ל שפיגל הנ"ל לעצמו ופטור מן תביעות היורשי'
9. הנ"ל על זה והנה אחרי שהצדדי' הנ"ל נתנו עינהם עלינו ב"ד לפשר
10. בינ[י]הם טוען כ' יוסף שלאס ותבע מן שאר היורשי' באם שיכרו הב"ד
11. שהצוואה הנ"ל יהי' {בתוקפו} בתקפו גם הוא תבע מה שנזכר בצוואה
12. שיתן לאשתו מ' יטלה והיינו כסף ביגל טעש וגם זהוב קעהט אם ימצא
13. בעזבון עדיין ושארי יורשים השיבו שגם בזה נתנו {על} עיניהם
14. עלינו לפשר ביניהם {ו}ולאחר שנזדקקנו גם בזה מצאנו ע"פ פשר דבר
15. שהכסף ביגל טעש יותן להאשה מ' יטלה אשת כה' יוסף שלאס הנ"ל
16. וישימו דמי שווים מ[ל]ביגלי[1] טעש הנ"ל וחלק שמינית מדמי שווי' תחזור
17. ותתן האשה מ' יטלה הנ"ל לעזבון במזו(מ)[2]נמים הנ"ל להוריש ולחלוק בו
18. כל היורשי' והיא גם היא תטול בזה חלק ירושתה מה שתגיע לה
19. וגם {הז הזהוב} הזהוב קעט הנ"ל אם המצא תמצא עדיין בעזבון
20. הנ"ל יותן לה ג"כ על אופן הנ"ל שתחזיר ותתן חלק שמינית מדמי
21. {שווי'} שווים בעזבון הנ"ל לירושת כל היורשי' ואף היא בכלל יצא
22. מאתנו אור ליו' ד' ב' דר"ח אדר שני תקמם לפק רנ"מ ורמ"ש ואני

No. 122

Kann v. Feitel of Kassel

Fols. 121b–122a; Tuesday 11 April 1780

In the spring of 1779, Isaac Kann sent Feitel of Kassel jewelry on consignment for sale to a local non-Jewish official. Unable to sell all of the items, Feitel returned a precious red coral piece to Isaac. Feitel claimed to have returned the piece in

---

1. לא ברור אם הסופר רצה למחוק את הלמד הראשונה
2. תוספת מעל השורה

perfect condition, but Isaac claimed that the piece was damaged when he received it. Since Isaac found no signs of breakage in the packaging in which it was shipped, he assumed the piece had been damaged in Feitel's possession and that Feitel bore responsibility for it. This led Isaac to withhold payment of 300 reichstalers from Feitel in another matter and prompted Feitel to approach the court and claim that Isaac had no right to deny him payment. The court examined both Isaac's and Feitel's testimony regarding the coral piece as well as the correspondence between them. It ordered Feitel to take an oath that he was unaware of any damage to the coral piece while it was in his possession. If he did so, he would be absolved of all claims and Isaac would be obliged to pay Feitel what he owed him.

A postscript notes that two days after the decision, Rabbi Gundersheim accompanied Feitel to the synagogue where he was to take his oath. He spoke to Feitel and convinced him to allow Rabbi Nathan Maas to help him and Isaac work out a compromise. They proceeded to Maas's home where a settlement was reached between the two sides according to which Feitel would pay Isaac 140 guldens. Then Isaac would pay Feitel what he was due.

קכא ע״ב

1. ע״ד שבא לפנינו ה״ה הו״ה פו״מ כ״ה פייטל מן ק״ק קאסיל יע״א ותבע מן ה״ה (הו״ה)[1] גץ[2]
2. כה איצק בכ״ה ליב קן יצו סך שלשה מאות רט שחייב לו כ״ה איצק הנ״ל ומחזיק עצמו
3. בהם על דבר חפצים ששלח לו ר׳ אציק הנ״ל לאחר יריד פסח תקלט העבר על פ״ע[3]
4. איזה גלאנטרי שטוקר להראותן ולימכר להשררה שחפץ ליקח חפצים חשובי׳ ואחת מהם
5. הי׳ בלוטקרעלרן בוים ואחר {שלא} שלא הי׳ יכול למוכרם שלח לו כה פייטל הנ״ל לחזרה על פ״ע
6. ולאח״כ כתב לו כ״ה איצק הנ״ל שקיבל החפצי׳ אצל הקרעללין בום מצא שהי׳ שבור ומש״כ
7. הי׳ מחזיק עצמו בשלשה מאות ר״ט שהעלה בכתבו דמי שווי׳ כ״כ בשעה ששלח לו וטוען
8. כ״ה פייטל הנ״ל שהוא בעצמו פתח השובלאט עם חפצי׳ הנ״ל בשעה שקיבל מן פ״ע
9. ולא מצא שברי׳ בתוך השובלאט וכל זמן שהי׳ ברשותו הי׳ תמיד תחת ידו וכן בשעה
10. שהחזירה הי׳ ג״כ בהשגחותו בכן הוא בעצמו אינו יודע באיזה אופן הוא נשבר
11. רק הוא החזיר כמו שקיבל ואפשר בשעה שנשלח לו הי׳ שבור ולא הי׳ משגיח בו וה״ה
12. התורני כ״ה משה אויך בהרשאות הו״ה ג״ץ כ״ה איצק הנ״ל וגם הוא בעצמו השיב
13. שקודם ששלח לו חפצי׳ הנ״ל דיבר עמו כאן שרוצה לשלוח לו החפצי׳ ואומר
14. לו כ״ה פייטל הנ״ל שישלח לו ובשעה ששלח לו הי׳ הוא בעצמו מסדר החפצי׳ וכרך
15. אותן בעצמו והי׳ שלם כראוי ומהיכי תיתי שישלח לו חפצי׳ הנשברי׳ למכור להשררה
16. יר״ה ובשעה שקיבל אותו לחזרה הי׳ הוא בעצמו פתח השובלאט ומצא שהי׳

---

1. תוספת מעל השורה
2. גבאי צדקה
3. לא ברור מה כוונת הראשי תבות. כנראה משהו שקשור לשליח או דואר. אולי 'Postamt'.

17. נשבר הקרעללין בוים וג"כ לא שברי' מונחי' בתוכה בכן הקילקול נעשה ברשותו
18. ואם לא על ידו אפשר ע"י אנשי ביתו בכן אין עליו לקבל ההפסד רק כ"ה
19. פייטל הנ"ל שנעשה הקילקול ברשותו עליו לסבול ההפסד חלק בלהקרעללין בוים
20. בשווי' שהעלה לו כה"א הנ"ל בעד סך שלשה מאות רט וכמו שהאריך בכמה אגרת
21. ששלח לו שהציע לפנינו ההעתקי' והאריכו בטענותיהם כמבואר בק"ה
22. המונח לפנינו ובאשר שחתמו הצדדי' הנ"ל עצמם בתוקף קומפרמיס
23. בח"ח ובקנסך[1] מסויים לאשר ולקיים כפי שיצא מאתנו נזדקקנו להם

קכב ע"א

1. ואחר שחקרנו היטיב בטענותיהם וגם באגרת שחלפו ביניהם מצאנו
2. שכ"ה פייטל הנ"ל ישבע על ד"ה וע"ד ב"ד בלי עו"מ ובלי שום הוראות היתר
3. שבעולם שכדבריו כן הוא שאינו יודע שנשבר הקרעללין בוים הנ"ל כל
4. זמן שהי' ברשותו הן ע"י עצמו והן ע"י אשתו ובניו ושאר בניביתו[2] וגם
5. ישבע שלא מצא השברי' מן הקרעללין בוים שנשבר הן בשעת אויז פא[רף]
6. או לאח"כ ושאינם ברשותו מן השברי' הנ"ל ולאחר שישבע כ"ה פייטל הנ"ל
7. כנ"ל מחויב כ"ה איצק הנ"ל לשלם לכ"ה פייטל הנ"ל סך שלשה מאות רט
8. הנ"ל יצא מאתנו יו' גימל ויו ניסן תק"מ רנ"מ ורמ"ש ואני
9. ביו' ה' ח ניסן (בערב לאחר יציאת מבה"כ)[3] הלכתי עם ר פייטל הנ"ל והמורשא ר משה אויך
10. והשמש ר' דוד ש"ש לבה"כ להשביע כה"פ הנ"ל ולאחר שדברתי
11. אליו בדברי רצוי' לפשר ביניהם התרצו שני הצדדי' שהדיין
12. רנ"מ [י]פשר ביניהם ויצאנו מבה"כ לבית רנ"מ הנ"ל ותקעו כפם לידו
13. לקיים הפשר ועשה פשר שכה[4] פייטל הנ"ל ישלם בההפסד סך
14. מאה וארבעי' זהו' וקרעללין בוים יוחזר לכה"א הנ"ל והמותרות מן סך
15. שלשה מאות רט ישלם לו כה"א הנ"ל

No. 123

Fol. 122b; undated

Five matchmakers argued over the fees due to each of them for arranging the marriage of the son of Zanvil Luria and the daughter of the late Herz Adler Katz. Among the disputants with conflicting claims were a father and son. The court

---

1. צ"ל 'ובקנס סך'
2. בני ביתו
3. תוספת מעל לשורה
4. שכבוד הרב

arranged a compromise between the parties and dictated how much each would receive.

קכב ע״ב

1. ב״ה
2. בהשידוך שנעשה שנתקשר בן של כ״ה זנוויל לורי׳ עם בת המנוח כהירץ[1] אדליר כץ ז״ל
3. התעצמו {כמה} שדכני׳ המבואר לפנינו ב״ד מחמת שכר שדכנות ועשינו פשר ביניהם
4. שכ״ה יוזפא מז יהי׳ לו שלשה זהו׳ וכ״ה יוזפא הירש בן ר יוקל מז שמונה זהו׳ ואבי׳
5. ר יוקל מז הנ״ל א זהוב ולהאשה מ׳ בריינלה אשת יודא שמואל ווירמש שבעה זהו׳ וכ״ה יוקב
6. שוויצר א זהוב אני ור״מ פאס[2] ורליזר[3] וואלה

No. 124

Fol. 123a; Sunday evening, 10 December 1780

Neta Wezlar owned a seat in the lower men's section of the synagogue. The non-Jewish authorities ordered that Wezlar's landed property, including the seat in the synagogue, be given to his wife, Rechle (see nos. 111, 112). Rechle subsequently sold the seat to Isaac Sinzheim for 900 guldens without the open bidding that was common in other sales of seats in the synagogue.

קכג ע״א

1. ב״ה
2. מקו׳ שלם בע״א (התחתונה)[4] שעומד עליו כעת ה״ה כ׳ זלמן בפו״מ כ״ה יודא שוסטר כץ שהי׳ שייך
3. לה״ה גץ[5] כ״ה נטע וועצלר ולאח״כ ע״י משפט פיסוטאציאהנש קומיסיאהן מאדונינו הקיסר
4. יר״ה בוועצלר נחלט כל הקרקעות לאשתו מ׳ רעכלה כמבואר מתוך כתב ראי׳ שיש ביד האשה
5. הנ״ל ע״ז אותו מקו׳ שלם הנ״ל מכרה האשה מ׳ רעכלה הנ״ל בפנינו ב״ד בלי הכרזה
6. לההי[6] גץ כ״ה איצק זינצהיים בעד תשעה מאות זהו׳ לשלם כפי תיקון הקהלה פה
7. נעשה אור ליו׳ ב׳ יג כסליו תקמ״א רנ״מ רמ״ש ואני

---

1. כבוד הירץ
2. = הרב מענדלי זאמשט (ר׳ ספר הזכרונות, תמה ע״א [שנת תקע״ה]).
3. ורב ליזר
4. תוספת מעל השורה
5. גבאי צדקה
6. להרב החכם

No. 125

Fol. 123a; Sunday evening, 17 December 1780

The record of the sale, by the community, of half a seat and the accompanying stand in the lower men's section of the synagogue to Moses Kassel for 420 guldens. The record notes that the other half of the seat was owned by the heirs of the late David Rapp. The seat was sold after the customary period of bidding.

קכג ע״א

8. חצי מקו׳ שלם בע״א התחתונה אשר (הי׳)[1] עומד עלי׳ פו״מ כ״ה זוסיל קולפא שהי׳ שייך
9. להאלופי׳ קציני׳ גובי׳ יצו אשר החצי׳ שניי׳ שייך ליתמי המנוח מה׳ דוד ראפף זצ״ל
10. והיינו המקו׳ עם השטענדר מלבד המקו׳ קטן הנעשה מאחורי שטענדר עם החריות[2]
11. השייכי׳ לזה ששייך לאנשי׳ אחרי׳ אותו חצי מקו׳ והשטענדר ששייך להגובי׳ יצו נמכר
12. בפני ב״ד לאחר הכרזה כנהוג לה״ה כ׳ משה בכ״ה בענדיט קאסיל סג״ל בעד סך
13. ארבע מאות ועשרי׳ זהו׳ לשלם כפי נ[ו]הג הקהלה פה אור ליו׳ ב׳ ך כסליו תקמ״א
14. רנ״מ ורמ״ש ואני

No. 126

Hammel v. Sichel

Fol. 123b; Tuesday evening, 19 December 1780

The guardians of the heirs of the late Isaac Hammel, through their representative, sued Yosle Sichel for back rent on property owned by the estate. Yosle had signed an agreement with the estate in 1773 to lease half a house for three years. Both sides agreed in writing that the lease would automatically be renewed at the end of three years, unless one of the parties expressly informed the other otherwise three months before the expiry date of the contract. Yosle continued to live in the house until late 1780. The estate claimed that Yosle's failure to notify them of his intentions to leave when the lease came up for renewal in 1779 meant that the contract had automatically been renewed for another three year period and that Yosle remained responsible for rent payments until 1782. The estate also maintained that Yosle was not permitted to sublet the space and that he was responsible for making some repairs. Through his representative Yosle countered that the agreement from 1773

---

1. תוספת מעל השורה
2. ר׳ שבת נ ע״א

only provided for one extension — not ongoing extensions every three years. He claimed that in 1779 the space had been shown to potential tenants, demonstrating that the guardians knew that the lease would not be renewed automatically. Yosle maintained that he was only responsible to pay rent for the period during which he lived in the house, no more. Moreover, he said that he had informed one of the guardians and one of the beneficiaries that he intended to leave the house once his own house was completed. The guardians responded that Yosle was lying and that he had twice told them that he intended to remain in the house at least until 1781. The parties asked the court to impose a compromise, which it did. The court required Yosle to pay the estate 25 reichstalers and make the repairs that had been requested of him. This done, he was free of further obligations.

קכג ע״ב

1. ע״ד שבא לפנינו ה״ה התורני כ״ה משה אויך בהרשאת האפטרופסי׳ דיתמי המנוח {כ׳ יצ
2. כ׳} איצק ב״כ מיכל הא[מ]יל ז״ל הו״ה האלוף והקצין כ״ה ליב אופנהיים יצו והו״ה כ׳ שלומה האמיל
3. סג״ל ותבע מן ה״ה כ׳ יוזלה זיכל ששכר החצי בית השייכי׳ ליתמי הנ״ל בר״ח סיון תקלג על שלשה שני׳
4. והוקמו שכירות הבית ע״ז בחתימות יד האפטרופס הנ״ל כ׳ שלמה האמיל הנ״ל ובתוכה מפורש
5. שרביעית שנה קודם כלות שלשה שני׳ מחויבי׳ להודיעם זה את זה באם אחד מהם אינו רוצה
6. להחזיק עד שכירות הנ״ל ובאם לא ידיעו נשאר השכירות בתקפו עוד שלשה שני׳ אחרי׳
7. ובשנת תקלויו כאשר כלו שלשה שני׳ נשאר כ׳ יוזלה הנ״ל בבית ולא תחדש כתב שכירות
8. הבית הנ״ל וגם לא נתן ח״כ רק נשאר בבית ודר בו עד חצי כסליו העבר שנת תקמ״א שפינה
9. הבית וטוען כ״ה משה הנ״ל באשר שבשנת תקל״ט חזרו ועברו שלשה שני משנת תקלויו ונשאר כ״י הנ״ל
10. מחויב להחזיק שכירות עוד שלשה שני׳ כימי שכירות הראשוני׳ והיינו עד סיון תקמב הבע״ל בכן מחויב
11. לשלם עוד דמי שכירות משנה וחצי עד חצי סיון תקמב הבע״ל ובכל זה לא יהי׳ רשות לכ׳ יוזלה הנ״ל
12. להשכירו לאחרים והאריך בזה בטענותי׳ עוד תבע שכ״י הנ״ל מחויב ללבן שני חדרי׳ כנז[כר]
13. בשכירות הנ״ל והתורני כ״ה בענדט הענא בהרשאת הו״ה כ׳ יוזל זיכל השיב שמה (שנזכר)[2] בכתב {ב} שכירו׳
14. שמחויב להודיע רביעית שנה מקודם ובאם לא נשאר השכירות עוד בתקפו על ג׳ שני׳ הוא

1. כבוד יוזלה
2. תוספת מעל השורה

15. רק על שלשה שני׳ והיינו עד שנת תקל ויו אבל לא יותר בכן נתבטל התוקף השכירות הבית
16. משנת תקלויו והלאה ומחויב לשלם רק המשך זמן שדר בו באשר שאיזה פעמי׳ אמר כ׳ יוזל הנ״ל
17. לכ׳ שלמה ויתום כ׳ משה בעצמו באם שנגמר הבנין בית חדש שלו רוצה לפנות את החצי
18. בית הנ״ל בכן כבר הודיע להם שיפנה (את)[1] הבית ועוד טען שכ״י הי׳ מראה לו מקו׳ לשכור חצי
19. הבית למאיר הענא כבר לפני איזה חדשי׳ וגם הי׳ מראה לו מקו׳ לשכור הבית לכ׳ שמואל
20. שוסטר[2] ונראה בעליל שהודיע לו שאין רוצה (לדור)[3] עוד בחצי בית הנ״ל וכ״ה משה השיב ע״ז
21. בהרשאת הנ״ל ששקר הוא אך להיפוך שבפירוש אמר כ׳ יוזל לכ׳ שלמה ולהיתום עצמו
22. בחודש סיון העבר וגם בימי הנוראי׳ העברו שרוצה להחזיק השכירות ורוצה לשלם השכירות
23. עד חדש סיון הבע״ל והאריכו הצדדי׳ הנ״ל בטענותיהם כמבואר באריכות בק״ה המונח לפנינו
24. ולאחר שחתמו עצמם בתוקף קומפרמיס בח״ח ובקנס סך מסוים לאשר ולקיים כפי מה שיצא מ
25. מאתנו נתנו עיניהם עלינו ב״ד לפשר ביניהם ומצאנו ע״פ פ״ד שכ׳ יוזל זיכל הנ״ל ישלם ל
26. להיתומי׳ הנ״ל סך חמשה ועשרי׳ רט וגם מחויב ללבן את שני חדרי׳ הנזכרי׳ בכתב שכירות
27. הבית הנ״ל ובזה הוא פטור ומסולק מכל תביעות הנ״ל יצא מאתנו אור ליו׳ ד׳ ך׳ כסליו
28. תקמ״א רנ״מ ורמ״ש ואני

No. 127

Fols. 124a–b; Tuesday 30 January 1781

In the late 1760s, Leb Kann bought a seat in the middle tier of the women's section of the synagogue and received a written confirmation of this from the court. Sometime thereafter, Leb lost the confirmation and he now came to the court requesting another. The court acceded to the request, but not before sending for the children of the previous owner (the owner himself had since died), the guardians of his younger children, and the younger children themselves to ascertain that this was indeed so and that Leb had paid for the seat in full. The court also

1. תוספת מעל השורה
2. לא ברור באיזה שמואל שוסטר מדובר. שמואל חיים בן ליפמן היה רווק ולכן יתכן שלא מדובר בו. בנוסף היו בתוך הקהילה שמואל בן הענלי שוסטר ושמואל בן יהודה שוסטר.
3. תוספת מעל השורה

checked the diary of the communal beadle who had noted that the seat had been offered for sale in both the old and new synagogues. The court was convinced that the sale had taken place no later than 1769 (there was uncertainty regarding the precise date) and issued a written confirmation of this to Leb.

קכד ע״א

1. בע״ה
2. במותב תלתא כחדא הוינא ואתא לקדמנא ה״ה התורני כ״ה וואלף בוריך סגל
3. בהרשאת הו״ה ג״ץ כה׳ ליב בן המנוח ג״ה כ״ה פער קן ז״ל ואמר מאחר שהוא
4. כה׳ ליב הנ״ל קנה לפני כמה שנים בפני ב״ד מקום שלם בע״נ האמצעי אשר
5. עומדות עלי׳ כעת אשת הו״ה כה׳ ליב הנ״ל ומצד ימין עומדת עלי׳ כעת
6. אשת הו״ה פ״ו כ׳ אברם האמיל סג״ל ומצד שמאל עומדות עלי׳ כעת
7. אל׳ המנוח [ג״ץ] כה׳ איצק בן המנוח כמהורר[1] משה קן זצ״ל בעד ששה עשר
8. {..} מאות זהו׳ שהי׳ שייך מקדמת ליתמי המנוח כה׳ אברהם בן המנוח פו׳[2] כה׳
9. יוסף האמיל סג״ל ז״ל והי׳ לו מעשה ב״ד על {.קניין} הקניות מקום שלם הנ״ל
10. ועכשיו נאבד ממנו בכן מבקש מאתנו ח״מ מעשה ב״ד מחדש על המקום שלם הנ״ל
11. והזדקקנו לו ושלחנו אחרי האחים כ׳ גומפיל וכ׳ {זלמן} זלמן בני המנוח כה׳ אברהם
12. הנ״ל ואחרי הו״ה כ׳ שלמה בן כ׳ מיכל האמיל ז״ל וה״ה כ׳ איצק בן כ״ה גומפ[יל]
13. ליזר שיף ז״ל אפוטרופסים של שאר יתמי המנוח {המנוח} כ״ה אברהם ז״ל הנ״ל
14. בני אל׳ מרת עדיל אל׳ המנוח הנ״ל והודו כולם בפנינו ב״ד ח״מ בהודאה
15. גמורה בדעת שלימה ומיושבת בלי שום אונס והכרח כלל רק מרצון נפשם
16. הטוב שמכרו לפני כמה שנים בפני ב״ד המקום שלם הנ״ל שהי׳ שייך מקדמת
17. לפני כמה שנים לאביהם המנוח כ׳ אברהם ז״ל הנ״ל לה״ה הו״ה ג״ץ כ׳ ליב
18. בן המנוח ג״ה כ׳ פער קן ז״ל בעד סך הנ״ל וקבלו הדמי מכירה מהמקום
19. שלם הנ״ל מהו״ה כ׳ ליב הנ״ל עד פרוטה אחרונה גם שלחנו אחרי היתומים
20. דהיינו כ׳ יוסף וכ׳ הירץ בני כ׳ אברהם הנ״ל ובאו בעצמם בפנינו ב״ד
21. ח״מ ואמרו {שה ..} שמה שהאפטרופסים הנ״ל אומרים בעסק זה הם
22. נאמנים עליהם גם שלחנו שלוחא דבי דינא אצל הבתולה רבקה בת כ״ה
23. אבר(הם)[3]ם (ז״ל)[4] הנ״ל ואמרה ג״כ שמה שהאפטרופסים הנ״ל אומרים בעסק זה נאמני׳
24. עלי׳ וכפי שחקרנו וראינו מהפנקס של השמש המנוח כ׳ משה פ״ב[5] ז״ל אש[ר]
25. שם נכתב זמן הכרזה בבה״כ ישן וחדש גם ראינו הכתב ההלאוה[6]
26. הנעשה על שכר בטילה מהמכירה הנ״ל בחתימת יד הדיין כה׳
27. אברהם טריר כץ נר״ו מתוכם הכרנו שהמכירה

---

1. כבוד מורנו הרב והגאון רב רבי
2. פרנס ומנהיג
3. תוספת מעל השורה
4. תוספת מעל השורה
5. פרידבורג
6. אולי צ״ל ׳ההלואה׳

קכד ע"ב

הנ"ל לא הי' מאוחר מיו' ה' א' דר"ח אדר שני תקכ"ח[1] לפק בכן אחרי החקירות וההודאות הנ"ל {וכתבנו} באנו אנחנו (ח"מ)[2] לעדות ולזכות ולראי' ובכח ב"ד יפה להיות ביד הו"ה כ"ה ליב הנ"ל וי"א וב"כ ששייך המקום שלם הנ"ל לחלוטין גמורין ולכמיתות[3] עלמין לה"ה הו"ה כ' ליב הנ"ל וי"א וב"כ עם כל זכות וחזקה כמו שהי' שייך מקדמת להמנוח כ' אברהם ז"ל הנ"ל בלי שום שיור כלל וכלל ורשאי כ' ליב הנ"ל וי"א ובכ' לעשות במקום שלם הנ"ל מה שירצה לבנות ולסתר להוריש ולהנחיל ולהחליף ולהשכיר ולהשכין ולמכור וליתן במתנה כאות נפשו ורצנו בכל איש דרשאי לעשות בשלו בלי שום {מוחכ} מוחה כלל בשופי גמור בלי שום עורר וטעון כלל יהי' המערער מי' שיהי' הן רבים או יחיד יהי' הטענה מה שהי' או בכל אופן שהי' מכל מה שהפה יוכל לדבר ולב לחשוב ולהרר[4] וכל מי שמערער אחר מכירה הנ"ל עד עולם יהי' מה שהי' או באיזה אופן שיהי' דבריו בטלין ומבוטלין לא שרירן ולא קיימן ולא יהי' חלין כלל וכלל כחרם[5] הנשבר וכאפס וכאין יחשב וכטעון אחר מעשה ב"ד הגדול ולא יזדקק שום קהל או ב"ד יצו או שום משפט שבעולם לדברי המערער הן בד[א"]ה או בד"י כי דברי הערער הן בטלים ומבוטלים ויהי' תוקף מעשה הלז כאילו הוא הגוף המעשה ב"ד הנעשה ביום המכירה ביד כ' ליב הנ"ל וכתוקף כל מעשה ב"ד דנהגין בישראל העשיון כתחכז"ל וכתבנו וחתמנו כל הנ"ל על פי ההודאות והחקירות הנ"ל בתוקף מעשה ב"ד ובכח ב"ד יפה להיות ביד כה' ליב הנ"ל וי"א וב"כ {לעשות} לעדות ולזכות ולראי' שיעמוד המקום שלם הנ"ל עם כל זכות וחזקה ביד כ' ליב הנ"ל וי"א וב"כ אבל לא למגביהי' לא ממשעב[דים] ולא מקום חרי רק להעמיד ביד כה' ליב הנ"ל וי"א וב"כ בשופי גמור בלי שום מוחה כלל ולראי' באנו על החתום יו' ג' ד' שב[ט] תקמא לפ[ק] אני ור"מענדלה[6] פאס ור' ליזר וואלא

---

1. שנת תרכ"ח לא היתה שנה מעוברת. שנת תקכ"ט כן היתה מעוברת ויום א' של ר"ח אדר שני (=ל' אדר ראשון) אכן נפל ביום ה'.
2. תוספת מעל השורה
3. צ"ל 'לצמיתות'
4. צ"ל 'ולהרהר'
5. צ"ל 'כחרס'
6. רבי מענדלה, הוא הרב מענדלי זאמשט (ר' לעיל, מס' 123, הערה 2).

No. 128

Fol. 125a; Tuesday evening, 6 February 1781

The guardians of Isaac Schwab-Öttingen came to the court to request that they be discharged from their responsibilities and that Isaac begin to run his affairs himself. Isaac, who appears to have been over 23 years of age at this time, declared of his own free will that he was ready to take charge of his affairs.[1] The court agreed to the request. Isaac also said that he had received all of his late father's assets from the guardians except for 10 guldens that would be used by the guardians to pay a certain tax for him. The court released the guardians from any future liability regarding the estate. Also see no. 113.

קדה ע״א

1. ב״ה
2. הן הקריבו לפנינו ב״ד ח״מ ה״ה הו״ה כ׳ אברהם בהמנוח[2] כ׳ זעליגמן איטינגין (ז״ל)[3] וה״ה הו״ה כ׳ זלמן
3. בהמנוח כ׳ קלמן רויטשילד ז״ל אפטרופסי׳ על היתום כ׳ איצק בהמנוח כ׳ קלמן רויטשילד ז״ל אפטרופסים
4. על היתום כ׳ איצק בהמנוח[4] כ׳ משה איטינגין ז״ל מכמה שני׳ באמרם שעתה הוא גדול ורוצי׳ לסלק
5. את עצמם מלהיות אפטרופסי׳ וליתן ליד היתום הנ״ל מה שנשאר בידם עדיין מעזבון אביו ז״ל
6. לפי חשבונם והיתום ישתדל בעצמו בצרכיו וביקשו האפטרופסי׳ הנ״ל מאתנו ב״ד ח״מ ליתן להם
7. רשות והרמנא לזה וליתן להם פטורי׳ אחר מסירתם ליד היתום הנ״ל מה שנשאר בידם כנ״ל ואחר
8. שהיתום כ׳ איצק הנ״ל עמד בעצמו לפנינו ואמר שהוא ג״כ מרוצה בכך בכן נזדקקנו לזה ומצא[נו]
9. שרשות ביד האפטרופסי׳ הנ״ל ליתן לכ׳ איצק הנ״ל את מה שנשאר בידם מעזבון אביו כנ״ל
10. ולסלק עצמם מאפטרופסות ובאשר שכ׳ איצק ג״כ הודה לפנינו אח״כ בהודאה גמורא
11. בלי אונס כלל שקיבל כל מה שנשאר בידם מעזבון אביו ז״ל חוץ מעשרה זהו׳ שיש עדיין ביד ר׳
12. זלמן הנ״ל לשלם להשרה יר״ה גרונדצונץ עבורו / בכן באנו אנחנו ב״ד ח״מ בתוקף מעשה

---

1. According to Dietz, p. 277, Isaac was born in 1757.
2. בן המנוח
3. תוספת מעל השורה
4. טעות סופר (השווה שורות 13-14); יש למחוק 'כ׳ קלמן רויטשילד ז״ל אפטרופסים על היתום כ׳ איצק בהמנוח'

13. ב"ד ובכח ב"ד יפה ופטרנו את האפטרופסי' הנ"ל וי"א וב"כ מן כ' איצק בהמנוח כ' משה
14. איטינגין ז"ל הנ"ל ויאי[1] וב"כ בפטור וסילוק גמור מכל טו"ת ודין ודברי' שבעולם מחמת אפטרו[פ]
15. =סות מעזבון אביו ז"ל כ' משה ז"ל הנ"ל מעתה ועד עולם ואין לכ' איצק הנ"ל ויא וב"כ שום טענה ותביע[ה]
16. מחמת עזבון אביו ז"ל על האפטרופסי' הנ"ל ויא וב"כ חוץ מעשרה זהו' שהם ביד כ זלמן הנ"ל וכנ"ל
17. יהי' טענה מה שיהי' או באיזה אופן שיהי' הן בע"פ או בכתב קרן ורווחי' מכל מה שהפה
18. יוכל לדבר והלב לחשוב ולהרהר ואל יזדקק שום קהל או משפט שבעולם לדבריו הן בד"י והן [ב]
19. בדא"ה רק האפטרופסי' הנ"ל וי"א וב"כ המה פטורי' ומסולקי' בלי שום תביעה או ג"ש וק"ה[2] וחרם
20. סתם וח"כ או לדור בחיי [רא]ש[ם] ובכל תוקף הנאמנות שבעולם ופטורי' הנ"ל לא יפסול ולא יגרע
21. כחם בשום ריעותא שבעולם אך תמ[י]ד יהי' בתקפם ובגבורתם ובחזקתם כי הכל נעש[ה]
22. בתוקף מעשה ב"ד ובכח ב"ד יפה וליתר תוקף בא כ' איצק הנ"ל גם כן על החתום נעשה
23. אור ליו' ד' יב שבט תקמ"א רנ"מ ורמ"ש ואני

No. 129

Mendler v. Esther, widow of Gershon Darum

Fols. 125b–126b; Tuesday evening, 6 February 1781

In 1714 Yuzpa Trier willed two equal halves in two seats in the upper women's section of the synagogue to his two daughters for their use on an annual rotating basis (i.e., one year one daughter would have the rights to one seat and the other daughter the other seat, the following year they would switch, the third year they would switch again, and so on). The seat on the south side of the synagogue was considered the better seat, and Yuzpa specified that if one of the daughters or her descendents chose to rent out the seat on the south side when it was her turn to sit there, the other daughter or her descendents had the right to pay 2 guldens less than had been offered and occupy the seat.

In 1746 the husband of one of Yuzpa's daughters sold their share in the seats to Anshel Mendler who eventually passed it on to his son, Mikhel. In 1781, Mikhel

1. ויורשיו אחריו
2. אולי 'וקנסי הקהילה' או 'וקונמי הקהילה'

came to the court and claimed that Yuzpa's granddaughter, Esther, had sat in the southern seat since 1746, and from 1775 had not paid him the 6 guldens that he was due (their practice was that if Esther exercised her right to sit in the south seat in alternate years then the Mendlers received rights to the other seat plus 2 guldens). Through his representative, Mikhel argued that as compensation he should be entitled to rent out the south seat for the next six years. If the court would not agree to this, he maintained that he should be paid the 6 guldens that he was owed for three of the past six years and that the court should impose a rotation with respect to future use of the seat.

Yuzpa's granddaughter, a widow, was represented before the court by her son. He argued that the terms of his great-grandfather's will were binding on those who purchased a portion of the seats. Therefore, so long as a family member owned a portion of the seats her rights preceded those of others and she had the right to use the southern seat. A note from 1746 seemed to suggest that Anshel Mendler had agreed to this arrangement, but Mikhel argued that the sides had never formally agreed to the terms of the note, an argument that the court accepted. Esther rejected Mikhel's claim to the seat for the next six years and maintained that she had made some payment for the previous six years but could not remember how much. Mikhel's counterclaim denying that Esther had any special rights to the southern seat was based on the contract of sale from 1746. Mikhel went further and requested that, if Esther's priority right to the seat was denied from 1746, she should pay him 36 guldens in damages for having sat in the seat during 18 of the past 35 years when it was really his to do with as he pleased.

The court examined the contract of sale from 1746 and confirmed Mikhel's full rights to half of the property without any need to give precedence to Yuzpa's descendents. The court ruled that the best way to share the property was to rent out both seats and then divide the rent equally, something that had been suggested as a contingency claim by Esther in case her original position was rejected. While the court denied Mikhel's request to have exclusive rights over the seat for the next six years, as well as his claim for 36 guldens, it did order Esther to pay Mikhel 3 guldens as a compromise for her use of the seat for 3 of the previous 6 years.[1]

1. The court specifically rejected Esther's claim to special rights after 1746, yet it failed to award Mikhel any compensation for these years. This seems somewhat contradictory. Mr. Richard Orzy, a lawyer with many years of court experience (and a life-long personal friend), suggested to me in an electronic letter of 27 October 2010 that the court may have been opposed to giving retrospective compensation since the party did not press for its rights all along. Mr. Orzy wrote, "if pressed earlier (as opposed to polite requests), the other party might have acquiesced (or lost in court) and courts do not like to penalize people in such cirucmstances or to reward others (here, the purchaser) for sitting on their hands. After all, unless the argument that the family member made was patently ridiculous, having relied on it was not necessarily

קכה ע"ב

1. ב"ה
2. ע"ד שבא לפנינו ה"ה התורני כ"ה משה אויך בהרשאת ובמעמד הב"ח כ' מיכל בהמנוח[1] כ'
3. אנשיל מענדלר ז"ל ותבע מן האשה מ' אסתר אל' המנוח כ"ה גרשון דארום ז"ל מאחר שכ' מיכל
4. הנ"ל והאשה מ' אסתר הנ"ל יש להם בשותפות שני מקומות בע"נ העליונה כל אחד מהם שייך ה
5. החצי משני מקומות הנ"ל מקו' אחד היא בצד דרום שעומדות עלי' כעת האשה מ' אסתר הנ"ל איין
6. לאך שטאט והשני' היא בצד צפון בחומה שעומדות עלי' כעת אשת כ' יוקב בן יוקב רינדשקופף
7. ועד שנת קהלת העבר היתה עומדות תמיד על המק' דרומית האשה מ' אסתר הנ"ל ומק' צפוני'
8. השכיר כ' מיכל לאחרי' ומחמת מה ששוה המק' דרומית יותר מצפונית נתנה האשה הנ"ל כל שני [ש]
9. שני' כשמגיע אותו מק' דרומית לכ' מיכל הנ"ל שני זהו' לכ' מיכל הנ"ל אבל משנת קהלת עד עתה לא
10. קיבל כלום ממנה בכן תבע ממנה שיכירו הב"ד אם אינו מגיע לכ' מיכל הנ"ל ג"כ המקו' דרומית
11. על ששה שני' לשכור אותו מקו' ובאם לא יזכה בזה עכ"פ תשלם לו ששה זהו' שכירות מחמת
12. שני' שעברו וגם טען שמכאן ולהבא לא יהי' המקו' דרומית להאשה תמיד רק יעשה הב"ד שיהיו
13. חלילה שנה אחר שנה ע"פ הגורל למי שיהי' המק' דרומית בשנה זו ולמי יהי' לו בשנה האח[רת]
14. וכן במקו' צפוני' שנה בשנה לפי ראות עיני ב"ד / וה"ה הו"ה כ"ה גרשון דארום[2] בהרשאת
15. אמו מ' אסתר הנ"ל השיב שאותו מקו' דרומית הנ"ל בא בכח מתנה מן המנוח כ"ה יוזפא [ט]
16. טריר ז"ל לשתי בנותיו החצי האחת להאשה מ' שאטלה אל' המנוח כמ"ה מיכל בינגא זצ"ל
17. אם של האשה מ' אסתר הנ"ל והחצי' השניי' לבתו האחרת מ' יענטלה אשת כ' וויבלמן
18. עמדין ז"ל וכמו שהציע שטר מתנה בפנינו ההוקם בג[3] אדר תע"ד לפק ושם נאמר בזה
19. הלשון הנני נותן מעכשיו לשתי בנותיי הנ"ל ביחד כנ"ל וכו' ולאחר מות[י] ומות אשתי הנ"ל
20. יעמדו בנותיי הנ"ל על המקו' הנ"ל שנה בעד שנה ואחרת תעמוד מאחרת דהיינו הינדר
21. שטאנד וכו' גם את זאת מחויבים בנותיי הנ"ל לעשות ולקיים באם שאחת מבנותי'

---

something for which compensation should be exacted." Yet a court would have no problem making its decision binding prospectively. Support for this understanding can be found in no. 151, fol. 141b, lines 8ff.

1. בן המנוח
2. גרשון בן גרשון דארום (ר' אבני זכרון, מס' 4681)
3. ב-ג' אדר תע"ד

22. תרצה להשכיר לאחרי׳ באותו שנה שיגיע לה לעמוד עליו ובתו השניי׳ תרצה לעמוד
23. עליו בעצמה או אחד מבנותי׳ אזי היא קודמות רק אפי׳ תהי׳ לה לשנה זו שני זהו׳
24. בדולר כמעשה אחרת רוצה ליתן וינכה מדמי שכירות שני זהו׳ לשנה עכ״ל וטוען כ״ה
25. גרשון שמכח אותו מתנה לאמו זקנתו מ׳ שאטלה הנ״ל קבלה אמו מ׳ אסתר חצי מקו׳ ד
26. דרומית

קדו ע״א

1. ב״ה
2. דרומית הנ״ל לנדן מאבי׳ מהו׳ מיכל הנ״ל וחצי׳ שניי׳ לקח המנוח כ׳ אנשיל מענדלר ז״ל מן כ׳ מאיר
3. [ע]מדין ז״ל בן המנוח כ׳ ווייבלמן הנ״ל שקיבל החצי בכח השטר הנ״ל בכן טען כ״ה גרשון הנ״ל שכ׳ מאיר
4. מכרה חצי מקו׳ הנ״ל דוקא על אופן ותנאי שהי׳ שייך לו וכמוזכר בשטר הנ״ל באם בנות או בנות
5. בנותיי של כ״ה יוזפא רוצה להעמיד בעצמם על המקו׳ אזי הם קודמי׳ לאחרי׳ ואפי׳ בפחות שני
6. זהו׳ לשנה כנ״ל בכן כל זמן שאמו מ׳ אסתר הנ״ל רוצה לעמוד בעצמה עלי׳ אינו רשאי כ׳ מיכל הנ״ל
7. להשכיר לאחרי׳ ומה מכר כ׳ מאיר הנ״ל לכ״אי[1] הנ״ל כל זכות שיש בידו אבל לא יותר / ועוד ה
8. הציע לפנינו כה״ג[2] הנ״ל כתב יד שיש ביד אמו מ״א[3] הנ״ל מן המנוח כ׳ אנשיל מענדלר ההוקם
9. יו׳ א טז שבט תק״ו ומשם רוצה להביא ראי׳ לזכותו שמחויב לקיים חריות (שטר)[4] ישן על לאך שטאט
10. שני שטעג הויך בעזרת הנשי׳ וטוען כה״ג הנ״ל שכ׳ מיכל שבא מכח אביו כ״א הנ״ל נמי צריך ל
11. לקיים התנאי הנ״ל בכן המקו׳ דרומית הנ״ל מגיע תמיד לאמו מ׳ אסתר לעמוד עליו בעצמה ואין
12. ביד כ׳ מיכל הנ״ל לשוכרו לאחרי׳ רק כפי מה שהי׳ עד עתה כן יהי׳ להבא שבכל שתי שני׳ כאשר
13. מגיע לו המקו׳ דרומית תהי׳ עומדות מ׳ אסתר הנ״ל על המקו׳ ההוא והיא תשלם שני זהו׳
14. פחות כפי מה ששוה שכירות המקו׳ הנ״ל ואם לא יזכה בדין בזה עכ״פ ישכירו השני מקומ׳
15. הנ״ל ויחלוקו השכירות ומה שטען שרוצה לזכות ששה שני׳ במקו׳ דרומית נגד מה שעמדה מ׳ א
16. אסתר הנ״ל השיב שאינו מחויב בכך אחר שלא מיחה והי׳ מרוצה בכך ומחמת השכירות
17. משלשה שני׳ שהוא ששה {שני} זהו׳ השיב ששילם לו מהם אבל אינו יודע כמה וטען עוד כה״ג

---

1. כבוד אנשיל
2. כבוד הרב גרשון
3. מרת אסתר
4. תוספת מעל השורה

18. הגם שיש לו תביעות ע"פ על כ' מיכל הנ"ל אינו רוצה לנכות תביעתו ולהזכירם כעת וכ' מיכ[ל]
19. השיב ע"ז שעל כתב יד הנ"ל לא נעשה שום קנין גם בהחלטה שיש לו לא נזכר שצריך לקיי'
20. שום זכות להאשה מ' אסתר ועוד הציע לפנינו שטר מכירה מכ' מאיר עמדין לאביו ז"ל ה
21. הנ"ל על אותו חצי מקו' דרומית הנ"ל הנעשה ך"ח אייר תק"ו ומשם הביא ראי' שמכח אותן
22. קניני' שנעשה בו ביו' הנ"ל שנתבטל כתב יד מאבי' הנ"ל עוד טען שאם יזכה בדין זה ש
23. שנתבטל זכויות של האשה מרת אסתר אזי הוא תבע שלשי' וששה זהו' מן שמונה עשרה שנה
24. באשר שהיא בטעות {שסבר} שהוא סבר שמחויב לקיים זכות זה שמחויב ליתן בזול
25. והאריכו הצדדי הנ"ל בטענותיהם זה מול זה כמבואר בק"ה המונח לפנינו ב"ד ובאשר
26. שהצדדי' הנ"ל חתמו עצמם בתוקף קומפרמיס בח"ח ובקנס סך מסויים לאשר ולקיי'

קכו ע"ב

1. ב"ה
2. את אשר יצא מאתנו נזדקקנו להם ואחר שהי' למראה עינינו השטר מכירה מכ' מאיר עמדין ז"ל
3. על מקו' דרומית הנ"ל לכ' אנשיל מענדלר ז"ל הנ"ל מצאנו שהדין עם כ' מיכל הנ"ל שהחצי מקו' דרומי'
4. דהיינו לאך שטאט הנ"ל שייך לו בכל זכיותיו בלי שום תנאי שבעולם ורשאי להשכיר חלקו לכל
5. מי שירצה ואינו מחויב לקיים התנאי הנ"ל להשכיר דווקא לאשה מ' אסתר ומה שטען כ"ה גרשון
6. מחמת כתיבת יד של כ' אנשיל מענדלר הנ"ל אין בו ממש ואכן אם כ' מיכל הנ"ל ישכור המקו' לאשה
7. אחרת והאשה מ' אסתר הנ"ל באה לזכות בה בתורת מצרנות אזי יקוב הדין ההר ביניהם אכן
8. בלא"ה יש לכ' מיכל כל זכיות כמו האשה מ' אסתר הנ"ל בשני המקומות הדרומית לאך שטאט
9. והצפוני מויער שטאט הנ"ל גם מצאנו שאופן החלוקה יהי' שישכירו שני המקומות הנ"ל יחד ב
10. בשותפות ודמי שכירות משניהם יוחלק כל שנה שוה בשוה כל אחד המחצה ומה שרוצה
11. לזכות כ' מיכל הנ"ל במקו' הדרומית לבד על ששה שני' רצופי' הבע"ל אין בו ממש ומחמת
12. דמי שכירות ששה זהו' מששה שני' העבר שתבע כ' מיכל הנ"ל מאחר שנתנו הצדדי' הנ"ל עיניהם
13. עלינו לפשר ביניהם על תביעות הלז מצאנו ע"פ פשר שתשלם האשה מ' אסתר הנ"ל לכ' מיכל הנ"ל
14. שלשה זהו' אבל מה שתבע שלשי' וששה זהו' מחמת שהי' השכירות בטעות הדין בזה עם האשה

15. מ' אסתר הנ"ל ואינה מחויבת לשלם יצא מאתנו אור ליו' ד' יב שבט תקמ"א רנ"מ
16. רמ"ש ואני

No. 130

Fol. 126b; Sunday evening, 11 February 1781

A record of the sale of a seat in the middle section of the women's section of the synagogue. The seat had belonged to the descendents of Herz Reinganum and was sold to Gedaliah Stiebel (Stiefel; both spellings appear here) for 456 guldens after the customary announcement of the availability of the seat was made in both the old and new synagogues. Gedaliah's wife had been using the seat prior to the sale.

17. ———
18. מקו' שלם בע"נ האמצעי אשר עומדות עלי' כעת אשת הו"ה כ' גדלי' שטיפל שהי' שייך ליתמי המנו'
19. כ"ה הירץ ריינגאנום נמכר בפנינו ב"ד לאחר הכרזה בבהכיו"ח כנהוג לה"ה כ' גדלי' שטיבל
20. בעד סך ארבע מאות וחמשי' וששה זהו' לשלם כפי תיקון הקהלה נעשה אור ליו' ב טוב שבט
21. תקמ"א רנ"מ ורמ"ש ואני

No. 131

Falk v. Cohen

Fol. 127a; Tuesday evening, 13 February 1781

Me'ir Falk sued Hirsch Cohen, a communal leader, for payment of fees for his services as an agent in the sale of unspecified items as well for funds that he had advanced him. Me'ir admitted that Hirsch had repaid some of the debt, but asserted that 37 guldens, 56 kreuzers remained outstanding. Through his representative, Hirsch admitted to some of the charges, challenged others, and outright denied the rest. Hirsch counterclaimed that Me'ir owed him 21 guldens for a purchase of goods made about four years earlier during a previous partnership. Me'ir is said to have answered these charges at length, but his statements are not included in the record here; they were, however, before the court in its record of claims and statements. Both sides asked the court to offer a compromise solution, which it did, and Hirsch was ordered to pay Me'ir 15 guldens.

קדז ע"א

1. ב"ה
2. ע"ד שבא לפנינו ה"ה הב"ח כ' מאיר בהמנוחי כ' זלמן פאלק כץ ז"ל ותבע מן ה"ה הו"ה פו"מ
3. כ"ה הירש כהן והציע לפנינו חשבן שנשאר לו כ"ה הירש הנ"ל חייב מחמת דמי סרסראות ומכירת
4. סחורת וגם מחמת מה שהוציא במזומני' בשבילו העולה אחר ניכוי מה שכבר שלם על חשבונו
5. עדיין סך שלשי' ושבעה זהו' נו"ץ[2] וה"ה התורני כ"ה אנשיל פפאן כץ בהרשאת פו"מ כ"ה הירש הנ"ל
6. השיב באריכות על חשבן כ' מאיר הנ"ל והודה על מקצת ועל מקצת לא הודה ועל מקצת אמר שאינו
7. מחויב לשלם לפי הדין עוד תבע כה"א[3] הנ"ל בהרשאת הנ"ל מן כ' מאיר הנ"ל מחמת חמשה שטוק צ[ט]ץ
8. שקנה כ"ה הירש הנ"ל בשותפות עם כ' מאיר הנ"ל לערך לפני ד' שני' מסוחר ש[מיהט] ושכ"ה הירש
9. לא יכול למוכרם בכן תבע מן כ' מאיר הנ"ל חלקו היזיק שמוטל עלי' העולה לסך אחד {וארבעי'}(ועשרי')[4] זהו'
10. וכ' מאיר הנ"ל חזר והשיב באריכות על תשובת ר אנשיל ותביעו שעשה כמבואר היטיב בק"ה ה
11. המונח אצלינו ואחרי שהצדדי' הנ"ל {חתמו עצמם} נתנו עיניהם עלינו ב"ד לפשר ביניהם ו
12. וחתמו עצמם בתוקף קומפרמיס בח"ח ובקנס סך מסויים לאשר ולקיים מה שיצא מאתנו ע"פ פשר
13. בכן נזדקקנו להם ומצאנו ע"פ פשר דבר שפו"מ כ"ה הירש הנ"ל מחויב לשלם לכ' מאיר הנ"ל סך
14. חמשה עשר זהו' ובזה פטורי' ומסולקי' זה מזה וזה מזה מחמת תביעות וחשבונות הנ"ל
15. יצא מאתנו אור ליו' ד' יט שבט תקמ"א רנ"מ ורמ"ש ואני

No. 132

Fol. 127a; Sunday evening, 25 February 1781

A seat in the lower portion of the men's synagogue was currently being used by

---

1. בן המנוח
2. 56 צל
3. כבוד הרב אנשיל
4. תוספת מעל השורה

Herz Flörsheim. The seat had multiple owners — Herz was not one of them — including the heirs of three different estates and three individuals. The owners sold the seat to Tevele Fulda for 475 guldens. Also see nos. 134, 136, 137, 157–59.

16. אור ליו' ב ב דר"ח אדר תקמ"א נמכר בפנינו ב"ד ח"מ מקו' של[ם]
17. בע"א התחתונה שעומד עלי' כעת כ' הירץ ב"מי[1] פלערשהיים
18. שהי' שייך [ל]משותפי' יתמי ג"ה כ"ה פער קן ז"ל ויתמי כ"ה מרדכי
19. בו"ו[2] אופנהיים ז"ל ויתמי כ' יוקב ב"מ[3] אופנהיים ז"ל ולכ"ה יוסף
20. טויב יצו ולכ' יום טוב אופנהיי' ולאחיו כ' אהרן בר"י[4] אופנהיי'
21. לכל אחד ואחד מהם (היה)[5] שייך חלק שישית מן המקו' שלם הנ"ל ונמכר
22. לה"ה כ' טעבלי בכ"ה מאיר פולדא יצו בעד סך ארבע מאות
23. ושבעי' וחמישה זהו' לשלם אין ק"מ כפי תיקון הקהלה
24. רנ"מ ורמ"ש ואני

No. 133

Fols. 127b–128a; Sunday evening, 4 February 1781

The court's decision in 1777 with respect to building on the so-called Heqdesh Platz (see no. 101) led to some disagreement about how to interpret the court's imposition of building codes. The court went to the site to see for itself what was involved and reviewed the language of its earlier decision. It then issued clarifications that favored the claims of those who lived on the neighboring Elefant lot. Those living next to the site also complained that the construction obstructed a drainage pipe. The builders agreed to correct the problem and install a new pipe. This done, the court specifically relieved the developers of any further liability for repairs to the pipe.

קכז ע"ב

1. ב"ה
2. אחרי שכבר יצא פס"ד מאתנו ב"ד ח"מ בר"ח מרחשון תקלחית לפק בין האלופי'
3. קציני' גובי' יצו מחזיקי הקדש פלאטץ באותו פעם ובין מחזיקי בתי' צום הירש
4. = הארן מנגד עליפאנד שכני' הקדש פלאטץ הנ"ל ואח"כ מכרו האלופי' גובי' יצו

---

1. בן משה
2. בן וואלף
3. בן מרדכי
4. בן רבי יוקב
5. תוספת מעל השורה

5. הקדש פלאטץ הנ״ל לקציני׳ הו״ה ג״ה כ׳ יעקב עמדין והו״ה גץ[1] כ״ה איצק זינצהיי׳ סגל
6. והמה בנאו ההקדש פלאטץ ובאו עכשיו לפנינו הלוקחי׳ הנ״ל עם מחזיקי בית
7. צום עליפאנד הנ״ל אודות מה שמבואר בפס״ד הנ״ל וז״ל ועוד יותר נתנו
8. רשות מחזיקי בית צום עליפאנד מאחר שלמעלה שלשה שטעג הויך ב
9. בעליפאנד נכנס בשטח ביתם לפני׳ לערך שני אמות בכן ניתן רשות
10. להאלופי׳ גובי׳ יצו וב״כ שרשאי להרחיב בניני׳ מן הקדש פלאטץ על אותו ב
11. בליטה הנכנס הנ״ל עד למעלה כפי שירצו עכל[2] פס״ד הנ״ל והנה מקודם שנבנה
12. הקדש פלאטץ הנ״ל הי׳ למחזיקי עליפאנד בשלשה ש[טע]ג הויך שלהם מן חוץ הב
13. הבית עד מחיצות החדר שלהם לערך שני אמות ברוחב סוכה בנוי עם
14. מחיצות וחלונות וגג שעלי{ה}׳ וכעת ע״י בנין הקדש פלאטץ הנ״ל נסתר כל ה
15. המחיצות וחלונות עם הגג שעלי׳ ובאו עכשיו הלוקחי׳ הנ״ל בשאלה לפנינו אם
16. רשאי לבנות או להעמיד שאנק על אותו בליטה שהי׳ מקודם הסוכה באשר שלפי
17. דעתם שגם זה נכלל מה שכתוב בפס״ד הנ״ל שרשאי להרחיב בניני׳ מן הקדש
18. פלאטץ על אותו בליטה ומחזיקי עליפאנד אומרי׳ שבוודאי לא {..צ} נתרצו
19. על מקו׳ הסוכה שיהי׳ שלהם רק הריצוי הי׳ למעלה שלשה שטעג הויך
20. על אויר הגג מן סוכה שהי׳ באותו פעם שיהי׳ רשות למחזיקי הקדש פ
21. פלאטץ לבנות עלי׳ והאריכו בדבריהם ולאחר שהלכנו בבית
22. עליפאנד והי׳ למראה עינינו בליטה הנ״ל גם הכרנו איך הי׳
23. מקודם שנסתר

קדח ע״א

1. ב״ה
2. מקודם שנסתר המחיצות והגג של הסוכה הנ״ל ואחר שאנחנו מעייני׳ היטיב בלשון הפס״ד הנ״ל
3. מצאנו שהדין עם מחזיקי עליפאנד הנ״ל ואין רשאי למחזיקי הקדש פלאטץ הנ״ל לבנות בש[ני] שטעג
4. הויך שלהם שום שאנק או בליטה שיהי׳ נכנס בתוך גבול של עליפאנד בסוכה שהי׳ להם
5. מקודם שלשה שטעג הויך בבית עליפאנד הנ״ל רק מאחר שכעת נסתר המחיצות וגג הסוכה כנ״ל
6. בכן לאחר שנבנה מחיצות וגג הסוכה רשאי מחזיקי הקדש פלאטץ לבנות או להרחיב בניני׳ על אויר
7. הגג הסוכה של עליפאנד הנ״ל לערך שני אמות כמבואר בפס״ד הנ״ל או לבנות שאנק או שום בליטה
8. על אויר הנ״ל / ומאחר שע״י בנין הקדש פלאטץ נסתר הגג והמחיצות של הסוכה הנ״ל וכנ״ל בכן על
9. המחזיקי הקדש פלאטץ הנ״ל לחזור ולבנותם כמקדם ומה שנשאר ממחיצה ישינה ביד

1. גבאי צדקה
2. עד כאן לשון

10. מחזיקי עליפאנד מחוּבי׳ המחזיקי׳ עליפאנד לחזור וליתן לזה הבנין / ומחמת מה שתבעו מ
11. מחזיקי עלי פאנד עבור מה שנזכר בפס״ד הנ״ל וז״ל ומחמת מי גשמי׳ של המגדול סביב השטעג
12. של עלי פאנד כמו שהי׳ נמשך עד עתה כן יהי׳ להבא וטועני׳ המחזיקי עלי פאנד שמכח הבנין חדש
13. מבית פנימי מן הקדש פלאטץ שהוא דבוק למגדול {לירד} הנ״ל נסתר הצנור שהי׳ חמשה שטעג הויך
14. בבית צום עליפאנד ואין יכולי׳ המי גשמי׳ של המגדול לירד כמו שהי׳ מקדם לזה התרצו
15. מחזיקי הקדש פלאטץ הנ״ל כדי לתקן קלקול הנ״ל לעשות צנור חדש הנכנס דרך המגדל ולחוץ
16. לאחורי המגדול עד למטה באופן שמי גשמי׳ יורדי׳ דרך צנור הנ״ל לתוך בתי כסאות
17. של עלי פאנד ובפירוש הותנה שלאחר שיתקנו המחזיקי הקדש פלאטץ הצנור חדש הנ״ל על
18. על אופן הנ״ל על הוצאתם שוב אין עליהם לתקן הקילקול מה שאירע אח״כ בצנור הנ״ל רק י
19. יהא על הוצאות מחזיקי עליפאנד יצא מאתנו אור ליו׳ ב יוד שבט תקמ״א רנ״מ ורמ״ש ואני

No. 134

Fol. 128a; Monday evening, 5 March 1781

The same estates and individuals mentioned in no. 132 each held one-sixth portions in a seat in the lower section of the men's section of the synagogue that was currently being used by Jacob Rindskopf. The owners collectively sold their shares to Abram Hahn for 220 guldens. Also see nos. 132, 136, 137, 157–59.

20. אור ליו׳ ג טית אדר (תקמ״א)[1] נמכר בפני ב״ד מקו׳ שלם בע״א התחתונה העומד עלי׳ כעת
21. כיוקב[2] ב״י[3] רינדשקאפף שהי׳ שייך למשותפי׳ ה״ה יתמי המנוח ג״ה כ״ה פער קן ז״ל ויתמי
22. המנוח כ״ה מרדכי בפ״ו כו״ו[4] אופנהיים (ז״ל)[5] ויתמי (המנוח)[6] כ יוקב ב״מ[7] אופנהיי׳ ולה״ה כ׳ יוסף טויב

1. תוספת מעל השורה
2. כבוד יוקב
3. בן יוקב
4. וואלף
5. תוספת מעל השורה
6. תוספת מעל השורה
7. בן מרדכי

23. ולה"ה כ' יום טוב ולאחיו כ' אהרן בהמנוח כה"י[1] אופנהיי' ז"ל כל אחד ואחד מהם (הי')[2] שייך
24. חלק שישית מהמקו' שלם הנ"ל ונמכר לה"ה כ' אברם ב"א[3] האן בעד סך שני מאות ועשרי'
25. זהו' לשלם כפי תיקון הקהלה רנ"מ ורמ"ש ואני

No. 135

Zunz v. Spanier

Fols. 128b–129a; Tuesday evening, 20 March 1781

Herz Zunz and his brother, Aaron, owned half of the "outer house" on the Frosch lot while the other half of the "outer house" was one-quarter owned by Moses, son of Isaac Spanier, and one-quarter owned by Ḥayyim Schuster, who was married to Sarah Rivkah, daughter of Samuel Spanier. Isaac and Samuel were brothers. The Zunz brothers claimed that they and they alone owned the property behind the house. To prove their claim they noted that their grandfather had bought half of the house and assumed that he received half of the property behind the house with it. They then produced a court document from 1736 according to which the elder Zunz purchased the second half of the property behind the house from Shinla Spanier. They further buttressed their point by noting that their father, the *dayyan* Anshel Zunz, had always lived in the lower section of the house and enjoyed use of the entire property behind the house.

Moses and Ḥayyim countered that they had each received one-quarter of the house and the property behind it as part of their dowries. They maintained that Isaac and Samuel Spanier had also received their shares in the house with property. In addition, they brought a contract from December 1733 that was held by another member of the community which made it clear that the Spaniers had rights to half of the property behind the house.

While each side made its claims and brought its proofs, it was the court that undertook the investigative work. Not only did it question people; it examined the communal records and found therein proof that the parties who had given Moses and Ḥayyim their shares in the house had rights to the area behind the house as well. Once this material was shown to the Zunz brothers they retracted their claim

---

1. בן המנוח כבוד הר' יוקב
2. תוספת מעל השורה
3. בן אנשיל

and recognized the rights of Moses and Ḥayyim. The court then clarified for the record that Moses and Ḥayyim had rights to half the property behind the house.

קכח ע"ב

1. בע"ה
2. ע"ד שבאו לפנינו ה"ה התורני כ"ה הירץ צונץ ואחיו כ' אהרן יצו מחזיקי חצי בית חיצון
3. צום פראש עם משותפי' שלהם בבית החיצון הנ"ל שהם הו"ה כ"ה משה שפאניער כ"ץ וה"ה
4. הו"ה כ"ה חיים שוסטר כ"ץ חתן המנוח כ' שמואל שפאניער שיש לכל או"א מהם רביעית בית
5. מן בית צום פראש הנ"ל וטוען כ"ה הירץ ואחיו כ' אהרן הנ"ל שהפלאטץ מה שאחורי הבית
6. החיצון הנ"ל לדעת[ם] שייך לולאחיו[1] לבד ואין לכהר"ם[2] וכ"ה חיים הנ"ל שום חלק בו והיינו
7. שכפי שהגיד לו אביו המנוח הדיין מהו' אנשיל זצ"ל לקח אביו כ"ה הירץ {הנ"ל} (ז"ל)[3] החצי
8. בית צום פארש הנ"ל מן כ"ה מאיר עלונגין ז"ל וטוען כ"ה הירץ הנ"ל שמס{..} שמסתמא
9. לקח באותו פעם ג"כ עם החצי בית הנ"ל החצי שאחורי הבית צום פראש הנ"ל שהפלטץ
10. שייך לבית החיצון ועוד הציע לפנינו מעשה ב"ד משנת תצ"ו שאביו זקנו כ"ה הירץ
11. ז"ל הנ"ל לקח חצי פלאטץ מהאשה מ' שינלה שפאניער בכן מעכשיו (הי')[4] שייך הפלאטץ שלם ל[א]
12. לאביו זקנו ז"ל לבד לפי דעתם ואין למורישם של כ"ה משה וכ"ה חיים הנ"ל שום חלק ב
13. בפלאטץ הנ"ל {וגם} והוסיף לטעון שכל ימי חיים חיותו של אביו המנוח מהו' אנשיל ז"ל
14. הנ"ל הי' דר בשטח מטה שמתוכה הוא מהלך לפלאטץ הנ"ל וגם הוא דר בשטח מטה
15. בכן הוא ואחיו הם המוחזקי' בפלאטץ שלם הנ"ל ועל כ"ה משה וכ"ה[5] ה[נ"ל] מוטל לברר
16. שמכח מה הם רוצי' ג"כ לזכות בחצי פלאטץ הנ"ל וה"ה כ"ה משה וכ"ה חיים הנ"ל השיבו
17. והציעו לפנינו כתב תנאי' שלהם שהם קבלו לנדן כל או"א מהם רביעית בית חיצון צום
18. פראש עם רביעית פלאטץ הפנימי שאחורי פראש וגם ת"ר מן כ' איצק שפניע[ר] אבי כ"ה
19. משה הנ"ל שגם הוא הכניס רביעית פלאטץ הנ"ל לנדן מזה ראיי' שמעולם הי' מורישם ש
20. שותפות בפלאטץ הנ"ל כמו בבית צום פראש הנ"ל והיינו לכל או"א מהאחי' כ' איצק וכ'
21. שמואל שפאניער ז"ל רביעית בית ורביעית פלאטץ והוסיפו להביא ראי' לדעתם מתוך
22. שטר שיש ביד הו"ה כ"ה הירץ שייאר יצו ההוקם דב כסליו תצ"ד לפק שמתוכה ניכר שהאחי'
23. המונחי' כ' איצק וכ' שמואל שפאניער הי' מחזיקי חצי פלאטץ הנ"ל והאריכו הצדדי' בטענותיה'
24. ולאחר שחתמו הצדדי' הנ"ל א"ע בתוקף קומפרמיס בח"ח ובקנס סך מסויים לאשר ולקיים

---

1. האות ו' משותפת לשתי המילים – 'לו ולאחיו'.
2. כבוד הרב משה
3. תוספת מעל השורה
4. תוספת מעל השורה
5. כנראה שהמילה 'חיים' חסרה כאן.

25. כפי

קדט ע״א

1. ב״ה
2. כפי מה שיצא מאתנו ב״ד ח״מ נזדקקנו להם / ולאחר חקירה ודרישה שהי׳ לנו על כל צדדי׳
3. מצאנו דאתא לידינו כמה העתקי׳ מפנקס הנאמני׳ מכמה ק״ס שנעשין כבר לפני כמה
4. שני׳ ומתוכם הי׳ הדברי׳ ניכרי׳ שהי׳ שייך להאחי׳ המונחי׳ כ׳ איצק וכ״ש[1] הנ״ל חצי פלאטץ
5. ולהמנוח כ״ה הירץ זונץ ז״ל הנ״ל החצי פלאטץ שניי׳ הנ״ל / ולאחר שהכרנו דבר זה הראינו
6. איזה העתקי׳ לה״ה כ״ה הירץ צונץ הנ״ל וכראותו הוא בעצמו כן מתוכם שוב אמר לפנינו
7. שיצא עכשיו הספק מלבו וחזר הוא ואחיו הנ״ל מטענותיהם והודה הוא ואחיו הנ״ל
8. בעצמם שחצי פלאטץ הנ״ל שייכי׳ לכ״ה משה שפניער וכ״ה חיים שוסטר הנ״ל והמה משותפ[י׳]
9. משותפי׳ יחד הוא ואחיו עם כהר״ם וכה״ח[2] הנ״ל בפלאטץ הנ״ל כמו בבית החיצון הנ״ל
10. לזאת באנו אנחנו ב״ד ח״מ בתוקף מעשה ב״ד ובכח ב״ד יפה לעדות ולזכות ולראי׳
11. שחצי פלאטץ שלם אחורי בית חיצון צום פראש הנ״ל שייך לכ״ה משה וכ״ה חיים הנ״ל
12. וי״א וב״כ לחלוטין גמורין ולצמיתת עלמין עם כל זכות וחזקה וכמו ששייך החצי פלאטץ
13. שניי׳ להאחי׳ ה״ה התו׳ כ״ה הירץ ואחיו כ׳ אהרן בני המנוח מהו׳ אנשיל צונץ זצ״ל בלי שו[ם]
14. שום שיור כלל וכלל ורשאי׳ ה״ה כ״ה משה וכ״ה חיים הנ״ל וי״א וב״כ לעשות עם חצי
15. [ה]פלאטץ הנ״ל להוריש ולהנחיל להחליף ולהשכן למכור ולהשכיר וליתן במתנה כאות
16. נפשם ורצונם ככל איניש דרשאי לעשות בשלו בלי שום מוחה ועורר וטוען יהי׳
17. מי שיהי׳ יחיד או רבי׳ יהי׳ הטענה מה שיהי׳ או בכל אופן שיהי׳ מכל מה שהפה יוכל
18. לדבר והלב לחשוב ולהרהר כולם בטלי׳ ומבוטלי׳ כאפס וכאין יחשב ולא יהי׳ חלין
19. כלל וכלל וכטוען אחר מעשה ב״ד הגדול יצא מאתנו אור ליו׳ ד׳ דד אדר תקמ״א לפק
20. רנ״מ ורמ״ש ואני

No. 136

Fol. 129b; Thursday 24 May 1781

A seat in the lower portion of the men's section of the synagogue that was being used by Moses Levi was jointly owned by four parties. Three-quarters of the seat was owned by the beneficiaries of the same estates mentioned in nos. 132, 134, and 137. The fourth quarter was owned by Solomon Oppenheim of Offenbach. The

---

1. וכבוד שמואל
2. וכבוד הרב חיים

quarter of the seat owned by Solomon was sold earlier in the year by the community to Leb Oppenheim, who now purchased the rest of the seat from the other parties. The record notes that Leb himself was a beneficiary of one of the estates that owned the seat and therefore could deduct his one-twelfth share in the seat from the total purchase price of 200 guldens.

An undated postscript notes that Solomon Oppenheim did not receive any funds for the sale of his portion because his late father had owed the community money and the proceeds of the sale went directly to the community to satisfy the debt. Also see no. 165.

קכט ע״ב

1. ב״ה
2. מקו׳ שלם בע״א התחתונה במיטל באנק עליונה אשר עומד עלי׳ כעת ה״ה כ׳ משה
3. לוי שהי׳ שייך בשותפות ליורשי המנוח ג״ה כ״ה פער קן ז״ל ויורשי ר מרדכי ב״פ[1] כו״ו[2]
4. אופנהיים ז״ל ויורשי׳ המנוח כ׳ יוקב (ב״מ)[3] אופנהיים ז״ל ולכ׳ שלמה ב״ל[4] אופנהיים מן
5. קק[5] אופיבאך יע״א והיינו שהי׳ שייך לכל או״א מהם רביעית מן מקו׳ שלם הנ״ל נמכר
6. ע״י נ״ה ביו׳ יט שבט העבר חלק של שלמה הנ״ל לכ[6] ליב ביוקב[7] אופנהיים חלק רביעי׳
7. שלו (כמבואר בק״ס)[8] וכהיו׳ דלמטה מכרו שארי משותפי׳ הנ״ל את חלקם שלשה רביעי׳ הנותרי׳ מן מ
8. מקו׳ שלם הנ״ל בפנינו ב״ד ח״מ לה״ה כ׳ ליב ב״י[9] אופנהיים הנ״ל ודמי מכירה
9. מכל ארבעה רביעית הוא יחד סך שני מאות זהו׳ והלוק[10] כ׳ ליב הנ״ל ינכה מסך
10. דמי מכירה הנ״ל בשביל חלק שנים עשר של מקו׳ שלם שהי׳ שייך לו מקדם סך שני׳ עשר
11. מסך דמי מכירה הנ״ל והנותרות ישלם הלוקח הנ״ל אין קונפונטציאהנש מינץ
12. אויף דעם {קונפונטציאהנש} דד זהו׳ פוס והיינו כמנהג הקהלה פה
13. נעשה יו׳ ה׳ ער״ח סיון תקמ״א רנ״מ ורמ״ש ואני
14. לזיכרון הק״ס נעשה מן כ׳ שלמה הנ״ל לבד קנין מכר בלי סכום דמי׳ הואיל שדמי מכירה
15. באו ליד הגובי׳ בשביל אביו ז״ל שנשאר חייב לגובי׳

---

1. בן פרנס (ע׳ אבני זכרון, מס׳ 2495)
2. כבוד וואלף
3. תוספת מעל השורה; בן מרדכי
4. בן לב (ר׳ מזכיר נשמות, מס׳ 486)
5. קהילת קודש
6. לכבוד
7. בן יוקב
8. תוספת מעל השורה
9. בן יוקב
10. צ״ל ׳והלוקח׳

No. 137

Fol. 129b; Wednesday 18 July 1781

A record of the sale of half a seat in the lower part of the men's section of the synagogue to Moses Kassel. The half-seat had been owned by the same three groups of beneficiaries mentioned in nos. 132, 134, and 136. The half- seat was sold by the court for 59 guldens after a period of open bidding. The purchaser was ordered to pay the entire sum in one payment. Also see nos. 158–59.

16. ———
17. חצי מקו׳ שלם בע״א התחתונה מן מקו׳ שלם קטן הדבוק באחורי שטענדר הוא אותו שטענדר
18. ששייך למקו׳ שעומד עלי׳ כעת הו״ה כ״ה יעקב בר״ל[1] האמיל סגל שהי׳ שייך בשותפות ליורשי
19. המנוח כהפ[2] קן ז״ל הנ״ל ו(ל)[3]יורשי המנוח כ״ה מרדכי אופנהיי׳ ז״ל הנ״ל וליורשי המנוח כ״י[4]
20. אופנהיים ז״ל הנ״ל לכל או״א מהם שליש מחצי מקו׳ הנ״ל מכרנו בפני ב״ד אחר הכרזה כנהוג
21. להו״ה כ׳ משה בן בענדיט קאסיל סגל בעד סך חמשי׳ ותשעה זהו׳ לשלם נגד מסירת חלטה
22. בפעם אחת אין קפ״מ אויף דעם כ״ד זהו׳ פוס נעשה יו׳ ד כ״ה תמוז תקמ״א
23. רנ״מ ורמ״ש ואני

No. 138

Yentela, widow of Moses Taub v. Taub

Fols. 130a–132a; Tuesday 3 July 1781

Yentela, the widow of Moses Taub, came to the court and requested that her late husband's estate pay her what she was due according to her marriage contract (*ketubbah*). She also asked to receive items of clothing and gifts that she had been given during the course of her engagement and marriage to her late husband. Yentela's father-in-law, Joseph Taub, who served as guardian for his grandchild, contested a number of his daughter-in-law's claims.

The court allowed Yentela to keep personal gifts that she had received from

---

1. בן ר׳ ליב
2. כבוד הרב פער
3. תוספת מעל השורה
4. כבוד יוקב

her relatives but, generally speaking, presents that she received from her husband during the marriage, gifts that Moses received, and items that they received as a couple belonged to the estate. The court granted Yentela a housing allowance and use of household items including a prayer book and a Yiddish Pentateuch. However, she was required to submit an inventory of what she kept in her possession to the guardians of the estate.[1] Should she remarry, she was required to return these items to the estate.

Yentela also asked for a living allowance and child support for the child that she had had with Moses. She received custody of her daughter at least until the age of twelve as well as support for food and the child's laundry. The allowance also included a provision for hiring a maidservant to care for her daughter. If Yentela chose not to hire a maidservant, the allowance would be reduced.

Yentela claimed that her father-in-law owed her daughter income from ownership of one-eighth of a house, a claim that the court upheld. At the same time, the court granted Joseph some relief on a debt owed to the estate.

The court was also asked to deal with the fact that two of the individuals named by Moses Taub in his will did not want to be executors of the estate. Yentela's representative suggested that the court pay off the marriage contract and that the remaining funds stay with the court until two executors were appointed. The court fundamentally accepted this view and appointed Anshel Pfann to work with Joseph on an interim basis. They were required to gather assets that Yentela did not have use of, liquidate them, and turn the funds over to the court.

קל ע"א

1. ב"ה
2. ע"ד שבאה לפנינו האשה מ' יענטלה אל' המנוח כ' משה ב"יוסף[2] טויב וביקשה מאתנו לסלק אותה
3. ולפרוע כתובת' ותוס' כפי השטרות שהציעה לפנינו ועוד תובעות שארי דברי'
4. מעזבון בעלה ז"ל מה שמגיע לה לפי טענותי' התור'[3] כ"ה כ"ה[4] בענדיט הענא סג"ל
5. בהרשאת שלה ({...})[5] גם תובעות מיגר אל' וה"ה התור' כ"ה משה אויך בהרשאת
6. כ' יוסף טויב אב זקנה ואפטרופס של היתומה שהניח כ' משה ז"ל ובמעמד כ' יוסף
7. הנ"ל בעצמו השיב באריכות נגד תביעות וטענות של האל' וכ"ה בענדיט הנ"ל כמבואר

1. Such postmortem inventories were well known in non-Jewish society in the south-eastern German lands from at least the sixteenth century. See David Sabean, *Property, Production, and Family in Neckarhausen, 1700–1870* (Cambridge: Cambridge University Press, 1990), 26.
2. בן יוסף
3. התורני
4. כפילות במקור
5. תוספת מחוקה מעל השורה

8. הכל בפראטיקאהל המונח לפנינו ולאחר שחתמו עצמם האל' וכ' יוסף הנ"ל בתוקף
9. קומפרמיס בח"ח ובקנס סך מסויי[1] לאשר ולקיים כפי אשר יצא מאתנו נזדקקנו להם
10. ומצאנו על כל [ל]פרט ופרט כמבואר להבא והיינו שיותן להאל' הנ"ל מעזבון בעלה
11. ז"ל הנ"ל לפירעון כתובת ותוס' שעולה כפי שטרות שיש בידה סך ששה מאות רט
12. רק שמחויבת להניח ויתר סך חמשי' רט לבתה היתומה כפי שהתחייב א"ע בת"א
13. שלה על אופן המבואר שם וטבעת קדושין אחרי שיש עדיין בעין בעזבון שייך להאל'
14. הנ"ל בלי ניכוי שום פרוטה מכתובה ותוספת' שלה ומחמת מלבושי של האל' הנ"ל
15. מצאנו ששייך לה כל מלבושי' בלי ניכוי שום פרוטה מכתובה ותוס' ומה שטוען כ"ה
16. משה הנ"ל שאפשר שיש מלבושי' שלא לובשות עדיין אין ממש בטענה גם אותו טבעת
17. שקיבל {הא.} האל' הנ"ל מחמותה מחמת ברכה ראשונה וישנו עדיין בעין תחת
18. ידה שייך להאל' הנ"ל בלי ניכוי גם מתנות איין ווארף מה שהי' נותני' בני {משפח}
19. משפחתה והוא עדיין בעין בעזבון שייך להאל' הנ"ל בלי ניכוי אבל מה שתבעה
20. מתנות שנתן לה בעלה במשך ימי הקנס שהם זהוב קעט טבעת' וקראנאזין וכסף
21. שנאלין וטוענת שהם בכלל מלבושי' אין בטענה זו ממש וכן מתנות שקיבל בעלה
22. ז"ל מאביו הן משך ימי הקנס והן לאחר ה[ח]תנה בשמי' ביקסכה מחמת ברכה
23. ראשונה והן הויז שטייער שקיבלה מאבי' וכן מה שנתן אחי' לבעלה במת[נ]ת
24. סנדק שייך הכל לעזבון ואין בתביעת אלמנה גם מה שתובעת לערך

קל ע"ב

1. ח' א[מ]ות זייטן צייג שנמצאי' בקופרט מעזבון וטוענת האל' הנ"ל שבעלה
2. נתן לה לעשות ממנה מלבוש ומחמת אונס לא הי' בידה לעשות מלבוש ממנה
3. מצאנו שהאל' הנ"ל ג"כ אינה יכולה להוציא מן היתומה ע"פ טענותי' בכן שייך
4. ליתומה ומחמת תביעות האל' שטוענת שנתן לה ({הכל})[2] בעלה {במתנה} ז"ל בכמה
5. ירידין מעות במתנה כשהי' מרוויח ממון ויש עדיין תחת ידה מצאנו שתכלול
6. זה בשבועת כתובת' שכדברי' כן הוא שנתן לה הכל בעלה במתנה ולאחר שנשבעו'
7. כנ"ל שייך לה בלי ניכוי מפרעון כתבתה ותוס' גם מה שטענת מחמת מתנת לויט
8. ווירטש שקיבלה מחמותה פעם אחת שני חגרים שישנו עדיין בעין תחת ידה
9. ופעם אחת קיבלה מחמותה ששה קונפינטציאהנש ר"ט והחליף לה בעלה שנתן
10. שני חגרים תמורת ששה קפי"ר שישנו ג"כ תחת ידה מצאנו שתכלול ג"כ בשבוע[ה]
11. כתובת ותוס' שכדברי' כן הוא שארבע חגרים שיש תחת ידה ששני'
12. מהן קיבלה בעין מחמותה מחמת לויט ווירטש ושני' אחרי' הם חליפין שנתן
13. לה בעלה תמורת ששה קפי"ר שקיבלה מחמותה ג"כ כנ"ל ולאחר שנשבעת כנ"ל
14. שייך לה ג"כ בלי ניכוי וכן מה שטוענות מחמת (פס..)[3] האר נאדל שהי' לה כבר
15. בעודה פנויי' תכלול ג"כ בשבוע שכדברי' כן הוא ואז שייך לה
16. כנ"ל עוד טוענת האל' הנ"ל לפנינו באשר שקצב לה ב"ד {שלה רט} שלשה רט
17. כל שבועה מחמת מזונות היא וב"ב והיא קימצה מכח שהאכילה אחי' על שלחנם

---

1. צ"ל 'מסוים'
2. תוספת מעל השורה
3. תוספת מעל השורה

18. בשבת ויטי[1] בלי תשלומי' באומרים שהם רוצים לוותר נגדה אבל לא נגד בתה
19. היתומה שיש לה מעות יותר ממנה בכן שואלת הנ"ל לצאת ידי שמים אם
20. רשאה לעכב לעצמה שעולה לסך [.״.][2] קרלין מצאנו שרשאה להחזיק לעצמה מה
21. שקימצה בלי ניכוי מפרעון כתובה [ותוס'] עוד תובעות האשה הנ"ל שנופטיכר
22. שהכניסה היא לבעלה בשעת חתנה ועכשיו ה[י]א מעורבת באותן ששייך

קלא ע"א

1. לבעלה ז"ל ואפשר שאבד בעלה מהם באשר ששימשו ביחד בהם שהם כעת
2. תחת מידה מצאנו שעל אותן שנופטיכר שיודעת בבירור שהכניסה לו ושהם עדיין
3. בעזבון נאמנות בשבועה שתיכלול בשבועת כתובה כנ"ל ומה שתובעות תפילה מחזור
4. סליחה טייטש חומש וגם קאמאהט שאנק יותן לה להי[3] בתורת כלי תשמיש משך ימי אל'
5. בתוך שארי כלי תשמישם כפי המבואר למטה ומחמת מיגר אל' יותן להאל' הנ"ל מן
6. עזבון בעלה כל זמן שלא תנשא לגברא אוחרן סך ארבעים זהו' מידי שנה בשנה ואם
7. רוצה האפטרופסי' ליתן לה מיד דמי מיגר אל' כדי שתפנה החצי בית שדרה בו כעת
8. מחויבת האל' לפנות את הבית ומחמת כלי תשמישי' על משך ימי אל' ינתן לה מעזבון בעלה כפי
9. רשימה הנמסר מאתנו ב"ד והיינו באופן שמחויבת האל' ליתן כתב ראי' לאפטרופסי'
10. על כל כלי תשמישי' שיש תחת ידה וכשתנשא לגבר אוחרן מחויבת להחזירם נגד כתב ראי'
11. הלז ומחמת סבלונות (שנכתב ג"כ בשטר כתובה ותוס' שלה רק אחרי שאותו סבלונות שנתן לה בעלה {ב...})[4] כל עת חתנה הי' שאלה בידן ואינו בעזבון ואותו סבלונות שנמצא
12. עכשיו בעזבון בעלה הוא סבלונת נשים ובעלה בעצמו נתן לה לעת חתנותו שתתן לו וטוענת
13. האל' שזאת הסבלונת הנמצא כעת בעזבון נתן לה בעלה תחת סבלונת אחרת שהחזיק למי
14. ששאל ממנו ובזה הטענה נתנה ה"א[5] הנ"ל עיני' על ב"ד (לפשר וגם מצאנו שהפשר הוא לטובת [...])[6] בכן פשרנו שרצו שישומה אותו סבלונת
15. הנמצא בעין בעזבון על דמי שווי' והחצי מדמי שווי' יותן להאל' במעות העזבון בלי ניכוי
16. מכתובה ותוס' ומחמת בתה הקטנה היתומה אצל מי יהי מכאן ולהבא מצאנו לטובת
17. היתומה שתהא היתומה אצל אמה עכ"פ עד שתגיע שנת עשתי עשר שנים ומחמת
18. דמי מזונת ולצורך כיבוס בגדי' של בתה מצאנו שכל זמן שתהי' להאל' הנ"ל משרתת יותן לה
19. מעזבון בעלה מידי שבועה ושבוע שני זהו' וחצי ובזה נתבטלה הטענה מה שתובעת

---

1. ויום טוב
2. יש כאן חור בנייר
3. כפילות במקור
4. תוספת מעל השורה
5. כנראה שר"ל 'האלמנה'
6. תוספת מעל השורה

20. האל׳ מחמת שכירות משרתת על זמן קיץ הלז שגם זה נכלל בתוך שני [זהו׳ (וחצי)[1]] הנ״ל שעליה
21. מוטל לשלם השכירות אכן כשאינה רוצה האל׳ להחזיק משרתת והיא בעצמה רוצה
22. לשמש את בתה או כשתנשא לגבר אוחרן והיא רוצה להחזיק בתה אצלה יותן לה
23. בשביל דמי מזונות וכיבוס בגדי׳ עד שתהי׳ יתומה {הן [...]
24. .ע.ל. מוטל על האפטרופסי׳ לשלם ממעות יתומה ומחמת מה שטוען כ״ה בענדיט
25. הנ״ל [...]} בת שתי׳ עשרה שנה מידי ש[בוע] בשבועה א׳ רט אבל שאר הוצאות של יתומה
26. הן כסדרן ושלא סדרן תמיד ולעולם מוטל על האפטרופסי׳ לשלם ממעות של יתומה
27. ומחמת

קלא ע״ב

1. ב״ה
2. ומחמת מה שטוען כ״ה בענדיט הנ״ל (בהרשאת הנ״ל)[2] שבצוואה {הנ״ל} בעלה ז״ל הי׳ ממנה אפטרופסי׳ אבי׳
3. כ׳ יוסף הנ״ל עם עוד שני׳ הו״ה כ״ה הירש ווירמש והו״ה כ׳ מכאל מאיי וכ״ה הירש הנ״ל אינו
4. רוצה להיות אפטרופס גם כ׳ מכאל מאיי הנ״ל אינו רוצה להיות אפטרופס עדיין
5. לפי שעה בכן יומסר כל העזבון ליד ב״ד והם יסלקו האל׳ בפרעון כתובה ותוס׳ ושארי ד
6. דברי׳ המגיע לה והמותרות יונח ביד ב״ד עד שיתמנה מקהל יצו עוד שני אפטרופסי׳
7. אחרי׳ שיהי׳ עם כ׳ יוסף הנ״ל והאריך בזה בטענותיו ומצאנו שהדין עמו / ואחר שהונח
8. אינפוטאריום מכל העזבון לפנינו מצאנו שיהי׳ באופן זה והיינו שאנחנו ב״ד העמדנו לפי
9. שעה עוד לאפטרופס נאמן הקהלה כ״ה אנשיל פפאן כץ עם כ׳ יוסף הנ״ל {ומה שנמצא ב}
10. ויהי׳ להם לפי שעה כל כח ותוקף כאילו נתמנה מקהל יצו ומה שנמצא בעזבון הנ״ל מעות ב
11. בעין או ח״כ יותן ביד ב״ד מחותם בחתימת של האפטרופס כ׳ יוסף הנ״ל וכ״ה אנשיל הנ״ל
12. ושארי מטלטלי׳ הן כסף וזהוב יובעלין נחושת וברזל בדיל ועופרת וויש גרעהט ושארי כלי
13. בית חוץ מה שניתן להאל׳ לכל תשמישה (על)[3] משך ימי אל׳ כנ״ל יומכר הכל ע״י מוקדם האפשרי ע״י כ׳
14. יוסף וכהר״א[4] הנ״ל ודמי מכירה מהנ״ל יומסר ג״כ ביד ב״ד מחותם בשני חתימת כנ״ל עד
15. שיתמנו שני אפטרופ[ס]י׳ מקהל יצו ואז יומסר להם מה שמונח מחותם ביד ב״ד עם כ׳ יוסף הנ״ל
16. עוד התעצמו לפנינו הצדדי׳ הנ״ל וטוענת האל׳ הנ״ל מחמת שמינית בית מבית שלם פנימי צור
17. ווייסה גנז שדר בו כ יעקב בוקסבוים שהי׳ שייך לחמיו כ׳ יוסף הנ״ל ונתן לחותנו ר׳ ליבמן

1. תוספת לא ברורה מעל השורה
2. תוספת מעל השורה
3. תוספת מעל השורה
4. כבוד הרב אנשיל

18. בשיור יד העליונה לו ולאשתו וכשנשרף הבית הנ"ל כנ"ל חזר ובנה בעלה על הוצאתו בריצוי
19. אביו כ' יוסף על אופן שהפירות מן שמינית בית (מהבית שלם פנימי צור וייסה גנז שדר בו
20. כ' יעקב בוקסבוים)[1] יהי' שלו כל ימי חיי אביו כ' יוסף הנ"ל ואשתו ששייך להם יד [ה] על[י]נ[ה][2]
21. עד תשלום הוצאות הבנין שמינית בית הנ"ל שהוציא גם גבה עד עת פטירתו שכירות ה
22. הבית ועכשיו שנפטר בעלה [ז"]ל וכתב הב"ד בפס"ד שהפירות משמינית בית הנ"ל יהי'
23. להיתומה עד תשלום הוצאות שהוציא אבי' ז"ל וכ' יוסף השיב שלא צווה לבנו הנ"ל לבנות ב
24. בשבילו ובאשר שכ' יוסף הנ"ל נתן עיניו עלינו לפשר ביניהם מצאנו ע"ד פשר שדמי שכירו'
25. מן שמינית בית הנ"ל שייך להיתומה משך זמן שיהי' כ' יוסף הנ"ל ואשתו בחיי' חיותם
26. עד

קלב ע"א

1. ב"ה
2. עד מיתת(ה)[3] א[ח]רון מהם ח"ו עד תשלום דמי בנין הבית שהוציא הנעדר כ' משה ז"ל
3. הנ"ל וכנ"ל נגד זה ינוכה שני זהו' לשנה מיו' דלמטה מדמי יד העליונה על חצי בית
4. פנימי צום קראך בוים שהתחייב א"ע כ' יוסף הנ"ל לשלם לבנו הנעדר ז"ל הנ"ל וי"א וב"כ כל
5. שנה סך עשרה זהו' לשנה כנזכר בת"א של בנו הנ"ל ומחויבי' רק לשלם שמונה זהו' לכל
6. שנה מיו' דלמטה יצא מאתנו יו' ג יוד תמוז תקמא לפק רנ"מ ורמ"ש ואני

No. 139

Fols. 132b–133a; Tuesday 16 October 1781

The Jewish community of Illereichen-Altenstadt did not want its cantor and religious leader, Isaac Lvov, to continue to serve the community. This led to a dispute between Isaac and the communal leadership. The matter came before the rabbi and head of the rabbinic court in Wallerstein, and his decision was brought before the non-Jewish authorities.[4] The non-Jewish authorities turned to the rabbinic court in Frankfurt for their assessment of whether the rabbi of Wallerstein had acted

1. הסוגריים בכתב היד
2. כנראה שר"ל 'העליונה'
3. תוספת מעל השורה
4. The rabbi of Wallerstein and its surrounding communities was probably Simḥah Bunim ben Ẓebi Hirsch Kohen Rappaport. Illereichen may not have had a rabbi at this time. See the introduction, 40–41, as well

according to the strictures of Jewish law. The Frankfurt court, which included the head of the rabbinic court and six *dayyanim*, refused to take a stand regarding some of the rabbi of Wallerstein's decisions, claiming that it did not know the rationales for the rabbi's rulings. The rabbis of Frankfurt were of the opinion that the community of Illereichen-Altenstadt could not be forced to employ the cantor. The court also noted that neither side could make financial claims against the other. The rabbi of Wallerstein had imposed a punishment on Isaac and demanded that Isaac ask for forgiveness which he appears to have done. Isaac appealed this decision but the Frankfurt court noted that in this regard what had already been done could not be changed and Isaac could not claim damages against the community for any humiliation that he may have suffered.

קלב ע"ב

1. בה
2. ע"ד קטטות ומריבות שבין המ"ץ וש"ץ דק"ק עלרייכה מה' איצק לבוב ובין הצד שכנג{..}
3. שכנגדו ה"ה מה' יוסף פו"מ דשמה עם צירופו שנשלחו האקטן שנשאו ונתנו
4. הצדדי' הנ"ל ביניהם הן בכתב עברי והן בכתב טייטש להשררה יר"ה דכאן
5. מן אדון רעגימענטש ראהט אונד לנד ריכטר אין אובר אונד נידרשוואבן
6. יר"ה גם הפס"ד מן הרב דק"ק וואלירשטיין נרו' והשררה יר"ה דכאן שלחו לנו[1]
7. כל האקטין ופס"ד הנ"ל ע"י ג"ק דכאן יצו ומתוך הדיקרעט של האדון רעגימענ'[2]
8. ראהט אונד לנדריכטר הנ"ל ראינו שבקש מאתנו ב"ד ח"מ לחוות דעתינו אם
9. יפה דן הרב דקק[3] וואלירשטיין לפי דין ישראל ובאם שטעה על איזה אופן יש
10. למלאות החסרון וטעות של פסק הנ"ל וזה תוכן דברי חפצו של האדון הנ"ל ולזה
11. ולזה נזדקקנו בעיון הדק היטיב בכל האקטין וגם בפס"ד הנ"ל ואחרי העיון ה
12. היטיב מצאנו שעל כל פני' אין להכריח את קהל עלרייכה להחזיק את מה' איצק ה
13. הנ"ל להיות ש"ץ ומ"ץ בעל כרחם / וגם אין לחייבם לשלם לו מן עבר עד עתה ש
14. שום פרוטה אחת / וגם להיפוך אין לקהל הנ"ל שום תביעה פרוטה אחת מהעבר
15. עד עתה על הש"ץ ומ"ץ הנ"ל / ועל אודות שארי דב[רי'] הנאמרי' בפס"ד הנ"ל דהיינו
16. העונשי' ובקשת מחילה ושארי דברי' שמוטל על המ"ץ וש"ץ הנ"ל בפס"ד הנ"ל מצאנו
17. מה שכבר[4] המ"ץ מאותן הדברי' כבר נעשה ואין יכול לתבוע עלבונו {.} על העבר
18. ומה שלא נתקיים עדיין / באם יבקשו צד שכנגדו הקיום ה[נ]ה מאחר שהרב
19. דק"ק וואלירשטיין כתב בפס"ד שלו הנ"ל בזה"ל להיות נקי מה' ומישראל כתב
20. = תי מיד קודם בובליציהרונג של פסק הנ"ל טעם הפסק והחקירות והעיון על כל

---

as Sendik, *Beyn din le-pesher*, p. 21 n. 97. On parallel archival material, see Gotzmann, *Jüdische Autonomie*, 270–71, n. 77.

1. כפילות במקור
2. רעגימענטש
3. דקהילת קודש
4. כנראה שהמילה 'קיים' חסרה כאן (ר' שורה 18)

21. פונקטן ופונקטין של טענות הצדדי' הנ"ל תוך פראטיקאהל המוסגר ומחותם
22. בחתימות הצדדי' להיות מוכן ומזומן לעת הצורך לפני כל יודעי דת ודין
23. {תורתינו שאין לנו לדון} להצ[...][1] זו בלי תוס' וגרעון עכ"ל / בכן
24. מצאנו לפי דת ודין תורתינו שאין לנו לדון בדבר באשר שאיננו ל
25. למראה עינינו

קלג ע"א

1. ב"ה
2. למרווה[2] עינינו הטעמי' של הרב הנ"ל הנזכרי' בפס"ד הנ"ל {וכן} וכל זמן
3. שאיננו למראה עינינו הטעמי' הנ"ל אין להכריח הש"ע ומ"ע הנ"ל לקיים
4. שום דבר מעונשי' ובקשת מחילה ושארי דברי' הנ"ל אשר לא נתקיימו ע
5. עדיין יצא מאתנו יו' ג דז תשרי תקמ"ב פה הק"ק פפורט[3] דמיין יע"א
6. ה"ק פנחס הלוי א[יש] הורוויץ אבד דקק[4] הנ"ל
7. הק' נתן בלא"א כ"ה שלמה מאַז ז"ל ראש ישיבה פה קק[5] פפ"ד יע"א
8. הק יעקב בלא"א המנוח כ' ישראל דוד טעבלי שמש ז"ל דיין דקק הנ"ל
9. הק אברהם טריר הכהן
10. הק זנוויל בלא"א כ"ה משה טרך ז"ל
11. הק מאיר בלא"א כ"ה זלמן שיף כץ ז"ל לה"ה
12. ואני

No. 140

Estate of Brynla, widow of Neta Orschel v. Trier

Fol. 133b–134a; Tuesday 20 November 1781

The executors of the estate of the late Brynla, widow of Neta Orschel, came to the court in a quandary. Brynla had willed that a perpetual fund be set up and that the proceeds be used for charitable purposes. However, in stating the amounts to be given to various causes each year, Brynla had assumed an annual return of 5% on the 4,000 guldens that she deposited with the community, yet the actual return was only 4.5% per annum. This left a shortfall between what Brynla had stipulated should be given out and what was on hand to be distributed. The executors asked

1. יש כאן חור בנייר
2. צ"ל 'למראה'
3. צ"ל 'פרנקפורט'
4. דקהילת קודש
5. קהילת קודש

the court to determine which of the donations should be reduced and by how much. In addition, Brynla's heirs had not delivered the money to create the fund immediately after her death, and thus the funds did not earn income for the full year. This resulted in a shortfall on the anniversary of Brynla's death, apparently the end of the fiscal year for the funds. With respect to the latter point, the court suggested that the executors simply recalibrate their fiscal year. As to the former, the court ordered that what remained to be cut would be reduced equally from all the charitable causes that she had listed. The question was also dealt with by the chief rabbi of Frankfurt, Rabbi Pinḥas Horowitz, in his responsa.[1]

In addition, Dayyan Abraham Trier sent a representative to the court claiming that Brynla had made a provision in her will that he be given 100 guldens on condition that he perform certain acts (rites?) during the first year after her passing, which he did. Brynla had also stipulated that the *dayyan* should receive 100 guldens towards the marriage of his son. Trier argued that both amounts were payable immediately upon Brynla's death and, since they had not yet been paid, he was entitled to the interest that had accrued. The executors countered that if the court examined the will carefully it would see that Trier was not entitled to the money for his son until his son was actually about to marry, a view accepted by the court.

Finally, there was a clause in the will that granted Trier 50 guldens in perpetuity from the income of the estate. Trier argued that he was entitled to the 50 guldens regardless of the rate of return that the estate received on its principal, and that the funds were due immediately upon the first anniversary of Brynla's death. The estate responded that the will stated Trier was to receive the aforementioned 100 guldens in the first year, and only in the following years was he to receive the 50 guldens. The court concurred with the *dayyan*'s claims for payment after the first year, but reduced his share in accordance with the reduced income of the estate.

קלג ע"ב

1. ב"ה
2. ע"ד שבא לפנינו ה"ה התור' כ"ה משה אויך בהרשאת אפטרופסי' מהעזבון אל' המנוח
3. מ' בריינלה אל' כ' נטע אורשל[2] ז"ל ה"ה הו"ה כ' זוסמן ריסלסהיים והו"ה כ"ה וואלף וויניג
4. יצו ונפשם בשאלתם בעזבון האל' על כמה דברי' טובי' הנפרטי' בצוואת האל' הנ"ל
5. לקיים מידי שנה בשנה מן רווחי' מסך ארבעה אלפי' זהו' שיונחו ביד האלופי' ג'
6. גובי' יצו לקרן קיימת על דורי דורות והנה מוכח מתוך הצוואה שחשבה וסברה

---

1. See introduction, 83–84.
2. ר' אבני זכרון, מס' 3683. מעשיה הטובים בתחום הצדקה רשומים במצבתה ושם כתוב, 'וגם הפרישה סך ממונה על קרן קיימת לדבר טוב'.

7. האל׳ ז״ל הנ״ל שהאלופי׳ גובי׳ יצו יתנו ה׳ למאה לשנה רווחי׳ וכעת אינם נותני׳
8. רק ד׳ למאה וחצי לכל שנה בכן נחסר עשרי׳ זהו׳ כל שנה בכן שאלתם של ה
9. האפטרופסי׳ הנ״ל שיכירו הב״ד ממי ינוכה אותן עשרי׳ זהו׳ / עוד שאל כהר״ם[1]
10. הנ״ל בהרשאת הנ״ל באשר שמכח עירעור בין היורשי׳ לא נתנו המעות סך ארבעה
11. אלפי׳ הנ״ל ליד הגובי׳ הנ״ל עד כ״ח אדר תקמא העבר בכן עדיין לא עלה עד יום
12. יארצייט שלה והוא ה כסליו הבע״ל הרווחי׳ לסך העולה לדב״ט הנפרטי׳ בצוואה
13. בכן יכירו הב״ד על מי ההפסד וה״ה התו׳ הדיין כה אברהם טריר נרו׳ שנזכר כמה
14. פעמי׳ בצוואת האל׳ הנ״ל שלח לפנינו ה״ה התו׳ כה {ש} וואלף שפייער בהרשאתו לטעון
15. בזכותו ותבע מן האפטרופסי׳ הנ״ל סך מאה זהו׳ הנאמרי׳ בצוואה וז״ל מלבד שיותן לו
16. ג״כ לסיועת נדן בנו סך מאה זהו׳ באשר שקיים כל [הד]ברי׳ המוטל עליו בצוואה הנ״ל
17. משנה ראשונה של העדרתה וטען כ״ה וואלף הנ״ל בהרשאת הנ״ל שתיכף אחר פ
18. פטירת האשה הנ״ל מגיע לו אותן מאה זהו׳ מאחר שנכתב בצוואה לשון תתן וגם
19. לסיועת נדן משמע תיכף ומיד וגם תבע הפירות מאותן מאה זהו׳ משנה שעבר
20. וה״ה התו׳ כ״ה משה הנ״ל בהרשאת האפטרופסי׳ הנ״ל השיב שייעיין הב״ד בצוואה
21. שמשמע מתוכה שלא ניתן לו מיד עוד תבע כ״ה וואלף בהרשאת הנ״ל משנה העבר
22. מיו׳ פטירתה עד עתה חמשי׳ זהו׳ שנזכר בצוואת[2] הנ״ל להדיין כ״ה אברהם ט
23. טריר יותן מרווחי׳ (הנ״ל)[3] כל שנה ושנה על כל ימי חייו סך חמשי׳ זהו׳ גם אינו משגיח
24. על רווחי׳ מה שנותני׳ הגובי׳ עכשיו פחות מה׳ למאה באשר שנזכר בצוואה סתם
25. ליתן לו מידי שנה בשנה חמישי׳ [זהו׳ בלי] תנאי מרווחי׳ / וה״ה כ״ה משה הנ״ל השיב
26. שייעיין הב״ד בצוואה המשמעות שבתוכה ששנה ראשונה לא יקבל רק מאה רט ולא
27. ג״כ חמשי׳ זהו׳ והביא הוכחה לזה מלשון הצוואה והאריכו בטענותיהם ולאחר
28. שחתמו

קלד ע״א

1. ב״ה
2. ולאחר שחתמו עצמם הדיין כ״ה אברהם טריר הנ״ל והאפטרופסי׳ הנ״ל בתוקף קומפרמיס בח״ח ו
3. ובקנס סך מסויים לאשר ולקיים כפי אשר יצא מאתנו ניזדקקנו להם ומצאנו על שאלה ראשונה
4. מן האפטרופסי׳ הנ״ל מחמת מה שנחסר מן הרווחי׳ עשרי׳ זהו׳ כל שנה שראוי להיות לפי הצוואה
5. שני מאות זהו׳ נמצא {נסח} נחסר כל שנה חלק עשיריות מן רווחי׳ בכן ינוכה מתחילה מן
6. שלשי׳ וששה זהו׳ הנפרטים לעניים קרובי׳ על חג הפסח חלק עשיריות העולה שלשה זהו׳
7. שלשי׳ וששה צל ונשאר עוד הפסד ששה עשר זהו׳ כד צל יחולק ההפסד בין הפרט ה

---

1. כבוד הרב משה
2. בכתב היד רשום ׳ה׳ ונראה שהסופר תיקן אותו ל-׳ת׳.
3. תוספת מעל השורה

8. הנאמר בצוואה לחלק לעניי' קרובי' על חג הפסח הנ"ל ובין כל שאר פרטי דברי' ד"ט[1] הנאמרי'
9. בצוואה הנ"ל לעשות מן הרווחי' על שנה דהיינו מן סך שלשי' וששה זהו' {ך. צל} לעניים ק
10. קרובי' על חג הפסח ינוכה עוד שמונה זהו' יב צל {.} נוסף על שלשה זהו' שלשי' וששה צל
11. נשאר לחלק לעני' קרובי' על חג הפסח מידי שנה בשנה סך עשרי' וארבעה זהו' יב צל
12. וחצי אחרת מן ששה עשר זהו' כד צל שהם סך שמונה זהו' יב צל ינוכה מכל שארי פרטי דברי'
13. הנאמרי' בצוואה והיינו לכל או"א לפי ערך ועל שאלה שניי' מן האפטרופסי' מצאנו שמחשבין ת
14. תחילת שנה מיו' שהונח המעות ליד הגובי' על קרן קיימת ואחר שמחשבין כך אין כאן
15. שום הפסד / ומחמת מה שתבע הדיין כ"ה אברהם נר"ו' מאה זהו' לנדן בנו מצאנו שכפי
16. ראינו בצוואה שא[ין מג]יע לו אותן מאה זהו' עדיין עד לעת נישואין בנו הנ"ל אבל מה
17. שתבע חמשי' זהו' מחמ[ת] שנה ראשונה הדין עמו ויותן לו ג"כ משנה ראשונה
18. חמשי' זהו' בניכוי לפי ערך כנ"ל יצא מאתנו יו' ג ג כסליו תקמ"ב לפק הג' אב"ד[2] נרו'
19. והדיין ור"י רנ"מ
20. והדיין רמש[3]
21. ואני

No. 141

Buchsbaum v. Adler

Fol. 134a; Wednesday evening, 19 December 1781

Feis Adler purchased one quarter of a plot on the Goldene Kopf lot from Jacob Buchsbaum for 300 reichstalers. Meʾir Buchsbaum, who must have owned adjacent property or had a share in this very land, objected to the sale and claimed abutter's rights (see B.T., *Babaʾ meziʿaʾ* 108a).[4] The court accepted Meʾir's claim, but obligated him to declare before the court that Jacob had never informed him of his intention to sell the lot for 300 reichstalers before having closed the deal with Feis. The court prohibited Meʾir from selling the lot for three years if no house was

1. כנראה שיש יתור לשון וצ"ל 'דברים טובים הנאמרים'.
2. ר' שו"ת גבעת פנחס, ס' עב.
3. רב מאיר שיף
4. Meʾir Buchsbaum lived in the Goldene Ente house, two doors from the Goldene Kopf lot (see Ettlinger, 23.12.1809). It is unclear when he began to live there and whether such proximity was considered close enough to invoke abutter's rights.

built on it. Me'ir was also obligated to pay Feis 1% of the selling price, apparently as a form of compensation. Cf., no. 182.

22. ע"ד[1] שקנה כ' פייס בהמנוח[2] כ' זעלקלי אדליר הרביעית
23. פלאטץ צום גולדנה קאפף מן כ' יעקב בכ"ה[3] בוקסבוים בעד שלשה מ
24. מאות רט וכ"ה מאיר בכאברלי[4] בוקסבוים (טוען)[5] שרוצה לזכות בו בדין
25. מצרנות מצאנו שמתחילה מחויב כהרם[6] הנ"ל לקבל בחרם בפנינו ב"[ד]
26. שלא אמר לו המוכר כ יעקב הנ"ל קודם שנעשה הקנין שרוצה למכור רביעית פלטץ ש[ל]ו ב
27. בעד שלשה מאות רט ואחר שקיבל כן כנ"ל זכה כהר"ם הנ"ל בדין מצרנות והנאמני' י
28. יכתבו השטר על שם המצרן אך אנחנו ב"ד קבענו זמן לכהר"ם שאין רשאי למכור הפלאטץ
29. משך זמן שלשה שני' מהיו' כל זמן שלא נבנות עלי' בית יצא מאתנו אור ליו' ה ג טבת תקמב לפק
30. ודמי מצרנות עשינו א פראצענט דהיינו שלשה רט שיתן המצרן ללוקח ולא יותר אפי' שכר ב[ש]ל[ש']
31. לב"ד אינו משלם ...
32. הדיין ור"י רנ"מ והדיין ר[מ"]ש [ואני]

No. 142

Fol. 134b; Tuesday evening, 13 November 1781

Hirsch Kohen, a communal leader, sent a message to the court asking that it divide the 30 guldens, 6 kreuzers in the estate of the late Leb Reinim among his various creditors. The nine creditors submitted their claims to the court and all signed a document in which they agreed to accept the court's compromises in the matter. The court examined the claims and spoke to the son of the deceased to find out what he knew about the creditors before dividing the assets. The record offers no hint as to the criteria used by the court in coming to its decision.

---

1. לאור זה שהשורות האחרונות של התעודה הקודמת היו קצרות (ראשי תבות שמות הדיינים), נשאר מקום ריק בדף והסופר החליט לנצל אותו. שלשת השורות הראשונות בתעודה זו הן באותן השורות אשר המילים האחרונות של התעודה הקודמת נמצאות בהן.
2. בן המנוח
3. בן כבוד הירץ
4. בן כבוד אברלי
5. תוספת מעל השורה
6. כבוד הרב מאיר

קלד ע"ב

1. ב"ה
2. ע"ד שהו"ה פו"מ כ"ה הירש כהן גבאי הקהל יצו שלח אלינו ב"ד ח"מ להזדקק בתביעות
3. הני {אשני} אנשי' המבוארי' למטה שיש להם על עזבון המנוח כ' ליב ריינום ז"ל שיש
4. תחת יד פו"מ הנ"ל שהוא סך שלשי' זהו' ויו צל ולעשות חלוקה ביניהם וכפי אשר
5. יצא מאתנו כן רוצה לחלוק ביניהם והנה אחרי שבעלי חובות המבוארי' למטה באו
6. לפנינו והציעו תביעתם וטענותם לפנינו באריכות מה שהי' לכל או"א מהם על
7. הנעדר ז"ל הנ"ל גם חתמו עצמם בתוקף קומפרמיס בח"ח ובקנס סך מסויים חצי
8. לשררה יר"ה וחצי להקדש לאשר ולקיים כפי הפשר שיצא מאתנו בחלוקה ביניהם
9. נזדקקנו להם ולאחר שדקדקנו הדק היטיב בתביעה של כל או"א מבעלי חובות
10. הנ"ל וגם חקרנו כפי האפשרי מה שידוע לכ' גדלי' בן המנוח כ' ליב ריינום ז"ל הנ"ל
11. מחמת בעלי חובות הנ"ל מצאנו ע"ד פשר דבר שיחלוק ה"ה פו"מ כ"ה הירש הנ"ל את
12. סך דמי עזבון הנ"ל כפי המבואר למטה והיינו שיתן להו"ה כ"ה ליב שאטן ומשות
13. ומשותפו הו"ה ג"ע כ' יחיאל כהן סך שני זהו' מעזבון הנ"ל להו"ה כ' טעבלי לנדוי[א]
14. סך שני זהו' להשמש כ"ה זיסקינד שטערן בשביל אחותו הינטלה[1] סך שלשה זהו'
15. לכ' שלמ[2] בר"ב[3] קאסיל חצי זהוב לכ' מרדכי בן [הירש] שטיפל זל[4] סך אחד עשר
16. זהו' להאשה מרת יהודית אשת כ' יוסף העכט [ס]ך ארבעה זהו' {שלשי' וששה צל
17. להאשה מ' בריינלה אלשטאט סך שני זהו' חמשי' צל לבן[ח] כ' אברלי} חמשי' צל
18. לכ' וואלף בר משה מינשטר סך שלשה זהו' שלשי' וששה צל להאשה מ' בריינלה
19. אלשטאט סך שני זהו' חמשי' צל לב"ח כ' אברלי האגנויא א' קש[5] יצא מאתנו
20. אור ליו' ד דו מרחשון תקמ"ב רמ"ש ואני ר מענדלי לילג

No. 143

Yachet, widow of Gumpel Mai v. Mai

Fol. 135a; Sunday evening, 23 December 1781

Through her legal counsel, Yachet, widow of Gumpel Mai,[6] asked the court to

---

1. אולי צ"ל 'מינדלה', שמה של אחותו של זיסקינד שטערן (ר' אלה תולדות 17.9.1762 [דף של אביו של זיסקינד שטערן, אברם שטערן]). אמנם, בספר הזכרון מוזכר אשה בשם הינדלה בת אברם שטערן שנפטרה בכ"ב אדר שני תקס"ב. אמנם ע"פ מצבתה (אבני זכרון, מס' 4386, עם תיקון השם ע"פ אלה תולדות) הינדלה היתה בתה של ליב שווארצשילד. אטלינגר (26.3.1802) הציע שאולי אברם שטערן היה אב חורג שלה.
2. כנראה 'שלמה'
3. בן בענדיט(?)
4. זכרונו לברכה
5. קופשטוק
6. Gumpel Mai (May) was murdered in late August 1781. For an account of his murder and the search for his

allow her to swear, as was customary, that she had received what was due to her according to her marriage contract and to declare her free and unencumbered by her husband's estate. The guardians of Gumpel Mai's children objected to the request. Through their representative, they noted that all assets of the estate were in Yachet's hands and that if the court allowed Yachet to swear, the guardians would have no way of receiving funds from her to support the children. The guardians suggested that the court state the amount due to Yachet, allow her to receive her due, and then permit her to swear. Presumably other funds would remain in the estate for the children. The court ordered Yachet to present an inventory of all assets in the estate. Once the inventory was certified to be true by the court, the court would see to it that she received what she was due, and she would be allowed to swear. See too no. 148.

קלה ע"א

1. ב"ה
2. ע"ד הטענות בין האשה מ' יאכט אל' המנוח כ' גומפל מאיי ז"ל ובין האפטרופסי' של ה
3. היתומי' ה"ה הו"ה כ' מכאל ואחיו כ' בענדיט מאיי סג"ל והיינו שה"ה התורני כ"ה משה
4. אויך בא בהרשאת האל' ותובע שרוצה לישבע על {שב} כתובת' כנהוג וה"ה כ"ה מ
5. מאיר מז בהרשאת האפטרופסי' הנ"ל השיב מאחר שכל העזבון הוא תחת ידה הם מתיראי'
6. שאם נשבעת אין יכולי' להוציא ממנה שום דבר בכן יכירו הב"ד מקודם מה שמגיע
7. לה ע"פ שטרותי' ואח"כ תשבע ורוצי' ליתן לה כתובת' והאריכו בטענותיהם ומאחר
8. שחתמו הצדדי' עצמם בקומפרמיס בח"ח ובקנס סך מסויים חצי לשררה יר"ה וחצי
9. להקדש לקיים כפי הפס"ד שיצא מאתנו נזדקקנו להם ומצאנו שהאל' הנ"ל מחויבת
10. להניח כל האינפוטאריום מעזבון בעלה ז"ל הן מטלטלין כסף וזהוב ואבני' טובות
11. [מ]זומני' ח"כ מכל מה שהפה יוכל לדבר והלב לחשוב מכל מה שיש בעזבון הנ"ל לפני ב"ד
12. וכסף וזהוב תכתב הכלי' והמשקל של כל או"א בתוך האינפוטאריום ואבנים טובו'
13. ומרגליות תוחתם בחתימת של הג'[1] אב"ד נר' וח"כ יונחו מחותם ביד הג' אב"ד נר'
14. עד לעת הסילוק ולאחר שתקיים האל' כל הנ"ל אזי אינם יכולי' האפטרופסי'
15. לעכבה מלהשבי'...[2] תשבע כתובת' כנהוג ואח"כ תציע שטרותי' לפני ב"ד
16. ואז אנחנו נעיין בהם ...[3]ק כמה מגיע לה ע"פ שטרותי' כל הנ"ל יצא מאתנו
17. בתורת קומפרמיס שבידינו אור ליו' ב זיין טבת תקמ"בלפק
18. הג' אב"ד נר'
19. וראש ישיבה רנ"מ

killer, see the Frankfurt *Memorbuch*, fol. 276b. Also see Horovitz, *Responsa*, no. 23, as well as the material — including archival items — cited by Ettlinger in his listing of Gumpel Mai (22.8.1781).

1. הגאון
2. יש כאן חור בנייר
3. יש כאן חור בנייר

20. ורמאירי[1] שיף
21. ואני

No. 144

Community v. Haas

Fols. 135b–136a; Wednesday 26 December 1781

The leaders of the community sued Zalman Haas for back rent resulting from his failure to pay for his use of a seat in the old synagogue which they had just sold to another party. According to the community, Zalman admitted to using the seat for twenty-one years, from 1758 until 1779. Based on the amount paid in rent by the person who had previously sat on the seat, the community reckoned that Zalman owed it 11.5 reichstalers for each year of use. Zalman countered that he certainly did not sit on the seat before 1761, and he was uncertain if he sat on the seat before 1763. According to Zalman, in 1763 one Moses Friedberg offered to act as an intermediary and said that the seat could be rented for 12 guldens a year. Zalman accepted this and claimed that he paid Moses for the seat every year thereafter until 1779, relying on Moses to transfer the funds to the community. The community countered that it never received any funds from Moses on Zalman's behalf and added that it was common knowledge that Moses was not a preceptor of the community. Moses himself could not be consulted, for he had died. Zalman acknowledged his obligation to pay for the seat for the period after Moses' death, during which he had paid no one. Finally, Zalman disputed the amount the community charged him and noted that the current cost of renting a seat was lower than he was being charged. The community conceded that seats were now less expensive than they had been but argued that Zalman should be charged according to the price of the seat during the period in which he used it.

The court rejected Zalman's claim that he had paid Moses Friedberg for the seat and had relied on him to transfer the money to the community. The court ordered Zalman to pay a compromise sum of 14 guldens per annum for his use of the seat between 1763 and 1779, the years that he admitted to using it, and a lump sum payment of 36 guldens for the years that were in dispute.

---

1. ורבי מאיר

קלה ע"ב

1. ב"ה
2. ע"ד שבא לפנינו ה"ה התורני כ"ה משה אויך בהרשאת האלופי' גובי' יצו ותבע מן הו"ה ג"ץ
3. כ' זלמן הז יצו דמי שכירות מקו' שלם בבהכ"י העומד עלי' כעת כ' טעבלי ווירמש שמכרו
4. הגובי' יצו בשנת תקלט העבר להו"ה כ' אנשיל פלערשהיים וטרם שמכרו הי' עומד עלי' כ' זלמן
5. הנ"ל משנת תקיח עד שנת תקלט וכפי שאמר כ' זלמן הנ"ל בעצמו לפניהם שמן שלשה שני' אחר
6. חתונתו הי' עומד עלי' עד שנת תקלט הנ"ל ולא שילם שכירות לגובי' בכן תבע ממנו דמי שכירו'
7. והיינו יא רט וחצי מן כל שנה ושנה כמו ששילם המנוח כ"ה נתן קולפא ז"ל שכירות
8. שהי' עומד עלי' מקדם ג"כ בשכירות ושילם כל כך וכפי שנמצא בפנקס הגובי' ששילם
9. ר נתן קולפא בעד שכירות המקו' הנ"ל וה"ה התורני כ"ה מאיר מז בהרשאת הו"ה ג"ץ
10. כ' זלמן הנ"ל השיב שברור לו משך ששה שני' ראשוני' אחר חתנותו שהי' בשנת תקטו
11. העבר לא הי' עומד על המקו' הנ"ל רק על מקו' אחר רק שמסופק עוד בשתי שני' שלאחר ששה
12. שני' הנ"ל אם הי' עומד על המקו' הנ"ל או לאו רק אח"כ בא אליו המנוח כ"ה משה פ
13. פרידבורג ז"ל לסרסור לו אותו מקו' הנ"ל בשכירות מן הגובי' יצו ושכרו ממנו וקצץ
14. עמו שכירות שני' עשר זהו' לשנה ושילם כ' זלמן כל שנה השכירות לכ"ה משה הנ"ל
15. וסמוך עליו שהי' שמש ונאמן הקהלה שיתן לגובי' ...[1] ר עוד חייב מן פטירת
16. ר משה ז"ל ואילך וזו רוצה לשלם ומה שטענו האלופ[ים גו]בי' שאמר לפניהם שמן שלשה
17. שני' אחר חתונתו הי' עומד על המקו' הנ"ל זה לא הי' דרך הודאה רק אמר כן במהירו' מ
18. מתוך כעסו שהי' תובעי' אותו משנת תקי"ג ע"ז השיב שבאותו פעם עדיין הי' פנוי ולא
19. נתן לב באותו פעם כמה הי' אחר חתנותו כשבא על אותו מקו' הנ"ל ומה שתבעו שכירו'
20. יא רט וחצי מן כל שנה השיב כה[2] מאיר הנ"ל שהשוכר שעומד עלי' כעת אינו משלם יותר
21. מן אחד עשר זהו' וגם כ' זלמן הנ"ל לא הי' נותן שכירות יותר באותו פעם רק יב זהו' וכ"ה
22. משה הנ"ל השיב שגובי' לא קיבלו כלום שכירות מן ר' משה פרידבורג ז"ל וגם ידוע שכ"ה
23. משה הנ"ל לא הי' השמש מן הגובי' בכן לא הי' לו לכ' זלמן הנ"ל לשלם לו רק לשמש דגובי' או
24. לפחות הי' לו להודיע לא' מן הגובי' ומדמי שכירות שנותן השוכר כעת אין ראי' ש
25. שעכשיו הם בזול ומקדם הי' מקומות ביוקר רק הם סמכו על פנקס הגובי' מה ששילם
26. השוכר מלפניו

קלו ע"א

1. ב"ה
2. והאריכו בטענותיהם ואחר שחתם עצמו הו"ה כ' זלמן הנ"ל בתוקף קומפרמיס וגם ה
3. האלופי' קציני' גובי' יצו התרצו עצמם לאשר ולקיים כפי אשר יצא מאתנו ב"ד נזדקקנו להם

---

1. יש כאן חור בנייר
2. כבוד הרב

4. ומצאנו שעל משך זמן שהודה כ' זלמן הנ"ל בעצמו שהי' עומד על מקו' שלם הנ"ל והיינו מחג ה
5. הפסח שנת תקק"ג עד (פסח)[1] שנת תקלט מחויב לשלם להאלופי' ק' גובי' יצו השכירות מקו' הנ"ל
6. ומה שטוען שכבר שילם לכ"ה משה פ"ב[2] ז"ל אינו מועיל כלום בטענתו לפטור את עצמו ומחו'
7. דמי שכירות מן כל שנה על משך זמן הנ"ל שהם שלשה עשר שני' ירדנו לשומא ע"פ פשר בריצוי
8. שני צדדי' הנ"ל ומצאנו שיחשבו השכירות מידי שנה בשנה לסך ארבע עשר זהו' עולה
9. יחד לששה עשר שני' הנ"ל לסך שני מאות וארבעה ועשרי' זהו' ועל השני' הנותרות דהיי'
10. דהיינו מפסח שנת תקיח עד פסח שנת תקדג שלא הודה כ' זלמן הנ"ל שעומד על מקו' זה
11. אך על שלשה שני' מהם טוען ברי שלא עומד עלי' ושני שני' שהוא בעצמו מסופק אם
12. עומד עלי' אם לאו מצאנו ע"פ פשר בריצוי שני צדדי' שמחויב לשלם כ' זלמן הנ"ל סך
13. שלשי' וששה זהו' נוסף על שני מאות ועשרי' וארבעה זהו' הנ"ל העולים יחד שני מאות וששי'
14. זהו' שמחויב לשלם הו"ה ג"ע כ' זלמן הנ"ל להאלופי' ק' גובי' יצו ובזה פטור מתביעות שכירות
15. מקו' הנ"ל יצא מאתנו יו' ד ט טבת תקמ"ב רנ"מ ורמ"ש ואני
16. ———

No. 145

Fol. 136a; Sunday evening, 6 January 1782

A record of the sale of half a seat in the upper women's section of the synagogue to Ḥayyim Halle for 230 guldens after the customary period of public bidding. The portion of the seat had been owned by a minor, the daughter of the late Getz Wittingin. The other half of the seat was owned by Simḥah Reiss, whose wife was currently using it. A postscript notes that according to the guardians of the daughter, it would be Ḥayyim's turn to enjoy the income from the (whole) seat the following year. Also see no. 146.

17. חצי מקו' שלם בע"נ העליונה שעומדו' עלי' כעת אשת כ' שמחה רייס שהי' שייך ליתומה בת
18. המנוח כ' געץ וויטינגין נמכר בפנינו בד[3] לאחר הכרזה כנהוג להו"ה כ' חיים בהמנוח[4] כ"ה הענוך

---

1. תוספת מעל השורה
2. פרידבורג
3. בית דין
4. בן המנוח

19. האלי בעד שני מאות ושלשי' זהו' לשלם כתיקון הקהלה נעשה אור ליו' ב' דא טבתקמ"בלפק[1]
20. רנ"מ ורמ"ש ואני והחצי' האחר מן אותו מקו' שייך לכ' שמחה רייס הנ"ל ושכרות שנה הב[ל][2]
21. מגיע לכ' חיים הנ"ל כפי שאמרו האפטרופסי' ר וואלף רופא וכ' משה [רי]סלסהיים לפנינו
22. ————

No. 146

Fol. 136a; Sunday evening, 6 January 1782

A record of the sale of half a seat in the upper women's section of the synagogue by the daughter of the late Getz Wittingin (see no. 145) to Me᾿ir Fulda for 310 guldens. The seat was currently being used by the wife of Isaac Heidelburg. Me᾿ir already owned the other half of the seat and this purchase gave him ownership of the entire seat. As in the previous case, the half-seat was sold after a period of open bidding.

23. חצי מקו' בע"נ העליונה אשר עומדות עלי' כעת אשת הו"ה כ' אייזק ב"י[3] היידלבורג יצו
24. שהי' שייך ליתומה הנ"ל[4] אשר חצי' האחרת שייך להו"ה כ"ה מאיר בו"ו פולדא
25. יצו נמכר בפנינו ב"ד לאחר הכרזה כנהוג להו"ה כ"ה מאיר בוו[5] פולדא הנ"ל בעד
26. סך שלשה מאות ועשרה זהו' לשלם כמנהג הקהלה נעשה אור ליו' ב דא
27. טבת תקמבלפק[6] רנ"מ ורמ"ש ואני

No. 147

Rivkah, widow of Mordecai Oppenheim v. Falk

Fol. 136b; Wednesday evening, 9 January 1782

Rivkah, widow of Mordecai Oppenheim, claimed that Mordecai Falk owed her late husband a silver candelabra and funds. Through her counsel, Rivkah stated that

1. טבת תקמ"ב לפרט קטן
2. הבאה לטובה
3. בן יוזבל
4. ההפניה היא ליתומה המוזכרת למעלה באותו עמוד בכתב היד (כאן מס' 145), בת המנוח כ' געץ וויטינגין.
5. בן וואלף
6. תקמ"ב לפרט קטן

her husband had told her of this debt on his deathbed. Oppenheim's son confirmed that his father had told him of the debt and added that the reason his father did not record the debt in his business diary was that he was afraid his wife would learn of the transaction and be angry with him. Mordecai Falk, represented by his son, refused to believe Oppenheim had said such a thing, and, if he had, Falk claimed that it was a lie, for he owed Oppenheim nothing and Oppenheim had never made such a claim against him.

The court ruled that Falk himself would have to appear before it and make his denial under threat of a rabbinic ban. Once he did so, he would be absolved of any liability.

קלו ע״ב

1. ב״ה
2. ע״ד שבא לפנינו ה״ה התורני כ״ה אנשיל פפאן בהרשאת האשה מ׳ רבקה אל׳ המנוח כ״ה
3. מרדכי בפו״מ כ׳ וואלף אופנהיים ז״ל ותבע מן הו״ה כ׳ מרדכי פאלק כץ א׳ קווארט רופל
4. שהוא ד אלטה ל״ד וגם א׳ באהר כסף לייכטר שאמר בעלה ז״ל הנ״ל כשהי׳ מוטל על ע״ד רנ״לי[1]
5. שכ׳ מרדכי עדיין חייב לו כנ״ל וגם הבן של כ״ה מרדכי ז״ל הנ״ל הב״ח כ׳ וואלף בעמדו לפנינו
6. ג״כ אמר ששמע מאביו ז״ל הנ״ל שכסף לייכטר הי׳ משקלם לה עד לו לויט[2] והוסיף לטעון מה
7. שלא נמצא כתוב בפנקס של אביו מזה החוב הוא מטעם שלא רצה אביו ז״ל לגלות לאמו
8. מפני שהי׳ מתיירא שלא {תעכ} תכעוס עליו והב״ח כ׳ זעלקלי בן הו״ה כמרדכי[3] פאלק כץ הנ״ל
9. השיב בהרשאת אביו שאינו מאמין שאמר כ״ה מרדכי ז״ל [ה]נ״ל כלל מזה החוב ואף אם אמר
10. כן שקר הוא שאינו (נשאר)[4] חייב לו כלום וגם כ״ה מרדכי לא תבע ממנו בעודו בחיי׳ כלום משום ..
11. והאריכו בטענותיהם ולאחר שחתמו עצמם בקומפרמיס נזדקקנו להם ומצאנו שכ׳ מרדכי
12. פאלק הנ״ל יקבל בחרם בפנינו ב״ד שכדבריו כן הוא שלא נשאר חייב כלום לכ״ה מ
13. מרדכי ז״ל הנ״ל ובזה פטור ומסולק מן תביעות הנ״ל יצא מאתנו אור ליו׳ ה׳ ך״ד טבתקמ״ב[5]
14. רנ״מ ורמ״ש ואני

---

1. אולי צ״ל ׳ר״ל׳ (רחמנא לצלן)
2. 1 לויט שווה בערך 15 גרם.
3. כבוד מרדכי
4. תוספת מעל השורה
5. טבת תקמ״ב

No. 148

Yachet, widow of Gumpel Mai v. Mai

Fol. 137a–138a; Tuesday evening, 15 January 1782

The dispute regarding the estate of Gumpel Mai continued (see no. 143). Representatives of Gumpel's widow, Yachet, and the children's guardians came to the court claiming rights to various parts of the estate. The court noted that Yachet was to receive 4000 reichstalers as part of her husband's direct obligation to her. During her marriage, Yachet had agreed to forgo an additional 500 reichstalers and give it to the children. The court ordered that this be carried out. Items that Yachet owned before her engagement to Gumpel remained hers, although she was ordered to give the children 40 guldens against them (the court offered no rationale for this ruling). Gifts received by Gumpel and Yachet during the period of their engagement from her father, Yudaʾ Kulp, and Gumpel's mother were awarded to the children. With respect to other gifts, the court favored the rights of the surviving children, although it granted Yachet some of the items. The court allowed Yachet to continue to live in the half of a house that she was currently occupying, as well as use household objects for the duration of her widowhood. However, she was obligated to pay an annual sum to the estate for the living space. The estate was responsible for repairs to the house and most of the taxes. Yachet's youngest daughter was to live with her for the next 6 years. During this time Yachet would bear all expenses for the child's care and maintenance, including her education. Extraordinary expenses that totaled more than 10 reichstalers annually would be borne by the estate. An older daughter was to live with Gumpel's brother, Michael, who assumed responsibility for her care and maintenance for six years.

קלז ע״א

1. ב״ה
2. ע״ד הטענות והפרשות בענין סילוק אל׳ המנוח כ׳ גומפל מאיי סג״ל ז״ל בהתחייבו׳
3. שיש בשטר כתובת׳ ותוספ׳ ותנאי׳ אחרוני׳ שלה שהציעו לפנינו והאריכו בטענותיהם
4. ה״ה התורני כ״ה משה אויך שבא בהרשאת האל׳ הנ״ל וה״ה התורני כ״ה מאיר מז הבא בהרשא׳
5. האפטרופסי׳ של יתמי המנוח ז״ל הנ״ל השיב נגדו בשביל זכות היתומי׳ הנ״ל כמבואר ה
6. הכל בקונטרס הטענות באריכות לפנינו ומאחר שהאל׳ הנ״ל וגם האפטרופסי׳ של יתמי
7. הנ״ל הו״ה כ״ה אייזק קולפא יצו והאחי׳ הו״ה כ׳ מכאל וכ׳ בענדיט מאיי סג״ל חתמו עצמם
8. בקומפרמיס בח״ח ובקנס לקיים כפי שיצא מאתנו בכן נזדקקנו להם ומצאנו על כל פרט
9. ופרט כמבואר להבא והיינו שקודם כל יותן להאל׳ הנ״ל מעזבון המנוח ז״ל הנ״ל סך ארבעת

10. אלפי' רט כפי השטרות שלה / ועוד שייך לה חמשה מאות רט בשביל תוספת' רק שמחויב'
11. להניח אותן חמש מאות רט בתורת ויתור ליתומי' שלה כפי שהתחייב את עצמה ב
12. בתנאי' אחרוני' שלה על אופן המבואר שם / ומחמת מתנות שתבע כ"ה משה והציע ל
13. לפנינו רשימה מה שניתן להזוג מתנות מיו' גמר השידוך עד שנת החתנה ובכלל הן
14. מאבי' והן מחמותה וטוען כ"ה משה הנ"ל ששייך להאל' הנ"ל כל מתנות ולפחות אותן
15. אב[י][1] שהם נכסי מלוג שלה מצאנו שכל מתנות שניתן לה משך ימי הקנס עד יו' החופה
16. הן מאבי' של האל' הנ"ל והן מחמותה שייך הכל ליתומי' / וגם מה שתבע כ"ה משה הנ"ל
17. איין גדול כסף בעכר עם טעקל פר גולד מה שנתן אבי' הו"ה כ' יודא קולפא מחמת
18. הויז שטרייער שייך ג"כ ליתומי' וגם מה שתבע ב' [פ]אהר אוהר הענג שנתן לה בעלה
19. אחר החתנה שייך ליתומי' ומחמת מה שתבע כ"ה משה הנ"ל והציע לפנינו רשימה
20. מה שניתן למתנות איין ווארף {..} לשעת החתנה מקרובי' של האל' הנ"ל כפי שהצי[ע]
21. רשימה לפנינו והיינו גדול בעכר איבר גולד מאבי' א' זאלץ פאס מן ר' ליזר קולפא
22. ב' לעפל מן ר אייזק קולפא ר אלחנן אופנהיים ב' זאלץ פעסר געלכה שפייער ב
23. פער גולדנר זאלץ פעסר ר משה רייס הויזמאן א' לעפל משה יעקב א' לעפל חברא ב
24. בבית אבי' א' לעפל המעות ביחד משני צדדי' פב זהו' נב צל עוד תבע כ"ה משה הנ"ל
25. שתי טבעתי' שנתן לה אבי' הנ"ל בשבת ראשונה אחר נישואין אחת יש בעין ואחת
26. נמכר / עוד נתן לה זהוב קוגיל אחר החתנה עוד נתן לה בפורי' ראשון אחר ה(ח)[2]תנה
27. כסף בוטשער עם בלעך עוד נתן לה אבי' משה חגרי' ברייט שטוך לשעת חתנות א
28. אחותה והם עדיין בעין עוד תבע והצי[ע] לפנינו רשימ[ה] מה שהי' להאל' הנ"ל בעודה פ
29. פנויי'

קלז ע"ב

1. ב"ה
2. פנויי' והיינו א' טאבאטיער ב' ביקסכר א' עטוויא א' שער הוגה עם קעט ב' ביקסכר
3. עם פינגר הוט אבאהר גרינה אָהרהענג א' באהר שטיינה אָהרהענג א נ"ב טבעת
4. א האר נאדל איבר גולד עם פערלי א איין הענגר שתולה {בצאוו} בצווארה כל הנ"ל טוען
5. כהרם[3] הנ"ל ששייך להאל' הנ"ל עוד תבע כהר"ם הנ"ל שני באהר כסף שנאלין שהם בעזבון
6. ואמר שהי' להאל' הנ"ל מאבי' א' באהר שטיין שנאלה חשובי' מאוד ובעלה ז"ל הי' לקחה ממנה
7. ונתן לשררה אחת ונתן לה תיכף א' באהר כסף קטן שנאלה {חדשי' בכן שייך} ולאחר זמן ע"פ
8. הפצרת' נתן לה עוד באהר כסף שנאלין חדשי' בכן שייך שני באהר הנ"ל להאל' הנ"ל תחת
9. באהר שטיין שנאלה שהי' לה ולאחר שנתנה האל' הנ"ל עיני' על הב"ד לפשר ביניהם

---

1. כנראה שצ"ל 'אותן שקבלה מאביה'
2. תוספת מעל השורה
3. כבוד הרב משה

10. על כל התביעות הנ"ל וגם אנחנו מצאנו שהפשר הוא לטובת היתומי' בכן ירדנו לפשר
11. ומצאנו בתורת פשר שמחמת מעות של איין ווארף הנ"ל אין להאל' שום תביעה על העזבון
12. וגם אותן באהר כסף שנאלין גדולי' חדשי' הנ"ל שייך ליתומי' אבל אותן באהר קטני' כסף
13. הנ"ל וגם זהוב קוגיל הנ"ל וגם טבעת שקיבלה מאבי' בשבת ראשונה אחר החתנה שהוא
14. עדיין בעין וגם כסף בוטשער עם פלעך שנתן לה בפורי' גם חמשה חגריים שנתן לה
15. אבי' ברייט שטוק לשעת חתנת אחותה וגם (כסף)[1] כל מה שנרשם ברשימה הנ"ל מן איין ווארף
16. חוץ המעות כנ"ל וכן מה שהי' לה בעודה פנויי' כפי רשימה הנ"ל שייך הכל להאל' הנ"ל בלי נ
17. ניכוי פרוטה אחת מכתובת' ותוספ' שלה רק שתתן האל' הנ"ל נגד כל הנ"ל סך ארבעי'
18. זהו' ליתומי' אבל מחמת אותו טבעת של ראזעטן שנמכר אין לה שום תביעה על היתומי'
19. ומחמת טבעת קדושין וסבלונות שניתן לה מהחתן ושנזכר בשטרות של האל' הנ"ל והאריכ[ו]
20. בטענותיהם / ובאשר שגם בזה נתנה האל' הנ"ל עיניה על הב"ד לפשר ביניהם מצאנו
21. עד"פ שהסבלונות שהוא עדיין בעין בעזבון שייך להאל' הנ"ל אבל מחמת טבעת קדושין
22. שאינו בעין בעזבון אין לה תביעה על העזבון ומחמת מיגר אל' גם בזה נתנו האל'
23. והאפטרופסי' הנ"ל עיניהם עלינו ב"ד לפשר ומצאנו שיהי' להאל' הנ"ל כל זמן שלא ת
24. תנשא לגבר אוחרא מיגר אל' בכל חצי בית שהיא דרה בו כעת על אופן המבואר והיינו
25. כל זמן שתדור בשטח שני שטעג הויך והוא עד ר"ח אלול הסמוך[2] מחויבת ליתן ליתומי'
26. לפי ערך שלשי' זהו' לשנה מלבד אותן [שכירות] שנותן השוכר בעד בית החורף התחתון
27. ששייך ג"כ ליתומי' וכאשר מגיע ל[ה] שטח איין שטאק הויך דהיינו מר"ח אלול הסמוך
28. הסמוך הבע"ל ואילך על משך שש [ש]ני' רצופי' א[זי] תשלם האל' הנ"ל לעזבון בעלה
29. מידי שנה

קלח ע"א

1. ב"ה
2. מידי שנה בשנה סך חמשי' וארבעה זהו' נגד זה יש רשות להאל' הנ"ל להשכיר איזה
3. חדרי' לאחרי' ודמי תיקון בדק הבית מחויבי' האפטרופסי' לשלם מעזבון הנ"ל / ומחמת
4. כלי תשמישי' על משך ימי אל' כל זמן שלא תנשא לגבר אוחרא ינתן לה מעזבון בעלה כפי רשימה
5. הנמסר לה מאתנו ב"ד והיינו באופן שמחויבת האל' הנ"ל ליתן כתב ראי' להאפטרופסי'
6. על כל כלי תשמישי' (שבידה גם הבלאות)[3] שיש תחת ידה וכשתנשא לגבר אוחרא מחויב'
7. להחזירם אותן כלי תשמישי' שבידה גם הבלאות שהם בעין / ומחמת מזונות האל' ויתומ[י]'
8. עד שעת הסילוק מצאנו שיותן לה מעזבון בעלה מיו' שהניחה אינפוטאריום לפנינו עד

1. תוספת מעל השורה
2. ר' לעיל, מס' 80.
3. הסוגריים במקור

9. שעת סילוק כל שבוע ושבוע סך חמשה רט ומחמת מזונות ושאר צרכי מן הילדי׳
10. יתמי המנוח ז״ל הנ״ל מן שעת סילוק ואילך התחייב את עצמה האל׳ הנ״ל להחזיק אצלה
11. בתה הקטנה מ׳ יטלה תי׳ מיו׳ דלמטה על משך ששה שני׳ בחנם והיינו שתהי׳ עלי׳ כל ה
12. הוצאות כסדרן והיינו אכילה ושתיי׳ מלבושי׳ שכר לימוד כסדר הבנות גם בהוצאות
13. שלא כסדרן חו׳[1] היא התחייבה את עצמה לשלם עד עשרה רט לכל שנה משך ששה שני׳
14. הנ״ל אבל מה שתוציאה יותר מעשרה רט להוצאות שלא כסדרן חו׳ מחויבי׳ האפטרופס[י׳]
15. לשלם לה מעזבון הנ״ל רק שמחויבת האל׳ לברר כמה הוציאה או שתשבע כמה הוציאה
16. ליטול היתרון מעשרה רט לשנה ובפי׳ הותנה שאף אם (לא)[2] יהי׳ לה הוצאות שלא כסדרן
17. בשנה ראשונה אפ״ה אינה מחויבת לשלם בשנה שניי׳ יותר מעשרה רט להוצאות
18. שלא כסדרן חו׳ וכן בכל שנה ושנה משך ששה שני׳ הנ״ל אינו מוטל עלי׳ לשלם יותר מעשורה
19. רט לכל שנה אף אם לא הוציאה כלום בשני׳ הקודמי׳ להוצאות שלא כסדרן חו׳ והא
20. והאפטרופס הו״ה כ׳ מכאל מאיי סג״ל הנ״ל התחייב את עצמו לפנינו להחזיק אצלו בחנם
21. היתומה הגדולה מ׳ בילה בת אחיו המנוח ז״ל הנ״ל ג״כ ששה שני׳ מיו׳ דלמטה בחנם
22. ולהיות כל הוצאות וצרכי היתומה מ׳ בילה הנ״ל עליו הן כסדרן והן שלא כסדרן על
23. משך ששה שני׳ מיו׳ דלמטה ומחמת (מה)[3] שטענו אודות קרונד צונץ מצאנו שיתומי׳ מחוי[בים]
24. לשלם ומה שטענו אודות שאצונג וק[יו]מי׳ והאל׳ הנ״ל נתנה עיני׳ עלינו ב״ד לפשר בזה
25. מצאנו ע״פ פשר שהיתומי׳ יתנו שאצונג עשרה קש[4] לכל שנה והיותר משאצונג
26. וקיומי׳ מוטל על האל׳ יצא מאתנו אור ליו׳ ד׳ רח שבט תקמ״ב הג׳ אב״ד נרו׳
27. והדיין ור״י מהו׳ נתן מז נרו׳ והדיין ר׳ מאיר שיף נרו׳ ואני 40[5]

No. 149

Rofe v. Widow of Wolf Burch

Fols. 138b–139a; Thursday evening, 24 January 1782

In late 1780, Wolf Burch and his here unnamed wife, Fagel, agreed that she would receive 900 guldens in satisfaction of her marriage contract if Wolf predeceased her. To this end they agreed that she would have the right to live in and have a lien on the one half of the house that Wolf owned on the Goldenes Faß lot so long as

---

1. חס ושלום
2. תוספת מעל השורה
3. תוספת מעל השורה
4. קופשטוק
5. לא ברור למה זה נמצא כאן

she did not remarry. After Wolf's death in November 1781, his widow approached the court and, through her representative, requested to be paid her due. She also asked to receive a number of items that had been listed as hers in the agreement, and made some other requests regarding the payment of what she thought she was entitled to but which are not itemized in this record.

The Burchs' son-in-law objected to this arrangement. Through his representative, Lipman Rofe claimed that his mother-in-law could not have the right to sell one-half of the house because she and Wolf had given Lipman that right on one-quarter of the house (i.e., half of their half) as part of a dowry. Without the house there were insufficient assets in the estate to meet the widow's claims, and Lipman suggested that he pay off his mother-in-law's marriage contract and provide her with a housing allowance as the court might see fit, in return for his receiving the right to live in the entire half house. The widow recognized her son-in-law's claim and did not want to move from the house. Through her representative she suggested that she relinquish her rights on a quarter of the house, and that it and some of the contents be sold to pay off her marriage contract.

The court ruled that the widow's rights encompassed the entire half house. It ordered that a quarter of the house be sold to the highest bidder. The widow maintained a lien on the property and it was understood that this reduced the value of the sale. The proceeds from the sale as well as the sale of books held by the estate were to be delivered to the head of the rabbinic court pending payment of the widow's marriage contract. Further decisions regarding the estate were held in abeyance until the value of the estate was realized. Also see no. 150.

קלח ע"ב

1. ע"ד הטענות והפרשות בענין סילוק אלמנת המנוח נאמן הקהלה כ"ה וואלף בוריך סג"ל ה"ה נ"ה התור'
2. כ"ה אנשיל פפאן שבא בהרשאת האל' והציע לפנינו שטר כתובה ותוספ'[1] מן רח[2] כסליו תקמ"א שמבואר
3. בתוכה שתקחי האל' תשעה מאות זהו' לפירעון כתובה ותוספ וגם יהי' לה יד העליונה על חצי בית
4. שלו צום גולדנה פאס כל זמן שלא תנשא לגבר אוחרא עוד נזכר שמה פרטי דברי' מה ששייך להאל'
5. הנ"ל ותבע לפנינו עוד כמה תביעות מה שנוגע לסילוק האל' הנ"ל וה"ה התורני כ"ה משה אויך ב

1. ותוספת
2. ראש חודש

6. בהרשאת ובמעמד חותנו של המנוח ז"ל הנ"ל הו"ה כ' ליפמן בהמנוח[1] כ"ה פער רופא ז"ל השיב על
7. כמה תביעות וגם תבע מן האל' הנ"ל באריכות וכמבואר הכל בק"ה המונח לפנינו גם הציע לפנינו
8. תנאי' ראשוני' בינו ובין חמיו ז"ל ושנעשה ק"ס ע"ז בשעת חופתו כנהוג מן חמיו ז"ל ואשתו האל' הנ"ל
9. שמבואר בתוכה שנתן לו חמיו ז"ל רביעית בית לנדן בשיור יד העליונה לו ולאשתו האל' הנ"ל וטו[ען]
10. וטוען באשר שעזבון חמיו ז"ל זולת חצי בית הנ"ל אינו מגיע לפרעון כתובה ותוס"פ לאל' הנ"ל ורביעי'
11. בית כבר נתן לו חמיו ז"ל לנדן שעשת' אל' ג"כ ק"ס ע"ז בשיור יד העליונה כנ"ל בכן אינו משועבד להאלמנה
12. הנ"ל רק רביעי[ת] בית לפירעון כתובה ומאחר שנשאר יד העליונה על רביעית בית להאל' הנ"ל כל ימי
13. מיגר אל' בכן אינם יכולי' למכור אותו רביעית בית לאחרי' רק בזול בכן רוצה כ' ליפמן הנ"ל ליקח
14. רביעית בית עם יד העליונה בעד תשעה מאות זהו' באופן ובתנאי שידור הוא בכל חצי בית הנ"ל
15. ורוצה לשלם להאל' הנ"ל דמי מיגר אל' כל מה שיכירו הב"ד שמגיע לה בעד מיגר אל' / וה"ה כהר"א[2]
16. הנ"ל הישב שהאל' הנ"ל אינה רוצה לצאת מן (חצי)[3] בית בעלה אחרי שנתן לה בעלה מזה יד העליונה
17. רק שיומכר רביעית בית בלי יד העליונה עם כל המטלטלי' חוץ מכלי תשמישי' שמגיע לה בתורת
18. מיגר אל' ומדמי מכירה יסולק לה מה שמגיע לפירעון כתובה ותוס"פ ושאר תביעות שיש לה על
19. העזבון והאריכו עוד בשאר טענות ותביעות כמבואר הכל בק"ה המונח לפנינו ובאשר ש
20. שהצדדי' הנ"ל חתמו עצמם בתוקף קומפרמיס בח"ח ובקנס סך מסויים לאשר ולקיים כפי אשר יצא
21. מאתנו ב"ד ח"מ בכן נזדקקנו להם ומצאנו על הראשונה הנ"ל שהדין עם האל' הנ"ל ששייך לה יד
22. העליונה בכל חצי בית הנ"ל כל ימי מיגר אל' כפי שטר כתובה ותוס"פ שיש בידה ומה שטוען כ'
23. ליפמן הנ"ל שהוא רוצה לפרוע תשעה מאות זהו' לידור בכל חצי בית ורוצה לשכור לה מיגר אל' אין

---

1. בן המנוח
2. כבוד הרב אנשיל
3. תוספת מעל השורה

24. ממש בטענה זו בכן יומכר רביעית מבית שלם צום גולדנ[י] פאַס הנ"ל בשיור יד העליונה להאל' הנ"ל
25. כנ"ל בהכרזה כנהוג עד שיפסקו המוסיפי[ם]...[1] ביו' ה' הסמוך הבע"ל וגם הספרי' שיש בעזבון
26. הנ"ל יומכרו ע"י המורשאי' כהר"א וכהר"ם[2] הנ"ל ודמי מכירה יונחו ביד ה"ג אב"ד נר"ו עד עת

קלט ע"א
1. ב"ה
2. עד עת סילוק ופריעות האל' הנ"ל / ומחמת שארי טענות שביניהם מאחר שעדיין אינה ידוע לנו
3. כמה עולה דמי מכירה של רביעית בית וספרי' הנ"ל אם מגיע לפירעון כתובת' ותוס"פ
4. או פחות או יותר בכן אין לנו להזדקק בשאר טענות עד שנמכרי' כנ"ל ונראה לפנינו
5. כמה עולה סכום העזבון הנ"ל ואח"כ יקוב הדין ההר ביניהם על הפרשות שיש ביניהם
6. בתורת קומפרמיס שבידינו יצא מאתנו אור ליו' ויו עש"ק יוד שבט תקמ"ב פק[3]
7. הג' אב"ד נר"ו ורנ"מ ורמ"ש ואני[4]

No. 150

Fol. 139a–140b; Monday 25 February 1782

Within a month of the court's order to liquidate assets of the Burch estate (see no. 149), Lipman Rofe and his mother-in-law appeared before the court. Apparently at his wife's urging, Lipman made a more generous offer to his mother-in-law. In addition to paying off her marriage contract (900 guldens), he offered to pay whatever the court determined to be appropriate to five (all?) of his mother-in-law's creditors. In return, he asked that his mother-in-law transfer her portion of the house on Goldenes Faß to him. The widow, whose name, again, is not mentioned, agreed to Lipman's proposal as did her creditors, all of whom are listed here. All the parties asked the court to impose a compromise, and after the sides agreed to be bound by the court's rulings the court agreed to do so.

The court ordered that the land on which one-quarter of the house sat be transferred to Lipman, leaving the widow with one-quarter of the house itself and

1. יש כאן חור בנייר
2. וכבוד הרב משה
3. פרט קטן
4. אחרי המילה 'ואני' יש שני קווים מקבילים, כנראה להפריד בין שתי התעודות בעמוד.

a primary lien on the entire half house as per her marriage contract. The court's compromise led Lipman to claim that he should be paid for the loss of his primary lien on a quarter of the house and that his mother-in-law should be responsible for taxes and repairs for the entire half house. The court rejected his claim for compensation and ordered that they share equally in the payment of taxes. As for repairs, the court instructed that neither side could force the other to make repairs. The court also awarded the widow various items of jewelry that were promised to her in her marriage contract. She also received the use of certain household items for the duration of her widowhood.

Lipman noted that one of the conditions of his marriage was that he and his wife were to be provided with room and board for 18 months by the Burchs, a condition that Lipman claimed his mother-in-law had specifically agreed to under the wedding canopy yet had not fulfilled. He added that Wolf had also promised certain gifts that had not been delivered. The widow, through her representative, counterclaimed that her agreement was not a personal obligation to fulfill the promise, but only allowed that assets she had a lien on through her marriage contract be given to her son-in-law. The court ordered the widow to continue providing the couple with a room, nothing more. The widow also wanted to rent out rooms in the house, but Lipman objected.[1] The court sided with Lipman in this matter, but noted that Lipman agreed that his mother-in-law could rent space to her widowed sister and provide space apparently rent free to Wolf's unmarried sister. There was also a dispute regarding a seat in the men's section of the synagogue. The court ruled that income from the seat belonged to Lipman since it was part of his dowry.

The court ruled that objects in the house (except those promised to the widow for the duration of her widowhood) belonged to Lipman. Since Wolf had no sons, Lipman inherited from him through his wife (Wolf's daughter). Lipman maintained that when the widow submitted an inventory of the estate, she had not reported all of Wolf's clothing. The widow countered that, with the consent of Lipman's wife, she had given some of Wolf's clothing to her brother who was saying Kaddish for Wolf. The court ruled that what the brother had already received could remain with him, but that all other items belonged to Lipman.

The court ordered Lipman to erect a gravestone on Wolf's grave within a year of Wolf's death. He was also to pay for a memorial light that was to burn for 11 months after Wolf's passing. The widow produced a number of receipts related to Wolf's death. These included the costs of memorial lights, hiring young men to study, recite Psalms, pray in a quorum, and having Wolf inscribed in the *memorbuch*.

---

1. Cf., no. 151.

In addition she requested payment of 5 reichstalers per week for living expenses from the time of Wolf's death until the time of this claim. Lipman contested the latter point but was ordered to make one payment of 19 guldens, 24 kreuzers for the sundry claims against him. The record also lists the claims of creditors against the estate and notes how much the widow and Lipman were to pay each one. Among the creditors were the doctor, Wolf Rofe, who was Lipman's younger brother and was owed money for treating Wolf during his illness, and the widow's maidservant.

8. אחרי שכבר יצא מאתנו פס״ד ביו׳ יוד שבט העבר שרביעית בית צום גולדנ[י] פאס

9. שהי׳ שייך להמנוח נ״ה כ״ה וואלף בוריך סג״ל ז״ל יומכר בהכרזה בשיור יד העליונה כדי

10. לפרוע ולסלק האל׳ המנוח הנ״ל שוב בא לפנינו הו״ה כ׳ ליפמן יצו חתן המנוח ז״ל הנ״ל בידיע

11. בידיעות וברצון אשתו בת המנוח הנ״ל ואמר שהוא רוצה לשלם להאל׳ הנ״ל סך דמי שטר

12. שטר כתובה ותוס׳ וגם רוצה לשלם את השט״ח שיש ביד הו״ה פו״מ כ׳ הירץ גייגר יצו קרן עם רווחי׳

13. שעלה עליו כדי לפצות את האל׳ מחוב הנ״ל וגם מחמת שארי טענות ותביעות שטענה

14. ותבעה האל׳ הנ״ל (על העזבון)[1] כמבואר בקונטרס הטענות הן מחמת עצמה והן מחמת אנשי׳ אחרי׳ רוצה

15. לשלם כ׳ ליפמן הנ״ל כפי מה שיכירו הב״ד ע״פ פשר נגד כל הנ״ל יחלטו הב״ד רביעית בית

16. הנ״ל לכ׳ ליפמן הנ״ל בשיור יד העליונה כנ״ל והאל׳ המנוח כ״ה וואלף ז״ל הנ״ל גם היא ה

17. התרצה עצמה לפשר ביניהם על אופן הנ״ל הן מחמת טענות ותביעות שיש לה על עזבון

18. הנ״ל והן מחמת אנשי׳ אחרי׳ וגם מה שיש לחתנה כ׳ ליפמן הנ״ל טו״ת עלי׳ כמבואר בק״ה

19. על כולם נתנה עיני׳ עלינו ב״ד לפשר ביניהם / ובאשר שחתמה האל׳ וחתנה הנ״ל

20. בקומפרמיס לקיים הפשר שיצא מאתנו / גם שארי תובעי׳ ה״ה כ״ה וואלף רופא יצו והו״ה

21. כ׳ משה עמדין והבתולה מרת יטכלה אחות המנוח ז״ל הנ״ל ומשרתת של האל׳ הנ״ל כולם

22. הי׳ לפנינו ונתרצו להב״ד לבשר[2] ולבצוע [ביני]הם וכן נתרצו כ׳ ליפמן והאל׳ הנ״ל בכן

23. נזדקקנו להם ומצאנו ע״פ פשר על כל פרט ופרט כפי המבואר למטה והיינו שרביעית

24. מבית צום גולדני פאס יהי׳ גוף הקרקע מהיו׳ דלמטה להו״ה כ׳ ליפמן הנ״ל נוסף על רביעית

25. מאותו בית שיש לו כבר שקיבל לנדן מחמיו המונח ז״ל הנ״ל והיינו בשיור יד העליונה

26. להאל׳ הנ״ל על כל חצי בית הנ״ל [כל זמן שלא תנשא לג]בר אוחרא ו(כ)[3]פי שטר כתובה ותוס״פ

1. תוספת מעל השורה
2. צ״ל ׳לפשר׳
3. תוספת מעל השורה

27. שבידה

קלט ע״ב

1. ב״ה
2. שבידה ומחויב כ׳ ליפמן הנ״ל לשלם להאל׳ הנ״ל סך תשעה מאות זהו׳ גם השט״ח מן פר״מ
3. כ׳ הירץ גייגר הנ״ל קרן ורווחי׳ וגם תקח האל׳ אותן תכשיטי׳ הנאמרי׳ בשטר כתובה
4. ותוס״פ בלי מגרעת מסך כתובת׳ ותוספ׳ והיינו זהוב קעט כסף ביגל טעש חד כסף
5. [ש]עהר עם קעט חד באהר טבעת גם יהי׳ לה יד העליונה על חצי בית הנ״ל וכנ״ל על
6. כל זמן שלא תנשא לגבר אוחרא / ומחמת כלי תשמישי׳ על משך ימי אל׳ כל זמן שלא ת
7. תנשא לגבר אוחרא ינתן לה מעזבון בעלה ז״ל הנ״ל כפי רשימה הנמסר לה מאתנו
8. ב״ד והיינו באופן שמחויבת האל׳ ליתן כתב ראי׳ לכ׳ ליפמן הנ״ל על כל כלי תשמישי׳
9. שיש תחת ידה וכשתנשא לגבר אוחרא מחויבת להחזיר אותן כלי תשמישי׳ שבידה
10. גם הבלאות שהם בעין / ומחמת מה שתבע התור׳ כ״ה משה אויך בהרשאת ובמעמד
11. כ׳ ליפמן הנ״ל {שיש} באשר שיש להאל׳ הנ״ל יד העליונה על כל חצי בית שתשלם היא לו דמי יד
12. העליונה על רביעית בית שנתן לו חמיו ז״ל כנהוג פה גם שתשלם האל׳ קרונדצינץ
13. ודמי תיקון בדק הבית מחצי בית הנ״ל והתור׳ כ״ה אנשיל פפאן כץ בהרשאת האל׳
14. הנ״ל השיב מחמת קרונדצונץ ובדק הבית יכירו הב״ד ודמי יד העליונה לא התחייב׳
15. היא א״ע לשלם מצאנו ע״פ פשר שדמי קרונדצונץ מן חצי בית הנ״ל ישלמו בן שניהם
16. דהיינו החצי האל׳ הנ״ל והחצי כ׳ ליפמן הנ״ל ודמי יד העליונה שתבע כ׳ ליפמן
17. האל׳ פטורה מלשלם ומחמת בדק הבית מצאנו שהאל׳ הנ״ל אינה יכולה לתבוע
18. את חתנה כ׳ ליפמן לתקן בדק הבית וגם להיפוך כ׳ ליפמן הנ״ל אינה יכול לכופה
19. לתקן בדק הבית / ומחמת שתבע כהרמ[1] הנ״ל שהנעדר כ״ה וואלף ז״ל הנ״ל פסק לחותנו
20. כ׳ ליפמן הנ״ל בתנאי׳ ראשוני׳ ליתן לו שנה וחצי אחר החתנה מזונות על שלחנו ודיר
21. {ב}דירה בחצי בית הנ״ל ובאשר שהאל׳ הנ״ל עשת׳ ק״ס תחת החופה על כל פרטי ד
22. דברי׳ הנאמרי׳ בתנאי׳ בכן תבע ממנה שהיא תשלם לו דמי מזונות עד כלות
23. הזמן הנ״ל וגם תניח לו דירה שיש לו עדיין בתוך חצי בית חדר אחד עד כלות
24. הזמן עוד תבע כהרם הנ״ל שחמיו ז״ל פסק שיתן לו מתנות וסבלונות ולא קיבל
25. כלום והיא עשת׳ ק״ס כנ״ל בכן היא מחויבת ...[2] וכהר״א[3] הנ״ל השיב שהקנין שעשת׳
26. האל׳ הנ״ל לא הי׳ רק לסלק שעבוד ...[4]ית שנתן לו בעלה ז״ל אבל היא לא
27. התחייבה עצמה כלום ואד ...[5] פנה חדרו באשר שיש לה יד
28. העליונה

1. כבוד הרב משה
2. יש כאן חור בנייר
3. וכבוד הרב אנשיל
4. יש כאן חור בנייר
5. יש כאן חור בנייר

קמ ע״א

1. ב״ה
2. העליונה על כל חצי בית / מצאנו ע״פ פשר שהאל׳ פטורה מלשלם דמי מזונות הנ״ל גם פטורה
3. מחמת מתנות וסבלונות הנ״ל אבל החדר שיש לכ׳ ליפמן עדיין בחצי בית הנ״ל יחזיק בו עד
4. כלות שנה וחצי מיו׳ חתונתו ולאח״כ יפנה החדר הנ״ל להאל׳ הנ״ל / ומחמת שרוצה
5. למחות כ׳ ליפמן הנ״ל להאל׳ הנ״ל להשכיר חדרי׳ מחצי בית הנ״ל מצאנו שאינה רשאי האל׳
6. הנ״ל להשכיר חדר לאחרי׳ אך את זה התרצה כ׳ ליפמן הנ״ל לאל׳ הנ״ל שתחזיק אצל
7. אצלה א׳[1] אחותה אל׳ ר׳ ליב שלאס ז״ל וליתן לה חדר נגד זה התחייב א״ע האל׳ ל
8. הנ״ל לפנינו בחיוב גמור להחזיק אצלה ג״כ את אחות בעלה ז״ל מ׳ יטלכה[2] וליתן
9. לה משכב לישן בביתה כל משך ימי אל׳ / ומחמת מקו׳ שלם בע״א התחתונה שנתן
10. המנוח ז״ל הנ״ל לכ׳ ליפמן הנ״ל לנדן בשיור יד העליונה לו ולאשתו האל׳ הנ״ל וכעת יש
11. המפתח תחת יד כ׳ ליפמן הנ״ל וכהר״א הנ״ל תבע ששייך להאל׳ יד העליונה מן מקו׳ הנ״ל
12. ותבע שיחזיר המפתח להאל׳ וכהרם הנ״ל השיב באשר שלא נזכר כלום בשטר כ
13. כתובה ותוס׳ מהמקו׳ הנ״ל (שייך לכ׳ ליפמן הנ״ל בתורת ירושה)[3] אינה יכולה להפקיע
14. הפירות מחזקת היורש מצאנו שהדין עם כ׳ ליפמן הנ״ל והפירות מן המקו׳ הנ״ל שייכי׳
15. לכ׳ ליפמן הנ״ל בתורת ירושה / ומחמת לומפט צעטל שנמצא בעזבון שייך לכ׳ ליפמן
16. והוא יפדה את המשכן והמותרות שייך לו גם כל הספרי׳ וכלי תשמישי׳ גם שמונה
17. ליטרות גארן שייך לכ׳ ליפמן הנ״ל זולת אותן כלי תשמישי׳ וספרי׳ הנרשם ברשימה
18. שיותן לה בתורת מיגר אל׳ על כל משך ימי אל׳ וכנ״ל / גם מה שתבעה האל׳ חד פאהר
19. כסף מעסר אונד גאבל שנמצא בעזבון שנתן לה בעלה בתוך ימי הקנס ושייך לה
20. בלי ניכוי מצאנו שאין בתביעה ממש רק ינתן לה בתורת מיגר אל׳ וכפי שנרשם
21. ברשימה ומחמת מה שתבע כהר״ם הנ״ל שהאל׳ העלימה מתוך אינפוטאריום
22. כל מלבושי בעלה ז״ל וכהרא[4] הנ״ל השיב שנתנה בגדי׳ לאחי׳ כ׳ ליב נייאגאס לא{..}ר
23. לאמור קדיש בשביל בעלה ז״ל שלא הניח בן ושכרה האל׳ את אחי׳ הנ״ל ליתום ונתנה
24. לו הבגדי׳ בריצוי אשת ליפמן הנ״ל ב..[5] בעלה ז״ל רק שיש לה עדיין [כל] מלבוש של בעלה
25. וגם כסף מאנטל שלא[ס] באם ו...[6] בד שלא תתנה לאחי׳ הנ״ל היא מרוצה
26. בכך מצאנו דרך פשר אותן...[7] לאח׳ כ׳ ליב הנ״ל ישאר בידו
27. אבל מה שיש

---

1. אולי צ״ל ׳את׳
2. ר׳ לקמן קמ ע״ב, שורה 21.
3. הסוגריים במקור
4. וכבוד הרב אנשיל
5. יש כאן חור בנייר
6. יש כאן חור בנייר
7. יש כאן חור בנייר

קמ ע״ב

1. ב״ה
2. אבל מה שיש עדיין ביד האל׳ הנ״ל מבגדי׳ גם כסף מאנטל שלאס מחויבת להחזיר
3. לכ׳ ליפמן הנ״ל / ומחמת מה שתבע כהר״א הנ״ל מחמת מצבה ונר תמיד לנעדר ז״ל הנ״ל
4. מצאנו ע״פ פשר שכ׳ ליפמן מחויב להעמיד מצבה לחמיו ז״ל על הוצאתו בתוך שנה ל
5. להעדרתו / וגם מחויב להדליק נר תמיד משמן עד כלות אחד עשר חדשי׳ לפטירתו
6. כנהוג / ומחמת מה שתבע כהרא הנ״ל והציע חשבן מה שהוציאה האל׳ הנ״ל מחמת
7. נר תמיד ושכירות בחורי׳ לאמר תהלי׳ ולהתפלל בעשרה וללמוד וגם לכתוב
8. בספר הזכרה[1] וגם עבור עץ שקנתה / עוד תבעה דמי מזונות מיו׳ פטירת
9. בעלה עד עכשיו כל שבועה חמשה רט וכהר״ם הנ״ל השיב על תביעות הנ״ל
10. ותבע ממנה מותר מעשה ידי׳ הן מחיי׳ בעלה והן מן לאחר מותו מצאנו ע״פ פ[ד]
11. שכ׳ ליפמן הנ״ל יתן להאל׳ הנ״ל מחמת כל תביעות הנ״ל סך תשעה עשר זהו׳
12. ךד צל ובזה פטור כ׳ ליפמן הנ״ל מחמת תביעות הנ״ל ומה שתבע כהרם
13. מותר מעשה ידי׳ הן מחיי בעלה והן לאח״כ אין בתביעתו ממש ומה שתבע
14. כהר״א הנ״ל והציע חשבן מן כה וואלף רופא שתבע שכירות שהלך אצלו בעת ח
15. חלי׳ כנ״ל סך עשרה זהו׳ ארבעי׳ וחמשה צל / מצא[נו] דרך פ״ד שכ׳ ליפמן הנ״ל
16. ישלם שני זהו׳ והאל׳ הנ״ל שלשה זהו׳ ומחמת תביעות הו״ה כ׳ משה ב״מ עמדי[ן]
17. שהלווה להאל׳ הנ״ל בחיי בעלה ובידיעתו סך שנים עשר זהו׳ ולאחר פטירת
18. בעלה לותה ממנו עוד שמונה זהו׳ ונתנה לו כסף בעכר למשכן מצאנו ע״פ פשר
19. שהברירה ביד כ׳ משה הנ״ל או שיעכב לעצמו כסף בעכר או שיחזיר להיורש
20. כ׳ ליפמן הנ״ל נגד זה יתן לו כ׳ ליפמן הנ״ל סך שלשה עשר זהו׳ וחצי / גם מ׳
21. תביעת הבתולה מ׳ יטכלה אחות המנוח ז״ל שהלוות לאחי׳ סך עשרי׳ זהו׳
22. מצאנו שישלם כ׳ ליפמן ארבעה זהו׳ והאל׳ תשלם {ששה זהו׳} שלשה זהו׳ ומחמ׳
23. תביעות משרתת של האל׳ הנ״ל שתבעה שכירות מן חמשה זמני׳ העולה עם
24. דמי [ש]וא העמד סך שלשי׳ זהו׳ מצ[אנו ע״פ] פשר שכ׳ ליפמן יתן למשרתת הנ״ל סך ש
25. ששה זהו׳ והאל׳ הנ״ל תתן עשרה...[2] בריצוי הצדדי׳ הנ״ל וגם אשת
26. כ׳ ליפמן הנ״ל בעצמה לפנינו...[3] [ב]כל מה שיעשו הב״ד שיהי׳ לבעלה
27. היו׳ יו׳ ב׳ י״א אדר תקמ[ב]...[4] ואני

---

1. ר׳ ספר הזכרונות, רעז ע״א.
2. יש כאן חור בנייר
3. יש כאן חור בנייר
4. יש כאן חור בנייר

No. 151

Yachet, widow of Me'ir of Fürth v. Oppenheim

Fols. 141a–143b; Wednesday evening, probably in the spring or summer of 1782

(the manuscript is damaged and the date is missing)

Yom Tov Oppenheim and Yachet, the widow of Me'ir of Fürth, each owned half of the Pfau house and approached the court through their representatives with specific complaints against each other. Yachet claimed that Yom Tov owed her back rent for space that he had rented in her section of the house. She asserted that in the fall of 1780 she told Yom Tov to vacate the room, but he did not and as a result she more than quadrupled the rent. Yom Tov denied that Yachet had ever told him to leave the space and claimed that he should be able to remain there at the original rate of 6 guldens per annum. The court ruled that Yachet must prove when it was she had informed Yom Tov that she wanted to him leave the space. From that point forward, Yom Tov would be obliged to pay an annual rent of 20 guldens. If she could not prove her point, she could take an oath to this effect and she would be believed.

Yachet also claimed that with the death of her husband the lottery that determined the rotation of space within the house was void and there was a need for a new lottery. Despite Yom Tov's objections, the court agreed with Yachet and held a new lottery that the parties agreed would go into effect in the fall of 1782.

There were also disputes with respect to repairs. Due to the collapse of a wall, Yom Tov had had repairs done without Yachet's knowledge and now asked the court to order Yachet to pay half the costs. Yachet objected, saying that there had been an agreement between Yom Tov and her husband that both sides had to agree to repairs before they were made. She also questioned whether the repairs were necessary and the receipts accurate. She added her own claim that repairs on her section of the house had also been made and Yom Tov should now pay her for half of these repairs. The court noted that it was now impossible to determine if the repairs had indeed been necessary, and the sides would have to swear regarding their claims and compromise with respect to payments. The court refused to deal with an additional claim from Yom Tov for carpentry repairs, noting that it would only deal with the claim when there was an actual receipt submitted.

Despite these improvements, the Pfau house was still in need of repair and Yom Tov requested that the court visit the house and decide how the expenses should be divided between the parties. The court did so and gave explicit instructions regarding the division of costs. In some instances the court was uncertain of the necessity of repairs and ordered the parties to call in a professional to determine if the repairs were necessary for the structural integrity of the house. If so, then the costs would be divided equally. The court stipulated that in instances in which payment was to be shared, the widow had to be present when the agreement with the repairmen was made. As for future repairs, they could only be made with mutual consent.

Finally, Yom Tov wished to prevent the widow from renting space in her section of the house to guests, including Sabbath guests for whom she would also provide meals, and a teacher of children. The court granted Yom Tov's request that Yachet not rent out space to Sabbath guests, but leasing space to the teacher and two (yeshiva?) students was allowed.

קמא ע״א

1. בה
2. ע״ד הטענות ותביעות שבין מחזיקי בית צור פפי[א] הו״ה כ׳ יום טוב אופנהיי׳ יצו ובין האשה מ״ י[אכט]
3. אל׳ המנוח כ״ מאיר פיורדא שיש לכל או״א החצי מבית הנ״ל שנתעצמו בטענותיהם לפנינו ה״ה התור׳
4. כ״ה בענדיט הענא סגל בהרשאות כ׳ י״ט[1] הנ״ל וה״ה התור׳ כ״ה פייס הענא בהרשאות ובמעמד
5. האל׳ הנ״ל שרבו בטענותיה׳ לפנינו ולאחר שחתמו עצמם כ״ י״ט והאל׳ הנ״ל בקומפרמיס בח״ח ובקנס סך
6. מסויים לקיים כפי הפס״ד אשר יצא מאתנו נזדקקנו להם ומצאנו על כל פרט ופרט כמבואר ו
7. והיינו שתבע כ״ה פייס בהרשאות הנ״ל וטוען באשר כפי כתוב חלקו וחלופי דירות ואקארדיש שיש
8. שבין מחזיקי בית כ״ י״ט ובעלה של האל׳ הנ״ל הית׳ האל׳ הנ״ל דרה בשטח מטה עם כל ה
9. השייכי׳ לזה רק החדר שני שטעג הויך לצד הרחוב דור בו כ״ י״ט בשכירות כפי
10. אקארד [ה]ישן שלהם (ובחודש חשון שנת תקמא״ל)[2]. שלהם וכ״ י״ט נשאור להאל׳ חייב עוד ששה
11. זהו׳ שכירות עוד שני זהו׳ עד ר״ח חשון שנת תקמא״ל שהי׳ נמשך עדיין אקארד ישן שלהם
12. ובחודש חשון הנ״ל הי׳ מיחת׳ בו האל׳ ואומרות לו שאינה רוצה להניח חדר הנ״ל בעד
13. שכירות ישן והוא לא השגיח בה ודר בו עדיין בכן תבעה ממנו עכשיו שכירות מאותו

---

1. יום טוב
2. תקמ״א לפק; הסוגריים והנקודה בשורה הזאת במקור.

14. חדר סך עשרים וחמשה זהו' לשנה [מי"ט] (..)[1] (......)[2] ועוד הוסיפה לטעון שמאחר שמת בעלה ז"ל
15. בטלה הגו(ר)[3]ל אקארד שנעשה מבעלה ורוצה האל' שנעשה אנחנו ב"ד גורל חדש ביניהם
16. [ו]"כ בענדיט בהרשאות כ' י"ט השיב שהיא לא מיחתו בו ונשאר חלוקת הגורל ואקארד ישן
17. בתקפו ומגיע לו עוד דירתו ארבעה שנים מחדש חשון שנת תקמא"ל העבר בכן
18. רוצה הוא להחזיק בדירתו וליתן לה ששה זהו' לשנה כפי אקארד ישן שלהם
19. האריכו בטענותיה' ואחר שדקדקנו בכתב גורל והתחלפות חלקי דירה ותנאי שכירות ש
20. שביניהם מצאנו שמחמת עשיות גורל חדש הדין עם האשה ומחויבי' לעשות גורל ביניהם
21. והתרצו שניהם לפנינו אחר שאמרנו להם דין זה שאנחנו ב"ד נעשה גורל אשר יתחיל מחודש
22. חשון שנת תקמג הבע"ל על משך ארבעה שנים רצופים (וכן עשינו הגורל לפניה')[4] למי
23. שיהי' שטח התחתון ולמי שטח עליון ובכלות ארב[ע] שנים מחשון שנת תקמג הבע"ל
24. יתחלפו הדירות ביניהם שוב על ...[5] [ארב]עה שנים רצופי' וכן עשינו הגורל לפניהם
25. ועלה הגורל שטח התחתון...[6] כי' לזה הדירה לכ' י"ט על משך א

קמא ע"ב

1. ארבע שנים רצופי' ר"ח מרחשון תקמג הבע"ל ושטח עליון עם כל החדרים השייכי' לה להאל'
2. הנ"ל על משך ארבעה שנים מ(ח)[7]שון תקמג"ל ובכלות ארבע שנים הנ"ל יחלפו דירתם על משך ארבע
3. שנים רצופי' וכמבואר היטיב חלקי הדירות בכתב גורל שיש לכל או"א הנחתם מ
4. מאתנו ב"ד ח"מ ומחמת מה שתבעות האל' שכירות מחדר שני שטעג הויך לצד ה
5. הרחוב מעבר מצאנו שמה שהודה כ' י"ט בעצמו שעדיין חייב לה והיינו עד חשון
6. שנת תקמא ששה זהו' ועוד שני זהו' מחויב לשלם ומחודש חשון תקמא העבר ואילך ש
7. שטוענת האל' שהיתה אומרת לו שיפנה חדרה ותובעות עשרי' וחמשה זהו' לשנה
8. מצאנו מאותו זמן ואילך שתוכל לברר האל' שמוח[תה] בו מחויב כ' י"ט הנ"ל לשלם
9. להאל' הנ"ל מיו' מחאתה ואילך עשרים זהו' לשנה בשביל החזקת דירתה ומה
10. שאינה יכולה לברר נאמנת בשבועה על אותו יום שמיחתה בו והיינו {באו...
11. יום ומחויב כ"י הנ"ל לשלם} שתשבע האל' הנ"ל {שבע} ע"ד המקום (ב"ה)[8] וע"ד ב"ד
12. בלי ערמה ומרמה ובלי שום הוראת היתר שבעולם שכדבריה כן הוא

1. תוספת מעל השורה
2. תוספת מתחת השורה
3. תוספת מעל השורה
4. הסוגריים במקור
5. יש כאן חור בנייר
6. יש כאן חור בנייר
7. תוספת מעל השורה
8. תוספת מעל השורה

13. שמיחתה בו באותו (יום)[1] ומחויב כ"י[2] הנ"ל לשלם (מאותו יו' ואילך)[3] מחמת דירתו עד חשון שנת תקמג"ל
14. {מאותו יום ואילך} לפי ערך עשרים זהו' לשנה וכ"ה בענדיט בהרשאות
15. כ"י הנ"ל תבע לפנינו והציע לפנינו קונטות מחותם מכמה בעלי מלאכות ששילם
16. להם מחמת בנין בדק הבית הנ"ל לאחר שנפל הכותל מכח הבנין חדש
17. שעל הקדש פלאטץ[4] שבצידה שעולה לערך קמג זהו' דב צל ותבע מן האל'
18. הנ"ל שתשלם החצי כפי המגיע ע"ח לערך שבעים ואחד זהו' נא צל וכל
19. זמן שלא שילמה לו הסך הנ"ל רוצה להחזיק עצמו בדירתו שדר בו עכשיו בשכירו'
20. שינכה ע"ז והאל' הנ"ל השיבה דרך כלל ע"פ כתב חילוקי דירות שבין כי"ט[5]
21. ובעלה ז"ל {אין} אין רשאי [ל"]א מהם [לבנות] שום דבר בלתי ידעות (חבירו)[6] גם טענה
22. ומי יודע אם (לא)[7] התקין כמה דברים ...[8] לצורך [עצמו] יהי' שיכירו הב"ד שהי'
23. מן הצורך מ"מ אינה מא...[9] כפי קונטות שהציע לפנינו
24. עוד

[קמב ע"א]

1. עוד השיבה שמחזיקי הקדש פלאטץ שילמו בשבילה כמה תיקוני' שתיקנו בעלי מלאכות בגבולה והיינו
2. טינכה ווייסן בשני חדרי' שלה תנור אחד זעצין גל[..]ט וגם שילמו חמשה זהו' לבית המוצנע וגם
3. וגם שילמו אבינד געלדר שהי' על כי"ט הנ"ל לשלם ג"כ החצי מתקוני' הנ"ל וזה ינוכה מתביעות
4. כ"י הנ"ל והמותרת שיכירו הב"ד רוצה לשלם אחת לאחת ושלא יחזיק כי"ט הנ"ל בחדרי' שלה
5. בשביל זאת והאריכו בטענותיהם ומצאנו שישבע כי"ט ע"ד המקו' ב"ה וע"ד ב"ד בלי
6. עו"מ ובלי שום הוראות היתר שבעולם ששילם כל כך כמו שאמר ובאשר אף לאחר ש
7. שישבע שהוציא כל כך על כל זה ע'פי[10] הדין (מוטל על כי"ט לברר על כל פרט ופרט שהי' בונה שהי')[11] מן הצורך וזה דבר שאי אפשר על כל
8. פרט ופרט שהי' בונה וגם מה ששילמו מחזיקי הקדש פלאטץ עבור גבול של האל' הנ"ל
9. ג"כ אינה באפשרי לבררו לעמוד עליו כמה שילמו בתוך בנין גדול שהי' להם כדי
10. לחשוב החצי המוטל על כי"ט הנ"ל ולנכות מתביעותיו הנ"ל בכן מצאנו שיש לנו כח לעשות

---

1. תוספת מעל השורה
2. כבוד יום טוב
3. תוספת מעל השורה
4. ר' לעיל, מס' 101.
5. כבוד יום טוב
6. תוספת מעל השורה
7. תוספת מעל השורה
8. יש כאן חור בנייר
9. יש כאן חור בנייר
10. על פי
11. תוספת מעל השורה

11. פשר ביניהם בשביל הנ״ל בכן לאחר שישבע כ״י הנ״ל כמה הוציא וכנ״ל ינוכה מסך תביעות
12. כי״ט הנ״ל וכנ״ל שמונה זהו׳ שכירות מחדר שני שעטג הויך שהודה כי״ט שחייב לה עדיין
13. עד חשון תקמא״ל עוד שני זהו׳ שהודה ג״כ שאינו רוצה לטעון ע״ז גם ינוכה שני זהו׳
14. וחצי ומה שמגיע ע״ח מחמשה זהו׳ ששילם מח[ז]יקי הקדש פלאטץ בשביל בנין בית המוצנע
15. שהודה ג״כ כי״ט עוד ינוכה מחמת מה שתבע האל׳ והציע ג״כ חשבונות מן שריינר
16. גלא[ס]ר ושארי דברי׳ ששילמה זמן רב קודם נפילת הכותל העולה לערך שמונה
17. עשר זהו׳ ומצאנו שגם היא תשבע כנ״ל כמה הוציאה בכן לאחר שתשבע תוכל
18. לנכות כל כך מה שמגיע על כי״ט הנ״ל ע״ח לשלם על מה שהוציאה עוד תנכה מה
19. שמחויב כי״ט הנ״ל לשלם לה בשביל חדר שני שטעג הויך לצד הרחוב מן יום
20. שתברר שמיחתו בו {או} מן היום ש...[1] והיינו סך עשרי׳ זהו׳ לשנה
21. ו{ס(י)[2][.]}רות מסך ע״א זהו׳ נ״א צל ...[3]ל מחויבת האל׳ לשלם לכי״ט הנ״ל

קמב ע״ב

1. וכל זמן שלא שילמה רשאוי להחזיק עצמו בחדר הנ״ל על אופן המבואר למטה ומחמת
2. מה שתבע כי״ט הנ״ל מה שתיקן צ[ימ]ר מאן שעדיין לא שילם החשבן מאחר שלא
3. קיבל עדיין איין קונטא מצאנו שלפי הוצעת דבריו וטעמיו שלא שילם עדיין
4. אין אנו יכולין לפסוק הדין עכשיו ולאחר שישלם אותו יקוב הדין ההר ש
5. שביניהם {בעת} (עוד)[4] התעצמו לפנינו לדין {ע..} ותבע כ״ה בענדיט הנ״ל בהרשאות
6. הנ״ל שיכירו הב״ד על כמה דברים שצריכי׳ לתקן עוד בבית הנ״ל הן
7. בגבולו והן בגבול שדר בו האל׳ שיבוא גם הוא בתוכה בהתחלפת הדירות
8. וביקשו מאתונו[5] ב״ד שנלכו בבית הנ״ל לראות מה הוא לצורך ולאחר שהלכנו
9. בבית הנ״ל וראינו הבית הנ״ל מדיוטא התחתונה לדיוטא העליונה לראות
10. מה הוא מן הצורך לבנות ודקדקנו בטענותיהם מצאנו על כל פרט ופרט
11. כמבואר והיינו למטה אין הויז עהרנד המחיצה חדשה עדיין צריך
12. להיות גטינכט ומה שנתקלקל במחיצה לתקן כדי שיהי׳ כמו מחיצה האחרת
13. יתוקן על הוצאות שניהם גם מה שנתקלקל הפלאטן למטה בהויז עהרנד
14. גם חורי׳ שבמחיצה יתוקן על הוצאות שניהם גם איין בלאט מברזל
15. על הכירה למטה על הוצאות שניהם אבל לעשות איין חדש פרשלאג
16. סביב הקיר למטה אינה מחויבת האל׳ לשלם חלקה ובבית {..} החורף למטה
17. מה שנתקלקל דער פוסבאדין יתוקן על הוצאות שניהם ומה שתבע
18. כי״ט הנ״ל לעשות גיס שטיין למטה גם חד שטעג הויך הדין עמו
19. ויתוקן על הוצאות שניהם אבל מה שתבע כי״ט לעשות גוס שטיין
20. גם שני שטעג הויך באשר שלמטה אינו ראוי לדירה בזה מצאנו

---

1. יש כאן חור בנייר
2. תוספת מעל השורה
3. יש כאן חור בנייר
4. תוספת מעל השורה
5. ר״ל ׳מאתנו׳

21. שהברירה בידו אם רוצה ...[1]ה שני שטעג הויך {אזי} יתוקן
22. למעלה נגד זה אינו מן הצ...[2] {שטיין למטה} בשטח מטה

[קמג ע"א]

1. בשטח מטה גם בשטח התחתן למעלה בתקרה נרקבו איזה קורת מצאנו שיובדק
2. ע"י אומן אם מן הצורך לעשות קורות חדשי' ואז מוטל על שניהם הוצאות התיקן
3. התנור שני שטעג הויך יש עומד עכשיו בחדר לצד החומה יתוקן עכשיו בחדר
4. לצד הרחוב על הוצאות שניהם גם (התיקל)[3] התיקל מה שנתקלקל בתקרה
5. של אותו חדר לצד הרחוב הוא על הוצאות שניהם אבל לעשות טעק חדש
6. אינה מחויבת הא"ל לשלם אם ע"פ אומן המושבע שיאמר שאי אפשר לתקן התקרה
7. בלא"ה כי אם לעשות טעק חדש גם יתוקן המחיצות והיינו טינכה צו לאזין
8. על הוצאות שניהם אבל אין מחויבת הא"ל לשלם בעשיות גטיפלש וגם אינה
9. מחויבת לשלם לעשות גיספאס שאנק אכן אם ידור למעלה שני שטעג הויך רשא{..}
10. לעשות בסיס מנסרי' להניח עליו גיספאס ומה שתבע כי"ט איין אייזרנה בלאט
11. לכירה קטנה אין האל' לשלם אכן אם ידור למעלה וע"פ אומן המושבע
12. {יתוקן} (שיאמר)[4] שיכולי' לעשות כירה (עם בלאט מברזל נגד זה)[5] קטנה שלא יצא תקלה
13. מזה ח"ו (אזי מחויבת הא"ל לשלם אכן)[6] אזי יתוקן על הוצאות שניהים כירה עם
14. בלאט מברזל נגד זה אינה מחויבת הא"ל לשלם בעשיות בלאט מברזל למטה בשטח
15. התחתון אין הויז עהרנד גם יתוקן בחדר שני שטעג הויך לצד החומה
16. בחלונות דהיינ{ה}(ו)[7] נייאה שייפן גם דיא ראמן מה שיאמר האומן שהוא
17. מן הצורך לתקן גם מה שנתקלקל במקו' דריסת רגלים הכל על הוצאות
18. שניהם גם יתוקן בחדר שלשה שטעג הויך לצד החומה החלונות שצריכין
19. תיקון גם גפעכר שנתקלקל יתוקן על הוצאות שניהם ומחמת הצנור מחוץ
20. לאותו חדר שלשה שטעג הויך שתבע כי"ט [ל]עשות צנור חדש ארוך שמשך עד
21. למטה בסוכה והא"ל אומרות...[8] שיש עדיין ב[ב]ית שיכולין

קמג ע"ב

1. בה
2. לתקן מצאנו שאם יאמר האומן שהוא מן הצורך גדול לבית לעשות צנור ארוך יתוקן
3. על הוצאות שניהם גם מחמת חדר שלשה שטעג הויך לצד הרחוב שטען כי"ט
4. הנ"ל מחמת מחיצות חדשה שלאבנים יזיע החומה מים בימי החורף מצאנו
5. שיתוקן בטיט על הכותל הנ"ל על הוצאות שניהם והנה אף שפסקנו על אותן

---

1. יש כאן חור בנייר
2. יש כאן חור בנייר
3. הסוגריים המקור
4. תוספת מעל השורה
5. הסוגריים במקור
6. הסוגריים במקור
7. תיקון מעל השורה
8. יש כאן חור בנייר

6. תיקוני׳ ובניני׳ הנ״ל שיתקן כי״ט הנ״ל יהי׳ על הוצאות שניהם מ״מ מחויב להודיע
7. להאל׳ הנ״ל שתהי׳ גם היא במעמד עם בעלי מלאכות בשעת אקארד מכל מה
8. שהוציא ושילם כי״ט לבעלי מלאכות כפי אקארד שלהם מחויבת היא לשלם
9. החצי כפי המגיע ע״ח וכל זמן שלא שילמה אזי רשאי כי״ט לדור בחדרי׳ שדר בו
10. עתה אף מחודש חשון שנת תקמב הבע״ל ואילך נגד שכירות עשרי׳ זהו׳
11. לשנה שינכה מתשלומין מה שמחויבת לשלם בשביל חלקה ולאחר גמר תשלומ[י׳]
12. מחויב כי״ט הנ״ל לפנות החדרי׳ שדר בו עתה ויכנוס לדור בשטח
13. התחתון אשר עלה עליו מגורל שנעשה ביניהם עד כלות ארבעה שני׳
14. מחדש חשון תקמג הבע״ל ולאח״כ יתחלפו דירתם ואין רשאי כי״ט
15. להחזיק עצמו בחדרי׳ ששייכי׳ לה אף אם רצה ליתן לה שכירות
16. עשרי׳ זהו׳ וזולת תיקוני׳ ובניני׳ הנ״ל מה שמבואר בפס״ד הנ״ל אם
17. יתקלקל עוד שום דבר בבית הנ״ל אינו רשאי ל״א מהם לבנות שום
18. שום דבר בלתי ידיעות חבירו ומה שטוען עוד כי״ט הנ״ל ורוצה
19. למחות ביד האל׳ הנ״ל להחזיק בגבולה מלמד תינוקת וגם להחזיק
20. ולהאכיל אורחי׳ בשבת בשכר ולהשכיר חדרי׳ לאחרי׳ בשכר
21. מצאנו שאינו יוכל למחות בידה מלהחזיק מלמד תינוקת אבל להשכר
22. חדרי׳ לאחרי׳ וגם להחזיק ולהאכיל אורחי׳ בשבת בשכר יוכל
23. למחות אך יותן לה רשו[ת] מאתונו להניח לישון שני בחורי׳
24. בע[לי] תורה בא...[1] השכר יצא מאתנו אור ליו׳ ה׳
25. ... ורמש[2] ואני

No. 152

No page number; no date

This page has been pasted into the collection without pagination. It is not included in the index at the end of the manuscript. The text deals with the timing of ritual immersion by women after childbirth. See no. 191 (which is basically identical to this document) for a fuller description including dating.

1. בע״ה
2. הערט צורבות[3] עז איזט בפאהלין ווארדין אויז צו רופין בשם הגאון אב״ד נר״ו ובצירוף שני ב״ד

---

1. יש כאן חור בנייר
2. ורב מאיר שיף
3. צ״ל ׳צורבותי׳

3. יצו באשר שידוע לכל שבמ[ד]ינתינו הי' אבותינו ואבות אבותינו נוהגין איסור שלא לטבול היולדת
4. עד ארבעים ואחד לזכר ועד שמונים ואחד לנ[ק]בה והמנהג הזה מבואר בש"ע בדברי רמ"א שאין
5. להתיר במקום שנוהגין איסור ובאשר ששמענו שאיזה נשים הי' עוברים על זה בכן לאזין הגאון אב"ד
6. נר"ו בצירוף שני ב"ד יצו הנ"ל מכריז ומזהיר באזהרה גדולה זיין דען זיך קיין אשה יולדת אונטר
7. שטיהן ווערד מכאן והלאה לטבול הן פה קהלתינו יע"א הן בסביבותינו עד ארבעים ואחד
8. לזכר ועד שמונים ואחד לנקבה ומי שיעבור ע"ז ווירד מאן איהם מפרסם ברבי' זיין מלבד
9. שארי ביושים ועונשים וועלש גשעין ווירד על עבריינות והשומע יונעם ותבוא עליו ברכת טוב

No. 153

Fols. 144a–b; Tuesday 30 July 1782

The rabbinic judges in Frankfurt were asked by the community to consider the case of a local cantor who was rumored to have performed unspecified but inappropriate acts. After an investigation of the charge, the judges prohibited the cantor from participating in any of the religious services connected with the upcoming High Holy Days. His case was to be reviewed the following year. The court imposed a number of limitations on him including distancing himself from women, staying in the *Judengasse*, and avoiding playing most games. It also required him to study ethical works daily. The case would be dealt with again by both the court (no. 224) and the community (see Appendix 3).[1]

קמד ע"א

1. בה
2. נתוועדנו יחד לעיין בדין החזן ר' שואל ע"פ רשות האלופי' קהל יצו על דבר
3. לא טובה השמועה שיצא עליו ואחר החקירות ובעיון הסכמנו יחד וזאת אשר מצאנו שבימי'
4. נוראים הבע"ל דהאי שתא דהיינו בר"ה ויו"כ ובסליחות שאומרים באשמורת הבקר
5. לא ירד לפני התיבה להתפלל בצבור הן בבה"כ ישן וחדש והן בשאר בה"כ גם
6. סדרנו לו הנהגות ישרות הראוי' בהכרח לכל שץ[2] שיתנהג בהן / ולא ישנה את ת

1. This material also appears in YIVO MS. RG 128 (folder 77–78) fol. 70a, without the signatures. Also see the discussion in Sendik, "Beyn din le-pesher," 75–78.
2. שליח ציבור

7. תפקידו כאשר נמסר לידו מאתנו בכתב רשום דבר אמת וכאשר המה בכתובי׳
8. אצלינו ואי״ה לשנה הבאה בר״ח אלול הבע״ל מחויב ר׳ שואל חזן הנ״ל לבוא לפני
9. הגאון אב״ד נ״י ושני ב״ד יצו לעיין בדינו לפי ראות עינינו אם התנהג ככל
10. אשר הושת עליו בלי מרמה ואם ראוי לעמוד לפני התיבה בימי׳ נוראי׳ היו׳
11. יו׳ ג׳ יט מנחם תקמ״ב הגאב״ד נר״ו ורנ״מ ורי״ש ורא״ט ורז״ט ורמ״ש ואני
12. א)[1] ירחיק עצמו בתכלית ריחוק מחבורות נשי׳ הן נשואות והן פנויות הן בבית והן בחוץ וכ״ש
13. שצריך לשמור עצמו שלא ליחד עם נשי׳ או פנויות ואפי׳ אם יהי׳ על שמחה חתנה או
14. ברית מילה ושארי שמחות לא יהי׳ בחבורות נשי׳ ומכ״ש שאסר לו לילך ולראות
15. במחולות ורקודים של בתולות גם לא ישב בסוד משחקי׳ במקו׳ שמשחקים נשי׳ או
16. בתולות ולהרחיק מהם ביותר (ב)[2] גם אסור לו לשחק כל מיני שחוק אפי׳ עם אנשי׳ לבד
17. הן כאן בקהלותינו יע״א והן חוץ לרחוב היהודים תוך ג׳ פרסאות מכאן בכל מיני
18. שחוק שבעולם חוץ שאָך צאבל אונד טאמה שפיהל ואפי׳ (ואף)[3] {אצל} יולדת וחולי׳ [ר]״ל {.}א
19. אסור לו לשחוק וגם אסור להניח [ב]תוך ביתו [ל]אחרי׳ [לש]חוק שום מיני שחוק חוץ מן שָאך
20. צאבל וטאמה הנ״ל ואף [חוץ] ל״ג[4] {פ.} פרסאות מכאן עכ״פ לא ישחוק

קמד ע״ב

1. בה
2. עם הנשי׳ ואף אשה אחת {בשע} במשמע (ג)[5] גם יזהר שלא להרבות לילך חוץ לרחוב
3. היהודי׳ ולטייל תוך מקו׳[6] כי אם לצורך (ד)[7] גם ילך בתמידות בבה״כ ישן וחדש (שחרית)[8] וערבית
4. ולא יעבור כאשר ראוי לשץ[9] להיות מן אנשי׳ זריזי׳ המקדמי׳ עצמם לתפלה (ה) גם מחויב
5. ללמוד בכל יום שיעור קבועה ובספרי מוסר אצל ב״ב אחד מבני קהלותינו יע״א
6. ————

1. חצי עיגול במקור
2. סוגריים במקור
3. תוספת מעל השורה
4. = לשלש
5. סוגריים במקור
6. זאת אומרת, בשאר חלקי העיר.
7. סוגריים במקור
8. תוספת מעל השורה
9. לשליח ציבור

No. 154

Fol. 144b; Monday 19 August 1782

The author noted that on this day he was present at the performance of a *ḥaliẓah* ceremony (see Deut. 25.5–10) involving Bunla, widow of Kalman Rothschild. As in almost all cases of *ḥaliẓah* mentioned in these records, the ceremony was carried out just over three months after the death of the husband. (Jewish law demands a 90 day waiting period to determine if the wife was pregnant by her deceased husband).[1] Kalman Rothschild died on 14 May 1782 (Horovitz, no. 3754). The record includes the names of the judges and witnesses who were present.

7. היו׳ יו׳ ב טית אלול שנת תקמ״ב הייתי אצל חליצה האל׳ מ׳ בונלה בת מהו׳ יעקב שמש נרו׳ אל׳
8. המנוח כ״ה קלמן בכ״ה אנשיל רויטשילד ז״ל שנחלץ מן היבום כ״ה משה בכ״ה אנשיל ז״ל הנ״ל ויהי רצון
9. שלא תבואנה עוד בנות ישראל לא לידי חליצה ולא לידי יבום מעתה וע״ע א״ס
10. והדייני׳ הי׳ ר״י מהו׳ נתן מז ור אברהם טריר {ורמאיר שי} ור זנוויל טרך ור מאיר שיף ואני
11. והעדי׳ השמשי׳ ר דוד שש[2] ור זיסקינד שטערן

No. 155

Fols. 144b–145a; Wednesday 21 August 1782

Leb Wezlar approached the court at the request of his mother, Rechle, asking that the court give its assurance that the Jewish community would accept her right to sell half of the Goldener Brunnen house. The house had come into Rechle Wezlar's possession through the intercession of the non-Jewish authorities, and she feared that the community would not recognize her right to sell the house unilaterally because her husband was still alive, albeit not well (see the introduction to no. 111; also see nos. 112 and 124). The court formally assured Rechle Wezlar that her rights would be recognized and added a note that the purchaser of the half-house should

1. A *ḥaliẓah* contract (*sheṭar ḥaliẓah*) from August 1797 notes that it was the custom in Frankfurt to perform the *ḥaliẓah* three months after the death of the husband (YIVO MS. RG 128 [folder 77–78], unpaginated section labeled "5 judgments of the rabbinical court in Frankfort /Main of 1759–1792," third and fourth documents in section).
2. שוואַרצשילד

receive a copy of this decision so no one would be able to challenge the validity of the transaction in the future.

12. הן היו׳ הקריב לפנינו ב״ד ח״מ הו״ה התור׳ כ״ה ליב בן הו״ה גע[1] כ״ה נטע וועצלר כץ
13. בהרשאת אמו מ׳ רעכלה אשת כהר״ן[2] הנ״ל והציע דבריו לפנינו שבדעת אמו
14. הנ״ל למכור חצי בית צו גולדני ברונן שנחלט לה ע״י פיסוטאציאהן קומיסיאהן בו
15. בוועצלר מאדוננו החסיד הקיסר ירה[3] כנהוג בק״ס עי[4] נאמני הקהלה יעא[5] רק ההיא
16. איתתא היא אמו הנ״ל בהאי פחדא יתיבה פן ואולי אינם רוצי׳ נאמני הקהלה
17. לקבל קנין ממנה לבד באשר שבעלה עדין בחיי חיותו בכן ביקשה מאתנו כתב ראי׳
18. ומעשה ב״ד על זה שיש כח בידה למכור החצי בית הנ״ל כדי להראות הנאמני׳ שברשות
19. ב״ד תמכר ואחר הוצעות דברי כהר״ל[6] הנ״ל נזדקקנו לדבריו גם הציע לפנינו ה
20. הכתבי׳ שיש לאמו הנ״ל מהשפט פיסוטאציאהכש קומיסיאהן הנ״ל ואחר שהי׳ למראה עינינו היינו
21. מעיינים בכתבי׳ הנ״ל ומצאנו שהדין עמה ויש כח ביד האשה מרת רעכלה {הנ״ל} אשת כהר״ן
22. הנ״ל למכור חצי בית הנ״ל ככל...[7] ואף בלא רשות בעלה כהרן[8] הנ״ל
23. ואין ש[..][9] ויכולת לשום אדם לערער שתע[לה] ע...[10] מכירת חצי בית הנ״ל
24. [והנא]מני׳ יקבלו

קמה ע״א

1. ב״ה
2. והנאמני׳ יקבלו ממנה ק״ס ע״ז כנהוג ויכתבו הקנין ובשטר מכירה שהב״ד נתנו
3. רשות להאשה הנ״ל למכור חצי בית הנ״ל ע״י שנחלט להאשה מ׳ רעכלה הנ״ל כפי כתבי׳ מפיסו
4. טאציאהנש קומיסיאהן מאדוננו החסיד הקיסר ירה כל הנ״ל יהא מאושר ומקוים בתוקף
5. מעשה ב״ד ובכח ב״ד יפה וכל מי שיערער אחר מכירה יהי׳ מי שיהי׳ או באיזה אופן
6. שיהי׳ דבריו בטלי׳ ומבוטלי׳ {כאפ} כחרס הנשבר כאפס וכאין יחשב לא שרירין ולא קיימין
7. ולא יהא חלין כלל וכלל ואל יזדקק שום קהל או ב״ד או שום משפט שבעולם הן בד״י והן
8. בדא״ה לדברי המערער כי הכל נעשה בתוקף מעשה ב״ד ובכח ב״ד יפה / וכדי
9. להיות עוד ללוקח לזכות ולמשמרת לדורי דורות מצאנו ג״כ שהנאמני׳ יתנו ה

---

1. גבאי צדקה
2. כבוד הרב נטע
3. ירום הודו
4. על ידי
5. יגן עליה אלהים
6. כבוד הרב ליב
7. יש כאן חורים בנייר
8. כבוד הרב נטע
9. יש כאן חור בנייר
10. יש כאן חור בנייר

10. העתקה ממעשה ב"ד הלז להיות בידו לראי' שהקנין מכירה עשת' האשה ברשות ב"ד
11. שאין לערער שוב אחרי' יצא מאתנו יו' ד[1] יב אלול תקמ"ב רנ"מ ורמ"ש ואני

No. 156

Fulda v. Yancha, wife of Abraham Fulda

Fol. 145a; Wednesday 2 October 1782

A domestic dispute between Abraham Fulda and his wife, Yatcha, was brought before the court. Yatcha claimed that she was unable to have sexual intercourse with her husband because she found unspecified things on his body to be disgusting. Nevertheless, she demanded financial support from him. Abraham denied that such things were on his body and noted that his wife used to be pleased with him. Abraham felt that Yatcha was simply making an excuse for not having intercourse with him for she regretted marrying him. He did not want to pay her support. The couple had married on 31 January 1781.[2] Neither husband nor wife had representation before the court, but both agreed to be bound by the court's decision. The court agreed that Abraham need not support his wife unless she was willing to live with him according to the traditional way of Jewish life. However, the court specifically noted that she was not to be compelled to do so. See no. 179.

12. על אודות דברי' שבין איש ואשה ה"ה כ' אברהם בהמנוח[3] כ"ה אהרן פולדא ז"ל ואשתו מרת
13. יטכה בת המנוח כ"ה פייבלמן עמדין ז"ל שהאשה מ' יטכה הנ"ל אינה רוצה להיות
14. עם בעלה הנ"ל להתנהג עמו כהלכות גוברין ונשין {ב}יהודאין ובאה בטענה ואומרות
15. שאי אפשר לה להיות עמו בצוותא חדא מפני דברי' מאוסי' שיש בגופו וטוענת מאיס
16. עלי' ותובעות מזונות מבעלה שיתן לה דמי מזונות והבעל כ' אברהם הנ"ל השיב שכל
17. דברי' ואמתלאות שאמרה מגופו הכל שקר שאינו בגופו מה שהיא אומרות וגם {בת}
18. בתחילה הית' מרוצה עמו ולאח"כ נתחרטה על הנישואין ומרדה בו בכן אינה רוצה
19. ליתן לה מזונות ושאר דברי' אם לא תתנהג עמו כראוי והאריכו בטענותיהם ובאשר
20. שהזוג הנ"ל חתמו עצמם בתוקף קומפרמיס בח"ח ובקנס לקיים כל אשר יצא מאתונו[4]
21. בכן נזדקקנו להם ואחר החקירה שיש לנו הסכמנו יחד שאין הבעל הנ"ל מחויב ליתן
לה מזונות

---

1. באותה השנה י"ב אלול נפל ביום ה' (22 באוגוסט) ולא ביום ד' כפי שרשום.
2. See JTS MS. 3672, fol. 2b. The month of Abraham's death as listed in the manuscript appears to be mistaken (cf., Horovitz, no. 4141, and Ettlinger, 26.8.1794).
3. בן המנוח
4. ר"ל 'מאתנו'

22. ולא כסות ושאר דברי' כל זמן שאינה דרה עמו ויתנהג עמו כדרך אשה עם בעלה כדת מו"י
23. ואף אין לכופה להיות עמו כדרך אשה עם בעלה בעל כרחה ואם תתרצה האשה הנ"ל
24. לחזור ממרדה ותדור עמו כדרך כל הארץ אזי מחוי[ב ל]זונה ולפרנסה כפי חיוב בעל לאשתו
25. ואודות שאר תביעות קטני' שביניהם לא פסקנ[ו][1]... הדין כעת / ובהגמר הדברי' יבוארו
26. על מכונם יצא מאתנו יו' ד אסר חג של סוכות שנת תקמ"ג ה"ג אב"ד [...] ורנ"מ[2]

No. 157

Fol. 145b; Sunday evening, 6 October 1782

The court produced a note affirming the identity of previous owners of two seats in the synagogue that had been sold in early 1781 (see nos. 132 and 134). The court noted that the total price received from the sale of the two seats was 695 guldens and that the three living sellers of their shares in the seats were each entitled to 115 guldens, 50 kreuzers from the sale. Also see nos. 158 and 159.

קמה ע"ב

1. ב"ה
2. כתב יושר דברי אמת שהמקו' שלם בע"א שנמכר בפנינו ב"ד לה"ה כ' טעבלי פולדא
3. בעד ארבע מאות ושבעי' וחמשה זהו' הי' שייך בשותפות ליורשי ג"ה כ"ה בער
4. קן ז"ל ויורשי כ"ה מרדכי בו"ו[3] אופנהיים ז"ל ויורשי כ' יוקב ב"מ[4] אופנהיים ז"ל
5. ולכ' יוסף טויב יצו ולכ' יט[5] אופנהיים ולאחיו כ' אהרן אופנהיים לכל או"א ממשותפי
6. הנ"ל הי' שייך חלק ששית ממקו' שלם הנ"ל וכן מקו' שלם שנמכר בפנינו לה"ה כ'
7. אברם האן בעד סך שני מאות ועשרי' זהו' הי' שייך ג"כ להני משותפי'
8. לכל או"א מהם חלק שישית כמבואר היטיב במעשה ב"ד שהם ביד הלוקחי'
9. הנ"ל בכן ניתן לכתוב שמן הסך דמי מכירות שני מקומות הנ"ל העולה יחד
10. ששה מאות ותשעי' וחמשה זהו' מגיע לכ' יוסף טויב הנ"ל חלק שישית
11. והוא סך מאה וחמשה עשר זהו' חמשי' צל וכן לכ' יט אופנהיי'
12. הנ"ל מאה וחמשה עשר זהו' חמשי' צל וכן לכ' אהרן אופנהיי' הנ"ל
13. מאה וחמשי' זהו' חמשי' צל ולראי' חתמנו אור ליו' ב דט תשרי תקמ"ג
14. רנ"מ ורמ"ש ואני

---

1. יש כאן חור בנייר
2. יש חתיכת נייר מודבקת לדף כדי לתקנו; יתכן שיש עוד שמות מתחתה.
3. בן וואלף
4. בן מרדכי
5. יום טוב

No. 158

Fol. 145b; Monday evening, 7 October 1782

The court affirmed that 135 guldens, 30 kreuzers were due to the descendents of Ber Kann after they sold their portions of seats in the synagogue (see nos. 132, 134, 137). The record notes that the proceeds of another sale were in dispute and that they would remain in the hands of the community until the matter was settled. Also see nos. 159 and 165. The record is damaged and some information is missing.

15. כתב יושר דברי אמת שמן המקו' שלם בע"א שנמכר בפנינו ב"ד לה"ה כ' טעבלי
16. פולדא (בעד סך {הנ"ל}ש[ע]ה זהו')[1] הי' שייך חלק שישית ליורשי המנוח ג"ה כ"ה פער קן ז"ל וגם מן מקו' שלם
17. בע"א שנמכר בפנינו לה"ה כ' אברם האן[2] (בעד סך {הנ"ל} [רך] זהו')[3] הי' שייך ג"כ חלק שישית ליורשי ר"פ[4] הנ"ל
18. ומן חצי מקו' קטן הדבוק בשטענדר בע"א שנמכר בפנינו לה"ה כ' משה בן בענדיט
19. ק[א]סיל[5] בעד סך חמשי' ותשעה זהו' הי' שייך ליורשי ר"פ קן הנ"ל חלק שליש
20. מן חצי מקו' קטן להנ"ל בכן ניתן לכתוב שמן הסך דמי מכירות שני מקומות
21. וחצי מקו' קטן הנ"ל מגיע ל[יור]שי המנוח ג"ה כה"פ[6] קן ז"ל הנ"ל סך מאה ושלשי'
22. וחמשה זהו' שלשי' צל מחמת דמי מכירות שלשה רביעית מקו' שנמכר בפנינו
23. לכ' ליב ב"כ יוקב אופ[נהיים בעד מ]אה רט כמבואר במעשה ב"ד שביד כ' ליב הנ"ל
24. ההוקם עם ... סך ...[7] אשר שיורשי ר פער קן ז"ל יש להם טענה ותביעה נגד
25. יורשי ר מרדכי אופנהיים ויורשי כ"י[8] ב"מ[9] אופנהיים בכן אותן מאה רט יונח
26. יונחו ...[10] ביד [הא]לופי' גובי' [י]צו עד [יקוב הדין] ההר ביניהם ולראי' חתמנו
27. אור ליו' [ג] א ד[רח מר]חשון [תקמג רנ"מ] רמ"ש ואני

---

1. תוספת מעל השורה; המקום נמכר בעד תע"ה זהובים (ר' לעיל, מס' 134) וכן החשיבו את הדבר בחישוב כאן.
2. ר' מס' 134.
3. תוספת מעל השורה
4. רבי פער
5. ר' מס' 137.
6. כבוד הרב פער
7. יש כאן חורים בנייר
8. כבוד יוקב
9. בן מרדכי
10. יש כאן חור בנייר

No. 159

Fol. 146a; Monday evening, 7 October 1782

An affirmation by the court that 135 guldens, 30 kreuzers were due to the descendents of Jacob Oppenheim from the sale of seats in the synagogue. Also see nos. 132, 134, 137, and 158.

קמו ע״א

1. ב״ה
2. גם חתמנו כתב ראי׳ ליורשי כ׳ יוקב ב״מ[1] אופנהיים שמגיע להם מסך דמי מכירת שני
3. מקומות וחצי מקו׳ קטן שלם הנ״ל סך קל״ה זהו׳ וחצי כמו ליורשי ר פער קן ז״ל וכנ״ל
4. אור ליו׳ ג א דר״ח מרחשון תקמ״ג רנ״מ ורמ״ש ואני

No. 160

Fol. 146a; Sunday evening, 10 November 1782

The community sold a seat in the upper section of the women's section of the synagogue to Solomon Luria for 620 guldens. Solomon was to pay one-third of the amount immediately and the remaining two-thirds in six semi-annual installments. The record notes that the seller maintained a lien on the property until the final payment was made. A comparison with YIVO MS. RG 128 (folder 77–78), fols. 168a–b (here Appendix 4) shows that this is an abbreviated record.

5. מקו׳ שלם בע״נ העליונה (בקצה מיטלבאנק למזרח מצד דרום)[2] שעומדות עלי׳
6. כעת אשת הו״ה כ׳ דוד בההמנוח[3] כ׳ מענדלי האמיל ז״ל שהי׳ שייך להאלופי׳
7. קציני׳ גובי׳ יצו נמכר בפנינו ב״ד להו״ה כ׳ שלמה בהמנוח כ׳ זנוויל לוריא ז״ל בעד
8. סך ששה מאות ועשרי׳ זהו׳ לשלם אין קונפונטציאהנש מינץ אויף דעם דך
9. זהו׳ פו״ס / והיינו לשלם שליש מסך דמי מכירה הנ״ל תיכף נגד מסירת מעשה
10. ב״ד ושני שלישי׳ הנותרי׳ מסך דמי מכירה הנ״ל לשלם על ששה חצאי שני׳ רצופי׳ זא״ז
11. מיו׳ מסירת מעשה ב״ד וכנהוג הקהלה גם נשאר מקו׳ שלם הנ״ל לאפותיקו מפורש
12. נעשה אור ליו׳ ב׳ ה כסליו תקמ״ג רנ״מ ורמ״ש ואני

---

1. בן מרדכי
2. הסוגריים במקור
3. בן המנוח

No. 161

Yuzpa of Bruchhausen v. Moses of Amelunxen

Fol. 146b–147b; Sunday 17 November 1782

Yuzpa of Bruchhausen claimed that Moses of Amelunxen owed him money for merchandise that he had taken (whether he purchased the items on credit or on consignment is unclear). Moses did not deny the debt, but noted that Yuzpa owed him almost five times as much because in 1781 Yuzpa had breached an agreement to purchase grain, a claim that Yuzpa denied. The case was not argued before the rabbinic court in Frankfurt but rather was brought before the head of the rabbinical court in Bruchhausen. The rabbi recorded each side's claim in the dispute and a copy of the protocol was sent to the rabbinic court in Frankfurt by the non-Jewish authorities in Corvey for a decision.

The Frankfurt court rejected Moses' claim but recognized that his efforts in the grain transaction were ultimately of benefit to Yuzpa and therefore ordered Yuzpa to pay Moses for his troubles, a payment that was almost equal to the amount that Yuzpa claimed from Moses. The matter of court costs was also raised. Yuzpa argued that since Moses' claim was unsuccessful he should be liable for court costs, as was customary, based on a ruling from the non-Jewish authorities. The court, however, decided that the parties would share the court costs equally since each party was partially successful in its claims.

קמו ע"ב

1. ב"ה
2. ע"ד טענות והפרשות בין ה"ה הו"ה פו"מ כ"ה יוזפא (סג"ל מן)[1] ברוכהויזן ובין ה"ה ה"ק כ' משה מאמלויג =
3. = דען שטענו הצדדי' הנ"ל בעצמם לפני הרב אב"ד דקק[2] ב"ה[3] ומ"ק[4] נרו' והרב כתב וסידר טענותם
4. בכתיבה תמה בפראטיקאהל ונשלח לנו ההעתק מן פראטיקאהל הנ"ל מן האך ליבליכה
5. יודן קומיסיאהן יר"ה צו קארבאיי לדון ב"ד[5] {בינהם} בין הצדדי' הנ"ל ותוכן טעונותיהם

---

1. תוספת מעל השורה
2. דקהילת קודש
3. ברוכהויזן
4. ומדינת קארבאיי(?)
5. כרנאה 'בית דינינו'

6. שה"ה פו"מ כ' יוזפא הנ"ל תבע מן ה"ה כ' משה הנ"ל סך שמוני' וחמשה רט יב ט"ג[1] בפשי'[2]
7. וה"ה כ' משה הנ"ל השיב באריכות שהאמת הוא שלקח סחורה כפי סך הנ"ל מן כ"ה יוזפא
8. הנ"ל אלא שיש לו תביעה על כ"ה יוזפא הנ"ל מן סך ארבע מאות ושבעה רט / לאחר ניכוי
9. {שמונה} שמוני' וחמשה רט שתבע כ"ה יוזפא הנ"ל נשאר עוד חייב סך שלשה מאות
10. ועשרי' ושניי' רט ח ט"ג ויו פשי' מכח מו"מ מדגן שהי' לו עם כ"ה יוזפא הנ"ל וכאשר הי'
11. בדעתו באמת לתבוע אותו / והיינו שמעשה כך הי' ביו' ה חי מנחם תקמ"א[3] באתי
12. לק"ק ברוכהויזן אצל האחי' הק[4] כ"ה אברהם וכ"ה יוזפא הנ"ל לעשות מקח עמהם מדגן
13. והשיבו האחי' שטרם כל מוכרח אני להביא איין צו לענגליכה [פ]רוב מן דגן
14. וגם כתב ראי' מן המוכר כדי שיכולי' לסמוך עליו ואח"כ רוצי' לעשות מקח עמי
15. [.".] הלכתי אצל השררה יר"ה שהי' לו למכור דגן ועשיתי מקח עמו / אחר זאת מיד
16. הבאתי איין פרוב מדגן הנ"ל גם כתב מן השררה כפי ההעתק שנמצא בפראטיקאהל
17. להראות האחי' הנ"ל שיש שורש ב{.}(ד)[5]ברי אשר ע"כ עשו האחי' הנ"ל מקח עמי כפי ש
18. שנראה מהעתק כתב נומרי ב שכתב כ"ה יוזפא הנ"ל בעצמו ונתרציתי לחתום כתב
19. הלז וליתן בידם / ובתוך כתב הנ"ל מיך פר בונדן צו שאפין להאחי' הנ"ל ד"ה מ
20. מאות שעפל דגן בעד למד ט"ג פער שעפל עם מדה גדול וכדי שאינם צריכי'
21. האחי' לעשות חשבן עמי מהוצאות ובעל עגלות הוסיפו האחי' הנ"ל ליתן לי א' רט
22. וחצי פער פודר נגד זה התחייבתי א"ע להביא דגן הנ"ל לנהר וועסר על הוצאתי והם
23. נקיים ומשופי' מכל הוצאות / אחר זמן באתי להאחי' הנ"ל ובקשתי מהם שיקחו הדגן
24. באשר שנדרשתי בגלל כן מן השררה יר"ה בכל יום ויו' והשיבו האחי' הנ"ל שאינם
25. יכולים לקבוע זמן על הקבלת דגן עד שיקבלו אורדר מן קרושפאנדעטץ שלהם ואני

קמז ע"א

1. ב"ה
2. ואני מוכרח להמתין עד אותו זמן שירצו / באשר שאינו נזכר שום זמן בכתב נומרי ב' הנ"ל
3. ע"ז הלכתי אצל השררה יר"ה ועשיתי עיכוב ואשתדל להניח הדגן עד זמן שארצה לקבלם
4. לאחר זאת ויו תשרי תקמ"ב לקחתי סחורה מהאחי' הנ"ל מדאגה פן ואולי ילכו האחי'
5. עמי ברמאות ויקחו הדגן בלי ידעתי מהשררה ירה[6] באשר שהראית להם המקו' שיש הדגן
6. הנ"ל / וכאשר יגורתי כן הי' שהאחים הנ"ל לקחו הדגן הנ"ל מן השררה יר"ה בלי ידיעתי

---

1. לא יודע לי מה כוונת הדברים. באותן השנים בקורביי 1 טאלר (Konventionstaler) = 32 גרושן (Konventionsgroschen) = 48 מריאנגרושן (Mariengroschen) = 2 גולדן (Konventionsgulden) = 2 חצי טאלר (Konventionshalbtaler) = 384 פשיטים (Pfennig) ר' Ilisch and Schwede, *Das Münzwesen im Stift Corvey*, 39. אולי הכוונה ל-gute Groschen ואם כן המילה 'טוב' תפסה את המילה 'gute'. Guter Groschen אחד = טאלר (ולא Konventionstaler). כנראה שכאן מדובר בטאלר של בראנשוויג. תודתי לד"ר מיכאל לענארז מהמוזיאון היהודי בפרנקפורט ולד"ר פרנק ברגר מהמוזיאן ההיסטורי בפרנקפורט על עזרתם בנושא.
2. כנראה שצ"ל 'ב פשי[טים]'
3. 9 באוגוסט 1781
4. הקצין
5. תוספת מעל השורה
6. ירום הודו

7. בכן תובע כ' משה ריווח ויו ט"ג מן כל שעפל ועלה חשבונו על ד"ה מאות שעפל לאחר
8. הוצאות וגם דמי סחורה שלקח מן האחי' הנ"ל על סך שלשה מאות ועשרי' ושניים רט
9. ח ט"ג ויו פשי' וכ"ה יוזפא השיב להד"ם רק כ' משה הנ"ל הוט זיך אופעריוט בכתב
10. למכור לנו {הדגן בשנת תקמא} וכי בשביל שרצה למכור לנו הדגן בשנת תקמא / שוב אינו
11. רשאי ליקח בשנה האחרת שנת תקמב דגן מן השררה שאינו ידוע לי ולא הי' בזכרוני
12. שזה הוא שהראה לי כ"מי הנ"ל / בכן תובע כ"ה יוזפא מן כ"מ הנ"ל סך פה רט יב טג [ב']
13. פשי' כנ"ל והאריכו בטענותיהם כמבואר באריכות בפראטיקאהל הנשלח לנו
14. מן האך ליבליכר קומיסיאהן ירה / ולאחר שדקדקנו ועיינו בטענותיהם מצאנו מה
15. שתבע כ' משה הנ"ל לערך ארבע מאות ושבעה רט לפי ערך פסיקה ממקח הנ"ל
16. אין לכ' משה הנ"ל שום תביעה בשביל טענה זו / אך עכ"פ יש לכ' משה הנ"ל טענה
17. ותביעה על פו"מ כ"ה יוזפא הנ"ל שעכ"פ נעשה לו סרסרות על ידו גם עשה לו פ
18. פעולה טובה הרבה שהודיע לכ' יוזפא הנ"ל אצל מי שהי' הדגן שהי' לוקח כ"ה יוזפא
19. בשנת תקמב גם עשה כבר כ' משה הנ"ל הפסקת דמי' של הדגן עם אותו מוכר שלקח
20. כ"ה יוזפא הנ"ל ממנו באותו סכום המקח / וגם עשה השתדלות אצל השררה ירה הנ"ל
21. שיעכב בידו הדגן הנ"ל שלא למכור לאחרי' בכן נעשה לכ"ה יוזפא הנ"ל ע"י כ' משה
22. הנ"ל טובה הרבה לזאת מצאנו בשביל שכר סרסראות ופעולה טובה שנעשה
23. לפו"מ כ"ה יוזפא הנ"ל ע"י כ' משה הנ"ל שמחוי[ב] כ"ה יוזפא הנ"ל לשלם לכ' משה הנ"ל
24. שכירות בשביל זה וירדנו לשומא כמה מגיע לכ' משה הנ"ל עבור זה ומצאנו
25. השומא שהוא חלק שישית מסך ארבע מאת ושבעה רט שתובע כ' משה הנ"ל
26. בכן

קמז ע"ב

1. ב"ה
2. בכן מחויב כה יוזפא הנ"ל לשלם לערך ששי' ושמונה רט וינוכה כ' משה הנ"ל סך
3. סח רט הנ"ל מן סך דמי סחורה שחייב כ' משה הנ"ל והוא לערך פה רט והמותר
4. ישלם כ' משה לכ"ה יוזפא הנ"ל ומחמת הוצאות המבואר בטענותיהם שטען כ"ה יוזפא
5. הנ"ל שכפי הנהוג שם ע"פ השררה ירה שכל מי שאינו זוכה בטענותיו אף בדיני
6. ישראל מחויב לשלם לכנגדו כל הוצאותיו / ובכן לפי המבואר לעיל שכל א' זוכה
7. במקצת טענותיו ממילא הוצאות חל על שני הצדדי' בשוה חלק כחלק ממש יצא
8. מאתנו יו' א יא כסליו תקמ"ג ה"ג אב"ד נרו' והדיין ור"י רנ"מ והדיין רמ"ש ואני

No. 162

Fol. 147b; Sunday evening, 17 November 1782

Half of a house on the Sonne lot was sold by the community to Anshel and

1. כבוד משה

Seligmann Schwarzschild for 2001 guldens. The brothers were to pay one-third of the amount immediately and the rest in six semi-annual installments. The record notes that the community maintained a lien on the house until the final payment was made.

9. ————
10. חצי בית פנימי צור הינטר זוהן שהי' שייך להאלופי' קציני' גובי' יצו נמכר
11. בפנינו ב"ד להאחי' כ' אנשיל וכ' זעליגמן בני המנוח כ' יוקב שווארצשילד
12. ז"ל בעד סך שני אלפי' ואחד זהו' לשלם אין קונפונטציאהנש מינץ כפי
13. מנהג הקהלה שליש (תיכף)[1] נגד כתב מעשה ב"ד ושני שלישי' על ששה חצאי שני'
14. רצופי' גם נשאר החצי בית לאפותקו מפורש ויתוקן ע"ז שטר אפותיקו עי[2] נ"ה כנהוג
15. נעשה אור ליו' ב יב כסליו תקמ"ג רנמ[3] ורמ"ש ואני

No. 163

Fols. 148a–b; Monday evening, 25 November 1782

Sussmann Rüsselsheim, his son Mikhel, and Sussmann's brother Feis jointly owned the Hellebarde house in which they each lived with their respective families. A court decision in early 1777 divided the house into three sections in a manner that was acceptable to all families, which is itemized here. The families now came to the court seeking a lottery to decide who should live where in the house when. The court agreed to the request and, on the basis of the lottery, apportioned the living spaces for a three year period. At the end of three years the families were to rotate living quarters, a rotation that was to be repeated after another three years, and again after another three years. The court suggested that after nine years the families return for a new lottery.

קמח ע"א

1. ב"ה
2. מחזיקי בית צום העליבאד הו"ה כ" זוסמן בן ה"ה המנוח כ" אייזק ריסלסהיים ז"ל
3. מחזיק שליש ואחיו הו"ה כ" פייס בן כ" אייזק הנ"ל מחזיק שליש / והו"ה כ" {פייס} (מיכל)[4] בן כ"

---

1. תוספת מעל השורה
2. על ידי
3. רב נתן מז
4. תוספת מעל השורה

4. זוסמן הנ"ל שאשה[1] בת המנוח כ" ברוך בן כ" אייזק הנ"ל מחזיק שליש המה חלק' ביתם
5. הנ"ל לשלשה דיורי' ע"פ המבואר בפס"ד שיצא ביניהם אור ליו' ויו ך"ד טבת
6. תקלזין לפק ואופן החלוקה נתרצו ה"ה כ" זוסמן וכ" פייס וכ" מיכל הנ"ל שיהי'
7. כמבואר והיינו שטח התחתון בית החורף למטה וחדר א" א" שטעג הויך לצד
8. הסוכה שאחורי בית הנ"ל וחדר אחד ארבע שטעג הויך לצד הרחוב
9. (וחדר אחד בזו השטח לצד הסוכה הצפוני)[2] וחדר אחד חמשה שטעג הויך לצד הסוכה
והמרתף החיצון כל זה יהי'
10. דירה אחת ודירה שניי' יהי' שטח האמצעי דהיינו בית החורף א" ש
11. שטעג הויך לצד הרחוב וחדר א" שני שטעג הויך לצד הסוכה / ו(ב)[3]מרתף
12. שתחת בית החורף התחתון ו(דירה שלישת יהי')[4] ו(א)[5]חדר א" שלשה שטעג
13. הויך לצד הסוכה ודירה שלישת יהי' שטח העליון דהיינו למעלה שני
14. שטעג הויך בית החורף לצד הרחוב / וחדר אחד שלשה שטעג הויך לצד
15. הרחוב וחדר אחד ארבע שטעג הויך לצד הסוכה הדרומה וחדר א"
16. חמשה שטעג הויך לצד הרחוב והמרתף שתחת הסוכה / ומאחר
17. שיש שני בתי המוצנע בסוכה הנ"ל בכן הקטן יהי' למי ששייך דירה
18. התחתונה והגדול יהי' בשותפות לשני דיורי העליונה ולכל הדיורי'
19. יהי' רשות לילך דרך בית החורף התחתון אל בית המוצנע הגדול
20. העומד בהסוכה הנ"ל והיינו להם ולנשיהם ולבניהם אבל לא לשאר בני
21. ביתם[6] גם יש לכל הדיורי' רשות ל[ה]שתמש בה[סו]כה הנ"ל כל ימי החג
22. כנהוג / וכהיו' הטלנו גורל ביניהם על משך תשעה שני' רצופי' מיו' ד
23. דלמטה ועלה שטח התחתון על משך שלשה שני' הראשוני' לכ"

קמח ע"ב

1. בה
2. לכ" פייס הנ"ל ושטח האמצעי לכ" מיכל ושטח העליון לכ" זוסמן הנ"ל /
3. ובכלות שלשה שנים הנ"ל יהי' שטח התחתון לכ" זוסמן הנ"ל ושטח האמצעי
4. לכ" פייס הנ"ל ושטח העליון לכ" מיכל הנ"ל כל משך שלשה שני' השניי'
5. ובכלות ששה שנים הנ"ל יהי' שטח התחתון לה"ה כ" מיכל הנ"ל
6. ושטח האמצעי לה"ה כ" זוסמן הנ"ל ושטח העליון לה"ה כ" פייס
7. הנ"ל כל משך שלשה שנים השלישיים מן משך תשעה שנים הנ"ל
8. ואחר כלות תשעה שנים הנ"ל יחזירו להפיל גורל מחודש כפי

---

1. כנראה שצ"ל 'שנשא' או 'שנשא לאשה'. על פי אלה תולדות 7.3.1817, מיכל ריסלסהיים נשא את ברענדלה, בתו של ברוך בן אייזק ריסלסהיים, בסביבות 1782.
2. תוספת מעל השורה
3. תוספת מעל השורה
4. הסוגרים במקור
5. תוספת מעל השורה
6. ר' לעיל, מס' 70.

9. שיתרצו עצמם יצא מאתנו אור ליו' ג" ך כסליו תקמ"ג
10. רנמ[1] ורמ"ש ואני

No. 164

Stern v. Steibel et al.

Fols. 149a–152a; Thursday evening, 28 November 1782

(the manuscript is damaged at the bottom of each page of this record except fol. 152a)

Siskind Stern, the community beadle (*shamash*), and David Gamburg acted as guardians for the late Ber, son of Leb Gans. During the period of guardianship, David Gamburg died leaving Siskind, who also attended to the estate of Ber's mother, to continue on alone. Siskind maintained a record of income and expenses, but Ber's costs were greater than his income. After Ber's death, Siskind claimed that the estate owed him almost 500 guldens, arguing that he had paid for Ber's food, clothing, taxes, house repairs, medical expenses, and burial costs out his own pocket. Ber was survived by two sisters who, through their representative, rejected Siskind's claims and did not accept his accounting. They maintained that there was no oversight of his books, that there were discrepancies in his record keeping, and that he had not recorded all of the estate's income. They also claimed that Siskind had no right to continue as a sole guardian and demanded that he turn over all materials that belonged to the estate to them. Siskind answered the various financial claims and noted that after David Gamburg's death he had approached a number of communal leaders asking that another guardian be appointed but, according to Siskind, they had told him that there was no need for another guardian since Ber had reached majority and trusted Siskind. Siskind was so upset by the lack of appreciation and trust shown by the sisters that he requested guardian's fees for eleven years of service and for dealing with their mother's estate. After both sides agreed in writing to a court-brokered compromise, the court rejected Siskind's demand for back fees but awarded him a large share of his expenses.

קמט ע"א

1. בה
2. ע"ד שבא לפנינו ה"ה התורני כ"ה הירץ אולף יצו בהרשאות ובמעמד השמש

---

1. רב נתן מז

3. דקהלותינו יע"א התור' כ"ה זיסקנד שטערן יצו שהי' אפטרופס על היתום המנוח
4. כ" פער בן ליב גנץ ז"ל ותבע מן היורשי' של היתום הנעדר כ" פער
5. הנ"ל ה"ה ה"ה כ"ה זעלקלי בהמנוחי[1] כ' יוסף שטיבל ז"ל שהוא בעל אחות הנעדר
6. היתום הנ"ל והאשה מ" יענטלה אשת ה"ה כ"ה בערמן הירש כץ מן קק[2] קאבלענץ
7. יע"א שהיא ג"כ אחות היתום הנ"ל הבאה בכח עצמה ובהרשאות בעלה
8. הן לדין והן לפשר וכמו שהציעה לפנינו ב"ד כו"ה מספקת מבעלה והציע ל
9. לפנינו כ"ה זיסקינד הנ"ל פנקס של אפטרופסית שלו ובתוכו חשבן מה ש
10. שקיבל (לאחר שנעשה אפטרופס הן מה שקיבל מעזבון אם [הי]תום הנ"ל והן מה שקיבל)[3] לאחר כך אחת לאחת בשביל היתום וגם מה שקיבל מהאלופי'
11. גובי' יצו סך מאה זהו' אחר פטירת הנעדר הנ"ל וגם נכתב ב
12. בתוכו חשבון הוצאות מה שהוציא הן בחיי' היתום הנ"ל בשביל
13. אם היתום מה שהיתה חייבת לאנשים אחרים ולשררה ירה[4] / אלף
14. זהו' ושאר הוצאת מ[עז]ב[ו]נה והן מה שהוציא עבור היתום והיינו ק
15. קאשט מעות מלבושי' שאצונג קרונד צינץ ובדק הבית שבועה מעות
16. להיתום וצרכי רפואת הן צרכי קבורה אחר פט[יר]תו והעלה בחשבונו
17. שהוצאות שהוציא על היתום הנעדר הנ"ל הם הוצאות יתירה ממה שקיבל
18. עבורו סך (ארבע)[5] מאת ושמוני' ותשעה זהו' כ"ב צל בכן תבע כ"ה זיסקינד הנ"ל
19. מן היורשי' הנ"ל שרוצים לירד בנחלת היתום הנעדר והוא רביעת בית
20. שהי' שייך להמנוח כ" פער הנ"ל מכרו אותו רביעת הבית הנ"ל
21. שישלמו לו מקודם סך ד' מאות [ופט] זהובים... כ"ה הירץ וכ"ה זיסקינד ה[נ"ל]
22. באשר שהקרקע הי' שייך לה ... כהי' אפטרופס' על
23. בכן הקרקע בחזקתו כל ...
24. [...]א[ל] מתחיל ...

קמט ע"ב

1. ב[ע]"ה
2. מה שהי' בעזבון של היתום הנ"ל הי' דעתנו ע"כ לגבות מן רביעת
3. בית הנ"ל והוא הי' מוכרח לעשות כן באשר שהיתום לא הי' תמיד
4. בקו הבריאה בכן הי' עשה לשם שמים לטובת היתום וה"ה התורני
5. כ"ה בענדיט הענא בהרשאות ובמעמד היורשי' הנ"ל וגם {עם שקיבל}
6. כ"ה זעלקלי עצמו השיב לא מיבעי' שאיני מאמין בתביעת כ"ה זיסקינד
7. הנ"ל מה שאמר שהוציא יותר ממה שהי' תחת ידו מעזבון היתום
8. הנ"ל והלווה מכיסו ע"פ פנקס שלו אלא שגם המה תבעו מן כ"ה זיסקינד
9. הנ"ל שיברר על כל מה שהי' בידו מן העזבון הנ"ל הן מקבלה והן

---

1. בן המנוח
2. קהילת קודש
3. תוספת מעל השורה
4. ירום הודו
5. תוספת מעל השורה

10. מהוצאת מתחילת אפטרופיסית שלו ואינו נותני' נאמנות על פנקס
11. שלו מכמה טעמי' שהאריכו ראשון שהפנקס שלו אינו כהוגן כפי שארי
12. פנקסאות של אפטרופסית גם אינו כמנהג שארי פנקסאות מאפטרופס'
13. אחרי' שהסדר כן הוא שאותו אפטרופס שיש בידו המעות אינו
14. כותב בפנקס אפטרופסית שלו הוצאות והכנסת הוא עצמו רק
15. מאפטרופסי' אחרו' שעמו הוא כותבם והפנקס שלו הכל מכתב
16. ידו ולא נמצא כלום בפנקס שלו מהאפטרופס שהי' עמו באותו פעם
17. המנוח כ"ה דוד גמבורג ז"ל ומה גם שהנאמנת של שטר אפטרופי'
18. הוא דוקא על שניהם יחד ולא עליו לבד וגם אינו מכוון הקבלה
19. שכתב ר' זיסקינד בפנקס שלו מה שקיבל מן כ"ה אברהם גנץ על
20. חלק היתום עם הפנקס של אברהם גנץ שכתב וחתם כה זיסקנד
21. הנ"ל בעצמו מה שה[י'] ... שקיבל ממנו כמו שטען על זה באריכות גם
22. נחסר בקבלת פנקס של ...[רו]ת הבית שקיבל ו[מ]כ"[ש]
23. {שה...שי'} (שהיורשי')[1] הנ"ל ... נ"ל להוציא
24. ה

קן ע"א

1. ב"ה
2. אפטרופסי' ובפרט שהוא רק חד אפטרופס ואינה רשאי להלוות אלא ברשות
3. ב"ד וגם הי' לו לר' זיסקנד לבקש עוד עוד[2] אפטרופס אחר במקו' ר' דוד
4. לאחר פטירתו וכ"ה זיסקנד הנ"ל השיב וטוען שהאפטרופס האחר לא הי'
5. כותב מעולם בתוך פנקס שלו ומן מה שנחסר בפנקס שלו בקבלה איזה ח"כ
6. מדמי שכירת הבית השיב ר' זיסקנד שכבר נכלל בתוך ל"ב מאות זהו'
7. שקיבל בתחילת אפטרופסות וכמבואר בתוך אינפורטאריום מעזבון
8. אם היתום הנ"ל ועל מה שחסר בדמי קבלה שקיבל מן כ" אברהם
9. גנץ הנ"ל השיב ג"כ באריכות ודרך כלל השיב שעל כל מה שנעשה בחיי'
10. האפטרופס האחר בודאי אין מחויב (ליתן חשבן גם)[3] יתר חשבונו ועל מה שנשאר א
11. אפטרופס יחידי השיב כ"ה זיסקנד שלאחר פטירת ר' דוד הנ"ל {הטען} (הת[אמ]ץ)[4]
12. את עצמו וביקש עוד אפטרופס מכמה פרנסי' והשיב לו הויאל[5] שהיתום פער
13. הוא גדול בשני' ואינו בקו הבריאה והוא ר' זיסקנד הנ"ל הי' משגיח עליו
14. ביותר שהיותם מרוצה עמו לבד אינו מן הצורך להעמיד עוד אפטרופס
15. אצלו באשר שהיתום הבטיח עליו והוא ונותן לו כל הנאמנות עוד השיב
16. שר' זעלקלי שהי' תמיד כאן מפני זה לא התאמץ הוא את עצמו וביקש עוד
17. אפטרופס אחר או להיות הוא עצמו אפטרופס עמו עוד תבע כ"ה זיסקינד

---

1. תוספת מעל השורה
2. כפילות במקור
3. תוספת מעל השורה
4. תיקון מעל השורה
5. צ"ל 'הואיל'

18. הנ״ל והציע ח״כ מסך קע״ה זהו׳ על כ״ (הירץ)[1] הירש הארן והיינו טערמינה בריב
19. וטוען כהרר[2] זיסקנד הנ״ל שהלווה להנ״ל מדמי עד ...
20. בשנת תקלב ולאח״כ בשנת תקל[ח ש] ...
21. זיסקינד עם הלווה ועשה עמו ...
22. קע״ה זהו׳ ואינו ...

קן ע״ב

1. ב״ה
2. פעמים רווחי׳ שקיבל בכן תבע כ״ה זיסקנד אותן קע״ה זהו׳ מן היורשי׳
3. הנ״ל ורוצה ליתן להם אותן ח״כ הנ״ל והיורשי׳ הנ״ל השיבו באשר שלא כתב
4. כ״ה כ״ה[3] זיסקינד בפנקס שלו לא בתחילה כשעשה הלוואה הנ״ל
5. ולא לבסוף כשהתפשר א״ע עם הלווה בכן מוכח שהלוואה הנ״ל
6. לא הי׳ מדמי העזבון היתום הנ״ל רק ממע[ו]ת ר׳ זיסקינד הנ״ל
7. עוד תבע כ״ה זיסקינד הנ״ל באשר שהיורשי׳ אינים[4] רוצים ליתן לו
8. נאמונת כמו אפטרופס אחר בכן תבע מהם שכר טירחה מה שעסק
9. והשגיח בעזבון היתום כל שנה סך חמשי׳ זהו׳ והיינו משנת תקלא
10. עד שנת תקמ״ב גם עבור מה שטרח בעזבון האל׳ מ׳ שינלה אם
11. היתום הנ״ל תבע שכר טרחתו סך ארבעי׳ זהו׳ באשר שאינו מחויב
12. להטריח עצמו בשביל היורשי׳ של היתום הנ״ל והיורשי׳ הנ״ל השיבו
13. שהאפטרופס אין יכול לתבוע שכר טרחתו עוד תבע היורשי׳ מן
14. כ״ה זיסקינד הנ״ל שיחזר להם כל מה שהי׳ תחת ידו מעזבון היתום
15. הנ״ל הן חשבונת וכתבי׳ פנקסאות יהי מה שיהי׳ מה ששייך לעזבון
16. היתום ואמו המונחת ז״ל שיש תחת ידו גם הפרוכת גם המלבושי׳
17. מהיתום הנ״ל וכ״ה זיסקינד הנ״ל השיב מן מלבושי׳ מהיתום כ׳
18. פער הנ״ל אינו בידו כלום והכתבים וחשבונות ופנקסאות שיש
19. בידו ... הם אחר שיצאת פס״ד נגד פטורי׳ עוד תבעו
20. ... פנקס של אפטרופסות מן כ״ה זיסקינד
21. ...ש לאינו [וימחלי׳] שהי׳ בעזבון
22. ...בר ידוע

קנא ע״א

1. בה
2. ידוע לר׳ זעלקלי הנ״ל שנמכרים אין אויזרוף לכ״ה פער ב[ר]״א[5] פפאן
3. ועדין לא קיבל הפירען ממנו והיורשי׳ יכולי׳ לתבוע ממנו והאריכו
4. הצדדים הנ״ל בטענותיהם ובתשבותיהם זה מול זה וזו מול זה על כל

---

1. תוספת מעל השורה
2. כבוד הרב רבי
3. כפילות במקור
4. צ״ל ׳אינם׳
5. בן ר׳ אנשיל

5. פרט ופרט כמבואר באריכות בק"ה המונח אצלינו ולאחר שחתמו
6. הצדדים הנ"ל א"ע בתוקף קומפרמיס בח"ח ובקנס מסויי' חצי לשררה ירה[1]
7. וחצי להקדש ה"ה כ"ה ר"ז[2] הנ"ל (ואשתו)[3] והאשה מרת יענטלה הנ"ל חתמה בעצמ[ה]
8. בכח עצמה ובכח (והרשאה מספקת)[4] מבעלה והרשאת מספקת מבעלה כ"ה פערמן הירש[5]
9. מקאבלענץ לאשר ולקיים כפי מה שיצא מאתונו[6] מתחילה (חתמו עצמם)[7] לפי הדין ואח"כ
10. נתנו הצדדי' עיניהם עלינו ב"ד ח"מ לפשר ביניהם (וקבלו עליהם)[8] ולחזק ולקיים
11. הפשר שיצא מאתונו (וקיבלו עליהם)[9] בכל חומרו בקנס הנ"ל וג"כ חתמו
12. עצמם בקומפרמיס כנ"ל בכן נזדקקנו להם ומצאנו מה שתבע כ"ה
13. זיסקינד מן היורשי' הנ"ל שכר טירחה שלו מיו' היותו אפטרופס והיינו
14. משנת תקלא עד (תוך)[10] שנת תקמב עת פטירת היתום הנ"ל כל שנה חמשי'
15. זהו' ונוסף ע"ז תבע ארבעי' בשביל מה שטרח בעזבון אם היתום הנ"ל
16. אין ממש בתביעת האלו אבל מה שתבע כ"ה זיסקינד הנ"ל ע"פ פנקס
17. אפטרופסות שלו והעלה בחשבונו [ש]הוציא עבור היתום הנ"ל סך
18. ארבע מאות ופ"ט זהו' יותר ממה שהי' תחת ידו מעזבון אחר ש
19. שראינו פנקס אינפוטואריום מאם היתום הנ"ל מה שהי' בעזבונה
20. וגם מה שראינו מה שנפרע לפ ...בונה בשביל אם היתום
21. החובת שהיתה חייב לשל ... שררה י[ר"ה]
22. (ושכירות הבית)[11] ושאר הוצאות (בעזבון אם היתום הנ"ל)[12] וקבלה תבע ...

קנא ע"ב

1. ב"ה
2. זה מול זה מצאנו ראינו כמה הי' מן ההכרח לפי ראות ענינו לשלם קאשט מעות
3. בשביל הנעדר היתום הנ"ל וגם מה שהי' מוכרח לשלם עבורו קרונד צונץ
4. ושאצונג בדק הבית אותן שנים שהי' כ"ה זיסקינד הנ"ל אפטרופס וגם מה
5. שהי' הוצאות מבנין הבית בשנת תקלד לאחר שריפה השם יצילנו
6. מכל פגע רע וירדנו עוד לשומא כמה הי' מוכרח לשלם כ"ה זיסקינד

1. ירום הודו
2. רבי זעלקלי
3. תוספת מעל השורה
4. תוספת מעל השורה
5. בערמן הירש
6. ר"ל 'מאתנו'
7. תוספת מעל השורה
8. תוספת מעל השורה
9. הסוגריים במקור
10. תוספת מעל השורה
11. תוספת מעל השורה
12. תוספת מעל השורה

7. הנ״ל בשביל היתום שבוע מעות ליתום הנ״ל מלבושי׳ בעטונג שכר
8. לימוד וצרכי רפואת כל שנה ושנה בהיותו אפטרופס גם צרכי
9. קבורה אחר פטירת היתום הנ״ל ואחר שחשבנו כל הנ״ל ודקדקנו בחשבונו׳
10. הנ״ל מצאנו בתורת פשר שמחויבי׳ היורשי׳ הנ״ל לשלם לכ״ה זיסקינד סך
11. שני מאות ושבעם וחמשה זהו׳ על [דבר] אותן מאה זהו׳ שקיבל כהרר
12. זיסקינד הנ״ל מהאלו{.} גובי׳ יצו בשביל יתום הנעדר ז״ל הנ״ל ש
13. שמחויבי׳ ג״כ היורשי׳ לשלם להאלופי׳ גובי׳ יצו ובתוך הסך שני מ
14. מאות ושבעי׳ וחמשה זהו׳ הנ״ל נכלל בתוכם אותן עשרה רט שהעלה כ״ה
15. זיסקינד הנ״ל בחשבונו שעדיין מחויב לשלם לשררה יר״ה בשביל שאצונג
16. וגם אויזצוטוהן שמחויב כ״ה זיסקינד הנ״ל לשלם העשרה רט הנ״ל והטרחה
17. בזה מצאנו שהוא ג״כ על כ״ה זיסקינד הנ״ל מאחר שהוא לטובת העזבון
18. אותן טערמינה ח״כ מסך מאה ושבעי׳ וחמשה זהו׳ שיש ביד כ״ה
19. זיסקינד הנ״ל על כ״ה הירץ הירש הארן יצו יחזיק לעצמו וכל מה
20. שיגבה כ״ה זיסקינד מן כ״ה הירץ הנ״ל מסך ח״כ הנ״ל הן כולה או
21. מקצותה שייך הכל לכ״ה זיס[קינד] הנ״ל / ומה שחייב כ״ה [פ]
22. פער בן כ״ה אנשיל [פפאן] ... כפי שאמר ר׳ זיסקינד
23. הנ״ל ... וגם מצאנו שכל מה

קנב ע״א

1. ב״ה
2. מה שיש תחת יד כהרר זיסקינד הנ״ל מן העזבון כ״ פער ז״ל הנ״ל הן
3. הפרוכת והן ח״כ פנקסאות חשבונות וכתבי׳ וכל מה שיש תחת ידו השי[י׳]
4. בעזבון הנ״ל יהי׳ מה שיהי׳ מחויב להחזיר ליורשי׳ ומחויבי׳ הצדדי׳ ה״ה
5. כ״ זעלקלי הנ״ל והאשה מרת יענטלה הנ״ל ובעלה כ׳ בערמן הירש הנ״ל
6. ליתן כתב {ראוי׳}(ראי׳)[1] לכ״ה זיסקינד שקיבלו מה שהי׳ תחת ידו וגם ר׳ זיסקינד
7. הנ״ל מחויב ליתן כתב שובר להיורשי׳ הנ״ל על המעות שקיבל מהם וכנ״ל
8. ולאחר שנעשה כל הנ״ל יהי פטורי׳ ומסולקי׳ כ״ה זיסקינד הנ״ל מצדדים
9. הנ״ל כ׳ זעלקלי הנ״ל והאשה מ׳ יענטלי הנ״ל ובעלה הנ״ל והצדדי׳ הנ״ל [מ]ן
10. ר׳ זיסקינד הנ״ל מחמת עזבון הנ״ל ואין לשום צד וצד מהצדדי׳ הנ״ל
11. שום טענה ותביעה שבעולם יהי׳ מה שיהי׳ מכל מה שהפה יוכל לדבר
12. והלב לחשוב להרהר אחר פירעון שני מאות ושבעי׳ וחמשה זהו׳ מ
13. מהצדדי׳ הנ״ל לכ״ה זיסקינד הנ״ל ואחר חזרת מה שיש תחת י״ד[2] כה
14. זיסקינד מהכתבים הנ״ל להצדדי׳ הנ״ל כ׳[3] כולם פטורים ומסולקי׳ בכא״ה כל
15. אחד מצד שכנגדו יצא מאתנו אור ליו׳ ויו עש״ק ד״ג כיסליו תקמ״ג
16. רנ״מ ורמ״ש ואני

---

1. תוספת מעל השורה
2. לא ברור למה יש גרשיים כאן; ר׳ גם סוף מס׳ 88.
3. כנראה שהאות מיותרת

No. 165

Fol. 152a; Thursday 19 December 1782

A disagreement among the heirs of a number of estates over the division of proceeds from the sale of three-quarters of a seat in the synagogue led the community to hold the disputed funds (see nos. 136 and 160). When a settlement was reached, the funds were distributed to the various parties and a record of the distribution was made by the court.

17. הדמי מכירה מן שלשה רביעי[ת] מן מקו' שלם שהי' עומד עליו כ' משה לוי ושנמכר
18. בפנינו ב"ד להו"ה כ' ליב בן המנוח כ' יוקב אופנהיים בעד סך מאה רט אשר הונח
19. ביד האלופי' גובי' יצו לאחר שהתפשרו המשותפי' יורשי כ' יוקב אופנהיי' ויורשי[.]
20. ר מרדכי אופנהיים עם יורשי ג"ה ר' פער קן ז"ל ניתן לכתוב שמגיע לכל או"א
21. {ממה שו} {מהשו} מהיורשי' המשותפי' הנ"ל דהיינו יורשי ר' פער קן ז"ל הנ"ל ויורשי
22. כ' יוקב ב"מ[1] אופנהיי' ויורשי ר' מ[רד]כי בו"ו[2] אופנהיי' ז"ל לכל או"א מגיע
23. סך חמשי' זהו' מן סך מאה (רט דמי)[3] מכירה הנ"ל וגם חתמנו כתב ראי' ע"ז ליורשי רפק[4] הנ"ל
24. יו' ה די טבת תקמ"ג
25. רנמ[5] ורמ"ש ואני

No. 166

Fol. 152b; Sunday evening, 26 January 1783

A record of the sale of a seat in the men's section of the synagogue to two brothers, Moses and Isaac Fulda. The brothers were nephews of the previous owner, Elijah Fulda, who had died. The record contains a blank space for a name. The name is not central to the case but was intended to be used as a point of reference for locating the seat in the synagogue (i.e., next to where *x* sat). The seat was sold for 184 guldens after a period of open bidding.

---

1. בן מרדכי
2. בן וואלף
3. תוספת מעל השורה
4. רבי פער קן
5. רב נתן מז

קנב ע"ב

1. ב"ה
2. מקו' שלם בעזרת אנשי' עליונה בכותל צפונה בחלון התחונה אשר עומד עלי' כעת הו"ה
3. כ"ה אהרן בהמנוח כ[1] וואלף פולדא ז"ל ומצד ימין על מקו' הסמוך עומד עלי' כעת הו"ה ג"ה כ"ה
4. מרדכי מז ומצד שמאל על מקו' הסמוך עומד כעת [2] אותו מקו' שלם הנ"ל שהי' שייך
5. להמנוח כ' אלי' בהמנוח כ"ה איצק פולדא ז"ל נמכר בפנינו ב"ד ע"פ הכרזה כנהוג {...}
6. בפקודת האלופי' גובי' יצו ויורשי המנוח כ' אלי' ז"ל להאחי' כ' משה וכ' ליב בהמנוח כ"ה אהרן
7. ב"ה איצק פולדא ז"ל בעד סך מאה ושמוני' וארבעה זהו' לשלם כפי תיקון הקהלה
8. נעשה אור ליו' ב דך שבט תקמ"ג רנ"מ ורמ"ש ואני

No. 167

Rothschild et al. v. Oppene et al.

Fol. 153a–b; Sunday evening, 23 February 1783

In about 1714, one-half of the Goldener Kopf house and one-third of the Eule house were combined into one house. The arrangement complicated tax payments to the non-Jewish authorities, and the rabbinic court of the day determined that the owner(s) of the Goldener Kopf house should pay a set amount to the owners of the Eule house, who would then transfer payment to the authorities. This arrangement was challenged in 1782 when the residents of the Goldener Kopf refused to transfer funds to the residents of the Eule house and questioned the validity of a 1750 copy of the 1714 ruling. The Eule residents came to the court demanding payment. The Goldener Kopf residents noted that their house had recently been announced for sale in the synagogue on three occasions, and yet the Eule residents failed to inform potential buyers of the obligation of Goldener Kopf residents to make tax payments through the owners of the Eule house. It was further claimed that according to community by-laws, the Eule residents' failure to announce this resulted in their forfeiting their rights to receive future payments. In their defense, the Eule residents claimed not to have heard the announcements of sale and reminded the court that the Goldener Kopf residents had made their tax payments through them

1. בן המנוח כבוד
2. מקום ריק בכתב היד

for years. The court offered a compromise in which the Goldener Kopf residents would continue to pay the Eule residents, but at a somewhat reduced rate.

קנג ע״א

1. ב״ה
2. ע״ד שבא לפנינו ה״ה התורני כ״ה פייס הענ[א] בהרשאת גיסו הו״ה כ׳
3. פייס בן זלמן רויט שילד יצו ובהרשאת הו״ה פו״מ כ׳ הירץ גייגר שיש לו כח
4. והרשאה מן הו״ה פו״מ כ״ה גבריאל האכעמס יצו מחזיקי חצי בית צו דער
5. אייהל ותבע מן מחזיקי בית צום גולדנקאפף והמה הו״ה כ״ה נתן א
6. אופנה והו״ה כ׳ פייס בן זעלקלי אדליר ששייך לכל או״א החצי מן הבית צו
7. גולדנקאפף הנ״ל והציע לפנינו כ״ה פייס הענא בהרשאת הנ״ל העתק
8. מקוים בחתימת יד הסופר דקהלתינו יע״א ה״ה התורני כ״ה ישראל סופר
9. יצו[1] מן י״ג סיון תק״יוד מגוף פסק ב״ד שיצא שנת תע״ד ושם נאמר
10. מאחר שנחלקו הבתי׳ של אייל ושל גולדן קאפף ונעשה מן חצי בית
11. גולדנ קאפף ומן שליש אייהל בית אחד וכו׳ בכן מחויב וכו׳ ו{..} ה
12. המחזיקו בבית הנ״ל עד עולם לשלם למחזיקו אייהל מידי שנה בשנה
13. כשפורעי המס לשררה יר״ה תשעה זהו׳ פחות רביעת שליש מס שמחויבי׳
14. לשלם מחזיקי אייהל להשררה יר״ה עכ״ל וגם עד הנה שילמו המחזיקי׳
15. צום גולדנ קאפף חלקם מס הנ״ל כמו שחתמו הם עצמם על ההעתק
16. הנ״ל הפרעון מכל שנה רק משנה העבר עדיין לא שילמו בכן תבע
17. משנה העבר וגם להבא ישלמו כל שנה תשעה זהו׳ פחות רביעת כנ״ל
18. וה״ה התורני כ״ה משה אויך בהרשאת מחזיקי בית גולדן קאפף הנ״ל
19. השיב שיכירו הב״ד באשר שהגוף פס״ד אין בידם רק העתק מחותם
20. בעד אחד אם יש כח להם להוציא על זה ומה ששילם כ״ה נתן הנ״ל עד
21. עכשיו מפני שלא הי׳ רוצה ליל[ך] יחידי בדינא ודיינא ומשותפו כ״ה
22. גרשון רינג לא הי׳ רוצה לילך עמו / ועוד הוסיף כ״ה משה הנ״ל לטעון
23. בהרשאת פייס אדליר הנ״ל שידועה היא שקנה חצי פלאטץ מן הבית
24. צום גולדן קאפף לפני איזה שנים מיורשי׳ האשה המונחת מ׳ יענטלה ב
25. בוקסבוים ז״ל והוכריז החצי פלאטץ שלשה פעמים בבה״כ כנהוג ב
26. באיבוד זכיות ומחזיקי בית צו אייהל הי׳ להם לתבוע זכיותי[ם] באו[תו]
27. פעם מה שמגיע על חלקו ומאחר שלא [ת]בעו איבד זכיות שלהם כפי
28. תיקון הקהלה / וכ׳ פייס הנ״ל השיב שלא שמע הכרוז וגם מ
29. משותפו פו״מ כ״ה גבריאל הנ״ל לא הי׳ ב...ע[2] הכרוז
30. וא...

1. כנראה ישראל בן מיכל שווארצשילד
2. יש כאן חור בנייר

קנג ע"ב

והאריכו בטענותיהם ולאחר שחתמו עצמם הצדדי' הנ"ל בתוקף קומפרמיס בקנס לאשר ולקיים כל אשר יצא מאתונו[1] גם נתנו עניהם בקומפרמיס הנ"ל עלינו ב"ד ח"מ לפשר ביניהם בכן נזדקקנו להם ומצאנו דרך פשר דבר תחת מה שנאמר בהעתק הנ"ל שמחויבי' כל המחזיקי' בית צום גולדן קאפף לשלם תשעה זהו' פחות רביעת [ו]יהי' מחויב עתה כ"ה נתן אופנה מחזיק חצי בית צום גולדן קאפף הנ"ל וי"א וב"כ לשלם רק ארבעה זהו' כל שנה ו"כ פייס אדליר מחזיק חצי בית האחרת מן גולדן קאפף הנ"ל ויא[2] וב"כ מחויב לשלם רק שלשה זהו' ד"ב צל לשנה וכן מחויבי' ג"כ לשלם מן שנת תקמ"ב העבר כנ"ל והיינו כ"ה נתן הנ"ל ארבעה זהו' וכ' פייס הנ"ל שלשה זהו' ד"ב צל וכל התשלומן יהי' בטוב מעות באותו מעות שפורעי' המס לשררה יר"ה ומחויבי' כ"ה נתן אופנה {הלז או לכתוב שובר} וכ" פייס אדליר הנ"ל ליכתוב הפירעון על גבי פסק הלז או לכתוב שובר בפני עצמו יצא מאתונו אור ליו' ב' ד"ב אדר ראשון תקמ"ג רנ"מ ורמ"ש {ואנ} ואני

No. 168

Sorle, widow of Samuel Schuster v. Frumet, widow of Sender Schuster

Fols. 154a–b; Wednesday 5 March 1783

Eight days before his death in 1776 Nathan Schuster Katz stipulated in his deathbed will that on his passing certain property be left to his son, Jacob.[3] Nathan, a widower (see Ettlinger, 16.8.1776), noted that Jacob was not to have full rights to this property until he married. An additional condition was that should Jacob die before having married the property would revert to Nathan's parents. Jacob died a bachelor in 1782 and, as a result, Nathan's mother, Sorle, claimed the property.[4] A counterclaim was entered by Frumet, widow of Nathan's brother, Sender Schuster. Through her representative, the widow argued that, based on the law of the Torah (Numbers 27.6–11), her husband should have inherited from his brother and there-

1. ר"ל 'מאתנו'
2. ויורשיהם אחריהם
3. The Frankfurt *Memorbuch* records Nathan's year of death as 1776 (fol. 254a). Cf. Horovitz, no. 3516, who mistakenly recorded the year of Nathan Schuster Katz's death as 1774. Nathan's gravestone states that he died on Friday 1 Elul. The first day of Elul fell on a Friday in 1776 while in 1774 it fell on a Sunday.
4. On Jacob's death, see Horovitz, no. 3776. Nathan's father died in 1778 (see Horovitz, no. 3619).

fore her children, through their father, were the rightful owners of the property. After both sides requested that the court impose a compromise and signed an agreement to accept its ruling, the court ordered that the property be sold and the majority of the funds be given to Nathan's mother.

קנד ע"א

1. ב"ה
2. ע"ד שבא לפנינו ה"ה התורני כ"ה מאיר מָז בהרשאות האשה מ' שרלה אל' המנוח כ" ש
3. שמואל שוסטר כץ ז"ל והציע לפנינו צואת (צ[וו]את)[1] שכ"מ מבנה המנוח כ' נתן ז"ל שנעשה
4. יו' ה ך"ג מנחם תקל"ו שנאמר בתוכה איך יתנהג בעזבונו וכו' ושהחצי בית
5. פנימה צום גולדן ברינן שהכניס לו אביו לנדן בשיור יד העליונה כנהוג והחצי
6. מקו' בעזרת נשים התיכונה שהכניס לו חמיו לנדן / זול בנו הילד יעקב שי'
7. ניט בפוגט זיין לעשות בהם שום דבר וכו' זונדרן באם שיזכה בנו
8. הנ"ל לנשואין / זול מאן איהם החצי בית והחצי מקו' הנ"ל מכניס לנדן זיין
9. אבר באם שיעדר ח"ו בעודו פנוי אזי יהי' החצי בית והחצי מקו' ה
10. הנ"ל לאביו ולאמו הנ"ל וכו' לחלוטין גמורין לאותו מהם שנשאר עדיין חי לאותו
11. הזמן / וטוען כ"ה מאיר הנ"ל באשר שנפטר הילד כ' יעקב הנ"ל ושבק
12. חיי' לכ"י בכן יקוים הצוואה הנ"ל שיהי' החצי בית וחצי מקו' הנ"ל
13. להאשה מ' שרלה הנ"ל אם של המנוח כ' נתן ז"ל הנ"ל / וה"ה התורני
14. כ"ה משה אויך בהרשאת אל' המנוח כ' סענדר שוסטר ז"ל[2] שהי' א
15. אחי המנוח כ' נתן הנ"ל השיב להפך לזכות היתומי' של המנוח
16. כ' סענדר הנ"ל יורשי דארייתא של המנוח כ' נתן ובנו הילד כ' יעקב
17. הנ"ל וטוען נגד הצוואה של כ' נתן הנ"ל כמבואר בקונטרס הטענות
18. המונח לפנינו / ושגם אנחנו ב"ד נעיין בזכות היתומי' הנ"ל כפי
19. הראוי ומוטל עלינו / ובאשר שהצדדי' הנ"ל נתנו עיניהם עלינו ב"ד ח"מ
20. לפשר ביניהם וחתמו עצמם בתוקף קומפורמיס בח"ח ובקנס לקיים ה
21. הפשר שיצא מאתנו / וגם היתום כ' משה נתן בן המנוח כ' סענדר
22. הנ"ל חתם א"ע עמהם / בכן נזדקקנו להם ומצאנו לטובת האל' מ'
23. שרלה והיתומי' הנ"ל דרך פשר דבר שהחצי בית הנ"ל יומכר
24. מיד לחלוטין בלי שיור יד העליונה כפי שהתחייבה א"ע האשה
25. מ' שרלה אל' כ' שמואל שוסטר ז"ל לפנינו וגם חצי מקו' הנ"ל יומכר
26. מיד / ומדמי מכירות קרקעות הנ"ל יהי' להאל' מ' שרלה הנ"ל מ
27. מחמת דמי יד העליונה שהי' לה על החצי בית הנ"ל סך חמשה
28. מאות ושבעי' זהו' והיינו שני מאות זהו' תגבה מיד ממעות מזומנים
29. שיתן הלוקח {על זמנים כנהוג דהיינו מאה ושמוני' וחמשה זהו'} נגד

---

1. תיקון מעל השורה
2. אלמנת סענדר שוסטר היתה פרומט בת מענדלי נאס מווינה. ר' הורוויץ, מס' 4560.

30. מסירת החלטה ושלשה מאות ושבעי' זהו' הנותרי' תגבה

קנד ע"ב

1. מאותן ח"כ שיתן הלוקח על זמני' כנהוג דהיינו מאה ושמוני' וחמשה
2. זהו' יגבה מדמי ח"כ הראשון שיתן הלוקח ועוד מאה ושמוני'
3. וחמשה זהו' מדמי ח"כ השני שיתן הלוקח / והמעות הנותרי' מדמי
4. מכירות החצי בית וחצי מקו' הנ"ל לאחר ניכוי חמשה מאות ושבעי' זהו'
5. הנ"ל ולאחר ניכוי תשלומי' לגובי' ושארי בעלי חובות מן כ' נתן הנ"ל
6. ובנו הילד כ' יעקב ז"ל הנ"ל יחולק המותרת לשלשה חלקים ויהי' להאל'
7. מ' שרלה הנ"ל שני שלישי' ולהיתומי' של המנוח כ' סענדר ז"ל הנ"ל
8. שליש אחד ויותן המעות שיגיע לחלק היתומי' ליד אפטרופסי' ש
9. שיתמנו ע"פ הח"ק יצו כנהוג יצא מאתנו יו' ד' ב דר"ח א"ש תקמ"ג
10. הגאב"ד מה' פנחס הלוי ורני[1] ורמש[2] ואני

No. 169

Schuster Katz v. Schuster

Fols. 155a–158b; Wednesday evening, 5 March 1783

Me᾿ir Schuster Katz and Neta Schuster each owned half of a house on the back of the Weiβe Kanne lot. In 1767, they signed an agreement on how to divide the house according to a three year rotation. As time passed, Me᾿ir agreed to waive his right to rotate and move into the lower section of the house as per the agreement in return for a fee from Neta. Similarly, he allowed Neta to use a large room upstairs for an additional sum. At a certain point, the arrangement broke down and Neta did not pay the said fee or relocate according to the rotation. Me᾿ir came to the court asking for back payments and also asking that the court order Neta to move to the space allotted to him by the rotation agreement. Me᾿ir also asked that Neta be forced to pay for home improvements made over the past fifteen years, as well as repair damage he had caused to the house. Neta disputed the charges and claimed that he too had made repairs that Me᾿ir had failed to reimburse him for, repairs that Me᾿ir deemed to have been unnecessary. Neta also claimed that Me᾿ir had not divided storage areas in the house fairly. There were other sundry disputes between the two owners, including a dispute regarding a stove that Me᾿ir had renovated to

---

1. ורב נתן (מז)
2. ורב מאיר שיף

allow him to keep coffee warm "to sell on the Sabbath." The two parties sought a compromise and the court obliged. It dealt with each of the financial claims and counterclaims, imposed payments, defined which areas of the house could be used by whom in the coming years, and ordered that in 1789 they return to observing the agreement made in 1767. They also ordered that future repairs be made only if both parties agreed to them. The court noted that future disagreements regarding the necessity of repairs be brought before the court for adjudication.

קנה ע״א

1. ב״ה
2. ע״ד שבא לפנינו ה״ה התורני כ״ה פייס הענא בהרשאת ובמעמד כ׳ מאיר ב״המנוח
3. פו״מ כ״ה יוסף שוסטר כץ ז״ל מחזיק חצי בית צור הינטר ווייסה קאן ותבע ממשותפו
4. הו״ה כ״ה נטע שוסטר מחזיקו חצי בית האחרת הנ״ל והציע לפנינו כתב חילוקו ד
5. דירות שיש ביניהם ההוקם ר״ח כסליו תקך״ח שמבואר בתוכה שהי׳ מגיע לפי
6. חוזר חלילה שביניהם הדירה התחתונה וכל השייכי׳ לזה הדירה מר״ח
7. כסליו שנת תקל״ב עד ר״ח כסליו תקלה העבר לכ׳ מאיר הנ״ל רק כ׳ מאיר הנ״ל
8. התרצה א״ע להניח כ״ה נטע הנ״ל בדירה התחתונה נגד דמי שכירות
9. סך חמשים רט לשלשה שנים הנ״ל שמחויב לשלם כה״נ[1] לכ״ מאיר הנ״ל {ו[בכלו]ת}
10. וכפי הכתב ההוקם ביניהם יוד טבת תקלב על שלשה שנים הנ״ל ובכלות השלשה
11. שנים והיינו משנת קהלת הי׳ מגיע לכה״נ הנ״ל הדירה התחתונה וכל השייכי׳
12. לה ושטח העליונה לכ״מ[2] הנ״ל ובתוך הדירה עליונה נכלל החדר גדול שלשה
13. שטעג הויך לצד הרחוב לכ״מ הנ״ל והניח לו כ״מ הנ״ל על שלשה שני׳ אותו חדר
14. שלשה שטעג הויך הנ״ל נגד שכירות שלשים רט לשלשה שנים שנתן כה״נ לכ׳ מאיר
15. הנ״ל והיינו עד שנת תקלח העבר ומשנת תקלח העבר שהי׳ מגיע שוב דירה
16. התחתונה לכ׳ מאיר על שלשה שנים והיינו עד שנת תקמ״א העבר אעפ״כ
17. נשאר כה״נ בדירה התחתונה ולא שילם כלום לכ״מ הנ״ל ומשנת תקמא עד
18. שנת תקמ״ד ר״ח כסליו כשמגיע לכה״נ הדירה התחתונה מגיע החדר הגדול
19. שלשה שטעג הויך לכ׳ מאיר וכה״נ החזיק חדר הנ״ל בכן תבע כ׳ מאיר שכירות
20. מן כה״נ הנ״ל סך חמשי׳ רט מן שלשה שני׳ ראשוני׳ מן שנת תקלח עד שנת תקמ״א בשביל
21. הדירה התחתונה שהחזיק בה שלא מן הראוי לו כפי פסיקה שביניהם מן שנת
22. תקלב עד שנת קהלת ומן שלשה שני׳ אחרוני׳ והיינו משנת תקמ״א עד כסליו שנת
23. תקמ״ד הבע״ל שהחזיק בחדר גדול שלשה שטעג הויך הנ״ל שאינו מגיע לו תבע
24. סך שלשים רט ג״כ כפי פסיקה שהי׳ ביניהם מן שנת קהלת עד שנת תקלח
25. עולה יחד שמוני׳ רט רק ינוכה מזה סך ארבעי׳ זהו׳ דמי טקרעט מן השררה
26. ירה[3] שמחויב לשלם כ׳ מאיר לכה״נ הנ״ל וכ״ה משה אויך בהרשאת הו״ה
27. כ״ה נטע הנ״ל השיב באריכות שדירה עליונה הוא מעולה מתחתונה ומה

---

1. כבוד הרב נטע
2. כבוד מאיר
3. ירום הודו

28. ששילם לו כה"נ שכירות לא הי' רק להשקיט הריב כמבואר בכתב ה
29. ההוקם ביניהם יוד טבת תקלב הנ"ל וגם כ' מאיר ...[1] תבע מן כ"ה נטע

קנה ע"ב

1. נטע הנ"ל דירה התחתונה כשהי' מגיע לו אותו דירה עוד תבע כ"מ הנ"ל שמן
2. ר"ח כסליו תקמד הבע"ל יפנה לו כה"נ הנ"ל דירה התחתונה על שלשה שנים ה
3. המגיע לו לפי חילוקי דירות הנ"ל וכ"ה משה הנ"ל השיב שיעיינו הב"ד בחלוקי
4. הדירות אם מגיע לכ' מאיר הנ"ל הדירה התחתונה עוד תבע כ"ה פייס
5. הנ"ל והציע חשבן מה שהוציא כ' מאיר הנ"ל עבור בנין בדק הבית אחת
6. לאחת משך חמשה עשר שנים משנת תקכ"ח עד עתה על איזה הוצאות הניח
7. כ"מ קונטא ל{ני}פנינו מבעלי מלאכות העולה על חלק של כ"ה נטע הנ"ל לשלם לו סך
8. שלשים ואחד זהו' ובתוכה נכלל חוב אחד סך שבעה זהו' ויו צלמר עבור
9. סחורה שמכר כ' מאיר הנ"ל לאשתו ראשונה של כ"ה נטע הנ"ל אחת לאחת כשהי'
10. כ' מאיר מוכר מיני מאכלי' וכה[2] משה הנ"ל השיב על כל פרט ופרט מן חשבן
11. שלו על איזה מהם השיב שאינו מאמין לו בלי קונטא ועל איזה מהן שכבר פרע
12. גם על אותו חוב של אשתו ראשונה ז"ל השיב שמא פרע וגם כ' מאיר הי'
13. לו לתבוע בשעת חתנותו עם אשתו שניי'[3] עוד תבע כה"פ[4] הנ"ל שמקדם
14. הי' בתוך הבית הנ"ל חור גדול הפונה מן המרתף החיצון תוך הויז ע
15. עהרנד למטה מכוסה בבנין אבני' כמין כיפה המושך לתוך הויז עהרנד
16. למטה לצד ימין וסמוך לאותו כיפה הי' עומד אותו שפייס שאנק המוזכר
17. בתוך חילוקי גורל שכל אחד ממחזיקו בית יהי' שני שענק שבתוכה ומקרוב
18. סותר כ"ה נטע הנ"ל אותו כיפה שהי' על החור שבמרתף ומכסה מקצת ה
19. החור באבני' ועל מקצת החור הפתוח עושה כיפה קטנה ואותו שפייס שאנק
20. שהי' מקדם חתך לשניי' וחלק של כ"מ הנ"ל העמיד על מקו' אחר בהויז
21. עהרנד מצד שמאל ולעצמו העמיד על אותו מקו' שהי' עומד מקדם אותו ש
22. שפייס שאנק הנ"ל חד קליידר שאנק גדול שמעכב ההילוך למדריגה מן הויז
23. עהרנד למעלה חד שטעג הויך שהי' אי אפשר לעמוד אותו קליידר שאנק זולת
24. סתירת אותו כיפה שהי' מקדם וטוען כה"פ שכה"נ הנ"ל קילקל המרתף
25. בסתימת החור הנ"ל שמתוך כך אי אפשר להתקיים מיני מאכל ב
26. במרתף מפ[נ]י שאין לו אויר כמקדם רק מדוחק גם קילקל האבני'

קנו ע"א

1. האביני' שסביבותיהם בכן תבע כה"פ שיעמוד כה"נ הנ"ל אותו חור עם
2. כיפה גדול כשהי' מקדם ויפנה אותו גדול קליידר שאנק שלו ויעשה איין שאנק
3. כפי המבואר בכתב חילוקי דירות גם יעשה כה"נ הנ"ל איין אן ריכט מעץ בתוך

---

1. יש כאן חור בנייר; יתכן שצ"ל 'לא'.
2. וכבוד הרב (משה אויך)
3. אשתו הראשונה, רייזלה בת אברלי בוקסבוים, נפטרה ב-5.10.1771 (אלה תולדות). בסביבות 1773 הוא נשא לאשה געלה בת וואלף אופנהיים-היידלברג (נפטרה 4.5.1812).
4. וכבוד הרב פייס

4. הויז עהרנד למטה שלא הי׳ שם מקדם בכן תבע כה״פ שיסלק אותו וכ״ה
5. משה הנ״ל השיב שאותו שפייס שאנק שהי׳ מקדם הי׳ נתקלקל והי׳ מן
6. הצורך לעשות אחר והי׳ כה״נ הנ״ל מתיעץ עם כ״מ הנ״ל ושאל לו על שרוצה
7. להעמיד חלק שאנק שלו על מקו׳ אחר ולעצמו רוצה להעמיד חלק קליידר שאנק
8. על אופן הנ״ל בסתירת כיפה ראשונה והרצה א״ע כ״מ הנ״ל לזה באופן
9. שהוצאות יהי׳ על כה״נ הנ״ל לבד וכן תקנו אותו ע״י בעלי מלאכות ב
10. במעמד כ״מ הנ״ל שהי׳ צווה כיצד יעשו בכן מחל כ״מ הנ״ל ע״ז וגם לא
11. קילקול כה״נ הנ״ל כלום במרתף שיש עדיין אויר הרבה במרתף
12. וכ״ה משה הנ״ל בהרשאת כ״ה נטע הנ״ל תבע מן כ״מ הנ״ל באשר
13. שכפי כתב חילוקי דירות הנ״ל שבין המחזיקי׳ הנ״ל נחלק המרתף
14. שלהם לארבעה מרתפות והיינו שני מרתיפות של יין לצד הרחוב
15. שיורדן לתוכם במדרגה חיצונה בכניסה לבית ושני מרתפות של
16. עץ לצד הסוכה בפנימה היורדן בתוכה במדריגה תחת הקוך ו
17. ומאותן ארבעה מרתפות יחזיק כל אחד שנים אחד מרתף של
18. עץ לצד הסוכה פנימה וחד מרתף של יין לצד הרחוב והכי[פ׳]
19. תחת הסוכה הפנימה אשר בתוכה דיא אנטוך ישתמשו שניהם בשוה
20. ככה הי׳ חילוקו מרתפות שביניהם רק לאח״כ כשהי׳ כ״מ הנ״ל מוכר
21. שכר הי׳ מבקש מן כה״נ שיתן לו שני מרתפות חיצוני׳ לצד הרחוב
22. ונתן לו כה״נ הנ״ל ולאח״כ כשתבע כה״נ הנ״ל מרתף החיצון שלו
23. ממנו השיב לו כ״מ הנ״ל שבתחילה [השכ]ירי[1] לו חדר שלו שמחזיק יותר על
24. ממה שמגיע לו על חלקו ובאשר שכה״נ הוכרח [מ]ש״כ לשכור מרתף
25. אצל א״נ בעד אחד עשר [רט לש]נה בכן [ת]בע כ״מ

קנו ע״ב

1. כ״מ שכירות מחמת דירה שני שטעג הויך אף הוא כה״נ תבע
2. מן כ״מ שכירות מרתף שהוציא י״א רט לשנה משנת תקלח העבר
3. וכ״ה פייס הנ״ל השיב ששקר הוא שכ״מ הנ״ל החזיק במרתפת
4. חיצוני׳ נגד רצון כה״נ הנ״ל רק כ״ה נטע הנ״ל הי׳ מבקש מן כ״מ הנ״ל
5. שיניח לו שלשה מרתפות הפנימי נגד שני מרתפות חיצוני׳ שיחזיק
6. כ״מ כדי שכל אחד מהם יהי׳ מרתפות ביחד מיוחד ומסוגר בלי שגם
7. חבירו יבוא ג״כ בגבולו ולא האמין לכ׳ מאיר לכנוס ג״כ דרך מדריגה
8. של מרתף שלו אדרבה כ׳ מאיר תבע ממנו באשר שכ״הנ הנ״ל הי׳
9. מחזיק שלשה מרתפות הפנימי׳ והוא רק שני׳ מרתפות חיצוני׳ בכן
10. תבע ממנו ששה זהו׳ לשנה מן שנת תקלב עד עכשיו והאריכו
11. בטענותיהם עוד תבע כה משה הנ״ל והציע חשבן לפנינו שהוציא
12. כה״נ הנ״ל עבור בדק הבית שני מאות ואחד עשר זהו׳ ותבע מן

---

1. יש כאן חור בנייר; ההשלמה על פי הקונטכסט.

13. כ"מ החצי זולת דמי טעקרעט מן השררה ירה[1] סך ארבעי' זהו' שהודה
14. כבר כ"מ הנ"ל והציע לפנינו קונטות מבעלי מלאכות מה ששילם להם
15. עבור בנין בדק הבית וכה"פ הנ"ל השיב באריכות על כל פרט
16. ופרט תשובה מיוחדת שיש מהם שנכלל כבר בתוך דמי טעקרעט
17. הנ"ל ויש מהם שהי' שלא לצורך ובלי ידיעתו כמו השאנק שני ש
18. שטעק הויך על השטעג בהויז עהרנד וגם שלשה שטעג הויך
19. בתוך החדר אותן שענק חדשי' והציע כ"ה פייס הנ"ל כתב יד
20. מן כה"נ הנ"ל מן ר"ח כסליו תקכ"ח שהותנה ביניהם באותו פעם
21. שמכאן והלאה שאם אחד מהם יבנה איזה דבר מחויבי' החבירו
22. ליתן לו תיכף חלקו נגד בויא שיין של חבירו כדי שלא יבוא לחשבון
23. בכן מה שתקן כה"נ הנ"ל מחדש בלי ידיעתו שייך לו לבד ואין
24. על כ"מ לשלם החצי וכה"מ חזר והשיב באריכות על דברי
25. כה"פ הנ"ל ...[2]

קנז ע"א

1. עוד תבע כה"מ הנ"ל שמקדם הי' חד שטעק הויך איין קוך סביב
2. הכירה ותחת הכירה הי' חלול כמין כיפה להניח עץ בתוכה
3. תחת הכירה וכשהתחיל כ"מ הנ"ל למכור קאפע בשבת סותר הקוך
4. הנ"ל וגם סותר אותו כירה שהי' מקדם ותיקן כירה חדשה כדי ש
5. שיכולין להעמיד קדרות של קאפע בתוכה בכן תבע כ"ה נטע הנ"ל
6. שיעמוד כ"מ הנ"ל הכירה עם הקוך על הוצאות לבד כמו שהי' מקדם
7. (וכ"מ התרתצה[3] להעמיד את הכירה כמו שהי' מקדם)[4] והקוך של עץ עדיין יש לו ברשותו ורוצה לתקן אותו והאריכו הצדדי'
8. הנ"ל מאד בטענותיהם ובתשובתיהם זה מול זה וזה מול זה כמבואר
9. היטב באריכות בקונטריס הטענות המונח לפנינו ובאשר שהצדדי'
10. הנ"ל חתמו א"ע בתוקף קומפורמיס בכל חומר ובקנס חצי לשררה ירה[5]
11. וחצי להקדש לקיים כל אשר יצא מאתנו גם נתנו עיניהם עלינו
12. ב"ד ח"מ לתווך השלום ביניהם ולפשר ביניהם על כל פרט ו
13. ופרט הנ"ל וקיבלו עליהם בתוקף הנ"ל לקיים הפשר שיצא מאתנו בכן
14. נזדקקנו להם ומצאנו דרך פשר דבר על כל פרט ופרט כמבואר והיינו
15. מחמת תביעות ממון שביניהם שכ"מ הנ"ל תבע מן כה"נ הנ"ל מחמת שכירות
16. מחדרי' מן שנת תקלח עד שנת תקמא סך חמשי' רט ומן שנת תקמא עד שנת
17. תקמד הבעל[6] סך שלשי' רט עולה יחד סך מאה ועשרי' זהו' ולאחר ניכוי

---

1. ירום הודו
2. יש כאן חתיכת נייר שמודבקת לכתב היד לחזקה שמכסה חלק מהשורה הזאת.
3. צ"ל 'התרצה'
4. תוספת מעל השורה
5. ירום הודו
6. הבא עלינו לטובה

18. סך ארבעי' זהו' דמי טעקרעט נשאר עוד סך שמוני' זהו' ועוד תבע
19. הוצאת מבדק הבית סך ל"א זהו' מדעי[1] עולה יחד לערך סך מאה ואחד
20. עשר זהו' (ממה שתבע)[2] וה"ה כה"נ {תבע} מכ"מ ע"ח החצי מן שני מאות ואחד עשר זהו'
21. עבור בנין הבית שהוציא שוב תבע סך אחד עשר רט לשנה מן מרתפות
22. מן תקלח עד עתה וכ"מ תבע בהיפך מצאנו על כל תביעות מזה על זה
23. ומזה על זה אחר שחשבנו ודקדקנו היטיב בטענותיהם ובחשבונת
24. שמחויב כה"נ הנ"ל לשלם לכ' מאיר הנ"ל סך ששים וחמשה זהו'
25. ובזה פטורי' ומסולקי' זה מזה [וזה] מזה ואי' ל[א]חד מהם שום

קנז ע"ב

1. שום תביעה על חבירו [ו]עב[ור] ומחמת חילוקו דירה שביניהם
2. מן ר"ח כסליו תקמד הבע"ל מצאנו דרך פשר שיהי' על אופן המבואר
3. והיינו שכל אחד ממחזיקי בית הנ"ל יחזיק בדירה כמו שהוא מחזיק
4. עד עתה דהיינו לכ"נ הנ"ל יהי' לו בית החורף למטה עם הסוכה
5. שאחורי בית והויז עהרנד הוילץ עק אונטר דעם שטעק ושני שענק
6. אונטר דער שטעג וגם ישת[ש]מש בקליודר[3] שאנק שנשאר עומד
7. על המקו' שעמד עד הנה כמו שהשתמש בו עד הנה וגם
8. רשאוי להשתמש דיא אן ריכט שמתוקן בהויז עהרנד כמו ש
9. שהשתמש עד הנה גם שני שטעג הויך שני חדרי' זה מול זה
10. בית החורף גם ישתמש בשאנק על השטעק ושלשה שטעג הויך
11. החדר לצד הרחוב וד' שטעג הויך חד קאמיר לצד א"נ וכ' מאיר
12. הנ"ל יחזיק וישתמש בדירה שלו כמו שהחזיק בו עד הנ[ה] והיינו
13. חד שטעק הויך שני חדרי' בית החורף זה מול זה עם הויז עה
14. עהרנד {למטה} ושאנק שעל השטעג משלשה שטעק הויך שני חדרי'
15. לצד א"נ ד' ש[ט]עק הויך קאמר לצד הרחוב וגם ישתמש בשני שענק
16. העומדת אין הויז עהרנד למטה הכל כמו שהחזיק בו עד עתה
17. וחילוקת מרתפות יהי' באופן הזה לכ"ה נטע הנ"ל יהי שני מרתפו'
18. חיצוני' ולכ"מ הנ"ל שלשה מרתפות הפנימי' ומחויב כ' מאיר הנ"ל
19. לפנות מיד {ש} תיכף אחר מסירת פסק הלז שני מרתפות חיצוני'
20. לכ"ה נטע הנ"ל וכן כה"נ הנ"ל מחויב לפנות עוד שלשה מרתפו'
21. הפנימי' לכ"מ הנ"ל וכה יהי' חלוקי [ד]ירות הנ"ל עד ר"ח כסליו שנת
22. תקנון הבע"ל נגד זה מחויב כה"נ הנ"ל לשלם שכירות לכ"מ הנ"ל
23. בשביל דירה שלו שעדיף הרבה יותר מדירה של כ"מ הנ"ל

---

1. מ"ד צל
2. תוספת מעל השורה
3. ר"ל 'קליידר'

קנח ע"א

1. כ"מ הנ"ל {ולפנות} על שלשה שנים ראשוני' והיינו מן ר"ח כסליו שנת תקמ"ד
2. הבע"ל עד ר"ח כסליו שנת תקמ"ז סך חמשי' רט ומחויב כה"נ הנ"ל לשלם
3. לכ"מ הנ"ל מיד אחר מסירת פסק הלז ועל שלשה שני' השניי' והיינו מן ר"ח
4. כסליו שנת תקמ"זין עד ר"ח כסליו שנת תקנון הבע"ל מחויב לשלם כה"נ
5. הנ"ל שכירות לכ"מ הנ"ל סך שלשים רט ומחויב לשלם כה"נ הנ"ל אותן שלשי'
6. רט הנ"ל ר"ח כסליו תקמ"ז הבע"ל ומחמת שכירות המרתפות שיש לכה"נ
7. עודפת על כ' מאיר הנ"ל מחויב כה"נ הנ"ל לשלם שכירות סך שלשה זהו'
8. לשנה והיינו שמחויב כה"נ לכ"מ הנ"ל תיכף השכירות של המרתפות מה
9. שמגיע לערך שכירו' הנ"ל עד ר"ח כסליו תקמ"ז הבע"ל ור"ח כסליו שנת
10. תקמז מחויב לשלם השכירות עד ר"ח כסליו שנת תקנון הבע"ל ומן ר"ח
11. כסליו שנת תקנון ואילך יחזור החילוקת דירת ביניהם משלשה לשלשה
12. שנים כפי חילוקי דירות שנעשה ביניהם ההוקם ר"ח כסליו שנת תקכ"ח
13. העבר והיינו ר"ח כסליו שנת תקנון עד ר"ח כסליו תקנג הבע"ל יהי'
14. דירה התחתונה עם כל השייך לה כפי חילוקו דירות שבינהם זולת
15. המרתפות וכמבואר למטה לכ"מ {ל} הנ"ל והדירה עליונה עם כל השייך לה
16. לכה"נ הנ"ל ומחויב כ"מ הנ"ל קודם שיפנה דירה עליונה לתקן הכירה
17. והקוך על הוצאות שלו לבד וכמו שהתרצה א"ע וכנ"ל ומן ר"ח כסליו שנת
18. תקנג עד ר"ח כסליו שנת תקנו הבע"ל יחליפו דירתם ויהי' לכה"נ הנ"ל
19. דירה התחתונה וכנ"ל ולכ"מ דירה העליונה וכנ"ל וככה יהי' חוזר
20. חוזר חלילה ביניהם משלשה לשלשה שני' עד עולם ואותן שענק חדשי'
21. שעומדי' בתוך חדר שלשה שטעג הויך לצד הרחוב יהי' ב
22. בשותפות לשני מחזיקו הנ"ל ולמי שיגיע אותו חדר ישתמש באותן
23. שענק וכן אותו שאנק ש[עומד] על השטעג ישתמשו בו אותו שדר
24. שני שטעג הויך וכן דיא אן ריכט אין הויז עהרנד למטה

קנח ע"ב

1. למטה יהי' בשותפות לשניהם ומי שדר בשטח מטה ישתמש בו ומחמת אותו קליידר
2. שאנק ששייך לכה"נ הנ"ל שעומד כעת בהויז עהרנד כשיגיע לכ' מאיר הנ"ל
3. דירה התחתונה והיינו מן ר"ח כסליו שנת תקנון הבע"ל ולכה"נ דירה עליונה
4. מחויב כה"נ הנ"ל לסלק אותו קליידר שאנק {ולהשתמש} ולהעמיד על מקומה איין שפייס
5. שאנק ולהשתמש בו לבד כמו אותו שפייס שאנק שעומד עתה בבית ש
6. שמשתמש בו כ"מ הנ"ל אך את זה מצאנו ג"כ בתורת פשר שחילוקת
7. מרתפות משנת תקנון ואילך לא יהי' באופן הנזכר בכתב חילוקי דירות
8. הנ"ל רק יהי' חילוקי' על אופן כמו שהוא עכשיו והיינו שהאחד מהם
9. יחזיק שני מרתיפות חיצונית והאחד שלשה פנימית משלשה לשלשה שנים
10. והיינו לאותו שדר בשטח התחתון יהי' לו שני מרתפות חיצוני' ולמי שדר
11. בשטח העליון יהי' שלשה מרתפות הפנימת ומחמת בנין בדק הבית

12. להבא אינו רשאו[1] כל אחד ממחזיק[י] בית הנ״ל לבנות שום דבר בלי
13. ידיעת חבירו ומה שבנה כל אחד בלי ריצו חבירו אינה מחויב האחר
14. ליתן חלק בהוצאות ואם האחד רוצה לבנות והשני אינו רוצה יכירו
15. הב״ד אשר יהי׳ בימי׳ ההם אם הוא מן הצורך ומחויבי׳ לקיימו הפס״ד
16. כפי קומפורמיס שבידינו יצא מאתנו אור ליו׳ ה׳ ב׳ א״ש תקמ״ג לפק
17. רנמ[2] ורמש[3] ואני

No. 170

Fol. 158b; Wednesday 26 March 1783

The court was asked, presumably by the community, about the community's authority to limit prayer quorums and the right of people to pray where they pleased. The tendency of people to pray outside of the two main synagogues resulted in a drop in charitable donations, left the main synagogues empty, and reduced the value of seats. The court noted that the community could not prevent prayer groups that had received formal permission from meeting, nor could it limit the rights of individuals to pray where they pleased unless a communal ordinance was enacted to this effect. However, those prayer quorums that did not enjoy official sanction could be prohibited from meeting. Also see Appendix 5.

18. המניני׳ שנעשו ברשות הקהל יצו אינם יכולי׳ למחות / ובפירוש אתמר נמי שהמניין
19. שקובע אדמ״ו הג׳ אב״ד נר״ו בביתו הוא נכלל בזה הכלל / אבל המנייני׳ שנעשו שלא
20. ברשות הקהל יצו הרשות ביד הקהל יצו למחות / ומחמת השאלה על אותן בתי כ
21. כניסיות שיש להם רשות מקהל יצו / אם רשאי׳ לכנוס בתוכם בעלי בתי׳ מקהלותנו
22. יע״א באשר שגורם הפסד לקופה של צדקה ובענין דמי המצות וגם שיש בזיון לבהכ״נ
23. שהמקומות עומדי׳ ריקנית וגם שדמי המקומות נזדלזל / מצאנו שאין רשות בידן
24. לימחות מליכנוס בתוכם הבעלי בתי׳ ואמנם רשאי׳ לעשות תקנה והיינו ע״פ
25. אסיפות וועד כמה יתן מי שלא ילך לבה״כ חדש וישן לג״ע יצו / ומה שיצא מפי הקהל
26. יצו בצירוף הוועד יותן להם תוקף מן הג׳ אב״ד נר״ו בצירוף שני ב״ד יצו שיסכימו ע
27. עמהם יצא מאתנו יו׳ ד׳ ד״ב א״ש תקמ״ג לפק הג״אבד נר״ו ור״י מ״ה נתן מז נר״ו ומ״ה
28. יעקב ש[מש] ...[4] ור מאיר שיף ואני

---

1. צ״ל ׳רשאי׳
2. רב נתן מז
3. והרב מאיר שיף
4. יש כאן חתיכת נייר שמודבקת לכתב היד לחזקו שמכסה חלק מהשורה הזאת.

No. 171

Binla, widow of Rabbi Samuel of Friedberg v. Schuster

Fols. 159a–160a; Wednesday evening, 26 November 1783

In 1759, the late Fiel, daughter of Isaac Schuster of Wassertrüdingen, left funds for charitable purposes. The money was to be administered by her nephew, Moses Schuster, who was to give the income from the funds to Rabbi Samuel Kohn Poppers of Friedberg for distribution.[1] Rabbi Samuel was to give three-quarters of the funds to help those studying Torah and, each year on the anniversary of Fiel's death, one-quarter of the money to needy brides. Brides who were related to the deceased were to have priority over others. After Rabbi Samuel's death in 1779, his widow, Binla, who was from a Frankfurt family, approached the court through her representative and claimed that Moses Schuster had not given her husband the correct amount for needy brides. Binla's claim was not made for totally altruistic reasons. Her own daughter was soon to be married and Binla wanted the funds for her. Moses Schuster responded without representation that while he had given funds to Rabbi Samuel in the past, he had recently taken it upon himself to distribute the funds. Moreover, he had a daughter of his own and he wanted to keep funds for her. Moses noted that while his sons were studying he had kept money allocated for those studying Torah to pay for his sons' expenses.

The widow also claimed that there were funds in Fiel's estate for free loans to the needy, and demanded that an accounting be given as to whom funds had been lent in the past. Moses responded that he had lent the funds to himself because he had been in need and, in a counterclaim, demanded an accounting of funds that had been left with Rabbi Samuel.

The court ruled that the funds had to be given annually to whomever the court appointed to replace Rabbi Samuel, and that Moses Schuster could not accumulate funds for his daughter. Funds that were to be distributed to those studying Torah were also to be given to Rabbi Samuel's replacement for distribution at his discretion. Moses' sons were eligible to receive such funds if the person distributing them deemed it appropriate. As for the free loan, Moses Schuster was allowed to continue the loan that he had given himself. Since Rabbi Samuel's estate was able

---

1. Samuel Kohn Poppers was the grandson of Rabbi Jacob Poppers (d. 1740) who served as rabbi of Frankfurt (see Horovitz, *Rabbaney Franqfurṭ*, 84–89). Rabbi Samuel served as rabbi of Friedberg from 1757 until his death in 1779 (see Cilli Kasper-Holtkotte, *Jüdisches Leben in Friedberg 16.–18. Jahrhundert, Kehilat Friedberg*, vol. 1, ed. Andreas Gotzmann [Friedberg: Bindernagel, 2003], 198).

to produce records of to whom he had distributed money, the court acquitted his estate of all claims against it. Also see no. 199.

קנט ע"א

ב"ה ע"ד שבא לפנינו ה"ה התורני כ"ה משה אויך בהרשאת הרבני' האשה מ' בינלה אל' המנוח הרב כמה"ז[1] שמואל זצ"ל אב"ד דק"ק פרידבוריג יע"א ותבע מן כ' משה ב"ל[2] שוסטר כץ והציע שטר הודאה לפנינו שנאמר בתוכה שעשה כ' משה ק"ס באשה והדר בעלה שחייבי' להרב ז"ל הנ"ל סך שלשה מאות וארבעי' ואחד זהו' על רווחי' חמשה למאה לשנה מחמת דמי דבר טוב שיש בידו מן דודתו המונחת האשה חשובה מ' פייאל בת כ"ה איצק שוסטר ז"ל שהי' הרב ז"ל הנ"ל אפטרופס ושמחויבי' ליתן הרווחי' לכמה"ו שמואל הנ"ל שיחלק אותן רווחי' שלשה רביעת מהם לסיועת תלמד תורה ורביעת מרווחי' יחלק ביום יארצייט מהאשה [ז]"ל הנ"ל לסיועת הכנסת כלה על אופן הנאמר בצוואה מן האשה מרת פייאל הנ"ל ההוקים ביום א' ה' אב תקיט לפק בק"ק וואסרטרילי[ב]ג[3] יע"א וטוען כהרם[4] הנ"ל בהרשאת הנ"ל שמהרווחי' המגיעי' לסיועת הכנסת כלה לא שילם כלום לבעלה הרב ז"ל הנ"ל באשר שלא נמצא שום חשבן בעזבון בעלה ששילם כ"מ[5] לבעלה ז"ל הנ"ל ובאשר שבת האל' הרבנית הנ"ל היא מקושרת להנשא וזמן נישואין קרובי' לבוא בכן יכירו הב"ד שיותן לה כל הרווחי' המגיע לצורך ה"כ כפי הצוואה שקרוב קרוב קודם ובתה הכלה היא קרובה להמונח מ' פיי[ע]ל ז"ל הנ"ל וכ' משה שוסטר הנ"ל בעצמו השיב שעד שנת תקלז העבר חישב עם הרב כמה"ו שמואל ז"ל הנ"ל ושני שנים שאחריו הוא הוציא בעצמו להכנסת כלה והציע קוויטונג לפנינו מן ארבעה זהו' רק מחודש תמוז תקמם העבר עד עתה עדיין לא הוציא הרווחי' וטוען כ' משה הנ"ל שרוצה להחזיק בידו לצורך בתו עד שיהי' ראוי לנישואין וטוען שהוא זוכה יותר ברווחי' מבת האל' ז"ל שהוא קרוב טפי לאשה המונח מ' {ש}פייאל ז"ל הנ"ל שהוא בן אחי' וכן להבא רוצה להניח אצל[ו] הרווחי' עד זמן שיגיע בתו לנשואין עוד טען כהר"ם הנ"ל מחמת הרווחי' המגיע ...[6] כפי השטר הנ"ל נשאר עדיין ביד כ' משה ...[7] תקלזין

1. צ"ל 'כמה"ו'; ר' לקמן שורה 8.
2. בן לעמלי, ע' מס' 199 וגם בתוכן העניינים.
3. ר' ס' 199 ששם כתוב 'וואסירטריליגען'.
4. כבוד הרב משה
5. כבוד משה
6. יש כאן חור בנייר
7. יש כאן חור בנייר

קנט ע"ב

לפק עד עתה [או] ליתן חשבון למי נתן אותם וכ' משה הנ"ל השיב שאותו שנה תקלז שילם להרב ז"ל הנ"ל ולאח"כ הוציא הרווחי' ללומדי' עם בניו שלו כל זמן שהי' בני' הולכים ולומדים בקביעת אצל רבם / ועכשיו שגדלו הנעורים ולומדי' רק שיער ע"ז[1] עשה שאלה לב"ד אם יש לו רשות לשלם מרווחי' הנ"ל באשר שהוא קרוב קודם / עוד טוען כהר"ם הנ"ל שנאמר בשטר הודאה הנ"ל שיש ביד כ' משה הנ"ל סך שמוני' וחמשה זהו' א' קש[2] מדמי דב"ט הנ"ל להלוות לעניים על המשכונת בלי רווחי' בכן יברר כ"מ הנ"ל למי הלווה אותן וכ' משה השיב שהוא החזיק אותן לעצמו בתורת הלוואה שהוא נצרך לכך כעת והוא הקרוב קודם וכ' משה הנ"ל טוען ותבע שהי' ביד הרב כמה"ש[3] הנ"ל סך חמשים ושנים זהו' השייכי' לדב"ט הנ"ל לקרן קיימת בכן תברר האל' היכן הם וכהר"ם[4] הנ"ל השיב והציע חשבן שהוציא הרב כמהו"ש[5] ז"ל הנ"ל אותן והארי{..} והאריכו בטענותיהם ולאחר שחתמו הצדדי' הנ"ל את עצמם בתוקף קומפרמיס בח"ח ובקנס חצי לשררה ירה[6] וחצי להקדש לאשר ולקיים כל אשר יצא מאתנו בכן נזדקקנו להם ומצאנו מחמת חלק הרווחי' השייכי' לצורך הכנסת כלה שעד שנת תקמם העבר אין בנו כח להוציא מידו רק יקבל בחרם לפנינו שבדבריו כן הוא שכבר חישב עם הרב ז"ל ואינ[ו] בידו כלום אבל אותן רווחי' העולי' משנת תקמם מן חודש תמוז עד ר"ח תמוז תקמ"ג העבר שהם ארבעה שנים מה שעולה הרווחי' הרביעת מקרן סך שמ"א זהו' הנ"ל השייכי' לסיועת הכנסת כלה שבתה הכלה הנ"ל וכן להבא מחויב כ' משה הנ"ל ליתן כל שנה כל הרווחי' המגיעי' לצורך הכנסת כלה מסך קרן הנזכר בשט"ח הודאה הנ"ל ליד האפטרופס ש...[7] תחת הרב ז"ל הנ"ל גם

קס ע"א

ב"ה

גם כפי מה שדקדקנו בלשון הצוואה אין לכ' משה הנ"ל שום זכות במעות הכנסת כלה מחמת מה שטען בקורבה שלו / ומחמת הרווחי' השייכי' לדבר טוב של תלמד תורה מצאנו על מה שעבר שטוען כ' משה הנ"ל שכבר הוציא ונתן למלמדי' עם בני' או שיברר כ' משה הנ"ל דבריו

1. על זה?
2. קופשטוק
3. כבוד מורנו הרב שמואל
4. וכבוד הרב משה (אויך)
5. כבוד מורנו הרב ורבנו שמואל
6. ירום הודו
7. יש כאן חור בנייר

6. למי הוציא ועל משך זמן שאומר שהוציא או יקבל בחרם ע"ז בפנינו ב"ד
7. שכדבריו כן הוא ומכאן ואילך מחויב כ' משה הנ"ל למסור ג"כ הרווחי'
8. המגיעי' על דב"ט של ת"ת מידי שנה בשנה ליד אפטרופס שיתמנה
9. מחדש תחת הרב ז"ל הנ"ל ורשות ביד אותו אפטרופס לשלם מאותן
10. רווחי' למלמדי' עם בני' של כ' משה הנ"ל שיעור כפי אומד דעת של
11. האפטרופס וכמבואר בצוואה / ומחמת מה שנזכר בשט"ח שיש ביד
12. כ' משה הנ"ל סך שמוני' וחמישה זהו' עשרי' צל מדמי דב"ט להלוותן
13. לענים בלי רווחי' וטוען כ' משה הנ"ל שהוא רוצה ללות לעצמו
14. שהוא נצרך לכך ובטוח עליהם שהוא עשה ק"ס בהודאה באשה והדר
15. בעלה מצאנו שכ' משה הנ"ל רשאי להחזיק אותן לעצמו בתורת הלוואה
16. וכל האחריות ושיעבוד הנזכר בשטר הנ"ל באשה והדר בעלה הוא בתקפו
17. כמקדם ג"כ על הסך שמוני' וחמשה זהו' א' ק"ש הנאמרי' שם ומה שטוען כ'
18. משה הנ"ל שהי' ביד הרב ז"ל הנ"ל סך חמשים ושניים זהו' מדמי
19. דבר טוב לקרן קיימת מצאנו מאחר שהציע לפנינו כ"ה משה הנ"ל חשבון
20. מה שהוציא הרב ז"ל הנ"ל שוב אין על היורשי' של הרב ז"ל
21. הנ"ל שום תביעה מחמת סך חמשי' ושני' זהו' מדמי דבר טוב
22. הנ"ל יצא מאתנו אור ליו' ה' ב' כסליו תקמד לפק רנ"מ ורמ"ש ואני

No. 172

Fol. 160b; Thursday evening, 8 January 1784

The beneficiaries of the late Mendele Speyer sold a number of seats in the local synagogues.[1] The seats were sold after the customary announcement of sale. The court noted the purchasers and the prices paid. In each of the four entries, the price that the seats were sold for are noted in Arabic numerals as well as spelled-out in Hebrew words.

קס ע"ב

1. ב"ה
2. אור ליו' ויו עש"ק טו טבת תקמ"ד נמכר בפנינו ב"ד המקומות שהי' שייך ליורשי'
3. המנוח כ"ה מענדלי שפייער ז"ל לשלם כתיקון הקהלה כנהוג אחר הכרזה כנהוג
4. ———
5. מקו' שלם בע"נ התיכונה שעומדות עלי' כעת אשת כ' שמואל ב"ר יודא שוסטר ז"ל
6. נמכר לכ"ה נטע פלערשהיים בעד סך תשעה מאות ואחד עשר זהו' 911*f*[2]

---

1. Mendele Speyer died on 24 April 1773 (Ettlinger, 24.4.1773).
2. *f* = פלורין (מטבע)

7. ———
8. החצי מקו' בע"נ התיכונה אשר עומדות עלי' כעת אשת פו"מ כ' אברם האמיל סג"ל
9. נמכר לכ' אברם הנ"ל בעד סך חמשה מאות ושני זהו' _ _ _502
10. וחצי' אחרת שייך ג"כ לכ' אברם הנ"ל
11. ———
12. *f*205 מקו' שלם בעזרת אנשי' התחתונה במיטל באנק התחתונה אשר עומד עלי' כעת
13. כ' טעבלי שפאניער נמכר לכ' פייבש בן כ' יעקב שלאס בעד סך שני מאות וחמשה זהו'
14. ———
15. שני חצאי מקומות סמוכי' זו אצל זו בבה"כ עליונה העומדי' עליהם כעת פו"מ כ"ה מ
16. מאדל ברונשוויג סג"ל וה"ה הו"ה כ' בענדיט מאי סג"ל ונמכרו להו"ה ג"ץ כ' הירש הז יצו
17. בעד סך ארבעה מאות ושמוני' זהו' וחצאי אחרות שייך ג"כ לכ' הירש הנ"ל 480[*f*]
18. ———
19. ר נתן מז וכה"מ[1] שיף ואני

No. 173

Fol. 160b; Monday evening, 19 January 1784

The court was ordered by the Bürgermeister to sell half of the outer house on the Kamel lot. The order directed the court to sell it according to the instructions of the Reiss family, who were creditors of the current owner, Herz Hirschorn. The court followed the directives and sold Herz's portion of the house to Aaron Zunz for 3550 guldens. Also see no. 174.

20. ———
21. חצי בית חיצון צום קאמעהל שהי' שייך לכ' הירץ בן המנוח כ' מאזוס הירשהארן ז"ל אשר נשלח
22. לנו בפקודת האדון בורגר מיינשטר עקסעלענץ יר"ה למכור ע"י ב"ד כנהוג / ואיכות ואופני
23. המכירה יהי' כמו שאמר רייסן[2] / ובא הו"ה כ"ה גומפל רייס לפנינו בפקודת אמו האשה
24. מ' רייזלה אל' המנוח ג"ה כ"ה אייזק רייס {יצו} ז"ל ובפקודת אחיו כ"ה ליב רייס שהם בעלי
25. חובות של כ' הירץ הנ"ל ואמר לנו שאיכות ואופני המכירה יהי' כמבואר והיינו שיומכר
26. ע"י ב"ד אותן החדרי' שדר בו כעת כ' הירץ הנ"ל והמה שני חדרי' זה מול זה חד שטאך
27. הויך / חדר אחד שלשה שטאך הויך לצד הרחוב ארבע שטאך הויך חדר אחד לצד לנגה
28. גאנג ועל העלי' איין יו' קעמרכה / וגם דען מיטלשטה קעלר וגם האחי' כ' דוד וכ' פייס

---

1. וכבוד הרב מאיר
2. כנראה משפחת רייס

29. בני המנוח כ׳ מענדלי האמיל ז״ל מחזיקי חצי בית האחרת הנ״ל רשאי׳ להחזיק מכירת
30. יין בגבולם בלי מוחה כלל / וגם אמר בפירוש שכל מי שלקח חצי בית הנ״ל ישתמש ימי החג בחג
31. בסוכה התחתון הוא וכל בני ביתו ועל אותן אופני׳ נמכר חצי בית הנ״ל בפנינו ב״ד ח״מ
32. להו״ה כ׳ אהרן צונץ בעד סך שלשת אלפי׳ וחמש מאות וחמשי׳ זהו׳ לשלם כתיקון הקהלה
33. נעשה אור ליו׳ ג דו טבת תקמ״ד רנמי[1] ורמש[2] ואני

No. 174

Fols. 161a–b; Sunday 1 February 1784

After the sale of a portion of the house on the Kamel lot mentioned in no. 173, the owners of the other half of the house, the Hammel brothers, and the new owner, Aaron Zunz, came to the court to have it sanction and record their agreements regarding the use of various areas of the house.

קסא ע״א

1. ב״ה
2. הן היו׳ הקריבו לפנינו מחזיקי בית צום קומעהל ה״ה האחי׳ הו״ה כ׳ דוד
3. וכ׳ פייס בני המנוח כ׳ מענדלי האָמיל ז״ל ששייך להם בשותפת החצי מן ה
4. הבית הנ״ל וה״ה הו״ה גבאי ת״ת כ׳ אהרן צונץ יצו שנמכר לו בפנינו ב״ד ח״מ
5. חצי בית האחרת והיינו החדרי׳ שדר בו ושהי׳ שייך לכ׳ הירץ הירש⸗
6. הארן יצו כמבואר במעשה ב״ד ההוקם אור ליו׳ ג׳ ד״ו טבת תקמ״ד וביקשו
7. מאתנו ב״ד ח״מ ליתן להם תוקף מעשה ב״ד על כל תנאי׳ ואופני׳ שהתרצו ה
8. האחי׳ הנ״ל לכ׳ אהרן הנ״ל בפנינו ב״ד והיינו באשר שבמעשה ב״ד
9. של מכירת חצי בית הנ״ל לכ׳ אהרן הנ״ל נמכר לכ׳ אהרן הנ״ל רק מרתף
10. האמצעי תחת השטוב שהשתמש בו מקדמת כ׳ הירץ ה״ה הנ״ל ועתה ה
11. התחייבו את עצמם האחי׳ הנ״ל ליתן לכ׳ אהרן הנ״ל עוד מהמרתף יין
12. שלהם משך חמשה בויא שוך אורך ברוחב המרתף והיינו לפני מרתף
13. של כ׳ אהרן הנ״ל מן מקו׳ המחיצה שעומד עכשיו במרתף הנ״ל תחת השטוב
14. יתחיל המדידה חמשה שוך הנ״ל ונמשך לצד הרחוב עד שכלה החמשה
15. שוך יהי׳ לכ׳ אהרן הנ״ל וי״א וב״כ מעתה ועד עולם לחלוטין גמורין ולצמית׳
16. עלמין והי׳ תוקף מעשה ב״ד הלז כאלו נעשה ע״י קנין סודר בב״ד חשוב ולאחר
17. שיתן לכ׳ אהרן הנ״ל חמשה שוך הנ״ל וכנ״ל מחויב כ׳ אהרן הנ״ל ליתן כתב

---

1. רב נתן מז
2. ורב מאיר שיף

18. ראי׳ להאחי׳ הנ״ל להיות בידם לראי׳ שקיבל כ׳ אהרן הנ״ל חמשה שוך הנ״ל
19. והתחייבו עוד את עצמם האחי׳ הנ״ל שאם ירצה כ׳ אהרן הנ״ל להניח יין
20. בחלקו מרתף חמשה שוך הנ״ל וצריך להכניס ולהוציא חביות ממרתף שלו וש[אי]
21. אפשר לו דרך פתח ומדרגה שלו למרתף שמחויבי׳ האחי׳ הנ״ל להניח לכ׳ אהרן
22. הנ״ל להכניס ולהוציא כל חביות וחביות דרך מרתף יין שלהם שמהלך ופתח
23. לתוכה הוא מיד בכניסת הבית והיינו דוקא כל חביות וחביות צריך להיות
24. מחזיק איין אוהם ולא יותר גם התחייבו א״ע האחי׳ הנ״ל מאחר שבמעשה ב״ד
25. של מכירת חצי בית לכ׳ אהרן הנ״ל נמכר לכ׳ אהרן הנ״ל ש...[1]

קסא ע״ב

1. ב״ה
2. חדר אחד לצד הרחוב לזאת התחייבו א״ע האחי׳ הנ״ל להחליף עמו וליתן לו
3. בחינם בלי שום פרוטה אחת החדר לצד אינו נימולים בשטח שלשה שטעג הויך
4. תחת החדר לצד הרחוב היהודי׳ להיות לכ׳ אהרן הנ״ל לדור בו ולהשתמש
5. בתוכה עם אשתו וב״ב כאות נפשו משך שני׳ עשר שנים רצופי׳ מיו׳ מכירת
6. חצי בית שלו בחדר לצד א״נ הנ״ל ובכלות שני׳ עשר שני׳ הנ״ל יוחזר החדרי׳
7. שלשה שטעג הויך ביניהם ויהי׳ אותו חדר שהוא לצד א״נ להאחי׳
8. הנ״ל עד עולם {ויהי שלו לחלוטין} והחדר שהוא לצד הרחוב היהודי׳ לכ׳
9. אהרן הנ״ל עד עולם ויהי׳ שלו לחלוטין כמבואר במעשה בד[2] ובפי׳ הותנה
10. ביניהם שאם יתקנו שום בנין בחדרי׳ שלשה שטעג הנ״ל משך שני׳ עשר
11. הנ״ל / הן דבר קטן או גדול הן כ׳ אהרן הנ״ל בחדר שמחזיק בו והוא
12. לצד א״נ והאחי׳ הנ״ל בחדר לצד הרחוב היהודי׳ שאין אחד
13. מהם רשאי לתבוע חלק הוצאות מחבירו רק יהי׳ על הוצאותו לבד / גם
14. הותנה ביניהם באם שיבנה שום אחד מהם בתוך שני׳ עשר שני׳ הנ״ל
15. בחדרי׳ הנ״ל בנין קבוע ומחובר בכותל הבית שאינו רשאי לחזור ולסתור
16. אותו בנין בכלות שני׳ עשר שני׳ כשפינה אותן חדר שבנה בו בנין מחובר
17. רק צריך להניח אותו כמות שהוא גם התחייבו א״ע האחי׳ הנ״ל והתרצו
18. א״ע שתלך משרתת של כ׳ אהרן הנ״ל בבית המוצנע שלהם העומד בתוך
19. הסוכה אחורי בית החורף התחתון והיינו כל היום ובתחילת הלילה
20. עד צעהן אויער והיינו דוקא לכ׳ אהרן הנ״ל התרצו האחי׳ הנ״ל א״ע ולא
21. לי״א וב״כ כל הנ״ל נעשה בפנינו ב״ד בריצוי האחי׳ הנ״ל בנפש
22. חפיצה שלא באונס כלל וכתבנו וחתמנו כל הנ״ל בתוקף ובמעשה ב״ד
23. ובכח ב״ד יפה להיות ביד הו״ה כ׳ אהרן הנ״ל והו״ה כ׳ דוד וכ׳ פייס
24. הנ״ל לראי׳ כדי שיקוים הכל כנ״ל בלי שום טענה ואמתלא שבעולם
25. נעשה יו׳ א׳ טית שבט תקמ״ד רנ״מ ורמ״ש ואני

---

1. יש כאן חור בנייר
2. בית דין

No. 175

Emden v. Kassel

Fol. 162a; Monday 2 February 1784

Through his representative, Jacob Emden brought suit against Moses Kassel for funds from a business deal involving lottery tickets.[1] Moses did not deny the charge, but, through his own representative, countered that Jacob owed him much more, a charge that Jacob denied. The court ruled that if Moses took an oath to the effect that Jacob owed him at least what he owed Jacob, he would be free of any and all claims against him. At the same time, the court instructed Jacob to take an oath that he had settled with Moses some time ago as he claimed. If he did so, he too would be absolved of the claims against him.

קסב ע"א

1. ב"ה
2. ע"ד טענות והפרשות שיש בין הו"ה ג"ה כ' יעקב עמדין יצו ובין הו"ה כ' משה ב"ההמנוח
3. כ' בענדיט קאסיל ז"ל שהאריכו בטענותיהם ה"ה התורני כ"ה משה אויך בהרשאת
4. כ' יעקב הנ"ל וה"ה התור' כ"ה אנשיל פפאן בהרשאת כ' משה הנ"ל ותוכן דבריהם
5. שכ' יעקב הנ"ל תבע מן כ' משה קאסיל הנ"ל סך תשעי' זהו' בץ[2] שנשאר לו רעשט מן
6. תשעה ושלשי' צעטל מן 37 לאטרע מן מענץ שמכר לו כ' יעקב הנ"ל וה"ה כ"ה
7. אנשל הנ"ל השיב שאמת הדבר שחייב לו סך תשעה[3] זהו' בץ הנ"ל אך הוא תובע
8. באשר שנתן לו כ משה לכ' יעקב אין ברוינה פעלש ד' אלטה ל"ד למשכן מחמת
9. די פרענד התשלומין בין מינץ וחדש רטי'[4] ואח"כ שילם לו הטיפרענד וכ' יעקב
10. הנ"ל לא החזיר לו אותן ארבע ל"ד הנ"ל ועוד תבע עשרי' קרלינר מחמת איין טרעפר
11. מן אוטרעכטר לאטרע נומרי 3788 שהי' לכ' משה מן כ' יעקב הנ"ל וועלכר עשרי'
12. אלפי' זהו' גוואהנין אונד כ' יעקב עדיין {ל.} חייב לו מחמת טרעפר הנ"ל
13. עשרי' קרלינר ובהצטרף ד' ל"ד הנ"ל עולה יתר שני מאות וחמשי' וששה זהו'
14. בכן תנכה מזה סך צ זהו' בץ הנ"ל בכן (תבע)[5] שישלם לו כ' יעקב הנ"ל המותר
15. שעלה סך קס"ה זהו' נח צל וכ"ה משה אויך בהרשאת הנ"ל השיב להדם[6]
16. שקיבל כ"י[7] הנ"ל ארבעה ל"ד וגם מחמת טרעפר כבר חישב לו כ' משה הנ"ל עמו

---

1. Regarding Moses Kassel and lottery tickets, see above, no. 68; with respect to Emden, see Schlick, "Zur Rolle der reichsstädtischen Gerichtsbarkeiten," 175–78.
2. ב צ"ל
3. צ"ל 'תשעים'; ר' שורות 5, 9.
4. וחדש רייכשטאלר (Konventionstaler כנראה)
5. תוספת מעל השורה
6. לא היו דברים מעולם
7. כבוד יעקב

17. וניכה לו כל מה שמגיע לו בתשלומין הקלאס שאחרי׳ כדרך התגרי׳ של קאלעקטע[רש]
18. ומצאנו שכ׳ משה הנ״ל ישבע ע״ד המקו׳ ב״ה וכו׳ שעכ״פ יש {לו} ביד כ״י הנ״ל כ״כ מחמת
19. התביעות שלו סך תשעי׳ זהו׳ בץ ובזה פטור כ׳ משה הנ״ל מחמת תביעות
20. הנ״ל ומחמת המותרות מצאנו שכ׳ יעקב הנ״ל ישבע באותו מעמד ג״כ
21. עדי[1] המקו׳ ב״ה וכו׳ שכדבריו כן הוא שלא קיבל ארבע ל״ד (הנ״ל)[2] מחמת טרעפר
22. כבר חישב עם כ׳ משה ונוכה לו כל מה שמגיע מאותו טרעפר הנ״ל
23. ולאחר שישבע כ״י כנ״ל גם הוא {ישבע} פטור מן כ׳ משה הנ״ל מחמת תביעות
24. הנ״ל יצא מאתנו יו׳ ב יוד שבט תקמ״ד רנ״מ ורמ״ש ואני

Fol. 162b is blank.

No. 176

Flörsheim et al. v. Spiegel et al.

Fols. 163a–169b; Sunday 15 February 1784

In early 1760 Meʾir Flörsheim stipulated in his will that upon his death his wife Glikhe (Glück) should administer his estate, something that was specifically allowed by Jewish law.[3] When Meʾir died in 1781, his sons and sons-in-law formally accepted the conditions of the will and Glikhe was given control of Meʾir's estate. It did not take long until her management was challenged, and already in 1781 an agreement was reached between Glikhe, her sons, and her sons-in-law limiting her right to give gifts or indebt herself to others.

Glikhe's death in 1783 brought about a family controversy as each of the beneficiaries made claims against the estate. The sons made substantial financial claims against their mother's estate, including demands for repayment of loans that they had extended to her during her lifetime, shares in the house that she had promised them, and partial ownership of a family business. The sons-in-law also had expectations. They each held "half a male's portion" contracts (see above, no. 99) but asked the court if they might not be entitled to more of the estate. One son-in-law

1. על דעת
2. תוספת מעל השורה
3. B.T., *Giṭṭin* 52a; *Shulḥan ʿaruk*, Ḥoshen mishpaṭ 290.1

had been promised two years of financial support after his marriage but had only received one; now he wanted the other.

Mistrust ran deep and there were concerns among the sons-in-law that the sons may have taken assets from the estate without reporting them. The sentiment must have been heightened by the fact that two sons held a "contract of belief" (*sheṭar ne'emanut*) from their mother which stated that they should be believed in all matters with respect to the estate and not be forced to swear or take an oath regarding their statements. There was particular resentment regarding the widow's attempt to pass assets on to her unmarried sons, thereby essentially trying to insure that they would be able to bring assets to their as yet unarranged marriages. While Glikhe's sons urged that her wishes be respected, the sons-in-law objected to the "contract of belief" and a number of Glikhe's gifts to her children.

The court examined Me'ir Flörsheim's will, the inventory of assets, and all the other documents produced by the parties and their representatives. The court explicitly noted that some of its decisions were based on compromises while others were founded on the law. Ultimately, the sons, including those with "contracts of belief," and sons-in-law were each required to swear that they had not taken assets from the estate. If they had made statements regarding the holdings of the estate, they also had to swear that their statements were accurate. The court established this as a prerequisite for the distribution of any assets and all parties obligated themselves to do so. Failure to do so carried a fine of 4000 guldens. A postscript notes that all parties fulfilled the court's rulings.

קסג ע"א

1. ב"ה
2. ע"ד טענות והפרשות שנתהוו בעזבון המנוח פו"מ כ"ה מאיר פלערשהיי'
3. ז"ל שציווה שתהא אשתו מ' גליקכה אפטרופסות ומושלת בעזבונו וכמבואר
4. בצוואה ההוקם ח' טבת תקד"ל וגם כל בני' וחתנה ר' ליב שפיגל וחתנה כ'
5. אנשיל קיבלו עליהם בק"ג לקיים צוואת אביהם וחמיו הנ"ל כמבואר
6. בק"ס ההוקם ביניהם ד"ב אייר תקמ"א לפק / ועתה שגם האשה מ' גליקכה
7. הנ"ל הלכה לעולמה ושבקה חיים לכל ישראל בא לפנינו כל הבנים
8. וחתני' עם המורשאים שלהם ה"ה האחים הו"ה התורני כ"ה משה והו"ה
9. כ"ה יעקב והו"ה כ"ה נטע עם התורני כ"ה משה אויך הביא בהרשאות כ"ה
10. כ"ה יעקב וכ"ה נטע הנ"ל והב"ח כ' לעמלי וב"ח כ' הירש יצו בני המנוח כהר"ר
11. מאיר הנ"ל והו"ה כ' ליב שפיגל כ"ץ עם התורני כ"ה וואלף שייאר יצו הבא בהרשא"
12. "תו והו"ה כ"ה אנשיל ב"כ משה פלערשהיי' עם ה"ה התורני כ"ה מאיר מַז ב
13. בהרשאת כ' אנשיל הנ"ל והציעה כל אחד ואחד מהם כל טענותיו וזכיותיו לפנינו
14. כמבואר להבא והיינו ה"ה התורני כ"ה משה בן המנוח כ מאיר פלערשהיי' ז"ל הנ"ל
15. הציע ל[פנ]ינו שני ח"כ מחתימת יד אמו ז"ל הנ"ל אחד מסך שלשת אלפים זהו' ואחד

16. מסך מאה רט ותבע שישולם לו קודם כל דמי ח"כ הנ"ל וכל היורשי' דהיינו האחי'
17. ר יעקב ור' נטע והאחים פנויים כ' לעמלי וכ' הירש בני ר' מאיר הנ"ל וגם חתניו
18. ר' ליב וכ' אנשיל הנ"ל הודו לפנינו שמרוצים המה שישולם לכ"ה משה הנ"ל את
19. דמי ח"כ הנ"ל / ועוד תבע כ"ה משה הנ"ל רווחי' מכל סך הנ"ל מר"ח כסליו ה
20. העבר עד עתה / עוד תבע כ"ה משה הנ"ל דמי יד העליונה מרביעת
21. בית שנתן לו אביו ז"ל לנדן וכמבואר בתנאים אחרונים שלי[1] מכל שנה חמשה רט ע[ולה][2]
22. יחד על שלשה עשר שנים סך ששים וחמשה רט והיורשי' השיבו שיכירו הב"ד
23. על זה / עוד תבע ח"כ משכירות הבית מן רביעת בית שלו הנ"ל הנמצאים
24. בעזבון ששייך לו רביעת בית הנ"ל לחלוטין מיו' פטירת אמו ז"ל הנ"ל ממה ש
25. שמגיע להעזבון הנ"ל מדמי ח"כ הנ"ל עד יום פטירת אמו ז"ל ינוכה ממה
26. שמגיע לו ע"פ תביעותיו הנ"ל / והו"ה כ"ה יעקב הנ"ל תבע סך שני מאות
27. וששים ואחד זהו' והיינו בראשון תבע מה שהלווה לאמו ז"ל

קסג ע"ב

1. הנ"ל במזומנים שהוא סך חמשים וששה זהו' גם תבע מה שנתן והלווה
2. לאחיו הפנויי' יצו לצורך מזונת שלהם סך מאה זהו' / עוד תבע דמי יד
3. העליונה מחצי בית שלו מיו' חתנותו עד עד[3] עתה שהוא לערך שמונה
4. ושלשה רביעת שנה כל שנה שמונה רט כמבואר בת"א שלו העולה
5. לערך סך שבעים רט / עוד תבע ג"כ שיוחזר לו מהעזבון כל ח"כ
6. משכירת הבית {עד עת} שניתן לו לנדן מאביו ז"ל ששייך לו לחלוטין
7. מיו' פטירת אמו ז"ל הנ"ל ומה שמגיע להעזבון מדמי שכירת עד
8. עת פטירת אמו ז"ל רוצה לנכות מתביעותיו הנ"ל / גם הודה
9. שיש בידו מעות השייך להעזבון הנ"ל מחמת שותפת מו"מ
10. של לאטר[י]ע שהי' לאמו ז"ל חלק שליש בו העולה לפי פנקס שלו
11. לאחר שינוכה חובת ישינים לסך שני מאות ותשעה עשר זהו'
12. כ"ה צל וזה ינוכה ג"כ מתביעותיו הנ"ל / והו"ה כ"ה נטע פלערש[היים]
13. הנ"ל תבע בעצמו וגם התורני כ"ה משה אויך בהרשאת כ"ה נטע
14. הנ"ל הציע לפנינו שטר הודאה מאמו ז"ל משותפת שהי' לו עם
15. אמו ז"ל הנ"ל בחנות של סחורת ההוקם ביו' ד"ג אייר תקמם לפק
16. ושם נאמר שהניח כ' נטע הנ"ל בשותפת סך ארבעת אלפים זהו'
17. מזומנים ומבואר שם שלעת החלוקת השותפת מסחורת הנ"ל יקח
18. כהר"ן[4] הנ"ל בראש כל אותן ארבעה אלפים זהו' {מזומני'} הנ"ל והיינו
19. שמחויב כהר"ן הנ"ל ליקח לדמי תשלומין סך ד' אלפי' זהו' הנ"ל שליש מסחורת
20. המונחין בעין בדמי קרן ראשון שלקחו הם ושליש מהמעות ושליש מ

---

1. אולי צ"ל 'שלו'
2. הנייר קטוע. ההצעה על פי השערה.
3. כפילות במקור
4. כבוד הרב נטע

21. מהחובת הן מהחובת הבטוחין והן מאינו בטוחין וטען כהרן[1] הנ"ל
22. באשר שעתה אינו מגיע השליש מן מזומנים והסחורת וכל החובת
23. הנ"ל לתשלום חובו סך ארבע אלופים זהו' הנ"ל רק שנחסר מזה
24. לאחר קבלת השליש מכל הנ"ל על חלקו סך שלשים קרלינר
25. בכן

קסד ע"א

1. ב"ה
2. בכן טען ראשון שהשליש מסחורת המונחים בחנות הנרשמים בתוך אינפוטאריום
3. המונח לפינו[2] וחובת ומזומנים שייכי' לו ועוד תבע אותן שלשה מאות ושלשים זהו'
4. בראש כל מן העזבון הנ"ל כמשמעות שטר הודאה שהציע לפנינו כהר"ן הנ"ל
5. עוד תבע רווחים על שלשים קרלינר הנ"ל סך שלשים זהו' / עוד תובע והציע
6. לפנינו שני ח"כ מח"י אמו ז"ל חד מסך ששים ק"ד[3] וחד מסך עשרים ק"ד ותבע
7. אותן סך שמונה מאות ושמונים זהו' ג"כ בראש כל מן העזבון הנ"ל
8. עוד תבע חלק רווח המגיע לו על חלקו מיריד פסח שנת תקמ"ג העבר
9. סך שני מאות ושלשה זהו' כמו שנרשום בפנקס שלו וטוען כהרן הנ"ל
10. שחלק ריווח של אמו כבר באת לידה שהיא הי' שולטת בחנות ותמיד
11. הי' הקאַ[סי] תחת ידה ומה שמגיע לו כנ"ל לא קיבל עדיין בכן תובע עתה
12. כנ"ל עוד תבע כהר"ן הנ"ל חלק ריווח המגיע לו מיריד ר"ה תקמ"ד
13. העבר העולה ע"ח סך מאה ושלשים ותשעה זהו' נ"ט צל וטוען שכל מה
14. שמונח בחנות הוא בחזקתו עד שיתפרע לו תביעתו עוד תבע מחמת
15. הוצאת אחת לאחת עבור אמו הנעדרת ז"ל עם הוצאות עשיות א
16. אינפוטאריום העולה לסך שני מאות ותשעה זהו' ל"ג צל כפי הנרשום
17. בפנקס שלו גם תבע דמי יד העליונה המגיע לו מארבע שנים מיו'
18. חתונתו ועד עתה מחצי בית הניתן לנדן מאביו ז"ל סך מ"ח זהו' דהיינו כל
19. שנה חית רט כמבואר בת"א שלו גם תבע שיותן לו מן העזבון ח"כ משכיר[ת]
20. חצי בית שלו ששייך לו לאחר פטירת (אמו ז"ל הנ"ל לחלוטין ומה שמגיע לה עזבון עד עת[ה])[4] ינוכה לו מתביעתו הנ"ל גם הציע
21. לפנינו האחי' כ"ה יעקב וכ"ה נטע הנ"ל שטר נאמונת שנתנה אמו ז"ל
22. לו ולאחיו כ"ה יעקב הנ"ל כל הנאמונת שבעולם בלי שבועה וג"ש וק"ח ות"כ ה
23. ההוקם יו' ה' ד"ב מנחם תקמ"ג בכן טען עתה בכח בכח[5] שטר
24. נאמונת הנ"ל שיש להם כל הנאמונת שבעולם בלי שבועה

---

1. כבוד הרב נטע
2. צ"ל 'לפנינו'
3. קרלינר (ר' דף קסז ע"ב שורה 12)
4. תוספת מעל השורה
5. כפילות במקור

קסד ע״ב

1. והאריכו בטענותיהם ליפוי כח ולחזיק שטר הנאמנות שלהם / וכל האחים
2. בני המנוח ר׳ מאיר ז״ל הנ״ל משיבי׳ שאין לטעון נגד השטר נאמונת אשר
3. להם מאמם ז״ל הנ״ל אך ה״ה הו״ה כ״ה ליב שפיגל כץ והו״ה כ׳ א
4. אנשיל ב״כ משה פלערשהיי׳ הציע לפנינו תנאים אחרונים שלהם עם
5. שטר חח״ז וגם טענו שיכרו ב״ד אם לא מגיע להם חלק זכר שלם
6. מכח צוואת חמיהם ההוקם ח׳ טבת תק״ך לפק וכנ״ל ומכח זכיות אלו
7. השיבו נגד תביעת כהרן הנ״ל ושטר נאמונת שלו וטענו שאין כח ביד
8. חמותה ליתן נאמונת באשר שבצוואת חמיו ז״ל נאמר בפירוש שגם
9. היא בעצמו[1] היתה מחויבת ליתן אינפוטאריום וגם גבאי הקהל
10. הי׳ מוחה לנאמני׳ שלא יקבלו ק״ס מן האשה הנ״ל וגם נאמר בפירוש
11. בשטר הנעשה מן כל הבנים הנ״ל וחתנה כ״ה ליב שפיגל הנ״ל
12. לאמם ז״ל ההקום ביו׳ ך״ב אייר תקמ״א שהאשה הנ״ל אין לה
13. רשות ליתן שט״ח או מתנה לשום אדם חוץ לבני׳ פנויי׳ לנדן גם
14. חוץ לבנה כ״ה משה וכמבואר שם בכן טענו שמכ״ש שאין לה רשות
15. ליתן נאמונת לאחרים ואין חוב גדול מזה ועוד האריכו בטענותיה׳
16. נגד שטר נאמונת הנ״ל והו״ה כ״ה ליב שפיגל הנ״ל הוסיף להשיב
17. על טענות כהרן הנ״ל שכפי השטר ערבות ופיצוי מחמת קוטציאהן[2]
18. שלו אצל השררה ירה[3] בשביל המשפט של חמיו ואביהם ז״ל מסך ששה
19. אלפי׳ זהו׳ מחמותה ז״ל הנ״ל כל הכתובה ותוספ׳ שלה משועבד לר׳
20. ליב הנ״ל כפי שטר ההוקם ביום ך״ב אייר תקמ״א בכן משועבד כל
21. העזבון בראש כל להערבות ופיצוי קויטציאהן שלו מסך הנ״ל שמגיע לו מחמת
22. שטר כתובה ותוספת והוא מוקדם לתשלומין ח״כ ושטר תביעות
23. של

קסה ע״א

1. ב״ה
2. של כהרן הנ״ל ופשיטא שאין לה כח ליתן שום נאמנות נגד שיעבוד קויטציאהן שלו ו
3. והאחי׳ הפנויים ה״ה כ׳ לעמלי וכ׳ הירש בני המנוח כהר״ם ז״ל הנ״ל הציעו לפנינו
4. שט״ח מאמם ז״ל ההוקם ביום ך״ה תשרי תקמ״ד מה שינתן להם לנדן ושאר צרכי נישואין
5. בכן תבעו מן העזבון שישלום להם סך דמי השט״ח הנ״ל והיינו לכ״א מהם סך
6. ארבעת אלפים זהו׳ לנדן ושאר דברי׳ ששייכו להם עוד מחמת שט״ח הנ״ל
7. ומחמת צוואת אביהם ז״ל הנ״ל וגם תובעים שיחליטו הב״ד להם את החצי
8. בית צום בונדין קן ושני מקומות א בע״א וא׳ בע״נ כמבואר בשט״ח הנ״ל
9. והאחים כ׳ משה וכ׳ יעקב וכ׳ נטע הנ״ל השיבו שאין להם טענה לטען נגד

---

1. צ״ל ׳בעצמה׳
2. פקדון, ערבון כספי (Kaution).
3. ירום הודו

10. שט"ח מהאחיהם הפנוי' הנ"ל לאחר שישולם תביעותיהם הנ"ל / וה"ה כ"ה
11. ליב שפיגל וכ' אנשיל הנ"ל ומורשאי' שלהם השיבו שאין כח ורשות ביד
12. חמותם ז"ל ליתן להאחים פנוי' הנ"ל שט"ח ואף שנזכר בשטר ההוקם
13. בניהם ביו' ך"ב אייר תקמ"א שיש רשות לאמם ז"ל ליתן להם
14. נדן הוא דוקא באופן אם הי' מגיע האחי' הנ"ל לנשואין בעודה בחייה
15. חיותה אבל לא נתנה כח בידה ליתן שטרות לגבות מן העזבון אחרי
16. מותה באשר שבפירוש הותנו שאין לה כח ליתן שט"ח ועוד טענו החתנים
17. הנ"ל אף אם יזכו הבני' מכח שט"ח שלהם אינם זוכי' כפי משמעות
18. שט"ח שלהם רק לזמן נישואין שלהם בכן יניח כל מה ששייך להאחים
19. מן העזבון הנ"ל מכ[ח] שט"ח הנ"ל ליד איש אמיד ובטוח המרוצה לכ[או"א][1]
20. וכ"ה {יעקב} ליב הנ"ל הוסיף לטעון ולהשיב על תביעות אחי' פנויים
21. הנ"ל אחרי שהציע לפנינו כנ"ל שטר פיצוי והערבות מחמותו ז"ל וגם
22. האחי' פנויי' ששיעבדו א"ע בכא"ה לפצות את כ"ה ליב הנ"ל מסך
23. קויטציאהן שלו סך ששה אלפים זהו' הנ"ל וממילה אחרי שמשועבד את
24. כל כתובה ותוספת מאמם ז"ל וכנ"ל וגם מה ששייך להאחים פ
25. פנויים משועבד לפצותו כנ"ל בכן טוען שעכ"פ יניח
26. סך

קסה ע"ב

1. סך ששה אלפים זהו' דמי קויטציאהן שלו ביד איש אמיד ובטוח המרוצה
2. לו באשר שהשיעבד שלו הוא מוקדש לירושה ושטרות של האחים פנויי'
3. ובפרט שהם עצמם שיעבדו א"ע בקויטציאהן שלו והאחי' הפנויי' ה
4. השיבו על מה שתבע שיותן מה שמגיע להם ביד איש אמיד ובטוח
5. שאינו מרוצים להניח את שלהם ביד אחר זולת ליד אחיהם כהרן הנ"ל
6. וכה"י[2] הנ"ל והמה יהי' אפטרופסי' שלהם וזה יהי' להם לטובה גדולה
7. מכמה טעמים עוד טען הב"ח כ' לעמלי הנ"ל אחרי שנמכר מתוך העזבון
8. טבעת אחת בעד סך ששים וששה זהו' וטען שדמי טבעת הלז שייך
9. לו לבד באשר שנתנה לו אמה ז"ל זה זמן רב במתנה גמורה ה
10. הטבעת הלז / וכ"ה ליב שפיגל השיב שאמו לא נתנה לו רק ל
11. להתקשט בו ולא למתנה בכן גם דמי אותו טבעת שייך להעזבון
12. הנ"ל והו"ה כ' ליב שפיגל כץ תבע אחרי שהציע לפנינו כנ"ל
13. שטר פיצוי מחמותו ומהבנוי'[3] פנויי' בכא"ה ההוקם ביום ך"ב אייר
14. תקמ"א מחמת ששיעבוד אצל השררה יר"ה שלשה רביעת בית
15. שלו בעד סך ששת אלפי' זהו' כנ"ל בכן תבע שיפצה לו
16. מן העזבון בראש כל כדי שאינו מגיע לו שום הזיק בשביל
17. ערבות שלו הנ"ל וכ"ה משה וכ"ה יעקב וכ"ה נטע השיבו

---

1. הנייר קטוע. הצעה על פי השערה.
2. כבוד הרב יעקב
3. צ"ל 'ומהבני'"

18. על זה שגם המה הי׳ יכולין לתבוע ג״כ פיצוי מכח קויטציאהן
19. שלהם שהעמידו גם המה את בתיהם בקויטציאהן ויכולין
20. לטעון נגד השט״ח של אחיהם פנויים הנ״ל שכל העזבון מ
21. משועבד להם קודם תשלם שט״ח להאחים פנויים הנ״ל וגם כל
22. הטענות שטען כ״ה ליב הנ״ל נגד שט״ח של האחים פנויים הנ״ל
23. גם המה יכולין לטעון לטובת עצמם רק שהמה מוחלין כל טענות אלו
24. הן מחמת קויטציאהן הן שאר טענות שטען כהר״ל[1] וכ׳ אנשיל הנ״ל
25. נגד

קסו ע״א

1. ב״ה
2. נגד האחים הפנויים כ׳ לעמלי וכ׳ הירש מחמת שט״ח שלהם ונותנם
3. תוקף לקיים השט״ח של האחים הפנויים הנ״ל ואינם מבקשים שום
4. פיצוי מהם לקויטציאהן שלהם באופן שלאחר שישולם להם ח״כ שלהם
5. ושאר תביעות של כל אחד מהם כנ״ל שייך כל העזבון הנמצא כעת
6. כפי האינפורטאריום שלפנינו הן מזומנים הן סחורת הן חובת הן
7. ספרים ושאר מטלטלין הכל כאשר לכל הנמצא כעת בלי שום שיור כלל
8. להאחים הפנויים הנ״ל ויכירו הב״ד כשיצטרכו לשלם מחמת
9. ערבות קויטציאהן שלהם אצל השררה יר״ה ערך התשלומין של כל א
10. אחת ואחת מה שישולם כ״א חלקו לפצות השתעבדות הנחלאות שלהם
11. אך בזאת נאותה להם שבאם יגיע איזה זכות לגיסם כ״ה ליב
12. שפיגל מחמת מחילה הנ״ל לא יחול מחילה זו נגד (כי לאחיה׳ הפנויי׳ הם מוחלי׳ ולא ל)[2] גיסם בכן ה
13. התביעות שלהם מחמת קויטציאהן הם בחזקתם נגד גיסם
14. וכ״ה משה הנ״ל הוסיף לטעון שאף שיש לו עוד תביעות אחרת על
15. העזבון מכח צוואת אביו מחוב מן סך אלף רט גם תביעה זו הוא
16. מוחל להאחים פנויים הנ״ל והיינו נמי על אופן הנ״ל שיזכו האחים
17. הנ״ל לעצמם אבל לא נגד גיסם כ״ה ליב שפיגל הנ״ל וכ״ה אנשיל הנ״ל
18. וגם הוסיפו האחים פנויים וטועני׳ באשר שהמה יתומים בכן
19. יהפכו הב״ד בזכתם ויטענו לטובתם כל מה שאפשרי לטעון לזכות
20. נגד טעון כ״ה ליב שפיגל הנ״ל וכ׳ אנשיל הנ״ל אחרי שכבר טענו [כ״א][3]
21. נגד שטר נאמנות של האחים כ״ה יעקב וכהרן הנ״ל בכן תבעו מן
22. כה״י וכהר״ן שבועת שותפות הן מחמת מו״מ של סחורת והן מ
23. מחמת מו״מ של לאטריע / עוד תבע אחרי שאינפוטאריום מעזבון
24. חמיהם וחמותם ז״ל הנ״ל גרו[ע] מאוד ממעמד שהעריכו אותו
25. בחיים חיותם וגם יודעים בבירור שנחסרו כמה וכמה כלי

---

1. כבוד הרב ליב
2. תוספת מעל השורה
3. הנייר קטוע. הצעה על פי השערה.

26. כסף

קסו ע״ב

1. כסף שאינם כעת בעזבון ושידוע להם בבירור שהי׳ ביד חמיהם
2. וחמותם ז״ל קודם מותם כאשר הניח כה״ל הנ״ל רשימה לפנינו
3. וגם טענו עוד כמה אומדנות והוכחת שחששו עי״כ שום הברחה
4. בעזבון הנ״ל הן קודם מיתת חמותם והן לאחר העדרתה
5. בכן יטילה הב״ד שבועה על כל הבנים הן הנשואין והן ה
6. הפנויים שלא העלימו ולא הבריחה ולא ידעו משום הברחה
7. שבעולם וכל האחים השיבו שהבנות ובעליהן הי׳ ג״כ
8. בבית אמם ז״ל עד שעת פטירתה שנסגר הכל וטועני׳
9. שיכירו הב״ד שאף המה מחויבם לישבע / וכ״ה יעקב
10. וכהר״ן הנ״ל הוסיפו עוד להשיב וסמכו עצמם על שט[ר][1]
11. נאמנות שלהם ואינם מחויבם לישבע שום שבועה עוד
12. תבעו כהר״ל וכה״א הנ״ל שיש להם זכות במלבושי נשים
13. מחמותם ז״ל / עוד תבע כ״ה מאיר מַז בהרשאת כ״ה
14. אנשיל הנ״ל דמי מזונת משנה אחת אחרי שלא אכל אצלה
15. אלא שנה אחת וחמותו התחייבה א״ע ליתן לו ולאשתו שתי
16. שנים מזונת / והאריכו הצדדים הנ״ל והמורשאים הנ״ל
17. כל או״א בתכלית אריכות כמבואר הכל בק״ה המונח לפנינו
18. ולפי שחתמו הצדדים הנ״ל א״ע בתוקף קומפרמיס בח״ח
19. ובקנס סך ארבעת אלפים חצי לשררה יר״ה וחצי להקדש
20. לקיים את אשר יצא מאתנו הן לדין והן לפשר נזדקקנו
21. להם ואחרי שהי׳ למראה עינינו הצוואה של כהרם[2] הנ״ל ו
22. וגם כל השטרות וזכיות שהציע כל או״א מהם לפנינו ו
23. ודקדקנו הדק היטיב בהם ובטענותיהם וגם ראינו את
24. כל האינפוטאריום מהעזבון הנ״ל הן ממה שנמצא
25. במזומני

קסז ע״א

1. בה
2. במזומנים מדמי מכירת כסף וזהוב ומרגליות ומטלטלין וכלי בית הן ממה
3. שנמצא עוד בעין והן ממה שנמצא בחנות הן סחורת וחובת הן בטוחין
4. והן אינן בטוחין / ולאחר שהי׳ לנו הכל למראה ענינו ושקלנו במאזני צדק
5. את כל ונוכחת מצאנו על כל פרט ופרט כמבואר להבא מקצתו על דרך פשר
6. ומקצתו ע״פ הדין והיינו שכ״ה משה בן המנוח כהר״ם ז״ל הנ״ל יקבל
7. בחרם לפנינו ב״ד שלא הבריח ולא תפס כלום מן העזבון הנ״ל ושאין

---

1. הנייר קטוע. הצעה על פי השערה.
2. כבוד הרב מאיר (פלערשהיים)

8. לו ידיעה משום הברחה הן מאחיו והן מאחיותיו והן מגיסיו הנ״ל והן משום
9. אדם יהי׳ מי שיהי׳ הן מקודם מיתת אמו ז״ל הנ״ל והן מלאחר העדרתה
10. והן ממעות מזומנים כסף ושוה כסף סחורת ואבנים טובת זהב ומרגליות
11. ח״כ שארי חובת משכנות על נימולם הן עא״נ מכל מה שהפה יוכל לדבר
12. והלב לחשוב ולאחר שיקבל כ״ה משה הנ״ל בחרם כנ״ל ישולם לו
13. את ח״כ מסך שלשת אלפים זהו׳ נוסף על דמי ח״כ מסך מאה רט שכבר
14. קיבל ומה שתבע כ״ה משה הנ״ל רווחים מר״ח כסליו העבר עד עתה
15. אין בו ממש גם ישולם לו מן העזבון הנ״ל סך ששים וחמשה רט דמי
16. יד העליונה גם יותן לו מן העזבון אותם ח״כ משכירת הבית על אותן
17. רביעת בית השייך מיו׳ מיתת אמו ז״ל לחלוטין ומה שמגיע לעזבון מדמי
18. ח״כ שכירת הנ״ל עד {עת} פטירת אמו ז״ל ינוכה לו מדמי תשלומין ה
19. הנ״ל / וה״ה הו״ה כ״ה יעקב הנ״ל ישבע במעמד שלשה דיינים
20. ע״ד המקו׳ ב״ה וע״ד ב״ד בלי שום עו״מ ובלי שום הוראות היתר
21. שבעולם שלא הבריח וכו׳ שבועת השותפות שאין בידו כלום מה ש
22. ששייך לעזבון מכ״ח מומי[1] לאטריע כי אם כפי מה שהודה לפנינו
23. כנ״ל וגם ישבע כנ״ל שבועת שותפות וכו׳ ולאחר שישבע כנ״ל
24. יותן לו מעזבון אותו ח״כ משכירת הבית מחצי בית שניתן לנדן
25. ושייך לו מיו׳ פטירת אמו ז״ל לחלוטין וגם מחויבי׳ העזבון לשלם
26. לו כפי תביעותיו הנ״ל סך שני מאות וששים ואחד זהו׳ הנ״ל
27. נגד

קסז ע״ב

1. נגד זה ינוכה מה שמגיע לעזבון כפי שהודה סך שני מאות ותשעה עשר
2. זהו׳ דמי לאטריע הנ״ל וגם ממה שמגיע לעזבון מדמי ח״כ של שכירת חצי
3. בית שלו עד עת העדרתו אמו ז״ל ויחשב זה מול זה / והו״ה כ״ה נטע
4. הנ״ל ישבע ג״כ במעמד שלשה דיינים ע״ד המקו׳ ב״ה וע״ד ב״ד כנ״ל
5. בלי עו״מ בלי שום הוראות היתר שבעולם שלא הבריח וכו׳ וגם ישבע
6. שבועת השותפים שאין בידו כלום ממה ששייך לעזבון הן מן מו״מ של
7. לאטר[י]ע והן מחמת מו״מ של סחורת בחנות הן סחורת מזומנים חובת ח״כ
8. יהי׳ מה שיהי׳ כי אם כפי מה שהודה לפנינו כפי אינפוטאריום ש
9. שהציע לפנינו וגם ישבע שחייב העזבון לו דמי ח״כ ושלשים קרלינר
10. ישבע כנ״ל וגם שמגיע לו מדמי ריוח מיריד פסח ושאר תביעות הנ״ל עכ״פ
11. כפי המבואר להבא ולאחר שישבע כנ״ל מצאנו ע״ד פשר דבר שישולם
12. לו שני {שליש} ח״כ מסך שמונים קרלינר {הנ״ל} גם שייך לו שליש בחנות
13. מחובת ומסחורת ומחובת מזומנים כפי טענותו גם ישולם לו שלשים
14. קרלינר המגיע לו לתשלום סך ארבעת אלפים זהו׳ שהניח בשותפו׳
15. גם ישולם לו מחמת דמי יד העליונה סך מ״ח זהו׳ גם ישולם לו ריווח

---

1. מקח וממכר

16. המגיע לו מיריד פסח תקמ״ג סך שני מאות ושלשה זהו׳ י״ד צל גם ישולם
17. לו מה שמגיע לו מחמת זה שהוציא אחת לאחת סך שני מאות ותשעה זהו׳ ל״ג
18. צל / ומחמת מה שתבע עוד רווחים משלשים קרלינר הנ״ל וגם מה
19. שטעון שמגיע לו מחלק ריווח מיריד ר״ה תקמ״ד העולה סך קל״ט זהו׳
20. כט צל מצאנו שאין לו תביעה בזה על העזבון וגם יותן לו ח״כ מ
21. משכירת הבית מחצי בית שלו שניתן לו לנדן מאביו ז״ל ושייך
22. לו לחלוטן מעת פטירת אמו ז״ל הנ״ל אך מה שמגיע לעזבון הנ״ל
23. מדמי שכירת חצי בית הנ״ל עד עת פטירת אמו ז״ל ינוכה לו מתשלום
24. תביעותיו הנ״ל והב״ח כ׳ לעמלי הנ״ל ישבע ג״כ במעמד שלשה
25. דייני׳ ע״ד המקו׳ ב״ה וע״ד הב״ד וכו׳ כנ״ל שלא הבריח
26. ולא

קסח ע״א

1. ב״ה
2. ולא תפס וכו׳ ואחיו כ׳ הירש יענה ויאמר אף אני כמוהו ולאחר שישבעו האחים
3. פנויים כנ״ל מצאנו שהשטר אשר להם מאמם ז״ל הנ״ל הוא בתוקפו ובגבורת[ו]
4. שלאחר שנשבעו שייך להאחים פנויים הנ״ל החצי בית צום בינדן קאן
5. ושני מקומות אחד בע״א ואחד בע״נ והיינו לכ׳ לעמלי רביעת בית ושני
6. חצאי מקומת הנ״ל (באשר שבפירש נאמר בשטר חח״ז של גיסיהם הנ״ל)[1]
7. ולכ׳ הירש ג״כ רביעת בית ושני חצאי מקומת הנ״ל באשר שבפירש נאמר
8. בשטר חח״ז של גיסיהם הנ״ל חוץ מקרקעת וגם בצוואת אביהם נאמר חוץ
9. מקרקעות בכן אין לכ׳ ליב וכ׳ אנשיל הנ״ל שום תביעה על זה מכח ירושה
10. והחלטנו מעתה הקרקעות הנ״ל להאחים פנויים הנ״ל כנ״ל אמנם שארי
11. דברים הנמצאים בעזבון הן מה שעדיין בעין והן מה שנמכר
12. כבר יהי׳ מה שיהי׳ כל מה שנמצא בעזבון בכל האינפוטאריום
13. המנוח לפנינו הן סחורת בחנות והן חובת בטוחים ושאינו בטוחים
14. הנרש[ומ]ים באינפוטאריום גם חלק שליש מחובת לאטרע שמגיע ע״ח
15. העזבון סך ל״ח זהו׳ לו צל כפי שהודה כ״ה יעקב הנ״ל יהי׳ הכל
16. משועבד להאחים הפנויי׳ הנ״ל מכח שט״ח שלהם הנ״ל שמצאנו שהוא
17. בתוקפו לאחר שנתפרע לאחיהם כפי המבואר בפס״ד הלז ובאשר
18. שלאחר פירעון כנ״ל אין כל העזבון כפי הנרשומים באינפוטאריום
19. מגיע לתשלום דמי שט״ח שלהם בכן יהי׳ כל מה שנמצא בעזבון כנ״ל
20. להאחים פנויים הנ״ל חצי לכ׳ לעמלי הנ״ל והחצי לכ׳ הירש הנ״ל אכן
21. מחמת מה שטעון כה״ל וכה״א הנ״ל ע״ז שאינו זוכה האחים פנוי׳
22. הנ״ל מכח שט״ח שלהם עד שעת נישואין וכ״ה ליב הנ״ל הוסיף
23. לטעון שכל מה שזכו האחים פנויים הוא משועבד לפצות
24. {הוא} אותו

1. הסוגריים במקור

קסח ע"ב

1. אותו מקויטציאהן כפי השטר שלו מצאנו שהשטר של ר"ל[1] שפיגל על האחים
2. הפנויים הוא בתוקפו וגבורתו שיפצו אותו מחלק קויטציאהן שלו כמבואר
3. שם רק מצאנו ע"ד פשר דבר שמחויב ליקבל כה"ל[2] הנ"ל בחרם בפנינו
4. ב"ד שלא הבריח ולא תפס כלום מן העזבון ושאין לו ידיעה משום הברחה
5. מאשתו ולאח"כ יונח ממעות העזבון הנ"ל השייך ליתומים סך שלשת
6. אלפים רייכשטאהליר ביד איש אמיד ובטוח יצריך[3] שיהי' אותו
7. איש אמיד ובטוח מרוצה לכ"ה ליב הנ"ל וליתומים הנ"ל והאחריות
8. משלשת אלפים רט הנ"ל יהי' על היתומים והרווחים עצ"ה שיעלה מסך
9. הנ"ל שייך ג"כ ליתומים לינתן להם בכל פעם אבל הקרן שלשת אלפים
10. רט הנ"ל יהא מונח כנ"ל ומשועבד לכ"ה ליב הנ"ל בשביל קויטציאהן שלו
11. כנ"ל וכל מה שמחויב ר' ליב לשלם עבור קויטציאהן יגבה מיד מן שלשת
12. אלפים רט הנ"ל ולאחר שיונח סך ג' אלפים רט כנ"ל יותן מה שנשאר
13. לאח"כ בעזבון הנ"ל ליתומם שיתעסקו בהם כאות נפשם בלי
14. שום מוחה ולהיות בידם לצרך נדן כמבואר בשטר שלהם ואין
15. לגיסיהם כ"ה ליב וכ"ה אנשיל על סך זה שום תביעה וחלק מחמת
16. ירושה וחח"ז שלהם בשום אופן שבעולם גם פסקנו דאם כ"ה ליב
17. הנ"ל מחויב לשלם בשביל קוטציאהן שלו עוד אלף רט נוסף על
18. שלשת אלפים רט הנ"ל כפי שהתחייב א"ע בקויטציאהן שלו
19. סך ששה אלפים זהו' יהי כל מה ששייך ליתומים הן קרקעות מטלטלין
20. כסף ושוה כסף הכל משועבד לכה[4] ליב הנ"ל ומחוייבי' היתומי'
21. לשלם גם אלף רט הנ"ל בשביל קויטציאהן כפי שהתחייבו א"ע היתומי'
22. בשטר התחייבות של הא"ר[מ][5] וכל שארי פרטות הדברים הנאמרי'
23. שם הכל יהי' מקוים בכל תוקף ועוז אכן אם לא יגיע ל[ר]"ל[6] הנ"ל
24. על

קסט ע"א

1. ב"ה
2. על חלקו לשלם שלשת אלפים רט הן מעט או הרבה פחות משלשת א<לפים>
3. רט אזי יהא מקוים כמבואר להבא שבתחילה יהא נפרע משלשת אלפים רט
4. הנ"ל המונח ביד איש אמיד כנ"ל כל מה שהי' מחויב ר"ל הנ"ל לשלם בשביל
5. חלקו ומהמותרת מצאנו שמתחילה יהא נפרע מזה כל מה שמגיע ע"ח היתומים
6. לשלם עבור קויטציאהן שלהם מחצי בית שלהם שנרשם ג"כ אצל השררה ירה

1. רב ליב
2. כבוד הרב ליב
3. צ"ל 'וצריך'
4. לכבוד הרב
5. אולי 'האב ר' מאיר'
6. לרב ליב

7. ובאם לאחר כך יש עוד מותרת ב"ג[1] אלפים רט הנ"ל יותן מזה ג"כ לאחים פנויים
8. הנ"ל כפי הסך ששילמו האחים כ"ה משה וכ"ה יעקב וכ"ה נטע הנ"ל על חלקם
9. בשביל קויטציאהן שהי' מגיע להם לשלם ג"כ מהעזבון הנ"ל רק האחים הנ"ל
10. הי' מוחלם חלקם לאחיהם הפנויים הנ"ל בכן יותן הסך הלז להאחים פנויים
11. הנ"ל להתעסק בהם ולהיות בידם לצורך נדן כמבואר בשטר שלהם ואין
12. לגיסיהם כ"ה ליב וכה"א הנ"ל על סך זה שום תביעה מחמת ירושה וחח"ז
13. שלהם בשום אופן שבעולם ואם לאחר ניכוי כל הנ"ל יהי' עוד מותר בסך
14. שלשת אלפי' רט הנ"ל אזי יונח ביד איש אמיד הנ"ל בחזקת כל היורשי'
15. הנ"ל עד זמן שיגיע להבנים פנויי' לנשואין ואז יותן לכל אחד מהם ש
16. שיגיע לנשואין החצי מסך המונח הנ"ל לנדן חלק כחלק ומחמת מה שתבעו
17. עוד כ"ה ליב וכה"א הנ"ל שיש להם זכות לבד במלבושי נשים מ
18. מאמותם ז"ל מצאנו שאין בדבריהם כלום ועל מה שתבע כ' אנשיל
19. מחמת דמי מזונת שנה אחת מצאנו שגם בזה אין בדבריו ממש
20. ומחמת מה שתובע הב"ח כ' לעמלי דמי טבעת שנמכר ששייך לו לבד שניתן
21. לו במתנה מאמו ז"ל מצאנו ע"ד פשר דבר ששייך להעזבן ובין האחי'
22. מצאנו שדמי טבעת הנ"ל שהוא ששים וששה זהו' יהי' לב"ח כ' לעמלי ארבעי'
23. וארבעה זהו' ולב"ח כ' הירש הנ"ל סך עשרים ושני' זהו' כל הנ"ל מצאנו
24. ע"פ הפשר לקיים ועשית הישר והטוב בעיני אלקים ואדם[2] ע"פ תוקף

קסט ע"ב

1. קונפערמיס שבידינו ומשיעבר ע"ז מחויב קנס סך ארבעת אלפים זהו' הנ"ל
2. המבואר בקומפרמיס מלבד שארי חומרת הנאמרים שם שקיבלו כל אחד עלי'
3. אופני' ואיכות הפרעון של קויטציאהן של כל האחי' אם המה מחויבם לשלם
4. בשביל משפט אביהם ז"ל הן ע"פ פס"ד מן הויך ליבליכה רייכש
5. גריכט מן וועצליר והן שמפשרי' עם הצדדי' שכנגדם יהי' על
6. אופן הזה שכל מה שנתפרע מהאחים כנ"ל מחויב כל או"א לשלם לפי שהתחייבו
7. כל או"א בקויטציאהן שלו על חלק ביתם של כל או"א אצל השררה ירה וגם האחים (פנויי' מחויבי' לשלם לזה לפי ערך שהשתעבד אביהם ז["ל])[3]
8. את חצי בית ששייך להם לנדן כמבואר בפסק דין הלז
9. ומאחר שהי[4] לאביהם ז"ל כתב יד התחייבות אורגינאהל מאדון שוויצר
10. מחמת המשפט הנ"ל וכעת הוא ביד האחי' כה"י וכהר"ן הנ"ל בכן
11. כל מה שיגבו וישולם להאחים הנ"ל מן האדון שווייצר יחזור ויחולק בין
12. האחים הנ"ל לפי ערך ששילם כל אוא[5] בשביל קוטציאהן שלו

---

1. בסך ג'
2. ר' דברים ו, יח
3. תוספת מתחת השורה
4. צ"ל 'שהיה'
5. אחד ואחד

13. יצא מאתונו[1] יו׳ א׳ ד״ג שבט תקמ״ד
14. הרב דקהלתנו מהורר[2] פנחס הלוי איש הורוויץ
15. והדיין מהורר נתן מאַז
16. והדיין ר׳ מאיר שיף
17. ואני
18. והיורשי׳ הנ״ל קיימו הפס״ד הנ״ל והאחי׳ הנ״ל נשבעי׳ וכה[3] ליב שפיגל קיבל בחרם כנ״ל

No. 177

Fols. 170a–b; perhaps 23 February 1784

In 1767 Herz Stiebel and his wife Bila made a formal agreement that if they remained married for three years and then Herz predeceased Bila, she would receive a lump sum payment of 2850 guldens from his estate plus half a seat in the synagogue that she had brought into the marriage. In addition, if they owned a house at the time of his death, Bila would have the right to live in the house for the balance of her widowhood. Herz died in the fall of 1783, predeceasing Bila. Through her representative, Bila approached the court to receive what was her due. Bila was required to present the court with an inventory of the assets that Herz had left and to swear that she had not taken anything from Herz's estate. Since the court was informed that the estate had insufficient assets to pay Bila the lump sum, it awarded her the entire estate, including half a house on the back of the Strauss lot she and Herz had purchased during their marriage. However, the court stipulated that Bila had to pay her maid back wages.

קעין ע״א

1. ב״ה
2. ע״ד שבא לפנינו ה״ה התורני כ״ה משה אויך יצו בהרשאות האשה מ׳ בילה אל׳
3. המנוח כ׳ הירץ שטיבל ז״ל והציע לפנינו שטר תנאים אחרונים ההוקם בין
4. האשה מ׳ בילה הנ״ל ובין בעלה כ׳ הירץ ז״ל הנ״ל ביו׳ ד׳ י״ב מרחשון תקך״ח
5. לפק ושם נאמר וז״ל ובשנה שלישת אחר החופה ומשם ואילך עד עולם
6. באם יעדר הוא ח״ו תקחי היא מחמת כתובה ותוספת משלם בין הכל יחד
7. סך עשרים ושמונה מאות וחמשים זהו׳ במעות מזומנים והחצי מקו׳ שהכניסה
8. לו וכו׳ גם באם יהי׳ לו בית לאותו זמן תהי׳ לה באותו בית מיגר אלמנותה

---

1. ר״ל ׳מאתנו׳
2. מורנו הגדול ורבנו רבי
3. וכבוד הרב

9. לפ"כ משך זמן ימי אלמנותה עכ"ל / וטען וביקש כהר"ם[1] הנ"ל בהרשאת
10. הנ"ל מאחר שבעלה כ' הירץ נפטר ושח"ל וכבר נשבעת האשה מ' בילה
11. הנ"ל ביו' [2] לפני הגאון אב"ד נר"ו כנהוג שבועת כתובה ותוס'
12. שאין לה בידה שום דבר יותר מהעזבון בעלה רק כפי הרשימה שהניח
13. לפנינו ממטלטלי' שהניח בעלה ז"ל הנ"ל והיינו כלי תשמישי' כסף ושוה כסף
14. בדיל נחושת ועופרת ווייששיג בעטונג גם הניח בעלה ז"ל אחריו חצי
15. בית פנימה צור הינטר שטרויס שקנה אחר חתנותו והחצי מקו' בע"א
16. שעומד עליו כעת הו"ה כ' אנשיל בן הו"ה כ' משה פלערשהיי' יצו שהכניסה
17. האשה הנ"ל לבעלה ז"ל הנ"ל לנדן כנ"ל ובאשר שכל העזבון מה שהניח
18. אחריו בעלה ז"ל הנ"ל אינו מגיע לתשלום דמי כתובתה ותוס' סך עשרים
19. ושמונה מאות וחמשי' זהו' הנ"ל חוץ ממה שצריכה לשלם עוד שכירות ל
20. למשרתת מכמה שנים לזאת נפשו בשלתו[3] מאתנו ב"ד ח"מ להחליט את כל
21. עזבון המנוח כ' הירץ ז"ל הנ"ל הן קרקעות והן מטלטלין הנ"ל לאל'
22. מ' בילה הנ"ל ולאחר שנזדקקנו לכך ומצאנו שדברי כהר"ם הנ"ל כני'
23. ואמיתי' שאינו מגיע כל עזבון המנוח כ' הירץ ז"ל הנ"ל לפירעון כתובה
24. ותוספ' של אלמנתו מ' בילה הנ"ל וכנ"ל בכן החלטנו לחלוטין גמורין
25. ולצמיתת עלמין את כל מה שהניח אחריו המנוח כ' הירץ שטיבל

קע ע"ב

1. בעז"ה
2. ז"ל הנ"ל הן חצי בית וחצי מקו' הנ"ל והן מטלטלין כפי הרשימה הנ"ל
3. להאל' מ' בילה הנ"ל וי"א וב"כ לפירעון כתובתה ותוס' ומעתה
4. יהי' כל העזבון מה שהניח אחריו המנוח כ' הירץ ז"ל הנ"ל
5. הן החצי בית פנימי צור הינטר שטרויז והן חצי מקו' בע"א הנ"ל
6. שעומד עליה כעת הו"ה כ' אנשיל ב"כ משה פלערשהיי' הנ"ל וכל
7. המטלטלין מה שהניח כ' הירץ ז"ל הנ"ל בעזבונו כפי הרשימה
8. הנ"ל לה"א מ' בילה הנ"ל וי"א וב"כ לעשות בכל עזבון בעלה
9. ז"ל הנ"ל כאות נפשה ורצונה ככל אינש דרשאי לעשות בשלו
10. בלי שום מוחה ועירעור שבעולם הן מיורשי בעלה וב"כ והן
11. משאר אדם יהי' מי שיהי' רק שתשלם למשרתת הנ"ל וכתבנו
12. וחתמנו כל הנ"ל בתוקף מעשה ב"ד ובכח ב"ד יפה להיות
13. ביד ה"א מ' בילה הנ"ל וי"א וב"כ לעדות ולזכות ול[רא]י'
14. שיהי' כל עזבון המנוח כ' הירץ ז"ל הנ"ל להאל' מ' בילה
15. הנ"ל וי"א וב"כ בלי שום מוחה כלל נעשה יו' ב' דר"ח שבט
16. תקמ"ד[4]

---

1. כבוד הרב משה
2. ריוח בין המילה הזו למילה 'לפני'; כנראה לא השלים.
3. צ"ל 'בשאלתו'
4. ראש חודש שבט הוא תמיד יום אחד (ובאותה השנה הוא נפל בשבת). אולי הכוונה ליום ב' דר"ח אדר שנפל

17. הגאון אב״ד נרו[1] והדיין מהורר[2] נתן מז ור׳ מאיר שיף ואני

No. 178

Sinzheim v. Scheyer

Fols. 171a–172b; Thursday 18 March 1784

Gele, widow of Moses Scheyer, enjoyed the right to live in half of a house that had belonged to her late husband for the duration of her widowhood.[3] Gele and Moses each had children from previous marriages and Gele chose not to exercise her right to live in Moses' home but rather to live with her son, Isaac Sinzheim. Beginning in 1778, Gele rented out the half of Moses' house that she was entitled to live in to Moses' son, Anshel. Anshel paid relatively high rent to Gele, 125 guldens per year, but he already lived in the other half of the house and at the time he needed the extra space for his family. Moreover, the rent included repairs and taxes which Anshel deducted from what he paid Gele. Through their representative, Gele and Isaac asked the court whether Gele was indeed responsible for taxes and repairs and, if not, asked that Anshel be ordered to refund to Gele the amount he had deducted all these years. Anshel's representative countered that Anshel had only agreed to pay such high rent because it included repairs and taxes. He countercharged that he had divided the house into two so Gele could live there and that she should be made to reimburse him for these costs. Anshel also announced that he no longer needed the extra space, and that from now on he would only agree to pay 50 guldens per annum. This prompted a request from Gele and Isaac's representative for a court ruling on whether Gele had the right to rent the space out to others. If the court ruled that she could not rent her half of the house to others, Gele asked that the court hold a lottery to determine who had the right to live in which section of the house when. She noted that her intention was to leave her section of the house empty if she could not rent it out.

The court ruled that Gele could not rent the house to anyone other than Anshel, nor could she leave it vacant. She could, of course, live in it herself and, if she decided to do so, there would be a lottery. If the space was rented to Anshel, he was

---

ביום ב׳ באותה השנה.

1. נטריה רחמנא ופרקיה
2. מורנו הגדול ורבנו רבי
3. Moses Scheyer died in 1775 (see Horovitz, no. 3530).

ordered to pay 90 guldens per year beginning with the next year of the contract. The court also ruled that Anshel was not liable for the earlier tax payments, but that in the future he would be. As for Gele's liability for repairs that Anshel had made in converting the house into a two family dwelling, the court ruled that the issue would only be decided if Gele returned to live in the house.

A further dispute within the family was whether an unmarried daughter of Moses Scheyer should be obliged to contribute to Gele's current and back tax payments to the authorities on her behalf. The heirs of the estate maintained that the division of taxation payments had been settled among them some time ago, and that the daughter owed Gele nothing. This view was sustained by the court.

קעא ע"א

בע"ה

הן הקריב לפנינו הו"ה התורני כהררי[1] מאיר מאז בהרשאת הו"ה ג"ץ כהרר איצק זינצהיים סג"ל ובהרשאת האל' הקצינה מרת געלה אל' המנוח ג"ה וג"ץ כ"ה משה שייאר סג"ל ז"ל וביקש מאתנו שיכירו הב"ד על אודת האל' מ' געלה הנ"ל שיש לה מיגר אלמנותה בחצי בית שהי' דר בו כהרר משה ז"ל הנ"ל רק באשר שהיא אצל בנו[2] כ"ה איצק זינצהיים הנ"ל השכירה החצי בית הנ"ל להו"ה ג"ץ כ"ה אנשיל שייאר סג"ל בעד סך מאה ועשרים וחמשה זהו' לשנה והתחיל השכירות מחדש טבת תקלח עד עתה וכ"ה אנשיל הנ"ל שילם לה כל שנה השכירות רק ה[ו]א מנכה לה כל שנה סך ידוע בעד דמי בדק הבית ודמי קרונדצונץ לזאת יכירו הב"ד אם האל' הנ"ל מחויבת לשלם דמי תיקון בדק הבית וקורנדצונז מחצי בית ובאם היא אינ['] מחויבת לשלם תבע כ"ה מאיר הנ"ל בהרשאת הנ"ל מן כ"ה אנשיל הנ"ל מן העבר שיחזר לה מה שנכה בשביל זה וגם להבא שלא לנכות עוד / והו"ה כ"ה משה אויך בהרשאת הו"ה ג"ץ כ"ה אנשיל שייאר סג"ל הנ"ל השיב שמתחילה אחר מיתת אביו כהרר משה ז"ל הנ"ל הי' בני ביתו מרובים והי' צריך לכל הבית שלם הנ"ל הי' מתרצה ליתן שכירות להאל' הנ"ל סך קכ"ה זהו' לשנה ועתה שאינו צריך לבית שלם הנ"ל אינו רוצה ליתן לה שכירת רק חמשים רט לשנה ובאם לא תדור היא בעצמה בחצי בית והי[י]נו היא לבדה זולת בנה כ"ה איצק הנ"ל וגם אין לה רשות להשכירה לאחרי[ם] ומחמת דמי בדק הבית וקרונדצונץ השיב שמחמת זה ששילמה חלקה הי' נותן לה כל כך שכירות וזולת זה לא הי' נותן לה כל כך ולהבא שאינו רוצה לשלם לה שכירות רק חמישים רט יכירו הב"ד אם היא אינה מחויבת לשלם חלקה בבדק הבית וקרונדצונץ

1. כבוד הרב רבי
2. צ"ל 'בנה' (וכן נמצא בשורה 20 בדף הזה)

25. עוד השיב כ"ה משה הנ"ל שהבית שלם הנ"ל לא הי' מתוקן
26. לשני דירות והיא האל' לא זכתה רק בחצי הנ"ל ו[כ"ה] אנשיל הנ"ל

קעא ע"ב

1. בע"ה
2. הנ"ל תיקון אותו בכמה תיקונים על הוצאותו שלו בכן תבע מן האל' דמי
3. תיקון הנ"ל / וכ"ה מאיר הנ"ל השיב שעכ"פ התחיל השכירות משנה הלז
4. מחדש טבת העבר בכן נשאר השכירות משנה זו לסך הקצב בינ[י]הם
5. כנ"ל עד חדש (טבת)[1] תקמה הבע"ל ומשם והלאה יכירו הב"ד אם אין רשות
6. להאל' הנ"ל להשכירה לאחירם[2] החצי בית המגיע לה במיגר
7. אלמנותה ובאם לא תזכה בזה עכ"פ יחולק הבית הנ"ל לשני
8. דירות ויטילו גורל בינהם על הדירת והדירת שמגיע על חלק האל'
9. רוצה להסגירה שלא ידור אחר בתוכה והאריכו בדבריהם
10. הצדדים הנ"ל (ולאחר שחתמו בתוקף בחח[3] ובקנס מסוים נזדקנו להם אחר)[4] שנתנו עיניהם על הב"ד לפשר ביניהם מצאנו
11. ע"ד הפשר דבר שעל מה שתבע כ"ה איצק הנ"ל בשביל אמו
12. האל' הנ"ל מן כ"ה אנשיל הנ"ל שיחזר לה דמי בדק הבית
13. וקרונדצנז שניכה כ"ה אנשיל הנ"ל בתשלומין שכירות חצי
14. הבית הנ"ל מצאנו שפטור כ"ה אנשיל הנ"ל מתביעה זו על עבר
15. אכן להבא כל זמן שאינה דרה האל' בעצמה בחצי בית הנ"ל
16. היא פטורה מלשלם כלום מחמת דמי בדק הבית וקרונדצונז
17. וכן פטורה האל' מה שתבא[5] כה"א[6] מחמת תיקון הבית כנ"ל
18. אמנם אם היא חוזרת ורוצה לדור בעצמה בתוך חצי בית
19. הנ"ל יקוב הדין ההר ביניהם מחמת דמי בדק הבית אבל
20. גרונדצונז לעולם היא פטורה ומחמת דמי שכירות חצי בית
21. מצאנו ע"ד פשר דבר שעל שכירת דהא שתא תקמ"ד לפק
22. עד חודש טבת תקמ"ה הבע"ל שכבר נכנס שנת השכירות

קעב ע"א

1. בעז"ה
2. מחויב כ"ה אנשיל הנ"ל לשלם דמי שכירות הקצוב ביניהם סך
3. מאה ועשרים וחמשה זהו' בלי נכוי שוה פרוטה אכן מחודש טבת
4. שנת תקמ"ה הבע"ל ואילך ישלם כ"ה אנשיל סך תשעים זהו' לשנה
5. עבור שכירות הבית ואין להאל' הנ"ל רשות להשכיר חצי בית

---

1. תוספת מעל השורה
2. צ"ל 'לאחרים'
3. בחרם חמור
4. תוספת מעל השורה
5. צ"ל 'שתבע'
6. כבוד הרב אנשיל

6. לאחירם[1] גם אין לה רשות לומר שתשאר חצי בית פנוי בלי דירות
7. שום אדם אלא יהי' מושכר לכ"ה אנשיל הנ"ל בעד דמי שכירות
8. תשעים זהו' לכל שנה כל ימי חיי' והיינו דוקא כל זמן שאינה רוצה
9. לדור היא בעצמה בתוכה אבל אם חוזרת ומתרצה לדור ב
10. בעצמה לתוכה אזי יחולק הבית לשני דיור[ים] ויטילו גורל על ה
11. הדירות ביניהם אכן אם היא התרצה לדור בעצמה בחצי
12. בית הנ"ל מחוייבת היא להודיע לכ"ה אנשיל הנ"ל עכ"פ רביעת
13. שנה קודם חדש טבת שהוא התחלת זמן השכירות של כל שנה
14. ושנה ובאם אינה מודיעה לו רביעת שנה קודם ר"ח טבת אזי
15. נשאר עכ"פ השכירות על אותו שנה מחדש טבת לכ"ה אנשיל
16. בעד סך תשעים זהו' דמי שכירות ושוב אין לה רשות על אותו
17. שנה לומר שתדור היא בעצמה לתוכה כ"ה[2] יהי' בכל שנה ושנה
18. על כל ימי חיי' שמחויבת (ה"א)[3] הנ"ל להודיע לו רביעת שנה מקודם כנ"ל
19. עוד התעצמו לפנינו לדין ותבע כ"ה מאיר הנ"ל בהרשאת הנ"ל
20. מן היורשים של כ"ה משה ז"ל הנ"ל מחמת בת הפנוי' של מ'[4]
21. ברענדלי בת המנוח כ"ה משה ז"ל הנ"ל שגם היא מחוייבת
22. לסייעו בתשלומין דמי שאצונג (#)[5] על שמה לאחר מיתת בעלה וע"י
23. פטורה הבת מליתן כלום ובלא"ה הי' הבת ג"כ מחוייבת
24. #ששילמה ה"א הנ"ל להשררה ירה[6] דיא פאלי שאצונג {מחויבת לסייע
25. בתשלומין לשלם} שהעמ[ידו] היורשם פנקס של [שאצונג]

קעב ע"ב

1. בע"ה
2. לשלם להשררה יר"ה בכן מחויבת הבת ג"כ לסייע לשלם מה
3. שמגיע על חלקה ותובע ג"כ מן העבר ליתן חלקה לערך במה ש
4. ששילמה כבר העבר / וה"ה כ"ה משה אויך השיב בהרשאות
5. כל היורשים שלאחר שסילקה היורשים האל' הנ"ל מן העזבון
6. הסכימו כלם יחד גם ר' איצק זינצהיים שהי' עומד בכח והרשאה
7. אמה[7] הנ"ל להעמיד פנקס שאצונג על אמה האל' הנ"ל בכן שוב
8. אינה מחויב לסייעה לה בפירעון שאצונג ואם האל' רוצה
9. לפחות ערכה אזי יראה הם אצל השררה יר"ה כדת מה לעשות
10. אם המה מחויבים לשלם בשביל ברענדלי הנ"ל באשר שלפי ד

---

1. צ"ל 'לאחרים'
2. לא ברור למה יש גרשיים כאן
3. תוספת מעל השורה
4. מרת
5. תוספת מעל השורה ויש לקרא את שורות 24-25 כאן.
6. ירום הודו
7. ר"ל אמה של ברענדלי בת משה

11. דעת[ו] אינה מחויבת לשלם אחר שהגיע לה רק הפירות מסך שהניח
12. אביהם וחמיו ז"ל והקרן שייך לכל היורשים והאריכו ב[ט]ענותיהם
13. ולאחר שחתמו עצמם הצדדים הנ"ל בתוקף קומפורמיס
14. לקיים את אשר יצא מאתנו נזדקקנו גם לזה ומצאנו שאין
15. להאל' מ' געלה הנ"ל שום תביעה על היורשים הנ"ל בשביל בת
16. פנוי' הנ"ל מחמת תשלומין שאצונג להשררה יר"ה הן מן העבר
17. והן מלהבא יצא מאתנו אור ליו' ויו דו אדר תקמ"ד
18. רנ"מ ורמ"ש ואני

No. 179

Fulda v. Yatcha, wife of Abraham Fulda

Fols. 173a–b; Monday 31 May or Tuesday 1 June 1784

Following an earlier court decision (see no. 156), Abraham Fulda and his wife, Yatcha, mutually agreed to divorce.[1] They came to the court asking that it rule on financial matters related to the divorce. Each had claims and counterclaims about who owed whom what. The court responded to their request and offered a division of assets. Yatcha was also required to participate in the costs associated with preparing the bill of divorce. The parties were ordered to deliver what they owed each other to a third party within thirty days. Any delay would lead to financial loss through fines or forfeit of assets.

קעג ע"א

1. ב"ה
2. אחרי שכבר יצא מאתנו פס"ד תקמ"ג העבר[2] על אודת דברים שבין
3. איש לאשה ה"ה כ' אברהם בהמנוח[3] כ"ה אהרן פולדא ז"ל ואשתו מ'
4. יטכה בת המנוח כ"ה פייבלמן עמדין ז"ל שוב חזרו הצדדים הנ"ל
5. וחתמו עצמם בתוקף קומפרמיס בח"ח ובקנס סך מסויים והתרצו בתוקף
6. הלז לעשות פירוד ביניהם בגט פטורין אכן מחמת תביעות ממון שביניה'
7. הן מחמת פירעון כתובה ותוספ' והן שארי טענות ותביעות נתנו עיניהם
8. עלינו ב"ד לפשר ביניהם לזאת התעצמו הצדדים שוב לפנינו ה"ה
9. התורני כ"ה משה אויך בהרשאת כ' אברהם ותבע מן האשה מ' יטכה
10. הנ"ל באריכת הן מעות בעין שיש בידה מן בעלה והן ממטלטלי' ומתנות

---

1. The divorce took place before 15 September 1784 (see JTS MS. 3672, fol. 120b).
2. כאן מס' 156
3. בן המנוח

11. שיש בידה והן מעות שכירות הבית שגבת והחזיקה לעצמה / והאשה הנ״ל
12. הכחישו על כמה דברים והודי׳ על כמה תביעותיו וגם היא תבע מן בעלה
13. כתובה ותוספ׳ והודית שהי׳ לא נתנה יותר לנדן רק סך שני מאות ושבעם (וחמשה)[1]
14. זהו׳ במזומנים ועוד ח״כ מן ר׳ גבריאל האכעמס מסך שבעה עשר רט וחלק
15. שישית מן בית פנוי לחלוטין עוד תבעה הוצאת ודמי מזונות וכ״ה משה
16. הנ״ל השיב שאינו מגיע לה תוספ׳ באשר שמיד לאחר החתונה לא היתה
17. מתנהגות עמו כראוי והיא הכחישה אותו והאריכו בטענותיהם כמבואר
18. באריכות בקה[2] המנוח לפנינו ובאשר שחתמו עצמם בקומפרמיס כנ״ל
19. נזדקקנו להם ומצאנו ע״פ פשר דבר[3] {(שלאחר שתקבל האשה מ׳ יטכה}
20. הנ״ל גט פטורין מבעלה כפי שהתרצו שניהם)[4] ומחויב כ׳ אברהם
21. הנ״ל לחזור לה הנדן שקבל ממנה והיינו סך שני מאות ושבעים וחמשה
22. זהו׳ רק ינוכה מזה מה שגבת קודם פסח סך עשרים וחמשה זהו׳
23. אבל מחמת תוספת אין עליו לשלם כלום גם יחזר לה ח״כ הנ״ל מסך
24. שבעה עשר רטי׳[5] מן ר׳ גבריאל הנ״ל והחלק שישית בית פנימי
25. שהכניסה מחויב הבעל להחזיר לה מנוקה ומשופה מכל ערעור וכמו
26. שהכניסה לו גם הזכיות ושטרות שיש תחת ידו הנוגע לשישת בית הלז
27. מחויב להחזיר לה ומחמת איין ווארף מצאנו שכלי כסף מן איין ווארף שנתנו
28. קרובים הבעל והם תי׳[6] הבעל יחזיק הוא לבד ואינה מגיע לה
29. כלום מזה והמעות שקיבלה היא מכח איינווארף תחזיק לעצמה

קעג ע״ב

1. ואין לבעל שום תביעה ע״ז ומתנות שנתן כ׳ אברהם הנ״ל להאשה מ׳
2. יטכה הנ״ל והיינו זהו׳ קעט וכסף ביקסכה מחויבת האשה הנ״ל
3. להחזר אבל המלבושי שעשת לה משל בעלה כאהנ״ל[7] והיינו א׳
4. זייטנה שורץ זייטה שני פטוך שני מיט שכר תחזיק לעצמה גם
5. המלבוש שעשתה מן יוד אמות צנטץ תחזיק לעצמה אך בשביל
6. זה ינוכה מסך דמי נדן הנ״ל חמשה זהו׳ גם ינוכה סך שמונה
7. עשר זהו׳ מחמת מה שהודית שגבתה שכירות הבית מאחים כ׳
8. זימלה מחדר אחד על שנה לשלשה רביעת וגם מה שגבתה מן המלמד
9. כ״ה יעקל טריר מן אופיבאך שעולה לערך שמונה עשר זהו׳ הנ״ל
10. גם מחויבת האשה מ׳ יטכה הנ״ל להחזיר לבעלה כאהנ״ל כל
11. כלי בית ומעבל שיש תחת ידה שהודית לפנינו וכפי רשימה

1. תוספת מעל השורה
2. בקונטרס הטענות
3. בסוף דף קעב ע״ב כתוב, ׳שכ׳ אברהם מחויב לגרש אשתו והיא תקבל הגט כפי שהתרצו שניהם׳ ויש הפניה להעבירו לכאן.
4. סוגריים במקור
5. כנראה ׳רייכשטאלרים׳
6. תחת יד(?)
7. כבוד אברהם הנזכר לעיל

12. המחותם ע"י שמש דב"ד גם מחויבת האשה לשלם סך עשרה
13. רט לסיועת הוצאות הגט (#)[1] ומחמת נת[י]נות עילום להאלופים גובים
14. יצו {מה שמוטל} מצאנו שעד נתינת הגט החיוב מוטל על כ'
15. אברהם הנ"ל לשלם לבד ומנתינות הגט והלאה מחויב כל
16. אחד מהם לשלם להאלופים גובים יצו מה שמוטל עליו לפי ערכו
17. זולת כל הנ"ל פטורים ומסולקים זה מזו וזו מזה מכל טו"ת
18. שבעולם יצא מאתנו יו' ב[2] יב סיון תקמ"ד
19. הגאב"ד (נר"ו)[3] רנ"מ ורמ"ש ואני (#)[4] ומחויב כ אברהם הנ"ל תוך שלשי' יו' מהיו' שיגיע
20. לו פס"ד הלז לידו להשליש בתחלה סך דמי נדן הנ"ל מה שעולה לאחר נכונות
21. הנ"ל ליד גבאי הקהל יצו ותכף אח"כ מחויבת האשה מ' יטכה ג"כ להשליש הזהוב קעט וכסף
22. ביקסכה הנ"ל ביד שליש הנ"ל ובאם תעכב היא מהשליש את החפצי' הנ"ל אזי יוחזר לבעלה
23. ממה שהניח כפי דמי שווי' של החפצי' הנ"ל ובאם יעכב כ' אברהם הנ"ל בכלות שלשים יו' ל
24. לקיים פס"ד הלז ולהשליש דמי נדן הנ"ל וכנ"ל אזי מחויב כ' אברהם לשלם להאשה הנ"ל כל שבוע
25. ושבוע בעד דמי מזונות ודירה סך שלשה זהו'

No. 180

Cerla, widow of Anshel Burch v. Deuz

Fols. 174a–175a; Tuesday 1 June 1784

Cerla, widow of Anshel Burch, arranged for the marriage of her daughter to Süssel Deuz, her brother. Although the two sides agreed to the match in the fall of 1782 and signed an agreement with respect to financial matters, disagreements between Cerla and Süssel lead the two sides to turn to the court. The claims of each side are not recorded here, but the record relates that the court spoke to both sides in the hope of achieving a compromise. This was deemed of special importance given the Talmud's specific praise of one who marries his sister's daughter.[5] Both sides agreed to accept the court's compromise, and the details of payment of the dowry,

---

1. תוספת מעל השורה. יש להכניס את המשפטים בשורה 19 מהסולמית ועד סוף התעודה לכאן.
2. בשנה זו י"ב סיון נפל ביום ג' בשבוע ולא ביום ב'.
3. תוספת מתחת השורה
4. תוספת מעל השורה
5. B.T., *Yeb.* 62b; *San.* 76b.

gifts, housing, and support are all itemized here. Cerla had financial difficulties and the court worked out a way for her to meet her obligations and marry off her daughter. While Süssel helped his sister with her debts, he exacted a price from her for his assistance. The court ordered that if all conditions were met, the wedding should take place during the Hebrew month of Ḥeshvan (between mid-October and mid-November) in the fall of 1784. The couple married on Wednesday 27 October 1784.[1]

קעד ע״א

1. ב״ה
2. ע״ד טענות והפרשות שיש בין האשה מ׳ צערלה אל׳ המנוח כ׳ אנשיל בוריך[2]
3. ז״ל ובין אחי׳ חתנה המקושר הב״ח כ׳ זוסיל בהמנוח[3] כ״ה מרדכי דייטץ
4. ז״ל אודת קשרי התנאים מבתה הכלה עם אחי׳ זוסיל הנ״ל ההוקים
5. יו׳ גימל דא מרחשון תקמ״ג ושהצדדים הנ״ל בעצמם עם המורשאי׳
6. שלהם ה״ה התורני כ״ה בענדיט הענא בהרשאת כ׳ זוסיל הנ״ל
7. וה״ה התורני כ״ה משה אויך בהרשאת האשה מ׳ צערלה הנ״ל
8. התעצמו בטענותיהם לפנינו כמבואר באריכות בק״ה המונח
9. לפנינו ואחרי שהצדדים הנ״ל חתמו עצמם בתוקף קומפרמיס
10. בח״ח ובקנס סך מסויים חצי לשררה יר״ה וחצי להקדש לאשר ולקיים
11. כל אשר יצא מאתנו נזדקקנו להם ודברנו על לב הצדדים
12. הנ״ל לתווך השל[ום] ביניהם ולקרב ולא לרחק ובפרט שזיווג
13. עם בת אחותו ועליו הכתוב אומר[4] אז תקרא ו״ה יענא והרכינו
14. את ראשם לדברינו והתרצו עצמם הצדדים הנ״ל על אופן
15. המבואר והיינו שהאשה מ׳ צערלה הנ״ל מחויבת להכניס לנדן
16. בתה הכלה המקושרת סך שלשה מאות רט כמבואר בת״ר הנ״ל
17. ועל אופן המבואר שהי׳ מחויבת להניח ביד שליש המרוצה
18. לשניהם עד זמן חצי אלול תקמ״ד הבע״ל סך שלשה מאות זהו׳
19. במזומנים גם מחויבת להניח לזמן הנ״ל ביד השליש הנ״ל המתנות
20. שיש בידה שנתן החתן הנ״ל לכלתו שהם עשרים קווארטקרלינר[5]
21. עם כסף טוהס על זה הותנה ביניהם בפי׳ בכא״ה שאם לא
22. תניח האל׳ הנ״ל לזמן הנ״ל הסך שלשה מאות זהו׳ הנ״ל עם ה
23. המתנות הנ״ל שיוחזר ליד החתן הנ״ל שני תנאים ראשוני׳ הנ״ל
24. אשר מונחים ביד ב״ד עד זמן הנ״ל ובטל ומבוטל יהי׳ הת

---

1. JTS MS. 3672, fol. 24b.
2. נפטר בשנת תקל״ה, ר׳ ספר הזכרונות, רסז ע״ב.
3. בן המנוח
4. ישעיה נח, ט (שם כתוב ׳יענה׳) ור׳ יבמות סב ע״ב, סנהדרין עו ע״ב.
5. Viertelkarolin

25. התקשרות השידוך הנ"ל ומחויבת הכלה להחזיר מת[נות]
26. הנ"ל ועל מאה רט ה...[1]

קעד ע"ב

1. להניח ביד שליש ארבעה ח"כ לאורדר החתן כ' זוסיל הנ"ל
2. כל אחד מסך חמשה ועשרים רט לשלם על ארבעה חצאי שנים
3. רצופים זא"ז מחצי אלול הבע"ל ולבטחון יותר יתוקן ע"ז בשעת
4. החופה שט"ח מן האשה הנ"ל בכא"ה על סך מאה רט הנ"ל עם
5. שיעבד ע"ז אותו רביעת בית ששייר לעצמה שלא פסקה ליתן
6. לחתן הנ"ל באופן שאם לא תשלם אפי' אחד מן ח"כ הנ"ל
7. שהרשות יותן ביד החתן הנ"ל למכור אותו רביעת
8. בית שלו לפרוע דמי ח"כ הנ"ל ומחמת מה שפסקה
9. האל' הנ"ל בת"ר הנ"ל להכניס לנדן בתה רביעת
10. פנימי צור ווייסר גאנז בשיור יד העליונה באשר
11. שנמצא כעת שהאל' הנ"ל עשה ק"ס על חצי בית הנ"ל
12. להאלופי' גובים יצו מחמת חוב מסך ארבעה מאות
13. זהו' עם רווחים ה' למאה לשנה וגם התחייבה א"ע
14. האל' בת"ר הנ"ל ליתן דירה להזוג הנ"ל ברביעת בית
15. הנ"ל על כל ימי חייו לזאת התרצו א"ע האשה הנ"ל להכניס
16. בשעת החופה לנדן בתה רביעת בית הנ"ל לחלוטין
17. במקום נתינת דירה הנ"ל נגד זה מחויב לקבל עליו החתן כ'
18. זוסיל הנ"ל לשלם סך מאה זהו' עם רווחים להאלופי' גובי' יצו
19. מהחוב סך ארבעה מאות זהו' המחויבת אחותו מ' צערלה הנ"ל
20. לשלם לגובים כנ"ל ולפצות אותו מסך מאה זהו' הנ"ל מחויבת
21. האשה מ' צערלה הנ"ל ליתן שט"ח ושיעבוד לחתנה הנ"ל מסך
22. {שלשה} מאה זהו' על רביעת בית אחרת הנ"ל ששיירה לעצמה
23. גם הותנה ביניהם כדי שלא להרבות החוב שלה אצל הגובי'

קעה ע"א

1. ב"ה
2. הגובי' מכח עיכוב פירעון רווחי' שמוטל עליו לשלם מסך שלשה מאות
3. זהו' הנשאר עליו לשלם כל שנה סך חמשה עשר זהו' לזאת התרצה
4. האל' הנ"ל וקיבלה על עצמה שבכלות שתי שנים רצופי' ומחצה שעבר
5. זמן השכירות מן רביעת בית שלה שהשכירה לאחרי' שהיא רוצה לשלם
6. כל שנה מן שכירות דלהבא כל שנה סך חמשה עשר זהו' לגובי' יצו רווחי'
7. הנ"ל ובאם תעכב בזה שיהא רשות ביד חתנה להשכיר רביעת ביתה
8. ולשלם לגובי' הרווחי' מידי שנה בשנה נגד זה קיבל על עצמו החתן כ'
9. זוסיל הנ"ל לשלם חלק רווחי' המוטל עליו להאלופי' גובי' יצו מידי שנה בשנה

---

1. סוף השורה חסרה

10. סך חמשה זהו' ובאשר שכפי המבואר שהאשה תכניס לנדן בשעת החופה
11. רביעת בית לחלוטין גמורי' לנדן בתה הנ"ל התרצה אע'[1] האשה הנ"ל להכריז
12. בבה"כ כנהוג חלטה על רביעת לנדן כדי להשקיטו מכל עירעור וטוען משאר
13. יחידי' אבל מה שנוגע מחמת האלופי' גובי' יצו ע"ז בענין החלטה מחמת
14. חוב הנ"ל אינה מקבל (עליו)[2] כלום ועוד התרצה עצמה האל' הנ"ל באשר ש
15. שהשכירה כבר מרביעת בית שתכניס לנדן שטוב אחד לאחרי' עד
16. ר"ח סיון תקמ"ה הבעל[3] ואינו פנוי רק חדר אחד ד שטעג הויך שאינו
17. ראוי לדירה לחתנה הנ"ל בכן מחויבת האשה הנ"ל לשכור לחתנה
18. מיו' חתנותו עד ר"ח סיון תקמ"ה עוד חדר בית (חורף)[4] אחרת בבית אחרת כדי
19. שיכול לדור בתוכה עד ר"ח סיון שכלה השכירות ומשם והלאה
20. יחזיק הוא ברביעת בית הנ"ל במקום זכיות דירה וכנ"ל ומחמת
21. מזונת שתי שני' על שלחנו[5] שפסקה האל' הנ"ל בתנאי' ראשוני'
22. הנ"ל והחתן הנ"ל אמר שאינו יכול לסבול ולילך בדירה שדרה
23. האל' הנ"ל כעת לזאת התרצה א"ע האל' הנ"ל לשלוח מזונת
24. להזוג בדירה שידור חתנה הנ"ל בתוכה לאחר החתנה והחתונה
25. תהי' למז"ט בחדש מרחשון שנת תקמ"ה הבעל[6] כל הנ"ל התרצו עצמם
26. הצדדי' הנ"ל בפנינו וכדי שקוים ויאושר כל הנ"ל ובל יפול שום דבר
27. ארצה באנו אנחנו ב"ד ח"מ ליתן תוקף מעשה ב"ד בכח בד[7] יפה
28. על כל הנ"ל יצא מאתנו יו' ג' יב סיון תקמ"ד
29. רנ"מ ורמ"ש ואני

Fol. 175b is blank.

No. 181

Fols. 176a–b; Wednesday 4 August 1784

Through her representative, Hendle Stiebel asked the court to discharge her

1. את עצמה
2. תוספת מעל השורה
3. הבא עלינו לטובה
4. תוספת מעל השורה
5. צ"ל 'שלחנה'
6. הבא עלינו לטובה
7. בית דין

from the estate of her late husband, Mordecai, who had died the previous year.[1] Hendle asked to be paid the amount stipulated in her marriage contract, as well as an additional sum that had been agreed to (totaling 1200 reichstalers), living expenses, and housing, all of which had been promised to her by Mordecai. She also requested possession of a certain gift that had been received during the course of the marriage. Moredcai's movable possessions were sold by the community, but they did not come close to meeting the amount promised to Hendle, and there was therefore a need to sell the real estate assets too. Before doing so, the court had to clarify whether Mordecai had sole possession of these assets or whether his brothers' heirs (his brothers themselves were deceased; Mordecai had no children) also had a share in them. This was complicated by the fact that not all of the brothers' children lived in Frankfurt and the court did not know their whereabouts. Even among those who did live in Frankfurt, not all agreed to come and cooperate with the court in dealing with Hendle's claims.

קעו ע״א

1. ב״ה
2. ע״ד שבא לפנינו ה״ה התורני כ״ה אנשיל פפאן כץ בהרשאת האשה מ׳ הענדלה
3. אל׳ המנוח כ׳ מרדכי בן הירש שטיבל ז״ל וביקש מאתנו לסלק האל׳ הנ״ל מע(ז)[2]בון
4. בעלה הנ״ל מכל תביעתה המבוארים להבא והציע לפנינו שטר כתובה ותוספ׳
5. ות״א ההוקם ביום החופה י״ב מרחשון תקך״ד שמבואר בתוכה שאם יעדר
6. בעלה הנ״ל בשנה השלישת אחר החופה ומשם ואילך שתקחי היא לפירעון
7. כתובה ותוספ׳ סך שנים עשר מאות רייכשטאהליר במזומני׳ ועתה שנעדר בעלה
8. הנ״ל תבע כ״ה אנשיל הנ״ל בהרשאת האל׳ הנ״ל סך הנ״ל אחרי שכבר נשבעת׳
9. האל׳ שבועת כתובה / עוד תבע מיגר אל׳ שנזכר בת״א ושטר כתובה ותוספ׳
10. הנ״ל ועוד תבעה אותן איין ווארף שנתנה בני משפחתה ועוד תבעה דמי מ
11. מזונת הן מקודם העדרת בעלה והן לאח״כ וטוען כ״ה אנשיל שיש מקו׳ לגבות
12. מן רביעת בית פנימי צור הינטר גרינ[י] טיהר ומקו׳ שלם בע״נ העליונה
13. שעומדת עלי׳ כעת האשה מ׳ הענדלה הנ״ל שהכניס בעלה לנדן שלה
14. כמבואר בת״א שהציע לפנינו והנה אחרי שקיבלה האל׳ הנ״ל על עצמה ל
15. לאשר ולקיים הפשר מה שיצא מאתנו ב״ד ח״מ נזדקקנו לטענותיה׳ ומצאנו
16. ע״ד פשר דבר שתקחי האל׳ הנ״ל מעזבון בעלה הנ״ל סך שנים עשר מאות
17. רט לפירעון כתובה ותוספ׳ כנ״ל ומחמת שארי תביעות שלה הנ״ל מצאנו שאין
18. בידה כח להוציא כלום מעזבון בעלה ובאשר שלא נמצא כעת בעזבון
19. בעלה בכסף ושוה כסף כי אם מ(ה)[3] שיש תחת ידה אל׳ הנ״ל כפי שהודית
20. אן בעטונג נעסל טוך וטבעת׳ וכסף טוהס השווי׳ לערך עם עשרה זהו׳

---

1. See Horovitz, no. 3808.
2. תוספת מעל השורה
3. תוספת מעל השורה

21. שוויתרה קודם שבועת' עולה יחד סך שישים זהו' וגם מדמי מכירת
22. שאר מטלטלים שהניח בעלה הנ"ל ונמכר ע"י נאמני' הקהלה נשאר אחרי
23. הרבה הוצאות סך עשרה זהו' חמשה וחמשים צל עולה יחד עם מה
24. שבידה כנ"ל לערך סך שבעי' זהו' נ"ה צל וזה יהי' להאל' הנ"ל לפירעון
25. כתובה ותוס' סך שנים עשר מאות רט הנ"ל כנ"ל ולאחר שקיבלה סך שבעי'
26. זהו' נ"ה צל מגיע לה עוד מעזבון בעלה סך אחד עשר מאות וחמיש' ושניי'
27. רט דד צלי[1] ולזה משועבד כל הקרקעות שהניח בעל[ה] ...[2]

קעו ע"ב

1. שבעלה הנ"ל לא הניח בני' ולא אחים רק בני אחים מהם שישנו פה בקהלותנו
2. יע"א ואיני' רוצים ליחד ולדון עמה לפנינו ומהם הרחיקו נדוד ואין אנו
3. יודעי' היכן הם לזאת הי' מוטל עלינו לחקור ולדרוש אם אנו רשאין לסלק
4. האל' מן רביעת בית ומקו' שלם הנ"ל כפי טענתה שהי' שייך לבעלה
5. כ' מרדכי הנ"ל לבד וכמבואר בת"א שהכניסם לנדן וכנ"ל והנה
6. אחר כמה חקירות ודרישות ידוע לנו שהי[3] להנעדר כ' מרדכי הנ"ל ארבעה
7. אחים שניים מהם הי' להם ג"כ לכל אחד רביעת בית מאביהם ז"ל
8. והאחד בשמו כ' ליפמן הי' נותן פטורי' להאפטרופסי' והי' מסלק
9. א"ע מכל הקרקעות של עזבון אביו ז"ל בפטורי' ההוקמו ויו תמוז
10. תפ"ט והאחד בשמו איצק שהי' דר בק"ק ווירמש נעדר ג"כ בלי
11. ז"ק ונודע לנו ג"כ ע"י כמה אומדנות ות"ר ממנו ואפטרופס שלו
12. שאין לו חלק בקרקועת אביו ז"ל לזאת מצאנו אחרי חקירות הנ"ל ואחרי
13. עוד כמה אומדנות דמוכח בענין קרקעות הנ"ל שכה יה[4] [ע]"י פשר
14. דבר שהרביע' בית צור הינטר גריני טיהר וחצי מקו' שלם הנ"ל ישתעבד
15. לתשלום סך שני' עשר מאות רט פירעון כתובה ותוס' של האל' הנ"ל כנ"ל
16. אבל חצי אחרת של מקו' שלו'[5] הנ"ל יהי' נשאר בחזקת בני האחי' של כ'
17. מרדכי הנ"ל ומצאנו שיומכר לפני ב"ד כנהוג הרביעת בית
18. וחצי מקו' הנ"ל ומדמי מכירה לאחר שינוכה מה שמחויבת האל' הנ"ל לשלם
19. להאלופי' גובי' יצו (וג"ץ יצו)[6] מה שמחויב בעלה כ' מרדכי הנ"ל תקחי האל' הנ"ל סך
20. אחד עשר מאות רט וחמשי' ושניי' רט סד[7] צל כנ"ל ובאם שנשאר מדמי
21. מכירה הנ"ל לאחר תשלום הנ"ל להאלופי' גובים וג"ץ יותר מסך שמגיע
22. להאל' כנ"ל אזי יהי' המותרת ג"כ בחזקת היורשי' הנ"ל
23. וכן אף אם לא תגיע מדמי מכירה הנ"ל לתשלום כל סך המגיע להאל'

---

1. 1200 ר"ט = 108000 צ"ל. 70 זהובים 55 צ"ל = 4255 צ"ל. 108000 צ"ל פחות 4255 צ"ל = 103745 צ"ל = 1152 זהובים 25 צ"ל.
2. סוף השורה חסר
3. צ"ל 'שהי"
4. צ"ל 'יה"
5. צ"ל 'שלם' (ר' לעיל, שורה 14)
6. תוספת מעל השורה
7. צ"ל 'כד'

24. הנ"ל וכנ"ל בכל זאת לא יהיי[1] להאל' הנ"ל שום תביעה על חצי
25. מקו' האחרת הנ"ל יצא מאתנו יו' ד טוב מנחם תקמד לפק
26. הגאו[ן][2]... [ורנ"מ] ורמ"ש ואני

No. 182

Maas v. Schuster

Fol. 177a; Wednesday 25 August 1784

Samuel Windmühl sold one-quarter of the inner house on Goldener Hirsch to Model Schuster (no price is mentioned). After the sale, Mordecai Maas, who had ownership in the house, approached the court asking that it invalidate the sale based on his claim of abutter's rights to the property (cf., no. 141). Model accepted Mordecai's claim and the court ordered the communal leadership to prepare a contract for the quarter of the inner house in Mordecai Maas's name.

קעז ע"א

1. ב"ה
2. ע"ד קנין מכירה שנעשה לפני נאמני הקהלה פה שמכר ה"ה כ' שמואל בהמנוח[3] כ' אהרן
3. ווינדמיהל כץ ז"ל רביעית בית פנימי צור גולדנר הירץ להו"ה כ' מאדל ב"כ שמואל ש
4. שוסטר כץ ובא לפנינו ה"ה הו"ה גע[4] וג"ה כ"ה מרדכי מז יצו וטען שרוצה לזכות
5. בקנין הנ"ל מכח מצרנות באשר שהוא משותף בבית הנ"ל והלוקח כ' מאדל הנ"ל
6. בא ג"כ לפנינו והתרצה את עצמו לפנינו שיזכה כ"ה מרדכי הנ"ל בכח מצרנות
7. שלו בכן מצאנו בכח מעשה ב"ד שיכתבו הנאמני' עידי קנין הנ"ל השטר מכירה
8. מן קנין רביעית בית הנ"ל על שם המצרן ה"ה ג"ה כ"ה מרדכי הנ"ל יצא
9. מאתנו יו' ד חית אלול תקמ"ד רמ"ש ואני ור ליזר וואלה

---

1. צ"ל 'יהי'
2. יש כאן חור בנייר
3. בן המנוח
4. גבאי צדקה

No. 183

Fol. 177a; Monday evening, 29 November 1784

One-third of a house on the Reuse lot that had been owned by Shirla, daughter of the late Ber Worms, was sold before the court to Süskind Hirschorn for 1450 guldens. The record notes that the availability of the house was announced publicly to insure that the highest bid was received for the property. There is an additional note that Süskind would not have rights to income from the property for about three and one half months from the time of sale.

10. ————
11. השליש מבית שלם החיצון צו דער רויס שהי' שייך להיתומה מ' שרלה בת
12. המנוח כ' פער בן יוזמן ווירמש ז"ל נמכר בפני ב"ד לאחר הכרזה כנהוג
13. להו"ה כ"ה זיסקינד בכ"ה אייזק הירש הארן יצו בעד סך ארבע עשר מאות
14. וחמשה זהו' לשלם כפי תיקון הקהלה ולוקח אין לו פירות רק מן חית
15. ניסן הסמוך הבע"ל והלאה נעשה אור לי[1] ג' יז כסליו תקמ"ה רנ"מ ורמ"ש ואני

No. 184

Fols. 177b–178a; Sunday evening, 14 November 1784

In the fall of 1779, Leb Schloss made a death bed will in which he appointed Wolf Heidelburg and Kalman Reiss as executors of his estate. Leb, who had no survivors, ordered that all his assets be liquidated and the proceeds used for "the benefit of his soul," paying off his debts, and as presents for relatives (in that order). Leb favored a particular great-niece and ordered that she receive more than the others. After his death on 25 December 1779 Leb's debts were paid off; however, there were insufficient funds in the estate to pay the relatives what they had been promised. The executors decided to reduce the amount given to each of the relatives and insure that everyone got something. The executors approached the court because two of Leb's great-nephews stated that they were willing to forgo their share in favor of their sister, Leb's great-niece. In light of this, the executors asked the court whether they could pay the great-niece this extra amount or if it would have to be added to the pool of funds available to all those mentioned in the will. The court ruled that the money could be given to the great-niece.

---

1. ליום

קעז ע״ב

1. ב״ה
2. ע״ד שבאו לפנינו ה״ה הו״ה כ׳ וואלף בהמנוחי[1] פו״מ כ״ה זעלקלי ה[ד]ל[2] ז״ל וה״ה הו״ה כ׳
3. קלמן רייס יצו והציעו לפנינו צוואת שכ״מ מן המנוח כ׳ ליב בן המנוח כ׳ מרדכי
4. שלאס ז״ל שנעשה ביו׳ ויו דן מרחשון תקמם לפק ובתוכה מבואר שהוא הי׳
5. ממנה אותם להיות אפטרופסי׳ על עזבונו והם יקחו כל עזבונו הן
6. קרקעותיו והן מטלטלי׳ וימכרו הכל ומהמעות יעשו כמבואר שם והיינו
7. בתחלה יקיימו הדברי׳ לטובת נשמתו המבואר שם ואח״כ ישלמו כל ה
8. החובות מה שהי׳ חייב לאחרי׳ הן לגובי׳ הן להקדש גבאי׳ והן ליחידי׳
9. ועוד נאמר שם וז״ל נכדי אחיו כ׳ משה ז״ל דהיינו בני׳ של ה״ה כ׳ זעליגמן
10. האן שהמה יורשי דאורייתא שלו זולין האבן בשביל ירושה דאורייתא
11. שלהם חמשה מאות רט וכו׳ ובאופן זה יתחלק חמשה מאות רט הנ״ל דהיינו
12. שני מאות {רט} וחמשי׳ רט יהי׳ לבת של כ׳ זעליגמן הנ״ל הבתולה מרת ע[ד]יל
13. ויניחו האפטרופסי׳ על רווחי׳ ולשעת נישואין של מרת עדיל י[ת]נו האפטרופסי׳
14. הנ״ל הקרן שני מאות וחמשי׳ רט הנ״ל עם רווחי׳ מה שעלה ע״ז עד זמן נישואין
15. לנדן שלה ושני מאות וחמשי׳ רט הנותרי׳ מחמשה מאות [רט] רט[3] הנ״ל
16. יניחו האפטרופסי׳ הנ״ל ג״כ על רווחי׳ ויחולק בין שארי בני׳ ובנות של
17. כ׳ זעליגמן הנ״ל שוה בשוה וכו׳ וכן יעשה לכל ארבעה בני׳ של כ׳ זעליגמן הנ״ל
18. כל זמן שיגיע לכלל נישואין יתן לו חלק המגיע לו קרן עם רווחי׳ אבל קודם שי
19. שיגיע לכלל נישואין לא יתנו להם שום פרוטה הן מהקרן והן מהרווחי׳
20. ואח״כ נאמר שם שיתנו האפטרופסי׳ לשארי קרובי׳ הנפרטי׳ שם שאינם
21. בני עירנו סך שני מאות וחמשי׳ זהו׳ וכו׳ והנשאר מעזבונו אחר שנעשה
22. ומקויים כל הנ״ל יניחו האפטרופסי׳ הנ״ל אצל האלופי׳ גובי׳ יצו לקרן קיימ[ת]
23. נגד רווחי׳ ומהרווחי׳ מבואר שם מה שיעשו מהנה האפטרופסי׳ נפשם
24. בשאלתם מאתנו אחרי שלא מצאנו בעזבון כ׳ ליב ז״ל הנ״ל אחר
25. תשלומין חובותיו רק לערך שלשה מאות רט שאינו מגיע לחצי פירעון
26. ממתנות הנפרטי׳ בצוואה הנ״ל וכנ״ל ומכ״ש שאינם יכולם לקיים
27. מה שנאמר שם מה שנעשו בעזבנו שנשאר לאחר שיקוים כנ״ל

קעח ע״א

1. ב״ה
2. כנ״ל לזאת הוכשר בעיני האפטרופסי׳ לחלוק אותן שלשה מאות רט בין בני
3. כ׳ זעליגמן הנ״ל ובין שארי קרובי׳ הנ״ל לפי ערך מתנה של כל או״א
4. ומה שמגיע לבני כ׳ זעליגמן הנ״ל שהמה יורשי׳ דארייתא של הנעדר הנ״ל
5. ונזכרים ראשונים בצוואת ש״מ הנ״ל כנ״ל עכ״פ לפי ערך מתנתם
6. סך לערך שלשה מאות ושלשי׳ ושבעה זהו׳ וחצי ורוצים האפטרופסי׳ הנ״ל

---

1. בן המנוח
2. היידלברג
3. כפילות במקור

7. להחזיק סך הנ"ל בידם עבור בני כ' זעליגמן הנ"ל וערך סך מאה ושנים עשר
8. זהו' וחצי הנשאר מסך מאות רט הנ"ל רוצים להחזיק האפטרופי' הנ"ל
9. בשביל שארי קרוביו הנ"ל אכן באשר שאותו סך המגיע לבני כ' זעליגמן
10. הנ"ל גם זה מוכרח עוד לחלק בין הבנים של כ' זעליגמן הנ"ל והיינו החצי
11. מסך הנ"ל לבתו מ' עדיל והחצי שניי' לשארי בניו שהם שני זכרים ושני
12. נקבות כפי הצוואה הנ"ל אמנם לפי דברי האפטרופסי' הנ"ל
13. שני בנים זכרים של כ' זעליגמן הנ"ל הב"ח כ' אנשיל וכ' מאיר
14. המה מרוצים בריצוי גמור למחול את כל מה שמגיע להם מעזבון דודם
15. כ' ליב ז"ל הנ"ל כנ"ל לאחותם הגדולה הבתולה מ' עדיל הנ"ל בכן
16. שאלו האפטרופסי' מאתנו ב"ד רשות אם רשאוי' המה ליתן לשעת
17. נישואן של מ'[1] עדיל הנ"ל מה שגיע[2] לה בשביל עצמה כנ"ל החצי מן סך
18. שלשה מאות ושלשי' ושבעה זהו' וחצי העולה ע"ח סך מאה וששי' ושמונה
19. זהו' מה צל ובשביל חלק שני אחים הנ"ל מה שמחלו לה סך פ"ז זהו'
20. ד"ה ע'[3] כנ"ל עולה יחד סך שני מאות וחמשי' ושלשה זהו' שמונה צל
21. ואחרי שבאו לפנינו האחי' כ' אנשיל וכ' מאיר בני כ' זעליגמן הנ"ל ואמרו
22. לפנינו שהמה מרוצים בכך ומחלו במחילה גמורה את חלקם הנ"ל לאחותם
23. מ' עדיל הנ"ל בכן מצאנו שיש רשות ביד האפטרופסי' הנ"ל
24. להניח בידם כפי הצוואה ערך סך שני מאות וחמשי' ושלשה זהו'
25. שמונה צל כנ"ל להבתולה מ' עדיל הנ"ל ליתן לה לנדן לעת נישואין
26. שלה יצא מאתנו אור ליו' ב ב' כסליו תקמ"ה
27. רנ"מ
28. ורמ"ש
29. ואני

No. 185

Fols. 178b–179a; Thursday 16 December 1784

Sorle daughter of Samuel came to Frankfurt and worked as a maidservant for a number of years. She died in Frankfurt leaving but one heir, a daughter, Reizla, who was married and lived in a different town.[4] Sorle left an estate of more than 1,000 guldens and stipulated that fifty guldens go to her daughter and 950 guldens

1. מרת
2. צ"ל 'שמגיע'
3. 25 צל
4. The community frowned on hiring married Jewish women as domestic help (see Kaplan, "Women and Worth," 97 with n. 18) but apparently a widow or single mother could be hired.

be divided among Reizla's children when each of them married. In the meantime, the funds were left with a trustee who was to invest the money. Profits that accrued over the years as the funds remained on hand waiting for the grandchildren to marry were to be given to Reizla.

Reizla's husband came to Frankfurt with three of his daughters and a letter from one of his sons and asked the court, without having any representation, to increase the amount to be given to Reizla because he could not support his wife and younger children. The four older children told the court that they were willing to give up their future share of the inheritance so that their father could support their mother and their younger siblings. The executor of the estate, Michael Mai, a communal leader in Frankfurt, urged the court to approve the request.

The court agreed to give Reizla a one time distribution of 100 guldens on condition that the share that each of the four older children receive at marriage be reduced by 25 guldens apiece. Also see no. 214.

קעח ע"ב

ב"ה

ע"ד שבא לפנינו כ' שמעון[1] ב"כ אהרן מק"ק בידונג[ן][2] יע"א וביקש מאתנו ב"ד ח"מ על אודת חמותו האשה מ' שרלה בת המנוח כ' שמואל ז"ל מוויל[מ]רשם שהיתה משרתת כאן כמה שנים[3] ונעדרת פה ושבקת חיים לכ"י ולא הניח שום יורשי' רק אשתו מ' ריזלה שהיא בת יחידה שלה ועזבונה היא ביד הו"ה פו"מ כ' מיכאל מאיי סג"ל ע"פ שט"ח ממנה ההוקם ח' אב תקמ"ם ושם נאמר שהודית בהודאה גמורה שחייבת לפרוע שעה אחת קודם מותה סך אלף זהו' לפו"מ כ' מיכאל מאיי הנ"ל ע"פ אופן בשביל בתה מ' ריזלה ונכדי' והיינו שסך חמשי' זהו' מהסך הנ"ל יתן כ' מיכאל לבתה הנ"ל וסך תשעה מאות וחמשי' זהו' הנותרי' יניח כ' מיכאל הנ"ל על רווחי' ע"צה כפי ראות עיניו וכל זמן שנכדי הנ"ל פנוים יתן כ' מיכאל הרווחי' העולי' כל שנה לבתה ולעת נשואין של נכדי הנ"ל יתן לכל אחד מהם לסיועת נדן מהקרן לפי ערך חלק המגיע לכל אחד מהם וכו' וכ' שמעון הנ"ל שאל מאתנו בכו"ה מן אשתו הנ"ל ראשון החמשי' זהו' ועוד אמר באשר שאשתו אינה יכולה לזוז ממקומה כנ"ל והי' גורם לו הוצאת יתירה שאין לו להתפרנס עצמו ובניו הקטני' המוטלי' עליו ובני' הגדולי' רוצים למחול לו מחלקם בכן יכירו הב"ד ליתן רשות להוסיף לו עוד יותר מחמשי' זהו' הנ"ל והו"ה פו"מ כ מיכאל מאיי סג"ל שלח אלינו השט"ח הנ"ל ורוצה שנזדקק אל דברי כ' שמעון הנ"ל וכל מה שיצא מאתנו הוא רוצה לאשר ולקיים והנה אחרי שהי' למראה עינינו השט"ח הנ"ל מצאנו באם המצא תמצא בעזבון האשה מ' שרלה הנ"ל אחר מכירת מלבושי' ובעטונג יותר

---

1. כנראה ששמו היה משה ולא שמעון; ר' סוף מס' 214 (דף רה ע"א, שורות 20-21).
2. אולי Büdingen (תודתי לפרופ' מיכאל ברוקי על ההצעה הזאת).
3. כראה שהיא עבדה עבור משפחת פלעגרן (ע' לוח העניינים בהפניה לדף רה).

21. מסך אלף זהו' דמי שט"ח הנ"ל שייך לבתה מ' ריזלה אשת כ' שמעון המותרו'
22. הנ"ל אכן אם לא יהי' עודפי' על סך אלף זהו' בעזבון הנ"ל אזי יותן לכ'
23. שמעון הנ"ל בכו"ה מספקת מן אשתו מ' ריזלה הנ"ל סך חמשי' זהו' הנ"ל
24. גם הרווחי' העולי' כל שנה וכפי שט"ח הנ"ל ועוד נוסף לזה מצאנו לטובת
25. הבנים קטנים של כ' שמעון נכדי של האשה מ' שרלה ז"ל באשר שבנות מן כ'
26. שמעון הנ"ל הי' לפנינו ה"ה מ' שרה ומ' מרים ומ' האנעל ואמרו בפנינו שהית מרוצי'
27. ברצונם הטוב שיותן לאביהם מחלק המגיע להם כדי שיוכל לפרנס עי"כ אמם
28. ובני' הקטני' וגם בנו כ' אהרן הי' לפנינו כתב ידו המקיים לפנינו

קעט ע"א

1. ב"ה
2. לפנינו שהוא מוחל ג"כ מחלקו לאביו בכן מצאנו שיותן לכ' שמעון הנ"ל עוד
3. נוסף על סך חמשי' זהו' הנ"ל סך מאה זהו' והיינו סך חמשה ועשרי' זהו'
4. מחלק של כל או"א משלשה בנותיו ובנו הנ"ל שמחלו לו לפנינו ולזמן נישואן שלהם
5. ינוכה מן כל או"א סך חמשה ועשרי' זהו' הנ"ל יצא מאתנו יו' ה' ג' טבת
6. תקמ"ה הגאון אב"ד נרו' ורנ"מ ורמ"ש ואני

No. 186

Stiebel v. Matla, daughter of Aaron Hecht

Fol. 179a; Thursday evening, 27 January 1785

Two unmarried sisters owned half of the Goldenes Einhorn house. One sister sold her share in the space, one-quarter of the house, to Meʾir Falk. This same sister later married Kalman Stiebel and he leased the space from Meʾir. This meant that Kalman now shared rights to half of the house with his sister-in-law, Matla, the daughter of Aaron Hecht. Given that Kalman did not think the space would be large enough for him, his wife, *and* his sister-in-law, he, through his counsel, invoked the talmudic principle that essentially stated that if two parties cannot share something, then one party can force the other either to be bought out or to buy out.[2] Kalman proposed that he rent the rest of the half-house from Matla for three years or that she sub-lease his quarter of the house. Matla did not have representation and simply said that she was willing to move into one unheated room in the house and sublease her share in the remaining sections of the house

1. נטריה רחמנא ופרקיה
2. See B.T., *Babaʾ batraʾ* 13a.

to her brother-in-law on condition that she had access to the lower kitchen/heated area. The court ruled that the talmudic rule did not apply in this instance, leaving Kalman's sister-in-law with her rights intact.

———

ע״ד שבא לפנינו ה״ה התורני כ״ה משה אויך יצו בהרשאות ובמעמד החתן כ׳ קלמן ב״המנוח כ״ה ישראל שטיבל ז״ל ותבע מן אחות כלה שלו הבתולה מ׳ מאטלה בת המנוח כ׳ אהרן העכט ז״ל באשר ששכר את רביעת בית צום גולד[י] איין האָרן מן כ׳ מאיר פאלק שקנה אותו מכלתו שהי׳ שייך לה ולאחותה מ׳ מאטלה הנ״ל החצי בית הנ״ל בשותפות ובאשר שאין אותו חצי בית הנ״ל ראוי לדור בו שניה׳ בכן טען כ׳ קלמן הנ״ל גוד או איגוד בשכירות על אופן המבואר או שהוא רוצה לשכור מן גיסתו מ׳ מ[אט]לה הנ״ל רביעת בית שלה על משך שלשה שנים רצופי׳ בעד סך עשרים רט לשנה או שהיא תשכר ממנו את רביעת בית הנ״ל ששכר מן כ׳ מאיר פאלק הנ״ל בעד שכירות הנ״ל על זמן הנ״ל אכן אם היא רוצה לשכור תהא מחויבת להעמיד ערבות מספקות על דמי שכירות על משך זמן הנ״ל והבתולה מ׳ מאטלה הנ״ל בעצמה השיבה באשר שהיא פנוי׳ יכולה היא לדור ברביעית בית שלה בלבד אך בזאת התרצה א״ע אם הניח לה חדר אחד בלי תנור אזי רוצה להשכיר לו שארי חדרי׳ המגיעי׳ לה על חלקה בעד עשרה רט לשנה באופן ובתנאי שתהי׳ לה רשות ליכנס ולצאת בחדר בית החורף התחתון והאריכו הצדדי׳ הנ״ל בטענותיה׳ כמבואר בפראטיקאהל המונח לפינונו ב״ד ולאחר שחתמו עצמם הצדדי׳ הנ״ל בתוקף קומפרמיס בח״ח ובקנס לאשר ולקיים כפי אשר יצא מאתנו נזדקקנו להם ודקדקנו היטב בטענותיהם ומצאנו שאין בנידן זה דין גוד או איגוד יצא מאתנו אור ליום ויו עשקי׳ טוב שבט תקמ״ה רנ״מ ורמ״ש ואני

No. 187

Stiebel v. Kulp

Fols. 179b–180a; Tuesday evening, 1 February 1785

Early in 1785, Isaac Stiebel rented half of the inner Eichhorn house for three years. Occupancy was to begin in the summer of 1785. Meanwhile, the space was being rented by Yudaʾ Kulp, who leased it from those who owned the other half of the house and currently presumably had rights to the space based on a lottery, or other

———

ערב שבת קדש

form of agreement, until the summer of 1785. Through his counsel, Yudaʾ disputed Isaac's lease and claimed abutter's rights to the space on the basis of his living there at the present time. The court upheld Yudaʾ's argument and awarded him the space for three years, albeit on condition that he sign a lease with the "new owner" that adhered to all conditions in the lease signed by Isaac. Yudaʾ was also required to pay Isaac's expenses related to drawing up the contract, and certain other costs connected to his rental agreement, including 4 guldens that Isaac paid to his servant for acting as an "agent" in finding the rental. Yudaʾ questioned whether Isaac actually paid his servant such a high agent's fee and the court ordered Isaac to confirm the payment.

קעט ע"ב

1. ע"ד {שבא} טענות והפרשות שיש בין הו"ה כ' יודא קולפא יצו ובין
2. הו"ה כ' איצק ב"אי שטיבל יצו שה"ה התורני כ"ה מאיר מאַז בהרשאות
3. כ' איצק שטיבל הנ"ל הציע לפנינו כתב שכירות ההוקם טוב שבט
4. תקמ"ה שמבואר בתוכה ששכר כ' איצק הנ"ל חצי בית
5. פנימי צום אייכהארן מן כ"ה יעקב בכ"ה מאיר פלערשהיי' והיינו
6. שטח התחתון עם החדרי' השייכי' להם כמבואר שם על שלשה
7. שנים רצופי' מן ר"ח תמוז הבע"ל וה"ה התורני כ"ה משה אויך
8. בהרשאות כ' יודא הנ"ל טען ורוצה לזכות בשכירות הנ"ל
9. מכח מצרנות מאחר שדר בשטח הנ"ל כעת בשכירות ממחזיקי
10. חצי בית האחרת / והאריכו הצדדי' הנ"ל בטענותיהם כ
11. כמבואר בק"ה המונח לפנינו ולאחר שחתמו הצדדי' הנ"ל
12. את עצמם בתוקף קומפרמיס בח"ח ובקנס סך מסוים חצי
13. לשררה ירה[2] וחצי להקדש לאשר ולקיים הפס"ד שיצא מאתנו
14. ב"ד ח"מ נזדקקנו להם ומצאנו שהדין עם כ' יודא הנ"ל
15. וזכה באותו חלק חצי בית שדר בו כעת בשכירות
16. מר"ח תמוז הבע"ל על שלשה שנים רצופי' דהיינו שטח
17. התחתון מדין מצרנות וה"ה כ' יודא הנ"ל מחויב להקים
18. מחדש כתב שכירות על שמו בינו ובין המשכיר כ"ה יעקב הנ"ל
19. ולקיים בכל אופנים הנאמרי' בכתב השכירות ההוקם בין
20. המשכיר ובין השוכר כ' איצק הנ"ל ומחמת מה שתבע כה
21. מאיר הנ"ל אם כ' יודא הנ"ל יזכה בדין שמחויב לשלם
22. כ' יודא הנ"ל לכ' איצק הנ"ל מה שהוציא והיינו חצי חדש
23. רט[3] מחמת כתובת כתב השכירות וארבעה זהו' שנתן
24. דמי סרסרנו' למשרת שלו וכ"ה משה השיב ששכר {כתיבה}

---

1. כנראה בן אברם (ר' אבני זכרון, מס' 3907, ואלה תולדות 18.7.1786).
2. ירום הודו
3. כנראה ה-Konventionstaler

קפ ע"א

1. חצי חדש רט מחמת כתבת כתב (שכירות)[1] רוצה ליתן לו אך שכר ס

2. סרסרנות ד' זהו' אינו מאמינו רק שיקבל כ' איצק הנ"ל בחרם שנתן

3. לו כל כך מצאנו שגם בזה הדין עמו וגם מצאנו שמחויב כ' יודא

4. הנ"ל ליתן לכ' איצק שכר שליחות סך ששה זהו' יצא מאתנו

5. אור ליו' ד' ך"ב שבט תקמ"ה רנ"מ ורמ"ש ואני

No. 188

Fol. 180a; Saturday evening, 5 February or Sunday 6 February 1785

The communal leadership addressed a question to the court regarding the rights of a child born during the first year of marriage to the assets of its deceased mother while its father was still alive. The question was an issue discussed in Jewish law.[2] The court offered no rationale for its position that the child had no claims on its deceased mother's assets unless there was a formal agreement made between the parents during their lives to the contrary. The question was written in Yiddish and the answer was recorded in Hebrew. According to the index compiled at the end of the collection, this question was addressed to the court from the Jewish community in Vienna at the request of the non-Jewish authorities. This is corroborated by a note in the margins of the YIVO MS. RG 128 (folder 77–78), fol. 56b. The italicized sections have been crossed out of the YIVO manuscript. Also see below nos. 190 and 194.

6. ———

7. ע"ד השאלה ששאלו {האלו} האלופי' קציני' פו"מ יצו אותנו[3] / בזה הלשון

8. איינע אורקונד דער יודן שאפט / דאש בייא איהנון דיא רעכטש רעגל

9. דאש וואן דש וייב שטירבט / אונד אין ערשטן יאַהר דער עהע איין

10. קינד פר האנדן איזט / דער מאן זיינה (פ[ר]ויא)[4] ערבַֿע / אונד דש קינד ייעדר

11. פאטרליך נאך מוטטרליכש פער מעגין ערבע / נאך איבר קאמָע עד

12. כאן לשון השאלה

13. תשובה דבר פשוט על השאלה הנ"ל / שאין להילד שום תביעה

14. מחמת ירושות אמו הן בחיי אביו הן לאחר שימות אביו / וכשימות

1. תוספת מעל השורה

2. See Isserles, *Shulḥan ʿaruk*, Eben ha-ʿezer 53.3, as well as the introduction, 72. A child conceived or born to the couple out of wedlock does not seem to have been the issue at hand.

3. בכתב יד יוו"א יש כאן הפנייה לשולי הדף שבו כתוב: 'שנשלח להם מווין ע"י שררה יר"ה כאן'.

4. תוספת מעל השורה

אביו הוא יורש את אביו *כדין כל בני׳ שיורשי׳ את אביהם /*
וזה הדין הוא אם לא התנו *בשעת נשואין בתנאי׳ אחרוני׳ כ*
כשנשא אביו את אשתו אֵם הבן / אבל אם התנו ביניהם בשעת
נשואין בתנאי׳ אחרוני׳ אזי יקויים כפי שהתנו ביניהם[1] היו׳
יו׳ א׳[2] כ״ה שבט תקמ״ה הגאון אב״ד נרו[3] ורנ״מ ורמ״ש
ואני

No. 189

Luria v. Oppenheim

Fols. 180b–182a; Thursday evening, 10 February 1785

Solomon Luria had a partnership with Wolfe Maas in the ownership of a house on the Weinsfass lot. According to Solomon, Wolfe still owed him 36 guldens, 40 kreuzers for repairs, but in 1779 Wolfe died without having paid his debt.[4] Wolfe was survived by his wife, Schönle, who passed away in late 1782 and was inherited by five of her nephews.[5] Seeking repayment, Solomon sued one set of nephews, the three sons of Mordecai Oppenheim, for their half of the debt. The nephews countered that after their uncle's death, their Aunt Schönle had come to the head of the rabbinic court to discharge her marriage contract. The head of the court granted the discharge and, given that there were insufficient assets in the estate to pay her marriage contract, relieved her of any further responsibility in the liabilities of her husband's estate. Since the nephews inherited Wolfe Maas's property through their aunt, they argued that as far as they were concerned they bore no responsibility for Wolfe's liabilities, for they had been discharged. Solomon Luria's counsel attempted to discredit the nephews' argument but without success.

The case engendered further legal activity. The sons of Mordecai Oppenheim sued their cousins, the two sons of Mordecai's brother, Kalman Oppenheim, with whom they shared Schönle's estate, for expenses incurred in dealing with their aunt's estate, including burial costs. In a rather ironic twist, one of Kalman's sons

1. החלק המסומן מחוק בכ״י יוו״א ובסוף כתוב, ׳בתנאי׳ ה[ר]אשים [אולי צ״ל: הראשונים] בזמן החופה כשנשא אב׳ את אשתו אם הילד אבל אם התנו ביניהם בזמן החופה אז יקוים כפי שהתנו ביניהם׳. אין שם תאריך. ברשות YIVO Institute for Jewish Research, New York
2. באותה שנה כ״ה שבט חל בשבת; אולי הכוונה למוצאי שבת.
3. נטריה רחמנא ופרקיה
4. See Horovitz, no. 3632.
5. Regarding Schönle's death, see Horovitz, no. 3785.

had sold his portion in the estate to Solomon Luria, and Solomon was now asked to pay his share of the costs, 21 guldens, 46 kruezers. While Solomon agreed to pay most of the expenses, he asked that Mordecai's sons who dealt with the estate take an oath regarding legal fees they had incurred and affirm they had not taken anything from the estate without the knowledge of others. Solomon was also asked to take an oath that he had not taken anything from Schönle Maas's estate, especially since he had a key to the storage area in the house where some of her things were kept, one item of which was known to be missing.

The court ultimately had the various parties swear that their statements were true and that they had not taken anything from the estate. That done, Kalman's son and Solomon Luria were each ordered to pay their shares.

קפ ע״ב

ב״ה

ע״ד שבא לפנינו הו״ה התורני כ״ה משה אויך בהרשאות הו״ה כ׳ שלמה לוריא ותבע מן האחי׳ בני המנוח כ״ה מרדכי בפו״מ כ׳ וואלף אופנהיי׳ ז״ל שלשי׳ וששה זהו׳ מם צל והציע לפנינו חשבן מה שהוציא כ׳ שלמה בבנין בית צום וויין פעסכה שהי׳ לו בשותפו׳ עם המנוח כ׳ וואלף מַז בעל דודתם המונחת מ׳ שינלה ז״ל העולה לסך שני מאות וששה זהו׳ נ״א צל ומגיע לכ׳ וואלף הנ״ל שהי׳ שייך לו חצי מבית הנ״ל החצי מסך הנ״ל אך התרצה שניהם על אופן המבואר ששכר כ׳ שלמה הנ״ל חדר אחד מחלק של כ׳ וואלף הנ״ל [מ]חדש {אחד} סיון שנת תקל״ח על ששה שנים כל שנה בעד עשרה רט שכירות ונתן לו כ׳ שלמה ד ח״כ ושני ח״כ אחרוני׳ החזיק בידו לתשלומין הנ״ל נמצא שנשאר לו חייב עוד כ׳ וואלף הנ״ל לאחר ניכוי שלשי׳ זהו׳ דמי ח״כ הנ״ל סך שבעי׳ ושלשה זהו׳ ך צל ועתה ש שנעדר כ׳ וואלף הנ״ל ואח״כ מתה אשתו מ׳ שינלה ז״ל ושבקה חיי׳ לכל ישראל ונפל החצי בית הנ״ל בירושה לבני אחי׳ ו[היי]נו רביעת מבית הנ״ל ליורשי׳ אחי׳ המנוח כמ׳[1] קלמן אופנהיי׳ ז״ל ורביעת בית ליורשי׳ אחי׳ המנוח כ״ה מרדכי ז״ל הנ״ל בכן תבע כהר״ם[2] הנ״ל בהרשאת כ׳ שלמה הנ״ל מן בני מרדכי ז״ל הנ״ל החצי מן החוב סך שבעי׳ ושלשה זהו׳ ך צל העולה על חלקם סך שלשי׳ ושלשה[3] זהו׳ מם צל והב״ח כ׳ קלמן הנ״ל בהמנוח[4] כ״ה מ מרדכי ז״ל הנ״ל השיב בשביל עצמו ובהרשאת אחיו הו״ה כ׳ וואלף יצו והו״ה כ׳ יודא יצו והציע לפנינו כתב ראי׳ שנשבעת דודתם

1. כבוד מר
2. כבוד הרב משה (אויך)
3. צ״ל ׳וששה׳
4. בן המנוח

23. מ׳ שינלה אחרי מיתת בעלה ז״ל הנ״ל לפני הגאון אב״ד נרו[1] {את כל
24. עזבון} השבעת כתובתה ותוספ׳ והחליט לה הגאון אב״ד נרו את כל
25. עזבון בעלה ז״ל הן קרקעות והן מטלטלין מכל מה שהפה יוכל לדבר
26. אחרי שביררה שאין כל עזבון בעלה מגיע לדמי פירעון כתובה
27. ותוספ׳ בכן אותו ה[חוב מ]דמי בנין בדק הבית אף שהי׳ על בעלה
28. מ״מ היא היתה פטורה מלשלם וממילא שגם המה היורשי׳
29. שלה ג״כ אינם מחויבם לשלם בשבילה וכהר״מ הנ״ל השיב

קפא ע״א

1. ב״ה
2. השיב אחרי שהחצי בית הנ״ל מן בעלה ז״ל הנ״ל {לגבות כתובה ובאשר
3. שבאם לא נבנה} הי׳ משועבד כבר בחיים חיותה לאשתו מ׳ שינלה ז״ל
4. הנ״ל לגביות כתובה ובאשר שבאם לא נבנה הבית באותו הפעם
5. התיקון כיפה של הבית הי׳ מפיל כל הבית וא״כ הקרקע הי׳ משובחת
6. באותו בנין הנ״ל בכן החוב מבנין הבית הנ״ל מוטל ג״כ על ה
7. האשה הנ״ל ועל יורשי׳ עוד תבע כ׳ קלמן וסומך עצמו על טענותיו הנ״ל
8. שפטורי׳ מתביעת בנין בית הנ״ל וכ׳ שלמה הנ״ל הודה ששני ח״כ
9. אחרוני׳ שנמשך זמן פירעון שלהם לאחר מיתת דודתם ז״ל הנ״ל והי׳
10. שייכי׳ לדודתם רק שטוען כהרם[2] הנ״ל שקיבלו כ׳ שלמה הנ״ל כבר
11. מן בעלה כ׳ וואלף ז״ל בעודו בחיים חיותו לתשלומן כנ״ל ובאשר
12. שאינו מאמין לכ׳ שלמה הנ״ל ע״ז בכן {יצא} ישבע כ׳ שלמה הנ״ל שכדבריו
13. כן הוא שקיבלו הח״כ הנ״ל מן כ׳ וואלף ז״ל הנ״ל לתשלומין כנ״ל /
14. וכ׳ שלמה הנ״ל הביא עד אחד שהעיד בפנינו ב״ד שגם הוא
15. יודע שקיבל כ׳ שלמה הנ״ל שני ח״כ הנ״ל מן כ׳ וואלף הנ״ל כנ״ל ו
16. והאריכו בטענותיהם ולאחר שחתמו הצדדי׳ הנ״ל א״ע בתוקף
17. קומפרמיס לקיים הפס״ד אשר יצא מאתנו נזדקקנו להם ולאחר שהי׳
18. למראה ענינו השבעות כתובתה מן האשה מ׳ שינלה ז״ל הנ״ל
19. (ובתוכה מבואר שנחלט לה את כל עזבון בעלה ז״ל הנ״ל)[3] מכל מה שהפה יוכל לדבר וכ׳ מצאנו שהדין עם האחי׳ בני המנוח
20. כ״ה מרדכי ז״ל הנ״ל ואין לכ׳ שלמה הנ״ל שום תביעה עליהם מחמת
21. הוצאות דמי בנין הבית הנ״ל ומחמת מה שתבע הב״ח כ׳ קלמן הנ״ל
22. מן כ׳ שלמה הנ״ל שישבע על טענותיו בשביל שני ח״כ אחרוני׳ מצאנו שפטו׳
23. כ׳ שלמה הנ״ל מתביעה זו / עוד התעצמו לדין והציע הב״ח כ׳ קלמן הנ״ל
24. בשביל עצמו ובהרשאות אחיו הנ״ל לפנינו חשבון מה שהוציאו אחיו
25. הנ״ל אחר מות דודתם הנ״ל בשבילה העולה לסך שמוני׳ ושבעה
26. [זהובי׳]

---

1. נטריה רחמנא ופרקיה
2. כבוד הרב משה
3. תוספת מעל השורה

קפא ע״ב

1. זין צל והם בשביל צרכ[י] קבורה ומהם להשררה יר״ה מס ורווחי׳ אין
2. פפאנטפויז וגם הוצאת משפט לטובת היורשי׳ נגד בענדט קאסיל
3. ונכלל בתוכם ג״כ משכן אחד שהי׳ בידם שהלווה לדודתם א׳ זהו׳
4. יוד צל ותבע כ׳ קלמן הנ״ל מן האחי׳ כ׳ אלי׳ וכ׳ גבריאל בני דודו ה
5. המנוח כמ״ה קלמן אופנהיי׳ ז״ל שגם המה יורשי׳ חצי עזבון דודתם
6. ז״ל הנ״ל שמוטל עליהם לשלם חצי מסך הנ״ל לזאת תבע מן כ׳
7. שלמה הנ״ל שקנה מן כ׳ גבריאל בן המנוח כמ״ה קלמן הנ״ל חלק ירושתו
8. מן דודתו מ׳ שינלה ז״ל הנ״ל הן חלק שמונת מבית הנ״ל וחלק שמונת
9. ממטלטלי׳ שהניח אחרי׳ האשה ז״ל הנ״ל נגד זה קיבל עליו כ׳ שלמה הנ״ל
10. לפרוע מה שמוטל על חלק של גבריאל הנ״ל לשלם בשביל דודתו הנ״ל
11. בכן ישלם כ׳ שלמה חלק רביעת מסך הנ״ל שהוציאו אחיו ומגיע ע״ח סך
12. עשרי׳ ואחד זהו׳ מו צל גם תבע כ׳ קלמן הנ״ל התביעה זו סך ד״א
13. זהו׳ מו צל הנ״ל מן הבחור כ׳ אלי׳ בן המנוחי[1] שמוטל עליו [ג״]כ לשלם
14. רביעת ממה שהוציא אחיו הנ״ל והב״ח כ׳ אלי׳ בא לפנינו והודה
15. על התביעה זו והתרצה א״ע לשלם מה שעלה על חלקו לשלם מהחוב
16. הנ״ל וכ״ה משה בהרשאות כ׳ שלמה הנ״ל השיב שמרוצה כ׳ שלמה
17. הנ״ל לשלם בשביל כ׳ גבריאל מה שמגיע ע״ח ממה שהוציא האחי׳ הנ״ל
18. לצורך צרכי קבורה ושאר הוצאות מה שנזכר בחשבונם אכן מה
19. שתבעו בחשבונם שהוציא לצורך {המשפן}(המשפט)[2] כנ״ל אינו מאמין להם
20. רק שישבעו האחי׳ הנ״ל על חשבונם שהוציאו כל כך וגם באשר
21. שהאחי׳ הנ״ל הי׳ עוסקי׳ בעזבון דודתם לאחר מיתתה בכן ישבעו
22. שלא לקחו ולא העל[י]מה כלום מעזבון דודתם ז״ל הנ״ל וכ׳ קלמן הנ״ל
23. השיב באשר שכ׳ שלמה הנ״ל רוצה להטיל שבועת על אחיו גם הוא
24. תבע מן כ׳ אלי׳ הנ״ל שעסק ג״כ בעזבון הנ״ל שגם הוא ישבע
25. שלא לקח ולא העלי׳ כלום מעזבון דודתו ז״ל הנ״ל וגם תבע שכ׳
26. שלמה הנ״ל שקנה חלק ירושת כ׳ גבריאל הנ״ל ישבע שלא

קפב ע״א

1. לקח הוא כלום מעזבון אשה הנ״ל ובפרט שהי׳ בידו המפתח מן חדר ד׳
2. שטעג הויך שהי׳ שם כלי בית וגם באשר שנחסר מן עזבון הנ״ל
3. איין טעש מן האשה ז״ל הנ״ל שבתוכה תכריך כתובי׳ בכן ישבע כ׳
4. שלמה הנ״ל כנ״ל שלא לקחו וגם שאינו ידוע לו שום ידיעה היכן הוא הטעש
5. עם כתבם הנ״ל והאריכו בטענותי׳ ולאחר שחתמו עצמם כל היורשי׳
6. מן האשה ז״ל והיינו האחי׳ בני המנוח כ״ה מרדכי הנ״ל והבחר
7. כ׳ אלי׳ בן המנוח כמ״ה קלמן ז״ל הנ״ל וכ׳ שלמה הנ״ל בהרשאות

1. כמ״ה קלמן אופנהיים
2. תיקון מעל השורה

8. כ' גבריאל בהמנוח כהמ"ק[1] הנ"ל בתוקף קומפרמיס בח"ח ובקנס לקיים כל
9. אשר יצא מאתנו נזדקקנו להם גם לזה ומצאנו שישבעו האחי' הוה[2] כ'
10. וואלף וכ'[3] יודא הנ"ל ע"ד המקו' ב"ה וע"ד ב"ד בלי עו"מ ובלי שום ה
11. הוראות היתר שבעולם שלא לקחו ולא העלימו כלום מעזבון דודתם
12. ז"ל גם ישבע האחי' הנ"ל כנ"ל שכדבריהם כן הוא שהוציא לצורך
13. המשפט הנ"ל כפי שכתבו בחשבונ' הנ"ל ולאחר שנשבעו האחי' כנ"ל
14. מחויבי' כ' אלי' הנ"ל לשלם חלק רביעת מסך שמוני' ושבעה זהו' זין צל
15. הנ"ל וגם כ' שלמה הנ"ל מחויב לשלם ג"כ בשביל חלק של גבריאל הנ"ל
16. חלק רביעי' מסך פ"ז זהו' זין צל הנ"ל וגם מחויבי' כל היורשי' לשלם
17. כפי שהתרצו לפנינו להעמיד מצבה על קבר דודתם ז"ל הנ"ל לפ"כ
18. על הוצאתם והיינו על יורשי כ"ה מרדכי ז"ל הנ"ל החצי ועל כ' אלי' וכ'
19. שלמה בשביל גבריאל הנ"ל החצי והב"ח כ' אלי' הנ"ל ישבע ג"כ ע"ד
20. המקו' ב"ה וע"ד הב"ד בלי עו"מ ובלי שום הוראות היתר שבעולם שלא
21. לקח ולא העלים כלום מעזבון דודתו ז"ל הנ"ל והו"ה כ' שלמה הנ"ל יקבל
22. בחרם בפנינו ב"ד שאין בידו כלום מה ששייך לעזבון האשה ז"ל
23. הנ"ל כלום ([ו]יכלול)[4] ושאין לו שום ידיעה שבעולם היכן הוא דיא טעש עם
24. תכריך כתבי' שבתוכה יצא מאתנו אור ליום ויו עש"ק ב' דר"ח
25. אדר תקמ"ה לפק רנ"מ ורמ"ש ואני

No. 190

Emmerich v. Fulda

Fols. 182b–184b; Monday 14 March 1785

The premature death of the here unnamed daughter of Gumpel Emmerich during the second year of her marriage to Moses Fulda led to a financial dispute between Gumpel and Moses.[5] Through his legal representative, Emmerich demanded that Fulda return to him half of the dowry plus numerous other items. Fulda, who had no legal counsel, did not deny the necessity to return funds to his former father-in-law. There was a medieval ordinance accepted in the German Jewish community that if a wife died early in the marriage assets had to be returned to the family of the

1. בן המנוח כבוד הרב מורנו קלמן
2. המפוארים והחשובים
3. וכבוד
4. תוספת מעל השורה
5. Gelche, daughter of Gumpel Emmerich and wife of Moses Fulda, died on 30 December 1784 (see Horovitz, no. 3856).

deceased if her family so requested.[1] It would seem that in Frankfurt this ordinance applied at least through the second year of marriage (see no. 194). Moses simply argued that he should be allowed numerous deductions from the amount that he was to repay, including burial costs (in keeping with the medieval ordinance) and the cost of clothing that he provided for his wife during her lifetime. Gumpel disputed many of the deductions Moses claimed and, in the course of the delibera-tions, added a number of items that he thought Moses should return. Ultimately, both sides asked the court to arrange a compromise, which it did on almost all issues. The court allowed Moses to repay Gumpel in installments.

קפב ע"ב

1. ב"ה
2. ע"ד הפרשות וטענות שנתהוו בין ה"ה הו"ה כ"ה גומפיל עמריך יצו
3. ובין ה"ה הו"ה כ"ה משה בהמנוח[2] כ"ה אהרן פולדא יצו בענין
4. עידור שמתה אשתו של כ"ה משה הנ"ל בת של כה"ג[3] הנ"ל בשנה
5. שני' לאחר החופה ושבקת חיי' לכ"י / ובא לפנינו ה"ה התורני כ"ה
6. מאיר מז יצו בהרשאות כ"ה גומפיל הנ"ל וכ"ה משה הנ"ל
7. בעצמו והאריכו בטענותיה' זה מול זה כמבואר בק"ה המונח
8. לפנינו ואחר שחתמו הצדדי' הנ"ל בתוקף קומפרמיס בח"ח
9. ובקנס לאשר ולקיים כפי הדין אשר יצא מאתנו ב"ד ח"מ ואח"כ
10. נתנו עינהם על הב"ד לפשר ביניהם וקיבלו עליהם בתוקף
11. קומפרמיס הנ"ל לקיים הפשר שיצא מאתנו בכן נזדקקנו להם
12. ומצאנו על כל פרט ופרט כמבואר והיינו מה שתבע כה"ג הנ"ל
13. מכ"ה משה הנ"ל לחזרה סך ששה מאות ועשרי' וחמשה זהו'
14. שהוא חצי דמי נדן שלו וכה"מ[4] הנ"ל השיב שאין צריך להחזיר
15. כלום כמו שטען לפנינו בקונטרס הטענות ואף אם מחויב להחזיר
16. מ"מ רוצה לנכות מחצי נדן הנ"ל סך מאה ועשרי' וחמשה זהו' שהוא
17. כל דמי מעשר מכל הנדן מצאנו שמחויב כ"ה משה הנ"ל להחזיר
18. לכה"ג הנ"ל החצי נדן הנ"ל ואינו רשאי לנכות מחמת המעשר
19. רק שישם ושנים זהו' וחצי דמי חצי מעשר מכל נדן שכבר
20. ניתן לכה"ג הנ"ל {החצי} בשעת החתנה ומחמת מה שרצה
21. כהר"מ הנ"ל לנכות עוד מדמי חצי נדן הוצאות החתנה הדין
22. בזה עם כה"ג ואינו רשאי כה"מ הנ"ל לנכות כלום ומחמת שרוצה
23. כהרם[5] הנ"ל לנכות הוצאות צרכי קבורה הן מה שהוציא

1. See Finkelstein, *Jewish Self-Government*, 163–65 (with an English translation and notes on 166–68), 191.
2. בן המנוח
3. כבוד הרב גומפיל
4. וכבוד הרב משה
5. כבוד הרב משה

24. כבר והן מה שעתי[ד] להוציא (עוד)[1] מצאנו שצרכי קבורה מוטל
25. על

קפג ע"א

1. ב"ה
2. על שניהם בשווה[2] בכן מה שמחוּיבי' עוד להוציא ע"ז והיינו
3. הוצאות עמידת מצבה יהי' על שניהם בשוה ומאחר שכה"ג הנ"ל
4. הוא בחברא יתעסק הוא בעמידת מצבה שהיא לפ"כ ולפ"כ בעלה וכן
5. נר תמיד כל י"א חדשי' החיוב מוטל על שניהם בשוה והיינו שמיו' העדרתה
6. עד כלות חמשה חדשי' וחצי מחויב כ"ה משה הנ"ל להדליק על הוצאותו וחמשה
7. חדשי' וחצי הנותרים מחויב כה"ג הנ"ל להדליק על הוצאותו והיינו בחול נר
8. של שמן ובשבת נר של שעוה ואמירת קדיש עד כלות אחד עשר חדשי' באשר
9. שכה"ג הנ"ל התרצה עצמו שיאמר הוא קדיש בעבור בתו ז"ל בכן כה יהי'
10. ומחמת הוצאות צרכי קבורה שכבר הוציא כה"רם הנ"ל ורוצה לנכותם
11. והציע חשבון לפנינו וכה"ג הנ"ל השיב על כל פרט ופרט מחשבן זה
12. עוד רוצה לנכות כהר"ם הנ"ל דמי סארלוב וראק שעשה לאשתו ז"ל
13. הנ"ל והיא הי' לבוש בהם בשעת מיתתה גם רוצה לנכות בשביל דמי
14. [מ]זונת משלושי' יום אחר העדרת אשתו ז"ל עוד רוצה לנכות כהרם הנ"ל
15. מה ש[הו]ציא צרכי {קבורה} חולי' מן כ"ד תשרי תקמ"ד וכה"ג הנ"ל השיב
16. באריכות ועייננו בחשבונ[ו'] ובטענות הנ"ל ומצאנו ע"ד פשר
17. שינכה כהר"ם הנ"ל בשביל כל התביעות האלו עוד סך ארבעי'
18. וחמשה זהו' שלשי' ושני' צל מתשלומין חצי נדן הנ"ל ומחמת מה שתבע
19. כה משה הנ"ל ורוצה לנכות מחמת שבדמי נדן שלו לקח סחורות
20. ומכרם בהקפה ועשה חובות לערך סך מאה זהו' שהם חצי יאוש
21. וכה"ג השיב ע"ז מצאנו ע"ד פשר שכהרם הנ"ל ינכה מחצי נדן
22. הנ"ל שיחזר לכה"ג הנ"ל עוד סך חמשה רט עוד תבע כ"המ[3] הנ"ל
23. ורוצה לנכות מחמת זהב קעט וכסף ביגל טעש וטבעת ששוה לערך
24. ארבעם זהו' שהכניסה אשתו ז"ל עוד לביתו בשעת החתנה
25. ואח"כ החזירה לאביה וטען כהר"ם הנ"ל שזכה בהן
26. ורוצה

קפג ע"ב

1. בה
2. ורוצה לנכות חצי דמי שווי' עוד תבע כהר"ם הנ"ל מחמת שלא נתן
3. לו חמיו כה"ג הנ"ל מתנות כראוי בשעת הקנס כפי שמוטל עליו וכמו ש
4. שנכתב בת"ר בכן רוצה לנכות אותם מדמי חזרה וכה"ג הנ"ל השיב

---

1. תוספת מעל השורה
2. ר' חלק מחוקק, אה"ע נה ס"ק יז. השווה בית שמואל שם ס"ק יא וגם דברי הפתחי תשובה שם.
3. כבוד הרב משה

5. על שני טענות באריכות מצאנו ע"ד פשר דבר שבשביל שני תביעות
6. הללו ינכה כהרם הנ"ל עוד סך עשרה זהו' מדמי חצי נדן שמחויב
7. להחזיר לכה"ג הנ"ל ומחמת מה שתבע כהר"מ[1] הנ"ל בהרשאת
8. כה"ג הנ"ל מן כ"ה משה הנ"ל לחזרה החצי מתנות מה שנתן הוא
9. קודם החופה כפי רשימה שהציע גם מתנות איין ווארף מה
10. שנתן בשעת החתנה הן מכה"ג הנ"ל והן ממשפחתו ואוהביו
11. כפי רשימה שהציע לפנינו וכה[2] משה הנ"ל השיב שאין
12. צריך להחזיר כלום מצאנו שכל מתנות שנתן להם הן קודם החתנה
13. והן בשעת חתנה מתנות איין ווארף מחויב כהרם הנ"ל להחזיר
14. לכה"ג הנ"ל {חלק רביעת} החצי אבל מתנות איין ווארף שנתנו בני
15. משפחתו וכן מה שנתן להם מסוחר אחד וכפי רשימה מצאנו ע"ד
16. פשר שמכסף כלים מחויב כה"רם הנ"ל להחזיר לכה"ג הנ"ל
17. חלק רביעת אבל ספרים ומעות מזומני' שייכי' לכהר"ם ואין
18. לכה"ג הנ"ל שום תביעה עליהם ומה שתבע כה"ג חצי טבעות
19. קידושין וסבלונות אין בו ממש עוד תבע כה"ג הנ"ל שיחזר
20. לו כהר"ם הנ"ל החצי ממלבושי' שהכניס לו בתו ז"ל וגם החצי
21. שני' ששייך לו יחזיר לו מפני עגמות נפש ורוצה ליתן לו דמי שווי'
22. כפי רשימת הב"ד וכהר"מ הנ"ל השיב שיומכר כל
23. המלבושי'

קפד ע"א

1. ב"ה
2. המלבושי' ודמי מכירה יחולק ביניהם מצאנו שכ"ה משה הנ"ל יחזיר לכה"ג הנ"ל
3. החצי ממלבושי' שהכניסה לו אשתו ז"ל כפי רשימה שהציע לפנינו והיינו שיחולקם
4. המלבושי' לשני חלקים שווי' ע"פ אומד דעתם ויעשה גורל ביניהם על החלקי'
5. הנ"ל אכן המלבשי' שעשה כ"ה משה הנ"ל לאשתו ז"ל והיינו אותן המלבושי'
6. שעשה מן שטוק צ[יט]ץ שקנה וגם איין וינר ראָק וגם איין ווייס דייטנה
7. ר"ה[3] יאקכה אין צריך להחזיר כלום עוד תבע כה"ג הנ"ל
8. סך שמונה זהו' שהלות' בתו פנוי'[4] לבתו נשואה ז"ל הנ"ל לעשות איין
9. יאקכה וכה משה השיב שלא ידע כלום מזה ואדרבה הוא תבע
10. שאשתו ז"ל הכניסה עמה לביתה איין דייטנה קונטעש ואחר החתנה
11. החזירה לאביה הנ"ל בכן טען כיון שהכניסה אשתו ז"ל לביתו זכה
12. הוא בחצי מצאנו ע"ד פשר שאין לזה על זה כלום מחמת תביעה זו עוד
13. תבע כהר"ם[5] בהרשאת כה"ג מן כה"ר משה הנ"ל לחזרה החצי מחצי

---

1. כבוד הרב מאיר (מז)
2. וכבוד הרב
3. ראש השנה(?)
4. כנראה בילה בת גומפיל (ר' אלה תולדות, 12.9.1793).
5. כבוד הרב מאיר (מז)

14. מקו׳ בע״נ שהכניס לו בשעת החופה והיינו רביעת ממקו׳ שלם
15. ששייך לו בתורת חזרה וברביעת מקו׳ האחרת ששייך לכהר״ם הנ״ל טוען כה״ג
16. שרוצה לזכות בו בדין גוד או איגוד וקצב סך מאה ועשרה זהו׳ שרוצה
17. ליתן מיד ברביעת מקו׳ הנ״ל וכהר״מ הנ״ל השיב באשר שנזכר בת״ר שהכניס
18. כה״ג החצי מקו׳ לחלוטין לא שייך בו תקנת חזרה ואף אם [י]זכה כה״ג ברביעת
19. מקו׳ הנ״ל גם הוא רוצה להחזיק בעד מאה ועשרה זהו׳ לשלם כפי תיקון
20. הקהלה על טערמישן מצאנו שהדין בזה עם ר׳ גומפיל הנ״ל ושייך לו רביעת
21. מקו׳ שלם הנ״ל בתקנת חזרה וברביעת מקו׳ אחרת יוכל לזכות בדין
22. גוד או איגוד בסך שקצב וכנ״ל עוד תבע כהר״מ הנ״ל מן כהר״ג הנ״ל
23. שכירות מחצי מקו׳ הנ״ל באשר שהכניס לו לחלוטין והוא גבה שכירות
24. בכן תבע משנה אחת וחצי וכה״ג הנ״ל השיב שכבר ניכה ממה שנשאר

קפד ע״ב

1. בה
2. שנשאר לו כהרם הנ״ל עוד חייב מהוצאת החתנה סך שבעה עשר
3. זהו׳ ותבע כה״ג עוד מן כהר״ם הנ״ל סך שמונה רט מצאנו ע״ד פשר
4. שאין לזה על זה כלום מחמת שני תביעות האלו עוד טען כהר״מ
5. באשר שדמי נדן שלו לקח סחורה בחנות שלו ואינה בעין בכן מה
6. שמחויב להחזיר מדמי נדן רוצה להחזיר בסחורת אבל לא במזומנ׳
7. ובאם יכירו הב״ד שיחזר במזומני׳ עכ״פ רוצה לשלם בזמני׳ וכהר״מ[1]
8. בהרשאת הנ״ל שבאם יכירו הב״ד שישלם לו כהרם[2] הנ״ל לזמני׳ עכ״פ
9. יתן ח״כ לשלם לזמן פירעון ומצאנו ע״ד פשר למה שמחויב כ״ה משה
10. הנ״ל להחזיר לכה״ג הנ״ל לאחר ניכוי׳ כל הנ״ל מחצי נדן הנ״ל יהי׳
11. התשלומן על אופן זה והיינו על ארבעה ירידם רצופי׳ זה אחר זה דהיינו
12. כל יריד בשבוע שלישת ישלם החלק הרביעת ממה שמוטל עליו
13. להחזיר והזמן פירעון הראשון יתחיל ביריד פסח הסמוך הב[על][3]
14. ומחויב כהרם הנ״ל ליתן לכה״ג הנ״ל תו״מ ארבעה ח״כ לאורדר
15. כה״ג לשלם לזמני׳ הנ״ל עוד תבע כה״ג שנחסר מן רשימה
16. א׳ גאסי שארץ שנתנה בתו פנויי׳ לבתו נשואה ז״ל דורן איין
17. ווארף אחר החתנה וגם נחסר מן רשימה ב בלייא שנופף טי{.}
18. טיכר א מולטונג ראק באהר ווייבר הויסן עוד תבע
19. תפילה ר׳ ישראל גר[4] שהכנסה בתו לבית בעלה וכהר״ם
20. הנ״ל השיב שגאסרשורץ נעשו בביתו לאחר החתנה ואיפשר
21. שלקחו ממעות שלו אונד דיא אונזר הויזן לבשה בשעת
22. מיתתה וגם המולטונג ראק אפשר ג״כ היתה לבוש בשעת

---

1. וכבוד הרב מאיר (מז)
2. כבוד הרב משה
3. הבא עלינו לטובה
4. התפילה הזאת לא מוכרת לי.

מיתה ושני שנופטיכר הם נאבד ומצאנו עד״פ שיחזר התפלה לכה״ג הנ״ל ובזה נפטר משאר התביעות שלו יצא מאתנו יו׳ ב ג ניסן תקמ״ה רנמי[1] ורמש[2] ואני

No. 191

Fol. 185a; Monday 2 May 1785

The rabbinic leadership of Frankfurt, represented by the chief rabbi and members of the two rabbinic courts, reminded residents that it was the established custom in Frankfurt not to allow post-partum women to immerse themselves in a ritual bath until forty-one days after the birth of a boy and eighty-one days after the birth of a girl (see Lev. 12.1–8). The court ordered that anyone who violated the custom was to be subject to a public announcement of their actions and warned of possible further punishment. The pronouncement made it clear that local custom was to be maintained not only in Frankfurt but in the surrounding areas as well. The announcement specifically noted that the court had heard that some local women were lenient in the matter.

קפה ע״א

ב״ה כרוז ביום ב דב אייר תקמ״ה הערט צו רבותי עז איזט בפאהלין ווארדין אויז צו רופין בשם הגאון אב״ד נרו[3] ובצירוף שני ב״ד יצו באשר שידוע לכל שבמדינתינו הי׳ אבותינו ואבות אבותינו נוהגין איסור שלא לטבול היולדת עד ארבעים ואחד לזכר ועד שמונים ואחד לנקבה והמנהג הזה מבואר בש״ע בדברי רמ״א שאין להתיר במקום שנוהגין איסור[4] ובאשר ששמענו שאיזה נשים הי׳ עוברים על זה בכן לאזין הגאון אב״ד נרו׳ בצירוף שני ב״ד יצו הנ״ל מכריז ומזהיר באזהרה גדולה זיין דש זיך קיין אשה יולדת אונזר שטיהן ווערד מכאן והלאה לטבול הן פה קהלותינו יע״א הן בסביבותינו עד ארבעים ואחד לזכר ועד שמונים ואחד לנקבה ומי שיעבור ע״ז ווירד מאן איהם מפרסם ברבים זיין על ב״ד שארי ביושי׳ ועונשים וועלכש גשעהן ווירד על עבריינות והשומע יונעם ותבוא עליו ברכת טוב

1. רב נתן מז
2. ורב מאיר שיף
3. נטריה רחמנא ופרקיה
4. רמ״א, שו״ע יו״ד, קצד ס׳ א.

No. 192

Fol. 185a; Sunday evening, 5 June or Monday evening, 6 June 1785

One-quarter of the inner house on the Krachbein lot was sold to Samuel Schotten for 900 guldens before the court. The house had belonged to the estate of the late Nathan Adler Katz and was auctioned for sale under the auspices of the community.

———

רביעת בית מבית שלם הפנימי צום קראך בוים שהי' שייך להמנוח כמ"ה נתן בכ"ה מרדכי אדליר כץ ז"ל נמכר בפנינו ב"ד ח"מ בפקודת האלופי' גובי' יצו לאחר הכרזה כנהוג להחתן כ' שמואל בהמנוחי כ"ה ליב שאטין ז"ל בעד תשעה מאות זהו' לשלם לפי תיקון הקהלה נעשה אור ליו' ב דט סיון תקמ"ה[2] רנ"מ ואני ורליזר[3] וואלה

No. 193

Fols. 185b–186a; Thursday 12 May 1785

Ber, son of Abraham Gans, died in 1774, leaving a wife, three daughters, and a son.[4] By 1785, the three daughters had all reached marital age and the executors of the estate approached the court asking that it award each of the daughters a portion of the estate so they could have dowries and find a suitable marriage partner. The request was supported by the children's mother, Freidche, who had since remarried. Freidche herself had given up 800 guldens of her own share in the estate in favor of the children when she was paid her marriage contract. She also had raised and supported three of the children, thus saving the estate significant sums in child support. After examining the status of the estate and earlier records, the court granted the request and ordered that each daughter receive 300 reichstalers from the estate at the time of marriage. The remainder of the estate was to be given to the son.

---

1. בן המנוח
2. באותה השנה חל יום ב' בכ"ח לחודש
3. ורב ליזר
4. Regarding his date of death, see Horovitz, no. 3514.

קפה ע״ב

1. ב״ה
2. הן היו׳ הקריבו לפנינו האפטרופסי׳ מיתמי המנוח כ׳ פער ז״ל בן הו״ה כ׳ אברהם
3. גנץ יצו ה״ה הו״ה כ׳ וואלף בן המנוח כ״ה זלמן שנאפיר סג״ל ז״ל[1] והו״ה כ׳
4. איצק בן המנוח כהרר[2] ליזר שיף כץ ז״ל והציע דבריהם לפנינו והיינו
5. באשר שהניח הנעדר כ׳ פער ז״ל הנ״ל אחריו ארבעה יתומי׳ שלשה
6. בנות ובן אחד[3] ומה שנמצא בעזבונו כעת היינו חצי בית בחצר קהל[4]
7. שדר בו כעת הו״ה כ׳ יוסף האמיל סג״ל גבר אוחרן של אם היתומי׳
8. הנ״ל ששייך ליתומי׳ הנ״ל רק שיש שיעבוד על החצי בית הנ״ל מחוב
9. סך שני מאות וחמשי׳ זהו׳ שנשאר עדיין חייב היתומי׳ הנ״ל לאמם הנ״ל
10. וכמבואר בפס״ד משנת קהלת לפק וממה שנכתב מפירעון מן יוד מנחם
11. תקלזין לפק וגם שייך עדיין היד עליונה מרביעת בית מחצי בית הנ״ל
12. לאבי זקנם של היתומי׳ הנ״ל כ׳ אברהם גנץ לו ולאשתו כל ימי חייהם
13. עוד יש בעזבון הנעדר הנ״ל מה ששייך ליתומי׳ הנ״ל חצי מקום בע״נ
14. ששייך היד העליונה לכ׳ אברהם הנ״ל [ול]אשתו עוד נמצא בעזבון
15. הנ״ל במזומני׳ לערך סך עשרה מאות זהו׳ והנה נפשם בשאלתם
16. אחרי שנתגדלו היתומי׳ הנ״ל שבנות הגיע לכלל נישואין שיכירו הב״ד
17. לפי ראות עיניהם הסך מה שמגיע להבנות יתומות הנ״ל מעזבון אביהם ז״ל
18. הנ״ל גם האשה מ׳ פראדכה אם של יתומים הנ״ל שלחה גכ[5] ה״ה התורנ[י]
19. כה פייס הענא יצו לפנינו וביקש מאתנו לפקח בטובת הנקבות היתומ׳
20. הנ״ל שייעינו הב״ד בפס״ד (הנ״ל)[6] יפה ושם נאמר מה שהטיבה האשה והניחה
21. ויתר סך שמונה מאות זהו׳ ליתומי׳ בעת סילוק האל׳ הנ״ל וגם מה שהרבת׳
22. עוד והחזיקה שלשה יתומי׳ אצלה מאותו זמן עד עכשיו וקיימה הכל כמבואר
23. בפס״ד הנ״ל בכן יכירו הב״ד שרוב ממה שיש עדיין בעזבון הנ״ל בא מטובתה
24. ולולי זאת הי׳ נחסר מן העזבון כמה מאות לצורך היתומי׳ בכן עתה שגידלה הבנות
25. שתגיע לנישואין יכירו הב״ד שגם הבנות תזכה בטובות שעשתה
26. בהם אמם בעזבן אביהן כמו הבן ויהפכו בזכותן שגם להן
27. יותן מעזבון אביהן לצורך נדן כדי שתבואו לכלל שידוך
28. [הגו]ן

קפו ע״א

1. ב״ה
2. הגון והנה אחרי שנזדקקנו לדבריהם עייננו הדק היטיב בפס״ד שיצא

---

1. וואלף שנאפיר היה אחיו של פראדכה, אשתו של פער גנץ.
2. כבוד הרב רבי
3. ר׳ אלה תולדות 5.8.1774, שבו מוזכר בן בשם וואלף ובת בשם בילה ותו לא.
4. ר׳ ספר הזכרונות, רמז ע״א, ושם מוזכר שפער גאנז היה גר ׳הינטר דער שול׳.
5. גם כן
6. תוספת מעל השורה

3. ביו' ה' ב' אדר ראשון שנת קהלת לפק מסילוק האל' מ' פראדכה
4. הנ"ל ומלשון וויתר שם גם ירדנו לשומא מה ששוה הק(ר)[1]יקעות שיש
5. בעזבון הנ"ל ולאחר שהי' לנו כל הנ"ל למראה עינינו ושקלנו במאזני
6. צדק את כל ונוכחת מצאנו לטובת היתומי' הבן עם הבנות הנ"ל שיותן
7. לכל אחת משלשה בנות יתומות של המנוח כ' פער ז"ל הנ"ל מעזבן
8. אביהן לעת נישואן שלהן סך שלשה מאות רט והשאר יהי' להבן
9. הנ"ל יצא מאתנו יו' ה' ג' סיון תקמ"ה (הגאון אב"ד נרו)[2] ורנמ[3] ורמש[4] ואני

No. 194

Fols. 186a–b; Monday 13 June 1785

The communal leadership in Frankfurt relayed a number of questions from the government in Vienna to the rabbinic court with respect to how conditions made at the time of marriage and inheritances between husband, wife, and children in Frankfurt were recorded. The leaders also asked the rabbis whether the ordinances made in the medieval communities of Worms and Mainz were followed in Frankfurt and the court replied that they were. The questions were addressed to the court in German and it responded in Hebrew. The Hebrew was then translated by a member of the community into German and recorded in the municipal records (see Appendix 6). Also see no. 188.

10. ע"ד השאלה שמסרו לנו האלופי' הקציני' גבאי הקהל יצו בלשון המבואר
11. מן רעגיהרונג דעיר מלוכה ווין
12. 1) אויך בייא הייאראהטש דען יודן אין פראנק פורט זיא ערשטן דיא יואהל אלז
13. צווייטן עהי פאקטן אין יעני האכצייטש ביכר וועלכה דיא שוהל קלעפפר
14. גווע[נליך] צו פיהרן פפלעגין גאנץ אונד פער עקסטענסום איין גטראגין ווערדן
15. ———
16. 2) אובש ניכט איינע אלגמיינעש יודישיס גזעץ באובאכטעט ווערדי דש
17. דער עהי מאן דעס אוניוורזאהל ערב זיינעש וויבש מיט אוש שלוס
18. דעם ער צייגטן קינדרביידרלייא גשלעכט זייאה
19. ———
20. 3) אויב איהם ניכט ווינגשטענס דש הייאראה[ט]ש גוטש זיינעש ווייבש

---

1. תוספת מעל השורה
2. תוספת מעל השורה
3. ורב נתן מז
4. ורב מאיר שיף

21. נאך איהרם אה[ר]די[1] פער בלייבה / אוהני דש איין בזונדרעש פאקטום
22. דער דוטא לוקראנדא היר צו ער פארדרט ווערדי
23. 4) ————
24. אויב אין פ"פורט[2] בייא שטערב פאלין דער יודן דיא איין ריכטונג דעם
25. שטעטן מענץ אונד ווירמש אין באויבאכטין אונד אויש איבונג זייאה

קפו ע"ב

1. תשובה
2. על שאלה א' תשובה כן כותבים השמשים בפנקס של חתנות שעשו
3. הצדדי' ק"ס לקיים התנאי' ראשוני' שהוקמו ביניהם אבל אין כותבין
4. פרטי דברי התנאי'
5. על שאלה ב' וג' תשובה כך הדין לפי דת תורתינו הקדושה
6. שהבעל יורש את אשתו במוחזק הן מה שהכניסה לו לנדן והן
7. מה שלא הכניס לו בכולם הבעל יורש אותן ואין הבנים הן
8. זכרים או נקבות יורשים כלום מאמם ואף שלא הוקים בין בעל
9. לאשתו שום כתב עז"ה שיירש אותה / אפ"ה הדין הוא
10. כך שהבעל יורש אותה אכן אם הותנה בין הבעל ואשתו
11. בתנאי' מפורשי' להיפך שלא יירש הבעל אותה הן הכל הן
12. מקצת אזי יקוים כפי שהותנה ביניהם
13. ————
14. על שאלה ד תשובה שנוהגין כאן תקנות שו"ם כל הנ"ל
15. יצא מאתנו פ"ה[3] פראנק פורט יו' ב' ה' תמוז תקמ"ה
16. הגאון אב"ד נרו[4] ורנ"מ ורמ"ש ואני

No. 195

Wallau v. Rothschild et al.

Fol. 187a; Wednesday 9 November 1785

Rabbi Meʾir Schiff, often a member of the rabbinic court, sold half of the Grünes Schild house to Meʾir (Meyer) Rothschild. Meʾir Maas and Rabbi Leser Wallau acted as agents in the transaction and each received payment for his services. Leser subsequently sued Maas and Rothschild for the entire agent's fee, claiming that

1. לא ברור; ע"פ המקור הגרמני (ר' נספח ו') צ"ל כאן 'טודה' (Tode).
2. פרנקפורט
3. אולי צ"ל 'פה'
4. נטריה רחמנא ופרקיה

he was the first agent to handle the matter and that he could have concluded the transaction without Maas. After both sides agreed to a compromise, Leser Wallau was awarded a payment by the court to be paid both by Rothschild and Schiff. Also see no. 208.

קפז ע״א

1. ב״ה
2. ע״ד שכר סרסרנות מן מכירת חצי בית צום גריני שילד שמכר הדיין
3. כ״ה מאיר שיף כץ להו״ה כ״ה מאיר רויטשילד ע״י סרסור התורני
4. כ״ה מאיר מז יצו וה״ה הדיין כ״ה ליזר וואלי סגל תבע לפנינו מן
5. כ״ה מאיר רויטשילד ומן כ״ה מאיר מז שמגיע לו כל שכר סרסרונות
6. באשר שהוא הי׳ סרסור ראשון והי׳ יכול לגמור וטעון לפנינו באריכות
7. כל אחד ואחד ובאשר שהצדדים הנ״ל חתמו עצמם בקומפרמיס
8. לקיים הפשר שיצא מאתנו נזדקקנו להם ומצאנו בתורת פשר
9. שכ״ה מאיר [ר]״ש הנ״ל מחויב ליתן לכ״ה ליזר הנ״ל חמשה חדש
10. ר״ט ומן התשעה חדש רטי׳ שמונח עדיין ביד הדיין ר׳ מאיר
11. שיף נר׳ יותן לו ארבע חדש רטי׳ יצא מאתנו יו׳ ד זין כסליו תקמ״ו
12. רנמ[1] אני ורמ״ל

No. 196

Trier v. Frumet, widow of Gershon Emden

Fols. 187a–b; Wednesday evening, 9 November 1785

After the death of Gershon Emden in the summer of 1785, his widow, Frumet, came to the court to discharge her marriage contract.[2] However, Jacob Trier of Offenbach approached the court with an obligatory note for 500 reichstalers that Gershon had given him in 1772, before Gershon married Frumet. Jacob argued that since Gershon indebted himself to him before he married Frumet, Jacob's claim against the estate preceded Frumet's. Frumet's counsel is reported to have made numerous attempts to support her claims to precedence but they are not itemized here.

Frumet was not the only beneficiary of the estate. Gershon's nephews were also to receive inheritances. To protect her interests, Frumet, with Jacob Trier's promise

1. רב נתן מז
2. Regarding Gershon Emden's death, see Horovitz, no. 3869.

of financial assistance, made a cash settlement with one of the nephews, who subsequently sent a note to the court stating that he withdrew his claim against the estate. The other three nephews maintained their claims. All five claimants signed an agreement to be bound by a court imposed compromise. The court ordered Frumet to pay 550 guldens to Jacob Trier within six months. Frumet and the nephews were prohibited from receiving their shares in the estate until Jacob was paid.

Gershon had also made provisions for the establishment of a perpetual fund to pay for ten men to study and pray in his memory during the first year after his death, and, subsequently, on the anniversary of his passing (*yahrzeit*). Jacob was to be included in the group but renounced his right to payment for his services, perhaps to ease the financial burden on Frumet. The court accepted this arrangement during the first year but ordered that Jacob be paid for study and prayer when the anniversary of Gershon's death was observed. Also see no. 197.

13. ————
14. ע"ד טענות והפרשות בענין סילוק האל' האשה מ' פרומט מעזבון בעלה
15. המנוח כ"ה גרשון עמדין ז"ל שה"ה התורני כ"ה יעקל טריר מק"ק
16. אויפיבאך יע"א הציע לפנינו שטר חוב מן המנוח כ"ה גרשון ז"ל הנ"ל
17. מסך חמשה מאות רט לשלם שעה אחת קודם מותו ההוקם ך"ב אדר
18. ראשון תקלב לפק ותבע באשר ששטר חוב שלו נעשה קודם החתנה
19. של האל' עם בעלה כ"ה גרשון הנ"ל בכן הוא מוקדם לגבות שטרו קודם
20. האל' הנ"ל / וכ"ה משה אויך בהרשאות האל' הנ"ל השיב באריכות
21. כמבואר בק"ה המונח אצלינו / ובאשר שהצדדים הנ"ל חתמו עצמם בתוקף
22. קומפרמיס בח"ח ובקנס סך מסוים חצי לשררה יר"ה וחצי להקדש לאשר
23. ולקיים הפשר שיצא מאתנו / גם יורשי דאורייתא מן המנוח
24. כ"ה

קפז ע"ב

1. בעז"ה
2. כ"ה גרשון הנ"ל המה שלשה בני יתומי' של המנוח כ' זעליג
3. עמדין ז"ל בן אחי המנוח כ"ה גרשון הנ"ל הי' לפנינו ונתנו
4. עיניהם על הב"ד וחתמו עצמם בקומפרמיס הנ"ל וכנ"ל / גם
5. הי' לפנינו פטורין מן היורש דאורייתא כ' גומפא וועצליר
6. בח"י מקוים / בכן נזדקקנו להם ומצאנו בתורת פשר
7. שמחויב' האל' הנ"ל לשלם מעזבון בעלה הנ"ל לכה[1] יעקל
8. הנ"ל סך חמשה מאות וחמשים זהו' במזומנים מהיו' דלמטה
9. תוך ששה חדשים ובזה נתפרע השט"ח הנ"ל מן כ"ה יעקל

———

1. לכבוד הרב

10. הנ"ל על כ"ה גרשון הנ"ל / ומשועבד כל עזבון ונכסי בעלה
11. {בעלה} הנ"ל לתשלומין סך הנ"ל לכ"ה יעקל הנ"ל ומחויבת האשה
12. אל' הנ"ל למכור הקרקעות הנ"ל מהיו' דלמטה תוך ששה [חד]שי'
13. לתשלומן סך הנ"ל לכ"ה יעקל הנ"ל / ולאחר תשלומין סך חמשה
14. מאות וחמשי' זהו' הנ"ל פטורה האל' הנ"ל ויא'[1] וב"כ מן כ"ה יעקל הנ"ל
15. וי"א וב"כ מחמת תביעות שט"ח הנ"ל / גם מצאנו בתורת פשר שפטור
16. כ"ה יעקל הנ"ל לשלם ארבעה קרלינר שהתרצה א"ע כ"ה יעקל לשלם
17. להאל' הנ"ל לסיועת דמי פשר שנתנה האל' הנ"ל ליורש בעלה ז"ל
18. ה"ה כ' גומפא ב"כ זימלן עמדין הנ"ל / ומה שמחל כ"ה יעקל הנ"ל
19. להאל' הנ"ל השכירות מן לימודו ואמירת קדיש בשנה ראשונה
20. להעדרת בעלה יקוים ופטורה האל' מלשלם לו שכירות / אכן מה
21. שנאמר בק"ס ובצוואת בעלה כ"ה גרשון הנ"ל שכ"ה יעקל הנ"ל יהי' בתוך
22. עשרה לומדים המתפללי' ולומדים בכל שנה ושנה ביארצייטן
23. הנזכרים שם יקוים ג"כ ומחויבי' לשלם לו שכרו כאחד מן לומדי'
24. אחרים יצא מאתנו אור ליו' ה' ח' כסליו תקמ"ו
25. הגאון אב"ד נר'
26. ורנ"מ
27. ורמ"ש
28. ואני

No. 197

Fols. 188a–189b; Wednesday evening, 9 November 1785

With the matter of a preceding lien against the estate of Gershon Emden settled (see no. 196), the very same evening Gershon's widow, Frumet, formally asked to be discharged from the estate. As in other cases, the court required the widow to provide it with an inventory of goods left by her husband, which she did. The court was informed that in 1776 Frumet had agreed to Gershon's request to set up a perpetual fund to hire ten men to study and pray in his and his son's memories on the anniversaries of their deaths.

There were insufficient assets in the estate to pay Frumet the 5,000 guldens stipulated in the marriage contract. Nevertheless, the court ordered Frumet to pay the obligation to Jacob Trier of Offenbach mentioned in no. 196, as well as to pay for those who studied and prayed in Gershon's memory during the first year after

---

1. ויוצאיה אחריה

his death, and to provide for the perpetual fund within a year. The court also ruled that obligatory notes held by Gershon against his late nephew, Selig, be canceled and that Selig's children, themselves beneficiaries of the estate, see the cancellation of these obligations as partial payment of what was due them from the estate. Frumet was also ordered to give Selig's sons a relatively modest cash payment to be divided among them. The rest of the estate was Frumet's to do with as she pleased.

קפח ע"א

1. בעז"ה
2. ע"ד שבא לפנינו ה"ה התורני כ"ה משה אויך בהרשאות ובמעמד האל' מ'[1] פרומט אל'
3. המנוח כ"ה גרשון עמדין ז"ל וביקש מאתנו לסלק האל' הנ"ל מעזבון בעלה הנ"ל ואמר
4. שאין לה שטרות תנאים אחרוינ'[2] רק הציע לפנינו ק"ס מן ר"ח אב ומן ויו אב
5. תקלו ושם נאמר שיותן להאשה מ' פרומט הנ"ל סך ארבעה עשר מאות זהו' לפירען
6. כתובה ותוספ' נגד זה התחייבה האשה מ' פרומט הנ"ל בק"ס הנ"ל וכמו שנאמר
7. שם בזה הלשון / ועוד התחייבה האשה מ' פרומט הנ"ל בק"ס הנ"ל כנ"ל להניח
8. ארבע מאות רייכש טאליר ממעות כתובה ותוספ' לזמן פרעון כתובה ותוספ'
9. אצל הו"ה הגובי' יצו על רווחים חמשה {מאו}רט מכל מאה ומאה רט לשנה
10. נגד קוויטונג מאתם לקרן קיימת עולמי עד לדבר טוב על שני יאהרצייטן / דהיינו
11. אחד ביאהר צייט של בנו המנוח כ' ליפמן ז"ל[3] בנו שכ"ה גרשון הנ"ל שהוא י"א כסליו
12. ואחד באם יעדר הוא ח"ו בעלה כ"ה גרשון הנ"ל בכל יאהרצייט של כאו"א ליקח עשרה
13. לומדים / תשעה מבני עירינו וקרוב קרוב קודם / והעשירי' יהי' התורני כ"ה יעקל טריר
14. מאויפיבאך שהוא יתום שלו[4] להתפלל ערב ובוקר / וגם לאחר התפלה ללמוד
15. פרק אחד משניות ולומר קדיש עליו / ויותן לכאו"א מעשרה לומדים הנ"ל בכל
16. יאהרצייט הנ"ל א רט וגם הציע לפנינו שטר וק"ס הנעשה ך"ז מנחם תק"מ שהוסיף
17. לה בעלה ופסק לה בשביל כתובה ותוס' שלה סך חמשת אלפים זה' / ועוד הציע
18. שטר מתנה לפנינו על החצי מקו' בע"נ ההוקם ד"י אלול תקלו / וגם הציע לפנינו
19. אינפודאריום מעזבון בעלה והיינו חצי בית צום נוס בוים ורביעת בית צום
20. צום שווארצואַדליר וחצי מקו' בע"נ ושטרות ואפותיקו / וח"כ ומטלטלין וכסף ושוה
21. כסף וספרים וכלי בית שהניח בעלה ז"ל / וטען כ"ה משה הנ"ל בהרשאות האל' הנ"ל
22. באשר שכל עזבון בעלה ז"ל הנ"ל אינו מגיע לפרעון כתובה ותוספ' סך חמשת
23. אלפי' זהו' הנזכר בשטר ההוקם ך"ז מנחם תק"מ / בכן יחליט לה הב"ד
24. כל עזבון בעלה הנ"ל באשר שכבר נשבעת שבועת כתובה לפני הגאון
25. אב"ד נר'ו / וה"ה התורני כ"ה יעקל מאויפיבאך יע"א הציע לפנינו שטר חוב
26. מסך חמשה מאות רייכש טאליר לשלם שעה אחת קודם מותו [מן] המנוח כ"ה גרשון

---

1. מרת
2. צ"ל 'אחרוני'"
3. לא היה לגרשון זרע בני קיימא להגיד עליו קדיש (ר' אלה תולדות 26.6.1785).
4. אולי בן חורג. לא מדובר ביעקב בן מאיר טריר שהיה שליח ציבור בפרנקפורט כ"ח שנה ונפטר בשנת תקס"ב (אבני זכרון, מס' 4383, וגם ספר הזכרון, שפח ע"ב).

27. הנ"ל ההוקם ך"ב אדר ראשון תקלב לפק וטען באשר שט"ח שלו נעשה קודם
28. חתנה

קפח ע"ב

1. בעז"ה
2. חתנה של האל' הנ"ל עם בעלה ז"ל הנ"ל / בכן הוא מוקדם לגבות שטרו
3. קודם אל' הנ"ל / וכ"ה משה הנ"ל השיב מה שהשיב באריכות על שטחי[1] מן כ"ה
4. יעקל הנ"ל וגם טען מה שטען נגד התחייבת של האל' הנ"ל בכל דמי דבר טוב
5. הנ"ל לזכות האל' הנ"ל באריכות כמבואר בק"ה / ויורשים דאורייתא מן המנוח
6. כ"ה גרשון הנ"ל המה בני אחיו מהם שישנו פה בקהלותינו יע"א והיינו שלשה
7. בנים מן המנוח כ' זעליג עמדין ז"ל באו לפנינו ונתנו עיניהם על הב"ד מה שיכירו
8. הב"ד הן בסילוק האל' הנ"ל הן בתשלומין כ"ה יעקל הנ"ל שמרוצם בכך /
9. ויורש אחד מן המנוח כ"ה גרשון הנ"ל הדר בק"ק וועצליר יע"א ה"ה כמר
10. גומפא בן כ' זימלן עמדין כבר סילוק א"ע מן העזבון הנ"ל ע"י פשר
11. שנעשה עם האל' הנ"ל וכמו שהציע האל' לפנינו פטורים בכא"ה מן
12. כ' גומפא הנ"ל ונתקיים חתימתו בפנינו ב"ד / והנה אחרי שהצדדי'
13. הנ"ל חתמו עצמם בתוקף קומפרמיס בח"ח ובקנס סך מסוים חצי לשררה יר"ה
14. וחצי להקדש לקיים מה שיצא מאתנו בתורת פשר נזדקקנו להם / ודקדקנו
15. בשט"ח מן ר' יעקל הנ"ל ובק"ס הנעשה מן ר' גרשון ואשתו הנ"ל בשנת תקלו
16. ובק"ס הנעשה תק"מ[2] / ודקדקנו הדק היטב בהם ובטענותיהם מה שטען
17. זה מול זה באריכות / וגם דקדקנו באינפודיאריום שהציע האל' לפנינו
18. ולאחר שעיינונו בכל הנ"ל / מצאנו בתורת פשר שמחויב האל' הנ"ל
19. לשלם מעזבון בעלה הנ"ל לכ"ה יעקל הנ"ל במזומנים סך חמשה
20. מאות וחמשים זהו' מיו' דלמטה תוך ששה חדשים / ובזה נתפרע
21. השט"ח הנ"ל מן כ"ה יעקל הנ"ל על כ"ה גרשון הנ"ל / ומשועבד
22. כל עזבון בעלה ונכסי בעלה הנ"ל לתשלומין סך חמשה מאות וחמשים
23. זהו' לכ"ה יעקל הנ"ל / ומחויבת האל' הנ"ל למכור הקרקעות הנ"ל מיו'
24. דלמטה תוך ששה חדשי' לתשלומן סך הנ"ל לכ"ה יעקל הנ"ל / ולאחר
25. התשלומין חמשה מאות וחמשים זהו' הנ"ל פטורה האל' ויא[3] וב"כ מן
26. כ"ה

קפט ע"א

1. בעז"ה
2. כ"ה יעקל הנ"ל ויא[4] וב"כ מחמת תביעות שט"ח הנ"ל / וגם מצאנו בתורת פשר
3. שפטר כ"ה יעקל הנ"ל לשלם להאל' הנ"ל סך ארבעה קרלינר שהתרצה א"ע

---

1. שטר חוב
2. ר' לעיל, דף קפח ע"א, שורה 16.
3. ויורשיה אחריה
4. ויורשיו אחריו

4. לשלם להאל' הנ"ל לסיועת דמי הפשר שנתנה האל' להיורש כ' גומפא הנ"ל
5. אבל מה שמחל כ"ה יעקל הנ"ל להאל' הנ"ל שכר לימודו ואמירת קדיש בשנה
6. ראשונה להעדרת בעלה ז"ל בתוך מנין עשה[1] לומדים יקוים ופטורה האל'
7. לשלם לו / ומה שנאמר בק"ס ובצוואה שכ"ה יעקל הנ"ל יהי' בתוך הלומדים ה
8. המתפללים בשני יאהר צייטן כל שנה ושנה כנ"ל יקוים ג"כ ומחויב'
9. לשלם לכה[2] יעקל הנ"ל שכרו כאחד מן שאר לומדים / ומחמת התחייבות האל'
10. הנ"ל לקיים דבר טוב הנ"ל להניח ארבע מאות רט אצל הו"ה גובי' יצו לצורך
11. דבר טוב הנ"ל מצאנו שמחויב האל' הנ"ל לקיים מה שהתחייבה א"ע לקיים דבר טוב
12. הלז להניח מיו' דלמטה תוך שנה אחת ארבע מאות רט אצל האלופי' גויב'[3] יצו
13. על אופן המבואר בצוואה הנ"ל / ומשועבד כל עזבון ונכסי בעלה הנ"ל לתשלומין
14. סך ארבע מאות רט הנ"ל / ומחויבת האל' הנ"ל למכור הקרקעות הנ"ל מהיו'
15. [דל]מטה תוך שנה אחת לתשלומין סך הנ"ל לדבר טוב הנ"ל וכל זמן שלא
16. הניח המעות דב"ט הנ"ל אצל הו"ה גובי' יצו כנ"ל מחויבת האל' לקיים שני
17. יאהר צייטן על אופן המבואר בצוואה לתועלת נשמת בעלה ז"ל ובנו כ' ליפמן
18. ז"ל ולשלם ללומדים מכיסה / וגם מצאנו מה שהתחילו האל' הנ"ל לקיים צוואת בעלה
19. לתועלת נשמתו שנה ראשונה מחויבת היא לגמור עד כלות שנה ראשונה
20. כמבואר בק"ס ההוקם ך"ז מנחם תק"מ / ומחמת יתומים של המנוח כ' זעליג
21. עמדין ז"ל הנ"ל בני אחיו של המנוח כ"ה גרשון ז"ל הנ"ל מצאנו בתורת
22. פשר שיקוים כל מה שנאמר בצוואה שנעשה ויו אב תקלו שכל השטרות וח"כ
23. הנמצאים בעזבון כ"ה גרשון הנ"ל על אביהם כ' זעליג ז"ל הם בחזקת
24. פרעון והם בטלין ומבוטלין ואין על אביהם שום חוב הן בע"פ או בכתב
25. מן

קפט ע"ב

1. בעז"ה
2. מן המנוח כ"ה גרשון הנ"ל ונוסיף לזה תתן האל' הנ"ל לשלשה יתומי' הנ"ל
3. מעזבון בעלה סך מאה זהו' / והיינו לכאו"א סך שלשים ושלשה זהו' ך
4. צ"ל וינוכה מן כאו"א מה שקיבל כבר ממנה לאחר מיתת בעלה ז"ל ובזה
5. {הוא} פטור ומסולק האל' הנ"ל וי"א וב"כ מן יתומי' הנ"ל וי"א וב"כ מכל טענות
6. ותביעות שבעולם מחמת העזבון בעלה כ"ה גרשון הנ"ל / ואחרי שיקוים
7. כל הנ"ל החלטנו מעכשיו את כל עזבון בעלה בעלה[4] הנ"ל להאל'
8. הנ"ל לחלוטין גמורין ולצמיתות עלמין / הן קרקעות הן מטלטלין משכונית
9. כסף ושוה כסף הן שטרות וח"כ על נימולי' והן על א"נ וכלי בית
10. וספרים מכל מה שהפה יוכל לדבר והלב לחשוב ולהרהר כולם
11. הוחלטנה להאל' הנ"ל וי"א וב"כ לעשות בכל עזבון בעלה הנ"ל

1. צ"ל 'עשרה'
2. לכבוד הרב
3. צ"ל 'גובי''
4. כפילות במקור

12. כאות נפשה ורצונה ככל אינש דרשאי לעשות בשלו בלי
13. שום מוחה וערעור שבעולם הן מיורשי בעלה והן משום אדם
14. יהי' מי שיהי' וכתבנו וחתמנו כל הנ"ל בתוקף מעשה ב"ד
15. ובכח ב"ד יפה להיות לעדות ולזכות ולראיי' שיהי'
16. כל עזבון המנוח כ"ה גרשון הנ"ל / להאל' הנ"ל וי"א וב"כ
17. לאחר שיקוים כל הנ"ל בלי שום מוחה כלל יצא מאתנו
18. אור ליו' ה חית כסליו תקמויו לפק
19. הגאון אב"ד נר'
20. ורנמ'[1]
21. ורמש[2]
22. ואני

No. 198

Fol. 190a; Sunday evening, 13 November 1785

Half a seat in the upper women's section of the synagogue that belonged to the community and was being used by the wife of Samuel Stern was sold to Yeḥiʾel Cohen for 340 guldens. The sale took place after the customary public announcement that the seat was for sale.

קצ ע"א

1. בעז"ה
2. אור ליו' ב' י"ב כסליו תקמ"ו מכרנו לפני ב"ד לאחר הכרזה כנהוג חצי מקו'
3. בע"נ עליונה שעומדת עליה כעת אשת כ"ה שמואל חיים שטערין יצו
4. שהי' שייך להו"ה גובי' יצו / להו"ה כמר יחיאל כהן בעד סך שלש מאות
5. וארבעים זהו' לשלם כפי תיקון הקהלה רנ"ש[3] ואני ורמ"ש

No. 199

Fols. 190a–b; Wednesday evening, 9 November 1785

Moses Schuster wanted to sell a here unspecified piece of property, but before the

1. והרב נתן מז
2. והרב מאיר שיף
3. אולי צ"ל 'רנ"מ' (רב נתן מז)

court would ratify the sale it checked to see that Moses had fulfilled a condition imposed upon him by the court two years earlier regarding a charitable matter (see no. 171). The court found that Moses had not properly fulfilled the will of his late aunt Fiel, daughter of Isaac Schuster, who had ordered that each year a sum of money be given by her estate to support poor brides and those studying Torah. The community had also failed in its responsibilities and had not appointed a guardian to oversee the charitable funds. To rectify this, the court appointed a communal official, Mikhl Geiger, as an interim overseer and ordered him to make sure that Moses made the appropriate payments, which Moses did. The court also instructed Moses about future payments and the distribution of funds to needy brides and scholars. Moses was to keep Mikhl informed of all transactions and, in any year in which there were no needy brides, to transfer that year's funds to Mikhl, presumably for investment or safe keeping.

6. ———
7. ע"ד שאנחנו ב"ד ח"מ עקלנו החלוטה על מכירות מקו' שמכר כ' משה בן לעמלי
8. שוסטר עד שנחקור אותו אם קיים הפס"ד שיצא מאתנו ויו כסליו תקמ"ד בענין הדבר
9. טוב הנאמר בצוואה של האשה המונחת מ' פייל בת כ"ה איצק שוסטר ז"ל ההוקם בק"ק
10. וואסירטריליגען ה' אב תקי"ט / ולאחר שבא לפנינו כ' משה הנ"ל וחקרנו אותו וראינו
11. שלא נתמנה עדיין אפטרופס ושלא קיים כ' משה הנ"ל הפס"ד כראוי הן במה שלא
12. קיבל החרם המוטל עליו בפס"ד הנ"ל מן העבר הן במה שעיכוב ולא שילם כל
13. שנה ארבעה זהו' לסיועת הכנסת כלה כפי הנאמר בפס"ד הנ"ל עד עתה /
14. לזאת מצאנו קצת ע"פ הדין וקצת ע"פ פשר שמחויב כ' משה הנ"ל לשלם שנים
15. עשר רט מחמת העבר ושייך עשרה רט לסיועת הכנסת כלה / ושני רט
16. לתלמוד תורה וכמבואר בצוואה / ובזה הוא פטור מכל קבלת חרם המוטל עליו
17. בפס"ד הנ"ל / וגם נתפרע בזה כל הרווחים עד ר"ח תמוז העבר / ובאשר
18. שלא נתמנה עדיין אפטרופס מקהל יצו בכן בירנו אנחנו ב"ד ח"מ בנתים
19. ה"ה התורני כ"ה מיכל גייגר נאמן הקהלה / להיות בידו שטר חוב מן כ' משה הנ"ל
20. אודת דבר טוב הנ"ל לגבות השנים עשר רט הנ"ל מן כ"ה משה הנ"ל / ובאשר
21. שנתברר לנו שכבר שילם שנים עשר רט הנ"ל לכ"ה מיכל הנ"ל / בכן הוא פטור
22. כ' משה הנ"ל מכל קבלת חרם הנ"ל ומן הרווחים הנ"ל וכנ"ל / וגם מצאנו לטובת
23. דבר טוב הנ"ל שמכאן והלאה יקוים הפס"ד הנ"ל על אופן המבואר שמחויב
24. כ' משה הנ"ל ליתן כל שנה ושנה דמי סיועת הכנסת כלה שעולה סך
25. ארבעה זהו' ד' פץ על אופן המבואר בפונקטה ב' בצוואה וז"ל
26. עוד

קצ ע"ב

1. בעז"ה
2. עוד מאה זהו' רייניש יוקח מעזבוני ויהא ג"כ קרן קיימת והרווחי' שיעלו כל
3. שנה מאלו מאה זהו' יותן כל שנה ביאהרצייט שלי לסיועת הכנסת כלה

4. לבת למדן הן בפפ״ד והן בפרידבוריג אונד וועז זיך פריאר אן
5. מעלט אצל האפטרופסי׳ יהי׳ זוכה ברווחי׳ האלו / והאפטרופסי׳ ישגיחו
6. ע״ז זולכש אויף צו שרייבן ווערר זיך פאהר אן גמעלט האט / ועכ״פ
7. הקרוב קרוב קודם עכ״ל וכזי[1] דקדקנו בלשון הצוואה מחויב להיות הבת
8. למדן מפפ״ד או מפרידבוריג / וגם מצאנו בפשר הנ״ל שמחויב הכלה
9. או אחר בחריקאה שביקש אותו מעות לילך אצל משה שוסטר הנ״ל ונתינה
10. יהי׳ בידיעת כ״ה מיכל הנ״ל נגד כתב ראיי׳ ממנו / ובאם לא
11. יזדמנה כלה אחת שתבקש סיועה ממנו עכ״פ ימסרם לכ״ה מיכל הנ״ל כל
12. שנה נגד כתב ראיי׳ ממנו וכה״ג הדמי רווחים לסיועת ת״ת העולה
13. כל שנה סך שנים עשר זהו׳ מ״ה צל מחויב כ׳ משה הנ״ל לשלם
14. כל שנה בידיעת כ״ה מיכל הנ״ל ולנגד כתב ראיי׳ ממנו ויקוים על
15. אופן המבואר בצוואה וז״ל בפונקטר ראשון והרווחי׳ שיעלו כל שנה
16. יחלקו כל שנה ושנה לתלמוד תורה כפי אומד דעתו של האפטרופס
17. הן בפראנקפורט דמיין או בפרידבורוג וואו וואהל אן גלעגט
18. זיין ועכ״פ הקרוב קרוב קודם יצא מאתנו אור ליו׳ ה׳ חית
19. כסליו תקמו לפק רנ״מ ורמ״ש ואני

No. 200

Fol. 190b; Monday 28 November 1785

A seat in the lower women's section of the here unspecified synagogue that was currently being used by the wife of Joseph Hammel was sold to Gumprecht Friedberg for 655 guldens. The seat had belonged to the late Aaron Ochs. Two-thirds of the proceeds of the sale went to charity and one-third to the beneficiaries of the estate of Aaron's widow, who is not named here. The record notes that the chief rabbi and members of both rabbinic courts were involved in the decision of how the funds should be divided. A court of three judges dealt with the actual sale of the seat.

20. מקו׳ שלם בע״נ התחתונה שעומדות עלי׳ אשת הו״ה גע[2] כ״ה יוסף האמיל סג״ל
21. שהי׳ שייך למנוח מה׳ אהרן אוקס ז״ל נמכר בפנינו ב״ד להה[3] כ״ה גומפריך
22. פרידבורג בעד סך ששה מאות וחמשי׳ וחמשה זהו׳ לשלם כתיקון הקהלה
23. ודמי מכירה (יחולק)[4] ושייך שני שלישי מהם לצדקה ושליש אחד ליורשי אל׳ המנוח

---

1. וכל זה
2. גבאי צדקה
3. להרב החכם
4. תוספת מעל השורה

24. הנ״ל שיש לכ״ה יוזלי באמבורג כח והרשאה ועומד בחריקאם יצא ע״פ פשר
25. עי[1] פסק ב״ד ביו׳ ד ערח[2] כסליו תקמ״ו החלוקה כנ״ל מה״ג אב״ד נרו[3] ושני ב״ד יצו
26. ועל מעשה ב״ד חתמו רנ״מ ורמ״ש ואני ביו׳ ב דן כסליו הנ״ל

No. 201

Fol. 191a; Sunday evening, 18 December 1785

A seat in the middle women's section of the here unspecified synagogue that had belonged to Yatcha, the wife of Herz Gans, and was being used by the wife of David Kassel, was sold by order of the community. As was customary, the availability of the seat was announced and the seat was eventually sold to Zanvil Stiebel for 577 guldens. Payment was made to the communal leadership in the customary installments. Also see document no. 202.

קצא ע״א

1. ב״ה
2. מקו׳ שלם בע״נ התיכונה אשר עומדות עלי׳ כעת אשת דוד קאסל יצו
3. שהי׳ שייך להאשה מ׳ יטכה אשת נאמן הקהלה כ״ה הירץ בהמנוח[4] כמ״ה
4. פער גנץ זצ״ל נמכר בפקודת קהל יצו לאחר הכרזה כנהוג בפנינו ב״ד
5. לכ׳ זנוויל ב״כ זעלקלי שטיבל בעד סך חמשה מאות ושבעי׳ ושבעה זהו׳ לשלם
6. כפי תיקון הקהלה להאלופי׳ גובי׳ יצו נעשה אור ליו׳ ב׳ חי טבת תקמם״ויו

No. 202

Fol. 191a; Monday evening, 2 January 1786

A seat in the lower men's section of the here unspecified synagogue that had belonged to the wife of Herz Gans and was being used by Herz Stern Katz was sold before the court. As in no. 201, the community ordered that the seat be sold and it receive the proceeds of the sale. The seat was sold to Solomon Luria for 166 guldens after the customary announcement of sale.

---

1. על ידי
2. ערב ראש חודש
3. נטריה רחמנא ופרקיה
4. בן המנוח

7. מקו׳ שלם בע״א התחתונה אשר עומד עלי׳ כעת כ״ה הירץ שטערן כץ שהי׳ שייך
8. לאשת כ״ה הירץ גנץ הנ״ל נמכר בפקודת הקהל יצו לאחר הכרזה כנהוג
9. בפנינו ב״ד לכ׳ שלמה בן כ׳ זנוויל לוריא בעד סך מאה וששים וששה זהו׳
10. {כפי} לשלם כפי תיקון הקהלה להאלופי׳ גובי׳ יצו נעשה אור ליו׳ ג
11. ד שבט תקמ״ו רנ״מ ורמשי[1] ואני

No. 203

Wetterhahn et al. v. Sorle, widow of Moses Deuz

Fols. 191a–194a; Wednesday 25 January 1786

After the death of Moses Deuz in April 1785 his sons continued to operate his business interests.[2] Abraham Deuz, one of Moses' sons, subsequently died, leaving a daughter. Her three guardians approached the court and demanded that Moses' widow, Sorle, present the court with an inventory of the estate and be paid her marriage contract. The remainder of the assets should then be divided and the granddaughter should receive her father's share in the estate, which was to be twice that of his brothers because he was the first born male (see Deut. 21.17).

Sorle replied through her representative that she had already given the court an inventory of all assets of the estate and had taken an oath before the head of the court with respect to its accuracy. She asked the court to discharge her marriage contract, pay her over 6000 guldens that she was due (an amount disputed by the guardians), and provide her with housing for the duration of her widowhood. Through their legal counsel, the guardians countered that based on what had been said of Moses, and given the size of the dowry that Sorle gave one of her daughters, the value of the estate had been significantly underestimated. As noted, they also questioned the amount due to Sorle as part of her marriage contract. They asked the court to investigate and compel the family to sell its silver, gold, and jewels, assuming that the value received through sale would be greater than the estimated value, a move vehemently contested by the defendants. The family asserted that, if anything, the inventory submitted to the court overvalued the estate and argued that a wholesale liquidation of assets would cause them loss.

Sorle's representative, who also represented Moses' young children, argued that the remaining assets of the estate should be divided among the beneficiaries, but

---

1. והרב מאיר שיף

2. On Moses' death, see Horovitz, no. 3865.

that Moses' unmarried children should be favored in the division since Abraham had received his fair share of familial wealth when he married and the other children deserved no less. They also noted Moses Deuz had left young children who needed to be provided for and they had yet to have guardians appointed for them. They maintained that the estate had a number of obligations and that nothing remained for the granddaughter.

The court offered a compromise solution that favored Moses' widow and children. Moses' children received five-sixths of the real estate assets and the granddaughter one-sixth. The widow was granted the right to live in the house as long as she did not remarry. She was also given rights to income from a seat in the synagogue but was obligated to pay her mother-in-law an annual sum.

12. ———
13. ע"ד טענות והפרשות בענין עזבון המנוח כ"ה משה בכ"ה אברהם
14. דייטץ ז"ל שבא לפנינו התורני כ"ה פייס הענא יצו בהרשאות הו"ה כ'
15. יוזפא וועטרהאן וה"ה התורני נאמן הקהלה כ"ה מיכל גייגר יצו והו"ה
16. כ' ליב ב"כ יוקב אופנהיים אפטרופסי' על היתומה בת של המנוח
17. כ' אברהם בכ"ה משה דייטץ ז"ל הנ"ל ותבע בשביל היתומה
18. הנ"ל מן האשה מ' צערלה אל' המנוח כ"ה משה דייץ ז"ל הנ"ל
19. שהניח לפנינו ב"ד ח"מ אינפוטאריום מכל עזבון בעלה
20. ז"ל הנ"ל שהניח אחריו ויסלקו הב"ד אותה מן העזבון והמותרת
21. שנשאר אח"כ בעזבון הנ"ל יחולק בין הבנים של כהרם[1] הנ"ל
22. וליתן ליתומה ג"כ מה שמגיע לה ע"ח מירושת אבי זקנה

קצא ע"ב

1. ב"ה
2. זקנה כהר"מ הנ"ל וה"ה התורני כ"ה משה אויך בהרשאות
3. האל' הנ"ל ובנים יתומי' של כהר"ם הנ"ל השיב שכבר הציע
4. האל' הנ"ל לפני הגאון אב"ד נרו' אינפוטאריום מכל מה
5. שהניח בעלה ז"ל אחריו הן קרקעות מעות מזומני' כסף ושוה כסף
6. אבנים טובות ומרגליות חובי' משכונו' מטלטלי' כלי בית ונשבעת
7. עליו לפני הגאון אב"ד נרו' שבועת כתובה ותוספ' ותבע
8. שמגיע להאל' הנ"ל קודם כל מן העזבון הנ"ל סך ששת
9. אלפים זהו' לפירעון כתובה ותוספ' ועוד מאה זהו'
10. עבור שהכניס לה אבי' לז"ק ראשון ועוד שלשה מאות זהו'
11. בשביל מתנות והציע לפנינו ת"ר מן האל' הנ"ל שמבואר ב[תוכה]
12. כל מה שפסק לה אבי' לבעלה ז"ל בכן יסלק הב"ד את האל' הנ"ל
13. כנ"ל גם יתן לה מיגר אל' בחצי בית שדרה בו האל'

1. כבוד הרב משה. בניו הנותרים היו יוסף, וואלף ואולי ראובן דייץ (אלה תולדות 26.4.1785, עם דייץ, עמ' 59).

14. הנ״ל וממה שנשאר עוד בעזבון אח״כ יכירו הב״ד ויהפכו
15. בזכות דיתמי בנים האל׳ הנ״ל באשר שאבי היתומה
16. כ׳ אברהם בן בעלה ז״ל כבר קיבל סך רב לנדן שלו
17. מאביו בעלה ז״ל וכמבואר בכתב פטורים שהציע לפנינו
18. מן המנוח כ׳ אברהם ז״ל הנ״ל בכן מגיע לכל אחד מבנים
19. ג״כ כל כך שקיבל אבי היתומה וכ״ה פייס הנ״ל
20. בהרשאות הנ״ל השיב וטען באריכות נגד אינפוטאריום
21. שהוא

קצב ע״א

1. בעז״ה
2. שהוא גרוע הרבה ממה שהעריכו אותו באשר שבעלה ז״ל
3. המנוח כהרמ הנ״ל הי׳ מוחזק בעיני כל לאיש אמיד ועשרי[1] והי׳ עוסק
4. במו״מ וגם הי׳ לו חובות על רווחים גם הי׳ לו ערך גדול אצל
5. בעלי מעריכם וגם בעודו בחיי׳ חיותו הי׳ רוצה להתקשר בתו הגדולה
6. וליתן לה איזה אלפי׳ זהו׳ לנדן / וגם האל׳ עצמה אחר מיתת
7. בעלה ז״ל התקשרה את בתה ופסקה לה {מכ} לנדן שני אלפי׳
8. זהו׳ מלבד שארי דברי׳ שפסקה לה / מכל הנ״ל נראה
9. לעין כל שבעלה ז״ל הניח אחריו הרבה יותר ממה שנמצא
10. באינפוטאריום בכן תבע כ״ה פייס הנ״ל שיכריזו הב״ד בהסכמת
11. הקהל יצו בבה״כ שמי שיש לו שום דבר תחת ידו ששייך לכ״ה
12. משה דייץ ז״ל הנ״ל הן שקיבל ממנו בעוד[ו] חיי׳ חיותו / והן מאל׳
13. הנ״ל ובנים לאחר העדרת כהרם הנ״ל הן בדרך הלוואה
14. והן בפיקדון שיודיע להג׳ אב״ד נר[ו] / וגם יכירו הב״ד שיתומי׳
15. גדולי׳ בני האל׳ הנ״ל ישבעו שלא העלימו ולא יבריחו כלום המה
16. מעזבון אביהם הנ״ל ושלא ידעו כלום מהברחה ובפרטות
17. בנה הגדול שעסק במו״מ ובמילי דאביו ז״ל עוד תבע כ״ה
18. פייס הנ״ל שתציע האל׳ הנ״ל כל פנקסאות שהי׳ לבעלה ז״ל
19. עוד תבע שיכירו הב״ד שיומכר בהכרזה כסף וזהב ואבנים
20. טובות ומרגליות שנמצא בעזבון הנ״ל שאפשר שיומכר בסך רב
21. יותר ממה שהעלה האל׳ את דמי שווי׳ בתוך אינפוטאריום הנ״ל
22. וכ״ה משה הנ״ל השיב שהוא בזיון והפסד גדול ליתומי׳
23. בנים של האל׳ הנ״ל שהם גדולים ועוסקי׳ במו״מ של אביהם
24. לעשות

קצב ע״ב

1. ב״ה
2. לעשות איין אויז רוף מעזבון אביהם ז״ל וגם יש לחוש שאין

---

1. צ״ל ׳ועשיר׳

3. נמכר כ"כ ביוקר כמו שהעריכו בתוך אינפוטאריום באשר
4. שהאל' ובנה העלו מטעם זה יותר מדמי שווי' אבני' טובו'
5. ומרגליות הנזכרים בתוך אינפוטאריום / עוד טען כ"ה
6. פייס הנ"ל שיכירו הב"ד באשר שאין להאל' הנ"ל תנאים אחרוני'
7. אם מגיע לה כלל תוספות כ"כ ומיגר אל' / עוד טען שנזכר
8. בת"ר שלה שאביה לא הכניס לה רק סך שלשת אלפי' וששה
9. מאות זהו' בכן אינה מגיעה לה רק שלשי' וששה מאות רט
10. לפירעון כתובה ותוספ' וגם אותן מאה זהו' שפסק
11. לה אביה בת"ר לז"ק אפשר שלא קיבל בעלה ז"ל בכן
12. יכירו הב"ד כמה מגיע להאל' הנ"ל לפירעון כתובה ותוספ'
13. והמותרת שנמצא בעזבון יחולק בין הבנים שהניח אחריו / גם טען
14. שלפי הנשמע שאבי היתומה המנוח כ' אברהם הנ"ל ז"ל
15. הי' בחזקת שהוא בן בכור לאביו בכן מגיעי ליתומה בת של כ'
16. אברהם הנ"ל שני חלקים מחמת חלק בכורה / ועל מה שטען כ"ה
17. משה הנ"ל שאבי יתומה כבר קיבל נדן שלו מאביו השיב
18. כה"פי[1] הנ"ל שמה שקיבל לנדן הי' מגיע לו בשביל ירושת אם
19. אמו ז"ל אבל מאביו לא קיבל כלום / וכ"ה משה הנ"ל הוסיף לטעון
20. שהב"ד יעיינו בזכות דיתמא בני' של האל' הנ"ל שעכ"פ מגיע
21. להם קודם כל כ"כ לנדן שקיבל אבי היתומה וביותר לבנותי' שמגיע
22. להם כפי אומדנא דעת אביהם ז"ל שהי' רוצה להתקשרה
23. בעודו

קצג ע"א

1. ב"ה
2. בעודו בחיי' חיותו וליתן להם שני אלפי' זהו' וגם משועבד טרם
3. כל העזבון לשלם להאלופי' גובי' יצו סך ארבעה מאות ועשרי'
4. זהו' לערך וגם מחויבי' לשלם כל שנה שלשים רט לאם אביהם כל
5. ימי חיי' כמבואר בק"ס שהציע לפנינו וגם נחסר מן העזבון כמה מאות
6. מיו' העדרת כהר"ם הנ"ל עד עתה בהוצאות רבות וכפי חשבונות
7. שהציע לפנינו בכן אינה מגיע כלום לירושת יתומה הנ"ל / וכ"ה
8. פייס הנ"ל השיב על מה שנחסר מן העזבון הנ"ל בהוצאות הבית
9. מיום העדרתו כהר"ם ז"ל הנ"ל שהי' שלא ברשות ב"ד וגם
10. היתומה לא נהנה עמהם כלום בכן אין לגרוע חלקה בשביל זה
11. והאריכו הצדדים הנ"ל בטענותיהם ובתשובתיהם זה מול זה בתכלית
12. האריכות כמבואר בק"ה המונח לפנינו / ובאשר שחתמו עצמם
13. הצדדים הנ"ל והיינו האפטרופסי' של היתומה הנ"ל / והאל'
14. הנ"ל ובני' ובנותי' הגדולים בתוקף קומפרמיס בח"ח ובקנס סך שנים

---

1. כבוד הרב פייס

15. עשר מאות רט חצי לשרה יר"ה וחצי להקדש לקיים מה שיצא מ
16. מאתנו דרך פשר דבר נזדקקנו להם ולאחר שראינו ודקדקנו
17. הדק היטיב בטענותיהם ובתשובתיה' ובתוך אינפוטאריום ואיזה
18. פנקסאות המונח לפנינו גם בת"ר של האל' הנ"ל וגם חשבנו במה
19. שמגיע לבנים של האל' הנ"ל מחמת ויתור כנהוג ובמה שמחויב
20. העזבון לשלם להאלופי' גובי' יצו ולאם של הנעדר כל ימי חיי'
21. כמבואר בק"ס הנ"ל וגם בהוצאות שנחסר מן העזבון כפי
22. חשבונות הנ"ל וגם לאחר שהי' לנו כמה דרישות וחקירות על
23. עניינ[י] עזבון הנ"ל בכל האפשר לנו לאחר כל הנ"ל מצאנו
24. דרך פשר דבר לטובת האל' הנ"ל ובני' יתומי' גדולי' הנ"ל

קצג ע"ב

1. ב"ה
2. הנ"ל ולטובת היתומה הנ"ל וגם לטובת יתומי' בנים קטני' של האל'
3. הנ"ל שאין להם עדיין אפטרופסי' שאנחנו ב"ד הפכנו לטובתם
4. בכח מעשה ב"ד יפה ומצאנו שכל מה שנמצא בעזבון המנוח
5. כ"ה משה דייץ ז"ל הנ"ל הן מזומני' כסף ושוה כסף אבנים
6. טובות ומרגליות חובות וח"כ ומשכונות על נימולים וא"נ ובפרט
7. שטר משכנות על מקו' שלם בע"נ התיכונה על שבעי' וחמשה
8. קרליהן[1] ספרי' ומטלטלי[ן] כלי בית נחושת ברזל בדיל ועופרת
9. בגדי' ווייסצייג בעטונג הכל כאשר לכל מה שנמצא בעזבון
10. הנ"ל זולת קרקעות יהי' הכל להאל' הנ"ל לחלוטין גמורין בתורת פרעון
11. כתובה ותוספ' ומחמת כל תביעות של האל' הנ"ל וגם יהי'
12. לה חצי מקו' בע"נ התיכונה שהכניס לה אביה בתר[2] הנ"ל לחלוטין
13. גמורין ומחויבת האל' הנ"ל לשלם להאלופי' גובי' יצו כל מה שמחויב
14. בעלה ז"ל הנ"ל לשלם עד יום דלמטה הן בשביל עצמו והן בשביל
15. אמו שהוא לערך ארבעה מאות ועשרים זהו' ובזה פטורה מן
16. החמשי' זהו' שוויתרה בשעת שבועה וכ"ש הויתר שמגיע
17. לבני' מן המנוח הנ"ל מתוספ' שלה כנהוג ובזה פטורי'
18. ומסולקי' היתומי' של כהר"ם הנ"ל מן תביעות האל' לפירעון
19. כתובה ותוספ' ושאר תביעות הנ"ל אכן הקרקעות שהניח
20. אחריו המנוח כהרם ז"ל הנ"ל והיינו בית חיצון וחצי מקו'
21. בע"א העליונה ומקו' שלם בע"נ העליונה שעומדו' עלי' כעת
22. אם של הנעדר הנ"ל יהי' גוף הקרקעות הנ"ל מעכשיו
23. ליורשי המנוח כהרם הנ"ל והיינו שיחולק החצי בית
24. ומקו' שלם

---

1. אולי צ"ל 'קרלינר'
2. בתנאים ראשונים

קצד ע"א
ב"ה
ומקו' של' וחצי מקו' הנ"ל לששה חלקים ויהי' לארבעה בני' של האל'[1] הנ"ל
ארבעה חלקים לכל או"א חלק אחד ולשתי בנותי' ביחדיו יהי' ג"כ
חלק אחד לשתיהן דהיינו לכל או"א מבנות הנ"ל חצי חלק שישת מכל
קרקעות הנ"ל וליתומה בת המנוח כ' אברהם ז"ל הנ"ל ג"כ יהי' לה
חלק שישת מקרקעות הנ"ל דהיינו מחצי בית חיצון הנ"ל וממקו' בע"נ
העליונה הנ"ל ומחצי מקו' בע"א העליונה ובזה פטורים ומסולקים
היתומי' הנ"ל והיתומה הנ"ל והאל' הנ"ל זה מזה וזה מזה מכל
תביעות הנ"ל הן מחמת תביעות כתובה ותוספ' לאל' הנ"ל והן מ'[2]
חלק בכורה ליתומה והן מ'[3] ויתר ליתומה ואין לזה ע"ז ולז'[4] ע"ז
כלום / אכן גם את זה מצאנו בתורת פשר לטובת הנ"ל שיהי'
להאל' הנ"ל הפירות ויד העליונה על חצי בית הנ"ל למיגר
אל' לה ולבנים על כל ימי חיי' האל' הנ"ל ועד כל זמן
שלא תנשא לגבר אוחרן נגד זה מחויבת האל' לשלם לחמותה
כל שנה שלשי' רט וכמבואר בקס'[5] הנ"ל וגם יהי' להאל' הנ"ל
כל ימי חיי' עד שתנשא לגבר אוחרין הפירות ממקו' שלם בע"נ
הנ"ל מלאחר העדרת חמותה ח"ו ומחצי המקום בע"א הנ"ל יהי'
להאל' הפירות מעכשיו על כל ימי חיי' כל זמן שלא
תנשא לגבר אוחרן וכנ"ל יצא מאתנו יו' ד כ"ז טבת
תקמו לפק הגאון אב"ד נר' ורנ"מ ורמ"ש ואני

No. 204

Fol. 194a; Sunday evening, 15 January 1786

Half a seat in the upper men's section of the synagogue was sold to Abraham Reiss for 150 guldens. The seat had belonged to Esther, widow of Rabbi Model Strauss, and was sold by the communal leaders to Abraham who had been using it. The proceeds of the sale went to the community.

חצי מקו' בע"א העליונה אשר עומד עלי' כעת כ' אברהם רייס יצו שהי' שייך

1. כנראה שהכוונה לבנים של משה דייטע (לא ידוע אם היו לצערלה, אלמנת משה דייץ, בנים [ר' אלה תולדות, 28.3.1793]). אם כן, אולי צ"ל כאן 'המנוח'.
2. מחמת
3. מחמת
4. ולזה
5. בקומפרומיס

22. להאשה מ' אסתר אל' המנוח הרב כמ"ה מאדל שטרויז יצו מכרו האלופי' גובי' יצו
23. לכ' אברהם רייס הנ"ל בעד סך מאה וחמשה זהו' לשלם לגובי' כפי תיקון הקהלה
24. ואנחנו ב"ד עשינו מעשה ב"ד על המכר כנ"ל אור ליו' ב טוב שבט תקמו
25. רנ"מ ורמ"ש ואני

No. 205

Sichel v. Halberstat

Fols. 194b–195b; Tuesday evening, 17 January 1786

Isaac Halberstat and Benedit Landau jointly owned half of an exterior house on the Grüne Tür lot and rented it out for three years beginning in late 1782. The renter paid with six post-dated notes that were deposited with Isaac, who collected the notes when they came due and then gave Benedit his share.

In the summer of 1784 Benedit transferred his share of the house to his daughter, Riska. Riska and her husband, Lima Sichel, came to the court claiming that they should receive from Isaac their share of the rent for a sixteen month period. Isaac replied that Benedit's share of the first two years of the rent had already been given to him directly and that his share of the last year's income had been paid to another of his sons-in-law who had bought the rights from Benedit himself. Thus, Isaac's counsel claimed, Halberstat did not owe the Sichels anything. Moreover, Isaac claimed not to know anything of the transfer of rights to Riska and her husband. Although the Sichels' counsel contested the claims, the court summoned the renter, Anshel Schwarzschild, for questioning and, after reviewing the matter and the document of transfer, dismissed the claim against Isaac.

קצד ע"ב

1. ב"ה
2. ע"ד שבא לפנינו ה"ה התורני כהררי[1] בענדט הענא בהרשאות
3. האשה מ' ריזכה ובעלה הו"ה כ' לימא בכ"ה משה זיכל ותבע
4. מן הו"ה כ"ה איצק הלברשטאט סך מאה וששה זהו' מם צל דמי
5. שכירות הבית מן שנה אחת וארבעה חדשי' מן רביעת בית
6. חיצון צור גריני טיהר שהי' שייך לחמיו ה"ה כ' בענדיט לאנדא
7. והשכיר חמיו הנ"ל עם ה"ה כ"ה איצק הנ"ל שהי' שייך לו

1. כבוד הרב רבי

8. ג"כ רביעית בבית הנ"ל בשותפת (את חצי בית הנ"ל)[1] להו"ה כ' אנשיל ב"כ
9. משה שווארץ שילד בשנת תקמג העבר בחדש כסליו על
10. שלשה שנים כל שנה בעד סך מאה וששים זהו' וע"ז נתן
11. השוכר הנ"ל ששה ח"כ על ששה חצאי שנים זא"ז לשלם לאורדר
12. הני משותפים ביחדיו כל אחד סך שמוני' זהו' וח"כ הנ"ל
13. הי' תמיד ביד ר' איצק הנ"ל שגבה אותן בשביל שניהם
14. והציע לפנינו כהרר בענדיט כתב יד מן כ' בענדיט
15. לנדויא הנ"ל (שמבואר בתוכה שנתן כ' בענדיט לאנדויא הנ"ל)[2] באוה"ב את רביעת בית הנ"ל לבתו מ'
16. ריזכה אשת כ' לימא הנ"ל ביו' ג ך"ח מרחשון שנת
17. תקמ"ג לפק בשיור יד העליונה כל ימי חיי האחרון מהם
18. בשטר מתנה / וביו' ב' ב דר"ח אדר ראשון שנת תקמ"ג
19. חזרו ונתנו כ' בענדיט הנ"ל באוה"ב במתנה גמור' אף
20. היד העליונה מן רביעית בית לבתם מ' ריזכה אשת כ'
21. לימא הנ"ל והיינו במעכשיו ולאחר נשואין בנם כ' יוסף סגל
22. וטוען באשר שכ' יוסף בן של כ' בענדיט הנ"ל עשה חתנה
23. בחדש

קצה ע"א

1. ב"ה
2. בחדש אב שנת תקמ"ד בכן מגיע לכ' לימא הנ"ל כבר הפירות מרביעית
3. בית הנ"ל מן חדש אב תקמ"ד עד חדש כסליו שנת תקמ"ו ובאשר
4. שכ"ה איצק הנ"ל גבה הדמי שכירות מחצי בית הנ"ל עד
5. חדש כסליו תקמ"ו בכן תבע כ' לימא הנ"ל שיחזור לו דמי שכירות
6. חלקו שנה אחת וארבעה חדשי' / וכהרר משה אויך בהרשאות כ"ה
7. איצק הנ"ל השיב אמת הוא שגבה כל דמי שכירות מן השוכר
8. כ' אנשיל הנ"ל רק ששכירות עד חדש כסליו תקמ"ה העבר
9. החזיר לכ' בענדיט הנ"ל עצמו חלק שכירות מה שמגיע עליו ודמי
10. שני ח"כ האחרוני' משנה אחת עד כסליו תקמ"ו נתן לחתנו
11. הו"ה כ' יודא אולמן יצו שקנה מן כ' בענדיט הנ"ל חלקו מן ח"כ
12. הנ"ל בניכוי רווחי' שפסקו ולאחר ששילם כ' יודא הנ"ל לכ'
13. בענדיט הנ"ל דמי פסיקה שבינהם הוט כ' בענדיט הנ"ל ח"כ
14. הנ"ל שארירט על כ' יודא הנ"ל בכן טוען כ"ה משה הנ"ל באשר
15. שכ"ה איצק הנ"ל כבר שילם כנ"ל בכן אינו מחויב כ"ה איצק הנ"ל
16. לשלם עוד לכ' לימא הנ"ל / עוד השיב כ"ה משה הנ"ל שכ"ה
17. איצק הנ"ל לא הי' יודע מן כתיבת יד הנ"ל שנתן כ"ה בענדיט

---

1. תוספת מעל השורה
2. תוספת לאורך השולים הימניים של הדף

18. הנ"ל היד עליונה ופירות לחותנו כ' לימא הנ"ל גם הי' לכ'
19. לימא הנ"ל למחות מזמן הנ"ל לשוכר הנ"ל או לכה[1] איצק הנ"ל
20. שלא ישלם לחמיו הנ"ל דמי שכירות הבית מה שמגיע ע"ח
21. וכ"ה בענדיט הנ"ל השיב שיברר כ"ה איצק הנ"ל שכדבריו
22. כן הוא ששילם את דמי שכירות הבית הנ"ל כנ"ל ומה שלא
23. מיחה כ' לימא הנ"ל לפי שלא הי' יודע כ' לימא שיש ביד
24. כ"ה

קצה ע"ב

1. ב"ה
2. כהרר איצק ח"כ משכירות הבית שיש לחמיו חלק בו רק הי' סבר
3. שחמיו כ' בענדיט הנ"ל יש לו בידו ח"כ מן חלקו שכירות
4. הבית והאריכו בטענותיהם זה מול זה וחקרנו את פי השוכר
5. כ' אנשיל שווארץ שילד הנ"ל והגיד לפנינו בת"ע אליו"ע כמבואר
6. בק"ה המונח לפנינו / ובאשר שחתמו הצדדים הנ"ל א"ע
7. בתוקף קומפרמיס בח"ח ובקנס סך מסוים חצי לשררה ירה[2]
8. וחצי להקדש לאשר ולקיים כל אשר יצא מאתנו נזדקקנו
9. להם ולאחר שעיינו הדק היטב בכתב יד הודאה שהציע
10. כ' לימא הנ"ל ובטענותיה' זה מול זה מצאנו שפטור כהרר
11. איצק הנ"ל מן האשה מ' ריזכה ובעלה כ' לימא הנ"ל מן
12. תביעו' הנ"ל יצא מאתנו אור ליו' ד יט שבט תקמ"ו
13. רנ"מ ורמ"ש ואני

No. 206

Fols. 196a–b; Wednesday 1 February 1786

Yatla, widow of Wolf Lechnich, approached the court with legal counsel asking that she receive what her husband had promised her in her marriage contract and subsequent agreements. Yatla had already taken an oath before the head of the rabbinic court that she had declared all that was in her possession from the estate. Since Wolf had promised her more than the value of the estate, Yatla asked that she be awarded all of the estate's assets. However, Wolf was also survived by a brother, Meʾir, who had a claim against the estate. Yatla and Meʾir signed an agreement stating that they would abide by the court's compromise. The court ordered Yatla

1. לכבוד הרב
2. ירום הודו

to make a lump sum payment to Meʾir, after which the rest of the assets would belong to her. Yatla assumed responsibility for paying off the remaining obligations of the estate.

קצו ע"א

1. ב"ה
2. ע"ד שבא לפנינו ה"ה התורני כ"ה משה אויך יצו בהרשאות האשה מ' יטלה אל'
3. המנוח כ' וואלף לעכניך כץ ז"לי[1] והציע לפנינו שטר תנאים אחרונים וגם שטר
4. תוספ' ההוקם בין האשה הנ"ל ובין בעלה ז"ל הנ"ל ביו' ד ך"ח תמוז תקמ"ב
5. ושם נאמר וז"ל הנני מוסיף לאשתי מ' יטלה הנ"ל וכו' עד באם שאעדר
6. אני ח"ו מהיו' ואילך תקחי היא מחמת כתובת ותוספ' דקמייתא ודהשתא
7. ביחד סך שני אלפי' וששה מאות ועשרים וחמשה זהו' אין קונפענס
8. יאָהנס מינץ אויף דעם ך"ד זהו' פוס וכו' גם תהי' לה היד עליונה
9. על חצי בית השייך לי צום הואף אייסן על כל זמן שלא תנשא לגבר
10. אוחרן עכ"ל וטען כהר"ם[2] הנ"ל בהרשאות האל' הנ"ל אחרי שנפטר בעלה
11. כ' וואלף הנ"ל וש"ח לכ"י וכבר נשבעת האל' שבועת כתובה ותוספ'
12. לפני הגאון אב"ד נרו' כנהוג שאין לה בידה שום דבר יותר מעזבון
13. בעלה רק כפי הרשימה מכלי בית שהניח לפנינו גם הניח בעלה
14. ז"ל את החצי בית הנ"ל צום הואף אייזן ובאשר שמגיע האל' מיגר
15. האל' בחנם בחצי בית כנ"ל בשטר תוספ' על כל זמן שלא תנשא לגבר
16. [או]חרן שוב אין מספיק כל מה שיש בעזבון בעלה לתשלם כתובה ותוספ'
17. ולתשלומין להאלופי' גובי' יצו ולשארי חובות הנרשמי' לפנינו לזאת ביקש
18. כהר"ם הנ"ל מאתנו להחליט להאל' הנ"ל את כל עזבון בעלה הן החצי בית
19. הנ"ל והן הכלי בית כפי רשימה הנ"ל ולאחר שחתמה האל' הנ"ל וגיסה כ'
20. מאיר לעכניך כץ בתוקף קומפרמיס בח"ח ובקנס חצי להקדש וחצי לשררה
21. יר"ה לקיים הפשר שיצא מאתנו ב"ד נזדקקנו להם ומצאנו שהאל'
22. הנ"ל תתן לגיסה כ' מאיר הנ"ל סך ארבעים זהו' ולאחר הפירעון סך
23. הנ"ל לגיסה הנ"ל שייך להאל' הנ"ל כל עזבון בעלה ז"ל הנ"ל לפירעון
24. כתובה ותוספ' ומעתה החלטנו לחלוטין גמורין ולצמיתת עלמין
25. את כל מה שהניח אחריו המנוח כ' וואלף לעכניך כץ הנ"ל
26. הן החצי בית חיצון הנ"ל והן מטלטלי' לאשתו מ' יטלה הנ"ל וי"א וב"כ
27. לעשות {..לו} בכל עזבון בעלה ז"ל הנ"ל כאות נפשה ורצונה
28. ככל אינש דרשאי לעשות בשלו בלי שום מוחה ועירעור
29. שבעולם

---

1. ר' אבני זכרון, מס' 3883, ששם רשום 'לעבניך'. כנראה שזו טעות (ע' במפתח שם וגם בדייץ, עמ' 181).
2. כבוד הרב משה

קצו ע״ב

שבעולם הן מיורשי בעלה וי״א וב״כ והן משארי אדם יהי׳ מי׳ שיהי׳ רק שהיא תשלם סך ארבעי׳ זהו׳ הנ״ל לגיסה הנ״ל וגם שארי חובות כפי רשימה הנ״ל וכתבנו וחתמנו כל הנ״ל בתוקף מעשה ב״ד ובכח ב״ד יפה להיות ביד האל׳ הנ״ל וי״א וב״כ לעדות ולזכות ולראי׳ שיהי׳ כל עזבון בעלה המנוח כ׳ וואלף הנ״ל להאל׳ מ׳ יטלה הנ״ל וי״א וב״כ בלי שום מוחה כלל יצא מאתנו יו׳ ד ג׳ אדר ראשון תקמ״ו רנמי[1] ורמש[2] ואני

No. 207

Rapp v. Schloss

Fols. 197a–198a; Monday evening, 6 March 1786

Feis Rapp and the here unnamed widow of Seligmann Ulf shared ownership in half an inner house and half an outer house on the front section of the Stuhl lot. To insure an equal sharing of assets, they rotated possession of the spaces every three years. Feis was supposed to receive possession of the outer home in just a few weeks, in late March 1786, and, in anticipation of this, he rented out the space for three years at 50 guldens per annum. However, the widow's agent, Leb Schloss, had rented that section of the house out until the fall of 1786, about seven months past the date that the space was to be transferred to Feis.

Feis came to the court with representation and demanded that the current renter be out on time or that Leb pay his losses. Leb, who had no representation, admitted to renting the space out until the fall of 1786, but said that he had been unaware of the arrangement between the widow and Feis. Leb claimed that once he learned of the problem he told Feis that he would reimburse him for the seven months of lost rent that he had incurred, but later thought better of his offer and turned to the court for a ruling. Moreover, Leb noted that Feis only rented out the space after he knew that it had been leased until the fall of 1786. Because of this, Leb claimed Feis had brought his loss upon himself and that Leb should not be liable for it.

The court spoke to Benedit Schwelm, Feis's potential tenant, in order to learn more details about the case. After considering the matter, the court formally

---

1. רב נתן מז
2. ורב מאיר שיף

canceled the lease that Leb had made, effective the first day of the Hebrew month of Nissan (30 March 1786), and ordered Leb to try and convince his tenant to vacate by then. If the tenant would not leave, Leb would have to pay Feis the rent that he would lose, except for a small deduction. Leb would also have to pay if Feis's potential tenant canceled his lease because of this misunderstanding. However, the court limited Leb's liability to the value of the approximately seven months of rent in question.

קצז ע"א

ב"ה ע"ד שבא לפנינו התורני כ"ה פייס הענא סג"ל {יצו} בהרשאות הו"ה כ"ה פייס ראפף יצו ותבע מן הו"ה גבאי ת"ת כ"ה ליב שלאס יצו שהשכיר לכ' מאיר קולפא בהרשאות האל' המנוח כ"ה זעליגמן אולף ז"ל[1] עד מרחשון תקמ"ז הבע"ל את החצי בית (צום)[2] פאדר שטוהל ששייך לכ"ה פייס הנ"ל בשותפות עם האל' הנ"ל / והיינו שיש להם בשותפות חצי בית החיצון וחצי בית פנימי וחלוקי דירות כבר נעשה ביניהם על אופן שיהי' לכל או"א מהם על משכ[3] שלשה שנים רצופי' או חצי בית פנימי לבד או חצי בית חיצון לבד ויחליפו ביניהם שמשכ[4] שלשה שני' שיהי' להאל' חצי בית חיצון יהי' לכ"ה פייס חצי בית הפנימי ובכלות שלשה שנים יחליפו ביניהם על שלשה שנים אחרים רצופים שהי' להאל' חצי בית פנימי / ולכ"ה פייס חצי בית החיצון / ובאשר שמן חדש ניסן (הסמוך)[5] הבע"ל מגיע לכ"ה פייס הנ"ל על שלשה שנים רצופים חצי בית החיצון וכבר השכיר כה"פ[6] הנ"ל את חצי בית חיצון הנ"ל עד ניסן תקמ"ט הבע"ל לכ' בענדיט שוועלים[7] בעד חמשים זהו' לשנה / בכן תבע כ"ה פייס מן כ"ה ליב הנ"ל שלא הי' לו רשות להשכיר מן ניסן הבע"ל עד ר"ח מרחשון לכ' מאיר הנ"ל / ותבע שישתדל כ"ה ליב הנ"ל שיפנה השוכר כ' מאיר הנ"ל את דירתו מחצי בית הנ"ל מחדש ניסן הסמוך הבע"ל כדי שיוכל להכניסו השוכר כ' בענדיט הנ"ל לתוכה / או שיקבל עליו לפצות כל ההפסד והוצאות מה שמגיע לו מן שוכר כ' בענדיט הנ"ל מפני שלא יכול להכניסו בבית שהשכיר לו / ולפחות תבע עוד כ"פ הנ"ל מן כ"ה ליב הנ"ל שבאם ע"י איחור שוב אינו רוצה שוכר שלו כ' בענדיט הנ"ל לקיים שכירות שלו והוא לא יוכל למצוא שוב שוכר אחר שמחזיק את חצי בית הנ"ל עד זמן הנ"ל בעד סך

1. פייגה בת גרשון ראפופורט (ר' אבני זכרון, מס' 3147).
2. תוספת בצד השורה
3. משך
4. שמשך
5. תוספת מעל השורה
6. כבוד הרב פייס
7. כנראה בענדיט בן מרדכי שוועלים שהיה רווק (ר' אלה תולדות 29.10.1791).

24. שכירות הנ״ל שמחויב כה״ל[1] הנ״ל להחזיק הבית בשכירות הנ״ל עד
25. זמן הנ״ל בסכום הנ״ל / וכ״ה ליב בעצמו השיב אמת שהוא
26. השכיר לכ׳ מאיר קולפא חצי בית הנ״ל עד חשון הבע״ל משום
27. שלא הי׳ יודע באותו פעם שיש לכ״ה פייס הנ״ל חלק בחצי
28. בית הנ״ל באשר שאותו פעם כשנסעה האל׳ הנ״ל מכאן ויצאה
29. מן הבית הנ״ל ביקשה האל׳ הנ״ל את כ״ה ליב הנ״ל לגמול חסד עמה
30. להשכיר חצי בית שלה בשביל יתומה שלה ולא הגידה לו שכה[2]
31. פייס הנ״ל יש חלק בבית הנ״ל והי׳ סבור כה״ל הנ״ל ששייך
32. לה

קצז ע״ב

1. לה לבד מש״כ השכר[ו] לכ׳ מאיר הנ״ל עד מרחשון הבע״ל בטעות ולאח״כ
2. כשנודע לו ששייך להאל׳ מחדש ניסן חצי בית פנימי / ולכה[3] פייס בית
3. חיצון דיבר כ״ה ליב הנ״ל עם כ״ה פייס הנ״ל שרוצה למלאות לו
4. היזיקא עד חשון הבע״ל / ולאח״כ נמלך את עצמו כ״ה ליב הנ״ל ולא
5. הי׳ רוצה ליתן לכ״ה פייס כלום בלי ידיעות ב״ד עכ״פ כבר
6. נודע לכ״ה פייס שהוא השכיר החצי בית חיצון לכ׳ מאיר הנ״ל
7. עד מרחשון הבע״ל ואעפ״כ השכיר כה״פ הנ״ל לפי דבריו
8. את החצי בית מן חדש אייר הבע״ל על שלשה שנים בעד סך חמשי׳
9. זהו׳ לשנה לכ׳ בענדיט שוועלים ב[כ]ן טוען כ״ה ליב דאיהו
10. הוא דאפסיד אנפשי / וגם אפשר שיוכל להחזיק השוכר
11. של כ״ה פייס כ׳ בענדיט שוועלים שכירות שלו באשר
12. שהוא יש לו דירה עוד בבית שדר בו כעת עד ר״ח תמוז
13. הבע״ל ובשביל איזה חדשי׳ אינו יכולי׳ להוציאו מן הבית / ועד
14. ר״ח חשון הבעל[4] יפנה השוכר כ׳ מאיר חצי בית הנ״ל ומחמת
15. איזה חדשי׳ אינם חוזרים משכירות הבית ואף גם שיהי׳ שהשוכר
16. כ׳ בענדיט אינו רוצה לקיים שכירותו / מ״מ יש עוד זמן עד
17. מרחשון למצוא שוכר אחר / וכל זמן שנשאר כ׳ מאיר בתוך הבית
18. הוא רוצה לשלם לו שכירות שלו / ואם לא ימצא אח״כ שוכר
19. אחר יכירו הב״ד אם הוא מחויב לשלם מאחר שהוא לא היזיקו
20. בידים רק גרמא בעלמא / והאריכו הצדדי׳ הנ״ל בטענותיהם
21. זה מול זה כמבואר בק״ה המונח לפנינו ובאשר שחתמו הצדדי׳
22. הנ״ל א״ע בתוקף קומפרמיס בח״ח ובקנס לקיים כל אשר יצא
23. מאתנו נזדקקנו להם ואחרי שדקדקנו הדק הטיב בטענותיה׳
24. גם שאלנו וחקרנו מן כ׳ בענדיט שוועלים הנ״[ל] על אופן

---

1. כבוד הרב ליב
2. שכבוד הרב
3. ולכבוד הרב
4. הבא עלינו לטובה

25. ומהות וזמן שכירות הבית שנעשה בינו ובין כ״ה פייס
26. הנ״ל ולאחר

קצח ע״א

1. ב״ה
2. הנ״ל ולאחר כל הנ״ל מצאנו שמן חדש ניסן הבע״ל ששייך החצי בית הנ״ל
3. לכ״ה פייס הנ״ל שוב נתבטל השכירות מן כ״ה ליב הנ״ל לכ״ה מאיר הנ״ל
4. ומחויב כ״ה ליב הנ״ל להשתדל כפי האפשרי שיפנה כ׳ מאיר הנ״ל
5. חצי בית הנ״ל מחדש ניסן הבע״ל ובאם אינו יכול להוציאו מחויב כ״ה
6. ליב הנ״ל לשלם לכה[1] פייס הנ״ל על כל משכ[2] זמן שנשאר כ׳ מאיר
7. הנ״ל בבית הנ״ל הדמי שכירות לערך חמשי׳ זהו׳ לשנה / ולאחר
8. שיפונה את כ׳ מאיר הנ״ל את הבית וע״י עיכובו בתוכה אינו
9. רוצה כ׳ בענדיט הנ״ל להחזיק את שכירות הנ״ל / וכה[3] פייס
10. אינו יכול להשכירו עוד בעד סך שכירות הנ״ל עד זמן
11. הנ״ל אזי מחויב כ״ה ליב הנ״ל למלאות את הפסדו כדי שיקבל
12. עד זמן הנ״ל לפי ערך חמשי׳ זהו׳ לשנה רק שינכה כה״ל
13. הנ״ל בשביל חדש אחד ארבעה זהו׳ עשרה צל / אבל יש
14. [ר]שות ביד כ״ה ליב הנ״ל לקבל עליו כל השכירות לפי ערך
15. חמשי׳ זהו׳ לשנה בניכוי הנ״ל וישכיר את חצי הבית לאיש
16. אחר אכן שאר היזיקות והוצאות מה שמגיע לכה״פ הנ״ל משוכר
17. שלו כ׳ בענדיט הנ״ל בשביל שלא יכול להכניסו בחצי בית הנ״ל
18. בזמן שקבע לו ע״י עיכוב כ׳ מאיר הנ״ל בתוכה / פטור כ״ה
19. ליב הנ״ל מלשלם כלום לכ״ה פייס הנ״ל יצא מאתנו אור
20. [ל]יו׳ ג׳ זין א״ש תקמ״ו רנמ[4] ורמש[5] ואני

No. 208

Schiff v. Rothschild

Fols. 198b–199b; Tuesday 13 June 1786

Dayyan Me᾿ir Schiff, who was often a member of the court, sold his half of a house on Grünes Schild to Me᾿ir Rothschild (see no. 195). Schiff and his brother,

---

1. לכבוד הרב
2. משך
3. וכבוד הרב
4. רב נתן מז
5. ורב מאיר שיף

Rabbi Tevele, who from 1765 was a rabbi in London, had inherited the house from their father, Solomon, who died in 1777.[1] From this record and no. 212, it seems that Me'ir Schiff acted as an agent for his brother Tevele and sold the second half of the house to Rothschild. The record assumes that Rothschild had acquired ownership of the house, but that the Schiffs had rights to use the house until Rosh Hashanah (23 September) 1786.[2] Schiff came to the court demanding payment of one of the notes that had come due. Rothschild claimed to be ready to pay what he owed on condition that once payment was made, Schiff would no longer have any claims against him. Schiff rejected this condition for he had other claims against Rothschild that he did not want to specify until after this payment was made. Rothschild responded that he was no longer willing to pay Schiff in *münz* but rather in "new" reichstalers. Rothschild also wanted to deduct taxes due on the entire house, taxes that Schiff was liable for until Rosh Hashanah of 1786, from the amount that he was to pay Schiff. However, Schiff preferred to pay the taxes himself, for this way he would have use of the funds until the taxes were due in September. Schiff noted that Rothschild had to make other payments and the value of the taxes could conceivably be deducted from these payments.

Both sides obligated themselves to be bound by the court's decision. The court ordered Rothschild to pay Schiff immediately in a currency to be determined by two bankers. It noted that Schiff's acceptance of payment did not impinge on his rights to make further claims against Rothschild. As for the taxes, the court allowed Rothschild to withhold half of the total tax due pending the outcome of other complaints by Schiff. Also see no. 212.

קצח ע"ב

1. ב"ה
2. ע"ד שבא לפנינו ה"ה התורני הדיין כ"ה (מאיר)[3] שיף כץ נרו' ותבע מן ה"ה
3. הו"ה כ"ה מאיר רויטשילד יצו שישלם לו א טערמיני ח"כ מקניית חצי בית
4. שלו / וכ"ה מאיר רויטשילד השיב שרוצה לשלם לו אם כ"ה מאיר שיף
5. מרוצה בתשלומין שלו / ושלא יתבע ממנו עוד שום דבר / וכ"ה מאיר
6. שיף השיב ע"ז שיש לו עוד תביעות עליו רק שאינו רוצה להציע
7. עתה עד לאחר הפירעון ח"כ שלו / וכ"ה מאיר ר"ש חזר והשיב ע"ז
8. מאחר שכ"ה מאיר שיף הנ"ל אינו מרוצה עדיין בתשלומין שלו שוב אינו
9. רוצה לשלם לו הדמי ח"כ הנ"ל אין מינץ רק אין חדש רטי' / עוד
10. השיב כ"ה מאיר רויטשילד הנ"ל ורוצה לנכות מפירעון ח"כ הנ"ל

1. See Duschinsky, *The Rabbinate of the Great Synagogue* (1971), 2, 74, 79. The two brothers stayed in contact with each other over the years (see Duschinsky, 88–89).
2. Cf. Dietz, p. 470, who notes that Rothschild purchased the house in 1780.
3. תוספת מעל השורה

11. דמי קרונד צונץ מן הבית שלם באשר שאותו דמי קרונד צונץ שעולה
12. על חלק חצי בית שהי׳ שייך להרב כמהו׳ טעבלי שיף כץ נרו׳
13. נזכר בפירוש בתוך מעשה ב״ד שלו שמחויב כה מאיר שיף הנ״ל
14. לשלם עד תשרי תקמ״ז הבע״ל ועל חלק חצי בית האחרת שהי׳
15. שייך לכ״ה מאיר שיף הנ״ל טוען כ״ה מאיר ר״ש הנ״ל שגם זה מחויב
16. כ״ה מאיר שיף הנ״ל לשלם עד תשרי תקמ״ז הבעלי[1] באשר שיש לו הפירות
17. עד זמן הנ״ל בכן רוצה כ״ה מאיר ר״ש הנ״ל לנכות דמי קרונד צונץ
18. כולה מן הפירעון ח״כ הנ״ל / וכ״ה מאיר שיף הנ״ל השיב לו
19. יהי׳ כדבריו שהתחייבות הפרעון יהי׳ עליו מ״מ אינו[2] לשלם
20. לכ״ה מאיר ר״ש הנ״ל רק להשררה יר״ה ועדיין יש לו זמן לשלם עד
21. חודש זעפטעמבר בכן אינו יכול לנכות מדמי פרעון ח״כ ושטר
22. אפותיקו שהוא חוב ברור שעבר זמנו דמי קרונד צונץ
23. שיוכל להחזיק עוד בידו עד חודש זעפטעמבר ובפרט שכ״ה
24. מאיר ר״ש יש עליו לשלם עוד שארי טערמינה ח״כ שיוכל להחזיק
25. בו על דמי קרונד צונץ הנ״ל / והנה הצדדי׳ הנ״ל התעצמו
26. מאוד בטענותיהם זה מול זה המה וה״ה התורני כ״ה מאיר
27. מז

קצט ע״א

1. ב״ה
2. מַז בהרשאות כ״ה מאיר ר״ש הנ״ל כמבואר היטיב בק״ה
3. המבואר לפנינו / ואחרי שחתמו עצמם הצדדי׳ הנ״ל בתוקף
4. קומפרמיס בח״ח ובקנס סך מסוים לקיים כל אשר יצא מאתנו
5. נזדקקנו להם / ומצאנו שמחויב הו״ה כ״ה מאיר ר״ש הנ״ל
6. לשלם לכ״ה מאיר שיף הנ״ל תיכף ומיד דמי ח״כ הנ״ל
7. כפי שהתרצו שניהם לפנינו שיהי׳ התשלומין כפי שיכירו
8. שני סוחרי׳ באנקיעהר זה שלא בפני זה במעמד ה״ה הו״ה
9. פו״מ כ״ה איצק שפייאר וכ״ה מאיר ר״ש הנ״ל האופן תשלומין
10. על לשון ח״כ הנ״ל אין מינץ אודער חדש רטי׳ / ומחמת
11. מה שיש לכ״ה מאיר שיף הנ״ל עוד לתבוע מן כ״ה מאיר
12. ר״ש הנ״ל ואינו רוצה להציע לפנינו עד לאחר הפירעון
13. ח״כ הנ״ל / מצאנו שהדין עמו שיכול לתבוע אח״כ לפנינו
14. [י]קוב הדין ההר ביניהם בתוקף קומפרמיס שלפנינו /
15. ומחמת מה שרוצה לנכות כ״ה מאיר ר״ש מדמי קרונדצונץ
16. מן הפירעון ח״כ הנ״ל מצאנו שאותו דמי חצי קרונדצונץ
17. שעולה על חלק חצי בית שהי׳ שייך להרב כמהו׳ טעבלי

---

1. הבא עלינו לטובה
2. כנראה שהמילה ׳חייב׳ חסרה כאן.

18. שיף נרו׳ / אינו יכול לנכותו מדמי פירעון ח״כ הנ״ל
19. כעת / אכן אותו חצי דמי קרונדצונץ מן חלק חצי בית
20. שהי׳ שייך לכ״ה מאיר שיף הנ״ל יש כח ביד כ״ה מאיר
21. ר״ש הנ״ל לנכותו מן הפירעון ח״כ הנ״ל ויהי׳ בידו עד
22. שיקוב הדין ההר ביניהם בתוקף קומפרמיס הנ״ל
23. אם החיוב {הו.} הוא על ה״ה הדיין כ״ה מאיר
24. שיף

קצט ע״ב

1. שיף כץ נרו׳ הנ״ל או על הו״ה כ״ה מאיר ר״ש יצו
2. יצא מאתנו יו׳ ג טוב סיון תקמ״ו רנ״מ ואני ורמ״ל

No. 209

Fol. 199b; Sunday 6 August 1786

The executors of a charitable fund came to the court seeking guidance. The late Leb Reiss had established a fund to distribute charity to members of his family on an annual basis.[1] Funds were currently being given to Libet, daughter of Moses Trier. Mindele, daughter of Zanvil Reiss and great-niece of Leb Reiss,[2] came to the executors and argued that she was a more appropriate recipient of the funds than the current beneficiary since she was more closely related to Leb Reiss. After both sides agreed to compromise, the court ruled that the 20 guldens distributed annually be divided equally between the two needy individuals.

3. ———
4. ע״ד השאלה שנשאל מאתנו ב״ד ח״מ מן האלופי׳
5. אפטרופסי׳ של הדב״ט של המנוח ג״ה כ״ה ליב
6. רייס ז״ל בענין חלוקת עשרי׳ זהו׳ לענים קרובי׳ כל
7. שנה[3] שהתעוררה האשה מ׳ מינדלה בת המנוח
8. כ׳ זנוויל רייס ז״ל להיות ג״כ מן המנוי׳ ורוצה
9. לדחות את האשה מ׳ ליבעט בת ר׳ משה טריר
10. מאיטשטיין באשר שהיא קרובה יותר למנדב ולאחר

---

1. With respect to the perpetual fund, see YIVO MS. RG 128 (folder 77–78), fols. 55a–56b.
2. Leb's father was Elijah Reiss (Horovitz, no. 2628). Elijah Reiss had a younger son, Jacob (Horovitz, no. 2577), who had a son Zanvil (Ettlinger, 15.2.1775). Mindele was one of Zanvil's daughters.
3. עיין אבני זכרון, מס׳ 3603, שבו רשום על הקרנות השונים שרייס השאיר. עיין גם בעמוד השער של ספרו של הרב מאיר שיף, דרך אני׳ בלב ים התלמוד, פיורדא תקנ״ח, וכן בספר הזכרונות, רנט ע״ב.

שהתרצו הנשים הנ"ל לפשר ביניהם מצאנו ע"ד פשר דבר שאותו חלק סך עשרי' זהו' יחולק ביניהן למחצה והיינו עשרה זהו' יהי' להאשה מ' ליבעט הנ"ל לשנה / ולהאשה מ' מינדלה הנ"ל ג"כ עשרה זהו' לשנה יצא מאתנו א' י"ב מנחם תקמו לפק הגאון אב"ד נר' ורנמ[1] ואני

No. 210

Fols. 200a–b; Sunday 6 August 1786

Me᾿ir and the recently engaged Wolf Fulda, sons of the late Herz Fulda, inherited a quarter of a house on the Holderbaum lot and four half seats in the women's section of the synagogue. Instead of further dividing the assets, the brothers decided to consolidate them. Wolf took the quarter of the house and Me᾿ir the seats in the synagogue. They approached the court asking that it recognize their distribution of the assets. The court questioned the brothers to insure that this arrangement was acceptable to the brothers' guardians and their mother. According to the agreement, their mother maintained her right to live in the house for the remainder of her widowhood and she maintained unspecified priority rights over the quarter of the house and two of the half seats. However, she relinquished her claim over all the property as surety for her marriage contract. This done, the court formally recognized the agreement. Also see no. 211.

ר ע"א

ב"ה

הן היו' הקריבו לפנינו ה"ה האחים הב"ח החתן היקר כ"ה וואלף ואחיו הב"ח כ' מאיר בני המנוח כ"ה הירץ בו"ו פולדא ז"ל ואמרו אחרי שיש להם בשותפות יחד מעזבון אביהם ז"ל הנ"ל ר רביעת בית צום האלדר בוים וארבעה חצאי מקומות בעזרת נשים / והיינו שלשה בע"נ התחתונה ואחת בעזרת העליונה בשיור יד העליונה לאמם הקצינה האל' מ' צערלה על כל ימי חיי' כל זמן שלא תנשא לגבר אוחרא על רביעת בית הנ"ל ושני חצאי ממקומות הנ"ל והאחים הנ"ל התרצו עצמם זה מול זה וזה מול זה לחלוק הקרקעות הנ"ל ביניהן על אופן זה והיינו שיהי' להב"ח החתן כ' וואלף הנ"ל הרביעת בית הנ"ל עם כל זכות וחזקה וכמו

1. ורב נתן מז

12. שהי׳ שייך לאביו כ׳[1] ז״ל לו לבד בשיור יד העליונה לאמו כנ״ל ולא
13. יהי׳ לאחיו כ׳ מאיר הנ״ל שום חלק בו / ונגד זה מסלק עצמו וזכותו
14. מן הארבעה חצאי מקומות ויהי׳ לאחיו כ׳ מאיר הנ״ל לבד עם
15. כל זכות וחזקה וכמו שהי׳ שייך לאביו ז״ל בשיור יד העליונה
16. לאמו הנ״ל וכנ״ל ונפשם בשאלתם מאתנו ב״ד ח״מ ליתן להם
17. תוקף מעשה ב״ד ע״ז / ו[ה]נה אחרי שנזדקקנו להם וחקרנו
18. אותם שאופן החלוקה הנ״ל ביניהם נעשה ברצונם הטוב ובנפשם
19. חפצה גם נעשה בידיעת וברצון אפטרופסי׳ שלהם ה״ה הו״ה
20. פו״מ כ׳ הירץ שוסטר כץ וה״ה הו״ה התורני כ״ה שמואל פולדא
21. יצו גם אמם האל׳ הקצינה מ׳ צערלה מרוצה בריצו גמור שיהי׳
22. הרביעת בית הנ״ל מעתה לבנה החתן הב״ח כ׳ וואלף הנ״ל
23. לו לבד בשיור יד העליונה לה לעצמה וכמו שהי׳ לה עד עכשיו
24. והארבעה חצאי מקומות הנ״ל לבנה כ׳ מאיר הנ״ל לבד בשיור
25. יד העליונה לה לעצמה על שני חצאי מקומות ומחלה שעבוד
26. כתובתה מן הרביעת בית הנ״ל ומן הארבעה חצאי מקומות
27. הנ״ל

ר ע״ב

1. הנ״ל ולאחר שברור לנו כל הנ״ל באנו גם אנחנו ב״ד ח״מ לטובת שני
2. היתומי׳ הנ״ל ליתן תוקף ועוז בכח מעשה ב״ד יפה על החלוקה
3. שביניהם על הקרקעות הנ״ל שיהי[2] בתקפו ובגבורתו / בלי שום
4. עורר וטוען מזה על זה ומזה על זה ומעתה יהי׳ הרביעת
5. בית חיצון צום האלדר בוים הנ״ל עם כל זכות וחזקה לב״ח
6. כ׳ וואלף הנ״ל ויא[3] וב״כ וכמו שהי׳ שייך לאביו המנוח כ׳
7. הירץ ז״ל הנ״ל והיינו בשיור יד העליונה לאמו הנ״ל וכמו
8. שהי׳ לה עד עכשיו ואין לאחיו כ׳ מאיר הנ״ל וי״א וב״כ
9. שום חלק וטו״ת שבעולם ברביעת בית הנ״ל ונגד זה יהי׳
10. הארבעה חצאי מקומות הנ״ל מעתה עם כל זכות וחזקה
11. לבח[4] כ׳ מאיר הנ״ל וי״א וב״כ וכמו שהי׳ שייך לאביו ז״ל
12. והיינו בשיור יד העליונה לאמו וכמו שהי׳ לה עד עתה ואין
13. להחתן כ׳ וואלף הנ״ל וי״א וב״כ שום חלק וטו״ת שבע[ולם]
14. בהם וכל מי שיערער אחר החלוקה הנ״ל יהי׳ מי שיהי׳
15. או באיזה אופן שיהי׳ יהי׳ טענה מה שיהי׳ מכל מה שהפה
16. יוכל לדבר והלב לחשוב ולהרהר יהי׳ בדבריו בטלים
17. ומבוטלים וכטוען אחר מעשה ב״ד הגדול כי נעשה הכל

---

1. או שצ״ל ׳כ׳ הירץ׳ או צריך למחוק את ה-׳כ׳״.
2. צ״ל ׳שיהי׳״
3. ויורשיו אחריו
4. לבחור חמד

18. בריצוי גמור מן כל הצדדים הנ"ל וכתבנו וחתמנו כל
19. הנ"ל בתוקף מעשה ב"ד ובכח ב"ד יפה להיות ביד
20. האחים הנ"ל לעדות ולזכות ולראי' שיעמדו הקרקעות
21. הנ"ל עם כל חזקות וזכיות ביד האחים הנ"ל וי"א
22. וב"כ וכנ"ל בלי שום מוחה כלל נעשה היו' יו' א י"ב
23. מנחם תקמ"ו לפק הגאב"ד נר"ו ורנ"מ ורמ"ש ואני[1]

No. 211

Fols. 201a–202a; Sunday 6 August 1786

Reichle, widow of Isaac Hahn, two of her daughters, and her son-in-law, Ḥayyim Halle, approached the court through their representatives asking that it ratify their division of familial assets.[2] Reichle had recently arranged for the marriage of a third daughter to Wolf Fulda (see no. 210) and had given her a substantial dowry in return for an obligation from the couple to work in the widow's store for three years. This was done with the agreement of the other sisters. However, the other sisters wanted assurances that they would not be denied their fair share of the estate. To this end, the family agreed on future distributions of assets, an agreement that they brought to the court. The court examined the agreement, insured that it was in the interests of all parties, and affirmed it, giving it the same validity as a court decision. A copy of the agreement was given to each party so that everyone would have a written record. Also see no. 233.

רא ע"א

1. ב"ה
2. הן היו' הקריבו לפנינו ה"ה התורני נאמן הקהלה כ"ה ליב שווארץ שילד יצו
3. בהרשאת האשה הקצינה מ' רייכלה אל' המנוח כ' אייזק האן ז"ל ובהרשאת
4. בנותי' הבתולה מ' בילה ואחותה האשה מ' עדל ובעלה הו"ה כ' חיים
5. האַלי יצו והציע לפנינו תנאים ראשונים ההוקים יו' ב' ד"ב סיון תקמ"ו
6. מהאשה מ' רייכלה הנ"ל שהתקשרה את בתה היתומה הבתולה מ'
7. בריינלה עם הב"ח היתום היקר כ"ה וואלף בהמנוח[3] כ"ה הירץ פולדא
8. ז"ל ומבואר בתוכה שהתחייבה א"ע האשה מ' רייכלה להכניס קה"ח לנדן
9. בתה מ' בריינלה מעזבון בעלה ז"ל סך ארבעה אלפים זהו' אין

---

1. החתימות נוספו בכתב יד אחר.
2. Isaac Hahn died in April, 1786 (see Horovitz, no. 3898).
3. בן המנוח

10. ד״ד זהו׳ פוס / גם התחייבה עצמה להכניס לבתה הנ״ל בשעת החופה
11. בק״ג א״ס בכא״ה כתחז״ל שליש בית מהבית שלם החיצון צום רויטה
12. האַנן עם כל זכות וחזקה מנוקה ומשופי מכל עורר וטוען רק בשיור
13. יד העליונה על השליש בית הנ״ל לה לעצמה על כל זמן שלא
14. תנשא לגבר אוחרא / גם מחויבת להלבישה מלבושי כבוד בגדי שבת
15. י״ט וחול וליתן מתנות וסבלונות הכל כראוי לפ״כ ולפ״כ הנדן
16. גם התחייבה עצמה מ׳ רייכלה הנ״ל ליתן להזוג הנ״ל תכוף ומיד
17. מיו׳ החופה ואילך על משך זמן שנה ומחצה רצופים ז׳א׳ז מזונות
18. על שלחנה ודירה בביתה משכי[1] זמן הנ״ל הכל בחנם / והזוג
19. מ׳ בריינלה והרר[2] וואלף הנ״ל התחייבו והשתעבדו עצמם בחוב
20. ובשיעבוד גמור בכא״ה שמחויבת מ׳ בריינלה על משכ שלשה שנים
21. רצופי׳ זא״ז מיו׳ החופה ואילך להתעסק ולהטריח עצמה לסייע
22. בעסק חנות מו״מ של אמה מ׳ רייכלה הנ״ל לטובת המו״מ מה דאפשרי
23. ואמה מ׳ רייכלה הנ״ל התחייבה עצמה ליתן להזוג הנ״ל משכ
24. שלשה שנים הנ״ל עבור שכר טרחתה מידי שבועה בשבועה
25. ארבעה זהו׳ אבל ההתחייבת[3] הלז הוא דוקא כל זמן שהזוג
26. הנ״ל יחד בחיים חיותה עכ״ל הת״ר הנ״ל ואמר כה ליב
27. הנ״ל

רא ע״ב

1. בהרשאת הנ״ל שכל מה שהתחייבה א״ע האשה מ׳ רייכלי הנ״ל
2. בת״ר הנ״ל להכלה מ׳ בריינלה הנ״ל נעשה ברצון ובהסכמת שארי
3. בנותי׳ מ׳ בילה הנ״ל ומ׳ עדל ובעלה חתנה כ׳ חיים הנ״ל
4. באופן ובתנאי שיותן ג״כ לבתה הבתולה מ׳ בילה הנ״ל מעזבון
5. אבי׳ לעת חתנותה בכל מילי כמו שפסקה אמה מ׳ רייכלה
6. הנ״ל לאחותה מ׳ בריינלה הנ״ל הן נדן הן חלק בית והן מזונות
7. ומתנות וסבלונות ומלבושים והוצאות החתנה וגם לבתה מ׳
8. עדל אשת הו״ה כ׳ חיים הנ״ל יותן מעזבון אבי׳ לעת חלוקת
9. העזבון הנ״ל יהי׳ באיזה זמן שיהי׳ הן בחיי׳ אחיותה וגיסה
10. והן לאחר מותה ח״ו סך אלף זהו׳ אין דד זהו׳ פוס כדי
11. למלאות ג״כ סך נדן שלה לסך ארבעה אלפי׳ זהו׳ גם יותן
12. להאשה מ׳ עדל הנ״ל אשת כ׳ חיים הנ״ל שליש בית מבית
13. שלם צום רויטה האַנן בשיור יד העליונה לאמה מ׳ רייכלה
14. והציע לפנינו כ״ה ליב הנ״ל כתב יד הודאה שהי׳ ביד האל׳
15. הנ״ל מן שתי בנותי׳ הבתולה מ׳ בילה והאשה מ׳ עדל ובעלה חתנה
16. ואחי׳ כ׳ חיים הנ״ל ההוקם ביו׳ ב׳ ד״ב סיון תקמ״ו ושם נאמר

---

1. משך
2. והרב רבי
3. צ״ל ׳ההתחייבות׳

17. דברים הנ"ל מריצוי שהתרצה {א}א"ע האחיות וכ' חיים
18. הנ"ל על אופן הנ"ל / גם נאמר שם לחזק הענין יותן ה"ג
19. אב"ד נרו' בצירוף הב"ד יצו תוקף ע"ז / בכן מבקש
20. כ"ה ליב הנ"ל בהרשאות הנ"ל מאתנו ב"ד תוקף על כל הנ"ל
21. והנה אחרי שנזדקקנו לדברי כ"ה ליב הנ"ל ועיינו הדק
22. הטיב בת"ר הנ"ל ובכתב יד הודאה שלהם / ומצאנו
23. שהמה דברי' כנים ולטובת האל' מ' רייכלה ולטובת בנותי'
24. וחתנה כ' חיים הנ"ל לזאת באנו אנחנו ח"מ בתוקף מעשה
25. ב"ד

רב ע"א

1. ב"ד ובכח ב"ד יפה ליתן חיזוק וקיום לכל הדברים הנ"ל שיקוים
2. הכל בכל אופני' הן מה שהתחייבה א"ע האשה מ' רייכלי הנ"ל בת"ר
3. הנ"ל ליתן לבתה הכלה מ' בריינלי הנ"ל והן מה שמבואר בתוך כתב
4. יד הודאה הנ"ל לכל מה שהותנו ביניהן דהיינו בין האל' הנ"ל
5. ובין שתי בנותיה מ' בילה ומ' עדיל וחתנה כ' חיים הנ"ל וכנ"ל
6. והיינו שיותן להבתולה מ' בילה בת המנוח כ' אייזק הנ"ל
7. מעזבון אבי' ז"ל הנ"ל ג"כ לעת חתנות' סך ארבעה אלפי'
8. זהו' אין ך"ד זהו' פוס ושליש בית מבית שלם הנ"ל צום רויט
9. האַנן ומזונות ומתנו' וסבלונו' ומלבושי' והוצאות החתנה
10. ג"כ כמו שהתחייבה א"ע האל' הנ"ל ותתן לבתה הכלה מ' בריינלי
11. הנ"ל וגם מחמת מה שפסק עוד האל' מ' רייכלי הנ"ל בת"ר
12. הנ"ל ליתן להזוג כל שבוע סך ארבעה זהו' על משכ שלשה
13. שני' לאחר החתנה נגד שכר טרחת' ובכתב יד הודאה
14. הנ"ל הותנו ביניהם / ונתנו עיניה' על הב"ד יצו שיכירו
15. אם יותן להבתולה מ' בילה ג"כ כל כך לאחר חתנותה
16. מצאנו שגם בזה לא יהי' הפרש ביניהן ובאם שתתחייבה
17. הבתולה מ' בילה הנ"ל א"ע ג"כ לעת התקשרות שלה להתעסק
18. ולהטריח עצמה בכל מה דאפשרי בחנות אמה מ' רייכלי
19. הנ"ל שגם היא תקבלי על משכ זמן הנ"ל כל שבוע סך ארבעה זהו'
20. הכל על אופן המבואר בתר[1] לאחותה הכלה מ' בריינלי הנ"ל
21. וגם להאשה מ' עדיל בת המנוח כ' אייזק הנ"ל ובעלה כ' חיים הנ"ל
22. יקוים הכל כמבואר בכתב יד הודאה הנ"ל והיינו שיותן
23. להאשה מ' עדיל אשת כ' חיים הנ"ל לעת חלוקת עזבון
24. אבי' ז"ל הנ"ל קודם שתרד לנחלה עם שאר אחיות' סך עשרה
25. מאות זהו' אין ך"ד פוס ושליש בית מבית שלם צום רויטה האַנן
26. וכתבנו וחתמנו כל הנ"ל בתוקף מעשה ב"ד ובכח ב"ד יפה להיו'

---

1. בתנאים ראשונים

27. ביד כל אחת מבנות׳ המנוח כ׳ אייזק ז״ל לעדות ולזכות ולראי׳
28. שלא יפול דבר ארצה מכל הנ״ל ויקוי׳ הכל בלי שום מוחה כלל נעשה יו׳
29. א י״ב מנחם תקמו לפק {רנ״מ ואני ורמ[.]} הגאב״ד [נרו] ורנ״מ ור״מ[1] ואני[2]

No. 212

Schiff v. Rothschild

Fols. 202b–204b; Tuesday evening, 22 August 1786

The sale of property by Rabbi Meʾir Schiff to Meʾir Rothschild (see nos. 195, 208) was wrought with problems. Schiff came to the court with his legal representative and claimed that Rothschild owed him funds because he had not paid in full in the currency specified in the contract. According to Schiff, Rothschild's decision to pay in a different currency cost Schiff about 3% as a result of currency fluctuations. Meʾir Rothschild's representative countered that it was the custom of merchants to pay in any currency that they wanted unless the parties had specified otherwise. Rothschild explained that the listing of a price solely in currency *x* was but a statement of price, not of the currency of payment. Rothschild also noted that Schiff had already accepted partial payment in a different currency and therefore did not now have the right to stipulate that payment had to be made in the currency noted in the contract. The court examined the contracts and made inquiries to learn what the accepted practice was. Ultimately, the court sided mainly with Schiff.

A further complication arose with respect to Schiff's tax liability, an issue that had previously been raised before the court (no. 208). Schiff claimed that he should not have to pay or even collect the taxes on the half of the house that his brother Tevele had owned. There were two renters there until Rosh Hashanah 1786, and Rothschild, as owner of the house, should collect directly from them. As for his own half of the house, Schiff claimed that he should be absolved from taxes altogether, for, although he had the benefit of using the space, Rothschild owned the land, and taxes fell on the owner, not the person who used it. Both sides agreed to a compromise given by the court according to which Schiff was given Rothschild's contract and forced to collect from the two renters. As for Schiff's half of the house, Schiff was ordered to pay two-thirds of the tax liability and Rothschild one-third.

1. כנראה ר׳ מאיר שיף
2. החתימות שאינן מחוקות כאן כתובות בכתב יד אחר.

רב ע"ב

1. ב"ה
2. אחרי שכבר יצא מאתנו ב"ד ח"מ פס"ד ביו' טוב סיון העבר[1]
3. חזרו ובאו לפנינו הצדדי' ה"ה התורני נאמן הקהלה כ"ה פייס
4. הענא בהרשאות ובמעמד התורני הדיין כה מאיר שיף נרו'
5. ותבע מן ה"ה הו"ה כ"ה מאיר רויטשילד וטוען אחרי שמכירת
6. חצי בית מן הדיין כ"ה מאיר שיף לכ"ה מאיר רויטשילד הנ"ל הי'
7. על אופן זה שהתשלומין שליש דמי מכירה נגד מסירת החלטה
8. וכמו כן התשלומין דמי שמונה טערמינן בריב מן השני
9. שלישי' הנותרי' יהי' הכל אין קרלינר א אחד עשר זהו'[2]
10. וכמבואר בשטר קנין ובשטר אפותיקו בפי' והלוקח כ"ה מאיר
11. ר"ש הנ"ל לא קיים את קנינו ומסר להתורני כ"ה בענדיט
12. הענא סג"ל שליח של המוכר הנ"ל דמי השליש אַן גאב נגד
13. מסירת החלטה מהם אין חדש רטי' ומהם אין מינץ ושמונה
14. טערמינה ח"כ כתב התשלומין אין ךּ"ד זהו' פוס וכאשר
15. הביאום כ"ה בענדיט הנ"ל לכ"ה מ"ש[3] הנ"ל הי' צועק
16. ככרוכי' היאך שינה הלוקח את התשלומין הנ"ל והשיב
17. ר"ב[4] שלא הי' ידע שהפירעון הוכרח להיות אין קרלין
18. א י"א זהו' ועל זה השיב הדי[י]ן כ"ה מאיר שיף הנ"ל לפי
19. שעה רוצה לקבל וכיו' מחר אצעק ע"ז שהוא עולה גדולה
20. ויען כי באותו הפעם לא הי' ההפרש בין קרלין ובין
21. התשלומין אשר נתן לו רק לערך חצי למאה לא רצה לירד
22. עמו לפני דינא ודיינא אך עתה שהזמין אותו הלוקח
23. הנ"ל לדינא תבע הדיין כ"ה מאיר שיף הנ"ל מן הלוקח
24. כ"ה מר"ש[5] הנ"ל ההפרש שיש בין הקרלין והתשלומין אן ג[אַ]ב
25. שעולה לערך עשרה זה' ומחמת טערמינ[י] ח"כ שנתן לו
26. שהעמידם אין מינץ תבע כ"ה מאיר שיף מן כהר"ם ר"ש[6]
27. הנ"ל

רג ע"א

1. ב"ה
2. הנ"ל שאותו ח"כ שישנו עדיין בידו גם מה שאינו בידו ואפשר להשתדל
3. להביאו תחת ידו עוד יכתוב לו ח"כ אחרי' מאותו זמן הנזכרי' בישנם

---

1. ע' לעיל, מס' 208.
2. ר"ל קרלינר אחד שהוא שווה י"א זהובים.
3. מאיר שיף
4. כנראה ר' בענדיט (עיין שורה 15 ובדף ר"ג ע"ב שורה 10)
5. מאיר רויטשילד
6. כבוד הרב מאיר רויטשילד

4. לשלם אין קרלין א אחד עשר זהו׳ ובשביל אותן ח״כ שאינם תחת ידו
5. ויהי׳ בלתי אפשר לשנותם / וגם בשביל אותן ח״כ ראשון שכבר שילם
6. לו כהר״ם ר״ש הנ״ל אין מינץ תבע כהרם[1] שיף הנ״ל שלשה למאה
7. באשר שכעת ההפרש בין קרלינר ובין מינץ עולה כ״כ וטוען
8. הדיין כ״הרם שיף הנ״ל שמשום כך נכתב בפירוש בשטרות אין
9. קרלינר אַ אחד עשר זהו׳ כדי אם שילם לו הלוקח במטבע
10. אחרת זולת קרלין אזי צריך להעלות לו כל הלאַשע שבין קרלינר
11. ואותו מטבע ועכשיו עולה הלאַשי ג׳ למאה בכן מחויב הלוקח
12. לשלם לו או אין קרלינר נאַטוראָ אָדער אין מינץ בעלוי ג׳ למאה
13. והאריך בטענותיה׳ כמבואר בק״ה המונח לפנינו / וה״ה התורני
14. כ״ה מאיר מַז בהרשאת ובמעמד הו״ה גבאי ת״ת כ״ה מאיר ר״ש
15. השיב שדרך הסוחרי׳ הוא {אין} אם כתובי׳ אין קרלן אַ אחד עשר
16. זהו׳ ולא כתוב אין זהוב אָודר אין נאַטורא אזי יכולין לשלם קרלינר
17. או חדש רַ[ט]י[2] אונד מינץ הוא כעת טוב יותר מחדש רטי בכן אינו
18. צריך לשלם לו לאַשע ולשנות ח״כ ובאם שכוונת השטר יהי׳ דוקא אין
19. קרלינר מפני מה כתוב בשטר אַ יא זהו׳ הי׳ לו לכתוב בתוך
20. שטר קנין סתם חמשה מאות וחמש[י]ם קרלינר ועוד טוען מה שעלה
21. כעת הקרלינר ג׳ למאה נגד מינץ מפני שצריך להיות
22. בתשלומין ח״כ כפי צוואות השררה יר״ה שטיין וויכטיג ובאותו
23. פעם בשעת קנין לא הי׳ מן הצורך להיות כך לתשלומין ח״כ רק
24. בחסרון חמשה ע[ס]ין ואף שלשון השטר יהי׳ דוקא אין קרלינר מ״מ
25. אחרי שכבר התרצה א״ע כהרם שיף הנ״ל בקבלת אן גאב בתשלומין
26. חדש רטי׳ רק הי׳ קפידא שלו מחמת מינץ בכן אין יכול לתבוע שוב
27. קרלינר באשר שמינץ הוא שוב יותר מחדש רטי׳ וכ״ה מאיר שיף
28. הנ״ל חזר והשיב שסומך עצמו על לשו[ן] אפותיקו שבידו שהפרעון

רג ע״ב

1. צריך להיות אין קרלין ולא בדבר אחר ומה שנאמר אַ יא זהו׳ כבר טוען שכדי
2. שהעילוי לאַשע יהי׳ שלו וכמשמעות לשון השטר הקרקע עומד עדיין בחזקת
3. מרא קמא כל זמן שלא נתפרע כפי התחייבות השטר והאריכו הצדדי׳
4. הנ״ל בטענותיה׳ ובתשובתיה׳ כמבואר באריכות בק״ה המונח לפנינו
5. והנה כפי קומפרמיס שבידנו שחתמו הצדדי׳ הנ״ל א״ע בח״ח
6. ובקנס סך שני מאות רט חצי לשררה יר״ה וחצי להקדש לקיים הפס״ד
7. שיצא מאתנו נזדקקנו להם ואחרי שדקדקנו הדק היטיב
8. ועניננו בלשון השטר הקנין שביד נאמני הקהלה יצו שנעשה
9. על מכירה הנ״ל וגם בלשון השטר קנין והשטר אפותקו ואחרי

---

1. כבוד הרב מאיר
2. רייכשטאלרים

10. שדרשנו את השליח כ״ה בענדיט הענא סג״ל הנ״ל וגם לאחר
11. חקירה מבעלי מו״מ בענין חלוקי מטבעות ודרך תשלומי ח״כ בלשון
12. ח״כ אחרי כל הנ״ל מצאנו שהברירה יהי׳ ביד הו״ה כ״ה מאיר ר״ש
13. הנ״ל אם רוצה להניח אותן טערמיני ח״כ ככתבם וכלשונם אויף
14. דעם ך״ד זהו׳ פוס ולא רצה לשנותם ולהעמידם הפירעון אי[ן]
15. קרלין אַ יא זה׳ אזי מחויב כהרמ ר״ש הנ״ל לשלם עוד להדיין כהרם
16. שיף הנ״ל מחמת תביעות לאַשע על כל סך דמי מכירה הנ״ל כנ״ל
17. סך חמשה עשר רייכט טאליר אין קונפונטציאהנש מינץ אַ כ״ד זהו׳
18. פוס ובזה נתפרע תביעות כהר״מ שיף הנ״ל הן ממה שכבר
19. שילם והן מחמת טערמיני בריף שעליו לשלם עדיין ובאם
20. ירצה כהר״מ ר״ש הנ״ל לשנות אותן טערמיני בריב שביד
21. הדיין כהר״מ שיף ויתן לו חדשי׳ {ן} מזמן הקנין לשלם לזמן
22. הראשוני׳ אין קרלין אַ יא זהו׳ אזי אינו מחויב (לשלם)[1] הלאַשע
23. רק על התשלומין אן גאב נגד מסירת החלטה וגם בשביל
24. תשלומין ח״כ אחד שכבר יפרע אין מינץ וגם על אותן
25. ח״כ שאי אפשר לכהר״מ שיף להביאו תחת ידו כדי
26. לשנות אותן וישלם כה[ר״מ] ר״ש הנ״ל הלאַשע מן כל אלו לפי ערך
27. מסך חמשה עשר רט על כל דמי מכירה הנ״ל

רד ע״א

1. עוד האריכו הצדדי׳ הנ״ל מחמת דמי קרונד צונץ שכבר מבואר
2. בפס״ד שיצא כבר מאתנו וכנ״ל שכהר״מ ר״ש הנ״ל רוצה לנכות
3. מפירעון טערמיני ח״כ מה שמוטל על כ״ה מאיר שיף הנ״ל לשלם דמי
4. קרונד צונץ מן הבית שלם עד ר״ה תקמ״ז הבע״ל באשר שאותו דמי
5. קרונד צונץ שעולה ע״ח חצי בית שהי׳ שייך להרב כמהו׳ טעבלי שיף
6. כץ נרו׳ נזכר בפירוש במעשה ב״ד שפטור כ״ה מאיר ר״ש הנ״ל
7. לשלם עד תשרי תקמ״ז והחיוב הוא על כה מאיר שיף הנ״ל במקום
8. הרב נרו׳ ועל חלק חצי בית האחרת שהי׳ שייך לכהר״מ שיף הנ״ל
9. טוען כ״ה מאיר {שיף} ר״ש הנ״ל שגם זה מחויב כהר״מ שיף לשלם
10. עד תשרי תקמ״ז הבע״ל באשר שיש לו עדיין הפירות מחצי בית
11. שלו עד זמן הנ״ל וכ״ה מאיר שיף הנ״ל השיב מחמת חלק דמי
12. קרונד צונץ מחצי בית שהי׳ שייך לאחיו הרב נרו׳ הנ״ל אף שהוא
13. מרוצה לשלם בשבילו היינו דוקא מה שמחויב אחיו הרב נרו׳
14. לשלם מכיסו אכן מה שמחוביב׳ השכני׳ מחזיקי בית ר״ז[2] שיף
15. וכ׳ יודא זיכל לשלם החצי מערך שני׳ עשר זהו׳ ט״מ מה שנזכר

---

1. תוספת מעל השורה
2. ר׳ זלמן

בק"צי[1] ביכל יותר מ'מ'ה[2] שנכתב בק"צ ביכל שלהם {החצי}
וכפי השטר שיש ביד כ"ה מאיר ר"ש הנ"ל מחויבי' המה לשלם החצי
וטוען רמ"ש הנ"ל שאינו מחויב עוד לתבוע מהם רק שכהר"ם ר"ש
שיש לו השטר בידו יכול לתבוע מהם מה שמוטל עליהם להשלי'
דמי קרונד צונץ של הרב ועל חלק דמי קרונד צונץ מן החצי בית
בית שהי' שייך לכ"ה מאיר שיף נרו' השיב כהרם שיף שהחיוב
דמי קרונד צונץ הוא על גוף הקרקע מי ששייך לו ולא על מי שיש לו
הפירות והא ראי' אפי' בית ותל עולם מחויבי' הבעלים
לשלם ק"צ וגם האלמנות שדרה בתורת מיגר אל' אין מחויבת
לשלם ק"צ והאריכו בטענותיה[3] גם בזה כמבואר בק"ה המנוח

רד ע"ב

לפנינו ובאשר שבענין דמי ק"צ הנ"ל נתנו הצדדי' הנ"ל עיניהם –
על הב"ד לפשר ביניהם ולקיים כפי הפשר שיצא מאתנו
נזדקקנו להם ומצאנו בפשר דבר שחלק קרונד צונץ מחצי
בית שהי' ששייך להרב נרו' מחויב הדיין כ"ה מאיר שיף נר'
לשלם עד ר"ה תקמ"ז הבעל[4] כפי החיוב הנזכר בביכל שלהם
והוא יתבע ממחזיקי ר' זלמן שיף הנ"ל מה שמוטל עליהם
וכ"ה מאיר ר"ש הנ"ל יתן לו השטר הנ"ל כדי שיוכל לתבוע
מהם ובאופן שלאחר הפירעון מחויב להחזיר לו
תיכף השטר הנ"ל ומחמת דמי ק"צ חצי בית שהי[5] שייך
להדיין כ"ה מאיר שיף הנ"ל מצאנו ע"ד פשר דבר שכהר"מ שיף
הנ"ל ישלם שני שלישם מסך דמי קרונד צונץ העולה
מיו' מכירה עד ר"ה תקמ"ז ה"בעל ועל כ"ה מאיר
ר"ש הנ"ל שליש אחד יצא מאתנו אור ליו' ד דט מנחם
תקמ"ו {הגא} רנ"מ ואני ורמ"ל

No. 213

Fol. 204b; Wednesday 21 March 1787

Rabbi Ḥayyim Gundersheim noted that he was present at the *ḥaliẓah* ceremony of Nenel, widow of Leb Schloss. During the ceremony, a question arose among the

1. קרונד צונץ
2. לא ברור למה יש גרשים כאן.
3. צ"ל 'טענותיהם'
4. הבא עלינו לטובה
5. צ"ל 'שהיה'

rabbis as to which hand the woman should use to remove the shoe. Normally the shoe was removed with the hand that the individual did most of her activities with, however, in this case the woman wrote and ate with her right hand but sewed and cut with her left. The court sent Rabbi Ḥayyim to the chief rabbi to ask what should be done. Rabbi Pinḥas Horowitz instructed that she should use her right hand.

15. ———
16. יו׳ ד ב ניסן (תקמ״ז)[1] הייתי אצל חליצה האשה מ׳ נענעל אל׳ המנוח כ״ה ליב שלאס ז״ל שלקחה
17. חליצה מן היבום מיכל שלאס והמסדר הי׳ ר״י ורב״ד מה׳ נתן מז והדייני׳ מה׳ אברהם טריר
18. ור׳ זנוויל טראך והנוספי׳[2] מאיר שיף ואני והשאלה הי׳ על אודות האל׳ הנ״ל שכותבת
19. בידה ימנית וגם אוכלות באותו יד ותופרות וחותכות מלאכת׳ (נשי׳)[3] בידה השמאלית
20. והי׳ דעת ר נתן הנ״ל שהיא איטרת יד (וחולצת בשמאלה)[4] דאזלינן אחר מלאכה דדוקא בתפילין אזלינן
21. [ב]תר כתיבה דכתיב וקשרתם וכתבתם אבל בחליצה לא ור׳ אברהם הנ״ל הי׳
22. אומר שנקראת שולטת בשתי ידים הואיל שנעשה איזה דבר ביד ימין ואיזה ביד
23. שמאל ונשלחתי אצל הג׳ אב״ד נרו׳ והי׳ מסכי׳ לדברי ר׳ אברהם הנ״ל הואיל שהוא ספק
24. [שראוי] לה[..] ביד ימין וגם בדיעבד חליצה בשמאל כשר בכן תהא חולצת בידה ימינית
25. וכן עשינו והעדי׳ הי׳ השמש ר׳ דוד שש[5] והבחור אברם בן השמש ר׳ זיסקינד שטערן

No. 214

Fol. 205a; Wednesday 9 May 1787

Sorle, a maidservant in Frankfurt, left a will in which she stipulated that each of her grandchildren receive an equal share in her estate when they married (see no. 185). She specifically stated that if a grandchild were to die before marrying, that portion would remain in the estate and be divided among the surviving grandchildren. Sorle's son-in-law, Moses, himself now a widower, came to the court after one of his sons died. Moses asked that the deceased child's portion in his grandmother's estate be given to him — even though the child had never married — to help Moses recover from the financial expenses related to the sickness and death of the

1. תוספת מעל השורה
2. על הצורך בנוספים, ר׳ שו״ע אה״ע קסט ס״ג.
3. תוספת מעל השורה
4. תוספת מעל השורה
5. שווארצשילד

child. The court asked Moses' three daughters, who lived with him and whom he supported, whether they agreed to this arrangement, and they asserted that they did. The court acceded to the request and noted that if Moses' two older children, who also lived with him, formally agreed to it, he could have their shares of the deceased child's portion of the estate as well, a total of 50 guldens.

רה ע״א

ב״ה שוב חזר ובא לפנינו כ׳ שמעון הנ״ל ושאל מאתנו ב״ד ואמר אחרי שנעדרו אשתו ובן אחד קטן ושבקו חיים לכ״י וכפי המבואר בשט״ח הנ״ל וז״ל ובאם שיעדר ח״ו אחד מהם בעודו פנוי אזי יותן כל הקרן להנשארים בחיי׳ בנים ובנות בשוה שיותן לכל א מחלקו לעת נישואן שלו מהקרן ובאשר שלפ״ז הי׳ לו על בנו הנעדר הוצאות הרבה שהוכרח לשלם לרופאים ולצרכי קבורה כפי אשר הציע לפנינו חשבונו לזאת תבע כ׳ שמעון הנ״ל שיותן לו מעזבון חמותו ז״ל הנ״ל כל מה שהי׳ מגיע לבתו הנעדרת[1] ז״ל ואמר שבניו המה מרוצים בכך / והנה לטובת בני׳ קטני׳ של כ׳ שמעון הנ״ל נכדי של האשה המונחת מ׳ שרלה הנ״ל המגודלי׳ אצל אביהם ומפרנס אותם נזדקקנו עוד לדברי כ׳ שמעון הנ״ל ומצאנו אחרי שהי׳ לפנינו שלש בנותיו הנ״ל ואמרו שהן מרוצות ברצונם הטוב שיותן לאביהם מחלקם / בכן יותן לכ׳ שמעון הנ״ל מעזבון חמותו ז״ל הנ״ל בשביל בנותיו הנ״ל סך שלשים זהו׳ מחלק המגיע להן מן אחיהם הנעדר הנ״ל דהיינו בשביל כל א עשרה זהו׳ / ובאם יביא כ׳ שמעון הנ״ל כתב מקוים מן אב״ד דק״ק בידונגין #[2] שבנו ובתו הגדולים שהם אצלו שגם המה מרוצים ליתן מחלקם לאביהם הנ״ל אזי יותן לכ׳ שמעון הנ״ל עוד עשרים זהו׳ עולה יחד חמשים זהו׳ מעזבון חמותו ז״ל הנ״ל יצא מאתנו יו׳ ד לו למב״י שנת תקמזין לפק הגאב״ד נר׳ ורנ״מ ורמ״ש ואני # וזאת לדעת שטעות נפל בפסק דין הלז להנ״ל בשם האיש אשר נקרא שמו משה במקו׳ שמעון

No. 215

Fol. 205a; Monday 4 June 1787

Rabbi Ḥayyim Gundersheim recorded that he was present at a *ḥaliẓah* ceremony

1. צ״ל ׳לבנו הנעדר׳
2. תוספת בשורה 20

involving Shinka, widow of Ber Kann, who died on 2 March 1787.[1] As in an earlier case (see no. 213), Rabbi Ḥayyim noted the names of the parties involved, the judges, and the witnesses.

22. היו׳ יו׳ ב חי סיון הייתי אצל חליצת האשה מ׳ שינכה אל׳ המנוח כ׳ פער קן
23. מן היבמה כ״ה גומפל בכ״ה ליב קן יצו והמסדר הי׳ הדיין ור״י ורב״ד רנ״מ
24. והדייני׳ מה׳ אברהם טריר ור זנוויל טראך והנוספי׳ ר מאיר שיף ואני ועדי׳
25. השמש ר דוד שש[2] והבחור כ׳ אברם בן השמש ר זיסקינד שטערן

No. 216

Fol. 205b; Monday 4 June 1787

The court confirmed the transfer of half a seat in the middle women's section of the synagogue that was currently being used by the wife of Benedit Mai. The seat came into the possession of the community as part of a here unspecified compromise between the community and Me᾽ir Hannover (also see nos. 219, 220). The communal leadership now awarded the place to Me᾽ir Kassel for his efforts in arranging the compromise. Kassel had to make a payment of 15 karoliners to the community as part of the transaction. There was no public auction of the seat.

רה ע״ב

1. ב״ה
2. היו׳ יו׳ ב׳ חי סיון עשינו מעשה ב״ד על מכירת חצי מקו׳ בע״נ התיכונה אשר עומד
3. עלי׳ כעת אשת כ׳ בענדיט מאיי שהי׳ שייך מקדמת להו״ה כ״ה מאיר הנובר סג״ל
4. והוחלט ע״י פשר להאלופי׳ גובי׳ יצו וכעת חזרו ומכרו האלופי׳ גובי׳ יצו חצי מקו׳
5. הנ״ל לה״ה כ׳ מאיר בן יוקל קאסיל [ס]ג״ל בעד התעסקות וטרחות שהי׳ לו בענין פשר
6. שנגמר על ידו בין האלופי׳ גובי׳ ובין כ״ה מאיר הנובר הנ״ל ונוסף לזה מחויב כ׳
7. מאיר הנ״ל לשלם להאלופי׳ גובי׳ יצו סך חמשה עשר קרלינר כפי תיקון הקהלה // בחתימות
8. רנ״מ ורמ״ש ואני

---

1. With regard to the date of Ber Kann's death, see C. Duschinsky, *Mazkir neshamot*, no. 435. Ettlinger (4.3.1787) noted that Ber and Shinka married in about 1782.
2. שווארצשילד

No. 217

Schiff v. Hammel et al.

Fols. 205b–206b; Sunday 24 June 1787

Isaac Schiff was a scribe for Leb Hammel and his associates. He was paid an annual salary of 200 guldens and ate at his employer's table. In December 1785 Isaac informed Leb that he could no longer eat with him for reasons that are not specified here. Leb accepted this and gave Isaac 2 guldens per week to buy meals on his own. According to Isaac, he informed Leb at the time that this amount was insufficient to cover his food expenses and he asked that Leb make payment directly to the cook who supplied Isaac's meals. Leb did not respond to the request. Isaac continued to work for Leb but his food allowance remained the same. Isaac now sued Leb and his associates for back payment of his food expenses, including extra expenses for Passover and holidays totaling 163 guldens.

Isaac stopped working for Leb in mid-May 1787 and demanded six months wages, claiming that he had missed a customary hiring period in the marketplace because he had continued to work for Leb. The business associates argued that they owed Isaac nothing for food since they had offered to let him eat at the table of a different associate but he had refused. Moreover, they informed the court they had told Isaac that if he was unhappy with the food arrangements he could leave. Regarding the wages, the associates agreed to make payment, but disputed the period of time to be covered. The two parties agreed to be bound by a court-imposed compromise with respect to both the meals and the lost hiring opportunity. The court ordered Leb Hammel and his associates to pay a total of 69 guldens to Isaac to settle all claims.

ע״ד שבא לפנינו ה״ה התורני כ״ה משה אויק בהרשאות הבחור כ׳ איצק בהמנוחי[1] כ׳ משה שיף ז״ל ותבע מן ה״ה הו״ה גץ[2] התורני כ״ה ליב האמיל סג״ל ומשותפי׳ סך מאה וששים ושלשה זהו׳ וטוען שכ׳ איצק הנ״ל הי׳ שרייבר אצלם כמה שנים בשכירות סך שני מאות זהו׳ לשנה ומזונות בחנם אצל ר׳ ליב האמיל הנ״ל ובשנה דאשתקד בר״ח טבת תקמויו אמר כ׳ איצק הנ״ל לכה[3] ליב הנ״ל שאי אפשר לו לאכול עוד על שלחנו מכמה טעמי׳ והשיב לו כ״ה ליב הנ״ל שרצה ליתן לו דמי מזונות כל שבועה שני זהו׳ שיוכל

1. בן המנוח
2. גבאי צדקה
3. לכבוד הרב

17. לילך אין דיא גאר קוך לאכול שם / והשיב לו כ׳ איצק הנ״ל שאינו
18. יכול לאכול בעד שני זהו׳ בתוכ[1] גאר קוך רק שהוא כ״ה ליב הנ״ל
19. יעשה אַקאָרד עם גאר קוך ומשלם לגאר קוך בשבילו כפי אשר השוה
20. עצמו ושתק כ״ה ליב הנ״ל ולא דיבר מאומה ובכלות הזמן לאחר פסח
21. שחישב כ׳ איצק עם כ״ה ליב הנ״ל ושילם כה״ל[2] לכ״א[3] הנ״ל דמי מזונות
22. שני זהו׳ לכל שבוע ושבוע צוח כ״א הנ״ל נגדו ואמר כל דמי שכירות
23. שקבלתי הכל יצא בדמי אכילה שהוכרחתי להוציא כל שבוע ארבעה
24. זהו׳ במזונות וע״ז ג״כ שתק ולא השיב כלום כה״ל ומשותפי׳ וכן בכל
25. חצי שנה הי׳ כיוצה בו בכן תבע כ״א הנ״ל מן כה״ל ומשותפי׳ דמי
26. מזונות מן שמונה עשר חדשי׳ דהיינו מן ר״ח טבת תקמויו עד ר״ח סיון
27. דהאי שתא כל חודש שמונה זהו׳ העולה לסך מאה וארבעים וארבעה זהו׳
28. מלבד דמי מזונות מן פסח משארי י״ט שהם במשך זמן הנ״ל שתבע עוד
29. סך תשעה עשר זהו׳ עולה [י]חד קסג זהו׳ כנ״ל
30. ועוד

רו ע״א

1. עוד תבע כה משה הנ״ל בהרשאת כ׳ א׳[4] הנ״ל שכירות מחצי שנה הלז מפסח
2. העבר עד ר״ה וטען באשר שכפי הנהוג מתחיל הזמן אן גלייטש טאג[5] לפני יריד
3. ובאשר שכ׳ איצק החזיק את עצמו מהם בחורף העבר ד״י יום קודם גלייטש
4. טאג ואמר שאי אפשר לו להיות עוד אצלם בשירות ע״ז השיב לו גץ[6] כ״ה
5. יוסף האמיל סגל באותו פעם שכעת עדיין לא עבר הזמן ולא צריך להחזיק
6. עצמו ומי יגרש אותו / וע״ז החזיר להם מה שהחזיק עצמו מהם / ובכלות
7. הזמן שתקו ולא אמרו לו כלום ומשום כך נשאר אצלם יריד העבר ולא
8. השכיר עצמו אצל אחרים ווילין איהם [נו]ט אויף גראגט האבין / בכן
9. תבע שכירות שלו מחצי שנה הלז שהם גרמו לו היזק שאין יוכל להשכיר
10. א״ע ובאם אינה זוכה בטענה שלו מכל הזמן עכ״פ תבע שכירות
11. עד ר״ח סיון העבר ואמר שהזמן שלו מתחיל תמיד אן גלייטש טאג כאשר
12. בא אצלם / וה״ה התורני כ״ה בענדיט הענא בהרשאת
13. המשותפי׳ הנ״ל השיב שהמה אינו מחויבי׳ ליתן לו כלום דמי מזונות
14. באשר שהמה הי׳ רוצה ליתן לו מזונות על שלחנם כפי שפסקו עמו רק
15. כ׳ איצק הנ״ל מסרב להיות אצלם על שלחן של ר׳ ליב הנ״ל ומבקש ממנו
16. דמי מזונות כל שבוע ושבוע סך שני זהו׳ כמו שארי משרתיו והשיב
17. לו ר״ל הנ״ל שדמי מזונות מוטל עליו לשלם מכיסו והוא יכול לאכול

---

1. בתוך
2. כבוד הרב ליב
3. לכבוד איצק
4. כבוד איצק
5. הוא יום הראשון של היריד. יש אחד בסתיו ואחד באביב. ר׳ *Frankfurter Wörterbuch*, s.v., "Geleitstag"
6. גבאי צדקה

18. אצלו וגם פו"מ כ לימא הענא אמר לו אם אינו רוצה להיות אצל חמיו
19. שלו על שלחנו רוצה הוא להחזיקו וליתן מזונות על שלחנו רק כ' איצק
20. לא רצה ג"כ להיות אצלו רק כל פעם קיבל דמי מזונות שלו כשחשב
21. עמו בשתיקה והוא הי' יכול לצאת מהם כל הזמן וגם בפירוש אמר
22. כ' לימא הנ"ל לכ"א הנ"ל בחורף העבר כשהחזיק עצמו ודיבר
23. עם כ"ה יוסף הנ"ל וכנ"ל שאם אינו מרוצה בדמי מזונות הנ"ל שיוכל
24. לילך למקו' אחר וכאשר החזיק עצמו בחודש אייר העבר שילם לו דמי
25. מזונות עד ר"ח סיון העבר בכן אין לו שום תביעה מדמי מזונות
26. רק דמי שכירות מגיע לו מהתחלת הזמן הלז שהוא לפי דיבורם מחודש אייר
27. כל פעם עד ר"ח סיון העבר שרוצים לשלם לו והאריכו בטענותיהם כמבואר
28. בק"ה ובאשר שחתמו עצמם הצדדי' הנ"ל בתוקף קומפרמיס בקנס לאשר ולקיים
29. כפי אשר יצא מאתנו גם קיבלו ע[צמם][1] לפשר בניהם בכן

רו ע"ב

1. נזדקקנו להם ומצאנו שמחויבי' המשותפי' הנ"ל לשלם לכ"א הנ"ל דמי
2. שכירות עד ר"ח סיון סך ששה עשר זהו' הקצוב ביניהם בשביל חדש
3. אחד א["כ] בשביל מה שתבע עוד כ"א הנ"ל שזמן שכירות התחיל
4. ביו' גלייטש טאג ותבע מן כל הזמן הלז וגם דמי מזונות מן
5. העבר וכנ"ל מצאנו ע"ד פשר דבר שמחויבי' המשותפי' הנ"ל
6. לשלם לכ"א הנ"ל בשביל כל תביעות הנ"ל סך חמשי' ושלשה זהו'
7. נוסף על סך ששה עשר זהו' הנ"ל ובזה פטורים ומסולקים מכל
8. תביעותיו הנ"ל יצא מאתנו יו' א חית תמוז תקמזין לפק
9. רנמ[2] ורמש[3] ואני

No. 218

Fol. 206b; Thursday 9 August 1787

Rabbi Ḥayyim Gundersheim noted that he was present at the *ḥaliẓah* ceremony of Breinla, widow of Aaron Dethmühl (Detmold) who had died in September 1786.[4] *Ḥaliẓah* was generally done 90 days after the death of the husband (exclusive of the day of death and the day of the *ḥaliẓah*), however, Aaron was not a native of Frankfurt and apparently none of his brothers was immediately available to

1. יש כאן חור בנייר. ההשלמה ע"פ ההשארה.
2. רב נתן מז
3. ורב מאיר שיף
4. Aaron died 26 September 1786 (see Horovitz, no. 3910). Ettlinger (26.9.1786) noted that he was not a native of Frankfurt.

perform the ceremony. It would seem that when the levir, Azriel, who lived in Homberg vor der Höhe, came to Frankfurt the ceremony took place. As in other such cases, the names of all parties involved are noted except the witnesses, who are referred to only with a cross reference, "mentioned above" (presumably no. 215).

היו' יו' ה דה מנחם (תקמ"ז)[1] הייתי אצל סידור חליצה של האשה מ' בריינלה אל'
המנוח כ"ה אהרן דעטמויהל {...} בת של המנוח ר' הענך האלי שחולצת
מיבמה כ' עזריאל ב"ר יוסף דיטמויעל הדר בק"ק הומבורג פר דער ה[א][2]
ומסדר הי' ר"י ורב"ד מהו' נ"מ והדייני' רא"ט ורזט[3] והוספות אני ור"מ[4] זאמשט
והעדי' הנ"ל

No. 219

Fol. 206b; Sunday 29 July 17[87]

The court confirmed the sale of half a house on the Knoblauch lot by the community to Ḥayyim Rofe (Doktor). The house had come into the community's possession as part of its compromise with Me'ir Hannover (see nos. 216 and 220) and was now sold for 2300 guldens. There is no mention of there having been a public auction of the property.

———
עשינו מעשה ב"ד על מכירת חצי בית פנימי צום קנויבליך שמכרו הגובי'
יצו לכ' חיים בהמנוח[5] כ"ה פער רופא[6] בעד סך עשרי' ושלשה מאות
זהו' לשלם שליש תיכף ושני שלישי' על שמונה טערמינן ביו' א יד מנחם תק[מ"ז]
שהי' שייך לכ"ה מאיר הנובר ועל ידי פשר הוחלט לגובי' רנ"מ ורמ"ש ואני

1. תוספת מעל השורה
2. Homberg vor der Höhe
3. ורבי זנוויל טראך
4. ורבי מענדלי
5. בן המנוח
6. בלוח העניינים (הפנייה לדף רו ע"ב) הוא רשום כ-'חיים טאקטער'.

No. 220

Fol. 206b; Monday 16 June 1788

The court confirmed the sale of half a house on the Glocke lot. As in the previous case and in no. 216, the property had belonged to Me'ir Hanover, but, as part of a compromise, the house had come into the possession of the community which now sold it to Me'ir Kassel for 4200 guldens. There is no mention of Kassel's role in the compromise or any hint that he received special treatment in the sale of the property (cf., no. 216). However, there is also no mention of the property being sold after a period of open bidding.

———

היו' יו' ב יא סיון תקמ"ח עשינו מעשה ב"ד על מכירת חצי בית צור גלאך שמכרו[1]
הגובי' יצו שהי' שייך לכ"ה מאיר הנובר הנ"ל וכעת שייך לגובי' ע"י פשר ומכרו הגוב'
להו"ה כ' מאיר בן המנוח כ' יוקל קאסל סג"ל בעד סך ארבעת אלפי' ושני מאות
זהו' לשלם כפי תיקון הקהלה וחתמנו רנ"מ ורמ"ש ואני

No. 221

Fol. 207a; Summer 1788

Rabbi Ḥayyim Gundersheim recorded a personal status case in which an unnamed woman was required to undergo *ḥaliẓah,* but, before she did, she married another man who was not a local resident. This was a violation of Jewish law since she had yet to be freed by her levir (see Deut. 25.5–10). As a result, the court forced the second husband to divorce his wife. She was then required to undergo *ḥaliẓah* from one of her late husband's brothers and then ordered to search out her husband's other brother to be released by him as well.[2] The case had an added complication in that there was a child from the wife's second marriage, but this issue is not addressed in this record.

1. כפילות במקור
2. See B.T., *Yebamot* 53a, and *Shulḥan ʿaruk*, Eben ha-ʿezer 170.5.

רז ע"א

ב"ה בקיץ תקמ"ח

יו' [1] הייתי אצל סידור חליצה מן האשה ארחי ופרכי[2] שנשאה אורח אחד

טרם שקיבל חליצה מן יבום שלה / והיבום שלה בא לכאן וגם בעלה בא עמה ומן בעלה

נולדה לה תינק אחד והזקיקו הגאב"ד (נרו')[3] ושני רב"ד יצו וסידרו לה גט מבעלה ולאח"כ

סדרנו חליצה מן יבום שלה / ובאשר שהיא חליצה שאינו ראוי ליבום ונקרא חליצה

פסולה לכן לא התרנו לה להתנשא לגבר אוחרא עד שחזרה על יבום אחר

שלה לחלוץ לה ג"כ רנ"מ ורז"ט ורמ"ש = אני ורמ"ז

No. 222

Fol. 207a; Sunday (20 July 1788)[4]

The court affirmed the sale of half a house on the Hufeisen lot by Yuzpa Maas to Leb Kassel for 1500 guldens. Yuzpa had owned the land that the house sat on, and his widowed mother, Feigel, had rights to the income from the house until her death, after which the income would to revert to her son. Yuzpa sold all his rights to Leb after the traditional announcement of sale and the bidding period. Leb also purchased half a seat in the men's section of the synagogue that was owned by Yuzpa and his mother according to the same arrangement as the house. The half seat was sold for 84 guldens.

יו' א טו תמוז עשינו מעשה ב"ד על מכירת חצי בית צום הוף אייזן

שמכרנו לאחר הכרזה כנהוג שהי' שייך גוף הקרקע לכ' יוזפא הירש

בן המנוח כ"ה יוקל מז ז"ל והפירות לאמו מ' פאגיל אל' המנוח כ"ה יוקל ז"ל הנ"ל

כל ימי חיי' ולאח"כ שייך אף הפירות לכ' יוזפא הירש הנ"ל ומכרנו גוף

קרקע הנ"ל מעכשיו והפירות בזמן הנ"ל לכ"ה ליב בן המנוח כ' מיכל קאסל

ז"ל בעד סך חמשה עשר מאות זהו' לשלם כפי תיקון הקהלה

———

וכה"ג מכרנו חצי מקו' בע"א עליונה שהי' שייך לכ' יוזפא הירש הנ"ל על

1. כנראה שהייתה כוונה למלא את התאריך אבל הדבר לא נעשה.
2. צ"ל 'ופרחי' (ר' כתבות סא ע"א)
3. תוספת מעל השורה
4. The date is recorded as Sunday 15 Tammuz, but no year is mentioned. The fifteenth of Tammuz fell on a Sunday in both 1787 and 1788. Given that the surrounding documents are from 1788, this seems the most reasonable possibility.

16. אופן הנ"ל ג"כ לכהי[1] ליב הנ"ל בעד סך שמוני' וארבעה זהו' על אופן
17. הנ"ל וחתמנו רנ"מ ורמ"ש ואני

No. 223

Levy v. Estate of Jacob Kann

Fol. 207b; 27 or 28 July 1788

In early 1775 Hanle, who less than two months earlier had been widowed by Jacob Kann, made a death bed will in which she ordered that her daughter Sprinẓ share equally in her estate with all male heirs (Sprinẓ's brothers).[2] In 1785 Hanle's son and Sprinẓ's brother, Samson, died without having married (see Horovitz, no. 3861). In 1787 Sprinẓ died in Mannheim, leaving a husband, Eliezer Levy of Mannheim, and a minor son.[3] Eliezer sent a representative before the Frankfurt court arguing that he and his son were entitled to a share in Samson's estate through Sprinẓ on the basis of Hanle's 1775 death bed will. The argument was rejected by guardians of Jacob Kann's son, Moses. They claimed that Sprinẓ and her husband had already received their share in Hanle's estate and that Hanle had no right to dictate anything with respect to Samson's estate. After examining Hanle's will, the court dismissed Eliezer's claim.

רז ע"ב

1. ע"ד שבא לפנינו התורני כ"ה מאיר בכ[4] אנשיל מז יצו ותבע בכח והרשאה מספקת
2. שהציע לפנינו מן ה"ה הו"ה כה אליעזר בכ' נתן לוי מן קק[5] מנהיי' יעא' לירד לפני ב"ד
3. לדון בשביל עצמו ובשביל בנו הילד כ' יעקב שי' מאשתו ראשונה שהי' לו המונחת מ'
4. שפרינץ בת פו"מ ר' יעקב קן ז"ל מפה לתבוע חלק ירושה מן עזבון גיסו הב"ח
5. המונח כ' שמשון בן של ר' יעקב קן הנ"ל אחי אשתו ז"ל הנ"ל שנפטר קודם פטירת
6. אשתו ז"ל וטוען באשר שחמותה של כ"ה ליזר הנ"ל היינו האשה מ' הנלא אל'
7. המנוח ר' יעקב קן ז"ל הנ"ל עשתה צוואת שכ"מ וציותה שבתה מ' שפרינץ הנ"ל
8. תקחי בעזבונה שוה בשוה חלק כחלק עם בניה הזכרים וטוען שהיתה כוונתה
9. ג"כ שבתה תהי' כבנים הזכרי' בכל מילי אף בירושת עזבון כ' שמשון הנ"ל

---

1. לכבוד הרב
2. Regarding the date of Jacob Kann's death, see Horovitz, no. 3522; Hanle died in early January 1775 (see Horovitz, no. 3523). Also see Pinqas Franqfurṭ, no. 476 (7 July 1776).
3. Mannheim *Memorbuch*, 73.
4. בן כבוד
5. קהילת קודש

בכן זכתה האשה מ' שפרינץ הנ"ל בשעת פטירת אחי' כ' שמשון הנ"ל בעזבונו כל כך כמו אחי' כ' משה שי' ולאחר פטירת האשה מ' שפרינץ ז"ל הנ"ל יורש כ"ה ליזר ובנו חלקה / וה"ה התורני נ"ה כה ליב שווארץ שילד בהרשאות הו"ה גע[1] כ' בענדיט מאיי סג"ל והו"ה גץ כה גומפיל רייס יצו אפטרופסי' של היתום כ' משה בן המנוח כ' יעקב קן ז"ל ובהרשאת האשה הקצינה מ' מרים אשת כה איצק בר יעקב קן ז"ל הנ"ל הציע לפנינו צוואת שכ"מ מן האשה מ' הנלא ז"ל הנ"ל והשיב שאינו מוזכר כלום בצוואה שתהי' בתה מ' שפרינץ יורשת בעזבון כ' שמשון ז"ל הנ"ל גם לא הי' כח בידה לצוות כן על דבר שלא בא לעולם רק כוונתה על עזבון שלה ומעזבונה כבר קיבלה באמת כל מה שהי' מגיע לה והציע לפנינו כתב פטורים שנתנה האשה מ' שפרינץ ז"ל הנ"ל להאפטרופסי' הנ"ל וגם כה ליזר הנ"ל חתם עצמו על פטורים שאין להם שום תביע שבעולם על עזבון האשה הנ"ל והאריכו בטענותיהם ולאחר שחתמו עצמם הצדדי' הנ"ל בתוקף קומפרמיס בח"ח ובקנס סך מסויים דהיינו כ"ה מאיר הנ"ל בתוקף כו"ה מספקת מן כה ליזר ובנו הנ"ל צד אחד והאפטרופסי' הנ"ל והאשה מ' מרים הנ"ל בעצמם לקיים הפסד[2] שיצא מאתנו בכן נזדקקנו להם והנה אחר שקיימנו את חתימת יד של הג[3] אב"ד נרו' דקק[4] מנהיים בכח והרשאה הנ"ל גם לאחר עיון הדק היטב בצוואת שכ"מ מן האשה מ' הנלא ז"ל הנ"ל מן יו' ד חי טבת קהלת לפק מצאנו שאין לכ"ה ליזר ובנו הילד כ' יעקב הנ"ל שום זכות בעזבון המנוח כ' שמשון ז"ל הנ"ל {יצא} והכל שייך לאחיו יורש דאורייתא של כ' שמשון הנ"ל יצא מאתנו יו' ב דב מנחם תקמ"ח הגאון אבד[5] נרו' ורנם[6] ורמש[7] ואני

No. 224

Fol. 208a; Wednesday 16 September 1789

A record of the agreement of all members of the Frankfurt rabbinic court not to allow the cantor to lead prayers until after Yom Kippur 1789. Even then, the cantor was not to be allowed to lead prayers until the matter was considered again by the communal leadership and the rabbinic courts. Also see no. 153 and Appendix 3.[8]

---

1. גבאי צדקה
2. הפסק דין
3. הגאון
4. דקהילת קודש
5. אב בית דין
6. ורב נתן מז
7. ורב מאיר שיף
8. The material also appears in YIVO MS. RG 128 (folder 77–78), fol. 70a, without the names of the members

רח ע"א

1. ב"ה
2. עלת' בהסכמה מהג' אב"ד נרו' עם שני ב"ד שחזן ר' שואל לא ירד לפני התיבה
3. להתפלל עד אחר יום כפור הבעלי[1] אפי' בחול / ומשם ואילך לא ירד ג"כ לפני תיבה
4. להתפלל בין בחול בין בשבת ויט[2] / עד שיתאספו יחד קהל יצו והג' אב"ד נרו'
5. ושני ב"ד יצו שידונו בדבר זה היו' יו' ד ך"ה אלול תקמ"ט הגאב"ד נרו' ורנ"מ
6. וראט[3] ורזט[4] ורמ"ש ואני ורמ"ז

No. 225

Fols. 208b–209a; Tuesday 17 November 1789

The administrators of a charitable trust for the support of needy brides set up by the late Ber Kann approached the court with questions regarding the eligibility of potential brides, including those who were pregnant but unwed.[5] They also asked about the amount of time that could pass between when a woman was awarded the funds until a suitable match was arranged (one year plus another six months for the wedding to take place) and what age women were eligible to enter the lottery for funds (eighteen to forty). The court examined Ber's will before answering each of the five questions addressed to it.

רח ע"ב

1. ב"ה
2. ע"ד שבא לפנינו ה"ה נ"ה התורני כ"ה פייס הענא סג"ל בהרשאות קציני'
3. ה"ה הו"ה פומ[6] כ"ה גומפיל קן יצו וההר[7] הו"ה כ"ה טעבלי ווינוג יצו אפטרופסי'
4. על דבר טוב שהניח אחריו המנוח כ"ה פער בפו"מ כ"ה ליב קן ז"ל והציע לפנינו
5. העתק מצוואת הנעדר כה"פ[8] ז"ל הנ"ל בגופן שלהם / ובתוכה מבואר
6. שהניח אחריו כה"פ ז"ל הנ"ל סך מה לקרן קיימת שיותן ביד האלופי'

---

of the court. It appears that in the YIVO manuscript the court's deliberations regarding Shoʾel (Saul?) the cantor were taken from a different source (or sources) and placed together on one page.

1. הבא עלינו לטובה
2. ויום טוב
3. ורב אברהם טריר
4. ורב זלמן טראך
5. This situation was not unknown in the Jewish community, even among leading families. See, for example, Pinqas Franqfurṭ, no. 498 (1788) as well as no. 497 (1796) with Segall's note.
6. פרנס ומנהיג
7. והרב החכם
8. כבוד הרב פער

7. קציני' גובי' יצו / ומהרווחי' יותן לסיועת הכנסת כלה סך חמשה מאות זהו'
8. על אופן המבואר שם באריכות / והנה נפשם בשאלתם מאתנו כיצד
9. ינהגו מחמת כמה ספיקות שיש להם על צוואה הנ"ל ואחרי שנזדקקנו
10. לדברי השאלות ששאל מאתנו כה פייס הנ"ל בהרשאות הנ"ל ועיינו
11. הדק היטב בהעתק צוואת הנ"ל מצאנו על כל שאלותנו כמבואר והיינו על
12. ראשון ראשון / אם אותה שהיא הרה לזנונים יש לה ג"כ הזכות לבוא ב
13. בתוך הגורל מצאנו אם אינה קרובה להנעדר הנ"ל קורבה של פסולי ע
14. עדות אף שהיא קרובה עמו קורבה שאין של פסולי עדות מכ"ש א
15. אם אינה קרובה כלל ואפי' היא מבנות קהלותינו אין לה זכות לבוא בתוך
16. הגורל אך אם יארע ח"ו בקרובה אחת שהיא של פסולי עדות עם הנעדר
17. הנ"ל שכפי הצוואה יש לקרובה פסולי עדות דין קדימה בלי עליית גורל / אזי
18. יפסקו הגאב"ד נרו' וב"ד הצדק שיהי' בימים ההם אם יש לה אותה זכות
19. המבואר שם ועל השאלה שיכירו הבד[1] עד כמה תקרא קרובה להנעדר ז"ל
20. הנ"ל / מצאנו שקרובה נקרא כל זמן שמבורר שהיא ממשפחתו אפי' למעלה עד
21. כמה דורות הן ממשפחות אביו והן ממשפחות אמו / ועל מה ששאל כמה זמן
22. יותן לאותה שעלתה מתוכ[2] הגורל להתקשר א"ע ולעשות שידוך לאחר ה
23. הגורל מצאנו שינתן לה זמן שנה תמימה מיו' שנעשה הגורל לעשות
24. שידוך והחתנה תהי' עכ"פ לזמן ששה חדשי' אח"כ וצריכי' להודיע
25. תיכוף ומיד כל זה לאותה שעלתה מגורל ולהזהירה וכמבואר להבא / שבאם
26. לא תעשה שידוך במשכ[3] שנה אחת אחר הגורל אזי יוגרל גורל אחר
27. ואותה אחרת שעלתה מתוך הגורל הזה יש לה קדימה ויותן לה אותה
28. המעות אשר הי' שייך לראשונה שעלה מגורל הראשון / והראשונה
29. תמתין

רט ע"א

1. בס"ד
2. תמתין עד שיגיע זמן לעשות גורל מחדש / ואז אם יש לבתולה ראשונה
3. שידוך יש לה דין קדימה בהמעות בלי שום גורל ובאם לא יהי'
4. להראשונה עדיין שידוך אבדה זכותה והרי היא כשארי בתולו'
5. לבוא בתוך הגורל ואין לה שום זכות יותר משאר בתולות ושלשי'
6. יום קודם זמן עשיות הגורל החדש הנ"ל יַתרו את הראשונה לחזור
7. אחר שידוך באיבוד זכיותיה / ועל השאלה ששאל שיכירו הב"ד
8. בת כמה שנים צריכה להיות הבתולה שראוי לבוא בגורל / מצאנו
9. מבת שמונה עשר עד בת ארבעי' ראוי' לבוא בגורל / ועל השאלה
10. חמישית אם אחד יש לו כמה בנות אם כולן באים בגורל מצאנו
11. שאין לו זכות רק בת אחת ממנו והגדולה יש לה קדימה וה"ה ביתומו'

1. הבית דין
2. מתוך
3. במשך

12. אחיות הדין כן יצא מאתנו יו׳ ג דח מרחשון תקנון לפק
13. הגאון אב״ד נרו׳ ורנ״מ ורמ״ש ואני

No. 226

Zunz v. Trier

Fols. 209b–211a; Tuesday 24 November 1789

The head of one of the rabbinic courts, Rabbi Abraham Trier, had held a position as rabbi of the private study hall (*kloysz*) of the late Elijah Scheyer. When Abraham was offered the position of rabbi in the study hall of the Wertheim family, Trier's son, Rabbi Zalman Katz, was appointed rabbi of the Scheyer study hall, an appointment that was challenged by Rabbi Herz Zunz. Herz had been "the second" rabbi in the Scheyer study hall for fourteen years and this, he argued through his representative, gave him the right to succeed Abraham. Moreover, Herz was related to Elijah Scheyer and maintained that in matters of making a living and charity not only could one assume that Elijah would have given preference to relatives over others, but that this could be inferred from his will. Zalman countered that a son always had the right to inherit the rabbinate of his father. Abraham himself noted that when he was first offered the position in the Wertheim study hall, he told the Wertheim family that he would only take the position if his son succeeded him in the Scheyer *kloysz*. To this end, members of the Wertheim family held discussions with a representative of the Scheyer study hall to insure that Zalman would succeed his father. A formal agreement to this effect was concluded. As such, argued Abraham, the deal had been made and there was nothing that Herz could do. Nevertheless, Herz challenged the agreement. A representative of the Scheyer *kloysz* testified before the court that the agreement with Abraham was made hastily and that, if he had thought of it, he would have made some sort of compromise with Herz.

The court tried to convince the sides to accept a compromise rather than a strict legal ruling, which they did. The court then decided that Rabbi Abraham Trier would move to the Wertheim study hall and that his son would assume his father's position as rabbi of the Scheyer study hall and live in the rabbi's quarters. With respect to the salary, the head of the *kloysz* was generally to receive 120 guldens more than the "second" in salary. The court decided that Rabbi Zalman Katz would receive only 40 guldens in additional salary and that the remaining 80 guldens would be given to Rabbi Herz Zunz.

רט ע"ב

1. ב"ה
2. ע"ד הטענות שבין ה"ה התורני כ"ה הירץ צונץ ובן[1] ה"ה הראש ב"ד
3. המופלא ומופלג מהורר[2] אברהם טריר כץ[3] נרו[4] ובנו התורני כה זלמן כץ
4. דהיינו שבא לפנינו ה"ה התורני כה משה אויך בהרשאות ובמעמד
5. התורני כה הירץ צונץ יצו וטענו באשר שכבר נתקבל ה"ה הרב"ד
6. מהורר אברהם טריר כץ נרו לרב בבהמ"ד של המנוח מהורר שמשון
7. ווירטהיים ז"ל ע"י הקציני' אפטרופסי' של משפחות ווירטהיימיר / ובנו
8. התורני כ"ה זלמן כץ רצה למלא מקומו בבהמ"ד של המנוח כ' אלי' שייאר
9. ז"ל בכל דבר לדור בדירתו אביו נרו ולקבל כל הסיפוק שהי' לאביו
10. לזאת תבע כה הירץ הנ"ל שיש לו קדימה בדירת שיש לר אברהם
11. טריר הנ"ל ובסיפוק שלו והוא כ"ה הירץ הנ"ל ימלא מקו' של ר' אברהם
12. הנ"ל ור' זלמן יקבל רק הסיפוק של ר הירץ מה שיהי' לו עד עכשיו
13. אבל לא הדירה שדר בו אביו גם (לא)[5] היתרון דמי' סיפוק מסך מאה ועשרי'
14. זהו' שהי' למהורר אברהם נרו' הנ"ל יותר ממנו באשר שכעת שנתקבל
15. בבהמ"ד אחר מגיע לר הירץ הנ"ל הדירה והסיפוק של מהורר אברהם
16. נרו ראשון מחמת חזקה שהוא נברר כבר בשנת תקל"ו לפק ע"פ שני
17. אפטרופסי' ה"ה הו"ה ג"ה גץ[6] כה משה שייאר סג"ל וה"ה[7] הו"ה גץ
18. כה ליב (בר"פ)[8] קן לבה"מ של ר' אלי ז"ל ללמד עם הבחורים והוחזק בכך זה
19. ארבעה עשר שנים בכן יש לו חזקה נגד ר' זלמן שנתמנא מחדש
20. וטוען שבכל דבר טובת והמנויי' בכל מקום המוחזק קודם נגד
21. אשר נתמנא מחדש עוד טוען ר' משה הנ"ל / בהרשאות הנ"ל באשר
22. שר' הירץ הנ"ל הוא קרוב עם הנעדר כה אלי' ז"ל דהיינו שלושה
23. בשני בכן יוכל לומר אומדנא דעת המת גבי פרנסי' וצדקה שיהיא
24. קרוב קרוב קודם ובמשמעות לשון הצוואה שכוונתו שקרוב קרוב קודם
25. ויעיין הב"ד בלשון הצוואה והה מהורר אברהם ובנו כה זלמן הנ"ל
26. השיבו שכבר ה{צוואה להה מהו' אברהם} בחודש אייר העבר כאשר
27. אמר

ר יו"ד ע"א

1. בה
2. אמר ה"ה כה זכרי' ווערטהיי' למהורר אברהם הנ"ל שבני משפחתו

---

1. צ"ל 'ובין'
2. מורנו הרב והגאון רבנו רבי
3. ר' אבני זכרון, מס' 4130, שבמצבה שלו רשום 'אב בית דין דקלויז'. ר' גם ספר הזכרונות, שמב ע"ב.
4. נטריה רחמנא ופרקיה
5. תוספת מעל השורה
6. גבאי צדקה
7. והרב החכם
8. תוספת מעל השורה; ראשי תבות: בן רב פער

3. נתנו עיניהם עליו למנות {.} אותו לרב בקלויז בבמד"ר של ר' שמשון וו
4. ווערטהיי' ז"ל השיבו שאם יכול להביא מכח אל הפועל שבנו ר' זלמן יהי'
5. במקומו בבהמ"ד של ר' אלי' שייאר ז"ל אזי מרוצה לעקור דירתו ולעלות
6. במעלות בהמ"ד של ר"ש[1] הנ"ל וע"ז דיבר עם האפטרופסי' של ר' אלי' שייאר
7. ה"ה הו"ה ג"ע וגה[2] כה אנשיל שייאר סג"ל ואיזה ימי' אחכ[3] נתרצה א"ע כ"ה
8. אנשיל הנ"ל שימלא בנו ר' זלמן במקומו לכל דבר / וע"ז הוקם כתב
9. ביניהם בחתימת יד של מהורר אברהם ובנו ר' זלמן הנ"ל וכ"ה א
10. אנשיל הנ"ל תקע כפו ליד ר' אברהם על גמר הדבר והציע ר' א
11. אנשיל הנ"ל כתב הנ"ל ההוקם ביניהם לפני קהל יצו והסכימו
12. ג"כ ע"ז בכן הדבר כבר נגמר ואין לר הירץ הנ"ל עוד טענה
13. בדבר וה"ה הו"ה ג"ה וגץ[4] כ"ה אנשיל שייאר סג"ל הנ"ל בא לפנינו
14. והציע לפנינו כתב ההוקם הנ"ל והעיד לפנינו בת"ע אמת שהמעשה
15. הי' כמו שאמר ר' אברהם נרו אך שהודה בעצמו שבאותו פעם
16. שנתרצה א"ע לכה[5] זלמן הנ"ל לא הי' בזכרונו לכה הירץ הנ"ל
17. ובאמת הי' קצת מהירות ממש ובאם הי' בזכרונו ר' הירץ הנ"ל הי'
18. עשה פשר בדבר ומחמת ת"כ לא ידע אם הי' ת"כ ממש או רק נתינת
19. יד והאריך בעדותו כאשר מונח לפנינו וכה[6] הירץ השיב ראשון
20. שר' אנשיל בעצמו אמר שהי' מהירות אחרי שמהורר[7] אברהם
21. נרו לא הניח אותו זמן שאמר ר' אנשיל להתישב בדבר גם ר'
22. אנשיל הוא רק אפטרופס אחד ואין כוחו למנות לבד רק צרי
23. צריכם[8] להיות שני אפטרופסי' כמו שהי' באותו פעם שנתמנה
24. ר' הירץ ומה' אברהם נר"ו שני אפטרופסי' בכן עומד בטענותו שמגיע
25. לו הקדימה בדירה הנ"ל ובסיפוק המותרות סך מאה ועשרים
26. זהו' מכח חזקה וקורבה וה"ה התורני כ"ה זלמן הנ"ל השיב
27. באריכות [שכ"ה] אנשיל לא יכול לחזור באשר שתקע כפו למר [א]בי[ו]
28. נרו

רי ע"ב

1. נר"ו ואף שהוא רק אפטרופס אחד מ"מ באשר שהי' לו הסכמה מקהל
2. שהם ממנם תמיד אפטרופסי' בכן הרי הם כמו אפטרופסי' ועל
3. טענות חזקה וקורבה של ר' הירץ הישב ר' זלמן באריכות ואדרבה
4. כ"ה זלמן טוען שמגיע לו הקדימה הואיל שהוחזק אביו לכך

---

1. רבי שמשון
2. וגבאי הקהילה
3. אחר כך
4. וגבאי צדקה
5. לכבוד הרב
6. וכבוד הרב
7. שמורנו הרב והגאון רב רבי
8. צ"ל 'צריכים'

5. ומי שהוחזק לרב בנו ובן בנו קודמין לאחרים אפילו הוא קרוב
6. ובפרט שהוא קרוב לאפטרופס המנוח ר׳ פער קן ז״ל שהוא הי׳
7. העיקור מתעסק בדבר טוב הנ״ל והאריכו הצדדי׳ הנ״ל מאוד
8. בטענותיהי׳ ואחר שחתמו עצמם הצדדי׳ הנ״ל בקומפרמיס המונח
9. לפנינו בח״ח ובקנס סך מסויים לאשר ולקיים הפס״ד שיצא מאתנו
10. גם לאחר שדברנו על לבם התרצה א״ע ונתנו עיניהם עלינו
11. בד[1] לפשר ביניהם וחתמו א״ע בקומפרמיס וגם האפטרופסי׳
12. הו״ה גץ וג״ה ר׳ אנשיל הנ״ל שהי׳ לפנינו כמה פעמי׳ מגלה
13. דעתו שניחה לי׳ ג״כ בפשרה מ״פ ב״ד בכן נזדקקנו להם
14. ולאחר שעיינו הדק היטיב בצוואת הנעדר והמנדב המנוח
15. כ״ה אלי׳ ז״ל הנ״ל ובשארי כתבי׳ וגם בכל טענות הצדדי׳
16. הנ״ל ובכתב ההוקם הנ״ל אחרי כל הנ״ל מצאנו לטובות שינהם
17. שכל זמן שכמה׳ אברהם נר׳ הנ״ל אינו עוקר דירתו מבהמ״ד
18. של ר׳ אלי׳ שייאר ז״ל הנ״ל הרי הוא עמוד בחזקתו הן בדירה
19. שלו והן בדמי סיפוקו (כאז)[2] וכמקדם ואין לכה הירץ שום תביעה
20. מכל מהתביעות הנ״ל אכן אם יעקור כמהורר אברהם הנ״ל
21. מדירה הנ״ל לדור בבה״מ של ר׳ שמשון ווירטהיי׳ הנ״ל אזי יהי
22. כמבואר והיינו לאחר שירדנו לשומא ערך שווי׳ דמי שכירות של
23. בהמ״ד של ר׳ אלי׳ ז״ל הנ״ל שדר בתוכה כמהו׳ אברהם טריר הנ״ל
24. לאחר {..כוי}(ניכוי)[3] שני חדרי׳ בית החורף מקו׳ לתלמיד לשני לומדי׳ ועוד חדר
25. אחד שכעת בתוכה הבחור כ׳ אלי׳ פרענקיל וגם חשבונו ה
26. ההפרש מה שיש למהו׳ אברהם נר״ו הנ״ל יותר מ[ל]כ״ה הירץ הנ״ל

ריא ע״א

1. בדמי ספיקו שהוא סך מאה ועשרי׳ זהו׳ כנ״ל ולאחר שחשבנו
2. כל (הנ״ל)[4] מצאנו עד[5] פשר שה״ה התורני כ״ה זלמן הנ״ל ידור בבהמ״ד
3. הנ״ל בכל הדירה שהי׳ דר בו אביו בתוכו בכל חזקותיו וזכיותיו
4. וכמו שהי׳ לאביו הנ״ל ומסך היתרון מאה ועשרי׳ זהו׳ דמי הספיקו
5. הנ״ל לכל שנה יותן להתורני כהרר הירץ צונץ הנ״ל סך שמונים
6. זהו׳ ולכה זלמן הנ״ל סך ארבעים זהו׳ יצא מאתנו יו׳ ג ו כסליו
7. תקנון לפק הגאן אב״ד נרו ורנמ[6] ורמש[7] ואני

---

1. בית דין
2. תוספת מעל השורה
3. תוספת מעל השורה
4. תוספת מעל השורה
5. על דרך
6. ורב נתן מז
7. ורב מאיר שיף

No. 227

Fol. 211b; Friday 4 December 1789

The community turned to the court for approval of recent measures taken by the tax assessors to improve assessments. The community sent the court previous ordinances regarding tax collection as well as recent measures that had been suggested. The court was asked whether it would agree with a decision to impose an oath on each and every householder who made a self-assessment of net worth, as had been done in the past (this would be the basis for determining a family's tax burden). The court agreed to the use of an oath, but limited it to those who would not accept a valuation imposed on them by the community's assessors. The court summoned all the assessors to warn them about the oath that they themselves had taken as assessors, and to inform them of other matters that the court deemed important for proper valuation (see no. 228). The court gave the assessors a document signed by the court to be read to all householders before making their self-assessment (see no. 229). The text stressed the importance of an honest statement of net worth. To emphasize the matter, the court prepared an announcement to be read in the synagogue (see no. 230). The record notes that this is a copy of the document that was sent to the communal leadership.[1] See Appendix 7 from which it is clear that the community had been facing difficult times from a financial perspective for a number of years.

ריא ע״ב

1. העתק מפסק לקהל וגובי׳ יצו
2. ע״ד שנשלח לנו מן האלופי׳ קציני׳ פו״מ וגובי׳ יצו ע״י גבאי הקהל יצו העתק
3. מתקנת ישני׳ בענין הנהגת אלופי׳ בעלי מעריכים יצו ונוסח השבועתם
4. גם מה שנעשה בענין זה מהאלופי׳ קציני׳ שנים עשר דעבוטיהרטע יצו
5. וגם מה שעלה במוסכם מקהל וגובי׳ יצו בענין הנ״ל ובקשו מאתנו לחוות
6. דעתינו ג״כ בענין הנ״ל אם גם אנחנו מסכימים ליתן לכל או״א מב״ב
7. דקהלותינו יעא[2] שבועת {על} הערך על אופן שהוסכם אצל דעפוטיהרטע הנ״ל
8. שהעלות עי״כ ערך של כל ב״ב על היושר שהוא עיקר מעמד ומצב קהלותינו
9. יע״א / ומה לעשות עוד לטובת הענין הנ״ל והנה אחרי שעיינו הדק היטיב
10. בכתובים הנ״ל ונושאין ונותני׳ אנחנו כמה פעמי׳ בדבר הזה מצאנו שאין
11. להטיל שבועת ערך על כל או״א מב״ב דקהלותינו / אלא אם אינו רוצה
12. לקיים הערך שנעשה מבעלי מעריכם אזי מחויב לשבע כפי תיקון
13. הישן אכן את זאת מצאנו לטוב׳ הענין הנ״ל לקרוא לפנינו האלופי׳

---

1. The material also appears in YIVO MS. RG 128 (folder 77–78), fol. 67a.
2. יגן עליה אלהים

בעלי מעריכים ולאיים עליהם באיום גדול להזהיר אותם על שבועתם ועל כמה דברים אשר נראה בעינינו שהוא מהכרחי לטובת ענין עשיות ערך באמת וצדק / ונוסף לזה מסרנו לבעלי מעריכים בכתב בחתימ' ידינו איום גדול על כל או"א מב"ב מה שמחוביב' לקרות לפני[1] {כל} כל או"א במלה במלה עד גמירא ואחכ[2] יעשו הבעלי מעריכים ערכו כפי תיקון הישן וכנהוג גם את זאת עשינו וסדרנו כרוז להכריז בשני בתי הכנסיות דקהלותינו להזהיר את העם ולהודיע להם גודל ההתחייב' ליתן ערך צדק שהוא עיקר מעמד ומצב דקהלותינו יעא כדי להעלות על לבו חומר ענין הזה לחשוב בתום וביושר כל מה שחנן ה' אותו בלי ערמה ומרמה שלא יעלם שום דבר בהגדת ערכו לפני אלופי' ב"מ בלי שום תחבולה והורא' היתר שבעולם נעשה יו' ו {ה} טז כסליו תקנון לפק הגאון אב"ד נר' ורנמ[3] ור' אברהם טריר ורז"ט ורמש[4] ואני ור' ליזר וואלי[5]

No. 228

Fols. 212a–b; no date (see no. 227)

The text of a letter from the head of the rabbinic court and the two rabbinic courts that functioned in Frankfurt on a semi-annual rotating basis to the communal assessors reminding them of the seriousness of their task and warning them to be impartial in estimating the value of each household.[6] According to the letter, local Jews believed that the assessors had acted unfairly in the previous assessment some six years earlier and had favored those with whom they had some sort of connection. The court reminded the assessors of the oath they had taken to do their job honestly and emphasized that they should not rely solely on the earlier assessment. The court also noted the need for discretion, and pointed out that people should not be told what others had been assessed.[7]

1. בכתב יד יוו"א כתוב 'לפנינו'
2. ואחר כך
3. ורב נתן מז
4. ורב מאיר שיף
5. בכ"י יוו"א כתוב 'וואלי סג"ל'
6. See Segall, Pinqas Frankfurṭ, no. 494 (4 March 1795), as well as the introduction, 45–46.
7. The material also appears in YIVO MS. RG 128 (folder 77–78), fols. 67a–b.

ריב ע"א

בה איום גדול לבעלי מעריכי' מן הגאבד[1] נר' ושני ב"דיץ וועלכה איהנ/פרגלייאני['] יוארד / מאחר דש ידוע לכל איזט / דש כל מעמד ומצב דקהלותינו יע"א טעפונטיהר' ונת[י]נת עולם ושאר ובלעטין מכל איש ואיש מבני קהלתינו יעא[2] / נאך דעם ערך דער איהנון מהאלופי' {גובי'} בעלי מעריכי' יצו גמאכט ווערד הקטן לפי קטנו והגדול לפי גדלו מחויב איזט נושא בעול צו זיין אונד כפי ערכו דמיו הקצובי עליו צו בצאהלין / ובאשר דש מאן האט פר נומן וויא רוב העולם דעהר מתרעם איזט / אויף דען מהבעלי מעריכים בששה שנים העברו גמאכטין ערך / דש זיא זעהר מיקיל העטן גוועזן לכמה ב"ב וועלכש אויך אין צווישן נ[גל]ה איזט ווארדן / דש סך עצום ורב מעהר הינטר לאסין האבין א[ול]ס בחייהם ערך גהאבט האבין / בכן התעוררנו אנחנו ה"ה הגאן אב"ד ושני ב"ד נרו' ומצאנו עצמנו מחויבי' בדבר להודיע ולאיים על האלופי' בעלי מעריכים יצו ולהזהר אותם על גודל עונש השבועה שהי' נשבעים ע"ד המקו' ב"ה ובלי ערמה ומרמה וה' יראה ללבב את אשר המה הבעלי מעריכים מושבעי' ועומדי' ומלבד זה דש דיא ח"ו נתפס ווערדן על עון השבועה / זיינין דיא נאך דא צו גורם גזל רבים ויתומי' ואלמנות וההריסות מעמד ומצב דקהלותינו יעא / אלזוא זיינין הבעלי מעריכים מחויב בחיוב גדול [ז]עהר גנויא השגחה צו האבין דש דיא ניכט מקיל זיינין חו[3] לשום אדם בעשיות הערך / מחמת שום פני' הן מ' קורבה או מ' אהבה או מ' יראה משום אדם או מ' שום הנאת כבוד או הנא' ממון / או מ' שום הרהור סיבו' הנאה שיעלה על לבם יהי' מחמת מה שיהי' גם דש אין בעל מעריך דען אנדרן בעל מעריך ניכט צו גפעליכקייט טוהט' רק בכל מגמותם ומחשבתם יהי' לשם שמים / כפי שיעלה על לבם ומכל שכן דש האלופי' בעלי מעריכים יצו קומן נאטיץ נעהמן זאלין אן דיא ב"ב איהרן שאהן גהאבטין ערך בששה שנים העברו / דא [ז]אך דער עולם בלאו הכי

ריב ע"ב

זעהר מתרעם איזט' אויף דעם ערך הנעשה לפני ששה שנים מיט היין אין להשגיח על הערך הקודם לבד / אלא יעשו כפי אומד דעתם עתה הין לגרוע או להוסיף כפלי כפלים / אף גם זאת מזהירם אנחנו באזהרה גדולה ובאיום גדול דש קיינר מהאלופי' בעלי מעריכים לשום אדם ומכ"ש אן דעם ב"ב זעלבשטן ניכט מגלה [זו]ל [זיי]ן בשום רמז

---

1. הגאון אב בית דין
2. יגן עליה אלהים
3. חס ושלום

הדיעות של כל אחד ואחד שהי' ביניה[ן] בענין הערך פון איינין
אודר דען אנדרן בב[1] דאמיט דש קיין ב"ב ניכט ווייסונד ווערד
וועהר איהם מקיל אודר מחמיר האט גוועזין בערך שלו / וע"ז
נאמר הולך רכיל מגלה סוד אויך ווערדן האלופי' בעלי מעריכי'
דארויף מוזהר מהגאון אב"ד ושני בתי דינן נרו[2] דש זיא אן
יעדן ב"ב אשר יקרא לבוא לפניהם אום ערך שלו צו מאכין
זולכן איום דער איהנון מהגאן אבד[3] ושני ב"ד נרו צו
גשטעלט איזט ווארדן מלה במלה במ[..]ן פאר צו לייאנין
כדי להיות כל אחד ואחד מהב"ב מוזהר בשעת מעשה
ומשים אל לבו זיין זאל גודל העונש וגזל הרבים וועלכר
דורך צו וויניג אן דאגונג ערך ענדשטיהט / ויראה לנפשו
ומאודו / זיין ערך בתום וביושר ניכט צו ווינוג אן צו זאגן
ומי שיעבור ח"ו על כל האזהרו' הנ"ל יהי' הקולר תלוי
בצווארו וכל השומע ומקיים דברי חכמי' ועוסק בצרכי הציבור
באמונה צדקתם יעמוד לעד ולעולם להם ולבניהם ויזכו
לראות בשוב שבות ישראל[4] לנויהם אמן

No. 229

Fols. 213a–b; Friday 4 December 1789[5] (see no. 227)

A letter from the head of the rabbinic court and the two courts that was to be taken by the assessors and read to each household before a self-assessment was made. The letter, in a mix of Hebrew and Yiddish, impressed upon listeners the importance of the assessment and of sharing the financial yoke of the community. It informed them which assets should be included in the assessment and used biblical verses to strengthen the call for an honest statement of self-worth. The material also appears in YIVO MS. RG 128 (folder 77–78), fol. 67b, with minor differences.

---

1. בעל בית
2. נטריהו רחמנא ופרקיהו
3. אב בית דין
4. ר' תפילת מוסף ליום טוב (ברכת רצה) וכן ירמיהו כג, ג; לא, כב; לג, ז; נ, יט.
5. The document notes the date as 15 Kislev, however, that date fell out on a Thursday in 1789. Since there is specific mention of the document having been prepared on the eve of the Sabbath, the correct date must be 16 Kislev. This is confirmed by the YIVO MS. where the date appears as 16 Kislev.

ריג ע״א

1. ב״ה
2. הן הן הדברי׳ אשר יצא מאתנו בד[1] ח״מ וועלכה אלופי׳ קציני׳ הבעלי׳ מעריכים
3. מחויב זיין / יעדם ב״ב פאר צו לייאנין / קודם ער זיין ערך אן זאגט
4. מאחר דש ידוע לכל איזט / דאש כל מעמד ומצב דקהלותינו יע״א דעפונטיהרט
5. מהערך של ב״ב מחמת נתינות עולם ושאר ובעלטין וועלכה יעדר ב״ב נאך דעם
6. ערך ווערכר איהם מהאלופי׳ ק׳ בעלי מעריכים גמאכט ווערד הקטן לפי
7. קטנו והגדול לפי גדלו / מחויב איזט נושא בעול צו זיין וכפי ערכו דמיו
8. הקצובי׳ לו צו בצאהלין / ובאשר שנתודע דש פילה ב״ב בשני׳ העברו האבין
9. מורה היתר לעצמם גווע[ז]ן / וכפי הנשמע ונראה כמה ב״ב סך עצום ורב
10. יותר פר לאזין האבין / אלז דיא ערך גהאבט / בכן התעוררו אנחנו ח״מ הרב
11. הגאון אב״ד ושני ב״ד נרו[2] ומצאנו עצמינו מחויבי׳ בדבר להודיע ולאיים
12. ולהביא מור[ה] בלב כל איש ואיש מבני קהלותינו יע״א דש יעדר יחיד וועלכר
13. לפני האלופי׳ בעלי מעריכי׳ גראפי[ן] וו[יר]ד אוהם ערך שלו אן צו זאגין
14. לדקדק ולחשוב כל אשר חנן ה׳ אותו אונד זיין ערך אן צו צאגין בהן
15. צדקו ע״ד המקו׳ ב״ה וע״ד ב״ד וע״ד האלופי׳ בעלי מעריכי׳ יצו בלי ערמה
16. ומרמה ותחבולה והוראות היתר שבעולם / דהיינו כפי תיקון ישן ומן מעות
17. מזומני׳ ח״כ בוך שולדן חובות בע״פ וסחורת יהי׳ מה שיהי׳ כסף וזהב
18. אונד תכשיטם וגם יינות מלבד ספרים וכלי קודש ומטלטלין וחובות
19. דיא איינר פר יאוש הלט אינם בכלל ערך אבר זונשטט אליס
20. גנויא צו רעכנין / דש ח״ו ניכט ווערד נכשול בעון גזל רבים יתומי׳ ואלמנות
21. אשר ממש אין לו תקנה בחזרה וכל הגוזל מחבירו אפי׳ פרוטה אחת
22. כאילו גוזל את נפשו ומלבד דש דער גאנצה אוהם רייסונג מעמד
23. ומצב דקהלותינו יעא[3] אן דעם פאלשר ערך הענגט / מיט הין זאל יעדר
24. זיך בדענקין אונד זאלכן עון גדול ניכט לייכט אויף נעדמין / אונד צו
25. בדענקין פן יג[רם][4] עי״כ הפסד לעצמו ובדברי׳ המסורי׳ ללב נאמר בו ויראת
26. מאלקיך וג׳[5] והשומע לדבר אזהרתינו אלה אונד זיך זיין ערך כחוב המוטל
27. עליו ריכטיג אן זאגין ווירד יברכהו ה׳ בנפשו ובמאודו ויהי כזית

ריג ע״ב

1. הודו[6] / ויתענג על רוב של׳ טובה וברכה עד עולם אמן נאך דעם
2. דש האלופי׳ ב״מ דעם ב״ב אויביגש הר גלייאניט האבין הירנאך

---

1. בית דין
2. נטריהו רחמנא ופרקיהו
3. יגן עליה אלוהים
4. יש כאן חור בדף; ההשלמה על פי ההשארה.
5. ויקרא יט, יד, לב; כה, יז, לז.
6. הושע יד, ז

זאללן האלופי' ק' בעלי מעריכי' דען ערך (מאכן)[1] כפי התיקון הישן וכנהוג אונד וויא דיא גטווארן האבין יצא מאתנו יו' ו עשק[2] טו[3] כסליו תקנון לפק הגאון אבד[4] נרו ושני ב"ד נר"ו כנ"ל

No. 230

Fol. 213b; Friday evening, [4 December 1789]

The rabbinic leadership composed a Hebrew-Yiddish language announcement to be read in the two synagogues on Friday night, 4 December 1789 (see no. 227). As in the previous texts regarding assessments (nos. 227–29) there was great concern that people make an honest declaration of their assets. The court acknowledged that householders did not trust the process, and attempted to impress upon listeners the importance of accurate self-assessment for political and religions reasons.[5]

כרוז שהוכרז בבכ"נ ישן וחדש ליל שק[6] יז כסליו תקנון לפק הערט צו רבותי עס איזט בפאהלין ווארדן אויש צו רופין בשם הגאב"ד ושני ב"ד נר"ו / מאחר שידוע לכל דש כל מעמד ומצב דקהלותינו יע"א דעפונדיהרט מהערך של כל הבעלי בתי' מחמת נתינת עולם ושאר ובלעטין ובאשר העולם מתרעם איזט על כמה ב"ב דש דיא איהר ערך צו וויניג אן זאגן / אונד ניכט ערך כראוי געבין / וגם דאס מאַן שויהן ערפאהרן האט דש פילע יותר פר לאסין האבין / אלס דיא בחייהם ערך גטראגין האבין / ועי"ז הריסו' מעמד ומצב דקהלתינו יע"א ענטשטיהט / דאהערא לאסין יושבי על מדין הרב הגאון אב"ד ושני ב"ד נרו[7] היר מיט מכריז זיין ומזהיר זיין דש יעדיר ב"ב קודם אן זאגונג זיין ערך להאלופי' בעלי מעריכי' יצו גנויא זיך צו ברעכנון / ולדקדק ולחוש לנפשו ומאודו / דש חו[8] ניכט נלכד וערד בעון גזל רבי' ויתומי' ואלמנות / אונד דען נוסח האיום ההוסכם ונעשה מהגאון אבד[9] ושני ב"ד נרו וועלכר יעדם ב"ב בבוא לפני האלופי'

1. תוספת מעל השורה
2. ערב שבת קדש
3. בכ"י יוו"א כתוב 'טז'
4. אב בית דין
5. The material is also found in YIVO MS. RG 128 (folder 77–78), fols. 67b–68a.
6. שבת קודש
7. נטריהו רחמנא ופרקיהו
8. חס ושלום
9. אב בית דין

20. בעלי מעריכי׳ פר גלייאנט ווערד ושם נאמר אלז מאן איהם זאל
21. פרלייאנון דער ניכט צו וויניג זיין ערך אַן צייגן זאל בהן
22. צדקו ע״ד המקו׳ ב״ה וע״ד הב״ד וע״ד האלופי׳ ב״מ יצו בלי ערמה ומרמה
23. ותחבולת והורא׳ היתר שבעולם זולכש אללעס ווירד יעדר משים אל
24. לכו׳[1] זיין אונד ניכט לייכט אכטין ולחוש לנפשו ומאודו ולחוש לתקנות
25. הצבור איהרן ערך ניכט צו וויניג אן צו זאגין / ויודה לה׳ על
26. ברכתו / ויתברך בבואו ובצאתו ולהשומעי׳ יונעם ותבא עליהם
27. ברכת טוב

No. 231

Fol. [214]a; Tuesday 29 December 1789

Rabbi Gundersheim recorded that he was present at the *ḥaliẓah* ceremony of the sister-in-law of Rabbi Nathan Maas. The record notes that a legal doubt led Nathan to have his brother, Ezekiel, perform the ceremony rather than Nathan himself. Since Nathan was related to one of the parties involved, he was replaced as head of the court by Rabbi Abraham Trier.

ריג ע״א[2]

1. ב״ה
2. יו׳ ג יב טבת תקן לפק הייתי בסדר חליצה של האל׳ מ׳ אסתר בת
3. המנוח מ[ר] אנשיל צונץ ז״ל אל׳ המנוח כ׳ מאיר בן המנוח כ״ה שלמה מז[3] ש[נח]לץ
4. מיבמה הבחור כ׳ יחזקאל בכ״ה שלמה מז ז״ל הנ״ל ובשביל שיבום הוא אחיו
5. של הר״י והרב״ד מה׳ נתן מז נרו׳ הי׳ המסדר הרב״ד מה׳ אברהם טריר נרו׳
6. והדייני׳ רזט[4] ורמ״ש נרו׳ והנוספי׳ אני ורמ״ש[5] ובשעת החליצה הי׳ מפרסם
7. המסדר הנ״ל הטעם שמהר׳ נתן מז הנ״ל לא חלץ הואיל שהוא מסופק
8. בעצמו אם הוא אטר רגל או לאו[6] לכך הניח לאחיו כ׳ יחזקאל הנ״ל לחלוץ

---

1. צ״ל ׳לבו׳
2. אע״פ שבדף הקודם רשום ׳ריג׳, גם בראש העמוד הזה מופיע המספר ׳ריג׳. אין דף שרשום בו ׳ריד׳.
3. מאיר מז נפטר ב׳ תשרי תק״ן (ר׳ אבני זכרון, מס׳ 4004).
4. רב זנוויל טראך
5. אולי טעות סופר ומדובר ברב מענדלי זאמשט (רמ״ז). יש לציין שבשנים אם לא בשלשה מקרים אחרים, הרב מאיר שיף והרב חיים גונדרשהיים היו הנוספים (ע׳ במס׳ 213, 215 וכנראה 244). אם הרב מאיר שיף היה הנוסף כאן, לא ברור מי היה בהרכב בית הדין. בי״ב אדר תקנ״ה (פנקס פרנקפורט, סימן 494), נמנה הרב משה בן ישראל שוורץ שילד (רמ״ש) לאחד הדיינים הנוספים אבל לא ידוע על מעמדו בשנת תק״ן.
6. ר׳ שו״ע אה״ע קסט ס׳ כ״ה.

No. 232

Hammel v. Sankwehrt

Fol. [214]a; Thursday 21 January 1790

Herz Sankwehrt leased the lower half of a house on the Goldener Strauss lot from the children of the late Leb Haas. Isaac Hammel, Herz's late mother's brother, who shared ownership in the house and currently lived on the lower floor, objected to Herz leasing the space, saying that as a co-owner of the house he (i.e., Isaac) should have the right of first refusal. It would appear that the argument stage of the dispute (for which the reader is referred to a court record that has not survived) included facts not found here that informed the court's decision. In the record below, the court obligated Herz to affirm that his version of the negotiations during the rental process was correct, and that he had not intended to prevent Isaac from exercising his abutter's rights. That done, Herz's lease was recognized by the court and he was obligated to make certain repairs to the house as per the contract. As for Isaac, he was ordered to vacate his living quarters in the lower section of the house.

9. ———
10. ע"ד טענות והפרשות שיש בין הו"ה כ"ה הירץ ז"ק ששכר חצי
11. בית צום גולדני שטרויז מן יתמי המנוח כ"ה ליב הַז ז"ל דהיינו שטח
12. התחתון / וה"ה התורני כ"ה משה אויך בהרשאות הו"ה כ"ה איצק
13. בכ"ה ליב האמיל ז"ל שהוא משותף בחצי בית ודר בשטח התחתון
14. עד עתה ורוצה לבטל השכירות ולזכות בו מדין מצרנות /
15. והאריכו בטענותיה' זה מול זה כמבואר בק"ה ולאחר שחתמו עצמם
16. בתוקף קומפרמיס בח"ח ובקנס סך שני מאות רט חצי לשררה יר"ה וחצי
17. להקדש בכן נזדקקנו להם ומצאנו שכ' הירץ הנ"ל יקבל בחר'
18. בפנינו ב"ד ע"ד המקו' ב"ה וע"ד ב"ד בלי ערמה ומרמה ובלי
19. שום הוראות היתר שבעולם שכדבריו כן הוא שהמשכיר' לא
20. הי' רוצי' להשכירו בעד מאה רט וכ' הירץ הנ"ל לא הי' רוצה
21. לשכור בעד יותר ממאה רט עד שהתרצה א"ע באופן שנזכר
22. בכתב שכירות שהוא מחויב לתקן כל מיני אוהרן וכמבואר שם
23. ושלא נעשה תנאי זה להערי' ולסלק המצרנות בכך ולאחר שיקבל כנ"ל
24. הוא זוכה בשכירות חצי בית שטח התחתון ואין לכ' איצק הנ"ל
25. טענות מצרנות ומחויב לפנות דירה שלו
26. {נעש}יצא מאתנו י' ה' ויו שבט תקן לפק רנ"מ ואני ורמ"ז

Fol. [214]b is blank.

No. 233

Hammel v. Reichle, widow of Isaac Hahn

Fols. 215a–217b; Tuesday 14 September 1790

Reichle, widow of Isaac Hahn, controlled her late husband's estate and ran a store with the help of her daughter Breinla, an arrangement that the court had agreed to some years earlier (see no. 211). Reichle now wanted to enter into a partnership in the store with Breinla's husband, Wolf Fulda. This raised objections from another of Reichle's sons-in-law, Mikhl Hammel, who argued that this violated an earlier signed agreement. Moreover, he maintained that, given Reichle's restricted legal status as a woman, she would be weakened in any dispute with Wolf and that assets Mikhl believed were part of the estate, an estate that he stood to benefit from through his wife, would be at risk. A partnership would also mean giving Wolf equal shares in profits instead of having them accrue to the estate. It could also result in increased liabilities as the partners tried to expand the business, another situation that Mikhl wanted to avoid. Accordingly, Mikhl argued through his legal counsel that if Reichle wanted to enter into a partnership in the store she would have to take what was due to her from her husband's estate and formally renounce any further rights to the assets of the estate. Only then would she be free to do as she pleased. Wolf Fulda, who represented his mother-in-law, argued that Reichle had every right to enter into a partnership that would benefit the estate. As a practical matter, Reichle had become dependent on Breinla's assistance in the store and, since Breinla's obligation to work in the store had ended, a partnership was the only way for the store to continue to operate. Wolf argued that Mikhl could not challenge Reichle's decision, for just as she could decide to stop working so too she could decide to expand the business.

Beyond contesting each other's claims, Wolf and Mikhl made numerous contingency claims in case they lost aspects of the case. For example, Wolf informed the court that if his mother-in-law's request to enter into a partnership was denied, Reichle would simply sell the inventory in the store to him at cost and then work for him. Mikhl objected that selling at cost did not reflect the current value of the goods. However, Mikhl acknowledged the possibility that Reichle might win on the point of selling the goods to Wolf, and responded that even if this might be allowed, Wolf should not simply receive the space where the store was. Mikhl argued that rights to continue to lease the space should be decided by a lottery involving Reichle's daughters. This elicited counterclaims from Wolf.

The court sided with Mikhl and did not allow Reichle to enter into a partnership with Wolf or sell the store to him unless she took an oath that she was selling all property at fair value without any intention of circumventing earlier agreements and creating a partnership. However, if Reichle decided to continue to run the store, Mikhl had no right to interfere in the business. In light of the ruling, Mikhl asked the court to prohibit Reichle from making a deathbed gift or debt that favored a particular party at the expense of other heirs. Regarding this the court ruled that only if Reichle dismissed herself from her late husband's estate was she was free to do as she pleased with her assets.

רטו ע"א

ב"ה ע"ד שבא לפנינו ה"ה התורני כ"ה משה אויך בהרשאת הו"ה כ"ה מיכל בן הו[״ה] גת"ת כ' גדלי' האמיל סג"ל ותבע מן חמותה[1] הקצינה מ' רייכלה אל' המנוח כ' אייזק האן ז"ל באשר שעד הנה היתה חמותו שולטת בעזבון בעלה ומוכרת ולוקחת סחורת בחנות בעלה ז"ל כפי רצונה וכמו שהתחייבו א"ע אשתו והוא כה"מ[2] הנ"ל בת"א שלהם וכפי שנאמר בקנין ובשטר ההוקם ע"ז ך' טבת תקנון לפ"ק ושם נאמר בזה הלשון ועל כל זמן שלא תנשא לגבר אוחרן זאל זיא בכל עזבון בעלה זיצן בלייבן וכו' ועכשיו שמע כה"מ הנ"ל שחמותו ר רוצת[3] לעשות שותפות עם חותנה הו"ה התורני כהו"ו[4] פולדא יצו בכן רוצה למחות כה"מ הנ"ל בידה שאין לה רשות לעשות כן מפני כמה וכמה היזיקות שמגיע לו עי"כ / כי הקנין הנ"ל לא הי' רק עלי' לבדה / אבל לא ליקח משותף עמה גם בלשון הקנין הנ"ל אין לה נאמנות לעולם רק כל זמן שאינה רוצת היא לסלקת א"ע ולגבות כתובה ותוס' אבל אם היא רוצת לגבות כתובתה ותוס' מחויבת לישבע כנהוג בכל הנשי' / והאיך רשאי האשה מ' רייכלה הנ"ל ליקח משותף אצלה וליתן לו נאמנת / ובאם באת לידי שבועה היאך תכול לשבע גם אינו מוכרח ליתן נאמנות למשותפה ו והאריך בזה בטענותיו / גם ע"י שותפות שנותנות חצי ריווח לכהו"[ו] נתבעת חלקה ולזה אין לה רשות וגם ע"י השותפות מוכרחי' להרבות החנות בסחורת ובחובת לבוא ריווח יותר ומתוך כך נתגדל ג"כ האחריות וזה אינו מחויב כה"מ לסבול מחמותו / ועוד כמה טעמי' ופסידת שחושש כה"מ הנ"ל שמגיע לו ע"י שותפות הנ"ל בכן טוען כה"מ הנ"ל שחמותו אינה ר

---

1. צ"ל 'חמותו'
2. כבוד הרב מיכל
3. ר"ל 'רוצה'
4. כבוד הרב וואלף

22. רשאי לעשות שותפות עד לאחר שתסלק א״ע מעזבון בעלה וגובה כתוב[ה]
23. ותוס׳ אבל לא כל זמן שהיא בעזבון בעלה אין לה כח לעשות הפרש בין הבנ[ים]
24. וליתן שותפת לכהו״ו לבד / ואף אם לא יזכה כה״מ הנ״ל בזה / ורשאי חמות[ו]
25. לעשות שותפות / מ״מ לא תהי׳ לה רשות להקי׳ שטר שותפות ולפרט
26. בתוכה מהות החנות בלי ידיעת שאר בנותי׳ וחותנה כה״מ וה״ה
27. התורני הו״ה כהו״ו פולדא בהרשאות חמותו הק׳ מ׳ רייכלה הנ״ל
28. השיב שחמותו

רטו ע״ב

1. ב״ה
2. שחמותו יש לה רשות לעשות שותפות עמו שהיא לטובת העזבון
3. באשר שאשתו מ׳ בריינלה הי׳ מתעסקות זה כמה שני׳ בחנות אמה
4. ובפרט בשלשה שני׳ העוברת אחר חתנותו כמוטל עליי וכמו שהתחייבו
5. א״ע כמבואר בת״א שלה על משך שלשה שני׳ ועתה שנשלם הזמן רוצת אשתו
6. מ׳ בריינלה להתחיל לעצמה חנות מסחורת ובאשר שהאשה מ׳ בריינלה
7. היא היודעת מו״מ של חנות׳ וזולתה אין יכולה חמותו להחזיק מו״מ של
8. חנותה כראוי מש״ה היא מוכרחת לעשות שותפות לטובת העזבון
9. כדי שתשאר האשה מ׳ בריינלה בחנות והיינו שחמותו תתן לו
10. חצי מכל סחורת בעד קרן ראשון נגד מעות התמורה שיניח כהו״ו
11. בחנות ויהי׳ לו חצי ריווח והציע לפנינו כהו״ו הנ״ל הלשון הקנין הנ״ל
12. מן כה״מ ואשתו ושם נאמר שהמה התרצו שהאשה מ׳ רייכלה זול בעזבון
13. בעלה זיצן בלייבן כאות נפשה ורצונה ואינה יכולי׳ לסלק אותה בשום
14. טענה ותביעה שבעולם וגם שלא לתבוע שום חשבון ואינפוטאריום –
15. מעזבון בעלה ובאשר שברירה ביד חמותה להחזיק חנותה כאות
16. נפשה ורצונה מי יוכל לימחות לה אם תרצה להתמעט הסחורת
17. של חנותה בלי עשיות שותפות שלא מגיע לה ג״כ ריווח כל כך
18. ותספוק א״ע בחצי ריווח או שברירה ג״כ בידה שלא לעסוק עוד
19. כלל במו״מ של סחורת / בכן גם זה אינו יוכל למחות חותנה כה״מ
20. הנ״ל לעשות שותפות כנ״ל / ומה שטוען כה״מ הנ״ל שע״י השותפות
21. יבוא העזבון לידי פסידא מכח שנתרבו בסחורת ובחובת –
22. כנ״ל השיב כהו״ו מי יוכל למחות בידה זולת עשיות השותפות
23. שלא תרבה בסחורת או שתמכור בהקפה למי שתרצה באשר
24. שברירה בידה להתעסק בחנותה כאות נפשה ועל מה שטוען
25. כה״מ שע״י שותפות הנ״ל שוב אינה יכולה חמותו לישבע אם –
26. תרצה לגבות כתובתה ולסלק א״ע מעזבון השיב כהו״ו מי יימר
27. שבאת לכלל שבועה / וגם זה אין מבטל שבועתה שלא העלימה
28. או הבריחה ועל מה שרוצה למחות כה״מ הנ״ל ביד חמותו

---

1. צ״ל ׳עליה׳

29. לעשות שטר

רטז ע״א

1. ב״ה
2. שטר שותפות בלי ידיעות שארי בנותי׳ השיב כהו״ו שחמותו אינה
3. מחויבת ליתן חשבון ואינפוטאריום מעזבון בעלה כמבואר בקנין הנ״ל
4. עוד תבע כה״מ שאם תזכה האשה מ׳ רייכלה בדין לעשות שותפות
5. אפ״ה מחויב׳ האשה מ׳ רייכלה הנ״ל לקיים התחייבות שלה ליתן כל
6. שבוע לבתה מ׳ בילה הנ״ל כל שבוע סך ארבע זהו׳ עד כלות שלשה
7. שנים מיו׳ חתנתה כמבואר בתאי[1] והיא אינה מחויבת לילך בחנות
8. ולסייע לה רק אם נשאר אמה לבד במו״מ כמו שהי׳ עד עתה כ[י] לה לבד
9. התחייבה א״ע לסייע לה הפועל אבל לא לגיסה ואחותה שבזיון היא
10. לה וכהו״ו הנ״ל השיב שיכירו הב״ד אם האשה מ׳ בילה רשאי לומר לאמה
11. לב״ד[2] מחויבת לעסוק בחנות ולסייע לה ולא אם יש לה משותף עמה הואל[3]
12. שמגיע עכ״פ לאמה ג״כ טובה מהתעסקות שלה / ואף אם תזכה בזה מ׳
13. בילה שאינה מחויבת להתעסק עוד / מ״מ אזי אינה זוכה בדמי שכירות
14. כל זמן שאינה הולכת בחנות לסייעה במו״מ כמשמעות לשון הת״א וקנין
15. שהיא האשה מ׳ בילה ובעלה השתעבדו והתחייבו א״ע שתלך האשה
16. מ׳ בילה בחנות אמה ולסייע לה במו״מ נגד זה התחייב[4] א״ע חמותו
17. מ׳ רייכלה ליתן לה כל שבוע ארבע זהו׳ אבל אם אינה הולכות
18. אזי אינה מגיע לה כלום עוד טען כהו״ו באם חמותו אינה זכת[5] בדין
19. שרשאה לעשות שותפות עמו אזי היא רוצה לימכור כל הסחורת
20. שבחנות לחתנה כהו״ו בעד דמי קרן ראשון של הסחורת והוא לבד
21. יהי׳ עוסק במו״מ וחמותו רוצות לילך ג״כ בחנותו לסייע לו נגד שכר
22. קצוב ביניהם או בחנם או בשארי אופני׳ שיתרצו ביניהם ואין
23. יוכל למחות לה כה״מ הנ״ל וכ״ה משה הנ״ל השיב על מה שטען כהו״ו הנ״ל
24. שחמותו רוצית למכור לו כל הסחורת שאין זה אלא ערמה ממנה
25. לעשות שותפת עמו אח״כ שבוודא לא תתן החנות ומו״מ לאחר בכן
26. תשבע האשה מ׳ רייכלה שלא תמכור לחתנה הנ״ל בערמה הנ״ל והוסיף
27. לטעון כה״מ הנ״ל באם תמכור כל סחורת לכהו״ו הנ״ל בעד דמי קרן
28. ראשון היא וויתרה לו דמי רווחי׳ שעלו על הסחורת מעת לקיחת

רטז ע״ב

1. ב״ה
2. לקיחת הסחורת עד שעת מכירתם וגם יש סחורת בחנות שנתיקרו

---

1. בתנאים אחרונים
2. לבד
3. צ״ל ׳הואיל׳
4. צ״ל ׳התחייבה׳
5. צ״ל ׳זוכה׳

3. בנתיי' ושווי' יותר עתה מעת לקיחתם בכן גם זה ערמה ותשבע גם ע"ז
4. אם רוצת לימכור לו כל סחורת שתעלה לו דמי רווחי' ויקרות על דמי
5. קרן ראשון מן סחורת / ובאם לאו מאי חזית שהאשה מ' רייכלה רשאי –
6. לימכור כל סחורת לכהו"ו לבד גם חתנה כה"מ רוצה לקנותם באשר
7. שגם הוא רוצה להתחיל חנות מסחורת בכן תמכרם האשה מ' רייכלה
8. בין לוקחי בנותי' למי שירבה בדמי סחורת עוד טען כ"ה משה הנ"ל אף
9. אם רשאי האשה מ' רייכלה הנ"ל למכור כל סחורת לכהו"ו הנ"ל לבד
10. מ"מ על מקו' החנות שמכרה חמותו בתוכה הסחורת יכירו הב"ד
11. שנעשה גורל בין לוקחי בנות למי שיהי' החנות בשכירות באשר
12. שכה"מ הנ"ל רוצה לקנות ג"כ סחורת ולהתחיל חנותה בתוכה
13. כמו שמנהג הוא בכל השותפי' כשיפרדו זה מזה שיעשו גורל –
14. ביניהם על מקו' החנות וגם באם יעלה הגורל לכה"מ שלא תגרום
15. חמותו שהמשכיר לא ישכיר החנות לכה"מ הנ"ל וכהו"ו הנ"ל חזר והשי'
16. בהרשאות הנ"ל שמכירת כל סחורת מן חמותה אינה ערמה רק היא
17. לטובת העזבון באם היא אינה רשאי לעשות שותפות עמו והיא
18. לבדה זולת בת[ה] מ' בריינלה אינה יכולה להחזיק חנותה כנ"ל –
19. בכן היא מוכרחת לימכר הסחורת ובריר[ה] בידה כפי הקנין הנ"ל
20. לימכר למי שתרצה בכן רוצית היא למכרם לחתנה כהו"ו ועל מה שטוען
21. שחמותו מחויבת להעלות על סחורה דמי רווחי' ויקרות שנתייקרו –
22. הסחורה בנתיי' השיב כהו"ו באריכות אדרבה שדרך התגרי' אם
23. מכרו כל סחורת ישני' מחנותם לימכר פחות מדמי קרן ולא להעלות
24. עליהן הרווחי' וגם היקרות לא הי' רק אלא בחד מין סחורה ומאותו
25. סחורה אין בחנותה הרבה וגם בלא"ה אין יוכל לצ[ו]ת עלי' כה"מ
26. כיצד תמכר סחורת שלה / ואף אם לא תזכה חמותו בזה למכור לו
27. כל סחורת אזי יחולק הסחורת בין לוקחי בנות והיינו ששתי בנותי'
28. מ' בריינלה ומ' בילה תעשה שומא וחלוקה מן כל סחורת ומהם יקח כה"מ
29. שליש אחד נגד תשלומין דמי שליש חלק סחורת שלו וכהו"ו הנ"ל יקח

ריז ע"א

1. ב"ה
2. יקח שני שלישי' הנותרי' נגד התשלומין דמי שני שלישי' שלו ועל מקו' החנו'
3. השיב כהו"ו הנ"ל באשר שחמותו שולטות בכל עזבון בעלה בכן רשאי
4. ליתן מקו' החנות למי שתרצה כמו בית' ומקומה בבה"כ שתוכל להשכיר
5. למי שתרצה בכן רוצה ליתנו לו ובפרט שהיא לטובתה ולטובת העזבו'
6. אם יהי' המקו' חנות לכהו"ו שעי"כ ירוויח יותר ויוכל ליתן יותר לחמות'
7. שהולכת בחנותו לסייע לו במו"מ וגם זולת זה מי יוכל למחות בידה
8. אף אם אינה עוסקת במו"מ במקו' החנות שאפ"ה רוצה להחזיק לעצמה
9. לצורך תשמישה בכן גם תהי' לה רשות ליתן לו מקו' החנות כדי שעי"כ
10. גם היא יכולה להשתמש בתוכה שאר צריכי' והאריכו הצדדי' הנ"ל –

11. בטענותיהם ובתשובתיהם זה מול זה כמבואר בקונטרס הטענות המונ׳
12. לפנינו ובאשר שהאשה מ׳ רייכלה וחתנה כ״ה מיכל הנ״ל חתמו עצמם
13. בתוקף קומפרמיס בח״ח ובקנס קצוב חצי להשררה ירה[1] וחצי –
14. להקדש לקיים הפס״ד שיצא מאתנו נזדקקנו להם ולאחר שעיינו ה
15. הדק היטיב בטענותיהם ובמעשה ב״ד ובקנין ובת״א שהציעו לפנינו
16. מצאנו מחמת עשיית השותפות שהדין עם כה״מ הנ״ל שחמותו מ׳ –
17. רייכלה הנ״ל אינה רשאי לעשות שותפות עם חתנה כהו״ו לבד וממילא
18. נסתלק הטענה שטען כהר״מ מחמת ארבע זהו׳ אם יזכה חמותה בדין בעשי׳
19. שותפות באשר שאין לה רשות לעשות כנ״ל ועל מה שטוען כהו״ו שיכירו ה
20. הב״ד אם חמותה אינה רצת׳ לעסוק עוד במו״מ של סחורת רק היא רצת׳
21. לימכר כל הסחורת לחתנה כהו״ו הנ״ל והוא יחזיק החנות והיא רוצה
22. לסייע לו בחנות נגד שכר קצוב או בשום אופן שיתרצו שניהם וכה״מ
23. הנ״ל מוחה בזה אם לא על אופן שהתרצה בזה בטענותיו כנ״ל מצאנו
24. שגם בזה הדין עמו והיינו שתשבע האשה מ׳ רייכלה טרם שמכרה סחורת
25. הנ״ל לכהו״ו הנ״ל ע״ד המקו׳ ב״ה וע״ד ב״ד בלי ערמה ומרמה ובלי שום ה
26. הוראת היתר שבעולם שלא יהי׳ לה ערמה במכירת זו כדי לעשות שותפ[ות]
27. אח״כ עי״ז עם חתנה כהו״ו הנ״ל ולאחר שנשבעת כנ״ל ורוצה למכור לכ״ה
28. וואלף הנ״ל על אופן שטען כה״מ הנ״ל להעלות על דמי קרן ראשון מסחורת הנ״ל
29. סך דמי רווחי׳ וגם עלייות דמי אותן הסחורה שנתייקרו ורוצה לישבע
30. גם ע״ז אזי רשאי לימכ׳

ריז ע״ב

1. ב״ה
2. רשאי לימכור לחותנה כהו״ו לבד / אכן אם אינה רוצת׳ לישבע או שכהו״ו
3. אינו מרוצה ליקח בדמי עילוי הנ״ל והאשה מ׳ רייכלה אינה רוצה להחזיק
4. עוד בחנות אזי יומכר הסחורת בין הני תלתא לוקחי בנותי׳ למי שיתן יותר
5. ומחמת מקו׳ החנות מצאנו שגם בזה הדין עם כה״מ הנ״ל שיוטל גורל בין
6. לוקחי בנותי׳ ולמי שיזכה בגורל לו יהי׳ המקו׳ חנות הנ״ל לשכור לעצמו
7. להחזיק חנותו בתוכה ואם יעלה הגורל לכה״מ הנ״ל אין האשה מ׳ רייכלה
8. הנ״ל {רוצה} (רשאי)[2] לגרום שלא ישכיר משכיר של חנות הנ״ל לכה״מ הנ״ל אכן כל
9. זמן שהאשה מ׳ רייכלה הנ״ל רוצה להחזיק במו״מ כמקדם אזי אין רשות לכה״מ
10. הנ״ל לימחות וכמו שהתחייב א״ע בקנין ובת״א ייקוים הכל כמו ש
11. שנאמר שם עוד התעצמו לפנינו בדין וטוען כה״מ הנ״ל בהרשאות הנ״ל
12. לימחות ביד האשה מ׳ רייכלה הנ״ל ליתן שטר {מתכ}מתנה או שט״ח לשום
13. אדם שיחול המתנה או החוב שעה אחת קודם מותה כל זמן שלא נשבעת
14. על כתובתה זולת ידיעות בנותי׳ ולוקחי׳ בנותי׳ וכהו״ו הנ״ל השיב –

---

1. ירום הודו
2. תוספת מעל השורה

שיכירו הב״ד אם יוכל כה״מ לימחות בידה / ומצאנו שאין רשות – ביד כה״מ הנ״ל לימחות בידה לעשות שטרות כנ״ל מתי שתרצה על סך מה שיגיע לה כפי שטרות כתובה ותוס׳ מבעלה ז״ל אכן אם תעדר ח״ו האשה הנ״ל קודם שנשבעת על כתובתה אזי עכ״פ מחאותו של כה״מ למפרע קיימת שלא יבוא לו שום הזיק ולא ינוכה לו מכח שטרות הנ״ל מחלק שליש המגיע לו מסך דמי כתו׳ ותוס׳ אבל אם נשבעת קודם שתעדר אזי אין מחאתו הועיל כלום ו[י]תפרע ג״כ מחלק שליש המגיע לכה״מ הנ״ל והנאמני׳ הלוקחי׳ הקנין מהאשה הנ״ל יקחו הקנין דווקא על אופן הנ״ל ולא על שום אופן אחר ויוכתב כן בשטר הנעשה על הקנין יצא מאתנו היו׳ יו׳ ג׳ וי״ו תשרי תקנ״א / רנ״מ ורמ״ש ואני /

No. 234

Fol. 218a; Monday 15 November 1790

A letter from the court to Rabbi Zalman Kahana of Fürth

A charitable trust had been established with funds from the late Leb Schloss to give money annually to needy brides.[1] Recipients of the funds were chosen by lot. The winner of one of the recent lotteries was not a resident of Frankfurt, but of Fürth, and this brought the executors of the trust to court. The terms of the endowment stated that the weddings of brides who received funds from the trust had to be held in Frankfurt, and the father of the bride had already written that this wedding would not be held in Frankfurt.

The court examined the document establishing the trust and ruled that the bride would only be eligible to receive the full 450 guldens (400 for her dowry and 50 for wedding expenses) granted by the trust if the marriage took place in Frankfurt. If the wedding could not take place in Frankfurt the bride would receive only 400 guldens, on condition that the marriage had already been contracted. The court specifically noted its concern that it should not be the cause of a disagreement between the two sides in any marriage agreement. The court wrote to Rabbi Zalman Kahana (Salomon Kohn) of Fürth asking him to confirm that the said marriage had been contracted as the father of the bride claimed. If the marriage had not been contracted then the bride would receive no funds unless they agreed to hold the wedding in Frankfurt.

1. See Frankfurt *Memorbuch*, fol. 305a.

ריח ע"א
לק"[ק] פירדא ב"ה פ"פ יו' ב' ח' כסליו תקנא לפ"ק
החיים והשל' לאוצר בלום / ספיר ויהלום / אהובנו הרב המופלא הג' הגדול
מעוז ומגדול נ[י]"י[1] ע"ה פ"ה המפורסם כבוד מה' זלמן כהנא[2] רבה נר' יזריח ויאיר
כאור בהיר יא"ק לד'
אחרי ד"ש וש"ת / לדבר מצוה קטרחנא מעכ"ת הרב הגאון נר' אודות בת
של כ"ה זנוויל ק"ד[3] על מה שזכתי' לעלות מגורל של דב"ט הכנסת כלה בקהלותינו
יע"א שהניח אחריו המנוח כ"ה ליב שלאס ז"ל ואבי' כ"ה זנוויל הנ"ל כתב
לכאן בי' א' כ' חשון[4] העבר שכבר נתקשר בתו עם הב"ח כ' מאיר בן יאיר
משנייטיך ל[5] ושאי אפשר לו להיות החתנה פה קהלותינו מחמת ריבוי ה
הוצאו' ובאו האפטרופסי' של דב"ט הנ"ל לפנינו ושאלו מאתנו אחרי ש
שנאמר בפי' בצוואת המנדב ז"ל הנ"ל שהחתנה צריך להיות דוקא
פה קהלותינו יע"א האיך יתנהגו אם רשאי ליתן את הנדן סך ד' מאות
זהו' ואת סך חמשי' זהו' לצורך החתנה הנזכרי' בצוואה הנ"ל לבת כ"ה
זנוויל הנ"ל אף אם לא יהי החתנה כאן או לא ולאחר שדקדקנו בלשון
צוואת המנדב ז"ל הנ"ל יצא מאתנו שבאם כבר נתקשרה הבת של
כ"ה זנוויל הנ"ל כפי כתב אגרת שלו אזי כדי שלא נעשה פירוד בין
הצדדי' יותן להכלה הנ"ל לשעת חתנותה סך ארבעה מאות זהו' לנדן
אבל לא הסך חמשי' זהו' לצורך החתנה אכן אם היא עדיין לא נתקשר[ה]
לא יהי לה אפי' סך נדן הנ"ל אם לא יתרצו א"ע שתהי' החתנה פה
כלשון הצוואה והנה אחרי שהודענא למעכ"ת הה"ג נר' את הדברי'
כהווייתן והפס"ד הנ"ל ימחול עכ"ת[6] הרמה ויודיענו נא מר אמיתת הדברי'
כהווייתן משמה אם כבר נתקשר הבת של כה"ז[7] הנ"ל או לאו ואף אם
אם כבר נעשה הקישור ידבר נא מעכ"ת במכ"ה על לב הצדדי' אולי
יהי באפשרי לקיים דברי המת להיות החתנה פה ויקבלו אז ג"כ
לצורך זה עוד חמשי' זהו' כנ"ל והי זה של' וחיים מעתה ועד עולם
כחפץ נפשו ונפש הד"ש ושל' תורתו ומצפי' לתשבתו המוכני'
לטובתו הק' רנ"מ ורמ"ש ואני

1. נר ישראל?
2. הרב משולם זלמן כהן (ר' לוינשטיין, *Zur Geschichte der Juden in Fürth*, כרך א, עמ' 203-209).
3. ראשי תבות לשם המשפחה. לא ברור מה שם השלם.
4. בשנת תק"ן כ' חשון חל ביום ב.
5. הכוונה לא ברורה. אולי טעות סופר.
6. נשפך כאן דיו. כנראה שצ"ל 'מעכ"ת' (ר' שורה 24).
7. כבוד הרב זנוויל

No. 235

Fol. 218b; Tuesday 25 January 1791

The leaders of the community approached the court regarding funds that had accrued in a charitable trust left by Treinle Schloss (d. 1779) and her sister, Malka Mez. The community wished to use funds from the trust to assist Yudaʾ Samuel Worms and his wife, Brinla, but they did not know if the rules of the trust allowed it. They came to the court not only for a ruling in the matter but, if necessary, a legal allowance that would permit the community to help the family. The court responded that, according to a 1782 decision, income from the trust could only be used for assisting poor orphan brides and therefore Yudaʾ Samuel Worms and his wife could not be helped.

The record notes that the daughter of the late Samuel Hanau was related to the sisters and in need of funds. The court ordered the community to make a public announcement that any orphan who was related to the sisters and in need of funds should come before the communal leadership within 30 days. If no one more closely related to the sisters than the daughter of Samuel Hanau came forward, the funds were to be given to her on condition that she enter into a marriage agreement within thirteen months from the date of this decision and marry no more than six months thereafter. The discussion makes reference to an earlier decision of the court in this matter from 1782, which appears in YIVO MS. RG 128 (folder 77–78), fols. 53b–54a (see here Appendix 8). The ruling of the court recorded below also appears in the YIVO manuscript on fol. 184a.

ריח ע״ב

1. ב״ה
2. ע״ד השאלה מאת האלופי׳ קציני׳ פרנסי׳ וגובי׳ יצו בענין הרווחי׳
3. המונחי׳ אצל האלופי׳ גובי׳ יצו מדבר טוב שהניח׳ אחרי׳ הרבנית
4. המונחת מ׳ מלכה בת המונח כ״ה אהרן מיץ ז״ל ששאלו ע״י השמש קהל
5. כ״ה זיסקינד שטערן וזה לשון השאלה לאמור להם שכל מה שיוכלו
6. להפוך בזכות מה״ה כ׳ יודא שמואל ווירמש ואשתו בריינלה תי׳ –
7. מחמת דבר טוב מה״ה אל׳ המונחת מרת טריינלה שלאס ואחותה –
8. המונחת מלכה ז״ל יראו ויהפכו בזכותם / ואם לא יוכלו ולא יראו
9. בעיניהם להפוך בזכות של כ׳ יודא שמואל {ווירמש} ואשתו בריינלה
10. הנ״ל מחמת הדין אזי קודם הפסק דין יראו ויעיינו אם יוכלו
11. אלופי כל הקהל ובצירוף אלופי׳ גובי׳ יצו לעשות דבר בעסק
12. הנ״ל לפנים משורת הדין ע״כ השאלה מצאנו באשר שבדבר
13. זה יצא כבר פסק דין ביו׳ ג׳ ד״ח שבט תקמ״ב וז״ל אודות הפירות

14. שעלה על הקרן קיימת מדבר טוב האשה המונחת מ' מלכה בת המנוח
15. כ"ה אהרן מיץ ז"ל מיו' פטירת אחותה מ' טריינלה ז"ל עד יו' הנ"ל
16. יתנו האלופי' גובי' לצורך הכנסת כלה יתומה וכל הקרוב –
17. קרוב קודם עכ"ל פסק דין בכן אין לזוז מפסק דין הנ"ל ויותן דוקא
18. ליתומה ואין כח בידינו וביד הקהל וגובי' יצ[1] לשנות פס"ד הנ"ל
19. (ולעשות לפנים משורת הדין)[2] אחרי שיש כאן יתומה אחת בת המנוח כ' שמואל הענא ז"ל שהיא
20. קרובה מהנעדרת הנ"ל ומפני שיש לחוש שמא תהי' יתומה אחרת
21. קרובה יותר ממנה לזאת מצאנו שיוכרז בבה"כ שכל יתומות שהיא
22. קרובה להנעדרת ז"ל הנ"ל ותרצה לזכות בה תבוא אצל האלופי' גובי'
23. יצו / תוך זמן שלשי' יום ובאם לאחר זמן שלשי' יום לא ימצא יתומה
24. שהיא קרובה יותר אזי זכת {...}(היתומה)[3] בת של כ' שמואל ז"ל הנ"ל
25. בהרווחי' הנ"ל באופן ובתנאים שתעשה שידוך משך שנה אחת מיו'
26. כלות שלשי' יו' מיו' דלמטה והחתנה צריך להיות לפחות אחר שנה –
27. ומחצה מיו' כלות שלשי' יום הנ"ל יצא מאתנו יו' ג' ד' שבט תקנ"א
28. הגאון אב"ד נר' ורנ"מ ורמ"ש ואני /[4]

No. 236

Sichel et al. v. Sichel

Fols. 219a–224b; Thursday 10 March 1791

The division of the estate of the late Zalman Sichel, who died in the spring of 1776, led to an ongoing dispute among his sons, Moses, Yosle, and Yudaʾ Sichel.[5] The brothers brought their dispute to a non-Jewish court, but later decided to come before the rabbinic court. The case involved more than fifteen claims, many of them by Moses against Yosle and Yudaʾ. Most of the claims stemmed from Moses' belief that there had been an inequitable division of assets and that his brothers had also improperly transferred assets. Moses also felt that a number of expenses had been unjustly charged to the estate, particularly by Yosle who was most active in collecting debts still owed to the estate.

---

1. ישמרם צורם
2. בשולי הדף מחוץ לשורה
3. תיקון מעל השורה. כנראה שמודבר בגוטלה בת שמואל הענא שבסוף לא הצליחה להתחתן (ר' אבני זכרון, מס' 4768, ואלה תולדות 11.1.1782).
4. קו הנטוי במקור. בכ"י יווא כל השמות, כולל של הרב גונדרשהיים, מופיעים בשלימותם (לא כראשי תבות).
5. On Zalman Sichel's death, see Horovitz, no. 3552.

An important piece of the discussion was a document from 1776 wherein Moses had signed a statement that the division of assets had been fair and could not be contested. Moses tried to have this admission dismissed, saying that he had not understood the contents of the note and had relied on the trustworthiness of his brothers, a trust that he now claimed was misplaced. The court dismissed this claim. Also see no. 237.

ריט ע"א

ב"ה ע"ד טענות והפרשות בין האחי' המשותפי' הו"ה גע[1] כ' יוזלי והו"ה כ' יודא זיכל ובין אחיהם הו"ה גת"ת כ' משה {ט} זיכל בני המנוח כ' זלמן זיכל ז"ל שהלכו למשפט אצל השררה יר"ה / ולאח"כ התרצו א"ע לילך בדיני ישראל לפני הב"ד אונד האבין משפטם מן השררה יר"ה אב גרופן כמבואר מתוך טעקרעט שהציע לפנינו ואח"כ באו הצדדי' הנ"ל ומורשאי' שלהם ה"ה התורני כ"ה משה אויך בהרשאות האחי' כ' יוזלי וכ' יודא הנ"ל וה"ה התורני נ"ה כה פייס הענא בהרשאות כ' משה הנ"ל לפנינו ב"ד ח"מ והאריכו מאוד בטענותיהם כמבואר היטב בקונטרס הטענות המונח לפנינו ולאחר שחתמו עצמם הצדדי' הנ"ל בתוקף קומפרמיס בח"ח ובקנס סך מסוים חצי להשררה יר"ה וחצי להקדש לאשר ולקיים הפס"ד שיצא מאתנו ח"מ נזדקקנו להם / ומצאנו על כל פרט ופרט כמבואר להבא והיינו מה שתבע הו"ה גע כ' יוזלי הנ"ל מן אחיו כ' משה הנ"ל סך ארבעה מאות זהו' באשר שאביו המנוח כ' זלמן ז"ל הנ"ל התחייב א"ע בקנין בשעת החופה של כ' יוזלי הנ"ל ליתן לכ' יוזלי הנ"ל כל שנה ושנה שני מאות רט על משך ששה שני' מיו' החתנה נגד זה מחויב כ' יוזלי הנ"ל לסייע לאביו בעסק מו"מ שלו וכ' יוזלי קיים התחייבת שלו ולא קיבל כלום כלום[2] מאביו ז"ל ומאחר שמבואר בכתב פשר שנעשה ע"י הר"י והרב"ד מהו' נתן מאז נר"ו מן ח"י סיון תקלויו לפק שמחויבי' האחים הנ"ל לשלם מן העזבון כל מה שחייב אביהם ז"ל בכן תבע כ' יוזלי הנ"ל מן אחיו (כ')[3] [מ]שה הנ"ל שישלם לו מה שמגיע ע"ח והיינו סך ארבעה מאות רט הנ"ל וכמר משה הנ"ל השיב אחרי שבאותו פעם שהי' עומדי' לדין לפני הר"י מה' נתן מאז נרו' הי' תובע כ' יוזלי הנ"ל כמה תביעות כמבואר בכתב פשר הנ"ל ולא תבע אותו תביעה מסך ארבעה מאות ר"ט וגם לאח"כ בשעת חלוקה לא תבע כלום / מזה מוכח או שכבר נפרע התחייבות הלז או שמתחילה ההתחייבות בת"ר לא הי' רק דרך ערמה כדי שנגמר השידוך שלו וראי' לזה שבתוך תנאים של כ' יוזלי נאמר שאביו התחייב א"ע ליתן לנדן שלו סך ששה מאות ק"ט ובאמת לא נתן רק חמשה מאות ק"ט בכן וודאי שגם ההתחייבות הנ"ל הי' בערמה מטעם הנ"ל והאריכו

---

1. גבאי צדקה
2. כפילות במקור
3. תוספת מעל השורה

29. בטענותיה׳

ריט ע״ב

1. בטענותיהם / ומצאנו שהדין עם כ׳ משה הנ״ל שאין עליו חיוב לשלם לכ׳ יוזלי
2. הנ״ל סך ארבעה מאות רט הנ״ל / ועל מה שתבעו האחי׳ כ׳ יוזלי וכ׳ יודא
3. הנ״ל מן כ׳ משה הנ״ל סך שלשה מאות זהו׳ שנתנו לו בחיי אביהם כשהי׳
4. להם קטטה עם אחיהם כ׳ מאיר וכ׳ משה אמר להם באותו פעם שרוצה
5. לשלם להם / בכן תבעו האחי׳ סך הנ״ל מן כ׳ משה הנ״ל וכ״ה משה השיב
6. שנתנו לו בשביל שלא הלך עם כ׳ מאיר במשפט נגדם / גם הי׳ צריך לו
7. באותו פעם לצורך מלבושיו ושארי צרכיו כמו שהוציאו גם המה בהיותם
8. פנוי מצאנו שגם בזה הדין עם כ׳ משה הנ״ל ופטור מתביעה הלז{ו}
9. ומחמת מה שתבעו עוד האחי׳ הנ״ל מן כ׳ משה הנ״ל שהמה הלווה לו
10. ביריד נומבוריג שנה חדשה שני זופרינה וחצי גם דמי פראכט
11. עולה יחד לערך סך ארבעי׳ זהו׳ / וכ׳ משה הנ״ל השיב שלא לוה
12. מהם כלום וגם דמי פראכט אינו חייב ועוד השיב אחרי שיש
13. להאחי׳ קוויטונג ממנו משנת תקמ״ז על איזה גביות חובות ישנו׳
14. ששילמו מפני מה לא הי׳ מנכי׳ סך ארבעי׳ זהו׳ הנ״ל וכ״ה משה
15. אויך הנ״ל השב בהרשאות האחי׳ הנ״ל שכ׳ משה ישבע ואז יהי׳
16. פטור מצאנו שמחויב כ׳ משה הנ״ל לישבע ע״ד המקו׳ בה ועדי[1] ב״ד
17. בלי ערמה ומרמה ובלי שום הוראות היתר שבעולם שכדבריו כן הוא
18. שלא לוה ממנו שני זופרינה וחצי הנ״ל וגם אינו חייב להם דמי פראכט
19. ולאחר שישבע כנ״ל פטור כ׳ משה הנ״ל מתביעה זו / וה״ה התורני כ״ה
20. פייס הנ״ל בהרשאות ובמעמד כ׳ משה הנ״ל בעצמו תבע מן האחי׳ הנ״ל
21. וטען שלא קיבל מן עזבון אביו את כל מה שמגיע לו על חלקו משולם הן
22. ממזומני׳ ח״כ סחורת וחובת שהניח אביהם אחריו בעזבונו באשר
23. שלא נתחלק כראוי ולא חילקו באותו פעם כי אם אותן סחורת שהניח
24. אחיו כ׳ יודא הנ״ל לחלוקה ובאשר שכ׳ יודא הנ״ל הי׳ לו לעצמו ג״כ
25. סחורת בחנות אביהם ז״ל ומי יודע אם לא הניח כ׳ יודא סחורת
26. של אביו

רך ע״א

1. ב״ה
2. של אביו בתוך שלו ואומר שלו הם / וגם מעות מזומני׳ שהי׳ שייך לאביו יוכל להיות
3. שהעלים כ׳ יודא הנ״ל וגם מחמת חלוקת ח״כ של אביהם ז״ל טוען {כ׳ יודא הנ״ל} שלא
4. נעשה גורל ע״ז והוא כמר משה לא קיבל רק שתי ח״כ וידוע ומפורסם שאביו הניח ח
5. חובות הרבה בעזבונו ובפרט שידוע לו שאביו ז״ל הי׳ לו מו״מ רב וגם חובות עם
6. המנוח כ׳ אברם שטיבל ועם הו״ה כ׳ משה ריסלסהיים בכן תבע כ׳ משה הנ״ל מן
7. אחיו הנ״ל שבועה {...} שלא העלימו כלום מכל הנ״ל גם מחמת חובות

---

1. ברוך הוא ועל דעת

8. שבפנקס אביהם אינו יודע אם כל החובות מפנקס אביהם נכתב׳ בתוך ג׳
9. עקסטראקטין ויוכל להיות שהעלים כ׳ יודא הנ״ל כמה חובות ולא כתבו בתוך
10. עקסטראקטין והנאמני׳ שעשאו גורל על עקסטראקטין רק כמו שהניח כ׳ יודא הנ״ל
11. לפניהם בכן תבע כמר משה הנ״ל מן אחי׳ הנ״ל שיתנו לו ג״כ העתק משני עקסטראקטן
12. שעלו על חלקם גם יראו לו כל הפנקסאות מאביהם ז״ל הויפט אונד גלידר
13. בוך לראות מתוכה כל החובות אביהם שלא העלימו כלום וטוען ג״כ שיודע
14. בבירור שהי׳ לאביו איין רעגיסטר בוך שלא הראה לו ושיציעו לפני הב״ד / וגם
15. מחמת / חובות שאינו בטוחי׳ הישנות נאמר בפסק פשר הנ״ל וז״ל יכתוב עקס=
16. טראקט משמות הבע״ח אשר הם עדיין חייב ויומסר לכ׳ משה הנ״ל אותו עקסטראקט
17. כדי שידע כמר משה ג״כ מי הם אותן הבע״ח וכו׳ והאחי׳ המשותפי׳ הנ״ל מחויב׳
18. ליתן תקיעת כף לכמר משה הנ״ל ע״ז שלא יעלימו שום דבר והיינו מה שבא לידי
19. גוביינא מהחובות הרעי׳ שיתנו שליש חלקו לאחי׳ כמר משה עכ״ל וטען כמר משה
20. הנ״ל שלא קיבל מאחיו הנ״ל לא עקסטראקט ולא ח״כ והביא ראי׳ לדבריו שלא קיבל עקס
21. טראקט מכתב הנאמני׳ שהציע לפנינו שהי׳ שלח {לאביו} לאחיו הנ״ל שיתנו לו עקסטרא
22. =קט והשיבו שמרוצי׳ ליתנו לו אם ישלם הוא הוצאות מזה משמע שעדיין לא קיבל ע
23. עקסטראקט מחובות הרעי׳ בכן תבע כ׳ משה אחרי שגבו האחי׳ הנ״ל כמה אלפ׳ מחובו׳
24. הרעי׳ ולא נתנו לו עדיין חלקו ועיכבו בידם זמן רב שלא כראוי בכן יבררו לפני ב״ד
25. האחי׳ הנ״ל כמה גבו ליתנו לו עתה חלקו גם יתנו לו עקסטראקט מחובות שישנו
26. עדיין בעזבון / עוד תבע כמר משה הנ״ל שיודע בבירור שיש עוד כלי בית מבדיל
27. תחת ידם ובפרט ש[מ]אלץ שטאנד מעזבון אביהם שלא נתחלק עדיין ויחקרו הב״ד
28. ע״י גביות עדות מן כ׳ משה בן המנוח כ׳ מיכל קאסיל ומן כ׳ גימפכה שהי׳ משרת
29. אצלם ויתוודע על ידם שהודו האחי׳ שיש עוד תחת ידם כלי בית ובדיל
30. מעזבון אביהם

רך ע״ב

1. ב״ה
2. מעזבון אביהם / בכן תובע עתה חלקו ועי״כ רוצה להחזיק טענות הנ״ל שהם העלימו
3. הרבה / עוד תבע כמר משה הנ״ל חלקו מן באך טוך רעיאהל שלעסיר קישטן שלא נתחלק עדיין
4. עוד תבע כמר משה מן האחי׳ הנ״ל שידוע לכל שהאחי׳ הנ״ל כ׳ יוזלי וכ׳ יודא הנ״ל הי׳ מבזבזי׳
5. יותר מאלף זהו׳ בחיי אביו ז״ל בשביל שידוך של כ׳ יוזלי הנ״ל בלי ידיעות אביו בכן תבע
6. עתה כמר משה הנ״ל שישבעו אחיו הנ״ל כמה הפריזו ויתן לו מה שהי׳ מגיע לו מזה
7. ע״ח / והאחי׳ הנ״ל השיבו באריכות לפנינו על כל פרט ופרט מתביעות כמר משה הנ״ל
8. והציע לפנינו כתב פטורי׳ מח״י של כ״מי הנ״ל מקויים בפני נ״ה מן ך סיון תקלויו לפק ו
9. ושם נאמר וז״ל הנני מודה בח״י וכו׳ באנו אנחנו שלשה אחי׳ הנ״ל ליחד בחשבן ב
10. בדיקדוק גדול וכו׳ על כל מה שנשאר לאחר כל הנ״ל בנחלת אבינו ז״ל הנ״ל בלי שום שיור
11. כלל וחלקנו הכל בינינו ע״פ אופן המבואר בפסק {דין} הנ״ל והיינו כל הסחורות וכו׳ ו

1. כבוד משה

12. והן כסף ושוה כסף מעות מזומני׳ ו{כו׳}(אבני׳ טובות ותכשיטין ושאר מטלטלי׳ יהי׳ מה שיהי׳ כו׳)[1] אבל זולת מה שנאמר בו חוץ הנ״ל חלקנו {הכל}
13. לשלשה חלקי׳ שוה בשוה ואח״כ נעשה גורל בינינו ואותו החלק שעלה לגורלי קבלתי
14. כבר מן אחי׳ שלי בלי שום שיור כלל ומחמת החובות שבפנקס וכו׳ נעשה ג״כ החלוקה
15. בינינו באופן המבואר בהפסק הנ״ל והיינו כל החובות הנמצאי׳ {באופן} בפנקס חלקנו
16. וכו׳ וכל מה שעלה לגורלי מאותן החובות קבלת[י] וכו׳ ומחמת חובות הישני׳ הן בפנקס והן
17. בח״מ או ח״כ שהם רעי׳ מאוד עד שלפי שעה הם כלאחר יאוש רק שיוכל להיות שיש
18. מהם יבואו בימי׳ מרובי׳ לידי גוביינא מן אותן חובות ישני׳ הנ״ל כתבנו עקס
19. =טראקט משמות הבע״ח שחייבי׳ עדיין וקבלת אותו עקסטראקט מאחי׳ שלי הנ״ל / בכדי
20. שיודע אני מי הם אותן הבע״ח / ואחר שהאחי׳ שלי הנ״ל הם עמדו בשותפות עדיין והם
21. מכירין אותן הבע״ח ישני׳ יותר מה שאני מכיר אותם וכו׳ בכן גוף הפנקס מהחובות
22. ישני׳ והח״כ וח״מ מחובות ישני׳ שהם רעי׳ יהי׳ מונחי׳ אצל האחי׳ שלי / ואם יבוא איזה
23. מהחובות הרעי׳ הנ״ל לידי גוביינא אזי מחויבי׳ האחי׳ ליתן לי מזה החל שליש והשני
24. אחי׳ שלי הנ״ל נתנו לי ע״ז ת״כ שלא יעלימו שום דבר וכו׳ אין לי זולת הנ״ל עוד שום ט
25. טענה ותביעה וזכות ודין ודברי׳ שבעולם על אחי שלי הנ״ל ויורשיהם וב״כ מעתה
26. ועד עולם והנני פוטר ומסלק ומוחל מעכשיו לשני האחי׳ שלי ויורשיהם וב״כ
27. בדא״ה ובד״י

רדא ע״א

1. ב״ה
2. בפטור וסילוק ומחילה גמורה בכא״ה בדא״ה ובכא״ה
3. בדא״ה ובד״י ממני ומיורשי וב״כ מעתה ועד עולם: כד״י על צד היותר מספיק לפתחז״ל ובמחילה
4. עולמית מחילת שמים ובני אדם מחמת כל הטענות ותביעת שאפשר לצייר בשום אופן מכל אופני׳
5. מיני צ[ו]רים בעולם שהי׳ אפשר להיות לי וליורשי וב״כ עוד עליהם ועל יורשיהם וב״כ הן
6. תביעות ממון או תביעות חשבון לא מחמת שום דבר הנוגע לעניני׳ עזבון אבינו ז״ל
7. ולא מחמת שום דבר מצד עצמותם וכו׳ ותמיד ולעולם יהי׳ על כל הנ״ל ועל כל עניני׳ כ
8. כל דין תורת נאמנות מפורש בכא״ה כתחז״ל לאחיי הנ״ל וי״א וב״כ מעתה וע״ע ב
9. בדא״ה ובד״י בדיבור הקל בלי שום אלה ושבוע וג״ש וק״ח ובכל תוקף הנאמנות ש
10. שבעולם כל הנ״ל קבלתי עלי מעכשיו בק״ס ובח״ח ובשד״א ובת״כ ובנדר גמור לאשר ולקיי׳
11. ונעשה ממנו בלי שום אונס והכרח כלל רק בלבב שלם ובנפש חפצה וכו׳ עכ״ל בכן
12. טוען כ״ה משה {הנ״ל} בהרשאות האחים הנ״ל שסמוך עצמו על פטורים הנ״ל שנכתב בכא״ה
13. שנסתלק כל תביעות שתבע כ״מר משה הנ״ל מהם הן מחמת עזבון אביהם הנ״ל באשר
14. שהודה כמר משה שנתחלק כל העזבון וקיבל מה שעלה על חלקו והן מחמת עצמם אין לו

1. תוספת מעל השורה

15. תביעה עליהם ושהוא מסלק ומוחל כל תביעות שבועלם[1] אכן יש עדיין תחת ידם מעזבון
16. אביהם שלא נתחלק איין קישט טֶעי שהודה כ"ה משה הנ"ל בהרשאות האחי' שיהי' לכמר
17. משה הנ"ל לבד ופאלנשע קליידר שעדיין לא נתחלק רוצי' האחים ליתן חלקו חלק שליש
18. מהם ממה שגבו מחובות הרעי' מעת חלוקת העזבון עד עתה הם מרוצים ליתן לו חלק
19. שליש המגיע על חלקו לאחר ניכו הוצאות והציע חשבון ורשימה לפנינו מהכנסה והוצאות
20. ועולה הכנסה לסך שלשת אלפים תשעי' ואחד זהו' נחץ[2] והוצאות משפטים כסדרן
21. ושלא כסדרן והוצאות הדרך ושאר הוצאות שהי' להם עד (עד עתה לצורך עזבון אביהם עולה לסך יג מאות)[3] ארבעי' ואחד זהו' ל
22. לצ[״ל] ולאחר ניכוי זה מזה נשאר עדיין בידם סך שבעה עשר מאות וחמשי' זהו' ד"א צל
23. וחלק שליש שהמגיע ע"ח רוצי' ליתן לכמר משה הנ"ל נגד קואיטונג והיינו שהב"ד יפרטו
24. בפס"ד אותן שמות אנשים ששילמו להאחים הנ"ל כפי שנרשם בחשבון ורשימה הנ"ל
25. שהציע ושנתנו לו שליש חלקו מאותן תשלומין או שכמר משה הנ"ל יתן קוויטונג על אופן הלז
26. וכ"ה פייס הנ"ל בהרשאת כמר משה הנ"ל האריך בטענותיו נגד הפטורים לבטלם
27. שכמר משה הנ"ל לא היה ידע בעת חתימתו מה שנכתב בפטורים רק כ"ה
28. אנשיל פפאן ז"ל הביא לו המעות סך אלף ושלשה ושבעי' ק"ט המגיע לו כפי
29. הפשר הנ"ל וגם הפטורים ואמר לו שמחויב מיד לחתום הפטורים אבל לא אמר לו
30. מהות וענין הפטורי' והוא לא הבינו וגם היה נחוץ לדרכו באותו פעם ליריד
31. נומבורג והיה סבור שאחיו הלכו עמו בנאמנות משום כך חתם עצמו בפטורים
32. והאריך בטענותיו שהפטורים הנ"ל הי' בטעות גמור ואף שנכתב בפטורי'
33. נאמנות מ[״מ] אח"כ נתגלה שאבדו נאמנות שלהם מחמת כמה וכמה דברים /
34. וגם יכירו הב"ד אם לא אבדו הנאמנו' שלהם במה שעיכב חלקו מדמי תשלומין
35. מחובת ישיני'

רדא ע"ב

1. ב"ה
2. מחובות ישינים כמה שנים בידם גם לא נעשה קנין על הפטורים אף שנכתב בתוכה
3. בק"ס מ"מ לא נעשה קנין על ידם וגם לא נכתב בתוכה שהנאמני' קראו לפניו הפטורים וגם מהבדיל וכלי ב
4. בית לא נתנו לו כל מה שמגיע לו כנ"ל בכן טוען שהפטורי' המה כחרס הנשבר ועומד בטענותיו ות
5. ותביעותיו כנ"ל וכ"ה משה בהרשאות האחים השיב שאין יוכל לטעון ולגרוע כח הפטורי' הנכתבי'
6. בכא"ה ועומד בטענותיו כנ"ל / ולאחר שדקדקנו הדק היטב בטענותיהם ובתשובותיהם בכתב פ

---

1. צ"ל 'שבעולם'
2. נ"ח צ"ל
3. תוספת בצד העמוד

7. פשר ובלשון הפטורים ובכתב{ה} הנאמנים מצאנו שהדין עם האחים כ׳ יוזלי וכ׳ יודא הנ״ל ש
8. שפטורים הנ״ל המה בתקפו ובגבורתי[ה]׳ ואין לכמר משה הנ״ל שום טענה נגד פטורים הנ״ל
9. ופטורי׳ האחים הנ״ל מתביעות כמר משה הנ״ל הן מה שתבע חלקו שלש מסך אלף זהו׳ שה
10. שהפרידו בחיי אביהן מחמת שידוך של כ׳ יוזלי הנ״ל הן מה שתבע שלא קיבל חלקו משולם מ
11. מעזבון אביו הן מסחורת ומזומני׳ ח״כ והן מה מחובות הפנקס שתבע שאינו יודע אם כל ה
12. החובות מפנקס אביהם נכתבי׳ בתוך שלשה עקסטראקטן וכנ״ל מכולם פטורים האחים הנ״ל
13. חוץ מן כלי בית ובדיל רעיאַל ובפראט שמאלץ שטאנד שלעסר באך טוך מצאנו שיש בידינו
14. כח לעשות פשר עד שיתנו לו האחים הנ״ל סך עשרים זהו׳ אכן כפי מה שראינו כתב
15. הנאמני׳ שהתרצו האחי׳ הנ״ל ליתן לו עקסטראקט מחובת הרעי׳ הנמצאי׳ עדיין בעזבון
16. אביהן ז״ל על הוצאות של כמר משה הנ״ל לבד בכן כה יהי׳ וכה יקום שמחויבי׳ האחי׳
17. הנ״ל ליתן לכמר משה הנ״ל עקסטראקט מחובת הרעי׳ הנמצאי׳ עדיין עוד בעזבון אביהם
18. ז״ל והיינו משמות אנשי׳ סך מה שמחויבי׳ כל או״א כפי הפנקס לשלם לעזבון אביהם והיינו
19. על הוצאות כמר משה לבד / וגם מחויבי׳ ליתן מה שהעלו האחי׳ בחשבונ׳ שנשאר בידם
20. מגבוי חובת הישיני׳ שכבר גבו מחובות הרעי׳ לאחר ניכוי הוצאות כפי מה שהעלו בחשבונם
21. סך שבעה עשר מאות וחמשי׳ זהו׳ ד״א צל שמחויבי׳ האחי׳ ליתנו לכמר משה הנ״ל חלק שליש
22. המגיע לו מזה נגד קוויטונג ע״פ אופן שיסדרו הב״ד אנחנו ח״מ / עוד טען כ׳ משה הנ״ל
23. נגד החשבן הרשימה שהציע לפנינו האחי׳ הנ״ל וכנ״ל מגביות תשלומין על חובת ישני׳
24. ומן הוצאות שהוציאו על זה הן מהוצאות המשפטי׳ שעל קצתם יש להם קוויטונג ועל קצתם
25. אין להם אין להם[1] הן כסדרן שעלו לערך סך שלשה מאות ושלשי׳ זהו׳ הן שלא כסדרן
26. שעלו לערך סך שני מאות ותשעי׳ זהו׳ והן מהוצאות הדרך שעלו לערך שלשה מאות
27. ושבעי׳ זהו׳ וטען כ׳ משה הנ״ל מי יודע שחשבונם צדק שהוציאו כל כך ובפרט ש
28. שהעלו בחשבונם הוצאות הדרך משלשה נסיעות בחורף שנת תקל״ז תקל״ח תקל״ט כל
29. פעם סך שבעים זהו׳ ומקיץ שנת תקלח תקלט שני נסיעות בכל פעם שמונים זהו׳
30. האיך אפשר לצמצם ולכווין כל כך ועוד טוען כמר משה מי יודע אם לא הי׳
31. רוב נסיעותיו והוצאות לטובת עצמו לגבות חובות שלהם וגם למכור על ידי כך
32. מה וכמה מיני סחורת מחנות וגם לא נתן כמר משה הנ״ל לכ׳ יוזלי הנ״ל כח הרשאה
33. לגבות חובות וליסע להוציא הוצאות על זה ובאם הי׳ האחי׳ הנ״ל נתנו לו כו״ה
34. גם הוא הי׳ רוצה ליסע ולגבות חובת הנ״ל בכן תבע כמר משה מן כ׳ יוזלי
35. הנ״ל

1. כפילות במקור

רדב ע״א

1. ב״ה
2. הנ״ל שבועה דאורייתא שכל הוצאות הי׳ רק לטובות העזבון ולא הי׳ בתוכה בשביל
3. טובות עצמו / וכ׳ יוזלי הנ״ל השיב ותובע מן כ׳ משה הנ״ל באשר שלא הי׳ {לו} נותן לו כו״ה
4. לגבות חובות {ולי[ס]ע להוציא הוצ}הי׳ גורם לו הפסד שהלכו כמה חובות לאיבוד / עוד
5. תובע כ׳ יוזלי הנ״ל באשר שהי׳ לו {כמה} טרחות ויגיעות הרבה בגיבוי חובות הנ״ל שהי׳
6. כמעט לאחר יאוש והי׳ כ׳ יוזלי כמה פעמי׳ על הדרך יומם ולילה בכן תובע כ׳ יוזלי מן כמר
7. משה הנ״ל שכר טרחתו על זה ורוצה לנכות ממה שמגיע על חלקו גיבוי חובות הנ״ל
8. והאריכו בטענותיהם / ומצאנו מחמת הוצאות כסדרן ושלא כסדרן שעולה ליחד לערך
9. סך ששה מאות ועשרי׳ זהו׳ ע״ז מחוייבי׳ האחי׳ כ׳ יוזלי וכ׳ יודא הנ״ל לשבע ע״ד המקו׳
10. ב״ה וע״ד ב״ד בלי עו״מ ובלי שום הוראות היתר שבעולם דהיינו כל אחד על מה שהוציא
11. ואח״כ רשאי׳ לנכות כפי חשבונם / ובאשר שכ׳ יוזלי הנ״ל הי׳ תמיד על הדרך מ
12. מצאנו שכ׳ יוזלי ישבע וכ׳ יודא יאמר אף אני כמו[1] / ומחמת מה שתבע כ׳ יוזלי הנ״ל
13. שכר טרחתו בגבוי החובות ישני׳ מצאנו שהדין עמו שישומו הב״ד שכר טרחתו כמה
14. מגיע לו ע״ז ומזה מחויב כ׳ משה הנ״ל לשלם שליש חלקו אבל מה שטען כ׳ יוזלי שגרם לו
15. כמר משה הנ״ל הפסד במה שלא נתן לו כו״ה על גביות חובות אין לו תביעה ומחמת
16. מה שתבע והעלו בחשבונם שהוציא כ׳ יוזלי בהוצאות הדרך כנ״ל מצאנו שלפי הדין
17. מחויב כ׳ יוזלי הנ״ל לשבע כנ״ל שהוציא כל כך כפי שהעלו בחשבונו וגם מחויב
18. לשבע כנ״ל שהוצאות לא הי׳ רק לטובות העזבון ולא לטובות עצמו / אכן מאחר
19. שכבר פסקנו כנ״ל שמחויב כמר משה הנ״ל לשלם לכ׳ יוזלי הנ״ל שכר טרחתו על חלקו כפי
20. שישומו הב״ד וכנ״ל לזאת מצאנו שיש בידינו כח לעשות פשר לטענות האלו ומ
21. ומצאנו בזה דרך פשר שינכה כ׳ יוזלי כפי שהעלו בחשבונם סך שלשה מאות ושבעי׳
22. זהו׳ מחמת הוצאות ומזונות הדרך בלי שום שבועה נגד זה פטור כמר משה הנ״ל
23. מן כ׳ יוזלי הנ״ל מלשלם שכר טרחתו מחמת גיבוי חובות ישני׳ הנ״ל אבל על מה שהוציא
24. הוצאות המשפט כסדרן ושלא כסדרן כנ״ל מחויבי׳ האחי׳ לישבע כנ״ל / עוד תבע
25. כמר משה הנ״ל מהאחי׳ הנ״ל אחרי שנמצאו עדיין תחת ידו פאלנישה קליידר שהם עדיין
26. {בעזבון} בשותפות מעזבון אביהם בכן ישבעו האחי׳ שלא לקחו מהם כלום לעצמם
27. והאחי׳ הנ״ל השיבו באשר שבתחילת חלוקת העזבון הי׳ בגדי׳ האלו תחת רשו[ת]ם
28. בחנות של כ׳ משה הנ״ל בכן ישבע כ׳ משה על זה שלא לקח כלום ומצאנו שיכללו האחי׳
29. הנ״ל

רכב ע״ב

1. ב״ה
2. הנ״ל בשבועתם הנ״ל שלא לקחו כלום מן פאלנישה בגדי׳ הנ״ל לעצמם וכ׳ משה הנ״ל יקבל בחרם
3. בפנינו ב״ד שגם הוא לא לקח לעצמו מן פאלנישה בגדי׳ הנ״ל / ולאח״כ יחולק הבגדי׳ הנ״ל

---

1. כמותו

4. על שלשה חלקי׳ ויתן לכ׳ משה הנ״ל שליש חלקו / עוד {תבע}(שאל)[1] כ׳ משה הנ״ל מאחיו הנ״ל אם לא גבו -[2]
5. יותר ממה שנאמר בחשבונם הנ״ל ופורט איזה אנשי׳ בעלי חובות מאביהם ז״ל נימולין
6. ואינו נימולין ששמע מהם ששילמו להם ולא העלו בחשבונם והשיבו האחי׳ על כל אחד ו
7. ואחד רק את זה מצאו בפנקס אביהם שהמה גבו מן המנוח ר׳ ליפמן חזן ז״ל מק״ק וויס⸗
8. ⸗באדן סך מאה ועשרי׳ {זהו׳} ותשעה זהו׳ וזה לא נזכר בחשבן שהוציע לפנינו באשר שאינם
9. יודעי׳ אם כבר גבה כמר משה הנ״ל בעצמו חלק שליש מן ר ליפמן חזן הנ״ל או שהמה שילמו
10. לו חלקו נגד קוויטונג ונאבד הקוויטונג מהם בכן אם כ׳ משה הנ״ל רוצה לקבל בחרם
11. שלא קיבל עדיין חלקו אזי רוצים המה לשלם#[3] כמר משה הנ״ל השיב שלא ידע אם קיבל חלקו
12. מן ר׳ ליפמן חזן הנ״ל רק את זה ידע כ׳ משה הנ״ל על תשלומין מן כ׳ הירץ פלערשהיים ומן
13. כ׳ משה בן ליב שלאס שקבל חלקו המגיע לו∞[4] ומצאנו שיכללו האחי׳ הנ״ל בשבועתם כנ״ל
14. שכדבריהם כן הוא שאינם יודעי׳ אם לא גבה כ משה הנ״ל בעצמו חלקו מן ר׳ ליפמן
15. חזן ואח״כ פטורי׳ המה ליתן לכ׳ משה הנ״ל מחמת תביעות של ר ליפמן חזן הנ״ל
16. ויכללו ג״כ בשבועתם הנ״ל שלא העלימו ולא גבו כלום מחובות הרעי׳ שלא נתחלקה
17. באותו פעם דהיינו בשעת חלוקה ונשארו עדיין בשותפות זולת מה שהעלו
18. והציעו בחשבן ובזה פטורי׳ המה ג״כ מתביעת יאהאן פילה פון געלם הנ״ל
19. #וגם על יאהאן פילה אין געלם השיבו שקבלו הפרעון ממנו וגם שילמו חלק שליש מסך
20. דמי פירעון דך רט דק[5] לכ׳ משה הנ״ל וכתבו ג״כ בתוך הפנקס אביהם ששילמו לו אך
21. אינם יודעי׳ אם קיבלו באותו פעם איין קוויטונג מן כ׳ משה או לאו ובאם כ׳
22. משה רוצה לישבע שלא קיבל רוצי׳ לשלם לו
23. ∞ ומחמת פילה פון געלם השיב שברי לו שלא קיבל חלקו שכל פעם שקבל נתן ק
24. קוויטונג אך הוא אינו רוצה לישבע רק הם ישבעו שנתנו לו כפי מה שאמרו
25. ויהי׳ פטורי׳ על זה (ומצאנו)[6] עוד טען כ׳ משה על הוצאת שהעלו בחשבונום מחמת מרתף על
26. חצי שנה סך ששה זהו׳ מ״ה צל שהוא אינו מחויב לשלם חלקו בזה באשר שגם הוא
27. הי׳ רוצה להחזיק לעצמו אותו מרתף בשכירות להניח בו יינו ולוותר על ידי כך
28. הוצאות לפנות את חלקו יין שקיבל מירושת אביהם למקום אחר והתרצו
29. ה[אחי]ם על זה לפטור אותו מדמי שכירות המרתף הנ״ל והחזיקו לעצמם ה
30. המרתף ב

---

1. תוספת מעל השורה
2. אולי הסופר רצה למלא רווח בסוף השורה.
3. תוספת שתבוא בהמשך (עיין שורה 19)
4. תוספת שתבוא בהמשך (עיין שורה 23)
5. כ צ״ל
6. תוספת מעל השורה

רדג ע"א

1. ב"ה
2. המרתף בשכירות והאחים השיבו על זה להד"ם ומצאנו שיכללנו האחים הנ"ל בשבועתם
3. שכדבריהם כן הוא שלא מחלו מס של מרתף לאחיו כ' משה ולאחר כך רשאים לנכות כמו
4. שהעלו בחשבונם סך מס הנ"ל עוד טען כ' משה הנ"ל על מה שהעלו בחשבונם בשביל מס של
5. החנות סך שמונים וחמשה זהו' שאינו מחויב לשלם רק עד חלוקת הסחורת והאחים השיבו על זה
6. ובירור שזמן של מס הנ"ל לא היה רק עד עת חלוקת העזבון והם תובעים מן כ' משה
7. {הנ"ל} מס מחדר אחד בחנות שהניח כ' משה הנ"ל סחורות שלו בתוכו והחזיק בו לבד לאחר
8. חלוקת העזבון לערך חצי שנה ותובעים ממנו שכירות סך עשרה זהו' וכ' משה הנ"ל הישיב
9. שבשעת חלוקת סחורות נתנו לו חדר ברצונם הטוב ומסרו לו המפתח וכאשר חזר מיריד
10. נומבורג ושכר לעצמו חנות במקום אחר החזיר להם המפתח בכן אין מחויב לשלם
11. להם בשביל החדר האחים הנ"ל הישיבו אמת הדבר שבשעת חלוקה נותנו לו המפתח
12. אכן סמך ליריד ר"ה הי' תובעי' אותו לפנות החדר ולא החזרים להם עד שיהי' מוכר'
13. לילך עמו בערכאות וע"י השררה יר"ה הי' כופין אותו לפנות החדר לאחר שנה חדשה
14. בכן אחר שהחזיק הוא לבדו בחדר מחויב הוא לשלם המה ותובען ממנו סך עשרה
15. זהו' הנ"ל והאריכו בטענותיהם ומצאנו שיכללו האחים הנ"ל בשבועתם כנ"ל
16. שכדבריהם כן הוא שהמה היה תובעים ממנו לפנות החדר והוא עיכבו מל
17. מלהחזירם ולאחר שישבעם האחים על זה ירדנו לשומא במס החדר הנ"ל ומצאנו על
18. דרך פשור דבר שרשאים לנכות עוד סך חמשה זהו' ממה שמחויבי' ליתן לו מן גיבו ח
19. חובות ישיני' שיש תחת ידם עוד תבע כ' משה הנ"ל מהאחים הנ"ל אחרי שהי' לו המשפט
20. עם קהל יצו בשעה שהי' רוצה איין שרייען לאזן אצל השררה יר"ה והי' תובעי' ממנו קהל
21. יצו סך חמשים קארלינר מחמת אביהם ז"ל ואחים הנ"ל אמרו לו שילך בערכאות נגד
22. הקהל יצו וכן עשה והוציא הוצאות המשפט לערך סך עשרים ושלשה רט ד[ג] צל
23. בכן תבע כ' משה הנ"ל מאחיו הנ"ל שני שלישי' מסך הוצאות המשפט הנ"ל / והאחים
24. השיבו להד"ם שהם לא הי' אומרם לשפוט בערכאות נגד הקהל יצו מצאנו שיכללו
25. האחי' הנ"ל בשבועתם כנ"ל שכדבריהם כן הוא שלא אמרו לכמר משה הנ"ל שישפוט
26. עם קהל יצו ולאחר כך הם פטורים מתביעות כ' משה הנ"ל עוד תבע כ' משה
27. הנ"ל מן כ' יוזלי הנ"ל לבד סך ששה עשר זהו' שהלווה לו במעות מזומני' בשעה
28. שהיתה אשת כ' יוזלי יולדת וכ' יוזלי הישב שלא לוה ממנו במזומני' כלום רק שנשאר
29. מחייב דרך שחוק והוא אסמכת' בעלמא ואינו מחויב לשלם / ומצא שכ' יוזלי הנ"ל יכלול
30. בשבועתו שכדבריו כן הוא שלא לוה {ממנו במזומני'} מן כ' משה הנ"ל סך ששה עשר זהו' הנ"ל
31. במעות מזומני' רק נשאר לו חייב דרך שחוק ולאחר כך פטור כ' יוזלי מן כ' משה הנ"ל מחמת
32. תביעות הנ"ל

רדג ע"ב

1. ב"ה
2. עוד טען כ' משה הנ"ל על מה שהעלו האחי' הנ"ל בחשבונם הנ"ל ששילמו לגובי' יצו סך שני מ
3. מאות וחמשי' זהו' שיכתבו האחי' ע"י פנקס הגובי' אם שלמו אותן במעות מזומני' ולא
4. נכו אותם בדמי רווחי' של דבר טוב של המנוח כ' זלמן קולפא ז"ל שגבה אביהם מן ה
5. הגובי' ועוד טען כ"ה פייס הנ"ל והציג לפנינו קוויטונג שיש ביד כ' משה מאחיו ה
6. הנ"ל מן ח חשון תקלז ששילם להם באותו פעם כמה הוצאות שחשבו המה שהוציאו ל
7. לצורך עזבון / בכן טען דרך כלל אותן הוצאות שהעלו עתה בחשבן הרשימה הנ"ל שהם
8. שהם מוקדמי' לח חשון הנ"ל אינו מחויב לשלם שאם הי' אמת כדבריהם למה לא הי'
9. מזכירם ג"כ בחשבן מן ח חשון הנ"ל / והאחי' השיבו שחשבונם מן הוצאות שלהם הם
10. שילמו לאחר ח חשון {הנ"ל} תקלז הנ"ל ומצאנו אחרי שכבר בירוו האחי' לפנינו עי[1] הגובי'
11. יצו ששילמו להם האחי' הנ"ל במעות מזומני' בכן אין בטענות של כ' משה הנ"ל בזה כלום
12. ומה שטוען על הוצאות שהציאו קודם ח חשון תקל"ז אינו מחויב לשלם גם אין בזה ממש
13. עוד טען כ משה הנ"ל שנזכר בתוך הכנסת מחשבונם הנ"ל וזל[2] {באינווייל ר} דען 28
14. דען יולי בשביל חוב פון דער זאנט באינווייל ר וועגין ערקויפטן הויז בשביל א
15. אונזרה פארדרונג אונד זאלכש אידרום אן הערן נעצאללע פרקויפט בעד 357 [*f*]
16. אונד אלזוא פולגנדש הירואיף ערהלטין אחת לאחת נמצא להחשבן יחד סך
17. קפט זהו' וחצי וטען כ"ה פייס הנ"ל שהאחי' הנ"ל מחויבי' לקבל אחריות מן מותרו'
18. דמי מכירה שלא קיבל עדיין העולה על סך קסז זהו' וחצי ושליש מזה מגיע על כ'
19. כ' משה הנ"ל שמחויבי' לשלם לו והאחי' הנ"ל השיבו שאין מחויבי' לשלם לו רק
20. ממה שגבו חלק שליש המגיע ע"ח אבל מה שלא גבו אין מחויבי' לקבל אחריות
21. עליהם באשר שכל מה שה' עושי' הי' לטובת העזבון ובאם לא הי' מוכרו לא הי' ג
22. גובה כלום / מצאנו שהדין עם האחי' ופטורי' מתביעה זו עוד תבע כ' משה הנ"ל
23. מן האחי' הנ"ל שהעלימו מחשבונם סך חמשי' קרלינר אשר הי' מונחי' בנייאשטאט פר קויטציאן
24. מאביהם ז"ל בשביל חוב טרויא מלא[וז]ום והאחי' הנ"ל השיבו שלא העלימו שזה הוא מה
25. שנזכר בחשבונם בתוך הכנסת וז"ל בנייאשטאט ממשפט טרויא חמשה מאות זהו'
26. וטענו שלא הי' מונחי' שם קויטציאהן / רק ר' ליברמן מנייאשטאט הי' ערב בשביל קויטציאהן
27. נגד זה הי' גובה המעות ולאחר יציאות משפט קיבלו האחי' המעות ממנו והעלו בחשבונם
28. כנ"ל ומצאנו שגם בזה אין לכ' משה הנ"ל שום תביעה כלל / עוד טען כ' משה הנ"ל אחרי ש
29. שמונח ביד נ"ה כ"ה הירץ גנץ יצו שטר חוב מן אביהם ז"ל על כ' אנשיל זיכל ששייך לו חלק
30. שליש

---

1. על ידי
2. וזה לשונו

רדד ע״א

1. ב״ה
2. מסך דמי שטר הנ״ל שהניחו המה שלשה אחי׳ הנ״ל אחר פטירת אביהם ז״ל לבטחון לקיים
3. הדבר טוב שקבלו עליהם שלשה אחי׳ הנ״ל על משך עשרי׳ שני׳ ליתן {ל} בכל שנה ביו׳ פ
4. פטירת אביהם ז״ל סך מה לענים וטוען כ׳ משה הנ״ל באשר שהוא הי׳ קיים עד עתה
5. הדבר טוב שקיבל עליו וחולק לענים מכיסו מה שמוטל עליו כמו כן רוצה לקיים עוד
6. עד תשלום עשר׳ שני׳ הנ״ל בכן תבע מאחיו הנ״ל שיוגבה שטר שטרי הנ״ל ויתן
7. לו חלק שליש המגיע לו מסך דמי שטר הנ״ל וכ״ה משה בהרשאת אחי׳ הנ״ל הישב
8. שאינם רוצי׳ לנגוש אשת כ׳ אנשיל זיכל הנ״ל שהיא עזובה מבעלה והוא הי׳ ק
9. קרוב עמהם / ואם כ׳ משה רוצה לנגוש אותה ולגבות ממנה יקח העתק משטר
10. הנ״ל ויגבה חלקו ומצאנו שהברירה ביד האחי׳ הנ״ל אם ירצה האחי׳ ליתן
11. לכ׳ משה הנ״ל העתק מקוים ע״י נ״ה משטר הנ״ל אזי רשות ביד האחי׳ הנ״ל ליקח
12. שטר הנ״ל מן כ״ה הירץ הנ״ל ויכתבו בחתימת ידם על אותו העתק שנתנו ליד כ׳
13. משה נ״ל שגוף השטר יש ביד האחי׳ הנ״ל ושייך לכ׳ משה הנ״ל חלק שליש מסך דמי שטר
14. הנ״ל ויקיימו הנאמני׳ הנ״ל חתימת ידם והוצאות מזה על האחי׳ הנ״ל לבד או
15. אם ירצו האחי׳ הנ״ל יתנו המה גוף השטר הנ״ל ליד כ׳ משה הנ״ל והוא יתן
16. העתק מזה להאחי׳ הנ״ל על אופן הנ״ל ושהוא יכתוב בחתימת ידו ששני שלישי׳ מסך
17. דמי שטר הנ״ל שייך להאחי׳ הנ״ל ושגוף השטר הוא בידו והוצאות מזה יהי׳ אז על
18. כ׳ משה הנ״ל לבד עכ״פ מחויבי׳ כל שלשה אחי׳ הנ״ל לקיים נדרם אשר קיבלו עליהם
19. ליתן כל אחד ואחד לענים בכל שנה ביו׳ פטירת אביהם ז״ל כמו שהתנהגו
20. עד עתה עד כלות זמן עשרי׳ שני׳ מיו׳ פטירת אביהם ז״ל / עוד תבע כ׳
21. כ׳ משה שיש עוד בעזבון אביהם ז״ל חלק רביעית ממקו׳ שלם בע״א העליונה שיומכר
22. ע״פ ב״ד למי שיתן יותר ודמי מכירה יחולק ביניהם ויתן לו השליש המגיע לו וכ״ה
23. משה בהרשאת הנ״ל השיב בתחלה שיומכר לפני ב״ד ואח״כ ח[ו]זר [מ]זה ויאמר ב
24. בהרשאתם שהם נחלת אבותם ואינם רוצי׳ למכור ומצאנו שיהי׳ כן כפי שהתרצו
25. בתחלה שיומכר לפני ב״ד ודמי מכירה יחולק ביניהם / עוד הניחו האחי׳ הנ״ל לפ
26. לפנינו חד בעקכה מחותם וטוען כ׳ משה הנ״ל שהב״ד יפתחו אותו בעקכה {מחותם}
27. ויחלקו בינינו מה שנמצא בתוכה ובפרט שמונח בתוכה ח״כ אחד מן השררה מוועכטרש
28. ⸗באך שהי׳ יכולי׳ לגבות מחוב זה למד למאה / והאחי׳ השיבו שאין יוד[עי׳] כלום מהחוב
29. מוועכסרשבאך

רכד ע״ב

1. ב״ה
2. מוועכטרשבאך רק בתוך הבעקכה יהי׳ מונחי׳ רק אגרת ישני׳ / ומצאנו שלאחר קיום
3. הפס״ד הנ״ל בכל פרט ופרט יבחרו הצדדי׳ הנ״ל שני אמצעי׳ שיפתחו הבעקכה לראו׳
4. מה יהי׳ בתוכה ומה שראוי לחלוקה יחולק ביניהם / ואם אינם יכולי׳ להשוות עצמם
5. אזי יוקב הדין ההר ביניהם / עוד טען כ׳ משה הנ״ל שגם הוא רוצה לזכות בטובות

---

1. כפילות במקור

6. הנאה מדבר טוב {של המנוח} שהניח אחריו אביו זקנו המנוח כ׳ זלמן קולפא ז״ל / והאחי׳
7. השיבו שקהל יצו ימנה אפטרופס תחת אביהם ז״ל / ומצאנו שהאחי׳ הנ״ל יבררו ה
8. הצוואת של כ׳ זלמן קולפא ז״ל הנ״ל לפנינו על אודות הדבר טוב שהניח אחריו היאך
9. יתנהגו ומי יהי׳ אפטרופס עליו ואז יופסק הדין ביניהם / ובאם לא יבררו ימנה ק
10. קהל יצו אפטרופס על הדבר טוב הנ״ל / עוד טען כמר משה הנ״ל שיותן לו כל הפנקסאו׳
11. מאביו ז״ל שיוכל לראות את כל ונוכחת ולפחות יותן לו חלק שליש מהם המגיע לו
12. לצור ע״פ צוואתו / ומצאנו שהפנקסאות נשארו ביד האחי׳ הנ״ל כפי פסק פשר הנ״ל
13. ואחרי שנתקיים כל {הפס״ד} פרטי דברי׳ מפסק דין הנ״ל פטורי׳ ומסולקי׳ האחי׳ הנ״ל
14. מן כ׳ משה הנ״ל וכ׳ משה הנ״ל מן האחי׳ הנ״ל ואין {לזה} להצדדי׳ הנ״ל לא זה על זה ולא
15. זה על זה כלום מכח טענות ותביעות הנ״ל יצא מאתנו יו׳ ה ד א״ש תקנא לפק
16. רנ״מ ורמ״ש ואני

No. 237

Fols. 225a–226b; Wednesday 16 March 1791

The court's previous decision (no. 236) regarding the Sichel brothers evoked a quick response from Yosle and Yudaʾ Sichel. Four days after the decision, the brothers sent their representative to the court to make some clarifications. Wary of taking an oath, the brothers asked to make adjustments to the sums that they were being asked to swear to. Concerned that they had benefited personally from some of the expenses made in collection of the debts, they asked that the total expenses they had claimed — and that they were now to take an oath regarding the accuracy of — be reduced. Similarly, since Yosle was often traveling, it was possible that he had collected some debts and failed to record them. With respect to this sum too, the brothers wished to reduce the amount they were being asked to swear to.

The negotiations over particulars continued on the following day. While the court accepted the request of the brothers to reduce the amounts that they were being asked to confirm through taking an oath, there were other claims that all three brothers withdrew because they did not want to asseverate regarding them. The court was also asked to resolve the matter of how payment to Moses Sichel was to be made. Yosle and Yudaʾ asked to pay a third party who would hold the money until a formal clarification was made regarding certain debts. Moses did not agree to this and it was his view that was accepted by the court.

A postscript noted that within a week after the court gave its decision in these matters Yosle and Yudaʾ sent the funds they owed Moses to the head of the rabbinic court, and the brothers went to the old synagogue and took their oaths. In the following few days the court divided the assets, gave them to each side, and the other rulings of the court were fulfilled.

רדה ע"א

1. ב"ה
2. אחרי שיצא פס"ד מאתנו ב"ד ח"מ י' ה ד' א"ש תקנא העבר בין הני אחי' הו"ה גץ[1] כ'
3. יוזלי זיכל יצו והו"ה כ' יודא זיכל ובין אחיהם הו"ה גת"ת כ' משה זיכל יצו וכבר יצא
4. הדין מאתנו על כל {פרט ופרט} טענות ותביעות שהם להצדדי' הנ"ל זה על זה כ
5. כמבואר שם באר היטיב בתוקף קומפרמיס שחתמו הצדדי' הנ"ל בח"ח ובכל שופרי
6. דשטרי ובקנס סך מסויים חצי לשררה יר"ה וחצי להקדש וביו' ב' העבר ח' א"ש חזר
7. ובא לפנינו התור' כ"ה משה אויך וטוען באשר בפסק דין הנ"ל נאמר שמחויבי' ה
8. האחי' כ' יוזלי וכ"י[2] הנ"ל לישבע על הוצאות כסדרן ושלא כסדרן שהעלו בחשבונם ש
9. שהוציאו בשביל גביות חובות אביהם כמה הוציאו בשביל זה / ע"ז טען כ"ה
10. משה בהרשאת האחי' הנ"ל באשר שאפשר הי' בידם לנכות מן טאקטארום [ב]שכרם
11. מן עשיות שריפטן והם לא הי' מנכוי[3] רק הי' נותני' שכרם משלם כדי שיהי' להם ט
12. טובות הנאה אם יצטרכו להם לטובות עצמם וגם מחמת הוצאות שלא כסדרן
13. ג"כ הי' יכולי' לנכות והמה לא הי' עושי' כן משום שיהי' להם ג"כ טובות הנאה
14. לזה והם רוצי' לצאת ידי שמים לישבע כהוגן / בכן הב"ד ישומו כמה שווה אותן
15. טובות הנאה וכפי השומה רוצי' לנכות מחשבן הוצאה שלהם / עוד טען כ"ה משה
16. הנ"ל שמבואר בפס"ד הנ"ל שמחויבי' האחי' לישבע שלא גבו מחובות הרעי' שלא
17. נתחלקו עדיין זולת אותן שהעלו בחשבונם ע"ז טוען כ"ה משה בהרשאת הנ"ל ב
18. באשר שכ' יוזלי שהי' תמיד על הדרך יוכל להיות שגבו איזה זהו' ונשכח ממנו
19. בכן רוצה לשלם סך ששים זהו' ועל השאר רוצה לשבע כמבואר בפסק הנ"ל / וכמר
20. משה זיכל הנ"ל בעצמו השיב ע"ז מחמת טובות הנאה מחל להם אך הוא טוען שמה
21. ששילם לטאקטארום וגם הוצאות שלא כסדרן נכלל גם בתוכה מחמת הוצאות מ
22. מחובות שלהם שלא שייך בעזבון אביהם ולזה וודאי אינו מחויב ליתן חלקו /
23. וע"ז חזר ובא לפנינו כ"ה משה הנ"ל יו' ג טית א"ש בהרשאת האחי' הנ"ל והשיב
24. שכדי לצאת ידי {שמים} שבועתם בלי ספק רוצי' לנכות מהוצאה שלהם הנ"ל סך
25. תשעי' זהו' / ומצאנו שכה יהי' וכה יקום שרשאי' האחי' הנ"ל לנכות מחשבן הוצאות
26. שלהם

רדה ע"ב

1. ב"ה
2. שלהם סך תשעי' זהו' וסך ששים זהו' כפי מה שטען כ"ה משה הנ"ל בהרשאת שלהם
3. ומחויב האחי' הנ"ל לשבע כמבואר בפסק דין הנ"ל שהוציאו עכ"פ כפי חשבונם

---

1. גבאי צדקה
2. כבוד יודא
3. ר' שורה 13.

4. מחמת הוצאות כסדרן ושלא כסדרן לצורך גביות חובות עזבון אביהם לערך סך
5. חמשה מאות ושלשי' זהו' וגם מחמת השבוע המוטלת עליהם בפס"ד הנ"ל שלא ג
6. גבו מחובות הרעי' זולת מה שהעלו והציע בחשבונם שעדיין מחויבי' ליתן לו ח
7. חלקו שליש ג"כ רשאי' לנכות שלא יהי' בכלל השבוע סך ששי' זהו' שהם ליחד סך
8. מאה רט / ומאחר שכפי חשבונם עולה כל הוצאות שלהם סך שבעה עשר מאות וחמשי'
9. זהו' דא צל בכן ינוכה מזה סך מאה רט ונשאר סך ששה עשר מאות זהו' דאץ[1] / עוד
10. טען כ"ה משה בהרשאת האחי' הנ"ל על מה שנאמר בפס"ד הנ"ל שמחויבי' האחי' ל
11. לשבע מחמת הוצאות שהעלה בחשבונם שהוציא מחמס[2] מס של מרתף סך ששה זהו'
12. מהץ[3] שהאחי' הנ"ל אינם רוצי' לשבע ורוצי' לוותר אותן ששה זהו' מהץ ומצאנו שיהי' כן
13. עוד טען כ"ה משה בהרשאת כ' יוזלי הנ"ל על מה שמוטל עליו בפס"ד הנ"ל שמחויב
14. לשבע על תביעות ששה עשר זהו' שתבע כ' משה הנ"ל ממנו וטוען (עתה)[4] כ"ה משה הנ"ל שכ'
15. יוזלי רוצה להפוך שבוע זו על כ' אחיו כ' משה הנ"ל באשר שכ' משה הנ"ל מחויב לשבע
16. בלא"ה כמבואר בפס"ד הנ"ל בכן ישבע ג"כ ע"ז ורוצה לשלם לו סך ששה עשר זהו' הנ"ל ו
17. וכ' מש"ה הנ"ל השיב שאינה רוצה לישבע שבועה המוטל עליו בפס"ד הנ"ל רק הוא
18. רוצה לשלם לאחיו התביעה לערך מסך ארבעי' זהו' שבא עליו שבוע זו ומחמת ה
19. השבוע של סך ששה עשר זהו' גם ע"ז אינה רוצה לישבע רק הם ישבעו ומצאנו שגם כ' י
20. יוזלי פטור משבוע זו רק כ' יוזלי הנ"ל יקבל בחרם שכדבריו כן הוא מחמת ששה עשר זהו'
21. ויהי' פטור מתביעה הלז וסך ארבעי' זהו' הנ"ל ינכו האחי' ממה שהמה מחויבי' ע
22. עדיין ליתן לכ' משה הנ"ל כפי חשבונם שהציע לפנינו / עוד טען כ"ה משה ב
23. בהרשאת האחי' הנ"ל שהם מוכני' לישבע שבועות המוטלות עליהם בפס"ד הנ"ל
24. בלי עיכוב אך מה שנאמר בפס"ד הנ"ל שמחויבי' האחי' ליתן מה שהעלו בחשבונם
25. שנשאר בידם מגבוי חובות הישני' לאחר ניכוי הוצאות סך שבעה עשר מאות ו
26. וחמשי' זהו' דאץ שמחויבי' האחי' ליתן לכ' משה הנ"ל חלק שליש המגיע לו מזה
27. נגד קוויטונג ע"פ אופן שיסדרו הב"ד אנחנו ח"מ ע"ז טוען כ"ה משה בהרשאת
28. הנ"ל

רדו ע"א

1. ב"ה
2. שהם רוצי' ליתן המעות הנ"ל ביד שליש עד שנעשה עקסטראקט מחובות הרעי' כמבואר
3. בפס"ד הנ"ל שהוא רק זמן קצר כדי שלאח"כ יסדרו הב"ד הפטורי' על כל קיום ה
4. הפס"ד בכל פרטות שלא יכול לתבוע אח"כ כ' משה מחמת עשיות עקסטראקט
5. והתור' נ"ה כ"ה פייס הענא סג"ל בהרשאת כ' משה זיכל הנ"ל השיב שהאחי' הנ"ל ישבעו
6. שבועות המוטלת עליהם מיד בלי עיכוב / וגם המעות הנ"ל מה שמחויבי' ליתן לו
7. כפי חשבונם וכפי פסק דין הנ"ל יתן לו ג"כ מיד בלי עיכוב ומכ"ש שהם עצמם

---

1. כ"א צ"ל
2. ר"ל 'מחמת'
3. מ"ה צ"ל
4. תוספת מעל השורה

8. מודי' שהם מחויבי' ליתן לו כל כך והוא אינו מחויב ליתן מעות ביד שליש ו
9. ולהמתין עד שנעשו עקסטראקט והוא אינו רוצה לעכב שום זמן מלעשות עקסטרא
10. ⸗קט והב"ד יקבעו לו זמן ע"ז ובאם יתרשל בזמן הזה שיהי' אחיו פטורי' עוד מליתן
11. ובלבד שלא יעכבו האחי' בשום אופן / והעתק עקסטראקט מפנקס יהי' באופן זה
12. שצריכי' האחי' להניח עקסטראקטין שלהם המחותם בחתימת יד הנ[א]מני' מכל חובו'
13. אביהם שעלו על חלקם כדי שנדע ע"י כך איזה הם חובות הרעי' שנשאר בפנקס ש
14. שלא נתחלק עדיין ולא גבו האחי' עדיין והאחי' השיבו ע"ז שאינם מחויבי' ואינם
15. רוצי' לעשות כן רק את זה מרוצי' לעשות שרוצי' להראות לו רק עשרה בעלי חובות
16. מחובות שעלו על חלקם ואח"כ רשאי הוא להעתק כל חובות שבפנקס והאריכו בטענותי'
17. ומצאנו שהאחי' הנ"ל מחויבי' ליתן המעות מיד בלי עיכוב דהיינו מה שעלה על
18. חלקו כפי חשבונם וכפי פס"ד הראשון ושני הלז שירדונו לחשבן ועלה לפי מה
19. שחשבנו סך ששה מאות וחמשה עשר זהו' מבע[1] וסך הנ"ל מחויבי' ליתן מיד נגד ק
20. קוויטונג מן כ' משה הנ"ל שקיבל סך הנ"ל (מהם)[2] כפי שיסדרו הב"ד לשון קוויטונג גם מחויבי'
21. האחי' הנ"ל לשבע מיד שבועות המוטלת עליהם כפי פס"ד / ולאחר שישבעו כנ"ל
22. יסדרו הב"ד אנחנו ח"מ בפרוטרוט כל שמות האנשי' בעלי חובות שגבו מהם האחי'
23. כפי הסך ורשימה שהציע לפנינו ויותן ביד האחי' הנ"ל לראי' שאין לכ' משה הנ"ל עוד
24. תביעה על האחי' הנ"ל בשביל זה / ומחמת סידור ועשיות עקסטראקט מחובות הרעי'
25. מצאנו שאין בידינו כח לחייב האחי' להראות לכ' משה שני עקסטראקטין משני חלקי'
26. חובות שלהם שהם מחותם בח"י הנאמני' / אך את זה מצאנו אם אינם רוצי' האחי'
27. הנ"ל להראות שני עקסטראקטין שלהם הנ"ל אזי מחויבי' לשבע ע"ד המקו' ב"ה וע"ד ב"ד בלי
28. עו"מ ובלי שום הוראות היתר שבעולם שרוצי' להראות [מ]פנקס כל חובות הרעי' שעדיין
29. לא נגבו

רכו ע"ב

1. ב"ה
2. עדיין לא נגבו גם ח"כ וח"מ מחובות הרעי' אם יש עדיין בידם ושלא יעלימו שום
3. חובות הרעי' ומחמת מה שטענו האחי' שכ' משה הנ"ל יעכב אותם בכתיבת עקסטראקטן
4. מצאנו {שאל} שלאחר קיום הפס"ד הנ"ל מנתינות המעות ומהשבועות המוטל עליהם לקיים
5. מיד כנ"ל יש לו זמן לעשיות עקסטראקט הנ"ל מהיו' עד שלשי' יו' לאחר יריד לייפסיגה
6. הסמוך הבע"ל / ובאם יתרשל כ' משה הנ"ל מלעשות עקסטראקט אזי לאחר זמן פטורי'
7. המה מליתן לו שום עקסטראקט אכן שלא יהי' העיכוב מהאחי' הנ"ל בשום אופן / וכל
8. הנ"ל נזדקקנו ופסקנו עפ"י תוקף קומפרמיס שיש בידינו שעדיין לא יצא מכחו עד
9. אשר יקיים כל צד מהנ"ל כפי פס"ד הראשון וכפי פס"ד הלז וכל צד שיעבור
10. ע"ז הוא נלכד בחומר קומפרמיס הנ"ל ובקנס הנאמר שם יצא מאתנו יו' ד יוד א"ש תקנ"[א]

---

1. מ"ב צ"ל
2. תוספת מעל השורה

11. רנ"מ ורמ"ש ואני
12. יו' ד י[ט] א"ש תקנא שלחו האחי' הנ"ל סך מעות הנ"ל ששה מאות וחמשה עשר זהו'
13. עוד ששה עשר זהו' מחמת תביעות של כ' משה הנ"ל מן כ' יוזלי שהלווה לו וכמבואר בפס"ד
14. הראשון ליד רב"ד מה' נתן מז נר' ליתן ליד כ' משה הנ"ל ג
15. גם נשבעו האחי' הנ"ל ביו' ד' במעמדי ובמעמד השמש כ"ה דוד ש"ש יצו בבהכ"י
16. כנהוג על הוצאות כסדרן ושלא כסדרן ועל פאלנישה קליידר ועל גביות חוב
17. מן ר' ליפמן חזן ועל שלא העלימו שאר גביות חובות הרעי' ועל הוצאות משפט
18. עם קהל הכל כפי שמוטלת עליהם בפס"ד ראשון {ושני} הנ"ל ומחמת שארי שבוע'
19. שבועות שילמו מה שעליהם
20. וגם כ' משה הנ"ל קיבל בחרם בפנינו ב"ד מחמת פאלנישה קליידר כפי המוטל עליו
21. ובי' ה שלאחריו ד[1] א"ש חלקנו אני והדיין ר מאיר שיף נר' דיא פאלנישה קליידר
22. ביניהם ע"פ גורל וקיבל כל אחד חלקו גם קיבל כ' משה הנ"ל דיא קישט טעה הנאמר
23. בכתב פשר הנ"ל גם פתחנו בריצוי הצדדי' הנ"ל במעמד ר' פייס הענא הנ"ל
24. ובמעמד הבחור כ' איצק הילסהיים שרייבר אצל האחי' הנ"ל הפעקכה וגם השאכטל
25. מחותם הנאמר בפס"ד הראשון {ואיזה}(ושני)[2] חובות שמצאנו בתוכה [א]חד מנהון על השררה
26. מן וועכטרשבאך מסך חמשה מאות זהו' וחד מסך ד' מאות ועשרי' וארבעה זהו'
27. וביו' א דא א"ש תקנא סדרנו אצל הרב"ד מה' נתן מז נר' (על השררה מן גיטרן)[3] הקוויטונג משמת ב"ח כ
28. כמבואר בפס"ד ראשון ושני הנ"ל שחתם עצמו כ' משה הנ"ל וקיבל המעות הנ"ל
29. והב"ד הנ"ל קיימו חתימתו

No. 238

Fols. 227a–b; Thursday 1 December 1791

Miriam, widow of Moses Rothschild Buseck, had two grandchildren from her son, Leb, who predeceased her.[4] In a will written in late 1781 she stipulated that her granddaughter and Leb's daughter, Shinka, should receive 1,000 reichstalers as an inheritance. However, Miriam's estate did not have sufficient assets to pay

1. כ' אדר שני חל בשבת באותה השנה; ר' גם שורה 27.
2. תיקון מעל השורה
3. תוספת מעל השורה
4. Moses Rothschild Buseck died in 1765 (Horovitz, no. 3214), Leb in 1775 (no. 3533), Leb's wife, Kele in 1781 (Ettlinger, 11.2.1781), and Miriam in August 1791 (10.8.1791). Leb and Kele had a number of other children who had either predeceased them or died soon after them (see Ettlinger, 22.7.1775).

Shinka this sum. To insure that Shinka received the maximum amount possible, an executor of the estate approached the court and asked that it transfer some of Miriam's liabilities to her grandson, Shinka's brother Isaac. The request focused on an obligation that Miriam, her son Leb, and his late wife Kele had made to Merle Braunschweig during their lifetimes. The executor argued that since Leb and his wife had been part of this obligation to Merle Braunschweig, their share in the obligation should pass on to their son who inherited from them. The executor also maintained that a loan Miriam had taken from the community should be paid in part by Isaac, because he and his mother had benefited from it while Shinka had not. In addition, he argued that Shinka should have some rights to the familial house. All these strategies were intended to increase the amount Shinka could receive from her grandmother's estate.

After Isaac agreed to be bound by the court's compromise, it was decided to take the assets of Miriam and her deceased daughter-in-law, pay off the debts, and give Isaac two-thirds and Shinka one-third of what remained. Shinka would receive a portion of her inheritance immediately and the rest only when she married. In the meantime, Isaac would enjoy the income from the funds earmarked for Shinka.

רדז ע"א

1. ב"ה
2. הן הקריב לפנינו ה"ה הו"ה התורני גע'[1] כ"ה ליב האמיל סג"ל ואמר
3. שהוא נבחר לאפטרופס מן האשה המונחת מ' מרים אל' המנוח כ"ה
4. משה רויט שילד פוסיק בצוואה שלה ט כסליו תקמ"ב על נכדי'
5. היתומי' כ' איצק ואחותו מ' שינכה בני המנוח כ"ה ליב פסוק ז"ל
6. וטוען כ"ה ליב הנ"ל לזכות היתומה מ' שינכה הנ"ל על אודות ש
7. שאם זקנת' מ' מרים ז"ל הנ"ל צוות' בצוואה שלה (שלאחר)[2] שנתפרע מ
8. מעזבונה להאלופי' גובי' יצו ושאר חוב' שהית' חייבת יותן
9. מעזבונה סך אלף רט לנכדה מ' שינכה הנ"ל גם עשת' ק"ס ע"ז
10. בחיוב גמור להאפטרופסים שלהם סך אלף רט בשביל היתומה הנ"ל
11. ובאשר שלא הניח אחרי' רק איזה מאות זהו' מדמי מטלטלין שנמכר
12. ועוד חצי בית צום גולדן בערן נגד זה מוטל על עזבונה לשלם ל
13. להאלופי' קציני' גובי' יצו לערך סך שני אלפי זהו' ועוד דמי שט"ח
14. ליורשי המונחת מ' מערלה{ב.} (ברונשוויג)[3] העולה קרן ורווחי' יותר משני מאות קרלינר
15. בכן טוען כ"ה ליב הנ"ל אם כל {..} החובות הנ"ל מוטל על עזבון האשה
16. מ' מרים לבד לא נשאר לשלם ליתומה מ' שינכה את שט"ח מסך אלף רט

---

1. גבאי צדקה
2. תוספת מעל השורה
3. תיקון בצד הימני של השורה

17. הנ"ל בכן [י]כ[י]רוי הב"ד באשר בתוך שט"ח הנ"ל מן האשה מ' מערלה
18. נאמר החיוב ג"כ על אם ואבי של היתומי' ונאמר שם בזה הלשון
19. זכרון עדות וכו' איך שבאו לפנינו היקרה מ' מרים אל' הנ"ל וכלתה
20. מ' קילה והדר בעלה בנה כ"ה ליב בן הר"ר משה ז"ל הנ"ל ואמרו לנו
21. הוו עלי' עדים וקנו מכל אחת ואחד מאתנו בק"ג א"ס מעכשיו וכתבו
22. וכו' איך אמת הוא שקבלנו מן האשה מ' מערלה תי' סך מאה {וחמש}
23. וחמשי' קרלינר וכו' ועל הסך דמי חוב קרן ורווחי' הנ"ל שעבדנו א
24. אנחנו מ' מרים וכלת' מ' קילה וה"ב בנה כ"ה ליב הנ"ל את החצי {בית}
25. מהבית שלם צום גולדן בערן דהיינו החצי ההוא אשר לא הוכנס
26. לנדן כ"ה ליב הנ"ל עכ"ל בכן חל חיוב מדמי שטר חוב גם (על)[2] אמם ואב{יה}
27. של היתומי' הנ"ל ובאשר שיתום כ' איצק הנ"ל יורש החצי בית
28. האחרת מהבית שלם הנ"ל שהניח אמו אחרי' בכן גם עליו מוטל לשלם
29. שט"ח הנ"ל לא מיבעי' בד[מ]י' הקרן ורווחי' מה שיש עדיין לשלם ליורשי'
30. מ' מערלה הנ"ל אלא אף גם ברווחי' ששילמה כבר האשה מ' מרים ז"ל
31. בעודה בחיים חיותה גם בזה מחויב היתום כ' איצק לשלם חלקו ועי"כ
32. נשאר עוד מותרות בחצי בית שהניח אחרי' האשה מ'

רדז ע"ב

1. ב"ה
2. מ' מרים ז"ל {לשלם} לשלם דמי שט"ח לנכדה מ' שינכה הנ"ל וטוען עוד
3. שגם החוב להאלופי' גובי' יצו מחויב ג"כ כ' איצק לשלם באשר שהחוב
4. הוא מקצת מחמת מה שלות' האשה מ' מרים על רווחים מהאלופי' גובי יצו
5. לצורך פרנסה ובאשר שהיתום כ' איצק הנ"ל ואמו הנ"ל הי' סמך על
6. שולחן אם זקנתו ז"ל הנ"ל והי' להם מזונות ממנה אבל לא אחות מ'
7. שינכה שלא הי' צריכה למזונותי' ממנה בכן גם הוא יסייע בפירעון ה
8. החוב לגובי' כדי שישאר מותרת בחצי בית שהניח אחרי מ' מרים לשלם
9. שט"ח ליתומה מ' שינכה הנ"ל / ועוד טוען כ"ה ליב הנ"ל שיכירו הב"ד
10. אם אינה מגיע לה עכ"פ בחצי בית שירש אחי' כ' איצק הנ"ל מ
11. {מאבותיהם} (מאמו)[3] עישור נכסי והאריך בטענותיו כה"ל[4] הנ"ל לטובת היתומה
12. מ' שינכה הנ"ל ובאשר שהאפטרופסי' ה"ה הו"ה כה"ל הנ"ל שנתמנה
13. כעת מהקהל יץ[5] על היתום והיתומה הנ"ל עם הו"ה כ' איצק בהו"ה כ'
14. גדלי' שטיבל גם הו"ה כ' אברהם רייז שנתמנה בצוואה של האשה
15. מ' מרים ט' כסליו תקמ"ב כולם נתנו עיניהם על הב"ד לפקח בעסקי
16. היתומי הנ"ל ולפשר ביניהם גם היתום כ' איצק הנ"ל בעצמו בא

---

1. ר' דף רכז ע"ב, שורה 9.
2. תוספת מעל השורה
3. תיקון מעל השורה
4. כבוד הרב ליב
5. ישמרה צורה

17. לפנינו וקיבל עליו לקיים הפשר שיצא מאתנו ונזדקקנו להם ואחרי'
18. שהי' למראה עינינו גוף השט"ח הנ"ל מן האשה מ' מערלה ב"ש[1] ז"ל ודקדקנו
19. הדק היטיב וגם בטענות כ"ה ליב הנ"ל מצאנו (מקצת)[2] ע"ד פשר לטובת שני
20. יתומי' הנ"ל שלאחר שנתפרע כל החובת המוטל על עזבון האשה
21. מ' מרים וכלתה מ' {מרים}(קילה)[3] ז"ל יחשבו האפטרופסי' דמי שווים של ה
22. העזבונות הנ"ל כפי שווי'{...}(עכשיו)[4] בעת הזאת / ומזה יהי['] שני ש
23. שלישי' להיתום כ' איצק הנ"ל ושליש אחד להיתומה מ' שינכה הנ"ל
24. ומהשליש של יתומה יהי' לה מעכשיו חמשי' קרלינר והפירות מזה יהי'
25. שלה מעכשיו והמותר עד תשלום שליש הנ"ל יותן לה לעת שתגיע
26. לנשואין והפירות מהמותר מעכשיו עד עת נשואין שייך להיות'
27. כ' איצק הנ"ל יצא מאתנו יו' ה' ה' כסליו תקנ"ב הגאון אב"ד ורנ"מ
28. ורמ"ש ואני

No. 239

Fol. 228a; Late October or November 1791

Rabbi Gundersheim noted that he was at a *ḥaliẓah* ceremony between Leb Stiebel and Gelche, widow of Tevele Stiebel, Leb's brother. Gelche was widowed on 30 June 1791.[5]

רדח ע"א
1. ב"ה
2. בחדש מרחשון תקנ"ב הייתי אצל סידור חליצה היבמה מ' געלכה (אל' כ' טעבלי ז"ל)[6] שטיבל מן היבום
3. הב"ח כ' ליב שטיבל שהוא אחי הגדול מן הנעדר רנ"מ רא"ט רזט[7] רמ"ש ואני

1. ברונשוויג
2. תוספת מעל השורה
3. תיקון מעל השורה
4. תיקון מעל השורה
5. See Horovitz, no. 4062.
6. תוספת מעל השורה
7. רב זנוויל טראך

No. 240

Fol. 228a; Tuesday evening, 10 January 1792

A servant in the community, Feis Kohl, and his son, Benedit, came before the court to request that it discredit unspecified but unfavorable rumors that had circulated about Benedit as a result of testimony that is not recorded in this record. The Kohls did not have legal representation. The court, composed of seven members rather than the usual three, declined to do so.

4. ————
5. ע"ד שבא לפנינו כ' פייס קהל משרת ובנו (כ' בענדיט)[1] וביקשו מאתנו ב"ד להעביר
6. קול השמועה לא טובה אשר יצא על בן של כ"מ פייס הנ"ל ע"י גביות
7. עדות ואחר אסיפה הג[2] אב"ד נר' ושני ב"ד יצו הסכמנו יחד
8. שאין להזדקק בדבר זה מכמה טעמי' כמוסי' יצא מאתנו אור ליו'
9. ד טז טבת תקנ"ב הגאב"ד נר' {ונ} ורנ"מ רא"ט רז"ט רמ"ש ואני ורמ"ש[3]

No. 241

Fol. 228a; Monday evening, 9 January 1792

A record of the community's sale of a seat in the women's section of the synagogue to Model Schuster. The seat, which was currently being used by the wife of Ḥayyim Stiebel, was sold for 441 guldens after the customary public announcement of sale.

10. אור ליו' גימל טו טבת (תקנ"ב)[4] מכרנו אחר הכרזה כנהוג מקו' שלם בע"נ{.}
11. התיכונה אשר {הי'} עומדות עלי' כעת אשת כ' חיים בהמנוח[5] כ' יוסף
12. שטיבל ז"ל והי' שייך להאלופי' גובי' יצו לה"ה כ' מאדל ב"כ שמואל
13. שוסטר כץ בעד סך ארבעה מאות וארבעי' ואחד זהו' לשלם אין
14. קונפונטציאהנש מינץ אויף דעם ך"ד זהו' פוס כפי תיקון הקהלה
15. רנ"מ ורמ"ש ואני

---

1. תוספת מעל השורה
2. הגאון
3. ר' לעיל, מס' 231 הערה 5.
4. תוספת מעל השורה
5. בן המנוח

No. 242

Gutle, widow of Benedit Schames[1] *v. Schames*

Fols. 228b–230b; (Sunday 15) January 1792[2]

(also see no. 243)

Benedit Schames passed away in 1791 without children, leaving his wife, Gutle, to undergo the *ḥaliẓah* ceremony with his brother, Ber (see no. 244).[3] Before the ceremony took place, Gutle made a number of claims against Ber and also against her late husband's estate. Through her legal representative, Gutle asked the court that Ber deposit 5,000 guldens with a third party to cover her marriage contract and other obligations. The request to deposit the funds with a third party was to insure that she could access the funds immediately after the *ḥaliẓah* ceremony. Ber had no objection to the request, but asked that he be considered the owner of the funds while they remained with the third party. Moreover, Ber wanted Gutle to be required to deposit the contracts that served as the basis of her claims against the estate with the third party.

The court gave Ber until the following Thursday to deposit the funds with the third party and ordered Gutle to deposit the contracts as well. No mention is made of a ruling with respect to ownership of the funds while they were in the hands of the third party. The court did, however, threaten Ber with having to support his sister-in-law if he delayed in depositing the funds as ordered.

Gutle also claimed support from Ber for the previous two weeks. Ber countered, saying that he had been ready to pay her what she was due and perform *ḥaliẓah* for the past two weeks and, if anything, she should be paying him money because he had supported her since his brother's death and had, in fact, overpaid her, a claim sustained by the court. Gutle also claimed that during her husband's lifetime she had been forced to take out a number of loans to pay for household expenses because her husband did not give her enough money. She now asked that her husband's estate pay off these loans. Ber, through his counsel, challenged these assertions, especially since his brother was relatively well-off and would have given her what she needed. In addition, Ber countered that Gutle may have taken such loans for her own needs, and also charged that she had taken assets belonging to

---

1. In this record her name appears as "Gitle" but in the next record (no. 243) she is referred to as "Gutle." The Frankfurt *Memorbuch* records that she was known as "Gutle" and therefore this has been used here.
2. With respect to the date, see the note at the beginning of no. 243.
3. Benedit Schames died on 22 September 1791 (Horovitz, no. 4064).

the estate which he wanted back. The court ordered Ber to swear that his claims were true. If he did so, the estate would owe Gutle nothing. She would also have to take an oath that she had not taken anything from the estate.

The court was asked to deal with a number of questions regarding what Gutle could and could not claim from the estate, including items that she maintained were her father's and had been inherited by her late husband (see no. 243). Gutle also asked the court to decide which household items she would have use of. Her husband had promised her that she would be provided for according to her station in life, and she now claimed that she had no silver household items as her station in life demanded. The court agreed with Gutle and ordered Ber to provide her with funds to purchase the appropriate silverware (see no. 243; silverware from the estate had been seized by the non-Jewish authorities). All the items that Ber was to provide her with were to return to the estate should Gutle remarry or die.

The question of who should pay taxes and repairs on the house she was living in was also addressed.

רקח ע"ב

ב"ה

ע"ד טענות והפרשות שיש בין האשה מ' גיטלה אל' המנוח כ' בענדיט שמש ז"ל ובין גיס[!] הו"ה כ' פער שמש בענין עזבון (בעלה ז"ל הנ"ל)[1] / ובא התורני כה בענדיט העניא סג"ל בהרשאות אל' {המנוח} הנ"ל / וה"ה התורני כה משה אויך בהרשאות כ' פער הנ"ל / וגם כ' פער הנ"ל בעצמו הי' לפנינו / והאריכו בטענותיהם כמבואר בק"ה המונח לפנינו / ולאחר שחתמו עצמם הצדדי' הנ"ל בתוקף קומפרמיס בח"ח ובקנס סך מסויים חצי לשררה ירה[2] וחצי להקדש לאשר ולקיים הפס"ד שיצא מאתנו ב"ד ח"מ נזדקקנו להם ולאחר שעיינו הדק היטיב בשטרות של האל' הנ"ל ובטענו זה מול זה מצאנו על כל פרט ופרט כמבואר / והיינו מחמת מה שתבע כה בענדיט הנ"ל בהרשאות האל' הנ"ל שיניח כ' פער הנ"ל תיכוף מעזבון בעלה סך חמשת אלפי' זהו' דמי כתובת ותוספת וירושת שלה כמבואר בשטרות שהציע לפנינו ויניח סך הנ"ל ביד שליש כדי שתוכל האל' הנ"ל לגבותם תיכף ומיד אחר חליצה / וה"ה כה משה הנ"ל בהרשאות הנ"ל השיב שהמעות דמי שטרות הנ"ל מוכן בידו וגם הוא מוכן לחליצה ואם יכירו הב"ד שמחויב להניח קודם חליצה מרוצה בכך רק שיונח על חזקה שלו וגם האל' תניח ג"כ השטרות ביד שליש אצל המעות ומצאנו שמחויב כ' פער הנ"ל להניח דמי שטרות הנ"ל מעזבון אחיו ז"ל הנ"ל ביד שליש ולא יאוחר מיר' {ד}ה הבע"ל / וגם

1. תוספת מעל השורה
2. ירום הודו

האל׳ תניח השטרות הנ״ל ביד אותו שליש ויהי׳ השליש איש מאומד ובטוח המרוצה לשניהם / ואם הצדדי׳ הנ״ל אינם יכולים להשוות עצמם מי יהי׳ השליש אזי יבחרו אנחנו בד חמ[1] מי יהי׳ השליש / ואם יעכב כ׳ פער הנ״ל מלהניח המעות הנ״ל מיו׳ [ד][2] ואילך או מעכב מליתן חליצה / אזי מחויב כ׳ פער הנ״ל ליתן להאל׳ הנ״ל משך ימי עיכובו דמי מזונות כפי שישומו הב״ד ולאחר החליצה יתן השליש הנ״ל סך הנ״ל להאל׳ הנ״ל ושטרות ליד כ׳ פער הנ״ל / ומה שתבע כ״ה בענדיט הנ״ל דמי מזונת מעזבון בעלה מן יו׳ א ויו טבת העבר

רדט ע״א

ב״ה

העבר / עד לאחר גמר המשפט והחליצה אחרי שפסק כ׳ פער הנ״ל מליתן לה עוד מאותו יו׳ הנ״ל וכה משה הנ״ל השיב אחרי שכבר הי׳ טוען שכ״פ[3] הנ״ל הי׳ מוכן לחליצה וגם דמי שטרות מוכן בידו ליתן לה שוב אינו צריך ליתן לה דמי מזונות והוא תבע להיפוך שינוכה ממה שמגיע לה דמי מזונות שנתן לה ממיתת בעלה עד יו׳ הנ״ל יותר מן הראוי לה / ומצאנו שאין להאל׳ הנ״ל על כ׳ פער הנ״ל שום תביעה מחמת זה וכן להיפוך לכ׳ פער הנ״ל על האל׳ הנ״ל בשביל דמי מזונות וכנ״ל עוד תבע כה בענדיט הנ״ל שבעלה ז״ל לא הי׳ נתן בחיי חיותו לאל׳ הנ״ל כדי צרכה מה שהיתה צריכה להוצאת צרכי הבית ומזונות לבני ביתו והיתה מוכרחת ללות מאחרים להוצאות הבית ומזונות וכמו שהציע רשימה לפנינו דמי הלוואה שלותה מאחירם {להוצאות} הנפרטים בשמם העולה לערך סך מאה ועשרי׳ ושמונה זהו׳ שהיא עדיין חייבת להם בכן תבע סך הנ״ל מעזבון בעלה מלבד דמי שטרות הנ״ל עוד טען שהיתה מוכרחת ג״כ למכור לצורך מזונות כנ״ל ממלבושי׳ שני כלה בגדי׳ בכן תבע כה בענדיט הנ״ל שגם דמי מלבושי׳ ישולם להאל׳ הנ״ל מעזבון בעלה ז״ל / וכה משה השיב שמסתמא אם היתה נצרכה למעות לצורך אנשי ביתה הי׳ נותן לה שהי׳ איש מאומד ויוכל להיות מה שלותה מאחרים הוצאה לצורך עצמה למותרת לעשות לה מלבושי׳ חשובי׳ יותר מן הראוי / או לשאר מותרת / אדרבה הוא תובעה וטוען שהי׳ מושלת בכל אשר יש לו וטוען בברי שכמה תכשיט׳ שהעלימה מביתה והפקידה ביד אחר ותובע איין זהו׳ אוהר עכ״פ אינו מגיע לה כלום מעזבון בעלה הן דמי

---

1. בית דין חתומי מטה
2. כנראה שלא תיקן (ר׳ לעיל שורה 19) וכן בדף רל ע״ב שורה 1.
3. שכבוד פער

26. הלוואה

רדט ע״ב

1. הלוואה שלותה / והן דמי בגדי׳ שמכרה / ומצאנו שכ׳ פער הנ״ל
2. יקבל בחרם בפנינו ב״ד או שלא ידע שהאל׳ הנ״ל לותה ומכרה בגדי׳
3. לצורך מזונות בחיי׳ בעלה או אם ידוע לו שלותה לצורך מזונות יקבל
4. בחרם שלא ידע שלא שילם לו בעלה מה שלותה / או אם ירצה ישבע כ׳
5. פער הנ״ל שידע בוודאי שהיא העלימה מנכסי בעלה כל כך
6. שעולה לדמי תביעתה כנ״ל ולאחר שקיבל כ׳ פער הנ״ל בחרם
7. או שנשבע כנ״ל שוב אין להאל׳ הנ״ל על עזבון בעלה שום תביעה
8. כנ״ל אכן אותו [שוא]באַך [או]הר שנרשם על רשימה ששייך לעזבון
9. בעלה והיא נתנה למשכון אצל משרת בעד ארבעה זהו׳ שלותה
10. ממנו מצאנו שהאל׳ הנ״ל אינה מחויבת לפדות אותה ממעות
11. שלה רק מעזבון בעלה ז״ל ומה שתבע כה בענדיט טבעת
12. קדושין וסבלונת ומתנות כלי כסף וטבעת שנתן לה בעלה
13. אחר מיתת אמו ז״ל מצאנו שאין לה תביע על עזבון בעלה גם
14. מה שהוציא׳ בשביל תיקון שטרות שלה וגם הוצאת לפתוח חותם
15. השררה ירה׳[1] ולהוציא איזה מלבושי׳ מצאנו שאין לה תביעה בשביל
16. טענות אלו על עזבון בעלה ז״ל ומה שתבע כה בענדיט הנ״ל מעזבון
17. בעלה כפי רשימה שהניח לפנינו כלים מכסף שירשה מאביה
18. והמה בתוך עזבון בעלה וגם איין כסף קימפכה שקיבל למתנה
19. איין ווארף ועוד איין שוויץ בעכיר אונד חרוסת שיסלכה
20. ממשפחתה / וטוען שהמה נמצאים בתוך עזבון בעלה ז״ל בעין
21. וכ״ה משה הנ״ל השיב שסומך עצמו על השטרות ושיעיין הב״ד
22. בתוכה ושם לא נאמר כלום מכסף שמגיע לה רק סך חמשת
23. אלפי׳ וגם אינו מאמין לה שקיבל בעלה כסף בירושה או למתנה
24. איין ווארף הנ״ל ומצאנו שכ׳ פער הנ״ל יקבל בחרם בפנינו ב״ד
25. שאינו ידוע לו כלל מכסף ירושה ומן מתנות איין ווארף הנ״ל
26. שקיבל

רל ע״א

1. שקיבל אחיו ז״ל או אם ידוע לו שקיבל כסף בירושה יקבל בחרם שאינו
2. ידוע לו שלא נכלל דמי ירושת כסף בדמי חמשת אלפי׳ זהו׳ שנזכר בשטרות
3. או אם ירצה כ׳ פער הנ״ל ישבע שידוע לו בוודאי שהעלימו האל׳ כל כך
4. שעולה לדמי כסף ירושה שנרשם ברשימה וגם לדמי איין ווארף הנ״ל
5. ולאחר שקיבל כ׳ פער הנ״ל בחרם כנ״ל או שנשבע כנ״ל שוב אין להאל׳ הנ״ל
6. שום תביע׳ בעזבון בעלה מחמת ירושה כסף ומתנות איין ווארף הנ״ל
7. הנ״ל / ומה שתבע כה בענדיט הנ״ל שיכירו הב״ד על מי לשלם דמי

---

1. ירום הודו

קרונדצונץ ובדק הבית מחצי בית שדרה בו האל׳ במיגר אל׳ מכח צוואת בעלה ז״ל ומצאנו מדמי בדק הבית אינה מחויבת האל׳ לשלם רק כפי המנהג מה שמחויב השוכר לשלם ומדמי קרונדצונץ מחויבת האל׳ לשלם רק חלק שליש עוד תבע כה בענדיט הנ״ל שיכירו הב״ד מה שמגיע לה מעזבון בעלה כלי בית לתשמישה לפ״כ במיגר אל׳ כמבואר בצוואת בעלה שיותן לה והציע לפנינו רשימה מכלי בית שיש תחת ידה מעזבון בעלה וטוען שאינה לפ״כ בכלי הבית שנרשם ברשימה לבד ותבע עוד בעטונג לייל טיכר טיש⸗טיכר האנד צווילן נוסף לזה על מה שיש כבר תחת ידה כפי רשימה וכלי כסף אין בידה מאומה בכן יכירו הב״ד מה שמחויבם שיתן לה / ומצאנו שכל מה שנרשם בתוך אינפוטאריום שהניחה ביד הגאון אב״ד נרו׳[1] בשעה שנשבעת עליו תהי׳ בידה למיגר אל׳ זולת איין קאמיזאהל וכסף אוהר שנרשם ברשימה מחויבת להחזיר וזולת כלי הבית הנרשמים ברשימה אינו מחויב ליתן לה עוד שום כלי תשמיש / ומחמת כלי כסף (יותן לה)[2] כפי הרשימה מאתנו ב״ד ומאחר שאין יכולים ליתן לה כסף מעזבון בעלה ז״ל שמחותם בחתימת השררה יר״ה בכן מחויב לקנות כפי רשימה הנ״ל ומחויב כ׳ פער הנ״ל

רל ע״ב

להניח הכלי כסף הנ״ל למיגר אל׳ ביד השליש הנ״ל ביו׳ ד הבע״ל עם סך חמשת אלפי׳ זהו׳ הנ״ל ואם לא ימצא לקנות תוך זמן הנ״ל יניח ביד השליש סך שני מאות זהו׳ נוסף על חמשת אלפי׳ זהו׳ לבטחון שיקנה תוך זמן שלשים יו׳ אחר חליצה כלי כסף הנ״ל ובאם לא {יקצה} יקנה כ׳ פער הנ״ל תוך זמן שלושי׳ יו׳ אחר חליצה אזי יתן השליש השני מאות זהו׳ ליד האל׳ הנ״ל שתקנה הי׳ כלי כסף הנ״ל ויהא נאמנות בדמי קניית כסף הנ״ל להאל׳ הנ״ל עכ״פ מחויבת האל׳ הנ״ל ליתן כתב ראיי׳ מידה לגיסה על מה שיש תחת ידה מעזבון בעלה לצורך מיגר אל׳ וכשתנשא לגבר אוחרא או לכשתעדר ח״ו שיוחזר ליורשי בעלה גם הבלאות הקיימים בעת ההיא ומה שטען כה משה הנ״ל שיוכל להיות שיש עוד עדיין בעין סחורת מה שקנה בחיי בעלה ששייך לעזבון בעלה ושאר תכשיטי׳ שהעלימה ששייך לעזבון בעלה מצאנו אחרי שנשבעת האל׳ הנ״ל אין בטענותיו ממש יצא מאתנו

---

1. נטריה רחמנא ופרקיה
2. תוספת מעל השורה

16. יו' א ך טבת תקנ"ב[1] לפק הגאן אבד[2] נרו'
17. ורנ"מ ורמ"ש ואני

No. 243

Fols. 231a–b; Sunday 15 January 1792[3]

Following the court's ruling in no. 242, the estate of Benedit Schames was required to supply Benedit's widow, Gutle, with silverware appropriate to her status. Before the court could say what was needed, it reviewed what was found in Benedit's home at the time of his death based upon a post mortem inventory that Gutle had supplied to the head of the court, as was standard procedure. While Benedit did have silverware, it was in the hands of the non-Jewish authorities and could not be retrieved. Therefore, the court listed what needed to be provided (see no. 242). Gutle was to have use of the objects for the rest of her life or until she remarried. Thereafter, the objects would return to her husband's beneficiaries.

רלא ע"א

1. רשימה מכלי בית מה שמחויב ליתן להאל' מ' גוטלי אל' בענדיט
2. שמש מעזבון בעלה ז"ל כפי הפס"ד שיצא מאתנו ח"מ יו' ה'
3. טוב[4] טבת תקנב לפק / והיינו כל הנזכר ברשימה שהי[5]
4. מונחת ביד הגאון אבד[6] נרו' ונשבעת עליו כנהוג / רשאה
5. להחזיק תחת ידה ולשמש בו כפי אות נפשה ורצונה
6. כל משך ימי מיגר אל' ובהרשימה הנ"ל נכתוב הכלי בית
7. כמבואר להלן . . . . .[7]
8. שני {..} טישכר חד אלטע קאמאט שאנק ששה אלטה שטיהל מן האלץ
9. דיטא ליין שטאהל פון האלץ חד מעסינגה לאמפף עם הויל /
10. חד מעסינגע לייכטר / חד קאפיע בריט דיטא / שני קופרה

---

1. ר' מס' 243.
2. אב בית דין
3. Nos. 242 and 243 are both dated Sunday 20 Tevet (5)552 (15 January 1792). However, lines 2–3 of this document refer to a previous decision regarding the silverware Benedit was obligated to provide for Gutle (=no. 242). That decision is said to have been given on Thursday 17 Tevet (5)552 (12 January 1792). This suggests that no. 242 should be dated 12 January.
4. י"ז טבת
5. צ"ל 'שהיתה'
6. אב בית דין
7. הנקודות במקור

11. קאפי קעננה / חד שפיגל / ששה גלאסנה וואנד לייכטר / שלשה
12. בארצילייניך קריגלכר / שלשה בלאטין דיטא / חד מעסינגה פיש
13. קעסלכה / חד שאהליט קעסיל דיטא / חד צינה בעט פלעש /
14. חד טֶע קעננה דיטא / חד מילך קעננה דיטא / חד צוקר
15. ביקס מן מעסינג / שלשה אלטי לייליטיכר עשרה צונה טעליר /
16. חד צינה קומפף / שני קלייני דיטא / ארבעה בלאטי דיטא /
17. שני ציני קאַנר דיטא / שבעה לעפיל דיטא / שני זאלץ פעסיר דיט[א] /
18. שני באטאַשע לעפיל דיטא / חד נאכט גשעהר דיטא / חד גיהס
19. פאס אונד בעקין דיטא / חד עשר טיש טיכר חד קאטון אובר
20. צוועהל ארבע טעק בעט ציכן דיטא (חד)[1] גאנץ אלטן / ששה קאפיצוכן
21. עשרה אלטי לייל טיכר / ששה אלטה האנד טיכר ששה סערפיעטן
22. ששה בלאט ווייסע פר הענג / דיטא ארבע בלאט בוך [ל]יי[ני]
23. עם קראנץ ארבע אלטע קאטוני חד באך טוך

רלא ע״ב

1. חד מעהלצוך שלשה סדר צי[ר]ע עם האנד צוויל שני גריכט דעטונג ע״כ הרשימה
2. שהיתה אצל הגאון אב״ד נרו׳ כנ״ל / וכל הנ״ל תחזיק בידה לצורך
3. תשמישה כנ״ל ועוד נוסף על זה מחויב ליתן להאל׳ הנ״ל מעזבון בעלה
4. ז״ל לצורך תשמישה כלי כסף כמבואר ארבע כסף מעסיר גאביל לעפיל
5. חד באהר כסף כסף לייכטר שלשה כסף כוסת / חד כסף
6. זאלץ פאס חד כסף באטאַשע לעפיל חד כסף רינג חד כסף
7. בשמי׳ ביקסכה חד חרוסת שיסלכה חד חומץ שיסלכה לצורך חג
8. הפסח / ומאחר שאין יכולים ליתן לה כסף מעזבון בעלה
9. זל[2] שמחותם בחתימת השררה ירה[3] בכן מחויב לקנות כפי
10. רשימה הנ״ל כל הנ״ל יהי׳ ביד האל׳ להשתמש בהם משך ימי
11. מיגר אל׳ ומחויבת האל׳ ליתן כתב ראי׳ מידה לגיסה
12. הו״ה כ׳ פער שמש על כל הנ״ל שקיבלה כן מעזבון בעלה
13. ז״ל וכשתנשא לגבר אוחרא מחויבת להחזיר את כל הנ״ל
14. ליורשי׳ בעלה גם הבלאות שהם בעין וכן אם תעדר היא
15. ח״ו מחויבת יורשי׳ להחזיר ליורשי בעלה את כל הנ״ל
16. יו׳ א ך טבת תקנ״ב יצא מאתנו הגאון אב״ד נר׳ ומהר״נ מַז ורמ״ש
17. ואני — — —[4]

---

1. תוספת מעל השורה
2. זכרונו לברכה
3. ירום הודו
4. הקווים במקור

No. 244

Fol. 231b; undated

A note by Rabbi Gundersheim that he was present at the *ḥaliẓah* ceremony of Gutle, widow of Benedit Schames (see nos. 242–43).

18. הייתי אצל חליצה אל׳ המנוח כ׳ בענדיט שמש ז״ל מיבמה כ׳ פער שמש יצו
19. ומסדר הי׳ הר״י ורב״ד רנ״מ והדייני׳ רזט[1] וראט[2] והוספות רמ״ש[3] ואני

No. 245

Fulda et al. v. Children of Leb Buseck

Fols. 232a–b; Tuesday evening, 17 January 1792

Three creditors approached the court asking that the children of Leb Buseck (see no. 238) pay debts that their father had either assumed from his father, Moses Rothschild Buseck, or had incurred himself. Each creditor had specific arguments as to why the children should have to repay him, including a procedural complaint against the head of the court. The children's guardian argued that the children should not be forced to pay these debts because Leb's now deceased widow had presented an inventory of assets and obligations before the head of the rabbinic court and the court had discharged her from further liabilities. Since the children inherited from their mother and she had been formally discharged of all obligations, there were no liabilities to pass on to her children.

The court ruled in favor of the children. However, it noted that for "the good of the community," if the children ever wanted to acquire residency rights in the community, the case would have to be reconsidered either by the court on the basis of communal legislation or by the communal leadership of the day.

רלב ע״א

1. ב״ה
2. ע״ד שבא לפנינו ה״ה התורני כ״ה אהרן בהמנוח[4] כמה׳ נתן פולדא

---

1. רב זנוויל טראך
2. ורב אברהם טריר
3. כנראה הרב מאיר שיף (ע׳ לעיל מס׳ 213, 215).
4. בן המנוח

3. זצ״ל והציע לפנינו ח״כ מכתיבת יד של המנוח כ״ה ליב פוסיק ז״ל
4. מסך שני מאות זהו׳ מן ר״ח אייר תקל״א ותבע כ״ה אהרן הנ״ל ב
5. בהרשאות ובמעמד אחיותיו[1] מן יתמי כ״ה ליב הנ״ל סך הנ״ל וטוען
6. שאביו ז״ל הלווה סך הנ״ל לכ״ה משה פוסיק ז״ל אבי של ר׳ ליב ה
7. הנ״ל ולאחר פטירת כ״ה משה ז״ל קיבל כ״ה ליב הנ״ל על עצמו חוב
8. הנ״ל ונתן ע״ז ח״כ הנ״ל / וה״ה התורני נ״ה כ״ה פייס הענא בהרשאו׳
9. אפטרופסי׳ דיתמי הנ״ל השיב והציע לפנינו השבועת כתוב
10. שנשבעת אם של יתמי אל׳ המנוח כ״ה ליב הנ״ל (על)[2] אינפוטאריום ל
11. (שהניח׳)[3] לפני הגאון אב״ד נר׳ והחליט לה הג׳ אב״ד נר׳ את כל עזבון בעלה
12. ז״ל וטוען שיתמי הנ״ל יורשי אמם ואין מחויבים לשלם ח״כ הנ״ל ועוד
13. טוען באשר שאין פראטעשט על ח״כ הנ״ל שמא פרע וכ״ה אהרן הנ״ל
14. השיב אם האל׳ של כ״ה ליב ז״ל הית׳ עדיין בחיי׳ חיותה יכולה
15. לפטור עצמה בכתיבת החלטה הנ״ל אבל עכשיו שמת׳ יורשי׳ אינם
16. יורשי׳ מה שמגיעי׳ לו מכח ח״כ הנ״ל ועל טענות שמא פרע השיב
17. מש״כ לא נעשה פראטעשט על הח״כ הנ״ל באשר ר׳ ליב ז״ל הנ״ל אצל
18. השררה ירה איין קומן איזט וגם הואיל שהח״כ הנ״ל העלה ר׳ ליב ז״ל
19. אויף דיא פאלאנס שהניח אצל השררה יר״ה שוב אין שייך לומר שמ[א]
20. פרע עוד בא לפנינו השמש התורני כ״ה זיסקינד שטערן בהרשאות ה״[ה]
21. כ״ה זלמן שאטין כץ והציע ח״כ אחד מכ״י ר׳ ליב הנ״ל לכ״ה אברלי איי[..][4]
22. מסך מאה וארבעה עשר זהו׳ מן ד״ד כסליו תקל״א ועוד הציע עוד (חצ[י])[5] ח״כ
23. ש[נ]קרע מן מאה זהו׳ מן כ״ה ליב ז״ל הנ״ל לכ״ה אברלי הנ״ל וטוען כ״ה זיסקינ[ד]
24. הנ״ל בהרשאות הנ״ל שכ״ה זלמן הנ״ל קיבל שני ח״כ מחמיו ר׳ אברלי ה
25. הנ״ל בתורת פרעון וואו רויף אויך חמי׳ שארית הוט בכן תבע סך
26. שני מאות וארבעה עשר זהו׳ הנ״ל מן יתמי כ״ה ליב פוסיק ז״ל הנ״ל
27. וטוען שחצי האחרת מן ח״כ הקרוע הנ״ל גם הוא תחת ידו רק שצריך
28. לחפש אחריו ואין לו זמן כעת ועל תשובת כ״ה פייס הנ״ל מכח
29. השבועת כתובה השיב כ״ה זיסקינד הנ״ל שבעלי חובת מן בעלה
30. לא הי׳ לפני הגאון אב״ד נר׳ בשעת השבועה שנשבעת האל׳ והי׳
31. לו

רלב ע״ב

1. ב״ה
2. לו להגאון אב״ד נר׳ להודיע לבעלי חובת אם יש סדר בכך וכ״ה פייס
3. הנ״ל השיב מסתמא עשה הג׳ אב״ד נר׳ כדינו עוד בא לפנינו כ״ה נתן

---

1. בעסלה אשת זלמן שוואב ופרומט אלמנת זעליג עמדין.
2. תוספת מעל השורה
3. תוספת מימין לשורה
4. ר׳ שורה 24. כנראה שמדובר באברלי איטנגן שהיה חמיו של זלמן שאטין כץ (ר׳ אלה תולדות 22.5.1793).
5. תוספת מעל השורה

אפני ותבע מן יתמי הנ"ל סך תשעה עשר זהו' חמשי' ושבעה צל {ל} להציע לפנינו חשבן מפנקס שלו שמכר לכ"ה ליב הנ"ל מן פ' נח עד פ' ויקהל שנת תקל"א לחם ולבן וחלב אחת לאחת כל יו' ויו' מזמן הנ"ל ה העולה לסך הנ"ל וטוען שחוב שלו חל ג"כ על אשתו שגם היא אכלה מ מסחורה שלו לשלם לו בכן דמי חוב שלו אינה נדחה מפני השבעת כ כתובת' והחלוטה מן הגאון אב"ד נר' וכ"ה פייס הנ"ל בהרשאות הנ"ל (השיב)[1] שחוב שלו אינו רק מפנקס שלו והשיב כנ"ל והאריכו הצדדי' ה הנ"ל בטענותיהם כמבואר בק"ה המונח לפנינו ולאחר שחתמו עצמם בתוקף קומפרמיס לקיים כל אשר יצא מאתנו נזדקקנו להם ומצאנו שהדין עם יתמי הנ"ל ואין לבעלי חובת הנ"ל לפי הדין שום תביעה על יתמי הנ"ל אכן מחמת תיקון הקהלה אם ירצה אחד מיתמי הנ"ל ל לעת נישואין שלו להיות לו חזקת עירונית בקהלותינו יע"א אזי יקוב הדין את ההר ביניהם ע"פ תיקון הקהלה על ידי ב"ד יצו או ע"פ קהל יצו אשר יהי' בימים ההם כי אדעת' דהכי חתמו הצדדי' הנ"ל א"ע בקומפרמיס הנ"ל יצא מאתנו אור לי' ד' ך"ג טבתקנ"ב[2] רנ"מ ורמ"ש ואני /[3]

No. 246

Fol. 232b; Monday 13 February 1792

Rabbi Gundersheim recorded that he was present at the *ḥaliẓah* ceremony of Sorle, widow of Leb Windmühl.[4]

היו' יו' ב ך שבט תקנ"ב הייתי אצל חליצה האשה מ' שרלה אל' המנוח כ' ליב ו ווינדמיהל ז"ל מיבמה כ"ה אברהם ווינדמיהל כץ ומסדר הי' רנ"מ והדייני' ראט[5] ורזט[6] והו(ס)[7]פות רמ"ש ואני

1. תוספת מימין לשורה
2. טבת תקנ"ב
3. קו נטוי במקור
4. Leb died 1 November 1791 (Horovitz, no. 3082, with correction of Ettlinger, 1.11.1791).
5. רב אברהם טריר
6. ורב זנוויל טראך
7. תוספת מעל השורה

No. 247

Fol. 232b; [Sunday 19 February 1792][1]

A record of the sale of a seat in the upper women's section of the synagogue that was currently being used by the widow of Leb Schotten. The seat had been owned by the community and was sold to Yuzpa Maas for 475 guldens after a public announcement that the seat was for sale. The terms of the sale allowed Yuzpa to make a down payment of 100 guldens and then repay the balance in eight payments over four years. This was a departure from the usual terms of six payments over three years. For a detailed description of the sale, see no. 248.

23. מקו' שלם בע"נ העליונה אשר עומדו' עליה כעת {אשת} אל' המנוח ר' ליב שאטין
24. ז"ל נמכר בפנינו ב"ד לאחר הכרזה לכ[2] יוזפא בכ"ה זנוויל מז ז"ל בעד סך ארבע
25. מאות {וחמשי' ושבעה זה'} ושבעי' וחמשה זהו' לשלם סך מאה זהו' נגד מסירת
26. מעשה ב"ד הלז ודמי מכירה הנותרי' לשלם על שמנה חצאי שני' רצופי' וסמוכי' זא"[ז]
27. מיו' מסירת מעשה ב"ד והמק' הנ"ל הי' שייך להאלופי' ק' גובי' יצ"ו
28. נעשה יו' א דה שבט תקנ"ב

No. 248

Unpaginated; Sunday 19 February 1792

A record of the same sale of a seat in the upper women's section of the synagogue as described in no. 247. This record of sale is far more detailed than other such records in Rabbi Gundersheim's diary and it may be that this is the court record that served as a basis for the summary that appears in no. 247. The document outlines the terms, and notes that the transfer of ownership was binding. The page is damaged along the left margin and some words are missing from this area. The suggested readings for this missing material are based on YIVO MS. RG 128 (folder 77–78; this section is unpaginated in the microfilm copy of the manuscript at The Central Archives for the History of the Jewish People and it does not appear in the microfilm at YIVO [MK 482.2]). The text in the YIVO MS. was specifically labeled a "copy" but what the source for the "copy" was remains uncertain.

1. The document is dated Sunday 25 Shevat (5)592. In that year 25 Shevat fell on a Saturday. See no. 248.
2. לכבוד

דף ללא עימוד

1. בע״ה
2. מקום שלם בעזרת נשים העליונה שעומד עלי׳ כעת אלמנת המנוח כ״ה ליב שאטין כץ
3. [מ]ימין על מקום הסמוך לה עומדת עלי׳ כעת אשת כ׳ מאיר הענא י״ץ ומצד שמאל ע[ל מקום הסמוך]
4. עומדת עלי׳ כעת אשת כהררי[1] יוזף שפייאר י״ץ אותו מקום שלם הנ״ל שהי׳ שייך [להאלופ׳]
5. קציני׳ גובי׳ י״ץ הוכרז בבה״כ ישן וחדש זמן זמני׳ טובא שכל מי שרוצה לקנותו י[בא פני ב״ד]
6. גם הוכרז לפנינו ב״ד ח״מ ולא הי׳ אחד שהי׳ פוסק כפי מה שפסק הו״ה כ׳ [יוזפא ב״כ]
7. המנוח כ״ה זנוויל מז ז״ל בכן מכרנו המקום שלם הנ״ל לה״ה כ׳ יוזפ[א] מַז הנ״ל בעד [סך]
8. ארבעה מאות ושבעים וחמשה זהו׳ לשלם אין קונפענציאהנש מי[נץ] אויף [דעם כ״ד זהו׳]
9. פוס והיינו לשלם סך מאה זהו׳ תיכף נגד מסירת מעשה ב״ד הלז ושל[שה מאות ושבעים]
10. וחמשה זהו׳ הנותרי׳ מסך דמי מכירה הנ״ל לשלם על שמנה חצאי שנים רצו[פי׳ וסמוכים זא״ז]
11. מיום מסירת מעשה ב״ד הנ״ל ומחויב הלוקח כ׳ יוזפא הנ״ל ליתן שמנה ח״כ ל[אורדרי האלופים גובים]
12. י״ץ לשלם לזמני׳ הנ״ל גם נשאר מקום שלם הנ״ל לאפותיקי מפורש שלא [יצא מחזקת מרא]
13. קמא כל זמן שלא נתפרע כל דמי מכירה הנ״ל ומעתה המקום שלם הנ״ל אשר הי׳ [שייך להאלופי׳]
14. גובי׳ י״ץ שייך מעכשיו לה״ה כ׳ יוזפא מאז הנ״ל וי״א וב״כ לחלוטין גמורין ולצמיתת [על מרן עם]
15. כל זכות וחזקה וכמו שהי׳ שייך מקדמת דנא להאלופי׳ גובי׳ י״ץ בלי שי[ור כלל]
16. וכלל ורשאי ה״ה כ׳ יוזפא מז הנ״ל וי״א וב״כ לעשות עם מקום שלם הנ״ל להוריש [ולהנחיל להחליף]
17. להשכין למכור ולהשכיר וליתן במתנה כאות נפשו ורצונו ככל אינ[ש דרשאי לעשות]
18. בשלו בלי מוחה כלל / ואחר שנתפרע כל דמי מכירה הנ״ל שייך מעכ[שיו המקום שלם]
19. הנ״ל לה״ה כ׳ יוזפא הנ״ל וי״א וב״כ בשופי גמור בלי שום עורר וטוען [יהי׳ המערער]
20. מי שיהי׳ הן רבי׳ או יחיד יהי׳ הטענה מה שיהי׳ או בכל אופן שיהי׳ מכל מ[ה שהפה]
21. יוכל לדבר והלב לחשוב ולהרהר וכל מי שיערער אחר מכירה הנ״ל יהי׳ מי [שיהי׳ או]
22. באיזה אופן שיהי׳ דבריו בטלין ומבוטלין כחרס הנשבר כאפס וכאין יחש[ב לא]
23. שרירין ולא קיימין ולא יהי׳ חלין כלל וכלל וכטוען אחר מעשה ב״ד הגדול וא[ל יזדקק]
24. שום קהל או ב״ד יצו או שום משפט שבעולם הן בדא״ה והן בד״י לדברי ה[מערער]
25. כי הם בטילים ומבוטלים ובאשר שכפי הנהוג בקהלתינו יע״א שעל [מכירת]

דף ללא עימוד, ע״ב

1. בעה
2. קרקעות ששייכי׳ להאלופי׳ גובי׳ יצו אינו בכי יותן להלוקח חלטה בפני עצמו

---

1. כבוד הרב רבי

3. [כ]נהוג בשארי מכירת הנעשי' מיחידי' בכן יהא תוקף מעשה ב"ד הלז כאלו יש
4. [ל]הלוקח כ' יוזפא הנ"ל גם שטר חלטה בפני עצמו וכתבנו וחתמנו כל הנ"ל בתוקף
5. [מ]עשה ב"ד ובכח ב"ד יפה להיות ביד לוקח כ' יוזפא הנ"ל וי"א וב"כ לעדות
6. [ול]זכות ולראי' שיעמוד המקום שלם הנ"ל ביד לוקח כ' יוזפא הנ"ל וי"א וב"כ בלי
7. שום מוח[ה] כלל נעשה פה פ"פ יום א' ך"ו שבט תקנ"ב לפק[1]

No. 249

Unpaginated; undated

This piece of paper was attached to the previous document. The first line seems to be a scribe's jotting to test the nib of his quill, for it states, "I will try my quill nib." The second section appears to be a receipt for a charitable gift to support the study of Torah, but it is too fragmentary to be understood fully. The third entry is only the opening three words of a document that seems to have been abandoned.

1. אנסה את הקולמושפעציע[2]

2. ב"ה[3]
3. קבלתי מן ה"ה הו"ה כ' אנשיל קולפא יצו א
4. זהו' ורביעות לסיועת ת"ת מן
5. ב"ה
6. ב"ה פפורט[4] יו'

No. 250

Fol. 233a; Sunday evening, [24 November 1793]

The court sold one-third of the Rindsfuss house that had belonged to the late Ẓipche, widow of Lipman Deuz, to the community for 1100 guldens. Proceeds from the sale were to be used to pay off Ẓipche's debt to the community. Line 2 of the

1. בכתב יד יו"א כתוב בסוף: הר"י והאב"ד מהר' נתן מז נר"ו
הדיין התורני כ"ה מאיר שיף כץ נר"ו
הדיין התורני כ"ה חיים גונדרשהיים נר"ו
2. דהיינו 'הקולמוס ושפעציע'
3. הדברים הבאים כתובים בצורה מהופכת בקצה השמאלי התחתון של הדף.
4. פרנקפורט(?)

text states that "today is Thursday." This opening seems to have been abandoned and a new document regarding the sale begins on line 3.

רלג ע"א

1. ב"ה
2. היו' יו' ה
3. אור ליו' ב דא כסליו[1] מכרנו בפני הב"ד יצו השליש בית צום רונד פוס
4. שהי' שייך להמונחת האשה מ' ציפכה אל' המנוח כ' ליפמן דייטץ ז"ל
5. בעד סך אחד עשר מאות זהו' {...} להאלופי' גובי' יצו והיינו שינכו ה
6. הגובי' את סך דמי מכירה הנ"ל מהחוב שהיית' האשה ז"ל הנ"ל חייב
7. להגובי' יצו רנ"מ ואני ורל[2] וואלי

Fol. 233b is blank.

No. 251

Eschwau v. Halle

Fol. 234a–235b; incomplete and undated but sometime after 28 July 1794

Leser Eschwau (or perhaps Eschwege), through his agent, Leb Schwarzschild, sued Joel Halle for payment of goods that Leser had supplied him with the previous winter. Joel disputed the charge, claiming that he did not receive as many goods as Leser claimed and that the price per unit that Leser charged was not the price that they had agreed upon. Leser noted that he had checked the number of goods himself. He also disputed Joel's countercharge with respect to the price. Not only were the two sides unable to come to any agreement, but Joel, who is said to have been the largest cloth dealer in the *Judengasse*, countersued Leser with respect to the materials shipped and currency values.[3]

The document is incomplete and does not include the court's decision. This

1. כ"א כסליו חל ביום ב' בשנת תקנ"ד
2. ורבי ליזר
3. On Joel Halle as a leading cloth dealer, see Dietz, no. 228 I.

document is not included in the index of Rabbi Gundersheim's diary found at the end of the manuscript.

רלד ע"א

1. ב"ה
2. ע"ד שבא לפנינו ה"ה התור' סופר ונ"ה כ"ה ליב ש"ש יצו בהרשאת ב"א[1]
3. הו"ה כ"ה ליזר עשווא[2] יצו ותבע מן הו"ה ג"ץ כ' יואל האלי יצו והציע לפנינו
4. קונטא קוראנט מן הסחורות ששלח לכ' יואל הנ"ל בחורף העבר / ונמצא לפי ה
5. החשבן הלז שמחויב כ' יואל הנ"ל לשלם לו עוד סך ארבעה מאות וארבעה עשר
6. רט יאץ[3] וה"ה הו"ה גץ[4] כ' יואל הנ"ל בעצמו וגם התור' כ"ה וואלף שפייער יצו
7. בהרשאת כ' יואל הנ"ל השיבו בתחלה ביו' א חית תמוז תקנ"ד שאינו מ
8. מחויב לשלם רק לערך חמשה קרלינר והציע ג"כ חשבונו לפנינו וטוען ב
9. באריכות נגד חשבן של ר' ליזר הנ"ל כמבואר / ראשון בסחורת שקיבל ממנו
10. דג חשון העבר שהי' מאה טאפלטה וג' חצי שטוך שמוכרחי' להחזיק כפי ר
11. רשימת ר"ל[5] שהעלה בחשבונו חמשת אלפי' ומאה ותשעה וחצי אמות וטוען
12. כ"י[6] הנ"ל שלא הי' מחזיקי' כ"כ רק שהי' חסר מהאמות הנ"ל שני מאות וחמשי' ושמונ[ה]
13. ושלשה רביעית אמות / גם בסחורה שקיבל כ"י אח"כ בר"ח טבת שהעלה
14. כה"ל[7] בחשבונו שהי' מחזיקי' אלף ושלשה אמות וטוען כ"י הנ"ל שחסר ארבעי'
15. אמות בכן מה שנחסר עולה יחד שני מאות ותשעי' וחמשה ושלשה רביעית
16. אמות[8] וזה רוצה לנכות מחשבן של כ"ל הנ"ל / עוד טען כ"י הנ"ל שר"ל הנ"ל העלה
17. בחשבונו הנ"ל הדמי מקח של כל אמה בעד ארבעי' וששה [צל][9] והוא כ"י הנ"ל
18. אינו מחויב לשלם רק ארבעי' ושנים צל והאריך כ"י ב[טענו]תיו[10] ואומר אחרי
19. שביריד ר"ה העבר הי' קנה ממנו בעד ארבעי' צל וכשהי' מבקש כ' יואל הנ"ל ב
20. בחורף העבר מן ר"ל הנ"ל לשלוח לו סחורות ולא כתב לו שום מקח לא הי' ד
21. דעתו ליתן לו יותר מארבעי' צל כמו ביריד הקודמו רק אחרי [ששלח] ר"ל הנ"ל את
22. סחורת הנ"ל וכתב ר"ל באגרת לכ"י הנ"ל שאי אפשר לו למכור ע"ז המקח שיהי' לו
23. היזיק וע"ז התרצה כ"י הנ"ל ליתן ארבעי' ושנים צל / וכה"ל הנ"ל השיב מחמת

---

1. אולי 'בעל אחותו'. על פי אלה תולדות 20.2.1794 (דף של ישראל שווארץ שילד), היו לליב שווארץ שילד שתי אחיות. אחת נשא את סענדר עמריך (ר' 13.3.1816) והשניה לא התחתנה ונפטרה בשנת תקמ"ו (ר' 24.4.1786). כנראה שליזר עשווא לא היה איש פרנקפורט (ולכן ההרשאה) ולאור זה אטלינגר לא ידע לא עליו ולא על אשתו.
2. ר' אלה תולדות 25.9.1753. שם אטלינגר תיקן את שם המשפחה באבני זכרון, מס' 2777, מ-'עשווא' ל-'עשווגי' (Eschwege) על פי ספר הקברנים.
3. י"א צ"ל
4. גבאי צדקה
5. ר' ליזר
6. כבוד יואל
7. כבוד הרב ליזר
8. על פי הנתונים שיש כאן, היה צריך לכתוב 298 ¾ אמות.
9. יש כאן חור בנייר
10. יש כאן חור בנייר

24. דמי מקח

רלד ע״ב

1. ב״ה
2. דמי מקח שהי׳ כותב לכ״י תיכף לאחר השלוח הסחורת קודם שקיבלם כ״י
3. הנ״ל בפירוש הדמי מקח בעד כל אמה חמשי׳ צל וגם בדעתו הי׳ שאינו מרוצה
4. בפחות מזה {רק אח״כ} כי אין הסחורת ואין הזמני׳ שווין רק אח״כ כשכותב
5. כ״י הנ״ל כמה פעמי׳ וצווח ככרוכי׳ ע״ז התרצה א״ע כה״ל הנ״ל בכתבו ביו׳[1] הנ״ל
6. מרחשון ליתן לו בעד מ׳גץ[2] אבל לא פחות ואף שכתב לו בזה״ל ער זולמיר
7. טרם כל שטען שני מאות וחמשי׳ קרלינר וואן איהם דיא סחורה ניט אהן ש
8. שטענדיג ווירדן מיר {איננג}(פערטיג)[3] ווירדן וז״ל / מ״מ כתב בפירוש באותו כתב
9. שלא מכר לו כי אם בעד מגץ[4] וגם סומך עצמו על מה שכתב לו אח״כ ביו׳ דח
10. מרחשון ושם נאמר בזה״ל בפירוש ליכר אובליגירע מיך דיא סחורה רעטוה׳
11. צו נעהמן געגין אסי גניהרונג דש געלט קיין אבצוג קן ניט לי[כ]טן זואהל
12. וואהל אין עהלין אלש אין געלט עד לאח״כ על כתבי׳ שוני׳ מן כ״י הנ״ל התרצ[ה]
13. גם בזה בכתבו מדח מרחשון ליקח עוד צ״ל פחות היינו מוץ[5] אבל לפחו׳
14. מזה לא התרצה מעולם להניח לו הסחורת הנ״ל כאשר נאמרו ונשנית בכתביו
15. הנ״ל והו״ה כ״י הנ״ל השיב אחרי שבכתבו מן כה״ל הנ״ל מיד[6] מרחשון בקש ממנו כ
16. כנ״ל שני מאות וחמשי׳ קרלינר נכתב לו מיר ווירטן פירטיג ווירדן וז״ל
17. וטוען שכוונת של וז״ל היינו שמסתא[7] יתרצה כה״ל הנ״ל לזה המקח וגם כאשר
18. שלח לו כמ[...][8]שו ח״כ על קאסיל מסך שני מאות וחמשי׳ קרלינר וכה״ל הנ״ל
19. קיבלו ולא שלח לו לחזרה גילוי מילתא שמרוצה בדמי מקח שכתב כ״י הנ״ל בעד
20. [מבץ][9] ואף שכתבו לו אח״כ כשקיבל כבר הח״כ הנ״ל ער וויל הסחורה אין
21. רעטוהר נעהמן געגין אסיגניהרונג / זה הי׳ בערמה יתירה שהי׳ לו ל
22. לבקשו תיכף קודם שיבקש שני מאות וחמשי׳ קרלינר שיחזור וישלח לו הסחורת
23. לחזרה וכה״ל הנ״ל השיב שעומד בטענותיו ובכתביו שכתב בפי׳ הנ״ל שאינו מכר
24. לו הסחורת

רלה ע״א

1. ב״ה
2. לו הסחורת פחות מן מט צל ומחמת מה שרצה לנכות כ״י הנ״ל מחמת חסרון

---

1. ביום י״ד במרחשון
2. מ״ג צ״ל (וצריך לומר ׳מ׳זץ׳ [= מ״ז צ״ל])
3. תיקון מעל השורה
4. מ״ג צ״ל (וצריך לומר ׳מ׳זץ׳ [= מ״ז צ״ל])
5. מ״ו צ״ל
6. ר״ל מיום י״ד במרחשון
7. צ״ל ׳מסתמא׳
8. יש כאן חור בנייר
9. מ״ב צ״ל

3. מדות האמות כנ"ל השיב כה"ל הנ"ל שכה"ל הנ"ל בעצמו מ[ס]ר הסחורת
4. וברר לו שמחזיקי' כ"כ אמות כמו שכתבו גם כתב כפי' לכ"י הנ"ל בך"ח מ
5. מרחשון בזה"ל לוזין דיא שטוך פרשטנג מעסין עז איזט קיין מאנקע אנונד
6. [ווא]ן איהנן דער טוך לעהרר דש עהלין מאס שיקט דש פיהל דאראהן פעהלט
7. זנא נעה עש ניכט אהן וויל ערשט איינם באורדרן דער בייא דעם מעסן
8. זיין זול / ליבר אלי מאהל וואן מן איינום שטוך וואש פיהלט אוהן בארית
9. ליגן גלאגט אויף מיינה רעכטונג וטוען כה"ל הנ"ל שכ' יואל הנ"ל הי' לו ל
10. להניח הסחורת כמו שכתב ר"ל הנ"ל והוא לא עשה כן אלא נתן לבעלי מלאכות
11. לצבוע ומכרם בכן מחויב לשלם הדמי מ[ח]ק (כמו)[1] שהתרצה כה"ל הנ"ל וגם המדות אמות
12. כמו שכתב כה"ל הנ"ל שהחזיקו הסחורת וכ"ה וואלף הנ"ל השיב שכבר
13. הי' לו הפרש בסכום המדות ביריד העבר עם כה"ל הנ"ל ואח"כ הודה כה"ל הנ"ל ב
14. בעצמו לכ"י שכני' דבריו וגם יוכל לברר עם כמה סוחרי' שהי' להם סכסוכי' עם ר"ל
15. הנ"ל מחמת חסרון שנמצא בסחורת שלו בכן עומד בטענותיו שרוצי' לנכות לו
16. כנ"ל / שוב ביו' ב' ר"ח אב התעצמו לדין וחזר ותבע כ' יואל הנ"ל מן כה"ל הנ"ל
17. סך שלשה מאות וחמשים ושבעה רט / והיינו שהב"ד יחקרו הסוחרי' ממיני הסחו'
18. הלז שכולם עוני' ואומרי' שדרך מין הסחורת הנ"ל שמחזיקי' לאחר גמר צביעה כל
19. שטוך ב אמות וחצי יותר מקודם הצבעה מכח וואַלקה ומשיכת בעל מלאכה
20. הצביעה בכלי אומנת שלהם ובאשר שהוא כ"י הנ"ל קיבלו וקנה הסחורת בעודו
21. לבן קודם הצביעה בכן מן הראוי להיותם אח"כ כל כך עודף שהוא מצא חסרון
22. כנ"ל בכן נודע שבעודם לבני' נחסר [כ]"כ כל שטוך ב אמות וחצי שעולה לסך שלשה
23. שלשה מאות וחמשי' ושבעה רט כנ"ל בכן מגיע ל[כ]"[י] הנ"ל לפי חשב[ונו]

רלה ע"ב

1. ב"ה
2. לפי חשבונו מן כה"ל הנ"ל סך שלשה מאות ועשרי' רט ך צ"ל / וכה"ל הנ"ל השיב
3. איך יעלה על דעת שר' ליזר הנ"ל נשאר {חיוב} חייב לכ' יואל הנ"ל כ"כ הלא
4. ביריד העבר שילם לו כ' יואל הנ"ל על חשבן עשרי' וחמשה קרלין
5. ולמה לא עיכבם על תביעת שלו ומאחר שכ' יואל הנ"ל הודה בעצמו
6. במקצת בטענותיו הראשוני' שעדיין חייב לכה"ל הנ"ל לערך חמשה ק"ט
7. וחייב שבועה דאורייתא בכן יגלגל עליו הב"ד (על)[2] כל מה שהכחיש את דברי
8. ר"ל הנ"ל עוד טען וחישב כ' יואל הנ"ל בחשבונו ורוצה לנכות מן
9. חשבן של ר"ל הנ"ל עוד חמשה רט מחמת פרייסיש מעות ששלח לכה"ל
10. הנ"ל סך חמשה מאות ושמוני' ואחד רט כל רט בעד א רט מאץ[3] לאשע על
11. כל קרלין {סך} ששה צל שעולה לסך ה רט נהץ[4] וכה"ל הנ"ל השיב שכתב לכ"י הנ"ל

1. תוספת מעל השורה
2. תוספת מעל השורה
3. מ"א צ"ל
4. נ"ה צ"ל

12. שהוא אינו יכול ליקח יותר כל רט רק בעד א רט לטץ[1] וכ״י הנ״ל חישב לו בעד
13. מאץ[2] ויוכל להיות שנכלל בזה כבר ה לאשע על קרטין וכ״י הנ״ל השיב שלא
14. חישב לו ביוקר ובאם כה״ל רוצה להחזירם עוד על אופן הנ״ל נגד חדש
15. רטי'[3] רוצה כ״י הנ״ל לקבלו לחזרה נגד ח״ר / עוד חישב כ יואל הנ״ל ב
16. בחשבונו ורוצה לנכות עוד בעד דמי נידר לאג סך שני רט זץ[4] וכה״ל
17. השיב שמעולם לא חישב לו כ יואל הנ״ל דמי נידר לאג וגם אינו מחויב לשלם
18. והאריכו הצדדי' הנ״ל מאוד בטענותיהם זה מול זה כמבואר באריכות
19. בק״ה המונח לפנינו ולאחר שחתמו עצמם הצדדי' הנ״ל בתוקף קומפרמיס
20. בח״ח ובקנס סך מסויי' לשררה ירה[5] ולהקדש לאשר ולקיים הפס״ד שיצא מאתנו
21. נזדקקנו להם ולאחר שעיינו הדק היטיב בחשבונם ובכתבי' אגרת שחלפ'
22. ביניהם גם בטענותיהם גם חקרנו את הו״ה גץ[6] כ' יואל הנ״ל לברר דבריו ה
23. היכן נודע את הדבר שהי' חסר מן הסחורת שקיבל מן כה״ל הנ״ל כפי טענותיו
24. הנ״ל ואמר כ' יואל הנ״ל שכל הסחורת שקיבל מן כה״ל הנ״ל והמה לבן
25. מניח בכל שט[וך][7]

Fols. 236–237 are blank.

No. 252

Fols. 238a–239b; Wednesday 28 August 1793

The construction of a new public building intended to serve as a hostel and hospice for the poor and elderly prompted communal leaders in charge of charitable funds to ask the court how the building should be built so that priests (*kohanim*) could enter the building both as visitors and users without becoming ritually impure (see Lev. 21.1–4).[8] Of concern was not only the ritual impurity conferred by the bodies

---

1. ל״ט צ״ל
2. מ״א צ״ל
3. רייכשטאלרים
4. ז' צ״ל
5. ירום הודו
6. גבאי צדקה
7. שני הדפים הבאים ריקים. שאר פסק הדין חסר.
8. Regarding the structure, see Deitz, p. 439, no. 10.

of those who died in the building, but the fact that the overhang of the north and east sides of the building extended over the Jewish cemetery.[1]

The court gave very specific instructions for construction and ordered that those responsible for building the structure adhere to the plans. The head of the court was to appoint someone to make sure that the court's orders were carried out. Eventually, some of the judges were to be shown the work so they could be sure it was satisfactory from the perspective of Jewish law. The court also gave instructions for dealing with the dead inside the building once it was built, so as to limit the spread of ritual impurity. Like the previous document, this text is not included in the index at the end of the manuscript. It is also not signed "and me" (referring to Rabbi Ḥayyim Gundersheim), but Rabbi Gundersheim's initials are listed at the end of the document as are those of the other rabbis on the court.

רלח ע"א

1. בה
2. ע"ד השאלה שנשאל מא{ת.} מאת האלופי' הקציני' גבאי צ[ד]קה המתעסקי'
3. בבנין חדש של הקדש איך לעשות תקנה שיוכלו הכהני' לכנוס ולצאת בתוך
4. הבנין הנ"ל / וכהני' החולי' ח"ו אשר ישכבו שמה שלא יטמאו טומאת מת / הן
5. מחמת טומאות אוהל אשר מצד צפון ומזרח שמאהל הבנין על הקברות
6. והן אם יהי' ח"ו בר מינן בתוך ההקדש מפני טומאת אהל / וגם שיוכלו הכהני'
7. לעמוד תחת בנין שעל העמודי' שבחצר ההקדש / ועוד לתקן החלונות של חדר
8. החברא דג"ח יצו עם שארי חלונות סמוכי' להני חלונות למטה סמוך לארץ
9. מצד צפון של ההקדש / את כל השאלות ותקנות הנ"ל בקשו מאתנו האלופי'
10. הקציני' הנ"ל לתקן את הכל כדין וכדת של תורתנו הקדושה
11. ולאחר עיון הדק היטיב מצאנו
12. א) תחלה צריך להעשות סביב ההקדש חדש מכל ארבעה צדדי' מזרח
13. מערב צפון ודרום גג אחת משופע קצת ומכוסה בשיפר שטיין שתהי'
14. רוחבו יותר מן הזיזין שלמעלה עם הצנור שעליהם לפחות שני צאָל / וגג
15. הזה יהי' מחובר בחבור גמור בתקרות התחתוני' אשר מונחי' על החומות
16. אשר ההקדש בנוי עליהם
17. ב) בפתח מצד מעריב אשר בו נכנסי' ויוצאי' לתוך ההקדש הנ"ל צריך להעשות
18. לפני הפתח מבחוץ מצד הפתח בימין / כותל מקורות ואבני' ביניהם מ
19. מחובר בחיבור גמור לחומה של דרום / מן הארץ עד שראשה תגיע לגג הנ"ל / מ
20. מהודק היטיב אל הגג בכל השיפוע בלי שום ריווח אפי' כל שהוא ומשך רוחב
21. כותל הלז כרוחב הגג הנ"ל / וכן יעשה כותל אחת בצד שמאל של הפתח
22. בלי שינוי כמו בצד ימין הנ"ל / ובחומה אשר היא מצד צפון של ההקדש לפני
23. ההקדש שהיא החומה מערבית של בית עלמין שהיא סמוכה לבאר / אשר לאחר

1. See Malkiel, "Law and Architecture," 268–69, 272–73.

24. עשיית הגג הנ"ל אינה מגעת עד הגג גם אותה החומה צריכה להעשות
25. גבוהה

רלח ע"ב

1. ב"ה
2. גבוהה יותר עד שתגיע אל הגג מהודק היטיב ברוחב הגג כמו שני הכותלים
3. שלפני פתח הנ"ל **ג**
4. גם שבפתח לצד מזרח נגד בית המטהר צריך להעשותן שני כותלי' אחת מימין
5. הפתח ואחת משמאלה לפני הפתח מבחוץ עד סוף משך הגג הנ"ל / הכל באופן
6. כמו שני הכותלים שבצד מערב כנ"ל וצריך לקצר את בית המטהר ובית צ[ד]וק
7. הדין כל מה דאפשר כדי שיהי' ריווח הר{..} הרבה בין הגג הנ"ל ובין הגג
8. של בית המטהר ובית צדוק הדין ועכ"פ יהי' הריווח יותר מן שני שוך:
9. ———
10. **ד**
11. ועוד בחלק ראשון של השטעג באותו חלק אשר המעלות קבועות בתוכה שהוא
12. בצד שמאל צריך להעשות בו דופן של נסרי' על פני כל החלק שתהי' גובהה
13. של הדופן עד למעלה במעזיבה סתום כולה וכן בחלק שני של השטעג באותו
14. צד שהוא פתוחה למטה על הארץ צריך להיות דופן קטן כמו כן מן נסרי' שתהי' סתום
15. כולה כמו חלק ראשון הנ"ל וגם צריך להעשות דופן מן נסרי' סתום כולה מן החתל[ת][1]
16. השטעג בצד שמאל עד מבחוץ לפתח המערב / ומבפנים לפתח תהי' א
17. אותו דופן גבוהה עד המעזיבה / ומבחוץ לפתח צריך שתמשוך הדופן ה
18. הלז עד המשך הכותל של צד ימין וגובהה עד הגג החדש כמו ש[ני] כותלי'
19. הנ"ל שבמערב **ה**
20. בחלונות אשר המה למטה בשטח החתתון[2] בתוך הקיר הצפוני של ההקדש הן בתוך
21. חדר החברא של ג"ח יצו והן בתוך שארי החדרי' צריך להעשות גג של נסר אחד
22. שהוא עב וחזק תחת חלונות ויהי' מן אייכן האלף רוחבו כרוחב הגג חדש
23. הנ"ל ומעט יותר לערך ב צאָל ורוחב גג נסר הלז תהי' בולט ומאהל על בית
24. עלמין ואורכו של גג נסר הלז יהי' במשך כל צד צפון ההקדש מתחלת חלון ר
25. ראשון עד סוף חלון אחרון אשר המה למטה מגג חדש הנ"ל / וצריך להיות
26. ריווח בין גג נסר הלז ובין קרקע של בית עלמין למטה מן הגג נסר הלז לפחות
27. חמשה טפחי' דהיינו שיפנה ויסולק את העפר שהוא תחת גג נסר הלז עד
28. שיהי' ריווח אויר בין קרקע של בית עלמין לגג הנסר הנ"ל חמשה טפחי' כנ"ל / ועל קרקע של
29. בית עלמין צריך להעשות בחבור גמור דף אחד במשך גג נסר הנ"ל בארכו וברחבו /
30. וצריך להשגיח שלא יפול עפר על אותו דף כי אם שיהי' הדף הלז תמיד מנוקה
31. מכל דבר

1. צ"ל 'התחלת'
2. צ"ל 'התחתון'

רלט ע"א

1. ב"ה
2. מכל דבר / ומצד ימין ומצד השמאל של אותו גג נסר יעשה בכל צד נסר אחד עב
3. וחזק רוחבו כרוחב גג הנסר הנ"ל שהוא ברוחב גג חדש הנ"ל ומעט יותר לערך
4. ב' צאל / וארכו של הנסר מכל צד יתחיל מן גג נסר הנ"ל ויגיע עד תחת גג חדש מ
5. מהודק ומחובר היטיב על גג חדש כמו כותלי של פתחי' הנ"ל וחיזוק של הד[ף ...]
6. הנ"ל אל הכותל יהי' ע"י יתדות של ברזל שקורין באנק אייזן
7. **ויו**
8. וזאת לדעת להח"ק של ג"ח וקברוני' יצו באם שיהי' ח"ו שני נעדרי' אזי כשנושאי'
9. המטה לחזרה בין לוי' של בר מינן הראשון לשני יהי' נושאי' את המטה מבית ה
10. המיטהר לתוך ההקדש / ומהקדש לחצר ההקדש / אבל לא מבית צדוק הדין לחצר
11. ההקדש **זיין**
12. ואם יהי' ח"ו בר מינן בתוך ההקדש אזי לא יניחו אותו בתוך המהלך אל ה
13. השטעג כי אם חוץ לדופן שהוא בתוך המהלך לבית המיטהר / וכל זמן ש
14. שגם בר מינן ח"ו בתוך המהלך לבית המיטהר ויצטרכו לפתוח פתח ש[ל]
15. הקאמין למטה על הארץ לבער אש בתוך התנור או לשום צורך / אזי צריך
16. להשגיח שהפתחי' של הקאמינן למעלה בכל החדרי' יהי' נעולי' וכן לא ילך
17. שום אדם ממהלך [ול]בין עמודי' לבית צדוק הדין או מבית צדוק הדין לבין עמוד
18. ופאַ[.ל.ֶ] פתוח בידו / וכן לא ישא שום דבר ארוך שם מה שיש ברחבו
19. טפח
20. כל התקנות הנ"ל עשינו לאחר שעיינונו היטיב בכל אופני' האפשריי'
21. מה שאפשר {ש}יהי' הבנין ח{.} חד[ש] עם ההקדש כולו מתוקן לצורך הכהנים
22. כנזכר למעלה בתוך השאלה / ומצאנו שהתקנות הנ"ל המה המובחרי' והישרי' ע[ל]
23. צד היותר טוב לפי דין ודת תורתנו הקדושה / בכן תוקף פקודתינו על ה
24. האלופי' קציני' גבאי צדקה אשר הי' מתעסקי' בבנין של ההקדש {הנ"ל} הלז להשגיח
25. {על כל פרט} בהשגחה יתירה ומעולה / וע"פ איש אחד מיוחד אשר הגאב"[ד]
26. נר' יעמוד

רלט ע"ב

1. ב"ה
2. נר' יעמוד לכך להשגיח על כל פרטי דברי התקנות הלז שלא להוסיף ושלא לגרוע
3. כי אם לעשות הדברי' כהווייתן הנאמרי' פה / גם מצאנו שיעתיקו הפסק הלז אות
4. באות תוך הפנקס של הקציני' גבאי צדקה ועכטר יצו שתהי' למשמרת לדורי ד
5. דורות / ולאחר שיוגמרו (את)[1] כל התקנות הנ"ל כראוי / יודיעם זאת להגאב"ד נר'
6. כדי שיוכלו איזה דייני' נר' לראות מה שנעשה / ולמראה עניהם ישפוטו שנעשה
7. הכל בלי שנוי כמבואר בתוך פסק הלז ואז יוכרז ההיתר לכהני' שרשאי' להשתמש

---

1. תוספת מעל השורה

8. ולילך בתוך ההקדש ההקדשי[1] ובין העמודי' / ותבער הטומאה מכל הארץ ב
9. במהרה בימינו / יצא מאתנו היו' יו' ד ך אלול תקנ"ג לפק
10. הגאבד[2] נר' רנ"מ ראטי[3] רזטי[4] רח"ג רמ"ז רל"ו

Fol. 240a is blank.

No. 253

Fol. 240b; copy of a document originally written on Friday 25 April 1749

A copy of a loan agreement made by Reichle and Jacob Mai, who borrowed 700 reichstalers from Feigl Scheyer at 6% per annum to be repaid in two installments. See no. 254.

(רמ ע"ב) קדח ע"ב

1. ב"ה ה[עת'] העתק מק"ס
2. האשה היקרה מ' רייכלה וה"ב כ' יעקב (הו"ה)[5] ב{א}המנוח[6] כ"ה מיכל מאַיי סגל (ז"ל)[7] עק"ס בכא"ה כתחז"ל והודו
3. מעכשיו שחייבי' להקצינה מ' פאגיל אשת הו"ה התורני פו"מ כ"ה ראובן שייאר סג"ל סך שבעה
4. מאות רייכשטאליר בת"ע עצ"ה כתחז"ל עם רווחי' ששה רט מכל מאה רט הנ"ל לשנה ולשלם ולפרוע
5. החצי מהקרן הנ"ל בתשעה חדשי' מהיום וחצי' שניי' מהקרן הנ"ל בשני' עשר חדשי' מהיום ומאחר
6. שנתנו הזוג הנ"ל ג"כ כהיום לאורדר הקצינ' מ' פאגיל ת"י הנ"ל שני ח"כ על הסך חוב

---

1. כפילות במקור (המילה הראשונה כתובה באופן מטושטש)
2. הגאון אב בית דין
3. רב אברהם טריר
4. רב זנוויל טראך
5. תיקון מעל השורה
6. בן המנוח
7. תוספת מעל השורה

7. הנ״ל עם הרווחי׳ הנ״ל ועל הזמני׳ הנ״ל בכן בהתפרע השטר הלז או השני ח״כ הנ״ל אזי גם
8. השני פרוע ובטל הוא נעשה היו׳ יו׳ ויו זיין אייר תקטית לפק ריב[1] ואני[2]

No. 254

Fol. 240b–241a; copy of a court decision from Wednesday 13 September 1758

A copy of an earlier case brought before the court in which the court agreed to make a new copy of the loan agreement mentioned in document no. 253 between Reichle and Jacob Mai and Feigl Scheyer after the original had been lost in a fire. There is a note at the end of this entry referring the user to fol. 48b (no. 43), which suggests that it was this case (and presumably no. 253 as well) that was referred to in the court's ruling in no. 43.

9. העתקהעתק מפסק
10. ה״ה כ״ה מאיר בהו״ה גע[3] כ״ה אהרן מאיי ז״ל ואשתו מ׳ אסתר ת״י הוציעו לפנינו העתק ק״ס
11. מפנקס הנאמני׳ מן האשה מ׳ רייכלה וה״ב כ׳ יעקב מאיי שעשאו ק״ס והודו שחייבי׳ להאשה
12. מ׳ פאגיל אמה של מ׳ אסתר הנ״ל סך שבעה מאות רט בת״ע עם רווחי׳ עצ״ה ששה למאה
13. לשנה לשלם החצי׳ מהקרן {בתעש} בתשעה חדשי׳ והחצי׳ השני בשנים עשר חדשי׳ וגם נתנו הזוג הנ״ל
14. שני ח״כ על שני זמני׳ הנ״ל וזמן הק״ס וח״כ הנ״ל המה ביו׳ אחד ז׳ אייר תק״ט ועל הק״ס הנ״ל נכתב
15. ונמסר השטר אמנם השטר וח״כ הנ״ל המה הי׳ בידה ורשות׳ של מ׳ פאג[י]ל בבית בעלה ה״ה
16. הו״ה פו״מ ר ראובן שייאר סגל ז״ל בעת שנשרף הבית הנ״ל וח״כ הנ״ל המה אוד מוצל מאש[4]
17. השריפה הנ״ל כאשר למראה עינינו אבל השטר נשרף לפי דיבורו בכן ביקשו מאתנו כ׳ מאיר
18. ואשתו הנ״ל לצוות לנאמני׳ הקהלה עידי השטר לתקן ולחדש להם השטר מח ש[5] מזמן הנ״ל
19. ובאשר שהח״כ הנ״ל המה ח״כ הראשוני׳ הנ״ל והמה ברוליגירט מן הזוג הנ״ל מזמן לזמן
20. עד ז׳ ניסן ד[ה]אי שתא תקי״ח העבר ומזמן הלז המה ברוליגירט על ששה חדשי׳ ממילא הוא
21. עכשיו עדיין בתוך זמן הפרעון וגם העדו לפנינו עדי׳ שח״י של הזוג הנ״ל בח״כ הנ״ל

---

1. לא ברור באיזה רב מדובר
2. לא מדובר בהרב חיים גונדרשהיים שבאותה השנה עדיין היה בגיל רך (אולי בן 10; ר׳ הקדמה).
3. גבאי צדקה
4. ר׳ זכריה ג, ב
5. כנראה שהסופר שכח לכתב את האות דלת וצ״ל ׳מחדש׳.

22. הוא ח"י ממש בכן הזדקקו לדבריהם ומצאנו ע"פ הדת והדין לתקי[1] ולהקי' על הק"ס הנ"ל שטר
23. מחדש {מזמן הנ"ל} כפי משמעות הק"ס הנ"ל מזמן {לזמן} הק"ס הנ"ל רק הנאמני' לא ימסרו {..}
24. השטר החדש ליד הזוג הנ"ל כ"א שיוכתב בפניהם על השטר [מ]ע"ל[ד][2] {פרען} (פרעון)[3] הרווחי'
25. כפי שנמצא כתוב על ח"כ הנ"ל ויהי' להשטר הלז כל תוקף ועוז בכא"ה כמו השטר
26. הראשון הנ"ל בלי שום פקפוק כלל והנאמני' יכתבו בתוך השטר קודם ו
27. וקנינא

(רמא ע"א) קכ"ט
1. וקנינא שנכתב ע"פ ב"ד תחת השטר שנשרף כנ"ל לראי' חתמנו היו'
2. י' ד' יוד אלול תקי"ח פק
3. הק' משה ראפף הומבורג
4. הק' נתן פולדאניי[מ]רק
5. הק' משה שווארץ שיל[ד]
6. עיין לעיל (דף מח ע"ב)[4] הטעם שהעתקתי פסק ב"ד הלז

Index to All Cases

Fols. 241b–247b

Rabbi Gundersheim or a copyist made a listing of all cases dealt with in the manuscript to ease the search for material. The list includes the subject matter of the first 34 cases that have been lost from the collection.

רמא ע"ב
סימני' למצוא בקל כל פסק על הצדדי'
דפי'
ש' תקכטל[5]

תקל

1. צ"ל 'לתקן'
2. אולי 'מעבר לדף'
3. תיקון מעל השורה
4. תוספת מעל השורה; ר' כאן מס' 43.
5. = שנת תקכ"ט לפ"ק
6. מילה מעל השורה

ד	פ׳ בין כ״ה יוזל גנץ ובין האחי׳ כ׳ ליב וכ׳ זוסל מַז
ה	פ׳ בין כ״ה ליב מז ובין הו״ה ג״ה כ״ה אייזק בכה״א רייס
ויו ע״ב	פ׳ בין האחי׳ כ׳ בענדיט וכ׳ פער שמש ובין כ׳ יעקב בוקסבוים
ז	פ׳ בין כ׳ אנשיל בהמנוח[1] כ׳ ליב זיכל ובין כ׳ לעמלי זיכל
ט	פ׳ בין האשה מ׳ יענטלה האל׳ איצק שפאניער ובין חותנה כ״ה דוד ב״ה ישראל ש״ש

תקלא

יוד	פ׳ בין האשה מ׳ צפר ובין בני׳ יתמי המנוח כ מאיר שוואווב ז״ל
יב	בין כה אנשיל פפאן ובין האשה מ׳ גוטלה אל׳ כ׳ יאקב ש״ש
יד ע״ב	בין כ״ה יודא שייאר ובין כ׳ הירש מן קינ[י]גשהויפן
טו	בין יתמי המנוח כ׳ ליב ב״כ משה שלאס ובין כ׳ קלמן ב״כ מאיר רויטשילד
ע״ב	השבעת כתובה מן האל׳ מ׳ פראדכה אשת המנוח כ׳ הירץ ווערהאַן

תקלב

טז ע״ב	פסק בין כ״ה אברלי ש״[ש] ובין כ״ה הירץ אופנהיי׳ מן אוביבאך
יז ע״ב	פסק בין כ״ה ליב פרענקל מק״ק פירדא ובין ה״[ג] כ״ה משה שייאר
יט	פ׳ בין כ״ה שמחה סופר ממנהיים ובין כ״ה אברלי איטינגין סג״ל
כ	פ׳ בין כ״ה וואלף פינטשוב ובין כ״ה איצק ווימפא
ע״ב	פ׳ בין כ״ה אברהם ברוינשוויג ובין כ׳ אברם האמיל

תקלג

כא	פ׳ בין כ״ה יוקב מאפ[ט] ובין האשה מ׳ אסתר אל׳ המנוח כ״ה יוקב ווימפא
כג ע״ב	פ׳ בין האשה מ׳ גיילכה בת המנוח כ׳ קאפל העכט ובין האשה אל׳ הירץ [ז][2]
כה	{פ׳} על דבר טוב שהניח הו״ה כ׳ [ז]נוויל שטערן ז״ל
כו	פ׳ על עזבון מן האשה המונחת מ׳ יטלה אל׳ ליב אלטירטה
כז	פ׳ בין כ״ה משה ב״כ גבריאל לאטר ובין כ״ה יעקב בהמנוח[3] כ״ה ליזר שלאס ז״ל
כח ע״ב	בין כ׳ הירש לעהרן ובין האשה מ׳ מיכלה אל׳ כ״ה וואלף כהן ז״ל

(רמב ע״א) קל

כט	פ׳ בין כ׳ אייזק בכ״מ קולפא וכ׳ וואלף ב״כ מיכל קולפא משותפ׳ בבית ובין ה״ה מאיר פלערשהיים
למד	פשר בין האשה מ׳ בריינלה אורשל ובין כ״ה זלמן שאטין
	פשר בין כ׳ אברהם עמריך ובין הבחור כ׳ אייזק בכ״ה וואלף שייאר
ע״ב	פ׳ בין כ׳ הירץ אדליר ובין כ׳ יודא שמואל ווירמש

1. בן המנוח
2. אולי הירץ זיכל (נפטר כ׳ אלול תקכ״ב [אבני זכרון, מס׳ 3112]). באלה תולדות (8.9.1762), לא מוזכר אישה ששרדה לאחר מותו.
3. בן המנוח

לג פ׳ בין האשה מ׳ טריינכה אל׳ כ׳ ליפמן פולדא ובין כ״ה יעסל כהן
לד פ׳ בין האשה מ׳ יטלה אל׳ כ׳ ליב קאסיל ובין היתום כ׳ איצק בה״ה כ׳ בענדיט קאסיל

תקלד
לה (ע״ב)[1] פ׳ על דבר טוב מן המנוח כ״ה ליב בכ״ה איצק קן ז״ל[2]
לו ע״ב פ׳ בין כ״ה זעליגמן ליכ[טן] שטאט מפ[י]רדא ובין האחי׳ כ׳ זוסמן וכ׳ ליב מַז
לז ע״ב פ׳ בין הב״ח כ׳ נטע פאפר[ט] ובין כ״ה אלי׳ וואו[ג]
לט [פ׳] בין כ״ה הירש לנדויא ובין כ״ה איצק ווימפא
מ ע״ב מעשה ב״ד קטן על חצי מקום בבהכ״י העליונה
מא מבד״ג על חצי מקום הנ״ל
עב הלווה על המוכר
מב העתק מפסק לענין בכור מפנקס הראש ב״ד כ״ה נתן מַז
מג פסק בין כ״ה מענדלי ווירטהיי׳ מווירמש ובין הב״ח כ״ה חיים ליב טראך מפירדא
ע״ב פשר בין השדכני׳ כ״ה נתן אופנה ה״ב כ׳ אלי׳ פולדא והאשה מ׳ יענטלה וואהל
מד פ׳ בין הו״ה כ״ה ליב אופנהיי׳ ובין הו״ה כ׳ יודא קולפא ובין כ׳ גומפל מאַיי
מה ע״ב פ׳ בין כ׳ יוזפא טריר ובין אחות אשתו הכלה מ׳ הי[נד]כה בת כ׳ ליזר ש״ש [ז״ל]
מז ע״ב פשר בין השדכני׳ כ׳ יוזפא ווערטהאן וכ׳ וואלף טרויב והבחור כ׳ יעקב מן פייערשטארף
{ובין} והאשה מ׳ קיילכה מפרידבורג
מח פ׳ לכ״ה מאיר לוי סג״ל שביקש מב״ד שטר חדש תחת שטר ש[נ]שרף לו ר״נ
מט פ׳ מענין שטר הנ״ל לכה״מ הנ״ל

רמב ע״ב ב״ה
מ״ט ע״ב פ׳ בין האח׳ בני המנוח כ׳ יעקב בוך ובין כ׳ לעמלי שוסטר כ״ץ
נ׳ פ׳ בין יורשי׳ מן כ״ה אנשיל קאסיל ובין יורשי׳ מן כ״י קאסיל [מד״ט] מאלף [ר״ט]
נא פ׳ בין הו״ה כ׳ טעבלי לנדויא סג״ל ובין כ׳ יוזפא ווערטהאַן משותפי׳ בבית

קהלת
נב ע״ב פ׳ בין כ׳ פער ר״ק ובין האשה מ׳ בילה אל׳ כ׳ קוסיל מן אופיבאך פלעגרן
נג ע״ב מעשה ב״ד ממכירת שני חצאי מקומות מן כ׳ אהרן אורשל ז״ל לכ׳ שמעון ר״ק
_____ חתימת מעשה ב״ד ממכירת חצי בית מן יתומי המנוח כ׳ אנשיל שטרוס
לכ׳ אנשיל ב״ה פלערשהיי׳
נד ע״ב פ׳ בין כ׳ אנשיל זיכל ובין האפטרופסי׳ מעזבון כ״ה יוזלי אופנהיים ז״ל
נו עב מעשה ב״ד בין האשה מרת אסתר אל׳ המנוח כ׳ הירץ אדליר כ״ץ ז״ל ובין י״ח וחתנה
אלחנן פוקס
נז עב מעשה ב״ד מלקיחת חצי בית החיצון צור טרום שלקח כ׳ אברלי ווימפא
נט מעשה ב״ד מלקיחת חצי בית (חיצון) צום טרופל שלקח פ״ה כ״ה ליב אופנהיים [יצ״ו]

---

1. מעל לשורה
2. אולי = כ״י יווא דף מו ע״ב-מז ע״א

סמך	מב״ד מלקיחת שליש פלאטץ צו הינטר קראנך שלקח האשה מ׳ מערלה ברונשוויג
ע״ב	מב״ד מלקיחת רביעית בית פנימי צור גולדני אפפיל שלקח {חתן}[1] כ׳ אייזק זינצהיים
סא ע״ב	פ׳ בין הב״ח מ״[ז] כ׳ ליזר בן (המנוח)[2] שלמה מז ז״ל ובין האשה מ׳ אסתר אל׳ המנוח כ״ה זנוויל מז ז״ל ובנ[ו] החתן כ׳ יוזפא [יצ״ו]
סד	מעשה ב״ד מלקיחת שישית פלאטץ צום הינטר קראניך שלקח האשה מ׳ מערלה אל׳ המנוח כ[מ]״ה משה ברונשוויג סג״ל ז״ל הנ״ל
סה ע״ב	פסק {עלה} בין דבט[3] ובין היתום הבח[4] כ׳ פער ב״ה כ״ה ליב קן ז״ל
סז ע״ב	פ׳ בין כ״ה אברלי ש״ש ובין כ׳ אלחנן פוקס בענין מצרנות
סט ע״ב	שטר אפטרופסיס מחמת דבר טוב של המנוח כ״ה ליב קן ז״ל הנ״ל
ע עב	פסק בין ה״ה כ׳ זלמן ווייסוויילר ובין המשרת פייס אדליר

עא עב	פשר בין ארבעה משרתת מחמת איין טרעפר
דיט[5]	פשר בין כ׳ פייס האַמיל ובין כ׳ אלי׳ אופנהיים
עב	פסק בין ה״ה [ל]יב קאסי[ל] ובין אנשיל ובנו זעליגמן בינגא
עג	פסק בין כ׳ פער ר״ק ובין האשה מ׳ רייכלה אל׳ כ׳ יעקב מייא[6] ז״ל
עה	פסק בין כ׳ הירץ בון ובניו ובין כ׳ יוזל זיכל

(רמ״ג ע״א) קלא

עז עב	פסק בין הבחור כ׳ שמעון אופנהיי׳ ובין כ׳ משה בהמנוח[7] כ׳ בענדיט קאסיל ז״ל
עח עב	פשר בין שדכנים ר׳ נתן אופנה שמאול סופר ליב עמריך קלערכה אויך
עט	פסק בין כ״ה ליב שאטין וכ׳ אברם האן ובין כ׳ מרדכי פאלק
פ	פ׳ בין החברא דבית הכנסת חדש עליונה ובין כ׳ משה בהמנוח כ״ב קאסיל
עב	פסק בין כ׳ שמואל בה״מ כ״ה הענלה שוסטר ובין האשה מ׳ רייצכה אל׳ כמ״ה פייס דייץ
פא עב	מעשה ב״ד ממכירת מקו׳ שלם לכ׳ טעבלי שטיפל מיתמי המנוח כ׳ משה שוואוב ז״ל
פב עב	פסק בין פ״מ כה הירץ ובנו ר׳ זלמן שיף ובין האשה מ׳ שינכה אל׳ כ׳ קאפל כהן ז״ל
פג עב	מעשה ב״ד [מ]לקיחת פלאטץ מן בית שלם צום הינטר קראניך שלקח כ׳ ישי וועטרהאן ולאח[יו]
	חתימת מעשה ב״ד קטן אמר שכ׳ הירץ גייגר יש לו החצי מן פלאטץ שלקח בשבלו[8] ובאשר שע...

---

1. כנראה שנפלה כאן טיפת דיו.
2. מעל השורה
3. דבר טוב
4. הבחור חמד
5. דיטה
6. = מאיי
7. בן המנוח
8. צ״ל ׳בשבילו׳

חתימת מעשה ב״ד הנ״ל לא הזכיר כלום מן כ׳ הירץ הנ״ל לכך לא ה[עמ]דנו מבד״ג רק על ר׳ ...

פד עב מב״ד מלקיחת חצי פלאטץ מבית שלם פנימי צום הינטר פלוג שלקחו האלופי׳ ק׳ גובי׳ יצו

פה פ׳ בין כ׳ יוזלי ב״כ איצק זיכל ובין החתן כ׳ משה בהמנוחי כ׳ לעמלה פלערשהיים

פו פ׳ בין כ׳ גומפל מאיי ובין משותפו בבית האשה מ׳ סערלה אל׳ כ׳ מאיר שוסטר [ז״ל]

פט ע״ב גורל וחלוקה בין הצדדי׳ הנ״ל

ה תקלז

צ ע״ב פסק בין יעקב מן אייבינגין ובין משרתת כאן ציפר בת משה

צא מעשה ב״ד גורל וחלוקה בין זלמן הז אברהם עמריך ר׳ שמואל לנדויא ר׳ סענדר ר״ק

צג פסק בין אל׳ כ׳ אנשיל בון ז״ל ובין אל׳ כ״ה ליפמן דייץ ז״ל בענין המרתף

ע״ב פסק בין אל׳ כ״ה שלמה מז ז״ל ובין אל׳ כ׳ יעקב בוך ז״ל

צד גורל על מקו׳ שלם בע״נ בין כ״ה הירש לנדויא ובין כ״ה משה פלערשהיים

ע״ב מעשה ב״ד וחלוקת בית צום שוועהרט בין כ׳ מאיר קאסל ובין כ׳ משה שמיטץ[2]

צו ע״ב מבד״ג מלקיחת שלשה רביעית פלאטץ שלקח כ׳ יואל האלי

צז פסק בין בעלי חובות של ר׳ יעקב קן ז״ל ובין כ״ה יוקב בן כ״ה ליב ממנהיי׳ בעל ציפר ש[וואב]

צח מעשה בד״ג מלקיחת רביעית בית צום וועטרהאן שלקח כ״ה אהרן פלעש

עוד מבד״ג מן מקו׳ שלם בע״נ התחתונה שלקח כ״ה הירץ פלעש

רמג ע״ב ב״ה

צ״ח ע״ב מעשה ב״ד ממכירת שמינית בית צור דרייא רעהמר שלקח כ׳ יוסף בכ״ה מרדכי האמל מן הגובי׳ [יצו]

עוד שם מעשה ב״ד מלקיחת רביעית בית צור הינדן שלקח כ׳ משה בכשלמה[3] אופנהיי׳ מן האלופי׳ גובי׳ יצו

צט ע״א מעשה ב״ד ממכירת שליש בית צור וויסה לאטר שלקח החתן כ׳ מאיר זיכל שהי׳ שייך לגובי׳ יצ[ו]

ע״ב מעשה ב״ד ממכירת שני רביעית מקומות בע״א שלקח כ״ה גומפל קן מן בעלי חובות של המנוח ר׳ יעקב קן

עוד שם מעב״ד ממכירת מקו׳ שלם בע״נ התיכונה שלקח כ׳ ליב מענץ מהנ״ל

ק הודאה שנעשה בפני ב״ד מן כ״ה גומפל קן על לקיחת שני רביעית מקומות הנ״ל לאחיו כ״פ קן

---

1. בן המנוח
2. צ״ל ׳שלאס׳
3. ב״כ (בן כבוד) שלמה

ע"ב מב"ד ממכירת שני חצאי פלעטץ שהי' עומדי' עליהם הבת' החיצוני' צור ענגי טיהר אונד צום (פאלקין)[1]

עוד שם מב"ד ממכירת חצאי פלאטץ שהי' עומד עליו הבית החיצון צור פאדר שוהל שלקח האשה מ' שינלה שוסט[ר]

קא פסק בין כ"מ זיסקינד במ["ה] אברם שטערן ובין גיסיו האחי' כ' דוד וכ פייס בני המנוח כ' מעדלה האמיל סג"ל ז"ל

קג עוד פסק אחד בין הצדדי' הנ"ל

תקל"ח

קד פסק בענין בית הכנסת שהי' בהקדש פלאטץ ששאלו האלופי' גובי' יצו

עב פסק בין הגובי' יצו ושכני הקדש פלאטץ המחזיקי בית צום הירש הארן כ' זעלקלי שטרויז וכ' מיכל וכ' הירץ ה"ה ומחזיקי בית פנימי צום עליפאנד האשה מ' שרלה אל' המנו' כ' אהרן ווירמש והאשה שרה אל' כ' קלמן פאלק וחותנה ברוך יפה

קו עב מעשה ב"ד ממכירת שישת בית פנימי צור הינטר זוהן שלקח ר' יחיאל שייער מן הגוב[י']

קז עא מעשה ב"ד ממכירת חצי מקו' בע"נ התחתונה שלקח ר' משה רינדשקאפף והי' שייך לר' זלמן (שיף)[2]

עוד שם פסק בין חברא ישן דביקור חולי' ובין דוד במשה[3] הירשהארן

עב פסק בין כ"ה יואל בינגא ובין יורשי המנוח כמ"ה מאיר שווארץ שילד ז"ל

קח ע"ב מעשה ב"ד ממכירת שבעה חלקי ששה עשר ממקו' שלם בע"א שלקח הדיין כ"ה מאיר שיף

[ק]ט {...} פסק ב"ד בין האשה מ' פערלכי אל' כ"ה דוד גמבורג ושארי בעלי חובות מבעלה [ז"ל]

ק יוד עב מעשה ב"ד ממכירת חצי בית חיצון צום פריהליכה מאן שלקח כ' יחיאל כהן מן הגובי'

תקלט מעשה ב"ד ממכירת חצי בית צום פאגלשגזאנג שלקח ר' מאיר פלערשהיי' מן הגובי'

קא מעשה ב"ד מרביעית בית פנימי צום רויטה טארן שלקח ר' זכריה ווירטהיי'

תקמם מעשה ב"ד מחצי בית החיצון צום רויטה טארן שלקח ר' גומפריכט פרידבורג

ע"ב רשוין להאפטרופסי' דיתמי המנוח כ' משה שוואוב למכור רביעית בית צור שייער

[ד]פי' ב"ה (רמ"ד ע"א) קלב

קיב פסק בין השדכני' בקשור חיתון הב"ח כ' פער קן עם בת הו"ה זוסמן ריסלסהיים

עב מעשה ב"ד על חלוקת פלאטץ אחורי שני בת' הסמוכי' צום פאפיגייא אונד צום פראש

---

1. מעל לשורה

2. מתחת לשורה

3. בן משה

קיד ע"ב מעשה ב"ד ממכירת מקו' שלם שלקח כ' קלמן רייס וחצי מקו' שלקח כה ישעי' בכ"ה אהרן לעה[רן]

מעשה ב"ד על מקו' שלם בע"נ שלקח כ' אברהם ע(מ)ריד[1] שהי' שייך לכ"ה שמעון זינצהיים

עוד על מקו' שלם בע"א העליונה שלקח כ' אנשיל בן אברם האן ושהי' שייך לכ"ה שמעון [הנ"ל]

קטו פ' בין אפטרופסי' על דבט[2] מן רליב[3] קן ז"ל ובניו ר גומפל ור פער קן

קטז פ' בין האלופי' גובי' יצו ובין ג"ה כ' יעקב עמדין ור איצק ווינר מחמת הקדש פלאטץ

קיט ע"ב פ' בין משרתת של האשה המונחת מ' שינלה מענץ ובין יורשי' שלה

קכא עב פ' בין ר' פייטל קאסיל ובין ר איצק בג"ה ליב קן

תקמא

קכג מעשה ב"ד על מקו' שלם בע"א התחתונה שהי' שייך לכ"ה נטע ווענלר ונמכר לכ"ה איצק זיצה[יים]

מעשה ב"ד על חצי מקו' בע"א התחתונה שהי' שייך להאלופי' גובי' יצו נמכר לכ' משה בן {....} (קאסיל)[4]

עב פסק בין כ' יוזלה זיכל ובין יתמי המנוח כ' איצק במיכל[5] האמיל ז"ל

קכד שטר מכירה על מקו' שלם בע"נ האמצית לכ"ה ליב בר"פ[6] קן {..} תחת שטרו שנאבד

קכה פטורי' להאפטרופסי מן היתום כ' איצק בן משה שוואוב ז"ל

עב פ' בין האשה אל' ר' גרשון דארום וב[י]ן היתום כ' מיכל בן אנשיל מענדלר

קכו ע"ב [מ]ב"ד על מקו' שלם בע"נ האמצעי שהי' שייך ליתמי ר' הירץ ריינגאנום נמכר לכ' גדלי' שטיבל

קכז פ' בין פו"מ כה הירש כהן ובין הב"ח כ' מאיר פאלק

מב"ד על מקו' שלם שעומד כ' הירץ פלערשהיי' נמכר לכ' טעבלי פולדא שהי' שייך לששה משותפי'

ע"ב פ' בין ג"ה יעקב עמדין וג"ץ ר' איצק זינצהיים מחזיקי הקדשפלאטץ ובין מחזיקי עלי פאנד

קכח מב"ד על מקו' שלם שעומד עלי' כ יוקב ב"י רינדשקאפף בעאה"ת נמכר לכ' אברם האן והי' שייך לששה משות[פי']

ע"ב פ' בין כה הירץ ואחיו כ' אהרן צונץ ובין כ"ה משה שפניער וכ"ה חיים שוסטר

קכט ע"ב מעשה ב"ד על מקו' שלם שעומד עלי' כ' משה לוי שיה' שייך למשותפי' ונמכר לכ' ליב ב"י אופנהיים

---

1. האות מ"ם מעל השורה
2. דבר טוב
3. ר' ליב
4. המילה מתחת לשורה
5. בן מיכל
6. בן רבי פער

עוד מב״ד על חצי מקו׳ הדבוק בשטענדר שעומד כ״ה יעקב האמיל נמכר לכ׳ משה ב[1] בענדיט קאסיל

קל פ׳ על סילוק האל׳ המנוח כ׳ משה טויב ז״ל

רמ״ד ע״ב[2]

תקמבלפק מז״ט ב״ה

דפי׳

קלב פסק על השץ ומץ[3] בעלרייכה על המשפט שנשלח לנו ע״י השררה ירה[4] פה

קלג ע״ב פסק בענין דבר טוב מן האל׳ בריינלה אשת נטע אורשל ז״ל

קלד פסק במצרנות על רביעית פלאטץ צום גולדנה קאפף בין כ״ה מאיר ב״ב וכ׳ פייס אדליר

ע״ב פסק בין בעלי חובות {וחלוקה} מן המנוח כ׳ ליב ריינום ז״ל וחלוקה שביניהם מן עזבון כ׳ ליב הנ״ל

[ק]לה פסק האל׳ המנוח הקדוש כ׳ גומפל [מ]איי ובין האפטרופסי׳ של בנותי׳ הו״ה כ׳ מכאל מאיי

פסק בין האלופי׳ קציני׳ גובי׳ יצו ובין הו״ה גץ[5] כ׳ זלמן הז יצו

[קל]ו מעשה ב״ד ממכירת שני חצאי מקומות שהי׳ שייכי׳ להיתומה בת כ׳ געץ איטינגין שנמכר בפני ב״ד חצי אחת לכ״ה מאיר ב״וו[6] פולדא יצו והאחת לכ׳ חיים בהמנוח[7] כ״ה הענוך האלי ז״ל

פ׳ בין אל׳ כ״ה מרדכי ב״וו אופנהיים ובין כ׳ מרדכי פאלק כץ

קלז פ׳ בין האל׳ המנוח כ׳ גומפל מאיי סג״ל ז״ל ובין האפטרופסי׳ מעזבון המנוח ז״ל בענין סילוק ה[נ]״ל

קלח עב פ׳ בין האל׳ המנוח כ״ה וואלף בוריך סגל ז״ל ובין חתנו כ׳ ליפמן טאקטר בענין סילוק

קלט פסק בין אל׳ המנוח כה וואלף בוריך ז״ל ובין חתנה הנ״ל בענין הנ״ל

[ק]מא פ׳ בין האל׳ המנוח כ׳ מאיר פירדא ובין כ׳ י״ט אופנהיים

קמד פ׳ על ר שואל חזן

עב חליצה {לאל׳} להאשה מ׳ בונלה בת כמ״ה יעקב שמש נר״ו אל׳ המנוח כ״ה קלמן בכה״א ר״ש[8]

פסק ורשיון להאשה מ׳ רעכלה אשת ר׳ נטע וועצלר למכור חצי בית חיצון צום גולדני בר[ונ]ן

תקמג

---

1. בן
2. חלק מצד הימין בדף נקרע וחסר
3. השליח ציבור ומורה צדק
4. ירום הודו
5. גבאי צדקה
6. בן וואלף
7. בן המנוח
8. בן כבוד הרב אנשיל רויטשילד

[ק]מה פסק בין הבעל כ' אברהם בר"א פולדא ובין אשתו מ' יטכה בת המנוח כ"ה פייבלמן עמד[ין]

עב כתב ראי' לכ' יט[1] אופנהיים וכ' יוסף טויב על חלק[ם] בשני מקומות שנמכר בפנינו

עוד ליורשי גץ[2] ר פער קן מה שמ[גיע] על חלקם בשני מקומות וחצי קלעפכי

קמו כתב ראי' ליורשי כ' יוקב ב"מ אופנהיים מה שמגיע להם משני מקומות וחצי הנ"ל
מעשה ב"ד ממכירת מקו' שלם בע"נ עליונה לכ' שלמה לורי' שהי' שייך לגובי' יצו

ע"ב פסק על טו"ת הנשלח לנו מן השררה יר"ה מן קארבאיי בין כ"ה יוזפא ברוכ//הויזן ובין כ' משה מאמלוינגזען

קמז ע"ב מעשה ב"ד ממכירת חצי בית פנימי צור הינטר זוהן להאחי' כ' אנשיל וכ' זעליגמן בני המנוח כ' יוקב שש[3] ז"ל שהי' שייך לגובי' יצו

מפתח מ"ט בע"ה (רמה ע"א) משנת תקמג

[ק]מח גורל ממחזיקי בית החיצון צום העליבאד

קמט פ' בין השמש התור' כ"ה זיסקינד שטערן ובין כ"ה זעלקלי שטיבל וגיסתו יענטלה מן קאבלענ[ץ]

קנב כתב ראי{'ל..} למחזיקי' ושותפי' מן {מקו'} שלשה רביעית מן מקו' שלם שלקח כ' ליב ב"י אופנהיי'

ע"ב מעשה ב"ד ממכירת מקו' שלם בע"א עליונה להאחי' כ משה וכ' ליב פולדא שהי' שייך להמנוח כ' אלי' פולדא

קנג פסק ב"ד בין מחזיקי בית צו דער אייהל ובין מחזיקי בית צום גולדן קאפף

קנד פסק בין אל' המנוח כ' שמואל שוסטר ז"ל ובין אל' כ' סענדר שוסטר ז"ל ויורשיו

קנה פסק בין כ' מאיר בהמנו'[4] פ"ה כ"ה יוסף שוסטר ובין כ"ה נטע בכ"ה שמואל שוסטר

קנח ע"ב פסק מחמת המנייני' מן ה"ג אב"ד נרו[5] ושני ב"ד יצו על פקודת הקהל יץ[6]

תקמד

קנט פסק בין האל' הרבני' (המנוח)[7] כמ"ה שמואל זצ"ל אב"ד דק"ק פרידבורג ובין כ' משה בלעמלי[8] שוסטר כץ

קס ע"ב מעשה ב"ד ממכירות מקו' שלם בענ[9] התיכונה לכ"ה נטע פלערשהיי' שהי' שייך ליורשי' כ"ה מענדלי שפ[ייער]
וגם חצי מקו' בע"נ התיכונה לפו"מ כ' אברם האמיל סג"ל שהי' שייך ליורשי' הנ"ל

---

1. יום טוב
2. גבאי צדקה
3. שווארץ שילד
4. בן המנוח
5. נטריה רחמנא ופרקיה
6. ישמרנו צורו
7. מעל לשורה
8. בן לעמלי
9. בעזרת נשים

וגם מקו' שלם בע"א התחתונה לכ' פייבל בן יעקב שלאס שהי' שייך להנ"ל
וגם שני חצאי מקומות בע"א העליונה להו"ה גץ[1] כ' הירש הז שי' שייך להנ"ל
וגם מעשה ב"ד ממכירות חצי בית צום קאמעהל לכ' אהרן צונץ שהי' שייך לכ' הירץ הירש הארן

קסא מעשה ב"ד בין מחזיקי בית צום ק[א]מעהל לכ' אהרן צונץ וכ' דוד וכ' פייס האמילי יצו

קסב פ[ס]ק בין גה[2] כ' יעקב עמדין ובין כ' משה ב"המנוח כ' בע[נ]דיט קאסיל

קסג פסק בין היורשי' של המנוח פו"[מ] כ"ה מאיר פלערשהיים ז"ל

קע סילוק להאל' מרת בילה אל' המנוח כ' הירץ שט[י]בל ז"ל

קעא פ' בין כ"ה אנשיל שייער סג"ל ובין אמו חורגתו אל' המנוח כ"ה משה שייער ז"ל

קעג פ[3] בין כ' אברהם ב"ה אהרן פולדא ואשתו מ' יטכה בת כ"ה פייבלמן עמדין ז"ל

קעד פ' בין החתן כ' זוסל דייטץ ובין אחותו אל' כ' אנשיל בוריך ז"ל

קעו פסק מסילוק האשה מרת הענדלה אל' המנוח כ' מרדכי שטיבל

קעז פסק על מצרנות מן רביעית בית פנימי לכ"ה מרדכי מז יצו

תקמה מעשה ב"ד ממכירות שליש בית חיצון צו דער רויס לכ"ה [זיסק]נד ה"ה[4] שהי' שייך ליתום של כ' פער [ווירמש]

עב פסק בע['] בני כ' ליב ב"מ[5] שלאס על בני כ' זעליגמן האן

קעח ע"ב פסק בע' בני האשה המונחת מ' שרלה [פלעגר]ן ז"ל

(רמה ע"ב)
תקמה
דפי'

קעט פסק בין כ' קלמן בכ"ה ישראל שטיבל ובין הבתולה מ' מאטלה ב"כ אהרן העכט ז"ל

ע"ב פ' בין כ' יודא קולפא ובין כ' איצק שטיבל

קפ פ' על השאלה שנשלח מק"ק ווין מהשררה יר"ה בענין תביעות מוטטרליך

עב פ' בין כ' שלמה לורי' ובין בני המנוח כ"ה מר(ד)כי[6] אופנהיי' בעזבון שינלה מז ז"ל

קפד עב פ' בין כ"ה גומפל עמריך ובין חתנו ר' משה פולדא משנת [...]

קפה כרוז מיו' כ[יל]ת (מ)יולדות {...}[7] מעשה ב"ד ממכירת רביעית בית פנימי צום קראך ביום שהי' שייך להמנוח כ"ה נתן אדליר ז"ל להחתן שמואל שאטין

ע"ב פסק בענין {.} יתמי בני המנוח כ' פער גנץ ז"ל בענין חלוקה [שב]ינהם

קפו על השאלה שנשלח מהשררה מווין על ענין הנ"ל

---

1. גבאי צדקה
2. גבאי הקהילה
3. פסק
4. הירש הארן
5. בן מרדכי
6. ד מעל לשורה
7. מעל לשורה

תקמו

קפ״ז פסק בין הדיין כ״ה ליזר וואלי ובין כ״ה מאיר רויטשילד ובעסק סרסרנות

פסק בין כ״ה יעקל טריר מאויפיבאך ובין האל׳ המנוח כ״ה גרשון עמדין

קפ״ח פסק בסילוק האל׳ המנוח כ״כ גרשון עמדין ז״ל

קץ מעשה ב״ד ממכירת חצי מקו׳ בע״נ {...}[1] העליונה לכ״ה יחיאל כהן שהי׳ שייך להו״ה גובי׳ יצו

פסק בענין דבר טוב של המונחת מ׳ פייל בר״א שוסטר מן וואסר טרקלוניגין (...)[2]

עב מעשה ב״ד ממכירת מקו׳ שלם בע״נ ל[כ״ה] גומפריך פ״ב שהי׳ שייך להמנו׳ כ׳ אהרן אוקס

קצא מעשה ב״ד ממכירת מקו׳ שלם בע״נ התיכונה לכ׳ זנוויל שטיבל

ומן מקו׳ שלם בע״א התחתונה לכ׳ שלמה לוריא שהי׳ שייכי׳ לאשת כ״ה הירץ גנץ

פסק בין אל׳ ובני׳ של כ״ה משה דייץ ובין היתומה של אברהם דייטץ

קצד מעשה בד[3] ממכירת חצי מקו׳ בע״א העליונה לכ׳ אברהם רייס שהי׳ שייך לאל׳ ר׳ מאדל שטרויז

עב פסק בין כ״ה איצק הלברשטאט ובין כ׳ לימא ב[ר״מ] זיכל יצו

קצו פסק וסילוק להאל׳ המנוח כ׳ וואלף לעכניך ז״ל

קצז פסק בין כ״ה פייס ראפף ובין כ״ה ליב שלאס יצו

קצח עב פסק בין הדיין כ״ה מאיר שיף נר״ו ובין גבאי ת״ת כ״ה מאיר רויטשילד יצו

צט עב פסק בענין דב״ט מן ר ליב רייס ז״ל

ר [תוק]ף מעשה ב״ד על חליפין שנעשה בין האחי׳ בני המנוח כ״ה הירץ פולדא ז״ל

רא [מ]גוף מעשה ב״ד של מה שנעשה בין האל׳ המנוח כ׳ אייזק האן ובין שלשה בנותי[ה] ... ו[חתנה כ׳ חי]ים האלי יצו

תק[מ״ז] בה (רמו ע״א)

[ר]ב ע״ב פסק בין הדיין כ״ה מאיר שיף נר״ו ובין הו״ה גב״תת כ״ה מאיר רויטשילד יצו

תקמז

רד ע״ב שאלה בענין חליצה

רה פסק בעזבון האשה משרתת פלעגרן מ׳ שרלה ז״ל לחותנה כ׳ שמען בידונגין יצו

בענין חליצה אל׳ מ׳ שינכה קן מן ר גומפל קן

עב מעשה ב״ד ממכירת חצי מקו׳ בע״נ התיכונה לכ׳ מאיר ק[אסי]ל מן האלופי׳ גובי׳ יצו

פסק בן כ׳ איצק שיף ובין ה[ו״ה] כ״ה ליב האמיל ומשותפיו

רו עב חליצה מן האשה בריינלה אל׳ ר אהרן דעטמוהל

מעשה ב״ד על מכירת חצי בית צום קנויבליך לכ׳ חיים טאקטר מן האלופי׳ גובי׳ יצו

---

1. מעל לשורה
2. יש מילה לא ברורה מתחת לשורה.
3. בית דין

תקמ"ח מעשה ב"ד על מכירת חצי בית צור גלאך לכ' מאיר קאסיל מן האלופי' גובי' יצו שהי'
שייך לכ' יוזפא הירש מז צו

רז בעניין חליצה עניי' שנשאה איש טרם שקיבלה חליצה מיבום שלה

מעשה ב"ד על מכירת חצי מקו' בע"[א] העליונה לכ' מאיר קאסיל מן כ' יוזפא הירש

עב פסק בין כ' אליעזר ב"כ נתן הלוי מן קק[1] מנהיים ובין היתום כ' משה קן

תקנון

רח עב פסק בענין דבר טוב של המנוח כה פער {.....} ב"ר ליב קן ז"ל

רט עב פסק בין ר הירץ צונץ ובין הרב"ד מהו' אברהם (נרו[2])[3] ובין ר' זלמן טרי[4] כץ בענין
בהמ"ד של המנוח ר' אלי' שייער ז"ל

ריא עב פסק לקהל וגובי' בענין עשיות בעלי מעריכי'

ריב בענין הנ"ל ע"ב כרוז בענין הנ"ל

ריג סדר חליצה להאשה מ' אסתר אל' המנוח כ' מאיר בר"ש מז ז"ל מן בחור יחזקאל מז

פסק בין הירץ זאנקוועהרט ובין כ' איצק בכ"ה ליב האמיל סגל

תקנ"א

רטו פסק בין האשה מ' רייכלה אל' כ' אייזק האן ובין חותנה כ"ה מיכל האמיל סג"ל

ריח אגרת להגאב"ד נר"ו דקק[5] פירדא יע"א מחמת דבר טוב של ר' ליב שלאס ז"ל

עב פסק על דבר טוב מן האשה המונחת מ' מלכה בת ר' אהרן מיץ מחמת בת של כ' יודא
שמואל

(רמו ע"ב) ב"ה

ריט פסק בין האחי' כ יוזל וכ' יודא זיכל ובין כ' משה זיכל

רדה פסק שני בין הצדדי' הנ"ל

רדו עב קיום הפס"ד מצדדי'

תקנ"ב

רדז פסק בין היתום והיתומה בני המנוח כ"ה ליב פוסיק ז"ל

רדח סדור חליצה להאשה מ' געלכה אל' המנוח כ' טעבלי שטיבל מיבום (הב"ח)[6] ליב יצו

שם פסק על בן של פייס ק"מ[7] /

מכירה על מקו' שלם בענ[8] העליונה שקנה כ' מאדל שוסטר

---

1. קהילת קודש
2. נטריה רחמנא ופרקיה
3. מעל לשורה
4. צ"ל 'טריר'
5. דקהילת קודש
6. מעל לשורה
7. כנראה 'קהל משרת' (ר' מס' 240).
8. בעזרת נשים

עב	פסק בין אל׳ כ׳ בענדיט שמש ובין כ׳ פער שמש
רלא	רשימה מכלי בית להאל׳ ל[מ]יגר אל׳ חליצה מן האל׳ הנ״ל
רלב	פסק בין יורשי׳ ר ליב פוסיק ובין בעלי חובות אביהם
עב	חליצה אל׳ המנוח כ׳ ליב ווינדמיהל מיבמה ר׳ אברהם ווינדמיהל
	מכירה על מקו׳ שלו׳[1] בענ[2] העליונה לכ׳ יוזפא מז מן האלופי׳ גובי׳ יצו

Fol. 247a is blank.

Fol. 247b

Rabbi Gundersheim listed the birth dates of his two children.

(רמז ע״ב)

1. ב״ה
2. בתי הנה[3] תי׳ נולד למ״ט יו׳ ג יט טבת תקנון לפק
3. בני משה שי׳ נולד למ״ט יו׳ ג דז תמוז תקנבל ה׳ יזכני לגדל אותם
4. לעבודתו וליראתו לתורה ולחופה ולמ״ט א״ס

---

1. צ״ל ׳שלם׳
2. בעזרת נשים
3. כנראה ׳חנה׳

Appendices

All of the material cited here from the Frankfurt community record book (*pinqas*) is copied directly from the unpublished transcription of and commentary on the Frankfurt *pinqas* prepared by the late Aryeh Segall and housed at The Central Archives for the History of the Jewish People, Jerusalem. Any additions beyond the correction of typographical errors and adaptations of style and bibliographic format have been noted. Transcriptions of all other material are my own unless otherwise stated.

Appendix 1

נספח א

מתוך פנקס דק"ק פרנקפורט בנושא החובות של יעקב קן ז"ל

[476] כ' תמוז תקל"ו (7.7.1776)

רמז ע"א

יום א', ך' תמוז תקל"ו לפ"ק, אחרי שנתהוו שהר"ר יעקב בהמנוח התורני מהור"ר איצק ז"ל הלך לעולמו וחלי"ש,[1] ולאחר ה[עד]רתו[2] נמצא בעזבונו שלא היה די סיפוק לשלם את חובותיו, גלל כן בא העזבון הנ"ל תחת ידי [ב"כ] בעלי חוב של הר"ר יעקב ז"ל הנ"ל. ובעלי חוב שלו המה אינו נימולים ונימולים. ואשתו מרת הנלי חי(!) אחרי מיתות בעלה כמו איזה חדשים.[3] ונתמנה על פי החברותא קדישא י"ץ שלשה אפטרופסים, דהיינו ה"ה התורני הדיין כהר"ר אברהם טריר כ"ץ יצ"ו וה"ה גובה צדקה כהר"ר יעקב בהר"ר פער קן ז"ל[4] וה"ה כהר"ר איצק בהו"ה ג"ץ כהר"ר ליב קן יצ"ו.[5] ותבעו האפטרופסים הנ"ל בשביל יתמי האשה מרת הנלי ז"ל הנ"ל את כתובתה ותוספתה של האשה הנ"ל,[6] והבעלי חוב מבני עמינו נתנו להם טרחה ויגיעה הרבה לפצות ולפייס את הבעלי חוב אשר לא מבני עמנו המה, לרצות בזה ליתן ליתמי הנ"ל מה שיגיע להם איברהויפט[7] לפני כתובתה ותוספת' 4500 *f* וגם על חלקם מיתמי אלף זהובים קרן נעבשט אלי רוקשטענדיגי אונד לויפנדי רווחים על אלף זהובים הנ"ל מן אבליגאציאן שעומדת אצל אדון לאנדגראף מדארמשטט יר"ה,[8] וגם מלבושים [ ][9] ווייס אונד שפיצין גרעהט[10] מה שנמצא בחדר שמת בה האשה מרת

1. יעקב בן יצחק קן, אחיינו של הרב משה קן ושל בער קן. פרנס, ולפי הרשום על מצבתו גם שתדלן הקהילה ואיני יודע בשל מה ניתן לו תואר זה. נפטר ביום ד' כסליו תקל"ה.
2. כתם המכסה 2-3 אותיות והשלמתי לפי התוכן.
3. הנלה בת אפרים דרעזין. היא היתה אשתו השלישית של יעקב קן לאחר שהיה נשוי לפני כן לשתי אחיותיה בזו אחר זו. לפי אטלינגר נערכו נישואין אלה בערך בשנת 1757. אין לדעת מי מבין ארבעת ילדיו של יעקב קן -יצחק, משה, בער ושמשון-נולדו ממנה.
4. בן דודו של יעקב קן.
5. ליב קן היה אחיו של יעקב בן בער קן ולכן היה גם הוא קרוב של יעקב קן.
6. לפי ההלכה יש לגביית כתובה קדימה לגבי גביית בעלי חוב אחרים רק אם יש לאלמנה שעבוד קודם להם, אחרת נדחה חיוב גביית הכתובה בפני בעל החוב שגובה תחילה (שו"ע, אה"ע סי' קב). במקרה שלפנינו מדובר בנסיון מצד בעלי החוב להגיע לידי פשרה עם האפוטרופסים של היתומים ולטענתם במטרה להבטיח את זכויותיהם והעניין לא הובא לפני בית דין, כנראה מאחר שבין בעלי החוב היו גם לא יהודים. ניסוח הדברים עמום ואין אפשרות לעמוד על כל פרטי המו"מ שהתנהל בין האפוטרופסים לבין בעלי החוב.
7. = בכלל. הכוונה, כנראה, שבעלי החוב הציעו לפצות את היתומים בסכום של 4,500 ר"ט ובחלקם בחוב שעמד לזכותו של הנפטר, לפני שידונו בעניין הכתובה והתוספת וזכותם לגביהם.
8. תרגום: 'וכן כל הרווחים (הרבית) המצטברים והשוטפים על אלף הזהובים הנ"ל משטר החוב העומד אצל הלאנדגראף מדרמשטט יר"ה'. הלנדגראף (לויס התשיעי – א.פ.) היה חייב כספים ליהודים רבים והיה במצב של פשיטת רגל מתמדת מאז 1730. רק בשנים 1778-1779 שולמו לבעלי החוב חלק מהכספים שהגיעו להם (ראה: דייץ, עמ' 163).
9. יש כאן כתם דיו ולא ברור אם יש מילה מחוקה או לא.
10. תרגום: 'כלי לבן ומעשי תחרה'.

הנלה הנ"ל, ונעשה האינפינדאריום[1] מכתב יד נאמני קהילתנו יע"א, ואמרנו להאפטרופסים הנ"ל שכך עלתה בהסכמת כל הבעלי חוב הנ"ל ליתן להם בשביל יתמי הנ"ל כנ"ל ובזה יתרצו, וכוונו לטובת יתמי הנ"ל. והאפטרופסים הנ"ל מסרבים וממאן בזה להתרצות ולפשר הנ"ל, ומדאגה בדבר פן ואולי שעל ידי כך יסתעף שיבוא במשפט בערכאות ויוכל להיות פן ואולי שלא לבד שיאבדו היתומים הנ"ל ח"ו כל זכיותיהם שיש להם מחמת כתובת אמם, אף גם זאת שיהיה ח"ו לדורי דורת לפוקה ולמכשול בכלל שיאבדו זכיותיהם ולא יהיה להם מחמת כתובתה קדימה נגד בעלי חוב, גלל כן באנו בעלי חוב, הלא הם הו"ה פ"ו כהר"ר אברהם ווייניג וה"ה הו"ה פ"ו כהר"ר יודא שוסטר וה"ה הו"ה גובה הקהל כ' הירץ בון וה"ה הו"ה גובה הקהל כ' רפאל האן סג"ל וה"ה הו"ה גובה הקהל כהר"ר ליב רייז[2] וכתבתנו זאת למשמרת לדורי דורת לבל תהיה האמת נעדרת שאין אשם תלוי בהבעלי חוב מבני עמנו, כי המה עשו כל הצטדקאות לעשות פשר דבר הנ"ל, ובאם שיסתעף להבא ח"ו קלקול בהנ"ל המה הצילו נפשם והאשם תלוי בהאפטרופסים הנ"ל שהיו מסרבים בדבר.

1. רשימת העזבון.
2. אין ספק שרק הודות לעובדה שבעלי החוב היו פרנסים וגובים רשמה תעודה זו שתוכנה בעל אופי פרטי והצהרתי בפנקס הקהל.

Appendix 2

נספח ב

מתוך פנקס דק"ק פרנקפורט בנושא ההקדש פלאטץ

[484] ח' סיון תק"ם (11.6.1780)

רנא ע"א

ב"ה

אחרי שנשמע קול העברה במחנה העברים[1] שהיתה בהמקום שנקרא הקדש פלאץ[2] השלכת אשפה לחוץ שנקרא אויז ווארף,[3] ובאים הקונים שקנו את המקום הנ"ל, דהיינו האלופים והקצינים גובה הקהל כ' יעקב עמדין יצ"ו וגובה צדקה כהר"ר איצק זינצהיים סג"ל יצ"ו[4] בקבלנא לפני החברותא קדישא יצ"ו באומרם שזה לא נודע להם מעולם וגם לא הודיע להם בשעת הקנין מקום הנ"ל שהיה שם באותו מקום השלכת אשפה לחוץ, ובוודאי יהי' ריעותא גדולה אם יהיה שם השלכת אשפה לחוץ, ואם היו יודעים מזה לא היו קונים אותו מקום הנ"ל. ומאחר שראו האלופים והקצינים גובים יצ"ו תוך הרשימה שמונח בחדר הגובים אשר שם נרשם המקומות שהוא השלכת אשפה לחוץ[5] ולא נמצא תוך הרשימה הנ"ל שיש באותו מקום שקנו הקצינים הנ"ל השלכת אשפה לחוץ, בכן עלתה בהסכמת החברותא קדישא יצ"ו דש תוך פנקס הקהל יצ"ו אינסירירט ולהאלופים קצינים גובים יצ"ו הנ"ל העתק דאפון געבין זאל ווירדן שאותו מקום הנ"ל שקנו כנ"ל פון אויז ווירפונג האשפה בפרייאט איזט.[6] ומחויבים הקהל יצ"ו לפצות את האלופים הקצינים קונים הנ"ל ויורשיהם ובאי כוחם מכל העוררים שיבואו ויערערו על זה ויאמרו שיש שם השלכת אשפה לחוץ, יהיה המערער מי שהוא, הן ערעור דיחיד או דרבים והן על ידי השררה יר"ה. וכל ההוצאות {ע"י} שיעלו מכח ערעור הנ"ל מחויבים הקהל לשלם מקופת הקהל אונד הקצינים קונים הנ"ל לגמרי דעס פאלס ניכטש צו לאשט גליגט זאל קעני ווירדן וקהל יצ"ו שולדיג גהאלטין זיא דעם פאלס שאדלאז צו האלטין.[7]

נעשה היום, יום א', ח' סיון תקמ"ם לפ"ק.

הק' יוזפא גונדרשהיים[8]
הק' מאיר בן משה פלערשהיים ז"ל

---

1. עפ"י הפסוק בשמואל א, ד ו.
2. המגרש שליד ההקדש שהיה בקצה הרחוב.
3. פסולת, אשפה.
4. יצחק בן רפאל זינצהיים
5. על סדרי הוצאת האשפה מה'רחוב' ראה: (סגל לא הספיק להשלים – א.פ.). המחבר אינו מזכיר את העובדה שהיה ברשות הגובים רשימה של המקומות בהם היה מותר להשליך את האשפה.
6. תרגום: 'שירשם בתוך פנקס הקהל יצ"ו ויינתן העתק מכך לאלופים הקצינים הגובים יצ"ו הנ"ל שאותו מקום הנ"ל שקנו כנ"ל משוחרר מהשלכת אשפה'.
7. תרגום: 'ושלא יהיה אפשר לחייב את הקצינים הקונים הנ"ל בנידון זה לגמרי והקהל יצ"ו יהיו חייבים לפצות אותם בעניין זה'.
8. חתימות מקוריות.

Appendix 3

נספח ג

מתוך פנקס דק"ק פרנקפורט בנושא החזן ר' שואל

[439] כ"א מרחשון תק"ן (10.11.1789)

ריד ע"א

ב"ה

דברי חכמים כדרבונות וכמסמרות נטועים בעלי אסופות, ה"ה האלופים קהל עדת ישורון הקצינים פ"ו בצירוף האלופים גובים יצ"ו ואסיפות הוועד, גזרו אומר להקים על החזן ר' שואל חזן יצ"ו,[1] להקים בקימה שיש בה הידור[2] ועיטור בכורים מראשית כל[3] את חמשת האזהרות אשר פקדו עליו שרי צבאות ישראל ומלכי רבנן ה"ה הגאון אב"ד קהלתינו ושני בתי דינים נר"ו, והן המה:[4]

א. ירחיק עצמו בתכלית הריחוק מחברת נשים, הן נשואות והן פנויות, הן בבית והן בחוץ, וכל שכן שצריך לשמור עצמו שלא ליחד עם נשים או פנויות, ואפילו אם יהיה על שמחות חתנה או ברית מילה ושארי שמחות לא יהיה בחברת נשים, ומכל שכן שאסור לו לילך ולראות המחולות ורקודים של בתולות, גם לא לישב בסוד משחקים במקום שמשחקים נשים או בתולות ולהרחיק מהם ביותר.

ב. גם אסור לו לשחוק בכל מיני שחוק,[5] אפילו עם אנשים לבד, הן כאן בקהלתינו יע"א והן חוץ לרחוב היהודים תוך ג' פרסאות מכאן,[6] בכל מיני שחוק שבעולם, חוץ שאך צאבל אונד דאמה שפיל,[7] ואפילו אצל יולדות וחולים ר"ל[8] אסור לו לשחוק, וגם אסור לו להניח בתוך ביתו

---

1. איננו יודעים מתי נתקבל ר' שאול (שואל) בן שלום שמוצאו היה מפולין כחזן וש"ץ בפפד"מ, אך התנהגותו הבלתי נאותה העסיקה את האב"ד ובית הדין כבר בשנת תקמ"ב, כפי שמתברר מפסק הדין משנת תקנ"ג (ר' [445] להלן). הסיבה שלמרות הכל המשיכו להעסיקו עד לשנת תקנ"ג ורק אז הוחלט לשלחו מפרנקפורט (ר' [446]) ניתן אולי למצוא בדברי פסק הדין 'מטעם אהבת קול זמרה' המורים על כך שהיה בעל קול נאה ומיטיב לשיר. (ר' ספר הזכרון, תכב ע"א – א.פ.)

2. עפ"י קידושין לב ע"ב: תקום והדרת לא אמרתי קימה אלא במקום שיש הידור.

3. עטור בכורים – ר' מסכת בכורים ג, י; מראשית כל – עפ"י הפסוק בדברים כו, ב בפרשת הבכורים. כל הפתיחה היא בלשון מליצית ביותר, אלא שהמליצות אינן נקשרות אחת לרעותה ונראה שנעשה נסיון מכוון לשוות להחלטה חגיגיות מבלי שמחברה נחון בידיעה ובלמדנות הדרושים.

4. Kracauer, *Geschichte der Juden in Frankfurt*, vol. 2, 110 n. 2, הניח בטעות על סמך תעודה זו שכל החזנים בפפד"מ היו נתונים בהגבלות חמורות כאלה ולא הבחין שהמדובר במקרה המיוחד של החזן ר' שואל שחטא ושב וחטא.

5. הכוונה למשחקי קלפים וקוביות או משחקי הימורים אחרים.

6. ר' (סגל לא הספיק להשלים – א.פ.)

7. משחק השח, שאך צאבל (Schach Zabel Mhd. [Mittelhochdeutsch] = Schachbrett) ומשחק הדמקה, שני משחקי לוח שהיו מקובלים בחברה הטובה.

8. להם היה מותר לשחק גם במשחקי קלפים ודומיהם, ר' (לא הספיק להשלים – א.פ.)

לאחרים לשחוק שום מיני שחוק חוץ משאך צאבל אונד דאמה כנ"ל, ואף חוץ לג' פרסאות מכאן על כל פנים לא ישחוק עם נשים ואף אשה אחת במשמע.

ג. גם יזהר שלא להרבות לילך חוץ לרחוב היהודים ולטייל תוך המקום[1] כי אם לצורך.

ד. גם ילך בתמידות בבית הכנסת ישן וחדש שחרית וערבית ולא יעבור, כאשר ראוי לש"ץ להיות מן אנשים זריזים המקדימים עצמם לתפלה.

ה. גם מחויב ללמוד בכל יום שיעור קבוע בספרי מוסר אצל בעל בית אחד מבני קהלתינו יע"א ועל פי הקהל י"ץ יוברר אותו הבעל בית, והברירה ביד הקהל לשלם מקופות הקהל או לנכות משכר החזן מה שינתן לבעל בית אחד שילמוד עם החזן.

וי"ו. גם נזרק מפי החברותא קדישא בצירוף האלופים גובים ואסיפות הוועד הנ"ל שלא לירד החזן ר' שואל הנ"ל לפני התיבה להתפלל עד ראש חודש מרחשון תקנ"א ל', אויך ניכט טלית צו בענשין בקול רם[2] עד ראש חודש מרחשון תקנ"א ל'[3] וגם שלא לירד לפני התיבה להתפלל מיום ראשון של סליחות עד ראש חודש מרחשון במשך ארבעה שנים והיינו עד שנת תקנ"ה לפ"ק.

נוסף על ששה נתיבי אמת ודרכי ישר אלו אשר יצאו מפי יושבי על מדין בי דינא רבה דקהלתינו יע"א עוד מצאו האלופים רוזנים קצינים פ"ו וגובים יצ"ו ואסיפות הוועד הנ"ל להוסיף הצוה והפקידה על ר' שואל חזן הנ"ל שלא ישנה מנהג קדמונים כאשר היה מאז ומעולם הנהוג פה קהלתינו יע"א שהחזן דמתא ילך תמיד, הן בשבתות וימים טובים אף בימי החול הן בבית הכנסת הן ברחוב גם בהמקום חוץ לרחובותינו, בבגדי שחורים. ולכל הדברים וששה סדרי הנהגות האלה הטה החזן ר' שואל הנ"ל שכמו לסבול לאשר ולקיים את הכל בלי שום מגרעת מעתה ועד עולם.

ולראיה ואות אמת בא החזן ר' שואל הנ"ל על החתום יום ג', ד"א מרחשון תקנו"ן לפ"ק.

לזכרון שגוף הנוסח דלמעלה אשר נחתם מהחזן ר' שואל הנ"ל ניתן למשמרת ביד הגאון אב"ד דקהלתינו נר"ו.

* * *

תגובת שואל החזן

[444] ללא תאריך[4]

ב"ה

שלומים אלומים, כטל וכרביבים, לכבוד אדוניי האלופים הקצינים פ"ו נטורי קרתא, ובצירוף אדוניי האלופי הקצינים גובים יצ"ו, כל חד וחד לפי מעלתו ומדרגתו יתברך בבואו ובצאתו.

---

1. המקום – העיר, בניגוד ל'רחוב'.
2. לברך את הברכה על עטיפת הטלית, מתפקידיו של הש"ץ, ר' (לא הספיק להשלים – א.פ.).
3. סעיף שישי זה, שנוסף כנראה רק לאחר שחמש ה"אזהרות" שצויינו בפתיחה נתקבלו, נראה תמוה. אם הכוונה היתה לאסור על החזן לירד לפני התיבה במשך שנה תמימה ובימים הנוראים למשך ארבע שנים נוספות, אם כן מה טעם לישיבתו בקהילה ולהמשך תשלום משכורתו בתקופה זו?
4. על דף כפול מודבק לתוך הפנקס

שמועני[!] אדוניי האלופים הקצינים מנהיגים יצ"ו דא איך אייניגה מאהלין לפני אסיפות הקהל יצ"ו פאר גשטאנדין בין, אבר נימאהלין וואש ערלאנגין קענין, איזט ערשטנס דיא שולד כי לא איש דברים אנכי, דש מיינה אהן זוכונג אונד רעכטי זוא צו וואָרט ברענגין קן וויא ווערקליך אין דער טאהט איזט, צווייטנש, דש האלופים מנהיגים יצ"ו ברוב עסקם וצרכי הקהלה זיך הזמן ניכט לאנג אב ברעכין קענין לשמוע דברי באריכות. דאהערא דענקי הירדורך שריפטליך תחנתי ובקשתי פאר צו שטעלין, בטרעפט דש דיא זעלבה פר לאנגין ממני ביום הכניסה מתפלל צו זיין. אהובי(?) אדוניי, איך האבי שוינט מינדליך פאר גשטעלט כי כבד ממני דבר זה, אבר ניכט וויא אייניגה דענקין דש חס ושלום אויש הויך מוהט אודר עצלנות זולכש ניכט טוהין וויל, לא כן, דא זולכש פאר קיינה מלאכה כבידה אן צו זעהן איזט, רק אין אדם יודע במטמונות של חבירו, ובפרט בדברים שבגופו של אדם, אונד וועגן זיינר גזונדהייט אוהן מיגליך איזט, וויא ווערקליך בש"ת(?) זה איזה שנים מיך מיט איינין אוהם שטאנד פון מיינר גזונדהייט אינקומדיהרט בפינדי, וועלכר מיר פילש ניכט ערלויבט אונד מיך דאפון ענטהאלטין מוז. אויך וואן מיך ווערקליך ניכט דאבייא בטראכטין וואולטי, וועהרי ניכט יוצא לפני אשתי וטפלי דתלו בי עטוואש צו אונטר נעהמין וואש לבריאות גופי שעדליך וועהר, וואוריבר אויך דיזוש אייניש דארונטר איזט בימי השבוע לפני העמוד מתפלל צו זיין, אבר חלילה צו דענקין, דש אויש מוהט וויל ממני צו רוק הלטי. מיט הין מובטח אני בתום וביושר צדקתם צו אבשטראגיהרן[1] אונד ניכט צו זוכין וואש מיר בלתי אפשר איזט צו מאנטוניהרן אודר איך מוזטי מיך ניכט אליין בנעימות הקול בסכנה זעצין זונדרין פיל מעהר חלילה וחס בבריאות כל גופי.

גם זאת אדרוש ואליהם אתודע, דא איך מידי שנה בשנה אב גרעכנט בקומי בשביל חובי מ"ם ר"ט, איזט ערשטנס לפי חשבוני החילוף כתב שלי ממש גנץ, אודר גוויש ביז אויף איין גאר וויניגש, בצאהלט. אלזוא ערזוכי ערשטליך דא החשבון מק"ק פירדא ניכט נור על שמי לבד שטיהט, זונדרן מפורש כל פרט ופרט וואש איך חייב אונד [ע"ב] וואש המשורר שלי שמואל פאס[2] חייב איזט, הן אמת הסך ממני לבד להאלופים גובים יצ"ו אויש גשטעלט, ווילין באותו פעם דאכטי דאש ניכט זוא גנויא אויף דער בצאהלונג דרינקין ווערדן, אויך דש פאר האפט האבי מעהר פר דינשט צו האבן, דא אבר ביידי ניכט כמחשבותי אויש פאלין, זוא ערזוכי האלופים הקצינים פ"ו וגובים יצ"ו החשבון מק"ק פרידא צו ספעפוריהרן, וואש שוינט בשביל המשורר כ' שמואל הנ"ל צאהלט האבי מיר צו פר גיהטן, ומכל שכן מיר ווייטר הין ניכטש בשבילו מהשכירות שלי צו דעקארטיהרן, מעהררש אבר חילוף כתב שלי מיר צו עקסטראדיהרן. אויך ערזוכי, בבקשה גדולה, לקיים דבריהם, וויא איך פר זיכרט בין ווארדן מהאלופים מנהיגים יצ"ו מיין שכירות כל פעם אויף שני חדשים פר אויש צו ערשטרעקין, כי לזה עיני מיחלות ומצפות. דיזוש אלליש ביטה כעבדא קמיה מריה בתחנונים ובבקשה גדולה וברוב חכמתם ויושר צדקתם ליתן מקום ולהטות אזנם לדברי התחנונים האלה, ובזכות זה תאריכו ימיכם ושנותיכם וה' ישלח ברכה במקהלכם. כה עתירות ותחנת עבדיכם הדובר שלום לכם ולכל קהלכם.

גם אבקש במטו מלפניכם, אויב צוואהר ניכט ווייש דש ח"ו כל ימי נגד האלופים הקצינים נטורי קרתא שום דבר נגד כבודם הרמה פאהרן האבי גלאזט, רק חושש אני דש על ידי שום רוכל בשקר וכזב וואש אן גבראכט איזט ווארדן, הנני מבקש מחילה מכל חד וחד מנהון וכבודם ויראתם

---

1. abstrahieren — abstraire (Fr.) = absehen
2. ר' אבני זכרון, מס' 4326, שבו הוא נקרא 'המשורר הגדול' – א.פ.

עלי תמיד כחובתי, והנני סר למשמעתם ודעתם הרמה כל ימי עולם, עד יקבץ שבות עמנו ויחיש להם מבשר טוב וגואלם אמן.

הק' שאול בן מהור"ר שלום כ"ץ ש"ץ דק"ק פ"פ דמיין

* * *

[445][1] כ"ד שבט תקנ"ג (6.2.1793)

ב"ה

על דבר השאלה ששאלו האלופים שני גבאים דקהל יצ"ו מאתנו חתומי מטה בנדון קול מפורסם שנשמע ברחובותינו על החזן ר' שואל שהמשרתת שלו נתעברה ממנו. גם אמרו שני גבאי הקהל הנ"ל שבאה לפניהם המשרתת הנ"ל וקובלה על החזן הנ"ל. והגידו לפנינו אלופי גבאי הקהל הנ"ל כל דברי הזונה בדברים המוכיחים על פי אומדנא שהוא כדבריה, כמבואר בפראטיקאהל[2] המונח לפנינו באריכות. ושאלו מאתנו חתומי מטה לעיין בדינו אם ראוי להיות ש"ץ או לאו. וגם באו לפנינו כמה אנשים והגידו ששמעו מפי הזונה שממנו נתעברה וגם הגידו האומדנות המוכיחות על כך שממנו נתעברה, כמבואר גם כן בפראטיקאהל המונח לפנינו. ושלחנו אחר ר' שואל הנ"ל והכחיש והביא עדיו שהזונה הודה לפניהם שהוא ובניו נקיים ומאחר נתעברה ולא נודע לה שמו והלך מכאן, כמבואר בפראטיקאהל המונח לפנינו. ולאחר שעיינו על פי דין ודת תורתינו הקדושה מצאנו באשר שנכתב בתקוני הקהל סי' ס"ה וזה לשונו: מחמת איזה פגם ממשועבדי הקהל יצ"ו אב צו זעצין וכו', יעיינו שם הקהל יצ"ו.[3] ובאשר שכבר יצא על החזן הנ"ל כמה פעמים קולי קולות של זנות וכבר היה ישיבת בית דין שני פעמים בשנת תקמ"ב ובשנת תקמ"ט ל' על הקולות שהיו באותם זמנים, ובכל פעם היה אומדנות מוכיחות בדבר, חוץ משארי קולות של זנות שנשמע על החזן הנ"ל, על כן מצאנו שמחויבים הקהל י"ץ לאשר ולקיים כפי התקנה הנ"ל ולעשות אסיפת הוועד כפי תקנות הקהל הנ"ל, ואם יסכימו כולם או רובם נקיי הדעת יראי ה' להעביר אותו לגמרי, הרשות בידם על פי הדין להעבירו ואין עליהם שום חיוב מחמת קבלתו מתחילה, כי אדעתא דהכי לא קבלהו, כי לא נשמע כזאת שיצא על ש"ץ כל כך קולות של זנות ובועל נדות ואין לך פגם גדול מזה והוא דבר מאוס לפני בשר ודם, על אחת כמה וכמה לפני מלך מלכי המלכים הקב"ה להתפלל לפני הציבור, גם כי חתם החזן הנ"ל את עצמו ד"א מרחשון תק"ן לפ"ק וחייב את עצמו לקיים הנהגות שהוטל עליו מפי הגאון אב"ד נר"ו ושני בתי דינין י"ץ ומקהל י"ץ ולא קיים אותם כפי הנשמע מרבים. אכן אם יסכימו האסיפות הוועד או רובם להחזיק את החזן הנ"ל מהיום והלאה, הן מטעם אהבת קול זמרה (ע"ב) או משארי טעמים, אנחנו נקיים כי אין בידינו כח על פי הדין לפסול אותו לגמרי על כרחם מלעמוד לפני התיבה כי לא היו עדים ברורים שראו המעשים הרעים. אך בימים נוראים, והיינו מיום א' של סליחות עד לאחר יום הכפורים ואפילו בימי חול שביניהם ותפלת טל וגשם ובהושענא רבה ותענית צבור פסול הוא לעולם מצד הדין לירד לפני התיבה. גם מצאנו שבאם יסכימו האסיפת וועד, כולם או רובם, להעבירו מלהיות ש"ץ

1. על דף מודבק לתוך הפנקס
2. זכרון הדברים.
3. ר' (לא הספיק להשלים – א.פ.).

ולעשות איזה סיפוק מקהלותינו או ליתן לו איזה סך מקופת הקהל לעקור דירתו מקהלותינו יע"א, אזי הרשות בידם. ועד שיתוועדו האסיפה הנ"ל בחדר הקהל כנ"ל לא ירד החזן הנ"ל לפני התיבה.

יצא מאתנו יום ד', ך"ד שבט תקנ"ג לפ"ק.

הק' פינחס הלוי איש הורוויץ[1]
הקטן נתן בלא"א כ"ה שלמה מאז זצ"ל
הקטן אברהם טריר כהן[2]
הק' זנוול בלא"א הר"ר משה טרך ז"ל[3]
הק' מאיר בלא"א כהר"ר זלמן שיף כ"ץ זצלה"ה[4]
הק' חיים בפ"ו כ"ה יוזפא גונדרשהיים שליט"א[5]
הקטן מנחם מענדלי בן המנוח מוהר"ר איצק זאמשט ז"ל לה"ה[6]

* * *

[446] כ"ח שבט תקנ"ג (10.2.1793)

ב"ה[7]

בהיום דלמטה התוועדנו אנחנו האלופים הק' פ"ו וגובים יצ"ו עם צירוף מהאלופים הק' עכטר[8] ויחידי סגולה יצ"ו כנהוג וכראוי לאסיפה זו. ואחרי אשר אנחנו כל אסיפות הוועד הנ"ל ועיינ׳נו בהפס"ד מהגאון אב"ד ושני בתי דינים נר"ו ושם ראינו את המעשה הרע[9] מר' שואל חזן ששנה ושילש באוולתו ונעשה מועד לעבירה, גם כי לא שת לבו לכל דברי אזהרת מהגאון אב"ד ושני בתי דינים דקהלתינו נר"ו זה פעמים ושלש. על כן יצא מפי כל אסיפות הוועד הנ"ל בדיעה אחת ושוה שיהיה ר' שואל הנ"ל מכאן ולהבא פסול להיות ש"ץ פה קהלתינו יע"א עד עולם, כי אין תקנה לאוולתו, אף אם יכובס בנתר נכתם עונו[10] מלהיות עוד ש"ץ פה וכמו זר נחשב. אף ביום יארצייט שלו אין לו רשות לבוא לפני התיבה באחת מבתי הכנסת דקהלתינו יע"א, ואף שלא יהא מעוטר בעטרת בגדי כבוד של בני קהלתינו בלבוש שבת מנדל וקראגן.[11] וממילא נשמע שפטורים האלופים מנהיגי הקהלה מליתן לו עוד פרוטה אחת סיפוק. אמנם לפני משורת הדין ולחוס על אשתו וביתו עלתה ההסכמה מאת אלופי אסיפות הוועד יצ"ו לוותר נגדו כמבואר והיינו, שמחויב

1. רבה של פרנקפורט. החתימות מקוריות.
2. הרב אברהם בן שמעון כ"ץ טריר, רב ואב"ד של הקלויז.
3. דיין וראב"ד.
4. אחיו של הרב טעבלי שיף, רבה של לונדון. ראב"ד וראש הישיבה בבית הכנסת של ר' אליה רייס. ר' הורוויץ, רבני פרנקפורט, ח"ד, עמ' 37-38, ובמהדורה העברית בנספחים ב' וג'.
5. דיין.
6. ר' ה' ר"פ, ח"ד עמ' 36-37, ובמהדורה העברית בנספחים ב' וג'.
7. על דף מודבק לתוך הפנקס
8. ר' (לא הספיק להשלים – א.פ.)
9. חמש מלים מחוקות.
10. עפ"י ירמיה ב, כב.
11. מעיל וצוואורן של שבת, ר' (לא הספיק להשלים – א.פ.).

ר' שואל הנ"ל לפנות את ביתו השייך להקהל י"ץ מהיום תוך זמן[1] עד ראש חודש אייר הסמוך הבע"ל וגם לבלי לבוא עוד מהיום על החזנים שטאט, לא הוא וגם לזוגתו תי' לא יהיה הזכות מהמקום בעזרת נשים רק בתורות נדבה יהיה לו {ולזוגתו} כל שבוע ושבוע חמשה זהובים כל ימי היותו פה. ובאם יגיע ראש חודש אייר הסמוך דהאי שתא הבע"ל ועדיין מחזיק את עצמו בבית הקהל, אזי לא יותן לו עוד מן ראש חודש הנ"ל אף פרוטה אחת. כל זאת הפריזו והפרישו אסיפות הוועד הנ"ל למען חיותו של ר' שואל הנ"ל. וממילא נשמע שמחויב ר' שואל הנ"ל להחזיק טובה ותשואות חן לבני קהלתינו יע"א על זאת, ומכל שכן שלא להחציף ולהרשיע לשום אחד מבני קהלתינו ומכל שכן נגד מנהיגי קהלתינו יע"א, ומכלל הן נשמע לאו.

נעשה בהסכמות כל אסיפות הוועד הנ"ל היום, יום א', ד"ח שבט תקנ"ג ל'.

הקטן אברהם ווינג

הק' יוזפא גונדרשהיים

הק' זלמן האז[2]

הק' זלמן בינגא[3]

הק' שמואל בהר"ר זעלקל לנדויא[4]

הק' זלמן בן המנוח מהור"ר משה ברונשוויג סג"ל ז"ל[5]

הק' יצחק איצק בהמנוח כהר"ר ליב קן בינגא זצ"ל[6]

הק' משה רויטשילד[7]

הק' טעבלי פולדא[8]

הק' זכריה ווערטהיים[9]

[הק' רפאל] הן[10]

הק' מרדכי בלא"א הר"ר מהו' נתן מאז שליט"א[11]

הק' פייבל ואס[12]

משה בן יוקב ר"ק[13]

הק' יוסף איצק בכרך[14]

הקטן אברם בהכ"ה ישראל כהן העכט

---

1. המלים 'תוך זמן' מעל לשורה.
2. הפרנס זלמן בן זעליגמן האז.
3. אולי הג"ץ זלמן בן ישראל בינגא.
4. פרנס (?)
5. פרנס
6. פרנס וג"ץ
7. הפרנס משה בן אנשיל רוטשילד
8. הפרנס
9. זכריה בן יצחק ווערטהיים
10. הגובה רפאל בן פער הן
11. גובה. נתמנה כמנהל ה'קלויז' של ר' אליה רייז.
12. אינו אצל אבני זכרון או אלה תולדות.
13. משה בן יעקב רינדסקופף
14. אינו אצל אבני זכרון או אלה תולדות.

הק׳ [ליזר] בלא״א המנוח כ׳ ליב עמריך[1]

הק׳ זעליג ש״ץ[2]

הק׳ קא[ל]מן שוסטר כ״ץ[3]

הק׳ איצק שוסטר כ״ץ[4]

יואל האלי[5]

הק׳ בענדיט מאיי סג״ל[6]

הק׳ יוזלי בן זלמן זיכל ז״ל

הק׳ איצקווימפא סג״ל[7]

הקטן גרשון קיסר[8]

הק׳ מיכל בלא״א המנוח כ׳ זלמן ראט שילד ז״ל[9]

הקטן הירץ שטערין[10]

הק׳ משה שיף[11]

הק׳ אייזק קולפא[12]

הקטן אברהם לאטיר[13]

הק׳ ליב קאסל[14]

הק׳ אייזק זינצהיים[15]

הק׳ משה אופנהיי׳[16]

* * *

1. גובה
2. לא מצאתיו
3. קלמן בן מאיר שוסטר־איטינגין כ״ץ
4. הפרנס יצחק בן הענדלי שוסטר כ״ץ
5. הגובה וג״ץ יואל בן הענך האלי
6. בענדיט בן אהרן מאי
7. יצחק בן טעבלי ווימפא סג״ל
8. גרשון קיסר בן אלחנן רינג
9. מיכל בן קלמן רוטשילד
10. הירץ בן מיכל שטערן כ״ץ
11. משה בן הירץ שיף כ״ץ
12. אייזק בן יודא קולפא
13. אברהם בן יצחק לאטר
14. לא מצאתיו
15. איצק (יצחק) בן רפאל זינצהיים
16. משה בן אהרן אופנהיים (אלה תולדות 2.5.1799) או משה בן שלמה אופנהיים (אבני זכרון, מס׳ 4110).

[447]

ריח ע"א

אותה תעודה כמו [445] בשינויי כתיב קלים וחסרי משמעות. בראש התעודה כתוב: העתק מפס"ד בעסק ר' שואל חזן.

בצד נרשם: 'גוף הכתב הלז מונח למשמרת ביד האלופים גובים יצ"ו'.

* * *

[449] ה' אדר תקנ"ג (17.2.1793)

ריט ע"א[1]

ב"ה

כהיום דלמטה באסיפות החברותא קדישא בצירוף האלופים גובים יצ"ו נמנו ורבו, אחרי שה"ה ר' שואל חזן מבקש ליסע ולעקור סוכו ומשכנו מכאן קהלתינו ולהרחיק מקום דירתו עם כל בני ביתו לארץ מולדתו היא מדינות פולין, גלל כן זוכט ער אן דש זיך האלופים מנהיגי הקהלה יצ"ו מיט איהן פער גלייכן זאללין, אונד קופות הקהל יצ"ו פון דיא איהמי בתורות נדבה וחסד כל ימי עיכובו עוד כאן להבא מידי שבוע בשבוע בוויליגטי חמשה זהובים זוא גלייך בסך מסוים צו בפרייאין, אום דאמיט זיין פאר האבנש ליסע עם כל בני ביתו לארץ מולדתו פולציגן צו קענין. לזאת עלתה ההסכמה מהאלופים פ"ו וגובים יצ"ו בדעת כולם שוה, דש מאן לר' שואל הנ"ל חמשה עשר מאות זהובים בוויליגן זאל אונד צוואהר באופן זה, דש ער עם אשתו ובניו בחודש אייר הסמוך דהאי שתא תקנ"ג ל' מכאן עוקר דירה זיין זאל וליסע לארץ מולדתו. אלזוא וואן עד הזמן הנ"ל מכאן אב ציהן וויל זאל איהם על הוצאות הדרך, נאך דעם דש ער הבית שהוא דר בו כעת גרוימט האט, איזה מאות זהובים מן אותן ט"ו מאות זהובים בהענדיגט[2] זאל ווערדן,[3] והמותרות עד חמשה עשר מאות זהובים הנ"ל זאל מאן איבר מאכין לק"ק ברלין יע"א, וועלכה ער בבואו לק"ק ברלין עם זוגתו וביתו עמפפאנגן זאל. דיזוש איזט איהם בוויליגט וואן ער עם זוגתו ובני ביתו בחודש אייר הסמוך הבע"ל מכאן עוקר דירה איזט. זוא אבר דש ר' שואל הנ"ל עם זוגתו ובני ביתו לענגר אלש חודש אייר הסמוך היר בלייבט ויבוא אחר זמן זה לעקור דירתו עם בני ביתו מכאן, זוא ווערד איהם פון זולכה בוויליגטי חמשה עשר מאות זהובים אב גיצאגן אותן חמשה זהובים לכל שבוע ושבוע מן ראש חודש אייר הסמוך דנא עד זמן נסיעתו ויוצא בגירעון כסף זה. כל הנ"ל הוסכם באסיפות החברותא קדישא וצירוף האלופים גובים יצ"ו, מיט דיזן אויש דרוק והסכמה גמורה שאין לשנות, דש אויך קיין גבאי קהל זולכש ווידרום פאר ברענגן זאל דערפן להוסיף או לגרוע, בקנס שני מאות ר"ט חצי להשררה יר"ה וחצי להקדש.

נעשה יום א', ה' אדר תקנ"ג ל'.

---

1. בצד הגליון: גוף הכתב הלז וגוף הכתב שבצד זה מונחים ביד האלופים גובים למשמרת.
2. היה כתוב 'בהענדיגן' ותוקן ל'בהענדיגט'.
3. המילה 'ווערדן' מעל לשורה.

הק' יוזפא גונדרשהיים[1]

הק' מרדכי [מאז]

הק' זלמן האז

הק' זלמן בינגא

הק' שמואל בהר"ר זעלקל לאנדויא

הק' זלמן בן המנוח מהור"ר משה ברונשוויג סג"ל זצ"ל

הק' משה רויט שילד

הק' טעבלי פולדא

הק' זכרי' ווערטהיים

...גלל כן הוא מבקש שהאלופים מנהיגי הקהילה יצ"ו יתפשרו אתו ושקופות הקהל ישחררו מיד סכום מסוים מתוך אותן חמשה זהובים שאושרו לו בתורת נדבה וחסד לכל שבוע ושבוע כל ימי עיכובו עוד כאן, כדי שעל ידי כך יוכל להוציא אל הפועל את תוכניתו ליסע עם כל בני ביתו לארץ מולדתו. לזאת עלתה ההסכמה מהאלופים פ"ו וגובים יצ"ו בדעת כולם שוה שיאשרו לר' שואל הנ"ל חמשה עשר מאות זהובים דהיינו באופן זה, שהוא ואשתו ובניו יעקרו דירתם מכאן בחודש אייר הסמוך דהאי שתא תקנ"ג ל' ויסעו לארץ מולדתו. לכן, אם ירצה לנסוע עד הזמן הנ"ל, ימסרו לו, לאחר שיפנה את הבית שהוא דר בו כעת, איזה מאות זהובים מן אותן ט"ו מאות זהובים, להוצאות הדרך, והמותרות עד חמשה עשר מאות זהובים הנ"ל יעבירו לק"ק ברלין יע"א והוא יקבלם בבואו לברלין עם זוגתו וביתו. כל זאת אושר לו אם יעקור הוא וזוגתו ובני ביתו דירתו מכאן בחודש אייר הסמוך הבע"ל. אבל עם ישארו ר' שואל הנ"ל עם זוגתו ובני ביתו כאן מעבר לחודש אייר הסמוך ויבוא אחר זמן זה לעקור דירתו עם בני ביתו מכאן, אזי ינכו לו מאותם חמשה עשר מאות זהובים שאושרו חמשה זהובים לכל שבוע ושבוע מראש חודש אייר הסמוך דנא עד זמן נסיעתו ויצא בגרעון כסף זה. כל הנ"ל הוסכם באסיפות החברותא קדישא וצירוף האלופים גובים יצ"ו בתנאי והסכמה גמורה שאין לשנות ששום גבאי קהל לא יהיה רשאי להעלות עניין זה שוב להוסיף עליו או לגרוע ממנו, בקנס שני מאות ר"ט, חצי להשררה יר"ה וחצי להקדש.

* * *

תיק 77-78, אוסף Collection of Rabbinical and Historical Manuscripts (RG 128) ארכיון ייוו"א, ניו יורק. ברשות YIVO Institute for Jewish Research, New York

ע ע"א

ב"ה

נתוועדו יחד לעיין בדין החזן ר' שואל ע"פ רשות האלופי' קהל יצו על דבר לא טובה השמוע שיצא עליו ואחר החקירות והעיון הסכמנו יחד / וזאת אשר מצאנו שבימי' נוראי' הבע"ל דהא שתא דהיינו בר"ה וי"ה ובסליחות שאומרים באשמורת הבוקר לא ירד לפני התיבה להת[פלל]

---

1. חתימות מקוריות

בציבור הן בבהכ"נ[1] ישן וחדש והן בשאר בהכ"נ / גם סדרנו לו הנהגות ישרות הראוי ב[הכרח] לכל שליח ציבור שיתנהג בהן ולא ישנה את תפקידו כאשר נמסר לידו מאתנו בכתב רש[ום] דבר אמת וכאשר המה בכתובי' אצלינו ואי"ה לשנה הבאה בר"ח אלול הבע"ל מחויב ר' שו[אל] חזן הנ"ל לבוא לפני הגאון אב"ד ושני ב"ד נר"ו לעיין בדינו לפי ראות עינינו אם התנהג כ[פי] אשר יושת עליו בלי ערמה ומרמה / ואם ראוי לעמוד לפני התיבה בימי' נוראי' היו' יו' ג' י["ט] מנחם תקמב"ל /

עלה בהסכמה מהגאון אב"ד נר"ו עם שני ב"ד יצו שר' שואל חזן לא ירד לפני התיבה להתפלל עד אחר י"כ הבע"ל אפי' בחול / ומשם ואילך לא ירד ג"כ לפני התיבה להתפלל בין בחול בין בשבת וי"ט עד שיתאספו יחד קהל יצו וכגאון אב"ד נר"ו ושני ב"ד יצו שידונו בדבר זה

היום יו' ד' ך"ה אלול תקמט"ל

על דבר ששלחו גבאי הקהל יצו להגאון אב"ד נר"ו ע"י שמש ר' זיסקניד שטערן להתאסף שני ב"ד יצו מ' החזן ר' שואל /

תשובה מהגאון אב"ד נר"ו ושני ב"ד יצו / כבר יצא מהגאון אב"ד נר"ו ושני ב"ד יצו קודם ר"ה העבר בכתב ליד ג"ק יצו שאף לאחר ימים נוראי' לא ירד ר' שואל חזן לפני התיבה עד שיתאספו הקהל יצו וגאון אב"ד נר"ו ושני ב"ד יצו יחד לדון בדבר זה / בכן אי אפשר לנו להשיב כלום עד שא[ס]אספו[2] כנ"ל ועד אותו אסיפה לא ירד לפני התיבה אור ליו' וי"ו עש"ק י"ב תשרי תק"ן לפ"ק

ע"ד הקול ורנון שיצא בקהלותינו יע"א ובסיבובות על החזן ר' שואל קלא דלא פסיק / וגם הגידו לפנינו אחרי החקירה ששמעו מפי הזונה שאמרי בפירוש עלי' שממנו נתעברה / בכן הסכמנו שר' שואל חזן לא יעבור לפני התיבה בימי' נוראי' דהיינו מיום א' של סליחות עד אחרי י"כ עד ר"ה שנת תקנ"ה לפ"ק ארבעה שנים וגם מחויב ר' שואל הנ"ל לקיים התקנות המבוארי' בפרטות ולאחר ארבעה שנים אזי יופסקו מפי הגאון אב"ד נר"ו ומפי שני ב"ד יצו אם הוא ראוי והגון לירד לפני התיבה בימים נוראי' אבל להעבירו לגמרי אין כח בידינו אם לא ע"פ תקנות הקהל ושם נאמר בסי' ס"ה[3] מחמת איזה פגם משועבדי קהל יצו אב צו זעטצין וכו' יעיינו שם ואם לא נעשה כפי תקנה הנ"ל תוך שלשי' יו' אין בידינו לפוסלו לירד לפני התיבה אם לא בימי' נוראי' וכנ"ל יצא מאתנו יום ה' ך"ה תשרי תק"ן לפ"ק לזכרון שנמנו וגמרו אצל האב"ד נר"ו ושני ב"ד יצו אם ישאלו אלופי' קהל יצו אם הם מחויבי' לעשות כפי התקנה הנ"ל או לא / אזי אנחנו משיבי' שהוא ע"פ דין שמחויבי' לקיים עם ר' שואל הנ"ל כפי התקנה הנ"ל /

* * *

---

1. בבתי הכנסת
2. ר"ל 'שאספו'
3. ר' כ"י ŻIH ,517, דף יג ע"ב. שם כתוב, 'מחמת איזה פגם ממשועבדי קהל ושארי דינצטן אב זעטצין / קן אנצרשט / ניט גשעהן / אלז אויף דער אַרט וויא זעלבה זיינין אן גנומן ווארדן /'.

מתוך כתב יד 3672, בית המדרש לרבנים

פב ע"א

ר' שואל חזן נ' בליל ש"ק פ' במדבר ונ' ביום א' הסמוך שלאחריו הוא ג' סיון תקסחית לפ"ק

* * *

ר' גם ספר הזכרון, תכב ע"א

http://jnul.huji.ac.il/dl/mss/heb1092/djvu/index.djvu?djvuopts&thumbnails=yes&zoom=page&page=422

Appendix 4

נספח ד

תיק 77-78, אוסף Collection of Rabbinical and Historical Manuscripts (RG 128), ארכיון ייוו"א, ניו יורק. ברשות YIVO Institute for Jewish Research, New York

קסח ע"א-ע"ב

13. ב"ה
14. העתק
15. מקו' שלם בעזרת נשי' הוא המקו' עליונה במיטל באנק למזרח מצד דרום שעומדות
16. עלי' כעת אשת הו"ה כ' דוד בהמנוח[1] כ' מענדלי האמיל ז"ל אשר מצד שמאול על מקו' ה
17. הסמוך עומדות עלי' כעט אשת הו"ה כ' געץ בן אייזק שוסטר כץ[2] אותו מקו' שלם הנ"ל ש
18. שהי' שייך להאלופי ק' גובי' יצו הוכרז לפנינו ב"ד עד שפסקו המוסיפי' ולא הי' אחד ש
19. שהי' פוסיק כפי מה שפסק הו"ה כ' שלמה בהמנוח כ' זנוויל לאריע ז"ל בכן מכרנו המקו'
20. שלם הנ"ל להו"כ כ' שלמה לוריא הנ"ל בעד סך ששה מאות ועשרי' זהו' לשלם אין קונפונטצ/
21. ≠יאהנש מינץ אויף דעם כ"ד זהו' פוס והיינו לשלם שליש מסך דמי מכירה הנ"ל תיכף
22. נגד מסירת מעשה ב"ד הלז ושני שלישי' הנותרי' מסך דמי מכירה הנ"ל לשלם על ששה ח
23. חצאי שני' רצופי' וסמוכי' זא"ז מיט מסירת מעשה ב"ד הלז ומחויב הלוקח כ' שלמה הנ"ל
24. ליתן ששה ח"כ לאורדר האלופי' גובי' יצו לשלם על זמני' הנ"ל גם נשאר מקו' שלם הנ"ל
25. לאפותיקי מפורש שלא יצא מחזקת מרי' קמא כל זמן שלא נתפרע {אפי'} כל ח"כ הנ"ל –
26. ומעתה המקו' שלם שיה' שייך מקדמת להאלופי' גובי' יצו שייך מעכשיו להו"ה כ' שלמה
27. לוריא הנ"ל ויא[3] וב"כ לחלוטין גמורין ולצמיתת עלמין עם כל זכות וחזקה וכמו שהי' שייך
28. מקדמת דנא להאלופי' גובי' יצו בלי שום שיור כלל וכלל / ואחר שנתפרע כל ח"כ הנ"ל שייך
29. מעכשיו המקו' שלם הנ"ל לכ' שלמה הנ"ל וי"א וב"כ בשופי גמור בלי שום עורר וטוען
30. יהי' המערער מי שיהי' הן רבי' או יחיד יהי' טענה מה שיהי' או באזי אופן שיהי'
31. מכל מה שהפה יוכל לדבר והלב לחשוב ולהרהר / וכל מי שיערער אחר מכירה הנ"ל

---

1. בן המנוח
2. ע"פ אלה תולדות (15.11.1793), געץ בן אייזק שוסטר כ"ץ התחתן עם רייזלה בסביבות 1785. ע"פ התעודה הזאת, יש להקדים את תאריך נישואיהם לפחות ל-1792.
3. ויורשיו אחריו

32. יהי׳ מי שיהי׳ או באיזה אופן שיהי׳ דבריו בטילי׳ ומבוטלי׳ כחרס הנשבר כאפס
33. וכאין יחשב לא שרירין ולא קיימין ולא יהי׳ חלין כלל וכלל וכטוען אחר מעשה ב״ד הגדול
34. ואל יזדקק שום קהל או ב״ד יצו או שום משפט שבעולם לדברי המערער באשר ש
35. שנעשה הכל ע״פ צוות האלופי׳ קציני׳ גובי׳ יצו / ובאשר שכפי הנהוג פה ק
36. קהלותנו יעאי[1] שהמכירה הנעשה מן האלופי ק׳ גובי׳ יצו אינו בכי יותן ל
37. להלוקח שטר חלטה בפני עצמו {על ...ן} כמו שארי מכירות הנעשין מאנשי׳
38. אחרי׳

1. ע״ב
2. אחרים בכן יהא תוקף מ[ע]שה ב״ד הלז כאילו יש להלוקח כ׳ שלמה הנ״ל גם ש[טר]
3. חלטה בפני עצמו על אותו מקום שלם הנ״ל וכתבנו וחתמנו כל הנ״ל בתוקף
4. מעשה ב״ד ובכח ב״ד יפה להיות ביד הלוקח הו״ה כ׳ שלמה הנ״ל ויא[2] וב״כ ל[עדות]
5. ולזכות ולראיה׳ שיעמוד המקו׳ שלם הנ״ל ביד הלוקח כ׳ שלמה הנ״ל ויא וב[״כ]
6. בלי שום מוחה כלל נעשה פה פפ״ד אור ליו׳ ב ה כסליו תקמם גמיל ל[פ״ק]
7. הדיין ור״י מה׳ נתן מז נר״ו
8. הדיין כ״ה מאיר שיף נר״ו
9. הדיין כ״ה חיים גונדרשהיים

---

1. יגן עליה אלהים
2. ויורשיו אחריו

Appendix 5

נספח ה

מתוך פנקס דק"ק פרנקפורט בנושא בתי תפילה

[482][1] י' אלול תקל"ט (22.8.1779)

רן ע"א

באשר שהתורני כ"ה נתן ב"ה שמעון אדליר כ"ץ ז"ל הנ"ל לא היה שומע להסכמת הקהל וגובים יצ"ו ולא היה ציית להכרזה הנ"ל מה שנכרז בפומבי בבית הכנסת ישן וחדש ואסף מנין בביתו והתפלל נגד תקנת הקהל וגובים יצ"ו הנ"ל, התאספו יחד החברא קדישא יצ"ו והאלופים גובים יצ"ו ובצירוף הגאון אב"ד נר"ו ושני בתי דינים יצ"ו ועלתה בהסכמה לשלוח לר' נתן הנ"ל שלא יתפלל {בביתו} עם מנין כלל וכלל, זולת בבתי כנסיות שיש להם רשות מקהל יצ"ו[2] בעונש חרם. וזה הנוסחא ששלחנו לו בהסכמת החברא קדישא יצ"ו והאלופים גובים יצ"ו ובצירוף (ע"ב) הגאון אב"ד נר"ו ושני בתי דינים יצ"ו איזט אונש שמשים מקהל יצ"ו בפאהלין ווארדן לילך אצל התורני כ"ה נתן ב"ה שמעון אדליר כ"ץ ז"ל אונד איהם צו זאגין בהסכמת כל הקהל וגובים יצ"ו ובצירוף הגאון אב"ד נר"ו ושני בתי דינים יצ"ו, דש ר' נתן הנ"ל בחרם בפאהלין ווארדן כלל וכלל קיין מנין צו מאכן להתפלל בעשרה.

היום, יום א', יו"ד אלול תקלטי"ת לפ"ק.

* * *

[483] י' אלול תקל"ט (22.8.1779)

רן ע"ב

באשר שר' נתן במ"ה שמעון אדליר כ"ץ ז"ל הנ"ל לא היה שומע להסכמת קהל וגובים יצ"ו הנ"ל ולא היה ציית להכרזה הנזכרת מעבר לדף מה שנכרז בפומבי בבית הכנסת ישן וחדש ואסף מנין בביתו להתפלל נגד תקנות הקהל וגובים יצ"ו, בכן התאספו יחד החברא קדישא יצ"ו והאלופים גובים יצ"ו ובצירוף הגאון אב"ד נר"ו ושני בתי דינים יצ"ו לשלוח לר' נתן הנ"ל שלא יתפלל בביתו או בשום {מנין} מקום במנין כלל, זולת בבתי כנסיות שיש להם רשיון כעת מקהל יצ"ו. וזה נוסחא ששלחנו בהסכמת החברא קדישא יצ"ו והאלופים גובים יצ"ו ובצירוף הגאון אב"ד נר"ו עם שני בתי דינים יצ"ו: איזא אונש שמשים מקהל יצ"ו בפאהלין ווארדן לילך אצל התורני כ"ה נתן במ"ה שמעון אדליר כ"ץ ז"ל הנ"ל אונד איהם צו זאגין בהסכמת כל הקהל וגובים יצ"ו ובצירוף הגאון אב"ד נר"ו ושני בתי דינים, דש ר' נתן הנ"ל בחרם בפאהלין ווארדן[3] שלא יתפלל בביתו או בשום מקום במנין כלל, זולת בבתי כנסיות שיש להם רשיון כעת מקהל יצ"ו.

---

1. תעודה זו נרשמה שנית, בשינויים קלים, באותו עמוד עם חתימות הרב, הדיינים והפרנסים וגובים, ר' [483].
2. המלים 'זולת... מקהל יצ"ו' הם תוספת מעל לשורה.
3. ...אנו השמשים נצטווינו על ידי הקהל יצ"ו לילך אצל התורני כ"ה נתן במ"ה שמעון אדליר כ"ץ ז"ל הנ"ל ולומר

היום, יום א׳, יו״ד אלול תקלטי״ת לפ״ק.

הק׳ פינחס הלוי איש הורויץ[1]

הקטן אליעזר ליזר לאטר

הקטון אברהםווינג

הק׳ יוזפא גונדרשהיים

הק׳ יודא שוסטר

גבריאל בן המנוח אאמ״ו כהר״ר יום טוב אופני׳ ז״ל מה״ע[2] (?)

הק׳ אברלי ווימפפא סג״ל

הירש בן שלמה כהן

הק׳ נפתלי הירץ בון

הק׳ רפאל הן סג״ל

הק׳ מרדכי בלא״א הר״י מה״ן מאז שליט״א

הק׳ ליב האז

הק׳ יעקב עמדין

הק׳ הירץ גייגר ג״ק

הק׳ מאיר בן משה פלערשהיים ז״ל ג״ק

הקטן נתן בלא״א כ״ה שלמה מז ראש ישיבה פה ק״ק פפ״ד יע״א[3]

הק׳ יעקב בלא״א המנוח כ׳ טעבלי שמש

הקטן אברהם טריר

הק׳ זנוויל בלא״א הר״ר משה טרך

הק׳ מאיר בלא״א כ״ה זלמן שיף כ״ץ זלה״ה

הק׳ חיים בפו״מ כ׳ יוזפא גונדרשהיים שלי״ט

* * *

[485] י״א אלול תק״ס (11.9.1800)

רנא ע״א

כהיום, יום ב׳, י״א אלול תקסמך לפ״ק איזט פולגנדר כרוז אויש גירופן ווארדן:

עש איזט בשם האלופים פ״ו וגובים בצירוף הגאון האב״ד נר״ו בפאהלין ווארדן אויז צו רופן. דעמי [נאך] בחודש אלול תקלטי״ת לפ״ק לר׳ נתן אדלר כ״ץ פר באטן ווארדן לעשות מנין להתפלל בביתו בעונש חרם אונד אויך כנ״ל אין גשריבן ווארדן, ואם אמנם דש ר׳ נתן הנ״ל דענאך מנין להתפלל בביתו גהאלטן האט, אין להרהר עליו ובוודאי טעמו ונימוקו עמו ושלא

לו בהסכמת כל הקהל וגובים יצ״ו ובצירוף הגאון אב״ד נר״ו ושני בתי דינים שר׳ נתן הנ״ל נצטווה בחרם שלא יתפלל...

1. חתימות מקוריות.
2. (אולי מהוהנאמס [Uffenheim] ע״פ סגל במספר [474] בפנקס. גם בכתב היד לא ברור שכתוב ׳מה״ע׳ אלא נראה שכתוב ׳מה״ס׳. – א.פ.)
3. מכאן והלאה טור שני של חתימות.

להיות חס וחלילה נלכד בעונש הנ"ל. בכל זאת, לצאת מכל הרהור עונש חרם הנ"ל, איזט מאן הירמיט[1] מודיע ומפרסם ברבים, דש כל הנעשה ונכתב בפנקס הקהל בשנת תקלטי"ת בטל ומבוטל ולהבא מותר זיין זאל.

הק' זכריה ווערטהיים ג"ק
הק' זלמן פלערשהיי' ג"ק

* * *

[488] א' ניסן תקמ"ג (3.4.1783)

רנד ע"ב

ב"ה

בהתאסף ראשי עם יחד ה"ה החברותא קדישא האלופים הקצינים פרנסים ומנהיגים וגובים יצ"ו, בצירוף ששה גבאי צדקה וששה בעלי בתים יחידי סגולה מבני קהלתינו יע"א עלה במוסכם הוועד הנ"ל בידיעות הגאון אב"ד נר"ו ושני בתי דינין כנראה מתוך ההעתק הנרשם גם כן למטה[2] שנמסר לנו מהגאון אב"ד נר"ו ושני בתי דינין נר"ו, לתקנה קבוע ויתד שלא תמוט,[3] מאחר חדשים מקרוב בא דש כמה וכמה בעלי בתים מבני קהלתינו ניכט בבית הכנסת ישן וחדש קומן זונדרן ניכט נור בבתי כנסיות קטנים גיהן, פיל מעהר מי שלבו רוצה בונה במה לעצמו[4] לאסוף עשרה להתפלל בביתו, וואורונט זוא וואהל היזק גדול להקדש גבאים פר אורזאכט ווערד, אלש אויך לחרפה ובזיון גדול לשני בתי הכנסיות הגדולים שבקהלתינו גרייכט. דא הערא האבן החברותא קדישא יצ"ו ובצירוף האלופים גובים ושארי קריאי העדה ובהסכמות הגאון אב"ד ושני בתי דינין נר"ו בשלאסן לתקנה קבוע כנ"ל, דש הבעלי בתים מקהלתינו יע"א וועלכה בעלי ערכים זיינין[5] ובבית הכנסת של הישיבה גיהן, מחויבים מידי שנה בשנה שלשה זהובים להגבאי דתלמוד תורה צו צאהלין.[6] וועלכר בעל ערך מבני קהלתינו יע"א דער בהקלויז[7] או בבית הכנסת של ר' זנוויל

1. כהיום... הוכרז הכרוז דלהלן: האלופים פ"ו וגובים בצירוף האב"ד נר"ר ציוו להכריז. מאחר שבחודש אלול תקל"ט לפ"ק נאסר על ר' נתן אדלר כ"ץ בעונש חרם לעשות מנין להתפלל בביתו והדבר גם נרשם (בפקנס), ואם אמנם שר' נתן הנ"ל בכל זאת קיים מניין להתפלל בביתו, אין להרהר אחריו... מכריזים ומודיעים בזאת ברבים שכל הנעשה והנכתב בפנקס הקהל בשנת תקל"ט בטל ומבוטל ויהיה מותר להבא.
2. ר' [490א]
3. על פי גיטין יז ע"א
4. חגיגה כב ע"א
5. 'בעל ערך' הוא מי שרכושו או הכנסתו מחייבים אותו לשלם מסים קבועים לקהילה.
6. לפי ההצעה המקורית כפי שנרשמה בכרוז (ר' [489]), היו גם המתפללים בישיבה חייבים בתשלום חמשה זהובים כמו בשאר בתי הכנסת המנויים להלן. ייתכן שהוחלט להקטין את הסכום מאחר שבית הכנסת בישיבה היה לו מעין מעמד רשמי של בית כנסת של הקהילה.
7. על הקלויז ר': [סגל לא הספיק להשלים. אפשר לעיין בהקדמה האנגלית כאן עמ' 27 הערה 50 – א.פ.]

הזי[1] או בבית הכנסת דהקדש[2] ובשני בתי הכנסיות של ר' מענדלי לילג ור' מיכל גייגר[3] בשבתות וימים טובים ויום הכניסה גיהן ווערדן, דיא זעלבה זיינין מחויב מידי שנה בשנה חמשה זהובים להגבאי צדקה צו בצאהלין בתורות התחייבות כמו שאר נתינות שבקהלתינו.

אותן בעלי ערכים מבני קהלתינו דיא אבר בבית הכנסת של ר' ליב רייס[4] או בבית הכנסת של הגאון אב"ד נר"ו ובבית הכנסת של ר' זלמן חסיד נר"ו[5] בשבתות וימים טובים ויום הכניסה גיהן ווערדן, מחויבים לשלם מידי שנה בשנה להגבאי צדקה עשרה ר"ט צו צאהלין.[6] אויך ווערכה אשה דש בעלה בעל ערך איזט או אלמנה בעלת ערך דיא בבית הכנסת נשים של ר' ליב רייס גיהן אונד קיינה שטאט קבוע באחד משלשה בתי הכנסיות של נשים האבן, דיא זעלבה מוזין כל שנה שלשה זהובים להגבאי צדקה צאהלין. אכן אותן הנשים דיא איינה שטאט קבוע באחת משלשה בתי הכנסיות של נשים האבן אונד דאך בבית הכנסת נשים של ר' ליב רייס געהן, ברויכן לא יותר אלש זהוב אחד מידי שנה בשנה להגבאי צדקה צו צאהלין. והתשלומין כנ"ל, פאלס דער זעלבה ניכט ברצונו הטוב להגבאי צדקה צאהלין וויל, זוא ווערדן זולכה רוק שטענדין מהאלופים גובים יצ"ו להגבאי צדקה בצאהלט אונד דעם זעלבן על דף שלו בפנקס האלופים גובים יצ"ו כמו תשלומן עולם שלו בלי שום נשיאות פנים כלל אויף גשריבן אונד צור בצאהלונג אויף דש שארפשטה אן גהאלטן.

שארי מנינים בבית בעלי בתים יהיו אסורים דרך כלל בלי שום נשיאות פנים, זולות על אופנים המבוארים להבא, אונד נעהמליך זקן או תש כח דער אצל החברותא קדישא יצ"ו אום רשות אן האלט לעשות מנין בביתו, מוז תיכף פאר אויש על שנה אחת חמשה רייכשטאהלר צאהלין, וואר געגן ערלויבט זיין זאל להתפלל בביתו בעשרה, אמנם בתנאי דש קיין בעל ערך מבני קהלתינו, זוא גאר אויך אחד מבניו הנשואים, במנין הנ"ל בשבתות וימים טובים ויום הכניסה מתפלל דערפין זיין אונד דער זעלבה בעל ערך מבני קהלתינו דער במנין הנ"ל {בשבתות} אויך נור שבת אחת גיהן ווערד, מחויב עשרה ר"ט להגבאי צדקה צו בצאהלין.

דער אבר {...} בלי שום מיחוש נור ברמות רוחו, צו זיינר (רנה, ע"א) קאמאדיטעט בביתו מנין הלטן וויל להתפלל בעשרה, יהיה מחויב מידי שנה בשנה פטר אויש להגבאי צדקה ארבעים

1. אינו מוזכר אצל אבני זכרון. אצל אטלינגר יש זנוויל בן זלמן האז (1.5.1760), אך לא מובא לגביו דבר העשוי לרמוז על כך שהקים בית כנסת פרטי בביתו.
2. בהקדש ששימש כבית חולים, בעיקר למחלות מידבקות, וכאכסניה לעוברי אורח עניים, היה בית כנסת שנועד כמקום תפילה לשוהים בו, אך כפי הנראה באו אליו גם תושבים אחרים.
3. הש"ץ והנאמן מיכל בן ליזר גייגר. בית הכנסת הנקרא כאן על שמו נוסד על ידי אביו, ליזר (אליעזר) בן הדיין זלמן גייגר. על מצבתו נרשם: 'והעמיד הרבה תלמידים מחוכמים וכ"א שנה לא מש מאוהל של תורה בית המדרש הגדול מחמיו המנוח מהר"מ (כצ"ל!) אופנהיים'. לפי הרשום על מצבתו של מיכל בן זנוויל אופנהיים היה "גאון מקובל... והעמיד תלמידים הרבה...'. יתכן, איפוא, שבית הכנסת היה קיים כבר מימיו של הרב מיכל אופנהיים, אך לפי רישום בספר הקברנים היה אברהם בייזלשטיין 'שמש בבית הכנסת ובבית המדרש של ליזר גייגר'. אלה תולדות 30.8.1780.
4. על ייסודו של בית המדרש מכספי עזבונו ועל פי צוואתו, ר': הורוויץ, רבני פרנקפורט, עמ' 64 ו-165.
5. על מצבתו (אבני זכרון, מס' 5855) רשום, 'הרב הגאון ו ה ח ס י ד... למד ולימד לאחרים והעמיד תלמידים הרבה...'.
6. ייתכן שהחמרה לגבי המתפללים בבתי כנסת 'פרטיים' אלה לעומת האחרים שנמנו בסעיף הראשון של התקנה נובעת מכך שמדובר בבתי תפילה שנוסדו בשנים האחרונות והיה חשש שמספרם ילך ויתרבה אם לא יחייבו את המתפללים בהם בסכום גבוה לקופת הצדקה. ראוי לציין שגם המניין בביתו של האב"ד לא הופלה לטובה בנידון זה.

זהובים צו צאהלין ובכל זאת דערף קיין בעל ערך מבני קהלתינו צו זולכם מנין קומן בחיוב תשלומין לכל שבת ושבת עשרה ר״ט, חוץ לשני הירידים יהיה מותר. בימי החול אבל לא בשבת ויום טוב[1] לעשות מנין בביתו להתפלל בעשרה. ועל כל המאורע,[2] אם יהיו הנעדרים חשוכי בנים,[3] זוא איזט דעם זעלבן ערלויבט על זמן י״א חדשים מנין צו האלטן, ואם יהיה להנעדר בנים ווערד ניכט לענגר אלש ימי השלושים ערלויבט מנין צו האלטן,[4] דש אבר בייא זולכה מנינים אויך קיין בעל ערך מבני קהלתינו דא צו קומן דערף בחיוב תשלומן עשרה ר״ט לכל שבת.

ההשכמות בבתים ומכל שכן לקרות בתורה אחר ההשכמה יהיו אסורים דרך כלל חוץ בהישיבה איזט ערלויבט להתפלל יוצר בהשכמה אבל לא לקרות בתורה בחיוב תשלומין מהבעל בית הנ״ל ומכל המתאספים לזה מכל אחד עשרה רייכשטאהלר.

גם הוסכם בהוועד הנ״ל דש הצדקות הן מהקלפות הקבועים בכותל בית הכנסת של ר׳ ליב רייס וגם מהקלפות הסובבים שם בבית הכנסת של ר׳ ליב רייס בשעת התפלה להגבאי צדקה דקהלתינו איין גליפרט מוזין ווערדן וגם יהיו המפתחות לקלפות הנ״ל ביד הגבאי צדקה נגד תשלומין להשמש של בית הכנסת של ר׳ ליב רייס שכר טרחתו בשביל הקלפות הנ״ל. אויך הספרי קודש הנקראים בבית הכנסת של ר׳ ליב רייס בשמחות תורה פר שטייגט זאלין ווערדן והשכר יפול להקדש, חוץ שיהיה היתר לאלמנת ר׳ ליב רייס לכתוב ספר תורה לעצמה ויהיה להספר תורה שלה הקדימה לקרות לספר ראשון בלי שום תשלומין.

ועל כל התחייבות התשלומין הנ״ל ווערדן הגבאי צדקה השגחה פרטיות האבין למסור אותן האנשים העוברים על אחת מכל הנ״ל להאלופים גובים יצ״ו, אונד איהרע בצאהלונג מהאלופים גובים יצ״ו רעשטאטיוויהרט בקומן זאלן ולאותן בעלי ערכים על דף שלהם, כמו שארי נתינות ותשלומן עולם שלהם, צור בצאהלונג אויף דש שארפשטה ובלי שום נשיאות פנים אן גהאלטן אונד גצוואונגין ווערדן זאלין.

כל הנ״ל איזט בהתוועדות החברותא קדישא יצ״ו ובצירוף האלופים גובים יצ״ו ואסיפות גבאי צדקה וגם יחידי סגולה ובהסכמות הגאון אב״ד נר״ו ושני בתי דינין לתקנה קבוע בשלאסן ווארדן צו בפאלגן מן פסח דהאי שתא תקמגימ״ל לפ״ק ואילך, בכל תוקף התחייבות תשלומין עולם ושארי נתינות מבני קהלתינו יע״א, וכאילו מועל בהקדש, כל הכפיות על התשלומין הנ״ל בלי שום נשיאות פנים גשעהן ווערד. כל הנ״ל נמנו וגמרו אסיפות הוועד הנ״ל, היום, יום ה׳, ראש חודש ניסן תקמגימ״ל לפ״ק והוכרז בשני בתי כנסיות דקהלתינו בשבת קודש ג׳ ניסן הנ״ל. ולראיה ואות אמת באו שני פרנסים ומנהיגים ושני גובים יצ״ו ושני גבאי צדקה ושני בעלי בתים על החתום.[5]

---

1. המלים ׳בימי החול אבל לא בשבת ויום טוב׳ הם תוספת מעל לשורה. בצד הגליון: ׳ובשבתות וימים טובים על עמדם בבתי הכנסיות הגדולים גיהן, זונדרן נור אן דיא וואוכין לבית הכנסיות׳. במשך הימים בהם התקיימו שני הירידים נהרו לפפד״מ סוחרים יהודים כה רבים שהקהילה היתה מחוייבת לאפשר להם תפילה בציבור גם במניינים פרטיים, אך גם כאן הוגבלה הרשות לימי החול בלבד.
2. כאן במובן של ׳פטירה׳. מלה זו, שבמקורה פירושה ׳מקרה׳, ׳דבר שאירע׳, קיבלה בספרות המאוחרת משמעות של ׳מקרה רע׳ (אולי על פי אותיות הסיום), ר׳: אליעזר בן־יהודה, מלון הלשון העברית, כרך ששי, 2759.
3. המלים ׳ועל כל... בנים׳ הם תוספת מעל לשורה.
4. כאשר הנעדר חשוך בנים מאפשרים קיום מניין בביתו במשך י״א חודשים כדי להבטיח שיאמרו קדיש עליו, אך כאשר יש בנים אין צורך בכך כי הם מחוייבים ממילא באמירת הקדיש עד גמר י״א חודשים לאחר הפטירה.
5. ...מאחר חדשים מקרוב באו שכמה וכמה מבעלי בתים מבני קהלתינו אינם באים לבית הכנסת הישן והחדש, אלא לא רק שהם הולכים לבתי הכנסת הקטנים אף גם זאת מי שלבו רוצה בונה במה לעצמו לאסוף עשרה להתפלל בביתו ועל ידי כך נגרם נזק גדול לגבאי ההקדש וכן מביא הדבר חרפה ובזיון גדול על שני בתי הכנסת

הקטן אברהם ווינג ג"ק
הק' הירש כהן ג"ק
הק' נפתלי הירץ בון
הק' מרדכי בלא"א הר"ר מה"ו נתן מאז שליט"א
הק' איצק שוסטר כ"ץ
הק' משה רויטשילד
הק' אהרן דעטמאלד

הגדולים שבקהלתינו. לכן החליטו החברותא קדישא יצ"ו בצירוף האלופים הגובים ושאר קריאי העדה ובהסכמת הגאון האב"ד נר"ו ושני בתי הדין נר"ו לתקנה קבועה כנ"ל שבעלי הבתים שהם בעלי ערך והולכים לבית הכנסת שבישיבה מחוייבים לשלם מדי שנה בשנה שלושה זהובים לגבאי התלמוד תורה. בעל ערך מבני קהלתינו יע"א שילך בשבתות וימים טובים ויום הכניסה לקלויז או לבית הכנסת של ר' זנוויל הז או לבית הכנסת בהקדש או לשני בתי הכנסת של ר' מענדל לילג ושל ר' מיכל גייגר חייב לשלם מדי שנה בשנה חמשה זהובים לגבאי הצדקה בתורת התחייבות כמו שאר נתינות שבקהלתינו.

אך אותן בעלי ערך מבני קהלתינו שילכו בשבתות וימים טובים ויום הכניסה לבית הכנסת של ר' ליב רייס או לבית הכנסת של הגאון אב"ד נר"ו או לבית הכנסת של ר' זלמן חסיד נר"ו מחוייבים לשלם מדי שנה בשנה עשרה ר"ט לגבאי הצדקה. גם האשה שבעלה הוא בעל ערך או אלמנה שהיא בעלת ערך ההולכות לבית הכנסת לנשים של ר' ליב רייס ואין להן מקום קבוע באחד משלושת בתי הכנסת של נשים, חייבות לשלם כל שנה שלושה זהובים לגבאי הצדקה. אכן אותן הנשים שיש להם מקום קבוע באחד משלושת בתי הכנסת של נשים ובכל זאת הולכות לבית הכנסת של ר' ליב רייס, אינן חייבות לשלם לגבאי הצדקה מדי שנה בשנה יותר מזהוב אחד. אם מישהו אינו רוצה לשלם את התשלומין הנ"ל לגבאי הצדקה מרצונו הטוב, אזי ישולמו חובות אלה מהאלופים הגובים יצ"ו לגבאי הצדקה וירשמו אותם על הדף שלו בפנקס הגובים יצ"ו כמו תשלומי עולים שלו, בלי שום נשיאות פנים כלל וידרשו ממנו את התשלום בכל החומרה.

שארי מניינים בבית בעלי בתים יהיו אסורים בדרך כלל, בלי שום נשיאות פנים, זולת על האופנים המבוארים להבא, דהיינו זקן או תש כח המבקש רשות מהחברותא קדישא יצ"ו לעשות מניין בביתו חייב לשלם תיכף מראש לשנה אחת חמשה ר"ט ותמורת זה יהיה מותר להתפלל בביתו בעשרה, אמנם בתנאי זה שאף בעל ערך מבני קהלתינו, אפילו לא אחד מבני הנשואים של בעל ערך, יהיה רשאי להתפלל במניין הנ"ל בשבתות וימים טובים ויום הכניסה ואותו בעל ערך שילך אפילו רק בשבת אחת למניין הנ"ל, מחוייב לשלם עשרה ר"ט לגבאי הצדקה.

אך מי שאין לו שום מיחוש ורק ברמות רוחו לנוחיותו רוצה לקיים מניין בביתו להתפלל בעשרה, יהיה מחוייב לשלם מראש מדי שנה בשנה ארבעים זהובים לגבאי הצדקה ובכל זאת אף בעל ערך מבני קהלתינו אינו רשאי לבוא למניין כזה בחיוב תשלומין עשרה ר"ט לכל שבת ושבת, חוץ מבשני הירידים שבהם יהיה מותר לעשות מניין בביתו להתפלל בעשרה בימי החול אבל לא בשבת ויום טוב. ובכל מקרה פטירה (מאורע), אם יהיו הנעדרים חשוכי בנים, מותר לו (לאבל) לקיים מניין בביתו במשך אחד עשר חודשים ואם יהיו לנעדר בנים, לא יהיה מותר לקיים מניין יותר מאשר במשך ימי השלושים, אך גם במניינים כאלה אסור שיבוא אליהם בעל ערך מבני קהלתינו בחיוב תשלומין של עשרה ר"ט לכל שבת... חוץ בהישיבה מותר להתפלל יוצר...

גם הוסכם בוועד הנ"ל שדמי הצדקה, הן מהקופות הקבועות בכותל בית הכנסת של ר' ליב רייס וגם מהקופות הסובבים שם בבית הכנסת של ר' ליב רייס בשעת התפילה, יש למסור לגבאי הצדקה של קהלתינו וגם שהמפתחות לקופות הנ"ל יהיו בידי גבאי הצדקה נגד תשלום לשכר הטרחה לשמש של בית הכנסת של ר' ליב רייס בשביל הקופות הנ"ל. יש גם למכור בהכרזה את ספרי הקודש בבית הכנסת של ר' ליב רייס בשמחת תורה והשכר יפול להקדש...

ועל כל התחייבות התשלומין הנ"ל תהיה לגבאי הצדקה השגחה פרטית למסור את אותם האנשים על אחת מכל הנ"ל לאלופים גובים יצ"ו והם יקבלו בחזרה את התשלום שלהם מהאלופים הגובים יצ"ו ולאותם בעלי ערך ירשם על דף שלהם כמו שאר נתינות ותשלום עולים שלהם והם ידרשו בכל החומרה וללא נשיאות פנים ויוכרחו לשלמם.

בהתוועדות... הוחלט לקיים את כל הנ"ל כתקנה קבועה מפסח דהאי שתא תקמ"ג לפ"ק ואילך...

הק' מ[יכאל][1] בן הר"ר אהרן מייא סג"ל

* * *

[489][2] א' ניסן תקמ"ג (3.4.1783)

דף מודבק לתוך הפנקס בין הדפים רנ"ד ורנ"ה

ב"ה

הערט צו רבותי, עש איזט בפאהלין ווארדן אויש צו ראפין[3] בשם החברותא קדישא יצ"ו ובצירוף האלופים גובים יצ"ו ובהסכמות הגאון אב"ד ושני בתי דינין נר"ו, מאחר חדשים מקרוב בא דש כמה וכמה בעלי בתים מבני קהלתינו ניכט בבית הכנסת ישן וחדש ... ניכט נור בבתי כנסיות קטנים גיהן, פיל מעהר מי שלבו רוצה בונה במה לעצמו לאסוף עשרה להתפלל בביתו, וואורונטר זוא וואהל היזק גדול להקדש גבאים פר אורזאכט ווערד, אלש אויך לחרפה ובזיון גדול לשני בתי הכנסיות הגדולים שבקהלתינו גרייכט. דאהערא האבן החברותא קדישא יצ"ו בצירוף האלופים גובים יצ"ו ושארי קריאי העדה מקהלתינו ובהסכמות הגאון אב"ד ושני בתי דינין נר"ו בשלאסן לתקנה קבוע ויתד שלא תמוט ושלא יזד ויסור דש הבעלי בתים מקהלתינו יע"א דיא בעלי ערכים זיינין ובבתי הכנסיות של הישיבה[4] או קלויז ובית הכנסת של ר' זנוויל הזו ובית הכנסת בהקדש ובשני בתי הכנסיות של ר' מענדלי לילג ור' מיכל גייגר בשבתות וימים טובים ויום הכניסה גיהן ווערדן, מידי שנה בשנה מחויב זיין להגבאי צדקה חמשה זהובים צו צאהלין בתורות התחייבות כמו שארי נתינות שבקהלתינו. אותן בעלי בתים בעלי ערכים דיא אבר בבית הכנסת של ר' ליב רייס או בבית הכנסת של הגאון אב"ד נר"ו ובבית הכנסת של ר' זלמן חסיד בשבת ויום טוב או ביום הכניסה גיהן ווערדן, מחויבים לשלם מידי שנה בשנה להגבאי צדקה עשרה ר"ט. אויך וועלכה אשה דש בעלה בעל ערך איזט אודר אלמנות בעלי ערכים דיא בבית הכנסת נשים של ר' ליב רייס גיהן אונד קיינה שטאט קבוע באחת משלשה בתי הכנסיות נשים שבקהלתינו האבן, דיא זעלבן מוזין מידי שנה בשנה להגבאי צדקה שלשה זהובים צאהלין. אכן אותן נשים דיא שטאט קבוע בשלשה בתי הכנסיות {גדולים} של נשים האבן[5] ובבית הכנסת של נשים בבית ר' ליב רייס גיהן, ברויכין לא יותר אלש זהוב אחד מידי שנה בשנה צו צאהלין לגבאי צדקה.[6] והשלומן כנ"ל פאלס דער זעלבה בעל ערך ניכט ברצונו הטוב צלין וויל להגבאי צדקה, ווערדן זולכה רוק שטענדן מהאלופים גובים יצ"ו להגבאי צדקה בצאהלט אונד דעם זעלבן על דף שלו בפנקס האלופים גובים

1. חור בנייר
2. נוסח הכרוז שהוכרז בבתי הכנסת שימש, כפי הנראה, בסיס לנוסח של ההחלטה של החברותא קדישא וצירופיה כפי שנרשם בפנקס ([488]). השינויים וההוספות נרשמו בצד הכרוז וכן הוספה בסופו. דברים אלה מובאים להלן בהערות לטקסט. הערות ענייניות ותרגום ניתנו לתעודה הנ"ל.
3. תרגום: שמעו, רבותי, ניתנה הוראה להכריז...
4. בצד הגליון: בהישיבה צ ולגבאי תלמוד תורה
5. בצד הגליון: ובשבתות וימים טובים על עמדם בבתי הכנסיות הגדולים גיהן, זונדרן נור אן דיא וואוכין לבית הכנסיות.
6. בצד הגליון: פירם ראפף(?) יהיה מותר לכנוס לר' זלמן חסיד בלי תשלומין.

יצ"ו כמו תשלומן עולם שלו בלי שום נשיאות פנים כלל אויף גשריבן אונד צור בצאהלונג אויף דש שארפשט אן גהאלטן.

שאר מנינים בבית בעלי בתים יהיו אסורים דרך כלל בלי שום נשיאות פנים, אמנם זקן או תש כח דער אצל החברותא קדישא יצ"ו אן האלט לעשות מנין בביתו, מוז תיכף פאר אויז על שנה אחת לגבאי הקהל {עשרה} חמשה[1] ר"ט צאהלין, וואורגעגן איהם ערלויכט זיין זאל להתפלל בביתו בעשרה, בתנאי דש קיין בעל בית בעל ערך, זוא גאר אויך אחד מבניו הנשואים, במנין הנ"ל אצלו מתפלל דערף זיין בשבתות וימים טובים ויום הכניסה. אונד דער זעלבה בעל בית בעל ערך דער במנין כנ"ל גיהט לכל שבת ושבת יו"ד ר"ט להגבאי צדקה צו צאהלין שולדיג ווערד. דער אבר בלי שום מיחוש, נור ברמות רוחו צו זיינר קאמאדעטיט בביתו מנין הלטן וויל להתפלל בעשרה, יהיה מחויב מידי שנה בשנה פאר אויש לגבאי צדקה ארבעים זהובים צו צאהלין, ובכל זאת דערף קיין בעל בית בעל ערך לאותו מנין קומין בחיוב תשלומן לכל שבת ושבת עשרה ר"ט.[2] ועל כל המאורע ח"ו, זוא הנעדר חשוכי בנים איזט אונד אצל הגבאי קהל יצ"ו אן הלט להתאסף מנין בביתו להתפלל בעשרה, זוא איזא ערלויבט על זמן י"א חדשים מנין צו הלטן, דש אבר קיין בעל בית בעל ערך במנין הלז גיהן דערף בחיוב תשלומין הנ"ל. זוא אבר הנעדר בנים האט, ווערד ניכט לענגר אלש ימי השלשים ערלויבט מנין צו האלטן, דש אבר אויך קיין בעל בית בעל ערך דא צו למנין הנ"ל קומן דערף בחיוב תשלומין הנ"ל.[3] ואצל ההשכמה בשבת ויום טוב, הן על הישיבה ומכל שכן בשארי בתים יהיה אסור לקרות בתורה בחיוב תשלומין לכל שבת ושבת עשרה ר"ט.

ועל כל התחייבות התשלומין הנ"ל ווערדן הגבאי צדקה השגחה פרטיות האבן למסור אותן האנשים העוברים על זה להאלופים גובים יצ"ו אונד איהרע בצאהלונג מהאלופים גובים רעשטאטיוויהרט בקומין זאלין ולאותן בעלי ערכים על דף שלהם כמו שארי נתינות ותשלומין עולם שלהם צו בצאהלין אויף דש שארפשטה ובלי שום נשיאות פנים אן גהאלטן אונד גצוואונגין ווערדן זאלין.

כל הנ"ל איזט בהתוועדות החברותא קדישא יצ"ו ובצירוף האלופים גובים יצ"ו ואסיפות כמה גבאי צדקה וגם יחידי סגולה ובהסכמות הגאון אב"ד ושני בתי דינין נר"ו לתקנה קבוע ובכל תוקף התחייבות תשלומן עולם ושארי נתינות מבני קהלתינו וכאלו מועל בהקדש, כל הכפיות על התשלומן הנ"ל בלי שום נשיאות פנים גשעהן ווערד ולהשומעם יונעם ותבוא עליהם ברכת טוב.[4]

כל הנ"ל נמנו וגמרו באסיפות וועד כנ"ל, יום ה', ראש חודש ניסן תקמגימ"ל לפ"ק.

הקטן אברהם ווינג
הק' הירש כהן
הק' נפתלי הירץ בון
הק' מרדכי מאז
הק' איצק שוסטר כ"ץ
הק' משה רויטשילד

1. המילה נמצאת מעל לשורה.
2. בצד הגליון: ימי היריד באמצע השבוע אינו בכלל.
3. מועבר קווי ביטול: השכמות בבתים ומכל שכן לקרות בתורה היה אסור דרך כלל חוץ בהישיבה יהיה מותר ההשכמה אבל לא לקרות בתורה בקנס עשרה ר"ט מאותו העברין וכל המתאסף בתוכו.
4. מכאן ועד לסוף בדיו וכתב יד אחר.

הק׳ מיכאל מייא סג״ל
הק׳ אהרן דעטמאלד

עד כאן דברי הכרוז. בפנקס הקהל מוז גזעצט ווערדן דש הצדקות הן מהקלפיות הקבועים בכותל בית הכנסת של ר׳ ליב רייס וגם מהקלפיות הסובבים בזמן תפלה בבית הכנסת של ר׳ ליב רייס להגבאי צדקה דקהלתינו איין גליפרט מוזין ווערדן, אויך דש המפתחות להקלפיות הנ״ל ביד הגבאי צדקה בהענדיגט זיין מוזן, וואורגעגן להשמש דבית הכנסת של ר׳ ליב רייס שכר טרחתו בשביל קלפיות הסובבים בבית הכנסת הנ״ל מהגבאי צדקה בצאהלט מוז ווערדן. אויך דש הספרי קודש הנקראים בבית הכנסת של ר׳ ליב רייס בשמחות תורה פר שטייגט זאלין ווערדן והשכר יהיה להגבאי צדקה. אמנם אם ירצה אלמנת ר׳ ליב רייס לכתוב ספר תורה לעצמה, יהיה להספר תורה שלה הקדימה להספר ראשון בלי שום תשלומין.

Appendix 6

נספח ו'[1]

Juden Akten 182

Juden Ugb D33#56 21 Bl. (CD 003 / 26.902 Fotostelle komplett digitalisiert), Nr. 6

Institut für Stadtgeschichte Frankfurt am Main

No 637

1) Ob bei Heirathen deren Juden in Franckfurth die ersten sowohl als zweyten Ehepacten in jenen Hochzeitsbüchern welche die Schulkläpperer gewöhnlich zu führen pflegen, ganz und per extensum eingetragen werden

2do) Ob es nicht ein allgemeines jüdisches Gesetz beobachtet werde, daß der Ehemann dem Universalerbe eines Weibes mit Ausschluss dem erzeugten Kind beiderlei Geschlecht sey

3) ob ihm nichts wenigstens das Heurathsgut seines Weibes nach ihrem Tode verbLebe, ohne daß ein besonderes Pactum de dote lucranda hierzu erfordert würde.

4) Ob in Franckfurth bei Sterbefällen deren Juden die Einrichtungen den Städten Maynz und Wormbs in Beobachtung und Ausübung sey

1 Frage. R[esponditur:]
Die Schulkläpperen schreiben in ihre Hochzeitsbücher ein, daß die Partheyen den Mantelgrief getan haben zu befolgen die erste errichtete Ehepacten, sie schreiben aber nicht die Puncten deren Ehepacten ein
Auf 2 et 3 Frage. R[esponditur:]
Es seinen die Rechte nach Ordnung unsere heilige Tohra, daß der Mann seine Frau erbt, in dem was er oder sie schon würcklich zur Zeit ihres Absterbens in Hand und Gewalt haben, es seyen das selbe, was sie ja zum Heurathsgut eingebracht hat, in allem erbt der Mann das selbe, und keine dessen Kinder, es seye dieselbe männlich- oder weiblichen Geschlechts, erben sie nichts von ihre Mutter.
Obschon zwischen dem Mann und seiner Frau kein schriftlich Pactum hierauf errichtet seye, dass er dieselbe erben soll, bei allen sind es folgende Rechte, dass der Ehemann sie erbt. Doch aber wann zwischen dem Mann und seiner Frau in

---

1. My thanks to Verena Kasper for alerting me to the existence of this document and to Dr. Johannes Wachten for transcribing it.

ihre Ehepacten deutlich das Contra vorbehalten und verabredet ist worden, dass der Mann nicht gänzlich auch nicht einiges Theil dieselben erben soll, als dann muß wie zwischen ihnen die Abrede geschehen sind, vollzogen werden.
Auf 4to Frage
R[esponditur:] Daß hier die Einrichtung den Stadten Maynz und Wormbs in Beobachtung und Ausübung sey. All obgeme[l]dtes ist von uns ergangen
Franckfurth an heute
Montag 5. Tag im Monat Tammuss 545 zur kleinen Zahl
L[oco] S[igelli] Pincas Levi Horvitz Ober Rabbiner
Natha[n] der Sohn Raby Schlomo Maas sel.[1] Oberjurist allhier in der Stadt Franckfurth
Mayer der Sohn R. Salomon Schiff Cahn sell.[2]
Hayum der Sohn des Baumeisters R. Joseph Gondersheim.
Daß vorstehende Übersezung mit dem Hebräischen Original gleichlautet, wird hiermit attestiert, so geschehen
Franckfurth am obigen Datum
L[oco] S[igelli] Wolf Jacob Speyer.

1. sel = ז"ל
2. sell = ז"ל

Appendix 7

נספח ז

מתוך פנקס דק"ק פרנקפורט בנושא הוצאות הציבור

[491] כ"ב סיון תקמ"ו (18.6.1786)

רנז ע"א

ב"ה

דא דיא רעדי מכל בני קהלתינו יע"א וביותר דיא עמפפינדונג ממנהיגי הקהלה ה"ה האלופים פרנסים ומנהיגים וגובים יצ"ו זעהר נאהי גיהט וויא ניהטיג זייאה מעמד ומצב דקהלתינו יע"א הן בהכנסות אף גם בהוצאות דיא ערפינדונג צו טרעפן לעזר ולהועיל לקיים ולחזק לכל, דא הערא עלה במוסכם כל המבואר להבא.[1]

א. דש להגאון אב"ד[2] עם שני בתי דינין נר"ו איבר געבן זאל ווערדן צור איין זיכט עד כמה תכבד העבודה, דש ההוצאות מדי שנה בשנה דערן הכנסות איבר טרעפין, והאוריבר הגאון אב"ד עם שני בתי דינין נר"ו איהרע גוט אכטונג מאכין זאלין, דאך אבר ניכט יושט להעמיד דבריהם על דין תורה, רק ברוב שכלם לפי הזמן והענין צו בטראכטין, אונד איהרע פראפאזטי ווידרום למנהיגי הקהלה אלופים קהל וגובים יצ"ו צו רוק געבן, וועלכה אחר כך בהסכמות אשר יבורר לכך, להגדיל או להקטין, אב שליסן זאלין, ובהסכמות הגאון אב"ד עם ב' בתי דינין נר"ו לתקנה קבועה עריכט זאל ווערדן על משך זמן אשר יוסכם מפיהם בצירוף הוועד.

ב. אויך איזט בשלאסין ווארדן, דש אויך על זמן המוסכם כנ"ל קיינה גבאי קהל במשך זמן שני חדשים ניכט יותר אן מתנות, הן לבני קהלתינו או לבאים ממרחקים, בכלל אויש געבן דערפין אלש שלשים זהובים, זולות לאיש נכבד והגון אשר ראוי לקבל טובה יתירה, זאל דער זעלבה

---

1. מצבה הכספי של הקהילה הלך והתערער במשך המחצית השנייה של המאה הי"ח והחובות הלכו וגדלו. פתיחת התעודה מורה על תופעה מעניינת של אי שביעות רצון מצד בני הקהילה מדרכי ניהול העניינים על ידי הפרנסים, דבר שהביאם לכך לפנות אל הרב ובתי הדין בבקשה שיאפשרו להם לערוך שינויים במערכת המיסוי. ראה: קראואר, *Geschichte der Juden in Frankfurt*, ח"ב, עמ' 308 ואילך, המצביע על ירידת קרנם של הפרנסים והגובים ואי הרצון לשאת בתפקידים אלה. דומה שראייתו של קראואר נכונה יותר בנידון זה מזו של הורוויץ, רבני פרנקפורט, ח"ד, עמ' 66, הכותב שענייני הקהילה היו באותן שנים בידיים הטובות ביותר.

2. הרב פינחס הלוי הורוויץ. כוונת הפרנסים והגובים בפנייה אל הרב ובית הדין הייתה, כפי הנראה, לקבל מהם הצעות כיצד להעלות את ההכנסות ממסים ולהקטין את ההוצאות המוטלות על קופת הציבור. לדעתו של הורוויץ (רבני פרנקפורט, עמ' 78-79) מוכיחה הפנייה בעניין כזה אל הרב את מעמדו של הרב שנבע מההערצה של בני הקהילה כלפיו ומהערכת כושרו גם בעניינים של מנהל וכספים. ניתן, עם זאת, לראות בכך סימן של חולשה של ההנהגה החילונית שביקשה לקבל גיבוי מהרב ומהדיינים להחלטות שבוודאי לא היו נוחות לציבור. כוונת הפונים היתה, מן הסתם, לקבל הצעות לשינויים מדברים עליהם הוחלט בדורות קודמים ושנתקדשו על ידי המסורת ולכן הדגישו שבקשתם היא לדון בנושא לאו דווקא רק לפי 'דין תורה' אלא בהתאם לתנאי הזמן ועל פי 'רוב שכלם'. אין בידינו התשובה של הרב ובית הדין, על אף שלפי הנאמר בסוף התעודה, הוחלט לא לדחות את הדבר מעבר לחודש טבת תקמ"ז. ייתכן שאמנם נתקבלו החלטות ואלה נרשמו בפנקס המוזכר בסעיף ה'.

לפני אסיפות הקהל פאר גבראכט ווערדן, אבר על ידי גבאי קהל אן קיינים, הן לענייי עירינו או לארחי ופרחי,[1] יותר משלשה זהובים צו געבן.

ג. גם דש מהאלופים פרנסים ומנהיגים וגובים יצ"ו אן איין בית דין כשר שאינם נוגעים בעדותן ודין זה איבר טראגן זאל ווערדן דיא רעדוציהרונג הרווחים מדבר טובות אודר זונשטן קאפיטאליען.[2]

ד. אף דש מהיום כל משך זמן המוסכם כנ"ל לשום אדם, יהיה מי שיהיה, קיין נייא סאלאריום ערשטאט זאל קענין ווערדן אונד כלל וכלל ניכט מגבאי קהל ניכט פאר צו ברענגן. דעש גלייכן קיין חזן משום קהלה שבעולם בבית הכנסת דפה מתפלל זיין צו לאזין אודר אויף הוצאות דענין זעלבן לושעמנט אן צו ווייזן.

ה. וואש פון איינין בלאנג צו עראכטין איזט אונד דאריבר פעם אחת מהאלופים הקהל יצ"ו איין שלום אב גפאסט איזט ווארדן, זוא זאל זולכש בפנקס מיוחד לזה איין גטראגן ווערדן להיות למשמרת לעת הצורך ולדורות הבאים דאנאך צו רעגוליהרן.[3]

כל הנ"ל נזרק והוסכם מפי החברותא קדישא ה"ה האלופים וגובים יצ"ו לקיים ולחזק לכל לטובות הכלל כולו, ולהיות כתוב בספר ופנקס הקהל הלז עם חתימות שני גבאי קהל המופקדים כעת עם שני גובים יצ"ו בשם ובהסכמות כולנו יחד כאיש אחד חברים, להיות למשמרת ולעד עולם, אונד דש פונקטן א' בבל תאחר עד ראש חודש טבת הסמוך תקמזי"ן הבע"ל אין גענצליכר אורדינונג גבראכט זאל ווערדן.[4] ולראיה ואות אמת באו השני פרנסים ומנהיגים ושני גובים כנ"ל על החתום פה קהלתינו יע"א, היום, יום א' ך"ב סיון תקו"ם לפ"ק.

---

1. כינוי לקבצנים הנודדים שכל הקהילות סבלו מהם ומהנטל הכספי שהטילו על קופות הצדקה.
2. דבר טוב הוא עזבון או מתנה שניתנים לקהל לצרכי ציבור תמורת ריבית קבועה המשתלמת לנותן או ליורשיו. שער הריבית המקובל לכספים כאלה וכן לכספים שהקהילה קיבלה לידיה היה ששה אחוזים לשנה. ראה: (סגל לא הספיק להשלים – א.פ.).
3. ייתכן שהכוונה ל'פנקס הקהל הקטן' המוזכר אצל אדלר, עמ' 200, הע' 3. פנקס זה לא נשתמר. (סגל לא השלים את ההפניה ואינני יודע למה הוא התכוין – א.פ.).
4. מאחר שהדברים הנאמרים על ידי כל בני קהילתנו יע"א וביותר ההרגשה של מנהיגי הקהילה, האלופים פרנסים ומנהיגים וגובים יצ"ו, מראים בעליל כמה דרוש למצוא דרך (לתיקון) מעמד ומצב קהילתנו יע"א הן בהכנסות אף גם בהוצאות כדי לעזור ולהועיל לקיים ולחזק לכל, לכן עלה במוסכם כל המבואר להבא:

למסור לעיון הגאון אב"ד עם שני בתי הדין נר"ו עד כמה תכבד העבודה, שההוצאות עולות מדי שנה בשנה על ההכנסות, כדי שהגאון האב"ד עם שני בתי הדין יתנו חוות דעתם על כך, אך שלא יעמידו דבריהם בדיוק על דין תורה רק יעיינו בדבר ברוב שכלם לפי הזמן והעניין ויחזירו את הצעותיהם למנהיגי הקהילה, לאלופים הקהל והגובים יצ"ו, והם יחליטו אחר כך בהסכמת מי שיבורר לכך, להגדיל או להקטין, והדברים ייקבעו לתקנה קבועה בהסכמות הגאון אב"ד עם שני בתי הדין נר"ו למשך זמן שיוסכם מפיהם בצירוף הוועד.

כמו כן הוחלט גם שבמשך הזמן המוסכם כנ"ל לא יוכלו גבאי קהל במשך זמן של שני חודשים לתת כמתנות, הן לבני קהילתנו והן לבאים ממרחקים, בסך הכל יותר מאשר שלושים זהובים, זולת לאיש נכבד והגון אשר ראוי לקבל טובה יתירה־אותו יביאו לפני אסיפת הקהל, אבל גבאי הקהל לא יהיו רשאים לתת לאף אחד, הן לענייי עירנו או לארחי פרחי, יותר משלושה זהובים.

גם שהאלופים פרנסים ומנהיגים וגובים יצ"ו יביאו לפני בית דין כשר שאינם נוגעים בעדותן ובדין זה את שאלת הורדת הרווחים מדברים טובים ומכספים מושקעים אחרים.

שמהיום, כל משך הזמן המוסכם כנ"ל, אסור יהיה לשלם משכורת חדשה לאף אדם, יהיה מי שיהיה, ושגבאי הקהל לא יביאו עניין כזה בכלל לדיון. כמו כן אין לתת לאף חזן משום קהילה שבעולם להתפלל בבית הכנסת דפה או להקציב לו אירוח על חשבון הקהל.

הק׳ אברליווימפפא סג״ל[1]
הק׳ איצק בן ג״ה הירץ בון
הק׳ רפאל הן סג״ל
הק׳ ליב האז

כל דבר שייחשב בעל חשיבות ושלגביו נתקבלה החלטה פעם אחת על ידי האלופים הקהל יצ״ו, יירשם בפנקס מיוחד לכך להיות למשמרת לעת הצורך ולמען ינהגו לפיו הדורות הבאים.

...ושאת האמור בסעיף א׳ יש להסדיר באופן מוחלט עד ר״ח טבת הסמוך תקמ״ז הבע״ל בעונש של בל תאחר...

1. חתימות מקוריות.

Appendix 8

נספח ח[1]

Folios 53b-54a, folder 77-78, Collection of Rabbinical and Historical Manuscripts (RG 128), YIVO Archives, New York. The material is reproduced with the permission of the YIVO Institute for Jewish Research, New York.

On the evening of 11 February 1782, the rabbinic court gave a ruling to the leaders of the community who had asked whether income from charitable trusts established by two sisters could be combined. Of particular interest is the fact that one of the sisters, Treinle, established her trust just before her husband, Jacob Schloss, died on 10 Novermber 1777 — in fact, on the very same day. The trust contained a provision for the hiring of teachers to study Torah with local orphans and for the saying of prayers, including Kaddish, on the anniversary of Treinle and Jacob's deaths. The Schlosses appear to have had at least one grown male child of their own at the time of Jacob's death (see Dietz, p. 262, with Ettlinger, 10.11.1777). However, neither her entry in the Frankfurt *Memorbuch* (fol. 265b) nor her gravestone (Horovitz, no. 3639) make mention of children, while both make extensive reference to her piety. The *Memorbuch* notes that the payment for the entry came from her estate.

דף נג ע"ב

1. ע"ד השאלה שנשאל מאתנו ח"מ מאת האלופי' הקציני' גובי' י"ץ מאחר שכבר מונח אצלם
2. קרן קיימת לדבר טוב מאת האשה הרבנית מ' מלכה בת ה"כ אהרן מיץ / א' הרב
3. הגאון אב"ד דק"ק בינגא מהור"ר אהרן תאומי' זצ"ל אשר ציוותה כן בצוואתה ה
4. הנעשה ט"ז אייר תקי"ח לפ"ק / ושם נאמר בזה"ל / אים איבר[ר]גין זאל מה ש[י]מצא בעזבוני
5. לד"ט אן גוועגדיט ווערדין / והיינו ענטוועדר יתומי' לערנין צו לאזין או יתומי' / אויז צו
6. געבין וכל הקרוב קרוב קודם עכ"ל / ובשנת תקל"ח יו"ד חשון עשה אחותה מ' טריינלה א' ר' יעקב
7. שלאָס ק"ס ונעשה ע"ד שטר התחייבות לה"ה האלופי' הנ"ל גובי' יצו מסך שני אלפי' זהו'
8. וכתוב שם וז"ל ומהרווחי' הנ"ל יהי' האלופי' הקציני' גובי' יצו שוכרי' מלמדי' כל שנה ללמוד עם
9. יתמי בני קהלתינו / ובכל יום היאָהר צייט של בעלה הנ"ל וכמו כן בכל יום יאָהרצייט
10. שלי יאמרו המלמדי' עם היתומי' הנ"ל יהי רצון אחר הלימוד לתועלת ותקון נשמתינו ויאמר

---

1. תודתי למשה פיירשטיין וחוה טורניאנסקי על עזרתם בפינוח מספר מילים בכתב היד.

11. א׳ מהיתומי׳ קדיש אחר הלימוד לזכות נשמתינו עכ״ל / ואח״כ ביום א׳ י״ב אדר תקל״ט לפ״ק
12. כתבה האשה מ׳ טריינלה הנ״ל בכתיבת ובחתימת ידה ממש בזה״ל / ווייל[ין] זיך פֿינדיט דש
13. לשון פֿון דען קנין הו״ה גובי׳ יצו ישכרו מלמדי׳ כל שנה ללמוד עם יתומי׳ בני קהלתינו וכו׳ הבי
14. ניט קענין בשיידליך זאגין וואש פֿר מלמדי׳ אלש מיין דעה איזט / אבר יעצונד זאגי איך מיינה
15. מיינ[ונ]ג איזט מלמדי׳ דיא גמר׳ וויא אויך הו״ת מיט קינדר לערנין כדי אלש מאן קאן מ[ג]דל לומדי׳
16. זיין וכו׳ / וויא זיך אויך פֿינדט אלש אחותי הרבנית מ׳ מלכה זצ״ל האט גמאכט איין ד״ט
17. וועלכיש המעות אויך אצל הגובי׳ יצו ליגט אויף רווחי׳ צו לערנין עניים יתומי׳ מבני קהלתינו
18. וועז מי[ג]ליך ווערי לאחר מאה שני׳ דיא רווחי׳ פון די שני ד״ט צו זאמין צו נעהמין כדי
19. אלש מאן איין ב״ב קאן מפרנס זיין מקהלתינו דער הלכה ותוס׳ עם קינדר לערנין
20. קאן / אונד רעכט השגחה צו הבין / אלש ער פֿלייסיג עם התלמודי׳ לערנט ווער מיר
21. זעהר ניחא / אונד ווען איין יתום איין קרוב איזט פֿון מיר אודר פון מיין מאן כ
22. כהר״ר יעקב שלאס ז״ל זאל זיין צום ערשטין אהן צו די[נ]ג[י]ן צו לערנין עכ״ל / ובאו הו״ה
23. גובי׳ עכשיו ושאלו אם יש לצרף הפירות משני ד״ט הנ״ל כפי כ״י הנ״ל או לא יצרפו יחד
24. ולהתנהג {ב.} בד״ט מן מ׳ מלכה הנ״ל כמ״ש בצוואתה הנ״ל זהו השאלה ששאלו הו״ה גובים
25. יצ[ו] מאתנו / ואחר שהוציעו לפנינו צוואת מ׳ מלכה הנ״ל {כמ״ש} ושט״ח וכתב יד של {ל} מ׳
26. טריינלה הנ״ל מצאנו עצמינו ב״ד ח״מ אחר שב״ד שבכל דור אבי יתומי׳ ויד עניים הם
27. שמחויבי׳ לעיין ג״כ מאחר שבצוואת מלכה נאמר ענטוועדר יתומי׳ לערנין צו לא[ז]ין
28. או יתומי׳ אויז צו געבין עכ״ל / בכן איזה מהם טוב יותר / גם מצאנו ש
29. שמחויבי׳ אנחנו לעיין אודת הרווחי׳ שעלו על הסך קרן קיימת מד״ט מהאשה מ׳
30. מלכה מעת פטירת מ׳ טריינלה הנ״ל עד עתה שלא נעשה מהם דבר / איזה ד״ט
31. יעשה בהם / והנה אחר שעיינינו ודקדקנו בצוואת הנ״ל ובשטר ובכ״י הנ״ל מצאנו
32. שהפירות שעלה על הקרן קיימת מד״ט האשה המנוחת מ׳ מלכה בת המנוח כ״ה אהרן
33. מיץ ז״ל מיום פטירת אחותה מ׳ טריינלה ע״ה עד היום דלמטה יתנו הו״ה גובי׳
34. י״ץ לצורך הכנסת כלה יתומה וכל הקרוב קרוב קודם / ולהבא יצורף יחד הפירות
35. שיעלה על הסך קרן קיימת מד״ט מהני שתי אחיות מ׳ מלכה ומ׳ טריינלה ע״ה הנ״ל /
36. ויתנהגו הו״ה גובי׳ יצו כפי המבואר להבא והיינו שהרווחי׳ שיעלה משני דברי׳ טובי׳
37. הנ״ל יהי׳ בכל לצורך ת״ת לנערי׳ יתומי׳ מאב ובאופן המבואר להבא / ומאחר שבשט״ח
38. של האשה מ׳ טריינלה מיוד מרחשון תקל״ח שם נזכר כל ההתחייבות על האלופי׳ גובי׳
39. יצו / וגם נאמר שם שהם ישכרו מלמדי׳ בכן כה יהי׳ וכה יקום שהו״ה גובי׳ י״ץ ישכרו ב״ב
40. אחד מתושבי קהלתינו ללמוד עם חמשה נערי׳ יתומי מאב מבני קהלתינו גמ׳ עם תו״ס כ
41. כדרך כל המלמדי׳ הו״ת ויתנו לו שכירות מחמשה נערי׳ הנ״ל מכל א׳ וא׳ עשרה ר״ט לחצי
42. שנה שעולה יחד מאה ר״ט לשנה / ויבחרו הו״ה גובי׳ י״ץ מלמד ראוי׳ והגון וכדאי למלאכה

---

1. ישמרם צורם

43. זו שהוא מלאכת שמים שיהי' טוב בעיני אלקי' ואדם / ויהיה' מהיר וזריז וחרד לדבר ה'
44. ויעשה מלאכתו באמונה / וע"ז נאמר ויראת מאלקיך / וגם יבחרו ויבחרו החמשה נערים
45. יתומי'

נד ע"א

1. יתומי' הנ"ל את מי שיוכ[שר] בעיניהם ללמוד ושיהא לימודו עולה יפה / ואם לא ימצא[ו]
2. חמשה נערי' יתומי' מבני קהלתינו שיוכלו ללמוד גמ' עם תו"ס / אזי יוקח נערי' יתומי'
3. כנ"ל הפחותי' במד[י]נה להשלים מספר החמשה / ואף שיהי' ראוי' רק ללמוד גמ'
4. לבד / ואם לא יהי' בנמצא שום מלמד מבני קהלתינו שירצה ללמוד עם שתי חברותות
5. דהיינו חבורה א' גמ' ותו"ס וחבורה א' לגמ' לבד / אזי יותן להמלמד כפי התלמידי' ש
6. שרוצה בחבורה א' מכל א' וא' עשרה ר"ט לחצי שנה כנ"ל / והחסר מן חמשה נערי'
7. כנ"ל יבחרו הפחותי' במדינה כנ"ל וישכרו להם מלמד אחר / ואותו רשאי להיות
8. ב"ב אחר אף שאינו מתושבי קהלתינו יע"א ויתנו מכל א' וא' מנערי' עשרה ר"ט לחצי שנה
9. והנותרת מהפירות משני ד"ט הנ"ל לאחר שיתנו הו"ה גובי' י"ע מאה ר"ט לשנה לצורך
10. מלמדי' הנ"ל / {..ן} כנ"ל ינתן לחמשה נערי' הנ"ל שוה בשוה לכל א' וא' כפי מה שיגיע
11. ע"פ חשבון מהמותרות מהפירות הנ"ל / ובחמשה נערי' הנ"ל כנ"ל הקדימה יהי' ל
12. להקרוב לשתי אחיות הנ"ל והקרוב קרוב קודם / אם הוא מוכשר ושוה לרחוק ואם אינו
13. בנמצא קרוב לשתי אחיות הנ"ל ויש קרוב להמנוח כ"ה יעקב שלאס ז"ל גם הוא יש
14. לו דין קדימה כמבואר בשט"ח של מ' טריינלה הנ"ל יצא מאתנו אור ליום ג'
15. ד"ח שבט לקמ"ב לפ"ק /

List of Abbreviations

ראשי תבות

א"א	אבי אדוני
אב"ד	אב בית דין
אדמ"ו	אדוננו מורנו ורבנו
או"א	אחד ואחד
א"ז	אביו זקנו
אי"ה	אם ירצה השם
א"ל	אלמנה
אל'	אלמנה
אל"א	אחד לאחד
אליו"ע	אם לא יגיד ונשא עונו
אמי"ה	אם ירצה השם
א"נ	אינו נימול, אינם נימולים
א"ס	אגב סודר, אמן סלה
א"ע	אותו עניין, את עצמה, את עצמו, את עצמי, את עצמם
אפ"ה	אפילו הכי
אפי'	אפילו
א"ר	אדר ראשון
א"ש	אדר שני
א"ת	אם תאמר
ב"א	באיש אחד
באוה"ב	באופן הברור, באשה והדר בעלה
ב"ב	בוקסבוים, בני ביתה, בני ביתו, בעל הבית, בעלי בתים
בבהכ"י	בבית הכנסת ישן
בבהכיו"ח	בבית הכנסת ישן וחדש
בבהמ"ד	בבית המדרש
בבמד"ר	בבית מדרש
בגוב"ר	בני גד ובני ראובן
ב"ד	בית דין
בדא"ה	בדיני אומות העולם
בד"י	בדיני ישראל
ב"דיץ	בתי דין ישמרם צורנו
ב"ה	בית המוצנע, בן המנוח, בניין הקנאהלין, בעזרת השם, ברוך הוא, ברוך השם
בהכ"ח	בית הכנסת חדש

בהכ"י	בית הכנסת ישן
בה"מ	בן המנוח
ב"המנוח	בן המנוח
בהר"ב	בן הרב
בו"ו	בן וואלף
בז"ה	בזה הלשון
בזה"ל	בזה הלשון
בח'	בחור
ב"ח	בחור חמד, בעל(י) חוב, בת(ה) חורגת
בח"ח	בחרם חמור
בח"י	בחתימת ידו
ב"כ	בא כוחו, באי כוחו, בן כבוד, בשביל כך
בכא"ה	בכל אופן המועיל
בכ"ה	בן כבוד הרב
בכו"ה	בכח והרשאה
בלא"א	בן לאדוני אבי
בלא"ה	בלאו הכי
ב"מ	בן מורנו, בעל מלאכה, בעלי מעריכים, בר מצרא
במב"ד	במעשה בית דין
במ"ה	בן מורנו הרב
במו"מ	בכל מקום ומקום, במשא ומתן
במכ"ה	במחילת כבוד הודו
בנגוב"ר	בני גד ובני ראובן
בעה"ת	בעל ספר התרומות
בעו"ה	בעונותיו הרבים, בעונותינו הרבים
בע"ח	בעל(י) חוב
בע"נ	בעזרת נשים
בפ'	בפירוש
ב"פ	בן פרנס
בפו"מ	בן פרנס ומנהיג
בפ"ז	בפני זה
בפ"מ	בפה מלא
בפס"ד	בפסק דין
בק"ג	בקניין גמור
בק"ה	בקונטרס הטענות
בק"ס	בקומפרמיס, בקניין סודר
ב"ר	בן רב(י)
ב"ש	ברונשוויג
בשד"א	בשבועה דאורייתא
בש"ע	בשלחן ערוך

בת"כ	בתקיעת כף
בתנ"ר	בתנאים ראשונים
בת"ע	בתורת עדות, בתורת עיסקא
בת"ר	בתנאים ראשונים
ג	גאון
גב"תת	גבאי תלמוד תורה
ג"ה	גבאי הקדש, גבאי הקהל, גבאי הקהילה, גדול הדור
ג"כ	גם כן
ג"ץ	גאון צדק, גבאי צדקה
ג"ק	גבאי קהילה, גובה קהילה
ג"ש	גלגול שבועה
גת"ת	גבאי תלמוד תורה
ד"א	דבר אחר
דאל"כ	דאם לא כן
דב"ט	דבר טוב
דג"ח	דגמילות חסד
דו"ד	דין ודברים
ד"ט	דבר טוב
דעכ"פ	דעל כל פנים
ד"פ	דרך פשר
דקפ"ד	דייני קהילת פרנקפורט דמיין
ד"ש	דרישת שלום
ה	הרב
ה"א	האלמנה
ה"ב	הבחור, הדר בעלה
הב"ל	הבא לטובה
הב"ע	הבא עלינו
הבע"ח	הבעל(י) חוב
הבע"ל	הבא עלינו לטובה
ה"ג	הגאון, הסגת גבול
הד"ש	הדורש שלומו
ה"ה	היה היה (ר' יחזקאל א, ג), הירש הארין, הרב החכם
הו"ה	הישרים והתמימים, המפואר(ים) והחשוב(ים)
הו"ת	הלכה ותוספות
ה"כ	הכנסת כלה
ה"מ	המנוח
הנ"ל	הנזכר(ים) לעיל, הנזכר(ים) לקמן
הנמע"ל	הנזכר(ים) מעבר לדף
הפס"ד	הפסק דין
הק'	הקטן, הקצין

ה"ק	הקטן, הקצין
הרב"ד	הראש בית דין
הר"י	הראש ישיבה
הר"ר	הרב רבי
ואפ"ה	ואפילו הכי
וג'	וגומר
וז"ל	וזה לשונו
וח"מ	וחובות מחותמים
וי"א	ויורשיה אחריה, ויורשיהם אחריהם, ויורשיו אחריו
ו"כ	וכבוד
וכה"ג	וכהאי גונא
וכנ"ל	וכן נראה לפרש
ומנ"ל	ומנא ליה
ומש"כ	ומשום כך
וע"ד	ועל דעת
וש"ח	ושבק חיים
ות"ר	ותוספת ראיות
ז"א	זה אינו
זא"ז	זה אחר זה
ז"ל	זה לשונו, זכרונו לברכה
זלה"ה	זכרונו לחיי העולם הבא
זצ"ל	זכר צדיק לברכה
ז"ק	זאנקוועהרט (Sankwehrt), זרע קיימא
חו"מ	חושן משפט
ח"ח	חרם חמור
חח"ז	חצי חלק זכר
ח"י	חתימת יד, חתימת ידה/ידו
ח"כ	חילוף כתבים
ח"מ	חתומים מטה
ח"ק	חברא קדישא
ח"ר	חדש רייכשטאלר
ט"ג	טוב(ים) גרושן(?) (= gute Groschen)
טו"ת	טענות ותביעות
ט"מ	טוב מעות
י'	יום
י"א	יורשיה אחריה, יורשיהם אחריהם, יורשיו אחריו
יו"ע	יגיד ונשא עונו
י"ח	יוצאי חלציה/חלציו
י"ט	יום טוב
י"כ	יום כיפור

יע"א	יגן עליה אלהים
י"ץ	ישמרהו צורו
יצ"ו, יצו	ישמרהו צורו וגואלו, ישמרם צורם וגואלם
יר"ה	ירום הודו
כ	כבוד
כ"א	כל אחד
כאו"א	כל אחד ואחד
כד"י	כדיני ישראל
כ"ה	כבוד הרב
כהר"ר	כבוד הרב רבי
כו"ה	כח והרשאה
כ"י	כתב יד
כ"כ	כל כך
כ"מ	כבוד מר
כמ"ה	כבוד מורנו הרב
כמה"ו	כבוד מורנו הרב ורבנו
כמהור"ר	כבוד מורנו הרב והגאון רב רבי
כ"מר	כבוד מורנו רבי
כנ"ל	כנזכר לעיל
כפ'	כפסק
כ"ש	כל שכן
כתחז"ל	כתיקון חכמינו זכרונם לברכה
ל'	לפרט קטן
ל"א	לא אחד
לא"נ	לאינם נימולים
לבה"מ	לבית המדרש
ל"ג	לשלש(ה)
ל"ד	לואי דאור (Louis d'or)
לד"ט	לדבר טוב
לדב"ט	לדבר טוב
לה"א	להאלמנה
להד"ם	לא היו דברים מעולם
לז"ק	לזרע קיימא
לכאו"א	לכל אחד ואחד
לכ"ה	לכבוד הרב
לכ"י	לכל ישראל
למב"י	למניין בני ישראל
למז"ט	למזל טוב
למ"ט	למזל טול, למעשים טובים
לפ"ז	לפי זה

לפ״כ	לפי כבודה, לפי כבודו
לפ״כ ולפ״כ	לפי כבודו ולפי כבודה
לפ״ע	לפי ערך, לפי ערכו
לפק, לפ״ק	לפרט קטן
לפתחז״ל	לפי תקנת חכמינו זכרונם לברכה
לש״ץ	לשליח ציבור
מ׳	מחמת, מרת, משום
מב״ד	מעשה בית דין
מבד״ג	מעשה בית דין גדול
מ״ה	מורה הדור, מורנו הרב
מהור״ר	מורנו הגדול ורבנו רבי
מהנ״מ	מורנו הרב נתן מז
מה״ר	מורנו הרב
מהר״נ	מורנו הרב נתן
מה״ת	מהיכא תיתי
מו״י	משה וישראל
מו״מ	מקח וממכר, משא ומתן
מז״ט	מזל טוב
מח״י	מחתימת ידו/ידה
מ״ט	מזל טוב
מעב״ד	מעשה בית דין
מעכ״ת	מעלת כבוד תורתו
מע״ל	מעבר לדף
מ״פ	מאשר פסק, מפסק
מ״ץ	מורה צדק
מש״ה	משום הכי, משורת הדין
מש״כ	מכל שכן, משום כך
נ״ה	נאמן הקהילה, נאמני הקהילה, נכבד(י) הקהילה
נ״י	נר ישראל
נ״ל	נזכר לעיל
נ״מ	נתן מז
נמע״ל	נזכר מעבר לדף
נר׳	נטריה רחמנא ופרקיה
נר״ו	נטריה רחמנא ופרקיה
סג״ל	סגן לויה
עאה״ת	עזרת אנשים התחתונה
עא״נ	על אינם נימולים
ע״ד	על דבר, על דעת, על דרך, ערש דוי
עד״פ	על דרך פשר
ע״ה	על החתום, עמוד הגולה, עמוד הימיני

עו״מ	ערמה ומרמה
ע״ז	עבר זמנו, עד זמן, על זה
עז״א	עזרת אנשים
עז״ה	על זה הדבר
ע״ח	על חלקה, על חלקו, על חשבון, על חשבונו
עי״כ	על ידי כך
ע״כ	עד כאן
עכ״ל	עד כאן לשונה/לשונו
עכ״פ	על כל פנים
ע״נ	עזרת נשים
ע״ע	עד עולם, עד עתה, על עצמם
ע״פ	על פה, על פי, על פרטים
ע״פי	על פי
עצ״ה	על צד היתר
ער״ח	ערב ראש חודש
עק״ס	עשו קניין סודר
עש״ק	ערב שבת קדש
פ׳	פסק, פרשת
פ״ב	פרידבורג
פ״ד	פשר דבר
פ״ה	פטיש החזק
פ״ו	פרנס ומנהיג
פו״מ	פרנס ומנהיג
פיר׳	פירות
פ״מ	פה מלא
פס״ד	פסק דין
פ״ע	(לא ברור מה כוונת הראשי תבות; אולי Postamt)
פ״פ	פרנקפורט
פפ״ד	פרנקפורט דמיין
פפדמיין	פרנקפורט דמיין
פק	פרט קטן (ר״ל לפרט קטן)
ץ	צלם (Kreuzer)
צ״ל	צלם (Kreuzer), צריך לומר
ק׳	קטן, קיין, קצין, קצינים
ק״ג	קנין גמור
ק״ה	קונטרס הטענות, קצין הקהילה
קה״ח	קודם החופה
ק״ח	קבלת חרם
ק״ט	קוניגטאלר (Königstaler)
ק״מ	קונפונטציאהנש מינץ

ק״ס	קומפרמיס, קניין סודר
קפי״ר	קונפונטציאהנש רייכשטאלר
קפ״מ	קונפונטציאהנש מינץ
ק״צ	קרונד צונץ (Grundzins)
ק״ק	קהילת קודש
ק״ש	קופשטוק (Kopffstück)
ר	רב, רבי
רא״ט	רב אברהם טריר
רב״ד	ראש בית דין
ר״ה	ראש השנה
רז״ט	רב זנוויל טראך
ר״ח	ראש חודש
רח״ג	רב חיים גונדרשהיים
רט	רייכשטאלר (Reichstaler)
רטי׳	רייכשטאלר
ר״י	ראש ישיבה
רי״ש	רב יעקב שמש
רל״ו	רב ליזר וואלוי
רמ״א	רב משה איסרלס
רמ״ז	רב מענדלי זאמשט
רמ״ל	רב מענדל לילג
רמ״ש	רב מאיר שיף
ר״נ	רחמנא ניצלן
רנ״מ	רב נתן מז
ר״ק	ראש קהילה, רינדסקוף (Rindskopf)
ר״ש	רויטשילד׳
ש״ד	שבועת דיינים
שו״ע	שלחן ערוך
ש״ח	שטר חוב
שח״ח	שטר חצי חלק
שחח״ז	שטר חצי חלק זכר
שח״ל	שבק חיים לכל
שחל״י	שבק חיים לכל ישראל
ש״ח לכ״י	שבק חיים לכל ישראל
שט״ח	שטר חוב
שטחח״ז	שטר חצי חלק זכר
שי׳	שיחיה
ש״כ	שכבוד
שכ״ה	של כבוד הרב
שכ״מ	שכיב מרע

של׳	שלום
שלהד״ם	שלא היו דברים מעולם
שלי״ט	שיחיה לאורך ימים טובים
שליט״א	שיחיה לאורך ימים טובים אמן
שלפ״ז	שלפי זה
ש״מ	שפל מעות
ש״ע	שלחן ערוך
ש״ץ	שליח ציבור
ש״ק	שבת קודש
ש״ש	שווארץ שילד, שווארצשילד
ש״ת	שלום תורתו
ת״א	תנאים אחרונים
תו״מ	תיכף ומיד
תו״ס	תוספות
תוס״פ	תוספת
תחז״ל	תקנת חז״ל
ת״י	תאריך ימים
ת״כ	תקיעת כף
ת״ע	תורת עדות, תורת עיסקא
ת״ר	תופסת ראיות, תנאים ראשונים
ת״ת	תלמוד תורה

Coins and Measurements

לוח המטבעות והמידות

מטבעות

1 קרליני[1] (Karolin)	=	11 זהובים (מסביבות שנת 1775)		
1 טאלר חדש (Koventionstaler)	=	2 זהובים (פרקנפורט)		
1 שפעציוס רייכשטאלר	=	2 גולדן		
1 רייכשטאלר (Reichstaler)	=	90 צלמר (צ"ל = Kreuzer)		
1 קוניגטאלר (Königstaler)	=	80 צ"ל (Kreuzer)		
1 זהב (Gulden)	=	1 Fl (פלורין)	=	60 צ"ל (Kreuzer)
1 ריניש (Rhenish gulden)	=	60 צ"ל (Kreuzer)		
חצי זהב	=	30 צ"ל (Kreuzer)		
1 ק"ש (Kopffstück)	=	20 צ"ל (Kreuzer)		
1 זופרינה (Sovereign)	=	20 שילניג (Schilling)		
1 שילניג (Schilling)	=	3 צ"ל (Kreuzer)		
1 פץ (בץ = Batzen)	=	4 צ"ל (Kreuzer)		
1 צ"ל (צלמר = Kreuzer)[2]	=	4 דינר (Denar)		
1 דינר (Denar)	=	1 פשי' (פשיט = Pfenning)		
1 דינר (Denar)	=	2 הלר (Heller)		

מידות

1 מנעל	=	1 שטאך (Schuh)	=	0.28461 מטר
1 שטאך	=	1 פֿוס (Fuss)		
1 פֿוס (Fuss)	=	12 צאל (Zoll)		

משקל

1 לויט (Lot)	=	בערך 15 גרם

נפח

1 שעפל (Scheffel)	=	בערך 45.8 ליטר
1 אוהם (Ohm)	=	1/6 פודר = בערך 150 ליטר
1 פודר (Fuder)	=	בערך 870 ליטר

1. בפרנקפורט היו קוראים למטבע 'Karliner'. ר' *Frankfurter Wörterbuch*, s.v. "Karlin"
2. היהודים לא רצו להשתמש במילה 'Kreuzer' ולכן תרגמו אותה ל'צלם' וקצרו אותה ל'צ"ל'. התופעה הזאת מוכרת גם בתחומים אחרים. ר' Carlebach, *Palaces of Time*, 130

Glossary of Non-Hebrew Words

מילים לועזיות

References in this and all other indices are to the case numbers as they appear in this volume.

אב גיצאגן (abgezogen), נספח ג
אב גפאסט (abfassen), נספח ה
אב גרופן (abgerufen), 236
אב צו ברעכין (aufzubrechen), 79
אב צו רייסין מוז (muß abreisen), 86
אב ציהן (absehen), נספח ג
אב שליסן (abschließen), נספח ה
אבינד געלדר (Abendgelder), 151
אבצוג (Abzug), 251
אָדער (oder), 212
אה[ר]ד (כנראה שצ"ל 'טודה'; Tode), 194
אָהרהענג (Ohrhaeng), 148
אובליגאצאהן, אובליגאציאהן (Obligation), 59, 61, נספח א
אובליגירע (obligieren), 251
אובר מאכין (über machen = übergeben), נספח ג
אובש (ob es), 194
אודער, אורדר (Order), 36, 51, 53, 54, 60, 75, 89, 91, 93, 161, 180, 205, 207, 253
אודר דען אנדרן (oder den anderen), 228
אוהם (Ohm), 174
אוהם רייסונג (Umreissung), 229
אוהן (ohn), 251
אוהני (ohne), 194
אוהר (Uhr), 242; [שוא]באַך [או]הר (Schwabach Uhr), 242
אוהר הענג (Ohrhaeng), 148
אוהרן = ארונות, 232
אוז צו בעשרן (auszubessern), 79
אוטרעכטר לאטרע (Utrechter Lotterie), 175
אויב (ob), 194
אויביגש (obiges), 229
אויז ווארף, אויז פא[רף] (Auswurf), 122, נספח ב
אויז ווירפונג (aus werfung) , נספח ב
אויז פא[רף], ר' אויז ווארף

בעטונג (Bettung), 164, 185, 203, 242
בעטונג נעסל טוך (Bettung nessel tuch), 181
בעכר (Becher), 148, 150
בעכר איבר גולד (Goldbecher), 148
בעקין (Becken), 243
בעקכה (Beckche), 236
בפאלין, בפאהלין (befehlen), 152, 191, 230, נספח ד
בפוגט זיין (befugt sein), 168
בפראט(?), 236
בפרייאט (befreit), נספח ב
בצאהלונג (Bezahlung), נספח ד
בקומט (bekommt), 86
בקלאזונג (?beglasung), 79
ברויכן (brauchen), נספח ד
ברויליגירט, ברוליגירט (proligare), 254
ברוך זהוב (?Bruchgold), 59
בריב (בריף) (Brief), 212
בריטר (breiter), 79
ברייט (breit), 120; ברייט שטוק (breiter Stock), 148
בשלאסין, בשלאסן (beschlossen), נספח ד, נספח ה
בשליגש (Beschläges), 79
גאבל, באביל (Gabel), 150, 243
גאגאטר (?Gegatter), 70
גאלדנר (Goldener), 121
גאנץ, גאנצה (ganz, ganze), 194, 229
גאסי שארץ (גאסרשורץ) (Gassenschürze), 190
גאר קוך (Garküch), 217
גארן (gern), 150
גבראכט (gebracht), נספח ה
גהאבט האבין (gehabt haben), 228
גהאלטן (gehalten), נספח ד
גוואהנין (gewonnen), 175
גווע[נליך] (gewöhnlich), 194
גוט (gut), 65, נספח ה
גוטש, ר' הייאראה[ט]ש גוטש
גולד (Gold), 148
גוסשטיין, גוס שטיין, גיס שטיין (Gussstein), 79, 80, 86, 151, 179
גזעצט ווערדין (gesetzt werden), נספח ד
גטינכט (getüncht), 151
גטיפלש (Getäfels), 79, 151
גטעבלט (getäfelt), 86
גטראגין (getragen), 230
גיהן (gehen), נספח ד

דורך (durch), 86, 228
דיזוש (dieses?), נספח ג
דיטא (ditto), 243
דיקרעט (Dekret), 139
דעבוטיהרטע (Deputierte), 227
דעמי נאך (nachdem), נספח ד
דענאך (dennoch), נספח ד
דעפונדיהרט, דעפונטיהרט (diffundiert או defundiert), 229, 230
דער עקצאין, דערעקצאין (Direktion), 68
דערפין (dürfen), נספח ג, נספח ד, נספח ה
דש פילע (dass viele), 230
האג"ישע (Haagische), 45
האוריבר (hierüber?), נספח ה
האט גוועזין (hat [ist] gewesen), 228
האכצייטש ביכר (Hochzeits Bücher), 194
האלץ (Holz), 243
האָלץ האף (Holzhof), 47
האנד טיכר (Handtücher), 243
האנד צוויל (Handzwehle), 242, 243
האר נאדל (Haarnadel), 138
האר נאדל איבר גולד (Haarnadel über Gold [= vergoldet?]), 148
הוט שארירט (hat scharriert), 205
הויבט (Haupt), 84
הויז (Haus), 66, 236
הויז טיהררן (Haustüren), 79
הויז עהרן, הויז עהרנד (Haus Ern), 47, 70, 79, 82, 86, 105, 151, 169
הויז שטייער (Haussteur), 138, 148
הויך (hoch), 47, 79, 82, 86, 101, 121, 129, 132; הויך ליבליכה רייכש גריכט (hoch löbliche Reichsgericht), 176
הויך שול (Hochschule), 49
הויל (Öl), 243
הוילץ עק (Holzeck), 169
הויפט אונד גלידר בוך (Haupt und Glieder- Buch), 236
הייראאה[ט]ש גוטש (Heiratsgut), 194
הינדן (hinten), 92
הינדר קעלר (hinter Keller), 86
הינדר שטאנד, הינטר שטאנד (hinter Stand), 72, 129
הינטר (hinter), 228; הינטר פלאטץ (hinter Platz), 120
היר (hier), 120, 230, נספח ג; היר נאך גיהטש ווידר גראד (hier nach gehts wieder grad), 120
היר זו (hierzu), 194
היראויף (hierauf), 236
הירמיט (hiermit), נספח ד
הירנאך (hiernach), 229

יעדם, יועדן, יעדיר, יעדר (jedem, jeden, jeder), 228, 229, 230
לא פפון וועלכר פיהלט (Lappen welcher fehlt), 121
לאט"ריע, לאטירע, לאטריע, לאטרע, לאטררע (Lotterie), 45, 63, 64, 68, 175, 176
לאָך (Loch), 86
לאך שטאט (Lachstatt), 129
לאמפף (Lampe), 243
לאסין (lassen), 196; לאסין האבין (haben lassen), 228
לאַשע (Lasse), 212, 251
לוזין (lassen), 251
לויט (Lot), 147
לויט ווירשט (Lot wertes), 138
לויפנדי (laufende), נספח א
לומפט צעטל (Zettel), 150
לושעמנט (logement), נספח ה
ליבליכה יודן קומיסיאהן (Löbliche Juden Kommission), 161
ליבר (lieber), 251
ליגן גלאזט (liegen gelassen), 251
לייכט (leicht), 229, 230
לייכטר (Leuchter), 147, 243
ליילטיכר (Leiltuch), 243
ליין שטאהל (Lehnstuhl), 243
ליכטן (leuchten), 251
לנד ריכט (Landricht), 139
לענגר (länger), נספח ג, נספח ד
לעפל (Leffel = Löffel), 148, 243
לעצטה (letzte), 68
מאכן (machen), 229
מאן (Mann), 188, 230
מאנטל שלאס (Mantel schloss), 150
מאנקע (Manko), 251
מאס (Maß), 251
מוטטרליכש (mutterlichs), 188
מויארער (Maurer), 79
מויער שטאט (Mauerstatt), 129
מולטונג (Molton), 190
מיט שפיצין (mit Spitzen), 121
מיטל באנק, מיטלבאנק (Mittelbank), 135, 136, 160, 172
מיטלשטה קעלר (Mittelste Keller), 173
מיטשכה גאלדנר (Goldener Mützche), 121
מילך קעננה (Milchkanne), 243
מינץ (Münz), 74 208, 212
מיר ווירטן פירטיג ווירדן (wir werden fertig werden), 251
מנדל (Mantel), נספח ג

ער קויפטן (erkauften), 236
ערב, ערבע (Erbe), 188, 194
ערהלטין (erhalten), 236
ערלויבט (erlauben), נספח ד
ערלויבט זיין (erlaubt sein), נספח ד
ערפאהרן (erfahren), 230
ערפינדונג (Erfindung), נספח ה
עררּיכט (erricht), נספח ה
ערשטאט (Erstatt), נספח ה
ערשטן (erst, ersten), 188, 194, 251
פאדער (vorder), 79
פאהר (bar), 148(?), 150
פאטרליך (väterlich), 188
פאלאנס (Balance), 245
פאלי שאצנוג (volle Schatzung), 178
פאלין, ר' שטערב פאלין
פאלנשע קליידר (פאלנישה קליידר) (Polnische Kleider), 236, 237
פאלס (Falls), נספח ד
פאלשר (falscher), 229
פאס (Fass), 79
פאסטן (fasten), 79
פאקטום (Paktum), 194
פאר אויש (voraus), נספח ד
פאר ברענגן (vorbringen), נספח ג
פאר גבראכט (vorgebracht), נספח ה
פאר האבנש (Vorhabens), נספח ג
פאר צו לייאנין (vorzulesen), 229
פארדרונג (Forderung), 236
פודר (Fuder), 161
פולגנדש (folgendes), 236
פולציגן (vollziehen), נספח ג
פון איינין (von einen), 228
פון אנדרי צייג (von andere Zeug), 121
פונפציג (fünfzig), 120
פונקטה, פונקטין, פונקטן, פונקטר (Punkte, Punkten), 139, 199, נספח ה
פוסבאדין (Fußboden), 151
פיהל, פיל (viel), 251, נספח ד
פיהלט (fehlt), 121, 251
פיהר (vier), 120
פייער ריכט, פייערריכט ([Feuer Richt[ung?), 79
פיל ר' פיהל
פילה, פילע (viele), 220, 229
פינגר הוט (Fingerhut), 148

פרלייאנ[י]ן (verleinen), 230
פרענד, ר׳ טיפרענד
פרשלאג (Vorschlag), 151
צאהל (Zahl), 115
צאָל (Zoll), 252
צו איבר ווארפן (zu überwerfen), 79
צו בדענקין ריכטיג (richtig zu bedenken), 229
צו בטראכטין, ר׳ בטראכטין
צו בענשין (= לברך, Segen sagen), נספח ג
צו בפרייאין (zu befreien), נספח ג
צו בצאהלין (zu bezahlen), 228, 229
צו ברענגן (zu bringen), נספח ה
צו גניסן (zu genießen), 65
צו גפעליכקייט טוהט (zu Gefälligkeit tut), 228
צו האבין (zu haben), 228
צו וויסן (zu weissen), 66
צו וויניג (zu wenig), 228, 230
צו זאגין (zu sagen), 228, 229, 230, נספח ד
צו זעצין (zu setzen), 79
צו טראגין (zu tragen), 86
צו טרעפן (zu treffen), נספח ה
צו לאזין (zu lassen), 66, 86, 151, 152, 191 נספח ה
צו לייאנין (= zu lesen), 228
צו לענגליכה פרוב (zulängliche Probe), 161
צו מאכין (zu machen), 79, 228, נספח ד, נספח ה
צו נעהמן (zu nehmen), 251
צו עראכטין (zu erachten), נספח ה
צו פיהרן (zu führen), 194
צו פרידרין (פרידרן; zu frieden), 79
צו צאהלין (zuzahlen), נספח ד
צו ציהן (zu ziehen), 79
צו קומן (zukommen), נספח ד
צו קענין (zu können), נספח ג
צו רופין (zu rufen), 230, נספח ד
צו רוק (zurück), נספח ג, נספח ה
צו רעגוליהרן (zu regulieren), נספח ה
צו רעכנין (zu rechnen), 229
צו רעפרירין (zu reparieren), 79
צו שאפין (zu schaffen), 161
צו שרייבן (zu schreiben), 199
צוג (Zug = Lotterie), 63, 64, 68
צוועהל (Zwehle), 243
צוועלפט (zwölft), 74

---

1. לאחר שנת 1766 היה מקובל שהיו 24 זהובים לקולנר מרק (Kölner Mark) בפרנקפורט וסביבותיה.

שטאָק (שטוק) (Stock), 47, 79, 101; שטאך, שטאק הויך (Stock hoch), 148, 173
שטוב (Stube), 80, 174, 180
שטופף (Stubb), 86
שטופף (Stuff), 86
שטוק (Stuck), 131, 190, 251; שטוק פר שטוק (Stuck für Stuck), 251
שטיהל (Stühl), 243
שטיהן (Stehen), 152, 191
שטיין (Stein), 212
שטיין שנאלה (stein schnalle), 148
שטיינה אָהרהענג (steine ohrhaeng), 148
שטיינה קענטל (steinernes Käntchen), 79
שטירבט (stirbt), 188
שטעג = שטעק (Steg), 70, 79, 82, 83, 86, 101, 129, 133, 169, 252; שטעג הויך (Steg hoch), 148, 151, 163, 169, 174, 180, 189
שטעטן (Städten), 194
שטען (stehen), 251
שטענדיג (ständig), 251
שטענדיג וויררן (ständing warden), 251
שטענדר (Ständer), 125, 137
שטעק (Stock), 47, 79, 169; ר' גם שטאק
שטערב פעלין (sterbefällen), 194
שייפן (Scheiben), 151
שיסלכה (Schüsselche), 242, 243
שיפט שטיין (Schieferstein), 252
שיקט (schickt), 251
שלאס (Schloss), 46
שלויט פיגר (Schlotfeger), 66
שלעסיר (Schlösser), 46, 236
שמאלץ שטאנד (Schmelz Stand), 236
שנאלין (Schnallen), 138, 148
שנופטיכר (שנופף טיכר) (Schnupftücher), 138, 190
שעהר (Schere), 150
שעהרר (Scherer), 251
שענק, ר' שאנק
שענקלכה (Schränkelche), 121
שעפל (Scheffel), 161
שפיגל (Spiegel), 121, 243; שפיגל שייפין (Spiegelscheiben), 79
שפייס = שפייז (Speise), 70; שפייס שאנק (Speis Schrank), 169
שפיצין גרעהט (Spitzengerät), נספח א
שרייבר (Schreiber), 217, 237
שריינר גלא[ס]ר (Schreiner Glaser), 151
שרייען לאזן (Schreien lassen), 236
שריפטן (Schriften), 237

Bibliography

Manuscripts

Bodleian Library, Oxford University.

MS. Mich. 465

MS. Opp. 730

Central Archives for the History of the Jewish People, Jerusalem.

Ettlinger, Shlomo. *Ēlē tōldōt*. P/237.

Segall, Aryeh, ed. and comp. Ḥomer le-pinqas ha-qahal (Franqfurṭ). Personal Papers of Aryeh Segall.

Institut für Stadtgeschichte Frankfurt am Main, Frankfurt.

*Ugb D33

Jewish Theological Seminary (JTS), New York.

Adler MS. 935

Duschinsky File (in process), Alexander Marx Collection, ARC 80

MS. 3672

MS. 3967

Leo Baeck Institute, New York.

*Mannheim Memorbuch 1673–1858

The National Library of Israel, Jerusalem.

*The Frankfurt *Memorbuch*, MS. Heb. 1092

*Pinqas Franqfurṭ, MS. 4°662

Staatsarchive, Hamburg.

*MS. AHW/121/3

YIVO Institute for Jewish Research (Archives), New York.

*Folder 77–78, Collection of Rabbinical and Historical Manuscripts (RG 128)

Żydowski Instytut Historyczny (ŻIH), Warsaw.

*MS. 517

* Viewed on microfilm or as an electronic image.

Primary Sources

Aleksander Suslin Ha-Kohen. *Sefer ha-aggudah*. 1571. New York: Abraham Cik, 1959.

———. *Sefer ha-aggudah*. Vol. 2. Edited by Eleazar Brizel. Jerusalem: n.p., 1966.

Anau, Yeḥiʾel ben Yequtiʾel. *Sefer tanyaʾ rabbati*. Edited by Shimʿon Horowitz. Warsaw: I. Goldman, 1879.

Aquinas, Thomas. *Summa Theologiae*. Vol. 40. Ed. & trans. T. F. O'Aleara and M. J. Duffy. London: Blackfriars, 1964.

Ashkenazi, Gershon. *Sheʾelot u-teshubot ʿabodat ha-gershuni*. Frankfurt: n.p., 1699.

Bachrach, Yaʾir. *Ḥavat Yaʾir*. Frankfurt: Johannes Faust, 1699.

Baḥye ben Asher. *Midrash Rabbeinu Bachya, Torah Commentary*. Vol. 4. Translated and annotated by Eliyahu Munk. Jerusalem: n.p., 1998.

———. *Rabbeynu Baḥye biʾur ʿal ha-Torah*. Vol. 2. Edited by Ḥayyim Dov Chavel. Jerusalem: Mossad Harav Kook, 1967.

Bible. *Deuteronomy (Debarim): The Traditional Hebrew Text with the New JPS Translation*. With commentary by Jeffrey Tigay. Philadelphia: Jewish Publication Society, 1996.

———. *Pentateuch with Targum Onkelos, Haphtaroth and Prayers for Sabbath and Rashi's Commentary (Exodus)*. Translated and annotated by M. Rosenbaum and A. M. Silbermann, in collaboration with A. Blashki and L. Joseph. London: Shapiro, Vallentine and Co., 1930.

Brocke, Michael. *Der alte jüdische Friedhof zu Frankfurt am Main: unbekannte Denkmäler und Inschriften*. Sigmaringen: J. Thorbecke, 1996.

Colon, Joseph. *Sefer sheʾelot u-teshubot Mahari"q ha-yeshanot*. Jerusalem: Oraysoh, 1988.

Dubnow, Simon, ed. *Pinqas ha-medinah o pinqas vaʿad ha-qehillot ha-raʾshiyyot bi-medinat Liṭaʾ: qobeẓ taqqanot u-pesaqim mi-shenat [5]383 ʿad shenat [5]521*. Berlin: Ayanot, 1925.

Duschinsky, Yaʿaqob Koppel. *Sefer mazkir neshamot de-q[ehillat] q[odesh] Offenbach ʿa[l] n[ahar] Meyn ve-ʿod qehillot aḥerot be-medinat Ashkenaz*. Frankfurt: J. Kauffmann, 1924.

Glikl bat Leb of Hamlen. *Glikl zikronot 1691–1719*. Edited and translated by Chava Turniansky. Jerusalem: Shazar, 2006.

Gundersheim, Sheneʾur Ziskind. *Sefer meqor ḥayyim ve-sefer tifʾeret Ẓebi*. Offenbach: Ẓebi Hirsch Segal and Son, 1798.

Hahn, Joseph Juspa Nordlingen. *Yosef omeẓ*. 1928. Jerusalem: n.p., 1965.

Halperin, Israel, ed. *Pinqas vaʿad arbʿa araẓot*. Revised and edited by Israel Bartal, with an introduction by Shmuel Ettinger. Jerusalem: Bialik Institute, 1990.

Horovitz, Markus. *Abney zikkaron: ha-ketab ve-ha-miktab*. Frankfurt: J. Kauffmann, 1901.

Horowitz, Pinḥas. *Sefer sheʾelot u-teshubot gibʿat Pinḥas*. Józefów: B. Zetzer, 1875.

Isserles, Moses. *Sheʾelot u-teshubot ha-Rem"aʾ*. Edited by Asher Siev. Jerusalem: Feldheim, 1970.

Joshua Höschel ben Joseph. *Sefer peney Yehoshuʿa ḥeleq sheni mi-sheʾelot u-teshubot.* L'viv: Zalman Leb Flekir, 1860.

Kupfer, Ephraim, ed. *Teshubot u-pesaqim meʾet ḥakhmey Ashkenaz ve-Ẓarefat.* Jerusalem: Mekize Nirdamim, 1973.

Landau, Ezekiel. *Sheʾelot u-teshubot nodaʿ be-Yehudah ha-shalem.* Oraḥ ḥayyim. Edited by Jacob Ehrnfeld et al. Ashkelon: Machon Yerushalayim, 1994.

Luria, Solomon. *Sheʾelot u-teshubot ha-Maharsha"l.* Jerusalem: Oẓar ha-sefarim, 1969.

Maas, Nathan. *Sefer binyan Shelomoh (Sanhedrin).* Offenbach: Abraham Poppers, 1784.

Meʾir ben Gedaliah. *Sheʾelot ut-teshubot.* Venice: Bragadin, 1618.

Mintz, Judah ben Eliezer ha-Levi and Meʾir ben Isaac Katzenellenbogen. *Sefer sheʾelot u-teshubot Mahar"i Minẓ ve-Mahara"m Padovah.* 1882. Jerusalem: n.p., 1980.

Mintz, Moses. *Sheʾelot u-teshubot Rabbeynu Mosheh Minẓ.* Edited by Yonatan Shraga Domb. Jerusalem: Machon Yerushalayim, 1991.

Molin, Jacob. *Sefer Mahari"l: Minhagim.* Edited by Shelomoh Spitzer. Jerusalem: Machon Yerushalayim, 1989.

Moses ben Naḥman. *Perush ha-Torah.* Edited by Ḥayyim Dov Chavel. Jerusalem: Mossad Harav Kook, 1962.

Nadav, Mordechai, ed. *Pinqas qahal Ṭiqṭin 381–566.* 2 vols. Jerusalem: Israel Academy of Sciences and Humanities, 1996–99.

Rappaport, Simḥah Bunim. *Sefer ḥiddushey halakot Rashba"z ʿal masseket Giṭṭin.* Fürth: Isaac ben Leb Buchbinder, 1779.

Reischer, Jacob. *Sefer sheʾelot u-teshubot shebut Yaʿaqob.* Vol. 1. Halle: Moses ben Abraham, 1709.

Wachstein, Bernhard. *Die Inschriften des alten Judenfriedhofes in Wien.* Quellen und Forschungen zur Geschichte der Juden in Deutsch-Österreich 4.2. Vienna: Braumüller, 1917.

Shabbetay ben Meʾir ha-Kohen. *Siftey kohen* (Yoreh deʿah). Cracow: Meisels, 1646.

Sirkes, Joel. *Sheʾelot u-teshubot ha-ba"ḥ ha-ḥadashot.* Koretz: Johan Anton Kreiger, 1785.

———. *Sheʾelot u-teshubot ha-bayit ḥadash.* Frankfurt: Johan Vost, 1697.

Slonik, Benjamin. *Sheʾelot u-teshubot masaʾat Binyamin.* Vilnius: Abraham Ẓebi Katzenellenbogen, 1894.

Sofer, Moses. *Sefer ḥata"m sofer* (Oraḥ ḥayyim). 1895. Jerusalem: Meqor, 1970.

Weil, Jacob. *Sheḥiṭot u-bediqot.* With notes by Ẓebi ben Isaac Jacob. Cracow: Isaac Prostitz, 1577.

Secondary Sources

Adler, Elkan Nathan. *Catalogue of Hebrew Manuscripts in the Collection of Elkan Nathan Adler.* Cambridge: Cambridge University Press, 1921.

Adler, Simon. "Aus den Judizialakten des XVIII. Jahrhunderts. Bilder aus dem täglichen

Leben der Juden in Prag," *Jahrbuch der Gesellschaft für Geschichte der Juden in der Čechoslovakischen Republik* 8 (1936): 411–20.

———. "Das älteste Judicial-Protokoll des jüdischen Gemeinde-Archives in Prag (1682)." *Jahrbuch der Gesellschaft für Geschichte der Juden in der Čechoslovakischen Republik* 3 (1931): 217–56.

Aschoff, Diethard. "Höxter." In *Germania Judaica*. Edited by Arye Maimon. Vol. 3.1, 567. Tübingen: Mohr, 1987.

Assaf, Simḥah. *Battey ha-din ve-sidreyhem aḥarey ḥatimat ha-talmud*. Jerusalem: n.p., 1924.

———. *Meqorot le-toledot ha-ḥinuk be-Yisra'el*. Vol. 1. Edited by Shmuel Glick. Jerusalem: Jewish Theological Seminary, 2002.

Assis, Yom Tov. *The Golden Age of Aragonese Jewry: Community and Society in the Crown of Aragon, 1213–1327*. London: Littman, 1997.

———. "Yehudey Sefarad be-ʿerkka'ot ha-goyyim (ha-me'ot ha-13 ve-ha-14)." In *Tarbut ve-ḥebrah be-toledot Yisra'el be-yemey ha-benayyim: qobeẓ ma'amarim le-zikro shel Ḥayyim Hillel Ben-Sasson*. Edited by Reuben Bonfil et al., 399–430. Jerusalem: Shazar, 1989.

Avneri, Zvi. "Peniyyah le-ʿerkka'ot." *Zion* 25 (1960): 57–61.

Baron, Salo. *The Jewish Community*. Vol. 1. Philadelphia: Jewish Publication Society, 1942.

Battenberg, Friedrich. "Zur Rechtsstellung der Juden am Mittelrhein in Spätmittelalter und früher Neuzeit." *Zeitschrift für Historische Forschung* 6 (1979): 129–83.

Baumann, Anette. "Jüdische Reichskammergerichtsprozesse aus den Reichsstädten Frankfurt und Hamburg. Eine quantitative Annäherung." In *Juden im Recht: Neue Zugänge zur Rechtsgeschichte der Juden im Alten Reich*. Edited by Andreas Gotzmann, Stephan Wendehorst. Zeitschrift für Historische Forschung Supplement 39, 297–316. Berlin: Duncker & Humblot, 2007.

Behringer, Wolfgang. *Thurn und Taxis: Die Geschichte ihrer Post und ihrer Unternehmen*. Munich: Piper, 1990.

Ben-Naeh, Yaron. *Jews in the Realms of the Sultans: Ottoman Jewish Society in the Seventeenth Century*. Tübingen: Morh Siebeck, 2008.

Berkovitz, Jay. "Acculturation and Integration in Eighteenth-Century Metz: The Circuitous Path to Modernity." *Jewish History* (2010). http://www.springerlink.com/content/rn54u021283115j1/fulltext.pdf.

———. "Civil Law and Justice in the Rabbinic Tribunals of 18th Century Metz." In *Iggud: Selected Essays in Jewish Studies*, 87–99. Jerusalem: Magnes, 2008.

———. *Protocols of Justice: The Pinkas of the Metz Rabbinic Court 1771–1789*. Leiden: Brill, forthcoming.

———. *Rites and Passages: The Beginnings of Modern Jewish Culture in France, 1650–1860*. Philadelphia: University of Pennsylvania Press, 2004.

Berman, Harold. *Law and Revolution: The Formation of the Western Legal Tradition*. Cambridge, Mass.: Harvard University Press, 1983.

Beyrer, Klaus. "The Mail-Coach Revolution: Landmarks in Travel in Germany between the Seventeenth and Nineteenth Centuries." *German History* 24, no. 3 (2006): 375–86.

Blanning, T.C.W. *The French Revolution in Germany*. Oxford: Clarendon, 1983.

Breuer, Mordechai. "The Early Modern Period." In *German-Jewish History in Modern Times*. Edited by Michael Meyer and Michael Brenner, translated by William Templer, 7–260. New York: Columbia University Press, 1996.

———. *Ohaley Torah: ha-yeshibah, tabnitah ve-toledoteyha*. Jerusalem: Shazar, 2003.

Brocke, Michael, and Julius Carlebach, eds. *Biographisches Handbuch der Rabbiner: Die Rabbiner der Emanzipationszeit in den deutschen, böhmischen und grosspolnischen Ländern 1781–1871*. Arranged by Carsten Wilke. Munich: K.G. Saur, 2004.

Brooks, C.W. *Pettyfoggers and Vipers of the Commonwealth: The "Lower Branch" of the Legal Profession in Early Modern England*. Cambridge Studies in English Legal History. Cambridge: Cambridge University Press, 1986.

Brundage, James. *Medieval Canon Law*. London: Longman, 1995.

Calvin, Jean. *Institutes of the Christian Religion*. Edited by John T. McNeill. Translated by Ford Lewis Battles, in collaboration with the editor, and a committee of advisers. The Library of Christian Classics 20. Philadelphia: Westminster Press, 1960.

Carlebach, Elisheva. *Palaces of Time: Jewish Calendar and Culture in Early Modern Europe*. Cambridge, Mass.: Belknap, 2011.

Cohen, Daniel J. "Irgguney 'beney ha-medinah' be-Ashkenaz be-meʾot ha-17 ve-ha-18." Ph.D. diss. Jerusalem: Hebrew University, 1967.

Cross, Rupert, and J.W. Harris. *Precedent in English Law*. 4th ed. Clarendon Law Series. Oxford: Clarendon Press, 1991.

Davis, Natalie. *Fiction in the Archives: Pardon Tales and Their Tellers in Sixteenth-Century France*. Stanford: Stanford University Press, 1987.

Dawson, John P. *A History of Lay Judges*. Cambridge, Mass.: Harvard University Press, 1960.

———. *Judges: Oracles of the Law*. Thomas M. Cooley Lectures. Ann Arbor: University of Michigan Law School, 1968.

Deventer, Jörg. *Das Abseits als sicherer Ort? Jüdische Minderheit und christliche Gesellschaft im Alten Reich am Beispiel der Fürstabtei Corvey (1550–1807)*. Forschungen zur Regionalgeschichte 21. Paderborn: Ferdinand Schöningh, 1996.

Dietz, Alexander. *The Jewish Community of Frankfurt: A Genealogical Study 1349–1849*. Translated by Frances Martin. Camelford: Vanderher, 1988.

———. *Stammbuch der Frankfurter Juden. Geschichtliche Mitteilungen über die Frankfurter jüdischen Familien von 1349–1849, nebst einem Plane der Judengasse*. Frankfurt: J. St. Goar, 1907.

Dinari, Yedidya. *Ḥakmey Ashkenaz be-shalhey yemey ha-beynayyim: darkeyhem ve-kitbeyhem be-halakah*. Jerusalem: Bialik Institute, 1984.

Dubin, Lois. "Jewish Women, Marriage Law, and Emancipation: The Civil Divorce of Rachele Morschene in Late Eighteenth-Century Trieste." In *Acculturation and Its*

Discontents: The Italian Jewish Experience Between Exclusion and Inclusion. Edited by David Myers et al., 119–47. Toronto: University of Toronto Press, 2008.

Duschinsky, Charles (Yaᶜaqob Koppel). "Rabbi David Oppenheimer: Glimpses of His Life and Activity, Derived from His Manuscripts in the Bodleian Library." *Jewish Quarterly Review* 20, no. 3 (1930): 217–47.

———. "Sefer maᶜaseh beyt din de-q[ehillat] q[odesh] Franqfurṭ y[agen] ᶜ[aleyha] e[lohim] mi-shannat [5]429 ᶜad [5]499." *Ha-ẓofeh le-ḥokmat Yisraʾel* 10 (1926): 106–15.

———. "The Rabbinate of the Great Synagogue, London, from 1756–1842." *Jewish Quarterly Review* 11, no. 3 (1921): 345–86.

———. *The Rabbinate of the Great Synagogue, London, from 1756–1842*. With a new bibliographical note by Ruth Lehmann. Farnborough: Gregg, 1971.

———. "Toledot R' David Oppenheymer." *Ha-ẓofeh le-ḥakmat Yisraʾel* 5 and 6 (1921–22): 39–45, 145–55; 26–37, 160–66, 205–56.

Duxbury, Neil. *The Nature and Authority of Precedent*. Cambridge: Cambridge University Press, 2008.

———. *Random Justice: On Lotteries and Legal Decision-Making*. Oxford: Clarendon, 1999.

Edrei, Arye. "Beyt din ke-avihem shel yetomim." *Diné Israel* 19 (1997–98): 5–40.

Elior, Rachel. "Natan Adler ve-ha-ᶜedah ha-ḥasidit be-Franqforṭ: ha-ziqah beyn ḥaburot ḥasidiyyot be-mizraḥ eyropah u-be-merkazah be-meʾah ha-18." *Zion* 59, no. 1 (1994): 31–64.

———. "Rabbi Nathan Adler of Frankfurt and the Controversy Surrounding Him." In *Mysticism, Magic, and Kabbalah in Ashkenazi Judaism: International Symposium Held in Frankfurt a.M.* Edited by Karl Erich Grözinger, Joseph Dan, 223–42. Berlin: W. de Gruyter, 1995.

Elon, Menachem. *Ha-mishpaṭ ha-ᶜibri toledotav, meqorotav, ᶜeqronotav*. 3d ed. Vol. 1. Jerusalem: Magnes, 1992.

Falk, Ulrich. *Consilia. Studien zur Praxis der Rechtsgutachten in der Frühen Neuzeit*. Frankfurt: Vittorio Klostermann, 2006.

Finaly, Robert. *Politics in Renaissance Venice*. New Brunswick, N.J.: Rutgers University Press, 1980.

Finkelstein, Louis. *Jewish Self-Government in the Middle Ages*. 2d ed. New York: Feldheim, 1964.

Fishman, Talya. "Forging Jewish Memory: *Besamim Rosh* and the Invention of Pre-Emancipation Jewish Culture." In *Jewish History and Jewish Memory: Essays in Honor of Yosef Hayim Yerushalmi*. Edited by Elisheva Carlebach, John Efron, and David Myers, 70–88. Hanover, New Hampshire: Brandeis University Press, 1998.

Flatto, Sharon. *The Kabbalistic Culture of Eighteenth-Century Prague: Ezekiel Landau and His Contemporaries*. Oxford: Littman Library of Jewish Civilization, 2010.

Fram, Edward. *Ideals Face Reality: Jewish Law and Life in Poland, 1550–1655*. Monographs of the Hebrew Union College 21. Cincinnati: Hebrew Union College Press, 1997.

———. *My Dear Daughter: Rabbi Benjamin Slonik and the Education of Jewish Women in*

Sixteenth-Century Poland. Monographs of the Hebrew Union College 33. Cincinnati: Hebrew Union College Press, 2007.

———. "Taqdim hilkati she-ʾeyno raʾuyi le-shemo." In *ʿAl pi ha-beʾer: meḥqarim be-hagut yehudit u-be-maḥshebet ha-halakah muggashim le-Yaʿaqob Blidstein*. Edited by Uri Erlich et al., 401–12. Beer Sheva: Ben-Gurion University Press, 2008.

Frank, Mosheh. *Qehillot Ashkenaz u-battey dineyhen*. Tel Aviv: Dvir, 1937.

Frankfurter Wörterbuch. 18 vols. Frankfurt: Waldemar Kramer, 1971–85.

Friedrichs, Christopher. *The Early Modern City, 1450–1750*. London: Longman, 1995.

———. "Politics or Pogrom? The Fettmilch Uprising in German and Jewish History." *Central European History* 19, no. 2 (June 1986): 186–228.

Fuchs, Ralf-Peter. "The Supreme Court of the Holy Roman Empire: The State of Research and the Outlook." *The Sixteenth Century Journal* 34, no. 1 (Spring 2003): 9–27.

Fuss, Abraham. "ʿEdut be-ketab be-diney mamonot." *Shenaton ha-mishpaṭ ha-ʿibri* 3–4 (1976–77): 327–39.

Gagliardo, John. *Reich and Nation: The Holy Roman Empire as Idea and Reality, 1763–1806*. Bloomington: Indiana University Press, 1980.

Garvía, Roberto. "Syndication, Institutionalization, and Lottery Play." *American Journal of Sociology* 113, no. 3 (November 2007): 603–52.

Gelber, N.M. *Toledot yehudey Brody*. Vol. 6 of *ʿArim ve-imahot be-Yisraʾel*. Edited by Y.L. Maimon. Jerusalem: Mossad Harav Kook, 1955.

Glick, Shmuel. "ʿAl shinuyyim hashmaṭot ve-ẓenzurah penimit be-sifrey sheʾelot u-teshubot." *Quntres* 1, no. 1 (2009): 40–76.

Godechot, Jacques. *La grande nation: l'expansion révolutionnaire de la France dans le monde de 1789 à 1799*. 2d ed. Paris: Aubier, 1983.

Goitein, S. D. *A Mediterranean Society: The Jewish Communities of the Arab World as Portrayed in the Documents of the Cairo Geniza*. Vol. 2. Berkeley: University of California Press, 1967.

Goldin, Simha. *Ha-yiḥud ve-ha-yaḥad: ḥidat hisardutan shel ha-qebuẓot ha-yehudiyyot be-yemey ha-beynayyim*. Tel Aviv: Hakibbutz Hameuchad, 1997.

Goodwin, Barbara. *Justice by Lottery*. 2d ed. Exeter: Imprint Academic, 2005.

Gotzmann, Andreas. "At Home in Many Worlds? Thoughts About New Concepts in Jewish Legal History." *Jahrbuch des Simon-Dubnow-Instituts* 2 (2003): 413–36.

———. *Jüdische Autonomie in der Frühen Neuzeit: Recht und Gemeinschaft im deutschen Judentum*. Hamburger Beiträge zur Geschichte der deutschen Juden 32. Göttingen: Wallstein, 2008.

Grossman, Avraham. *Ḥakmey Ashkenaz ha-riʾshonim*. 2d ed. Jerusalem: Magnes, 1989.

———. *Ḥakmey Ẓarefat ha-riʾshonim: qoroteyhem, darkam be-hanagat ha-ẓibbur, yiẓiratam ha-ruḥanit*. Jerusalem: Magnes, 1995.

Grünfeld, Richard. *Geschichte der Juden in Bingen am Rhein: Festschrift zur Einweihung der neuen Synagoge in Bingen (21. September 1905)*. Frankfurt: J. Kaufmann, 1905.

Haas, Peter. *Responsa: Literary History of a Rabbinic Genre*. Atlanta: Scholars Press, 1996.

Hacker, Yosef. "Gebulteyha shel ha-ʾoṭonomyah ha-yehudit: ha-shippuṭ ha-ʿaẓmi ha-yehudi be-ʾimperyah ha-ʿotmaʾnit be-meʾot ha-16 —ha-18." In *Transition and Change in Modern Jewish History, Essays Presented in Honor of Shmuel Ettinger*. Edited by S. Almog et al., 349–88. Jerusalem: Shazar, 1987.

Hacohen, Aviad. "Parshanut taqqanot ha-qahal be-mishpaṭ ha-ʿibri." Ph.D. diss. Jerusalem: Hebrew University, 2003.

Haferkamp, Hans-Peter. "The Science of Private Law and the State in Nineteenth Century Germany." *American Journal of Comparative Law* 56, no. 3 (Summer 2008): 245–67.

Heather, Peter. *The Fall of the Roman Empire: A New History of Rome and the Barbarians*. New York: Oxford University Press, 2006.

Horovitz, Markus. *Frankfurter Rabbinen: ein Beitrag zur Geschichte der israelitischen Gemeide*. 2d ed. With supplement by Josef Unna. Hildesheim: Georg Olms, 1972.

———. *Die Frankfurter Rabbinerversamlung vom Jahre 1603*. Frankfurt: M. Slobotzky, 1897.

———. *Rabbaney Franqfurṭ*. With supplement by Joseph Unna, translated by Joshua Amir. Jerusalem: Mossad Harav Kook, 1972.

Horowitz, David H. "Fractures and Fissures in Jewish Communal Autonomy in Hamburg, 1710–1782." Ph.D. diss. Columbia University, 2010.

Houtman-De Smedt, Helma. "North-West Europe Under the Spell of Lotteries and Lotto in the Eighteenth and Nineteenth Centuries." In *Lotteries in Europe: Five Centuries of History*. Edited by Bernard Bruno et al., 137–85. Brussels: Belgian National Lottery, [1994].

Hsia, R. Po-chia. "The Jews and the Emperor." In *State and Society in Early Modern Austria*. Edited by Charles Ingrao, 71–80. West Lafayette: Purdue University Press, 1994.

Ilisch, Peter, and Arnold Schwede. *Das Münzwesen im Stift Corvey 1541–1794*. Studien und Quellen zur Westfälischen Geschichte 58, Veröffentlichungen der Historischen Kommission für Westfalen 11, Arbeiten zur Geld- und Münzgeschichte Westfalens 3. Paderborn: Bonifatius, 2007.

Johanek, Peter. "Imperial and Free Towns of the Holy Roman Empire City-States in Pre-Modern Germany." In *A Comparative Study of Thirty City-State Cultures: An Investigation Conducted by the Copenhagen Polis Centre*. Edited by Mogens Herman Hansen. Historik-Filosofiske Skrifter 21, 295–319. Copenhagen: Kongelige Danske Videns Kabernes Selskab, 2000.

Kagan, Richard L. *Lawsuits and Litigants in Castile, 1500–1700*. Chapel Hill: University of North Carolina Press, 1981.

Kahana, Maoz. "Me-Praʾg le-Presburg: ketibah hilkatit be-ʿolam mishtaneh me-ha-'Nodaʿ be-Yehudah' el ha-'Ḥata″m sofer' 1720–1839." Ph.D. diss. Hebrew University, 2010.

Kanarfogel, Ephraim. "Religious Leadership During the Tosafist Period: Between the Academy and the Rabbinic Court." In *Jewish Religious Leadership: Image and Reality*, vol. 1. Edited by Jack Wertheimer, 265–305. New York: Jewish Theological Seminary, 2004.

Kaplan, Debra. "Kooperation und Konflikt. Elässische Juden, Herrschaft und Recht im Spiegel der Reichskammergerichtsprozesse des 16. Jahrhunderts." In *Juden im Recht: Neue Zugänge zur Rechtsgeschichte der Juden im alten Reich*. Edited by Andreas Gotzmann and Stephan Wendehorst. Zeitschrift für Historische Forschung Supplement 39, 333–46. Berlin: Dunckert & Humblot, 2007.

———. "Women and Worth: Female Access to Property in Early Modern Urban Jewish Communities." *Leo Baeck Institute Yearbook* 55 (2010): 93–113.

Kaplan, Yosef. "Pesaqim mi-beyt ha-din shel ha-qehillah ha-sefardit — ha-porṭugaʾlit be-ʾAmsṭerdam be-meʾah ha-shemonah ʿesreh u-mashmaʿutam ha-hisṭorit — ḥebratit." *Studies on the History of Dutch Jewry* 5 (1988): 1–54.

Kasper, Verena. "Die Frankfurter Judengemeinde und der Reichshofrat unter Joseph II. (1765–1790)." Ph.D. diss. Graz: Karl-Franzens-Universität, 2009.

Kasper-Holtkotte, Cilli. *Die jüdische Gemeinde von Frankfurt/Main in der Frühen Neuzeit: Familien, Netzwerke und Konflikte eines jüdischen Zentrums*. Göttingen: De Gruyter, 2010.

———. *Jüdisches Leben in Friedberg 16.–18. Jahrhundert*. Vol. 1 of *Kehilat Friedberg*. Edited by Andreas Gotzmann. Friedberg: Bindernagel, 2003.

Katz, Jacob. *Masoret u-mashber: ha-ḥebrah ha-yehudit be-moẓaʾey yemey ha-beynayyim*. Jerusalem: Bialik Institute, 1958.

Kirschenbaum, Aaron. "Representation in Litigation in Jewish Law." *Diné Israel* 6 (1975): xxv-xli.

Kisch, Guido. *The Jews in Medieval Germany: A Study of Their Legal and Social Status*. 2d ed. New York: Ktav, 1970.

———. "Relations Between Jewish and Christian Courts in the Middle Ages." In *Louis Ginzberg Jubilee Volume on the Occasion of His Seventieth Birthday*. Edited by Alexander Marx et al., 201–25 (English section). New York: Jewish Publication Society, 1945.

Klein, Birgit. "Erbinnen in Norm und Praxis: Fiktion und Realität im Erbstreit der Familien Liebmann-von Geldern." In *Juden im Recht: Neue Zugänge zur Rechtsgeschichte der Juden im Alten Reich*. Edited by Andreas Gotzmann and Stephan Wendehorst. Zeitschrift für Historische Forschung Supplement 39, 175–205. Berlin: Duncker & Humblot, 2007.

———. "Die 'Frankfurter Rabbinerversammlung' von 1603: Vorgeschichte, Verordnungen, Folgen." In *Die Frankfurter Judengasse: Jüdisches Leben in der frühen Neuzeit*. Edited by Fritz Backhaus et al., 161–70. Frankfurt: Societäts, 2006.

Klein, Elka. *Jews, Christian Society, and Royal Power in Medieval Barcelona*. Ann Arbor: University of Michigan Press, 2006.

Klemperer, Gutmann. "The Rabbis of Prague: A History of the Rabbinate of Prague from the Death of Rabbi Loewe b. Bezalel ('The High Rabbi Loew') to the Present (1609–1879)." *Historia Judaica* 12–13 (1950–51): 33–66, 143–52, 55–82.

Kober, Adolf. "Die Reichsstadt Köln und die Juden in den Jahren 1685–1715: Ein Beitrag zur Geschichte der jüdischen Hoffaktoren." *Monatsschrift für Geschichte und Wissenschaft des Judentums* 75 (1931): 412–28.

Kochan, Lionel. *The Making of Western Jewry, 1600–1819*. London: Palgrave, 2004.

Koren-Loeb, Tzvia. "Das Memorbuch zu Frankfurt am Main: Erschließung und Kommentierung ausgewählter Themenkreise." Ph.D. diss. Universität Duisburg-Essen, 2008.

Kowaleski, Maryanne. "Singlewomen in Medieval and Early Modern Europe: The Demographic Perspective." In *Singlewomen in the European Past, 1250–1800*. Edited by Judith Bennett and Amy Froide, 38–81, 325–44. Philadelphia: University of Pennsylvania Press, 1999.

Kracauer, I. "Beiträge zur Geschichte der Frankfurter Juden im dreißigjährigen Kriege." *Zeitschrift für die Geschichte der Juden in Deutschland* 3 (1889): 130–58, 337–72.

———. *Geschichte der Juden in Frankfurt a.M. (1150–1824)*. Vol. 2. Frankfurt: Kauffmann, 1927.

———. "Die Kulp-Kannschen Wirren. Ein Beitrag zur Geschichte der jüdischen Gemeinde in Frankfurt a.M. im XVIII. Jahrhundert." *Archiv für Frankfurts Geschichte und Kunst* Series 3, no. 10 (1910): 135–212.

Kriegk, Georg Ludwig. *Frankfurter Bürgerzwiste und Zustände im Mittelalter: Ein auf urkundlichen Forschungen beruhender Beitrag zur Geschichte des deutschen Bürgerthums*. Frankfurt: J. D. Sauerländer, 1862.

Kupfer, Franciszka (Ephraim), and Stefan Strelcyn. *Katalog rękopisow orientalnych ze zbiorów polskich*. Vol. 4. Rękopisy hebrajskie i aramejskie. Zakład Orientalistaki PAN. Warsaw (typescript).

Lackey, Jennifer. "Introduction." In *The Epistemology of Testimony*. Edited by Jennifer Lackey and Ernest Sosa, 1–21. Oxford: Clarendon, 2006.

Leesch, Wolfgang. *Inventar des Archivs der Stadt Höxter*. Inventare der nichtstaatlichen Archive Westfalens. Neue Folge 1. Münster: Aschendorff, 1961.

Libson, Gideon. *Jewish and Islamic Law: A Comparative Study of Custom During the Geonic Period*. Harvard Series in Islamic Law. Cambridge, Mass.: Islamic Legal Studies Program, Harvard Law School, 2003.

Löwenstein, Leopold. *Geschichte der Juden in der Kurpfalz*. Beiträge zur Geschichte der Juden in Deutschland 1. Frankfurt: J. Kauffmann, 1895.

———. *Zur Geschichte der Juden in Fürth*. 1909–13. Hildesheim: Olms, 1974.

Malkiel, David. "Law and Architecture: The Pollution Crisis in the Italian Ghetto." *European Journal of Jewish Studies* 4, no. 2 (2010): 255–84.

Masud, Muhammed Khalid, Brinkely Messick, and David S. Powers. "Muftis, Fatwas, and Islamic Legal Interpretation." In *Islamic Legal Interpretation: Muftis and their Fatwas*. Edited by Muhammed Khalid Masud, Brinkely Messick, and David S. Powers. Harvard Studies in Islamic Law, 3–32. Cambridge, Mass.: Harvard University Press, 1996.

Mauersberg, Hans. *Wirtschafts- und Sozialgeschichte zentraleuropäischer Städte in neuerer Zeit*. Göttingen: Vandenhoeck & Ruprecht, 1960.

Michałowska-Mycielska, Anna. *The Jewish Community: Authority and Social Control in Poznań and Swarzędz, 1650–1793*. Translated by Alicja Adamowicz. Bibliotheca Judaica 3. Wrocław: Wydawnictwo Uniwersytetu Wrocławskiego, 2008.

Milgrom, Jacob. *Leviticus 1–16: A New Translation with Introduction and Commentary*. The Anchor Bible, vol. 3. New York: Doubleday, 1991.

Morell, Samuel. *Precedent and Judicial Discretion: The Case of Joseph ibn Lev*. South Florida Studies in the History of Judaism 26. Atlanta: Scholars Press, 1991.

Nadav, Mordechai. "Pinqas qahal Franqfurṭ de-Mayn." *Kiryat Sefer* 31 (1955–56): 507–16.

Ogilvie, Sheilagh. *A Bitter Living: Women, Markets, and Social Capital in Early Modern Germany*. Oxford: Oxford University Press, 2003.

Ortlieb, Eva. "Frankfurt vor dem Reichshofrat." In *Die Reichsstadt Frankfurt als Rechts- und Gerichtslandschaft im Römisch-Deutschen Reich*. Edited by Anja Amend et al., 57–75. Munich: Oldenbourg, 2008.

Paton, G.W., and G. Sawer. "Ratio Decidendi and Obiter Dictum in Appellate Courts." *The Law Quarterly Review* 68 (October 1947): 461–85.

Pazdro, Zbigniew. *Organizacya i praktyka żydowskich sądów podwojewodzinskich w okresie 1740–1772 r.* L'viv: Nakładem Funduszu Konkursowego, 1903.

Pollack, Herman. *Jewish Folkways in Germanic Lands (1648–1806)*. Cambridge, Mass.: M.I.T. Press, 1971.

Pinqas ha-qehillot: enẓiqlopediyah shel ha-yishubim ha-Yehudiyyim le-min hivvasdam ve-ʿad le-ʾaḥar shoʾat milḥemet ha-ʿolam ha-sheniyyah. Vol. 1, *Germanyah — Baʾvʾaryah*. Edited by Baruch Z. Ophir in collaboration with Chasia Turtel-Aberzhanska and Shlomo Schmiedt. Jerusalem: Yad Vashem, 1972.

Press, Volker. "Kaiser Rudolf II. und der Zusammenschluß der deutschen Judenheit: Die sogenannte Frankfurter Rabbinerverschwörung von 1603 und ihre Folgen." In *Zur Geschichte der Juden im Deutschland des späten Mittelalters und der frühen Neuzeit*. Edited by Alfred Haverkamp, 243–93. Stuttgart: Anton Hiersemann, 1981.

Preuss, Monika. *Gelehrte Juden: Lernen als Frömmigkeitsideal in der frühen Neuzeit*. Hamburger Beiträge zur Geschichte der Deutschen Juden 31. Göttingen: Wallstein, 2007.

Putík, Alexandr. "The Prague Jewish Community in the Late 17th and Early 18th Centuries." *Judaica Bohemiae* 35 (1999): 4–140.

Rakover, Nahum. *Ha-sheliḥut ve-ha-harshaʾah be-mishpaṭ ha-ʿibri*. Jerusalem: Mossad Harav Kook, 1972.

Reiner, Avraham (Rami). "Battey ha-din be-Ẓarefat be-meʾah ha-shetaym ʿesreh: beyn rikkuz le-bizzur." In *ʿAl pi ha-beʾer: meḥqarim be-hagut yehudit u-be-maḥshebet ha-halakah muggashim le-Yaʿaqob Blidstein*. Edited by Uri Erlich et al., 565–91. Beer Sheva: Ben-Gurion University Press, 2008.

———. "Eben she-katub ʿaleha: toʾarey ha-nifṭarim be-maẓebot beyt ha-ʿalmin be-Wirẓburg 1147–1346." *Tarbiz* 78, no. 1 (December 2008): 123–52.

Reiner, Elchanan. "Hon, maʿamad ḥebrati ve-talmud Torah: ha-qeloyz be-ḥebrah ha-yehudit be-mizraḥ eyropah ." *Zion* 58, no. 3 (1993): 287–328.

———. "Maʿaseh she-ʾirʿa be-q[ehillat] q[odesh] Virmaysaʾ be-raʿash ha-gadol shenat [5]396." *Haaretz* 6 October 2006: 4 (Culture and Literature Section).

Rixen, Carl. *Geschichte und Organisation der Juden im ehemaligen Stifte Münster*. Münster: Westfälischen Vereinsdruckerei, 1906.

Rosenfeld, Mosche. "Fürther jüdische Kalender." *Israelitische Kultusgemeinde Fürth*, September 1989, 26–36.

Rosman, Moshe. "The Role of Non-Jewish Authorities in Resolving Conflicts within Jewish Communities in the Early Modern Period." *Political Studies Review* 12, no. 3–4 (Fall 2000): 53–65.

Roth, Cecil. *The Frankfurt Memorbuch*. Jerusalem: Jewish National and University Library, 1965.

Rubinstein, Nicolai. *The Government of Florence Under the Medici (1434 to 1494)*. 2d ed. Oxford: Clarendon, 1997.

Rustow, Marina. *Heresy and the Politics of Community: The Jews of the Fatimid Caliphate*. Ithaca: Cornell University Press, 2008.

Salfeld, Siegmund. *Das Martyrologium des Nürnberger Memorbuches*. Berlin: Leonhard Simion, 1898.

Schacht, Joseph. *An Introduction to Islamic Law*. Oxford: Clarendon, 1964.

Schedlitz, Bernd. *Leffmann Behrens: Untersuchungen zum Hofjudentum in Zeitalter des Absolutismus*. Hildesheim: August Lax, 1984.

Schlick, Gabriela. "Zur Rolle der reichsstädtischen Gerichtsbarkeiten in den Alltagsbeziehungen der Frankfurter Juden im 18. Jahrhundert." In *Die Frankfurter Judengasse: Jüdisches Leben in der frühen Neuzeit*. Edited by Fritz Backhaus et al., 171–85. Frankfurt: Societät, 2006.

Schmädel, Judith von. "The History of Marriage Law in Austria and Germany: From Sacrament to Civil Contract." *Hitotsubashi Journal of Law and Politics* 37 (2009): 41–47.

Schochetman, Eliav. "Ḥobat ha-hanmaqah be-mishpaṭ ha-ʿibri." *Shenaton ha-mishpaṭ ha-ʿibri* 6–7 (1979–80): 319–97.

Schudt, Johann Jacob. *Jüdische merckwürdigkeiten: Vorstellende was sich curieuses und denckwurdiges in den neuern Zeiten bei einigen Jahr-hunderten mit denen in alle IV. Theile der Welt sonderlich durch Teutschland zerstreuten Juden zugetragen*. Vol. 3. 1714. Berlin: Louis Lamm, 1922.

Sendik, Rivka. "Beyn din le-pesher: peʿiluto shel beyt ha-din be-qehillat Franqfurṭ ʿa[l] n[ahar] Mayn be-maḥaẓit ha-sheniyyah shel ha-meʾah ha-shemonah ʿesreh." M.A. thesis. Ben-Gurion University of the Negev, 2000.

Shaw, James E. *The Justice of Venice: Authorities and Liberties in the Urban Economy 1550–1700*. Oxford: Oxford University Press, 2006.

Shazar, Shneur Zalman. "Gebiyyot ᶜedut be-lashon yidish be-sheʾelot u-teshubot." In *Orey dorot: meḥqarim ve-heʾarot le-toledot Yisraʾel be-dorot ha-ʾaḥaronim*. 1929, 239–319. Jerusalem: Mossad Bialik, 1971.

Shohet, Azriel. *ᶜIm ḥilufey tequfot: reʾshit ha-haskalah be-yahadut Germanyah*. Jerusalem: Mosad Bialik, 1960.

Shohet, David. *The Jewish Court in the Middle Ages*. 1931. Studies in Jewish Jurisprudence. New York: Hermon, 1974.

Shweka, Aharon. "Ha-pulmus ᶜal taqqanot Ṭoliṭulah be-yerushat ha-baᶜal et ishto." *Tarbiz* 68, no. 1 (December 1998): 87–127.

Simonsohn, Uriel I. "Overlapping Jurisdictions: Confessional Boundaries and Judicial Choice Among Christians and Jews Under Early Muslim Rule." Ph.D. diss. Princeton University, 2008.

Skovgaard-Petersen, Jakob. *Defining Islam for the Egyptian State: Muftis and Fatwas of the Dār al-Iftā*. Social, Economic, and Political Studies of the Middle East and Asia 59. Leiden: Brill, 1997.

Soliday, Gerald. *A Community in Conflict: Frankfurt Society in the Seventeenth and Early Eighteenth Centuries*. Hanover, N.H.: University Press of New England, 1974.

Soloveitchik, Haym. "Responsa: Literary History and Basic Literacy." Review of *Responsa: The Literary History of a Rabbinic Genre* by Peter Haas. *AJS Review* 24, no. 2 (1999): 343–57.

———. *Shu"t ke-meqor hisṭori*. Jerusalem: Shazar, 1990.

Sorkin, David. *The Transformation of German Jewry, 1780–1840*. New York: Oxford University Press, 1987.

Speiser, E. A. "The Stem *PLL* in Hebrew." *Journal of Biblical Literature* 82, no. 3 (September 1963): 301–6.

Staudinger, Barbara. "'Gelangt an eur kayserliche Majestät mein allerunderthenigistes Bitten' Handlungsstrategien der jüdischen Elite am Reichshofrat im 16. und 17. Jahrhundert." In *Hofjuden und Landjuden: Jüdisches Leben in der Frühen Neuzeit*. Edited by Sabine Hödl, Barbara Staudinger, and Peter Rauscher, 143–83. Berlin: Philo, 2004.

Stern, Selma. *The Court Jew*. Translated by Ralph Weiman. Philadelphia: Jewish Publication Society, 1950.

———. *Der Preussische Staat und die Juden*. Vol. 3.1. Tübingen: Mohr Siebeck, 1971.

Thomas, Keith. *Religion and the Decline of Magic: Studies in Popular Beliefs in Sixteenth and Seventeenth Century England*. London: Weidenfeld and Nicholson, 1971.

Unna, Josef. *Statistik der Frankfurter Juden bis zum Jahre 1866*. Frankfurt: Israelitischen Gemeide Frankfurt, 1931.

Vierhaus, Rudolf. *Germany in the Age of Absolutism*. Translated by Jonathan B. Knudsen. Cambridge: Cambridge University Press, 1988.

Weinberg, M. *Die Memorbücher der jüdischen Gemeinden in Bayern*. 2 vols. Frankfurt: S. Neumann, 1937.

Wendehorst, Stephan. "Imperial Spaces as Jewish Spaces — The Holy Roman Empire, the Emperor and the Jews in the Early Modern Period. Some Preliminary Observations." *Jahrbuch des Simon-Dubnow-Instituts* 2 (2003): 437–74.

Wettstein, P.H. "Dibrey ḥefeẓ mi-pinqasey ha-qahal be-Qeraʾqaʾ." *Meʾasef* (St. Petersburg) 1 (1902): 7–78.

———. *Mi-pinqasey ha-qahal be-Qeraʾqaʾ*. Breslau: S. Schottländer, 1900.

White, James Boyd. *Justice as Translation: An Essay in Cultural and Legal Criticism*. Chicago: University of Chicago Press, 1990.

———. "An Old-Fashioned View of the Nature of Law." *Theoretical Inquiries in Law* 12, no. 1 (January 2011): 381–402.

Whitman, James Q. *The Legacy of Roman Law in the German Romantic Era: Historical Vision and Legal Change*. Princeton, N.J.: Princeton University Press, 1990.

Yuval, Israel. "Ha-hesdarim ha-kaspiyyim shel ha-nesuʾin be-Ashkenaz be-yemey ha-beynayyim." In *Dat ve-kalkalah*. Edited by Menahem Ben-Sasson, 191–207. Jerusalem: Shazar, 1995.

———. *Ḥakamim be-doram*. Jerusalem: Magnes, 1988.

———. "Taqqanot neged ribbuy gerushin be-Germanyah be-meʾah ha-15." *Zion* 48 (1983): 177–215.

Zimmer, Eric (Yitzhak). *Harmony and Discord: An Analysis of the Decline of Jewish Self-Government in 15th Century Central Europe*. New York: Yeshiva University Press, 1970.

———. *Jewish Synods in Germany During the Late Middle Ages*. New York: Yeshiva University Press, 1978.

———. "Yemey ha-ṭohar shel ha-yoledet." In *ʿOlam ke-minhago noheg*, 220–39. Jerusalem: Shazar, 1996.

Index of Place Names

מפתח מקומות

1. ר' טורניאנסקי, גליקל, עמ' 2, הערה 5.

Index of Houses, Lots, and Streets in the Judengasse

בתים ורחובות ברובע היהודי בפרנקפורט

Index of Personal Names

מפתח שמות

All references are to the case numbers as they appear in this volume. Men have been listed according to their family names. Those who did not have family names are noted by personal name (e.g., Jacob ben [= son of] Herz Ḥayyim). Individuals whose names reflect their status in the Jewish community, for example *kohen* or *levi*, are recorded according to their personal or family names and not by the descriptive term unless it served as the person's main family name (e.g., Spiegel Katz, Solomon — and not Katz, Solomon Spiegel; but Kohen, Yeḥiʾel — and not Yeḥiʾel Kohen). Women are listed by their personal names (e.g., Sarah bat [=daughter of] Aaron Hecht, wife of Kalman Steibel). In instances where women are not explicitly named in Gundersheim's diary, but referred to as the wife of so and so, widow of *x*, or daughter of *y*, wherever the name of the individual is known from other sources there is a blind entry at "wife of so and so" or "widow of *x*" directing readers to the person.

At the beginning of my work on this project, M. Horovitz's *Abney zikkaron* was the most accessible reference work for the period and it therefore became the default reference in this index. References include two numbers (e.g., 5306 d. [5]587). The first represents the entry in Horovitz's book and the second the Hebrew year of the person's death. References to other works are noted.

Recently, both Horovitz's *Abney zikkaron* and Shlomo Ettlinger's *Ēlē tōldōt* have been made freely available on the internet. Horovitz's book is available at http://www.hebrewbooks.org/36587 and Ettlinger's work has been digitized by the Leo Baeck Institute in New York and can be accessed through their website (http://www.lbi.org/research/family-research/).

Subject Index of Cases

מפתח נושאים

המפתח אינו כולל מילים לועזיות כמו 'אינפנטאריום'. אפשר לאתר אותן במפתח למילים לועזיות.